Psychology

Core Concepts

by Philip G. Zimbardo, Robert L. Johnson,
and Vivian McCann
Second Custom Edition
for Citrus College

Taken From:

Psychology: Core Concepts, Sixth Edition
by Philip G. Zimbardo, Robert L. Johnson, and Vivian McCann

Keys to Colege Success in College, Career, and Life, Third Edition
By Carol Carter, Joyce Bishop, Sarah Lyman Kravits, and Judy Block

Custom Publishing

New York   Boston   San Francisco
London   Toronto   Sydney   Tokyo   Singapore   Madrid
Mexico City   Munich   Paris   Cape Town   Hong Kong   Montreal

Cover Art: Courtesy of Photodisc, Stockbyte/Getty Images

Taken from:

Psychology: *Core Concepts,* Sixth Edition
Copyright © 2009, 2006, 2003, 2000 by Allyn & Bacon
A Pearson Education Company
Upper Saddle River, New Jersey 07458

Keys to Success in College, Career, and Life, Third Edition
Copyright © 2003 by Prentice Hall
A Pearson Education Company
Upper Saddle River, New Jersey 07458

This special edition published in cooperation with Pearson Custom Publishing.

Printed in the United States of America

10 9 8 7 6 5 4 3 2 1

2009500082

BW

Pearson
Custom Publishing
is a division of

www.pearsonhighered.com

ISBN 10: 0-558-30455-9
ISBN 13: 978-0-558-30455-3

Welcome to Citrus Psychology 101

PSYCHOLOGY COURSES AT CITRUS COLLEGE

Below are some of the courses that may be offered in Psychology within the Behavioral Sciences Department at Citrus College. For a more complete course description along with prerequisites and Credit information, please consult the Citrus College Catalog for the most up to date information.

PSY 101—Introduction to Psychology—an introduction to the field of psychology through involved learning, motivation, intelligence, and personality.

PSY 102—Psychobiology—Study of the effects of biology upon behavior, the relationship between psychological processes and the nervous system, muscular, and glandular features of the response mechanism, and the structure and functions of the sense organs.

PSY 103—Elementary Statistics—An Elementary course in basic statistical concepts designed especially for students in the social science area.

PSY 110—Psychology of Religion—This course explores the connection between psychology and religion. It focuses on how different schools of psychological thought view and interpret religious concepts.

PSY 111—Psychology of Religion II—This course expands on the concepts introduced in Psy 110.

PSY 133—Personal and Social Growth—This course aims to assist students in achieving a foundation in the study of personal and social growth behavior and a better understanding of themselves and human relationships.

PSY 152—Psychology of Human Relations—This course deals with the various problems that arise in the manifold relationships which exist between human beings.

PSY 203—Research Methods In Behavioral Sciences—An introductory course in research methodology designed for students in the behavioral and social sciences.

PSY 205—Developmental Psychology—Developmental Psychology is the scientific study of progressive changes in behavior, cognition, and abilities.

PSY 206—Child Growth and Development—Students will critically examine theories of child development in the physical, intellectual and social-emotional areas as they pertain to the various ages and states in a child's life from the prenatal development through adolescence.

PSY 212—Abnormal Psychology—The purpose of this course is two fold: 1) A description of the various mental disorders as listed in current DSM 2) An investigation of the various therapies used in treatment for these disorders.

PSY 213—Survey of Drug and Alcohol Use and Abuse—Psychological, sociological, and biological perspectives regarding alcohol and drug abuse are examined.

PSY 225—Survey of Human Sexuality—An introductory survey of the psychological bases and dimensions of human sexuality with emphasis on the socio-cultural factors involved in intimate relating, sexuality, and loving.

PSY 226—Psychology of Women—A bio-cultural anaysis of women. Emphasis will be placed on biological, psychological and sociological factors influencing the development of women from birth to death.

PSY 250—Honors Topics Seminar

WEB LINKS FOR STUDENT ASSIGNMENTS

Here are some websites that may be of interest to you as a student of psychology. The following links are organized by chapter so that you may visit the sites that correspond to any topics of interest to you.

Chapter 1

American Psychological Association
http://www.apa.org/
As noted on their Web site, "Based in Washington, DC, the American Psychological Association (APA) is a scientific and professional organization that represents psychology in the United States."

American Psychological Society
http://www.psychologicalscience.org/
As noted on their Web site, "The Society's mission is to promote, protect, and advance the interests of scientifically oriented psychology in research, application, teaching, and the improvement of human welfare." This organization is focused on research in the field.

The History of Psychology
http://www.ship.edu/~cgboeree/historyofpsych.html
Dr. C. George Boeree wrote an e-book on the history of psychology.

The Association for Women in Psychology
http://www.awpsych.org/
As noted on their Web site, "AWP is a not-for-profit scientific and educational organization committed to encouraging feminist psychological research, theory, and activism."

Marky Lloyd's Careers in Psychology Page
http://www.psywww.com/careers/
This site contains information for undergraduate students interested in careers in psychology.

Chapter 2

The Human Brain: Dissections of the Real Brain
http://www.vh.org/adult/provider/anatomy/BrainAnatomy/BrainAnatomy.html
This site allows you to virtually dissect real pictures of a human adult brain.

Institute for Behavioral Genetics
http://ibgwww.colorado.edu/
This is the official website for the Institute for Behavioral Genetics. According to their site, their mission is to, "conduct and facilitate research on the genetic bases of individual differences in behavior."

Mind and Brain
http://wl.middlebury.edu/fysmindandbrain/stories/storyReader$41
This site provides some interesting (and fun!) links to sites that explore the split brain issue.

National Institute of Neurological Disorders and Stroke
http://www.ninds.nih.gov/index.htm
The National Institute of Neurological Disorders and Stroke website highlights current research and discoveries in the field.

Medline Plus Health Information
http://www.nlm.nih.gov/medlineplus/endocrinesystem hormones.html
This site contains helpful information about the endocrine system and hormones.

Chapter 3

Dr. P's Dog Training
http://www.uwsp.edu/psych/dog/dog.htm
A virtual library for people interested in dog training and behavior. Maintained by Dr. Mark Plonsky at the University of Wisconsin-Stevens Point.

Interactive Classical Conditioning
http://www.uwm.edu/~johnchay/cc.htm
This computer simulation allows you to classically condition a virtual dog.

B.F. Skinner Foundation
http://bfskinner.org/index.asp
This is the official website for the B.F. Skinner Foundation. It contains background information, publications, pictures, and media clips of B.F. Skinner and his work.

The Psi Café — Ivan Pavlov
http://www.psy.pdx.edu/PsiCafe/KeyTheorists/Pavlov.htm
Part of The Psi Café: A Psychology Resource Site, this page contains information about Ivan Pavlov, as well as various links containing information about him and classical conditioning.

Albert Bandura
http://www.ship.edu/~cgboeree/bandura.html
This site, written by C.G. Boeree, contains information on Albert Bandura's life and theory.

Chapter 4

Memory Enhancement
http://www.ec-online.net/Knowledge/Articles/memoryenhancement.html
An article containing many practical techniques for improving memory, from the ElderCare Online site.

Alzheimer's Association
http://www.alz.org/
This site has abundant information on memory loss, including Alzheimer's Disease and similar illnesses.

Remembering Dangerously
http://faculty.washington.edu/eloftus/Articles/witchhunt.html
This article, written by Elizabeth Loftus, was published in the Skeptical Inquirer. It describes false memory syndrome and the problems that it can cause.

Exploratorium: Memory
http://www.exploratorium.edu/memory/index.html
This page on the Exploratorium website contains links to various memory lectures, tricks and tests.

Chapter 5

Cognitive Science Society
http://www.cognitivesciencesociety.org/
This society, "brings together researchers from many fields who seek to understand the nature of the human mind."

Psycholinguistics Research Group
http://www.york.ac.uk/res/prg/
This research group, based in New York, conducts research, "into the mental structures and representations underlying human language processing."

Central Washington University — The Chimpanzee and Human Communication Institute
http://www.cwu.edu/~cwuchci/links.htm
This institute "is a sanctuary for a unique family of chimpanzees who have acquired the signs of American Sign Language (ASL) and use those signs in conversations with each other and their human companions." Several links are also provided at this site.

Society for Judgment and Decision Making
http://www.sjdm.org/
This society, "is an interdisciplinary academic organization dedicated to the study of normative, descriptive, and proscriptive theories of decision."

Non-Sexist Language
http://owl.english.purdue.edu/handouts/general/gl_nonsex.html
This site, created by the Purdue University Online Writing Lab, assists writers to reduce or eliminate the use of sexist language.

Chapter 6

Medline Plus — Pregnancy
http://www.nlm.nih.gov/medlineplus/pregnancy.html
This site links to the latest news about pregnancy and prenatal development.

What you need to know about: Pregnancy/Birth
http://pregnancy.about.com/cs/laborbirth/
This is a commercial site, but it contains many articles about pregnancy, labor, and birth.

Jean Piaget Archives
http://www.unige.ch/piaget/Presentations/presentg.html
This site offers a description of the Jean Piaget Archives and its activities.

Raising Children to Resist Violence
http://www.apa.org/pubinfo/apa-aap.html
Research has shown that violent or aggressive behavior is often learned. This brochure on the APA's public information web site is designed to help parents work within the family, school, and community to prevent and reduce youth violence.

Alzheimer's Disease Education & Referral Center
http://www.alzheimers.org/
This organization was created to disseminate information about Alzheimer's disease to the public.

Chapter 7

Perception – From the Exploratorium in San Francisco
ttp://www.exploratorium.edu/exhibits/f_exhibits.html
This site has several online vision experiments that you can try.

Tutorials in Sensation and Perception
http://psych.hanover.edu/Krantz/sen_tut.html
This site was published by Dr. John Krantz and offers tutorials from Hanover University.

Vision Science
http://www.visionscience.com/
An Internet Resource for Research in Human and Animal Vision.

Color Laboratory
http://colorlab.wickline.org/colorblind/colorlab/
This color laboratory allows you to select colors and see how they appear next to one another, and in various foreground/background combinations. It also allows you to see those colors as they might appear to color-blind users.

Laurent Clerc National Deaf Education Center
http://clerccenter.gallaudet.edu/InfoToGo/index.html
Gallaudet University's Laurent Clerc National Deaf Education Center shares the concerns of parents and professionals about the achievement of deaf and hard of hearing students in different learning environments across the country.

Spinning Wheels
http://www.coc.cc.ca.us/users/rafterm/SpinningWheels.htm
This is a wonderful visual illusion. Although none of the wheels are moving, it is practically impossible to view all of them as stationary.

ColorQuiz
http://www.colorquiz.com/
This interactive site tests your color/reading ability.

Chapter 8

The Association for the Study of Dreams
http://www.asdreams.org/
The Association for the Study of Dreams is a nonprofit, international, multidisciplinary organization dedicated to the pure and applied investigation of dreams and dreaming.

Journal SLEEP
http://www.journalsleep.org/
The official publication of the Associated Professional Sleep Societies, LLC, a joint venture of the American Academy of Sleep Medicine and the Sleep Research Society. This site allows you to read the current edition of their journal.

National Institute on Drug Abuse (NIDA)
http://www.nida.nih.gov/
NIDA's mission is to lead the Nation in bringing the power of science to bear on drug abuse and addiction.

Neuroscience for Kids — Ecstasy (MDMA)
http://faculty.washington.edu/chudler/mdma.html
Part of the award-winning "Neuroscience for Kids" site, this section presents basic information about MDMA in a friendly, easy-to-read format.

Hypnosis.com
http://hypnosis.com/index.html
The website for the American Board of Hypnotherapy. Their site contains Frequently Asked Questions about hypnosis, as well as training programs in hypnotherapy.

Chapter 9

Weight-control Information Network
http://win.niddk.nih.gov/index.htm
A national information service of the U.S. National Institutes of Health. WIN was established in 1994 to provide health professionals and consumers with science-based information on obesity, weight control, and nutrition.

National Eating Disorders Association
http://www.edap.org/p.asp?WebPage_ID=337
"NEDA is dedicated to expanding public understanding of eating disorders and promoting access to quality treatment for those affected along with support for their families through education, advocacy and research."

Sexual Orientation and Homosexuality
http://www.apa.org/pubinfo/answers.html
This American Psychological Association page answers frequently asked questions about sexual orientation and provides links for further information.

Controlling Anger
http://www.apa.org/pubinfo/anger.html
This American Psychological Association page answers frequently asked questions about anger.

Affective Computing
http://affect.media.mit.edu/
This MIT site links together technology, research, and emotions.

Chapter 10

Links to Personality and Assessment Sites
http://www.oklahoma.net/~jnichols/perth.html
Maintained by Prof. John Nichols, this is a useful jumping off point for information about personality theories and tests.

The Origin and Development of Psychoanalysis
http://psychclassics.yorku.ca/Freud/Origin/index.htm
Sigmund Freud's five lectures on how he developed the original theory of psychoanalysis. From the "Classics in the History of Psychology" site, maintained by Prof. Christopher Green of York University.

Searching for genes that explain our personalities
http://www.apa.org/monitor/sep02/genes.html
This article from the APA Monitor describes the search for information on genes and their link to personality.

The Personality Project
http://personality-project.org/personality.html
This is a link for those interested in personality theory and research into current personality literature. Most information cited should be available from university libraries.

Personality Theories
http://www.ship.edu/%7Ecgboeree/perscontents.html
This site, maintained by Dr. C. George Boeree, contains information about many of the famous personality theories.

The Jung Typology Test
http://www.humanmetrics.com/cgi-win/JTypes2.asp
This test differentiates 16 personality types based on responses to 72 statements that are quickly answered by YES or NO.

Chapter 11

Current Research in Social Psychology
http://www.uiowa.edu/~grpproc/crisp/crisp.html
"Current Research in Social Psychology (CRISP) is a peer reviewed, electronic journal covering all aspects of social psychology."

Social Psychology Network
http://www.socialpsychology.org/
A wonderful site on social psychology, with a huge number of links to other resources. Created and maintained by Dr. Scott Plous of Wesleyan University.

Persuasive Disciplines
http://www.workingpsychology.com/persdisc.html
This site describes persuasion and social psychology.

Anti-Defamation League
http://www.adl.org/adl.asp
This site provides many articles, information, and links with regard to discrimination and combating racial hatred.

stanleymilgram.com
http://flockhart.com/milgram/main.html
This is a site devoted to Stanley Milgram, the psychologist who conducted the classic obedience experiment.

Chapter 12
National Alliance for the Mentally Ill (NAMI)
http://www.nami.org/
This site provides resources and information for individuals and others affected by mental illness.

Depression Central
http://www.psycom.net/depression.central.html
Dr. Ivan Goldberg maintains this website which contains a lot of information on many mood disorders, including depression, bipolar disorder, and others.

DSM-IV Made Easy
http://mysite.verizon.net/res7oqx1/index.html
Dr. James Morrison has practically placed his entire book online. This site summarizes much of the information contained in the DSM-IV-TR.

Schizophrenia.com
http://www.schizophrenia.com/
This site provides information and personal web journals on schizophrenia.

Attention Deficit Disorder Association
http://www.add.org/
This association helps to build connections among those with the disorder.

Chapter 13
Behavior OnLine
http://www.behavior.net/
Calling itself "The Gathering Place for Mental Health and Applied Behavioral Science Professionals," Behavior OnLine has articles about psychological issues (including many disorders and their treatment), discussion groups for professionals, and links to other behavioral science and mental health practice sites.

National Institute of Mental Health
http://www.nimh.nih.gov/about/index.cfm
This is a comprehensive site, covering current understandings and ongoing research into mental health and psychological disorders.

Online Dictionary of Mental Health
http://www.shef.ac.uk/~psysc/psychotherapy/
This is an online dictionary of mental health to answer questions about psychotherapy. There are also numerous links to related sites.

American Psychoanalytic Association
http://apsa.org/index.htm
This is the official web site for the American Psychoanalytic Association. On this site you will find new and old information about psychoanalysis.

Electroconvulsive Therapy — E.C.T.
http://www.psycom.net/depression.central.ect.html
This site has the National Institute of Health's conference statement of Electroconvulsive Therapy (ECT), among other detailed information.

Chapter 14
American Heart Association
http://www.americanheart.org/
This is the official website for the American Heart Association. Among other information, you will find hints for a healthy lifestyle.

Mind Tools: Stress Management Techniques
http://www.mindtools.com/smpage.html
This site contains links to various articles that describe stress and stress management techniques.

Health Psychology and Rehabilitation
http://www.healthpsych.com/
This site provides, "[r]esearch, viewpoints and practical suggestions about the practice of health psychology in medical and rehabilitation settings."

Occupational Health Psychology: Stress at Work
http://www.cdc.gov/niosh/ohp.html
This site provides information on an emerging field in psychology, occupational health psychology. This field is concerned with, "the primary prevention of organizational risk factors for stress, illness, and injury at work."

National Center for PTSD
http://www.ncptsd.org/
"This website is provided as an educational resource concerning PTSD and other enduring consequences of traumatic stress."

LEARNING STYLES—AN IMPORTANT PART OF SUCCESSFUL STUDYING

It happens in nearly every college course: Students listen to lectures throughout the semester. Each student hears the same words at the same time and completes the same assignments. However, after finals, student experiences will range from fulfillment and high grades to complete disconnection and low grades or withdrawals.

Many causes may be involved in this scenario—different levels of interest and effort, for example, or outside stresses. Another major factor is *learning style* (any of many particular ways to receive and process information). Say, for example, that a group of students is taking a freshman composition class that is often broken up into study groups. Students who are comfortable working with words or happy when engaged in discussion may do well in the course. Students who are more mathematical than verbal, or who prefer to work alone, might not do as well. Learning styles and capacities play a role.

There are many different and equally valuable ways to learn. The way each person learns is a unique blend of styles resulting from distinctive abilities, challenges, experiences, and training. In addition, how you learn isn't set in stone; particular styles may develop or recede as your responsibilities and experiences lead you to work on different skills and tasks. The following assessment and study strategies will help you explore how you learn, understand how particular strategies may heighten your strengths and boost your weaknesses, and know when to use them.

MULTIPLE INTELLIGENCES THEORY

There is a saying. "It is not how smart you are, but how you are smart." In 1983, Howard Gardner, a Harvard University professor, changed the way people perceive intelligence and learning with his Multiple Intelligences Theory. This theory holds that there are at least eight distinct *intelligences* possessed by all people, and that every person has developed some intelligences more fully than others. (Gardner defines an "intelligence" as an ability to solve problems or fashion products that are useful in a particular cultural setting or community.) According to the Multiple Intelligences Theory, when you find a task or subject easy, you are probably using a more fully developed intelligence; when you have more trouble, you may be using a less developed intelligence.

Following are descriptions of each of the intelligences, along with characteristic skills. The *Multiple Pathways to Learning* assessment, based on Gardner's work, will help you determine the levels to which your intelligences are developed. You will find the assessment on p. xxiv.

PUTTING ASSESSMENTS IN PERSPECTIVE

Before you complete the *Multiple Pathways to Learning* assessment, remember: No assessment has the final word on who you are and what you can and cannot do. An intriguing but imperfect tool, its results are affected by your ability to answer objectively, your mood that day, and other factors. Here's how to best use what this assessment, or any other, tells you:

Use Assessments for Reference Approach any assessment as a tool with which you can expand your idea of yourself. There are no "right" answers, no "best" set of scores. Think of it in the same way you would a set of eyeglasses for a person with blurred vision. The glasses will not create new paths and possibilities, but will help you see more clearly the ones that already exist.

Use Assessments for Understanding Understanding the level to which your intelligences seem to be developed will help prevent you from boxing yourself into categories that limit your life. Instead of saying "I'm no good in math," someone who is not a natural in math can make the subject easier by using appropriate strategies. For example, a learner who responds to visuals can learn better by drawing diagrams of math problems. The more you know yourself, the more you will be able to assess and adapt to any situation—in school, work, and life.

Face Challenges Realistically Any assessment reveals areas of challenge as well as ability. Rather than dwelling on limitations (which often results in a negative self-image) or ignoring them (which often leads to unproductive choices), use what you know from the assessment to look at where you are and set goals that will help you reach where you want to be.

Following the assessment, you will see information about the typical traits of each intelligence, and more detailed study strategies geared toward the four intelligences most relevant for studying this text. During this course you should make a point to explore a large number of new study techniques, considering all of the different strategies presented, not just the ones that apply to your strengths. Why?

Change Because you have abilities in all areas, though some are more developed than others, you may encounter useful suggestions under any of the headings. Furthermore, your abilities and learning styles change as you learn, so you never know what might work for you.

Strategies Help Weaknesses, Build Strengths Knowing learning styles is not only about guiding your life toward your strongest abilities; it is also about choosing strategies to use when you face challenges. Strategies for your weaker areas may help when what is required of you involves tasks and academic areas that you find difficult. For example, if you are not strong in logical-mathematical intelligence and have to take a math course, the suggestions geared toward logical-mathematical learners may help you build what skill you have.

As you complete the assessment, try to answer the questions objectively—in other words, answer the questions to best indicate who you are, not who you want to be (or who your parents or instructors want you to be). Then, enter your scores on p. xxiv. Don't be concerned if some of your scores are low—that is true for almost everyone.

Intelligence	Description	Characteristic Skills
Verbal/Linguistic	Ability to communicate through language through listening, reading, writing, speaking.	• Analyzing own use of language • Remembering terms easily • Explaining, teaching, learning, & using humor • Understanding syntax and meaning of words • Convincing someone to do something
Logical/Mathematical	Ability to understand logical reasoning and problem solving, particularly in math and science.	• Recognizing abstract patterns and sequences • Reasoning inductively and deductively • Discerning relationships and connections • Performing complex calculations • Reasoning scientifically
Visual/Spatial	Ability to understand spatial relationships and to perceive and create images.	• Perceiving and forming objects accurately • Manipulating images for visual art or graphic design • Finding one's way in space (using charts and maps) • Representing something graphically • Recognizing relationships between objects
Bodily/Kinesthetic	Ability to use the physical body skillfully and to take in knowledge through bodily sensation.	• Connecting mind and body • Controlling movement • Improving body functions • Working with hands • Expanding body awareness to all senses • Coordinating body movement
Intrapersonal	Ability to understand one's own behavior and feelings.	• Evaluating own thinking • Being aware of and expressing feelings • Taking independent action • Understanding self in relationship to others • Thinking and reasoning on higher levels
Interpersonal	Ability to relate to others, noticing their moods, motivations, and feelings.	• Seeing things from others' perspectives • Cooperating within a group • Achieving goals with a team • Communicating verbally and non-verbally • Creating and maintaining relationships
Musical/Rhythmic	Ability to comprehend and create meaningful sound and recognize patterns.	• Sensing tonal qualities • Creating or enjoying melodies and rhythms • Being sensitive to sounds and rhythms • Using "schemas" to hear music • Understanding the structure of music and other patterns
Naturalistic	Ability to understand features of the environment.	• Deep understanding of nature, environmental balance, ecosystem • Appreciation of the delicate balance in nature • Feeling most comfortable when in nature • Ability to use nature to lower stress

STUDY STRATEGIES FOR DIFFERENT LEARNING STYLES

Finding what study strategies work best for you is almost always a long process of trial and error, often because there is no rhyme or reason to the search. If you explore strategies in the context of learning style, however, you give your-self a head start.

Rate each statement: rarely 5 1,   sometimes 5 2,   often 5   3,   almost always 5   4
Write the number of your response on the line next to the statement and total each set of 6 questions.

1. _____ I enjoy physical activities.
2. _____ I am uncomfortable sitting still.
3. _____ I prefer to learn through doing rather than listening.
4. _____ I tend to move my legs or hands when I'm sitting.
5. _____ I enjoy working with my hands.
6. _____ I like to pace when I'm thinking or studying.
_____ **TOTAL for Bodily-Kinesthetic**

7. _____ I use maps easily.
8. _____ I draw pictures or diagrams when explaining ideas.
9. _____ I can assemble items easily from diagrams.
10. _____ I enjoy drawing or taking photographs.
11. _____ I do not like to read long paragraphs.
12. _____ I prefer a drawn map over written directions.
_____ **TOTAL for Visual-Spatial**

13. _____ I enjoy telling stories.
14. _____ I like to write.
15. _____ I like to read.
16. _____ I express myself clearly.
17. _____ I am good at negotiating.
18. _____ I like to discuss topics that interest me.
_____ **TOTAL for Verbal-Linguistic**

19. _____ I like math.
20. _____ I like science.
21. _____ I problem-solve well.
22. _____ I question why things happen or how things work.
23. _____ I enjoy planning or designing something new.
24. _____ I am able to fix things.
_____ **TOTAL for Logical-Mathematical**

25. _____ I listen to music.
26. _____ I move my fingers or feet when I hear music.
27. _____ I have good rhythm.
28. _____ I like to sing along with music.
29. _____ People have said I have musical talent.
30. _____ I like to express my ideas through music.
_____ **TOTAL for Musical**

31. _____ I like doing a project with other people.
32. _____ People come to me to help them settle conflicts.
33. _____ I like to spend time with friends.
34. _____ I am good at understanding people.
35. _____ I am good at making people feel comfortable.
36. _____ I enjoy helping others.
_____ **TOTAL for Interpersonal**

37. _____ I need quiet time to think.
38. _____ When I need to make a decision, I prefer to think about it before I talk about it.
39. _____ I am interested in self-improvement.
40. _____ I understand my thoughts, feelings, and behavior.
41. _____ I know what I want out of life.
42. _____ I prefer to work on projects alone.
_____ **TOTAL for Intrapersonal**

43. _____ I enjoy being in nature whenever possible.
44. _____ I would enjoy a career involving nature.
45. _____ I enjoy studying plants, animals, forests, or oceans.
46. _____ I prefer to be outside whenever possible.
47. _____ When I was a child I liked bugs, ants, and leaves.
48. _____ When I experience stress I want to be out in nature.
_____ **TOTAL for Naturalist**

Write your 8 Multiple Intelligences in the table below according to your scores.

Scores 20–24 5 Highly Developed	Scores 14–19 5 Moderately Developed	Scores below 14 5 Underdeveloped

Now that you have completed the Multiple Pathways to Learning assessment, you will be able to look at the following material with a more informed view of what may help you most.

The strategies presented here are linked to four intelligences, selected because they have the most relevance to your study in this course—Verbal/Linguistic, Logical/Mathematical, Visual/Spatial, and Interpersonal. Although they are written in the context of strength, remember that the strategies can also help you build up an area of weakness. Try strategies from all different areas and evaluate them. Do the ones that match your strengths work best for you? Do the ones that correspond to your weaker areas help you improve? Does a winning strategy come from an unexpected intelligence area? What might that help you learn about yourself?

Note Taking Because it is virtually impossible to take notes on everything you hear or read, the act of note taking encourages you to evaluate what is worth writing down and remembering. Note taking keeps you actively involved with the material and helps organize your thinking. Knowing how you learn will help you decide how to take notes in class and from the textbook.

Learners with Verbal/Linguistic Strength Words are your thing, and notes are words, so you generally take comprehensive notes. In fact you may often overdo it by trying to write down everything that you hear. Your challenge is to be choosy, and organized, with what you write.

- Rewrite notes to cut out unnecessary material and focus on the important ideas.
- Summarize the main ideas and supporting points of chapters.
- Avoid writing out every word—use abbreviations and other "personal shorthand."

Learners with Logical/Mathematical Strength You prefer organized notes that flow logically. Unfortunately, not all classes and instructors make it possible for you to take the kind of notes you prefer. You often need time to convert your notes into a more structured format.

- On your own time, rewrite notes and organize the material logically.
- Write outlines of class notes or text material.
- Leave one or more blank spaces between points, in case making your notes more logical requires filling in missing information later.

Learners with Visual/Spatial Strength You retain best what is presented in some sort of graphic, visual format. Courses that primarily consist of lectures don't make the most of your abilities. Look for materials that tap into your strength—or create them when none exist.

- Take notes in a visual style—for example, use a "mind map" or "think link" that connects ideas and examples using shapes and lines.
- Use different colors—either during class or after—to organize your notes.
- Start a new page for a new topic.

Learners with Interpersonal Strength Material stays with you best when you learn it and review it actively with others. Some classes give you the opportunity to interact—and some don't. Make your notes come alive by making interaction a part of your note taking experience.

- Go over notes with one or more fellow students, helping one another fill in the gaps.
- Solidify your understanding of your notes by teaching concepts to someone else.
- If you tend to talk with classmates and get distracted, try not to sit with your friends.

Reading Research has shown that it is far more effective to break your reading into several steps than to spend the same amount of time going through the material once. SQ3R is a textbook reading technique that will help you grasp ideas quickly, remember more, and review effectively for tests. The symbols S-Q-3-R stand for survey, question, read, recite, and review. Following is a brief overview of SQ3R:

Survey *Surveying* refers to the process of previewing, or pre-reading, a book before you actually study it. When you survey, pay attention to frontmatter (table of contents and preface); chapter elements (title, outline or list of objectives, headings, tables and figures, quotes, summary, other features); and backmatter (glossary, index, bibliography).

Question *Questioning* means reading the chapter headings and/or objectives and, on a separate piece of paper or in the margins, writing questions linked to them. If your reading material has no headings, develop questions as you read. These questions focus your attention and increase your interest, helping you build comprehension and relate new ideas to what you already know.

Read Your questions give you a starting point for *reading*, the first R in SQ3R. Learning from textbooks requires that you read *actively*—engaging with the material through questioning, writing, note taking, and other activities. As you read, focus on your Q-stage questions, look for important concepts, and make notations in your textbook (marginal notes, highlighting, circling key ideas). Read in segments and make sure you understand what you read as you go.

Recite Once you finish reading a topic, stop and answer the questions you raised in the Q stage of SQ3R. You may decide to recite each answer aloud, silently speak the answers to yourself, tell or teach the answers to another person, or write your ideas and answers in brief notes. Writing is often the most effective way to solidify what you have read because writing from memory checks your understanding.

Review *Review* soon after you finish a chapter. Reviewing, both immediately and periodically in the days and weeks after you read, solidifies your understanding. Reviewing techniques include rereading, answering study questions, summarizing, group discussion, quizzing yourself, and making flash cards. Reviewing in as many different ways as possible increases the likelihood of retention.

This text has features that fit into the SQ3R steps and reinforce your learning. The Table above shows how you can use specific features as you move through the steps of SQ3R. Here are some reading tips geared toward the intelligences:

Learners with Verbal/Linguistic Strength You tend to function well as a reader. Set yourself up for success by being as critical as you can be when you read.

- As you read the text, highlight no more than 10%.
- Mark up your text with marginal notes while you read.
- Recite information by rewriting important ideas and examples.

Learners with Logical/Mathematical Strength When reading material is organized and logical, you tend to do well. When it is not, you may run into trouble.

- Look for patterns and systems in your reading material.
- Read material in sequence.
- Think about the logical connections between what you are reading and the world at large.

Learners with Visual/Spatial Strength Textbooks with tables, figures, and other visuals help you to retain the concepts in your reading. You can make your own when there are few or none.

Survey	Question	Read	Recite	Review
A **Chapter Outline** begins each chapter	**Questions** appear after each major chapter heading and also in the **Psychological Detective** features	The text is designed to flow, minimizing interruptions to the reader	**Check Your Progress** quizzes appear at the end of each main section of each chapter	**Review Summaries** appear at the end of each main chapter section: **Study Charts** appear in many chapters

- As you read, take note of all visuals—photos, tables, figures, other visual aids.
- Reconstruct what you have read using a visual organizer (mind map, timeline, chart).
- Take time out to visualize concepts as you read.

Learners with Interpersonal Strength Since reading is solitary, not your strongest setting, you need to find group situations that can enhance your understanding of what you read.

- Start a study group that discusses assigned class readings.
- Have a joint reading session with a friend and take turns summarizing sections for each other.
- Teach someone else selected concepts from your reading.

Memory In one theory, the human memory is compared to a computer, with an encoding stage, a storage stage (with three storage levels—sensory, short-term, and long-term), and a retrieval stage. Taking this view, memory improvement involves rehearsing information in order to move it from short-term to long-term memory. Another theory proposes that there are different levels of processing information that lead to varying degrees of memory. From this perspective, improving your memory requires using increased effort when processing information. You can learn more about some of the following strategies in Chapters 7 and 8 of the text.

Learners with Verbal/Linguistic Strength Use words to rehearse information.

- Write summaries of your text passages and notes.
- Rewrite notes, working to make them neater, more concise, easier to understand.
- Make up word-based mnemonics, such as acronyms.

Learners with Logical/Mathematical Strength Organizing your material will help you remember.

- Impose structure on information—write outlines, use grouping or chunking techniques.
- Put dates and events into timelines.
- Review systematically—for example, for 30 minutes at a particular time every day.

Learners with Visual/Spatial Strength Make your material visual.

- Draw mind maps and fill them in with important information.
- Turn information into charts or graphs.
- Use imagery—visualize items as you learn them.

Learners with Interpersonal Strength Reviewing with others helps you cement what you learn.

- Discuss material in a group; make quizzes for one another; teach one another.
- Work together to create mnemonic devices.
- Perform songs or poems for others that contain the information you need to remember.

Test Taking Test taking is about learning. Tests are designed to show what you have learned and to help you figure out where you need to work harder. The best test takers understand that they train not just for the test but to achieve a solid level of competence. Using a learning styles-based approach to studying for and taking tests will boost your ability—if you learn the material in the way that suits you best, you will best be able to retain it and communicate it in a testing situation.

Learners with Verbal/Linguistic Strength Put your focus on words to good use.

- Think of and write out questions your instructor may ask on a test—and write answers.
- Pay attention to important words—directions that tell you how to answer, for example, or negatives that sway the meaning of a question ("Which of the following is *not* …").
- For math and science tests, do word problems first—and translate the words into formulas.

Learners with Logical/Mathematical Strength Find a sequential system.

- Devise and use a system that you prefer—going through the test in its exact order, for example, or doing all the simple problems first and then coming back to harder ones.
- Outline the key steps involved in topics on which you may be tested.
- If you don't know the right answer to a multiple-choice question, look for patterns that may lead to the right answer. For example, when there are two similar choices, one of them is usually correct.

Learners with Visual/Spatial Strength Do what you can to make the test appeal to the visual.

- Underline key words and phrases in the test questions.
- Make drawings to illustrate concepts you are being tested on.
- Create mind maps to organize your thoughts before completing an essay question.

Learners with Interpersonal Strength Testing, usually a solitary enterprise, rarely makes use of your strengths. Do what you can to prepare in setings that provide interaction.

- Study for tests in pairs and groups.
- In your group, write possible test questions and ask each other questions in an oral-exam type format.
- Debrief with others—talk about the test, how you answered questions, what you wish you had done differently, and what you will do differently next time.

These study tips and the "Pathways to Learning" assessment are from *Keys to Success. Third Edition* (© 2002, Prentice Hall), by Carol Carter, Joyce Bishop, and Sarah Lyman Kravits.

brief contents

contents

CHAPTER 6 Development Over the Lifespan 229

CHAPTER 7 Sensation and Perception 287

CHAPTER 11 Social Psychology 477

CHAPTER 12 Psychological Disorders 529

There is one simple formula for academic success, and the following demonstration will show you what it is. Study this array of letters for a few seconds:

IBMUFOFBICIA

Now, without peeking, write down as many of the letters as you can (in the correct order).

Most people remember about 5 to 7 letters correctly. A few people get them all. How do these exceptional few do it? They find a pattern. (You may have noticed some familiar initials in the array above: IBM, UFO, FBI, CIA.) Finding the pattern greatly eases the task because you can draw on material that is already stored in memory. In this case, all that needs to be remembered are four "chunks" of information instead of 12 unrelated letters.

The same principle applies to material you study for your psychology class. If you try to remember each piece of information as a separate item, you will have a difficult time. But if instead you look for patterns, you will find your task greatly simplified—and much more enjoyable.

USING PSYCHOLOGY TO LEARN PSYCHOLOGY

So, how can you identify the patterns? With a little help from your friendly authors, who have developed several learning features that will make meaningful patterns what you are reading in this text stand out clearly:

Core Concepts We have organized each major section of every chapter around a single, clear idea called a Core Concept. For example, one of the four Core Concepts in Chapter 4, "Memory," says:

Human memory is an information processing system that works constructively to encode, store, and retrieve information.

core concept

The Core Concept, then, becomes the central idea around which about 10 pages of material—including several new terms—are organized. As you read each chapter, keeping the Core Concept in mind will help you encode the new terms and ideas related to that concept, store them in your memory, and later retrieve them when you are being tested. To borrow an old saying, the Core Concepts become the "forest," while the details of the chapter become the "trees."

Key Questions Each Core Concept is introduced by a Key Question that also serves as a main heading in the chapter. Here, for example, is a Key Question from the "Memory" chapter:

4.4 KEY QUESTION
WHY DOES MEMORY SOMETIMES FAIL US?

Key Questions such as this will help you anticipate the most important point, or the Core Concept, in the section. In fact, the Core Concept always provides a brief answer to the Key Question. Think of the Key Question as the high beams on your car, helping you focus on what lies ahead. Our key questions should also serve as guides for you to be posing questions of your own about what your are reading.

Both the Key Questions and the Core Concepts later reappear as organizing features of the Chapter Summary.

Psychology Matters Psychology has many connections with events in the news and in everyday life, and we have explored one of these connections at the end of each major section in every chapter. What makes psychology so fascinating to us and to our students are all the ways in which things learned in this course directly apply to events and experiences in the real world. To illustrate, here are some examples from the "Memory" chapter:

- Would You Want a "Photographic" Memory?
- "Flashbulb" Memories: Where Were You When . . . ?
- On the Tip of Your Tongue

Such connections—practical, down to earth, and interesting—link your reading about psychology with your real-life experiences. They also help you critically evaluate many of the psychological ideas you encounter in the media. Also, begin to notice how often you read news stories that make statements that begin with "research shows that . . . " By the end of this course, you will become a much wiser consumer of such information—some of which is often false or misleading.

Psychology Matters: Using Psychology to Learn Psychology A special Psychology Matters section in every chapter explains how you can apply your new knowledge of psychology to make your studying more effective. For example, in Chapter 2, "Biopsychology, Neuroscience, and Human *Nature*," we tell you how to put your understanding of the brain to work for more efficient learning. Similarly, at the end of Chapter 9, "Emotion and Motivation," we explain how to use a new psychological concept of "flow" to boost your own academic motivation. Thus, Using Psychology to Learn Psychology not only reinforces points that you have studied, it brings the material home with immediate and practical applications to your life in college.

Do It Yourself! We have scattered active-learning demonstrations (such as the one at the beginning of this student preface) throughout the book. Besides being fun, these activities have the serious purpose of illustrating principles discussed in the text. In Chapter 4, for example, one Do It Yourself! box helps you find the capacity of your short-term memory; another lets you test your "photographic memory" ability.

Check Your Understanding Whether you're learning psychology, soccer, or the saxophone, you need feedback on your progress, and that's exactly what you will get from the Check Your Understanding quizzes. These quizzes appear at the end of every major section in the chapter, offering you a quick checkup indicating whether you have gotten the main points from what you just read. Some questions call for simple recall; others call for deeper analysis or application of material. Some are multiple-choice questions; some are short-answer essay questions. These exercises will help you determine how well you have mastered the material.

CONNECTION • CHAPTER 10
Extraversion-Introversion is one of the basic Big Five personality dimensions that seem to apply to people all over the world.

Connection Arrows Important topics in other chapters are often cross-referenced with an arrow in the margin, as you can see in the sample here. The accompanying reference gives you either a preview or reminder of concepts covered in other chapters. This feature helps you connect ideas from different chapters.

Marginal Glossaries The most important terms appear in boldface, with their glossary definitions readily accessible in the margin. Then, at the end of the book, a comprehensive Glossary gathers together all the key terms and definitions from each chapter.

Chapter Summaries We have written our Chapter Summaries to provide you with an overview of main points in each chapter—to help you preview and review the chapter. The summaries are organized around the Key Questions and Core Concepts introduced within the chapter to facilitate review and mastery of chapter material. But we offer one caution: Reading the Chapter Summary will not substitute for reading the entire chapter! Here's a helpful hint: We recommend that you read the summary before you read the rest of the chapter to get a flavor of what's ahead, then reread the summary after you finish the chapter. Reading the summary before will help you organize the material so that it can be more easily encoded and stored in your memory. And, naturally, reviewing the summary after reading the chapter will reinforce what you have just learned so that you can retrieve more of it in the future.

THINKING LIKE A PSYCHOLOGIST

Learning all the facts and definitions of psychology won't make you a psychologist. Beyond the facts, *thinking like a psychologist* requires learning some *problem-solving* skills and some *critical thinking* techniques that any good psychologist should possess. To do so, we have added two unique features to this book.

Chapter-Opening Problems Each chapter asks an important problem that you will learn how to solve with the tools you acquire in the chapter. Examples of the chapter-opening problems include testing the idea that sweet treats give children a "sugar high," evaluating claims of recovered memories, and judging the extent to which the people we call "geniuses" are different from the rest of us.

Critical Thinking Applied At the end of each chapter, you will be asked to actively consider issues in dispute among psychologists and issues raised in the media, such as the nature of the unconscious and subliminal persuasion. Each of these issues requires a skeptical attitude and the application of a special set of critical thinking skills that we will provide in Chapter 1.

DISCOVERING PSYCHOLOGY VIDEOS

At the end of each chapter, you will notice viewing guides for Discovering Psychology, a 26-part video series produced by WGBH and Annenberg Media, and narrated by the lead author of this textbook, Phil Zimbardo. The videos provide an overview of historic and current theories of human behavior, and feature many of the researchers and studies introduced in this textbook. You can access the Discovering Psychology videos and additional viewing resources through MyPsychLab (www.mypsychlab.com), the online companion to this textbook.

We have one final suggestion to help you succeed in psychology: This book is filled with examples to illustrate the most important ideas, but you will remember these ideas longer if you generate your own examples as you study. This habit will make the information yours, as well as ours. And so, we wish you a memorable journey through the field we love.

Phil Zimbardo
Bob Johnson
Vivian McCann

to the instructor . . .

Psychological knowledge continues to explode. As a result, many introductory textbooks have grown to daunting proportions. Meanwhile, our introductory courses remain the same length—with the material ever more densely packed. We cannot possibly introduce students to all the concepts, and our students cannot possibly remember everything in the standard, encyclopedic introductory text.

We also realize that the problem is not just one of sheer volume and information overload; it is also a problem of meaningfulness. To be clear, our textbook is briefer than most encyclopedic texts, but we did not want to write a watered-down brief textbook, either. To make the material more meaningful for students who use *Psychology: Core Concepts*, we have found inspiration in a classic study of chess players. Researchers showed that experts did no better than novices at remembering the locations of pieces on a chessboard when the pieces were placed at random (de Groot, 1965). Only when the patterns made sense—because they represented actual game situations—did the experts show an advantage. Clearly, meaningful patterns are easier to remember than random assignments. In applying this to *Psychology: Core Concepts*, our goal has been to present a scientific overview of the field of psychology within meaningful patterns that will help students better remember what they learn so that they can apply it in their own lives. Thus, we have organized each major section of every chapter around a single, clear idea that we call a Core Concept, which helps students focus on the big picture so they don't become lost in the details.

From the beginning, our intention in writing *Psychology: Core Concepts* has been to offer students and instructors a textbook that combines a sophisticated introduction to the field of psychology with pedagogy that applies the principles of psychology to the learning of psychology, all in a manageable number of pages. Our goal was to blend great science with great teaching, to provide an alternative to the overwhelmingly encyclopedic or skimpy essentials books that have been traditionally offered. We think you will like the introduction to psychology presented in this book—both the content and the pedagogical features. After all, it's a text that relies consistently on well-grounded principles of psychology to teach psychology.

NEW TO THIS EDITION

As you would expect, we have updated this sixth edition *Psychology: Core Concepts* with the latest in cutting-edge theory and research. Much of the new material comes from neuroscience—for example, mirror neurons, new roles for glial cells, and pioneering studies of brain implants. But you will also find brand new work on cognitive-behavioral therapy, emotion and politics, cultural differences in perception, evolutionary psychology, the "tyranny of choice," and much more.

In addition to current references and topics, we have made the following improvements to the sixth edition.

Increased Emphasis on Thinking Like a Psychologist Two groundbreaking studies have helped guide our development of this new edition of *Psychology: Core Concepts*. In parallel research on the characteristics of master teachers at nearly 100 American colleges and universities, Bill Buskist (2004) and Ken Bain (2004) found that outstanding teachers have many different teaching styles. Yet despite this diversity in approaches, the best teachers share some important characteristics—most of which won't surprise you:

- The best teachers are enthusiastic about teaching.
- The best teachers are also scholars who keep up with new developments in their disciplines.
- The best teachers like their students and make themselves available to them.
- The best teachers use a variety of teaching techniques, including the lecture method—although none lecture exclusively. (Nor are they necessarily the ones with the drop-dead PowerPoints or other electronic wizardry.)

But one more factor wasn't quite so obvious:

- Both Buskist and Bain found that *the best teachers engage their students in solving problems that require thinking like experts in their disciplines.*

For those of us who teach psychology, encouraging students to develop expertise in solving problems in our discipline means helping them *think like psychologists*. For this sixth edition of *Psychology: Core Concepts* we have made two important additions to the pedagogy that are designed to help students develop these problem-solving skills: chapter-opening *problems* and end-of-chapter *Critical Thinking Applied* boxes.

Every chapter in the book now begins with a vignette that leads the reader to a *problem*—a real and substantive psychological problem that will be resolved with tools developed in the chapter. Here are some examples of these chapter-opening problems:

- How could you test the claim that sugar makes children hyperactive?
- How can our knowledge about memory help us evaluate claims of recovered memories?
- What produces "genius," and to what extent are the people we call "geniuses" different from others?
- How can psychologists examine objectively the worlds of dreaming and other subjective mental states?

As you can see, finding the answer to each problem requires learning to apply new and important ideas presented in the chapter. For example, the answer to the "sugar-high" problem leads to an understanding and application of the scientific method, whereas solving the "recovered memory" problem involves learning how memory works. We invite you, as you peruse this book, to see how we use other examples of this problem-based approach.

A second pedagogical addition to the sixth edition also aims to help students think like psychologists by applying critical thinking skills that are especially important in psychology: In a "Critical Thinking Applied" section at the end of every chapter, we address significant issues with which we psychologists also wrestle, such as:

- The person-situation controversy
- The evidence-based practice debate
- The nature of the unconscious
- The source of group differences in intelligence and other abilities

Other critical thinking sections take on some of the most egregious misconceptions that students encounter in "pop" psychology, such as:

- Left brain/right brain differences
- Facilitated communication
- Subliminal persuasion

What do we mean by *critical thinking?* That's the question, of course, that has dogged those who would teach their students to evaluate evidence and come to reasoned conclusions. Broadly, we take critical thinking to mean a skeptical approach to new ideas and old assumptions. Beyond that, we have developed a "tool kit" of six critical thinking questions that students are expected to apply to these end-of-chapter issues:

1. What is the source?
2. Is the claim reasonable or extreme?
3. What's the evidence?
4. Could bias contaminate the conclusion?
5. Does the reasoning avoid common fallacies?
6. Does the issue require multiple perspectives?

Of course, the book itself cannot make students good problem solvers and critical thinkers. That's why we have packed the *Instructor's Manual* with ideas for teaching problem solving and critical thinking. We hope that you, the instructor, will incorporate some of these ideas in your classes.

Expanded Coverage of Cross-Cultural, Multicultural, and Gender Research
Reflecting the increasing diversity and global reach of psychology, we have made a special effort to weave more material on gender, culture, and ethnicity throughout the text. The result is that every chapter of the book contains material on cross-cultural or multicultural psychology and diversity. Here's a sampling of such topics:

- What cultural differences are found in people's earliest memories?
- Do other cultures mean the same thing by "intelligence"?
- Research shows that dream content varies by culture, gender, and age. So, was Freud wrong about dreams?
- How can Bandura's social learning theory be applied to combat AIDS, promote safe sex, and enhance the status of women in developing countries?
- There are significant differences among groups in intelligence test scores, but do they stem from nature or from nurture?
- Is the Big Five trait theory valid across cultures?
- How does stereotype threat influence on test scores and classroom performance?
- How does the incidence of mental disorder vary by gender and culture?
- What are the differences between male and female brains? And what do these differences mean?
- Are males and females more alike in their thinking (as Janet Hyde's nurturist position suggests) or different (as Roy Baumeister's nativist position claims)?
- What differences have been discovered in the way Asians and Americans perceive their worlds?
- What are four important ways that men and women are different in their sexuality?

- How did Mary Calkins beat the odds to become the first woman president of the American Psychological Association—even though Harvard wouldn't give her the doctorate she earned?

New Coverage of the Impact of Social Systems on Human Behavior Philip Zimbardo is, of course, known for his Stanford Prison Experiment. Most recently, he has published a detailed description and analysis of this famous experiment in *The Lucifer Effect: Understanding How Good People Turn Evil*. We are pleased that some of Zimbardo's groundbreaking insights in *Lucifer*—particularly the notion of the effect of *social systems* on human behavior—are included in the extensively revised Chapter 11, "Social Psychology" appearing in this edition of *Psychology: Core Concepts*.

Integration of *The Discovering Psychology* Video Programs We are thrilled to be able to fuse the wildly successful video series, *Discovering Psychology: Updated Edition*, with our textbook. Author Phil Zimbardo narrates the video series, as leading researchers, practictioners, and theorists probe the mysteries of the mind and body and bring psychology to life for introductory students. Each chapter of the text ends with a Viewing Guide that contains program review questions that draw attention to key information presented in the videos.

Improved Chapter Organization With the sixth edition, we have resequenced some of the chapters with several goals in mind:

- We brought forward Chapter 3, "Learning and Human *Nurture*," and Chapter 4, "Memory," so that concepts in those chapters could be used to emphasize early on how students can *use psychology to learn psychology*.
- We also brought forward Chapter 11, "Social Psychology," to capitalize on students' intrinsic interest in this material.
- We tried to even out the pace of the material presented throughout the book.

TEACHING AND LEARNING PACKAGE

The following supplements will also enhance teaching and learning for you and your students:

New Expanded *Instructor's Manual* (ISBN: 0-205-59730-0) Written and compiled by Diane L. Finley, Prince George's Community College, with dozens of new resources pulled together by a team of master teachers, the expanded *Instructor's Manual* is an invaluable tool for new and experienced instructors alike. First-time instructors will appreciate the detailed introduction to teaching the introductory psychology course, with suggestions for preparing for the course, sample syllabi, and current trends and strategies for successful teaching. Each chapter offers integrated teaching outlines to help instructors seamlessly incorporate all of the ancillary materials for this book into their lectures, and all *Key Questions, Core Concepts*, and *Key Terms* for each chapter are listed for quick reference. For the sixth edition, the *Instructor's Manual* offers a substantially enhanced bank of lecture launchers, handouts, and activities, and new categories of materials have been added, including new crossword puzzles, suggestions for integrating third-party videos and web resources, a guide written by Sonya Lott-Harrison of Community College of Philadelphia with tips for integrating music into lesson plans, and cross-references to transparencies and hundreds of multimedia and video assets found in the *Psychology: Core Concepts* MyPsychLab course.

Print Test Bank and *MyTest* Computerized Test Bank (Print ISBN: 0-205-59737-8) Nicholas Greco IV, College of Lake County, has provided an extensively updated test bank containing over 2000 accuracy-checked questions, including multiple choice, completion (fill-in-the-blank and short answer), conceptual matching sequences, and critical essays. Test item questions have been also written to test student comprehension of select multimedia assets found with MyPsychLab, for instructors who wish to make MyPsychLab a more central component of their course. In addition to the unique questions listed previously, the Test Bank also includes all of the *Check Your Understanding* questions from the textbook and all of the test questions from the *Discovering Psychology* Telecourse Faculty Guide for instructors who wish to reinforce student use of the textbook and video materials. All questions include the correct answer, page reference, difficulty ranking, question type designation, and correlations to American Psychological Association (APA) Learning Goal/Outcome. A new feature of the Test Bank is the inclusion of a *Rationale* that explains why the correct answer is, in fact, the correct answer. This product is also available in the MyTest computerized version for use in creating tests in the classroom.

PowerPoint Presentation Written by Beth M. Schwartz, Randolph College, the PowerPoint lecture slides offer detailed outlines of key points for each chapter supported by selected visuals from the textbook. A separate *Art and Figure* version of these presentations contain all art from the textbook for which Pearson has been granted electronic permissions.

MyPsychLab (www.mypsychlab.com) The APA strongly recommends student self-assessment tools and the use of embedded questions and assignments (see www.apa.org/ed/eval_strategies.html for more information). In response to these demands, Pearson's *MyPsychLab* offers students useful and engaging self-assessment tools, and provides instructors flexibility in assessing and tracking student progress. To instructors, *MyPsychLab* is a powerful tool for assessing student performance and adapting course content to students' changing needs—without investing additional time or resources. Students benefit from an easy-to-use site on which they can test themselves on key content, track their progress, and utilize individually tailored study plans. *MyPsychLab* includes an e-book plus multimedia tutorials, audio, video, simulations, animations, and controlled assessments to completely engage students and reinforce learning.

MyPsychLab is designed with instructor flexibility in mind—you decide the extent of integration into your course—from independent self-assessment for students tracked in a gradebook to total instructor-driven course management. By transferring faculty members' most time-consuming tasks—content delivery, student assessment, and grading—to automated tools, *MyPsychLab* enables faculty to spend more quality time with students. Instructors are provided with the results of student diagnostic tests in a gradebook and can view performance of individual students or an aggregate report of their class. Instructors can access the remediation activities students receive within their customized study plans, and can also link to extra lecture notes, video clips, and activities that reflect the content areas their class is struggling with. Instructors can bring into these resources to class, or easily post them on-line for students to access. For sample syllabi with ideas on incorporating *MyPsychLab*, see www.mypsychlab.com.

With the sixth edition of *Psychology: Core Concepts* comes a new generation of *MyPsychLab*, with dozens of of improvements and new features that make *MyPsychLab* both more powerful and easier to use. Some highlights of the new *MyPsychLab* course include:

- New *peerScholar* On-Line Peer Grading (available only in the course management version of *MyPsychLab*): Class-tested for five years at the Psychology Department of the University of Toronto, with over 8000 students participating so far, peerScholar is an elegant peer-grading system that enables instructors to implement writing assignments into even large classroom settings and that encourages the students to reassess and think critically about their own work.

- A new, more flexible, powerful, and intuitive platform for the course management version of *MyPsychLab*.
- A redesigned *e-book* that gives students the option to highlight passages and access media content directly from the e-book page.
- A new interactive *Timeline* tool that vividly illustrates key dates in the history of psychology through text, audio, and video.
- A new *Survey* tool that allows instructors to poll students anonymously.
- Redesigned *Flash Cards* for reviewing key terms, with audio to help students with pronunciation of difficult terminology.
- A new *Podcasting* tool that allows instructors to quickly and easily create their own Podcasts.
- Dozens of new video clips, animations, and podcasts, including footage of classic experiments in psychology from Pennsylvania State Media, edited by Dennis Thompson, Georgia State University.
- Continued improvements to design, course content, and grading system based on direct customer feedback

Please contact your local Pearson representative for more information on MyPsychLab. For technical support for any of your Pearson products, you and your students can contact http://247.pearsoned.com.

Pearson Teaching Films Introductory Psychology Video Library with Annual Updates (Five DVD Set ISBN: 0-13-175432-7 / Update DVD for 2008 ISBN: 0-205-65280-8) This multi-DVD set of videos offers qualified adopters over 100 short video clips of 5 to 15 minutes in length, organized by course topic for easy lecture integration. Videos come from many of the most popular video sources for psychology content, such as ABCNews, the Films for the Humanities series, ScienCentral, as well as videos from the Pearson video library. Additional videos will be added to the library on an annual basis.

Discovering Psychology **Telecourse Videos** Written, designed, and hosted by Phil Zimbardo and produced by WGBH Boston in partnership with Annenberg Media, this perfect complement to *Psychology: Core Concepts. Discovering Psychology* is a landmark educational resource that reveals psychology's contribution not only to understanding the puzzles of behavior but also to identifying solutions and treatments to ease the problems of mental disorders. The video series has won numerous prizes and is widely used in the United States and internationally. The complete set of 26 half-hour videos is available for purchase (DVD or VHS format) from Annenberg Media. The videos are also available online in a streaming format that is free (www.learner.org), and, for the convenience of instructors and students using *Psychology: Core Concepts*, links to these online videos have been included in the *MyPsychLab* program that accompanies the textbook. A student Viewing Guide is found at the end of every chapter within *Psychology: Core Concepts*, with additional Viewing Guide resources also available online within *MyPsychLab*.

Discovering Psychology **Telecourse Faculty Guide (ISBN: 0-205-69929-4)** The Telecourse Faculty Guide provides guidelines for using *Discovering Psychology* as a resource within your course. Keyed directly to *Psychology: Core Concepts*, the faculty guide includes the complete Telecourse Study Guide plus suggested activities; suggested essays; cited studies; instructional resources, including books, articles, films, and websites; video program test questions with answer key; and a key term glossary. Test questions for *Discovering Psychology* also reappear in the textbook's test bank and MyTest computerized test bank.

The Allyn & Bacon Introduction to Psychology Transparency Set (ISBN: 0-205-39862-6) This set of approximately 200 full-color transparencies is available upon adoption of the text from your local Allyn & Bacon sales representative.

Grade Aid Study Guide (ISBN: 0-205-58217-6) This robust study guide, written by Jane P. Sheldon, Ph.D., University of Michigan-Dearborn, is filled with guided activities and in-depth exercises to promote student learning. Each chapter includes worksheets that give you a head start on in-class note taking; a full list of key terms with page references; a collection of demonstrations, activities, and exercises, and three short practice quizzes; and one comprehensive chapter exam with critical thinking essay questions and concept maps to help you study for your quizzes and exams. The appendix includes answers to all of the practice activities, tests, and concept maps.

A NOTE OF THANKS

Nobody ever realizes the magnitude of the task when taking on a textbook-writing project. Stephen Frail, our Acquisitions Editor, deftly guided (and prodded) us through this process. The vision of the sixth edition confronted reality under the guidance of Julie Swasey and Deb Hanlon, our tenacious Developmental Editors, who made us work harder that we had believed possible. Associate Editor Angela Pickard managed our spectacular ancillaries package.

The job of making the manuscript into a book fell to Roberta Sherman, our Production Manager, Lynda Griffiths, our Project Manager, and Margaret Pinette, our puckish copyeditor. We think they did an outstanding job—as did our tireless photo researcher, the tenacious Kate Cebik.

We are sure that none of the above would be offended if we reserve our deepest thanks for our spouses, closest colleagues, and friends who inspired us, gave us the caring support we needed, and served as sounding-boards for our ideas. Phil thanks his wonderful wife, Christina Maslach, for her endless inspiration and for modeling what is best in academic psychology. He has recently passed a milestone of 50 years of teaching the introductory psychology course, from seminar size to huge lectures to more than 1000 students. Phil continues to give lectures and colloquia to college and high school groups throughout the country and overseas. He still gets a rush from lecturing and from turning students on to the joys and fascination of psychology.

Bob is grateful to his spouse and best friend, Michelle, who has for years put up with his rants on topics psychological, his undone household chores, and much gratification delayed—mostly without complaint. She has been a wellspring of understanding and loving support and the most helpful of reviewers. His thanks, too, go to Rebecca, their daughter, who has taught him the practical side of developmental psychology—and now, much to her own astonishment, possesses her own graduate degree in psychology. In addition, he is indebted to Mary Bagshaw, Linda Denney, Emerson Hall, Claudia Johnson, Cheryl Okonek, and (again) Michelle, none of whom are psychologists but who were nevertheless always eager to raise and debate interesting issues about the applications of psychology to everyday life. Readers will find topics they have raised throughout the book and especially in the chapter-opening "problems" and in the critical thinking sections at the end of each chapter.

Both Phil and Bob welcome their new coauthor, Vivian McCann, to the project. Vivian brings not only the perspective of a teacher but also expertise on gender and culture issues. She has also brought a strong emphasis on critical thinking to this sixth edition of *Psychology: Core Concepts.*

Vivian's thanks go first to her family, starting with her amazing husband and best friend Shawn, who has not only been a wonderful source of love and support, but who even hung in there when she had to edit a chapter while on their honeymoon! Her stepsons Storm and Blaze never complained about the missed baseball games or family time, and found creative ways to amuse themselves during some long weekends of writing. She also thanks her father for encouraging her love of learning from her earliest years, and for being a role model of resilience, optimism, and grace. And finally, Vivian thanks the many students who have inspired and challenged her over the years, as well as her dear friend and colleague Lauren Kuhn, who continues to serve as a model of excellence, creativity, and humanity in teaching.

M any experts and teachers of introductory psychology also shared their constructive criticism with us on every chapter and feature of the sixth edition of this text:

Susan Cloninger, The Sage Colleges

Lenore Frigo, Shasta College

Jonathan Grimes, Community College of Baltimore County

Karen Hayes, Guilford College

Deana Julka, University of Portland

Jean Mandernach, University of Nebraska, Kearney

Laura O'Sullivan, Florida Gulf Coast University

Mary Ellen Dello Stritto, Western Oregon University

Alan Whitlock, University of Idaho

W e also thank the reviewers of the previous editions of *Psychology: Core Concepts* and hope that they will recognize their valued input in all that is good in this text:

Gordon Allen, Miami University

Beth Barton, Coastal Carolina Community College

Linda Bastone, Purchase College, SUNY

Susan Beck, Wallace State College

Michael Bloch, University of San Francisco

Michele Breault, Truman State University

John H. Brennecke, Mount San Antonio College

T. L. Brink, Crafton Hills College

Jay Brown, Southwest Missouri State University

Sally S. Carr, Lakeland Community College

Saundra Ciccarelli, Gulf Coast Community College

Wanda Clark, South Plains College

John Conklin, Camosun College (Canada)

Michelle L. Pilati Corselli (Rio Hondo College)

Sara DeHart-Young, Mississippi State University

Janet DiPietro, John Hopkins University

Diane Finley, Prince George's Community College

Krista Forrest, University of Nebraska at Kearney

Rick Froman, John Brown University

Arthur Gonchar, University of LaVerne

Peter Gram, Pensacola Junior College

Lynn Haller, Morehead State University

Mary Elizabeth Hannah, University of Detroit

Jack Hartnett, Virginia Commonwealth University

Carol Hayes, Delta State University

Michael Hillard, Albuquerque TVI Community College

Peter Hornby, Plattsburgh State University

Brian Kelley, Bridgewater College

Sheila Kennison, Oklahoma State University

Laurel Krautwurst, Blue Ridge Community College

Judith Levine, Farmingdale State College

Dawn Lewis, Prince George's Community College

Deborah Long, East Carolina University

Margaret Lynch, San Francisco State University

Marc Martin, Palm Beach Community College

Richard Mascolo, El Camino College

Steven Meier, University of Idaho

Nancy Mellucci, Los Angeles Community College District

Yozan Dirk Mosig, University of Nebraska

Melinda Myers-Johnson, Humboldt State University

Michael Nikolakis, Faulkner State College

Cindy Nordstrom, Southern Illinois University

Ginger Osborne, Santa Ana College

Vernon Padgett, Rio Hondo College

Jeff Pedroza, Santa Ana College

Laura Phelan, St. John Fisher College

Faye Plascak-Craig, Marian College

Skip Pollock, Mesa Community College

Chris Robin, Madisonville Community College

Lynne Schmelter-Davis, Brookdale County College of Monmouth

Mark Shellhammer, Fairmont State College

Christina Sinisi, Charleston Southern University

Patricia Stephenson, Miami Dade College

Mario Sussman, Indiana University of Pennsylvania

John Teske, Elizabethtown College

Stacy Walker, Kingwood College

Robert Wellman, Fitchburg State University

Finally, we offer our thanks to all of the colleagues whose feedback has improved our book. Thanks also to all instructors of this most-difficult-to-teach course for taking on the pedagogical challenge and conveying to students their passion about the joys and relevance of psychological science and practice.

If you have any recommendations of your own that we should not overlook for the next edition, please write to us! Address your comments to Dr. Robert Johnson, bjohnson@dcwisp.net.

about the authors

Philip Zimbardo, Ph.D., Stanford University professor, has been teaching the Introductory Psychology course for 50 years and has been writing the basic text for this course, as well as the Faculty Guides and Student Workbooks, for the past 35 years. In addition, he has helped to develop and update the PBS-TV series, *Discovering Psychology,* that is used in many high school and university courses both nationally and internationally. He has been called "The Face and Voice of Psychology" because of this popular series and his other media presentations. Phil also loves to conduct and publish research on a wide variety of subjects, as well as teach and engage in public and social service activities. He has published more than 300 professional and popular articles and chapters and 50 books of all kinds. He recently published a trade book on the psychology of evil, *The Lucifer Effect,* that relates his classic Stanford Prison Experiment to the abuses at Iraq's Abu Ghraib Prison. His new projects include the Time Paradox and the psychology of ordinary heroes. Please see these websites for more information: www.zimbardo.com, www.prisonexp.org, www.PsychologyMatters.org, and www.theTimeParadox.com.

Robert Johnson, Ph.D, taught introductory psychology for 28 years at Umpqua Community College. He is especially interested in applying psychological principles to the teaching of psychology and in encouraging linkages between psychology and other disciplines. In keeping with those interests, Bob founded the Pacific Northwest Great Teachers Seminar, of which he was the director for 20 years. He was also one of the founders of Psychology Teachers at Community Colleges (PT@CC), serving as its executive committee chair during 2004. That same year he also received the Two-Year College Teaching Award given by the Society for the Teaching of Psychology. Bob has long been active in APA, APS, the Western Psychological Association, and the Council of Teachers of Undergraduate Psychology.

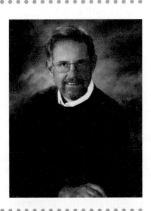

Vivian McCann, a senior faculty member in psychology at Portland Community College in Portland, Oregon, teaches a wide variety of courses, including introductory psychology, human relations, intimate relationships, and social psychology. Born and raised in the California desert just 10 miles from the Mexican border, she learned early on the importance of understanding cultural backgrounds and values in effective communication and in teaching, which laid the foundation for her current interest in teaching and learning psychology from diverse cultural perspectives. She loves to travel and learn about people and cultures, and to nurture the same passions in her students. She has led groups of students on three trips abroad, and in her own travels has visited 20 countries so far. Vivian maintains a strong commitment to teaching excellence, and has developed and taught numerous workshops in that area. She currently serves on the APA's Committee for Psychology Teachers at Community Colleges (PT@CC), and is an active member of the Western Psychological Association and APS. She is also the author of *Human Relations: The Art and Science of Building Effective Relationships.*

Critical Thinking Applied **Facilitated Communication**

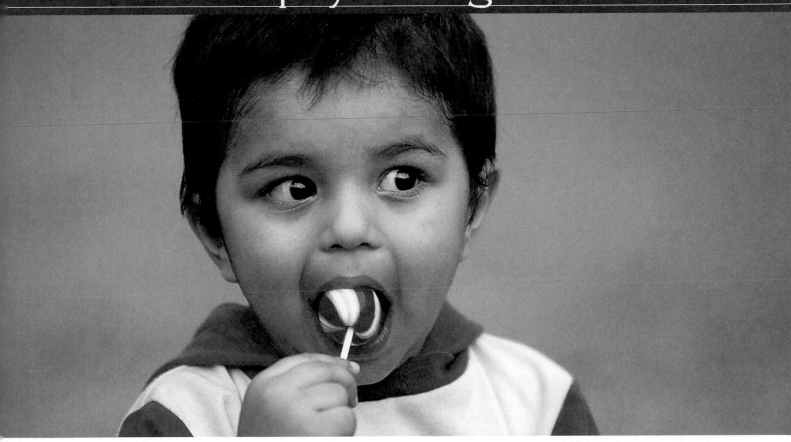

chapter 1

mind, behavior, and psychological science

"After the kids had all that sugar—the cake, ice cream, punch, and candy—they were absolutely bouncing off the walls!" said one of our friends who was describing the recent birthday party for her 8-year-old daughter.

I must have had a skeptical look on my face, because she stopped her story short and asked, "You don't believe it?" Then she added, "You psychologists just don't believe in common sense, do you?"

I responded that what people think of as "common sense" can be wrong, reminding her that common sense once held that Earth was flat. "Perhaps," I suggested, "it might be wrong again—this time about the so-called sugar high that people think they observe."

"It could have been just the excitement of the party," I added.

"*Think* they observe?" my friend practically shouted. "Can you *prove* that sugar doesn't make children hyperactive?"

3

"No," I said. Science doesn't work that way. "But what I *could* do," I ventured, "is perform an experiment to test the idea that sugar makes children 'hyper.' Then we could see whether your claim passes or fails the test."

My timing wasn't the best for getting her involved in a discussion of scientific experiments, so let me pose the problem to you.

—RJ

PROBLEM: How would you test the claim that sugar makes children hyperactive?

We invite you to think how we might set up such an experiment. We could, for example, give kids a high-sugar drink and see what happens. But because people often see only what they expect to see, our expectations about sugar and hyperactivity could easily influence our observations. So, how could we design an experiment on the sugar problem that also accounts for our expectations? It is not an easy problem, but we will think it through together in this chapter.

Every chapter in the book will begin with a problem such as this—a problem aimed at getting you actively involved in learning psychology and thinking critically about some important concept in the chapter. Thinking these issues through with us, rather than just passively reading the words, will also help you develop a *schema* (a mental framework) that will make each of these concepts more meaningful and more easily remembered.

The important concept illustrated by the "sugar high" problem in this chapter is one of the most fundamental concepts in all of psychology: using the *scientific method* to explore the mind and behavior. But before we get into the nitty and gritty of the scientific method, let's be more specific about what we mean by the term *psychology* itself.

1.1 KEY QUESTION
WHAT IS PSYCHOLOGY—AND WHAT IS IT *NOT?*

"I hope you won't psychoanalyze me," says the student at the office door. It is a frequent refrain, and an occupational hazard for professors of psychology. But students need not worry about being psychoanalyzed—for two reasons. First, not all psychologists are trained to diagnose and treat mental problems, and they are in the minority among professors of psychology. Second, only a few psychologists are actually *psychoanalysts*. The term *psychoanalysis* refers to a highly specialized and not-very-common form of therapy. You will learn more about the distinction between psychologists and psychoanalysts later in the chapter—but, in the meantime, don't fret that your professor will try to find something wrong with you. In fact, your professor is much more likely to be interested in helping you learn the material than in looking for signs of psychological disorder.

So, you might wonder, if psychology is not all about mental disorders and therapy, what *is* it all about?

The term **psychology** comes from *psyche*, the ancient Greek word for "mind," and the suffix *-ology*, meaning "a field of study." Literally, then, *psychology* means "the study of the mind." Most psychologists, however, use the broader definition given in our Core Concept for this section of the chapter:

Psychology The science of behavior and mental processes.

core concept

Psychology is a broad field, with many specialties, but fundamentally psychology is the science of behavior and mental processes.

One important point to note about this definition: Psychology includes not only *mental processes* but *behaviors*. In other words, psychology's domain covers both the *internal* mental processes that we can observe only indirectly (such as thinking, feeling, and desiring) and *external,* observable behaviors (such as talking, smiling, and running). A second important part of our definition concerns the *scientific* component of psychology. In brief, the science of psychology is based on objective, verifiable evidence—not just the opinions of experts and authorities, as we often find in nonscientific fields. A more complete explanation of what we mean by "the science of psychology" will occupy the second part of this chapter.

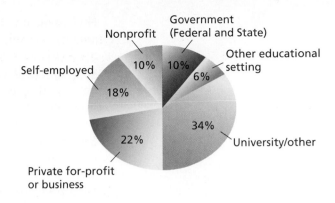

FIGURE 1.1
Work Settings of Psychologists

(*Source:* Updated information from *Employed Doctoral Scientists and Engineers, by Sector of Employment, Broad Field of Doctorate and Sex: 2001,* National Science Foundation.)

Psychology: It's More than You Think

Psychology covers more territory than most people realize. As we have seen, not all psychologists are therapists. Some work in education, industry, sports, prisons, government, churches and temples, private practice, and in the psychology departments of colleges and universities. (See Figure 1.1.) Other psychologists work for engineering firms, consulting firms, and the courts (both the judicial and the NBA variety). In these diverse settings, they perform a wide range of tasks, including teaching, research, assessment, and equipment design—as well as psychotherapy. In fact, psychology's specialties are too numerous to cover them all here, but we can give you the flavor of the field's diversity by first dividing psychology into three broad categories.

Three Ways of Doing Psychology   Broadly speaking, psychologists cluster into three main categories: *experimental psychologists, teachers of psychology,* and *applied psychologists.* Some overlap exists among these groups, however, because many psychologists take on multiple roles in their work.

Experimental psychologists (sometimes called *research psychologists*) constitute the smallest of the three groups. Nevertheless, they perform most of the research that creates new psychological knowledge (Frincke & Pate, 2004). While some experimental psychologists can be found in industry or in private research institutes, the majority work at a college or university, where most also teach.

Teachers of psychology are traditionally found at colleges and universities, where their assignments most often involve not only teaching but research and publication. Increasingly, however, psychologists can be found at community colleges and high schools, where their teaching load is higher because these institutions generally do not require research (American Psychological Association, 2007b; Johnson & Rudmann, 2004).

Applied psychologists use the knowledge developed by experimental psychologists to tackle human problems, such as equipment design, personnel selection, and psychological treatment. They work in a wide variety of places, such as schools, clinics, factories, social service agencies, airports, hospitals, and casinos. All told, some 64 percent of the doctoral-level psychologists in the United States work primarily as applied psychologists, and that percentage has been steadily increasing since the 1950s (Kohout & Wicherski, 2000).

Applied Psychological Specialties   Some of the most popular applied specialties include:

- *Industrial and organizational psychologists* (often called *I/O psychologists*) specialize in personnel selection and in tailoring the work

Experimental psychologists
Psychologists who do research on basic psychological processes—as contrasted with applied psychologists; also called research psychologists.

Teachers of psychology   Psychologists whose primary job is teaching, typically in high schools, colleges, and universities.

Applied psychologists   Psychologists who use the knowledge developed by experimental psychologists to solve human problems.

environment to maximize productivity and morale. Some I/O psychologists also develop programs to train and retain employees; others may do market research.

- *Sports psychologists,* as you might expect, work with athletes to help them improve their performance by planning practice sessions, enhancing motivation, and learning to control emotions under pressure. Many major sports franchises have sports psychologists on staff.

- *Engineering psychologists* work at the interface between people and equipment. Some design airplane instrument displays or control panels, for easy and reliable human use. Some do psychological detective work to discover what went wrong in accidents attributed to "human error." Others may consult with architects or road builders to design conditions that will optimize traffic flow. Engineering psychologists usually work in private industry or in government—often on a team with other scientists.

- *School psychologists* have expertise in the problems of teaching and learning. Most school psychologists work for a school district, where they spend a good deal of time administering, scoring, and interpreting psychological tests. They also may diagnose learning and behavior problems and consult with teachers, students, and parents.

- *Rehabilitation psychologists* work with physicians, nurses, counselors, and social workers on teams that may treat patients having both physical and mental disorders, such as stroke, spinal cord injury, alcoholism, drug abuse, or amputation. Some work in a hospital setting. Others work for social service agencies and for sheltered workshops that provide job training for people with disabilities.

CONNECTION • CHAPTER 13

Clinical and counseling psychologists help people deal with mental disorders and other psychological problems.

- *Clinical psychologists* and *counseling psychologists* provide services for people having problems with social and emotional adjustment or those facing difficult choices in relationships, careers, or education. About half of all doctoral-level psychologists list clinical or counseling psychology as their specialty (American Psychological Association, 2003b). Clinicians are more likely to have a private practice involving psychological testing and long-term therapy, while counseling psychologists are more likely to work for an agency or school and to spend fewer sessions with each client.

More information on the career possibilities in psychology can be found in *Careers in Psychology for the Twenty-First Century,* published by the American Psychological Association (2003a).

Psychiatry A medical specialty dealing with the diagnosis and treatment of mental disorders.

Psychology Is Not Psychiatry

Just as beginning psychology students may think that all psychologists are clinical psychologists, they may not know the distinction between *psychology* and *psychiatry.* So let's clear up that confusion— just in case you encounter a test question on the topic.

Virtually all psychiatrists, but only some psychologists, treat mental disorders—and there the resemblance ends. **Psychiatry** is a medical specialty, not a part of psychology at all. Psychiatrists hold MD (Doctor of Medicine) degrees and, in addition, have specialized training in the treatment of mental and behavioral problems, typically with drugs. Therefore, psychiatrists are licensed to prescribe medicines and to perform other medical procedures. Consequently, psychiatrists tend to view patients from a *medical* perspective, as persons with mental "diseases."

By contrast, psychology is a much broader field that encompasses the whole range of human behavior and mental processes, from brain

Applying psychological principles of learning and motivation, sports psychologists work with athletes to improve performance.

function to social interaction and from mental well-being to mental disorder. For most psychologists, graduate training emphasizes research methods, along with advanced study in a specialty such as those listed earlier. Moreover, while psychologists usually hold doctoral degrees, their training usually is not *medical* training, although an exception involves a few clinical psychologists who have recently, under new laws in a handful of states, acquired the medical qualifications for prescribing drugs specifically for psychological problems. Most states, however, have yet to open the door to prescription privileges for psychologists (Holloway, 2004a,b; Practice Directorate Staff, 2005).[1]

So, now you know that psychiatry is not psychology. Now let's look at something else that often gets confused with psychology: *pseudopsychology*.

Fortune tellers, astrologers, and other practitioners of pseudopsychology don't bother to verify their claims with careful research—nor do their clients engage in critical thinking about such practices.

PSYCHOLOGYMATTERS
Thinking Critically about Psychology and Pseudopsychology

The TV series *Sci Fi Investigates* continues a long tradition that also included such programs as *The X Files* and *Unsolved Mysteries*. All have played on people's fascination with the fantastic and the paranormal—especially claims of mysterious powers of the mind and supernatural influences on our personalities. So does the horoscope in your daily newspaper. Never mind that astrology has been thoroughly debunked (Schick & Vaughn, 2001). The same goes for the supposed power of the full moon to encourage crime and mental disorder (Berman, 2003). Nor is there any factual basis for graphology (the bogus science of handwriting analysis), fortune telling, or the purported power of subliminal messages to make us buy products or vote for certain politicians. All these fall under the heading of **pseudopsychology**: unsupported psychological beliefs masquerading as scientific truth.

Certainly horoscopes and paranormal claims can be fun as pure entertainment, but it is important to keep pseudopsychology in perspective. Thus, one of the goals we have for this text is to help you *think critically* about extraordinary claims made about behavior and mental processes.

What Is Critical Thinking?   Those who talk about "critical thinking" often find themselves in the position of Supreme Court Justice Potter Stewart, who famously was unable to define *pornography* but concluded, "I know it when I see it." Like Justice Stewart, your fearless authors (Phil, Bob, and Vivian) cannot offer a definition of critical thinking with which everyone will agree. Nevertheless, we are willing to jump into the fray with a list of the six **critical thinking skills** that we wish to emphasize in this book. Each is based on a question that we believe should be asked when confronting new ideas.

1. *What Is the Source?*   Does the person making the claim have real expertise in the field? Suppose, for example, that you hear a newscast on which a politician or pundit declares that juvenile lawbreakers can be "scared straight" by a program in which they receive near-abusive treatment by felons who try to scare them away from a delinquent lifestyle with tales of the harsh life in prison. Such programs have, in fact, been tried in several states (Finckenauer et al., 1999). The first thing to ask is whether the person making the claim has

Pseudopsychology   Erroneous assertions or practices set forth as being scientific psychology.

Critical thinking skills   This book emphasizes six critical thinking skills, based on the following questions: What is the source? Is the claim reasonable or extreme? What's the evidence? Could bias contaminate the conclusion? Could the reasoning avoid common fallacies? Does the issue require multiple perspectives?

---

[1]Throughout this book you will find that we use brief citations in parentheses, calling your attention to a complete bibliographic reference found in the "References" section, beginning on p. R-1, near the end of this book. These brief in-text citations give the authors' last names and the publication date. With the complete references in hand, your library can help you find the original source.

any real knowledge of corrections—or, at the very least, has sought the counsel of someone with the necessary expertise.

Additionally, one should ask whether the source has something substantial to gain from the claim. If it's a medical breakthrough, does the claimant stand to make money from a new drug or medical device? In the case of a "scared straight" program, is the source trying to score political points?

2. *Is the Claim Reasonable or Extreme?* Life is too short to be critical of everything, of course, so the trick is to be selective. How? Critical thinkers are skeptical of claims touted as "breakthroughs" or "revolutionary." Likewise, claims that conflict with well-established knowledge should raise a red flag. In the case of "scared straight" programs—or any other quick fix for a difficult problem—one should be wary because simple solutions to complex problems rarely exist.

3. *What's the Evidence?* As the famous astronomer Carl Sagan once said about reports of people being abducted by aliens, "Extraordinary claims require extraordinary evidence" (Nova Online, 1996). Returning to our "scared straight" example, we should ask: Is there extraordinary evidence supporting the "scared straight" approach? Often those touting a new program will offer anecdotes and testimonials suggesting that the program has had a dramatic effect. Critical thinkers, though, know that testimonials and anecdotes, no matter how compelling, are not *evidence*. They merely represent the experiences of some individuals. But it would be risky to assume that what seems true for some people must also be true for everyone. To know for sure, scientific studies must be conducted. In fact, studies have shown not only that "scared straight" programs do not work but that they may actually inoculate juveniles against fears about prison. Surprising as it may seem, the hard evidence suggests that juveniles exposed to such treatments, on the average, subsequently get in *more* trouble than do those not given the "scared straight" treatment (Petrosino, Turpin-Petrosino, & Buehler, 2003).

4. *Could Bias Contaminate the Conclusion?* Critical thinkers know the conditions under which biases are likely to occur, and they are able to recognize common types of bias that we will examine in this chapter. For example, they would question whether medical researchers who are involved in assessing new drugs can be unbiased if they are receiving money from the companies whose drugs they are testing (McCook, 2006).

The form of bias most applicable to our "scared straight" example is **emotional bias:** People not only fear crime and criminals, but they are often in favor of harsh treatments for criminal behavior, as we can see in the spate of "three strikes" laws passed by state legislators in recent years. Accordingly, the "scared straight" approach may appeal to people simply because of its presumed harshness, rather than because it works.

Another especially common form of bias is **confirmation bias,** the all-too-human tendency to remember events that confirm our beliefs and ignore contradictory evidence (Halpern, 2002; Nickerson, 1998). Confirmation bias explains why believers in astrology remember the predictions that seemed accurate and forget about the ones that missed the mark. Confirmation bias also explains why gamblers have better recollections for the times they won than for those when they lost. And here's one more example: In an amazing brain-scan study done just before a recent presidential election, people with strong political opinions listened to contradictory statements made by one of their favorite politicians. When they did so, the brain circuits associated with reasoning suddenly shut down, while those parts of the brain most involved with emotion remained active (Shermer, 2006; Westen et al., 2006). It was as though the brain was saying, "I don't want to hear anything that conflicts with my beliefs." This brain-scan study, then, offers strong evidence that the

Emotional bias The tendency to make judgments based on attitudes and feelings, rather than on the basis of a rational analysis of the evidence.

Confirmation bias The tendency to attend to evidence that complements and confirms our beliefs or expectations, while ignoring evidence that does not.

brain itself can physically switch into a "confirmation bias mode," when it confronts contradictory evidence.

5. *Does the Reasoning Avoid Common Fallacies?* We will study several common logical fallacies in this book, but the one most applicable to the "scared straight" example is the assumption that "common sense" is a substitute for data. No matter how sensible the program may sound, there is no substitute for gathering some objective evidence.

6. *Does the Issue Require Multiple Perspectives?* The "scared straight" intervention makes the simplistic assumptions that (a) fear of punishment is the major deterrent to delinquency and (b) delinquent youth will respond positively to realistic threats of punishment. A more sophisticated view sees delinquency as a complex problem that demands scrutiny from several perspectives. Psychologists, for example, may look at delinquency from the standpoints of learning, social influence, or personality traits. Economists would be interested in the financial incentives for delinquency. And sociologists would focus on such things as gangs, poverty, and community structures. Surely such a multifaceted problem will require a more complex solution than a scary program.

Harmful Effects of Pseudopsychology But, you might ask, what's the big deal if people want to believe in pseudopsychological claims? Let's look at a few serious problems that such *un*critical thinking can cause.

In 1949, the Nobel Prize in medicine went to the inventor of the "lobotomy," a crude brain operation that disconnected the frontal lobes from the rest of the brain. The procedure had no careful scientific basis, yet it became popular because people who *wanted* it to work didn't ask critical questions. Originally intended as a treatment for severe mental disorders, the operation led instead to thousands of permanently brain-injured patients. Only after drugs for psychiatric disorders came into wide use in the 1950s did most of the world recognize the folly in this procedure.

For a modern example of pseudopsychology's harmful effects, we offer the widespread belief that positive thoughts can cure dire diseases, such as cancer. What could possibly be wrong with that idea? For one thing, the evidence doesn't support the notion that a person's state of mind affects the chances of recovery from a serious physical illness (Cassileth et al., 1985; Coyne et al., 2007). For another, the attitude-can-make-you-well belief can lead to blaming patients who do not get well for not having an attitude that was sufficiently optimistic (Angell, 1985; Becker, 1993).

Yet, countering pseudopsychological beliefs is not easy—and can even be dangerous. To see why, we have only to look back a few decades in parts of the United States, where a person who dared to question the widespread belief in the inferiority of African Americans risked being beaten, jailed, or lynched. Even today, in many regions of the world, posing critical questions about the status of women or ethnic prejudices can carry dire consequences.

In this book we will take a less dangerous approach—but still one that we hope will be productive. We will emphasize critical thinking in two ways. One involves the "problem" presented at the beginning of each chapter: For its solution, each of these problems will require both the critical thinking skills we have just described and some new knowledge to be developed in the chapter. The second way we will encourage you to think critically involves a special section at the end of every chapter, where we will model the critical thinking process as we consider a "hot button" issue related to the material in the chapter. If you disagree or have evidence that you think we should consider on one of these issues, we urge you to contact us and give us your critical take on the matter.

Now, let's put a sampling of your psychological beliefs to the test. Some of the following statements are true, and some are false. Don't worry if you get a few—or all—of the items wrong: You will have lots of company. The point is that what so-called common sense teaches us about psychological processes may not withstand the scrutiny of a scientific test. Mark each of the following statements as "true" or "false." (The answers are given at the end.)

1. _____ It is a myth that most people use only about 10% of their brains.

2. _____ During your most vivid dreams, your body may be paralyzed.

3. _____ Psychological stress can cause physical illness.

4. _____ The color red exists only as a sensation in the brain. There is no "red" in the world outside the brain.

5. _____ Bipolar (manic–depressive) disorder is caused by a conflict in the unconscious mind.

6. _____ The newborn child's mind is essentially a "blank slate" on which everything he or she will know must be "written" (learned) by experience.

7. _____ Everything that happens to us leaves a permanent record in memory.

8. _____ You were born with all the brain cells that you will ever have.

9. _____ Intelligence is a nearly pure genetic trait that is fixed at the same level throughout a person's life.

10. _____ Polygraph ("lie detector") devices are remarkably accurate in detecting physical responses that, in the eye of a trained examiner, reliably indicate when a suspect is lying.

Answers The first four items are true; the rest are false. Here are some brief explanations for each item; you will find more detail in the chapters indicated in parentheses. **1.** True: This is a myth. We use all parts of our brains every day. (See Chapter 2, "Biopsychology, Neuroscience, and Human Nature.") **2.** True: During our most vivid dreams, which occur during rapid eye movement sleep (REM), the voluntary muscles in our body are paralyzed, with the exception of those controlling our eyes. (See Chapter 8, "States of Consciousness.") **3.** True: The link between mind and body can make you sick when you are under chronic stress. (See Chapter 14, "Stress, Health, and Positive Psychology.") **4.** True: Strange as it may seem, all sensations of color are created in the brain itself. Light waves do have different frequencies, but they have no color. The brain interprets the various frequencies of light as different colors. (See Chapter 7, "Sensation and Perception.") **5.** False: There is no evidence at all that unconscious conflicts play a role in bipolar disorder. Instead, the evidence suggests a strong biochemical component. The disorder usually responds well to certain drugs, hinting that it involves faulty brain chemistry. Research also suggests that this faulty chemistry may have a genetic basis. (See Chapter 12, "Psychological Disorders," and Chapter 13, "Therapies for Psychological Disorders.") **6.** False: Far from being a "blank slate," the newborn child has a large repertoire of built-in abilities and protective reflexes. The "blank slate" myth also ignores the child's genetic potential. (See Chapter 6, "Psychological Development.") **7.** False: Although many details of our lives are remembered, there is no evidence that memory records all the details of our lives. In fact, we have good reason to believe that most of the information around us never reaches memory and that what does reach memory often becomes distorted. (See Chapter 4, "Memory.") **8.** False: Contrary to what scientists thought just a few years ago, some parts of the brain continue to create new cells throughout life. (See Chapter 2, "Biopsychology, Neuroscience, and Human Nature.") **9.** False: Intelligence is the result of both heredity and environment. Because it depends, in part, on environment, your level of intelligence (as measured by an IQ test) can change throughout your life. (See Chapter 5, "Thinking and Intelligence.") **10.** False: Even the most expert polygrapher can incorrectly classify a truth-teller as a liar or fail to identify someone who is lying. Objective evidence supporting the accuracy of lie detectors is meager. (See Chapter 9, "Emotion and Motivation.")

CheckYourUnderstanding

1. **RECALL:** In what way is modern psychology's scope broader than the Greek concept of *psyche*?

2. **RECALL:** Name two types of *applied* psychologists.

3. **RECALL:** Why is the notion that the full moon encourages crime and mental disorder an example of pseudopsychology?

4. **APPLICATION:** Which critical thinking questions discussed in this section would be most applicable to the

argument that harsher sentences are the best way of dealing with crime, because "punishment is the only language that criminals understand"?

5. **RECALL:** Give an example of the potentially harmful effects of pseudopsychology.

6. **UNDERSTANDING THE CORE CONCEPT:** How is psychology different from psychiatry and other disciplines that deal with people?

Answers 1. Modern psychology studies behavior, as well as the mind. **2.** There are many sorts of applied psychologists. The ones mentioned in this chapter are I/O psychologists, sports psychologists, engineering psychologists, school psychologists, clinical psychologists, rehabilitation psychologists, and counseling psychologists. **3.** The idea that the moon causes mental disorder is based on anecdote, but it has no scientific basis. The persistence of this belief is also a good illustration of confirmation bias. **4.** Probably the most applicable for this claim would be these: "What is the evidence?" and "Could bias contaminate the conclusion?" But we wouldn't disagree with any of the other critical thinking questions that you may have listed because, just as with the "scared straight" issue, they could all apply to a critical analysis of the claim. **5.** The ones listed in this section were lobotomies, use of "lie detectors," and the belief in the intellectual inferiority or superiority of some races. **6.** Psychology is a broader field, covering all aspects of behavior and mental processes.

HOW DO PSYCHOLOGISTS DEVELOP NEW KNOWLEDGE?

As early as 1880, psychologists were challenging the claims of spiritualists and psychics (Coon, 1992). And today, psychology continues to dispute the unfounded claims of pseudoscience—which seem to blossom far faster than they can be nipped in the bud. Modern sources of such nonsense include astrologers, palm readers, and graphologists, along with an assortment of psychics, seers, and prophets who claim to have special insights into people's personalities and the ability to predict their futures.

So, what makes psychology different from these pseudopsychological approaches to understanding people? Answer: None of them have survived trial by the *scientific method,* which is a way of testing ideas against observations. Instead, pseudopsychology is based on speculation, confirmation bias, anecdote—and on human gullibility.

You might think this a snobbish view for psychologists to take. Why can't we make room for many different ways of understanding people? In fact, we do. Psychologists welcome sociologists, anthropologists, psychiatrists, and other scientists as partners in the enterprise of understanding people. We reject only those approaches that claim to have "evidence" but offer only anecdotes and testimonials.

So, what makes psychology a real science? Again, it's the *method.* As our Core Concept for this section says:

Psychologists, like all other scientists, use the scientific method to test their ideas empirically.

core concept

What is this marvelous method? Simply put, the **scientific method** is a way of putting ideas to an objective pass–fail test. The essential feature of this testing procedure is **empirical investigation,** the collection of objective information by means of careful measurements based on direct experience. Let's unpack this important concept a little more.

Literally, *empirical* means "experience based"—as contrasted with speculation based solely on reason, hope, authority, faith, or "common sense." Investigating a question empirically means collecting evidence carefully and systematically. From these empirical investigations, psychological science ultimately seeks to develop comprehensive explanations for behavior and mental processes. In science we call these explanations *theories,* a commonly misunderstood word.

"It's only a theory," people may say. But to a scientist, *theory* means something special. In brief, a scientific **theory** is a testable explanation for a set of facts or observations (Allen, 1995; Kukla, 1989). Obviously, this definition differs from the way people customarily use the term. In everyday language, *theory* can mean wild speculation or a mere hunch—an idea that has no evidence to support it. But to a scientist, a good theory has two attractive attributes: (a) the power to explain the facts and (b) the ability to be tested. Some theories have a great deal of evidence to support them, while others are highly speculative. Examples of well-supported theories include Einstein's theory of relativity, the germ theory of disease, and Darwin's theory of natural selection. And as you will see throughout this text, psychology has many well-supported theories, too.

Now, to illustrate the scientific method in action, let's return to the problem we posed at the beginning of the chapter: How would you go about testing whether sugar causes hyperactivity in children? As we go through the steps of designing a scientific experiment to answer this question, please remember that there is usually more than one good way to perform an empirical investigation. Your ideas, even if they differ from ours, can be good ones, too, as long as they follow the requirements of good science.

Scientific method   A five-step process for empirical investigation of a hypothesis under conditions designed to control biases and subjective judgments.

Empirical investigation   An approach to research that relies on sensory experience and observation as research data.

Theory   A testable explanation for a set of facts or observations. In science, a theory is not just speculation or a guess.

FIGURE 1.2
Five Steps of the Scientific Method

1. Developing a hypothesis

2. Performing a controlled test

3. Gathering objective data

4. Analyzing the results

5. Publishing, criticizing, and replicating the results

The Five Steps of the Scientific Method

Testing any scientific assertion requires five basic steps that we can illustrate by our experiment on the behavioral effects of sugar. (See Figure 1.2.) All scientists follow essentially the same steps, no matter whether their field is psychology, biology, chemistry, astronomy, or any other scientific pursuit. Thus, it is the *method* that makes these fields scientific, not their subject matter.

Developing a Hypothesis   The scientific method first requires a testable idea, or prediction. Scientists call this prediction a **hypothesis.** The term literally means "little theory" because it often represents only one piece of a larger theoretical explanation. For example, a hypothesis suggesting that introverted people are attracted to extraverted people might be part of a theory tying together all the components of romantic attraction. Alternatively, a hypothesis can just be an interesting idea that piques our curiosity—as in our experiment on the effects of sugar on children.

To be testable, the hypothesis must be potentially *falsifiable*—that is, stated in such a way that it can be shown to be either correct or incorrect. So, if our hypothesis states that sugar causes children to become hyperactive, we could test it by having children consume sugar and then observing any effect on their activity level. If we find none, the hypothesis is falsified. (The hypothesis would *not* be falsifiable if we were merely to state a value judgment—for example, that sugar is "bad" for children.)

Next, the scientist must consider precisely how the hypothesis will be tested, which means specifying all aspects of the experiment in concrete terms called **operational definitions.** This requires that we specify the procedures (operations) to be used in conducting the experiment and measuring the results. The following examples, which could serve as operational definitions for our experiment, will help you understand this important idea.

● *Operational definition of children.*   We can't test all the children in the world, of course. So, our operational definition of "children" might be all the third graders in one class at a nearby elementary school.

Hypothesis   A statement predicting the outcome of a scientific study; a statement describing the relationship among variables in a study.

Operational definitions   Objective descriptions of concepts involved in a scientific study. Operational definitions may restate concepts to be studied in behavioral terms (e.g., fear may be operationally defined as moving away from a stimulus). Operational definitions also specify the procedures used to produce and measure important variables under investigation (e.g., "attraction" may be measured by the amount of time one person spends looking at another).

- *Operational definition of sugar.* Likewise, we could specify what we mean by "sugar" as the amount of sugar in a commercial soft drink. If we decide, for example, to use 7Up as our sugar source, we could operationally define "sugar" as the 38 grams available in one can of 7Up. (Using a noncaffeinated beverage, such as 7Up, avoids the possibly confounding effects of caffeine on the children's behavior.)
- *Operational definition of hyperactive.* This one will be a bit more complicated. Suppose we have observers who will rate each child's behavior on the following 5-point scale:

passive		moderately active		very active
1	2	3	4	5

So, if our experimental design specifies giving some children a sugar-sweetened drink and others the same drink containing artificial sweetener, we can operationally define *hyperactive* as a significantly higher average rating for the group getting the sugared drink.

With our hypothesis and operational definitions in hand, we have taken the first step in our scientific study. But there is more to do: We still need to perform the actual experiment. (The great failing of pseudosciences like astrology or fortune-telling is that they never actually take this step of verifying or rejecting their assertions.)

Performing a Controlled Test To be ethical, our experiment should include only those children whose parents give permission for their participation. So, we might begin by explaining to parents and the teacher the broad outline of the experiment in the following way:

> We propose to examine the supposed effect of sugar on children's activity level. To do so, we have planned a simple study of the children in your child's third-grade classroom—subject to the permission of their parents. The procedure calls for dividing the children into two groups: At lunchtime, one group will be given a commercial soft drink (7Up) sweetened with sugar, while the other group will be given the same drink sweetened with an artificial sweetener (Diet 7Up). The children will not be told to which groups they have been assigned. For the rest of the school day, observers will rate the children's activity level. The ratings should show whether the group receiving the sugar-sweetened drink was more active than the other group. We will share the results with you at the end of the study.

Psychologists use special terms as a shorthand way of referring to the two groups to be compared in an experiment such as ours and to the two different treatment conditions to which they will be exposed. Those receiving the special treatment of interest are said to be in the *experimental condition.* (In our study, the experimental condition involves the high-sugar drink.) Individuals exposed to the experimental condition, then, make up the **experimental group.** Meanwhile, those in the **control group** enter the *control condition,* where they do *not* receive the special treatment. (In our study, the control group will get the artificially sweetened drink.) Thus, the control group serves as a standard against which to compare those in the experimental group. (See Figure 1.3.)

In the most basic experimental design, the researcher varies one factor and holds all the other experimental conditions constant. Scientists call that one variable factor the **independent variable.** (In our experiment, the different amounts of sugar given to the two groups constitute the independent variable.) By manipulating the independent variable in this way, the experimenter can determine whether that factor *causes* any observed effect. You can think of the independent variable as a factor that the experimenter changes *independently* of all the other carefully controlled experimental conditions.

Experimental group Participants in an experiment who are exposed to the treatment of interest.

Control group Participants who are used as a comparison for the experimental group. The control group is not given the special treatment of interest.

Independent variable A stimulus condition so named because the experimenter changes it independently of all the other carefully controlled experimental conditions.

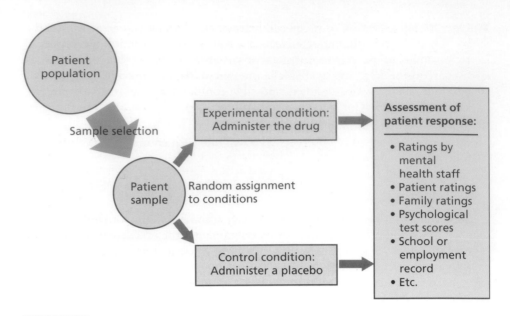

....
FIGURE 1.3
Experimental Groups and Control Groups in a Drug Study

Well-designed experiments often compare the responses of an experimental group and a control group, as in this design for evaluating a new drug.

One more issue to consider in designing and conducting an experiment involves the selection of participants in such a way that the experimental and control groups are essentially the same—except for the experimental treatment they receive. The important thing is that we don't want to mistake some preexisting difference between the two groups for the effects of the independent variable. So, in our study of sugar and activity level, it wouldn't do to put all the girls in one group and all the boys in the other. (Why not? There could be gender differences in their physical reactions to sugar. In addition, one sex might be better than the other at controlling their reactions.) Nor would it be a good idea to have shy children in one group and outgoing children in the other (because the shy children are likely to be less active in the first place). In brief, experimenters must find a way to avoid systematic bias in assigning individuals to the experimental or control group. A good solution involves **random assignment,** where participants are assigned to each group by chance alone. One way to do this would be to list the children alphabetically and then assign alternating names to the experimental and control groups. In this way, chance minimizes any potential differences between the two groups. This, in turn, assures that any differences in activity level are truly due to sugar rather than some other factor.

Gathering Objective Data   In the third step of the scientific method, the scientist collects objective **data:** information gathered by direct observation. In our experiment, the data will consist of the observers' ratings of the children's activity level. Scientists refer to such data as the **dependent variable.** The term comes from the expectation that the responses of participants in an experiment will *depend* directly on the conditions to which they have been exposed. (You might think of the independent variable as the *stimuli* you are studying and the dependent variable as the *responses* made by the participants in your experiment.)

Analyzing the Results and Accepting or Rejecting the Hypothesis   In the fourth step of the scientific method, the researcher examines the results (the data) to see whether the hypothesis survived the test or whether it must be rejected.

Random assignment   A process used to assign individuals to various experimental conditions by chance alone.

Data   Pieces of information, especially information gathered by a researcher to be used in testing a hypothesis. (Singular: datum.)

Dependent variable   The measured outcome of a study; the responses of the subjects in a study.

This step usually requires some special mathematical analysis, particularly if the data require a close call. Statistics can tell the researcher whether the observed results are likely due to the independent variable or merely due to chance. A detailed explanation of statistics lies beyond the scope of this book. In fact, it's a subject for a whole course in itself. But to give you a glimpse of this world, we have provided a brief introduction to statistics in the Appendix, which can be found online.

In our experiment, the statistical analysis will be relatively straightforward, because we merely want to know whether scores for the children receiving sugar are higher than those taking the sugar-free drink. If so, we can declare that our hypothesis has been supported. If not, we will reject the hypothesis.

Publishing, Criticizing, and Replicating the Results   In the final step of the scientific method, researchers find out whether their work can withstand the scrutiny and criticism of the scientific community. To do so, they communicate their results to colleagues by publishing them in a professional journal, making a presentation at a professional meeting, or writing a book. Then the researchers must wait for the critics to respond.

If colleagues find the study interesting and important—and especially if it challenges other research or a widely held theory—the critics may look for flaws in the research design: Did the experimenters choose the participants properly? Were the statistical analyses done correctly? Could other factors account for the results? Alternatively, they may decide to check the study by *replicating* it. To **replicate** the experiment they would redo it, to see whether they would get the same results.

In fact, our study of the effects of sugar on children is a simplified replication of research done previously by Mark Woolraich and his colleagues (1994). Their study lasted three weeks and compared an experimental group of children who ate a high-sugar diet with a control group given a low-sugar diet with artificial sweeteners. Contrary to folk wisdom, the researchers found no differences between the groups in behavior or cognitive (mental) function. So, if our study were to find a "sugar high" effect, it would contradict the Woolraich findings, and you can be sure that it would receive careful scrutiny and criticism.

Criticism also goes on behind the scientific scenes to filter out poorly conceived and executed research prior to publication. Journal editors and book publishers (including the publishers of this book) routinely seek the opinions of expert reviewers. As a result, authors usually receive helpful, if sometimes painful, suggestions for revision. Only when a hypothesis has cleared all these hurdles will editors put it in print and scholars tentatively accept it as scientific "truth."

We should emphasize, however, that scientific findings are always tentative. As long as they stand, they stand in jeopardy from a new study that requires a new interpretation or sends earlier work to the academic scrap heap. Consequently, the results of both our sugar study and the Woolraich sugar study could be eventually replaced by better, more definitive knowledge. Obviously, then, the scientific method is an imperfect system, but it is the best method ever developed for testing ideas about the natural world. As such, it represents one of humankind's greatest intellectual achievements.

Five Types of Psychological Research

We're not out of the scientific woods yet—even though we have covered the basic steps of science's experimental method. We still need to consider other forms that psychological research may take. Aside from *experiments*, scientists do *correlational studies*, *surveys*, *naturalistic observations*, and *case studies*. Each, we will see, has its advantages, limitations, and special applications.

Replicate   In research, this refers to doing a study over to see whether the same results are obtained. As a control for bias, replication is often done by someone other than the researcher who performed the original study.

Experiments   In a well-designed **experiment**, all the conditions that could potentially influence the results come under the researcher's control. Thus, we sought to control the other conditions under which the children were tested in our "sugar" study: By using children in a single classroom and randomly assigning them to the two experimental conditions, we were able to assure that all the variables for both groups were the same—except for the amount of sugar they ingested. This allows us to be confident that the results were due to the effects of sugar, rather than any other factors.

Correlational Studies   Sometimes scientists cannot gain enough control over the situation to allow them to conduct a true experiment. Here's an example: Suppose that you wanted to test the hypothesis that children who ingest lead-based paint (common in older homes, especially in low-income urban housing) run an increased risk of learning disabilities. You couldn't do an experiment to verify this hypothesis. Why? In an experiment you would have to manipulate the independent variable—which would mean giving toxic material to a group of children. Obviously, this would be harmful and unethical.

Fortunately, you can find a way around the problem—but at the expense of some control over the research conditions. The solution takes the form of a **correlational study.** In correlational research you, in effect, look for a "natural experiment" that has already occurred by chance in the world outside the laboratory. So, in a correlational study on the effects of ingesting lead-based paint, you might look for a group of children who had already been exposed to leaded paint. Then, you would compare them to another group who had not been exposed. As a further control, you should try to match the groups so that they are comparable in every conceivable respect (such as age, family income, and gender)—except for their exposure to leaded paint.

The big drawback of a correlational study is that you can never be confident that the groups are really comparable, because you did not randomly assign people to test groups or manipulate the independent variable. In fact, the groups may differ on some important variables (such as access to health care or nutrition) that you may have overlooked. Thus, you cannot say with certainty that the condition of interest was the *cause* of the effects you observed. So, even if you observe more learning disabilities among children who were exposed to lead-based paint, you cannot conclude that exposure to the paint *caused* the disabilities. The most you can say is that lead-based paint is *correlated* or associated with learning disabilities. Scientists often put the general principle this way: *Correlation does not necessarily mean causation.* In fact, confusing correlation with causation is one of the most common critical thinking errors, and is an example of a fallacy in reasoning.

Researchers usually express the degree of correlation as a number known as the *correlation coefficient*, often symbolized in formulas by the letter *r*. The size of the correlation coefficient summarizes the relationship between the two variables: It can range from a negative number (as low as −1.0) to a positive number (as high as +1.0). We won't go into the details of calculating the correlation coefficient here, but any introductory statistics book will tell you how to do it. You can also find more information about correlations in the Appendix online.

The important thing is for you to develop a feeling for what *positive correlation, negative correlation,* and *zero correlation* mean. (See Figure 1.4.) If the variables have *no relationship* at all, their correlation is zero. You would expect a zero correlation between height and GPA, for example. If, however, the two variables show a relationship in which they vary in the same direction (as one variable increases, so does the other) then we say they have a **positive correlation.** An example of a positive correlation is the moderate relationship between SAT scores and college grades (which is approximately +0.4). In other words, as SAT scores increase, grades in college also increase.

Experiment   A kind of research in which the researcher controls all the conditions and directly manipulates the conditions, including the independent variable.

Correlational study   A form of research in which the relationship between variables is studied, but without the experimental manipulation of an independent variable. Correlational studies cannot determine cause-and-effect relationships.

Positive correlation   A correlation coefficient indicating that the variables change simultaneously in the same direction: As one grows larger or smaller, the other grows or shrinks in a parallel way.

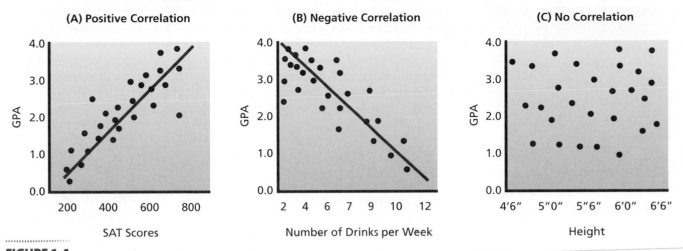

FIGURE 1.4

Three Types of Correlation

The graphs illustrate the three main types of correlation, with data points for 27 individuals. (A) shows a *positive correlation* between SAT scores and GPA; (B) shows a *negative correlation* between alcohol consumption and GPA; and (C) shows *no correlation* between height and GPA.

But when one variable decreases as the other increases, they have a **negative correlation,** and their correlation coefficient would have a negative sign. You would probably find a negative correlation between the amount of alcohol consumed by college students and their grade-point averages (as college students increase their consumption of alcohol, their grade-point averages decrease). In our earlier example, we might have predicted a negative correlation between lead levels in the blood and IQ scores.

It is also important to understand that *a correlation can show a strong relationship even when it is negative.* (*Note:* Professors often ask test questions about this!) Let us suppose that we find a negative correlation of –0.7 between some measure of anxiety and time spent studying. In other words, more anxiety is correlated with less studying. Even though this is a negative correlation, it shows a *stronger* relationship than, for example, the positive correlation between SAT scores and grades (+0.4) that we cited earlier.

Surveys   If you want to know people's attitudes, preferences, or other characteristics, you don't need to perform an experiment or a correlational study. Instead, you can simply ask them for the information, using a **survey.** It is a method widely used by political pollsters and marketing consultants, as well as by many researchers in psychology and sociology. Surveys typically ask people for their responses to a prepared set of questions. The survey method offers the advantage of generating large numbers of respondents with relative ease. But the value of a survey is only as good as the honesty of the respondents' reports (Schwarz, 1999). Two other important factors affecting survey results include the *wording of the questions* (Are they clear? Are they biased?) and the *sample* (How well do the respondents represent the group of interest to the pollsters?).

Naturalistic Observations   In her classic studies showing that chimpanzees have a complex, tool-making culture, Jane Goodall just observed chimps in their natural jungle setting. Likewise, when psychological researchers want to know how people act in their natural surroundings (as contrasted with the artificial conditions of a laboratory), they use the same method of **naturalistic observation.** This approach might also be a good choice for studying child-rearing practices, shopping habits, or how people flirt in public. Thus, the setting for a naturalistic

Negative correlation   A correlation coefficient indicating that the variables change simultaneously in opposite directions: As one becomes larger, the other gets smaller.

Survey   A technique used in descriptive research, typically involving seeking people's responses to a prepared set of verbal items.

Naturalistic observation   A form of descriptive research involving behavioral assessment of people or animals in their home surroundings.

Jane Goodall used the method of naturalistic observation to study chimpanzee behavior.

In his book Even the Rat Was White, *Robert Guthrie called attention to the neglect of contributions by African Americans in psychology.*

Case study   Research involving a single individual (or, at most, a few individuals).

Expectancy bias   The researcher allowing his or her expectations to affect the outcome of a study.

observation could be as varied as a home, a shopping mall, a lunchroom, or a remote wilderness. This is the point to remember: Naturalistic observations are made under far less controlled conditions than are experiments because the researcher merely observes and records behaviors, rather than manipulating the environment. We should be clear, however, that the best naturalistic observations follow a carefully thought-out plan. Nevertheless, when doing this sort of research, the scientist must be especially cautious about jumping to cause-and-effect conclusions.

Case Studies   How might you do a study to find out what factors shaped comedian Eddie Murphy's sense of humor? You can't have an experimental and a control group, because you have only one Eddie Murphy. A well-controlled study is obviously out of the question, so the researcher will probably turn to yet another kind of research, the **case study**, which focuses on only a few individuals—sometimes just one. Scientists usually reserve this approach for the in-depth study of unusual people with rare problems or unusual talents. For example, in his book *Creating Minds,* Howard Gardner (1993) used the case study method to explore the thought processes of several highly creative individuals, including Einstein, Picasso, and Freud. Therapists who use case studies to develop theories about mental disorder sometimes call this the *clinical method.* By either name, the disadvantages of this approach lie in its subjectivity, its small sample size, and the lack of control over the variables that could affect the individuals under study. These limitations severely restrict the researcher's ability to draw conclusions that can be applied with confidence to other individuals. Nevertheless, the case study can sometimes give us valuable information that could be obtained in no other way.

Controlling Biases in Psychological Research

Assisted suicide. Abortion. Capital punishment. Do you have strong feelings and opinions on any of these issues? Emotion-laden topics such as these can bring out biases that make critical thinking difficult, as we have seen. The possibility of bias, then, poses problems for psychologists interested in studying such issues as child abuse, gender differences, or the effects of racial prejudice—topics that may interest them precisely because of their own strong opinions. Left uncontrolled, researchers' biases can affect the ways they design a study, collect the data, and interpret the results. Let's take a look at two forms of bias that require special vigilance in research.

Emotional bias, which we discussed earlier in connection with critical thinking, involves an individual's cherished beliefs, strong preferences, unquestioned assumptions, or personal prejudices. Often these are not obvious to the individual who has such biases. For example, in his book *Even the Rat Was White,* psychologist Robert Guthrie (1998) points out the bias in the long psychological tradition of using mainly white participants (usually college students) in research—without even realizing that they were introducing bias with their sample-selection procedures. This practice, then, diminished the applicability of the research results to people-in-general. Fortunately, the scientific method, with its openness to peer criticism and replication, provides a powerful counterbalance to an experimenter's emotional bias. Still, scientists would prefer to identify and control their biases before possibly erroneous conclusions hit print.

Expectancy bias can also affect scientists' conclusions when they observe only what they *expect* to observe. (You can see a close kinship here with *confirmation bias,* also discussed earlier.) For example, we can see expectancy bias at work in a study in which psychology students trained rats to perform behaviors such as pressing a lever to obtain food (Rosenthal & Lawson, 1964). The experimenters told some students that their rats were especially bright; other students heard that their rats were slow learners. (In fact, the experimenters had randomly selected both groups of rats from the same litters.) Sure enough, the students' data showed that rats believed to be bright outperformed their supposedly duller littermates—in accord with the students' expectations. How could this be? Apparently, rats perform better for an enthusiastic audience! Follow-up questionnaires showed that the students with the "bright" rats were "more enthusiastic, encouraging, pleasant, and interested in their rat's performance."

Not only can these sources of bias lead to erroneous conclusions, but they can also produce expensive or even dangerous consequences. Imagine that you are a psychologist working for a pharmaceutical company that wants you to test a new drug. With millions of dollars riding on the outcome, you may not be thinking with complete objectivity. And what about the doctors who are going to be prescribing the drug to patients in your study? Surely those doctors will have high hopes for the drug, as will their patients. And so the stage is set for your own bias to creep into the study along with the expectations of other involved.

A common strategy for controlling expectancy bias in drug studies is to keep participants in the research experimentally "blind," or uninformed, about whether they are getting the real drug or a **placebo** (a sham "drug" with no medical value). An even better strategy is a **double-blind study**, which involves keeping *both* the participants and the experimenter clueless about which group receives which treatment. In a drug study, this would mean that neither the researchers nor the participants would know (until the end of the study) which individuals were getting the new drug and which were getting the placebo. This scientific trick controls expectations by assuring that the experimenters will not inadvertently treat the experimental group differently from the control group. It also controls for expectations of those receiving treatment, because they are also "blind" to which group they have been assigned.

As you can imagine, expectancy bias could affect the response of the children in our sugar study. Similarly, the expectations of the observers could color their judgments. To prevent this, we should incorporate a double-blind procedure into our experimental design.

CONNECTION • CHAPTER 7

For many people, the brain responds to placebos in much the same way that it responds to pain-relieving drugs.

Placebo *(pla-SEE-bo)* Substance that appears to be a drug but is not. Placebos are often referred to as "sugar pills" because they might contain only sugar, rather than a real drug.

Double-blind study An experimental procedure in which both researchers and participants are uninformed about the nature of the independent variable being administered.

© The New Yorker Collection 1993. Ronald Reilly from Cartoonbank.com. All Rights Reserved.

Ethical Issues in Psychological Research

Research also can involve serious ethical issues, such as the possibility of people being hurt or unduly distressed. No researcher would want this to happen, yet the issues are not always clear. Is it ethical, for example, in an experiment on aggression, to deliberately provoke people by insulting them? What degree of stress is too high a price to pay for the knowledge gained from the experiment? Such ethical issues raise difficult, but important, questions, and not all psychologists would answer them in exactly the same way.

To provide some guidelines for researchers, the American Psychological Association (APA) publishes *Ethical Principles of Psychologists and Code of Conduct* (2002). This document not only deals with the ethical obligation to shield research participants from potentially harmful procedures, but it also admonishes researchers that information acquired about people during a study must be held confidential (Knapp & VandeCreek, 2003; Smith, 2003a,b).

Deception   The use of *deception* poses an especially knotty problem for researchers in psychology. The *Ethical Principles* document states that, under most circumstances, participation in research should be voluntary and informed. That is, we should advise volunteers of what challenges they will face and give them a real opportunity to opt out of the study. But the issue can be more complicated than it first appears. What if you are interested in the "good Samaritan" problem: the conditions under which people will help a stranger in distress? If you tell people that you have contrived a phony emergency situation and ask them whether they are willing to help, you will spoil the very effect that you are trying to study. Consequently, the guidelines do allow for deception under some conditions, provided that no substantial risks are likely to accrue to the participants.

You might well ask, "Who judges the risks?" Most places where research is done now have watchdog committees, called *institutional review boards* (IRBs) that make these judgments by examining all studies proposed to be carried out within an institution, such as a college, university, or clinic. Further, when a researcher uses deception, the APA guidelines require that participants be informed of the deception as soon as is possible without compromising the study's research goals. Individuals used in deceptive research must also be *debriefed* after the study to make sure that they suffer no lasting ill effects. Despite these precautions, some psychologists stand opposed to the use of deception in any form of psychological research (Baumrind, 1985; Ortmann & Hertwig, 1997).

Animal Studies   Another long-standing ethical issue surrounds the use of laboratory animals, such as rats, pigeons, and monkeys. Animals make attractive research subjects because of the relative simplicity of their nervous systems and the ease with which a large number of individuals can be maintained under controlled conditions. Animals also have served as alternatives to humans when a procedure was deemed risky or outright harmful, such as implanting electrodes in the brain to study its parts.

With such concerns in mind nearly 100 years ago, officers of the American Psychological Association established a Committee on Precautions in Animal Experimentation, which wrote guidelines for animal research (Dewsbury, 1990). More recently, the APA's *Ethical Principles* document reiterated the experimenter's obligation to provide decent living conditions for research animals and to weigh any discomfort caused them against the value of the information sought in the research. Additional safeguards appear in a 1985 federal law that regulates animal research (Novak & Suomi, 1988).

TABLE 1.1   What Questions Can the Scientific Method *Not* Answer?

The scientific method is not appropriate for answering questions that cannot be put to an objective, empirical test. Here are some examples of such issues:

Topic	Question
Ethics	Should scientists do research with animals?
Values	Which culture has the best attitude toward work and leisure?
Morality	Is abortion morally right or wrong?
Preferences	Is rap music better than blues?
Aesthetics	Was Picasso more creative than Van Gogh?
Existential issues	What is the meaning of life?
Religion	Does God exist?
Law	What should be the speed limit on interstate highways?

Although science can help us understand such issues, the answers ultimately must be settled by logic, faith, legislation, consensus, or other means that lie beyond the scope of the scientific method.

Recent years have seen a renewal of concern, both inside and outside of psychology, about the use of animals as research subjects, particularly when the research involves painful or damaging procedures, such as brain surgery, electrode implants, or pain studies. Some people feel that the limitations should be more stringent, especially on studies using humanlike animals, such as chimpanzees. Others believe that limitations or outright bans should apply to all animal research, including studies of simple animals such as sea slugs (which are often used in neurological studies). While many psychologists support animal research under the APA guidelines, the issue remains a contested one (Bird, 2005; Plous, 1996).

Questions Science Cannot Answer

You should understand that we are *not* saying that science can give us answers to every important question in our lives. Even scientists themselves don't take a scientific approach to everything. The scientific method is simply the best way to find answers to testable questions about the natural world—the world of atoms and animals, of stones and stars, and of behavior and mental processes. So, what are science's boundaries and limitations? Science is *not* appropriate for answering questions that cannot be empirically tested—such as questions of ethics, morality, religious beliefs, or preferences. For some examples of questions that science can never answer, please see Table 1.1.

PSYCHOLOGYMATTERS
Using Psychology to Learn Psychology

In this book, your authors have attempted to help you find meaningful patterns that will aid you in making a mental map (sometimes called a *cognitive map* or *concept map*) of every chapter. To do so, we have built in many learning devices. Among the most important are numbered Key Questions and Core Concepts. Let us show you how using these features can make your study of psychology easier.

The Key Questions, which act as the main headings in each chapter, give you a "heads up" by signaling what to watch for as you read. For example,

Key Question 1.2 for this section of the chapter asked, HOW DO PSYCHOLOGISTS DEVELOP NEW KNOWLEDGE? This should alert you to the idea that psychologists must have a special method for developing new knowledge and that you should be alert to what the method is. The larger point is that you are much more likely to remember new concepts if you approach them with an appropriate Key Question in mind (Glaser, 1990). You can also use the Key Question as a review-check of your understanding of each section before the next test. If you have a study partner, try asking each other to give detailed answers to the Key Questions.

You can think of Core Concepts as brief answers to the Key Questions. (In fact, each one is numbered to match its Key Question.) A Core Concept also highlights the central idea in each chapter section—much like a preview of coming attractions. It is important to realize that a Core Concept is not a complete answer but a capsule summary of ideas to be fleshed out. As you come to understand the meaning of a Core Concept, you will see that the details of the section—the terms, names, and important research—will fall easily into place. And to reinforce your understanding, it is a good idea to revisit the Core Concept after you have finished reading the section. In fact, this is precisely what the brief end-of-section quizzes (Check Your Understanding) are designed to do.

Another good way to use the Core Concepts is to see whether you can explain how the terms in boldface link to the Core Concepts. Let's take Core Concept for this section, which says:

Psychologists, like all other scientists, use the scientific method to test their ideas empirically.

This should alert you that there are two especially important ideas that will be described in this section: *scientific method* and *testing ideas empirically*. Knowing this will help you find the important ideas and organize them in your mind.

In summary, then, the Key Questions and Core Concepts are designed to pose important questions that lead you to the big ideas in the chapter. They will help you step back from the details to see meaningful patterns—as the saying goes, to distinguish the forest from the trees.

CheckYourUnderstanding

1. **RECALL:** What is the difference between a scientific theory and a mere opinion?

2. **APPLICATION:** Which of the following could be an operational definition of "fear"?
   a. an intense feeling of terror and dread when thinking about some threatening situation
   b. panic
   c. a desire to avoid something
   d. moving away from a stimulus

3. **ANALYSIS:** Identify the only form of research that can determine cause and effect. Why is this so?

4. **ANALYSIS:** Why would an experimenter randomly assign participants to different experimental conditions?

5. **ANALYSIS:** Which one of the following correlations shows the strongest relationship between two variables?
   a. +0.4
   b. +0.38
   c. -0.7
   d. .05

6. **ANALYSIS:** What would be a good method for controlling expectancy bias in research on a new drug for depression?

7. **RECALL:** Why does research using deception pose an ethical problem?

8. **UNDERSTANDING THE CORE CONCEPT:** What do scientists mean by *empirical observation*?

Answers 1. A scientific theory is a testable explanation for the available facts or observations. An opinion is not necessarily testable, nor does it necessarily attempt to explain all the relevant information. **2.** d. (because it is the only one couched in terms of behaviors that can be observed objectively) **3.** Only the experiment can determine cause and effect, because it is the only method that involves manipulation of the independent variable. **4.** Random assignment helps insure that the experimental and control groups are comparable. **5.** c. **6.** A double blind study, because it controls for the expectations of both the experimenter and the participants who receive the drug. **7.** Deception involves a conflict with the principle that participants in research should give their informed consent. (Deception is, however, permitted under certain circumstances specified in the Ethical Principles document.) **8.** Empirical observation requires making careful measurements based on direct experience.

1.3 KEY QUESTION
WHAT ARE PSYCHOLOGY'S SIX MAIN PERSPECTIVES?

The shape of modern psychology has been molded by its history, which dates back some 25 centuries to the Greek philosophers Socrates, Plato, and Aristotle. These sages not only speculated about consciousness and madness; they also knew that emotions could distort thinking and that our perceptions are interpretations of the external world. Even today, people would probably agree with many of these ancient conjectures—and so would modern psychology.

But the Greeks also came up with some psychological notions that seem odd to the modern mind. They believed, for example, that emotions flowed from the heart, the liver, and the spleen and that mental disorder could be caused by excess bile. Strange as these ideas now sound, we still use the metaphor of "heartfelt" emotions and may even speak of "venting the spleen," as a figure of speech for anger.

Yet, the Greeks get only partial credit for laying the foundations for psychology. At roughly the same time, Asian and African societies were developing their own psychological ideas. In Asia, followers of Yoga and Buddhism were exploring consciousness, which they attempted to control with meditation. Meanwhile, in Africa, other explanations for personality and mental disorder were emerging from traditional spiritual beliefs (Berry et al., 1992). Based on these *folk psychologies*, shamans (healers) developed therapies rivaling in effectiveness the treatments used in psychology and psychiatry today (Lambo, 1978). It was, however, the Greek tradition and, later, the Church that most influenced the winding developmental path of Western psychology as a science.

Oddly, it never occurred to any of the ancient thinkers to put their speculations to a test in the same way that we planned the test for our hypothesis about sugar and hyperactive behavior. In the Greek mind, truth came from simple observation, logic, and the authority of experts. The breakthrough idea of a controlled experiment wouldn't appear for more than two thousand years.

Fast forwarding just a dozen centuries, we find the medieval Church in control of Europe, with its clerics actively suppressing inquiry into human nature. Why? Part of the answer was an attempt to discourage interest in the "world of the flesh." The other part of the answer lay in the conviction that the mind and soul were inseparable, operating outside the natural laws that govern worldly objects and events. For medieval Christians, the human mind—like the mind of God—presented a mystery that mortals should never try to solve.

Change of this entrenched viewpoint did not come easily. It took a series of radical new ideas, spaced over several hundred years, to break the medieval mindset and lay the intellectual foundation for modern psychology—which brings us to our Core Concept for this section:

> **Six main viewpoints dominate the rapidly changing field of modern psychology— the biological, cognitive, behavioral, whole-person, developmental, and socio- cultural perspectives—each of which grew out of radical new concepts about mind and behavior.**

core concept

Separation of Mind and Body and the Modern Biological Perspective

The 17th-century philosopher René Descartes *(Day-CART)* proposed the first of these radical new concepts that eventually led to modern psychology. (See Table 1.2.) His idea involved *a distinction between the spiritual mind and the physical body*. The genius of Descartes's insight was that it allowed the Church to keep the mind off limits for scientific inquiry but still allowed the study of human sensations and behaviors because they were based on physical activity in the

TABLE 1.2   The Big Ideas on which Psychology's Six Perspectives Are Based

Perspective	Big Idea	Sources
Biological perspective	The body can be studied separately from the mind.	René Descartes
Cognitive perspective	The methods of science can be used to study the mind.	Wilhelm Wundt
Behavioral perspective	Psychology should be the science of observable behavior—not mental processes.	John Watson
Whole-person perspective	*Psychodynamic psychology:* Personality and mental disorders arise from processes in the unconscious mind.	Sigmund Freud
	Humanistic psychology: Psychology should emphasize human growth and potential, rather than mental disorder.	Abraham Maslow Carl Rogers
	Trait and temperament psychology: Individuals can be understood in terms of their basic temperaments and enduring personality traits.	Originally from the ancient Greeks
Developmental perspective	People change as the influences of heredity and environment unfold over time.	Many psychologists
Sociocultural perspective	The power of the situation: Social and cultural influences can overpower the influence of all other factors in determining behavior.	Many psychologists

nervous system. His proposal fit well with exciting new discoveries about the biology of nerve circuits in animals, where scientists had just shown how the sense organs convert stimulation into the nerve impulses and muscular responses. Such discoveries, when combined with Descartes' separation of mind and body, allowed scientists, for the first time, to demonstrate that biological processes, rather than mysterious spiritual forces, lay behind sensations and simple reflexive behaviors.

The Modern Biological Perspective   The tradition of studying the biological bases of psychological processes, which began with Descartes, can still be seen in the **biological perspective** found in modern psychology. In this view, our personalities, preferences, behavior patterns, and abilities all stem from our physical makeup. Accordingly, biological psychologists search for the causes of our behavior in the nervous system, the endocrine (hormone) system, and the genes. They are also interested in the psychological effects of environmental trauma, such as accidents or disease.

Modern biological psychologists, no longer constrained by the dictates of the medieval Church, have rejoined mind and body (although they leave issues of the soul to religion). Biological psychologists now view the mind as a product of the brain. While they don't deny the value of other perspectives on mind and behavior, biological psychologists see their mission as learning as much as possible about the physical underpinnings of psychological processes.

Two Variations on the Biological Theme   As you might imagine, the biological view has strong roots in medicine and biological science. In fact, the emerging field of **neuroscience** combines biological psychology with biology, neurology, and other disciplines interested in brain processes. Thanks to spectacular advances in computers and brain-imaging techniques, neuroscience is a hot area of research. Among their achievements, neuroscientists have begun to unravel the mystery of how our eyes and brain convert light waves into vision. They have also learned how damage to certain parts of the brain can destroy specific abilities, such as speech, social skills, or memory. And, as we will see in Chapter 8,

Biological perspective   The psychological perspective that searches for the causes of behavior in the functioning of genes, the brain and nervous system, and the endocrine (hormone) system.

Neuroscience   The field devoted to understanding how the brain creates thoughts, feelings, motives, consciousness, memories, and other mental processes.

they have used brain wave patterns to open up the hidden world of sleep and dreams.

Another important variant of biological psychology sprouted recently from ideas proposed by Charles Darwin some 150 years ago. This new **evolutionary psychology** holds that much human behavior arises from inherited tendencies, and it has been given a substantial boost by the recent surge of research in genetics. In the evolutionary view, our genetic makeup—including our most deeply ingrained behaviors—were shaped by the conditions our remote ancestors faced thousands of years ago.

According to evolutionary psychology, environmental forces have pruned the human family tree, favoring the survival and reproduction of individuals with the most adaptive mental and physical characteristics. Darwin called this process *natural selection*. Through it, the physical characteristics of our species have evolved (changed) in the direction of characteristics that gave the fittest organisms a competitive advantage.

Some proponents of evolutionary psychology have made highly controversial claims. In their view, even the most undesirable human behaviors, such as warfare, rape, and infanticide, may have grown out of biological tendencies that once helped humans adapt and survive (Buss, 2008). This approach also proposes controversial biological explanations for certain gender differences—why, for instance, men typically have more sexual partners than do women. More of this controversy will have to wait until our discussion of sexuality in Chapter 9.

The Founding of Scientific Psychology and the Modern Cognitive Perspective

Another radical idea that shaped the early science of psychology came from chemistry, where scientists had noticed patterns in properties of the chemical elements, leading them to develop the famous *periodic table*. At one stroke, the periodic table made the relationships among the elements clear. This revolutionary discovery particularly intrigued one Wilhelm Wundt, a German scientist (who, incidentally, later became the first person to call himself a "psychologist"). Wundt wondered if he could simplify the human psyche in the same way the periodic table had simplified chemistry. (See Table 1.2.) Perhaps he could discover "the elements of conscious experience"! Although Wundt never realized his dream of a periodic table for the mind, he did have this breakthrough insight: *The methods of science could be used to study the mind, as well as the body.*

Introspecting for the Elements of Conscious Experience

"Please press the button as soon as you see the light," Professor Wundt might have said, as he readied to record the *reaction time* between the light stimulus and student's response. Such experiments were common fare in the world's first psychology laboratory where Wundt and his students also performed studies in which trained volunteers described their sensory and emotional responses to various stimuli—a technique called **introspection**— based on an elaborate classification scheme Wundt had devised. There, at the University of Leipzig, in 1879, Wundt and his students began history's first psychology experiments: studies on what they proposed to be "elements" of consciousness, including sensation and perception, memory, attention, emotion, thinking, learning, and language. All our mental activity, they asserted, consists of different combinations of these basic processes.

Wundt's Legacy: Structuralism

Wundt's pupil, Edward Bradford Titchener, brought the quest for the elements of consciousness to America, where Titchener began calling it **structuralism**. Titchener's term was fitting, because his goal—like

Evolutionary psychology A relatively new specialty in psychology that sees behavior and mental processes in terms of their genetic adaptations for survival and reproduction.

Introspection The process of reporting on one's own conscious mental experiences.

Structuralism A historical school of psychology devoted to uncovering the basic structures that make up mind and thought. Structuralists sought the "elements" of conscious experience.

E. B. Titchener brought Wundt's quest for the "elements of conscious experience" to America. These elements included the terms you see superimposed on Titchener's image.

In 1879, Wilhelm Wundt (1832–1920) founded the first formal laboratory devoted to experimental psychology. He's shown here (center) in his laboratory in Leipzig in 1912.

that of Wundt—was to reveal the most basic "structures" or components of the mind (Fancher, 1979). So, even though Wundt never used the term, he is considered the "father" of structuralism.

From the outset, both Wundt and Titchener became magnets for critics. Objections especially targeted the introspective method as being too subjective. After all, said the critics, how can we judge the accuracy of people's description of their thoughts and feelings?

But, Wundt and Titchener have had the last laugh. Even though psychologists sometimes view their ideas as quaint, they still rely on updated versions of the old structuralists' methods. For example, you will see introspection at work when we study sleep and dreaming. And you will experience introspection yourself in the upcoming "Do It Yourself!" box. Finally, we can guess that Wundt and Titchener, if they were alive today, would still be laughing for one more reason: The topics that they first identified and explored can be found as chapter headings in every introductory psychology text, including this one.

James and the Function of Mind and Behavior   One of Wundt's most vocal critics, the American psychologist William James, argued that the German's approach was far too narrow. (James also said that it was boring—which didn't help his already strained relationship with Wundt.) Psychology should include the *function* of consciousness, not just its *structure*, James argued. Appropriately, his brand of psychology led to a "school"[2] that became known as **functionalism** (Fancher, 1979).

James and his followers found Charles Darwin's ideas far more interesting than Wundt's. Like Darwin, James had a deep interest in emotion that included its relation to the body and behavior (not just as an element of con-

Functionalism   A historical school of psychology that believed mental processes could best be understood in terms of their adaptive purpose and function.

---

[2]The term *school* refers to a group of thinkers who share the same core beliefs.

sciousness, as in Wundt's system). Recurring bouts of depression probably added to his concern with problems and emotions of everyday living (Ross, 1991; Viney, 2006). James also liked Darwin's emphasis on organisms *adapting* to their environments. James therefore proposed that psychology should explain how people adapt—or fail to adapt—to the real world outside the laboratory.

This sort of thinking led the functionalists to become the first *applied* psychologists—interested in how psychology could be used to improve human life. James himself wrote extensively on the development of learned "habits," the psychology of religion, and teaching. Incidentally, he was also probably the first American professor ever to ask for student evaluations (Fancher, 1979). His follower, John Dewey, founded the "progressive education" movement, which emphasized learning by *doing*, rather than by merely listening to lectures and memorizing facts.

Introspection was the point on which structuralism and functionalism agreed. Ironically, their point of agreement was also their greatest point of vulnerability: The introspective method was subjective, leaving them open to the criticism that their versions of psychology were not really scientific. Overcoming this problem took over a half century and the cooperation of experts from several disciplines that came together to form the *cognitive perspective*.

The Modern Cognitive Perspective The development of the computer—which became the new metaphor for the mind—gave psychology an irresistible push toward a new synthesis: the

William James spoke of the "stream of consciousness," which portrayed consciousness as an active, ever-changing process. This metaphor, James argued, was much more apt than Wundt's image of consciousness composed of many separate elements.

DO IT YOURSELF! A Demonstration from Gestalt Psychology

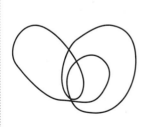 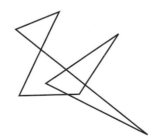

....
FIGURE 1.5
Takete or Maluma?

Without reading further, decide quickly which one of the two figures above you would name "Takete" and which you would call "Maluma." You might want to see if your friends give the same answer.

According to an early 20th-century group of German psychologists, known as the *Gestalt psychologists,* the names you give to

these figures may reflect the associations wired into your brain. Indeed, most people think that the soft-sounding term *Maluma* is more appropriate for the rounded left-hand figure, while the sharp-sounding term *Takete* better fits the pointy figure on the right (Köhler, 1947). This was just one of many simple tests they developed in their

quest to understand how we perceive our world.

For such demonstrations, the Gestalt psychologists borrowed Wundt's method of introspection, but they objected to his emphasis on the parts, or "elements," of consciousness. Instead, the Gestalt psychologists sought to understand how we construct "perceptual wholes," or *Gestalts*. How do we, for example, form the perception of a face from its component lines, shapes, colors, and textures? Their ultimate goal was even grander: They believed that understanding perception would lead them to an understanding of how the brain creates perceptions. You will get to know the Gestalt psychologists better in Chapter 7, when we take an in-depth look at sensation and perception.

Strict behaviorists, such as B. F. Skinner, believe that psychology should focus on the laws that govern behavior—that is, on the relations between stimuli (S) and responses (R)—rather than on the subjective processes of the mind.

CONNECTION • CHAPTER 3

John Watson and his colleague Rosalie Rayner performed a notorious experiment in which they taught a young boy, Albert, to fear furry objects.

Cognitive perspective Another of the main psychological viewpoints distinguished by an emphasis on mental processes, such as learning, memory, perception, and thinking, as forms of information processing.

Behaviorism A historical school (as well as a modern perspective) that has sought to make psychology an objective science that focused only on behavior—to the exclusion of mental processes.

Behavioral perspective A psychological viewpoint that finds the source of our actions in environmental stimuli, rather than in inner mental processes.

modern **cognitive perspective**, which emphasizes *cognition*, mental activity such as sensation, perception, learning, thinking, and memory. All such activities involve the processing of information, say the cognitive psychologists. From this viewpoint, our thoughts and actions arise when our computer-like brains interpret our experiences and generate responses. For a brief comparison of the cognitive perspective with the other five main psychological perspectives, see Table 1.2.

You might consider cognitive psychologists as heirs to the best of the structuralist, functionalist, and Gestalt traditions. They have appropriated ideas from other sources, as well. From linguistics they took the notion that our most basic language abilities are wired into our brains at birth (Pinker, 2002). From medicine they have borrowed the technology that now allows visualizing the activity of the brain and connecting it to mental processes. And it was from computer science that they borrowed the metaphor of the brain as a biological computer—a processor of information (Gardner, 1985; Gazzaniga, 1998a). Those who are especially interested in the biological underpinnings of mind and behavior are known as *cognitive neuroscientists*.

The Behavioral Perspective: Rejection of Introspection and a Focus on Observable Behavior

Early in the 1900s, a particularly radical and feisty group, known as the *behaviorists*, made a name for themselves by disagreeing with nearly everyone. Most famously, they proposed the idea that the mind should not be a part of psychology at all! John B. Watson, an early leader of the behaviorist movement, argued that a truly objective science of psychology should deal solely with observable events: *stimuli* from the environment and the organism's *responses*. Behaviorism, said Watson, should be the science of *behavior* and environmental conditions that influence behavior. (See Table 1.2.)

Behavioral Psychology Loses Its Mind   In general, the behaviorists rejected any science of subjective mental processes. And, in particular, they objected to *introspection*, the practice of reporting on mental experiences—a technique that the structuralists, functionalists, and Gestalt psychologists all used. But Watson and his followers cared nothing about what people were thinking or feeling. Instead, they wanted to know how people would *act*—for example, whether a child would recoil from a rabbit that earlier had been paired with a sudden loud noise.

B. F. Skinner, the most influential American behaviorist since Watson, argued that the seductive concept of "mind" has led psychology in circles. The mind, he said, is something so subjective that it cannot even be proved to exist (Skinner, 1990). (Think about it: Can you prove that you have a mind?) As Skinner noted wryly, "The crucial age-old mistake is the belief that . . . what we feel as we behave is the cause of our behaving" (Skinner, 1989, p. 17).

And so, the behaviorists rejected a science of inner experience, choosing instead to study the person entirely from the outside, based only on what they could observe directly: the effects of people, objects, and events on behavior. We can summarize the radical new idea that drove behaviorism this way: *Psychology should be the study of observable behavior and the stimuli that shape behavior.* This **behavioral perspective** called attention especially to the way our actions are modified by their consequences, as when a child is praised for saying, "Thank you." Perhaps the behaviorists' greatest contribution to psychology consists of a detailed understanding of how the environment affects learning. The behaviorists have also given us powerful methods of changing behavior by altering the environment (Alferink, 2005; Roediger, 2004). We will examine all of these ideas more closely in Chapter 3.

The Whole-Person Perspectives: Psychodynamic, Humanistic, and Trait and Temperament

At the dawn of the 20th century, another challenge to Wundt and structuralism came from the Viennese physician Sigmund Freud and his disciples, who were developing a method of treating mental disorders based on yet another radical idea: *Personality and mental disorders arise mainly from processes in the unconscious mind, rather than from consciousness.* (See Table 1.2.) Moreover, Freud's *psychoanalytic theory* purported to explain the *whole person,* not just certain components (such as attention, perception, memory, or emotion), as the other schools of psychology had done. His goal was to explain every aspect of mind and behavior in a single, grand theory.

Although Freud was not the first to recognize that we are unaware of some mental processes, neither structuralism nor functionalism nor Gestalt psychology nor behaviorism had imagined that unconscious processes could dominate the personality and cause mental disorders. And Freud's ideas were revolutionary in another respect: None of the earlier "schools" of psychology had proposed a comprehensive method of psychotherapy.

Sigmund Freud taught that the mind had three parts: the unconscious reservoir of energy, needs, and desires (the id), the guardian of morals and values (the superego), and the conscious executive of the personality (the ego).

Psychodynamic Psychology

Freud could be a difficult mentor, provoking many of his followers to break ranks and develop their own theories. We use the term *psychodynamic* to refer to all these *neo-Freudian* formulations that arose from Freud's idea that the mind (psyche), especially the unconscious mind, is a reservoir of energy (dynamics) for the personality. This energy, says **psychodynamic psychology,** is what motivates us. Practitioners specializing in psychotherapy have found such a view especially attractive.

The first and best-known representative of the psychodynamic approach is, of course, Sigmund Freud, whose system is called **psychoanalysis.** Originally conceived as a medical technique for treating mental disorders, psychoanalysts emphasize the analysis of dreams, slips of the tongue (the so-called "Freudian slip"), and a technique called *free association* to gather clues to the unconscious conflicts that are thought to be censored by consciousness. Even today, most psychoanalysts are physicians with a specialty in psychiatry and advanced training in Freudian methods. (And now, as we promised earlier, you know the difference between a *psychologist* and a *psychoanalyst.*)

But Freud and his followers were not the only ones aspiring to explain the whole person. Two other groups shared an interest in a global understanding of the personality, *humanistic psychology* and *trait and temperament psychology.* Here we group all three under the heading of the **whole-person perspectives.**

Humanistic Psychology

Reacting to the psychoanalytic emphasis on sinister forces in the unconscious, **humanistic psychology** took a different tack. The radical new idea developed by the humanistic therapists was *an emphasis on the positive side of our nature that included human ability, growth, and potential.* (See Table 1.2.) In the humanistic view, your self-concept and your physical and emotional needs have a huge influence on your thoughts, emotions, and actions.

Led by the likes of Abraham Maslow and Carl Rogers, humanistic psychologists also rejected what they saw as the cold and mechanical approach of scientific psychology. In its place, they offered a model of human nature emphasizing the free will that people can use to make choices affecting their lives (Kendler, 2005). As you might have suspected, humanistic psychologists have not produced a great deal of scientific research, although their voluminous writings have had a major impact on the practice of counseling and psychotherapy.

Psychodynamic psychology A clinical approach emphasizing the understanding of mental disorders in terms of unconscious needs, desires, memories, and conflicts.

Psychoanalysis An approach to psychology based on Sigmund Freud's assertions, which emphasize unconscious processes. The term is used to refer broadly both to Freud's psychoanalytic theory and to his psychoanalytic treatment method.

Whole-person perspectives A group of psychological perspectives that take a global view of the person: Included are *psychodynamic psychology, humanistic psychology,* and *trait and temperament psychology.*

Humanistic psychology A clinical approach emphasizing human ability, growth, potential, and free will.

Trait and Temperament Psychology   The ancient Greeks, who anticipated so many modern ideas, proclaimed that our personalities are ruled by four body *humors* (fluids): blood, phlegm, melancholer, and yellow bile. Depending on which humor was dominant, an individual's personality might be sanguine (dominated by blood), slow and deliberate (phlegm), melancholy (melancholer), or angry and aggressive (yellow bile).

We no longer buy into the ancient Greek typology, of course. But their notion of *personality traits* lives on in modern times as **trait and temperament psychology**. The fundamental idea distinguishing this group says: *Differences among people arise from differences in persistent characteristics and dispositions called traits and temperaments.* (See Table 1.2.)

You have probably heard of such traits as *introversion* and *extraversion*, which seem to be fundamental characteristics of human nature. Other traits that psychologists have identified in people all over the world include a sense of anxiety or well-being, openness to new experiences, agreeableness, and conscientiousness. We will examine these "Big Five" personality traits more closely in Chapter 10. Some psychologists also propose that we differ on an even more fundamental level called *temperament*, thought to account for the different dispositions observed among newborn babies (and among adults, as well).

The Developmental Perspective: Changes Arising from Nature and Nurture

Change may be the only constant in our lives. According to the **developmental perspective**, psychological change results from an interaction between the *heredity* written in our genes and the influence of our *environment*. (See Table 1.2.) A big question mark, however, stands over the relative contributions made by these two forces. So, developmental psychologists ask: Which counts most heavily, *nature* or *nurture* (heredity or environment) in shaping who we become? As you might expect, biological psychologists emphasize *nature,* while behaviorists emphasize *nurture.* But developmental psychology is where the two forces come together.

The big idea that defines the developmental perspective is this: *People change in predictable ways as the influences of heredity and environment unfold over time.* In other words, humans think and act differently at different times of their lives. Physically, development can be seen in such predictable processes as growth, puberty, and menopause. And psychologically, development can be observed in the acquisition of language, logical thinking, and the assumption of different roles at different times of life.

In the past, much of the developmental research has focused on children—in part because they change so rapidly and in rather predictable ways. More recently, however, developmental psychologists have increasingly turned their attention to teens and adults—showing that developmental processes continue throughout our lives. In Chapter 6, we will explore the common patterns of psychological change seen across the entire lifespan, from before birth to old age. The developmental theme will appear elsewhere throughout this text, too, because development affects all our psychological processes, from biology to social interaction.

The Sociocultural Perspective: The Individual in Context

Who could deny that people exert powerful influences on each other? The **sociocultural perspective** places the idea of *social influence* center stage. From this viewpoint, *social psychologists* have long probed the mysteries of liking, lov-

---

CONNECTION • CHAPTER 10

People's personalities differ on five major trait dimensions, cleverly called the *Big Five.*

Trait and temperament psychology
A psychological perspective that views behavior and personality as the products of enduring psychological characteristics.

Developmental perspective   One of the six main psychological viewpoints, distinguished by its emphasis on nature and nurture and on predictable changes that occur across the lifespan.

Sociocultural perspective   A main psychological viewpoint emphasizing the importance of social interaction, social learning, and a cultural perspective.

ing, prejudice, aggression, obedience, and conformity. And more recently, many have become interested in how these social processes vary from one *culture* to another. (See Table 1.2.)

Culture, a complex blend of human language, beliefs, customs, values, and traditions, exerts profound influences on all of us. We can see culture in action by comparing people, for example, in the California–Mexican culture of San Diego and the Scandinavian-based culture of Minnesota. Psychology's earlier blindness to culture was due, in part, to the beginnings of scientific psychology in Europe and North America, where most psychologists lived and worked under similar cultural conditions (Lonner & Malpass, 1994; Segall et al., 1998). But now the perspective has broadened. Although nearly half of the world's half-million psychologists still live and work in the United States, it is encouraging to note that interest in psychology is also growing in countries outside of Europe and North America (Pawlik & d'Ydewalle, 1996; Rosenzweig, 1992, 1999). Even so, most of our psychological knowledge still has a North American/European flavor. Recognizing this bias, **cross-cultural psychologists** have begun the long task of reexamining the "laws" of psychology across cultural and ethnic boundaries (Cole, 2006).

Proponents of the sociocultural view, of course, do not deny the effects of heredity or learning or even of unconscious processes. Rather they bring to psychology a powerful additional concept: *the power of the situation*. From this viewpoint, then, *the social and cultural situation in which the person is embedded can overpower all other factors that influence behavior.*

To summarize the perspectives we have just covered, please have a look at Figure 1.6. There you will find a thumbnail overview of the main viewpoints that make up the spectrum of modern psychology. A few moments taken to fix these perspectives in your mind will pay big dividends in your understanding of the chapters that follow, where we will refer to them often, as we shift from one perspective to another.

The Changing Face of Psychology

Modern psychology is a field in flux. Over the last several decades, the biological, cognitive, and developmental perspectives have become dominant. And increasingly, adherents of once-conflicting perspectives are making connections and joining forces. So we now see such new and strange hybrid psychologists as "cognitive behaviorists" or "evolutionary developmentalists." At the same time, nearly all specialties within psychology seem eager to make a connection with neuroscience, which is rapidly becoming one of the pillars of the field. Yet another trend has appeared among psychologists taking a sociocultural perspective: Those who put the emphasis on culture are gaining ascendancy. Meanwhile, the Freudian camp seems to be losing ground among those holding a whole-person perspective.

We also call your attention to an especially noteworthy shift in the proportion of psychologists who are women and members of minority groups. Ethnic minorities—especially Asians, African Americans, and Latinos—are becoming psychologists in increasing numbers (Kohout, 2001). Even more striking is the new majority status of women in psychology. In 1906, only 12% of American psychologists listed were women, according to a listing in *American Men of Science* (named with no irony intended). By 1921 the proportion had risen above 20%. And now, women receive more than two-thirds of the new doctorates awarded in the field each year (Cynkar, 2007; Kohout, 2001).

Dr. Phil Zimbardo, one of your authors, is a social psychologist who studies the "power of the situation" in controlling our behavior. You will see how strongly social situations affect our behavior when you read about his Stanford Prison Experiment in Chapter 11.

Culture   A complex blend of language, beliefs, customs, values, and traditions developed by a group of people and shared with others in the same environment.

Cross-cultural psychologists   Those who work in this specialty are interested in how psychological processes may differ among people of different cultures.

Cross-cultural psychologists, such as this researcher in Kenya, furnish important data for checking the validity of psychological knowledge.

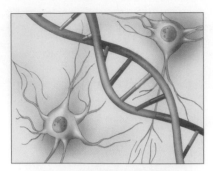

The Biological Perspective focuses on:
- nervous system
- endocrine system
- genetics
- physical characteristics

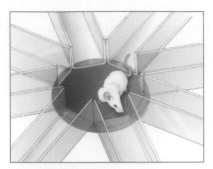

The Behavioral Perspective focuses on:
- learning
- control of behavior by the environment
- stimuli and responses—but not mental processes

The Developmental Perspective focuses on:
- changes in psychological functioning across the life span
- heredity and environment

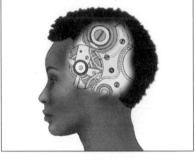

The Cognitive Perspective focuses on:
- mental processes, such as thought, learning, memory, and perception
- the mind as a computer-like "machine"
- how emotion and motivation influence thought and perception ("hot cognition")

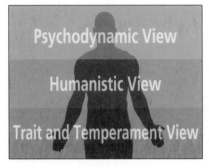

The Whole-Person Perspective includes:
- the *Psychodynamic view*, which emphasizes unconscious motivation and mental disorder
- the *Humanistic view*, which emphasizes mental health and human potential
- the *Trait and Temperament view*, which emphasizes personality characteristics and individual differences

The Sociocultural Perspective focuses on:
- social influences on behavior and mental processes
- how individuals function in groups
- cultural differences

FIGURE 1.6
Summary of Psychology's Six Main Perspectives

CONNECTION • CHAPTER 10

The opening vignette in the "Personality" chapter gives more detail about Mary Calkins's life.

Although psychology has always included a higher proportion of women than any of the other sciences, women have too often found gender biases blocking their career paths (Furumoto & Scarborough, 1986). For example, G. Stanley Hall, one of the pioneers of American psychology, notoriously asserted that academic work would ruin a woman's health and cause deterioration of her reproductive organs. Nevertheless, as early as 1905 the American Psychological Association elected its first female president, Mary Whiton Calkins.

Ironically, Calkins had earlier been denied a doctorate by Harvard University because of her sex even though she had completed all the requirements. In those early days of psychology, as in all fields of science, women were pressured to choose between marriage and career; those who managed to have a career were usually limited to less prestigious positions at women's colleges. Still, they made important contributions to their developing field, as you can see in a sampling presented in Table 1.3.

TABLE 1.3 Early Contributions Made by Women in Psychology

	Research Area	Institutional Affiliation
Mary Calkins	Memory, psychology of the self	Wellesley College
Christine Ladd Franklin	Logic and color vision	Johns Hopkins University
Kate Gordon	Memory and attention	Mount Holyoke, Carnegie Tech
Julia Gulliver	Dreams and the subconscious self	Rockford University
Alice Hinman	Attention and distraction	University of Nebraska
Lillien Martin	Psychophysics	Wellesley College
Anna McKeag	Pain	Bardwell School
Naomi Norsworthy	Abilities of the child	Columbia Teachers College
Millicent Shinn	Child development	Unaffiliated
Helen Thompson	Mental traits	Mount Holyoke College
Margaret Washburn	Perception	Vassar College
Mabel Williams	Visual illusions	Unaffiliated

Source: The 1906 edition of *American Men of Science.*

DO IT YOURSELF! An Introspective Look at the Necker Cube

The cube in Figure 1.7A will trick your eye—or, more accurately, it will trick your brain. Look at the cube for a few moments, and suddenly it will seem to change perspectives. For a time it may seem as if you were viewing the cube from the upper right (Figure 1.7B). Then, abruptly, it will shift and appear as though you were seeing it from the lower left (Figure 1.7C).

It may take a little time for the cube to shift the first time. But, once you see it change, you won't be able to prevent it from alternating back and forth, seemingly at random. Try showing the cube to a few friends and asking them what they see. Do they see it shifting perspectives, as you do?

This phenomenon was not discovered by a psychologist. Rather, Louis Necker, a Swiss geologist, first noticed it nearly 200 years ago while looking at cube-shaped crystals under a microscope. Necker's amazing cube illustrates two important points.

First, it illustrates the much-maligned process of *introspection*, pioneered by Wundt and his students. You will note that the only way we can demonstrate that the Necker cube changes perspectives in our minds is by introspection: having people look at the cube and report what they see. And why is this important to psychology? Only the hardest of the hard-core behaviorists would deny that something happens mentally within a person looking at the cube. Moreover, as the Gestalt psychologists noted, this shifting perspective obviously involves more than seeing lines on a page. In fact, the Necker cube demonstrates that we add meaning to our sensations—a process called *perception*, which will be a main focus of a later chapter.

The second important point is this: The Necker cube can serve as a metaphor for the multiple perspectives in psychology. Just as there is no single right way to see the cube, there

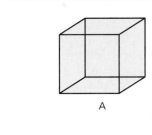

FIGURE 1.7
Different Perspectives of the Necker Cube

is no single perspective in psychology that gives us the whole "truth" about behavior and mental processes. Put another way, if we are to understand psychology fully, we must alternately shift our viewpoints among multiple perspectives.

Necker cube An ambiguous two-dimensional figure of a cube that can be seen from different perspectives: The Necker cube is used here to illustrate the notion that there is no single "right way" to view psychological processes.

PSYCHOLOGYMATTERS:
Psychology as a Major

Becoming a fully fledged psychologist requires substantial training beyond the bachelor's degree. In graduate school, the psychology student takes advanced classes in one or more specialized areas while developing general skills as a scholar and researcher. On completion of the program, the student receives a master's or doctor's degree, typically a PhD (Doctor of Philosophy), an EdD (Doctor of Education), or a PsyD (Doctor of Psychology).

Satisfying careers are available, however, at various levels of education in psychology, although by far the best choices are available to holders of a doctorate (Smith, 2002b). In most states, a license to practice psychology requires a doctorate, plus a supervised internship. Most college and university teaching or research jobs in psychology also require a doctorate.

A master's degree, typically requiring two years of study beyond the bachelor's level, may qualify you for employment as a psychology instructor at the high school level or as an applied psychologist in certain specialties, such as counseling. Master's-level psychologists are common in human service agencies, as well as in private practice (although many states do not allow them to advertise themselves as "psychologists").

Holders of associate's degrees and bachelor's degrees in psychology or related human services fields may find jobs as psychological aides and technicians in agencies, hospitals, nursing homes, and rehabilitation centers. If this is your goal, however, you should know that salaries at this level are relatively low (Kohout, 2000). A bachelor's degree in psychology, coupled with training in business or education, can also lead to interesting careers in personnel management or education.

If you would like further information about job prospects and salary levels for psychologists, search the U.S. Department of Labor's *Occupational Outlook Handbook* (2008–2009 edition). You can find it on the Web at www.bls.gov/oco/home.htm.

CheckYourUnderstanding

1. **RECALL:** René Descartes made a science of psychology possible when he suggested that _____.

2. **APPLICATION:** "The differences between men and women are mainly the result of different survival and reproduction issues faced by the two sexes." Which of the main viewpoints in psychology would this statement represent?

3. **RECALL:** Which of the early schools of psychology is most closely associated with developing the method of *introspection?*

4. **APPLICATION:** If you were a teacher trying to understand how students learn, which of the following perspectives would be most helpful?
   a. the cognitive view
   b. the psychodynamic view
   c. structuralism
   d. the trait and temperament view

5. **RECALL:** To which of the structuralists' and functionalists' ideas did the behaviorists object?

6. **RECALL:** Which of the "whole-person" views focuses on understanding the unconscious mind?

7. **APPLICATION:** "Soldiers may sometimes perform heroic acts, not so much because they have heroic personality traits but because they are in a *situation* that encourages heroic behavior." Which perspective is this observation most consistent with?

8. **APPLICATION:** If you wanted to tell whether a friend had experienced a perceptual shift while viewing the Necker cube, you would have to use the method of _____, which was pioneered by Wundt and the structuralists.

9. **UNDERSTANDING THE CORE CONCEPT:** Which of the following sets of factors is all associated with the perspective indicated?
   a. memory, personality, environment: the behavioral perspective
   b. mental health, mental disorder, mental imagery: the trait and temperament perspective
   c. heredity, environment, predictable changes throughout the lifespan: the developmental perspective
   d. neuroscience, evolutionary psychology, genetics: the cognitive perspective

Answers 1. Descartes declared that sensations and behaviors are the result of activity in the nervous system. **2.** the biological perspective—in particular the viewpoint of evolutionary psychology **3.** structuralism **4.** a **5.** They particularly objected to the concept of the *mind* as an object of scientific study. They also objected to introspection as a subjective, and therefore unscientific, method. **6.** the psychodynamic view, especially psychoanalysis **7.** the sociocultural perspective **8.** introspection **9.** c

34   **CHAPTER 1 ●** MIND, BEHAVIOR, AND PSYCHOLOGICAL SCIENCE

Critical Thinking Applied: Facilitated Communication

Autism is a developmental disorder that can cause severe impairments in attention, cognition (thinking and related mental processes), communication, and social functioning. In the most extreme forms, persons with autism often seem encapsulated in their own worlds, disconnected from people around them. Consequently, the psychological resources they require can impose a heavy burden on parents and teachers. It is no wonder, then, that a technique known as "facilitated communication" was heralded as a dramatic "breakthrough" when it was touted as a means of communicating with individuals who have *autism*.

What Is the Issue?

Here's how facilitated communication was said to work: A *facilitator* attempts to help the person with autism converse by helping him or her answer questions by pointing to letters on a letter board or keyboard. (You can see how this is done in the accompanying photo.) The technique rests on the unfounded belief that untapped language abilities lie hidden by the mask of autism. You may have already identified the problem with this method: How can we be sure that the individual, rather than the facilitator, is the one responding?

Parents and teachers enthusiastically received the initial reports on facilitated communication. But many psychologists remained skeptical. The real issue, they said, was this: Can we find evidence to show that this method really works—or not? They pointed out that testimonials are not acceptable scientific evidence. They

When skeptical psychologists tested the claims for facilitated communication, they found that it wasn't the autistic children who were responsible for the messages.

also suggested that the helper might be consciously or unconsciously guiding the child's hand to produce the messages.

What Critical Thinking Questions Should We Ask?

On its face, the claim that a person with autism is, somehow, ready but unable to communicate—and that this simple pointing technique could break through the barrier of autism—sounded too good to be true. Such extreme claims should be a cue for critical thinkers to ask two other questions. First, "Is there a possibility of bias?"—perhaps because the facilitators and the parents want so much to find an effective therapy for this disorder. Second, then, is the critical thinking question, "What is the evidence?"

Sure enough, evidence in the form of scientific studies showed that, when the facilitator knew the questions, the child with autism would seem to give sensible answers. But when "blinders" were applied—by hiding the questions from the facilitator—the responses were inaccurate or nonsensical (American Psychological Association, 2003; Lilienfeld, 2007).

Sadly, although facilitated communication had extended hope to beleaguered parents and teachers, a scientific look presented a picture showing how uncritical belief could lead to consequences far worse than false hopes. Not only were more effective treatments delayed, but parents blamed themselves when their children did not respond to the treatment as expected (Levine et al., 1994). Worst of all were the false accusations of sexual abuse based on messages thought to have come from children with autism (Bicklen, 1990; Heckler, 1994). The research left little doubt, however, that these messages had originated wholly in the minds of the facilitators. In light of such findings, the American Psychological Association (2003b) denounced facilitated communication as a failure and relegated it to the junk pile of ineffective therapies.

What Conclusions Can We Draw?

So, what lessons about critical thinking can you, as a student of psychology, take away from the facilitated communication fiasco? After all, you won't be able to run your own scientific test on every fantastic-sounding claim that comes along. We hope that it will help instill a skeptical attitude about reports of extraordinary new treatments, dramatic psychological "breakthroughs," and products that claim to help you develop "untapped potential." And, we hope you will always pause to ask: What is the evidence? Is there another possible explanation? Has someone done a controlled test? Could the claims be merely the result of people's expectations—that is, of *expectancy bias*? Confirmation bias and emotional biases were undoubtedly at work, too: Parents and teachers desperate for an effective treatment uncritically grabbed onto the anecdotal reports of success. Perhaps this summarizes the big lesson to be learned: No matter how much you want to believe, and no matter how many anecdotes and testimonials you have, none of it ever adds up to real evidence.

Chapter Summary

1.1 What Is Psychology—And What Is It *Not?*

Core Concept 1.1: Psychology is a broad field, with many specialties, but fundamentally psychology is the science of behavior and mental processes.

All psychologists are concerned with some aspect of behavior and mental processes. Unlike the pseudo-sciences, scientific **psychology** demands solid evidence to back up its claims. Within psychology there are many specialties that fall within three broad areas. **Experimental psychologists** primarily do research, but they often teach as well. Those who are primarily **teachers of psychology** work in a variety of settings, including colleges, universities, and high schools. **Applied psychologists** practice many specialties, such as engineering, school, rehabilitation psychology, clinical psychology, and counseling. In contrast with psychology, **psychiatry** is a medical specialty that deals with mental disorder.

In the media, much of what appears to be psychology is actually **pseudopsychology**. Telling the difference requires development of **critical thinking skills**—which this book organizes around the following questions that should be asked when confronting new claims that purport to be scientifically based:

- What is the source?
- Is the claim reasonable or extreme?
- What is the evidence?
- Could bias contaminate the conclusion?
- Does the reasoning avoid common fallacies?
- Does the issue require multiple perspectives?

Unchecked, pseudopsychology can have harmful effects, as seen in the use of the "lobotomy" and the "lie detector." People are attracted to pseudopsychology for many reasons, but one of the most important is **confirmation bias,** which can also blind them to more credible alternatives.

Applied psychologists (p. 5)	**Pseudopsychology** (p. 7)
Confirmation bias (p. 8)	**Psychiatry** (p. 6)
Critical thinking skills (p. 7)	**Psychology** (p. 4)
Emotional bias (p. 8)	**Teachers of psychology** (p. 5)
Experimental psychologists (p. 5)	

MyPsychLab Resources 1.1:

Watch: Cultural Biases: Robert Guthrie

Explore: How to Be a Critical Thinker

1.2 How Do Psychologists Develop New Knowledge?

Core Concept 1.2: Psychologists, like all other scientists, use the scientific method to test their ideas empirically.

Psychology differs from the pseudosciences, such as astrology, in that it employs the scientific method to check its ideas empirically—based on direct observations. The **scientific method** consists of five steps: (1) developing a hypothesis, (2) performing a controlled test, (3) gathering objective data, (4) analyzing the results and accepting or rejecting the **hypothesis**, and (5) publishing, criticizing, and replicating the results. Variations on this scientific method include **experiments, correlational studies,** and several kinds of descriptive research, such as **surveys, naturalistic observations,** and **case studies.** Each differs in the amount of control the researcher has over the conditions being investigated. Everyone, including the scientist, has biases. Researchers can fall prey to **personal bias** and **expectancy bias.** One way that scientists control for bias in their studies involves the double-blind control method. Using the experimental method in large and well-controlled double-blind studies, researchers have failed to find evidence that links sugar to hyperactivity in children.

Psychologists must conduct their work by following a code of ethics, established by the American Psychological Association, for the humane treatment of subjects. Still, some areas of disagreement remain. These especially involve the use of deception and the use of animals as experimental subjects. And, despite the power of science to help us learn about the natural world, there are many important nonscientific questions that science simply cannot answer.

Case study (p. 18)	**Independent variable** (p. 13)
Control group (p. 13)	**Naturalistic observation** (p. 17)
Correlational study (p. 16)	**Negative correlation** (p. 17)
Data (p. 14)	**Operational definitions** (p. 12)
Dependent variable (p. 14)	**Placebo** (p. 19)
Double-blind study (p. 19)	**Positive correlation** (p. 16)
Empirical investigation (p. 11)	**Random assignment** (p. 14)
Expectancy bias (p. 18)	**Replicate** (p. 15)
Experiment (p. 16)	**Scientific method** (p. 11)
Experimental group (p. 13)	**Survey** (p. 17)
Hypothesis (p. 12)	**Theory** (p. 11)

MyPsychLab Resources 1.2:

Simulation: Distinguishing Independent and Dependent Variables

Simulation: Ethics in Psychological Research

Watch: The Complexity of Humans: Phil Zimbardo

- -

1.3 What Are Psychology's Main Perspectives?

Core Concept 1.3: Six main viewpoints dominate the rapidly changing field of modern psychology—the biological, cognitive, behavioral, whole-person, developmental, and social-cultural perspectives—each of which grew out of radical new concepts about mind and behavior.

Psychology has its roots in several sometimes-conflicting traditions stretching back to the ancient Greeks. René Descartes helped the study of the mind to become scientific, based on his assertion that sensations and behaviors are linked to activity in the nervous system—a step that ultimately led to the modern **biological perspective,** which looks for the causes of behavior in physical processes such as brain function and genetics. Biological psychology itself has developed in two directions: the emerging fields of **neuroscience** and **evolutionary psychology.**

The formal beginning of psychology as a science, however, is traced to the establishment by Wundt of the first psychological laboratory in 1879. Wundt's psychology, which American psychologists morphed into **structuralism,** advocated understanding mental processes such as consciousness by investigating their contents and structure. Another early school of psychology, known as **functionalism,** argued that mental processes are best understood in terms of their adaptive purposes and functions. Also in opposition to structuralism, Gestalt psychology focused on perceptual "wholes," rather than parts of consciousness. Each of them was criticized for the use of **introspection,** which some psychologists found too subjective. Nevertheless,

elements of these three "schools" can be found in the modern **cognitive perspective,** with its interest in learning, memory, sensation, perception, language, and thinking and its emphasis on information processing.

The **behavioral perspective** emerged around 1900, rejecting the introspective method and mentalistic explanations, choosing instead to analyze behavior in terms of observable stimuli and responses. Proponents of **behaviorism,** such as John Watson and B. F. Skinner, have exerted a powerful influence on modern psychology, with their emphasis on objective methods, insights into the nature of learning, and effective techniques for the management of undesirable behavior.

Three rather different viewpoints make up the **whole-person perspectives,** which all take a global view of the individual. Sigmund Freud's psychoanalytic approach, with its emphasis on mental disorder and unconscious processes, led to **psychoanalysis** and modern **psychodynamic psychology.** In contrast, **humanistic psychology,** led by Abraham Maslow and Carl Rogers, have emphasized the positive side of human nature. Meanwhile, **trait and temperament psychology** sees people in terms of their persistent characteristics and dispositions.

The **developmental perspective** calls attention to mental and behavioral changes that occur predictably throughout the lifespan. Such changes result from the interaction of heredity and environment. Likewise, the **sociocultural perspective** calls attention to the fact that each individual is influenced by other people and by the culture in which they are all embedded.

Modern psychology has changed rapidly over the past decades, as the biological, cognitive and developmental perspectives have become dominant. At the same time, adherents of different perspectives are joining forces. Another major change involves the increasing number of women and minority-group members entering the field.

While careers in psychology are available at various educational levels, becoming a fully fledged psychologist requires a doctorate. Those with less than a doctorate may find work in various applied specialties as aides, teachers, and counselors, although salaries are usually low.

Behavioral perspective (p. 28)

Behaviorism (p. 28)

Biological perspective (p. 24)

Cognitive perspective (p. 28)

Cross-cultural psychologists (p. 31)

Culture (p. 31)

Developmental perspective (p. 30)

Evolutionary psychology (p. 25)

Functionalism (p. 26)

Humanistic psychology (p. 29)

Introspection (p. 25)

Necker cube (p. 33)

Neuroscience (p. 24)

Psychoanalysis (p. 29)

Psychodynamic psychology (p. 29)

Sociocultural perspective (p. 30)

Structuralism (p. 25)

Trait and temperament psychology (p. 30)

Whole-person perspectives (p. 29)

MyPsychLab Resources 1.3:

Explore: Diversity in Psychological Inquiry

Watch: Even the Rat was White: Robert Guthrie

Watch: Women and the Field of Pychology: Florence Denmark

The Six Modern Perspectives in Psychology

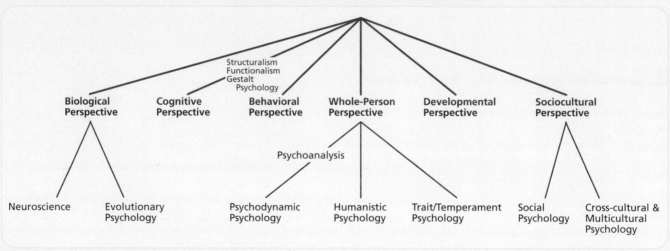

FIGURE 1.8
The Six Modern Perspectives in Psychology

Discovering Psychology Viewing Guide

Watch the following videos by logging into MyPsychLab (www.mypsychlab.com). After you have watched the videos, complete the activities that follow.

 PROGRAM 1:
PAST, PRESENT, AND PROMISE

 PROGRAM 2:
UNDERSTANDING RESEARCH

PROGRAM REVIEW

1. What is the best definition of psychology?
   a. the scientific study of how people interact in social groups
   b. the philosophy explaining the relation between brain and mind
   c. the scientific study of the behavior of individuals and of their mental processes
   d. the knowledge used to predict how virtually any organism will behave under specified conditions

2. As scientists, psychologists do which of the following?
   a. develop methods of inquiry that are fundamentally at odds with those of physics and chemistry
   b. test their theories under carefully controlled experimental circumstances
   c. ignore their own observational biases when collecting data
   d. rely completely on introspective techniques

3. What is the main goal of psychological research?
   a. to cure mental illness
   b. to find the biological bases of the behavior of organisms
   c. to predict and, in some cases, control behavior
   d. to provide valid legal testimony

4. Who founded the first psychology laboratory in the United States?
   a. Wilhelm Wundt
   b. William James
   c. G. Stanley Hall
   d. Sigmund Freud

5. Which of the following psychologists was the first to study people's sensory processing, judgment, attention, and word associations?
   a. G. Stanley Hall
   b. William James
   c. Wilhelm Wundt
   d. Sigmund Freud

6. Which of the following is desirable in research?
   a. having the control and experimental conditions differ on several variables
   b. interpreting correlation as implying causality
   c. systematic manipulation of the variable(s) of interest
   d. using samples of participants who are more capable than the population you want to draw conclusions about

7. What is the main reason the results of research studies are published?
   a. so researchers can prove they earned their money
   b. so other researchers can try to replicate the work
   c. so the general public can understand the importance of spending money on research
   d. so attempts at fraud and trickery are detected

8. Why does the placebo effect work?
   a. because researchers believe it does
   b. because participants believe in the power of the placebo
   c. because human beings prefer feeling they are in control
   d. because it is part of the scientific method

9. What is the purpose of a double-blind procedure?
   a. to test more than one variable at a time
   b. to repeat the results of previously published work
   c. to define a hypothesis clearly before it is tested
   d. to eliminate experimenter bias

10. A prediction of how two or more variables are likely to be related is called a
    a. theory.
    b. conclusion.
    c. hypothesis.
    d. correlation.

11. Imagine a friend tells you that she has been doing better in school since she started taking vitamin pills. When you express disbelief, she urges you to take vitamins too. Why might the pills "work" for her but not necessarily for you?

a. Healthy people don't need vitamins.

b. A belief in the power of the vitamins is necessary for any effect to occur.

c. She is lying.

d. They would work for her and not for you if she was a poor student and you were a straight-A student.

12. In which experiment would a double-blind test be most appropriate?

a. a lab experiment by a technician who does not understand the theory under scrutiny

b. a study designed to test the researcher's own controversial theory

c. a survey asking subjects how many siblings they have

d. an experiment on the effect of a drug on maze running ability in rats

13. Why would other scientists want to replicate an experiment that has already been done?

a. to have their names associated with a well-known phenomenon

b. to gain a high-odds, low-risk publication

c. to ensure that the phenomenon under study is real and reliable

d. to calibrate their equipment with those of another laboratory

14. What is the main focus of Donchin's research involving the P-300 wave?

a. the relation between brain and mind

b. the role of heredity in shaping personality

c. the development of mental illness

d. the role of situational factors in perception

15. The reactions of the boys and the girls to the teacher in the *Candid Camera* episode were essentially similar. Professor Zimbardo attributes this reaction to

a. how easily adolescents become embarrassed.

b. how an attractive teacher violates expectations.

c. the way sexual titillation makes people act.

d. the need people have to hide their real reactions.

16. Which cluster of topics did William James consider the main concerns of psychology?

a. reaction times, sensory stimuli, word associations

b. consciousness, self, emotions

c. conditioned responses, psychophysics

d. experimental design, computer models

17. The amygdala is an area of the brain that processes

a. sound.

b. social status.

c. faces.

d. emotion.

18. How did Wundtian psychologists, such as Hall, react to William James's concept of psychology?

a. They accepted it with minor reservations.

b. They expanded it to include consciousness and the self.

c. They rejected it as unscientific.

d. They revised it to include the thinking of Sigmund Freud.

19. Who wrote *Principles of Psychology* and thereby became arguably the most influential psychologist of the last century?

a. G. Stanley Hall

b. Wilhelm Wundt

c. William James

d. Sigmund Freud

20. What assumption underlies the use of reaction times to study prejudice indirectly?

a. People of different ethnic backgrounds are quicker intellectually than people of other ethnicities.

b. Concepts that are associated more strongly in memory are verified more quickly.

c. Prejudice can't be studied in any other way.

d. People respond to emotional memories more slowly than emotionless memories.

QUESTIONS TO CONSIDER

1. Although psychologists are involved in many different kinds of research and professional activities, there are certain fundamental issues that form the basic foundation of psychology. What are they?

2. Why would the study of normal behavior be more important to the science of psychology than an understanding of abnormal behavior?

3. How do your culture, age, gender, education level, and past experience bias your observations about events, your own actions, and the behavior of others?

4. Imagine the year 2500. How do you think the boundaries of psychological and biological research

might have become redefined by then? Do you think the two fields will have become more integrated or more distinct?

5. What is your reaction to the guidelines prohibiting research if it would require deception and if distress is a likely result? Are there studies you think would be valuable to perform but that could not be? Could the same research questions be answered in some other way?

ACTIVITIES

1. Start a personal journal or a log. Make a daily practice of recording events, thoughts, feelings, observations, and questions that catch your attention each day. Include the ordinary and the unusual. Then speculate on the possible forces causing your behavior. As you progress through the course, review your notes and see how your observations and questions reflect what you have learned.

2. As you go through your day-to-day life, watching the news, battling traffic, and making decisions about how to spend your time and money, consider all the ways that psychologists might be interested in studying, facilitating, or intervening in human behavior.

3. Design an experiment that would allow you to show whether a two-week-old child knows who her mother is. Be sure your experimental design can eliminate alternative explanations for your data.

Critical Thinking Applied: Left Brain vs. Right Brain

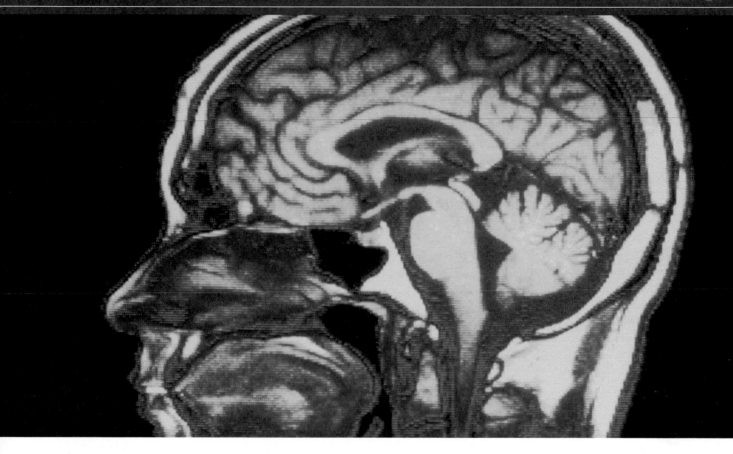

chapter 2
biopsychology, neuroscience, and human *nature*

To visualize the human brain, make two fists and put them together. Your fists represent the two **cerebral hemispheres,** which make up the bulk of the brain and house the neural circuits that give us our powers of learning, memory, thinking, and feeling. The two hemispheres communicate with each other over a connecting band of fibers, known as the **corpus callosum,** shown in Figure 2.1.

Now imagine what your world might be like if the two hemispheres could *not* communicate—if your brain were, somehow, "split" in two. Would you be, literally, "of two minds"? This is not an idle question, because there *are* people with "split brains," the result of a last-resort surgical procedure used to treat a rare condition of almost continuous epileptic seizures.

What could be the rationale for such a drastic procedure? In these patients, abnormal electrical bursts of brain waves seem to "echo" back and forth between the hemispheres, quickly building into a seizure—much as feedback through a microphone

Cerebral hemispheres The large symmetrical halves of the brain located atop the brain stem.

Corpus callosum The band of nerve cells that connects the two cerebral hemispheres.

FIGURE 2.1
The Corpus Callosum

Only the corpus callosum is severed when the brain is "split." This medical procedure prevents communication between the cerebral hemispheres. Strangely, split-brain patients act like people with normal brains under most conditions. Special laboratory tests, however, reveal a duality of consciousness in the split brain.

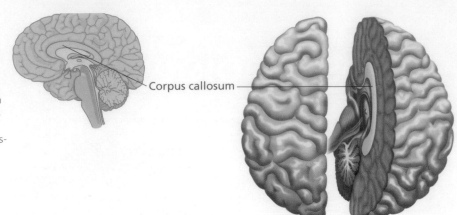

Corpus callosum

generates a loud screeching noise. So the idea is to cut the corpus callosum and thereby prevent the seizure from ranging out of control.

In fact, this neurosurgical trick works quite well. Some patients even become seizure free after the split-brain operation. But what is the psychological price they pay? Curiously, split-brain patients appear mentally and behaviorally unaffected by this extreme procedure under all but the most unusual conditions.

Those unusual conditions involve clever tests contrived by Nobel Prize winner Roger Sperry (1968) and his colleague Michael Gazzaniga (2005). When holding a ball in the left hand, as shown in Figure 2.2, their split-brain patients could not identify it by feel, even though they had no trouble saying what it was when the ball was transferred to the right hand. In another test, split-brain patients said they saw nothing when an image of a spoon flashed briefly on the left side of the visual field. Yet, they could reach around a visual barrier with the right hand and easily pick the spoon out of an array of other objects.

PROBLEM: Why does it make a difference which hand a split-brain patient uses to identify an object by touch?

Finding an answer to this problem requires several pieces of information about the brain that we will assemble throughout this chapter. In the process

FIGURE 2.2
Testing a Split-Brain Patient

Split-brain patients can name unseen objects placed in the right hand, but when an object is placed in the left hand, they cannot name it. Why?

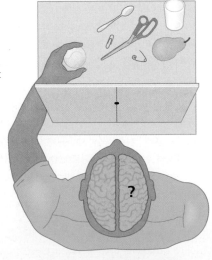

could *not* identify verbally

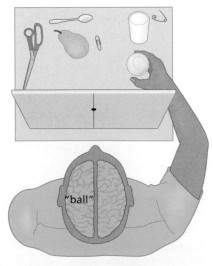

could identify verbally

of understanding why split-brain patients respond as they do, you will gain a broad knowledge of the brain and how it interacts with the rest of the nervous system.

• •

What do we know about the human brain? In the simplest terms, it is about the size of a grapefruit, it weighs about 3 pounds, and it has a pinkish-gray and wrinkled surface. But such bald facts give us no hint of the brain's amazing structure and capabilities. Some 100,000,000,000 nerve cells, each connecting with up to 10,000 other nerve cells, make the human brain the most complex structure known. Our largest computers seem primitive by comparison with its intricate circuitry.

At birth, you had far more nerve cells than you do now. Many of them have been pruned away, probably from disuse in the first few years of your life. (Don't worry: It happens to everyone!) By adolescence the number stabilized. So, while your brain generates some new nerve cells throughout life, and some more cells die along the way, the total remains essentially the same throughout adulthood (Gage, 2003). Even so, it is sobering to realize that some 200,000 brain cells will die every day of your adult life (Dowling, 1992).

As for its capabilities, the human brain uses its vast nerve circuitry to regulate all our body functions, control our behavior, generate our emotions and desires, and process the experiences of a lifetime. Most of this brain activity operates unconsciously behind the scenes—much like the electronics in your TV. Yet, when disease, drugs, or accidents destroy brain cells, the biological basis of the human mind becomes starkly apparent. Then we realize that biology underlies all human sensation and perception, learning and memory, passion and pain, reason—and even madness.

Most remarkable of all, perhaps, the human brain has the ability to think about itself. This fact fascinates specialists in **biopsychology,** who work in a rapidly growing field that lies at the intersection of biology, behavior, and mental processes. Biopsychologists often collaborate with cognitive psychologists, biologists, computer scientists, chemists, neurologists, linguists, and others interested in the connection between brain and mind—how the circuitry of the brain produces mental processes and behavior. The result is a vibrant interdisciplinary field known as *neuroscience* (Kandel & Squire, 2000).

Looking at mind and behavior from a *biological perspective,* as we will throughout this chapter, has produced many practical applications. For example, we now know that certain parts of the brain control sleep patterns—with the result that we now have effective treatments for a number of formerly untreatable sleep disorders. Likewise, the effects of certain psychoactive drugs, such as cocaine, heroin, and methamphetamine, make sense now that we understand how these drugs interact with chemicals made by the brain. And, as we will see, recent discoveries involving "mirror neurons," the genetic code for human life, brain implants, and the biological basis of memory promise many more benefits for people who suffer from brain disease.

We begin our exploration of biopsychology and neuroscience at the most basic level—by considering the twin domains of *genetics* and *evolution,* both of which have shaped our bodies and minds. Next, we will examine the *endocrine system* and the *nervous system,* the two communication channels carrying messages throughout the body. Finally, we will focus on the brain itself. As we follow this path, please keep in mind that we are not asking you to undertake a mere academic exercise: You will come to understand the odd communication patterns of the split brain. More important, you will learn how biological processes also shape your every thought, feeling, and action.

CONNECTION • CHAPTER 8
Neuroscientists have discovered the causes and treatments for many sleep disorders.

Biopsychology   The specialty in psychology that studies the interaction of biology, behavior, and mental processes.

2.1 KEY QUESTION
HOW ARE GENES AND BEHAVIOR LINKED?

Just as fish have an inborn knack for swimming and most birds are built for flight, we humans also have *innate* (inborn) abilities. At birth, the human brain emerges already "programmed" for language, social interaction, self-preservation, and many other functions—as we can readily see in the interaction between babies and their caregivers. Babies "know," for example, how to search for the breast, how to communicate rather effectively through coos and cries, and, surprisingly, how to imitate a person sticking out her tongue. We'll look more closely at the menu of innate human behaviors in our discussion of human development (Chapter 6), but for now, this is the question: How did such potential come to be woven into the brain's fabric?

The scientific answer rests on the concept of **evolution,** the process by which succeeding generations of organisms change as they adapt to changing environments. We can observe evolution in action on a microscopic level, when an antibiotic fails to work on a strain of bacteria that has evolved a resistance. When it comes to larger and more complex organisms, change occurs over much longer time spans, as they adapt to changing climates, predators, diseases, and food supplies. In our own species, for example, change has favored large brains suited to language, complex problem solving, and social interaction.

Our Core Concept for this section makes this evolutionary process the link between genetics and behavior.

core concept | Evolution has fundamentally shaped psychological processes because it favors genetic variations that produce adaptive behavior.

The idea of evolution is both simple and powerful. It also suggests explanations for some otherwise mysterious psychological processes, as you will see. Our explanation of evolution begins in this section with the story of Charles Darwin, who gave the idea of evolutionary change to the world. Following that, we will build on Darwin's insight with a look at *genetics,* which involves the molecular machinery that makes evolution work—and ultimately influences all our thoughts and behaviors.

Evolution and Natural Selection

Although he had trained for careers in both medicine and the ministry, Charles Darwin decided that biology was his calling. So, in 1831, he signed on as a naturalist aboard HMS *Beagle,* a British research vessel commissioned to survey the coastline of South America. Returning five years later with numerous specimens and detailed records of the many unusual life-forms he had found, Darwin also brought home the radical idea of a relationship among species. Struck by the similarities among the various animals and plants he studied, Darwin concluded that all creatures, including humans, share a common ancestry.

He knew this notion flew in the face of accepted scholarship, as well as the religious doctrine of creationism. So, in his famous book *On the Origin of Species* (1859), Darwin carefully made the case for the evolution of life. And controversial it was. The essential features of his argument, however, withstood withering attacks, and eventually the theory of evolution created a fundamental change in the way people saw their relationship to other living things (Keynes, 2002; Mayr, 2000).

The Evidence That Convinced Darwin
What was the evidence that led Darwin to his radical conclusion about the evolution of organisms? Again and again on the voyage, he had observed organisms that were exquisitely adapted to their environments: flowers that attracted certain insects, birds with beaks perfectly suited

Evolution The gradual process of biological change that occurs in a species as it adapts to its environment.

to cracking certain seeds. But he had also observed *variation* among individuals within a species—just as some humans are taller than others or have better eyesight (Weiner, 1994). It occurred to Darwin that such variations could give one individual an advantage over others in the struggle for survival and reproduction. This, then, suggested a mechanism for evolution: a "weeding out" process that he called **natural selection.** By means of natural selection, those individuals best adapted to the environment are more likely to flourish and reproduce; those that are poorly adapted will tend to leave fewer offspring, and their line may die out. (You may have heard this described as *survival of the fittest,* a term Darwin disliked.) Through natural selection, then, a species gradually changes as it adapts to its environment.

Application to Psychology This process of adaptation and evolution helps us to make sense of many observations we make in psychology. For example, human *phobias* (extreme and incapacitating fears) almost always involve stimuli that signaled danger to our ancestors (snakes, lightning, or blood). In the same way, the fact that we spend about a third of our lives asleep makes sense in evolutionary terms: Sleep kept our ancestors out of trouble in the dark. Evolution also explains our innate preferences and distastes, such as the attractiveness of sweets and fatty foods (good sources of valuable calories for our ancestors) and a dislike for bitter-tasting substances (often a sign of poisons).

Evolution is, of course, an emotionally loaded term, and, as a result, many people have a distorted understanding of its real meaning. For example, some believe that Darwin's theory says humans "come from monkeys." But neither Darwin nor any other evolutionary scientist has ever said that. Rather, they say people and monkeys had a common ancestor millions of years ago—a big difference. Evolutionary theory says that, over time, the two species have diverged, with each developing different sets of adaptive traits. For humans, this meant developing a big brain adapted for language (Buss et al., 1998).

We should be clear that the basic principles of evolution, while still controversial in some quarters, have been accepted by virtually all scientists for more than a century. That said, we should also note that evolutionary theory is a controversial newcomer to psychology. It is not that psychologists dispute Darwin— most do not. Rather, the controversy centers on whether an evolutionary approach places too much emphasis on *nature*, the biological basis of psychology, and not enough emphasis on *nurture*, the role of learning. As we saw in Chapter 1, this *nature–nurture issue* has a long history in psychology, and it is an issue that we will meet again and again throughout this book.

Natural selection The driving force behind evolution, by which the environment "selects" the fittest organisms.

In later chapters we will discuss specific evolutionary theories that have been advanced to explain aggression, jealousy, sexual orientation, physical attraction and mate selection, parenting, cooperation, temperament, morality, and (always a psychological hot potato) gender differences. But for now, let us turn our attention to genetics and the biological underpinnings of heredity and evolutionary change.

Genetics and Inheritance

In principle, the genetic code is quite simple. Much as the microscopic pits in a CD encode information that can become pictures or music, your *genes* encode information that can become inherited traits. Consider your own unique combination of physical characteristics. Your height, facial features, and hair color, for example, all stem from the encoded genetic "blueprint" inherited from your parents and inscribed in every cell in your body. Likewise, genetics influences psychological characteristics, including your basic temperament, tendency to fears, and certain behavior patterns (Pinker, 2002).

Yet, even under the influence of heredity, you are a unique individual—different from either of your parents. One source of your uniqueness lies in your experience: the environment in which you grew up—distinct in time and, perhaps, in place from that of your parents. Another source of difference between you and either of your parents arises from the random combination of traits, both physical and psychological, that each parent passed on to you from past generations in their own family lines. This hybrid inheritance produced your unique **genotype**, the genetic pattern that makes you different from anyone else on earth. Still, as different as people may seem, 99.9 percent of our genetic material is the same (Marks, 2004).

If the genotype is the "blueprint," then the resulting structure is the **phenotype**. All your physical characteristics make up your phenotype, including not only your visible traits (for instance, your height or your hair color) but also "hidden" biological traits, such as the chemistry and "wiring" of your brain. In fact, any *observable* characteristic is part of the phenotype—so the phenotype includes *behavior*. We should quickly point out that, while the phenotype is based in biology, it is not completely determined by heredity. Heredity never acts alone but always in partnership with the environment, which includes such biological influences as nutrition, disease, stress, and experiences that leave a lasting mark in the form of learning. We can easily see the influence of environment in, for example, poor medical care that results in a birth defect.

Now, with these ideas about heredity, environment, genotypes, and phenotypes fresh in mind, let's turn to the details of heredity and individual variation that were yet to be discovered in Darwin's time.

Chromosomes, Genes, and DNA   The blockbuster film *Jurassic Park* and its sequels relied on a clever twist of plot in which scientists recovered the genetic code for dinosaurs and created an island full of reptilian problems. The stories, of course, are science fiction, yet the films rest on an important scientific fact: Every cell in the body carries a complete set of biological instructions for building the organism. For humans, these instructions are spelled out in 23 pairs of *chromosomes*, which, under a high-powered microscope, look like tiny twisted threads. Zooming in for an even closer look, we find that each chromosome consists of a long and tightly coiled chain of **DNA** (deoxyribonucleic acid), a molecule that happens to be especially well suited for storing biological information.

Genes are the "words" that make up each organism's instruction manual. Encoded in short segments of DNA, each gene contributes to the operation of an organism by specifying a single protein. Thousands of such proteins, in turn, serve as the building blocks for the organism's physical characteristics (part of the phenotype) and the regulation of the body's internal operations. Genes,

CONNECTION • CHAPTER 10

Infants differ on their tendency to be shy or outgoing, which is believed to be an aspect of *temperament* that has a strong biological basis.

Genotype   An organism's genetic makeup.

Phenotype   An organism's observable physical and behavioral characteristics.

DNA   A long, complex molecule that encodes genetic characteristics. DNA is an abbreviation for deoxyribonucleic acid.

Gene   Segment of a chromosome that encodes the directions for the inherited physical and mental characteristics of an organism. Genes are the functional units of a chromosome.

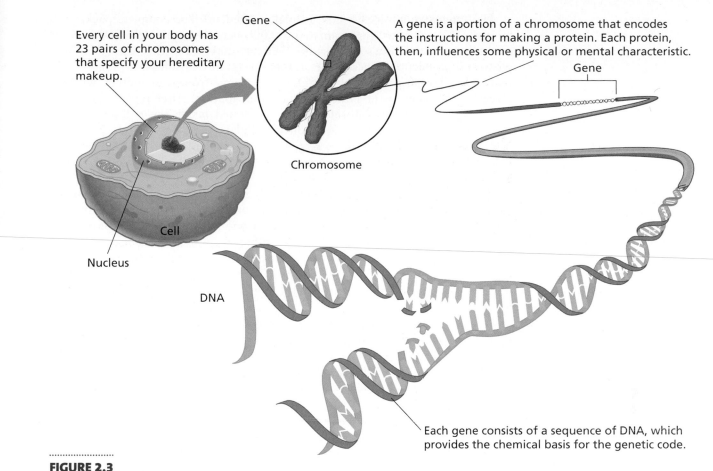

Every cell in your body has 23 pairs of chromosomes that specify your hereditary makeup.

Gene

A gene is a portion of a chromosome that encodes the instructions for making a protein. Each protein, then, influences some physical or mental characteristic.

Gene

Chromosome

Cell

Nucleus

DNA

Each gene consists of a sequence of DNA, which provides the chemical basis for the genetic code.

FIGURE 2.3

DNA, Genes, and Chromosomes

A chromosome is composed mainly of a tightly coiled strand of DNA, an incredibly long molecule. Each chromosome contains thousands of genes, along with instructions for the "when" and "how" of gene expression. Genes themselves are segments of DNA. Each gene contains instructions, coded in the four-nucleotide alphabet, for making a protein. The Human Genome Project has identified the sequence of nucleotides in all 23 pairs of our chromosomes.

because they differ slightly from one individual to another, provide the biological source for the variation that caught Darwin's attention.

Like the string of words in this paragraph, genes occur in sequence on the **chromosomes.** But the chromosomes are much more than strings of genes. Like paragraphs, they also contain "punctuation" that indicates where each gene begins and ends, along with commands specifying how and when the genes will be expressed (Gibbs, 2003). Sometimes, however, these commands are wrong, or the genes themselves have defects. The resulting errors in gene expression can cause physical and developmental problems, such as cerebral palsy and mental retardation.

On a still smaller scale (now we're getting beyond the power of microscopes to resolve), genes are composed of even tinier molecular units called *nucleotides* that serve as individual "letters" in the genetic "words." Instead of a 26-letter alphabet, the genetic code uses just four nucleotides. Consequently, a particular gene may require hundreds of nucleotides to specify a particular protein.

Physically, the nucleotides fit together in pairs, rather like the opposing teeth in a zipper. Then, when a protein is needed, the nucleotides in the appropriate segment of DNA "unzip," forming a jagged pattern, or template, from which the protein is built. (See Figure 2.3.)

Chromosome Tightly coiled threadlike structure along which the genes are organized, like beads on a necklace. Chromosomes consist primarily of DNA.

How many genes does it take to make a human? The complete package of human DNA contains approximately 30,000 genes—surprisingly few, in view of the human organism's complexity (Marcus, 2004). Together with their supplemental instructions, these genes reside on 46 chromosomes, arranged in 23 pairs. One in each pair of your chromosomes came from your mother, with the remaining 23 being your father's genetic contribution. After repeated duplication, copies of all this information are crammed inside the trillions of cells throughout your body, where they direct cellular operations. In this way, your body, with all its cells, is like a large corporation that relies on many individual computers—each of which requires its own copy of the operating system software.

Two of the 46 chromosomes warrant special mention: the **sex chromosomes.** Named X and Y for their shape, these chromosomes carry genes encoding for a male or a female phenotype. We all inherit one X chromosome from our biological mothers. In addition, we receive either an X or a Y from our biological fathers. When they pair up, two X chromosomes (XX) contain the code for femaleness, while an XY pair codes for maleness. In this sense, then, the chromosome we get from our fathers—either an X or a Y—determines our biological sex.

It is important to note that you do not inherit copies of *all* your father's and mother's genes. Rather you get half of each, randomly shuffled—which explains why siblings all have slightly different genotypes (unless they are identical twins). This random shuffling and recombining of parental genes produces the variation that Darwin viewed as the raw material for evolution.

Genetic Explanations for Psychological Processes Most of the foregoing discussion of heredity and genetics could apply equally to fruit flies and butterflies, hollyhocks and humans. All organisms follow the same basic laws of heredity. The differences among different species arise, then, from different genetic "words"—the genes themselves—"spelled" with the same four letters of life's universal four-letter alphabet.

And what does all this have to do with psychology? Simply put, genes influence our psychological characteristics as well as our physical traits. In later chapters we will explore the extent to which genes affect such diverse human attributes as intelligence, personality, mental disorders, reading and language disabilities, and (perhaps) sexual orientation. Even our fears can have some genetic basis (Hariri et al., 2002). But, because genetic psychology is still a field in its infancy, we don't yet know exactly how or to what extent genes are involved in most psychological processes (Rutter, 2006).

In only a few cases can we hold a single gene responsible for a specific psychological disorder. For example, just one abnormal gene has been linked to a rare pattern of impulsive violence found in several members of a Dutch family (Brunner et al., 1993). Most other genetically influenced disorders appear to involve multiple genes, often on more than one chromosome (Plomin, 2000). Experts think it likely that multiple genes contribute, for example, to schizophrenia, a severe mental disorder, and to Alzheimer's disease, a form of dementia. (See St. George-Hyslop, 2000).

So, does this mean that heredity determines our psychological destiny? Will you grow up to be like your Uncle Henry? Not to worry. Although you share many of his genes, your heredity never acts alone. Heredity and environment always work together to influence our behavior and mental processes (Pinker, 2002). Even identical twins, who share the same genotype, display individual differences in appearance and personality that result from their distinct experiences, such as exposure to different people, places, chemicals, and diseases. Moreover, studies show that, when one identical twin acquires a psychological disorder known to have a genetic basis (schizophrenia, for example), the other twin does not necessarily develop the same disorder. This is the takeaway mes-

CONNECTION • CHAPTER 12
Schizophrenia is a psychotic disorder that affects about 1 out of 100 persons.

Sex chromosomes The X and Y chromosomes that determine our physical sex characteristics.

sage: *Never attribute psychological characteristics to genetics alone* (Ehrlich, 2000a,b; Mauron, 2001).

An example of the interaction between heredity and environment—and one of the rays of hope that has come from biopsychology—can be seen in a condition called *Down's syndrome*. Associated with an extra chromosome 21, this disorder includes markedly impaired physical development, as well as mental retardation. Only a few years ago, people with Down's syndrome faced bleak and unproductive lives, shut away in institutions, where they depended almost wholly on others to fulfill their basic needs. Now, a better understanding of the disorder, along with a deeper appreciation for the interaction between genetics and environment, has changed that outlook. Although no cure has been found, today we know that people with Down's syndrome are capable of considerable learning, despite their genetic impairment. With special programs that teach life skills, those with Down's syndrome now can learn to care for themselves, work, and establish some personal independence.

"Race" and Human Variation   Certain features of skin color and other physical characteristics are more (or less) common among people who trace their ancestry to the same part of the world. Tropical ancestry is often associated with darker skin, which affords some protection from the sun, and lighter skin frequently identifies people from high latitudes, which receive less sun. While it is common to speak of "race" in terms of these superficial characteristics, biologists tell us that there are no physical characteristics that divide people cleanly into distinct "racial" groups. We are all one species.

In reality, the physical characteristics of the so-called "races" blend seamlessly one into another. We should think of "race," therefore, as a socially defined term, rather than a biological one. Alternatively, the concept of *culture* serves as a far better explanation for most—perhaps all—the group differences that are important to psychologists (Cohen, 1998).

In this chapter, where we talk about the brain, we should be especially clear that there is no physical characteristic that reliably distinguishes the brain of a person of one geographic region, skin color, or ethnic origin from that of another. Inside the skull are many physical differences—even some gender differences—but no race-based differences.

Just because race is not a precise biological concept, however, doesn't mean that its social meaning is unimportant. On the contrary, race as a socially defined category can exert powerful influences on behavior. We will see, for example, that social conceptions of race influence expectations and prejudices. Please keep this notion in mind when we look at studies in which people who identify with different racial or ethnic groups are compared, for example on intelligence and academic achievement (Eberhardt & Randall, 1997; Hirschfeld, 1996).

PSYCHOLOGYMATTERS
Choosing Your Children's Genes

Scientists already have the ability to control and alter the genetics of animals, like Dolly, the late and famous fatherless sheep, cloned from one of her mother's cells. But what about the prospects for genetic manipulation in people? Thanks to the scientists working on the Human Genome Project, the human genetic code has been cracked: We now know the sequence of nucleotides on all the human chromosomes (Pennisi, 2001).

Psychologists expect this information to teach us something about the genetic basis for human differences in abilities, emotions, and resistance to stress (Kosslyn et al., 2002). The rest of the 21st century will see us mining the data for insight into the genetic basis for many physical and mental difficulties. High on the list will be disorders that affect millions: cancer, heart disease, schizophrenia, and Alzheimer's disease. But not all the promise of human genetics lies in the future. We can already sample fetal cells and search for certain genetic problems, such as Down's syndrome.

Right now, with a little clinical help, parents can select the sex of a child with a fair degree of certainty. And, within your lifetime, parents may be able to select specific genes for their children, much as you select the components of a deli sandwich. Most probably we will learn to alter the DNA in a developing fetus in order to add or delete certain physical and mental traits (Henig, 1998). This might be done by infecting the fetus with a harmless virus containing desirable genes that will alter or replace the genetic blueprint in every cell of the body. Another approach might involve injecting *stem cells* ("generic" cells that have not fully committed themselves to becoming a particular type of tissue) that have desirable genetic characteristics (Doetsch, 2002). But what will be the price of this technology?

Undoubtedly, parents in this brave new genetic world will want their children to be smart and good looking—but, we might wonder, by what standards will intelligence and looks be judged? And will everyone be able to place an order for their children's genes—or only the very wealthy? You can be certain that the problems we face will be simultaneously biological, psychological, political, and ethical (Patenaude et al., 2002).

Already, psychologists are called on to provide guidance about how genetic knowledge can best be applied (Bronheim, 2000), particularly in helping people assess genetic risks in connection with family planning. We invite you to grapple with these issues by answering the following questions:

CONNECTION • CHAPTER 5
While intelligence is influenced by heredity, the relative contributions of nature and nurture are hotly debated.

- If you could select three genetic traits for your children, which ones would you select?

- How would you feel about raising children you have adopted or fostered but to whom you are not genetically related?

- If a biological child of yours might be born disabled or fatally ill because of your genetic heritage, would you have children anyway? What circumstances or conditions would affect your decision?

- If you knew you might carry a gene responsible for a serious medical or behavioral disorder, would you want to be tested before having children? And would it be fair for a prospective partner to require you to be tested before conceiving children? Would it be fair for the state to make such a requirement?

These questions, of course, have no "right" answers; but the answers you give will help you define your stand on some of the most important issues we will face in this century. When answering these questions, consider how the critical thinking guidelines from Chapter 1 might affect your responses. For instance, to what degree might your own emotional bias color your reaction to these questions?

CheckYourUnderstanding

1. **RECALL:** Explain how natural selection works to increase certain genetic characteristics with a population of organisms.

2. **APPLICATION:** Name one of your own characteristics that is a part of your phenotype.

3. **RECALL:** Which of the following statements expresses the correct relationship?
   a. Genes are made of chromosomes.
   b. DNA is made of chromosomes.

   c. Nucleotides are made of genes.
   d. Genes are made of DNA.

4. **ANALYSIS:** In purely evolutionary terms, which one would be a measure of your own success as an organism?
   a. your intellectual accomplishments
   b. the length of your life
   c. the number of children you have
   d. the contributions that you make to the happiness of humanity

2.2 KEY QUESTION
HOW DOES THE BODY COMMUNICATE INTERNALLY?

You are driving on a winding mountain road, and suddenly a car comes directly at you. At the last instant, you and the other driver swerve in opposite directions. Your heart pounds—and it keeps pounding for several minutes after the danger has passed. Externally, you have avoided a potentially fatal accident. Internally, your body has responded to two kinds of messages from its two communication systems.

One is the fast-acting *nervous system*, with its extensive network of nerve cells carrying messages in pulses of electrical and chemical energy throughout the body. This first-responder network comes quickly to your rescue in an emergency, carrying the orders that accelerate your heart and tense your muscles for action. The other communication network, the slower-acting *endocrine system*, sends follow-up messages that support and sustain the response initiated by the nervous system. To do this, the endocrine glands, including the pituitary, thyroid, adrenals, and gonads, use the chemical messengers we call *hormones*.

The two internal message systems cooperate not only in stressful situations but in happier circumstances of high arousal, as when you receive an unexpected "A" on a test or meet someone especially attractive. The endocrine system and nervous system also work together during states of low arousal, to keep the vital body functions operating smoothly. Managing this cooperation between the endocrine system and the nervous system is the body's chief executive, the brain—which brings us to our Core Concept:

The brain coordinates the body's two communications systems, the nervous system and the endocrine system, which use similar chemical processes to communicate with targets throughout the body.

core concept

Why is this notion important for your understanding of psychology? For one thing, these two communication systems are the biological bedrock for all our thoughts, emotions, and behaviors. Another reason for studying the biology behind the body's internal communications is it can help us understand how drugs, such as caffeine, alcohol, heroin, and Prozac, can change the chemistry of the mind. Finally, it will help you understand many common mental and behavioral disorders, such as stroke, Alzheimer's disease, and schizophrenia.

Our overview of the body's dual communication systems first spotlights the building block of the nervous system: the *neuron*. Next, we will see how networks of these neurons work together as modular components of the great network of the *nervous system* that extends all through the body. Then, we will shift our attention to the *endocrine system*, a group of glands that operates together and in parallel with the nervous system—again throughout the body.

The Neuron: Building Block of the Nervous System

Like transistors in a computer, *neurons* or *nerve cells* are the fundamental processing units in the brain. In simplest terms, a **neuron** is merely a cell special-

Neuron Cell specialized to receive and transmit information to other cells in the body—also called a *nerve cell*. Bundles of many neurons are called *nerves*.

FIGURE 2.4
Sensory Neurons, Motor Neurons, and Interneurons

Information about the water temperature in the shower is carried by thousands of *sensory neurons* (afferent neurons) from the sense organs to the central nervous system. In this case, the message enters the spinal cord and is relayed, by *interneurons,* to the brain. There, the information is assessed and a response is initiated ("Turn the water temperature down!"). These instructions are sent to the muscles by means of *motor neurons* (efferent neurons). Large bundles of the message-carrying fibers from these neurons are called *nerves.*

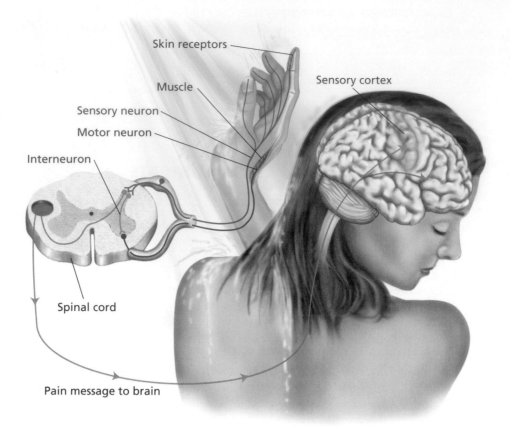

Skin receptors

Muscle

Sensory neuron

Motor neuron

Interneuron

Sensory cortex

Spinal cord

Pain message to brain

ized to receive, process, and transmit information to other cells. And neurons do that very efficiently: A typical nerve cell may receive messages from a thousand others and, within a fraction of a second, decide to "fire," passing the message along at speeds up to 100 meters per second to another thousand neurons— sometimes as many as 10,000 (Pinel, 2005).

Types of Neurons   While neurons vary in shape and size, all have essentially the same structure, and all send messages in essentially the same way. Nevertheless, biopsychologists distinguish three major classes of neurons according to their location and function: *sensory neurons, motor neurons,* and *interneurons.* (See Figure 2.4.) **Sensory neurons,** or *afferent neurons,* act like one-way streets that carry traffic from the sense organs *toward* the brain. Accordingly, afferent neurons treat the brain to all your sensory experience, including vision, hearing, taste, touch, smell, pain, and balance. For example, when you test the water temperature in the shower with your hand, afferent neurons carry the message toward the brain.

In contrast, **motor neurons,** or *efferent neurons,* form the one-way routes that transport messages *away* from the brain and spinal cord to the muscles, organs, and glands. Motor neurons, therefore, carry the instructions for all our actions. So, in our shower example, the motor neurons deliver the message that tells your hand just how much to move the shower control knob.

Sensory and motor neurons rarely communicate directly with each other, except in the simplest of reflexive circuits. Instead, they usually rely on the go-between **interneurons** (also shown in Figure 2.4), which make up most of the billions of cells in the brain and spinal cord. Interneurons relay messages from sensory neurons to other interneurons or to motor neurons, sometimes in complex pathways. In fact, the brain itself is mostly a network of billions of intricately connected interneurons. To see how fast these neural circuits work, try the demonstration in the accompanying "Do It Yourself!" box.

Sensory neuron   A nerve cell that carries messages *toward* the central nervous system from sense receptors. Also called *afferent neurons.*

Motor neuron   A nerve cell that carries messages *away* from the central nervous system toward the muscles and glands. Also called *efferent neurons.*

Interneuron   A nerve cell that relays messages between nerve cells, especially in the brain and spinal cord.

How Neurons Work   A look at Figure 2.5 will help you visualize the neuron's main components. The "receiver" parts, which accept most of the incoming messages, consist of finely branched fibers called **dendrites.** These dendritic fibers extend outward from the cell body, where they act like a net, collecting messages received by direct stimulation of the sense organs (e.g., the eyes, ears, or skin) or from other neurons.

Significantly, neuroscientists have discovered that learning can cause subtle changes in our dendrites (Barinaga, 2000). As you might imagine, this discovery has launched a search for drugs that may one day improve learning. While students will probably never be able to take a pill instead of a psychology class, a more realistic possibility involves a chemical that will help them remember what they have read or heard in class. For the moment, the best we have to offer is coffee or tea—the caffeine in which actually acts as a mild, but temporary, stimulus to the dendrites (Julien, 2005). (Whether or not caffeine actually promotes learning is controversial.)

Dendrites complete their job by passing messages on to the central part of the neuron, called the *cell body* or **soma.** Not only does the soma contain the cell's chromosomes, it must also assess the messages received by the cell. Input from a single nerve cell carries little weight in this process, because a typical neuron may receive stimulation from hundreds or even thousands of other neurons. Making the assessment even more complex, some of these messages received by the neuron can be *excitatory* (saying, in effect, "Fire!") or *inhibitory* ("Don't fire!"). The "decision" made by the cell body depends on its overall level of arousal—which depends, in turn, on the sum of all the incoming messages.

When sufficient excitation triumphs over inhibition, the neuron initiates a message of its own, sent along a single "transmitter" fiber, known as the **axon.** In some cases, these axons can extend over considerable distances: In a college basketball player, the axons connecting the spinal cord with the toes can be more than a meter in length. At the other extreme, the axons of interneurons in the brain may span only a tiny fraction of an inch.

The Action Potential   When arousal in the cell body reaches a critical level, it triggers an electrical impulse in the axon—like the electronic flash of a camera—and, as we said, the cell "fires." Much like a battery, the axon gets the electrical energy it needs to fire from charged chemicals, called *ions.* In its normal, resting state, the ions within the axon give it a negative electrical charge, appropriately called the **resting potential.** But this negative state is easily upset. When the cell body becomes excited, it triggers a cascade of events, known as the **action potential,** that temporarily reverses the charge and causes an electrical signal to race along the axon. (See Figure 2.5.) This happens when tiny pores open in a small area of the axon's membrane adjacent to the soma, allowing a rapid influx of positive ions. Almost immediately, the internal charge in that part of the axon changes from negative to

Dendrite   Branched fiber that extends outward from the cell body and carries information into the neuron.

Soma   The part of a cell (such as a neuron) containing the nucleus, which includes the chromosomes. Also called the *cell body.*

Axon   In a nerve cell, an extended fiber that conducts information from the soma to the terminal buttons. Information travels along the axon in the form of an electric charge, called the *action potential.*

Resting potential   The electrical charge of the axon in its inactive state, when the neuron is ready to "fire."

Action potential   The nerve impulse caused by a change in the electrical charge across the cell membrane of the axon. When the neuron "fires," this charge travels down the axon and causes neurotransmitters to be released by the terminal buttons.

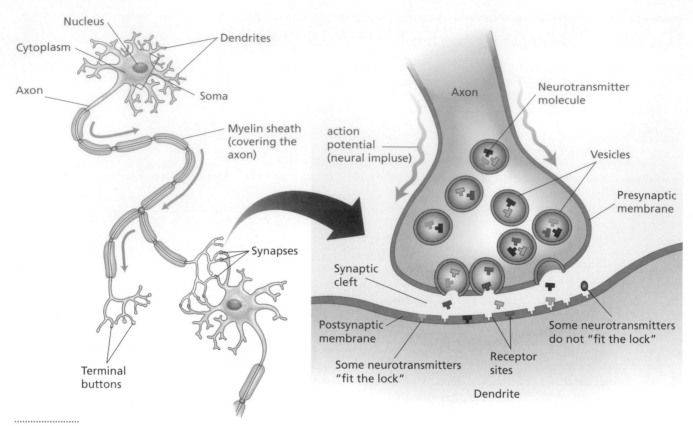

FIGURE 2.5
Structure and Function of the Neuron

A typical neuron receives thousands of messages at a time through its *dendrites* and *soma* (cell body). When the soma becomes sufficiently aroused, its own message is then passed to the *axon*, which transmits it by means of an *action potential* to the cell's *terminal buttons*. There tiny vesicles containing *neurotransmitters* rupture and release their contents into the *synapse* (synaptic cleft). Appropriately shaped transmitter molecules arriving at the postsynaptic membrane can dock at *receptors*, where they stimulate the receiving cell. Excessive transmitter is taken back into the "sending" neuron by means of *reuptake*.

All-or-none principle Refers to the fact that the action potential in the axon occurs either completely or not at all.

Synapse The microscopic gap that serves as a communications link between neurons. Synapses also occur between neurons and the muscles or glands they serve.

Terminal buttons Tiny bulblike structures at the end of the axon that contain neurotransmitters that carry the neuron's message into the synapse.

Synaptic transmission The relaying of information across the synapse by means of chemical neurotransmitters.

positive. (We're talking 1/1000 of a second here.) Then, like a row of falling dominoes, these changes in the cell membrane progress down the axon. The result is an electrical signal that races from the soma toward the axon ending. There's no halfway about this action potential: Either the axon "fires" or it doesn't. Neuroscientists call this the **all-or-none principle**. Incidentally, when this process careens out of control, with very large numbers of neurons becoming hypersensitive and firing too easily, the result can be an epileptic seizure.

Almost immediately after firing, the cell's "ion pump" flushes out the positively charged ions and restores the neuron to its resting potential, ready to fire again. Incredibly, the whole complex cycle may take place in less than a hundredth of a second. It is an amazing performance—but this is not the end of the matter. Information carried by the action potential still must traverse a tiny gap before reaching another cell.

Synaptic Transmission The microscopic gap between nerve cells, called the **synapse,** acts as an electrical insulator in most neurons. (See Figure 2.5.) This *synaptic gap* (or *synaptic cleft*) prevents the charge from jumping directly from the axon to the next cell in the circuit (Dermietzel, 2006). To pass a message across the synaptic gap, the neuron must stimulate tiny bulblike structures called **terminal buttons,** found at the ends of the axon. There, in a remarkable sequence of events known as **synaptic transmission,** the electrical message morphs into a chemical message that easily flows across the synaptic cleft between neurons.

Neurotransmitters When the electrical impulse arrives at the terminal buttons, it causes bursting of tiny bubblelike *vesicles* (sacs) located next to the synapse. This causes the vesicles to release their contents, consisting of chemical **neurotransmitters,** into the synapse. These neurotransmitters, expelled from the vesicles, then carry the neural message across the gap to the next neuron in the chain. (Again, see Figure 2.5.)

Each ruptured vesicle releases about 5000 neurotransmitter molecules into the synapse (Kandel & Squire, 2000). There, if they have the right shape, the neurotransmitters can fit into special *receptors* in the receiving neuron—much as a key fits into a lock. This lock-and-key process stimulates the receiving neuron, which passes the message onward.

After the transmitter molecules have done their work, other chemicals break them down and recycle them back to vesicles inside the terminal buttons for reuse. Many of the transmitter molecules, however, don't make it across the synapse. Through a process called *reuptake,* a large fraction of transmitters are intercepted within the synapse and drawn back into vesicles. Reuptake, then, has the effect of "turning the volume down" on the message being transmitted between neurons. Certain drugs—such as the well-known Prozac—interfere with the reuptake process, as we will see in more detail when we later discuss drug therapy for mental disorders (in Chapter 13).

The brain uses dozens of different neurotransmitters, and Table 2.1 describes several that have proved especially important in psychological functioning. Neuroscientists believe that imbalances in these neurotransmitters underlie certain disorders, such as depression. It shouldn't surprise us, then, that most drugs used to treat mental disorders act like neurotransmitters or otherwise affect the action of neurotransmitters on nerve cells. Similarly, drugs of abuse (heroin, cocaine, methamphetamine, for example) either mimic, enhance, or inhibit our brains' natural neurotransmitters. We will talk more about neurotransmitters and their relation to drug action in the "Psychology Matters" section, coming up.

Synchronous Firing Over the last decade, neuroscientists have discovered that some neurons—a small minority—don't play by the customary rules of synaptic transmission. That is, instead of using neurotransmitters to send messages across the synapse, they forego the chemical messages and communicate directly through electrical connections (Bullock et al., 2005; Dermietzel, 2006). Scientists have found these exceptional neurons with electrical synapses concentrated in special parts of the brain that orchestrate synchronized activity in a large number of other neurons, such as those involved in the coordinated beating of the heart. These synchronized bursts may also underlie the greatest mystery of all in the brain: how the brain combines input from many different modules into a single sensation, idea, or action.

Plasticity Regardless of the communication method—electrical or chemical—neurons have the remarkable ability to *change.* That is, neurons can make new connections or strengthen old ones, a hugely important property known as **plasticity.** This means that the nervous system, and especially the brain, has the ability to adapt or modify itself as the result of experience (M. Holloway, 2003; Kandel & Squire, 2000). Earlier we discussed one form of plasticity that involves changes within dendrites when we learn. Another form involves making new synapses, a process also believed to be involved in learning. In addition, plasticity may account for the brain's ability to compensate for injury, as when one region takes on a new task, pinch-hitting for another site that can has been injured—as in a stroke or head trauma (Pinel, 2005). In all these ways, then, plasticity is a property that allows the brain to be restructured and "reprogrammed" by experience.

Here is a more subtle point: Because of the brain's neural plasticity, interactions with the outside world can change its physical structure (LeDoux, 2002). For example, as a violin player gains expertise, the motor area linked to the fingers of the left hand becomes larger (Juliano, 1998). Likewise, the brain dedicates more neural real estate to the index finger used by a blind Braille reader

Neurotransmitter Chemical messenger that relays neural messages across the synapse. Many neurotransmitters are also hormones.

Plasticity The nervous system's ability to adapt or change as the result of experience. Plasticity may also help the nervous system adapt to physical damage.

TABLE 2.1   Seven Important Neurotransmitters

Neurotransmitter	Normal Function	Problems Associated with Imbalance	Substances That Affect the Action of This Neurotransmitter
Dopamine	A transmitter used in brain circuits that produce sensations of pleasure and reward Used by CNS neurons involved in voluntary movement	Schizophrenia Parkinson's disease	Cocaine Amphetamine Methylphenidate (Ritalin) Alcohol
Serotonin	Regulates sleep and dreaming, mood, pain, aggression, appetite, and sexual behavior	Depression Certain anxiety disorders Obsessive–compulsive disorder	Fluoxetine (Prozac) Hallucinogenics (e.g., LSD)
Norepinephrine	Used by neurons in autonomic nervous system and by neurons in almost every region of the brain Controls heart rate, sleep, stress, sexual responsiveness, vigilance, and appetite	High blood pressure Depression	Tricyclic antidepressants Beta-blockers
Acetylcholine	The primary neurotransmitter used by efferent neurons carrying messages from the CNS Also involved in some kinds of learning and memory	Certain muscular disorders Alzheimer's disease	Nicotine Black widow spider venom Botulism toxin Curare Atropine
GABA	The most prevalent inhibitory neurotransmitter in neurons of the CNS	Anxiety Epilepsy	Barbiturates "Minor" tranquilizers (e.g., Valium, Librium) Alcohol
Glutamate	The primary excitatory neurotransmitter in the CNS Involved in learning and memory	Release of excessive glutamate apparently causes brain damage after stroke	PCP ("angel dust")
Endorphins	Pleasurable sensations and control of pain	Lowered levels resulting from opiate addiction	Opiates: opium, heroin, morphine, methadone

CONNECTION • CHAPTER 14

Extremely threatening experiences can cause *posttraumatic stress disorder,* which can produce physical changes in the brain.

(Elbert et al., 1995; LeDoux, 1996). While these changes in the brain usually have beneficial effects, plasticity also allows traumatic experiences to alter the brain's emotional responsiveness in detrimental ways (Arnsten, 1998). Thus, the brain cells of soldiers who experience combat or people who have been sexually assaulted may undergo physical changes that can produce a hair-trigger responsiveness that can cause them to overreact to mild stressors and even to merely unexpected surprises. Taken together, such findings indicate that neural plasticity can produce changes both in the brain's function and in its physical structure in response to experience.

Brain Implants   Plasticity, of course, cannot compensate for injuries that are too extensive. Driven by this problem, neuroscientists have been experimenting with computer chips implanted in the brain, where they offer the hope of restoring some motor control in paralyzed patients. In one recent case, a 26-year-old paralyzed male received such a chip as an implant in his motor cortex. By merely thinking about movement, the patient learned to send signals from his brain to a computer, controlling a cursor by thought, much as he might have used a computer's mouse by hand. In this cerebral way, he could play video games, draw circles, operate a TV set, and open e-mails—all of which his paralysis would have made impossible without the implant (Dunn, 2006; Hochberg et al., 2006).

Glial Cells: A Support Group for Neurons   Interwoven among the brain's vast network of neurons is an even greater number of *glial cells* that were once thought to "glue" the neurons together. (In fact, the name comes from the Greek word for "glue.") Now we know that glial cells provide structural support for neurons, as well as help in forming the new synapses needed for learning (Fields, 2004; Gallo & Chittajallu, 2001). In addition, the **glial cells** form the *myelin sheath,* a fatty insulation that covers many axons in the brain and spinal cord. Like the sheath covering on an electrical cable, the myelin sheath on a neuron insulates and protects the cell. It also helps speed the conduction of impulses along the axon (see Figure 2.5). Certain diseases, such as multiple sclerosis (MS), attack the myelin sheath, especially in the motor pathways. The result is poor conduction of nerve impulses, which accounts for the increasing difficulty some MS patients have in controlling movement.

So there you have the two main building blocks of the nervous system: *neurons,* with their amazing plasticity, and the supportive *glial cells,* which protect the neurons and help to propagate neural messages. But, wondrous as these individual components are, in the big picture of behavior and mental processes, a single cell doesn't do very much. It takes thousands upon millions of neurons flashing their electrochemical signals in synchronized waves back and forth through the incredibly complex neural networks in your brain to produce thoughts, sensations, and feelings. Similarly, all your actions arise from waves of nerve impulses delivered to your muscles, glands, and organs through the nervous system. It is to this larger picture—the nervous system—that we now turn our attention.

The Nervous System

If you could observe a neural message as it moves from stimulus to response, you would see it flow seamlessly from one part of the nervous system to another. The signal might begin, for example, in the eyes, then travel to the brain for extensive processing, and finally reemerge from the brain as a message instructing the muscles to respond. In fact, the **nervous system,** consisting of all the nerve cells in the body, functions as a single, complex, and interconnected unit. Nevertheless, we find it convenient to distinguish among divisions of the nervous system, based on their location and on the type of processing they do. The most basic distinction recognizes two major divisions: the *central nervous system* and the *peripheral nervous system.* (See Figure 2.6.)

The Central Nervous System   Comprised of the *brain* and *spinal cord,* the **central nervous system (CNS)** serves as the body's "command central." The brain, filling roughly a third of the skull, makes complex decisions, coordinates our body functions, and initiates most of our behaviors. The spinal cord, playing a supportive role, serves as a sort of neural cable, connecting the brain with parts of the peripheral sensory and motor systems.

Reflexes   The spinal cord has another job, too. It takes charge of simple, swift **reflexes**— responses that do not require brain power, such as the reflex your physician elicits with a tap on the knee. We know that the brain does not become involved in these simple reflexes, because a person whose spinal cord has been severed may still be able to withdraw a limb reflexively from a painful stimulus—even though the brain doesn't sense the pain. *Voluntary* movements, however, do require the brain. That's why damage to the nerves of the spinal cord can produce paralysis of the limbs or trunk. The extent of paralysis depends on the location of the damage: The higher the site of damage, the greater the extent of the paralysis.

Contralateral Pathways   Significantly, most of the sensory and motor pathways carrying messages between the brain and the rest of the body are *contralateral*—that

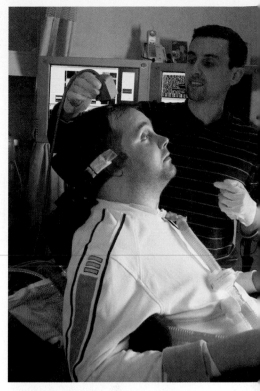

By means of a chip implanted in his motor cortex, this man can use his brain waves to control a computer that helps him operate other electronic devices. In this way, he can play video games, make simple drawings, and select TV programs.

Glial cell   One of the cells that provide structural support for neurons. Glial cells also provide an insulating covering (the myelin sheath) of the axon for some neurons, which facilitates the electrical impulse.

Nervous system   The entire network of neurons in the body, including the central nervous system, the peripheral nervous system, and their subdivisions.

Central nervous system   The brain and the spinal cord.

Reflex   Simple unlearned response triggered by stimuli—such as the knee-jerk reflex set off by tapping the tendon just below your kneecap.

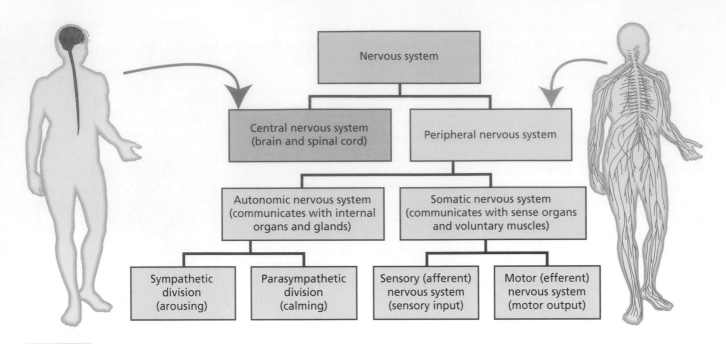

FIGURE 2.6
Organization of the Nervous System

This figure shows the major divisions of the nervous system. The figure on the left shows the *central nervous system,* while the figure on the right shows the *peripheral nervous system.*

is, they cross over to the opposite side in the spinal cord or in the brain stem. The result is that each side of the brain communicates primarily with the opposite side of the body or the opposite side of the environment. This fact is important in understanding how damage to one side of the brain often results in disabilities on the opposite side of the body. (See Figure 2.7.)

The crossover of communication pathways is also an important piece of the puzzle of the split-brain patients' performance on the special laboratory tests devised by Sperry and Gazzaniga. As you will recall, a crucial part of those tests involved presenting visual or tactile (touch) information to only one hemisphere. Because the sensory pathways cross to the opposite side, each hemisphere perceives touch sensation from the hand on the opposite side of the body. The visual pathways are more complicated, as we will see, but the result is simple: Information from one side of the visual field of each eye is processed in the hemisphere on the opposite side of the brain.

The Peripheral Nervous System   Also playing a supportive role, the **peripheral nervous system (PNS)** connects the central nervous system with the rest of the body through bundles of sensory and motor axons, called *nerves.* The many branches of the PNS carry messages between the brain and the sense organs, the internal organs, and the muscles. In this role, the peripheral nervous system carries the incoming messages that tell your brain about the sights, sounds, tastes, smells, and textures of the world. Likewise, it carries the outgoing signals that tell your body's muscles and glands how to respond.

You might think of the PNS as a pick-up-and-delivery service for the central nervous system. If, for example, an aggressive dog approaches you, your PNS picks up the auditory information (barking, growling, snarling) and visual information (bared teeth, hair standing up on the neck) for delivery to the brain. Quickly, perceptual and emotional circuits in the brain assess the situation (Danger!) and communicate with other circuits that dispatch orders for a hasty retreat. The PNS then delivers those orders to mobilize your heart, lungs, legs, and other body parts needed in response to the emergency. It does this through

Peripheral nervous system   All parts of the nervous system lying outside the central nervous system. The peripheral nervous system includes the autonomic and somatic nervous systems.

its two major divisions, the *somatic nervous system* and the *autonomic nervous system*. One deals primarily with our external world, the other with our internal responses. (A few moments spent studying Figure 2.6 will help you understand these divisions and subdivisions.)

The Somatic Division of the PNS   Think of the **somatic nervous system** as the brain's communications link with the outside world. Its sensory component connects the sense organs to the brain, and its motor component links the CNS with the skeletal muscles that control voluntary movements. (We met these two divisions earlier in our discussion of sensory and motor neurons.) So, for example, when you see a slice of pizza, the visual image is carried by the somatic division's *afferent* (sensory) system. Then, if all goes well, the *efferent* (motor) system sends instructions to muscles that propel the pizza on just the right trajectory, into your open mouth.

The Autonomic Division of the PNS   The other major division of the PNS takes over once the pizza heads down your throat and into the province of the **autonomic nervous system** (*autonomic* means self-regulating or independent). This network carries signals that regulate our internal organs, as they perform such jobs as digestion, respiration, heart rate, and arousal. And it can do so without our having to think about it—all unconsciously. The autonomic nervous system also works when you are asleep. Even during anesthesia, autonomic activity sustains our most basic vital functions.

And—wouldn't you know?—biopsychologists further divide the autonomic nervous system into two subparts: the *sympathetic* and *parasympathetic divisions* (as shown in Figure 2.8). The **sympathetic division** arouses the heart, lungs, and other organs in stressful or emergency situations, when our responses must be quick and powerfully energized. Often called the "fight-or-flight" system, the sympathetic division carries messages that help us respond quickly to a threat either by attacking or fleeing. The sympathetic system also creates the tension and arousal you feel during an exciting movie or a first date. Perhaps you can recall how the sympathetic division of your autonomic nervous system made you feel during your last oral presentation. Was it hard to breathe? Were your palms sweaty? Did your stomach feel queasy? All these are sympathetic division functions.

The **parasympathetic division** does just the opposite: It applies the neural brakes, returning the body to a calm and collected state. But even though it has an opposing action, the parasympathetic division works cooperatively with the sympathetic system, like two children on a teeter-totter. Figure 2.8 shows the most important connections made by these two autonomic divisions.

Now, having completed our whirlwind tour of the nervous system, we return our attention briefly to its partner in internal communication, the *endocrine system*.

The Endocrine System

Perhaps you had never thought of the bloodstream as a carrier of *information*, along with oxygen, nutrients, and wastes. Yet, blood-borne information, in the form of *hormones*, serves as the communication channel among the glands of the **endocrine system**, shown in Figure 2.9. (*Endocrine* comes from the Greek *endo* for "within" and *krinein* for "secrete.")

Playing much the same role as neurotransmitters in the nervous system, **hormones** carry messages that influence not only body functions but behaviors and emotions (Damasio, 2003; LeDoux, 2002). For example, hormones from the pituitary stimulate body growth. Hormones from the ovaries and testes influence sexual development and sexual responses. Hormones from the adrenals

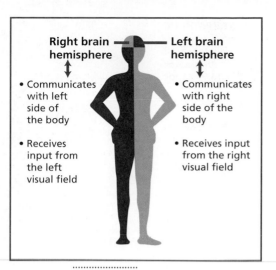

Right brain hemisphere
- Communicates with left side of the body
- Receives input from the left visual field

Left brain hemisphere
- Communicates with right side of the body
- Receives input from the right visual field

FIGURE 2.7
Contralateral Connections

For most sensory and motor functions, each side of the brain communicates with the opposite side of the body. (This is known as *contralateral* communication.) The case of vision is a bit more complicated: The visual cortex on one side "sees" the opposite side of the external world, as the text will explain.

Somatic nervous system   A division of the peripheral nervous system that carries sensory information to the central nervous system and also sends voluntary messages to the body's skeletal muscles.

Autonomic nervous system   The portion of the peripheral nervous system that sends communications between the central nervous system and the internal organs and glands.

Sympathetic division   The part of the autonomic nervous system that sends messages to internal organs and glands that help us respond to stressful and emergency situations.

Parasympathetic division   The part of the autonomic nervous system that monitors the routine operations of the internal organs and returns the body to calmer functioning after arousal by the sympathetic division.

Endocrine system   The hormone system—the body's chemical messenger system, including the endocrine glands: pituitary, thyroid, parathyroid, adrenals, pancreas, ovaries, and testes.

Hormones   Chemical messengers used by the endocrine system. Many hormones also serve as neurotransmitters in the nervous system.

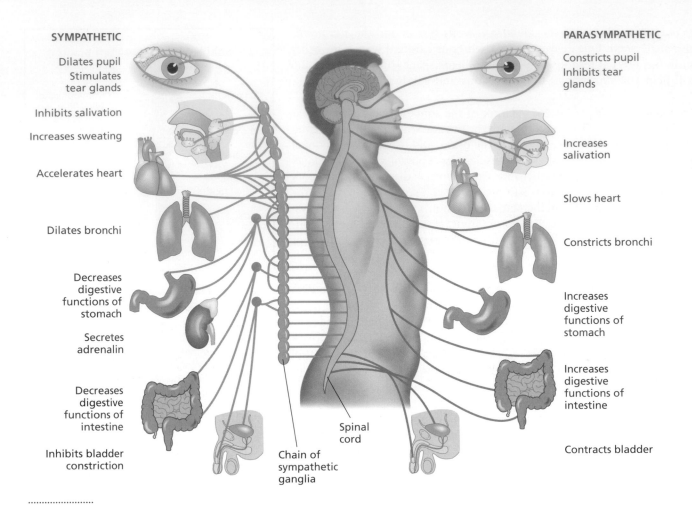

SYMPATHETIC

Dilates pupil
Stimulates tear glands

Inhibits salivation

Increases sweating

Accelerates heart

Dilates bronchi

Decreases digestive functions of stomach

Secretes adrenalin

Decreases digestive functions of intestine

Inhibits bladder constriction

PARASYMPATHETIC

Constricts pupil
Inhibits tear glands

Increases salivation

Slows heart

Constricts bronchi

Increases digestive functions of stomach

Increases digestive functions of intestine

Contracts bladder

Spinal cord

Chain of sympathetic ganglia

FIGURE 2.8
Divisions of the Autonomic Nervous System

The *sympathetic nervous system* (at left) regulates internal processes and behavior in stressful situations. On their way to and from the spinal cord, sympathetic nerve fibers make connections with specialized neural clusters called *ganglia*. The *parasympathetic nervous system* (at right) regulates day-to-day internal processes and behavior.

produce the arousal accompanying fear. And hormones from the thyroid control metabolism (rate of energy use). Once secreted into the blood by an endocrine gland, hormones circulate throughout the body until delivered to their targets, which may include not only other endocrine glands but muscles and organs. Table 2.2 outlines the major endocrine glands and the body systems they regulate.

How Does the Endocrine System Respond in a Crisis? Under normal (unaroused) conditions, the endocrine system works in parallel with the parasympathetic nervous system to sustain our basic body processes. But in a crisis, it shifts into a different mode, in support of the sympathetic nervous system. So, when you encounter a stressor or an emergency (such as the speeding car headed at you), the hormone *epinephrine* (sometimes called *adrenalin*) is released into the bloodstream, sustaining the body's defensive reaction that we call "fight or flight." In this way, the endocrine system finishes what your sympathetic nervous system has started by keeping your heart pounding and your muscles tense, ready for action.

Later in the book we will see what happens when this stressful state gets out of control. For example, people who have stressful jobs or unhappy relationships may develop a chronically elevated level of stress hormones in their blood, keeping them in a prolonged state of arousal. The price your mind and body pays for this extended arousal can be dear.

CONNECTION • CHAPTER 14

Prolonged stress messages can produce physical and mental disorders by means of the *general adaptation syndrome*.

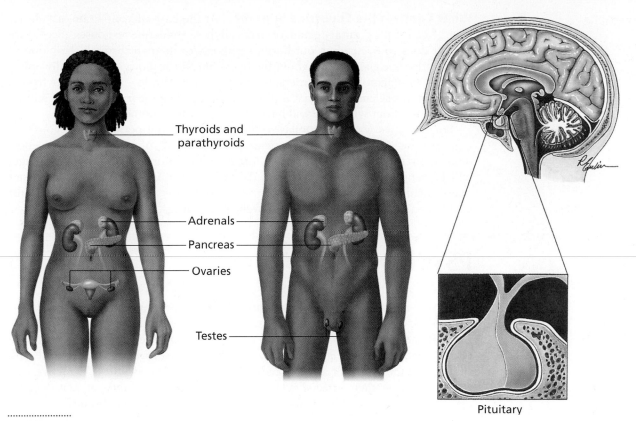

Thyroids and parathyroids

Adrenals

Pancreas

Ovaries

Testes

Pituitary

FIGURE 2.9
Endocrine Glands in Females and Males

The pituitary gland (shown at right) is the "master gland," regulating the endocrine glands, whose locations are illustrated at left. The pituitary gland is itself under control of the hypothalamus, an important structure that regulates many basic functions of the body.

TABLE 2.2	Hormonal Functions of Major Endocrine Glands
These Endocrine Glands ...	**Produce Hormones That Regulate ...**
Anterior pituitary	Ovaries and testes
	Breast milk production
	Metabolism
	Reactions to stress
Posterior pituitary	Conservation of water in the body
	Breast milk secretion
	Uterus contractions
Thyroid	Metabolism
	Physical growth and development
Parathyroid	Calcium levels in the body
Pancreas	Glucose (sugar) metabolism
Adrenal glands	Fight-or-flight response
	Metabolism
	Sexual desire (especially in women)
Ovaries	Development of female sexual characteristics
	Production of ova (eggs)
Testes	Development of male sexual characteristics
	Sperm production
	Sexual desire (in men)

What Controls the Endocrine System? At the base of your brain, a "master gland," called the **pituitary gland,** oversees all these endocrine responses. (See Figure 2.9.) It does so by sending out hormone signals of its own through the blood to other endocrine glands throughout the body. But the pituitary itself is really only a midlevel manager. It takes orders, in turn, from the brain—in particular from a small neural nucleus to which it is physically appended: the *hypothalamus,* a brain component about which we will have more to say in a moment.

For now, we want to emphasize the notion that the peripheral nervous system and the endocrine system provide parallel means of communication, coordinated by their link in the brain. Ultimately, the brain decides which messages will be sent through both networks. We will turn our attention to this master "nerve center"—the brain—right after exploring how the concepts we have just covered can explain the effects of psychoactive drugs.

PSYCHOLOGYMATTERS
How Psychoactive Drugs Affect The Nervous System

The mind-altering effects of marijuana, LSD, cocaine, narcotics, tranquilizers, and sedatives attract millions of users. Millions more jolt their brains awake with the caffeine of their morning coffee, tea, or cola and the nicotine in an accompanying cigarette; then at night they may attempt to reverse their arousal with the depressant effects of alcohol and sleeping pills. How do these seductive substances achieve their effects? The answer involves the ability of *psychoactive drugs* to enhance or inhibit natural chemical processes in our brains.

Agonists and Antagonists The ecstasy and the agony of psychoactive drugs come mainly from their interactions with neurotransmitters. Some impersonate neurotransmitters by mimicking their effects in the brain. Other drugs act less directly by enhancing or dampening the effects of neurotransmitters. Those that enhance or mimic neurotransmitters we call **agonists.** Nicotine, for example, is an agonist because it acts like the neurotransmitter acetylcholine. (See Table 2.1.) This has the effect of "turning up the volume" in the acetylcholine pathways (the acetylcholine-using bundles of nerve cells controlling the muscles and connecting certain parts of the brain). Similarly, the well-known antidepressant Prozac (fluoxetine) acts as an agonist in the brain's serotonin pathways, where it makes more serotonin available (see Figure 2.10).

In contrast, those chemicals that dampen or inhibit the effects of neurotransmitters we refer to as **antagonists.** So, curare and botulism toxin are antagonists because they interfere with the neurotransmitter acetylcholine—effectively "turning the volume down." So-called beta blockers act as antagonists against both epinephrine and norepinephrine, thereby counteracting the effects of stress. In general, agonists facilitate and antagonists inhibit messages in parts of the nervous system using that transmitter.

Why Side Effects? Why the occasional unwanted side effects of drugs? The answer to that question involves an important principle about the brain's design. The brain contains many bundles of neurons—**neural pathways**—that interconnect its components, much as rail lines connect major cities. Moreover, each pathway employs only certain neurotransmitters—like rail lines allowing only certain companies to use their tracks. This fact allows a drug affecting a particular transmitter to target specific parts of the brain. Unfortunately for the drug-takers, different pathways may employ the same neurotransmitter for widely different functions. Thus, serotonin pathways, for example, affect not only mood but sleep, appetite, and cognition, just as the same railroad serves many cities. So, taking Prozac (or one of its chemical cousins with other brand names) may treat depression but, at the same time, have side effects on other psychological processes involving serotonin. That is, because serotonin's effects are not limited

Pituitary gland The "master gland" that produces hormones influencing the secretions of all other endocrine glands, as well as a hormone that influences growth. The pituitary is attached to the brain's hypothalamus, from which it takes its orders.

Agonists Drugs or other chemicals that enhance or mimic the effects of neurotransmitters.

Antagonists Drugs or other chemicals that inhibit the effects of neurotransmitters.

Neural pathways Bundles of nerve cells that follow generally the same route and employ the same neurotransmitter.

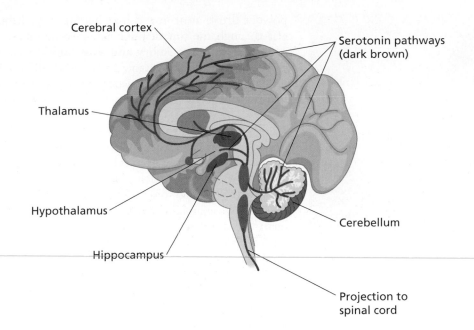

FIGURE 2.10
Serotonin Pathways in the Brain

Each neurotransmitter is associated with certain neural pathways in the brain. In this cross section of the brain you see the main pathways for serotonin. Drugs that stimulate or inhibit serotonin will selectively affect the brain regions shown in this diagram.

Cerebral cortex

Serotonin pathways (dark brown)

Thalamus

Hypothalamus

Cerebellum

Hippocampus

Projection to spinal cord

to the pathways involved in mood, fluoxetine can also cause changes in sleep patterns, appetite, and thinking.

In fact, no psychoactive drug exists that acts like a "magic bullet" that can strike only one precise target in the brain, to work its wonders without causing collateral effects.

CheckYourUnderstanding

1. **RECALL:** Of the body's two main communication systems, the _____ is faster, while the _____ sends longer-lasting messages.

2. **APPLICATION:** You are touring a "haunted house" at Halloween, when suddenly you hear a blood-curdling scream right behind you. The _____ division of your autonomic nervous system quickly increases your heart rate. As you recover from your fright, the _____ division slows your heart rate to normal.

3. **RECALL:** Explain how a neural message is carried across the synapse.

4. **RECALL:** Which gland takes orders from the brain but exerts control over the rest of the endocrine system?

5. **RECALL:** Make a sketch of two connecting neurons, indicating the locations of the dendrites, soma, axon, myelin sheath, terminal buttons, and synapse. Which part of the neuron sends messages by means of a brief electric charge?

6. **UNDERSTANDING THE CORE CONCEPT:** The chemical messengers in the brain are called _____, while in the endocrine system they are called _____.

Answers 1. nervous system/endocrine system **2.** sympathetic/parasympathetic **3.** When the electrical impulse arrives at the axon ending, it causes neurotransmitters to be released into the synapse. Some of those neurotransmitters lodge in receptor sites on the opposite side of the synapse, where they stimulate the receiving neuron. **4.** the pituitary gland **5.** Your diagram should be similar to the one on the left side in Figure 2.5. The burst of electric energy (the action potential) occurs in the axon. **6.** neurotransmitters/hormones

2.3 KEY QUESTION
HOW DOES THE BRAIN PRODUCE BEHAVIOR AND MENTAL PROCESSES?

News flash: In September of 1848, a 25-year-old American railroad worker named Phineas Gage sustained a horrible head injury when a charge of blasting

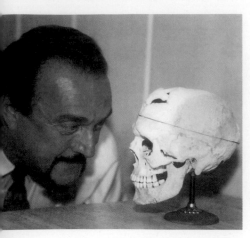

Author Phil Zimbardo (left) with the skull of Phineas Gage.

powder drove an iron rod into his face, up through the front of his brain, and out through the top of his head. (See accompanying photo.) Amazingly, Gage recovered from this injury and lived another 12 years—but as a psychologically changed man (Fleischman, 2002; Macmillan, 2000). Those who knew him remarked that Gage, once a dependable and likeable crew boss, had become an irresponsible and rowdy ruffian. In essence, he was no longer himself. "Gage was no longer Gage," remarked his former companions (Damasio, 1994, p. 8). We cannot help but wonder: Had the site of his injury—the front of his brain—been the home of Phineas Gage's "old self"?

Gage's accident raises another question: What is the connection between mind and body? Humans have, of course, long recognized the existence of such a link—although they didn't always know the brain to be the organ of the mind. Even today we might speak, as they did in Shakespeare's time, of "giving one's heart" to another or of "not having the stomach" for something when describing revulsion. But today we know that love doesn't really flow from the heart, nor disgust from the digestive system. We now know that emotions, desires, and thoughts originate in the brain. (The news hasn't reached songwriters, who have yet to pen a lyric proclaiming, "I love you with all my brain.")

At last, neuroscientists have begun unraveling the deep mysteries of this complex organ of the mind. They now see the brain as a collection of distinct modules that work together like the components of a computer. This new understanding of the brain, then, becomes the Core Concept for this final section of the chapter:

core concept | **The brain is composed of many specialized modules that work together to create mind and behavior.**

As you study the brain, you will find that each of its modular components has its own responsibilities (Cohen & Tong, 2001). Some process sensations, such as vision and hearing. Some regulate our emotional lives. Some contribute to memory. Some generate speech and other behaviors. What's the point? The specialized parts of the brain act like members of a championship team: each doing a particular job, yet working smoothly together. Happily, many of these brain modules perform their tasks automatically and without conscious direction—as when you simultaneously walk, digest your breakfast, breathe, and carry on a conversation. But, when something goes awry with one or more of the brain's components, as it does in a stroke or Alzheimer's disease—or as happened to Phineas Gage—the biological basis of thought or behavior comes to the fore.

Let's begin the story of the brain by seeing how neuroscientists go about opening the windows on its inner workings. As you will see, much of what we know about the brain's secrets comes from observing people with brain disease and head injuries—people like Gage.

Windows on the Brain

Isolated within the protective skull, the brain can never actually touch velvet, taste chocolate, have sex, or see the blue of the sky. It only knows the outside world secondhand, through changing patterns of electrochemical activity in the peripheral nervous system, the brain's link with the world outside. To communicate within the body, the brain must rely on the neural and endocrine pathways that carry its messages to and from the muscles, organs, and glands throughout the body.

But what would you see if you could peer beneath the bony skull and behold the brain? Its wrinkled surface, rather like a giant walnut, tells us little about the brain's internal structure or function. For that, technology—especially *EEG*, *electrical stimulation*, and various types of *brain scans*—has opened new windows on the brain.

Sensing Brain Waves with the EEG   For nearly one hundred years, neuroscientists have been using the **electroencephalograph (or EEG)** to record the extremely weak voltage patterns called *brain waves*, sensed by electrodes pasted on the scalp. Much as the city lights can tell you which parts of town are most "alive" at night, the EEG senses which parts of the brain are most active. The EEG can identify, for example, regions involved in moving the hand or processing a visual image. It can also reveal abnormal waves caused by brain malfunctions, such as *epilepsy* (a seizure disorder that arises from an electrical "storm" in the brain). You can see the sort of information provided by the EEG in Figure 2.11.

Useful as it is, however, the EEG is not a very precise instrument, indiscriminately recording the brain's electrical activity in a large region near the electrode. Because there may be fewer than a dozen electrodes used, the EEG does not paint a detailed electrical picture of the brain. Rather, it produces a coarse, moment-to-moment summary of the electrical activity in millions of neurons—making it all the more amazing that we can sometimes read the traces of mental processes in an EEG record.

Mapping the Brain with Electric Probes   Half a century ago, the great Canadian neurologist Wilder Penfield opened another window on the brain by "mapping" its pinkish-gray surface. During brain surgery, using a pen-shaped electric probe, Penfield stimulated patients' exposed brains with a gentle electric current and recorded the responses. (His patients were kept awake, but under local anesthesia, so they felt no pain.)

This was not just an experiment born of curiosity. As a surgeon, Penfield needed to identify the exact boundaries of the diseased brain areas, to avoid removing healthy tissue. In the process, he found that the brain's surface had distinct regions, with distinct functions. Stimulating a certain spot might cause the left hand to move; another site might produce a sensation, such as a flash of light. Stimulating still other sites occasionally provoked a memory from childhood (Penfield, 1959; Penfield & Baldwin, 1952). Later, other scientists followed his lead and probed structures deeper in the brain. There they found that electrical stimulation could set off elaborate sequences of behavior or emotions. The overall conclusion from such work is unmistakable: Each region of the brain has its own specific functions.

CONNECTION • CHAPTER 8
Sleep researchers use *brain waves*, recorded by the EEG, to distinguish REM sleep, which is characterized by dreaming.

Electroencephalograph (EEG)   A device for recording brain waves, typically by electrodes placed on the scalp. The record produced is known as an electroencephalogram (also called an EEG).

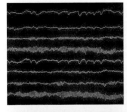
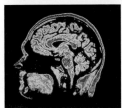
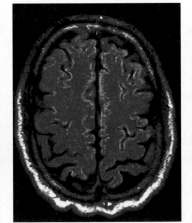
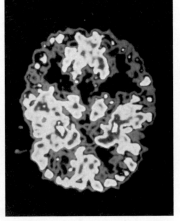
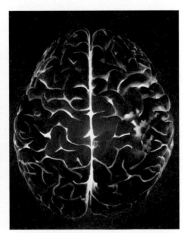

FIGURE 2.11
Windows on the Mind

Images from brain-scanning devices. *Top:* EEG; *Bottom:* MRI; *From left:* CT scan, PET, and fMRI. Each scanning and recording device has strengths and weaknesses.

HOW DOES THE BRAIN PRODUCE BEHAVIOR AND MENTAL PROCESSES?   **67**

Computerized Brain Scans Advances in brain science during the last few decades have given us more detailed views of the brain by employing sophisticated procedures collectively known as *brain scans*. Some types of scans make images with X-rays, others use radioactive tracers, and still others use magnetic fields. Thanks to such scanning methods, scientists can now make vivid pictures of brain structures without opening the skull. In medicine, brain scans help neurosurgeons locate brain abnormalities such as tumors or stroke-related damage. And in psychology, the images obtained from brain scans can show where our thoughts and feelings are processed. How? Depending on the scanning method used, specific regions of the brain may "light up" when, for example, a person reads, speaks, solves problems, or feels certain emotions (Raichle, 1994).

The most common brain-scanning methods currently employed are *CT, PET, MRI,* and *fMRI:*

CT scanning, or **computerized tomography,** creates digital images of the brain from X-rays passed through the brain at various angles, as though it were being sliced like a tomato. By means of sophisticated computer analysis, this form of tomography (from the Greek *tomos,* "section") reveals soft-tissue structures of the brain that X-rays alone cannot show. (See Figure 2.11.) CT scanning produces good three-dimensional images, and it is relatively inexpensive; the downside is that it employs X-rays, which can be harmful in high doses. CT scans are often used in hospitals for assessing traumatic brain injuries.

PET scanning, or **positron emission tomography,** produces an image showing brain *activity* (rather than just brain *structure*). One common PET technique does this by sensing low-level radioactive glucose (sugar), which concentrates in the brain's most active circuits. Areas of high metabolic activity show up as brightly colored on the image. (See Figure 2.11.) Thus, researchers can use PET scans to show which parts are more active or less active during a particular task.

MRI, or **magnetic resonance imaging,** uses brief, powerful pulses of magnetic energy to create highly detailed pictures of the structure of the brain. (Again, see Figure 2.11.) The MRI technique makes exceptionally clear, three-dimensional images, without the use of X-rays, which favors its use in research despite its higher cost.

fMRI, or **functional magnetic resonance imaging** is a newer technique that can also distinguish brain *activity* as well as the *structure* shown in standard MRI images (Alper, 1993; Collins, 2001). By monitoring the blood and oxygen flow in the brain, it can also identify more active brain cells from less active ones. Thus, fMRI allows neuroscientists to determine which parts of the brain are at work during various mental activities, much the same as PET, except that the fMRI technique produces more detailed images. (See Figure 2.11.)

Which Scanning Method Is Best? Each type of brain scan has its particular strengths and weaknesses. For example, both PET and fMRI are good at showing which parts of the brain are active during a particular task, such as talking, looking at a picture, or solving a problem. Standard MRI excels at distinguishing the fine details of brain structure. But none of these methods can detect processes that occur only briefly, such as a shift in attention or a startle response. To capture such short-lived "conversations" among brain cells requires the EEG—which, unfortunately, is limited in its detail (Raichle, 1994). Currently, no single scanning technique gives biopsychologists a perfectly clear "window" on all the brain's activity.

Three Layers of the Brain

What one sees through these windows on the brain also depends on the brain one is examining. Birds and reptiles manage to make a living with a brain that consists of little more than a stalk that regulates the most basic life processes

CT scanning or **computerized tomography** A computerized imaging technique that uses X-rays passed through the brain at various angles and then combined into an image.

PET scanning or **positron emission tomography** An imaging technique that relies on the detection of radioactive sugar consumed by active brain cells.

MRI or **magnetic resonance imaging** An imaging technique that relies on cells' responses in a high-intensity magnetic field.

fMRI or **functional magnetic resonance imaging** A newer form of magnetic resonance imaging that reveals different activity levels in different parts of the brain.

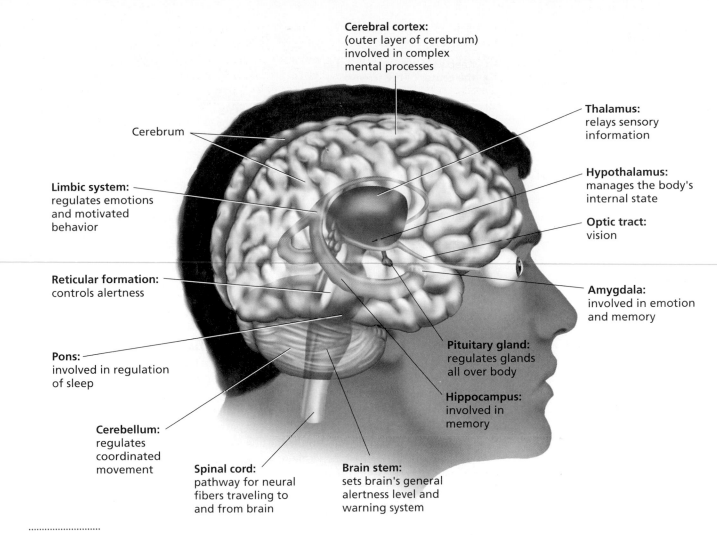

Cerebral cortex:
(outer layer of cerebrum) involved in complex mental processes

Cerebrum

Thalamus:
relays sensory information

Hypothalamus:
manages the body's internal state

Limbic system:
regulates emotions and motivated behavior

Optic tract:
vision

Reticular formation:
controls alertness

Amygdala:
involved in emotion and memory

Pons:
involved in regulation of sleep

Pituitary gland:
regulates glands all over body

Hippocampus:
involved in memory

Cerebellum:
regulates coordinated movement

Spinal cord:
pathway for neural fibers traveling to and from brain

Brain stem:
sets brain's general alertness level and warning system

....

FIGURE 2.12
Major Structures of the Brain

From an evolutionary perspective, the brain stem and cerebellum represent the oldest part of the brain; the limbic system evolved next; and the cerebral cortex is the most recent achievement in brain evolution.

and instinctual responses. Our own more complex brains arise from essentially the same stalk, called the **brain stem.** From an evolutionary perspective, then, this is the part of the brain with the longest ancestry and most basic functions. On top of that stalk, we and our mammalian cousins have evolved two more layers, known as the *limbic system* and the *cerebrum,* that give us greatly expanded brain powers. (See Figure 2.12.)

The Brain Stem and Its Neighbors If you have ever fought to stay awake in class, you have struggled with your brain stem. Most of the time, however, it does its many jobs less obviously and less obnoxiously. We can infer one of the brain stem's tasks from its location, linking the spinal cord with the rest of the brain. In this position, it serves as a conduit for nerve pathways that carry messages traveling up and down the spinal pathway between the body and the central processing areas of the brain. Significantly, as we have seen, the sensory and motor pathways between the brain and our sense organs and skeletal muscles cross over to the opposite side, with many of them doing so in this region. This fact has the following extremely important consequence that bears reiterating: *Each side of the brain connects to the opposite side of the body.*

Brain stem   The most primitive of the brain's three major layers. It includes the medulla, pons, and the reticular formation.

FIGURE 2.13
Communicating with the Opposite
Hemisphere

Sensory pathways from the left hand
cross over to the right hemisphere of
the brain. Likewise, visual information
from the left side of the visual field
of both eyes is sent to the right
hemisphere.

Keep your eyes on the dot in
the center of the screen.

Then, when you see an object
flashed on the screen, find the
object with your left hand.

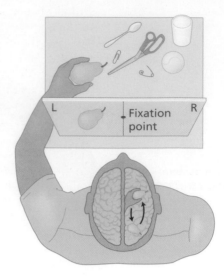

The Brain Stem in Split-Brain Patients: A Piece of the Puzzle The crossover of sensory
and motor pathways gives us a clue that can help us explain the puzzling responses
of the split-brain patients described at the beginning of the chapter. It is important
to realize that the surgeons did *not* cut these cross-over pathways when they severed the corpus callosum in these patients. That is, they left the brain stem and
spinal cord intact. Thus, the sensory-motor pathways in the brain stem and spinal
cord could still carry information from one side of the body to the hemisphere on
the opposite side. In their experiments, Sperry and Gazzaniga cleverly used these
intact pathways to send information selectively to one hemisphere or the other in
these patients. Figure 2.13 shows what they did. When the experimenters flashed
the image of the pear on the left side of the visual field, the patient perceived it in
the right hemisphere—which also communicates with the left hand. Similarly, the
left hemisphere processes information from the right side of the visual field and
communicates with the right hand.

Brain Stem Components and Connections More than just a conduit, the brain stem
also connects several important information-processing regions, three of which are
contained in the brain stem itself—the *medulla,* the *pons,* and the *reticular formation*—along with two adjacent parts of the brain, the *thalamus* and the *cerebellum*
(Pinel, 2005). From an evolutionary standpoint, they are all ancient structures that
can be found in the brains of creatures as diverse as penguins, pigs, pandas, pythons,
porcupines, and people. You can see their location in Figure 2.14.

The **medulla,** appearing as a bulge low in the brain stem, regulates basic body
functions, including breathing, blood pressure, and heart rate. It operates on
"automatic pilot"—without our conscious awareness—to keep our internal
organs operating. An even bigger bulge called the **pons** (meaning *bridge*) appears
just above the medulla, where it houses nerve circuits that regulate the sleep and
dreaming cycle. True to its name, the pons also acts as a "bridge" that connects
the brain stem to the *cerebellum,* a structure involved in making coordinated
movements.

The **reticular formation,** running through the center of everything, consists of
a pencil-shaped bundle of nerve cells that forms the brain stem's core. One of
the reticular formation's jobs is keeping the brain awake and alert. Others include
monitoring the incoming stream of sensory information and directing attention
to novel or important messages. And—don't blame your professor—it is the reticular formation you struggle with when you become drowsy in class.

Medulla A brain-stem structure that
controls breathing and heart rate. The
sensory and motor pathways
connecting the brain to the body cross
in the medulla.

Pons A brain-stem structure that
regulates brain activity during sleep
and dreaming. The name pons derives
from the Latin word for "bridge."

Reticular formation A pencil-shaped
structure forming the core of the brain
stem. The reticular formation arouses
the cortex to keep the brain alert and
attentive to new stimulation.

The **thalamus,** a pair of football-shaped bodies perched atop the brain stem, receives nerve fibers from the reticular formation. Technically part of the cerebral hemispheres, not the brain stem, the thalamus acts like the central processing chip in a computer, directing the brain's incoming and outgoing sensory and motor traffic. Accordingly, it receives information from all the senses (except smell, oddly enough) and distributes this information to appropriate processing circuits throughout the brain. The thalamus also has a poorly understood role in focusing attention—which seems appropriate for a structure with its connections to almost everything.

The **cerebellum,** tucked beneath the back of the cerebral hemispheres and behind the stalk formed by the brain stem, looks very much like a neural knot stuck on the brain as an evolutionary afterthought. (It will help to locate its position visually in Figure 2.14.) Although not counted as a part of the brain stem by many anatomists, the cerebellum works cooperatively with processing units in the brain stem and the cerebral hemispheres to coordinate the movements that we perform without thinking (Spencer et al., 2003; Wickelgren, 1998b). It is your cerebellum that allows you to run down a flight of stairs without being conscious of the precise movements of your feet. The cerebellum also helps us keep a series of events in order—as we do when listening to the sequence of notes in a melody (Bower & Parsons, 2003). Finally, the cerebellum gets involved in a basic form of learning that involves habitual responses we perform on cue—as when you learn to wince at the sight of the dentist's drill (Hazeltine & Ivry, 2002).

Taken together, these modules associated with the brain stem control the most basic functions of movement and of life itself. Note, again, that much of their work is automatic, functioning largely outside our awareness. The next two layers, however, assert themselves more obviously in consciousness.

The Limbic System: Emotions, Memories, and More We're sorry to report that your pet canary or goldfish doesn't have the emotional equipment that we mammals possess. You see, only mammals have a fully developed **limbic system,** a diverse collection of structures that wraps around the thalamus deep inside the cerebral hemispheres. (See Figures 2.12 and 2.15.) Together, these ram's-horn-shaped structures give us greatly enhanced capacity for emotions and memory, facilities that offer the huge advantage of mental flexibility. Because we have limbic systems, we don't have to rely solely on the instincts and reflexes that dominate the behavior of simpler creatures.

The limbic layer houses other modules as well. Certain parts of the limbic system regulate basic motives, such as hunger and thirst. Others regulate body temperature. In general, you can think of the limbic system as a brain's multitasking command central for emotions, motives, memory, and maintenance of a balanced condition within the body.

Two especially important limbic structures take their names from their shapes. One, the **hippocampus,** is shaped (vaguely) like a sea horse—hence its name, again from Greek. (Actually, the brain has one hippocampus on each side, giving us two *hippocampi*. See Figures 2.12 and 2.15.) One of its jobs is to help us remember the location of objects, as when you remember where you left your car in a large parking lot (Squire, 2007). Its other main task is also a memory function, originally revealed by the notorious case of H. M.

H. M.: The Man Who Lost His Hippocampus In 1953, when he was in his early 20s, H. M. underwent a radical and experimental brain operation, intended to treat the frequent seizures that threatened his life (Hilts, 1995). The surgery, which removed most of the hippocampus on both sides of his brain, indeed succeeded in reducing the frequency of his seizures. But in another sense, it proved a total failure: Ever

CONNECTION • CHAPTER 7
The sense of smell has a unique ability to invoke memories.

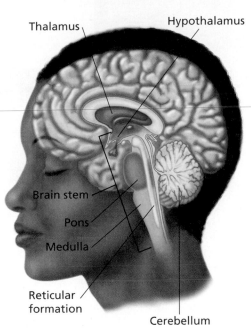

Thalamus

Hypothalamus

Brain stem

Pons

Medulla

Reticular formation

Cerebellum

FIGURE 2.14
The Brain Stem and Cerebellum

These structures in the central core of the brain are primarily involved with basic life processes: breathing, pulse, arousal, movement, balance, and early processing of sensory information.

Thalamus The brain's central "relay station," situated just atop the brain stem. Nearly all the messages going into or out of the brain go through the thalamus.

Cerebellum The "little brain" attached to the brain stem. The cerebellum is responsible for coordinated movements.

Limbic system The middle layer of the brain, involved in emotion and memory. The limbic system includes the hippocampus, amygdala, hypothalamus, and other structures.

Hippocampus A component of the limbic system, involved in establishing long-term memories.

Fear and apprehension:
Amygdala

Hunger and eating:
Hypothalamus

Learning and memory:
Hippocampus

FIGURE 2.15
The Limbic System

The structures of the limbic system are involved with motivation, emotion, and certain memory processes.

since the operation, new experiences disappear from H. M.'s memory almost as soon as they happen. Now, when he tries to search his memory for the years since 1953, H. M. draws a blank. He doesn't even recognize those who care for him every day in a nursing home near Boston. In fact, he continues to believe he is living in 1953. Later in the text, we will return to H. M., but suffice it for now to note that his tragic case illustrates the important role played by the hippocampus in storing our experiences in long-term memory.

The Amygdala and Emotion Another limbic structure, the **amygdala,** also takes its name from its shape: *amygdala* (again in Greek) means "almond." Your brain has two amygdalas, one extending in front of the hippocampus on each side. (See Figure 2.15.)

In a classic experiment designed to find out what the amygdala does, Heinrich Klüver and Paul Bucy (1939) surgically snipped the connections to the amygdala on both sides of the brain in normally foul-tempered rhesus monkeys. Postsurgically, the beasts became so docile and easy to handle that even Klüver and Bucy were surprised. Since then, many studies have shown that the amygdala is involved not only in aggression but in fear—and probably in other emotional responses (Damasio, 2003).

Pleasure and the Limbic System In addition to the amygdala and hippocampus, the limbic system contains several so-called "pleasure centers" that create good feelings when aroused by electrical stimulation or by addictive drugs like cocaine, methamphetamine, and heroin (Olds & Fobes, 1981; Pinel, 2005). But you don't have to take drugs to stimulate these limbic pleasure circuits. Sex will do it, too. So will eating and drinking or otherwise exciting activities, such as riding a roller coaster. Even a serving of rich chocolate can arouse the same rewarding brain circuits (Small, 2001).

Amygdala A limbic system structure involved in memory and emotion, particularly fear and aggression. Pronounced *a-MIG-da-la.*

And one more thing: Psychologists Vinod Goel and Raymond Dolan (2001) have found indications that the brain's reward circuits also participate in our response to humor. For most people, having a brain scan is not the most pleasant experience—largely because of the cramped spaces and strange, loud noises made by the machine. But by telling jokes during the fMRI scan, Goel and Dolan got a few laughs from volunteers with their heads in the scanner. (Sample: "Why don't sharks bite lawyers?" Punch line: "Professional courtesy.") And, sure enough, for those who thought it was funny, parts of the brain's reward circuitry "lit up." Other researchers have corroborated these findings and, depending on the type of humor involved, implicated other brain areas, such as those involved in language and emotion (Watson, Matthews, & Allman, 2007).

The Hypothalamus and Control over Motivation In passing, we have already met the **hypothalamus,** another limbic structure that performs multiple tasks related to maintaining the body in a stable, balanced condition. (See Figure 2.14.) Rich with blood vessels, as well as with neurons, the hypothalamus serves as your brain's blood-analysis laboratory. By constantly monitoring the blood, it detects small changes in body temperature, fluid levels, and nutrients. When it detects an imbalance (too much or too little water, for example), the hypothalamus immediately responds with orders aimed at restoring balance.

The hypothalamus makes its influence felt in other ways, as well. Although much of its work occurs outside of consciousness, the hypothalamus can send neural messages to "higher" processing areas in the brain—making us aware of the needs it senses (hunger, for example). It also can control our internal organs through its influence on the pituitary gland, attached to the underside of the hypothalamus at the base of the brain. Thus, the hypothalamus serves as the link between the nervous system and the endocrine system, through which it regulates emotional arousal and stress. Finally, the hypothalamus also plays a role in our emotions by hosting some of the brain's reward circuits, especially those that generate the feel-good emotions associated with gratifying the hunger, thirst, and sex drives.

The Cerebral Cortex: The Brain's Thinking Cap

When you look at a whole human brain, you mostly see the bulging *cerebral hemispheres*—a little bigger than your two fists held together. The nearly symmetrical hemispheres form a thick cap that accounts for two-thirds of the brain's total mass and hides most of the limbic system. The hemispheres' thin outer layer, the **cerebral cortex,** with its distinctive folded and wrinkled surface, allows billions of cells to squeeze into the tight quarters inside your skull. Flattened out, the cortical surface would cover an area roughly the size of a newspaper page. But because of its convoluted surface, only about a third of the cortex is visible when the brain is exposed. For what it's worth: Women's brains have more folding and wrinkling than do men's, while, as we have seen, men's brains are slightly larger than women's, on the average (Luders et al., 2004). And what does the cerebral cortex do? The locus of our most awesome mental powers, it processes all our sensations, stores memories, and makes decisions—among many other functions that we will consider in our discussion of its lobes, below.

Although we humans take pride in our big brains, it turns out that ours are not the biggest on the planet. All large animals have large brains—a fact more closely related to body size than to intelligence. Nor is the wrinkled cortex a distinctively human trait. Again, all large animals have highly convoluted cortexes. If this bothers your self-esteem, you can take comfort in the fact that we do have more massive cortexes for our body weight than do other big-brained creatures. Although no one is sure exactly how or why the brain became so large in our species (Buss, 2008; Pennisi, 2006), the comparisons with other animals show that human uniqueness lies more in the way our brains operate, rather than in their size.

CONNECTION • CHAPTER 9

The *hypothalamus* contains important control circuits for several basic motives and drives, such as hunger and thirst.

Hypothalamus A limbic structure that serves as the brain's blood-testing laboratory, constantly monitoring the blood to determine the condition of the body.

Cerebral cortex The thin gray matter covering the cerebral hemispheres, consisting of a ¼-inch layer dense with cell bodies of neurons. The cerebral cortex carries on the major portion of our "higher" mental processing, including thinking and perceiving.

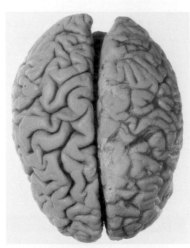

The cerebral hemispheres of the human brain.

Lobes of the Cerebral Cortex

In the late 1700s, the famous Austrian physician Franz Joseph Gall threw his considerable scientific weight behind the idea that specific regions of the brain control specific mental faculties, such as hearing, speech, movement, vision, and memory. Unfortunately, he carried this sensible idea to muddle-headed extremes. In his theory of *phrenology*, Gall claimed that the brain also had regions devoted to such traits as spirituality, hope, benevolence, friendship, destructiveness, and cautiousness. Moreover, he asserted that these traits could be detected as bumps on the skull, the "reading" of which became a minor scam industry.

Gall's ideas captured the public's attention and became enormously popular, even though his theory was mostly wrong. But he was absolutely right on one important point: his doctrine of *localization of function*. Stated simply, localization of function means that *different parts of the brain perform different tasks.* The discoveries made by modern neuroscience have helped us to correct Gall's picture of the cerebral cortex. As we discuss the geography of the cortex, please keep in mind that, while the lobes are convenient features, the functions we will ascribe to each (see Table 2.3) do not always respect the precise boundaries of the lobes.

The Frontal Lobes   Your choice of major, your plans for the summer, and your ability to answer test questions all depend heavily on the cortical regions at the front of your brain, aptly named the **frontal lobes.** (See Figure 2.16.) Here, especially in the foremost regions, known as the *prefrontal cortex,* we find circuitry that contributes to our most advanced mental functions, such as planning, deciding, and anticipating future events (Miller, 2006; O'Reilly, 2006). The biological underpinnings of personality, temperament, and our sense of "self" seem to have important components here, too, as the case of Phineas Gage suggested (Bower, 2006).

At the back of the frontal lobe lies a special strip of cortex capable of taking action on our thoughts. Known as the **motor cortex,** this patch of brain takes its name from its main function: controlling the body's motor movement by sending messages to the motor nerves and on to the voluntary muscles. As you can see in Figure 2.17, the motor cortex contains an upside-down map of the body, represented by the *homunculus* (the distorted "little man" in the figure). A closer look at the motor homunculus shows that it exaggerates certain parts of the body, indicating that the brain allots a larger amount of cortex to those body parts. Note especially the areas representing the lips, tongue, and hands. Perhaps the most exaggerated areas represents the fingers (especially the thumb), reflecting the importance of manipulating objects. Another large area connects to the muscles of the face, used in expressions of emotion. Please remember, however, that commands from the motor cortex on one side of the brain control muscles on the opposite side of the body. So a wink of your left eye originates in your right motor cortex, while the left motor cortex can wink your right eye.

Mirror Neurons Discovered in the Frontal Lobes   Recently, neuroscientists have discovered a new class of neurons, called *mirror neurons*, scattered throughout the brain

Frontal lobes   Cortical regions at the front of the brain that are especially involved in movement and in thinking.

Motor cortex   A narrow vertical strip of cortex in the frontal lobes, lying just in front of the central fissure; controls voluntary movement.

TABLE 2.3	**Major Functions of the Cortical Lobes**
Lobe	**Functions**
Frontal	Movement, producing speech, abstract thought
Parietal	Sensations of touch, body position, understanding speech
Temporal	Hearing, smell, recognizing faces
Occipital	Vision

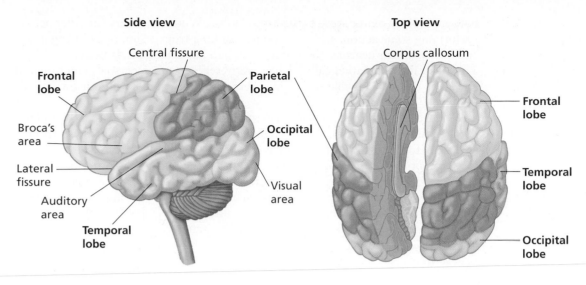

Side view

Central fissure

Frontal
lobe

Broca's
area

Lateral
fissure

Auditory
area

Temporal
lobe

Parietal
lobe

Occipital
lobe

Visual
area

Top view

Corpus callosum

Frontal
lobe

Temporal
lobe

Occipital
lobe

Left
hemisphere

Right
hemisphere

....

FIGURE 2.16

The Four Lobes of the Cerebral Cortex

Each of the two hemispheres of the cerebral cortex has four lobes. Different sensory and motor functions have been associated with specific parts of each lobe. The two hemispheres are connected by a thick bundle of fibers called the *corpus callosum*.

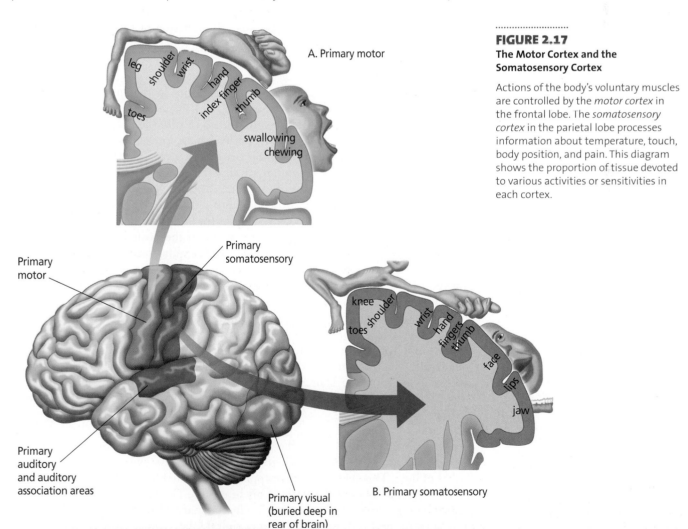

A. Primary motor

Primary motor

Primary somatosensory

Primary auditory and auditory association areas

Primary visual (buried deep in rear of brain)

B. Primary somatosensory

FIGURE 2.17

The Motor Cortex and the Somatosensory Cortex

Actions of the body's voluntary muscles are controlled by the *motor cortex* in the frontal lobe. The *somatosensory cortex* in the parietal lobe processes information about temperature, touch, body position, and pain. This diagram shows the proportion of tissue devoted to various activities or sensitivities in each cortex.

but especially in motor areas of the frontal lobes. When we observe another person performing some action, such as waving, drinking from a cup, or swinging a golf club, these **mirror neurons** fire, just as if we had performed the same act ourselves. They also fire "empathetically" when we observe another person's emotions. In effect, we do and feel what we see in others—but in the privacy of our own minds (Dobbs, 2006a).

What could be their purpose? For one thing, mirror neurons may help children mimic—and therefore learn—language. But more than that, these specialized cells form part of a brain network that allows us to anticipate other people's intentions, says Italian neuroscientist Giacomo Rizzolatti, one of the discoverers of mirror neurons (Rizzolatti et al., 2006). Because they connect with the brain's emotional circuitry, mirror neurons allow us to "mirror" other people's emotions in our minds. From an evolutionary perspective, observing and imitating others is a fundamental human characteristic, so mirror neurons may even turn out to be the biological basis of culture. Finally, some researchers believe that deficits in the mirror system may underlie disorders, such as autism, that involve difficulties in imitation and in understanding others' feelings and intentions (Ramachandran & Oberman, 2006).

The Frontal Lobes' Role in Speech … and the Split-Brain, Again   In most people, the left frontal lobe has yet another important function: the production of speech. So, damage to this region on the left side of the brain can leave a person without the ability to talk—although, if other areas are spared, the ability to understand speech may be unimpaired. This offers us another clue that can help us understand the split-brain patients' inability to *name* an unseen object held in the left hand, which connects to the right hemisphere: Because the left side of the brain usually has greater language ability, it makes sense that the right hemisphere would have trouble naming objects.

The Parietal Lobes

To the rear of each frontal lobe lie two large patches of cortex that specialize in sensation. (See Figure 2.16.) These **parietal lobes** allow us to sense the warmth of a hot bath, the smoothness of silk, the poke of a rude elbow, and the gentleness of a caress. A special parietal strip, known as the **somatosensory cortex,** mirrors the adjacent strip of motor cortex that we found in the frontal lobe. This somatosensory cortex has two main functions. First, it serves as the primary processing area for the sensations of touch, temperature, pain, and pressure from all over the body (Graziano et al., 2000; Helmuth, 2000). Second, it relates this information to a mental map of the body to help us locate the source of these sensations.

Other maps in the parietal lobes keep track of the position of body parts, so they prevent you from biting your tongue or stepping on your own toes. And, when your leg "goes to sleep" and you can't feel anything but a tingling sensation, you have temporarily interrupted messages from the nerve cells that carry sensory information to body maps in the parietal lobe.

Besides processing sensation and keeping track of body parts, the parietal lobes—especially the one in the right hemisphere—allow us to locate, in three-dimensional space, the positions of external objects detected by our senses. Meanwhile, the left hemisphere's parietal lobe has its own special talents. It specializes in locating the source of speech sounds, as when someone calls your name. It also works with the temporal lobe to extract meaning from speech and writing.

The Occipital Lobes

During the Apollo 11 mission to the moon, lunar module pilot Edwin Aldrin reported back to Earth that he was experiencing mysterious flashes of light. This celestial display apparently resulted from cosmic rays penetrating the **occipital lobes** at the back of his brain (see Figure 2.16). Similarly—if less pleasantly—you, too, will "see stars" when a sharp blow to your head bounces your brain around and stimulates your occipital lobes. Under more normal circum-

Mirror neuron   A recently discovered class of neuron that fires in response to ("mirroring") observation of another person's actions or emotions.

Parietal lobes   Cortical areas lying toward the back and top of the brain; involved in touch sensation and in perceiving spatial relationships (the relationships of objects in space).

Somatosensory cortex   A strip of the parietal lobe lying just behind the central fissure. The somatosensory cortex is involved with sensations of touch.

Occipital lobes   The cortical regions at the back of the brain, housing the visual cortex.

stances, the occipital lobes receive stimulation relayed from the eyes. There the **visual cortex** constructs our moving picture of the outside world.

Specialized Visual Processing Regions in the Cortex   To create our pictures of the outside world, the brain divides up the incoming visual input and sends it to separate cortical areas for the processing of color, movement, shape, and shading—as we will see in more detail in Chapter 7. But the occipital lobes do not do all this work alone. As we have noted, they rely on adjacent association areas in the parietal lobes to locate objects in space. They also work with temporal regions to produce visual memories (Ishai & Sagi, 1995; Miyashita, 1995). There is even a distinct patch of temporal cortex dedicated to the recognition of faces and another for perception of the human body (Kanwisher, 2006; Tsao, 2006). In one patient, neurosurgeons found a neuron that responded *only* to images of Halle Berry (Quiroga, 2005)! To complete the picture, we should note that congenitally blind people recruit the visual cortex to help them read Braille (Amedi et al., 2005; Barach, 2003).

Visual Pathways in Split-Brain Patients   Now let's return again to the split-brain patients described at the beginning of the chapter. As we have said, they were able to name objects seen in the right visual field, but not on the left. A look at the visual pathways, shown in Figure 2.18, will show you why.

Notice in Figure 2.18 that everything to the left of the point of eye fixation goes to the *right* side of the retina *of each eye*. Similarly, everything to the *right* goes to the *left side of each eye*. This happens because the lenses of the eyes flip everything backward (whether or not the individual has a split brain). As the information flows back to the visual cortex from each eye, it splits into two streams because the optic nerve separates into two pathways here (again, whether or not the corpus callosum has been cut). The result is that *everything a person sees on the right gets processed in the left hemisphere's visual cortex*, while *the right visual cortex processes everything to the left* of the point on which the eyes are fixed.

How can we apply this schema to the odd responses of the split-brain patients? Because language is usually a left hemisphere function, it makes sense that these patients could name objects that were "seen" by the left hemisphere—coming from the right visual field. The right hemisphere, on the other hand (so to speak), cannot produce speech and so cannot name objects seen in the left visual field—which are processed by the right hemisphere. Studying how the visual pathways cross over in Figure 2.18 should make this clear.

The Temporal Lobes   When the phone rings or a horn honks, the sound registers in your **temporal lobes,** on the lower side of each cerebral hemisphere (see Figure 2.16). There lies the *auditory cortex,* which helps you make sense of the sounds, especially speech. In most people, a specialized section of auditory cortex on the brain's left side helps process the meaning of speech sounds.

But the temporal lobes take responsibility for more than just hearing. As we have seen, portions of the temporal lobes "subcontract" from the visual cortex the work of recognizing faces. Other temporal regions work with the hippocampus on the important task of storing long-term memories. (And, when you think of it, this makes a lot of sense, because the hippocampus, which has a central role in forming memories, lies directly beneath the temporal lobes.) Finally, we should note that deaf individuals apparently recruit the speech areas of the temporal lobes for understanding sign language (Neville et al., 1998).

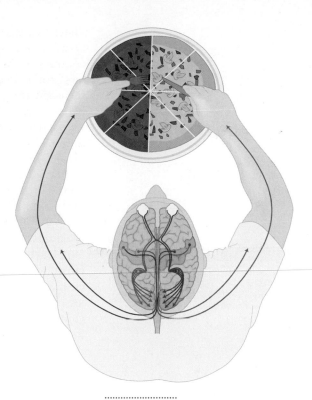

....

FIGURE 2.18
The Neural Pathways from the Eyes to the Visual Cortex

There are two things to notice in this illustration, in which the person is looking at the center of the pizza. First, the information from the left side of the retina in each eye corresponds to the right side of the pizza. Conversely, the right visual field senses the left side of the pizza. (This happens because the lens of the eye reverses the image.) Second, please notice that the left sides of both retinas in the eyes send images to the brain's left visual cortex, while the right sides of the retinas send images to the right visual cortex. As a result, when the eyes are fixated in the center, each side of the brain "sees" the pizza.

Visual cortex   The visual processing areas of cortex in the occipital and temporal lobes.

Temporal lobes   Cortical lobes that process sounds, including speech. The temporal lobes are probably involved in storing long-term memories.

The Cooperative Brain   No single part of the brain takes sole responsibility for emotion, memory, personality, or any other complex psychological characteristic—contrary to the beliefs of Gall and his phrenologists. There are no single "brain centers" for any of the major faculties of the mind—attention, consciousness, learning, memory, thinking, language, emotion, or motivation. Rather, every mental and behavioral process involves the coordination and cooperation of many brain networks, each an expert at some highly specialized task (Damasio, 2003; LeDoux, 2002). For example, when you do something as simple as answer a ringing telephone, you hear it in your temporal lobes, interpret its meaning with the help of the frontal lobes, visually locate it with your occipital lobes, initiate grasping the phone on the orders of your frontal and parietal lobes, and engage in thoughtful conversation, again using frontal-lobe circuitry. Even the cortex cannot do its work without communicating with circuits lying deep beneath the surface: the limbic system, thalamus, brain stem, cerebellum, and other structures.

Clearly, the brain usually manages to "put it all together" in a coordinated effort to understand and respond to the world. Exactly *how* it does so is not clear to neuroscientists—and, in fact, this constitutes one of the biggest mysteries of modern psychology. Some clues have appeared in recent work, however. Constantly active, even when we are asleep, our brains produce pulses of coordinated waves that sweep over the cortex that are thought, somehow, to coordinate activity in far-flung brain regions (Buzsáki, 2006). Stay tuned for further developments.

With the brain's democratic division of labor in mind, it shouldn't surprise you to learn that we use the largest proportion of the cortex for integrating and interpreting information gathered from the sensory parts of the brain and from memory. Collectively, we call these regions the **association cortex.** Diverse parts of the association cortex, then, interpret sensations, lay plans, make decisions, and prepare us for action—precisely the mental powers in which we humans excel and which distinguish us from other animals.

We have seen that the four lobes in each hemisphere have specialized functions and that we depend on them working cooperatively with the rest of the brain. Now, let's turn to some additional evidence that the two cerebral hemispheres themselves are not strictly mirror images of each other but specialize in different tasks. These differences fall under the heading of *cerebral dominance*—a commonly misunderstood concept.

Cerebral Dominance

In the mid 1800s, at about the same time that Phineas Gage lay recovering from his accident, a French neurologist named Paul Broca occupied himself studying patients who had speech impairments that resulted from brain injuries. An especially important case involved a man known in the medical books as "Tan"—a name derived from the only word he was able to speak. After Tan's death, an autopsy revealed severe damage in the left front portion of his brain. This clue prompted Broca to study other patients who had developed *aphasia*—the loss of speech caused by brain injury. Again and again, Broca found damage to the same spot, later named *Broca's area*, that had been damaged in Tan's brain, as well. (This is the frontal lobe speech area we mentioned earlier. You can see its location in Figure 2.16.) Broca's discovery was one of the early suggestions that the two sides of the brain specialize in different tasks. Subsequent work has confirmed and extended his findings:

- Brain-damaged patients suffering paralysis on the right side of their bodies often develop speech disturbances, suggesting that speech production involves the frontal lobe, usually in the *left* hemisphere. (Again, please recall that the left hemisphere controls the right side of the body.)

CONNECTION • CHAPTER 7

The puzzle of how the brain "puts it all together" is known as *the binding problem*.

Association cortex   Cortical regions throughout the brain that combine information from various other parts of the brain.

- Damage to the left parietal and left temporal lobes commonly causes problems in understanding language.

What about damage to the right hemisphere? People with right-sided brain injuries less often have speech problems, but they are more likely to have difficulties with *spatial orientation* (locating themselves or external objects in three-dimensional space). They may, for example, feel lost in a previously familiar place or be unable to assemble a simple jigsaw puzzle. Musical ability is also associated with the right hemisphere, particularly with the right-side counterpart to Broca's area (Janata et al., 2002; Zatorre & Krumhansl, 2002).

Thus, while the two hemispheres superficially appear to be near mirror images of each other, they assume somewhat different functions. This tendency for the hemispheres to take the lead in different tasks is called **cerebral dominance,** an often-misunderstood concept. What many people don't realize is this: While some processes are more under the control of the left hemisphere, and others are predominantly right-hemisphere tasks, *both hemispheres work together to produce our thoughts, feelings, and behaviors.*

Some People Are Different—But That's Normal Just to complicate your picture of cerebral dominance, you should know that the dominance pattern is not always the same from one person to another. Research demonstrating this fact uses a technique called *transcranial magnetic stimulation* (TMS) to deliver powerful magnetic pulses through the skull and into the brain. There the magnetic fields interfere with the brain's electrical activity, temporarily disabling the targeted region but without causing permanent damage. The experiments found that, when the left-side language areas receive TMS, language abilities remain unaffected in some people. Oddly enough, most of these people are left-handers. In general, these studies show that about one in ten individuals process language primarily on the *right* side of the brain. Another one in ten—again, mostly left-handers—have language functions distributed equally on both sides of the brain (Knecht et al., 2002).

Other studies have shown that, while one hemisphere usually dominates language functions, both sides of the brain get involved to some extent. Typically, the left side is more dominant in processing the "what," or *content,* of speech. The right hemisphere, by contrast, assumes the role of processing the *emotional tone* of speech and relating it to social expectations (Vingerhoets, 2003). In fact, the right hemisphere is generally more involved than the left in interpreting the emotional responses of others. As for our own emotions, the control of *negative* emotions, such as fear and anger, usually stems from the right frontal lobe, while the left frontal lobe typically regulates the *positive* emotions, such as joy (Davidson, 2000b).

Different Processing Styles Different though they may be, the two hemispheres don't compete with each other—as is sometimes supposed—except under the most unusual conditions, which we will describe in a moment. Rather, they make different contributions to the same task, except in split-brain patients, of course. In the lingo of neuroscience, the two hemispheres have different *processing styles.* For example, the left hemisphere groups objects analytically and verbally—as by similarity in function (*knife* with *spoon*)—while the right hemisphere might match things by form or visual pattern—as in matching *coin* to *clock,* which are both round objects (Gazzaniga, 1970; Sperry, 1968, 1982). In general, we can describe the left hemisphere's processing style as more *analytic* and *sequential,* while the right hemisphere interprets experience more *holistically, emotionally,* and *spatially* (Reuter-Lorenz & Miller, 1998).

Male and Female Brains In a culture where bigger is often seen as better, the undeniable fact that men (on the average) have slightly larger brains than do women has caused heated debate. The real question, of course, is: What is the meaning of the size differential? Most neuroscientists think it is simply the result of the male's larger body size—and not of much other importance (Brannon, 2008).

Cerebral dominance The tendency of each brain hemisphere to exert control over different functions, such as language or perception of spatial relationships.

Within the brain, certain structures exhibit sex differences, too. A part of the hypothalamus commonly believed to be associated with sexual behavior and, perhaps, gender identity, is larger in males than in females. Some studies have suggested that male brains are more *lateralized*, while females tend to distribute abilities, such as language, across both hemispheres. This claim is disputed by the results of a recent study (Sommer et al., 2004). If true, however, the difference in lateralization may explain why women are more likely than men to recover speech after a stroke. Other than that, what advantage the difference in lateralization may have is unclear.

At present, no one has nailed down any psychological difference that can be attributed to physical differences between the brains of males and females. The research continues, but your authors suggest interpreting new claims with a liberal dose of critical thinking, being especially wary of bias that may influence the way results are interpreted.

The Split Brain Revisited: "I've Half a Mind to . . . "

We now have all the important pieces of the split-brain puzzle presented at the beginning of the chapter:

- When the corpus callosum has been cut, the two brain hemispheres cannot communicate. As a result, information going into one side of the brain cannot be accessed by the other side of the brain.
- Split-brain patients can verbally identify objects when the information is available only to the left hemisphere. They fail to do so when the information goes only to the right hemisphere.
- The left hemisphere is dominant for language (in most people).
- Because the sensory pathways cross over to the opposite side as they ascend to the cortex, each side of the body communicates with the opposite side of the brain.
- The visual pathways constitute an exception: Information coming from the right side *of the visual field of both eyes* goes to the left side of the retina and on to the left visual cortex; information coming from the left visual field ends up in the right visual cortex.

The Clueless Hemisphere   We can now piece together an explanation for the odd symptoms displayed by people with split brains: The hemisphere doing the talking doesn't have a clue when the information has been presented solely to the other hemisphere. Under everyday conditions outside the laboratory, however, people with split brains get along surprisingly well, because they can scan a scene with their eyes, which sends essentially the same visual information to both sides of the brain. Only when the two hemispheres of split-brain patients get entirely different messages does the bizarre psychological reality of the split brain show itself—as it did in the Sperry and Gazzaniga experiments. Under those conditions, the patient can name only objects sensed by the left hemisphere.

Now, to test your understanding of these concepts, look at Figure 2.19 and see if you can explain why the split-brain patient responds as indicated. Why is he able to match, using the left hand, the image seen on the left side of the screen? And, why does he fail the same test when he uses the right hand?

The patient in the figure has been asked to identify an object that had been visualized only by the brain's right hemisphere because the image had been flashed only on the left side of the screen. The identification task was easily performed by the left hand, which is connected to the right hemisphere, but impossible for the right hand, which communicates with the left hemisphere.

Some unexpected effects of having a split brain also showed up in patient reports of their everyday experiences. For example, one told how his left hand would unzip his pants or unbutton his shirt at most inappropriate times, espe-

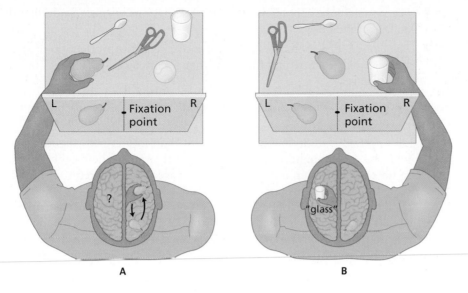

A

B

When the split-brain patient uses his left hand to find a match to an object flashed briefly in the left visual field, he is successful because both the visual and tactile (touch) information are registered in the right hemisphere, as shown in A. Nevertheless, the patient cannot *name* the object, because speech is mainly a *left*-hemisphere function. Now consider the same patient asked to perform the same task with the *right* hand, as shown in B. In this case, he is unsuccessful in picking out the object by touch, because the visual information and the tactile information are processed in different hemispheres. In this test, however, the patient is able to name the object in his hand!

cially when he felt stressed. But why? Sperry theorized that the right hemisphere—which has little language ability, but which controls the left hand—was merely trying to find a way to communicate (Sperry, 1964). It's almost as if the right hemisphere were saying, "I'm here! Look at me!"

Two Consciousnesses Such cerebral antics point to the most interesting finding in Sperry and Gazzaniga's work: the *duality of consciousness* observed in split-brain patients. When the two hemispheres received different information, it was as if the patient were two separate individuals. So, in the experiment shown in Figure 2.19, the right hemisphere might direct the left hand to select a pear, and the left hemisphere might tell the right hand to select a glass. In other tests, they found that right-hemisphere responses tended to be more emotional, while the left hemisphere responses were more analytic. As expected, the left hemisphere typically had much more language fluency than did the right.

We must be cautious about generalizing such findings from split-brain patients to individuals with normal brains, says Gazzaniga (1998a,b). He suggests that we think of the human mind as neither a single nor a dual entity but rather as a *confederation of minds*, each specialized to process a specific kind of information. For most people, then, the corpus callosum serves as a connecting pathway that helps our confederation of minds share information. And so we come full circle to the Core Concept that we encountered at the beginning of this section: The brain is composed of many specialized modules that work together to create mind and behavior (Baynes et al., 1998; Strauss, 1998).

What's It to You? Nearly everybody knows someone who has suffered brain damage from an accident, a stroke, or a tumor. Your new knowledge of the brain and behavior will help you understand the problems such people must face. And if you know what abilities have been lost or altered, you can usually make a good guess as to which part of the brain sustained the damage—especially if you bear in mind three simple principles:

1. Each side of the brain communicates with the opposite side of the body. Thus, if symptoms appear on one side of the body, it is likely that the other side of the brain was damaged. (See Figure 2.20.)

2. For most people, speech is mainly a left-hemisphere function.

3. Each lobe has special functions:
   - The occipital lobe specializes in vision;
   - The temporal lobe specializes in hearing, memory, and face recognition;

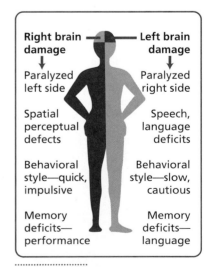

....
FIGURE 2.20
Contralateral Effects of Damage to the Cerebral Hemispheres

- The parietal lobe specializes in locating sensations in space, including the surface of the body;
- The frontal lobe specializes in motor movement, the production of speech, and certain higher mental functions that we often call "thinking" or "intelligence."

Here's how one of your authors (Bob) applied his knowledge of the brain:

I hadn't noticed Dad dragging the toe of his right foot ever so slightly as he walked. But my Mom noticed it on their nightly tour of the neighborhood, when he wasn't keeping up with her brisk pace. I just figured that he was slowing down a bit in his later years.

Dad, too, casually dismissed his symptom, but Mom was persistent. She scheduled an appointment with the doctor. In turn, the doctor scheduled a brain scan that showed a remarkably large mass—a tumor—on the left side of Dad's brain. You can see what the neurologist saw in Figure 2.21—an image taken ear-to-ear through the head.

When I saw the pictures, I knew immediately what was happening. The tumor was located in an area that would interfere with tracking the position of the foot. I knew that each side of the brain communicates with the opposite side of the body—so it made sense that the tumor showing so clearly on the left side of Dad's brain (right side of the image) was affecting communications with his right foot.

The neurologist also told us that the diseased tissue was not in the brain itself. Rather, it was in the saclike layers surrounding the brain and spinal cord. That was good news, in an otherwise bleak report. Still, the mass was growing and putting pressure on the brain. The recommendation was surgery—which occurred after an anxious wait of a few weeks.

During this difficult time, I remember feeling grateful for my professional training. As a psychologist, I knew something about the brain, its disorders,

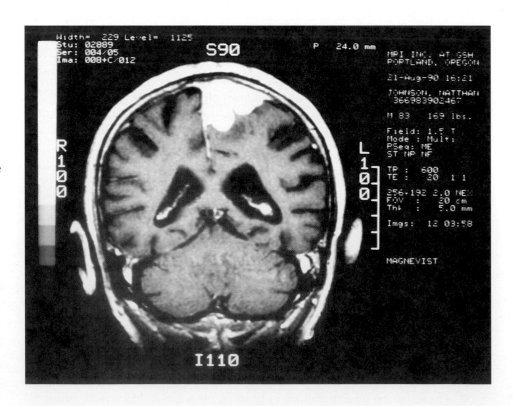

FIGURE 2.21

MRI Image of a Brain Tumor

This image, showing a side-to-side section toward the back of the head, reveals a large mass on the left side of the brain, in a region involved with tracking the position of the right foot. Visible at the bottom is a cross section of the cerebellum. Also visible are the folds in the cerebral cortex covering the brain. Near the center, you can see two of the brain's ventricles (hollow spaces filled with cerebrospinal fluid), which are often enlarged, as they are here, in Alzheimer's disease. The scan is of the father of one of your authors.

and treatments. This allowed me to shift perspectives—from son to psychologist and back again. It helped me deal with the emotions that rose to the surface when I thought about the struggle for the organ of my father's mind.

Sadly, the operation did not produce the miraculous cure for which we had hoped. Although brain surgery is performed safely on thousands of patients each year—many of whom receive immense benefits in the quality and lengths of their lives—one has to remember that it is a procedure that is usually done on very sick people. In fact, the operation did give Dad some time with us that he may otherwise not have had.

PSYCHOLOGYMATTERS
Using Psychology to Learn Psychology

The old idea that we use only 10 percent of our brains is bunk that probably came from a time when neuroscientists hadn't figured out the functions of many cortical areas. We have since filled in the blanks. Every part of the brain has a known function, and they all get used every day—but not necessarily for intellectual purposes. We now know that much of the brain merely deals with basic biological needs. Therefore, simply finding a way to engage *more* of the brain is not the royal road to increased brainpower.

Have neuroscientists found anything that you can use to improve your memory, especially for the concepts you are learning in your classes? The fact that we employ many different regions of the cerebral cortex in learning and memory may be among their most practical discoveries (Kandel & Squire, 2000). Accordingly, if you can bring more of this cerebral circuitry to bear on your studies (about biopsychology, for example), your brain will lay down a wider web of memories.

Reading the material in this book will help you form verbal (language) memories, parts of which involve circuits in the temporal cortex. Taking notes brings the motor cortex of the frontal lobes into play, adding a "motor memory" component to your study. Scanning the accompanying photos, charts, and drawings adds visual and spatial memory components in the occipital and parietal lobes. Listening actively to your professor's lectures and discussing the material with a study partner will engage the auditory regions of the temporal cortex and lay down still other memory traces. Finally, study time spent anticipating what questions will appear on the exam will involve regions of the frontal lobes in your learning process.

In general, the more ways that you can engage with the material—the more sensory and motor channels you can employ—the more memory components you will build in your brain's circuitry. As a result, when you need to remember the material, you will have more possible ways of accessing what you have learned.

CheckYourUnderstanding

1. **APPLICATION:** Suppose that you are a neuroscientist interested in comparing what parts of the brain are most active when people are driving and when they are talking on a cell phone. Which imaging technique would be best for your research?

2. **RECALL:** Name the three main layers of the human brain discussed in the text: _____, _____, and _____.

3. **APPLICATION:** An fMRI or a PET scan would show activity in a person's _____ during an emotional response.

4. **RECALL:** Make a sketch showing the four lobes of the cerebral cortex. Indicate the main functions of each lobe. Indicate which hemisphere of the brain controls language in most people. Which hemisphere of the brain controls the left hand?

5. ANALYSIS: The split-brain patient in Figure 2.13 would have trouble using his _____ hand to select the object flashed on the left side of the screen. (*Hints:* Which hemisphere controls each hand? Which hemisphere processes information from the left side of the visual field?)

6. UNDERSTANDING THE CORE CONCEPT: The brain is composed of many specialized and interconnected modules that work together to create mind and behavior. Can you name at least two specialized parts of the brain that are known to work together?

ANSWERS: 1. The best would be fMRI, because it not only gives detailed three-dimensional images but also shows different activity levels in different parts of the brain. The driving task, however, would have to be modified so that it could be performed while in the fMRI machine. **2.** the brain stem and cerebellum, the limbic system, the cerebrum **3.** limbic system **4.** See the location of the four lobes in Figure 2.16. The left hemisphere controls language, and the right hemisphere controls your left hand. **5.** right **6.** Examples include the interaction of regions in the four lobes of the cerebral cortex when answering the phone. There are many other examples mentioned in this section.

Critical Thinking Applied: Left Brain vs. Right Brain

The split-brain studies and the resulting discovery that the two sides of the brain process information differently have captured the public's interest in recent years. The press reports claiming that the left hemisphere is logical and the right hemisphere is emotional might easily lead to the mistaken conclusion that your friend Joe, a guy with an analytic bent, lives mostly in his left hemisphere, while his wife Barbara, more sensitive to people's emotions, filters her experience mainly on the right side of her brain.

Knowing a fad when they see it, pseudoscientists have classified people as "right-brained" or "left-brained" and developed workshops to help plodding analytical types get into their "right minds." But is this distinction really accurate?

What Are the Issues?

The idea that people fall neatly into one category or another has a lot of popular appeal, but the facts seldom bear this out. More commonly, we find that people are distributed from one extreme to the other, with most somewhere in the middle. (Think, for example, of intelligence or athletic ability.) So, one issue we should address involves seeing whether people tend to be *either* analytical *or* emotional, but not both. When a claim, such as this, conflicts with prior knowledge, we should be skeptical.

A second issue is whether the brain actually functions as proponents of the left-brain/right-brain claims say it does. That is, do some people mainly use the left side of the brain, while others mainly use the right?

What Critical Thinking Questions Should We Ask?

Is the claim reasonable or extreme? As we have noted, the idea that we can categorize people into neat, either-or categories doesn't fit with what we know about most other psychological characteristics, such as intelligence. This alerts us that we need to look carefully at the evidence.

Neuroscience should be able to tell us how the left and right brain interact—and whether people differ in the activity of one hemisphere or the other. The primary critical thinking question we should ask, then, is: What is the evidence?

What Conclusions Can We Draw?

The evidence—both from the split-brain studies and research on the intact brain—by no means warrants categorizing people in this way. As we have seen, the two hemispheres have somewhat different *processing styles,* but the actual differences between the two hemispheres do not outweigh their similarities (Banich, 1998; Trope et al., 1992). Most important—and what the right-brain/left-brain faddists overlook—is the fact that the two hemispheres of the intact brain cooperate with each other, each by making its own complementary contribution to our mental lives. (See Figure 2.22.)

Unless you have a split brain, you bring the abilities of both sides of your brain to bear on everything you do. Why, then, do people have such obvious differences in the way they approach the same tasks? Some people *do* seem to approach things in a more analytical, logical fashion; others operate from a more "intuitive" and emotional perspective. But now that you know something of how the brain works, you can understand that we cannot account for these differences among people simply by suggesting that they employ one side of the brain or the other. Even split-brain patients use both sides of their brains! A better explanation involves different combinations of experience and brain physiology. People are different because of different combinations of nature and nurture—not because they use opposite sides of the brain.

Left hemisphere

- Regulation of positive emotions
- Control of muscles used in speech
- Control of sequence of movements
- Spontaneous speaking and writing
- Memory for words and numbers
- Understanding speech and writing

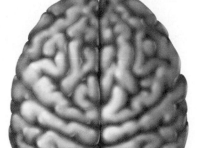

Right hemisphere

- Regulation of negative emotions
- Responses to simple commands
- Memory for shapes and music
- Interpreting spatial relationships and visual images
- Recognition of faces

FIGURE 2.22
Specialization of the Cerebral Hemispheres

While each hemisphere communicates with the opposite side of the body, the hemispheres each specialize in controlling different functions. For most people, the left hemisphere specializes in speech and other functions performed in sequence (such as walking, throwing, and reading). The right hemisphere specializes in synthesis: gathering many pieces of information and synthesizing it as a unified whole (as in recognizing faces or shapes).

Chapter Summary

2.1 How Are Genes and Behavior Linked?

Core Concept 2.1 Evolution has fundamentally shaped psychological processes because it favors genetic variations that produce adaptive behavior.

Charles Darwin's theory of evolution explains behavior as the result of **natural selection.** Variation among individuals and competition for resources lead to survival of the most adaptive behavior, as well as the fittest features. This principle underlies human behavior, as well as that of other animals. Genetics has clarified the biological basis for natural selection and inheritance. Our **chromosomes** contain thousands of **genes,** carrying traits inherited from our parents. Each gene consists of a **DNA** segment that encodes for a protein. Proteins, in turn, serve as the building blocks for the organism's structure and function, including the functioning of the brain. While a draft of the human genome has been completed, we do not yet know precisely how specific genes influence behavior and mental processes. Genetic research may be nearing the point at which we may alter our genetic makeup or select certain genetic traits for our children. This new knowledge brings with it choices that humans have never had to face before.

Biopsychology (p. 45)   **Gene** (p. 48)

Cerebral hemispheres (p. 43)   **Genotype** (p. 48)

Chromosome (p. 48)   **Natural selection** (p. 47)

Corpus callosum (p. 43)   **Neuroscience** (p. 45)

DNA (p. 48)   **Phenotype** (p. 48)

Evolution (p. 46)   **Sex chromosomes** (p. 50)

MyPsychLab Resources 2.1:

Explore: Building Blocks of Genetics

Watch: How the Human Genome Map Affects You

2.2 How Does the Body Communicate Internally?

Core Concept 2.2 The brain coordinates the body's two communications systems, the nervous system and the endocrine system, which use similar chemical messengers to communicate with targets throughout the body.

The body's two communication systems are the **nervous system** and the **endocrine system. Neurons** receive messages by means of stimulation of the **dendrites** and **soma.** When sufficiently aroused, a neuron generates an **action potential** along the **axon. Neurotransmitter** chemicals relay the message to receptors on cells across the **synapse.** The nervous system has two main divisions: the **central nervous system** and the **peripheral** nervous system. The peripheral nervous system, in turn, comprises the **somatic nervous system** (further divided into sensory and motor pathways) and the **autonomic nervous system**, which communicates with internal organs and glands. The **sympathetic division** of the autonomic nervous system is most active under stress, while the **parasympathetic division** attempts to maintain the body in a more calm state. The glands of the slower endocrine system also communicate with cells around the body by secreting **hormones** into the bloodstream. Endocrine system activity is controlled by the **pituitary gland,** attached to the base of the brain, where it receives orders from the hypothalamus. Psychoactive drugs affect the nervous system by influencing the effects of neurotransmitters by acting as **agonists** or **antagonists.** Unfortunately for people taking psychoactive drugs, many neural pathways in the brain may employ the same neurotransmitter, causing unwanted side effects.

MyPsychLab Resources 2.2:

Explore: The Structure of a Neuron

Explore: Neuronal Transmission

Explore: Action Potential

Explore: The Synapse

2.3 How Does the Brain Produce Behavior and Mental Processes?

Core Concept 2.3 The brain is composed of many specialized modules that work together to create mind and behavior.

In modern times, researchers have opened windows on the brain, using the **EEG** to sense the brain's electrical activity. In recent years, computer technology has led to brain-scanning techniques, such as **CT, PET, MRI,** and **fMRI**—each having its advantages and disadvantages. We can conceive of the brain as being organized in three integrated layers. The **brain stem** and associated structures (including the **medulla, reticular formation, pons, thalamus,** and **cerebellum**) control many vital body functions, along with influencing alertness and motor movement. The **limbic system** (including the **hippocampus, amygdala,** and **hypothalamus**) plays vital roles in motivation, emotion, and memory. The **cerebral cortex** contains highly specialized modules. Its **frontal lobes** control motor functions, including speech, and higher mental functions. The **parietal lobes** specialize in sensation, especially the senses of touch and body position, as well as the understanding of speech. The **occipital lobes** deal exclusively with vision, while the **temporal lobes** have multiple roles involved in face recognition, hearing, and smell. Even though the functions of the brain are highly localized within specific modules, they normally work seamlessly together: Every mental and behavioral process involves the coordination and cooperation of many brain networks. The **association cortex** integrates the output of the sensory networks and of memory. One of psychology's major mysteries centers on how the brain manages to coordinate these processes. The two cerebral hemispheres are differently specialized with language, analytical thinking, and positive emotions regulated by circuits in the left hemisphere. The right hemisphere specializes in spatial interpretation, visual and musical memory, and negative emotions. The two hemispheres communicate across the corpus callosum. If the hemispheres are surgically severed, as when the corpus callosum is cut in split-brain patients, a duality of consciousness emerges. Because each side of the body has sensory and motor links to the opposite side of the brain, a split-brain patient who "sees" an object in only one hemisphere of the brain will only be able to locate that object by touch, using the hand linked to the same hemisphere.

MyPsychLab Resources 2.3:

Explore: The Limbic System

Explore: The Visual Cortex

Simulation: Split-brain Experiments

Discovering Psychology Viewing Guide

 Watch the following videos by logging into MyPsychLab (www.mypsychlab.com). After you have watched the videos, complete the activities that follow.

 PROGRAM 3: THE BEHAVING BRAIN

 PROGRAM 4: THE RESPONSIVE BRAIN

 PROGRAM 25: COGNITIVE NEUROSCIENCE

PROGRAM REVIEW

1. What section of a nerve cell receives incoming information?
   a. the axon
   b. the terminal button
   c. the synapse
   d. the dendrite

2. In general, neuroscientists are interested in the
   a. brain mechanisms underlying normal and abnormal behavior.
   b. biological consequences of stress on the body.
   c. comparison of neurons with other types of cells.
   d. computer simulation of intelligence.

3. Which section of the brain coordinates body movement and maintains equilibrium?
   a. the brain stem
   b. the cerebellum
   c. the hippocampus
   d. the cerebrum

4. Which brain structure is most closely involved with emotion?
   a. the cortex
   b. the brain stem
   c. the limbic system
   d. the cerebellum

5. Which method of probing the brain produces actual pictures of the brain's inner workings?

    a. autopsies

    b. lesioning

    c. brain imaging

    d. electroencephalograms

6. Research related to acetylcholine may someday help people who

    a. have Alzheimer's disease.

    b. have Parkinson's disease.

    c. suffer spinal cord trauma.

    d. suffer from depression.

7. When we say the relationship between the brain and behavior is reciprocal, we mean that

    a. the brain controls behavior, but behavior can modify the brain.

    b. behavior determines what the brain will think about.

    c. the brain and behavior operate as separate systems with no interconnection.

    d. the brain alters behavior as it learns more about the world.

8. Which of the following is true about how neurons communicate with each other?

    a. All neuronal communication is excitatory.

    b. Neurons communicate with each other by sending electrical discharges across the connecting synapse.

    c. Neurons of any given type can communicate only with other neurons of the same type.

    d. The sum of excitatory and inhibitory signals to a neuron determines whether and how strongly it will respond.

9. Which part of the brain controls breathing?

    a. cerebellum

    b. brain stem

    c. hypothalamus

    d. limbic system

10. The cerebrum

    a. consists of two hemispheres connected by the corpus callosum.

    b. relays sensory impulses to the higher perceptual centers.

    c. releases seven different hormones to the pituitary gland.

    d. controls temperature and blood pressure.

11. After a rod was shot through Phineas Gage's skull, what psychological system was most strongly disrupted?

    a. his emotional responses

    b. his ability to sleep and wake

    c. his language comprehension

    d. his ability to count

12. Which of the following does not provide information about the structure of the brain?

    a. CAT

    b. EEG

    c. MRI

    d. fMRI

13. Which of the following provides the highest temporal and spatial resolution in brain imaging?

    a. ERP

    b. MRI

    c. PET

    d. fMRI

14. Stimuli that pass through the right eye are processed by

    a. the left side of the brain.

    b. the front of the brain.

    c. the right side of the brain.

    d. the brain stem.

15. The process of learning how to read shows that the brain is plastic. What does this mean?

    a. The brain is rigid in what it is designed to do.

    b. Learning how to read reorganizes the brain.

    c. The brain cannot be damaged simply by attempting new mental feats.

    d. The brain can be damaged when it attempts new mental feats.

16. If a scientist was studying the effects of endorphins on the body, the scientist would be likely to look at a participant's

    a. memory.

    b. mood.

    c. ability to learn new material.

    d. motivation to compete in sports.

17. What is the relationship between the results of Saul Schanberg's research and that of Tiffany Field?

    a. Their results are contradictory.

    b. The results of Schanberg's research led to Field's research.

    c. Their results show similar phenomena in different species.

    d. Their results are essentially unrelated.

18. What physical change did Mark Rosenzweig's team note when it studied rats raised in an enriched environment?

a. a thicker cortex

b. more neurons

c. fewer neurotransmitters

d. no physical changes were noted, only functional changes

19. A scientist who uses the methodologies of brain science to examine animal behavior in natural habitats is a

a. naturalist.

b. bioecologist.

c. neuroethologist.

d. cerebroetymologist.

20. With respect to the neurochemistry of the brain, all of these are true, *except* that

a. scopolamine blocks the establishment of long-term memories.

b. opioid peptides are naturally occurring chemicals in the brain.

c. physostigmine is responsible for information transmission in the perceptual pathways.

d. endorphins play a major role in pleasure and pain experiences.

QUESTIONS TO CONSIDER

1. Different technologies for measuring brain activity help psychologists view structures and functioning of the brain. What advantages do these advanced techniques offer?

2. Imagine that you were a relative of Phineas Gage. How do you think you would have reacted to the changes in his behavior in the years following his accident at the railroad construction site? Would you have been willing to believe that the changes were permanent, or that they weren't under Gage's control?

3. Given the advances being made in the imaging of brain activity, will it ever be possible for scientists to "read someone's mind" or to control someone's thoughts?

4. Imagine that you were designing an animal brain. Why would you want to design neurons to have an all-or-none response rather than a graded potential? Why would you want to create a brain that responded to several different neurotransmitters rather than creating one all-purpose neurotransmitter that affected all cells equally?

5. If we have developed techniques that can eventually allow us to fully understand the various pathways of the brain and its neurochemistry, are we close to being able to build a brain from scratch?

ACTIVITIES

1. Can you feel the effects of your hormones? Try this: Imagine yourself falling down the stairs, stubbing your toe, or suddenly losing control of your car on a busy highway. Did your heart skip a beat? Did you catch your breath or feel a tingle up your back? Did the hair on your neck stiffen? Your imagination has caused a biochemical reaction in your brain, and you are feeling the effect of the hormones it produces. Can you name the hormones involved?

2. As science enters an era of allowing researchers to study the brain's activities, our imaginations about what is possible run much faster than the development of neuroimaging and simulation techniques. Watch films such as *The Cell, The Matrix,* and *AI,* and identify several ways in which the "science" they portray is impossible given the current state of the field. Think about which aspects will likely remain impossible even hundreds of years from now.

3. Check out a textbook for a neuroscience or medical course that shows brain images of normal people and various clinical populations such as patients with schizophrenia, patients with Alzheimer's disease, or victims of accidents. Which areas of loss are associated with the loss of which functions?

Critical Thinking Applied: **Do Different People Have Different "Learning Styles"?**

learning and human *nurture*

I n 1924, John Watson boasted, "Give me a dozen healthy infants, well-formed, and my own specified world to bring them up in and I'll guarantee to take any one at random and train him to become any type of specialist I might select—doctor, lawyer, artist, merchant-chief, and, yes, even beggar-man and thief, regardless of his talents, penchants, tendencies, abilities, vocations, and race of his ancestors." Decades later, the assumption behind Watson's boast became the bedrock on which the community called Walden Two was built: *Nurture* trumps *nature*. Or, to put it another way: Environment carries far more weight than heredity in determining our behavior.

So at Walden Two, residents can enter any sort of profession that interests them. And in their leisure time, they can do whatever they like: attend concerts, lie on the grass, read, or perhaps drink coffee with friends. They have no crime, no drug problems, and no greedy politicians. In exchange for this happy lifestyle, community members must earn four "labor credits" every day, doing work needed by the community.

(That's about four hours work—fewer hours for unpleasant tasks, such as cleaning sewers, but more for the easiest work, perhaps pruning the roses.) Following Watson's vision, the founder of Walden Two, a psychologist named Frasier, believed that people could have happy, fulfilling lives in an environment psychologically engineered to reward people for making socially beneficial choices. To reap these benefits, all a community need do is change the way it deals out rewards.

We should say *where* this community was built: all in the mind of behaviorist B. F. Skinner. You see, *Walden Two* is the name of a novel, written by Skinner (1948) to promote his ideas on better living through behavioral psychology. But so alluring was the picture he painted of this mythical miniature society that many real-world communes sprang up, using *Walden Two* as the blueprint.

None of the real communities based on *Walden Two* ran so smoothly as the one in Skinner's mind. Yet at least one such group, Twin Oaks, located in Virginia, thrives after 40 years—but not without substantial modifications to Skinner's vision (Kincade, 1973). In fact, you can visit this group electronically, through their website at www.twinoaks.org/index.html (Twin Oaks, 2007).

Nor was behaviorism's fate exactly as Skinner had envisioned it. Although the behaviorist perspective dominated psychology during much of the 20th century, its fortunes fell as cognitive psychology grew in prominence. But what remains is behaviorism's substantial legacy, including impressive theories of behavioral learning and a valuable set of therapeutic tools for treating learned disorders—such as fears and phobias. To illustrate what behaviorism has given us, consider the problem that confronted Sabra.

A newly minted college graduate, Sabra had landed a dream job at an advertising firm in San Francisco. The work was interesting and challenging, and she enjoyed her new colleagues. The only negative was that her supervisor had asked her to attend an upcoming conference in Hawaii—and take an extra few days of vacation there at the company's expense. Why was that a negative? Sabra had a fear of flying.

PROBLEM: Assuming that Sabra's fear of flying was a response that she had learned, could it also be treated by learning? If so, how?

A common stereotype of psychological treatment involves "reliving" traumatic experiences that supposedly caused a fear or some other symptom. Behavioral learning therapy, however, works differently. It focuses on the here-and-now, instead of the past: The therapist acts like a coach, teaching the patient new responses that can replace old problem behaviors. So, as you consider how Sabra's fear might be treated, you might think along the following lines:

● What behaviors would most likely be seen in people like Sabra, who are afraid of flying?

● What behaviors could Sabra learn that could replace or conflict with her fearful behavior?

● How could these new behaviors be taught?

While the solution to Sabra's problem involves learning, it's not the sort of hit-the-books learning that usually comes to the minds of college students. Psychologists define the concept of **learning** broadly, as *a process through which experience produces a lasting change in behavior or mental processes.* Accord-

Learning A lasting change in behavior or mental processes that results from experience.

ing to this definition, then, Sabra's "flight training" would be learning—just as much as taking golf lessons or reading this book are learning experiences.

To avoid confusion, two parts of our definition need some elaboration. First, we underscore the idea that learning may lead to a *lasting change in behavior*. Suppose that you go to your doctor's office and get a particularly unpleasant injection, during which the sight of the needle becomes associated with pain. The result: The next time you need a shot, you wince when you first see the needle. This persistent change in responding involves learning. In contrast, a simple, reflexive reaction, such as jumping when you hear an unexpected loud noise, does *not* qualify as learning because it produces no lasting change—nothing more than a fleeting reaction, even though it does entail a change in behavior.

Second, let's focus on the part of our definition that says learning affects *behavior* or *mental processes*. In the doctor's office example above, it is easy to see how learning affects behavior. But mental processes are more difficult to observe. How could you tell, for example, whether a laboratory rat had simply learned the behaviors required to negotiate a maze (turn right, then left, then right . . .) or whether it was following some sort of mental image of the maze, much as you would follow a road map? (And why should we care what, if anything, was on a rat's mind?) Let's venture a little deeper into our definition of learning by considering the controversy surrounding mental processes.

The "instinctive" behavior of these turtles returning to the sea is driven in part by heredity, but such behavior also relies on environmental cues. Scientists usually shun the term instinct, *preferring the term* species-typical behavior, *for reasons discussed in the text.*

Behavioral Learning versus Cognitive Learning

The problem of observing mental events, whether in rats or in people, underlies a long-running controversy between the behaviorists and the cognitive psychologists that threads through this chapter. For over 100 years, the behaviorists have maintained that psychology could be a true science only if it disregarded subjective mental processes and focused solely on observable stimuli and responses. On the other side of the issue, cognitive psychologists have contended that the behavioral view is far too limiting and that understanding learning requires that we make inferences about hidden mental processes. In the following pages, we will see that both sides in this dispute have made important contributions to our knowledge.

Learning versus Instincts

So, what does learning—either behavioral or cognitive learning—do for us? Nearly all human activity, from working to playing to interacting with family and friends, involves some form of learning. Without learning, we would have no human language. We wouldn't know who our family or friends were. We would have no memory of our past or goals for our future. And without learning, we would be forced to rely on simple reflexes and a limited repertoire of innate behaviors, sometimes known as "instincts."

In contrast with learning, instinctive behavior (more properly known as *species-typical behavior*) is heavily influenced by genetic programming. It occurs in essentially the same way across different individuals in a species. We see instincts at work in bird migrations, animal courtship rituals, and a few human behavior patterns, such as nursing in newborns. All these examples involve responses in which experience plays a small role, as compared to learned behaviors like operating a computer, playing tennis, or wincing at the sight of a needle. In general, human behavior is much more influenced by learning and much less influenced by instincts than that of other animals. For us, learning confers the flexibility to adapt quickly to changing situations and new environments. In this sense, then, learning represents an evolutionary advance over instincts.

CONNECTION • CHAPTER 9

Instinct refers to motivated behaviors that have a strong innate basis.

Simple and Complex Forms of Learning

Some forms of learning can be quite simple. For example, if you live near a busy street, you may learn to ignore the sound of the traffic. This sort of learning, known as **habituation**, involves learning *not to respond* to stimulation. Habituation occurs in all animals that have nervous systems, from insects and worms to people. It helps you focus on important

Habituation Learning not to respond to the repeated presentation of a stimulus.

stimuli, ignoring stimuli that need no attention, such as the feel of the chair you are sitting on or the sound of the air conditioning in the background.

We find another relatively simple form of learning most obviously in humans: When everything else is equal, we have a preference for stimuli to which we have been previously exposed, as contrasted with novel stimuli. This **mere exposure effect** occurs whether or not the stimulus was associated with something pleasurable or even whether we were aware of the stimulus. The mere exposure effect probably accounts for the effectiveness of much advertising (Zajonc, 1968, 2001). It may also account for young children being less interested in a present than in the box in which the present came.

Other kinds of learning can be more complex. One type involves learning a connection between two stimuli—as when a school child associates the 12 o'clock bell with lunch. And another occurs when we associate our actions with rewarding and punishing consequences, such as a reprimand from the boss or an A from a professor. The first two sections of the chapter will emphasize these last two especially important forms of **behavioral learning**, which we will call *classical conditioning* and *operant conditioning*.

In the third section of the chapter, we shift the focus from external behavior to internal mental processes. There our look at *cognitive learning* will consider how sudden "flashes of insight" and imitative behavior require theories that go beyond behavioral learning—to explain how we solve problems or why children imitate behavior for which they see other people being rewarded. We will also discuss the acquisition of concepts, the most complex form of learning and the sort of learning you do in your college classes. Finally, the chapter will close on a practical note, by considering how to use the psychology of learning to help you study more effectively—and enjoy it.

Let's begin with a form of behavioral learning that accounts for many of your own likes and dislikes: *classical conditioning*.

3.1 KEY QUESTION
WHAT SORT OF LEARNING DOES CLASSICAL CONDITIONING EXPLAIN?

CONNECTION • CHAPTER 1

Structuralism and *functionalism* were two of the early "schools" of psychology.

Mere exposure effect   A learned preference for stimuli to which we have been previously exposed.

Behavioral learning   Forms of learning, such as classical conditioning and operant conditioning, that can be described in terms of stimuli and responses.

Ivan Pavlov (1849–1936) would have been insulted if you had called him a psychologist. In fact, he had only contempt for the structuralist and functionalist psychology of his time, which he saw as being hopelessly mired in speculation about subjective mental life (Todes, 1997). Pavlov and the hundreds of student researchers who passed through Pavlov's Russian research "factory" were famous for their work on the digestive system—for which Pavlov eventually snared a Nobel prize (Fancher, 1979; Kimble, 1991).

Unexpectedly, however, the experiments on salivation (the first step in digestion) went awry, sending Pavlov and his crew on a detour into the psychology of learning—a detour that occupied Pavlov for the rest of his life. The problem they encountered was that their experimental animals began salivating even before food was put in their mouths (Dewsbury, 1997). In fact, saliva would start flowing when they saw the food or even when they heard the footsteps of the lab assistant bringing the food. (Normally, salivation occurs after food is placed in the mouth.)

This response was a puzzle. What, after all, was the biological function of salivating before receiving food? When Pavlov and his associates turned their attention to understanding these "psychic secretions" they made a series of discoveries that would change the course of psychology (Pavlov, 1928; Todes, 1997). Quite by accident, they had stumbled upon an objective model of learn-

To study classical conditioning, Pavlov placed his dogs in a restraining apparatus. The dogs were then presented with a neutral stimulus, such as a tone. Through its association with food, the neutral stimuls became a conditioned stimulus eliciting salivation.

ing that could be manipulated in the laboratory to tease out the connections among stimuli and responses. This discovery, now known as **classical conditioning**, forms the Core Concept of this section:

Classical conditioning is a basic form of learning in which a stimulus that produces an innate reflex becomes associated with a previously neutral stimulus, which then acquires the power to elicit essentially the same response.

core
concept

In the following pages we will see that classical conditioning accounts for some important behavior patterns found not only in animals but in people. By means of classical conditioning, organisms learn about cues that help them anticipate and avoid danger, as well as cues alerting them to food, sexual opportunity, and other conditions that promote survival. First, however, let's examine some of the fundamental features that Pavlov identified in classical conditioning.

Classical conditioning   A form of behavioral learning in which a previously neutral stimulus acquires the power to elicit the same innate reflex produced by another stimulus.

The Essentials of Classical Conditioning

Pavlov's work on learning focused on manipulating simple, automatic responses known as *reflexes* (Windholz, 1997). Salivation and eye blinks are examples of such reflexes. They commonly result from stimuli that have biological significance: The blinking reflex, for example, protects the eyes; the salivation reflex aids digestion.

Pavlov's great discovery was that his dogs could associate these reflexive responses with *new* stimuli—*neutral stimuli* that had previously produced no response. Thus, they could *learn* the connection between a reflex and a new stimulus. For example, Pavlov found he could teach a dog to salivate upon hearing a certain sound, such as the tone produced by a striking a tuning fork or a bell. You have experienced the same sort of learning if your mouth waters when you read the menu in a restaurant.

To understand how these "conditioned reflexes" worked, Pavlov's team employed a simple experimental strategy. They first placed an untrained dog in a harness and set up a vial to capture the animal's saliva. Then, at intervals, they sounded a tone, after which they gave the dog a bit of food. Gradually, over a number of trials, the dog began to salivate in response to the tone alone.

off the mark.com   by Mark Parisi

(*Source:* © Mark Parisi. Reprinted by permission of Atlantic Feature Syndicate.)

FIGURE 3.1
Basic Features of Classical Conditioning

Before conditioning the food (UCS) naturally elicits salivation (UCR). A tone from a tuning fork is a neutral stimulus and has no effect. During conditioning (the acquisition phase), the tone is paired with the food, which continues to elicit the salivation response. Through its association with the food, the previously neutral tone becomes a conditioned stimulus (CS), gradually producing a stronger and stronger salivation response.

(*Source:* P. G. Zimbardo and R. J. Gerrig, *Psychology and Life,* 15th ed. Published by Allyn and Bacon, Boston, MA. Copyright © 1999 by Pearson Education. Reprinted by permission of the publisher.)

Neutral stimulus   Any stimulus that produces no conditioned response prior to learning. When it is brought into a conditioning experiment, the researcher will call it a conditioned stimulus (CS). The assumption is that some conditioning occurs after even one pairing of the CS and UCS.

Unconditioned stimulus (UCS)   In classical conditioning, UCS is the stimulus that elicits an unconditioned response.

Unconditioned response (UCR)   In classical conditioning, the response elicited by an unconditioned stimulus without prior learning.

Acquisition   The initial learning stage in classical conditioning, during which the conditioned response comes to be elicited by the conditioned stimulus.

Conditioned stimulus (CS)   In classical conditioning, a previously neutral stimulus that comes to elicit the conditioned response. Customarily, in a conditioning experiment, the neutral stimulus is called a conditioned stimulus when it is first paired with an unconditioned stimulus (UCS).

Conditioned response (CR)   In classical conditioning, a response elicited by a previously neutral stimulus that has become associated with the unconditioned stimulus.

In general, Pavlov and his students found that a **neutral stimulus** (one without any reflex-provoking power, such as a tone or a light), when paired with a natural reflex-producing stimulus (food), will by itself gradually begin to elicit a learned response (salivation) that is similar to the original reflex. It's essentially the same conditioning process behind the association of romance with flowers or chocolate.

Figure 3.1 illustrates the main features of Pavlov's classical conditioning procedure. At first glance, the terms may seem a bit overwhelming. Nevertheless, you will find it immensely helpful to study them carefully now so that they will come to mind easily later—when we analyze complicated, real-life learning situations, as in the acquisition and treatment of fears, phobias, and food aversions.

Acquisition   Classical conditioning always involves an **unconditioned stimulus** (**UCS**), a stimulus that automatically—that is, without conditioning—provokes a reflexive response. Pavlov used food as the UCS, because it reliably produced the salivation reflex. In the language of classical conditioning, then, this is called an *unconditioned reflex* or, more commonly, an **unconditioned response** (**UCR**). It is important to realize that the UCS–UCR connection is "wired in" and so involves no learning. Dogs don't have to learn to salivate when they receive food, just as you don't have to learn to cry out when you feel pain: Both are unconditioned responses.

Acquisition, the initial learning stage in classical conditioning, pairs a new stimulus—a neutral stimulus (the tone produced by a tuning fork, for example)— with the unconditioned stimulus. Typically, after several trials the neutral stimulus will elicit essentially the same response as does the UCS. So, in Pavlov's experiment, when the sound alone began to produce salivation, this formerly neutral stimulus has become a **conditioned stimulus** (**CS**). Although the response to the conditioned stimulus is essentially the same as the response originally produced by the unconditioned stimulus, we now refer to it as the **conditioned response** (**CR**). The same thing may have happened to you in grade school, when your mouth watered (a conditioned response) at the sound of the lunch bell (a conditioned stimulus).

With those terms firmly in mind, look at the graph of acquisition in a typical classical conditioning experiment, which appears in the first panel of Figure

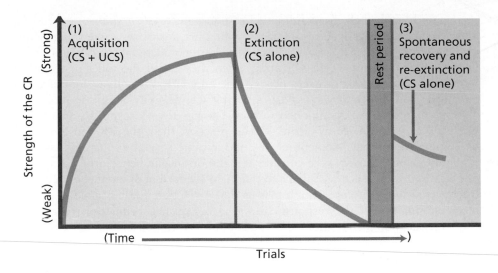

FIGURE 3.2
Acquisition, Extinction, and Spontaneous Recovery

During acquisition (CS + UCS), the strength of the CR increases rapidly. During extinction, when the UCS no longer follows the CS, the strength of the CR drops to zero. The CR may reappear after a brief rest period, even when the UCS is still not presented; only the CS alone occurs. The reappearance of the CR is called "spontaneous recovery."

(*Source:* P. G. Zimbardo and R. J. Gerrig, *Psychology and Life,* 15th ed. Published by Allyn and Bacon, Boston, MA. Copyright © 1999 by Pearson Education. Reprinted by permission of the publisher.)

3.2, where gradual acquisition of the conditioned response is reflected in the upward sweep of the line. Note that, at first, only weak responses are elicited by the conditioned stimulus. With continued CS–UCS pairings, however, the conditioned response increases in strength.

In conditioning, as in telling a joke, timing is critical. In most cases, the CS and UCS must occur *contiguously* (close together in time) so that the organism can make the appropriate connection during acquisition. The range of time intervals between the CS and UCS that will produce the best conditioning depends on the type of response being conditioned. For motor responses, such as eye blinks, a short interval of one second or less is best. For visceral responses, such as heart rate and salivation, longer intervals of 5 to 15 seconds work best. Conditioned fear optimally requires even longer intervals of many seconds or even minutes between the CS and the UCS. Taste aversions, we will see, can develop after even after several hours' delay. (Why these time differentials exist is not known with certainty, but they probably have survival value. For example, in the case of taste aversions, rats seem to be genetically programmed to eat small amounts of an unfamiliar food and, if they don't get sick, return to the food after a few hours.)

These, then, are the building blocks of classical conditioning: the CS, UCS, CR, UCR, and the timing that connects them. So, why did it take Pavlov three decades and 532 experiments to study such a simple phenomenon? There was more to classical conditioning than first met Pavlov's eyes. Along with *acquisition,* he also discovered the details of *extinction, spontaneous recovery, generalization,* and *discrimination*—which we will now explore.

Extinction and Spontaneous Recovery Suppose that, as a result of your grade-school experience with lunch bells, your mouth still waters at the sound of a bell at a school in your neighborhood. But, does this conditioned response have to remain permanently in your behavioral repertoire? The good news, based on experiments by Pavlov's group, suggests that it does not. Conditioned salivation responses in Pavlov's dogs were easily eliminated by withholding the UCS (food) over several trials in which the CS (the tone) was presented alone. In the language of classical conditioning, we call this **extinction**. It occurs when a conditioned response disappears after repeated presentations of the CS without the UCS. Figure 3.2 shows how the conditioned response (salivation) becomes weaker and weaker during extinction trials.

Now for the bad news: Let's imagine that your mouth-watering conditioned response to the lunch bell has been extinguished. (The cafeteria repeatedly ran out of food just before you got there.) But, after a time (summer vacation), when

Extinction (in classical conditioning) The weakening of a conditioned response in the absence of an unconditioned stimulus.

you again hear the bell, the conditioned response makes a *spontaneous recovery,* and you find yourself again drooling on your shirt. Much the same thing (without the shirt) happened with Pavlov's dogs: After undergoing extinction training, they would again begin salivating when they heard the tone. In technical terms, this **spontaneous recovery** occurs when *the CR reappears after extinction and after a period without exposure to the CS.* Happily, when spontaneous recovery happens, the conditioned response nearly always reappears at a lower intensity, as you can see in Figure 3.2. In practice, then, the CR can gradually be eliminated, although sometimes this may require several extinction sessions.

Spontaneous recovery is of considerable importance in behavioral therapy for phobias and fears, such as Sabra's aversion to flying. But spontaneous recovery has theoretical importance, too. It tells us that extinction does not involve a complete elimination of the response from the organism's behavioral repertoire. Rather, extinction merely suppresses the conditioned response. During extinction, the organism actually learns a competing response *not to respond* to the conditioned stimulus (Adelson, 2004; Travis, 2004).

CONNECTION • CHAPTER 13

Behavioral therapies are based on classical conditioning and operant conditioning.

Generalization   Now, switching to a visual CS, suppose you have developed a fear of spiders. Most likely, you will probably respond the same way to spiders of all sizes and markings. We call this **stimulus generalization**: giving a conditioned response to stimuli that are similar to the CS. Pavlov demonstrated stimulus generalization in his laboratory by showing that a well-trained dog would salivate in response to a tone of a slightly different pitch from the one he had used during conditioning. As you would expect, the closer the new sound was to the original, the stronger the response.

In everyday life, we find stimulus generalization in people who have acquired fears as a result of traumatic events. So, a person who has been bitten by a dog may develop a fear of all dogs, rather than a fear of the specific dog responsible for the attack. Likewise, stimulus generalization accounts for an allergy sufferer's sneeze upon seeing a paper flower. In short, by means of stimulus generalization we learn to give old responses in new situations.

Discrimination Learning   When you were in grade school, you may have learned to salivate at the sound of the lunch bell, but—thanks to *stimulus discrimination—*your mouth probably didn't water when the doorbell rang. Much the opposite of stimulus generalization, **stimulus discrimination** occurs when an organism learns to respond to one stimulus but not to stimuli that are similar. Pavlov and his students demonstrated this experimentally when they taught dogs to distinguish between two tones of different frequencies. Once again, their procedure was simple: One tone was followed by food, while another was not. Over a series of trials, the dogs gradually learned the discrimination, evidenced in salivation elicited by one tone and not the other. Beyond the laboratory, stimulus discrimination is the concept that underlies advertising campaigns aimed at conditioning us to discriminate between particular brands, as in the perennial battle between Pepsi and Coke.

Conditioning an Experimental Neurosis   If you have ever had a class in which you couldn't figure out what the teacher wanted, you have faced a vexing problem in discrimination learning. Transposing this problem to the laboratory, Pavlov confronted dogs with the seemingly simple task of distinguishing between a circle and an ellipse. One stimulus was always paired with food, and the other was always paired with a painful electric shock. The task became more difficult, however, over a series of trials, when Pavlov gradually changed the ellipse to become more and more circular—to the point that the dogs could not tell the images apart. And how did they respond? As the discrimination became increasingly difficult, their responses grew more erratic. Finally, as the animals became more confused between the circle and the ellipse, they would snarl and snap at the handlers. Because such agitated responses resemble behavior of "neurotic" people who become irritable and defensive when they have difficult choices to make, this behavior pattern was

Spontaneous recovery   The reappearance of an extinguished conditioned response after a time delay.

Stimulus generalization   The extension of a learned response to stimuli that are similar to the conditioned stimulus.

Stimulus discrimination   Learning to respond to a particular stimulus but not to stimuli that are similar.

dubbed **experimental neurosis**. Even today, this pattern stands as a model for the deterioration of behavior seen in both people and animals under stress.

Applications of Classical Conditioning

The beauty of classical conditioning is that it offers a simple explanation for many behaviors, from cravings to aversions. But it offers more than an explanation: It also gives us the tools for eliminating unwanted human behaviors—although Pavlov himself never attempted any therapeutic applications. Instead it fell to the American behaviorist, John Watson, to apply classical conditioning techniques to people.

John Watson and Rosalie Rayner conditioned Little Albert to fear furry objects like this Santa Claus mask (Discovering Psychology, 1990).

The Notorious Case of Little Albert   Over 80 years ago, John Watson and Rosalie Rayner first demonstrated conditioned fear in a human (Brewer, 1991; Fancher, 1979). In an experiment that would be considered unethical today, Watson and Rayner (1920/2000) conditioned an infant named Albert to react fearfully to a white laboratory rat. They created the fear response by repeatedly presenting the rat, paired with an aversive UCS—the loud sound of a steel bar struck with a mallet. It took only seven trials for "Little Albert" to react with distress at the appearance of the rat (CS) alone. After Albert's response to the rat had become well established, Watson and Rayner showed that his aversion readily generalized from the rat to other furry objects, such as a Santa Claus mask and a fur coat worn by Watson (Harris, 1979).

Most likely, the experiment caused Albert only temporary distress, because his fear response extinguished rapidly, making it necessary for Watson and Raynor to renew the fear conditioning periodically. In fact, the need to recondition Albert nearly ended the whole experiment when Watson and Rayner were attempting to show that the child's fear could be generalized to a dog, a rabbit, and a sealskin coat. Watson decided to "freshen the reaction to the rat" by again striking the steel bar. The noise startled the dog, which began to bark at Albert, frightening not only Little Albert but both experimenters (Harris, 1979).

Unlike Little Albert's short-lived aversion to furry objects, some fears learned under highly stressful conditions can persist for years (LeDoux, 1996). During World War II, the Navy used a gong sounding at the rate of 100 rings a minute as a call to battle stations. For combat personnel aboard ship, this sound became strongly associated with danger—a CS for emotional arousal. The persistent effect of this association was shown in a study conducted 15 years after the war, when Navy veterans who had experienced combat still gave a strong autonomic reaction to the old "call to battle stations" (Edwards & Acker, 1962).

◄ **CONNECTION • CHAPTER 2**
The *autonomic nervous system* regulates the internal organs.

Like those veterans, any of us can retain a readiness to respond to old emotional cues. Fortunately, however, classical conditioning also provides some tools for eliminating troublesome conditioned fears (Wolpe & Plaud, 1997). A good strategy combines extinction of the conditioned fear response with learning a relaxation response to the CS. This *counterconditioning* therapy, then, teaches patients to respond in a relaxed manner to the conditioned stimulus. The technique has been particularly effective in dealing with phobias. As you may have been thinking, we will want to consider counterconditioning as part of the treatment plan to help Sabra conquer her fear of flying.

CONNECTION • CHAPTER 13 ►
Behavioral therapies based on *counterconditioning* are effective ways of treating phobias.

Conditioned Food Aversions   All three of your authors have had bad experiences with specific foods. Phil got sick after eating pork and beans in the grade school lunchroom, Bob became ill after a childhood overdose of olives, and Vivian became queasy after eating chicken salad (formerly one of her favorite meals!). In all three cases, we associated our distress with the distinctive sight, smell, and taste of the food—but not to anything else in our environment. Even today, the taste, smell, or appearance of the specific food is enough to cause a feeling of nausea.

Unpleasant as it can be, learning to avoid a food associated with illness has survival value. That's why humans and many other animals readily form an association between illness and food—much more readily than between illness and

Experimental neurosis   A pattern of erratic behavior resulting from a demanding discrimination learning task, typically one that involves aversive stimuli.

A conditioned taste aversion can make a coyote stop killing sheep.

a nonfood stimulus, such as a light or a tone. And, while most forms of classical conditioning require only a short delay between the CS and the UCS, food aversions can develop when a distinctive taste has been separated by hours from the onset of illness. "Must have been something I ate!" we say.

John Garcia and Robert Koelling (1966) first recognized this highly selective CS–UCS connection when they noticed that rats avoided drinking from the water bottles in the chambers where they had previously been made nauseous by radiation. Could it be the taste of the water in those bottles that the rats were associating with being sick? Subsequent experiments confirmed their suspicions and led to yet another important discovery. Rats readily learned an association between flavored water and illness, yet the rats could *not* be conditioned to associate flavored water with the pain of an electric shock delivered through a grid on the floor of the test chamber. This makes good "sense" from an evolutionary perspective, because illness can easily result from drinking (or eating) poisonous substances but rarely occurs following a sharp pain to the feet. Conversely, the experimenters found that rats easily learned to respond fearfully when bright lights and noise signaled an electric shock—but could *not* learn to connect those light and sound cues with subsequent illness.

Biological Predispositions: A Challenge to Pavlov The problem that the Garcia and Koelling experiments pose for classical conditioning is that conditioned aversions involve both nature and nurture. That is, the tendency to develop taste aversions appears to be "wired in" as a part of our biological nature, rather than purely learned. It is this biological basis for taste aversions that has caused psychologists to question some aspects of Pavlov's original theory of classical conditioning (Rescorla & Wagner, 1972).

Unlike conditioning dogs to respond to a tone, food aversions seem to be grounded in an innate (and therefore *unlearned*) disposition to associate sickness with food. We know this because people who develop food aversions don't normally make the same association to other stimuli that accompanied the food. For example, when Bob developed an aversion to olives, he developed no such aversion to other objects in the room at the time, such as a light or a book on the table. It was solely the olives that became an effective conditioned stimulus. Such observations suggest that organisms have an inborn preparedness, to associate certain stimuli with certain consequences, while other CS–UCS combinations are highly resistant to learning.

Moreover, food aversions can develop even when the time interval between eating and illness extends over several hours—as compared with just a few seconds in Pavlov's experiments. Again, this suggests that in food aversions we are not dealing with a simple classically conditioned response as Pavlov understood it but, instead, with a response that is based as much in nature (biology) as it is in nurture (learning).

Such biological predispositions go far beyond taste and food aversions. Psychologists now believe that many of the common fears and phobias arise from *genetic preparedness*, built into us from our ancestral past, disposing us to learn fears of things associated with harm: snakes, spiders, blood, lightning, heights, and closed spaces. We can even see how concern over mutilation or other bodily harm contributes to fears of seemingly modern objects or situations, such as injections, dentistry, or flying.

Conditioning Coyotes: An Application Returning to conditioned food aversions, let's see how psychologists have applied their knowledge to a practical problem in the world outside the laboratory. Specifically, John Garcia and his colleagues have demonstrated how aversive conditioning can dissuade wild coyotes from attacking sheep. They did so by wrapping toxic lamb burgers in sheepskins and stashing them on sheep ranches: When roaming coyotes found and ate these meaty morsels, they became sick and—as predicted—developed a distaste for lamb meat. The result was a 30 to 50% reduction in sheep attacks. So powerful was this aversion for conditioned coyotes that, when captured and placed in a cage with a sheep, the coyotes would not get close to it. Some even vomited at the sight of a sheep (Garcia, 1990). Perhaps the most amazing result was this: Despite their success with conditioning coyotes, the scientists have been unable to modify the behavior of sheep ranchers to get them to apply the research. Apparently, sheep ranchers have a strong aversion to feeding lamb to coyotes!

So, what is the big lesson coming out of all this work on learned aversions and fears? *Conditioning involves both nature and nurture.* That is, conditioning depends not only on the learned relationship among stimuli and responses but also on the way an organism is genetically attuned to certain stimuli in its environment (Barker et al., 1978; Dickinson, 2001). What any organism can—and cannot—learn in a given setting is to some extent a product of its evolutionary history (Garcia, 1993). And that is a concept that Pavlov never understood.

PSYCHOLOGY**MATTERS**

Taste Aversions and Chemotherapy

Imagine that your friend Jena is about to undergo her first round of chemotherapy, just to make sure that any stray cells from the tumor found in her breast will be destroyed. To her surprise, the nurse enters the lab, not with the expected syringe, but with a dish of licorice-flavored ice cream. "Is this a new kind of therapy?" she asks. The nurse replies that it is, indeed, explaining that most patients who undergo chemotherapy experience nausea, which can make them "go off their feed" and quit eating, just when their body needs nourishment to fight the disease. "But," says the nurse, "We have found a way around the problem. If we give patients some unusual food before their chemotherapy, they will usually develop an aversion only to that food." She continued, "Did you ever hear of Pavlov's dogs?"

Conditioned food aversions make evolutionary sense, as we have seen, because they helped our ancestors avoid poisonous foods. As is the case with some of our other evolutionary baggage, such ancient aversions can cause modern problems. Cancer patients like Jena often develop aversions to normal foods in their diets to such an extent that they become malnourished. The aversions are nothing more than conditioned responses in which food (the CS) becomes associated with nausea. Chemotherapy personnel trained in classical conditioning use their knowledge to prevent the development of aversions to nutritive foods by arranging for meals not to be given just before the chemotherapy. And, as in Jena's case, they also present a "scapegoat" stimulus. By consuming candies or ice cream with unusual flavors before the treatments, patients develop taste aversions only to those special flavors. For some patients, this practical solution to problems with chemotherapy may make the difference between life and death (Bernstein, 1988, 1991).

CheckYourUnderstanding

1. **APPLICATION:** Give an example of classical conditioning from your everyday life and identify the CS, UCS, CR, and UCR.

2. **RECALL:** Before a response, such as salivation, becomes a conditioned response, it is a(n) _____.

3. **APPLICATION:** If you learned to fear electrical outlets after getting a painful shock, what would be the CS?

4. **UNDERSTANDING THE CORE CONCEPT:** Which one of the following could be an *unconditioned* stimulus (UCS) involved in classical conditioning?
   a. food
   b. a flashing light
   c. music
   d. money

HOW DO WE LEARN NEW BEHAVIORS BY OPERANT CONDITIONING?

With classical conditioning, you can teach a dog to salivate, but you can't teach it to sit up or roll over. Why? Salivation is a passive, involuntary reflex, while sitting up and rolling over are much more complex responses that we usually think of as voluntary. To a behavioral psychologist, however, such "voluntary" behaviors are really controlled by *rewards* and *punishments*. And because rewards and punishments play no role in classical conditioning, another important form of learning must be at work. Psychologists call it *operant conditioning*. (An *operant*, incidentally, is an observable behavior that an organism uses to "operate" in, or have an effect on, the environment. Thus, if you are reading this book to get a good grade on the next test, reading is an operant behavior.) You might also think of **operant conditioning** as a form of learning in which the *consequences* of behavior can encourage behavior change. The Core Concept of this section puts the idea this way:

core concept

> In operant conditioning, the consequences of behavior, such as rewards and punishments, influence the probability that the behavior will occur again.

Common rewarding consequences include money, praise, food, or high grades—all of which can encourage the behavior they follow. By contrast, punishments such as pain, loss of privileges, or low grades can discourage the behavior with which they are associated.

As you will see, the theory of operant conditioning is an important one for at least two reasons. First, operant conditioning accounts for a much wider spectrum of behavior than does classical conditioning. And second, it explains *new* behaviors—not just reflexive behaviors.

Skinner's Radical Behaviorism

The founding father of operant conditioning, American psychologist B. F. Skinner (1904–1990), based his whole career on the idea that the most powerful influences on behavior are its *consequences:* what happens immediately after the behavior. Actually, it wasn't Skinner's idea, originally. He borrowed the notion of behavior being controlled by rewards and punishments from another American psychologist, Edward Thorndike, who had demonstrated how hungry animals would work diligently to solve a problem by trial and error to obtain a food reward. Gradually, on succeeding trials, erroneous responses were eliminated and effective responses were "stamped in." Thorndike called this the **law of effect**. (See Figure 3.3.) The idea was that an animal's behavior leads to pleasant or unpleasant results that influence whether the animal will try those behaviors again.

The first thing Skinner did with Thorndike's psychology, however, was to rid it of subjective and unscientific speculation about the organism's feelings, intentions, or goals. What an animal "wanted" or the "pleasure" it felt was not important for an objective understanding of the animal's behavior. As a radical behaviorist, Skinner refused to consider what happens in an organism's mind, because such speculation cannot be verified by observation. For example, eating can be observed, but we can't observe the inner experiences of hunger, the desire for food, or pleasure at eating.

The Power of Reinforcement

While we often speak of "reward" in casual conversation, Skinner preferred the more objective term **reinforcer**. By this he meant any stimulus that *follows* and

Operant conditioning A form of behavioral learning in which the probability of a response is changed by its consequences—that is, by the stimuli that follow the response.

Law of effect The idea that responses that produced desirable results would be learned, or "stamped" into the organism.

Reinforcer A condition (involving either the presentation or removal of a stimulus) that occurs after a response and strengthens that response.

strengthens a response. Food, money, and sex serve this function for most people. So do attention, praise, or a smile. All are examples of **positive reinforcement**, which strengthens a response by occurring after the response and making the behavior more likely to occur again.

Most people know about positive reinforcement, of course, but fewer people understand the other main way to strengthen operant responses. It involves the reinforcement of behavior by the *removal* of an unpleasant or aversive stimulus. Psychologists call this **negative reinforcement**. (The word *negative* here is used in the mathematical sense of *subtract* or *remove*, while *positive* means *add* or *apply*.) So, using an umbrella to avoid getting wet during a downpour is a behavior learned and maintained by negative reinforcement. That is, you use the umbrella to avoid or remove an unpleasant stimulus (getting wet). Likewise, when a driver buckles the seat belt, the annoying sound of the seat-belt buzzer stops, providing negative reinforcement. Remember, it is the "subtraction" or removal of the unpleasant stimulus that creates negative reinforcement.

Reinforcing Technology: The "Skinner Box"

One of B. F. Skinner's (1956) important innovations consisted of a simple device for studying the effects of reinforcers on laboratory animals: a box with a lever that an animal could press to obtain food. He called this device an **operant chamber**. Nearly everyone else called it a "Skinner box," a term he detested. Over the years, thousands of psychologists have used the apparatus to study operant conditioning.

The virtue of the operant chamber lay in its capacity to control the timing and the frequency of reinforcement, factors that exert important influences on behavior, as you will soon see. Moreover, the Skinner box could be programmed to conduct experiments at any time of day—even when the researcher was home in bed.

Contingencies of Reinforcement

The timing and frequency of reinforcement determines its effect on behavior. So, while college and university students receive some reinforcement for their studying from grade reports delivered two or three times a year, such a schedule has little effect on their day-to-day behavior. Many professors realize this, of course, so they schedule exams and assignments and award grades periodically throughout their courses, as a means of encouraging continual studying, rather than making one big push at the end of the semester.

Here's the point: Whether we're talking about college students, Fortune 500 CEOs, or laboratory rats, any plan to influence operant learning requires careful consideration of the timing and frequency of rewards. How often will they receive reinforcement? How much work must they do to earn a reinforcer? Will they get a reward for every response or only after a certain number of responses? We will consider these questions below in our discussion of **reinforcement contingencies**, involving the many possible ways of associating responses and reinforcers.

Continuous versus Intermittent Reinforcement

Suppose you want to teach your dog a trick—say, sitting up on command. It would be a good idea to begin the training program with

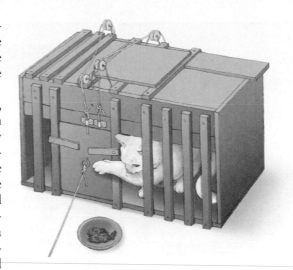

FIGURE 3.3
A Thorndike Puzzle Box

Unlike Pavlov's dogs, Thorndike's cats faced a problem: how to open the door in the puzzle box to get a food reward lying just outside. To solve this problem, the animals used *trial-and-error learning*, rather than simple reflexive responses. At first, their responses seemed random, but gradually they eliminated ineffective behaviors. And when the effects of their behavior were desirable (that is, when the door finally opened and the animals got the food), they used this strategy on subsequent trials. This change in behavior based on outcome of previous trials is called the *law of effect*. Much the same trial-and-error learning occurs when you learn a skill, such as shooting a basketball.

Positive reinforcement A stimulus presented after a response and increasing the probability of that response happening again.

Negative reinforcement The removal of an unpleasant or aversive stimulus, contingent on a particular behavior. Compare with *punishment*.

Operant chamber A boxlike apparatus that can be programmed to deliver reinforcers and punishers contingent on an animal's behavior. The operant chamber is often called a "Skinner box."

Reinforcement contingencies Relationships between a response and the changes in stimulation that follow the response.

(*Source:* Hi & Lois © King Features Syndicate.).

B. F. Skinner is shown reinforcing the animal's behavior in an operant chamber, or "Skinner box." The apparatus allows the experimenter to control all the stimuli in the animal's environment.

Just to set the record straight, we'd like to mention a bit of trivia about the "baby tender" crib that Skinner devised for his daughter, Deborah (Benjamin & Nielsen-Gammon, 1999). It consisted of an enclosed, temperature-controlled box that unfortunately bore a superficial resemblance to the operant chambers used in his experiments. The public learned about the "baby tender" from an article by Skinner in the magazine Ladies' Home Journal. *The story took on a life of its own, and, years later, stories arose about Deborah Skinner's supposed psychotic breakdown, lawsuits against her father, and eventual suicide—none of which were true. In fact, Deborah grew up to be a well-adjusted individual who loved her parents.*

Positive reinforcement exerts a powerful influence on our behavior. This competitor, for example, must train for years to achieve this reinforcement. What schedule of reinforcement was she on? Is the trophy a primary or secondary reinforcer?

Continuous reinforcement A type of reinforcement schedule by which all correct responses are reinforced.

Shaping An operant learning technique in which a new behavior is produced by reinforcing responses that are similar to the desired response.

Intermittent reinforcement A type of reinforcement schedule by which some, but not all, correct responses are reinforced; also called *partial reinforcement.*

a reward for every correct response. Psychologists call this **continuous reinforcement**. It's a useful tactic early in the learning process, because rewarding every correct response and ignoring the incorrect ones provides feedback on how well each response was performed. In addition, continuous reinforcement is useful for **shaping** complex new behaviors. Shaping, which is often used in animal training, involves the deliberate use of rewards (and sometimes punishments) to encourage better and better approximations of the desired behavior. (You have experienced shaping in school, as a teacher taught you to read, write, or play a musical instrument by gradually setting higher standards.) By means of shaping, the teacher can continually "raise the bar," or increase the performance level required for earning a reward. This tells the learner when performance has improved. In general, then, we can say that *continuous reinforcement is a good strategy for shaping new behaviors.*

Continuous reinforcement does have some drawbacks. For one thing, a failure to reward a correct response on one trial could easily be misinterpreted as a signal that the response was not correct. For another, continuous reinforcement loses its reinforcing quality as the organism becomes satiated, as you can imagine if someone were training you to shoot free throws by rewarding you with big slices of chocolate cake. Your first piece of cake may be highly rewarding, but by the time you have had 10 or 12 servings, the reward value dissipates.

Happily, once the desired behavior becomes well established (for example, when your dog has learned to sit up), the demands of the situation change. The learner no longer needs rewards to discriminate a correct response from an incorrect one. It's time to shift to **intermittent reinforcement** (also called *partial* *reinforcement*), the rewarding of some, but not all, correct responses. A less frequent schedule of reward—perhaps, after every third correct response—can still serve as an incentive for your dog to sit up on command. In general, whether we're dealing with people or animals, *intermittent reinforcement is the most efficient way to maintain behaviors that have already been learned* (Robbins, 1971; Terry, 2000). As a practical matter, the transition to intermittent reinforcement can be made easier by mixing in social reinforcement ("Good dog!") with more tangible rewards (food, for example).

A big advantage of intermittent reinforcement comes from its resistance to *extinction*. The operant version of **extinction** occurs when reinforcement is withheld, as when a gambler stops playing a slot machine that never pays off. So, why do responses strengthened by partial reinforcement resist extinction more strongly than do responses that have been rewarded continuously? Imagine two gamblers and two slot machines. One machine inexplicably pays off on every trial, and another, a more typical machine, pays on an unpredictable, intermittent schedule. Now, suppose that both devices suddenly stop paying. Which gambler will catch on first? The one who has been rewarded for each pull of the lever (continuous reinforcement) will quickly notice the change, while the gambler who has won only occasionally (on partial reinforcement) may continue playing unrewarded for a long while.

Continuous reinforcement is useful for training animals, but intermittent reinforcement is better for maintaining their learned behaviors.

Schedules of Reinforcement   Now that we have convinced you that intermittent reinforcement has considerable power, you should know that it occurs in two main forms or **schedules of reinforcement**. One, the **ratio schedule**, rewards a subject after a certain *number of responses*. The other, known as an **interval schedule**, provides a reward after a certain *time interval*. Let's look at the advantages and disadvantages of each.

Ratio Schedules   Suppose that you own a business and pay your employees based on the amount of work they perform: You are maintaining them on a *ratio schedule* of reinforcement. That is, ratio schedules occur when rewards depend on the *number of correct responses*. (See Figure 3.4.) Psychologists make a further distinction between two subtypes of ratio schedules, *fixed ratio* and *variable ratio* schedules.

Fixed ratio (FR) schedules commonly occur in industry, when workers are paid on a piecework basis—a certain amount of pay for a certain amount of production. So, if you own a tire factory and pay each worker a dollar for every ten tires produced, you are using a fixed ratio schedule. Under this scheme the amount of work (the number of responses) needed for a reward remains constant, but the faster people work, the more money they get. Not surprisingly, management likes FR schedules because the rate of responding is usually high (Terry, 2000; Whyte, 1972).

Variable ratio (VR) schedules are less predictable. Telemarketers work on a VR schedule, because they never know how many phone calls they must make before they get the next sale. Slot machine players also respond on a variable ratio schedule. In both cases continually changing the requirements for reinforcement keeps responses coming at a high rate—so high, in fact, that the VR schedule usually produces more responding than any other reinforcement schedule. In a demonstration of just how powerful a VR schedule could be, Skinner showed that a hungry pigeon would peck a disk 12,000 times an hour for rewards given, on the average, for every 110 pecks!

Extinction   (in operant conditioning) A process by which a response that has been learned is weakened by the absence or removal of reinforcement. (Compare with *extinction in classical conditioning*.)

Schedule of reinforcement   A program specifying the frequency and timing of reinforcements.

Ratio schedule   A program by which reinforcement depends on the number of correct responses.

Interval schedule   A program by which reinforcement depends on the time interval elapsed since the last reinforcement.

Fixed ratio (FR) schedule   A program by which reinforcement is contingent on a certain, unvarying number of responses.

Variable ratio (VR) schedule   A reinforcement program by which the number of responses required for a reinforcement varies from trial to trial.

What schedule of reinforcement encourages this man to buy lottery tickets?

Interval Schedules   Time is of the essence on an interval schedule. That is, with an interval schedule, reinforcement depends on responses made within a certain *time period* (rather than on the total number of responses given). (See Figure 3.4.) Psychologists distinguish two kinds of interval schedules: *fixed interval* and *variable interval* schedules.

Fixed interval (FI) schedules commonly occur in the work world, where they may appear as a periodic paycheck or praise from the boss at a monthly staff meeting. A student who studies for a weekly quiz is also on a fixed interval schedule. In all such cases, the interval does not vary, so the time period between rewards remains constant. You may have already guessed that fixed interval reinforcement usually results in a comparatively low response rate. Ironically, this is the schedule most widely adopted by business. Even a rat in a Skinner box programmed for a fixed interval schedule soon learns that it must produce only a limited amount of work during the interval to get its reward. Pressing the lever more often than required to get the food reward is just wasted energy. Thus, both rats and humans on fixed interval schedules may display only modest productivity until near the end of the interval, when the response rate increases rapidly. (Think of college students facing a term paper deadline.) Graphically, in Figure 3.4 you can see the "scalloped" pattern of behavior that results from this flurry of activity near the end of each interval.

Variable interval (VI) schedules are, perhaps, the most unpredictable of all. On a VI schedule, the time interval between rewards (or punishments) varies. The resulting rate of responding can be high, although not usually as high as for the VR schedule. For a pigeon or a rat in a Skinner box, the variable interval schedule may be a 30-second interval now, 3 minutes next, and a 1-minute wait later. In the classroom, pop quizzes exemplify a VI schedule, as do random visits by the boss on the job. Fishing represents still another example: The angler never knows how long it will take before the fish start biting again, but the occasional, unpredictable fish delivers reward enough to encourage fishing behavior over long intervals. And watch for responses typical of a VI schedule while waiting for an elevator: Because the delay between pressing the call button and the arrival of the elevator varies each time, some of your companions will press the button multiple times, as if more responses within an unpredictable time interval could control the elevator's arrival.

Primary and Secondary Reinforcers   You can easily see why stimuli that fulfill basic biological needs or desires will provide reinforcement: Food reinforces a hungry animal, and water reinforces a thirsty one. Similarly, the opportunity for sex becomes a reinforcer for a sexually aroused organism. Psychologists call such stimuli **primary reinforcers**.

But money or grades present a different problem: You can't eat them or drink them. Nor do they directly satisfy any physical need. So why do such things reinforce behavior so powerfully? Neutral stimuli, such as money or grades, acquire a reinforcing effect by association with primary reinforcers and so become **conditioned reinforcers or secondary reinforcers** for operant responses. The same thing happens with praise, smiles of approval, gold stars, "reward cards" used by merchants, and various kinds of status symbols. In fact, virtually any stimulus can become a secondary or conditioned reinforcer by being associated with a primary reinforcer. With strong conditioning, secondary reinforcers such as money, status, or awards can even come to be ends in themselves.

Piggy Banks and Token Economies   The distinction between primary and secondary reinforcers brings up a more subtle point: Just as we saw in classical conditioning, operant conditioning is not pure learning, but it is built on a biological

Fixed interval (FI) schedule   A program by which reinforcement is contingent upon a certain, fixed time period.

Variable interval (VI) schedule   A program by which the time period between reinforcements varies from trial to trial.

Primary reinforcer   A reinforcer, such as food or sex, that has an innate basis because of its biological value to an organism.

Conditioned reinforcer or **secondary reinforcer**   A stimulus, such as money or tokens, that acquires its reinforcing power by a learned association with primary reinforcers.

base; hence our "wired-in" preferences for certain reinforcers—to which "junk" food manufacturers pander with their sweet and fatty treats.

Biology is also seen on the behavioral side of operant conditioning. And that's why Keller and Marian Breland, two psychologists who went into the animal training business, had so much trouble with their trained pigs. As you probably know, pigs are very smart animals. Thus, the Brelands had no difficulty teaching them to pick up round wooden tokens and deposit them in a "piggy bank." The problem was that, over a period of weeks, these porcine subjects reverted to piggish behavior: They would slow down, repeatedly dropping the token, root at it, pick it up and toss it in the air, and root it some more. And this happened in pig after trained pig. What was happening? The Brelands (1961) called this **instinctive drift**, which they defined as the tendency for innate response tendencies to interfere with learned behavior. The Brelands found similar patterns of instinctive drift in critters as diverse as raccoons and chickens. No wonder, then, that people can't make their cats refrain for long from scratching the furniture.

Happily, psychologists have had better luck in using tokens with people than with pigs. Mental institutions, for example, have tapped the power of conditioned reinforcers by setting up so-called *token economies* to encourage desirable and healthy patient behaviors. Under a **token economy**, the staff may reinforce grooming or taking medication with plastic tokens. Patients soon learn that they can exchange the tokens for highly desired rewards and privileges (Ayllon & Azrin, 1965; Holden, 1978). As an adjunct to other forms of therapy, token economies can help mental patients learn useful strategies for acting effectively in the world (Kazdin, 1994).

Preferred Activities as Reinforcers: The Premack Principle

The opportunity to perform desirable activities can reinforce behavior just as effectively as food or drink or other primary reinforcers. For example, people who exercise regularly might use a daily run or fitness class as a reward for getting other tasks done. Likewise, teachers have found that young children will learn to sit still if such behavior is reinforced later with the opportunity to run around and make noise (Homme et al., 1963).

The principle at work here says that the opportunity to engage in a preferred activity (active, noisy play) can be used to reinforce a less preferred one (sitting still and listing to the teacher). Psychologists call this the **Premack principle**, after its discoverer. David Premack (1965) first demonstrated this concept in thirsty rats, which would spend more time running in an exercise wheel if the running were followed by an opportunity to drink. Conversely, another group of rats that were exercise deprived, but not thirsty, would increase the amount they drank, if drinking were followed by a chance to run in the wheel. In exactly the same way, then, parents can use the Premack principle to get children to engage in otherwise unlikely behavior. For example, the opportunity to play with friends (a preferred activity) could be used to reinforce the less-preferred activity of making the bed or doing the dishes.

Reinforcement across Cultures

The laws of operant learning apply to all animals with a brain. The biological mechanism underlying reinforcement is, apparently, much the same across species. On the other hand, exactly what serves as a reinforcer varies wildly. Experience suggests that food for a hungry organism and water for a thirsty one will act as reinforcers because they satisfy basic needs related to survival. But what any particular individual will choose to satisfy those needs may depend as much on learning as on survival instincts—especially in humans, where secondary reinforcement is so important. For us, culture plays an especially powerful role in determining what will act as reinforcers. So, while people in some cul-

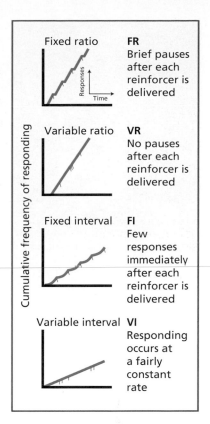

FIGURE 3.4
Reinforcement Schedules

The graphs show typical patterns of responding produced by four different schedules of reinforcement. (The hash marks indicate when reinforcement is delivered.) Notice that the steeper angle of the top two graphs shows how the ratio schedules usually produce more responses over a given period of time than do the interval schedules.

Instinctive drift The tendency of an organism's innate (instinctive) responses to interfere with learned behavior.

Token economy A therapeutic method, based on operant conditioning, by which individuals are rewarded with tokens, which act as secondary reinforcers. The tokens can be redeemed for a variety of rewards and privileges.

Premack principle The concept, developed by David Premack, that a more-preferred activity can be used to reinforce a less-preferred activity.

Foods that many people around the world enjoy may not be a source of reinforcement for the typical North American.

tures would find eating a cricket reinforcing, most people of Euro-American ancestry would not. Similarly, disposing of a noisy cricket might seem both sensible and rewarding to a Baptist, yet aversive to a Buddhist. And, just to underscore our point, we note that watching a game of cricket would most likely be rewarding to a British cricket fan—although punishingly dull to most Americans.

So, culture shapes preferences in reinforcement, but reinforcement also shapes culture. When you first walk down a street in a foreign city, all the differences that catch your eye are merely different ways that people have found to seek reinforcement or avoid punishment. A temple houses cultural attempts to seek rewards from the deity. Clothing may reflect attempts to seek a reinforcing mate or to feel comfortable in the climate. And a culture's cuisine evolves from learning to survive on the native plants and animals. It is in this sense, then, that we can see culture broadly as a set of behaviors originally learned by operant conditioning and shared by a group of people.

The Problem of Punishment

Punishment as a means of influencing behavior poses several difficulties, as schoolteachers and prison wardens will attest. In some respects, punishment acts as the opposite of reinforcement. Thus, **punishment** is an *aversive* consequence used to *weaken* the behavior it follows. But, like reinforcement, punishment comes in two main forms. One, called **positive punishment**, requires the *application of an aversive stimulus*—as, when you touch a hot plate, the painful consequence reduces the likelihood of your repeating that behavior. The other main form of punishment, known as **negative punishment**, results from the *removal of a reinforcer*—as when parents take away a misbehaving teen's car keys. Technically—in the strictest meaning of the term—an aversive stimulus is punishing only if it actually weakens the behavior it follows. In this sense, then, spankings or speeding tickets may or may not be punishment, depending on the results.

Unlike reinforcement, however, punishment must be administered consistently. Intermittent punishment is far less effective than punishment delivered after every undesired response. In fact, *not punishing* an occurrence of unwanted behavior can have the effect of rewarding it—as when a supervisor overlooks the late arrival of an employee.

Punishment versus Negative Reinforcement   You have probably noted that punishment and negative reinforcement both involve unpleasant stimuli. So, to avoid confusion, let's see how punishment and negative reinforcement differ, using the following examples (Figure 3.5). Suppose that an animal in a Skinner box can turn off a loud, unpleasant noise by pressing a lever. This response produces negative reinforcement. Now compare that with the other animal in Figure 3.5 for which the loud noise serves as a punishment for pressing the lever.

Please note that punishment and negative reinforcement lead to opposite effects on behavior (Baum, 1994). Punishment *decreases* a behavior or reduces its probability of recurring. In contrast, negative reinforcement—like positive reinforcement—always *increases* a response's probability of occurring again.

Don't forget that the descriptors "positive" and "negative" mean "add" and "remove." Thus, both positive reinforcement and positive punishment involve administering or "adding" a stimulus. On the other hand, negative reinforcement and negative punishment always involve withholding or removing a stimulus. For a concise summary of the distinctions between positive and negative reinforcement and punishment, please see Table 3.1.

The Uses and Abuses of Punishment   Our society relies heavily on punishment and the threat of punishment to keep people "in line." We fine people, spank them, and give them bad grades, parking tickets, and disapproving looks. Currently, American jails and prisons contain more than 2 million people (Benson, 2003),

Punishment   An aversive consquence which, occurring after a response, diminishes the strength of that response. (Compare with *negative reinforcement*.)

Positive punishment   The application of an aversive stimulus after a response.

Negative punishment   The removal of an attractive stimulus after a response.

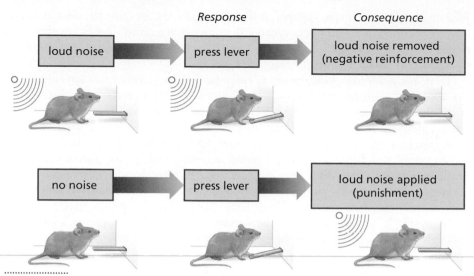

Response   Consequence

FIGURE 3.5
Negative Reinforcement and Punishment Compared

while the United States currently maintains one in every 32 of its citizens in jail or prison or on probation or parole (Bureau of Justice Statistics, 2007).

One reason we use punishment so often is that it can produce an immediate change in behavior—which, incidentally, reinforces the punisher. Several other factors also encourage a punishment habit. For one, punishers may feel good while delivering the punishment, sensing that they are "settling a score" or "getting even" or making the other person "pay." This is why we speak of revenge as being "sweet," a sentiment that seems to underlie public attitudes toward the punishment of lawbreakers (Carlsmith, 2006).

But, punishment—especially the sort of punishment involving pain, humiliation, or imprisonment—usually doesn't work as well in the long run (American Psychological Association, 2002b). Punished children may continue to misbehave; reprimanded employees may sabotage efforts to meet production goals.

TABLE 3.1   **Four Kinds of Consequences**

		Apply (add) Stimulus (positive)	Remove (subtract) Stimulus (negative)
What is the effect of the stimulus (consequence) on behavior?	The probability of the behavior increases.	**Positive reinforcement** Example: An employee gets a bonus for good work (and continues to work hard).	**Negative reinforcement** Example: You take aspirin for your headache, and the headache vanishes (so you take aspirin the next time you have a headache).
	The probability of the behavior decreases.	**Positive punishment** Example: A speeder gets a traffic ticket (and drives away more slowly).	**Negative punishment** Example: A child who has stayed out late misses dinner (and comes home early next time).

Three important points to keep in mind as you study this table:

1. "Positive" and "negative" mean that a stimulus (consequence) has been added (presented) or subtracted (removed). These terms have nothing to do with "good" or "bad."

2. We can often predict what effect a particular consequence will have, but the only way to know for sure whether it will be a reinforcer or a punisher is to observe its effect on behavior. For example, although we might guess that a spanking would punish a child, it might actually serve as a reinforcer to strengthen the unwanted behavior.

3. From a cognitive viewpoint, we can see that reinforcement consists of the presentation of a pleasant stimulus or the removal of an unpleasant one. Similarly, punishment entails the presentation of an unpleasant stimulus or the removal of a pleasant one.

And in the United States, people still commit crimes, despite the fact that we imprison criminals in numbers greater than any other nation on Earth (International Centre for Prison Studies, 2007). So, why is punishment so difficult to use effectively? There are several reasons.

First, *the power of punishment to suppress behavior usually disappears when the threat of punishment is removed* (Skinner, 1953). Drivers will observe the speed limit when they know the highway patrol is watching. Johnny will refrain from hitting his little brother when his parents are within earshot. And you will probably give up your wallet to a mugger who points a gun at you. That is, most people will comply with a demand accompanied by the threat of strong and certain punishment. But they may act quite differently when they know punishment is unlikely. This explains why motorists rarely slow down for "construction speed" signs on the highways: They know that the police rarely enforce these zones. In general, you can be certain of controlling someone's behavior through punishment or threat of punishment only if you can control the environment all of the time. Such total control is usually not possible, even in a prison.

Second, *the lure of rewards may make the possibility of punishment seem worth the price.* This seems to be a factor that encourages drug dealing—when the possibility of making a large amount of money outweighs the possibility of prison time (Levitt & Dubner, 2005). And, in a different way, the push-pull of punishment and rewards also affects dieters, when the short-term attraction of food may overpower the unwanted long-term consequences of weight gain. Again, if you attempt to control someone's behavior through punishment, you may fail if you do not control the rewards, as well.

Third, *punishment triggers escape or aggression.* When punished, organisms usually try to flee from or otherwise avoid further punishment. But if escape is blocked, they are likely to turn aggressive. Corner a wounded animal, and it may savagely attack you. Put two rats in a Skinner box with an electrified floor grid, and the rats will attack each other (Ulrich & Azrin, 1962). Put humans in a harsh prison environment, and they may riot—or, if they are prison guards, they may abuse the prisoners (Zimbardo, 2004b, 2007).

Further, in a punitive environment, whether it be a prison, a school, or a home, people learn that punishment and aggression are legitimate means of influencing other. The punishment–aggression link also explains why abusing parents so often come from abusive families and why aggressive delinquents so often come from homes where aggressive behavior toward the children is commonplace (Golden, 2000). Unfortunately, the well-documented fact that punishment so often leads to aggression remains widely unknown to the general public.

Here's a fourth reason why punishment is so often ineffective: *Punishment makes the learner apprehensive, which inhibits learning new and more desirable responses.* Unable to escape punishment, an organism may give up its attempts at flight or fight and surrender to an overwhelming feeling of hopelessness. This passive acceptance of a punitive fate produces a behavior pattern called *learned helplessness* (Overmier & Seligman, 1967). In people, this reaction can produce the mental disorder known as depression (Terry, 2000).

CONNECTION • CHAPTER 12

Depression is one of the most common mental disorders.

If you want to produce a constructive change in attitudes and behavior, then learned helplessness and depression are undesirable outcomes. The same goes for aggression and escape. Moreover, punishment fails to help learners see what to do because it focuses attention on what *not* to do. All of these outcomes interfere with new learning. By contrast, individuals who have not been punished feel much freer to experiment with new behaviors.

And a fifth reason why punitive measures may fail: *Punishment is often applied unequally,* even though that violates our standards of fair and equal treatment. For example, parents and teachers punish boys more often than girls.

Then, too, children (especially grade school children) receive more physical punishment than do adults. And, to give one more example, our schools—and probably our society at large—more often punish members of minority groups than members of the majority (Hyman, 1996).

Does Punishment Ever Work?   In limited circumstances, punishment can work remarkably well. For example, punishment can halt the self-destructive behavior of children with autism, who may injure themselves severely, in some cases, by banging their heads or chewing the flesh off their fingers. A mild electric shock or a splash of cold water in the face can quickly put a stop to such unwanted behavior, although the effects may be temporary (Holmes, 2001). It can also be combined effectively with reinforcement—as when students receive good grades for studying and failing grades for neglecting their work.

Prison riots and other aggressive behavior may result from highly punitive conditions.

Punishment is also more likely to be successful if it involves a *logical consequence:* a consequence that is closely related to the undesirable behavior—as contrasted with an *un*related punishment, such as spanking or grounding. So, if a child leaves a toy truck on the stairs, a logical consequence might be that the toy "disappears" for a week. To give another example, a logical consequence of coming home late for dinner is getting a cold dinner.

Rather than a purely punitive approach to misbehavior, we suggest you consider some combination of logical consequences, extinction, and the rewarding of desirable alternative responses. And when you do decide to use punishment, it should meet the following conditions:

● *Punishment should be swift*—that is, immediate. Any delay will impair its effectiveness, so "You'll get spanked when your father gets home" is a poor punishment strategy.

● *Punishment should be certain*—consistently administered every time the unwanted response occurs. When "bad" behavior goes unpunished, the effect can actually be rewarding.

● *Punishment should be limited in duration and intensity*—just enough to stop the behavior but appropriate enough to "make the punishment fit the crime."

● *Punishment should clearly target the behavior* and be a *logical consequence of the behavior,* rather than an attack on character of the person (humiliation, sarcasm, or verbal abuse) or physical pain.

● *Punishment should be limited to the situation in which the response occurred.*

● *Punishment should not give mixed messages* to the punished person (such as, "You are not permitted to hit others, but I am allowed to hit you").

● *The most effective punishment is usually negative punishment,* such as loss of privileges, rather than the application of unpleasant stimuli, such as a spanking.

A Checklist for Modifying Operant Behavior

Think of someone whose behavior you would like to change. For the sake of illustration, let's consider your nephew Johnny's temper tantrums, which always seem to occur when you take him out in public. Operant conditioning offers a selection of tools that can help: positive reinforcement, punishment, negative reinforcement, and extinction.

- *Positive reinforcement* is a good bet, if you can identify and encourage some desirable behavior in place of the unwanted behavior. The most effective parents and teachers often do this by distraction—by shifting the child's attention to some other reinforcing activity. And don't overlook the Premack principle, by which Johnny gets to do something he likes if he refrains from temper outbursts.

- *Punishment* may be tempting, but we have seen that it usually produces unwanted effects, such as aggression or escape. In addition, punishment usually has a bad effect on the relationship between punisher and the person being punished. Moreover, punishment is difficult to employ with unfailing consistency. If you do decide to punish Johnny for his tantrums, consider making it a logical consequence, such as "time out" in his room while he is making his scene—doing so swiftly, certainly, but without undue harshness.

- *Negative reinforcement* carries many of the same drawbacks as punishment, because it involves unpleasant stimulation. In its most common form, the parents attempt to use nagging (an aversive stimulus) until the desired behavior occurs, whereupon the nagging presumably stops (negative reinforcement). Such tactics rarely work to anyone's satisfaction. The only time negative reinforcement really works well is when the aversive conditions were imposed naturally and impersonally—as when you have headache and take aspirin, which produces negative reinforcement when your headache goes away. In Johnny's case, if he were required to take his temper tantrum to his room (a punishment), then being allowed to come out of his room when his misbehavior stops could be an effective negative reinforcement.

- *Extinction* guarantees solution, but only if you control all the reinforcers. In Johnny's case, extinction simply means not giving in to the temper tantrum and not letting him have what he wants (attention or candy, for example). Instead, you simply allow the tantrum to burn itself out. This can be embarrassing, because children intuitively pick the most public places for such displays—a good sign that they are doing so for attention. Another problem with extinction, however, is that it may take a while, so extinction is not a good option if the subject is engaging in dangerous behavior, such as playing in a busy street.

The best approach—often recommended by child psychologists—combines several tactics. In Johnny's case, this might involve both reinforcing his desirable behaviors and using extinction or logical consequences on his undesirable ones.

We recommend memorizing the four items on this checklist: *positive reinforcement, punishment, negative reinforcement,* and *extinction.* Then, whenever you are dealing with someone whose behavior is undesirable, go through the list and see whether one or more of these operant tactics might do the trick. And remember: The behavior you may want to change could be your own!

Operant and Classical Conditioning Compared

Now that we have looked at the main features of operant and classical conditioning, let's compare them side by side. As you can see in Table 3.2, the *consequences* of behavior—especially, rewards and punishments—distinguish operant conditioning different from classical conditioning. But note this point of potential confusion: As the example in Figure 3.6 shows, food acts as a reward in operant conditioning, but in classical conditioning, food acts as an unconditioned stimulus. The important thing to note is that in classical conditioning the food comes *before* the response—and therefore it cannot serve as a reward.

Because classical conditioning and operant conditioning differ in the order in which the stimulus and response occur, classically conditioned behavior is largely a response to *past stimulation.* (Think of Pavlov's dogs salivating after hearing a bell.) Operant behavior is directed at attaining some *future* reinforcement or

TABLE 3.2   Classical and Operant Conditioning Compared

Classical Conditioning	Operant Conditioning
Behavior is controlled by stimuli that precede the response (by the CS and UCS).	Behavior is controlled by consequences (rewards, punishments, and the like) that *follow* the response.
No reward or punishment is involved (although pleasant and aversive stimuli may be used).	Often involves reward (reinforcement) or punishment.
Through conditioning, a new stimulus (the CS) comes to produce "old" (reflexive) behavior.	Through conditioning, a new stimulus (a reinforcer) produces new behavior.
Extinction is produced by withholding the UCS.	Extinction is produced by withholding reinforcement.
Learner is passive (responds reflexively): Responses are involuntary. That is, behavior is *elicited* by stimulation.	Learner is active (operant behavior): Responses are voluntary. That is, behavior is *emitted* by the organism.

avoiding a punishment. (Think of a dog sitting up to get a food reward.) To say it another way, operant conditioning requires a stimulus that follows the response, whereas classical conditioning ends with the response. (See Figure 3.7.)

Another difference between the two types of conditioning lies in the kinds of behaviors they target. Operant conditioning encourages *new behaviors*—whether they be pulling slot machine levers, making beds, brushing teeth, going to work, or studying for an exam. Classical conditioning, on the other hand, emphasizes eliciting *old responses to new stimuli*—such as salivating at the sound of a bell or flinching at the sound of a dentist's drill.

You may have also noticed that extinction works in slightly different ways in the two forms of learning. In classical conditioning, extinction requires with-

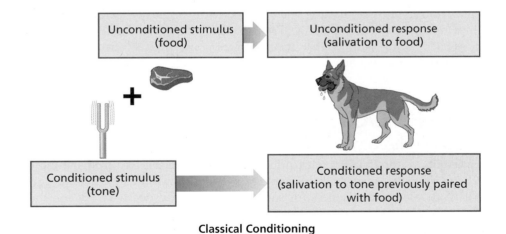

Classical Conditioning

Operant Conditioning

FIGURE 3.6

The Same Stimulus Plays Different Roles in Classical Conditioning and Operant Conditioning

The same stimulus (food) can play vastly different roles, depending on which type of conditioning is involved. In classical conditioning, it can be the UCS, while in operant conditioning it can serve as a reinforcer for operant behavior. Note also that classical conditioning involves the association of two stimuli that occur *before* the response. Operant conditioning involves a reinforcing (rewarding) or punishing stimulus that occurs *after* the response.

FIGURE 3.7
Classical and Operant Conditioning
Can Work Together

A response originally learned through
classical conditioning can be maintained and strengthened by operant
reinforcement.

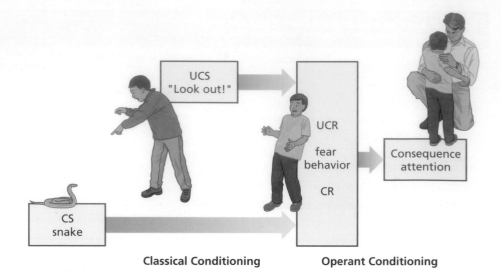

Classical Conditioning   **Operant Conditioning**

holding the unconditioned stimulus. In operant conditioning, extinction results
from withholding the reinforcer.

Operant conditioning and classical conditioning differ in several other important ways that you see in Table 3.2. For one, operant behavior is not based on
an automatic reflex action, as was the dog's salivation or Little Albert's crying.
Accordingly, operant behavior seems more "voluntary"—more under the control
of the responder. To paraphrase a proverb: You can stimulate a dog to salivation (a reflex), but you can't make it eat (an operant behavior).

But don't make the mistake of thinking that classical and operant conditioning are competing explanations for learning. They can be complementary. In fact,
responses that were originally learned by classical conditioning will often be
maintained later by operant conditioning. How might this happen? Consider a
snake phobia. Suppose that the fear of snakes was originally learned by classical conditioning when a snake (CS) was paired with a frightening UCS (someone yelling, "Look out!"). Once the phobic response is established, it could be
maintained and strengthened by operant conditioning, as when bystanders give
attention to the fearful person (Figure 3.7).

PSYCHOLOGYMATTERS
Using Psychology to Learn Psychology

You may have tried the Premack principle to trick yourself into studying more,
perhaps by denying yourself TV time or a trip to the refrigerator until your
homework was done. It works for some people, but if it doesn't work for you,
try making the studying itself more enjoyable and more reinforcing.

For most of us, getting together with people we like is reinforcing, regardless
of the activity. So, you can make some (not all) of your studying a social activity. That is, schedule a time when you and another classmate or two can get
together to identify and clarify important concepts and to try to predict what
will be on the next test.

Don't focus just on vocabulary. Rather, try to discover the big picture—the overall meaning of each section of the chapter. The Core Concepts are a good place
to start. Then you can discuss with your friends how the details fit in with the
Core Concepts. You will most likely find that the social pressure of an upcoming
study group will help motivate you to get your reading done and identify murky
points. When you get together for your group study session, you will find that
explaining what you have learned reinforces your own learning. The real reinforcement comes, however, from spending some time—studying—with your friends!

CheckYourUnderstanding

1. **APPLICATION:** Give an example of a response that a pet dog or cat might learn that could be explained by Thorndike's *law of effect*.

2. **APPLICATION:** Give an example of *negative reinforcement* from your own life.

3. **APPLICATION:** Suppose that you have taught your dog to roll over for the reward of a dog biscuit. Then, one day you run out of dog biscuits. Which schedule of reinforcement would keep your dog responding the longest time?
   a. continuous reinforcement
   b. intermittent reinforcement
   c. negative reinforcement
   d. noncontingent reinforcement

4. **RECALL:** Give an example of something that serves as a conditioned reinforcer for most people.

5. **APPLICATION & ANALYSIS:** Suppose that you are trying to teach Stevie not to hit his sister. What operant techniques would you use? Also, explain why neither extinction nor negative reinforcement would be wise in this case.

6. **UNDERSTANDING THE CORE CONCEPT:** What is a feature of operant conditioning that distinguishes it from classical conditioning?

Answers 1. Any response that was learned by being rewarded—such as sitting up for a food reward or scratching at the door to be let in the house—involves Thorndike's law of effect. **2.** Negative reinforcement occurs any time that your behavior causes an unpleasant stimulus to stop bothering you. Examples include taking aspirin to stop a pain, going to the dentist for a toothache, or opening an umbrella in the rain. **3.** b **4.** Money is probably the most common example. **5.** The best approach is probably some combination of reinforcing alternative responses and "time out" for hitting behavior. Under extinction alone, Stevie would still continue to hit his sister for a period of time, until the behavior is extinguished, which might inflict an undue hardship on the sister. Negative reinforcement would also be undesirable, because it would require contriving for Stevie an unpleasant or painful stimulus that you would remove when his behavior improved. This would have all the disadvantages of punishment. **6.** In operant conditioning, learning depends on stimuli that occur after the response. These stimuli include rewards and punishments. By contrast, classical conditioning focuses on stimuli that occur before the response.

3.3 KEY QUESTION
HOW DOES COGNITIVE PSYCHOLOGY EXPLAIN LEARNING?

According to biologist J. D. Watson's (1968) account in *The Double Helix*, he and Francis Crick cracked the genetic code one day in a flash of insight following months of trial and error. You may have had a similarly sudden, if less famous, insight when solving a problem of your own. Such events present difficulties for strict behaviorists because they obviously involve learning, but they are hard to explain in terms of Pavlovian or Skinnerian conditioning.

Many psychologists believe that an entirely different process, called *cognitive learning*, is responsible for such flashes of insight. From a cognitive perspective, learning does not always show itself immediately in behavior. Instead, learning can be reflected in mental activity alone—as the Core Concept for this section says:

> **According to cognitive psychology, some forms of learning must be explained as changes in mental processes, rather than as changes in behavior alone.**

core concept

Let's see how cognitive psychologists have approached this task of examining the covert mental processes behind learning. To do so, we first take you on a trip to the Canary Islands, off the coast of northern Africa.

Insight Learning: Köhler in the Canaries with the Chimps

Isolated on the island of Tenerife during World War I, Gestalt psychologist Wolfgang Köhler *(KER-ler)* had time to think long and hard about learning. Disenchanted with the behaviorists' explanation for learning, Köhler sought to develop his own theories. To his way of thinking, psychology had to recognize mental processes as an essential component of learning, even though mental events had

CONNECTION • CHAPTER 7

Gestalt psychology is best known for its work on perception.

The ruins of Köhler's old laboratory, known as La Casa Amarilla (the Yellow House), can still be seen near the town of Puerto de La Cruz (Johnson, 2007). You can see a satellite view of it, using the following coordinates in Google Earth: latitude 28° 24′ 52.23″ N and longitude 16° 31′ 47.93″ W. If you enjoy historical mysteries, you might read A Whisper of Espionage, *a book exploring the possibility that Köhler was not only studying chimpanzee behavior but also spying on allied shipping from his laboratory's vantage point on the coast of Tenerife during World War I (Ley, 1990).*

Insight learning A form of cognitive learning, originally described by the Gestalt psychologists, in which problem solving occurs by means of a sudden reorganization of perceptions.

been spurned as subjective speculation by the behaviorists. To press his point, Köhler took advantage of a primate research facility, constructed by the German government on Tenerife. There he contrived experiments designed to reveal cognitive learning in observable behavior (Sharps & Wertheimer, 2000; Sherrill, 1991).

In a series of famous studies, Köhler showed that his chimps could learn to solve complex problems, not just by trial-and-error (an explanation favored by behaviorists), but by "flashes of insight" that combined simpler responses learned previously. One such experiment involved Sultan, a chimp that had learned to pile up boxes and scramble on top of them to reach fruit suspended high in his cage and to use sticks to obtain fruit that was just out of reach. When Köhler presented Sultan with a novel situation that combined the two problems—with fruit suspended even higher in the air—the chimp first attacked it unsuccessfully with sticks, in trial-and-error fashion. Then, in apparent frustration, Sultan threw the sticks away, kicked the wall, and sat down. According to Köhler's report, the animal then scratched his head and began to stare at some boxes nearby. After a time of apparent "thinking," he suddenly jumped up and dragged a box and a stick underneath the fruit, climbed on the box, and knocked down his prize with the stick.

Remarkably, Sultan had never before seen or used such a combination of responses. This behavior, Köhler argued, was evidence that the animals were not mindlessly using conditioned responses but were learning by *insight*: by reorganizing their *perceptions* of problems. He ventured that such behavior shows how apes, like humans, learn to solve problems by suddenly perceiving familiar objects in new forms or relationships—a decidedly mental process, rather than a merely behavioral one. He called this **insight learning** (Köhler, 1925). Insight learning, said Köhler, results from an abrupt reorganization of the way a situation is perceived.

Behaviorism had no convincing explanation for Köhler's demonstration. Neither classical nor operant conditioning could account for Sultan's behavior in stimulus–response terms. Thus, the feats of Köhler's chimps demanded the cognitive explanation of perceptual reorganization.

The sort of learning displayed by Köhler's chimps defied explanation by the behaviorists—in terms of classical conditioning and operant conditioning. Here you see Sultan, Köhler's smart animal, solving the problem of getting the bananas suspended out of reach by stacking the boxes and climbing on top of them. Köhler claimed that Sultan's behavior demonstrated insight learning.

Cognitive Maps: Tolman Finds Out What's on a Rat's Mind

Not long after Köhler's experiments with chimpanzees, the rats in Edward Tolman's lab at Berkeley also began behaving in ways that flew in the face of accepted behavioral doctrine. They would run through laboratory mazes as if following a mental "map" of the maze, rather than mindlessly executing a series of learned behaviors. Let's see how Tolman managed to demonstrate these "mindful" responses.

Mental Images—Not Behaviors   If you have ever walked through your house in the dark, you have some idea what Tolman meant by "cognitive map." Technically, a **cognitive map** is a mental image that an organism uses to navigate through a familiar environment. But could such a simple-minded creature as a rat have such complex mental imagery? And, if so, how could the existence of these cognitive maps be demonstrated? A cognitive map, Tolman argued, was the only way to account for a rat quickly selecting an alternative route in a maze when the preferred path to the goal is blocked. In fact, rats will often select the shortest detour around a barrier, even though taking that particular route was never previously reinforced. Rather than blindly exploring different parts of the maze through trial and error (as behavioral theory would predict), Tolman's rats behaved as if they had a mental representation of the maze. (Figure 3.8 shows the arrangement of such a maze.)

In further support of his claim that learning was *mental*, not purely behavioral, Tolman offered another experiment: After his rats had learned to run a maze, he flooded it with water and showed that the rats were quite capable of swimming though the maze. Again, this demonstrated that what the animals had learned was a *concept*, not just behaviors. Instead of learning merely a sequence of right and left turns, Tolman argued, they had acquired a more abstract mental representation of the maze's spatial layout (Tolman & Honzik, 1930; Tolman et al., 1946).

Learning without Reinforcement   In yet another study that attacked the very foundations of behaviorism, Tolman (1948) allowed his rats to wander freely about a maze for several hours. During this time, the rats received no rewards at all—they simply explored the maze. Yet, despite the lack of reinforcement, which behaviorists supposed to be essential for maze learning, the rats later learned to run the

Cognitive map   In Tolman's work a cognitive map was a mental representation of a maze or other physical space. Psychologists often used the term *cognitive map* more broadly to include an understanding of connections among concepts. (Note that your *Grade Aid* study guide uses the related term *concept map* for the diagrams showing the relationships among concepts in every chapter.) Thus, a cognitive map can represent either a physical or a mental "space."

....

FIGURE 3.8
Using Cognitive Maps in Maze Learning

Rats used in this experiment preferred the direct path (Path 1) when it was open. When it was blocked at A, they preferred Path 2. When Path 2 was blocked at B, the rats usually chose Path 3. Their behavior indicated that they had a cognitive map of the best route to the food box.

(*Source:* From "Degrees of Hunger, Reward and Nonreward, and Maze Learning in Rats," by E. C. Tolman and C. H. Honzik, *University of California Publication of Psychology*, Vol. 4, No. 16, December 1930.)

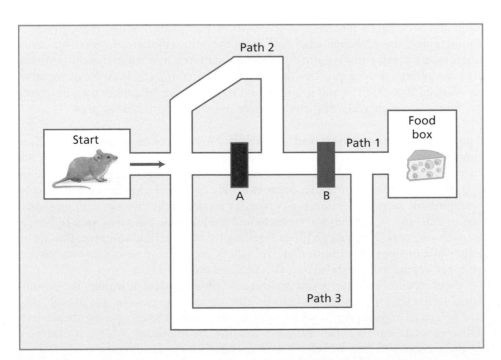

In the BoBo doll experiment, a boy and girl imitate the aggressive behavior that they have seen from an adult.

maze for a food reward more quickly than did other rats that had never seen the maze before. Obviously, they had learned the maze during the exploratory period, even though no hint of learning could be seen in their behavior at the time. Tolman called this *latent learning*.

The Significance of Tolman's Work As with Köhler's experiments, what made Tolman's work both significant and provocative was its challenge to the prevailing views of Pavlov, Watson, and the other behaviorists. While Tolman accepted the idea that psychologists must study observable behavior, he showed that simple associations between stimuli and responses could not explain the behavior observed in his experiments. Tolman's *cognitive* explanations, therefore, presented a provocative challenge to behaviorism (Gleitman, 1991).

Subsequent experiments on cognitive maps in rats, chimpanzees, and humans have broadly supported Tolman's work (Olton, 1992). More recently, brain imaging has pointed to the hippocampus as a structure involved in "drawing" the cognitive map in the brain (Jacobs & Schenk, 2003). So, it seems clear that Tolman was on target: Organisms learn the spatial layout of their environments by exploration, and they do so even if they are not reinforced for exploring. From an evolutionary perspective, the ability to make cognitive maps would be highly adaptive in animals that must forage for food (Kamil et al., 1987).

In the following section we shall see that Albert Bandura followed in Tolman's footsteps by toppling yet another pillar of behaviorism: the idea that rewards and punishments act only on the individual receiving them. Bandura proposed that rewards and punishments can be effective even if we merely see someone else get them. (This is why casinos make such a fuss over jackpot winners.) Bandura's work, then, suggests that the consequences of behavior can operate indirectly, through *observation*. Let's see how he demonstrated this idea.

Observational Learning: Bandura's Challenge to Behaviorism

Does observing violent behavior make viewers more likely to become violent? A classic study by Albert Bandura suggests that it does—at least in the children he invited to his lab for a simple experiment. All it took to bring out aggressive behavior in these children was watching adults seeming to enjoy punching, hitting, and kicking an inflated plastic clown (a BoBo doll). When later given the opportunity, the children who had seen the adult models showed far more aggressive behavior toward the doll than did children in a control condition who had not observed the aggressive models (Bandura et al., 1963). Subsequent studies showed that children will similarly imitate aggressive behaviors they have seen on film—yes, even when the models were merely cartoon characters.

Learning by Observation and Imitation An important implication of Bandura's BoBo doll study is that learning by observation and imitation can affect our behavior in situations where we have had no previous opportunity for personal experience. Thus, learning can occur not only by direct experience but also by watching the behavior of another person, or *model*. If the model's actions appear successful—that is, if the model seems to find it reinforcing—we may seek to behave in the same way. You can think of learning by observation and imitation as an extension of operant conditioning, by which we observe someone else getting rewards but act as though we had also received a reward.

Psychologists call this *social learning* or **observational learning**. It accounts for children learning aggressive behavior by imitating aggressive role models who are perceived as successful or admirable or who seem to be enjoying themselves. Observational learning also accounts for how people learn athletic skills, how to drive a car, and how to behave with friends and then shift roles in a job inter-

Observational learning A form of cognitive learning in which new responses are acquired after watching others' behavior and the consequences of their behavior.

view. And it accounts for changes in clothing fashions and the rapid spread of slang expressions.

Observational learning occurs in nonhuman species, too, as when a mother cat teaches her kittens how to hunt. One study demonstrated that even a creature as simple-brained as the octopus can learn by example from watching the behavior of other octopi (Fiorito & Scotto, 1992). And, not to be outdone, a clever bowerbird in an Australian national park has achieved some notoriety through observational learning by fooling tourists with its imitation of a cell phone ringing (Winters, 2002).

Effects of Media Violence   As you might have guessed, much of the research on observational learning has focused on the impact of violence in film and video (Huesmann et al., 2003). Predictably, the issue is a controversial one, because much of the evidence is *correlational* (Anderson & Bushman, 2002). That evidence makes a credible case, based on more than 50 studies showing that observing violence is associated with violent behavior. But does observing violence *cause* violent behavior? Or is it the other way around? Or, could it be that violent people are drawn to violent films and videos?

Thanks to more than 100 *experimental* studies, however, the experts have concluded that observing violence increases the likelihood of violent behavior (Huesmann & Moise, 1996; Primavera & Heron, 1996). And if that were not sufficient, we have experimental evidence that viewers of media violence show less emotional arousal and distress, when they subsequently observe violent acts—a habituation-like condition known as *psychic numbing* (Murray & Kippax, 1979). Finally, psychologist Elliot Aronson makes a case that extensive media violence is one important factor contributing to violent tragedies, such as the Columbine High School shootings (Aronson, 2000).

CONNECTION • CHAPTER 1
Only an *experimental* study can determine cause and effect.

Not all imitation is harmful, of course. We also learn by imitation about charitable behavior, comforting others in distress, and driving on the legal side of the road. In general, we can say that people learn much—both prosocial (helping) and antisocial (hurting) behaviors—through observation of others. This capacity to learn from watching enables us to acquire behaviors efficiently, without going through tedious trial and error. So, while observational learning seems to be a factor in violent behavior, it also enables us to learn socially useful behaviors by profiting from the mistakes and successes of others.

Observational Learning Applied to Social Problems around the Globe

Television is one of the most powerful sources of observational learning—and not necessarily of the undesirable sort that we have just noted. Here at home the long-running children's program, *Sesame Street,* uses such well-loved characters as Big Bird and the Cookie Monster to teach language, arithmetic, and courtesy through observational learning. And in Mexico, TV executive Miguel Sabido has deliberately drawn on Bandura's work in creating the popular soap opera *Ven Conmigo* (Come with Me), which focuses on a group of people who connect through a literacy class. After the initial season, enrollment in adult literacy classes in the broadcast area shot up to nine times the level in the previous year (Smith, 2002b).

The idea was taken up by a nonprofit group, Populations Communications International, which has promoted it worldwide. As a result, television dramas are now aimed not only at literacy but at promoting women's rights and safe sex and at preventing HIV and unwanted pregnancies. Such programs can be wildly popular, reaching large numbers of devoted fans in dozens of countries and regions around the world, including Latin American, Africa, South and East Asia, the Middle East, the Caribbean, and the Philippines. In China observers learn about the value of girls; in Tanzania they learn that AIDS is transmitted by people, not by mosquitoes; and in India the programs question the practice of child marriages. In the Caribbean, soap operas now promote responsible environmental practices.

Does it work? Very well, say professors Arvind Singhal and Everett Rogers (2002), who are currently gathering data on such projects. Because of a soap opera broadcast in India, a whole village signed a letter promising to stop the practice of child marriages. Similarly, Tanzanians now increasingly approve of family planning. And in rural villages in India, the enrollment of girls in school has risen between 10 and 38%. Overall, it appears that the use of television as a means of producing positive social change is a success story, showing that psychological theory and research can make a significant difference in people's lives.

Rethinking Behavioral Learning in Cognitive Terms

In the last few decades of the 20th century, a new breed of *cognitive-behavioral psychologists* ventured deep into the territory of classical and operant conditioning, giving those behavioral theories a cognitive tweak (Leslie, 2001). One of the big issues they raised focuses on the survival value of classical conditioning for an animal (Hollis, 1997). Specifically, Leon Kamin (1969) has shown that the crucial feature of the conditioned stimulus is its *informativeness*. In his landmark conditioning experiments, Kamin presented an animal with multiple stimuli, such as lights and sounds—sometimes alone and sometimes in pairs. He found that only those stimuli that reliably helped the animal predict the unconditioned stimulus would become conditioned stimuli and so produce a conditioned response—which explains why the most effective CS is one that *precedes* the UCS. We also saw another version of CS informativeness a few pages ago, when we discussed conditioned food aversions—where a *taste,* but not other stimuli present at the time, could serve as a warning of toxic food and, therefore, come to produce nausea as a conditioned response. As Robert Rescorla (1988), another leader of the cognitive-behavioral movement, has noted:

> Pavlovian conditioning is not a stupid process by which the organism willy-nilly forms associations between any two stimuli that happen to co-occur. Rather, the organism is better seen as an information seeker using logical and perceptual relations among events . . . to form a sophisticated representation of the world. (p. 154)

Cognitive-behavioral psychologists argue that operant conditioning also demands a cognitive explanation. As evidence, they point to Tolman's rats, following cognitive maps through a maze, and to the children pummeling the BoBo doll in Bandura's experiment. Reinforcement, they point out, changes not only behavior but the individual's *expectations* for future rewards or punishments in similar situations. Perhaps an example will help clarify this point: If you learn something in class that helps you get a better grade on the next exam, this affects your subsequent class attendance, because you now *expect* rewards for doing so. (See Table 3.3.)

Brain Mechanisms and Learning

What do we know about the biology behind learning? On the level of neurons, learning apparently involves physical changes that strengthen the synapses in groups of nerve cells—a process called **long-term potentiation** (Antonova et al., 2001; Kandel, 2000). Initially, the neurons in different brain areas involved in the learning task work very hard—for example, as a person learns the location of various objects, cells in the visual and parietal cortex may fire rapidly. But as learning progresses, the connections among the different cortical regions become stronger, and the firing pattern becomes less intense (Büchel et al., 1999).

In operant conditioning, the brain's reward circuitry also comes into play, especially parts of the frontal cortex and the limbic system, with its circuits rich

Long-term potentiation A biological process involving physical changes that strengthen the synapses in groups of nerve cells that is believed to be the neural basis of learning.

| TABLE 3.3 | Behavioral Learning and Cognitive Learning Compared |

Behavioral Learning	Cognitive Learning
Focus is on observable events (stimuli and responses) only.	Inferences are made about mental processes that are not directly observable.
Learning consists of associations among stimuli and responses.	Learning as information processing: The learner seeks useful information from stimuli.
Main forms of learning are habituation, classical conditioning, and operant (instrumental) conditioning.	Learning also involves insight, observational learning, cognitive maps, and other more complex forms of learning.
Developed as a rebellion against the subjective methods of structuralism and functionalism: Behaviorism became the dominant perspective for much of the 20th century.	Developed as a rebellion against the narrow perspective of behaviorism: Cognitive psychology became the dominant perspective at the end of the 20th century.
Big names include Pavlov, Thorndike, Watson, Skinner.	Big names include Köhler, Tolman, Bandura, Kamin.

in dopamine receptors (O'Doherty et al., 2004; Roesch & Olson, 2004). Many experts now believe that the brain uses this circuitry to sense the rewards that are the essence of positive reinforcement (Fiorillo et al., 2003; Shizgal & Avanitogiannis, 2003). The limbic system also helps us remember the strong emotions, such as fear, so often associated with classical conditioning (Miller, 2004). And, in the next chapter, when we talk about memory, you will learn about some other parts of the brain that get involved in learning the places of objects in space and remembering events.

The Brain on Extinction   While it can be important for our survival to remember emotion-laden events, it's also important to *forget* associations that turn out to be unimportant. So, just as wild animals need to forget about a water hole that has run dry, you must learn to deal with a change in train schedules or traffic laws. These examples, as you will remember, involve *extinction* of responses learned previously. And, recently, neuroscientists have found that extinction occurs when certain neurotransmitters, including glutamate and norepinephrine, block memories (Miller, 2004; Travis, 2004). These discoveries have stimulated the search for drugs that can block unwelcome memories of emotional experiences. One day, perhaps, such drugs can be given to people who have undergone extreme trauma in the hope of avoiding posttraumatic stress disorders—which are common among accident victims, rape survivors, and combat veterans. However, ethical questions remain about who decides which memories should be suppressed.

Linking Behavioral Learning with Cognitive Learning   Neuroscientists Eric Kandel and Robert Hawkins (1992) have made a proposal that may connect behavioral learning and cognitive learning at the level of brain pathways. Their theory rests on the discovery that animals with relatively simple nervous systems have a single type of nerve circuit that enables them to learn simple behavioral responses. In the more complex brains of mammals, however, neuroscientists have found a second type of learning circuitry that apparently facilitates higher forms of learning, such as memory for events.

What is the significance of these findings? Kandel and Hawkins speculated that the two types of learning circuits may divide the task of learning along the same line that has long separated behavioral psychologists and cognitive psychologists. Some other psychologists now tentatively agree (Clark & Squire, 1998; Jog et al., 1999). The simpler circuit seems to be responsible for the sort of "mindless" learning that occurs when a dog drools at the sound of a bell or when a person acquires a motor skill, such as riding a bike or swinging a golf club. This kind of learning occurs slowly and improves with repetition over many trials. Significantly, classical conditioning and much of operant learning fit this description. By contrast, the second type of learning circuit seems to be responsible for more complex forms of learning that require conscious processing—the sort of learning that interests cognitive psychologists: concept formation, insight learning, observational learning, and memory for specific events. If further research verifies that this division reflects a fundamental distinction in the nervous system, we will be able to say that those on the behavioral and cognitive extremes were both (partly) right. They were talking about fundamentally different forms of learning.

Observational Learning and Mirror Neurons   People obviously learn from their observations of others, as we saw in Bandura's "BoBo doll" studies. Similarly, if you see someone at the dinner table take a bite and grimace with disgust, you will be reluctant to taste the same dish—again, a form of observational learning. But the mystery has always been to understand how our brains respond to somebody else's rewards or punishments. The recent discovery of mirror neurons suggests a neurological basis for observational learning. The "mirror cells" in our brains apparently are finely tuned to help us "mirror" other people's sense of being rewarded or punished by activating the same circuits in our own brains (Jaffe, 2007).

CONNECTION • CHAPTER 2

Mirror neurons help us imitate other people's behavior.

"Higher" Cognitive Learning

It now seems clear that much of the complex and abstract learning required in college classes is fundamentally different from the learning that Pavlov, Watson, and Skinner studied. Acquiring knowledge about the field of psychology, for example, involves building mental images, assimilating concepts, and pondering ways they can be related. It's not that behavioral conditioning isn't involved in human learning—after all, students do work for grades and salivate when they see a pizza—but the principles of behavioral learning don't tell the whole story of "higher" cognitive learning.

The following chapters will take us deeper into this realm of cognitive learning, where we will discuss memory, thinking, concept formation, problem solving, and intelligence. There you will find out more about the mental structures that underlie cognition. The problem we will face is exactly the one that the behaviorists were hoping to avoid: In studying cognition, we must make inferences about processes that we cannot measure directly. We will find, however, that cognitive psychologists have developed some very clever methods for obtaining objective data on which to base their inferences. The newest of these—coming fully on line in the last decade or so—is brain imaging, which, as we will see, has brought psychologists very close to an objective glimpse at private mental processes.

But, before we move on to these topics in the next chapter, let's return to the problem with which we began the chapter: Sabra's fear of flying.

PSYCHOLOGYMATTERS
Fear of Flying Revisited

Which kind of learning—operant conditioning or classical conditioning—do you suppose lay behind Sabra's aversion to flying? Although we may never know exactly what caused her fear in the first place, we can guess that both forms of conditioning were involved. Fears commonly arise through direct experience involving classical conditioning. Alternatively, fears can be learned through observational learning, perhaps from a fearful parent or peer. And once the fear has been learned, operant conditioning can maintain it, because people are rewarded by avoiding the feared object.

These assumptions have led some airlines to experiment with a hybrid treatment known as *cognitive-behavioral therapy*, aimed at helping people overcome their fear of flying. Happily, Sabra located one of these programs a few weeks before the conference started. She contacted the airline and signed up for three weekend sessions to be held at a nearby airport.

She arrived at the appointed time, full of expectations and apprehensions. Would the therapist probe her childhood experiences and fantasies? Would she have to take tranquilizers? Or would she have to undergo some sort of terrifying treatment, such as flying upside-down in a small airplane?

Her worst expectations turned out to be unfounded. The treatment sessions were organized by a behavioral psychologist who gathered the nine participants in a small conference room. He began by saying that such fears are learned—much as you might learn to cringe when you hear a dentist's drill or the scraping of fingernails on a blackboard. But, because it is not important how such fears originated, this fear-of-flying program would focus on the present, not on the past, he said. Sabra began to feel more relaxed.

The conditioning-based therapy program combined several learning strategies. A classical conditioning component would involve extinction of her fear through gradual exposure to the experience of flying. Operant conditioning would play a role through social reinforcement from the therapist and other members of the group. In addition, a cognitive component would involve learning more about how airplanes work.

After a brief overview of the process they would experience over the next three weeks, the group took a tour of the airport, including the cabin of a passenger jet parked on the Tarmac. Then they went back to the conference room to learn about how a pilot controls an airplane and about the physical forces that keep it in the air. The group also watched some videos involving routine flights in a commercial jet. All in all, this first session went smoothly, and everyone seemed much more at ease than when they started.

The second weekend began with more classroom discussion. Then, the class went back into the airliner, where they took seats and went through a series of relaxation exercises designed to extinguish the participants' fears and to learn a new and more relaxed response to the experience of being in an airplane. This training included deep breathing and progressive relaxation of specific muscle groups all over the body. When everyone in the group reported feeling relaxed, they again watched videos of flight on the plane's TV monitors. This was followed by more relaxation exercises. The final activity for the second weekend involved starting the engines and going through the preflight routine—all the way up to takeoff . . . and more relaxation exercises.

The final weekend session was almost identical to the previous one. The only difference was that "graduation" involved an actual flight—a 20-minute trip out over the local countryside and back to the airport. It was, of course, voluntary, but only one of the nine people in the class chose not to go. Sabra went, but not without some anxiety. The therapist, however, encouraged the group to focus on the relaxation exercises they had learned, rather than on their feelings of fear. To the amazement of all who participated, these learning-based techniques helped them through the flight exercise without losing control of their emotional responses. Although no one's fear had vanished completely, everyone on board was able to bring it under control.

The happiest result was that Sabra was able to go to her meeting in Hawaii—where, by the way, she had a productive conference and a wonderful time. For our purposes we should also note that she has flown several times since then. Each trip gets just a little easier, she says—just as the psychology of learning would predict.

CheckYourUnderstanding

1. **ANALYSIS:** Why was *insight*, rather than *trial-and-error*, the best explanation for Sultan's solution to the problem of reaching the food reward?

2. **RECALL:** What evidence did Tolman have that his rats had developed cognitive maps of a maze?

3. **APPLICATION:** If you were going to use Bandura's findings in developing a program to prevent violence among middle school children, you might
   a. have children watch videos of children who are responding constructively to aggressive acts on the playground.
   b. punish children who are aggressive and reward those who are not aggressive.
   c. have children punch a BoBo doll, to "get the aggression out of their system."
   d. punish children for aggressive acts performed at school.

4. **APPLICATION:** Mirror neurons seem to explain how observational learning works. So, looking at your answer to the previous question: What would the observers' mirror neurons be responding to?

5. **UNDERSTANDING THE CORE CONCEPT:** Pick one experiment described in this section of the chapter and discuss why it is difficult to explain in purely behavioral terms.

Critical Thinking Applied: Do Different People Have Different "Learning Styles"?

Without a doubt, people differ in the ways that they approach learning. As you can see by observing your classmates, everyone brings a different set of interests, abilities, temperamental factors, developmental levels, social experiences, and emotions to bear on learning tasks. But, can we say that these constitute distinct "learning styles"? For example, are some people "visual learners," who need to *see* the material, rather than hearing it, as, perhaps, an "auditory learner" must do?

Educators have been drawn to the concept of learning styles, in the hope that schools might be able to encourage learning by tailoring instruction to a student's learning styles. (A Google search, revealing over a half-million hits, shows just how compelling this idea has become.) The excitement about learning styles has, in turn, led to a proliferation of learning-styles inventories, each purporting to diagnose how each student learns best, with implications for how to fit each learner to the optimum teaching environment. Perhaps you have taken one such test. But is all this buzz based on fact or fantasy?

What Are the Issues?

From a critical perspective, the principal issue centers on the meaning of "learning styles." The term may seem intuitively clear—but does it mean same thing to everyone? And, are learning styles really *requirements*, or mere *preferences* for learning? In other words, if you are a "visual learner," to what extent does this truly impact your ability to learn when visuals are not available? One further issue centers on whether learning styles are unchangeable (like eye color) or whether people can adjust their approach to learning to fit the demands of the subject matter (say, literature, psychology, dentistry, or music).

What Critical Thinking Questions Should We Ask?

We need to ask about both the *source* and the *evidence*. That is, we need to know whether the sources of information on learning styles are credible. And we need to know whether their work is based on solid research or mere speculation. We also need to ask if any *biases* might have contaminated the research conclusions. Is there a possibility that those who profit from developing tests that identify different learning styles could have biases?

Finally, we should wonder whether advocates of the "learning styles" concept might not be guilty of the logical error of oversimplifying a complex problem. Learning involves an interaction of many factors: the learner, the material, the medium in which the material is presented, the organization of the presentation, the personalities of the teacher and learner, and the environment in which learning takes place, to name a few. So, you may not be able to learn in a distracting or dangerous environment (think of children in substandard inner city schools), no matter how the material is presented. Even if it is valid, the concept of "learning styles" may be simplistic.

What Conclusions Can We Draw?

Unfortunately, most of the publications on learning styles come from sources that have not taken the trouble to do the controlled studies needed to support their claims (Stahl, 1999). Further, even among learning-style enthusiasts, we find no agreed-upon list of distinct learning styles. So, although educators commonly talk about "verbal learners," "visual learners," and "kinesthetic (movement) learners," some inventories also claim to assess some combination of the following styles: tactile (touch), logical, social, solitary, active/reflective, sensing/intuitive, thinking/feeling, judging/perceiving, sequential/global.

Moreover, we have no evidence that any of these is any more than a preference (Krätzig & Arbuthnott, 2006). Nor is there evidence suggesting that different "styles" are equally effective with different learning tasks. (Imagine, for example, taking a "visual learner" approach to studying piano.) Regarding the tests for assessing students' learning styles, most such schemes have little supporting data for their claim that people with different scores learn the same material in different ways (Krätzig & Arbuthnott, 2006).

Some educators have also made claims about learning styles that confound learning styles with the popular, but mistaken, notion of "left-brained" and "right-brained" thinkers (Terry, 2000). But, as we saw in Chapter 2, this dichotomy is based on a fundamental misinterpretation of split-brain research: In a person with an intact corpus callosum, both hemispheres work cooperatively. What the proponents of left-brain/right-brain learning styles usually mean is that some people *prefer* learning verbally, while others *prefer* materials that are more visual–spatial. And, like all typologies, this one assumes that people fall neatly into distinct groups, even though it would be more accurate to see people as gradually shading from one end of the spectrum to the other. This questionable assumption may be one reason why little solid evidence exists to show that people who are described as having different learning styles actually do learn differently.

Many other learning style theories have been proposed, and with them tests have appeared on the market for assessing students' learning styles. Again, we should ask: What is the evidence? And is there a possibility that those who profit from the tests could have biases? Again, most such schemes have little supporting data for their claim that people with different scores learn the same material in different ways (Kratzig & Arbuthnott, 2006).

An exception may be an ambitious program developed by Sternberg and Grigorenko to assess students on their abilities for logical, creative, and practical thinking—arguably, three distinct forms of "intelligence" (Sternberg, 1994; Sternberg & Grigorenko, 1997). Students in an introductory psychology course were divided into groups that received instruction emphasizing the form of intelligence on which they had scored highest. (A control group of students was deliberately mismatched.) Tests at the end of the course indicated that students did best when the teaching emphasis matched their intellectual style. As a practical matter, however, such a fine-tuned approach is probably not feasible for implementation on a wide scale.

Cross-cultural research may also provide another reason to keep our minds open about learning styles (Winerman, 2006b). For example, studies by Richard Nisbett (2003) and his colleagues have shown that Asians and Americans often perceive the world quite differently, with Americans focusing on central objects and Asians taking in a scene more globally. (The difference is cultural: Americans of Asian ancestry perceive in essentially the same way as other Americans.) To illustrate the difference in these two styles of "seeing," picture in your mind a tiger against a jungle background. Nisbett's group found that the typical American spends more mental energy on putting prominent elements of the scene—the tiger—into logical categories, while Asians usually pay more attention to the context and background—the jungle.

Culture can also influence the way people approach classroom learning. For example, Americans generally believe that academic success is the result of innate intelligence, while East Asians emphasize discipline and hard work (Li, 2005). Which belief system would you guess might encourage most children to do well in school?

Other cultural differences can play a role in academic achievement, says Korean-born psychologist Heejung Kim. After struggling with classes that required group discussion, which was rare in her Korean educational experience, Kim (2002) decided to look for differences between the ways Asians and Americans approach academic tasks. As she predicted, when Asian and American college students were given problems to solve, the Americans usually benefited from talking over the problems with each other, while such discussion often inhibited problem solving by Asian students.

The lines on this image, used by Nisbett's team, show one individual's eye movements when scanning the scene. Americans spent more time looking at the tiger and other prominent objects in the picture, whereas Asians spent more time scanning details of the context and background.

In general, while we might best be cautious about most claims about "learning styles," we should remain open to new developments that may come out of cross-cultural research and from work on Sternberg's three-intelligences theory. Beyond that, we should acknowledge that interest in "learning styles" has encouraged teachers and professors to present the material in a variety of ways in their classes—including media, demonstrations, and various "active learning" techniques. Further, the available research suggests everyone learns better when the same material can be approached in more than one way—both visual and verbal, as well as through hands-on active learning (McKeachie, 1990, 1997, 1999).

But back to our main point: Your authors recommend a big dose of skepticism when interpreting the results of tests that purport to identify your learning style. And beware of people who might tell you that you are a visual learner, a reflective learner, or some such other type. Just because you prefer images to words, for example, does not mean that you should avoid reading and just look at the pictures. This sort of thinking erroneously suggests that each person learns in only one way. It also erroneously suggests that the way we learn is fixed and unchanging. Thus, we need to learn how to adapt the way we learn to the type of material to be learned: You wouldn't learn about music in exactly the same way you would learn about math. In fact, your college experience presents a wonderful opportunity to learn to think in new and unaccustomed ways.

Chapter Summary

Learning produces lasting changes in behavior or mental processes, giving us an advantage over organisms that rely more heavily on **reflexes** and **instincts**. Some forms of learning, such as **habituation**, are quite simple, while others, such as classical conditioning, operant conditioning, and cognitive learning, are more complex.

Behavioral learning (p. 94)   **Learning** (p. 92)

Habituation (p. 93)   **Mere exposure effect** (p. 94)

3.1 What Sort Of Learning Does Classical Conditioning Explain?

Core Concept 3.1: Classical conditioning is a basic form of learning in which a stimulus that produces an innate reflex becomes associated with a previously neutral stimulus, which then acquires the power to elicit essentially the same response.

The earliest learning research focused on **classical conditioning**, beginning with Ivan Pavlov's discovery that **conditioned stimuli** (after being paired with **unconditioned stimuli**) could elicit reflexive responses. His experiments on dogs showed how **conditioned responses** could be **acquired** and **extinguished** and undergo **spontaneous recovery** in laboratory animals. He also demonstrated **stimulus generalization** and discrimination learning. John Watson extended Pavlov's work to people, notably in his famous experiment on the conditioning of fear in Little Albert. More recent work, particularly studies of taste aversions, suggests, however, that classical conditioning is not a simple stimulus–response learning process but also has a biological component. In general, classical conditioning affects basic, survival-oriented responses. Therapeutic applications of Pavlovian learning include the prevention of harmful food aversions in chemotherapy patients.

Acquisition (p. 96)   **Neutral stimulus** (p. 96)

Classical conditioning (p. 96)   **Spontaneous recovery** (p. 98)

Conditioned response (CR) (p. 99)   **Stimulus discrimination** (p. 98)

Conditioned stimulus (CS) (p. 96)   **Stimulus generalization** (p. 98)

Experimental neurosis (p. 99)   **Unconditioned response (UCR)** (p. 96)

Extinction (in classical conditioning) (p. 94)   **Unconditioned stimulus (UCS)** (p. 96)

MyPsychLab Resources 3.1:

Explore: Three Stages of Classical Conditioning

Explore: Process of Extinction and Spontaneous Recovery

Explore: Process of Stimulus Generalization and Stimulus Discrimination in Classical Conditioning

---

3.2 How Do We Learn New Behaviors By Operant Conditioning?

Core Concept 3.2: In operant conditioning, the consequences of behavior, such as rewards and punishments, influence the probability that the behavior will occur again.

A more active form of learning, called **instrumental conditioning**, was first explored by Edward Thorndike, who established the **law of effect**, based on his study of trial-and-error learning. B. F. Skinner expanded Thorndike's work, now called **operant conditioning**, to explain how responses are influenced by their environmental consequences. His work identified and assessed various consequences, including **positive** and **negative reinforcement**, **punishment**, and an operant form of **extinction**. The power of operant conditioning involves producing new responses. To learn how this works, Skinner and others examined **continuous reinforcement**, as well as several kinds of **intermittent reinforcement** contingencies, including **FR, VR, FI,** and **VI schedules.** As for punishment, research has shown that it is more difficult to use than reward because it has several undesirable side effects. There are, however, alternatives, including operant extinction and rewarding of alternative responses, application of the **Premack principle,** and prompting and shaping new behaviors. These techniques have found practical use in controlling behavior in schools and other institutions, as well as in behavioral therapy for controlling fears and phobias.

Conditioned reinforcer or secondary reinforcer (p. 106)   **Fixed ratio (FR) schedules** (p. 105)

Continuous reinforcement (p. 104)   **Instinctive drift** (p. 107)

Extinction (in operant conditioning) (p. 105)   **Intermittent reinforcement** (p. 105)

Fixed interval (FI) schedules (p. 106)   **Interval schedule** (p. 105)

   Law of effect (p. 102)

   Negative punishment (p. 108)

MyPsychLab Resources 3.2:

Explore: Learned Helplessness: An Experimental Procedure

Simulation: Schedules of Reinforcement

Explore: The Shaping Process

3.3 How Does Cognitive Psychology Explain Learning?

Core Concept 3.3 According to cognitive psychology, some forms of learning must be explained as changes in mental processes, rather than as changes in behavior alone.

Much research now suggests that learning is not just a process that links stimuli and responses: Learning is also cognitive. This was shown in Köhler's work on **insight learning** in chimpanzees, in Tolman's studies of **cognitive maps** in rats, and in Bandura's research on **observational learning** and **imitation** in humans—particularly the effect of observing aggressive models, which spawned many studies on media violence and, recently, applications dealing with social problems, such as the spread of AIDS. All of this cognitive research demonstrated that learning did not necessarily involve changes in behavior nor did it require reinforcement. In the past three decades, cognitive scientists have worked on reinterpreting behavioral learning, especially operant and classical conditioning, in cognitive terms, as well as searching for the neural basis of learning. Some educators have, however, taken new developments in learning far beyond the evidence: Specifically, there is little empirical support for most of the claims in the "learning style" literature.

MyPsychLab Resources 3.3:

Watch: Bandura's BoBo Doll Experiment

Simulation: Latent Learning

Watch the following video by logging into MyPsychLab (www.mypsychlab.com). After you have watched the video, complete the activities that follow.

PROGRAM 8: LEARNING

PROGRAM REVIEW

1. Which of the following is an example of a fixed-action pattern?
   a. a fish leaping at bait that looks like a fly
   b. a flock of birds migrating in winter
   c. a person blinking when something gets in her eye
   d. a chimpanzee solving a problem using insight

2. What is the basic purpose of learning?
   a. to improve one's genes
   b. to understand the world one lives in
   c. to find food more successfully
   d. to adapt to changing circumstances

3. How have psychologists traditionally studied learning?
   a. in classrooms with children as participants
   b. in classrooms with college students as participants
   c. in laboratories with humans as participants
   d. in laboratories with nonhuman animals as participants

4. In his work, Pavlov found that a metronome could produce salivation in dogs because
   a. it signaled that food would arrive.
   b. it was the dogs' normal reaction to a metronome.
   c. it was on while the dogs ate.
   d. it extinguished the dogs' original response.

5. What is learned in classical conditioning?
   a. a relationship between an action and its consequence
   b. a relationship between two stimulus events
   c. a relationship between two response events
   d. classical conditioning does not involve learning

6. What point is Professor Zimbardo making when he says, "Relax," while firing a pistol?
   a. There are fixed reactions to verbal stimuli.
   b. The acquisition process is reversed during extinction.
   c. Any stimulus can come to elicit any reaction.
   d. Unconditioned stimuli are frequently negative.

7. What point does Ader and Cohen's research on taste aversion in rats make about classical conditioning?
   a. It can be extinguished easily.
   b. It takes many conditioning trials to be effective.
   c. It is powerful enough to suppress the immune system.
   d. It tends to be more effective than instrumental conditioning.

8. What is Thorndike's law of effect?
   a. Learning is controlled by its consequences.
   b. Every action has an equal and opposite reaction.
   c. Effects are more easily changed than causes.
   d. A conditioned stimulus comes to have the same effect as an unconditioned stimulus.

9. According to John B. Watson, any behavior, even strong emotion, could be explained by the power of
   a. instinct.
   b. inherited traits.
   c. innate ideas.
   d. conditioning.

10. In Watson's work with Little Albert, why was Albert afraid of the Santa Claus mask?
    a. He had been classically conditioned with the mask.
    b. The mask was an unconditioned stimulus creating fear.
    c. He generalized his learned fear of the rat.
    d. Instrumental conditioning created a fear of strangers.

11. What was the point of the Skinner box?
    a. It kept animals safe.

b. It provided a simple, highly controlled environment.

c. It set up a classical conditioning situation.

d. It allowed psychologists to use computers for research.

12. Skinner found that the rate at which a pigeon pecked at a target varied directly with

a. the conditioned stimulus.

b. the conditioned response.

c. the operant antecedents.

d. the reinforcing consequences.

13. Imagine a behavior therapist is treating a person who fears going out into public places. What would the therapist be likely to focus on?

a. the conditioning experience that created the fear

b. the deeper problems that the fear is a symptom of

c. providing positive consequences for going out

d. reinforcing the patient's desire to overcome the fear

14. When should the conditioned stimulus be presented in order to optimally produce classical conditioning?

a. just before the unconditioned stimulus

b. simultaneously with the unconditioned response

c. just after the unconditioned stimulus

d. just after the conditioned response

15. Operant conditioning can be used to achieve all of the following, *except*

a. teaching dogs to assist the handicapped.

b. teaching English grammar to infants.

c. teaching self-control to someone who is trying to quit smoking.

d. increasing productivity among factory workers.

16. Which psychologist has argued that in order to understand and control behavior, one has to consider both the reinforcements acting on the selected behavior and the reinforcements acting on the alternatives?

a. E. Thorndike

b. J. Watson

c. B. F. Skinner

d. H. Rachlin

17. If given a choice between an immediate small reinforcer and a delayed larger reinforcer, an untrained pigeon will

a. select the immediate small one.

b. select the delayed larger one.

c. experiment and alternate across trials.

d. not show any signs of perceiving the difference.

18. In order to produce extinction of a classically conditioned behavior, an experimenter would

a. reward the behavior.

b. pair the behavior with negative reinforcement.

c. present the conditioned stimulus in the absence of the unconditioned stimulus.

d. model the behavior for the organism.

19. In Pavlov's early work, bell is to food as

a. unconditioned response is to conditioned response.

b. conditioned stimulus is to unconditioned stimulus.

c. unconditioned response is to conditioned stimulus.

d. conditioned stimulus is to conditioned response.

20. Howard Rachlin has discovered that animals can be taught self-control through

a. reinforcement.

b. operant conditioning.

c. instrumental conditioning.

d. all of the above.

QUESTIONS TO CONSIDER

1. Approximately 2% of Americans are hooked on gambling, which experts claim can be just as addictive as drugs. Is compulsive gambling a disease or a learned behavior? Consider the kind of reinforcement gamblers get. Using the terms you learned in this program, how would you characterize the nature of the reinforcement and the reinforcement schedule? What techniques do you predict would work best to help compulsive gamblers change their behavior?

2. You are a school principal, and you are trying to get your students to help clean up the school. Given what you now know about the control of behavior, what sorts of techniques would you use in order to get students to comply?

3. What role does intention to learn play in classical and operant conditioning? Would these techniques work on people who do not know they are being used? Would they work on people who oppose their use?

4. Is it possible that children learn their native language through operant conditioning? When parents and young children interact, do the parents reinforce the use of some grammar and punish others? Are some aspects of language, such as the

rules of politeness, more likely to be taught through conditioning than other aspects?

ACTIVITIES

1. Design your own behavior change program based on the learning principles described in Program 8. First, identify a specific behavior. Instead of setting a broad goal, such as becoming more fit, design a strategy to reinforce a desired behavior—going for jogs, cutting out midnight snacks, or taking the stairs rather than the elevator. Analyze the specific behavior you would like to change in terms of antecedents-behavior-consequences. Then get a baseline measurement of the target behavior, try out your plan for a predetermined amount of time, and evaluate the results.

2. Have someone teach you something new, such as how to juggle, play basic guitar chords, or serve a tennis ball. Analyze the teacher's method. How does he or she apply principles of theories of learning? How would you change the teacher's method to be more effective?

3. Choose a member of your family and some trivial behavioral detail, such as standing still. See if you can train the person to reliably perform the behavior without having him or her catch on to what you're doing.

Key Questions/ Chapter Outline	Core Concepts	Psychology Matters

4.1 What Is Memory?

Metaphors for Memory
Memory's Three Basic Tasks

- Human memory is an information processing system that works constructively to encode, store, and retrieve information.

Would You Want a "Photographic" Memory?

This ability is rare, and those who have it say that the images can sometimes interfere with their thinking.

4.2 How Do We Form Memories?

The First Stage: Sensory Memory
The Second Stage: Working Memory
The Third Stage: Long-Term Memory

- Each of the three memory stages encodes and stores memories in a different way, but they work together to transform sensory experience into a lasting record that has a pattern or meaning.

"Flashbulb" Memories: Where Were You When...?

These especially vivid memories usually involve emotionally charged events. Surprisingly, they aren't always accurate.

4.3 How Do We Retrieve Memories?

Implicit and Explicit Memory
Retrieval Cues
Other Factors Affecting Retrieval

- Whether memories are implicit or explicit, successful retrieval depends on how they were encoded and how they are cued.

On the Tip of Your Tongue

It is maddening when you know the word, but you just can't quite say it. But you're not alone. Most people experience this about once a week.

4.4 Why Does Memory Sometimes Fail Us?

Transience: Fading Memories Cause Forgetting
Absent-Mindedness: Lapses of Attention Cause Forgetting
Blocking: Access Problems
Misattribution: Memories in the Wrong Context
Suggestibility: External Cues Distort or Create Memories
Bias: Beliefs, Attitudes, and Opinions Distort Memories
Persistence: When We Can't Forget
The Advantages of the "Seven Sins" of Memory
Improving Your Memory with Mnemonics

- Most of our memory problems arise from memory's "seven sins"—which are really by-products of otherwise adaptive features of human memory.

Using Psychology to Learn Psychology

In studying psychology there isn't much you will need to memorize. Instead, you will need mnemonic techniques that will help you learn and remember concepts.

Critical Thinking Applied: The Recovered Memory Controversy

chapter **4**
memory

Can memory play tricks on us? Or does memory make an accurate and indelible record of our past? In fact, the truth about memory encompasses some of both of those extremes. Memory *does* sometimes play tricks on us. And many of our memories are quite accurate. The difficulty lies in knowing when to rely on memory, as the following cases will illustrate.

Case 1 Twelve-year-old Donna began to suffer from severe migraine headaches that left her sleepless and depressed. Concerned, her parents, Judee and Dan, agreed to find help for her. Over the next year, Donna was passed from one therapist to another, ending up with a psychiatric social worker who specialized in the treatment of child abuse. It was to that therapist that Donna disclosed—for the first time—having been sexually molested at the age of 3 by a neighbor. The therapist concluded that memories of the assault, buried in her mind for so long, were probably responsible for some of Donna's current problems, so she continued to probe for details and for other possible instances of sexual abuse.

Eventually, the therapist asked her to bring in a family photo album, which included a photo of Donna, taken at age 2 or 3, wearing underpants. The therapist suggested that this might be evidence that Donna's father had a sexual interest in her and, possibly, had molested her. Moreover, the therapist contacted the authorities, who began an investigation (ABC News, 1995).

For two years, Donna felt intense pressure to blame her father, but consistently denied that he had molested her. Finally, amid increasing confusion about her childhood memories, she began to believe that she suffered from "repressed memory syndrome" and that her father had abused her repeatedly during her childhood. Eventually, Donna was hospitalized. While in the hospital she was placed on medication, hypnotized repeatedly, and diagnosed with *multiple personality disorder* (now called *dissociative identity disorder*).

As for her father, Dan was arrested and tried on charges of abuse based solely on his daughter's recovered memory. When his two-week trial ended in a hung jury, Dan went free. Shortly after the trial, Donna moved to another state with a foster family. In new surroundings and far away from the system that had supported her story, she began to believe that her memories were false. Eventually, her doctor recommended she be sent back to her family, where they began the slow process of rebuilding lost relationships and trust.

Case 2   Ross is a college professor who entered therapy because he was unhappy with his life. Describing his condition, he said, "I felt somehow adrift, as if some anchor in my life had been raised. I had doubts about my marriage, my job, everything" (Schacter, 1996, p. 249). Then, some months after entering therapy, he had a dream that left him with a strong sense of unease about a certain camp counselor whom he had known as a youth. Over the next few hours, that sense of unease gradually became a vivid recollection of the counselor molesting him. From that point on, Ross became obsessed with this memory, finally hiring a private detective who helped him track down the counselor in a small Oregon town. After numerous attempts to talk with the counselor by telephone, Ross at last made contact and taped the phone conversation. The counselor admitted molesting Ross, as well as several other boys at the camp. Strangely, Ross claimed that he had simply not thought about the abuse for years—until he entered therapy.

PROBLEM: How can our knowledge about memory help us evaluate claims of recovered memories?

Keep in mind that there is no sure way to "prove a negative." That is, without some independent evidence, no one could ever prove conclusively that abuse or some other apparently long-forgotten event did *not* occur. Instead, we must weigh the claims against our understanding of memory. In particular, we will need to know the answers to the following questions:

● Does memory make an accurate record of everything we experience?

● Are traumatic experiences, such as those of sexual abuse, likely to be *repressed* (blocked from consciousness), as Sigmund Freud taught? Or, are we more likely to *remember* our most emotional experiences, both good and bad?

- How reliable are memories of experiences from early childhood?

- How easily can memories be changed by suggestion, as when a therapist or police officer might suggest that sexual abuse occurred?

- Are our most vivid memories more accurate than less vivid memories?

You will find the answers to these questions and many more in this chapter. Let's begin with the most fundamental question of all.

4.1 KEY QUESTION
WHAT IS MEMORY?

Without doubt, memory does play tricks on us. Our best defense against those tricks comes from an understanding of how memory works. So, let's begin building that understanding with a definition: Cognitive psychologists view **memory** as a system that encodes, stores, and retrieves information—a definition, by the way, that applies equally to an organism or a computer. Unlike a computer's memory, however, we humans have a *cognitive* memory system that takes information from the senses and selectively converts it into meaningful patterns that can be stored and accessed later when needed. These memory patterns, then, form the raw material for thought and behavior. Such memory patterns allow you to recognize a friend's face, ride a bicycle, recollect a trip to Disneyland, and (if all goes well) recall the concepts you need during a test. More generally, our Core Concept characterizes memory this way:

CONNECTION • CHAPTER 1

Cognitive psychology is one of the six main perspectives in psychology.

> **Human memory is an information processing system that works constructively to encode, store, and retrieve information.**

core concept

And how is memory related to *learning*, the topic of the last chapter? Learning and memory are different sides of the same coin. You might think of memory as the cognitive system that first processes, encodes, and stores the information we learn and, later, allows us to retrieve that information. So, this chapter is really an extension of our discussion of cognitive learning in Chapter 3. The focus here, however, will be on more complex *human* learning and memory, as contrasted with the simpler forms of animal learning and conditioning that we emphasized earlier.

Metaphors for Memory

We often use metaphors to help us understand complicated things. One such metaphor compares human memory to a library or a storehouse, emphasizing the ability of memory to hold large amounts of information (Haberlandt, 1999). Another, as we've just described, compares memory to a computer. Some metaphors for memory, however, can be misleading. That's certainly the case with the "video recorder" metaphor for memory, which leads people to believe that human memory makes a complete and accurate record of everything we experience.

Experiments have shown that this video-recorder metaphor is wrong. And especially in some cases of "recovered memories," believing in the unfailing accuracy of memory can be dangerously wrong. Instead, cognitive psychologists see human memory as an *interpretive* system that takes in information and, much

Memory Any system—human, animal, or machine—that encodes, stores, and retrieves information.

Memory encodes the best records for information on which we have focused attention.

like an artist, discards details and organizes the rest into meaningful patterns. As a result, our memories represent our *perceptions* of events, rather than being accurate representations of the events themselves.

When remembering, you retrieve fragments of memory—like pieces of a jigsaw puzzle. Then, from these fragments, you *reconstruct* the incident (or idea, emotion, or image) by filling in the blanks *as you think it was*, rather than the way it actually was. Most of the time this works well enough that you don't realize just how much of remembrance is reconstruction.

A look at Figure 4.1 should convince you of this reconstructive process. Which image in the figure is the most accurate portrayal of a penny? Although pennies are common in our everyday experience, you will probably find that identifying the real penny image is not easy. Unless you are a coin collector, you probably pay little attention to the details of these familiar objects. The result is a vague memory image that serves well enough in everyday life but is sparse on details. So, when retrieving the image of a penny, you automatically fill in the gaps and missing details—without realizing how much of the memory image you are actually creating. (The right answer, by the way, is A.)

Some memories are sketchier than others. In general, psychologists have found that we make the most complete and accurate memory records for:

● Information on which we have *focused our attention*, such as a friend's words against a background of other conversations

● Information in which we are *interested*, such as the plot of a favorite movie

● Information that *arouses us emotionally*, such as an especially enjoyable or painful experience (unless the material also brings our biases into play, as when we listen to a highly partisan political presentation)

● Information that *connects with previous experience*, such as a news item about the musician whose concert you attended last week

● Information that we *rehearse*, such as material reviewed before an exam

The rest of the chapter will unfold this cognitive approach to memory, known as the **information-processing model**. It emphasizes how information undergoes systematic changes on its way to becoming a permanent memory—quite differ-

Information-processing model A cognitive understanding of memory, emphasizing how information is changed when it is encoded, stored, and retrieved.

FIGURE 4.1
The Penny Test

(*Source:* From "Long-Term Memory for a Common Object," by Nickerson and Adams in *Cognitive Psychology*, Vol. 11, Issue #1, 1979, pp. 287–307. Copyright © 1979. Reprinted by permission of Elsevier.)

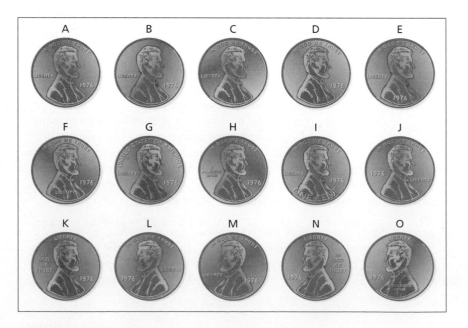

ent from the naïve video recorder model. The information-processing model also emphasizes that memory is *functional*—that is, it performs some useful functions for us. The most basic of these, we will see below, are the *encoding, storage,* and *retrieval* of information.

Memory's Three Basic Tasks

In simplest terms, human memory takes essentially meaningless sensory information (such as the sounds of your professor's voice) and changes it into meaningful patterns (words, sentences, and concepts) that you can store and use later. To do so, memory must first *encode* the incoming sensory information in a useful format.

Encoding requires that you first *select* some stimulus event from among the vast array of inputs assaulting your senses and then make a preliminary classification of that stimulus. Is it a sound, a visual image, or an odor? Next you *identify* the distinctive features of that input. If it's a sound, is it loud, soft, or harsh? Does it fit some pattern, such as a car horn, a melody, a voice? Is it a sound you have heard before? Finally, you mentally tag, or *label,* an experience to make it meaningful. ("It's Dr. Johnson. He's my psychology professor!")

For many of our everyday experiences, encoding is so automatic and rapid that we have no awareness of the process. For example, you can probably recall what you had for breakfast this morning, even though you didn't deliberately try to make the experience "stick" in your mind. Emotionally charged experiences, such as an angry exchange with a colleague, are even more likely to lodge in memory without any effort on our part to encode it (Dolan, 2002).

On the other hand, memories for concepts, such the basic principles of psychology that you are learning about in this book, usually require a deliberate encoding effort, called *elaboration,* to establish a usable memory. During elaboration, you attempt to connect a new concept with existing information in memory. One way to do this is to link the new material with concrete examples, as when you associated the term *negative reinforcement* with the removal of pain when you take an aspirin. (As an aid to elaboration, this book deliberately provides many such examples that, we hope, will connect new concepts with your own experiences.)

Storage, the second essential memory task, involves the retention of encoded material over time. But it's not a simple process. As we get deeper into the workings of memory, you will learn that memory consists of three parts, or *stages,* each of which stores memories for different lengths of time and in different forms. The trick of getting difficult-to-remember material into long-term storage, then, is to recode the information in the way long-term memory "likes" it, before the time clock runs out. For example, while listening to a lecture, you may have just a few seconds to encode a pattern or meaning in the sound of your professor's voice before new information comes along and the old information is lost.

Retrieval, the third basic memory task, becomes the payoff for your earlier efforts in encoding and storage. When you have a properly encoded memory, it takes only a split second for a good cue to access the information, bring it to consciousness, or, in some cases, to influence your behavior at an unconscious level. (Let's test the ability of your conscious retrieval machinery to recover the material we just covered: Can you remember which of the three memory tasks occurs just before *storage?*)

Alas, retrieval doesn't always go well, because the human memory system—marvelous as it is—sometimes makes errors, distorts information, or even fails us completely. In the last section of the chapter, we will take a close look at these problems, which memory expert Daniel Schacter (1996) calls the "seven sins of memory." The good news is that you can combat memory's "sins" with a few simple techniques that you will also learn about in the following pages.

Encoding   The first of the three basic tasks of memory, involving the modification of information to fit the preferred format for the memory

Storage   The second of the three basic tasks of memory, involving the retention of encoded material over

Retrieval   The third basic task of memory, involving the location and recovery of information from memory.

Look at the dot pattern on the left in the figure for a few moments and try to fix it in your memory. With that image in mind, look at the dot pattern on the right. Try to put the two sets of dots together by recalling the first pattern while looking at the second one. If you are the rare individual who can mentally combine the two patterns, you will see something not apparent in either image alone. Difficult? No problem if you have eidetic imagery—but impossible for the rest of us. If you want to see the combined images, but can't combine them in your memory, look at Figure 4.2.

 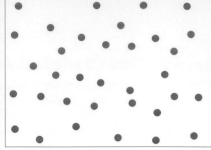

A Test of Eidetic Imagery

People with good eidetic imagery can mentally combine these two images to see something that appears in neither one alone.

PSYCHOLOGY**MATTERS**
Would You Want a "Photographic" Memory?

Suppose that your memory were so vivid and accurate that you could use it to "read" paragraphs of this book from memory during the next psychology exam. Such was the power of a 23-year-old woman tested by Charles Stromeyer and Joseph Psotka (1970). One of the amazing things she could do would be to look at the meaningless configuration of dots in the left-hand pattern in the "Do It Yourself!" box above and combine it mentally with the right-hand image. The result was the combined pattern shown in Figure 4.2. (Did you see the number "63" before you looked at the solution?) So, wouldn't it be great to have such a "photographic" memory? Not entirely, it turns out.

The technical term for "photographic memory" is **eidetic imagery.** Psychologists prefer this term because eidetic images differ in many important respects from images made by a camera (Haber, 1969, 1980). For example, a photographic image renders everything in minute detail, while an eidetic image portrays the most interesting and meaningful parts of the scene most accurately.

Eidetic memories also differ in several respects from the normal memory images that most of us experience. For one thing, *eidetikers* describe their memory images as having the vividness of the original experience (Neisser, 1967). For another, eidetic images are visualized as being "outside the head," rather than inside—in the "mind's eye." (Yet, unlike a person who is hallucinating, eidetikers recognize these images as *mental* images.) Further, an eidetic image can last for several minutes—even for days, in some cases. For example, the woman tested by Stromeyer and Psotka could pass the dot-combining test even when the two patterns were shown to her 24 hours apart. But, remarkable as this is, the persistence of eidetic images can be a curse. Eidetikers report that their vivid imagery sometimes clutters their minds and interferes with other things they want to think about (Hunter, 1964).

Eidetic imagery appears most commonly in children but only rarely in adults. One estimate says that up to 5% of children show some eidetic ability—although in most instances it's not good enough to pass the dot-combining test (Gray & Gummerman, 1975). While no one knows why eidetic imagery tends to disappear in adults, it may follow some sort of developmental sequence—like losing one's baby teeth. Possibly its disappearance is related to the child's development of abstract thought, which often begins to develop at about age 11 or 12.

Eidetic imagery An especially clear and persistent form of memory that is quite rare; sometimes known as "photographic memory."

CONNECTION • CHAPTER 6

In Piaget's theory, the formal operational stage, which often begins at about age 11 or 12, marks the appearance of abstract thought.

Case studies also suggest a connection between the decline of eidetic imagery and the development of language skills: Eidetikers report that describing an eidetic image in words makes the image fade from memory, and they learn to exploit this fact to control their intrusive imagery (Haber, 1969, 1970). Oddly enough, forensic psychologists have found that, for ordinary people (non-eidetikers), giving verbal descriptions of suspects' faces interferes with later memories for those faces. Likewise, trying to describe other hard-to-describe perceptions, such as a voice or the taste of a wine, impairs most people's abilities to recall those perceptions later (Bower, 2003; Dodson et al., 1997).

A study from Nigeria further supports the idea that the loss of eidetic ability may result from a conflict between language skills and visual imagery. This research found eidetic imagery to be common not only among children but also among illiterate adults of the Ibo tribe who were living in rural villages. Although many of the Ibo adults could correctly draw details of images seen sometime earlier, further testing found that members of the same tribe who had moved to the city and had learned to read showed little eidetic ability (Doob, 1964).

Whatever eidetic memory may be, it is clearly rare—so rare, in fact, that some psychologists have questioned its existence (Crowder, 1992). The few existing studies of "photographic memory" have portrayed it as different from everyday memory, as we have seen. But the fact is that we know relatively little about the phenomenon, and few psychologists are currently studying it.

Eidetic imagery presents not only a practical problem for those rare individuals who possess it but also a theoretical problem for cognitive psychologists. If eidetic imagery exists, is a known component of memory responsible? On the other hand, if it proves to be a unique form of memory, how does it fit with the widely accepted three-stage model of memory—which we will discuss next?

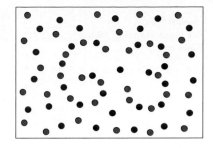

FIGURE 4.2
What an Eidetiker Sees

The combined images from the "Do It Yourself!" box form a number pattern.

(*Source:* From *Human Memory: Structures and Processes* by Roberta Klatzky. Copyright © 1975, 1980 by W. H. Freeman and Company. Used with permission.)

CheckYourUnderstanding

1. **ANALYSIS:** What is a major objection to the "video recorder" model of human memory?

2. **RECALL:** What are the three essential tasks of memory?

3. **ANALYSIS:** Suppose that you have just gotten a new cat. You note her unique markings, so that you can remember what she looks like in comparison with other cats in the neighborhood. What would a cognitive psychologist call this process of identifying the distinctive features of your cat?

4. **UNDERSTANDING THE CORE CONCEPT:** Which one of the following memory systems reconstructs material during retrieval?
   a. computer memory
   b. human memory
   c. video recorder memory
   d. information recorded in a book

Answers 1. Unlike a video recorder, which makes an accurate and detailed record, memory stores an interpretation of experience. **2.** Encoding, storage, and retrieval **3.** Encoding **4.** b

4.2 KEY QUESTION
HOW DO WE FORM MEMORIES?

If the information in a lecture is to become part of your permanent memory, it must be processed in three sequential stages: first in *sensory memory,* then in *working memory* (also called short-term memory), and finally in *long-term memory.* The three stages work like an assembly line to convert a flow of incoming stimuli into meaningful patterns that you can store and later recall. This three-stage model, originally developed by Richard Atkinson and Richard Shiffrin (1968), is now widely accepted—with some elaborations and modifications. Figure 4.3 shows how information flows through the three stages. (Caution: Don't get these three *stages* confused with the three basic *tasks* of memory that we covered earlier.)

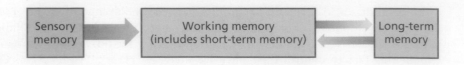

FIGURE 4.3

The Three Stages of Memory (Simplified)

The "standard model," developed by Atkinson and Shiffrin, says that memory is divided into three stages of processing. Everything that eventually goes into long-term storage must first be processed by sensory memory and working memory.

Sensory memory, the most fleeting of the three stages, typically holds sights, sounds, smells, textures, and other sensory impressions for only a fraction of a second. Although we are usually not aware of sensory memory, you can see its effects in the fading luminous trail made by a moving flashlight or a twirling Fourth-of-July sparkler. You can also hear the effects of fading sensory memories in the blending of one note into another as you listen to a melody. In general, these short-lived images allow us to maintain incoming sensory information just long enough for it to be screened for importance by working memory.

Working memory, the second stage of processing, takes information selectively from the sensory registers and makes connections with items already in long-term storage. (It is this connection we mean when we say, "That rings a bell!") Working memory holds information for only a few seconds, making it a useful buffer for temporarily holding a name you have just heard or a phone number you have just looked up. Originally, psychologists called this stage *short-term memory (STM),* a term still in use. The newer term *working memory* emphasizes some refinements of the original Atkinson and Shiffrin model that we will discuss in more detail shortly.

It is worth noting that everything entering consciousness passes into working memory. The opposite is also true: We are conscious of everything that enters working memory—although some information may not be the focus of our attention. Because of this intimate relationship, some psychologists have suggested that working memory is actually the long-sought seat of consciousness (Engle; 2002; LeDoux, 1996).

Long-term memory (LTM), the final stage of processing, receives information from working memory and can store it for much longer periods—sometimes for the rest of a person's life. Information in long-term memory constitutes our knowledge about the world. It includes material as varied as an image of your mother's face, the lyrics to your favorite song, and the year that Wilhelm Wundt established the first psychology laboratory. (You remember: That was in 18??.)

Our Core Concept captures the three stages in brief:

core concept

Each of the three memory stages encodes and stores memories in a different way, but they work together to transform sensory experience into a lasting record that has a pattern or meaning.

Our focus in this section will be on the unique contributions each stage makes to the final memory product. (See Table 4.1.) More specifically, we will look at each stage in terms of its storage *capacity,* its *duration* (how long it retains information), its *structure and function,* and its *biological basis.*

Sensory memory The first of three memory stages, preserving brief sensory impressions of stimuli.

Working memory The second of three memory stages, and the one most limited in capacity. It preserves recently perceived events or experiences for less than a minute without rehearsal.

Long-term memory (LTM) The third of three memory stages, with the largest capacity and longest duration; LTM stores material organized according to meaning.

The First Stage: Sensory Memory

Your senses take in far more information than you can possibly use. While reading this book, they serve up the words on the page, sounds in the room, the feel of your clothes on your skin, the temperature of the air, the slightly hungry feeling in your stomach. . . . And how does the brain deal with all of this sensory information?

It's the job of sensory memory to hold the barrage of incoming sensation just long enough (about 1/4 second) for your brain to scan it and decide which stream of information needs attention. But just how much information can sensory

TABLE 4.1   The Three Stages of Memory Compared

	Sensory Memory	Working Memory (STM)	Long-Term Memory (LTM)
Function	Briefly holds information awaiting entry into working memory	Involved in control of attention Attaches meaning to stimulation Makes associations among ideas and events	Long-term storage of information
Encoding	Sensory images: no meaningful encoding	Encodes information (especially by meaning) to make it acceptable for long-term storage	Stores information in meaningful mental categories
Storage capacity	12–16 items	"Magic number 7" ± 2 chunks	Unlimited
Duration	About $1/4$; second	About 20–30 seconds	Unlimited
Structure	A separate sensory register for each sense	Central executive Phonological loop Sketchpad	Procedural memory and declarative memory (further subdivided into semantic and episodic memory)
Biological Basis	Sensory pathways	Involves the hippocampus and frontal lobes	Involves various parts of the cerebral cortex

memory hold? Cognitive psychologist George Sperling answered this question by devising one of psychology's simplest and most clever experiments.

The Capacity and Duration of Sensory Memory   In brief, Sperling demonstrated that sensory memory can hold far more information than ever reaches consciousness. To do so, he first asked people to remember, as best they could, an array of letters flashed on a screen for a fraction of a second. (You might try glancing briefly at the array below and then trying to recall as many as you can.)

```
D     J     B     W
X     H     G     N
C     L     Y     K
```

There was no surprise here: Most people could remember only three or four items from a fraction-of-a-second exposure.

But, Sperling hypothesized, it might be possible that far more information than these three or four items might enter a temporary memory buffer but vanish before it can be reported. To test this conjecture, he modified the experimental task as follows. Immediately after the array of letters flashed on the screen, an auditory cue signaled which row of letters to report: A high-pitched tone indicated the top row, a medium tone the middle row, and a low tone meant the bottom row. Thus, immediately after seeing the brief image and hearing a beep, respondents were to report items *from only one row*, rather than items from the whole array.

Under this *partial report* condition, most people achieved almost perfect accuracy—no matter which row was signaled. That is, Sperling's volunteers could accurately report *any single row*, but *not all rows*. This result suggested that the actual storage capacity of sensory memory can be 12 or more items—even though all but three or four items usually disappear from sensory memory before they can enter consciousness (Sperling, 1960, 1963).

Would it be better if our sensory memories lasted longer, so we would have more time to scan them? Probably not. With new information constantly flowing in, old information needs to disappear quickly, lest the system become overloaded. We are built so that sensory memories last just long enough to dissolve into one another and give us a sense of flow and continuity in our experience. But they usually do not last long enough to interfere with new incoming sensory impressions.

FIGURE 4.4
Multiple Sensory Stores

We have a separate sensory memory for each of our sensory pathways. All feed into working (short-term) memory.

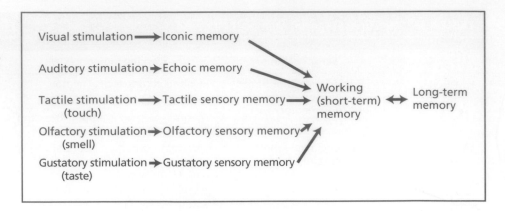

The Structure and Function of Sensory Memory

You might think of sensory memory as a sort of mental "movie screen," where images are "projected" fleetingly and then disappear. In fact, this blending of images in sensory memory gives us the impression of motion in a "motion picture"—which is really just a rapid series of still images.

But, not all sensory memory consists of visual images. We have a separate *sensory register* for each sense, with each register holding a different kind of sensory information, as shown in Figure 4.4. The register for vision, called *iconic memory,* stores the encoded light patterns experienced as visual images. Similarly, the sensory memory for hearing, known as *echoic memory,* holds encoded auditory stimuli.

Please note that the images in sensory memory have no meaning attached to them—just as an image on photographic film has no meaning to a camera. It's the job of sensory memory simply to store the images briefly. Then, as we will see, it's in the next stage, working memory, where we add meaning to sensation.

The Biological Basis of Sensory Memory

The biology of sensory memory appears to be relatively simple. Psychologists now believe that, in this initial stage, memory images take the form of neural activity in the sense organs and their pathways to the brain. In this view, sensory memory consists of the rapidly fading trace of stimulation in our sensory systems (Bower, 2000b; Glanz, 1998). Working memory then "reads" these fading sensory traces and decides which ones to admit into the spotlight of attention and which to ignore and allow to disappear.

The Second Stage: Working Memory

In the second stage of processing, working memory serves as the buffer in which you put the new name you have just heard. It also acts as the temporary storage site for the words in the first part of this sentence while you read toward the end. More broadly, working memory is the processor of conscious experience, including information coming from sensory memory, as well as information being retrieved from long-term memory (Jonides et al., 2005).

Additionally, working memory provides a mental "work space" where we sort and encode information before adding it to more permanent storage (Shiffrin, 1993). In doing so, it makes experiences meaningful by blending them with information from long-term memory. To give a concrete example: Working memory is the register into which you retrieve the information you learned in yesterday's class, as you review for tomorrow's test.

You might think of working memory, then, as the "central processing chip" for the entire memory system. In this role, it typically holds information for about 20 seconds—far longer than does sensory memory. If you make a special effort to rehearse the material, it can keep information active even longer, as when you repeat a phone number to yourself before dialing. It is also the mental work space in which we consciously mull over ideas and images pulled from long-term storage, in the process that we call "thinking." In all of these roles, then, working memory acts much like the main processing chip in a computer—as not only the center of mental action but as a go-between for the other components of memory.

The Capacity and Duration of Working Memory   Psychologist George Miller (1956) famously suggested that this second stage of memory is associated with the "magic number" seven. What he meant was that working memory holds about seven items—a fact that caused lots of distress when phone companies began requiring callers to add an area code to the old seven-digit phone number. Working memory's storage capacity does vary slightly from person to person, so you may want to assess how much yours can hold by trying the test in the "Do It Yourself!" box. In addition, STM has different capacities for different kinds of material, with some psychologists suggesting that it has a practical limit of only about three or four items (Cowan, 2001). The take-away message is that working memory has a limited capacity.

When we overload working memory, earlier items usually drop away to accommodate more recent ones. Yet, when working memory fills up with information demanding attention, we may not even notice new information streaming through our senses. That's why, in the opinion of some experts, this limited capacity of working memory makes it unsafe to talk on your cell phone while driving (Wickelgren, 2001).

You will note that working memory's meager storage capacity is significantly smaller than that of sensory memory. In fact, working memory has the smallest capacity of the three memory stages. This limitation, combined with a tendency to discard information after about 20 seconds, makes working memory the information "bottleneck" of the memory system. (See Figure 4.5.) As you may have surmised, the twin problems of limited capacity and short duration present obstacles for students, who must process and remember large amounts of information when they hear a lecture or read a book. Fortunately, there are ways to work around these difficulties, as we will see.

Chunks and Chunking   In memory, a *chunk* can be any pattern or meaningful unit of information. It might be a single letter or number, a name, or even a concept. For example, the letters P-H-I-L could constitute four chunks. However, you probably recognize this sequence as a name (in fact, the name of one of your authors), so you can combine the four letters into a single chunk in STM. Thus, by **chunking,** you can get more material into the seven slots of working memory.

Chunking   Organizing pieces of information into a smaller number of meaningful units (or chunks)—a process that frees up space in working memory.

FIGURE 4.5
The STM Bottleneck

Caught in the middle, with a much smaller capacity than sensory and long-term memories, working memory (short-term memory) becomes an information bottleneck in the memory system. As a result, much incoming information from sensory memory is lost.

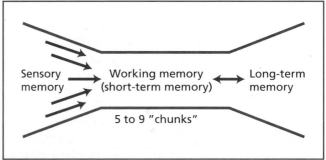

Sensory memory → Working memory (short-term memory) ↔ Long-term memory

5 to 9 "chunks"

The phone company discovered chunking years ago—which is why they put hyphens in phone numbers. So, when they group the seven digits of a phone number (e.g., 6735201) into two shorter strings of numbers (673-5201), they have helped us arrange seven separate items into two chunks—which leaves room for the area code. The government uses the same chunking principle to help us remember our nine-digit Social Security numbers.

The Role of Rehearsal Speaking of phone numbers, suppose that you have just looked up the phone number mentioned in the preceding paragraph. To keep it alive in working memory, you can repeat the digits to yourself over and over. This technique is called **maintenance rehearsal,** and it serves us well for maintaining information temporarily in consciousness. Maintenance rehearsal keeps information fresh in working memory and prevents competing inputs from crowding it out. But repetition is not an efficient way to transfer information to long-term memory, even though people often attempt to do so. Sadly, the student who tries to learn the material for a test by using simple repetition (maintenance rehearsal) probably won't remember much.

A better strategy for transferring material into long-term memory involves **elaborative rehearsal.** With this method, information is not merely repeated but is actively connected to knowledge already stored. So, suppose that you are an ophthalmologist, and you want your patients to remember your phone number. Because numbers are notoriously difficult to remember, you can help your customers with their elaborative rehearsal by using a "number" that makes use of the letters on the phone buttons, such as 1-800-EYE-EXAM. The same principle can be used with more complex material, such as you are learning in psychology. For example, when you read about echoic memory, you may have elaborated it with a connection to "echo," which is also an auditory sensation.

The Structure and Function of Working Memory
Figure 4.6 shows several components of working memory. Alan Baddeley and Graham Hitch (1974) originally proposed a *central executive* that directs your attention to important input from sensory memory, such as someone calling a name, or to material retrieved from long-term memory, as when you are taking a test. In addition, they proposed a *phonological loop* that temporarily stores sounds—helping you to remember the mental "echo" of a name or to follow a melody. A third part of working memory, that they dubbed the *sketchpad,* stores and manipulates visual images, as when you are imagining the route between your home and class.

Are there other components in the working memory system? Baddeley has, more recently, proposed an *episodic buffer* (Figure 4.6) that may help us remember events or "episodes" (Baddeley, 2000). Others have posited a *semantic buffer,* or language-processing module, that seems to help us attach meaning to words that we see or hear (Martin, 2005). Indeed, it would not be surprising if there were other components associated with other cognitive functions. Because the episodic and verbal buffers are not so well established, let's focus on the three components of working memory in the original Baddeley and Hitch model.

The Central Executive The information clearinghouse for working memory, the *central executive* is perhaps the most important and most poorly understood component of working memory. We do know that it serves as the interface between sensory memory, long-term memory, and the brain's voluntary (conscious) response system. In that role, the central executive is also part of the process that directs attention. Think of the central executive, then, as the heart and soul of the working memory system. Even now, as you sit reading this book, the central executive in your working memory is helping you decide whether to attend to these words, or to other stimuli flowing into working memory from your other senses, along with thoughts from long-term memory.

Maintenance rehearsal A working-memory process in which information is merely repeated or reviewed to keep it from fading while in working memory. Maintenance rehearsal involves no active elaboration.

Elaborative rehearsal A working-memory process in which information is actively reviewed and related to information already in LTM.

144 CHAPTER 4 ● MEMORY

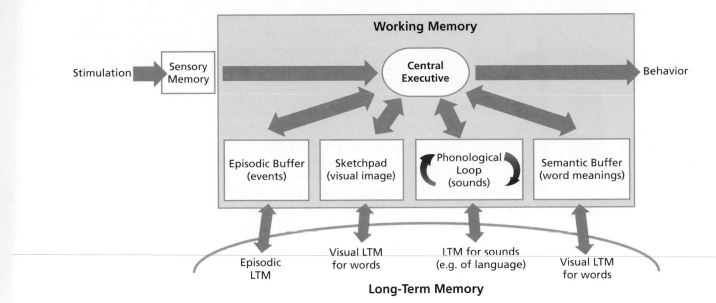

FIGURE 4.6
A Model of Working Memory

Atkinson and Shiffrin's original model divided memory into three stages. Events must first be processed by sensory memory and short-term memory (now called *working memory*) before they finally go into long-term memory storage—from which they can later be retrieved back into working memory. Baddeley's (2001) updated version of working memory includes a *central executive* that directs attention, a *sketchpad* for visual and spatial information, a *phonological loop* for sounds, and an *episodic buffer* that can combine many kinds of information into memories of events. More recently, neuroscience research has pointed to a *semantic buffer* that draws on the meaning of words in LTM (Martin, 2005). This drawing includes all of these refinements to the original model of working memory.

(*Source:* Adapted from "Episodic Buffer: A New Component of Working Memory?" by A. Baddeley, *Trends in Cognitive Sciences* [2000], 4, pp. 417–423, American Psychological Association.)

Acoustic Encoding: The Phonological Loop   If you were reading poetry, containing words like "whirr," "pop," "cuckoo," and "splash," you could hear in your mind the sounds they describe. This **acoustic encoding** also happens with words that don't have imitative sounds. That is, working memory converts all the words we encounter into the sounds of spoken language and shuttles them into its phonological loop—whether the words come through our eyes, as in reading, or our ears, as in listening to speech (Baddeley, 2001). There, working memory maintains the verbal patterns in an acoustic (sound) form as they are processed.

Acoustic encoding in working memory can cause some interesting memory errors. When people recall lists of letters they have just seen, the mistakes they make often involve confusions of letters that have similar sounds—such as D and T—rather than letters that have a similar look—such as E and F (Conrad, 1964). Mistakes aside, however, acoustic encoding has its advantages, particularly in learning and using language (Baddeley et al., 1998; Schacter, 1999).

Visual and Spatial Encoding: The Sketchpad   Serving much the same function for visual and spatial information, working memory's *sketchpad* encodes visual images and mental representations of objects in space. It holds the visual images you mentally rummage through when you're trying to imagine where you left your car keys. It also holds the mental map you follow from home to class. Neurological evidence suggests that the sketchpad requires coordination among several brain systems, including the frontal and occipital lobes.

Levels of Processing in Working Memory   An important tip for students: The more connections you can make with new information in working memory, the more likely you are to remember it later. Obviously this requires an interaction between working memory and long-term memory. According to the **levels-of-processing theory** proposed by Fergus Craik and Robert Lockhart (1972), "deeper"

Acoustic encoding   The conversion of information, especially semantic information, to sound patterns in working memory.

Levels-of-processing theory   The explanation for the fact that information that is more thoroughly connected to meaningful items in long-term memory (more "deeply" processed) will be remembered better.

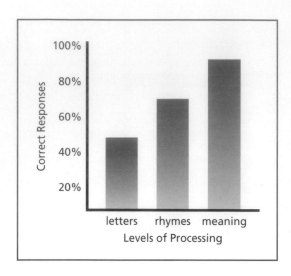

FIGURE 4.7
Results of Levels-of-Processing Experiment

In the Craik and Tulving (1975) experiment, words that were processed more deeply (for meaning) were remembered better than words examined for rhymes or for target letters.

processing—establishing more connections with long-term memories—makes new information more meaningful and more memorable. A famous experiment will illustrate this point.

Craik and Tulving (1975) had volunteer subjects examine a list of 60 common words presented on a screen one at a time. As each word appeared, the experimenters asked questions designed to influence how deeply each word was processed. For example, when BEAR appeared on the screen, the experimenters would ask one of three questions: "Is it in capital letters?" "Does it rhyme with *chair*?" "Is it an animal?" Craik and Tulving theorized that merely thinking about capital letters would not require processing the word as deeply as would comparing its sound with that of another word. But the deepest level of processing, they predicted, would occur when some aspect of the word's *meaning* was analyzed, as when they asked whether BEAR was an animal. Thus, they predicted that items processed more deeply would leave more robust traces in memory. And, sure enough, when the participants were later asked to pick the original 60 words out of a larger list of 180, they remembered the deeply processed words much better than words processed more superficially, as the graph in Figure 4.7 shows.

The Biological Basis of Working Memory   Although the details remain unclear, working memory probably holds information in the form of messages flashed repeatedly in nerve circuits. Brain imaging implicates brain regions in the frontal cortex (Beardsley, 1997b; Smith, 2000). Moreover, these regions also project to all the sensory parts of the brain and to areas known to be involved in long-term storage—just as we might expect from our three-stage model of memory. Brain imaging also suggests that the frontal lobes house some anatomically distinct "executive processes" that focus attention on information in short-term storage (Smith & Jonides, 1999). Together, these brain modules direct attention, set priorities, make plans, update the contents of working memory, and monitor the time sequence of events.

The Third Stage: Long-Term Memory

Can you remember who discovered classical conditioning? What is the name of a play by Shakespeare? How many birthdays have you had? Such information, along with everything else you know, is stored in your long-term memory (LTM), the last of the three memory stages.

Given the vast amount of data stored in LTM, it is a marvel that we can so easily gain access to so much of it. Remarkably, if someone asks your name, you don't have to rummage through a lifetime of information to find the answer. The method behind the marvel involves a special feature of long-term memory: Words and concepts are encoded by their meanings. This connects them, in turn, with other items that have similar meanings. Accordingly, you might picture LTM as a huge web of interconnected associations. As a result, good retrieval cues (stimuli that prompt the activation of a long-term memory) can travel though the web and help you quickly locate the item you want amid all the data stored there. Information scientists would very much like to fully understand this feature of LTM and use it to increase the search and retrieval speed of computers.

The Capacity and Duration of Long-Term Memory   How much information can long-term memory hold? As far as we know, it has unlimited storage capacity. (No one has yet maxed it out, so you don't have to conserve memory by cutting back on your studying.) LTM can store the information of a lifetime: all the experiences, events, information, emotions, skills, words, categories, rules, and judgments that have been transferred from working memory. Thus, your LTM contains your total knowledge of the world and of yourself. This makes long-term memory clearly the champion in both duration and storage capacity among the three stages of memory. But how does LTM manage to have unlimited capacity? That's another unsolved mystery of memory. Perhaps we might conceive of LTM as a sort of mental "scaffold," so the more associations you make, the more information it can hold.

Procedural memory allows experts like pitcher Josh Beckett to perform complex tasks automatically, without conscious recall of the details.

The Structure and Function of Long-Term Memory
With a broad overview of LTM in mind, let's look at some of the details of its two main components. One, a register for the things we know how to *do,* is called *procedural memory.* The other, which acts as storage for the information that we can *describe*—the facts we know and the experiences we remember—is called *declarative memory.* We know that procedural and declarative memory are distinct because brain damaged patients may lose one but not the other (as we will see).

Procedural Memory We call on **procedural memory** when riding a bicycle, tying shoelaces, or playing a musical instrument. Indeed, we use procedural memory to store the mental directions, or "procedures," for all our well-practiced skills (Schacter, 1996). Much of procedural memory operates outside of awareness: Only during the early phases of training, when we must concentrate on every move we make, must we think consciously about the details of our performance. Later, after the skill is thoroughly learned, it operates largely beyond the fringes of awareness, as when a concert pianist performs a piece without consciously recalling the individual notes. (Figure 4.8 should help you clarify the relationship between the two major components of long-term memory.)

Declarative Memory We use **declarative memory** to store facts, impressions, and events. Recalling the directions for driving to a certain location, such as the grocery store, depends on declarative memory (although knowing *how* to drive a car requires procedural memory). In contrast with procedural memory, using declarative memory more often requires conscious mental effort, as you can tell when people roll their eyes or make facial gestures while trying to recall facts or experiences.

To complicate matters, declarative memory itself has two major subdivisions, *episodic memory* and *semantic memory.* One deals with the rich detail of personal experiences (your first kiss), while the other simply stores information, without an "I-remember-when" context—information like the multiplication tables or the capital of your state.

Episodic memory is the division of declarative memory that stores personal experiences: your memory for events, or "episodes," in your life. It also stores *temporal coding* (or time tags) to identify *when* the event occurred and *context coding* that indicates *where* it took place. For example, you store memories of your recent vacation or of an unhappy love affair in episodic memory, along with codes for where and when these episodes occurred. In this way, episodic memory acts as your internal diary or *autobiographical memory.* You consult it when someone says, "Where were you on New Year's Eve?" or "What did you do in class last Tuesday?"

Semantic memory is the other division of declarative memory. (Again, refer to Figure 4.8, if this is becoming confusing.) It stores the basic meanings of words and concepts. Usually, semantic memory retains no information about the time and place in which its contents were acquired. Thus, you keep the meaning of *cat* in semantic memory—but probably not a recollection of the occasion on which you first learned the meaning of *cat.* In this respect, semantic memory more closely resembles an encyclopedia or a database than an autobiography. It stores a vast quantity of facts about names, faces, grammar, history, music, manners, scientific principles, and religious beliefs. All the facts and concepts you know are stored there, and you consult its registry when someone asks you, "Who was the third president?" or "What are the two major divisions of declarative memory?"

Procedural memory A division of LTM that stores memories for how things are done.

Declarative memory A division of LTM that stores explicit information; also known as *fact memory.* Declarative memory has two subdivisions, episodic memory and semantic memory.

Episodic memory A subdivision of declarative memory that stores memory for personal events, or "episodes."

Semantic memory A subdivision of declarative memory that stores general knowledge, including the meanings of words and concepts.

FIGURE 4.8
Components of Long-Term Memory

Declarative memory involves knowing specific information—knowing "what." It stores facts, personal experiences, language, concepts—things about which we might say, "I remember!" *Procedural memory* involves knowing "how"—particularly motor skills and behavioral learning.

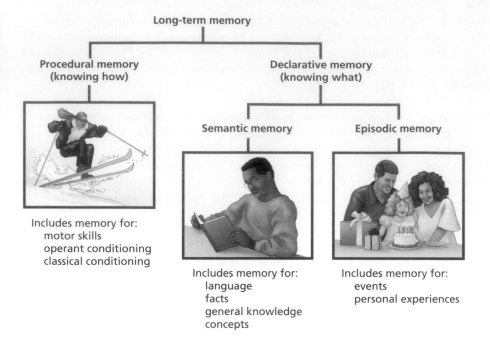

Long-term memory

Procedural memory (knowing how)

Declarative memory (knowing what)

Semantic memory

Episodic memory

Includes memory for:
motor skills
operant conditioning
classical conditioning

Includes memory for:
language
facts
general knowledge
concepts

Includes memory for:
events
personal experiences

Schemas When you attend a class, have dinner at a restaurant, make a phone call, or go to a birthday party, you know what to expect, because each of these events involve familiar scenarios. Cognitive psychologists call them **schemas**: clusters of knowledge in semantic memory that give us a context for understanding events (Squire, 2007). The exact contents of your schema depend, of course, on culture and personal experience, but the point is that we invoke our schemas to make new experiences meaningful.

Schemas allow us quick access to information. So, if someone says "birthday party," you can immediately draw on information that tells you what you might expect to be associated with a birthday party, such as eating cake and ice cream, singing "Happy Birthday," and opening presents. Just as important, when you invoke your "birthday party" schema, you don't have to sort through irrelevant knowledge in your memory—such as the information contained in your "attending class" schema or your "dinner at a restaurant" schema.

The details of how memory constructs its schemas are still murky—and, incidentally, of great interest to designers of computers and software—again, because human memory has such quick and efficient access to information. The main point, however, is that semantic long-term memory seems to be organized around schemas that make new experiences meaningful. We will have a closer look at schemas in the next chapter, when we discuss thinking.

Early Memories Most people have difficulty remembering events that happened before their third birthday, a phenomenon called **childhood amnesia**. This suggests to us that younger children have limited episodic memory ability. Learning clearly occurs, however, long before age 3, perhaps from the moment of birth. We see this in a baby that learns to recognize a parent's face or in a toddler learning language. Thus, we know that very young children have, at least, a semantic memory and a procedural memory.

Until recently, however, psychologists thought that childhood amnesia occurs because young children's brains have not yet made the neural connections required for episodic memory. New research, however, finds that the brain has created the necessary circuits by the end of the first year of life. Moreover, cognitive scientists have found that children as young as 9 months do show some signs of episodic memory—in the ability to imitate behaviors they have observed after a delay (Bauer et al., 2003). So why can't you remember your first birthday party? Part of the answer probably involves rudimentary language skills (for

Schema Cluster of related information that represents ideas or concepts in semantic memory. Schemas provide a context for understanding objects and events.

Childhood amnesia The inability to remember events during the first two or three years of life.

verbal encoding of memories) and the lack of the complex schemas older children and adults use to help them remember.

Other studies suggest that culture also influences people's early memories. For example, the earliest memories of Maori New Zealanders go back to 2.5 years, while Korean adults often do not remember anything before the age of 4. The difference seems to depend on how much the culture encourages children to tell detailed stories about their lives. "High elaborative" parents spend a lot of time encouraging children to talk about their daily experiences. This seems to strengthen early memories, which allows them to persist into adulthood (Leichtman, 2006; Winerman, 2005).

The Biological Basis of Long-Term Memory   Scientists have searched for the **engram,** the biological basis of long-term memory, for more than a century. One of their tactics involves looking for the neural circuitry that the brain uses to forge memories. Another approach goes to the level of synapses, looking for biochemical changes that might represent the physical *memory trace* within nerve cells. A tragic figure, known as H. M., represents the first of these two approaches.

On the TV show, Are You Smarter Than a 5th Grader?, *host Jeff Foxworthy's questions call for facts stored in semantic memory.*

Clues from the Case of H. M.   As a young man in 1953, H. M. lost most of his ability to form new memories—the result of an experimental brain operation performed as a last-ditch effort to treat his frequent epileptic seizures (Corkin, 2002; Hilts, 1995). Since that time, he has been almost completely unable to create new memories of the events in his life. At this writing, H. M. lives in a nursing home in Connecticut, where he has resided for decades. So profound is his memory impairment that he has never even learned to recognize the people who have taken care of him in the ensuing 55-plus years after his surgery.

Remarkably, H. M.'s memory for events prior to the operation remains normal, even as new experiences slip away before he can store them in long-term memory. He knows nothing of the 9/11 attacks, the moon landings, or the computer revolution. He cannot remember what he had for breakfast or the name of a visitor who left two minutes ago. Ironically, one of the very few things he has been able to retain is that he has a memory problem. Even so, he is mildly surprised to see an aging face in the mirror, expecting the younger man he was in 1953 (Milner et al., 1968; Rosenzweig, 1992). In brief, H. M. is a man caught in the present moment—which quickly fades away without being captured by memory. Yet, throughout this long ordeal, he has maintained generally good spirits and has worked willingly with psychologist Brenda Milner, whom he still cannot recognize.

H. M.'s medical record lists his condition as **anterograde amnesia**—which means a disability in forming new memories. To put the problem in cognitive terms, H. M. has a severe impairment in his ability to transfer new concepts and experiences from working memory to long-term memory (Scoville & Milner, 1957). From a biological perspective, the cause was removal of the hippocampus and amygdala on both sides of the brain. (See Figure 4.9.)

What have we learned from H. M.? Again speaking biologically, he has taught us that the hippocampus and amygdala are crucial to laying down *new* episodic memories, although they seem to have no role in retrieving *old* memories (Bechara et al., 1995; Wirth et al., 2003). Further, as we will see in a moment, H. M.'s case helps us understand the distinction between *procedural* memories and *declarative* memories. Surprisingly, H. M. is upbeat about his condition— even joking about his inability to remember—although, ironically, the removal of his amygdalas may have contributed to his positive disposition (Corkin, 2002).

Parts of the Brain Associated with Long-Term Memory   In the last two decades, neuroscientists have added much detail to the picture that H. M. has given us of human memory. We now know that the hippocampus (Figure 4.9) is implicated in Alzheimer's disease—which also involves loss of ability to make new declarative memories. And we have learned about a process called **consolidation,** whereby new memories

New Zealand Maoris often remember events from when they were 2½ years old—probably because their culture encourages children to tell stories about their lives.

Engram   The physical changes in the brain associated with a memory. It is also known as the *memory trace.*

Anterograde amnesia   The inability to form new memories (as opposed to retrograde amnesia, which involves the inability to remember information previously stored in memory).

Consolidation   The process by which short-term memories are changed to long-term memories over a period of time.

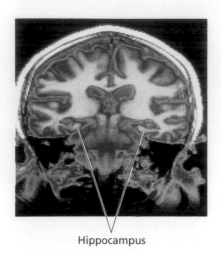

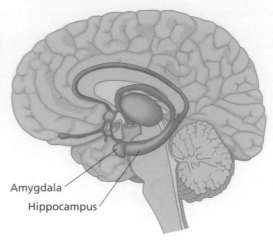

Amygdala

Hippocampus

Hippocampus

FIGURE 4.9
The Hippocampus and Amygdala

The hippocampus and amygdala were surgically removed from both sides of H. M.'s brain. To help yourself visualize where these structures lie, compare the drawing with the MRI image. The MRI shows the brain in cross section, with a slice through the hippocampus visible on each side.

> **CONNECTION • CHAPTER 14**
>
> Lasting biological changes may occur in the brains of individuals having posttraumatic stress disorder.

processed in the hippocampus gradually form permanent memories in the cortex. But, in a discovery just out of the lab, researchers report that new experiences can consolidate much more rapidly if they are associated with existing memory schemas (Squire, 2007; Tse et al., 2007). For rats this might mean solving a familiar maze problem. For you it might mean connecting what you learned about the hippocampus in Chapter 2 with the new information about its role in consolidation that you are learning here.

Neuroscientists have also discovered that the hippocampus's neural neighbor, the amygdala, processes memories that have strong emotional associations (Bechara et al., 1995). These emotional associations, it seems, act as an aid for quick access and retrieval (Dolan, 2002). The amygdala, then, is probably the mechanism responsible for the persistent and troubling memories reported by soldiers and others who have experienced violent assaults. In some cases, these memories can be so disturbing that they constitute a condition known as *posttraumatic stress disorder.*

But the amygdala and hippocampus aren't the whole memory show. When you bring to mind the colors of the flag, memory draws on the same visual circuits used when you see a real flag (Paller, 2004). Likewise, when you imagine riding a bicycle or hitting a ball, the image in your mind arises from the same motor pathways you would use if you were actually performing the action. That is, the brain uses some of the same circuits for memory that it uses for sensation, perception, and motor responses (Kandel & Squire, 2000; Packard & Knowlton, 2002). Under some conditions, neuroscientists have even learned to identify specific patterns of activity in the brain that correspond to certain memories (Polyn et al., 2005).

Memories, Neurons, and Synapses   A standard plot in soap operas and movies depicts a person who develops *amnesia* (loss of memory) after a blow or injury to the head. But does research support this soap-opera neuroscience? In the modern picture of memory at the level of individual neurons, memories form initially as fragile chemical traces at the synapse and consolidate into more permanent synaptic changes over time. During this consolidation process, memories are especially vulnerable to interference by new experience, certain drugs, or a blow to the head (Doyère et al., 2007). The diagnosis, in the event of significant memory loss, would be **retrograde amnesia,** or loss of prior memory. (Note that retrograde amnesia is the opposite of H. M.'s problem, *anterograde* amnesia, which was the inability to form *new* memories.)

Memories can be strengthened, as well as weakened, during consolidation—especially by a person's emotional state. Research shows, however, that positive and negative emotions have vastly different effects on attention and therefore on memory. So, if you are happy, you tend to look at situations broadly and remember the "big picture." But if you are being robbed at gunpoint, you will most likely attend to the gun while giving less notice to details of the robber's appearance. In general, we can say that emotional arousal accounts for our most vivid memories, but the scope of happy memories tends to be larger, while negative emotions tend to restrict the focus of our memories (Dingfelder, 2005; Levine & Bluck, 2004).

Retrograde amnesia   The inability to remember information previously stored in memory. (Compare with anterograde amnesia.)

From an evolutionary perspective, emotion plays a highly adaptive role in memory. If you survive a frightening encounter with a bear, for example, you are quite likely to remember to avoid bears in the future. The underlying biology involves emotion-related chemicals, such as epinephrine (adrenalin) and certain stress hormones, which act to enhance memory for emotion-laden experiences (McGaugh, 2000).

PSYCHOLOGYMATTERS

"Flashbulb" Memories: Where Were You When . . . ?

The closest most people will come to having a "photographic memory" is a **flashbulb memory,** an exceptionally clear recollection of an important and emotion-packed event (Brown & Kulik, 1977). You probably harbor a few such memories: a tragic accident, a death, a graduation, a big victory. It's as though you had made a flash picture in your mind of the striking scene. (The term was coined in the days when flash photography required a disposable "flashbulb" for each picture.)

Cognitive psychologists have taken advantage of the fact that large numbers of people form flashbulb memories of certain emotionally charged events in the news, such as the September 11 attacks, Princess Diana's death, the shootings at Columbine high school, or the O. J. Simpson murder trial verdict (Pillemer, 1984; Schmolck et al., 2000). These memories usually record precisely where the individuals were at the time they received the news, what they were doing, and the emotions they felt.

Remarkably, flashbulb memories can be quite accurate. Further, studies show that the more personally involved a person is at the time, the more accurate and durable these memories will be later (Berntsen & Rubin, 2007). Still, flashbulb memories can become distorted over time (Neisser, 1991). For example, on the morning after the Challenger space shuttle explosion, psychology professors asked their students to describe the circumstances under which they had heard the news. Three years later the same students were again asked to recall the event. Of the latter accounts, about one-third gave substantially different stories, mostly about details on which they had previously not focused their attention at the time. It is noteworthy that students whose recollections were seriously flawed reported a high level of confidence in their memories (Winograd & Neisser, 1992). The general pattern appears to be this: Up to a year later, most flashbulb memories are nearly identical to reports given immediately after the event, while recollections gathered after two or three years show substantial distortions (Schmolck et al., 2000). What doesn't change, oddly enough, is people's confidence in their recollections.

The attacks on the World Trade Center and the Pentagon were shocking events, and many Americans have "flashbulb" memories that include where they were and what they were doing when they learned of the attacks.

Flashbulb memory   A clear and vivid long-term memory of an especially meaningful and emotional event.

CheckYourUnderstanding

1. **RECALL:** Which part of memory has the smallest capacity? (That is, which part of memory is considered the "bottleneck" in the memory system?)

2. **RECALL:** Which part of long-term memory stores autobiographical information?

3. **RECALL:** To get material into permanent storage, it must be made meaningful while it is in _____.

4. **APPLICATION:** As you study the vocabulary in this book, which of the following methods would result in the deepest level of processing?

a. learning the definition given in the marginal glossary
b. marking each term with a highlighter each time it occurs in a sentence in the text
c. thinking of an example of each term
d. having a friend read a definition, with you having to identify the term in question form, as on the TV show *Jeopardy*

5. **UNDERSTANDING THE CORE CONCEPT:** As the information in this book passes from one stage of your memory to the next, the information becomes more _____.

Answers 1. Working memory or short-term memory **2.** Episodic memory **3.** Working memory or short-term memory **4.** c **5.** meaningful or associated with other information in LTM

HOW DO WE FORM MEMORIES?   **151**

4.3 KEY QUESTION
HOW DO WE RETRIEVE MEMORIES?

Memory has several surprising tricks that it can play during retrieval. One involves the possibility of retrieving a memory that you didn't know you had—which tells us that some memories can be successfully encoded and stored without full awareness. Another quirk involves our being both quite confident of a memory and quite wrong—as we saw in flashbulb memories. Our Core Concept summarizes the retrieval process this way:

core concept | Whether memories are implicit or explicit, successful retrieval depends on how they were encoded and how they are cued.

Implicit and Explicit Memory

We will begin our exploration of retrieval with another lesson from H. M. Surprisingly, he has retained the ability to learn new motor skills, even though he has lost most of his ability to remember facts and events. For example, H. M. learned the difficult skill of mirror writing—writing while looking at his hands in a mirror (Milner et al., 1968; Raymond, 1989). In fact, his *procedural* memory for motor tasks is quite normal, even though he cannot remember learning these skills and doesn't even know that he knows how to perform them.

But you don't have to have brain damage like H. M. to have memories of which you are unaware. A normal memory has disconnected islands of information, too. For over a hundred years psychologists have realized that people with no memory defects can know something without knowing that they know it. Psychologist Daniel Schacter (1992, 1996) calls this **implicit memory**: memory that can affect your behavior without coming into full awareness. By contrast, **explicit memory** requires conscious awareness.

Procedural memories are often implicit, as when golfers remember how to swing a club without thinking about how to move their bodies. Likewise, H. M.'s mirror writing was an implicit memory. But implicit memories are not limited to procedural memory—nor is explicit memory the same as declarative memory. Information in your semantic store can be either *explicit* (such as in remembering the material you have studied for a test) or *implicit* (such as knowing the color of the building in which your psychology class is held). The general rule is this: A memory is implicit if it can affect behavior or mental processes without becoming conscious. Explicit memories, on the other hand, always involve consciousness during storage and retrieval.

In some striking new studies, Brian Skotko and his colleagues (2004) have shown that H. M. can learn some new semantic material through implicit channels—that is, even though he doesn't know he has learned it. To do this, Skotko's group exploited H. M.'s favorite pastime of doing crossword puzzles. They devised crosswords that linked knowledge H. M. had already acquired at the time of his operation with new information: For example, H. M. knew that polio was a dread disease, but the polio vaccine was not discovered until after his surgery, and so he had no knowledge of it. Yet by working on a specially designed crossword puzzle over a 5-day period, H. M. learned to respond correctly to the item, "childhood disease successfully treated by Salk vaccine." Similarly, he was able to learn that Jacqueline Kennedy, wife of assassinated President John Kennedy, subsequently became Jacqueline Onassis. This technique, then, shows that H. M.'s problem is primarily one of explicit memory.

Retrieval Cues

For accurate retrieval, both implicit and explicit memories require good cues. You have some feeling for such cues if you've ever used search terms in Google

Implicit memory   A memory that has not deliberately learned or of which you have no conscious awareness.

Explicit memory   Memory that has been processed with attention and can be consciously recalled.

or another Internet search engine: Make a poor choice of terms, and you can come up either with nothing—or with Internet garbage. Things work in much the same way in long-term memory, where a successful search requires good mental **retrieval cues,** the "search terms" used to recover a memory. Sometimes the only retrieval cue required to bring back a long-dormant experience is a certain odor, such as the smell of fresh-baked cookies that you associated with visiting Grandma's house. At other times the retrieval cue might be an emotion, as when a person struggling with depression gets caught in a maelstrom of depressing memories.

On the other hand, some memories, especially semantic ones, are not so easily cued. During a test, for example, you can draw a blank if the wording of a question doesn't jibe with the way you framed the material in your mind as you were studying. In other words, your memory may fail if the question isn't a good retrieval cue. In general, whether a retrieval cue is effective depends on the type of memory being sought and the web of associations in which the memory is embedded.

In the following paragraphs, we will illustrate how retrieval cues can activate, or *prime,* implicit memories. Then we will return to the more familiar territory of explicit memory to show how recognition and recall are cued. Later in the chapter, we will discuss the failure of retrieval cues in the context of forgetting.

Retrieving Implicit Memories by Priming A quirk of implicit memory landed former Beatle George Harrison in court (Schacter, 1996). Lawyers for a singing group known as the Chiffons claimed that the melody in Harrison's song "My Sweet Lord" was nearly identical to that of the Chiffon classic "He's So Fine." Harrison denied that he deliberately borrowed the melody but conceded that he had heard the Chiffons's tune prior to writing his own. The court agreed, stating that Harrison's borrowing was a product of "subconscious memory." Everyday life abounds with similar experiences, says Daniel Schacter (1996). You may have proposed an idea to a friend and had it rejected, but weeks later your friend excitedly proposed the same idea to you, as if it were entirely new.

In such real-life situations it can be hard to say what prompts an implicit memory to surface. Psychologists have, however, developed ways to "prime" implicit memories in the lab (Schacter, 1996). To illustrate, imagine that you have volunteered for a memory experiment. First, you are shown a list of words for several seconds:

assassin, octopus, avocado, mystery, sheriff, climate

Then, an hour later, the experimenter asks you to examine another list and indicate which items you recognize from the earlier list: twilight, assassin, dinosaur, and mystery. That task is easy for you. But then the experimenter shows you some words with missing letters and asks you to fill in the blanks:

c h _ _ _ _ n k, o _ t _ _ _ u s, _ o g _ y _ _ _ , _ l _ m _ t e

It is likely that answers for two of these pop readily into mind, *octopus* and *climate.* But chances are that you will be less successful with the other two words, *chipmunk* and *bogeyman.* The reason for this difference has to do with **priming,** the procedure of providing cues that stimulate memories without awareness of the connection between the cue and the retrieved memory. Because you had been primed with the words *octopus* and *climate,* they more easily "popped out" in your consciousness than did the words that had not been primed.

Retrieving Explicit Memories Anything stored in LTM must be "filed" according to its pattern or meaning. Consequently, the best way to add material to long-term memory is to associate it, while in working memory, with material already stored in LTM. We have called that process *elaborative rehearsal.* Encoding many

CONNECTION • CHAPTER 8
Priming is also a technique for studying nonconscious processes.

Retrieval cue Stimulus that is used to bring a memory to consciousness or to cue a behavior.

Priming A technique for cuing implicit memories by providing cues that stimulate a memory without awareness of the connection between the cue and the retrieved memory.

such connections by elaborative rehearsal gives you more ways of accessing the information, much as a town with many access roads can be approached from many directions.

Meaningful Organization One way of retrieving information from explicit memory involves getting just the general idea or *gist* of an event, rather than a memory of the event as it actually occurred. We saw this earlier in the penny demonstration, but let's look at another example of gist. Suppose you hear the sentence, "The book was returned to the library by Mary." Later, when asked if you heard the sentence, "Mary returned the book to the library," you may indeed mistakenly remember having heard the second sentence. This happens because we tend to remember the meaning or sense of the words—the **gist**— rather than the exact words themselves.

If you'll forgive us for repeating ourselves, your authors want to underscore the practical consequences of LTM being organized by meaning. *Storing new information in LTM usually requires that you make the information meaningful while it is in working memory.* This means that you must associate new information with things you already know. Sometimes it is important to remember all the details accurately (as in memorizing a mathematical formula), while at other times the important thing is to remember the gist (as when you read the case study of H. M.). In attempting to remember the gist, it is especially important to think of personal examples of the concepts and ideas you want to remember. (So, can you think of another example of *gist?*)

Recall and Recognition The cues we use to search for explicit memories come in two main forms. One involves the kinds of retrieval cues used on essay tests, the other involves the cues found on multiple choice tests. Essay tests require **recall,** a task in which you must retrieve a memory from minimal retrieval cues. That is, on an essay test, you must create an answer almost entirely from memory, with the help of only minimal cues from a question such as, "What are the two ways to cue explicit memories?"

Recognition, on another hand, is the method required by multiple-choice tests. In a recognition task, you merely identify whether a stimulus has been previously experienced. Normally, recognition is less demanding than recall because the cues available for a recognition task are much more complete. Incidentally, the reason people say, "I'm terrible with names, but I never forget a face," is because recall (names) is usually tougher than recognition (faces).

The police use recognition when they ask an eyewitness to identify a suspected robber in a lineup. The witness is required only to match an image from memory (the robber) against a present stimulus (a suspect in the lineup). And what would be a comparable recall task? A witness working with a police artist to make a drawing of a suspect must recall, entirely from memory, the suspect's facial characteristics.

Other Factors Affecting Retrieval

We have seen that the ability to retrieve information from explicit declarative memory depends on whether information was encoded and elaborated to make it meaningful. You won't be surprised to learn that alertness, stress level, drugs, and general knowledge also affect retrieval. Less well known, however, are the following influences related to the context in which you encoded a memory and also the context in which you are remembering.

Encoding Specificity The more closely the retrieval cues match the form in which the information was encoded, the better they will cue the appropriate memory. For example, you may have encountered your psychology professor at the grocery store, but you needed a moment to recognize who she or he was, because the context didn't cue you to think "psychology professor." On the other hand, you may have

Gist (pronounced *JIST*) The sense or meaning, as contrasted with the exact details.

Recall A retrieval method in which one must reproduce previously presented information.

Recognition A retrieval method in which one must identify present stimuli as having been previously presented.

been talking to a childhood friend, and your conversation cued a flood of memories that you hadn't thought about for years. These two experiences are examples of the **encoding specificity principle,** which says that successful recall depends on how well the retrieval cues match the cues present at the time a memory was encoded and stored.

As far as studying for your classes is concerned, one of the most important things you can do is to anticipate the retrieval cues you will get on the test and organize your learning around those probable cues. Students who merely read the material and hope for the best may have trouble. In fact, this is such a common problem for students that psychologist Robert Bjork (2000) has suggested that teachers introduce "desirable difficulties" into their courses to encourage students to encode the material in multiple ways. By desirable difficulties, Bjork means that students should be given assignments that make them come to grips with the material in many different ways—project, papers, problems, and presentations—rather than just memorizing the material and parroting it back. By doing so, the professor would help students build more connections into the web of associations into which a memory is embedded—and the more connections there are, the easier it becomes to cue a memory.

Mood and Memory Information processing isn't just about facts and events, it's also about emotions and moods. We use the expressions "feeling blue" and "looking at the world through rose-colored glasses" to suggest that moods can bias our perceptions. Likewise, our moods can also affect what we remember, a phenomenon called **mood-congruent memory.** If you have ever had an episode of uncontrollable giggling, you know how a euphoric mood can trigger one silly thought after another. And at the other end of the mood spectrum, people who are depressed often report that all their thoughts have a melancholy aspect. In this way, depression can perpetuate itself through retrieval of depressing memories (Sakaki, 2007).

Not just a laboratory curiosity, mood-congruent memory can also have important health implications. Says memory researcher Gordon Bower, "Doctors assess what to do with you based on your complaints and how much you complain" (McCarthy, 1991). Because depressed people are likely to emphasize their medical symptoms, they may receive treatment that is much different from that dispensed to more upbeat individuals with the same disease. This, says Bower, means that physicians must learn to take a person's psychological state into consideration when deciding on a diagnosis and a course of therapy.

Prospective Memory One of the most common memory tasks involves remembering to perform some action at a future time—such as keeping a doctor's appointment, going to lunch with a friend, or setting out the garbage cans on the appointed day. Psychologists call this **prospective memory.** Surprisingly, this important process of remembering-to-remember has received relatively little study. We do know that a failure in prospective memory can have consequences that range from merely inconvenient and embarrassing to horrific:

> After a change in his usual routine, an adoring father forgot to turn toward the day care center and instead drove his usual route to work at the university. Several hours later, his infant son, who had been quietly asleep in the back seat, was dead. (Einstein & McDaniel, 2005, p. 286)

How could such a terrible thing happen? The father probably became distracted from his intended task and fell into his customary routine. In situations like this, where people have to remember to deviate from their customary routine, they usually rely on *continuous monitoring,* which means trying to keep the intended action in mind. Continuous monitoring, however, can be easily

Because mood affects memory, depressed people may remember and report more negative symptoms to a physician. As a result, their treatment may differ from that given to patients with the same condition who are not depressed.

Encoding specificity principle The doctrine that memory is encoded and stored with specific cues related to the context in which it was formed. The more closely the retrieval cues match the form in which the information was encoded, the better it will be remembered.

Mood-congruent memory A memory process that selectively retrieves memories that match (are congruent with) one's mood.

Prospective memory The aspect of memory that enables one to remember to take some action in the future—as remembering a doctor's appointment.

derailed by distraction or by habit. So, if you find yourself faced with an important task requiring a change in a long-established routine, your best bet is to use a more reliable prompt, such as note on the dashboard. Another good technique involves thinking of a specific cue you expect to encounter just before you must perform the required task. In the case of the father who intended to take his son to the day care center, he might have imagined a prominent landmark that he would see just before the turn off his accustomed route and then imagined that landmark as a memory cue.

The Washington Monument is an example of a tapered stone object that is topped by a pyramid-shaped point. Can you recall the name for such objects? Or, is it "on the tip of your tongue"?

PSYCHOLOGYMATTERS
On the Tip of Your Tongue

Try to answer as many of the following questions as you can:

- What is the North American equivalent of the reindeer?
- What do artists call the board on which they mix paints?
- What is the name for a tall, four-sided stone monument with a point at the top of its shaft?
- What instrument do navigators use to determine latitude by sighting on the stars?
- What is the name of a sheath used to contain a sword or dagger?
- What is the name of a small Chinese boat usually propelled with a single oar or pole?

If this demonstration works as expected, you couldn't remember the answer, but you had a strong sense that you had it somewhere in memory. We might say that the answer was "on the tip of your tongue." Appropriately enough, psychologists refer to this sort of a near-miss memory as the **TOT phenomenon** (Brown, 1991). Surveys show that most people have a TOT experience about once a week. Among those who watch *Jeopardy* or play the board game Trivial Pursuit, it may occur even more frequently. And, according to a recent study, deaf persons who use sign language sometimes have a "tip of the fingers" (TOF) experience, in which they are sure they know a word, but cannot quite retrieve the sign (Thompson et al., 2005). Obviously, then, some fundamental memory process underlies both the TOT and the TOF phenomena.

The most common TOT experiences center on names of personal acquaintances, names of famous persons, and familiar objects (Brown, 1991). About half the time, the target words finally do pop into mind, usually within about one agonizing minute. Most reports suggest that the experience is uncomfortable (Brown & McNeill, 1966).

What accounts for the TOT phenomenon? One possibility—often exploited in laboratory studies—involves inadequate context cues. This was probably what made you stumble on some of the items above: We did not give you enough context to activate the schema associated with the correct answer.

Another possibility involves *interference*: when another memory blocks access or retrieval, as when you were thinking of Jan when you unexpectedly meet Jill (Schacter, 1999). And, even though you were unable to recall some of the correct words in our demonstration of TOT (caribou, palette, obelisk, sextant, scabbard, sampan), you would probably have spotted the right answer in a recognition format. It's also likely that some features of the sought-for words abruptly popped to mind ("I know it begins with an *s!*"), even though the words themselves eluded you. So, the TOT phenomenon occurs during a recall attempt, when there is a weak match between retrieval cues and the encoding of the word in long-term memory.

And we'll bet you can't name all seven dwarfs.

TOT phenomenon The inability to recall a word, while knowing that it is in memory. People often describe this frustrating experience as having the word "on the tip of the tongue."

CheckYourUnderstanding

1. **APPLICATION:** Remembering names is usually harder than remembering faces because names require _____, while faces merely require _____.

2. **APPLICATION:** At a high school class reunion you are likely to experience a flood of memories that would be unlikely to come to mind under other circumstances. What memory process explains this?

3. **APPLICATION:** Give an example of mood-congruent memory.

4. **APPLICATION:** Give an example of a situation that would require prospective memory.

5. **RECALL:** A person experiencing the TOT phenomenon is unable to _____ a specific word.

6. **UNDERSTANDING THE CORE CONCEPT:** An implicit memory may be activated by priming, and an explicit memory may be activated by a recognizable stimulus. In either case, a psychologist would say that these memories are being
   a. cued.
   b. recognized.
   c. encoded.
   d. chunked.

4.4 KEY QUESTION
WHY DOES MEMORY SOMETIMES FAIL US?

We forget appointments and anniversaries. During today's test you can't remember the terms you studied the night before. Or a familiar name seems just out of your mental reach. Yet, ironically, we sometimes cannot rid memory of an unhappy event. So, why does memory play these tricks on us—making us remember what we would rather forget and forget what we want to remember?

According to memory expert Daniel Schacter, the blame falls on what he terms the "seven sins" of memory: *transience, absent-mindedness, blocking, misattribution, suggestibility, bias,* and *unwanted persistence* (Schacter, 1999, 2001). Further, he claims that these seven problems are really the consequences of some very useful features of human memory. From an evolutionary perspective, they are features that stood our ancestors in good stead and so are preserved in our own memory systems. Our Core Concept puts this notion more succinctly:

> **Most of our memory problems arise from memory's "seven sins"—which are really by-products of otherwise adaptive features of human memory.**

core concept

While looking into the "seven sins," we will have the opportunity to consider such everyday memory problems as forgetting where you left your car keys or the inability to forget an unpleasant experience. Finally, we will look at some strategies for improving memory by overcoming some of Schacter's "seven sins"—with special emphasis on how certain memory techniques can improve your studying. We begin with the frustration of fading memories.

Transience: Fading Memories Cause Forgetting

How would you do on a rigorous test of the course work you took a year ago? We thought so—because memories seem to weaken with time. Although no one has directly observed a human memory trace fade and disappear, much circumstantial evidence points to this **transience,** or impermanence, of long-term memory—the first of Schacter's "sins."

Ebbinghaus and the Forgetting Curve   In a classic study of transience, pioneering psychologist Hermann Ebbinghaus (1908/1973) first learned lists of

Transience   The impermanence of a long-term memory. Transience is based on the idea that long-term memories gradually fade in strength over time.

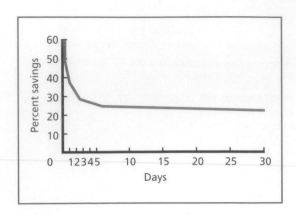

FIGURE 4.10
Ebbinghaus's Forgetting Curve

Ebbinghaus's forgetting curve shows that the savings demonstrated by relearning drops rapidly and reaches a plateau, below which little more is forgotten.

(*Source:* P. G. Zimbardo and R. J. Gerrig, *Psychology and Life*, 15th ed. Published by Allyn and Bacon, Boston, MA. Copyright © 1999 by Pearson Education. Reprinted by permission of the publisher.)

◄ **CONNECTION • CHAPTER 2**

PET and fMRI are brain scanning techniques that form images of especially active regions in the brain.

Forgetting curve A graph plotting the amount of retention and forgetting over time for a certain batch of material, such as a list of nonsense syllables. The typical forgetting curve is steep at first, becoming flatter as time goes on.

nonsense syllables (such as POV, KEB, FIC, and RUZ) and tried to recall them over varying time intervals. This worked well over short periods, up to a few days. But to measure memory after long delays of weeks or months, when recall had failed completely, Ebbinghaus had to invent another method: He measured the number of trials required to *relearn* the original list. Because it generally took fewer trials to relearn a list than to learn it originally, the difference indicated a "savings" that could serve as a measure of memory. (If the original learning required 10 trials and relearning required 7 trials, the savings was 30%.) By using the *savings method*, Ebbinghaus could trace what happened to memory over long periods of time. The curve obtained from combining data from many experiments appears in Figure 4.10. There you can see how the graph initially plunges steeply and then flattens out over longer intervals. This, curve, then, represents one of Ebbinghaus's most important discoveries: *For relatively meaningless material, we have a rapid initial loss of memory, followed by a declining rate of loss.* Subsequent research shows that this **forgetting curve** captures the pattern of transience by which we forget much of the verbal material we learn.

Modern psychologists have built on Ebbinghaus's work, but they now have more interest in how we remember *meaningful* material, such as information you read in this book. Meaningful memories seem to fade, too—just not as rapidly as did Ebbinghaus's nonsense syllables. Modern work sometimes uses brain scanning techniques, such as fMRI and PET, to visualize the diminishing brain activity that characterizes forgetting (Schacter, 1996, 1999).

Not all memories, however, follow the classic forgetting curve. We often retain motor skills, for example, substantially intact in procedural memory for many years, even without practice—"just like riding a bicycle." The same goes for especially memorable emotional experiences, such as "flashbulb" incidents.

Interference   Schacter tells us that one of the most common causes of transience comes from *interference*—when one item prevents us from forming a robust memory for another item. This often occurs when you attempt to learn two conflicting things in succession, such as if you had a French class followed by a Spanish class.

What is likely to cause interference? Three main factors top the list:

1. *The greater the similarity between two sets of material to be learned, the greater the interference between them is likely to be.*   So, French and Spanish classes are more likely to interfere with each other than are, say, psychology and accounting.

2. *Meaningless material is more vulnerable to interference than meaningful material.*   Because LTM is organized by meaning, you will have more trouble remembering two locker combinations than you will two news bulletins. (The exception occurs when you experience a direct conflict in meaning, as when two of your professors seem to be telling you conflicting things.)

3. *Emotional material can be an especially powerful cause of interference.*   So, if you broke up with your true love last night, you will probably forget what your literature professor says in class today.

Interference commonly arises when an old habit gets in the way of learning a new response, as we saw in the case of the father who forgot to stop at the day care center. Interference can also happen when people switch from one word-processing program to another. And, of course, interference accounts for the legendary problem old dogs have in learning new tricks. Everyday life offers many more examples, but interference theory groups them in two main categories, *proactive interference* and *retroactive interference*.

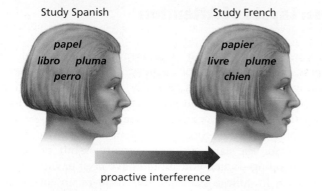

Study Spanish
papel
libro pluma
perro

Study French
papier
livre plume
chien

Recall French

French 101
Midterm exam

papier_____

livre_____

plume_____

chien_____

proactive interference

Study Spanish
papel
libro pluma
perro

Study French
papier
livre plume
chien

Recall Spanish

Spanish 101
Midterm exam

papel_____

libro_____

pluma_____

perro_____

retroactive interference

FIGURE 4.11
Two Types of Interference

In proactive interference, earlier learning (Spanish) interferes with memory for later information (French). In retroactive interference, new information (French) interferes with memory for information learned earlier (Spanish).

Proactive Interference   When an old memory disrupts the learning and remembering of new information, **proactive interference** is the culprit. An example of proactive interference occurs every January, when we all have trouble remembering to write the correct date on our checks. *Pro-* means "forward," so in proactive interference, old memories act forward in time to block your attempts at new learning.

Retroactive Interference   When the opposite happens—when new information prevents your remembering older information—we can blame forgetting on **retroactive interference.** *Retro-* means "backward"; the newer material reaches back into your memory to push old material out of memory. (See Figure 4.11.) In a computer, retroactive interference occurs when you save a new document in place of an old one. Much the same thing happens in your own memory when you meet two new people in succession, and the second name causes retroactive interference that makes you forget the first one.

The Serial Position Effect   You may have noticed that the first and last parts of a poem or a vocabulary list are usually easier to learn and remember than the middle portion. In general, the *primacy effect* refers to the relative ease of remembering the first items in a series, while the *recency effect* refers to the robustness of memory for the most recent items. Together, with diminished memory for the middle portion, we term this the **serial position effect.** To illustrate, when you are introduced to several people in succession, you are more likely to remember the names of those you met first and last than you are those you met in between. (That's assuming other factors are equal, such as the commonness of their names, distinctiveness of their appearance, and their personalities.)

How does interference theory explain the serial position effect? Unlike the material at the ends of the poem or list, the part in the middle is exposed to a double dose of interference—both retroactively and proactively. That is, the middle part receives interference from both directions, while material at either end gets interference from only one side. So, in view of the serial position effect, perhaps it would be helpful to pay special attention to the material in the middle of this chapter.

Proactive interference   A cause of forgetting by which previously stored information prevents learning and remembering new information.

Retroactive interference   A cause of forgetting by which newly learned information prevents retrieval of previously stored material.

Serial position effect   A form of interference related to the sequence in which information is presented. Generally, items in the middle of the sequence are less well remembered than items presented first or last.

Absent-Mindedness: Lapses of Attention Cause Forgetting

Misplacing your car keys results from a shift in attention. Which of the seven "sins" does this represent?

When you misplace your car keys or forget an anniversary, you have had an episode of **absent-mindedness,** the second "sin" of memory. It's not that the memory has disappeared from your brain circuits. Rather, you have suffered a retrieval failure caused by shifting your attention elsewhere. In the case of a forgotten anniversary, the attention problem occurred on the retrieval end—when you were concentrating on something that took your attention away from the upcoming anniversary. And as for the car keys, your attentive shift probably occurred during the original encoding—when you should have been paying attention to where you laid the keys. In college students, this form of absent-mindedness commonly comes from listening to music or watching TV while studying.

This kind of encoding error was also at work in the "depth of processing" experiments we discussed earlier: People who encoded information shallowly ("Does the word contain an *e?*") were less able to recall the target word than those who encoded it deeply ("Is it an animal?"). Yet another example can be found in demonstrations of *change blindness:* In one study, participants viewed a movie clip in which one actor who was asking directions was replaced by another actor while they were briefly hidden by two men carrying a door in front of them. Amazingly, fewer than half of the viewers noticed the change (Simons & Levin, 1998). Much the same thing may happen to you in the magic trick demonstration in Figure 4.12.

Blocking: Access Problems

Blocking, the third of Schacter's seven "sins" of memory, occurs when we lose access to the information we have in memory. You may have experienced blocking when you see familiar people in new surroundings and can't remember their names. The most thoroughly studied form of blocking, however, involves the maddening "tip-of-the-tongue" (TOT) experience: when you *know you know* the name for something but can't retrieve it. As we saw earlier, the TOT phenomenon often results from poor context cues that fail to activate the necessary memory schema.

Stress, too, can produce blocking, perhaps through failure to sustain one's focus of attention. Similarly, distraction has been shown to cause blocking on prospective memory tasks, such as remembering to perform a certain action at a certain time. Age plays a role, too, with blocking becoming a greater problem as one grows older.

Studies of brain-injury patients who exhibit blocking point to specific regions of the brain that, when damaged, seem especially likely to interfere with memory. These include the frontal lobes, hippocampus, and temporal lobe. These studies suggest that blocking involves many different brain circuits, because damage in different regions produces different kinds of blocks, such as loss of proper names, but not the names of objects.

Misattribution: Memories in the Wrong Context

All three "sins" discussed so far make memories unavailable in one way or another. But these are not the only kinds of memory problems we experience. For example, we can retrieve memories, but associate them with the wrong time, place, or person. Schacter (1999) calls this **misattribution.** It stems from the reconstructive nature of long-term memory. In the penny demonstration at the beginning of the chapter, you learned that we commonly retrieve incomplete memories and fill in the blanks so as to make them meaningful to us. This paves the way to mistakes that arise from connecting information with the wrong, but oh-so-sensible, context.

Absent-mindedness Forgetting caused by lapses in attention.

Blocking Forgetting that occurs when an item in memory cannot be accessed or retrieved. Blocking is caused by interference.

Misattribution A memory fault that occurs when memories are retrieved but are associated with the wrong time, place, or person.

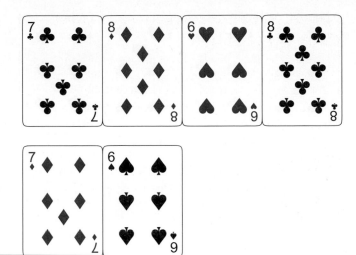

FIGURE 4.12A
The "Magic of Memory"

Pick one of the cards. Stare at it intently for at least 15 seconds, being careful not to shift your gaze to the other cards. Then turn the page.

Here's an example of misattribution: Psychologist Donald Thompson was accused of rape, based on a victim's detailed, but mistaken, description of her assailant (Thompson, 1988). Fortunately for Thompson, his alibi was indisputable. At the time of the crime he was being interviewed live on television—about memory distortions. The victim, it turned out, had been watching the interview just before she was raped and had misattributed the assault to Thompson.

Misattribution also can cause people to believe mistakenly that other people's ideas are their own. This sort of misattribution occurs when a person hears an idea and keeps it in memory, while forgetting its source. Unintentional plagiarism comes from this form of misattribution, as we saw earlier in the case of Beatle George Harrison.

Yet another type of misattribution can cause people to remember something they did not experience at all. Such was the case with volunteers who were asked to remember a set of words associated with a particular theme: *door, glass, pane, shade, ledge, sill, house, open, curtain, frame, view, breeze, sash, screen,* and *shutter.* Under these conditions, many participants later remembered *window,* even though that word was not on the list (Roediger & McDermott, 1995, 2000). This result again shows the power of context cues in determining the content of memory. And it demonstrates yet again how people tend to create and retrieve memories based on meaning.

Suggestibility: External Cues Distort or Create Memories

Suggestion can also distort or even create memories, a possibility of particular concern to the courts. Witnesses may be interviewed by attorneys or by the police, who may make suggestions about the facts of a case—either deliberately or unintentionally—that might alter a witness's memory. Such concerns about **suggestibility** prompted Elizabeth Loftus and John Palmer to find out just how easily eyewitness memories could be distorted.

Memory Distortion   Participants in the Loftus and Palmer study first watched a film of two cars colliding. Then, the experimenters asked them to estimate how fast the cars had been moving (Loftus, 1979, 1984; Loftus & Palmer, 1973). Half of the witnesses were asked, "How fast were the cars going when they *smashed* into each other?" Their estimates, it turned out, were about 25% higher than those given by respondents who were asked, "How fast were the cars going when they *hit* each other?" This distortion of memory caused by misinformation has been dubbed, appropriately, as the **misinformation effect**.

Clearly, the Loftus and Palmer study showed that memories can be distorted and embellished by cues and suggestions given at the time of recall. But memories

Suggestibility   The process of memory distortion as the result of deliberate or inadvertent suggestion.

Misinformation effect   The distortion of memory by suggestion or misinformation.

FIGURE 4.12B
The "Magic of Memory" (continued)

Your card is gone! How did we do it? We didn't read your mind; it was your own *reconstructive memory* and the "sin" of *absent-mindedness* playing card tricks on you. If you don't immediately see how the trick works, try it again with a different card.

can also be *created* by similar methods. And it can be done without the individual's awareness that memory has been altered.

Fabricated Memories   The famed developmental psychologist, Jean Piaget, described a vivid memory of a traumatic event from his own early childhood:

> One of my first memories would date, if it were true, from my second year. I can still see, most clearly, the following scene in which I believed until I was about fifteen. I was sitting in my pram, which my nurse was pushing in the Champs Elysées [in Paris], when a man tried to kidnap me. I was held in by the strap fastened round me while my nurse bravely tried to stand between me and the thief. She received various scratches, and I can still see vaguely those on her face. . . .

Piaget's nurse described the alleged attack in vivid detail and was given an expensive watch from his parents as a token of their thanks for her bravery. However, years later, the former nurse sent a letter to Piaget's family confessing that the story had been fabricated and returning the watch she had received as a reward. From this, Piaget concluded:

> I, therefore, must have heard, as a child, the account of this story, which my parents believed, and projected into the past in the form of a visual memory. (Piaget, 1951)

Are we all susceptible to laying down fabricated memories such as the one Piaget described? To find out, Elizabeth Loftus and her colleagues decided to do an experiment. They first contacted the parents of a group of college students, obtaining lists of childhood events, which the students were then asked to recall. But, embedded in those lists were plausible events that never happened, such as being lost in a shopping mall, spilling the punch bowl at a wedding, meeting Bugs Bunny at Disneyland (impossible because Bugs is not a Disney character), or experiencing a visit by a clown at a birthday party (Loftus, 2003a). After repeated recall attempts over a period of several days, about one-fourth of the students claimed to remember the bogus events. All that was required were some credible suggestions. (This experiment may remind you of Donna's case, with which we began our chapter: Repeated suggestions by the therapist led to Donna's fabricated memory.) New research also suggests that doctored photographs can also create false memories, perhaps even more powerfully than the stories used by Loftus and her colleagues. For example, in a variation of the lost-in-the-mall technique, adults viewed altered photographs purporting to show them riding in a hot air balloon. After seeing the photos several times over a period of two weeks, half of the participants "remembered" details about the fictitious balloon ride (Wade et al, 2002). Even in this age of digital cameras and image-altering software, people don't always stop to question whether a photograph may have been modified (Garry & Gerrie, 2005).

Factors Affecting the Accuracy of Eyewitnesses   So, to what extent can we rely on eyewitness testimony? Obviously, it is possible in laboratory experiments to distinguish false memories from true ones. But what about in real-life situations in which people claim to have recovered long-forgotten memories?

As we saw in our second case at the beginning of the chapter, Ross's recollection was independently verified by the confession of a camp counselor, but such objective evidence doesn't always materialize. In such cases, the best we can do is look for evidence of suggestion that may have produced the memory—as we see in false-memory experiments. If suggestion has occurred, a healthy dose of skepticism is warranted, unless objective evidence appears. Specifically, we should beware of eyewitness reports tainted by the following factors (Kassin et al., 2001):

The way mug shots are presented can bias the recollections of witnesses. Realizing this, the U.S. Department of Justice has published guidelines for interrogating eyewitnesses.

- *Leading questions* ("How fast were the cars going when they *smashed* into each other?") can influence witnesses' recollections. But such questions have less effect if witnesses are forewarned that interrogations can create memory bias.

- *The passage of substantial amounts of time,* which allows the original memory to fade, makes people more likely to misremember information.

- *Repeated retrieval:* Each time a memory is retrieved, it is reconstructed and then restored (much like a computer document that is retrieved, modified, and saved), increasing the chances of error.

- *The age of the witness:* Younger children and older adults may be especially susceptible to influence by misinformation in their efforts to recall.

- *Unwarranted confidence:* Confidence in a memory is not a sign of an accurate memory. In fact, misinformed individuals can actually come to believe the misinformation in which they feel confidence.

Based such concerns, the U.S. Department of Justice (1999) has published national guidelines for gathering eyewitness testimony, available on its website.

Bias: Beliefs, Attitudes, and Opinions Distort Memories

The sixth memory "sin," which Schacter calls *bias,* refers to the influence of personal beliefs, attitudes, and experiences on memory. Lots of domestic arguments of the "Did not! Did too!" variety owe their spirited exchanges to bias. While it's easier to see another person's biases than our own, here are two common forms that you should especially guard against.

Expectancy Bias   An unconscious tendency to remember events as being congruent with our expectations produces *expectancy bias.* To illustrate, suppose that you are among a group of volunteers for an experiment in which you read a story giving details about the relationship between Bob and Margie, a couple who plan to get married. Part of the story reveals that Bob doesn't want to have children, and he is worried about how Margie is going to take this disclosure. When he does tell her, Margie is shocked, because she desperately wants children. Then, suppose that, after reading the story you are informed, contrary to your expectations, that Bob and Margie did get married. Meanwhile, another group of volunteers read the same story, but they are told that the couple ended their relationship. Other than the ending, will people in those two groups remember the Bob and Margie story differently?

In a laboratory experiment using this same story, those who heard the unexpected ending (the condition in which Bob and Margie decided to get married) gave the most erroneous reports. Why? Because of their expectancy biases, they recalled distorted information that made the outcome fit their initial expectations (Schacter, 1999; Spiro, 1980). One person, for example, "remembered" that Bob and Margie had separated but decided their love could overcome their differences. Another related that the couple had decided on adoption, as a compromise.

Self-Consistency Bias People abhor the thought of being inconsistent, even though research suggests that they are kidding themselves. This Schacter calls the **self-consistency bias.** For example, studies have found people to be far less consistent than they realized in their support for political candidates, as well as on political issues such as the equality of women, aid to minority groups, and the legalization of marijuana (Levine, 1997; Marcus, 1986).

Of particular interest for the study of memory, the self-consistency bias can affect what we remember (Levine & Safer, 2002). So, in a study of dating couples who were interviewed twice, two months apart, memories about the course of the relationship would change, depending on how well the relationship had progressed over the two-month interval, although the participants generally did not recognize their inconsistencies. Those who had grown to like each other more remembered their initial evaluations of their partners as more positive than they had before, while those whose relationships had become more negative had the opposite response (Scharfe & Bartholomew, 1998). In all of these studies, whether they involve attitudes, beliefs, opinions, or emotions, we see that our biases act as a sort of distorted mirror in which our memories are reflected, but without our awareness that our memories had been altered.

Persistence: When We Can't Forget

The seventh "sin" of memory, **persistence,** reminds us that memory sometimes works all too well. We all experience this occasionally, when a persistent thought, image, or even a melody cycles over and over in our minds. Such intrusive memories are usually short lived. Yet they can become a problem when we have persistent thoughts colored by intense negative emotions. At the extreme, the persistence of memories for unpleasant events creates a downward emotional spiral whereby people suffering from *depression* or *posttraumatic stress disorder* can't stop ruminating about unhappy events or traumas in their lives. Similarly, patients with *phobias* may become obsessed by fearful memories about snakes, dogs, crowds, spiders, or lightning. All of this again points to the powerful role that emotion plays in memory.

The Advantages of the "Seven Sins" of Memory

Despite the grief they cause us, the "seven sins" arise from adaptive features of memory, argues Daniel Schacter (1999). Thus, transience—maddening as it can be to the student taking a test—is actually a way the memory system prevents itself from being overwhelmed by information that it no longer needs. Similarly, blocking is helpful when it allows only the most relevant information—the information most strongly associated with the present cues—to come to mind. Again, this is a process that prevents us from a flood of unwanted and distracting memories.

Absent-mindedness, too, is the by-product of the useful ability to shift our attention. Similarly, misattributions, biases, and suggestibility result from a mem-

CONNECTION • CHAPTER 12
People with *phobias* have extreme and unreasonable fears of specific objects or situations.

Self-consistency bias The commonly held idea that we are more consistent in our attitudes, opinions, and beliefs than we actually are.

Persistence A memory problem in which unwanted memories cannot be put out of mind.

ory system built to deal with *meaning* and discard details: The alternative would be a computer-like memory filled with information at the expense of understanding. And, finally, we can see that the "sin" of persistence is really a feature of a memory system responsive to emotional experiences, particularly those involving dangerous situations. In general, then, the picture that emerges of memory's "failures" is also a picture of a system well adapted to the conditions people have faced for thousands of years.

Improving Your Memory with Mnemonics

To improve your memory, your authors recommend a tool kit of mental strategies known as *mnemonics* (pronounced *ni-MON-ix*, from the Greek word meaning "remember"). **Mnemonic strategies** work by helping you encode new information to be remembered by associating it with information already in long-term memory. To illustrate, we will take a detailed look at two mnemonic strategies, the *method of loci* and *natural language mediators,* both of which are especially useful for remembering lists. Then, we will offer some tips that can help with the common problem of remembering names.

The Method of Loci   Dating back to the ancient Greeks, the **method of loci** (pronounced *LOW-sye*, from *locus*, or "place"), is literally one of the oldest tricks in this book. Greek orators originally devised the method of loci to help them remember the major points of their speeches.

To illustrate, imagine a familiar sequence of places, such as the bed, desk, and chairs in your room. Then, using the method of loci, mentally move from place to place in the room, and as you go imagine putting one item from a list in each place. To retrieve the series, you merely take another mental tour, examining the places you used earlier. There you will "see" the item you have put in each locus. To remember a grocery list, for example, you might mentally picture a can of *tuna* on your bed, *shampoo* spilled on your desktop, and a box of *eggs* open on a chair. Bizarre or unconventional image combinations are usually easier to remember—so a can of tuna in your bedroom will make a more memorable image than tuna in your kitchen (Bower, 1972).

The mental images used in the method of loci work especially well because they employ both verbal and visual memories (Paivio, 1986). It's worth noting, by the way, that visual imagery is one of the most effective forms of encoding: You can easily remember things by associating them with vivid, distinctive mental pictures. In fact, you could remember your grocery list by using visual imagery alone. Simply combine the mental images of tuna, shampoo, and eggs in a bizarre but memorable way. So, you might picture a tuna floating on an enormous fried egg in a sea of foamy shampoo. Or you might imagine a politician you dislike eating tuna from the can, hair covered with shampoo suds, while you throw eggs at her.

Natural Language Mediators   Memory aids called **natural language mediators** associate meaningful word patterns with new information to be remembered. Using this method to remember a grocery list, you would make up a story. Using the same list as before (tuna, shampoo, and eggs), the story might link the items this way: "The cat discovers I'm out of *tuna* so she interrupts me while I'm using the *shampoo* and meows to *egg* me on." (OK, we know it's hokey—but it works!) Similarly, advertisers know that rhyming slogans and rhythmic musical jingles can make it easier for customers to remember their products and brand names ("Oscar Mayer has a way with . . ."). The chances are that a teacher in your past used a simple rhyme to help you remember a spelling rule ("*I* before *E* except after *C*") or the number of days in each month ("Thirty days has September . . ."). In a physics class you may have used a natural language mediator in the form of an *acronym*—a word made up of initials—to learn the colors of the visible spectrum in their correct

Mnemonic strategy   Technique for improving memory, especially by making connections between new material and information already in long-term memory.

Method of loci   A mnemonic technique that involves associating items on a list with a sequence of familiar physical locations.

Natural language mediator   Word associated with new information to be remembered.

order: "Roy G. Biv" stands for red, orange, yellow, green, blue, indigo, violet.[1]

Remembering Names   The inability to remember people's names is one of the most common complaints about memory. So, how could you use the power of association to remember names? In the first place, you must realize that remembering names doesn't happen automatically. People who do this well must work at it by making deliberate associations between a name and some characteristic of the person—the more unusual the association, the better.

Suppose, for example, you have just met the authors of this book at a psychological convention. You might visualize Bob's face framed in a big *O*, taken from the middle of his name. To remember Vivian, think of her as "Vivacious Vivian," the liveliest person at the convention. And, as for Phil, you might visualize putting a hose in Phil's mouth and "fill"-ing him with water. (While unusual associations may be easier to remember than mundane ones, it is best not to tell people about the mnemonic you have devised to remember their names.)

In general, the use of mnemonics teaches us that memory is flexible, personal, and creative. It also teaches us that *memory ultimately works by meaningful associations.* With this knowledge and a little experimentation, you can devise techniques for encoding and retrieval that work well for you, based on your own personal associations and, perhaps, on your own sense of humor.

Mnemonic strategies help us remember things by making them meaningful. Here, Wangari Maathai, the Nobel Peace Prize laureate from Kenya, tries her hand at learning the chinese character for "tree"—which bears a resemblance to a stylized tree. Many chinese and Japanese characters originally were drawings of the objects they represented.

PSYCHOLOGY**MATTERS**
Using Psychology to Learn Psychology

Mnemonic strategies designed for learning names or memorizing lists of unrelated items won't help much with the material you need to learn in your psychology class. There the important material consists of concepts—often abstract concepts, such as "operant conditioning" or "retroactive interference"—ideas for which you need to learn the *gist,* rather than merely memorize. Such material calls for different mnemonic strategies geared both to concept learning and to avoiding the two memory "sins" feared most by college students, *transience* and *blocking.* So, let's see what advice cognitive psychologists would give to students for avoiding these two quirks of memory.

Studying to Avoid Transience

- *Make the material personally meaningful.*   Many studies have shown that memories will remain stronger if the information is approached in a way that makes it meaningful, rather than just a collection of facts and definitions (Baddeley, 1998; Haberlandt, 1999). One good strategy for doing this is the **whole method,** a technique often used by actors who must learn a script in a short time. With this approach, the learner begins by getting an overview of all the material to be learned—the "big picture" into which the details can be assimilated. Suppose, for example, that you have a test on this chapter coming up next week. Using the whole method, you would look over the chapter outline and summary, along with all the Key Questions and Core Concepts on the chapter opening page, before beginning to read the details of the chapter.

Whole method   The mnemonic strategy of first approaching the material to be learned "as a whole," forming an impression of the overall meaning of the material. The details are later associated with this overall impression.

---

[1]Schacter's "seven sins" of memory are a pun on the famous seven sins of medieval times. You can remember them by the acronym WASPLEG, which refers to Wrath, Avarice, Sloth, Pride, Lust, Envy, and Gluttony.

This approach erects a mental framework on which you can hang the details of encoding, interference, retrieval, and other memory topics.

- *Spread your learning out over time.* A second way to build strong memories that resist transience involves **distributed learning**. In less technical terms, you would study your psychology repeatedly and at frequent intervals, rather than trying to learn it all at once in a single "cram" session (called *massed learning*). Distributed learning not only avoids the lowered efficiency of massed learning, which causes fatigue, but it also strengthens memories that are in the process of consolidation. One study found that students could double the amount of information they learned in a given amount of time and also increase their understanding of the material by studying in two separate sessions, rather than in one session (Bahrick et al., 1993). Studies have also shown that distributed learning results in the material being retained longer (Schmidt & Bjork, 1992).

- *Take active steps to minimize interference.* You can't avoid interference altogether, but you can avoid studying for another class after your review session for tomorrow's psychology test. And you can make sure that you understand all the material and that you have cleared up any potentially conflicting points well before you go to the test. If, for example, you are not sure of the difference between *declarative memory* and *semantic memory*, you should discuss this with your instructor.

Studying to Avoid Blocking on the Test The strategies mentioned above will help you get to the test with a strong memory for the material you need to know. But you also will want to avoid blocking, the inability to find and retrieve what you have in memory. To help you achieve this, we suggest some techniques that apply two ideas you have learned in this chapter, *elaborative rehearsal* and *encoding specificity:*

- *Review and elaborate on the material.* Students often think that, just because they have read the material once and understood it, they will remember it. With complex concepts and ideas, you probably need to review what you have learned, perhaps several times. But your review should not be mindless and passive—merely looking at the words in the book. Rather, you should employ the technique of *elaborative rehearsal.* One of the best ways of doing this when studying for a test is to create your own examples of the concepts. So, as you study about proactive interference, think of an example from your own experience. And don't forget to think of examples involving the Core Concepts, too. This approach will help to prevent blocking because adding associations to the material you are learning adds more ways that the material can be accessed when you need it.

- *Test yourself with retrieval cues you expect to see on the examination.* By using the principle of *encoding specificity*, you can learn the material in a form that is most likely to be cued by the questions your psychology professor puts on the test. To do this it is helpful to work with a friend who is also studying for the same test. We recommend that you get together for this purpose a day or two before the exam, after both of you have studied the material thoroughly enough to feel you understand it. Your purpose, at this point, will not be to learn new material but to anticipate the most likely test items. Does your professor prefer essay questions? Short-answer questions? Multiple choice? Try to think of and answer questions of the type most likely to appear on the test. Don't overlook the Key Questions throughout the chapter.

And please don't overlook the other mnemonic features we have included throughout this book to guide you in your study. These include the "Check Your Understanding" quizzes and the "Do It Yourself!" demonstrations. All these mnemonic devices are based on well-established principles of learning and memory. Studying this way may sound like a lot of work—and it is. But the results will be worth the mental effort.

Distributed learning A technique whereby the learner spaces learning sessions over time, rather than trying to learn the material all in one study period.

CheckYourUnderstanding

1. **ANALYSIS:** What happens to memory over time, as described by Ebbinghaus's forgetting curve?

2. **APPLICATION:** Which kind of forgetting is involved when the sociology I studied yesterday makes it more difficult to learn and remember the psychology I am studying today?

3. **RECALL:** What is the term for the controversial notion that memories can be blocked off in the unconscious,

where they may cause physical and mental problems?

4. **RECALL:** Which one of the seven "sins" of memory was responsible for Piaget's fabricated memory of an attempted kidnapping?

5. **UNDERSTANDING THE CORE CONCEPT:** Which one of the "sins" of memory probably helps us avoid dangerous situations we have encountered before?

Critical Thinking Applied: The Recovered Memory Controversy

Let's return now to the case studies with which we began the chapter. All involved claims of recovered memories: Ross's memory of molestation by a camp counselor was clearly accurate, and Donna's memory of abuse by her father was eventually repudiated. So where does that leave us when we hear about other such claims?

What Is the Issue?

The controversy centers on the accuracy of claims of recovered memories—*not* on the reality of sexual abuse. Is it possible that recovered memories could be false? If so, we must decide how to judge the accuracy of recovered memories, especially memories of traumatic events.

What Critical Thinking Questions Should We Ask?

Let's begin by asking: Is the notion of recovered memories of sexual abuse reasonable or outrageous? That is, does it fit with what we know, both about memory and about sexual abuse? Let's see what the evidence can tell us.

Sexual Abuse Does Occur   We need to emphasize that sexual abuse of children *does* occur and poses a serious problem. How widespread is it? While estimates vary considerably, it appears that from 4% to 20% of children in the United States have experienced at least one incident of sexual abuse (McAnulty & Burnette, 2004; Terry & Tallon, 2004). Accurate figures are difficult to obtain, of course, because people can be reluctant to discuss these experiences. And *if* it is true that sexual abuse can be blocked out of consciousness for long periods, the actual numbers could be much higher.

We should also say that most claims of sexual abuse do *not* involve "recovered" memories. In general, we have no reason to doubt people who say they have been molested and have always remembered. The controversy centers on memories said to have been "recovered" after having been forgotten for long periods of months or even years.

Do People Forget Traumatic Events?   The general public harbors a strong, but unfounded, belief that the most common response to trauma is *repression*, the blocking of memories in the unconscious, as first described by Sigmund Freud. But, in fact, most people who have traumatic experiences remember them vividly, rather than forgetting them (McNally, 2003). Unwelcome remembering of disturbing experiences is precisely the problem in posttraumatic stress disorder (PTSD). Nevertheless, such cases don't eliminate the possibility that some people may react differently by repressing a memory of a particularly unpleasant experience—although it is difficult to get credible data on how often this might occur.

Only a few studies have addressed the question of how common repression may be, and the resulting data do not give us a very precise picture: Anywhere from 20 to 60% of people who remember being abused also report a period of time during which they did not remember (Schacter, 1996). None of these studies cited corroborating evidence for the memories, so a critical look at these data raises the question as to how many of those forgotten-then-recovered recollections might be false memories. Again, we are left without definitive evidence.

The Role of Suggestion   We have seen that memory does not make a complete record of our experiences. Nor is it always accurate. On the other hand, we do sometimes recover memories—accurate memories—of long-forgotten events. A chance remark, a peculiar odor, or an old tune can cue vivid recollections that haven't surfaced in years. These more common "recovered" memories, however, are not typically the sort of threatening memories that might have been blocked from consciousness. Rather, they are likely to be memories that we have not had occasion to think about for years—such as the name of a pal in the fourth grade.

Of special relevance to the recovered memory controversy is the research we discussed earlier in the chapter, showing that memories can rather easily be modified, or even created, by suggestion. As a result, participants not only reported false memories but came to believe them (Bruck & Ceci, 2004). Such experiments should make us skeptical of memories recovered during therapy or interrogation involving suggestive techniques. Memory expert Elizabeth Loftus argues that therapists who assume that most mental problems stem from childhood sexual abuse commonly use suggestive practices, although she does not say how widespread the problem might be (Loftus, 2003a, b). And in the book *Making Monsters,* social psychologist Richard Ofshe and his coauthor describe how clients can unknowingly tailor their recollections to fit their therapists' expectations. He adds that "therapists often encourage patients to redefine their life histories based on the new pseudomemories and, by doing so, redefine their most basic understanding of their families and themselves" (Ofshe & Watters, 1994, p. 6). As you can imagine, the issue has provoked deep divisions within psychology.

We are *not* saying that all, or even most, therapists use suggestive techniques to probe for memories of sexual abuse, although some certainly do (Poole et al., 1995). Nevertheless, patients should be wary of therapists who go "fishing" for repressed memories of early sexual experiences, using such techniques as hypnosis, dream analysis, and suggestive questioning. No evidence exists in support of these methods for the recovery of accurate memories.

Another source of suggestion that pops up in a surprisingly large proportion of recovered memory cases is a book: *The Courage to Heal.* This book argues that forgotten memories of incest and abuse may lie behind people's feelings of powerlessness, inadequacy, vulnerability, and a long list of other unpleasant thoughts and emotions (Bass & Davis, 1988). The authors state, "If you . . . have a feeling that something abusive happened to you, it probably did" (pp. 21–22). None of these assertions, however, rests on anything more solid than speculation. Thus, say memory experts Elizabeth Loftus and Katherine Ketcham (1994), it seems likely that *The Courage to Heal* has contributed to many false memories of sexual abuse.

A Logical Error: The Post Hoc Fallacy?   When we observe that things are associated, we have a natural tendency to suspect that one might cause the other—as we associate overeating with gaining weight or spending time in the sun with a sunburn. Most of the time this logic serves us well, but occasionally it leads us to the wrong conclusions—as when we conclude that a chill causes a cold or that eating sweets causes a "sugar high." Experts call this the post hoc fallacy: *Post hoc* literally means "after the fact," and the idea is that looking back at events occurring in succession (e.g., sugar followed by excitement) we may erroneously conclude that the first event is the cause of the second.

How could the post hoc fallacy contribute to the "recovered memory" controversy? When people "look back" in their memories and find a memory (accurate or not) of abuse that seems to be associated with their current unhappiness, they assume that the abusive event (again, whether real or erroneously remembered) is the cause of their current mental state. But, as we have seen, this conclusion may be faulty. Ironically, this can reinforce one's belief in the memory—through confirmation bias.

Emotional Biases   We should also note that the issue of recovered memories is both complex and charged with emotion—always a worrisome influence on critical thinking. Not only does the issue of sexual abuse strike many people close to home, but none of us wants to turn our back on those who believe they have been victims of sexual abuse. Yet what we know about memory tells us that we should not accept long-forgotten traumatic memories without corroborating evidence.

What Conclusions Can We Draw?

So, where does this leave us? You should weigh the evidence yourself on a case-by-case basis, mindful of the possibility that emotional biases can affect your thinking. Keep in mind the following points, as well:

- Sexual abuse of children *does* occur, and it is more prevalent than most professionals had suspected just a generation ago (McAnulty & Burnette, 2004).

- On the other hand, memories cued by suggestion, as from therapists or police officers, are particularly vulnerable to distortion and fabrication (Loftus, 2003a). So, without independent evidence, there is no way to tell whether a recovered memory is true or false.

- Remember that people can feel just as certain about false memories as accurate ones.

- Although traumatic events can be forgotten and later recalled, they are much more likely to form persistent and intrusive memories that people cannot forget. Nevertheless, cases such as that of Ross show us that recovered memories of abuse can be true.

- Early memories, especially those of incidents that may have happened in infancy, are quite likely to be fantasies or misattributions. As we have seen, episodic memories of events before age 3 are rare (Schacter, 1996).

- One should be more suspicious of claims for memories that have been "repressed" and then "recovered" years later than for memories that have always been available to consciousness.

Chapter Summary

4.1 What Is Memory?

Core Concept 4.1: Human memory is an information processing system that works constructively to encode, store, and retrieve information.

Human memory, like any **memory** system, involves three important tasks: **encoding, storage,** and **retrieval.** Although many people believe that memory makes a complete and accurate record, cognitive psychologists see human memory as an information processing system that interprets, distorts, and reconstructs information. **Eidetic imagery,** however, is a rare and poorly understood form of memory that produces especially vivid and persistent memories that may interfere with thought. It is not clear how eidetic memory fits with the widely accepted three-stage model of memory.

Eidetic imagery (p. 138)   Memory (p. 135)

Encoding (p. 137)   Retrieval (p. 137)

Information-processing model   Storage (p. 137)
(p. 136)

MyPsychLab Resources 4.1:

Explore: Encoding, Storage, and Retrieval in Memory

4.2 How Do We Form Memories?

Core Concept 4.2: Each of the three memory stages encodes and stores memories in a different way, but they work together to transform sensory experience into a lasting record that has a pattern or meaning.

The memory system is composed of three distinct stages: *sensory memory, working memory,* and *long-term memory.* The three stages work together sequentially to convert incoming sensory information into useful patterns or concepts that can be stored and retrieved when needed later.

Sensory memory holds 12 to 16 visual items for about ¼; second, making use of the sensory pathways. A separate sensory register for each sense holds material just long enough for important information to be selected for further processing.

Working memory, which has the smallest storage capacity of the three stages and a duration of a few seconds, draws information from sensory memory and long-term memory and processes it consciously. Theorists have proposed at least five components of working memory: a *central executive,* a *phonological loop,* a *sketchpad,* an *episodic buffer,* and a *semantic buffer.* We can cope with its limited duration and capacity by **chunking, rehearsal,** and **acoustic encoding.** The biological basis of working memory is not clear, but it is believed to involve actively firing nerve circuits, probably in the frontal cortex.

Long-term memory has apparently unlimited storage capacity and duration. It has two main partitions, **declarative memory** (for facts and events) and **procedural memory** (for perceptual and motor skills). Declarative memory can be further divided into **episodic memory** and **semantic memory.** Semantic information is encoded, stored, and retrieved according to the meaning and context of the material. The case of H. M. showed that the hippocampus is involved in transferring information to long-term memory. Other research has found long-term memories associated with relatively permanent changes at the synaptic level.

Flashbulb memories are common for highly emotional experiences. While most people have a great deal of confidence in such vivid memories, studies have shown that these memories can become distorted over time, especially the material that was not the focus of attention.

MyPsychLab Resources 4.2:

Explore: Key Processes in Stages of Memory

Simulation: Digit Span

4.3 How Do We Retrieve Memories?

Core Concept 4.3: Whether memories are implicit or explicit, successful retrieval depends on how they were encoded and how they are cued.

H. M.'s case also demonstrated that information can be stored as **explicit** or **implicit memories.** The success of a memory search depends, in part, on the **retrieval cues.** Implicit memories can be cued by **priming.** Explicit memories can be cued by various **recall** or **recognition** tasks, although some tasks require remembering the **gist,** rather than exact details. The accuracy of memory retrieval also depends on **encoding specificity** and **mood.** Relatively little is known about the conditions required for successful **prospective memory.** When there is a poor match between retrieval cues and the encoding, we may experience the **TOT** phenomenon.

MyPsychLab Resources 4.3:

Watch: The Effects of Sleep and Stress on Memory

4.4 Why Does Memory Sometimes Fail Us?

Core Concept 4.4: Most of our memory problems arise from memory's "seven sins"—which are really by-products of otherwise adaptive features of human memory.

Memory failures involve the "seven sins" of memory. These include forgetting, resulting from weakening memory traces (**transience**), lapses of attention (**absent-mindedness**), and inability to retrieve a memory (**blocking**). Much forgetting can also be attributed to a cause of transience known as **interference.** Memory can also fail when recollections are altered through **misattribution, suggestibility,** and **bias.** An important example involves eyewitness memories, which are subject to distortion. Suggestibility can also produce false memories that seem believable to the remember. The final "sin" of **persistence** occurs when unwanted memories linger in memory, even though we would like to forget them.

The "seven sins" of memory, however, are by-products of a memory system that is well suited to solving problems of day-to-day living. Some of these problems can be overcome by **mnemonic strategies,** such as the method of loci, natural language mediators, and other associative methods. The learning of concepts, however, requires special strategies geared to learning the *gist* of the material and to avoiding the two memory "sins" of transience and blocking.

MyPsychLab Resources 4.4:

Simulation: Creating False Memories

Simulation: Experiencing the Stroop Effect

Simulation: Serial Position Effect

Watch: Elizabeth Loftus

Watch the following video by logging into MyPsychLab (www.mypsychlab.com). After you have watched the video, complete the activities that follow.

PROGRAM 9: REMEMBERING AND FORGETTING

PROGRAM REVIEW

1. What pattern of remembering emerged in Hermann Ebbinghaus's research?
   a. Loss occurred at a steady rate.
   b. A small initial loss was followed by no further loss.
   c. There was no initial loss, but then there was a gradual decline.
   d. A sharp initial loss was followed by a gradual decline.

2. The way psychologists thought about and studied memory was changed by the invention of
   a. television.
   b. electroconvulsive shock therapy.
   c. the computer.
   d. the electron microscope.

3. What do we mean when we say that memories must be encoded?
   a. They must be taken from storage to be used.
   b. They must be put in a form the brain can register.
   c. They must be transferred from one network to another.
   d. They must be put in a passive storehouse.

4. About how many items can be held in short-term memory?
   a. three   c. eleven
   b. seven   d. an unlimited number

5. Imagine you had a string of 20 one-digit numbers to remember. The best way to accomplish the task, which requires increasing the capacity of short-term memory, is through the technique of
   a. selective attention.   c. rehearsing.
   b. peg words.   d. chunking.

6. According to Gordon Bower, what is an important feature of good mnemonic systems?
   a. There is a dovetailing between storage and retrieval.
   b. The acoustic element is more important than the visual.
   c. The learner is strongly motivated to remember.
   d. Short-term memory is bypassed in favor of long-term memory.

7. According to Sigmund Freud, what is the purpose of repression?
   a. to protect the memory from encoding too much material
   b. to preserve the individual's self-esteem

c. to activate networks of associations
   d. to fit new information into existing schemas

8. In an experiment, people spent a few minutes in an office. They were then asked to recall what they had seen. They were most likely to recall objects that
   a. fit into their existing schema of an office.
   b. carried little emotional content.
   c. were unusual within that particular context.
   d. related to objects they owned themselves.

9. The paintings Franco Magnani made of an Italian town were distorted mainly by
   a. repression, causing some features to be left out.
   b. a child's perspective.
   c. sensory gating, changing colors.
   d. false memories of items that were not really there.

10. What was Karl Lashley's goal in teaching rats how to negotiate mazes and then removing part of their cortexes?
    a. finding out how much tissue was necessary for learning to occur
    b. determining whether memory was localized in one area of the brain
    c. discovering how much tissue loss led to memory loss
    d. finding out whether conditioned responses could be eradicated

11. What has Richard Thompson found in his work with rabbits conditioned to a tone before an air puff?
    a. Rabbits learn the response more slowly after lesioning.
    b. Eyelid conditioning involves several brain areas.
    c. The memory of the response can be removed by lesioning.
    d. Once the response is learned, the memory is permanent, despite lesioning.

12. Patients with Alzheimer's disease find it almost impossible to produce
    a. unconditioned responses.
    b. conditioned stimuli.
    c. conditioned responses.
    d. unconditioned stimuli.

13. The best way to keep items in short-term memory for an indefinite length of time is to
    a. chunk.
    b. create context dependence.

c. use the peg-word system.

d. rehearse.

14. Long-term memory is organized as

a. a complex network of associations.

b. a serial list.

c. a set of visual images.

d. a jumble of individual memories with no clear organizational scheme.

15. You remember a list of unrelated words by associating them, one at a time, with images of a bun, a shoe, a tree, a door, a hive, sticks, Heaven, a gate, a line, and a hen. What mnemonic technique are you using?

a. method of loci   c. link

b. peg-word   d. digit conversion

16. What did Karl Lashley conclude about the engram?

a. It is localized in the brain stem.

b. It is localized in the right hemisphere only.

c. It is localized in the left hemisphere only.

d. Complex memories cannot be pinpointed within the brain.

17. Long-term memories appear to be stored in the

a. cortex.   c. hippocampus.

b. occipital lobe.   d. parietal lobe.

18. How has Diana Woodruff-Pak utilized Richard Thompson's work on eyeblink conditioning?

a. as a precursor to early-onset dementia

b. as a predictor of musical genius

c. as a mechanism for growing brain cells in intact animals

d. as a tool for training long-term visual memories

19. Which neurotransmitter(s) is/are disrupted in Alzheimer's patients?

a. scopolamine   c. both of the above

b. acetylcholine   d. none of the above

20. Alzheimer's disease is associated with the loss of

a. memory.   c. life itself.

b. personality.   d. all of the above.

QUESTIONS TO CONSIDER

1. What memory strategies can you apply to help you better retain the information in this course? Why is rote rehearsal not the optimal strategy?

2. What is your earliest memory? How accurate do you think it is? Can you recall an experience that happened before you could talk? If not, why not? How does language influence what people remember?

How do photographs and other mementos aid memory?

3. Most American kids learn their ABCs by singing them. Why does singing the ABCs make it easier to remember the alphabet?

4. Many quiz shows and board games, such as Trivial Pursuit, are based on recalling items of general knowledge that we do not use every day. Why is it so much fun to recall such trivia?

5. As a member of a jury, you are aware of the tendency to reconstruct memories. How much weight do you give to eyewitness testimony? Is it possible ever to get "the whole truth and nothing but the truth" from an eyewitness? Do you think memory distortions (for details of what was said during a trial) occur in jurors as well?

ACTIVITIES

1. Do you have an official family historian? In individual interviews, ask family members to recall and describe their memories of a shared past event, such as a wedding or holiday celebration. Perhaps a photograph or memento will trigger a story. Compare how different people construct the event and what kind of details are recalled. What do different people reveal about their personal interests, needs, and values when they describe the experience?

2. Try to recall an experience from your childhood that at least one friend or family member also recalls. Have each person write down details of his or her memory, and then compare notes. Are there any details you hadn't remembered that you now do, based on other people's mention of them? Are there any details that you have contradictory memories for? How do you resolve the disagreement?

3. Make up a list of ten unrelated words. Have five friends study the list for one minute with only the instruction to "remember as many of them as you can." After one minute, have your friends write down as many as they can remember. Have another five friends learn the list for one minute after you teach them the peg-word mnemonic. Do they outperform the control group? What sort of strategies, if any, did the control group tend to use?

Key Questions/ Chapter Outline	Core Concepts	Psychology Matters
5.1 What Are the Components of Thought? Concepts Imagery and Cognitive Maps Thought and the Brain Intuition	• Thinking is a cognitive process in which the brain uses information from the senses, emotions, and memory to create and manipulate mental representations, such as concepts, images, schemas, and scripts.	**Schemas and Scripts Help You Know What to Expect** But sometimes they fill in the blanks—without your realizing it.
5.2 What Abilities Do Good Thinkers Possess? Problem Solving Judging and Making Decisions Becoming a Creative Genius	• Good thinkers not only have a repertoire of effective strategies, called algorithms and heuristics, they also know how to avoid the common impediments to problem solving and decision making.	**Using Psychology to Learn Psychology** Psychologists have learned the secrets of developing expertise—in psychology or any other subject.
5.3 How Is Intelligence Measured? Binet and Simon Invent a School Abilities Test American Psychologists Borrow Binet and Simon's Idea Problems with the IQ Formula Calculating IQs "on the Curve" IQ Testing Today	• Intelligence testing has a history of controversy, but most psychologists now view intelligence as normally distributed and measurable by performance on a variety of tasks.	**What Can You Do for an Exceptional Child?** In both mental retardation and giftedness, children should be encouraged to capitalize on their abilities.
5.4 Is Intelligence One or Many Abilities? Psychometric Theories of Intelligence Cognitive Theories of Intelligence Cultural Definitions of Intelligence Animals Can Be Intelligent— But Do They Think?	• Some psychologists believe that intelligence comprises one general factor, g, while others believe that intelligence is a collection of distinct abilities.	**Test Scores and the Self-Fulfilling Prophecy** An IQ score can create expectations that have a life of their own.
5.5 How Do Psychologists Explain IQ Differences among Groups? Intelligence and the Politics of Immigration What Evidence Shows That Intelligence Is Influenced by Heredity? What Evidence Shows That Intelligence Is Influenced by Environment? *Heritability* (not *Heredity*) and Group Differences	• While most psychologists agree that both heredity and environment affect intelligence, they disagree on the source of IQ differences among racial and social groups.	**Stereotype Threat** Just a reminder that you belong to a minority group may be enough to lower your test scores.

Critical Thinking Applied   **The Question of Gender Differences**

chapter 5
thinking and intelligence

Follow your passions and you, too, may become a multimillionaire. At least that's what happened to Sergey Brin and Larry Page, graduate students in computer science at Stanford University. Both were deeply interested in finding a quicker way to search the World Wide Web and extract specific information from its abundance of informational riches.

It was January of 1996, and both Brin and Page had some creative ideas about how to search the Web more efficiently than the existing "search engines" could do the job. After deciding to combine forces, the first thing this duo did was to build a computer in Larry's dorm room, equipping it with as much memory as they could afford.

The first-generation search engine to come out of their collaboration was Back-Rub, so called because it could identify and follow "back links" to identify which websites were listing a particular page—giving them an index of how valuable users had found a site to be. And, while their search engine performed well, Brin and Page couldn't get any of the big computer companies or existing Internet entrepreneurs to buy their design. So, they started their own business—with a little financial help from their family and friends. One friend of a Stanford faculty member saw so much promise in their enterprise that he wrote them a check for $100,000. The check sat in a drawer in Page's desk for two weeks because they hadn't yet set up a company that could cash the check.

In most respects, Brin and Page's search engine worked like any other web-searching software. It sent out electronic "spiders" that crawl across web pages, looking for important terms and lists these in an index, along with their web addresses. It also followed links on the web pages it scans (both forward and backward) and lists more terms. The main secret ingredient for their success remains as closely guarded as the formula for Coca-Cola. It involves the way results are ranked for presentation to the user. More often than not, it manages to put the sites users want near the top of a list that can stretch to millions of possible sources. Thus, the software is designed to serve as the link between a concept in the user's mind and billions of words on the web. That is, Brin and Page had to organize their search engine to "think" as much as possible like a person—which is what this chapter is about.

The public seemed to like their search engine. In fact, the public liked it far better than did the big companies that had turned it down. And over the next decade it became "the little engine that could." First it outgrew Page's dorm room and—in the great tradition of American inventors and rock bands—into a garage. Now it has its own Silicon Valley building complex, with 1000 employees. It also has a reputation as the most comprehensive of search engines, indexing key words from billions of web pages. Every day it processes hundreds of millions of search requests. Things got so busy that Brin and Page had to take a leave from graduate school to run the company—which they renamed after the term mathematicians use for the number 1 followed by 100 zeros. They called it Google.

In some respects, Brin and Page are like other legendary pioneers in the computer field: the two Steves, Jobs and Wozniak, who started Apple Computers in a garage, and Bill Gates who, with his friend Paul Allen, launched Microsoft on a shoestring. All could be called "geniuses," a term that frames our initial problem for this chapter:

PROBLEM: What produces "genius," and to what extent are the people we call "geniuses" different from others?

As we consider this problem, here are some additional questions worth pondering:

- Thomas Edison once said that genius is 1% inspiration, 99% perspiration. If so, does that mean genius is mainly a matter of high motivation, rather than aptitude or talent?
- Is genius a product mainly of nature or nurture?
- Do geniuses think differently from the rest of us? Or do they just use the same thought processes more effectively?
- Could Einstein (for example), whose specialty was physics, have been a genius in painting or literature or medicine, if he had chosen to do so? That is, are there different kinds of genius? And is the potential for genius specific to a particular field?

We will address all of these questions in the following pages. But first, let's return to Google and the computer metaphor for the human mind, as we begin our inquiry into thinking and intelligence.

Despite its phenomenal success, Google is only a pale imitation of the human mind. Sure, it can scan its memory, amassed from 4 billion web pages, and return 12 million links on, say, the term "search engine" in about a half second. But ask it what food to serve at a birthday party, and it will merely serve up (at this writing) 7,500,000 links to the terms "birthday" and "party" and "food." Unlike most human minds, Google and its network of supportive hardware is clueless. So is the computer on your desk. Computers just don't index information by *meaning*.

Nevertheless, computers in the hands of cognitive scientists can be powerful tools for studying how we think—for three reasons. First, these scientists use computers in brain imaging studies, which have shown the brain to be a system of interrelated processing modules, as we have seen. Second, researchers use computer simulations that attempt to model human thought processes. And third, while they haven't yet made a computer function exactly like a brain, cognitive scientists have adopted the computer as a metaphor for the brain as a processor of information.

This **computer metaphor**—the brain as an information processor—suggests that thinking is nothing more, or less, than information processing. The information we use in thought can come from the raw data we receive from our senses, but it can also come from the meaningful *concepts* that we retrieve from long-term memory. As you can see, then, the psychology of thinking deals with the same processes that we discussed in connection with learning and memory.

To be sure, the computer metaphor is not perfect. Computers can't deal with meaning. And, as we will see, they are not very good at abstract thought or humor (although they are *very* good at transmitting the millions of jokes shared on e-mail each day). Consequently, some psychologists have called for moving beyond the computer metaphor to talk about the sort of modular, parallel information processing that we now know the brain really does when it thinks. Says David Rubin (2006): "Instead of viewing the mind as a general-purpose computing machine, we should view it as a collection of more specialized systems or devices, each with properties tuned for the problems it is to process." Nevertheless, the computer metaphor is a good place to begin our thinking about thought.

In the first two sections of this chapter, we will focus on the processes underlying thought, especially in decision making and problem solving. This discussion will examine the building blocks of thought: *concepts*, *images*, *schemas*, and *scripts*. Our excursion into thinking will also give us the opportunity to return for a closer look at that mysterious quality known as "genius."

In the second half of the chapter, we will turn to the form of thinking we call **intelligence**. There you will learn about IQ tests, conflicting perspectives on what intelligence really is, and what it means to say that IQ is "heritable." In the "Using Psychology to Learn Psychology" feature, you will learn how to apply the knowledge in this chapter to become an expert in psychology—or any other field you choose. Finally, our critical thinking application will look at the hot-button issue of gender differences in thought.

5.1 KEY QUESTION
WHAT ARE THE COMPONENTS OF THOUGHT?

Solving a math problem, deciding what to do Friday night, and indulging a private fantasy all require *thinking*. We can conceive of thinking as a complex act of *cognition*—information processing in the brain—by which we deal with our world of ideas, feelings, desires, and experience. Our Core Concept notes that this information can come from within and from without, but it always involves some form of mental representation:

Computer metaphor The idea that the brain is an information-processing organ that operates, in some ways, like a computer.

Intelligence The mental capacity to acquire knowledge, reason, and solve problems effectively.

Read the following passage carefully:

Chief Resident Jones adjusted his face mask while anxiously surveying a pale figure secured to the long gleaming table before him. One swift stroke of his small, sharp instrument and a thin red line appeared. Then the eager young assistant carefully extended the opening as another aide pushed aside glistening surface fat so that the vital parts were laid bare. Everyone stared in horror at the ugly growth too large for removal. He now knew it was pointless to continue.

Now, without looking back, please complete the following exercise.

Circle below the words that appeared in the passage:

patient scalpel blood tumor
cancer nurse disease surgery

In the original study, most of the subjects who read this passage circled the words *patient, scalpel,* and *tumor.* Did you? However, none of the words were there! Interpreting the story as a medical story made it more understandable, but also resulted in inaccurate recall (Lachman et al., 1979). Once the subjects had related the story to their schema for hospital surgery, they "remembered" labels from their schema that were not present in what they had read. Drawing on a schema not only gave

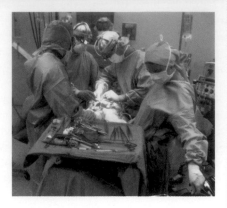

people an existing mental structure to tie the new material to but also led them to change the information to make it more consistent with their schema-based expectations.

core concept

Thinking is a cognitive process in which the brain uses information from the senses, emotions, and memory to create and manipulate mental representations, such as concepts, images, schemas, and scripts.

These mental representations, then, serve as the building blocks of cognition, while thinking organizes them in meaningful ways. The ultimate results can be the higher thought processes that we call reasoning, imagining, judging, deciding, problem solving, expertise, creativity, and—sometimes—genius.

Concepts

Have you ever visited a new place only to feel like you had been there before? Or had a conversation with someone and felt that the experience was uncannily familiar? If so, you have experienced a phenomenon known as *déjà vu* (from the French for "seen before"). The term refers to the strange feeling that your present experience jibes with a previous experience, even though you cannot retrieve the explicit memory. This feeling reflects the brain's ability to treat new stimuli as instances of familiar categories, even if the stimuli are slightly different from anything it has encountered before. Here's the point: The ability to assimilate experiences, objects, or ideas into familiar mental categories—and to take the same action toward them or give them the same label—is regarded as one of the most basic attributes of thinking organisms (Mervis & Rosch, 1981).

The mental categories that we form in this way are known as **concepts**. We use them as the building blocks of thinking, because they enable us to organize our knowledge (Goldman-Rakic, 1992). Concepts can represent classes of objects, such as "chair" or "food." Concepts can also represent living organisms, such as "birds" or "buffaloes," as well as events, like "birthday parties." They may also represent properties (such as "red" or "large"), abstractions (such as "truth" or "love"), relations (such as "smarter than"), procedures (such as how to tie your shoes), or intentions (such as the intention to break into a conversation) (Smith & Medin, 1981). But because concepts are mental structures, we cannot observe them directly. For the cognitive scientist, this means inferring concepts from their influence on behavior or on brain activity. For example, you

Concepts Mental groupings of similar objects, ideas, or experiences.

cannot be sure that another person shares your concept of "red," but you can observe whether he or she responds in the same way you do to stimuli that you both call "red."

Two Kinds of Concepts

Everyone conceptualizes the world in a unique way, so our concepts define who we are. Yet behind this individual uniqueness lie similarities in the ways that all of us form concepts. In particular, we all distinguish between *natural concepts* and *artificial concepts* (Medin et al., 2000).

Natural concepts are rather imprecise mental categories that develop out of our everyday experiences in the world. You possess a natural concept of "bird" based on your experiences with birds. You probably also have natural concepts associated with artichokes, elephants, your mother's face, and the Statue of Liberty. While each of these examples may involve words, natural concepts also can involve visual images, emotions, and other nonverbal memories.

Your natural concept of "bird" invokes a mental **prototype**, a generic image that represents a typical bird from your experience (Hunt, 1989). To determine whether some object is a bird or not, you can quickly compare the object to your bird prototype. The more sophisticated your prototype, the less trouble you will have with flightless birds, such as ostriches and penguins; or with birdlike flying creatures, such as bats; or with egg-laying creatures like turtles and platypuses. Natural concepts are sometimes called "fuzzy concepts" because of their imprecision (Kosko & Isaka, 1993).

Empirical support for the idea of a prototype comes from studies showing that people respond more quickly to typical members of a category than to more unusual ones—that is, their reaction times are faster. For example, it takes less time to say whether a robin is a bird than to say whether an ostrich is a bird, because robins resemble most Americans' prototype of a bird more closely than ostriches do (Kintsch, 1981; Rosch et al., 1976).

Your natural concept of "bird" involves a prototype *that is probably more like a robin than an ostrich. Biology majors, however, may also have an artificial concept of "bird" that works equally well for both.*

By comparison, **artificial concepts** are defined by a set of rules or characteristics, such as dictionary definitions or mathematical formulas. The definition of "rectangle" that you learned in math class is an example. Artificial concepts represent precisely defined ideas or abstractions, rather than actual objects in the world. So, if you are a zoology major, you may also have an artificial concept of "bird," which defines it as a "feathered biped." In fact, most of the concepts you have learned in school are artificial concepts. "Cognitive psychology" is also an artificial concept; so is the concept of "concept"!

Concept Hierarchies

You organize much of your declarative memory into **concept hierarchies**, arranged from general to specific, as illustrated in Figure 5.1. For most people, the broad category of "animal" has several subcategories, such as "bird" and "fish," which are divided, in turn, into specific forms, such as "canary," "ostrich," "shark," and "salmon." The "animal" category may itself be a subcategory of the still larger category of "living beings." We can think of these concepts and categories as arranged in a hierarchy of levels, with the most general and abstract at the top and the most specific and concrete at the bottom. They are also linked to many other concepts: Some birds are edible, some are endangered, some are national symbols.

Culture, Concepts, and Thought

Concepts can carry vastly different meanings in different cultures. For example, the concepts of "democracy" and "freedom," so dear to Americans, may have the connotation of chaos, license, and rudeness in parts of Asia and the Middle East.

Americans also differ with many Asians in the ways they deal with conflicting ideas and contradictions (Peng & Nisbett, 1999). We can see this in the way the Chinese have dealt with the conflicting ideologies of capitalism and communism by allowing elements of both to flourish in their economy, an approach that many Americans find difficult to understand. The Chinese culture encour-

Natural concepts Mental representations of objects and events drawn from our direct experience.

Prototype An ideal or most representative example of a conceptual category.

Artificial concepts Concepts defined by rules, such as word definitions and mathematical formulas.

Concept hierarchies Levels of concepts, from most general to most specific, in which a more general level includes more specific concepts—as the concept of "animal" includes "dog," "giraffe," and "butterfly."

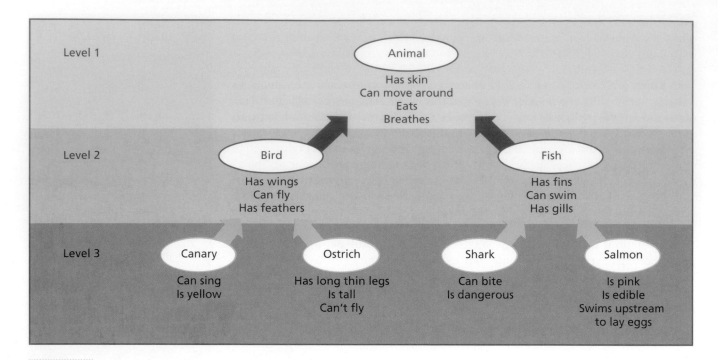

FIGURE 5.1
Hierarchically Organized Structure of Concepts

ages thinkers to keep opposing perspectives in mind and seek a "middle way," while American culture tends toward thinking in more polarized "either-or" terms—capitalism *or* communism.

Another big cultural difference involves the use of logic: Many cultures do not value the use of logical reasoning as much as do Europeans and North Americans (Bower, 2000a; Nisbett et al., 2001). Some seek "truth" by comparing new ideas with the wisdom of sacred writings, such as the Koran, the Bible, or the Upanishads. Even in the United States, many people place higher value on qualities variously known as "common sense," which refers to thinking based on experience, rather than on logic.

What is the lesson to be learned from these cultural differences? While there are some universal principles of thought that cut across cultures, they involve very basic processes, such as the fact that everyone forms concepts. But when it comes to *how* they form concepts or the *meaning* they attach to them, we should be cautious about assuming that others think as we do.

Imagery and Cognitive Maps

We think in words, but we also may think in pictures and spatial relationships or other sensory images. Taking a moment to think of a friend's face, your favorite song, or the smell of warm cookies, makes this obvious. Visual imagery adds complexity and richness to our thinking, as do images that involve the other senses (sound, taste, smell, and touch). Thinking with sensory imagery can be useful in solving problems in which relationships can be grasped more clearly in an image rather than in words. That is why books such as this one often encourage visual thinking by using pictures, diagrams, and charts.

A cognitive representation of physical space is a special form of visual concept called a *cognitive map*. Cognitive maps help you get to your psychology class, and they enable you to give another person directions to a nearby theater or deli. By using cognitive maps, people can move through their homes with their eyes closed or go to familiar destinations even when their usual routes are blocked. As you can see in Figures 5.2 and 5.3, people's cognitive maps can be vastly different.

CONNECTION • CHAPTER 3

Learning theorist Edward C. Tolman suggested that we form cognitive maps of our environment, which we use to guide our actions toward desired goals.

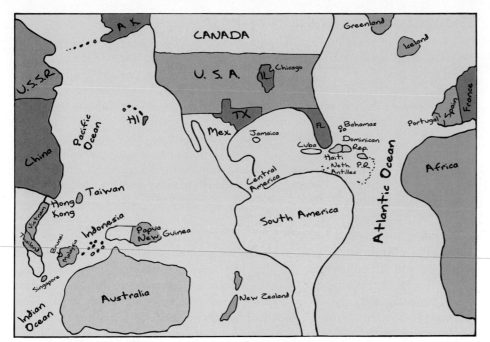

FIGURE 5.2
Chicagocentric View of the World

How does this student's sketch compare with your view of the world?

(*Source:* From Robert L. Solso, *Cognitive Psychology*, 5th ed. Published by Allyn and Bacon, Boston, MA. Copyright © 1998 by Pearson Education. Reprinted by permission of the publisher.)

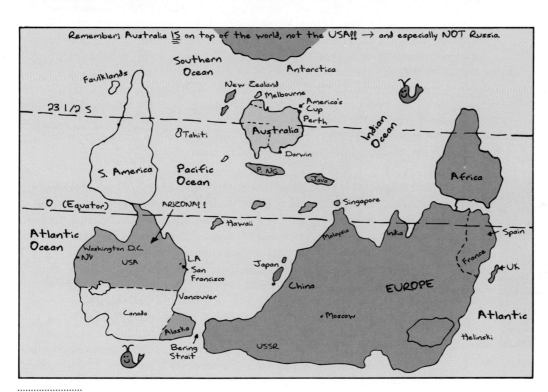

FIGURE 5.3
Australiocentric View of the World

Now who's "down under"? It probably would not occur to most Americans to draw a map "upside down" like this one drawn by an Australian student, placing Australia near the center of the world.

The maps we carry in our minds mirror the view of the world that we have developed from the perspective of our own culture. The maps you see here and in the previous figure came from a study aimed at understanding how nearly 4000 students from 71 cities in 49 countries visualize the world. The majority of maps had a Eurocentric world view: Europe was placed in the center of the map and the other countries were arranged around it—probably due to the dominance for many centuries of Eurocentric maps in geography books. But the study also yielded many interesting culture-biased maps, such as the one by a Chicago student in Figure 5.2 and this one by an Australian student. American students, incidentally, performed especially poorly on this task, often misplacing countries. Students from the former Soviet Union and Hungary made the most accurately detailed maps (Saarinen, 1987).

(*Source:* From Robert L. Solso, *Cognitive Psychology*, 5th ed. Published by Allyn and Bacon, Boston, MA. Copyright © 1998 by Pearson Education. Reprinted by permission of the publisher.)

Thought and the Brain

Developments in brain imaging have allowed cognitive researchers to begin mapping the mind itself (Ashby & Waldron, 2000). With the help of the computer, scientists can connect certain thoughts, such as "dog" or "pencil," with specific electrical wave patterns in the brain (Garnsey, 1993; Osterhout & Holcomb, 1992). They do this by repeatedly presenting a stimulus (such as the word *dog* flashed on a screen) to a volunteer "wired" to record the brain's electrical responses. While the brain waves on just one trial may show no clear pattern, a computer can average many brain wave responses to a single, repeated stimulus (such as a tone or a visual image), eliminating the random background "noise" of the brain and isolating the unique brain wave pattern evoked by that stimulus (Kotchoubey, 2002). These EEG patterns associated with particular stimuli are called **event-related potentials**.

Thinking in Modules   Other methods can also tell us which parts of the brain switch on and off while we think. With PET scans and magnetic resonance imaging (MRI), neuroscientists have identified brain regions that become active during various mental tasks. Two broad conclusions have come from this work. First, *thinking is an activity involving widely distributed areas of the brain—not just a single "thinking center."* Second, *neuroscientists now see the brain as a community of highly specialized modules, each of which deals with different components of thought* (Cree & McRae, 2003). Moreover, the brain generates many of the images used in thought with the same circuitry it uses for sensation. Thus, visual imagery drawn from memory activates the visual cortex, while auditory memories engage the auditory cortex (Behrmann, 2000). And thinking with language may involve different regions, depending on the topic. One brain-imaging study found that most jokes tickle us mainly in the language processing areas of the cortex, while sound-alike puns activate the brain's sound-processing circuits, as well (Goel & Dolan, 2001). In general, the picture of thought coming out of this work reveals thinking as a process composed of many modules acting in concert.

Frontal Lobe Control   The frontal lobes of the brain play an especially important part in coordinating mental activity when we make decisions and solve problems (Helmuth, 2003a; Koechlin et al., 2003). To do so, the prefrontal cortex performs three different tasks: keeping track of the *episode* (the situation in which we find ourselves), understanding the *context* (the meaning of the situation), and responding to a specific *stimulus* in the situation. Here's how it works. Suppose that the phone rings (the stimulus). Normally—at your own house—you would answer it. But suppose that you are at a friend's house (a different context). Under this condition, you would probably let the phone ring without answering it. But if your friend, who has just hopped into the shower, has asked you to take a message if the phone happens to ring (the episode), you will answer it. From a neuroscience perspective, the interesting thing is that each of these tasks is performed cooperatively by different combinations of brain modules. It's an impressive and sophisticated system.

Intuition   Another fascinating discovery involves the location of brain circuits associated with what we often call "common sense," or the ability to act on "intuition." Psychologists have long known that when people make decisions—whether about buying a house or selecting a spouse—they may make quick judgments that draw on feelings, as well as reason (Gladwell, 2005; Myers, 2002). This emotional component of thinking apparently involves regions of the frontal lobes just above the eyes. These structures allow us unconsciously to add emotional "hunches" to our decisions in the form of information about past rewards and punishments. Indi-

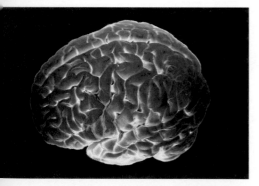

Different thoughts and actions make different parts of the brain "light up" on brain scans. This image shows the brain areas used in thinking about words and producing speech.

Event-related potentials   Brain waves shown on the EEG in response to stimulation.

viduals with severe damage to this area of the brain may display little emotion. They may also have impairments in **intuition**—the ability to make judgments without consciously reasoning. Such persons frequently make unwise choices when faced with decisions (Damasio, 1994).

But not all intuitive thinking draws on emotion. Much of what we know "intuitively" comes from implicit memory. Says psychologist Seymour Epstein, "Intuition is just the things we've learned without realizing we've learned them. And sometimes they're useful. Sometimes they're maladaptive" (Winerman, 2005d, p. 5). Nor is intuition always right—sometimes our intuitive snap judgments, which may feel like truth, are merely our prejudices and biases (Myers, 2002). That has been shown to be true of executives, who commonly overestimate the power of their intuition by believing that they are especially good judges of other people's abilities and character. Accordingly, executives often rely exclusively on in-person interviews as the basis for hiring, even though studies show that they usually make better judgments by factoring in some more objective data, such as educational levels and test scores (Dawes, 2001).

Sometimes, however, quick intuitive judgments can be surprisingly on target. Dr. Nalini Ambady has found that people make remarkably accurate judgments of a person's personality traits after viewing only a six-second video clip. Similarly, students' quick judgments about a professor's teaching effectiveness correlate highly with end-of-course ratings (Ambady & Rosenthal, 1993; Greer, 2005). Daniel Kahneman suggests that intuition is an evolutionary invention that helped our ancestors make snap judgments in difficult and dangerous situations (2003).

So, where do the seemingly contradictory findings about intuition leave us? Much of the time our "instincts" about personality are correct—but, notes psychologist Frank Bernieri, the serial killer Ted Bundy made a good first impression (Winerman, 2005c). Kahneman notes that one of the most unreliable aspects of intuition concerns statistical judgments. (How many English words end with *r*? Or how likely is it that I will be killed by a terrorist?)

It is important for us to realize when we are making intuitive judgments and to realize that they can be wrong: As we saw in our discussion of memory, confidence is not a reliable indicator of accuracy. For psychologists, the task that lies ahead is to help us learn to use intuition more accurately (see Haslam, 2007). This is particularly important for people who must make rapid life-and-death decisions: police officers, soldiers, pilots, air traffic controllers, and medical personnel.

PSYCHOLOGY**MATTERS**
Schemas and Scripts Help You Know What to Expect

Much of your knowledge is stored in your brain as *schemas* (Oden, 1987). We can define a *schema* as a cluster of related concepts that provides a framework for thinking about objects, events, ideas, or even emotions. So, you probably have schemas that represent "cat," "Internet," "classical conditioning," "music," and "fear." Some of your schemas could even contain an entire hierarchy of other concepts. Let's look at some important ways that these schemas are used.

Expectations Schemas are one of the attributes that Google and other search engines lack, so they have no real understanding of "birthday" or "psychology" or "nonfat mocha." But for us, schemas provide contexts and expectations about the features likely to be found when you encounter familiar people, situations,

CONNECTION • CHAPTER 4
Implicit memory holds information that can affect behavior without becoming fully conscious.

CONNECTION • CHAPTER 6
Piaget said that cognitive development involves changes in *schemas*.

Intuition The ability to make judgments without consciously reasoning.

images, and ideas (Baldwin, 1992). For example, to an airline passenger, the word *terminal* probably conjures up a schema that includes scenes of crowds, long corridors, and airplanes. For a heart attack victim, however, the schema for *terminal* might include feelings of anxiety and thoughts of death. And for an auto mechanic, *terminal* might mean a connection for a battery cable.

Making Inferences New information, which is often incomplete or ambiguous, makes more sense when you can relate it to existing knowledge in your stored schemas. So schemas enable you to make inferences about missing information. Consider this statement:

> Tanya was upset to discover, on opening the basket, that she'd forgotten the salt.

With no further information, what can you infer about this event? *Salt* implies that the basket is a picnic basket containing food. The fact that Tanya is upset that the salt is missing suggests that the food in the basket is food that is usually salted, such as hard-boiled eggs or vegetables. You automatically know what other foods might be included and, equally important, what definitely is not: Everything in the world that is larger than a picnic basket and anything that would be inappropriate to take on a picnic—from a boa constrictor to bronze-plated baby shoes. Thus, the body of information you now have has been organized around a "picnic-basket" schema. So by relating the statement about Tanya to your preestablished schema, the statement has meaning.

How important are schemas to you? According to researchers Donald Norman and David Rumelhart, schemas are the primary units of meaning in the human information-processing system (1975). You comprehend new information by integrating new input with what you already know, as when your favorite pizza parlor advertises a new spicy Thai chicken curry pizza that you had never even dreamed of before. (Psychologists call this process of blending the new with the old *assimilation*.) If you find a discrepancy between new input and existing schemas, you may deal with it by changing your schema (a process called *accommodation*), as most of us did when the concept of "telephone" was revolutionized by the introduction of cell phones.

In a practical application of schema theory, researchers taught low-achieving math students how to classify word problems into just a few different types. For example, one type involved a "change" schema. The students learned that all "change" problems involve a story, such as this one: "Rudy had three pennies, and his mother gave him four more. How many does he now have?" They also learned some common strategies for solving "change" problems. After several months of schema-based instruction, test results showed that these low-achieving students had made tremendous gains in their math scores—enough to move into the "above average" ranks (Jitendra et al., 2007).

Schemas and Humor Schemas also serve as the foundation for much of our humor (Dingfelder, 2006). We often find things funny when they invoke two or more incongruous or incompatible schemas at once. Consider this joke:

> A horse walks into a bar, and the bartender says, "Why the long face?"

This brief (and possibly lame) joke features several incongruous schemas, including (a) our knowledge that horses don't frequent bars and (b) the confusion over the horse's long nose and the "long face" as a metaphor for sadness.

Not everything we find incongruous is funny, however. A person being struck by a car on the sidewalk is not humorous. Generally, if the conflicting frames of reference involve threat or if the situation holds a cherished belief up to ridicule, we won't find it funny. If, however, schemas in a joke serve to demean someone who we consider threatening, we may well find it humorous. This accounts for much humor that we call racist, sexist, or political.

Scripts as Event Schemas We have schemas not only about objects and events but also about persons, roles, and ourselves. These schemas help us to decide what to expect or how people should behave under specific circumstances. An *event schema* or **script** consists of knowledge about sequences of interrelated, specific events and actions expected to occur in a certain way in particular settings (Baldwin, 1992). We have scripts for going to a restaurant, using the library, listening to a lecture, going on a first date, and even making love.

Cultural Influences on Scripts Scripts used in other cultures may differ substantially from ours. For example, American women living in conservative Arab countries often report that many behaviors they might take for granted at home—such as walking unescorted in public, wearing clothing that showed their faces and legs, or driving a car—are considered scandalously inappropriate by citizens of their host country. To maintain good relations, these women have had to change their habits and plans to accommodate local customs. We can see from such examples that the scripts found in diverse cultures have developed from distinct schemas for viewing the world.

When people from the same culture get together, they may feel comfortable because they follow the same scripts, helping them to comprehend the "meaning" of the situation in the same way and have the same expectations of each other (Abelson, 1981; Schank & Abelson, 1977). When people do not all follow similar scripts, however, they may be made uncomfortable by a script "violation" and may have difficulty understanding why the scene was "misplayed" by others. Unfortunately, when scripts from different cultures clash, people may say, "I tried to interact, but it was so awkward that I don't want to try again" (Brislin, 1993).

CheckYourUnderstanding

1. **APPLICATION:** A dictionary definition would be an example of which kind of concept?

2. **APPLICATION:** Give an example of a concept hierarchy.

3. **APPLICATION:** Give an example of a script.

4. **UNDERSTANDING THE CORE CONCEPT:** All of the following are components of thought, except
   a. concepts.
   b. images.
   c. schemas.
   d. stimuli.

Answers 1. An artificial concept. **2.** Our example is animal, mammal, dog, cocker spaniel. Any such series forms a concept hierarchy, provided that each category includes the one that follows. Another example would be food, Italian food, pasta, spaghetti. **3.** Knowing how to check out a book at the library is an example of a script. So is any other procedure, such as knowing how to study for a test or how to boil an egg. **4.** d

5.2 KEY QUESTION
WHAT ABILITIES DO GOOD THINKERS POSSESS?

The popularity of lotteries and casino games, in which the chances of winning are small, shows us that human thought is not always purely logical. Instead, we might say that thinking is *psycho*logical—which has some advantages. Departures from logic allow us to fantasize, daydream, act creatively, react unconsciously, respond emotionally, and generate new ideas.

We are, of course, capable of careful reasoning. After all, our species did invent that most logical of devices, the computer. Still, the psychology of thinking teaches us that we should not expect people to behave always in a strictly logical manner or that good judgment will be based on reason alone. This

Script A cluster of knowledge about sequences of events and actions expected to occur in particular settings.

ability to think *psychol*ogically enhances our ability to solve problems. And, as we will see, good thinkers also know how to use effective thinking strategies and the avoidance of ineffective or misleading strategies. We will also see that *psychol*ogical thinking is more useful than mere logic because it helps us make decisions rapidly in a changing world that usually furnishes us incomplete information. Our Core Concept puts all this in more technical language:

core concept | Good thinkers not only have a repertoire of effective strategies, called algorithms and heuristics, they also know how to avoid the common impediments to problem solving and decision making.

Problem Solving

Artists, inventors, Nobel Prize winners, great presidents, successful business executives, world-class athletes, and high-achieving college students—all must be effective problem solvers. And what strategies do these effective problem solvers use? No matter what their field, those who are most successful share certain characteristics. They, of course, possess the requisite knowledge for solving the problems they face. In addition, they are skilled at (a) *identifying the problem* and (b) *selecting a strategy* to attack the problem. In the next few pages we will examine these two skills, with the aid of some examples.

Identifying the Problem   A good problem solver learns to consider all the relevant possibilities, without leaping to conclusions prematurely. Suppose that you are driving along the freeway, and your car suddenly begins sputtering and then quits. As you coast to the shoulder, you notice that the gas gauge says "empty." What do you do? Your action in this predicament depends on the problem you think you are solving. If you assume that you are out of fuel, you may hike to the nearest service station for a gallon of gas. But you may be disappointed. By representing the problem as "out of gas," you may fail to notice a loose battery cable that interrupts the supply of electricity both to the spark plugs and to the gas gauge. The good problem solver considers all the possibilities before committing to one solution.

Selecting a Strategy   The second ingredient of successful problem solving requires selecting a strategy that fits the problem at hand (Wickelgren, 1974). For simple problems, a trial-and-error approach will do—as when you search in the dark for the key to open your front door. More difficult problems require better methods. Problems in specialized fields, such as engineering or medicine, may require not only specialized knowledge but special procedures or formulas known as *algorithms*. In addition, expert problem-solvers have a repertoire of more intuitive, but less precise, strategies called *heuristics*. Let's look more closely at both of these methods.

Algorithms   Whether you are a psychology student or a rocket scientist, selecting the right algorithms will guarantee correct solutions for many of your problems. And what are these never-fail strategies? **Algorithms** are nothing more than formulas or procedures, like those you learned in science and math classes. They can help you solve particular kinds of problems for which you have all the necessary information. For example, you can use algorithms to balance your checkbook, figure your gas mileage, calculate your grade-point average, and make a call on your cell phone. If applied correctly, an algorithm always works because you merely follow a step-by-step procedure that leads directly from the problem to the solution.

Despite their usefulness, however, algorithms will not solve every problem you face. Problems involving subjective values or having too many unknowns (Will you be happier with a red car or a white car? Which is the best airline to take to Denver?) and problems that are just too complex for a formula (How

Algorithms   Problem-solving procedures or formulas that guarantee a correct outcome, if correctly applied.

can you get a promotion? What will the fish bite on today?) do not lend themselves to the use of algorithms. And that is why we also need the more intuitive and flexible strategies called *heuristics*.

Heuristics   Everyone makes a collection of heuristics while going through life. Examples: "Don't keep bananas in the refrigerator." "If it doesn't work, see if it's plugged in." "Feed a cold and starve a fever" (or is it the other way around?). Heuristics are simple, basic rules—so-called "rules of thumb" that help us cut through the confusion of complicated situations. Unlike algorithms, heuristics do not guarantee a correct solution, but they often give us a good start in the right direction. Some heuristics require special knowledge, such as training in medicine or physics or psychology. Other heuristics, such as those you will learn in the following paragraphs, are more widely applicable—and well worth remembering.

Some Useful Heuristic Strategies   Here are three essential heuristics that should be in every problem-solver's tool kit. They require no specialized knowledge, yet they can help you in a wide variety of puzzling situations. The common element shared by all three involves getting the problem solver to approach a problem from a different perspective.

Working Backward   Some problems, such as the maze seen in Figure 5.4, may baffle us because they present so many possibilities we don't know where to start. A good way to attack this sort of puzzle is by beginning at the end and *working backward*. (Who says that we must always begin at the beginning?) This strategy can eliminate some of the dead ends that we would otherwise stumble into by trial and error. In general, working backward offers an excellent strategy for problems in which the goal is clearly specified, such as mazes or certain math problems.

Searching for Analogies   If a new problem is similar to another you have faced before, you may be able to employ a strategy that you learned previously. The trick is to recognize the similarity, or *analogy*, between the new problem and the old one (Medin & Ross, 1992). For example, if you are an experienced cold-weather driver, you use this strategy to decide whether to install tire chains on a snowy day: "Is the snow as deep as it was the last time I needed chains?" Even very complex problems may yield to this strategy. The cracking of the genetic code was assisted by the analogy of the DNA molecule being shaped like a spiral staircase, as you can see in the accompanying photos.

Breaking a Big Problem into Smaller Problems   Are you facing a huge problem, such as an extensive term paper? The best strategy may be to break the big problem down into smaller, more manageable steps, often called *subgoals*. In writing a paper, for example, you might break the problem into the steps of selecting a topic, doing your library and Internet research, outlining the paper, writing the first draft, and revising the paper. In this way, you will begin to organize the work and develop a plan for attacking each part of the problem. And, by tackling a problem in a step-by-step fashion, big problems will seem more manageable. Any large, complex

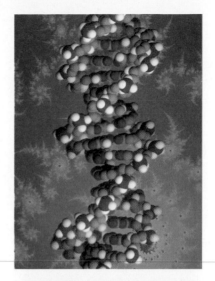

Watson and Crick used the analogy of a spiral staircase to help them understand the structure of the DNA molecule and crack the genetic code.

Heuristics   Cognitive strategies or "rules of thumb" used as shortcuts to solve complex mental tasks. Unlike algorithms, heuristics do not guarantee a correct solution.

FIGURE 5.4
Working Backward

Mazes and math problems often lend themselves to the heuristic of working backward. Try solving this maze, as the mouse must do, by starting at what would normally be the finish (in the center) and working backward to the start.

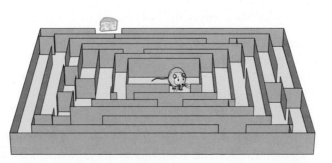

problem—from writing a paper to designing an airplane—may benefit from this approach. In fact, the Wright Brothers deliberately used this heuristic to break down their problem of powered human flight into its components. By using a series of kites, gliders, and models, they studied the component problems of lift, stability, power, and directional control. Later they put their discoveries together to solve the larger problem of powered human flight (Bradshaw, 1992).

Obstacles to Problem Solving   Having a good repertoire of strategies is essential to successful problem solving, but people often get stuck because they latch onto an ineffective strategy and won't let go. For this reason, problem solvers must learn to recognize when they have encountered an obstacle that demands a new approach. Becoming a successful problem solver has as much to do with recognizing such obstacles as it does with selecting the right algorithm or heuristic. Here are some of the most troublesome of the obstacles problem solvers face.

Mental Set   Sometimes you may persist with a less-than-ideal strategy simply because it has worked on other problems in the past. In psychological terms, you have an inappropriate **mental set**—the tendency to respond to a new problem in the same way you approached a similar problem previously. You have "set" your mind on a single strategy, but this time you've chosen the wrong analogy or algorithm. Let's illustrate this with the following puzzle.

Each of the groups of letters in the columns below is a common, but scrambled, word. See if you can unscramble them:

nelin	frsca	raspe	tnsai
ensce	peshe	klsta	epslo
sdlen	nitra	nolem	naoce
lecam	macre	dlsco	tesle
slfal	elwha	hsfle	maste
dlchi	ytpar	naorg	egran
neque	htmou	egsta	eltab

Check your answers against the key on page 190.

Most people, whether they realize it or not, eventually solve the scrambled word problem with an algorithm by rearranging the order of the letters in all the words in the same way, using the formula 3-4-5-2-1. Thus,

$$n e l i n \text{ becomes } l i n e n$$
$$1\,2\,3\,4\,5 \qquad\qquad 3\,4\,5\,2\,1$$

Notice, however, that by using that algorithm, your answers for the last two columns won't agree with the "correct" ones given on page 190. The mental set that you developed while working on the first two columns prevented you from seeing that there is more than one answer for the last 14 items. The lesson of this demonstration is that a mental set can make you limit your options, without realizing that you have done so. While a mental set often does produce results, you should occasionally stop to ask yourself whether you have slipped into a rut that prevents your seeing another answer. (Now can you find some other possible answers to the scrambled words in the last two columns?)

Functional Fixedness   A special sort of mental set occurs when you think you need a screwdriver, but you don't realize that you could tighten the bolt with a dime. Psychologists call this **functional fixedness**. Under this condition, the function of a familiar object becomes so set, or fixed, in your mind that you cannot see a new function for it. To illustrate, consider this classic problem:

Your psychology professor has offered you $5 if you can tie together two strings dangling from the ceiling (see Figure 5.5) without pulling them down.

Mental set   The tendency to respond to a new problem in the manner used for a previous problem.

Functional fixedness   The inability to perceive a new use for an object associated with a different purpose; a form of mental set.

◀ CONNECTION • CHAPTER 4

Compare *functional fixedness* with *proactive interference.*

But when you grab the end of one string and pull it toward the other one, you find that you cannot quite reach the other string. The only objects available to you in the room are on the floor in the corner: a Ping-Pong ball, five screws, a screwdriver, a glass of water, and a paper bag. How can you reach both strings at once and tie them together?

Read the following if you want the answer: In this problem you may have had functional fixedness with regard to the screwdriver. Did you realize that you could use the screwdriver as a pendulum weight to swing one of the strings toward you?

Self-Imposed Limitations   We can be our own worst enemies when we impose unnecessary limitations on ourselves. The classic nine-dot problem in Figure 5.6 illustrates this neatly. To solve this one, you must connect all nine dots with no more than four connecting straight lines—that is, drawn without lifting your pencil from the paper. The instructions allow you to cross a line, but you may not retrace a line.

Hint: Most people who confront this problem impose an unnecessary restriction on themselves by assuming that they cannot draw lines beyond the square made by the dots. Literally, they don't "think outside the box." Figure 5.7 gives two possible correct answers. Translating this into personal terms, we can find many instances in which people impose unnecessary restrictions on themselves. Students may assume that they have no talent for math or science—thereby eliminating the possibility of a technical career. Or because of gender stereotypes a man may never consider that he could be a nurse or a grade school teacher, and a woman may assume that she must be a secretary, rather than an administrator. What real-life problems are you working on in which you have imposed unnecessary limitations on yourself?

Other Obstacles   There are many other obstacles to problem solving that we will simply mention, rather than discuss in detail. These include lack of specific knowledge required by the problem, lack of interest, low self-esteem, fatigue, and drugs (even legal drugs, such as cold medicines or sleeping pills). Arousal and the accompanying stress represent another important stumbling block for would-be problem solvers. When you study emotion and motivation later in this book, you will see that there is an optimum arousal level for any task, be it basketball, brain surgery, or making a presentation in class. Beyond that critical point, further arousal causes performance to deteriorate. Thus, moderate levels of arousal actually facilitate problem solving, but high stress levels can make problem solving impossible.

In general, our discussion of problem solving shows that we humans are thinkers who readily jump to conclusions, based on our knowledge and biased by our motives, emotions, and perceptions. In view of this, it is surprising that our thinking so often serves us well in day-to-day life. Yet, from another perspective it makes perfect sense: Most of our problem-solving efforts draw on past experience to make predictions about future rewards or punishments. This, of course, is exactly what operant conditioning is all about—which suggests that this mode of thinking is a fundamental part of our nature. Many of the "flaws" in our reasoning abilities, such as functional fixedness, are actually part of an adaptive (but necessarily imperfect) strategy that helps us use our previous experience to solve new problems.

Judging and Making Decisions

Whether you are a student, a professor, or a corporate president, you make decisions every day. "How much time do I need to study tonight?" "What grade does this paper deserve?" "How much should I invest?" You can think of each decision as the solution to a problem—a problem for which there may not be a

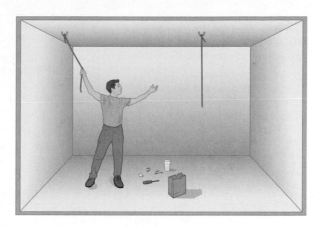

FIGURE 5.5
The Two-String Problem

How could you tie the two strings together, using only the objects found in the room?

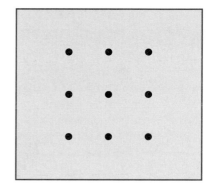

FIGURE 5.6
The Nine-Dot Problem

Can you connect all nine dots with four connecting straight lines without lifting your pencil from the paper?

(*Source:* Adapted from "Can You Solve It?" in *How to Solve Mathematical Problems: Elements of a Theory of Problems and Problem Solving* by Wayne A. Wickelgren. Copyright © 1974 by W. H. Freeman and Company. Reprinted by permission of Dover Publications.)

CONNECTION • CHAPTER 3

Operant conditioning involves the control of behavior by rewards and punishments.

FIGURE 5.7
Two Solutions to the Nine-Dot Problem

(*Source:* Adapted from "Can You Solve It?" in *How to Solve Mathematical Problems: Elements of a Theory of Problems and Problem Solving* by Wayne A. Wickelgren. Copyright © 1974 by W. H. Freeman and Company. Reprinted by permission of Dover Publications.)

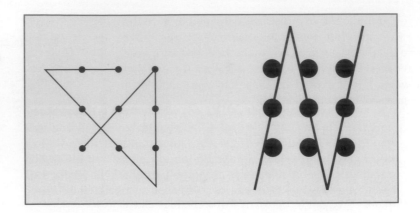

clearly right answer, but a problem requiring judgment. Unfortunately, especially for those who have not studied the psychology of decision making, judgment can be clouded by emotions and biases that interfere with critical thinking. Let's examine the most common of these causes of poor judgment.

Confirmation Bias   Suppose that Tony has strong feelings about raising children: "Spare the rod and spoil the child," he says. How do you suppose Tony will deal with the news that punishment can actually encourage aggressive behavior? Chances are that he will be swayed by *confirmation bias* to ignore or find fault with information that doesn't fit with his opinions and to seek information with which he agrees. He will probably tell you tales of spoiled children who didn't get much punishment for their transgressions or of upstanding adults, like himself, who owe their fine character to harsh discipline. A great deal of evidence shows that the confirmation bias is a powerful and all-too-human tendency (Aronson, 2004; Nickerson, 1998). In fact, we all act like Tony sometimes, especially on issues on which we hold strong opinions.

> ◀ **CONNECTION • CHAPTER 1**
>
> *Confirmation bias* makes us pay attention to events that confirm our beliefs and ignore evidence that contradicts them.

Hindsight Bias   A friend tells you that she lost money investing in "dot-com" stocks. "I thought the Internet was the wave of the future," she says. And you reply, "I knew the boom in Internet stocks would turn into a bust." You are guilty of the **hindsight bias**, sometimes called the "I-knew-it-all-along effect" (Fischhoff, 1975; Hawkins & Hastie, 1990). Just as guilty of hindsight bias are the Monday morning quarterbacks who know what play should have been called at the crucial point in yesterday's big game. This form of distorted thinking appears after an event has occurred and people overestimate their ability to have predicted it. Hindsight bias can flaw the judgment of jurors, historians, newscasters, and anyone else who second-guesses other people's judgments after all the facts are in.

Hindsight bias   The tendency, after learning about an event, to "second guess" or believe that one could have predicted the event in advance.

Unscrambled Words (from page 188)

The words you found to solve the scrambled word problem may not jibe with the ones listed here—especially the third and fourth columns. Most people, whether they are aware of it or not, develop an *algorithm* as they work on the first two columns. While the formula will work on all the words, it becomes a *mental set* that interferes with the problem solver's ability to see alternative solutions for the words in the last two columns.

linen	scarf	pears	stain
scene	sheep	talks	poles
lends	train	melon	canoe
camel	cream	colds	steel
falls	whale	shelf	meats
child	party	groan	anger
queen	mouth	gates	bleat

Anchoring Bias   Ask a few of your friends, one at a time, to give a quick, off-the-top-of-the-head guess at the answer to the following simple math problem:

$$1 \times 2 \times 3 \times 4 \times 5 \times 6 \times 7 \times 8 = ?$$

Make them give you an estimate without actually doing the calculation; give them only about five seconds to think about it. Then, pose the problem in reverse to some other friends:

$$8 \times 7 \times 6 \times 5 \times 4 \times 3 \times 2 \times 1 = ?$$

Are the results different for the two groups?

Nobody will give precisely the right answer, of course, but it's likely that your friends will respond as volunteers did in Daniel Kahneman and Amos Tversky's (2000) experiment. It turns out that the answers to such questions, where people usually don't have a good "ballpark" answer, depend on whether the problem begins with larger or smaller numbers. Those who saw the first problem gave a lower estimate than did those who were given the second problem. In Kahneman and Tversky's study, the average answer for the first group was 512, while the average for the second group was 2250. Apparently, their "first impression"—larger or smaller numbers at the beginning of the problem—biased their responses. Incidentally, the correct answer (40,320) was larger than either group had imagined.

Kahneman and Tversky have explained the difference between the two groups on the basis of an **anchoring bias**. That is, people apparently use this flawed heuristic to "anchor" their thinking to the higher or lower numbers that appear at the beginning of the problem. The anchoring bias can affect our real-world decisions, as those who sell automobiles and real estate well know: What we ultimately decide to pay for a car or a house depends on the price and condition of the first item we are shown.

Representativeness Bias   If you assume that blondes are mentally challenged or ministers are prudish or math professors are nerdish, you not only have some prejudices, but your judgment has been clouded by **representativeness bias**. One reason people succumb to such prejudices is because the representativeness bias simplifies the task of social judgment. Once something is "categorized," it shares all the features of other members in that category. The fallacy in this heuristic, of course, is that people, events, and objects do not "belong" to categories simply because we find it mentally convenient to give them labels. By relying on category memberships to organize our experiences, we risk ignoring or underestimating the tremendous diversity of individual cases and complexity of people.

When estimating the likelihood that a specific individual belongs to a certain category—"vegetarian," for example—we look to see whether the person possesses the features found in a typical category member. For example, is your new acquaintance, Holly, a vegetarian? Does she resemble your prototype of a "typical" vegetarian? Perhaps you believe that most vegetarians wear sandals, ride bicycles, and support liberal social causes. If so, you might judge that Holly represents enough of the characteristics of your concept of "vegetarians" to belong to the same group.

But such an analysis is not entirely reasonable. Although some—perhaps many—vegetarians wear sandals, ride bicycles, and hold liberal views, the opposite may not be true: Because vegetarians are a minority group in the general population, it is unlikely that any particular individual who supports liberal social causes, wears sandals, and rides a bicycle is also vegetarian. That is, by ignoring the base rate information—the probability of a characteristic occurring in the general population—you have drawn an erroneous conclusion. Holly may in fact be an omnivore like most of your acquaintances, although if you invite her to dinner she will probably accept the cheese pizza and salad you offer her

Anchoring bias   A faulty heuristic caused by basing (anchoring) an estimate on a completely irrelevant quantity.

Representativeness bias   A faulty heuristic strategy based on the presumption that, once people or events are categorized, they share all the features of other members in that category.

Shoppers face the tyranny of choice *when they must decide among similar products. Psychologist Barry Schwartz suggests quickly settling on one that is "good enough," rather than wasting time on "maximizing" a choice of little importance.*

without complaint. While your representativeness bias—judging Holly by what seems to be her "type"—may not have dire consequences in this case, the same error underlies the more serious stereotypes and prejudices that result when people classify others solely on the basis of group membership.

Availability Bias   Yet another faulty heuristic comes from our tendency to judge probabilities of events by how readily examples come to mind. Psychologists call this the **availability bias.** We can illustrate this by asking you: Do more English words begin with *r* than have *r* in the third position? Most people think so because it is easier to think of words that begin with *r.* That is, words beginning with *r* are more available to us from long-term memory. Similarly, the availability bias affects people who watch a lot of violent crime on television. Why? They have violent images readily *available* in their memories. Studies show that fans of violent TV shows usually judge their chances of being murdered or mugged as being much higher than do people who watch little television (Singer et al., 1984).

The Tyranny of Choice   Not all decision problems stem from faulty heuristics; they can also come from factors outside the person. To illustrate: Have you ever had trouble deciding among a bewildering array of choices—perhaps in buying a car, a computer, or even a tube of toothpaste? Too many choices can interfere with effective decision making, sometimes to the point of immobilizing us. For example, when Sheena Sethi-Iyengar and her colleagues (2004) studied the choices employees made concerning matching contributions to retirement funds, they found that too many alternatives could, in effect, make people throw away free money. If employers offered to match employees' contributions and give them only two alternatives, 75% elected to participate. But when allowed to select among 59 possibilities, the participation rate fell to 60%. Apparently some people just gave up. Psychologist Barry Schwartz (2004) calls this the **tyranny of choice.**

Schwartz says that the tyranny of choice can also become a source of stress, not to mention a big waste of time, especially for those who feel compelled to make the "correct" decision or get the very "best buy." The antidote, he says, is "satisficing," rather than "maximizing." Satisficers, says Schwartz, scan their options until they find one that is merely "good enough," while maximizers stress themselves out by trying to make certain they have made the very best choice.

Decision-Making and Critical Thinking   Much of the foregoing discussion should have a familiar ring, because it involves critical thinking. In fact, one of the critical thinking questions we have posed in this book deals with the possibility of biases, such as confirmation bias, anchoring bias, and availability bias. In other words, critical thinkers are alert to the common obstacles to problem solving.

In addition, we should now add a few more items to the list of critical-thinking skills that we have discussed in previous chapters. Specifically, the critical thinker should know how to identify a problem (which is exactly what we do when we ask, "What is the issue?"), select a strategy, and apply the most common algorithms and heuristic strategies. All of these skills can help those who want to take their thinking the next level: to become an expert—or even a creative genius.

Becoming a Creative Genius

Everyone would agree that Einstein was a creative genius. So were Aristotle and Bach. And we can make a case that Brin and Page, the Google guys, are geniuses, too. But what about your Aunt Elisa, who does watercolors? Such questions illustrate the big problem in creativity research: The experts cannot agree on an exact definition of **creativity.** Most, however, would go along with the slightly fuzzy notion that creativity is a process that produces novel responses that contribute to the solutions of problems. Most would also agree that a "genius" is someone whose insight and creativity are so great that they set that individual

Availability bias   A faulty heuristic strategy that estimates probabilities based on information that can be recalled (made available) from personal experience.

Tyranny of choice   The impairment of effective decision making, when confronted with an overwhelming number of choices.

Creativity   A mental process that produces novel responses that contribute to the solutions of problems.

apart from ordinary folk. As with the idea of creativity, the boundary for genius is not well defined.

Let's follow the lead of psychologist Robert Weisberg, who offers a view of "genius" that goes against the commonly held assumption that geniuses are completely different from the rest of us. In brief, he argues that geniuses are merely good problem solvers who also possess certain helpful—but entirely human—characteristics.

Creative Genius as Not So Superhuman   Here's how Weisberg (1986) characterized most people's assumptions about the quality we call "genius":

> Our society holds a very romantic view about the origins of creative achievements. . . . This is the genius view, and at its core is the belief that creative achievements come about through great leaps of imagination which occur because creative individuals are capable of extraordinary thought processes. In addition to their intellectual capacities, creative individuals are assumed to possess extraordinary personality characteristics which also play a role in bringing about creative leaps. These intellectual and personality characteristics are what is called "genius," and they are brought forth as the explanation for great creative achievements. (p. 1)

There was no question but that Albert Einstein was bright. He also had an independent streak, a sense of humor, an intense interest in the complex problem of gravity, and a willingness to restructure the problem. And he sought the stimulation of other physicists. But he probably did not use thought processes that were altogether different from those used by other thinkers.

But, according to Weisberg and some other scholars in this area (Bink & Marsh, 2000), there is surprisingly little evidence supporting this view. In fact, the notion that creative geniuses are a breed apart may actually discourage creativity by making people feel that real creativity lies out of their reach. A more productive view, suggests Weisberg, portrays the thinking of people we call geniuses as "ordinary thought processes in ordinary individuals" (p. 11). What produces extraordinary creativity, he says, is extensive knowledge, high motivation, and certain personality characteristics—not superhuman talents.

Knowledge and Understanding   Everyone agrees with Weisberg on one point: The most highly creative individuals have *expertise,* defined as a highly developed understanding of the knowledge in their fields (Ericsson et al., 2006). In fact, you cannot become highly creative without first becoming an **expert**: having extensive and organized knowledge of the field in which you will make your creative contribution. But such mastery is not easily achieved, because it requires a high level of motivation that can sustain years of intense training and practice. Studies indicate that about ten years of work are required to master the knowledge and skills required for full competence in virtually any field, whether it be skiing, sculpture, singing, or psychology (Ericsson et al., 1993; Sternberg & Lubart, 1991, 1992). Oh, yes, and this rule also applies to the field of computing, as in the case of Google founders Brin and Page. Meanwhile, such factors as time pressures or an overly critical supervisor, teacher, or parent can suppress the creative flow (Amabile et al., 2002).

Aptitudes, Personality Characteristics, and Creativity   In opposition to Weisberg, psychologist Howard Gardner (1993) argues that the extraordinary creativity that we see in the work of Freud, Einstein, Picasso, and others is a combination of several factors that include not only expertise and motivation but also certain patterns of abilities and personality characteristics. Highly creative individuals, he says, have **aptitudes**—largely innate potentialities—specific to certain domains. (These potentialities, of course, must be developed by intensive study and practice.) Freud, for example, had a special facility for creating with words and understanding people; Einstein was remarkably good at logic and spatial relationships; and Picasso's creativity arose from a combination of aptitudes comprising spatial relationships and interpersonal perceptiveness.

But at the same time, creative people usually possess a common cluster of personality traits, including the following ones (Barron & Harrington, 1981; Csikszentmihalyi, 1996):

Experts   Individuals who possess well-organized funds of knowledge, including the effective problem-solving strategies, in a field.

Aptitudes   Innate potentialities (as contrasted with abilities acquired by learning).

- *Independence.* Highly creative people have the ability to resist social pressures to conform to conventional ways of thinking, at least in their area of creative interest (Amabile, 1983, 1987; Sternberg, 2001). That is, they have the confidence to strike out on their own. Because of this, perhaps, some creative people describe themselves as loners.

- *Intense interest in a problem.* Highly creative individuals also must have an all-consuming interest in the subject matter with which they will be creative (Amabile, 2001). They are always tinkering, often just in their minds, with problems that fascinate them (Weisberg, 1986). External motivators, such as money or a Nobel Prize, may add to their motivation, but the main motivators are internal, otherwise they could not sustain the long-term interest in a problem necessary for an original contribution.

- *Willingness to restructure the problem.* Highly creative people not only grapple with problems, but they often question the way a problem is presented (Sternberg, 2001). (Recall our earlier discussion about identifying the problem.) For example, students from the School of the Art Institute of Chicago who later became the most successful creative artists among their class members had one striking characteristic in common: They were always changing and redefining the assignments given by their instructors (Getzels & Csikszentmihalyi, 1976).

- *Preference for complexity.* Creative people seem drawn to complexity—to what may appear messy or chaotic to others. Moreover, they revel in the challenge of looking for simplicity in complexity. Thus, highly creative people may be attracted to the largest, most difficult, and most complex problems in their fields (Sternberg & Lubart, 1992).

- *A need for stimulating interaction.* Creativity of the highest order almost always grows out of an interaction of highly creative individuals. Early in their careers, creative people usually find a mentor—a teacher who brings them up to speed in their chosen field. Highly creative individuals go on to surpass their mentors and then find additional stimulation from the ideas of others like themselves. Often, this means leaving behind family and former friends (Gardner, 1993).

So, what is the take-home message for our understanding of creativity? Those who have looked closely at this domain agree on two main points. First, creativity requires well-developed knowledge of the field in which the creative contribution will be made. Second, high-level creativity requires certain personal characteristics, such as independence and the motivation required to sustain an interest in an unsolved problem over a very long period of time. That is your formula for becoming a creative genius.

The Role of Intelligence in Creativity   Is a high IQ necessary for creativity or genius? The answer is a bit complicated. Low intelligence inhibits creativity—although, we will see that there are some special cases, known as *savants,* who may have a highly developed skill, despite their mental handicaps. On the other end of the IQ spectrum, we find that having high intelligence does not necessarily mean that the individual will be creative: There are lots of very bright people who never produce anything that could be called groundbreaking or highly original and insightful. In general, we can say that intelligence and creativity are distinct abilities. We can find plodding, unimaginative persons at all IQ levels, and we can find highly creative persons with only average IQ scores.

Robert Sternberg (2001) argues that creativity lies a step beyond IQ. In his view, creativity requires a decision to go against the expectations of the crowd. This makes creativity potentially achievable for everyone who chooses to adopt a creative attitude. Most people will not do so, he says, for a variety of reasons, including an unwillingness to take the necessary risks.

But we are again getting ahead of ourselves. To understand more deeply how creativity and intelligence are different, it will be helpful to know what intelligence is and how it is measured . . . coming up in a couple of pages.

PSYCHOLOGYMATTERS
Using Psychology to Learn Psychology

Obviously, *experts* are people who know a lot about a particular subject. Unlike a novice, an expert confronting a problem does not have to start from scratch. Experts can often see a solution quickly because they have seen many similar problems before. That is, they are especially good at finding analogies.

Their secret lies in the way their knowledge is organized (Ericsson et al., 2006; Ross, 2006). Characteristically, the novice possesses knowledge that is both limited and unorganized, while experts have extensive knowledge organized into elaborate "chunks" and schemas. We can see this quite clearly in a famous study of world-class chess players.

A Study of Chess Experts   Dutch psychologist Adriaan de Groot found some striking differences when he compared how well a group of grand master chess players and another group of merely good players could remember to a chess problem. When allowed five seconds to view a configuration of pieces as they might appear on a chessboard during a match, the grand masters could reproduce the pattern far more accurately than those with less proficiency (de Groot, 1965). Does that mean that the grand masters had better visual memories? No. When confronted with a random pattern of pieces on the chess board—a pattern that would never happen in a match—the grand masters did no better than the others. This suggests that the experts were better able to draw on familiar patterns in memory, rather than trying to recall individual pieces and positions.

Expertise as Organized Knowledge   How do experts organize their knowledge? There is no easy formula. Through study and practice they develop both a fund of knowledge to apply to a problem and a familiarity with the field's common problems and solutions. That is, they know not only the facts but how the facts are interrelated and used (Bédard & Chi, 1992). Aside from facts and specific skills they must learn, would-be-experts must also acquire a repertoire of heuristics, also known as "tricks of the trade," that are unique to their field of expertise. These heuristics help them find solutions more quickly, without having to follow so many blind leads (Gentner & Stevens, 1983; Simon, 1992).

Practice versus Talent   Are experts born, or is expertise learned? The highest levels of skilled performance requiring speed and accuracy of movement, as in athletics or music, seem to depend in part on native ability (Ackerman, 2007; Simonton, 2001). Expertise in a field requiring the mastery of a body of knowledge (think psychology, medicine, or medieval literature) clearly requires considerable study. There is evidence that people have differing aptitudes for performing at the highest levels in any given field, but it is impossible to predict in advance who has the requisite ability for a particular endeavor. At this point, the important variables seem to be motivation and practice—much as we saw with creativity (Ericsson & Charness, 1994).

Eventually, perhaps, the theories of multiple intelligences that we will study can give us some practical assistance. But for now, especially if you are at the beginning of your college career, the best advice would be to explore as many fields as you can, to find out where your passions lie. You are much more likely to do the necessarily long and hard work on something you love.

So, How Do You Become an Expert?   A supportive environment, with good teachers and mentors, helps (Barab & Plucker, 2002). Beyond that, it's study and practice! But don't just focus on the details. Learn the important schemas and problem-solving strategies in your chosen field, too. How long will it take? Research shows that achieving world-class status in any of a wide gamut of fields—from athletics to academics to chess to music—requires about ten years of intensive study and practice (Ericsson et al., 1993; Gardner, 1993).

What does this suggest for your learning of psychology and other disciplines? You can take the first steps in developing your expertise in any subject by attending to the way your professor and your text organize the information they present (Gonzalvo et al., 1994). Consider such questions as the following:

● What are the terms that your psychology professor keeps mentioning over and over? These might be such concepts as "cognitive science," "behaviorism," "developmental," or "theoretical perspectives." For you they may be, at first, unfamiliar and abstract, but for the professor they may represent the core of the course. Make sure you know what the terms mean and why they are important.

● What concepts does the course syllabus emphasize? What terms are associated with the main topics?

● Around what concepts is the textbook organized? You may be able to tell this quickly by looking at the table of contents. Alternatively, the authors may lay out the organizing points in the preface at the beginning of the book. (In this book, we have attempted to help you identify the organizing principles of each chapter in the form of Core Concepts.)

If you can identify the organizing principles for the course, they will simplify your studying. This makes sense, of course, in light of what you learned earlier about memory. Long-term memory (as you will remember!) is organized by meaningful associations. Accordingly, when you have a simple and effective way of organizing the material, you will have a framework that will help you store and retain it in long-term memory.

CheckYourUnderstanding

1. **APPLICATION:** From your own experience, give an example of an algorithm.

2. **RECALL:** Good problem solvers often use "tricks of the trade" or "rules of thumb" known as _____.

3. **APPLICATION:** Which one of the following would be an example of the confirmation bias at work?
   a. Mary ignores negative information about her favorite political candidate.
   b. Aaron agrees with Joel's taste in music.
   c. Natasha refuses to eat a food she dislikes.

   d. Bill buys a new RV, even though his wife was opposed to the purchase.

4. **RECALL:** List four personality characteristics commonly found in highly creative people.

5. **UNDERSTANDING THE CORE CONCEPT:** Heuristic strategies show that our thinking is often based on
   a. logic rather than emotion.
   b. experience rather than logic.
   c. trial and error rather than algorithms.
   d. creativity rather than genius.

Answers 1. The mathematical formula for finding the area of a triangle is an example of an algorithm—as is any formula or procedure that always gives the correct answer. **2.** heuristics **3.** a **4.** Any four of the following are correct: independence, intense interest in a problem (high motivational level), willingness to restructure problems, preference for complexity, need for stimulating interaction. **5.** b

5.3 KEY QUESTION
HOW IS INTELLIGENCE MEASURED?

Psychologists have long been fascinated by the ways in which people differ in their abilities to reason, solve problems, and think creatively. The assessment of individual differences, however, did not begin with modern psychology. Historical records show that sophisticated mental testing methods were used in ancient China. Over 4000 years ago, the Chinese employed a program of civil service testing that required government officials to demonstrate their competence every third year at an oral examination. Later, applicants were required to pass written civil service tests to assess their knowledge of law, the military, agriculture, and geography. British diplomats and missionaries assigned to China in the early 1800s described the selection procedures so admiringly that the British, and later the Americans, adopted modified versions of China's system for the selection of civil service personnel (Wiggins, 1973).

Unlike the historical Chinese, however, modern Americans seem to be more interested in how "smart" people are, as opposed to how much they have learned. It is the interest in this sort of "native ability" that spurred the development of intelligence testing as we know it today. But, despite the long history of mental testing and the widespread use of intelligence tests in our society, the exact meaning of the term *intelligence* is still disputed (Neisser et al., 1996). Still, most psychologists would probably agree with the general definition that we gave at the beginning of the chapter—that intelligence involves abilities to acquire knowledge, reason, and solve problems. They would also agree that a complete picture of an individual's intelligence must be obtained from measurements across a variety of tasks. However, they disagree on exactly what these abilities are or whether they are many or few in number.

Everyone does acknowledge that intelligence is a relative term. That is, an individual's level of intelligence must be defined in relation to the same abilities in a comparison group, usually of the same age range. Everyone also agrees that intelligence is also a *hypothetical construct:* a characteristic that is not directly observable but must be inferred from behavior. In practice, this means that intelligence is measured from an individual's responses on an intelligence test. The individual's scores are then compared to those of a reference group. Exactly what these tests should assess is the source of much controversy—and the focus of this section of this chapter.

Intelligence testing has a history of controversy, but most psychologists now view intelligence as a normally distributed trait that can be measured by performance on a variety of tasks.

core concept

We begin our survey of intelligence and intelligence testing by introducing you to the people who founded the field of intelligence testing.

Binet and Simon Invent a School Abilities Test

Alfred Binet *(Bi-NAY)* and his colleague Théodore Simon stepped into history in 1904. At that time, a new law required all French children to attend school, and the government needed a means of identifying those who needed remedial help. Binet and Simon were asked to design a test for this purpose. They responded with 30 problems sampling a variety of abilities that seemed necessary for school (Figure 5.8). The new approach was a success. It did, indeed, predict which children could, or could not, handle normal schoolwork.

Four important features distinguish the Binet-Simon approach (Binet, 1911):

1. They interpreted scores on their test as an estimate of *current performance* and not as a measure of innate intelligence.

2. They wanted the test scores to be used to identify children who needed special help and not merely to categorize or label them as bright or dull.

3. They emphasized that training and opportunity could affect intelligence, and they wanted to pinpoint areas of performance in which special education could help the children identified by their test.

4. They constructed the test *empirically*—based on how children were observed to perform—rather than tying the test to a particular theory of intelligence.

On the original Binet-Simon test, a child was asked to perform tasks such as the following:

- Name various common objects (such as a clock or a cat) shown in pictures.
- Repeat a 15-word sentence given by the examiner.
- Give a word that rhymes with one given by the examiner.
- Imitate gestures (such as pointing to an object).
- Comply with simple commands (such as moving a block from one location to another).
- Explain the differences between two common objects.
- Use three words (given by the examiner) in a sentence.
- Define abstract terms (such as "friendship").

FIGURE 5.8
Sample Items from the First Binet-Simon Test

Binet and Simon assessed French children of various ages with this test and computed the average for children at each age. Then, they compared each child's performance to the averages for children of various ages. Finally, they gave each child a score expressed in terms of **mental age (MA)**: the average age at which individuals achieve a particular score. So, for example, when a child's score was the same as the average score for a group of 5-year-olds, the child was said to have a mental age of 5, regardless of his or her **chronological age (CA)**, the number of years since birth. Binet and Simon decided that those most needing remedial help were students whose MA was two years behind CA.

American Psychologists Borrow Binet and Simon's Idea

Less than a decade after the French began testing their school children, American psychologists imported the Binet-Simon test of school abilities and changed it into the form we now call the *IQ test*. They did this by first modifying the scoring procedure, expanding the test's content, and obtaining scores from a large normative group of people, including adults. Soon "intelligence testing" was widely accepted as a technique by which Americans were defining themselves—and each other.

The Appeal of Intelligence Testing in America   Why did tests of intelligence become so popular in the United States? Three forces changing the face of the country early in the 20th century conspired to make intelligence testing seem like an orderly way out of growing turmoil and uncertainty. First, the United States was experiencing an unprecedented wave of immigration, resulting from global economic, social, and political crises. Second, new laws requiring universal education—schooling for all children—were flooding schools with students. And third, when World War I began, the military needed a way of assessing and classifying the new recruits. Together, these events resulted in a need for large numbers of people to be assessed (Chapman, 1988). Intelligence was seen not only as a way to bring some order to the tumult of rapid social change but also as an inexpensive and democratic way to separate those who could benefit from education or military leadership training from those who could not.

One consequence of the large-scale group-testing program in America was that the public came to accept the idea that intelligence tests could accurately differentiate people in terms of their mental abilities. This acceptance soon led to the widespread use of tests in schools and industry. Another, more unfortunate, consequence was that the tests reinforced prevailing prejudices. Specifically, Army reports suggested that differences in test scores were linked to race and country of origin (Yerkes, 1921). Of course, the same statistics could have been used to demonstrate that environmental disadvantages limit the full development of people's intellectual abilities. Instead, immigrants with limited facility in English (the only language in which the tests were given) or even little understanding of how to take such tests were labeled as "morons," "idiots," and "imbeciles" (terms used at the time to specify different degrees of mental retardation).

While these problems are more obvious to us now (with the help of hindsight), at the time they were obscured by the fact that the tests did what most people wanted: They were simple to administer, and they provided a means of assessing and classifying people according to their scores. Never mind that there were

Mental age (MA)   The average age at which normal (average) individuals achieve a particular score.

Chronological age (CA)   The number of years since the individual's birth.

some biases and that some people were treated unfairly. In general, the public perceived that the tests were objective and democratic.

The Stanford-Binet Intelligence Scale   The most respected of the new American tests of intelligence came from the laboratory of Stanford University professor Lewis Terman. His approach was to adapt the Binet and Simon test for U.S. schoolchildren by standardizing its administration and its age-level norms. The result was the Stanford-Binet Intelligence Scale (Terman, 1916), which soon became the standard by which other measures of intelligence were judged. But, because it had to be administered individually, Terman's test was less economical than the group tests. Nevertheless, it was better suited for spotting learning problems. Even more importantly, the Stanford-Binet test was designed both for children and adults.

With his new test Terman introduced the concept of the **intelligence quotient (IQ)**, a term coined originally by German psychologist William Stern in 1914. The IQ was the ratio of mental age (MA) to chronological age (CA), multiplied by 100 (to eliminate decimals):

$$IQ = \frac{\text{Mental Age}}{\text{Chronological Age}} \times 100$$

Please follow us through the IQ equation with these examples: Consider a child with a chronological age of 8 years, whose test scores reveal a mental age of 10. Dividing the child's mental age by chronological age (MA/CA = 10/8) gives 1.25. Multiplying that result by 100, we obtain an IQ of 125. In contrast, another 8-year-old child who performs at the level of an average 6-year-old (MA = 6) has an IQ of 6/8 × 100 = 75, according to Terman's formula. Those whose mental age is the same as their chronological age have IQs of 100, which is considered to be the average or "normal" IQ.

Within a short time, the new Stanford-Binet test became a popular instrument in clinical psychology, psychiatry, and educational counseling. With the publication of this test Terman also promoted his belief that intelligence is largely innate and that his IQ test could measure it precisely. The message was that an IQ score reflected something fundamental and unchanging about people.

Although the Stanford-Binet became the "gold standard" of intelligence testing, it had its critics. The loudest objection was that it employed an inconsistent concept of intelligence because it measured different mental abilities at different ages. For example, 2- to 4-year-olds were tested on their ability to manipulate objects, whereas adults were tested almost exclusively on verbal items. Test makers heeded these criticisms; and, as the scientific understanding of intelligence increased, psychologists found it increasingly important to measure multiple intellectual abilities at all age levels. A modern revision of the Stanford-Binet now provides separate scores for several mental skills.

Problems with the IQ Formula

A problem in calculating IQ scores became apparent as soon as psychologists began to use their formula with adults. Here's what happens: By the mid- to late teenage years, gains in mental age scores usually level off, as people develop mentally in many different directions. Consequently, mental growth, as measured by a test, appears to slow down. As a result, Terman's formula for computing IQs makes normal children appear to become adults with mental retardation—at least as far as their test scores are concerned! Note what happens to the average 30-year-old's score if mental age, as measured by a test, stays at the same level as it was at age 15:

$$IQ = \frac{\text{Mental Age}}{\text{Chronological Age}} = \frac{15}{30} \times 100 = 50$$

Intelligence quotient (IQ)   A numerical score on an intelligence test, originally computed by dividing the person's mental age by chronological age and multiplying by 100.

FIGURE 5.9

An (Imaginary) Normal Distribution
of Women's Heights

The level of the curve at any point
reflects the number of women with
that height.

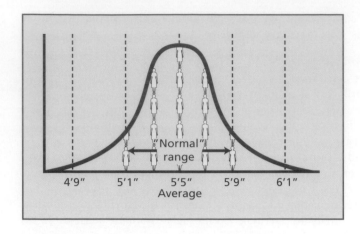

Psychologists quickly realized that this paints an erroneous picture of adult mental abilities. People do not grow less intelligent as they become adults (even though their children sometimes think so). Rather, adults develop in different directions, which their IQ scores do not necessarily reflect. Prudently, psychologists decided to abandon the original IQ formula and to find another means of calculating IQs. Their solution was similar to the familiar practice of "grading on the curve." This famous curve demands some explanation.

Calculating IQs "on the Curve"

Behind the new method for calculating IQs lay the assumption that intelligence is *normally distributed*. That is, intelligence is assumed to be spread through the population in varying degrees in such a way that only a few people fall into the high or low ranges, while most people cluster around a central average. In this respect, intelligence is presumed to be like many physical traits, including height. weight, and shoe size. If you were to measure any of these variables in a large number of people, you would probably get a set of scores that follow the same "curve" teachers use when they grade "on the curve." Let us take women's heights as an example.

Imagine that you have randomly selected a large number of adult women and arranged them in single-file columns, according to their heights (everybody 5′ tall in one column, 5′ 1″ in the next, 5′ 2″ in the next, and so on). You would find most of the women standing in the columns near the group's average height (See Figure 5.9.) Only a few would be in the columns containing extremely tall women or extremely short women. We could easily describe the number of women at each height by a curve that follows the boundary of each column. We call this bell-shaped curve a **normal distribution** (or **normal curve**).

Applying this same concept to intelligence, psychologists find that people's IQ test scores (like the women's heights we considered above) fit a normal distribution. (See Figure 5.10.) More precisely, when IQ tests are given to large numbers of individuals, the scores of those at each age level are normally distributed. (Adults are placed in their own group, regardless of age, and the distribution of their scores also fits the bell-shaped curve.) Instead of using the old IQ formula, IQs are now determined from tables that indicate where test scores fall on the normal curve. The scores are statistically adjusted so that the average for each age group is set at 100. Scores near the middle of the distribution (usually between 90 and 110) are considered to be in the **normal range**. (See Figure 5.10.) At the extreme ends of the distribution, scores below 70 are often said to be in the *mentally retarded range,* while those above 130 are sometimes said to indicate *giftedness.*

Normal distribution (or **normal curve**)
A bell-shaped curve, describing the spread of a characteristic throughout a population.

Normal range   Scores falling near the middle of a normal distribution.

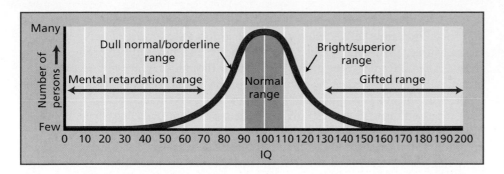

FIGURE 5.10
The Normal Distribution of IQ Scores among a Large Sample

(*Source:* from *Weschler's Measurement and Appraisal of Adult Intelligence*, 5th ed., by Joseph D. Matarazzo. Reprinted with permission of the Helen Reid Educational Foundation. Published by Heldref Publications, 1319 Eighteenth St., NW, Washington, DC 20036-1802. Copyright © 1974.)

Thus, IQ scores are no longer calculated by dividing mental age by chronological age. The concept of a "ratio" expressed as a multiple of 100 (a percentage-like number that is easy to understand) is retained, however. This solves the problem of calculating adult IQs by comparing adults with adults.

But one more problem has surfaced—and remains unsolved. Much to everyone's chagrin, James Flynn has pointed out that the average IQ score has risen gradually, at the rate of about 3 points per decade, ever since the tests were invented, a fact obscured by "renorming" of the tests every few years to keep the average IQ at 100 (Flynn, 1987). If taken at face value, this *Flynn effect* would mean that a person scoring in the average range in your great-grandparents' time might be considered to have mental retardation today! Flynn, along with most other observers, believes that such a conclusion is absurd. Yet, there is no agreed-upon explanation (Flynn, 2003; Neisser et al., 1996). The truth may well involve a combination of factors, including increasing test-taking skills, greater "complexity" of society (everything from movies, to games, to computers, to cell phones), more schooling, and better nutrition. Flynn himself (2007) points out that different components of intelligence have accelerated at different rates (with vocabulary, for example, hardly having budged at all), so part of the IQ gain can be explained in terms of societies valuing and encouraging certain factors that contribute to intelligence, such as the abstract thinking skills involved in identifying similarities: "How are a dog and a rabbit alike?" A century ago, says Flynn, the answer would have been: "You use dogs to hunt rabbits." Now, he notes, the correct answer would be "They are both mammals." Whatever the causes may be, they affect problem-solving ability more than they do general knowledge. In the meantime, test makers must keep adjusting the average scores every few years to keep up with the "IQ creep."

IQ Testing Today

The success of the Stanford-Binet test encouraged the development of other IQ tests. As a result, psychologists now have a wide choice of instruments for measuring intelligence. The most prominent of these alternatives are the Wechsler Adult Intelligence Scale (WAIS), the Wechsler Intelligence Scale for Children (WISC), and the Wechsler Preschool and Primary Scale of Intelligence (WPPSI). With these instruments, psychologist David Wechsler offers a family of tests that measure many skills that are presumed to be components of intelligence, including vocabulary, verbal comprehension, arithmetic ability, similarities (the ability to state how two things are alike), digit span (repeating a series of digits after the examiner), and block design (the ability to reproduce designs by fitting together blocks with colored sides). As our Core Concept noted, these tests measure intelligence by assessing performance on a variety of tasks.

Like the Stanford-Binet, the Wechsler tests are *individual* tests. That is, they are given to one person at a time. Also available are *group* tests of intelligence

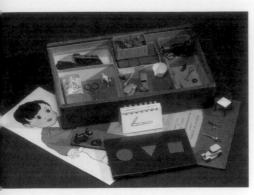

The Stanford-Binet intelligence test kits contains objects used in assessing the intelligence of children.

that can be administered to large numbers of students simultaneously. Unlike the Stanford-Binet and the Wechsler tests, these group tests consist of paper-and-pencil measures, involving booklets of questions and computer-scorable answer sheets. The convenience of group tests—even though they are not as precise as individual tests—has made IQ testing, along with other forms of academic assessment, widespread. It is quite likely that you have taken such tests several times as you passed through grades 1 to 12, perhaps without realizing what they were. The items in the "Do It Yourself!" box are similar to items in many of these commonly used group tests of mental abilities.

What are IQ tests used for today? An IQ score assumes almost overwhelming importance in determining whether a child has "mental retardation" or is "gifted"—concepts we will examine more closely in the next Psychology Matters feature. Aside from those uses, IQ tests figure most prominently in the diagnosis of learning disabilities. The problem with that, says Dr. Jack Naglieri, is that IQ scores don't tell us much about which intervention strategies are likely to be effective with a given child (Benson, 2003a). To remedy this, Naglieri and others are developing tests that place less emphasis on a single number, such as IQ, and more on classifying people in ways that suggest helping strategies, such as identifying reading problems, perceptual problems, or attention disorders.

PSYCHOLOGYMATTERS
What Can You Do for an Exceptional Child?

As we have noted, mental retardation and giftedness lie at the opposite ends of the intelligence spectrum. As traditionally conceived, **mental retardation** occupies the IQ range below IQ 70—taking in the scores achieved by approximately 2% of the population (see Figure 5.11). Arbitrarily, **giftedness** begins 30 points above average, at 130 IQ points, comprising another 2% of the population. Now, bearing in mind all we have learned about the limitations of IQ tests, let's take a brief look at these two categories.

Mental Retardation The most current view of mental retardation deemphasizes IQ scores by focusing on practical abilities to get along in the world (Robinson et al., 2000). In fact, the American Association of Mental Retardation now offers a definition of mental retardation that does not even mention an IQ cut-off score. According to this new perspective, mental retardation involves "significantly subaverage intellectual functioning" that becomes apparent before age 18. It also involves limitations in at least two of the following areas: "communication, self-care, home living, social skills, community use, self-direction, health and safety, functional academics, leisure and work" (Turkington, 1993, p. 26).

Causes of Mental Retardation Mental retardation has many causes (Daily et al., 2000; Scott & Carran, 1987). Some are known to be genetic because we can point to a specific genetically controlled defect. This is the case in people who have *Down's syndrome,* a chromosome disorder that produces multiple physical defects, as well as mental retardation. Some causes are purely environmental, as in *fetal alcohol syndrome,* which involves brain damage incurred before birth, resulting from the mother's abuse of alcohol during pregnancy. Other environmental causes include postnatal accidents that damage the cognitive regions of the brain. Still other causes involve conditions of deprivation or neglect, which fail to give the developing child the experiences needed for advancement up the intellectual ladder. Some cases have no known cause.

Dealing with Mental Retardation We have no cures, although research has found some preventive measures for certain types of mental retardation. For example, a simple test performed routinely on newborn babies can identify a hidden genetic disorder known as PKU. If detected early, the mental retardation usually associated with PKU can be prevented by a special diet. More generally, genetic

Mental retardation Often conceived as representing the lower 2% of the IQ range, commencing about 30 points below average (below about 70 points). More sophisticated definitions also take into account an individual's level of social functioning and other abilities.

Giftedness Often conceived as representing the upper 2% of the IQ range, commencing about 30 points above average (at about 130 IQ points).

CONNECTION • CHAPTER 2

Down's syndrome produces both physical symptoms and mental retardation; it arises from a chromosomal defect.

counseling, pregnancy care services, and education of new parents are other preventive strategies (Scott & Carran, 1987).

Aside from prevention, special education programs can help those who develop mental retardation to learn vocational and independent living skills. Meanwhile, biological scientists hope that one day they will be able to treat genetically based forms of mental retardation with therapies that are just now being conceived. As noted in Chapter 2 genetic treatment may involve splicing a healthy gene into a benign virus that would "infect" all of the cells of a person with mental retardation and replace the defective gene. At present, genetic therapy is being tried experimentally for the treatment of certain physical diseases, but it is at least a few years away in the treatment of mental retardation.

For now, what can you do if you have a child with mental retardation? Dealing with mental retardation usually means making the best of a difficult situation. Parents of a child with mental retardation should realize that, because the nervous system is so immature at birth and because so much physical and mental development occurs during the first years of life, interventions that begin early will have the greatest payoffs. Realistically, however, the most intellectual improvement one can expect from an optimal educational program is an IQ gain of about 15 points (Robinson et al., 2000).

Psychological approaches that involve sensory stimulation and social interaction can be enormously important. In fact, an enriched environment may be just as helpful to a child with mental retardation as it is to a gifted child. Teams of special education teachers, speech therapists, educational psychologists, physicians, and other specialists can devise programs that allow persons with mental retardation to capitalize on the abilities they have, rather than being held prisoner of their disabilities (see Schroeder et al., 1987). Behavior modification programs have been especially successful. As a result, many citizens with mental retardation have learned to care for themselves and have acquired vocational skills that enable them to live independently (Landesman & Butterfield, 1987).

Giftedness At the other end of the intelligence spectrum we find the "gifted," with their especially high IQs, typically defined as being in the top 1 or 2% of

The Special Olympics offers children with mental retardation (and others with disabilities) an opportunity to capitalize on their abilities and to build self-esteem.

CONNECTION • CHAPTER 13

Behavior modification therapies are based on behavioral learning principles derived from operant and classical conditioning.

the population (Robinson et al., 2000). But, you might wonder, what do such people eventually do with their superior intellectual abilities? Does a high IQ give its owner an advantage in life? A long look at gifted individuals suggests that it does.

Terman's Studies of Giftedness   The most extensive project ever undertaken to study gifted individuals began in 1921 under the direction of Lewis Terman, the same person who brought Binet and Simon's IQ test to the United States (Leslie, 2000). From a large pool of children tested in the California schools, Terman selected 1528 children who scored near the top of the IQ range. His longitudinal research program followed these children as they went through school and on into adulthood. Periodically through their lives, Terman retested them and gathered other information on their achievements and adjustment patterns. The resulting decades of data have taught us much about the nature of giftedness. Almost uniformly, Terman's gifted children excelled in school—as one might expect from the strong correlation between IQ and academic achievement. Terman also remarked on the good health and happiness of the children in his sample, although newer evidence suggests that highly gifted children are susceptible to certain physical and psychological disorders (Winner, 2000).

As they moved into adulthood, the gifted group continued on the path of success. An unusually high number of scientists, writers, and professionals emerged from its ranks. Together they published more than 2000 scientific articles, patented 235 inventions, and wrote 92 books. By middle age, more than 86% of the men in Terman's sample had entered high-status professions (Terman & Oden, 1959).

Yet, for all their achievements, no one in this high-IQ sample achieved the level of an Einstein, a Picasso, or a Martha Graham. Nor did a high IQ turn out to be a guarantee of wealth or stature. In fact, many from Terman's sample led ordinary, undistinguished lives. The ones who were most visibly successful seemed to have, in addition to their high IQs, extraordinary motivation and someone at home or at school who was especially encouraging to them (Goleman, 1980; Oden, 1968). You will remember that we previously found these same characteristics to be markers of "genius."

Dealing with Giftedness   Imagine that you are the parent of a child with a very high IQ score, say 145. Which one of the following would be the best course of action?

● Enroll your child in special after-school classes.
● Hire a tutor to help the child with his or her homework.
● Send the child to a private school.
● Do nothing special.

What do the experts say?   Don't rush out to enroll your child in special classes or provide other "help" because of his or her IQ score (Csikszentmihalyi et al., 1993; Wong & Csikszentmihalyi, 1991). Parents can destroy the spark of curiosity by pushing a child toward goals that do not hold the child's interest. Chances are you have already provided an environment in which your child's native ability could thrive. So do not make any rash and radical changes.

Above all, avoid making the child feel like a freak because of his or her unusual abilities and high IQ score. In part because of the personality traits common in gifted children—especially a tendency to spend time alone, working on their interests—they are more likely than other children to suffer social and emotional disorders (Winner, 2000). Nor should you feel smug about your genetic contribution to your child's intellect. Remember that intelligence involves a nature–nurture interaction—and, besides, IQ tests sample only a small fraction of human abilities. Other people's kids may have equally amazing abilities in untested regions of their intellects. In fact, many gifted individuals may go unrecognized by the schools because they have an outstanding talent that shows up primarily in art or music—domains in which formal abilities testing is rarely done.

Remember, also, that a high IQ is no guarantee of high motivation, high creativity, or success in life. All it guarantees is an intellectual opportunity.

So, what should you do with a bright child? Nothing special that you would not have done before you knew the IQ score.

CheckYourUnderstanding

1. RECALL: One of Binet's great ideas was the concept of *mental age,* which he defined as

_____

_____.

2. APPLICATION: You have tested a 12-year-old child and found that she has a mental age of 15. Using the original IQ formula, what is her IQ?

3. RECALL: A problem with the original IQ formula is that it

gave a distorted picture of the intellectual abilities of
  a. adults.
  b. children.
  c. persons with mental retardation.
  d. gifted students.

4. UNDERSTANDING THE CORE CONCEPT: If intelligence is a normally distributed characteristic, in what part of the distribution would you expect to find most people's scores on a test of intelligence?

Answers 1. Mental age on an IQ test is the average age at which individuals achieve a particular score. Or, in different words: Mental age is determined by the average score achieved by individuals of a particular chronological age. **2.** 125. **3.** a **4.** near the middle of the distribution

5.4 KEY QUESTION
IS INTELLIGENCE ONE OR MANY ABILITIES?

People who show aptitude in one area—language, for example—often score high on tests of other domains, such as mathematics or spatial relationships. This fact argues for the idea of a single, general intellectual ability. But there are some glaring exceptions. Persons with **savant syndrome** represent the most extreme exceptions of this sort. These rare individuals have a remarkable-but-limited talent, such as the ability to multiply numbers quickly in their heads or to determine the day of the week for any given date, even though they are mentally slow in other ways (Treffert & Wallace, 2002). Typically, they also show symptoms of autism (Winner, 2000), as you may remember from Dustin Hoffman's classic portrayal of one such person in the film *Rain Man.* Such cases raise a serious question about the whole concept of a single, general intelligence factor. Obviously, there is no simple solution to the question of one or many intelligences. Different psychologists have dealt with the issue in different ways, as our Core Concept suggests:

> **Some psychologists believe that intelligence comprises one general factor, *g*, while others believe that intelligence is a collection of distinct abilities.**

| core
| concept

We will first examine this issue from the viewpoint of psychologists in the *psychometric tradition:* those who have been interested in developing tests to measure mental abilities. Following that excursion, we will look at intelligence from the standpoint of cognitive psychologists who have recently brought a fresh perspective to the problem.

Psychometric Theories of Intelligence

Psychometrics is the field of "mental measurements." It is the psychological specialty that has given us most of our IQ tests, achievement tests, personality tests,

Savant syndrome Found in individuals having a remarkable talent (such as the ability to determine the day of the week for any given date) even though they are mentally slow in other domains.

the SAT, and a variety of other assessment instruments. Many pioneers in psychology carved their professional niches with contributions to psychometrics, including Alfred Binet and Lewis Terman. Yet another famous figure in this field was Charles Spearman, a psychologist who is best known for his work suggesting that intelligence is a single factor.

Spearman's *g* Factor By the 1920s, there were many tests of intelligence available, and British psychologist Charles Spearman was able to show that individuals' scores on different tests tend to be highly correlated (1927). These correlations, he said, point to a single, common factor of general intelligence underlying performance across all intellectual domains. Spearman did not deny that some people have outstanding talents or deficits in certain areas. But, he said, these individual differences should not blind us to a single *general intelligence* factor at work behind all our mental activity. Spearman called this general intellectual ability the ***g* factor**. He assumed that this general factor is innate, and most psychologists at the time agreed with him (Tyler, 1988, p. 128).

Recently, neuroscientists have found some support for Spearman's theory. Various tests of *g* all involve certain gray-matter regions, especially in the brain's frontal lobes (Duncan et al., 2000; Haier et al., 2004). This suggests that a small group of brain modules, working together, control various forms of intelligent behavior. Could these be the loci of *g*? Although some neuroscientists think so, others believe this explanation oversimplifies both the nature of intelligence and of the brain (McArdle et al., 2002; Sternberg, 1999, 2000).

Cattell's Fluid and Crystallized Intelligence Using sophisticated mathematical techniques, Raymond Cattell (1963) determined that general intelligence can be broken down into two relatively independent components that he called *crystallized* and *fluid intelligence*. **Crystallized intelligence**, said Cattell, consists of the knowledge a person has acquired, plus the ability to access that knowledge. Thus, crystallized intelligence relates to the person's ability to store and retrieve information from semantic memory. It is measured by tests of vocabulary, arithmetic, and general information. In contrast, Cattell proposed **fluid intelligence** as the ability to see complex relationships and solve problems—abilities that involve using algorithms and heuristics, which we discussed earlier in this chapter. Fluid intelligence is often measured by tests of block design and spatial visualization, tests that do not rely on the individual possessing certain "crystallized" background information to solve a problem. For Cattell, both types of intelligence were essential to adaptive living.

Cognitive Theories of Intelligence

Late in the 20th century, when the cognitive view emerged as a major force in psychology, it produced some radical new ideas about intelligence. In brief, the cognitive view of intelligence went well beyond the emphasis on vocabulary, logic, problem solving, and other skills that had been measured to predict school success (see Table 5.1). Intelligence, said cognitive psychologists, involves cognitive processes that contribute to success in many areas of life—not just school (Sternberg, 2000). We will focus on two of these cognitive theories.

Sternberg's Triarchic Theory You may know someone who seems to have plenty of "book smarts" but who has never been very successful in life. Such people often don't know how to "read" others or to deal with unexpected events. Psychologist Robert Sternberg says that they lack **practical intelligence**: the ability to cope with the people and events in their environment. Practical intelligence is sometimes called "street smarts," although it applies just as well at home, on the job, or at school as it does on the street. We might even infer from one study that it can be thought of as "horse sense": Researchers found that, among regular visitors to racetracks, those who were most successful at picking winning horses had IQs no higher than those who were less successful. This suggests that the very practical ability to pick

CONNECTION • CHAPTER 4
Much of our general knowledge is stored in *semantic memory*, a partition of long-term memory.

***g* factor** A general ability, proposed by Spearman, as the main factor underlying all intelligent mental activity.

Crystallized intelligence The knowledge a person has acquired, plus the ability to access that knowledge.

Fluid intelligence The ability to see complex relationships and solve problems.

Practical intelligence According to Sternberg, the ability to cope with the environment; sometimes called "street smarts."

TABLE 5.1 — Theories of Intelligence Compared

Spearman	Cattell	Sternberg	Gardner
g factor	Crystallized intelligence		
	Fluid intelligence	Analytical intelligence	Naturalistic intelligence
			Logical-mathematical intelligence
		Creative intelligence	Linguistic intelligence
			Spatial intelligence
			Musical intelligence
			Bodily-kinesthetic intelligence
		Practical intelligence	Interpersonal intelligence
			Intrapersonal intelligence
			Spiritual intelligence
			Existential intelligence

Note: Different theorists see intelligence as having different components, as shown in the columns of this table. The rows show roughly comparable components of intelligence described by various theories (although the reader should be aware that the correspondences are not exact). For example, Sternberg's practical intelligence is similar to Gardner's two components, called interpersonal intelligence and intrapersonal intelligence, while Spearman's g ignores these abilities.

winners is something different from the form of intelligence measured on standard IQ tests (Ceci & Liker, 1986).

In contrast with practical intelligence, Sternberg refers to the ability measured by most IQ tests as **analytical intelligence** (also called *logical reasoning*). Analytical intelligence includes the ability to think problems through and find correct answers. Your grades in college are likely to be closely related to this logical reasoning ability.

Creative intelligence, a third form of intelligence described by Sternberg's theory, helps people develop new ideas and see new relationships among concepts. Creative intelligence is what Picasso used to develop the form of painting called *Cubism* and what Einstein used to formulate his theory of relativity. It is also the form of intelligence that Sternberg used to develop his new theory of intelligence.

Sternberg's three-part formulation is often called the **triarchic theory** of intelligence, because it combines three (*tri* = three) different kinds of intelligence. For Sternberg each one in this trio of abilities—practical intelligence, analytical intelligence, and creative intelligence—is relatively independent of the others. That is, a person's ability in one of the three areas doesn't necessarily predict his or her intelligence in the other two. Each represents a different dimension for describing and evaluating human performance. This theory reminds us that it is inaccurate to think of a single IQ score as summarizing all that is important or valuable about people's mental abilities (Sternberg, 1999; Sternberg et al., 1995).

Gardner's Multiple Intelligences
Like Sternberg, Harvard psychologist Howard Gardner also believes that traditional IQ tests measure only a limited range of human mental abilities. But he argues that we have at least seven separate mental abilities, which he calls **multiple intelligences** (Ellison, 1984; Gardner, 1983, 1999b):

1. *Linguistic intelligence.* Often measured on traditional IQ tests by vocabulary tests and tests of reading comprehension

Analytical intelligence According to Sternberg, the ability measured by most IQ tests; includes the ability to analyze problems and find correct

Creative intelligence According to Sternberg, the form of intelligence that helps people see new relationships among concepts; involves insight and creativity.

Triarchic theory The term for Sternberg's theory of intelligence; so called because it combines three ("tri-") main forms of intelligence.

Multiple intelligences A term used to refer to Gardner's theory, which proposes that there are seven (or more) forms of intelligence.

2. *Logical-mathematical intelligence.* Also measured on most IQ tests with analogies, math problems, and logic problems

3. *Spatial intelligence.* The ability to form mental images of objects and to think about their relationships in space

4. *Musical intelligence.* The ability to perform, compose, and appreciate musical patterns, including patterns of rhythms and pitches

5. *Bodily-kinesthetic intelligence.* The ability for controlled movement and coordination, such as that needed by a dancer or a surgeon

6. *Interpersonal intelligence.* The ability to understand other people's intentions, emotions, motives, and actions, as well as to work effectively with others

7. *Intrapersonal intelligence.* The ability to know oneself, to develop a satisfactory sense of identity, and to regulate one's life

Each of these intelligences arises from a separate module in the brain, Gardner claims. The latter two, interpersonal and intrapersonal intelligence, are similar to a capacity that some psychologists call *emotional intelligence* (sometimes referred to as "EQ"). People who are high in emotional intelligence are good at "reading" other people's emotional states, as well as being especially aware of their own emotional responses.

CONNECTION • CHAPTER 9

Emotional intelligence involves the ability to understand and use emotions effectively.

In addition to these, Gardner's book *Intelligence Reframed* (1999a) proposes three more intelligences. *Naturalistic intelligence* allows people to classify living things as members of diverse groups (e.g., dogs, petunias, bacteria). *Spiritual intelligence* involves the ability to think in abstract spiritual terms and to put oneself in a spiritual frame of mind. And, finally, *existential intelligence* permits individuals to think about the largest and smallest components of the universe, the purpose of existence, and the meaning of death, and to deal with profound emotional experiences such as love. The evidence that these latter three involve independent abilities based in specific brain modules, however, is not as strong as for the previous seven intelligences.

Assessing these newly recognized kinds of intelligence demands more than the usual paper-and-pencil tests. Gardner's approach requires that examinees be observed and assessed in a variety of life situations. On its face, the notion of multiple intelligences appears to be sound, but it awaits verification through tests that are still in the process of development.

Cultural Definitions of Intelligence

Like Sternberg, Gardner sees each component of intelligence as equally important. Yet the value of each is also culturally determined, according to what is needed by, useful to, and prized by a given society. Gardner notes that Western society (including those from the Euro-American traditions) promotes the first two intelligences, while many other societies value one or more of the other kinds of intelligence. For example, in small isolated communities, people often place a high value on getting along with others (Gardner's *interpersonal ability*). In these restricted social settings, people have no place to go if they get into a quarrel and want to escape or part ways. In such societies, people generally avoid quarrels by recognizing potential problems at an early stage and modifying behaviors to solve problems quickly.

If you had been socialized in a Pacific island culture, which would matter more, your SAT scores or your ability to navigate a boat on the open ocean? With such examples, cross-cultural psychologists have called our attention to the notion that "intelligence" can have quite different meanings in different cultures (Sternberg, 2000, 2004). In fact, many languages have no word at all for intelligence as we conceive of it: the mental processes associated with logic, vocab-

The popular TV show, Survivor, *emphasizes practical intelligence. This scene is from the sixth episode in Micronesia.*

ulary, mathematical ability, abstract thought, and academic success (Matsumoto, 1996).

African Concepts of Intelligence
Still, people in all cultures prize certain mental abilities—although those abilities are not the same in different cultures. In rural Kenya, Robert Sternberg found that children with the greatest practical intelligence skills actually scored lower on traditional IQ tests that measure academic success. Sternberg says, "In Kenya, good grades don't get you anywhere. You're better off getting an apprenticeship or learning to mine or fish—those will allow you to support a family" (Winerman, 2005b). So, the kids with the best minds don't learn academic skills, but concentrate on practical skills that will get them ahead in life.

Western cultures typically associate intelligence both with school success and with quick solutions to problems. This contrasts with the Buganda people in Uganda, who associate intelligence with slow and thoughtful responses. Yet another view is found among the Djerma-Sonhai in Niger (West Africa), who think of intelligence as a combination of social skills and good memory. And for the Chinese, intelligence involves, among other things, extensive knowledge, determination, social responsibility, and ability for imitation.

A Native American Concept of Intelligence
John Berry (1992) has extensively studied the kinds of mental abilities considered valuable among Native Americans. He began by asking adult volunteers among the Cree in northern Ontario to provide him with Cree words that describe aspects of thinking, starting with examples like "smart" or "intelligent." The most frequent responses translate roughly to "wise, thinks hard, and thinks carefully."

Although Cree children attend schools introduced by the dominant Anglo (English-European) culture, the Cree themselves make a distinction between "school" intelligence and the kind of "good thinking" valued in the Cree culture. Such thinking seems to center on being "respectful." As one respondent explained, intelligence "is being respectful in the Indian sense. You need to really know the other person and respect them for what they are" (Berry, 1992, p. 79). This attitude of "respect for others" is widespread in Native American cultures, Berry found.

For this Native American teacher and his students, "intelligence" may have a different meaning from that used by Anglo Americans. In the Cree culture, intelligence involves wisdom and respect for others.

One term Berry's respondents offered as an example of the opposite of intelligence translates as "lives like a white." This refers disparagingly to behaviors the Cree have observed among some Anglo people. The Cree define "lives like a white" as a combination of being "stupid" and having "backwards knowledge." A "stupid" person does not know the necessary skills for survival and does not learn by respecting and listening to elders. One who has "backwards knowledge" disrupts relationships, creating disharmony instead of encouraging smooth interactions with others. Such disruption is not necessarily intentional or malicious. For example, an English teacher may ask Cree students to write an essay that would persuade others to change certain behaviors. However, in the Cree culture the concept of "persuading" can interfere with the traditional Cree value of "accepting others as they are." By encouraging such questioning of elders and traditions—a common practice in Anglo education—the teacher promotes disruption, which may be a path to "wisdom" in Anglo culture, but is "backward" in Cree views of intelligence.

As you can see from these examples, different cultures may define intelligence quite differently. To understand and cooperate with people of diverse heritages, we would be most "intelligent" if we resisted the impulse to impose our own definition of "intelligence" on others. Within psychology, cross-cultural psychologists have led the way in urging us to see what is valued—and devalued—in other people's experience.

Animals Can Be Intelligent—But Do They Think?

Animals can be taught to perform amazing tricks, as anyone who has ever been to the circus can attest. In the wild, groups of wolves or lions or a pod of killer whales commonly cooperate in making a kill—or in raising their young. And even your cat may sometimes seem to be acting with skill and cunning as she herds you toward the kitchen in the apparent hope of being fed. But do animals really *think?*

Speaking of cats, you may remember that Thorndike's cats were rather clever, when it came to escaping from his "puzzle boxes." Likewise, the rats in Tolman's lab developed *cognitive maps* of his mazes and were sometimes purported (in a sarcastic remark by one of Tolman's adversaries) to be "lost in thought." And, of course, in a lab on the island of Tenerife, Wolfgang Köhler's chimpanzees solved problems in flashes of "insight."

Despite such evidence, many scientists dismissed the idea of animal cognition as a mere trained-animal tricks—until some startling new reports came trickling in from scientists like Jane Goodall. Willing to risk her career in the jungles of Tanzania, Goodall spent 30 years watching and recording the behavior of wild chimpanzees, a highly intelligent species about whose behavior in the wild very little was known (1986). And her career gamble paid off handsomely. To give just one example from the long list of her discoveries, Goodall reported that chimps would strip leaves from twigs and use them to extract tasty morsels from a termites nest. And why was that amazing? She had discovered that chimpanzees could make and use tools! Previously, tool-making was an ability believed to set humans apart from the rest of the animal kingdom. So, Goodall's work raised the question of human uniqueness. (You can learn more about this work at the Jane Goodall Institute at www.janegoodall.org/).

What Abilities Make Humans Unique?   If not tool-making, what distinctive cognitive abilities might we humans possess? One possibility is a **theory of mind:** the ability to know that our own thoughts may be different from someone else's thoughts. For example, a poker player uses a theory of mind when bluffing. So does a child who tells a lie about raiding the cookie jar. But recent animal research shows

CONNECTION • CHAPTER 3

Thorndike, Tolman, and Köhler showed that animals can learn to solve complex problems.

Theory of mind   An awareness that other people's behavior may be influenced by beliefs, desires, and emotions that differ from one's own.

that the lowly Western scrub jay (a relative of the crow) also shows signs of having a theory of mind. Amazingly, a scrub jay that sees another bird watching while it is hiding a grub for a later meal will return later and rehide the grub in another location (Dally et al., 2005). So much for human-only theory of mind conjecture!

So, perhaps it is *language* that distinguishes humans from animals. But alas for human pride! Animal behaviorist Karl Von Fritsch (1974) showed that a honeybee discovering a new source of nectar uses a language consisting of a "waggle dance," performed along a wall inside the hive, that conveys the direction and distance of the food. Other scientists pointed out that many other animals use distinctive sounds to communicate different "ideas," such as the approach of a predator. But such animal communications have a limited repertoire: Do they qualify as true language?

Language of the Apes   An answer to that question came from Allen and Beatrice Gardner, who decided to take a 10-month-old chimpanzee named Washoe into their home and raise it like a human child. The crux of their experiment, however, was an attempt to teach Washoe to communicate. Because chimps do not have the vocal apparatus required for complex spoken language—but they do have excellent finger dexterity—the Gardners (1969) attempted to communicate with Washoe using American Sign Language. Remarkably, by the time Washoe was 5, she had learned some 160 signs. Eventually she learned about 250. Even more remarkably, she was able to put the signs together to make phrases or even "sentences," as when she would declare, "Me Washoe" or request, "Please tickle more." Some of her signs were even novel, as when she first saw a swan and signed "water bird."

Washoe's remarkable accomplishments were followed during the next decade by a parade of other primates that communicated with sign language, with plastic tokens of various shapes, and even with computers. Some outstripped Washoe by achieving vocabularies of up to 500 words (Savage-Rumbaugh, 1990). Kanzi, a pygmy chimp, demonstrated an understanding of spoken words—even sentences that he had not heard before (Rumbaugh & Savage-Rumbaugh, 1994; Savage-Rumbaugh & Lewin, 1994). Sarah, another articulate chimp, was able to construct complex sentences like these: "If Sarah take apple, then Mary give Sarah chocolate. If Sarah take banana, then Mary no give Sarah chocolate." And a gorilla named Koko has been caught signing lies (Patterson & Linden, 1981). On occasion, Koko has even "sworn" at her handler in ASL, making the signs for "dirty toilet."

The work on ape language was not enthusiastically accepted by everyone, however. Chief skeptic Herbart Terrace (1979, 1985), who also trained a chimp to use sign language, concluded that chimps can learn to use signs, but that they imitate without real understanding and that many cases of so-called novel expressions might be most charitably ascribed to impressions in their handlers' minds, rather than real language in the minds of apes. Koko's nasty outbursts notwithstanding, Terrace claims that most apes merely ape what they have seen, repeating sequences of gestures that they have learned.

The pro-chimp-language people, to their credit, paid attention to their critics and have since taken care to make their experiments more objective. And, although the issue is still not settled to everyone's satisfaction, most observers are convinced that chimpanzees have learned at least the rudiments of language, perhaps at the level of a 2½-year-old human.

In the meantime, channels of communication have reportedly been opened to a variety of species. Dolphins have been taught to interpret and respond to complex strings of gestures and sounds. An African gray parrot, who answered to the name of Alex, could not only speak but could count up to six objects and give the correct answers to simple problems ("Which one is bigger?"). And, not to be outdone, a border collie named Rico has learned to fetch some 200 different objects by name (Kaminski et al., 2004).

Pigeons have remarkable problem-solving abilities. Here a pigeon moves a block so that it can reach a food reward—much like Köhler's chimpanzee Sultan.

Alex, an African gray parrot, could count up to six objects and solve simple problems posed by his trainer, Dr. Irene Pepperberg.

What Are the Lessons of Research on Animal Language and Intelligence? Without doubt, animals are capable of intelligent behavior, and all but the strictest of behaviorists would say that many animals are capable of cognition—thought. But we must see these abilities in an evolutionary perspective: Most animals are exquisitely adapted to a particular biological niche, which makes them very intelligent about certain things (hunting down an antelope, catching a salmon, or protecting a clutch of eggs) but not so well adapted to other tasks, such as arithmetic or language. The main exception seems to be humans, who have become generalists.

Nevertheless, the study of language in nonhuman animals has pulled us down from our self-constructed pedestal by demonstrating that other creatures are capable of using language at a surprising level of sophistication. Those who worry about maintaining our feelings of species superiority can take comfort in this fact: Human language displays far more grammatical structure and productivity than do the languages of other animals. More than anything else, our language abilities have allowed us to grapple with abstract problems and to pass our solutions on to other members of our species.

But then, Washoe has taught her adopted son to use sign language.

PSYCHOLOGY**MATTERS**
Test Scores and the Self-Fulfilling Prophecy

If you have ever been called "dumb" or "slow," "shy," "plain," "bossy," or "uncoordinated," you know, first hand, the powerful effect that labels and expectations can have. An IQ score is a label, too; and, in our test-conscious society, an IQ score can alter the course of a life. As a nation of test takers, we sometimes forget that test scores are, at best, statistical measures of current functioning. People too often think of themselves as being "an IQ of 110" or "a B student," as if scores or grades were labels stamped permanently on their brains. Such labels may become barriers to advancement, as people come to believe that their mental and personal qualities are unchangeable—that they dictate their lot in life. Two classic studies will bring this fact into stark relief.

Expectations Influence Rat Performance Robert Rosenthal and Lenore Jacobson (1968a,b) asked psychology students to run rats through a maze and record their times. The experimenters told some students that their rats were especially bright; other students heard that their rats were slow learners. (In fact, Rosenthal and Jacobson had randomly assigned rats to the "bright" and "dull" groups.) Amazingly, the students' data showed that rats that were believed to be bright outperformed their supposedly duller littermates. Obviously, expectations had influenced the students' observations.

Expectations Also Influence Student Performance After seeing the results of their experiment with rats, Rosenthal and Jacobson wondered: Could a teacher's expectations similarly affect evaluations of a student's performance in school? To find out, they arranged to give grade school teachers erroneous information about the academic potential of about 20% of their students (approximately five in each classroom). Specifically, the teachers heard that some students had been identified by a standardized test as "spurters," who would blossom academically during the coming year. In fact, testing had revealed no such thing; the "spurters" had been randomly selected by the experimenters.

Knowing what happened with the rats, you can guess what happened in the classroom. Those children whom the teachers expected to blossom did so. Rosenthal and Jacobson didn't watch what actually happened to the children, although it seems likely that the teachers were more attentive and supportive of the students who were supposed to become "spurters." The data merely showed that teachers rated the "spurters" as being more curious and having more potential for success in life than the other children. Socially, the teachers saw these children as happier, more interesting, better adjusted, more affectionate, and needing less social approval. Significantly, when the children again took the original test (actually an IQ test) a year later, the children in the experimental group (who had been arbitrarily assigned a high expectation of mental growth) made substantial gains in IQ points. The gains were especially pronounced among first and second graders. Rosenthal and Jacobson call this effect a **self-fulfilling prophecy**. You can see it operating anywhere that people live up to the expectations of others—or of themselves.

The Effects of Negative Expectations   Did the self-fulfilling prophecy apply to the students not labeled as possible academic "spurters"? Many of these children also gained IQ points during the year of the experiment, but they gained fewer points, and they were rated less favorably by their teachers. Apparently, not receiving a promising prophecy can create negative expectations, just as a positive label can create positive expectations.

CheckYourUnderstanding

1. **APPLICATION:** In Cattell's theory, the ability to use algorithms and heuristics would be called _____ intelligence.

2. **APPLICATION:** A friend tells you that he has found a way to improve his grades by stopping by his psychology professor's office once a week to ask questions about the reading. In Sternberg's triarchic theory, which of the three kinds of intelligence is this?

3. **RECALL:** Name one of Gardner's seven intelligences that is also measured on standard IQ tests.

4. **RECALL:** Why does a self-fulfilling prophecy come true?

5. **UNDERSTANDING THE CORE CONCEPT:** Sternberg, Gardner, and others maintain that there are multiple intelligences. What is the position taken by Spearman and others on the opposite side of this argument?

Answers 1. fluid **2.** practical intelligence **3.** Either linguistic intelligence or logical-mathematical intelligence would be correct. (Some intelligence tests also assess spatial intelligence.) **4.** Expectations: We frequently observe what we expect to see, even when our expectations are erroneous. So, if we expect someone to be smart (obnoxious, stupid, pleasant, lazy, and so on), the chances are good that this "prophecy" will fulfill itself. **5.** Although they do not deny that different abilities exist, Spearman and others have argued intelligence involves a single general, or *g*, factor underlying all these special abilities.

5.5 KEY QUESTION
HOW DO PSYCHOLOGISTS EXPLAIN IQ DIFFERENCES AMONG GROUPS?

While we can find the full range of IQ scores in every ethnic group, we also find differences among groups in average IQ scores (Rushton & Jensen, 2005). In the United States, Americans of Asian extraction score higher, on the average, than do Euro-Americans. Hispanics, African Americans, and Native Americans—again, on the average—score lower. Curiously, children from middle-income homes also score higher on IQ tests than do their counterparts from low-income homes (Jensen & Figueroa, 1975; Oakland & Glutting, 1990). Nobody disputes that these differences exist. What the experts disagree about are the causes of these IQ discrepancies. As we will see, the disagreement is another example of the nature–nurture controversy. Our Core Concept describes the issue this way:

| While most psychologists agree that both heredity and environment affect intelligence, they disagree on the source of IQ differences among racial and social groups. | core concept |

The controversy over the source of intelligence is potentially of great importance for people's lives—and a politically hot issue. And when race becomes involved, such issues can become even hotter. Never mind that the concept of

Self-fulfilling prophecy   Observations or behaviors that result primarily from expectations.

distinct human "races" has no precise biological meaning, but rather a social one (Cooper, 2005; Sternberg et al., 2005)

If we assume that intelligence is primarily the result of innate (hereditary) factors, we will most likely conclude that it is fixed and unchangeable. This easily leads some to the conclusion that a group (usually a "racial" group) having low IQ scores must be innately inferior and, perhaps, should be treated as second-class citizens. On the other hand, if we conclude that intelligence is shaped largely by experience (environment), we are more likely to make a range of educational opportunities available for everyone and to view people of all ethnic, cultural, and economic groups as equals. Either way, our conclusion may become a self-fulfilling prophecy.

In actuality, neither the hereditarian nor environmentalist view is completely right. Repeatedly in this text we have seen that psychologists now recognize that both heredity and environment play a role in all our behavior and mental processes. But there is more to the issue of group differences than this. In this chapter, we will add another important complication to the heredity–environment interaction: While each *individual's* intelligence is determined, in part, by heredity, this fact does not mean that the IQ differences *among groups* have some biological basis. On the contrary, many psychologists have argued that group differences are totally environmental—although this, too, is disputed, as our Core Concept suggests. As we will see, however, the idea that group differences stem from biology has historically garnered the most support.

Intelligence and the Politics of Immigration

In the early 1900s, Henry Goddard, an influential psychologist who believed that intelligence is a hereditary trait, proposed mental testing of all applicants for immigration and the exclusion of those who were found to be "mentally defective" (Strickland, 2000). With encouragement from Goddard and some other assessment-minded psychologists, Congress passed the 1924 Immigration Restriction Act, designed to restrict immigration of groups and nationalities in which people had been "proven" to be of inferior intellect—based largely on Goddard's data. Among the groups restricted were Jews, Italians, and Russians. What Goddard and the U.S. Congress ignored was the fact that the tests were given in English—often to people with little familiarity with the English language and the culture in which the tests were conceived. Of course many of these immigrants received low scores!

Today we are more aware of the shortcomings of intelligence tests. We also know that, while heredity has an effect on an individual's intelligence, experience does, too. And we know that Goddard used faulty reasoning when he concluded that heredity accounts for group differences in intelligence. To understand how heredity could affect individual differences but not group differences, we need to look first at the evidence supporting the hereditarian and environmentalist arguments.

What Evidence Shows That Intelligence Is Influenced by Heredity?

Many lines of research point to a hereditary influence on intelligence. Studies comparing the IQ scores of identical twins with fraternal twins and other siblings show a strong genetic correlation. But the gold standard for differentiating the effects of heredity and environment involves looking at children who have not been raised by their biological parents. This means studying adopted children and the rare instances of twins who have been separated at birth. Such studies reveal that the correlation between the IQs of children and their biological parents is greater than that with their adoptive parents (Plomin & DeFries, 1998). Work coming out of the Human Genome Project has also lent support

TABLE 5.2 Correlation of IQ Scores with Genetic Relationship

Genetic relationship	Correlation between IQ scores
Identical twins	
Reared together	0.86
Reared apart	0.72
Fraternal twins	
Reared together	0.60
Siblings	
Reared together	0.47
Reared apart	0.24
Parent/child	0.40
Foster parent/child	0.31
Cousins	0.15

Note: A correlation shows the degree of association between variables—in this case, between the IQs of pairs of individuals. The closer to 1.0, the closer the connection. For example, we can see that the IQ scores of identical twins reared together are more closely correlated (.86) than the IQs of mere siblings reared together (.47). The data strongly suggest a genetic component that contributes to intelligence.
(*Source:* From Bouchard and McGue, 1981, "Familial Studies of Intelligence: A Review," in *Science,* Vol. 212, pp. 1055–1059. Adapted with permission from AAAS.)

to the notion that intelligence has a genetic component. Scientists are careful to point out, however, that the genetic basis of intelligence is complex because it involves the interaction of many genes (Chorney et al., 1998). In general, however, the closer the genetic relationship—from cousins to siblings to twins—the closer the relationship of IQ scores, as Table 5.2 shows. In fact, studies of twins and adopted children reveal genetic influences on a whole range of attributes as diverse as heart functioning (Brown, 1990), personality traits (Tellegen et al., 1988), hypnotizability (Morgan et al., 1970), and intelligence (Sternberg et al., 2005).

While psychologists agree that heredity plays an important part in determining an individual's IQ scores, they also agree that it remains difficult to estimate the relative weights of heredity and environment (Sternberg et al., 2005). One reason for this is that children who live in the same family setting do not necessarily share precisely the same psychological environment. First-born children, for example, are treated differently from the youngest. You probably are aware of this fact if you have siblings.

What Evidence Shows That Intelligence Is Influenced by Environment?

The evidence that the environment influences intellectual development is persuasive, too. This is seen in a longitudinal study of 110 children from impoverished homes, done over a period of about 10 years (Farah, 2008). The researchers assessed children on both language ability and memory (two important aspects of intelligence). They also assessed the children's home environment on two factors: (a) How stimulating was it? (judged by the child's access to such things as books and musical instruments) and (b) How nurturing was it? (rated according to observations of positive emotional climate, along with attention and praise given by parents). What the study revealed was a combination of the expected and the unexpected:

- A strong association between a stimulating environment and language ability (but not memory)
- An unexpected association between nurturance and memory (but not language ability)

How can we explain these results? The answer is not clear. But, says Martha Farah, lead author of the study, "Our results show that poverty affects different neurocognitive systems in different ways."

The effects of environment show themselves even when we look for genetic effects: We find greater similarities of IQ among people who have been reared together than those reared apart. And, in laboratory animals, a stimulus-enriched habitat early in life results in a more complex, complete development of brain cells and cortical regions. The superior performance of these animals on a range of tasks persists through life. In other experiments, we find that young monkeys who are trained to solve problems and are also offered the companionship of other monkeys display more active curiosity and higher intelligence than those reared without this environmental stimulation.

Such findings in animals hint that we might boost the intellectual functioning of human infants by enriching their environments. Indeed, we will see that early intervention programs can raise children's IQ scores (Barlow, 2008). Schooling also may boost IQ scores. In fact, the total amount of schooling children receive correlates well with their IQ scores (Ceci & Williams, 1997). Even in adulthood, environmental factors, such as the cognitive complexity and intellectual demands of one's job, can influence mental abilities throughout life (Dixon et al., 1985).

Recently, William Dickens and James Flynn reported the first evidence that the black–white IQ gap is narrowing—solid evidence that environment rather than heredity is the culprit. Citing data from large groups on four different IQ tests over the past three decades, they find that the gap has narrowed by up to 50%—which translates into nearly eight IQ points (Dickens & Flynn, 2006, Krakovsky, 2007.) Meanwhile, the hereditarians have not conceded, arguing that the research ignored data showing no change. Dickens and Flynn have rebutted these charges, but some critics remain unconvinced.

There is more evidence for the environmental side of the nature–nurture debate about intelligence, but to understand that evidence we must pause to explore a most important—and often misunderstood—concept: *heritability.*

Heritability (not Heredity) and Group Differences

Let us acknowledge that intelligence has a hereditary component. But, just because intelligence can be influenced by heredity—perhaps even by a substantial amount—does not mean that the environment has no impact (Dickens & Flynn, 2001; Neisser et al., 1996). Moreover, the influence of heredity on intelligence does not mean that heredity accounts for the differences we observe *between* groups. To understand why this is so, we need to distinguish *heredity* from another important term: *heritability.* Specifically, **heritability** refers to the amount of trait variation within a group that can be attributed to genetic differences.

To illustrate, suppose that we examine a group of children who were all raised in an intellectually stimulating environment, with devoted parents who spent lots of time interacting with them and reading to them—things we know improve intellectual abilities. Among these children, we would find variation in intellectual abilities. Because they were all treated in essentially the same fashion, however, we could attribute much of the differences in their IQ scores to the effects of heredity. *In this group, IQ would have high heritability.*

In contrast, suppose that we examine a group of children who had been raised under conditions of neglect—given mere custodial care in an orphanage, with no intellectual stimulation from their caregivers. We would most likely find that

Heritability The amount of trait variation within a group, raised under the same conditions, that can be attributed to genetic differences. Heritability tells us nothing about between-group differences.

these children have relatively little variability among their IQ scores because they are all intellectually stunted. *For this group, IQ would have low heritability*—because the poor environment did not offer an opportunity for these children's genetic potential to be realized.

Now, what about the differences *between* the two groups? The IQ differences would be real. But—this is the important part—*our observations could tell us nothing about the genetic differences (if any) between the groups.* For all we know they might have the same genetic potential. But because the environments were so different we cannot tell what role genetics played in determining the differences in their IQ scores.

In view of the fact that people are exposed to different cultural traditions and experience different levels of wealth or discrimination, you can see that we have no way to evaluate what proportion of the differences *between* the groups should be attributed to heredity or to environment. To reiterate: *Heritability* is a concept that refers to within-group differences, not between-group differences. Thus, it is important to realize that *we can speak of heritable differences only within a group of individuals who have shared essentially the same environment* (Sternberg et al., 2005).

And finally, we must reiterate another important point: Biologists tell us that "race" is not a valid biological concept (Cooper, 2005; Sternberg et al., 2005). There are no biological boundaries defining different races. And even if we use a social definition, where people define their own racial group, the differences between the gene pools of people who claim to be of different racial groups are very small compared to the genetic differences among individual members of the same group (Bamshad & Olson, 2003). For all these reasons, then, we can*not* say that the evidence supports the notion of genetic differences producing the IQ discrepancies we observe among "racial" groups.

The Jensen Controversy   Despite the concerns we have just cited, some psychologists remain unconvinced that environment can account for group differences in IQ (Nisbett, 2005; Rushton & Jensen, 2005). The most recent controversy has its roots in the contention by Harvard psychologist Arthur Jensen (1969) that racial differences in IQ have a substantial genetic basis. We can boost IQ scores to some extent, said Jensen, by helping the poor and disadvantaged, but there are limits imposed by heredity.

In support of his thesis, Jensen cited several studies showing a strong influence of heredity on IQ. He also presented a complex statistical argument that showed only a weak environmental effect on IQ and achievement. Then, turning his attention to government programs that had attempted to give extra help to disadvantaged black children, Jensen claimed that, while most had shown some positive effects, none had erased racial differences in performance. What remained must be a genetic difference in abilities, he maintained.

Over the next five years more than 100 published articles responded to Jensen's challenge. Sometimes it seemed that the Jensen controversy had generated far more heat than light. The protest occasionally became ugly, with charges of bigotry and racism nearly drowning the scientific debate. Nevertheless, it did have the positive effect of stimulating a new wave of research and theory aimed at gaining greater understanding of black–white IQ differences.

Critics pointed out several factors that Jensen had minimized or ignored, including the effects of racism, lower teacher expectations for black children, lack of opportunity, low self-esteem, and a white, middle-class bias built into IQ and achievement tests (Neisser, 1997; Neisser et al., 1996). While Jensen holds to his original position (Jensen, 1998, 2000), many (but not all) psychologists now agree that a combination of environmental factors can explain the differences on which Jensen built his case. Let us now look at some of the post-Jensen discoveries, beginning with a study of children whose environment had been altered by adoption.

The Scarr and Weinberg Adoption Study A monumental study by Sandra Scarr and Richard Weinberg confronted the issue head-on by comparing black and white children who had been adopted into similar home environments (1976, 1978). Their research focused on educational records and IQ test scores from both the biological families and the adoptive families of 115 white children and 176 black children who had been adopted in Minnesota during the 1950s. All the children had been adopted into white families. For both groups of children, the biological parents had average IQ scores (near 100), while the adoptive parents' IQs were somewhat higher, averaging above 115.

What did Scarr and Weinberg find when they reexamined the IQ scores of these two groups of adoptees in late adolescence? There were no differences! Both the black group and the white group of adoptees had scores that averaged about 110, significantly higher than their biological parents, although not quite as high as their adoptive parents. Such results testify to a powerful effect of the environment on IQ. The results also contradict Jensen's claim that group differences are genetic.

Social Class and IQ Research on the relationship between social class and IQ shows similar environmental effects. Socioeconomic class (as reflected in an individual's financial status and lifestyle) clearly correlates with IQ. While affluence is associated with higher IQ scores, groups with the lowest average IQ scores are those for whom poverty, illiteracy, and hopelessness are most widespread. Supporters of the environmental position claim that racism and discrimination initially landed many minorities in impoverished neighborhoods, and these same factors continue to keep them there today.

How does social class affect IQ? The relationship is not a simple one: The negative effects of growing up in a disadvantaged home far outweigh the benefits of growing up in a wealthy family (Turkheimer et al., 2003). In fact, poverty creates circumstances that limit individual potential in many ways, particularly in terms of nutrition, health care, and education (Brown & Pollitt, 1996; Neisser et al., 1996). Poverty also means less-adequate health care, so it should not surprise you that researchers have traced poor health during pregnancy and low birth weight to low mental ability in children. Research also shows that a significant proportion of children with low IQs have been adversely affected by "environmental insults," such as living in homes with lead-based paint chips peeling from walls, causing toxic lead levels in children who ingest this material (Needleman et al., 1990). And poverty also means less of other factors known to promote intellectual development. Poor nutrition, lack of access to books and computers, and job schedules that leave parents little time to stimulate a child's intellect all correlate with poverty and can be detrimental to performance on tasks such as those demanded by IQ tests (for example, vocabulary or sentence comprehension).

Poverty has other crippling effects, too. In most parts of the United States, public schools are funded by revenue from local property taxes. Thus, wealthy neighborhoods can provide bigger and better school facilities and amenities, while poorer districts may suffer from crowding, physically deteriorating structures, threats to personal safety, poorly prepared teachers, and lack of access to computers. In such environments, even children with the aptitude to learn may find it difficult to rise above their circumstances. Proponents of the view that environment has a strong influence on intelligence usually support equal-opportunity legislation, better schools, and intervention programs that help disadvantaged children build self-confidence and learn the skills necessary to succeed in school (Tirozzi & Uro, 1997).

Head Start: A Successful Intervention Program One such intervention program is *Head Start,* originally implemented some 40 years ago to provide educational enrichment for disadvantaged children. It grew from the assumption that many children from deprived families need an intellectual boost to prepare them for school. The program is intended to head off problems on several fronts by serving children's physical as well as mental needs with nutritional and medical support, plus a year or two of preschool education. Wisely, Head Start also involves parents in making policy, planning programs, working in classrooms, and learning about parenting and child development. Head Start centers around the country currently serve about 800,000 children yearly—estimated to be 40% of the number who need it (Ripple et al., 1999).

Does it work? Again, there is some controversy (Jensen, 1969; Kantrowitz, 1992), although a great deal of research suggests that Head Start does, indeed, help disadvantaged children get ready for school (Garces et al., 2002; Ripple & Zigler, 2003). Children who were enrolled in the program score higher on IQ tests and have higher school achievement during the early grades than a matched control group who received no such intervention (Zigler & Styfco, 1994). More important, their head start lasts. Although the differences between the Head Start children and the control group diminish over time, the effects are still detectable in adolescence. Among other things, Head Start children are less likely to be placed in special education classes, less likely to fail a grade, more likely to graduate from high school, and less likely to have trouble with the law.

It now appears, however, that such attempts to raise IQ by special environmental interventions may not start early enough. Studies indicate that early educational intervention, starting in the first months of life, can raise infants' scores on intelligence tests by as much as 30% compared to control groups (Ramey & Ramey, 1998a,b; Wickelgren, 1999). Although the gains may diminish with time, especially if supportive programs are withdrawn, significant differences remain when intervention starts in infancy. The best way to summarize these and other relevant findings is to say that the earlier the individual is immersed in an enriched environment, the stronger the effects.

Test Biases and Culture-Fair Tests   Still other forces influence IQ scores and contribute to differences among groups. A portion of the difference between the average IQ scores of black and white children may reside in problems with the IQ tests themselves. Many psychologists have argued that IQ test questions have built-in biases toward a middle- or upper-class background—biases that favor the white child (Helms, 1992). For an opposing view, however, that holds that test bias does *not* contribute to group differences in IQ scores, see Jensen (2000) and Reynolds (2000).

One source of possible bias stems from the fact that most IQ tests rely heavily on vocabulary level. This gives a big advantage to children who have been read to and who are encouraged to read. We can see a related bias in a well-known IQ test that asks for a definition of *opulent* (rich), a term one is far less likely to hear in a poor household. To their credit, however, test makers have been working hard to rid their tests of items that discriminate against people of minority cultural backgrounds (Benson, 2003).

Yet another source of bias has to do with the examiner. Not only does the examiner's attitude influence IQ scores, but so do his or her gender and race. Studies have found that black children receive higher scores when tested by a black examiner (Bodmer & Cavalli-Sforza, 1970; Sattler, 1970). In brief, test takers do best when they perceive the examiner to be similar to themselves.

Finally, Janet Helms (1992) has pointed out that the attempt to explain why African American children deviate from the Caucasian norm may, itself, rest on the biased assumption that one culture is superior to another. Specifically, she says, it "assumes that white-American culture defines the most intellectually rich environment" (p. 1086). Seldom do we ask how well white children learn the norms of other cultures. Helms asks: Why should the Caucasian American norm be the standard by which everyone else is judged?

Psychologists realize that a culture-free test of ability or achievement is an impossibility. Nevertheless, most agree that we should strive for *culture-fair* tests that minimize cultural biases, insofar as possible. Many of the built-in biases in ability and achievement tests arise from language. After all, how could we expect most people to perform well on a test in their nonnative language? To get around this problem, several attempts have been made to develop nonverbal intelligence tests involving mazes and the manipulation of shapes.

Critics of culture-fair tests make two main points. First, not all minority groups do poorly on traditional intelligence tests. For example, we have seen that Asian-Americans often do better than Americans of European ancestry (Sue & Okazaki, 1990). Second, culture-fair tests do a poorer job of predicting academic success, which is the main strength of traditional IQ tests (Aiken, 1987; Humphreys, 1988). The main reason that culture-fair tests are relatively poor predictors of academic success is that they deemphasize verbal skills, which are an important component of success in school.

The Bell Curve: Another Hereditarian Offensive   The dispute over causes of racial differences in IQ flared again in 1994. At issue was a book, *The Bell Curve: Intelligence and Class Structure in American Life,* by Richard Herrnstein and Charles Murray. The name echoes the bell-shaped "normal distribution" of IQ scores (see shape of the graph in Figure 5.11). In this volume, Herrnstein and Murray argued that racial differences in IQ have a strong genetic basis. If these innate differences were accepted, the nation could move on to more enlightened and humane social policies, they said. Critics immediately identified not only a racist bias but pointed to questionable science at the core of *The Bell Curve*.

How is *The Bell Curve*'s argument flawed? The answer will be familiar to you by now: While there is no doubt that heredity influences individual intelligence, Herrnstein and Murray, like hereditarians before them, have offered no proof that differences *between groups* exposed to different environments have a hereditary basis (see Coughlin, 1994; Fraser, 1995). Further, much of the "evidence" they offer is suspect (Kamin, 1994). One study cited by Herrnstein and Murray claimed to document the low IQs of black Africans, but it employed tests given in English—a language in which the Zulu subjects of the study were not fluent (Kamin, 1995). The test used in that study also assumed that subjects were familiar with electrical appliances found in urban middle-class homes (rather than Zulu villages) and equipment, such as microscopes, not typically found in Zulu schools.

Compounding the problems in their analysis of the evidence, Herrnstein and Murray commit another critical thinking error that we have emphasized in this book: They confuse correlation with causation. In fact, the Herrnstein and Murray argument is just as plausible when turned around: Poverty and all of the social and economic disadvantages that go with it could just as well be important causes of low IQ scores.

Despite its flaws, *The Bell Curve* has struck a chord with many Americans. It resonates with the preference for simple genetic "causes" for behavior rather than more complex explanations. But not every culture holds this viewpoint. We can see a different perspective in a study that asked Americans and Asians to account for a child's academic success: American respondents emphasized "innate ability," whereas Asian respondents emphasized the importance of "studying hard" (Stevenson et al., 1993). Thus, the idea that individual differences, as well as group differences, in performance have an innate basis is a widespread belief in American culture. In fact, Carol Dweck's (2007/2008) work shows that the parents and teachers who adopt an approach similar to the Asian view find that their children are more interested in school, learn more, and achieve higher grades.

PSYCHOLOGYMATTERS
Stereotype Threat

Can you get smarter? Or is your IQ a fixed number? As we have seen, many people believe that their level of "smarts" is a given. But, as Shakespeare once observed, there's the rub: If you think your intelligence is fixed, you will probably live up to your expectations. This is, of course, the expectancy bias and the self-fulfilling prophecy at work.

Psychologists have argued that members of some groups harbor low expectations about the abilities of everyone in their group. These expectations, as you might guess, can adversely affect IQ scores, especially when people are reminded of the stereotype (Schwartz, 1997). Psychologist Claude Steele calls this **stereotype threat**, and he has amassed a lot of evidence that it has a negative effect on many members of minority groups, particularly in academic situations (Steele, 1997; Steele et al., 2002). One study found that merely being asked to identify their race resulted in lower scores for minority students on a test of academic abilities (Steele, 1997). In another study, a group of black women taking an IQ test were told that white women usually do better on the test. As a result of this stereotype threat, these black women received scores that averaged a full 10 points lower than a comparison group who were told that black women usually receive high scores (Thomas, 1991).

Stereotype threat is not necessarily a racial or ethnic issue. We find it also in the domain of gender, where girls may learn to feel inferior in science and math, or boys may be taught that they have lesser verbal skills. Stereotype threat can also intimidate older persons who worry about memory failure or that as "old dogs" they cannot learn "new tricks." Anyone who believes that he or she is part of an inferior group is vulnerable to these feelings of anxiety, intimidation, and inferiority.

Is there a way to combat stereotype threat? Social psychologist Joshua Aronson and his colleagues (2001) found that grades improved for college students who were encouraged to think of intelligence as being influenced by experience and expectations, rather than a fixed trait. The grades of African American students actually rose more than those of white students and those in a control group. Apparently, those who may have felt themselves targets of stereotype threat reaped the most benefits from this program. It remains to apply Aronson's findings to stereotype threat in the domains of gender and aging.

More information on intelligence and on stereotype threat is available under "Education" on the American Psychological Association's "Psychology Matters" website at www.psychologymatters.org/education.html.

Stereotype threat An expectation of being judged by the standard of a negative stereotype. Such expectations can adversely affect performance.

CheckYourUnderstanding

1. **RECALL:** Did Goddard's view of intelligence place more emphasis on nature (heredity) or nurture (environment)?

2. **ANALYSIS:** What is the position taken by most modern psychologists with regard to intelligence and the heredity-environment issue?

3. **APPLICATION:** Cite one piece of evidence showing that intelligence is influenced by heredity and one piece of evidence that intelligence is influenced by the environment.

4. **RECALL:** Put the words *between* and *within* in the appropriate places in the following statement: Heritability may account for differences _____ groups but not for differences _____ groups.

5. **APPLICATION:** Give an example of the conditions under which you would you expect stereotype threat to occur.

6. **UNDERSTANDING THE CORE CONCEPT:** Although everyone agrees that heredity produces differences in intelligence among individuals, there is no evidence that it accounts for differences among _____.

Answers 1. Goddard, along with most of the early American psychologists interested in intelligence, believed that heredity was the most powerful influence on intelligence. **2.** Neither heredity nor environment acts alone: intelligence involves an interaction of heredity and environmental factors. **3.** Evidence for hereditary influence includes: twin studies and correlations of IQs among biological relatives. Evidence for environmental influence includes: comparison of siblings reared together versus those reared apart, animals reared in stimulus-rich environments, the correlation of IQ scores with amount of schooling, and the recent narrowing of the black–white IQ discrepancy. **4.** Heritability may account for differences within groups, but not for differences between groups. **5.** Stereotype threat occurs any time people have low expectations of the group to which they belong, especially when they are reminded of those expectations. One example involves women who believe that they have low aptitude for math and who are taking a math class, particularly if the teacher raises the issue of gender differences in math. **6.** racial or ethnic groups

Critical Thinking Applied: The Question of Gender Differences

In June of 2006 Dr. Larry Summers, the president of Harvard University, lost his job, in part because he opined that factors other than socialization—most notably innate intellectual differences—may account for the undisputed fact that men outnumber women in most scientific fields. (Psychology, incidentally, is an exception!) So, what is really going on? A look at the evidence requires some interpretation—based on your critical thinking skills.

What Is the Issue?

It's the nature–nurture controversy: Are the undisputed gender differences we see the result of different ways men and women are socialized? Are they the result of prejudice, discrimination, and lack of opportunity for women who go into science? Or are they the result of different ways that men's and women's brains process information?

What Critical Thinking Questions Should We Ask?

Certainly the first thing that comes to mind is the possibility of bias—on both sides of the issue. In addition to potential problems of "political correctness," we all have a vested interest in making sure that our gender doesn't come off looking less smart than the other.

Beyond bias, we should be willing to judge the evidence on its merits and, perhaps, be willing to look at the issue from multiple perspectives. After all, it may be that both sides have a piece of the truth.

The Evidence from the "Nurture" Perspective
After an extensive review of the literature on gender, Janet Shibley Hyde (2007) points out that men and women are far more similar than different on nearly all dimensions studied—a view that she calls the *gender similarities hypothesis.* The similarities include such diverse characteristics as mathematical ability, problem-solving, reading comprehension, leadership effectiveness, and moral reasoning. But there are a few exceptions, most of which won't surprise you. These include greater male aggression, acceptance of casual sex, and throwing velocity—differences that she allows may have biological roots. In general, however, Hyde favors an explanation that emphasizes the different ways that males and females are socialized. One factor may be the whole set of expectations (and limitations) that society offers girls as they are growing up. Hyde says that the few physical differences

between men and women "are important mainly because they are amplified by cultural beliefs and roles."

Further, Hyde cautions, many people tend to believe that any male–female differences we may find in the brains of men and women are "hard wired" and unchangeable. Instead, she urges us to see such differences as rooted in the brain's *plasticity,* by which the very fabric of the brain is altered by experience. In fact, brains seem to be changing: The number of women entering scientific fields has surged dramatically in the last decade, with women now making up, for example, half of the graduating classes at U.S. medical schools (Halpern et al., 2007/2008).

The Evidence from the "Nature" Perspective
Taking quite a different approach, Roy Baumeister (2007) calls our attention to a different set of facts. He notes that men, as a group, are more *variable* and *extreme* than women—with more men lying at the opposite poles of virtually all mental and behavioral dimensions. Men, he says, seem to outnumber women among both the biggest losers and the biggest winners. Thus, we find more men than women in prisons and homeless shelters and among those with mental retardation—as well as among jazz musicians, scientists (except in psychology), members of Congress, and people whom we call "geniuses." If men go to extremes more than women, says Baumeister, we would find these gender differences, *and yet the averages could be the same.*

Baumeister is quick to point out that he doesn't see one gender as being better than the other—merely that evolution selected different traits in men and women. In general, he says, cultures give the highest payoffs to men who take risks and have the most extreme skills. These extremists, the risk-takers, are also the ones who tend to have the most children, who perpetuate the trend. The situation is quite different for women, Baumeister argues. The evolutionary pressures for women have emphasized playing it safer than men do—which is the smart thing when your opportunities for leaving offspring are biologically much more limited than are men's.

What Conclusions Can We Draw?

Which side to believe? As we noted earlier, both sides may have part of the truth. Both agree that the gender differences in abilities are small. Baumeister suggests that the gender differences have more to do with motivation (particularly the male willingness to take risks) than with ability, while Hyde maintains that the differences are mainly cultural and, therefore, can be shaped. You will have to decide the issue for yourself, but we urge you, as a critical thinker, to be mindful of your own biases. In the end, this issue may have to be seen from multiple perspectives—rather like the changing views of the Necker cube.

Chapter Summary

5.1 What Are the Components of Thought?

Core Concept 5.1: Thinking is a cognitive process in which the brain uses information from the senses, emotions, and memory to create and manipulate mental representations, such as concepts, images, schemas, and scripts.

Cognitive scientists often use the **computer metaphor** to conceive of the brain as an information-processing organ. Thinking is a mental process that forms new mental representations by transforming available information coming from various sources, including the senses, emotions, and memory. **Natural concepts** and **artificial concepts** are building blocks of thinking; they are formed by identifying properties that are common to a class of objects or ideas. Concepts are often arranged in *hierarchies*, ranging from general to specific, but the way they are organized varies across cultures.

Other mental structures that guide thinking include **schemas**, **scripts**, visual imagery, and cognitive maps. In recent years, neuroscientists have used brain imaging techniques to learn about the connections between thought processes and the brain—particularly the frontal lobes. At the same time, other scientists have emphasized the role of emotions in thinking, especially in **intuition**. Schemas and scripts assume special importance in understanding thought because they are mental structures that organize concepts, helping us make sense of new information and events—and underlie a sense of humor. Our schemas and scripts are influenced by culture.

Artificial concepts (p. 179)	**Intelligence** (p. 177)
Computer metaphor (p. 177)	**Intuition** (p. 183)
Concept hierarchies (p. 179)	**Natural concepts** (p. 179)
Concepts (p. 178)	**Prototype** (p. 179)
Event-related potentials (p. 182)	**Script** (p. 185)

MyPsychLab Resources 5.1:

Simulation: Intuition and Discovery in Problem Solving

Simulation: Schemas

5.2 What Abilities Do Good Thinkers Possess?

Core Concept 5.2: Good thinkers not only have a repertoire of effective strategies, called algorithms and heuristics, they know how to avoid the common impediments to problem solving and decision making.

Two of the most crucial thinking skills involve *identifying the problem* and *selecting a problem-solving strategy*. Useful strategies include **algorithms**, which produce a single correct answer, and **heuristics**, or "rules of thumb." Among the most useful heuristics are *working backward, searching for analogies*, and *breaking a bigger problem into smaller problems*.

Common obstacles to problem solving include **mental set**, **functional fixedness**, and *self-imposed limitations*.

Judgment and *decision making* can be flawed by biases and faulty heuristics. These include the *confirmation bias*, **hindsight bias, anchoring bias, representativeness bias**, and **availability bias**. Judgment can also be affected by factors outside the person, such as the **tyranny of choice**. In general, good decision makers are those who use good critical thinking skills.

People who are often called "creative geniuses" are highly motivated **experts** who often have a certain cluster of traits, such as independence and a need for stimulating interaction. They appear, however, to use ordinary thinking processes, although the role of natural talent is the subject of dispute.

5.3 How Is Intelligence Measured?

Core Concept 5.3: Intelligence testing has a history of controversy, but most psychologists now view intelligence as a normally distributed trait that can be measured by performance on a variety of tasks.

The measurement of *intelligence* is both common and controversial. Assessment of mental ability has an ancient human history but was not based on scientific practice until the 20th century. In 1904, Binet and Simon developed the first workable test of intelligence, based on the assumption that education can modify intellectual performance.

In America, IQ testing became widespread for the assessment of Army recruits, immigrants, and schoolchildren. The original IQ calculation was abandoned in favor of standard scores based on the **normal distribu-** tion. Today, IQ tests come in both individual and group forms. They are typically used to diagnose learning disabilities and to assess whether a child is eligible for special education classes. In particular, IQ scores are a key ingredient in identifying **mental retardation** and **giftedness**, which are often seen as occupying the extremes of the IQ distribution.

5.4 Is Intelligence One or Many Abilities?

Core Concept 5.4: Some psychologists believe that intelligence comprises one general factor, *g*, while others believe that intelligence is a collection of distinct abilities.

Among the first *psychometric theories* of intelligence, Spearman's analysis emphasized a single, common factor known as *g*. Later, Cattell separated *g* into two components: **fluid intelligence** and **crystallized intelligence**. Modern cognitive psychologists have conceived of intelligence as a combination of several abilities.

In particular, Gardner and Sternberg have taken the lead in extending the definition of intelligence beyond school-related tasks. Sternberg's **triarchic theory** proposes **analytic**, **creative**, and **practical intelligences**, while Gardner's theory of **multiple intelligences** has claimed seven components of intelligence—and possibly three more. Meanwhile, cross-cultural psychologists have shown that "intelligence" has different meanings in different cultures. A century of research shows that animals, too, are capable of intelligent behavior, as in chimpanzees that make tools and use language. Recent work also shows that certain birds have a rudimentary **theory of mind**.

In the United States much emphasis is placed on mental tests. In such a climate, however, a big danger lies in test scores becoming mere labels that influence people's behavior through the **self-fulfilling prophecy**.

5.5 How Do Psychologists Explain IQ Differences among Groups?

Core Concept 5.5: While most psychologists agree that both heredity and environment affect intelligence, they disagree on the source of IQ differences among racial and social groups.

Hereditarian arguments maintain that intelligence is substantially influenced by genetics, a belief endorsed at one time by the U.S. government, which used IQ tests to restrict immigration early in the 20th century. *Environmental* approaches argue that intelligence can be dramatically shaped by influences such as health, economics, and education. While most psychologists now agree that intelligence is *heritable,* they also know that **heritability** refers to variation within a group and does not imply that between-group differences are the result of hereditary factors.

The dispute over the nature and nurture of group differences in intelligence flared again in 1969, when Jensen argued that the evidence favored a strong genetic influence. This argument was echoed in the 1994 book *The Bell Curve.* Critics have pointed out that much of the research cited by those taking the extreme hereditarian position is flawed. In addition, intelligence testing itself may be biased in favor of those with particular language and cultural experiences. Hereditarian claims, however, have stimulated much research, such as Scarr and Weinberg's research on adopted children and follow-up studies of the Head Start program. This research suggests that the racial and class differences in IQ scores can be attributed to environmental differences and to the influence of low expectations and negative stereotypes, as found in stereotype threat.

Heritability (p. 216)   **Stereotype threat** (p. 221)

MyPsychLab Resources 5.5:

Watch: Demographics and Intelligence Testing: Robert Guthrie

Watch: Gender Difference: Robert Sternberg

Watch: Correlations Between IQ Scores of Persons of Varying Relationships

Discovering Psychology Viewing Guide

 Watch the following videos by logging into MyPsychLab (www.mypsychlab.com). After you have watched the videos, complete the activities that follow.

PROGRAM 10: COGNITIVE PROCESSES

 PROGRAM 11: JUDGEMENT AND DECISION MAKING

 PROGRAM 16: TESTING AND INTELLIGENCE

PROGRAM REVIEW

1. Michael Posner's work on brain imaging showed
   a. major differences between the brains of young and old adults, with cognitive processes more localized in brains of the elderly.
   b. that blood flow decreases in the brain as thinking becomes more efficient.
   c. that electrical stimulation of the brain can enhance performance on logic puzzles reliably.
   d. that patterns of brain activity differ in predictable ways when people see words, versus read them aloud, versus name the function of the objects to which they refer.

2. A cognitive psychologist would be most interested in which one of the following issues?
   a. how you decide which answer is correct for this question
   b. how pain stimuli are processed
   c. maturation of the efferent system
   d. how to distinguish mania from schizophrenia

3. What is one's prototype of a tree most likely to be similar to?
   a. a maple tree   c. a Christmas tree
   b. a palm tree   d. a dead tree

4. According to the program, why do people assume that Montreal is farther north than Seattle?

	Core Concepts	Psychology Matters
6.1 What Innate Abilities Does the Infant Possess? Prenatal Development The Neonatal Period: Abilities of the Newborn Child Infancy: Building on the Neonatal Blueprint	• Newborns have innate abilities for finding nourishment, avoiding harmful situations, and interacting with others—all of which are genetically designed to facilitate survival.	**Psychological Traits in Your Genes** When genes contribute to your thoughts and behaviors, you shouldn't assume that biology is solely responsible
6.2 What Are the Developmental Tasks of Childhood? How Children Acquire Language Cognitive Development: Piaget's Theory Social and Emotional Development	• Nature and nurture work together to help children master important developmental tasks, especially in the areas of language acquisition, cognitive development, and development of social relationships.	**The Puzzle of ADHD** New research sheds light on the prevalence, causes, and treatments of attention-deficit/hyperactivity disorder.
6.3 What Changes Mark the Transition of Adolescence? Adolescence and Culture Physical Maturation in Adolescence Adolescent Sexuality Cognitive Development in Adolescence Moral Development: Kohlberg's Theory	• Adolescence offers new developmental challenges growing out of physical changes, cognitive changes, and socioemotional pressures.	**Using Psychology to Learn Psychology** Our thinking processes continue to grow and develop in a predictable pattern as we pursue higher degrees of education.
6.4 What Developmental Challenges Do Adults Face? Early Adulthood: Explorations, Autonomy, and Intimacy The Challenges of Midlife: Complexity and Generativity Late Adulthood: The Age of Integrity	• Nature and nurture continue to interact as we progress through a series of transitions in adulthood, with cultural norms about age combining with new technology to increase both the length and quality of life for many adults.	**A Look Back at the Twin Studies** Remarkable reports of similarities in twins raised apart from each other may grab our attention, but do they necessarily point to genetics as the primary cause of human thinking and behavior?

Critical Thinking Applied: **The Mozart Effect**

development over the lifespan

chapter 6

What could grab media interest more effectively than a story of twins separated at birth and reunited as adults? Many such tales have emerged from psychologist Thomas Bouchard's famous twin-study project at the University of Minnesota. But what really attracts journalists are the reports of uncanny similarities between identical twins who were raised by different parents, taught by different teachers, influenced by different peers and siblings, and sometimes even raised in different cultures.

Take, for example, the "Jim Twins." Separated just a few weeks after they were born, identical twins Jim Springer and Jim Lewis were adopted separately and raised apart. Yet something drove them on parallel paths, even though those paths didn't cross again for 39 years. At their reunion, the "Jim twins" discovered some remarkable correspondences in their habits, preferences, and experiences. Some examples:

● They achieved nearly identical scores on tests of personality, intelligence, attitudes, and interests.

- Medically, both have mildly high blood pressure and have had spells that they mistakenly thought were heart attacks; both have had vasectomies; both suffer from migraine headaches.
- Both chain-smoke Salem cigarettes and drink Miller Lite beer.
- Both had been indifferent students: Jim Lewis had dropped out in the tenth grade, while Jim Springer had managed to graduate from high school.
- Both had been married twice, and both of their first wives were named Linda. Both of their second wives were named Betty. Both men like to leave love notes around the house.
- Lewis had three sons, including one named James Alan. Springer had three daughters, plus a son named James Allan.
- Both had owned dogs named Toy.
- Both drive Chevrolets, chew their fingernails, like stock-car racing, and dislike baseball.
- Both had been sheriff's deputies.
- Both do woodworking as a hobby. Lewis likes to make miniature picnic tables, and Springer makes miniature rocking chairs. Both had built white benches around trees in their yards.

When he first read about the two Jims in a newspaper, Bouchard knew their case presented a rare opportunity to study the relative effects of heredity and environment and how they unfold over time in the process we call development (Holden, 1980a,b; Lykken et al., 1992). The Jims agreed to participate and so became the first of some 115 pairs of reunited twins (plus four sets of reared-apart triplets) to be studied over the next 20 years at the University of Minnesota.

Another remarkable pair, Oskar Stör and Jack Yufe, was also separated at birth, and from that point on their lives went in almost unbelievably different directions. Stör was raised by his grandmother in Czechoslovakia and attended a Nazi-run school during World War II, while Yufe was taken to Trinidad, where he was raised as a Jew by his biological father. Oskar is now married, a strong union man, and a devoted skier, while Jack is separated, a businessman, and a self-styled workaholic. Still, alongside these huge differences, the researchers again found some striking similarities in seemingly trivial behavior patterns. Both twins wear neatly clipped moustaches; both read magazines from back to front; both have a habit of storing rubber bands on their wrists; both flush the toilet before using it; both like to dunk buttered toast in coffee; and both think it is funny to sneeze loudly in public.

PROBLEM: Do the amazing accounts of similarities in twins reared apart indicate that we are primarily a product of our genes? Or do genetics and environment work together to influence growth and development over the lifespan?

As compelling as these stories are, we must interpret them with care (Phelps et al., 1997). Let's begin that interpretation by putting on our critical thinking caps and asking some important questions:

- Are these twin stories representative of all twins reared apart, or are they exceptional cases?

- When we notice striking similarities between biological relatives—whether they be twins, siblings, or parent–child relationships—what factors other than genetics might account for these similarities?
- Are there methods by which we can reliably tease out the differences between the genetic contributions and the influences of the environment to make an accurate determination of the relative contribution of each?

These fascinating questions are just part of what we'll explore in our study of development across the lifespan. Broadly speaking, **developmental psychology** is the psychology of growth, change, and consistency from conception to death. It asks how thinking, feeling, and behavior change through infancy, childhood, adolescence, and adulthood. It examines these changes from multiple perspectives—physical, emotional, cognitive, and sociocultural. Furthermore, it seeks to understand how both heredity and environment influence these changes. *The primary questions for developmental psychologists, then, are these: How do individuals predictably change throughout the lifespan, and what roles do heredity and environment play in these changes?*

This issue of heredity and environment is important, so let's take a closer look at it. Psychologists call this the **nature–nurture issue:** As you know from the two previous chapters, nature refers to the contribution of our heredity, whereas nurture refers to the role of our environment. In earlier years, the nature–nurture question was an either-or question, but modern researchers have a more sophisticated understanding of this complex issue (Bronfenbrenner & Ceci, 1994; Dannefer & Perlmutter, 1990). Today the nature–nurture issue recognizes that both nature and nurture play a role in almost all aspects of human behavior (de Waal, 1999), and questions (1) what the relative weight of each of these factors is and (2) how the two factors might interact to ultimately produce a given characteristic.

What do we mean by interact? Simply put, *nature–nurture interaction* means that we are all born with certain predispositions *(nature)* that, if exposed to the proper experiences in our environment *(nurture),* can reach their full potential. If you are good at, say, math or music, your ability is really the result of a combination of genetic potential and experience. Heredity establishes your potential, but experience determines how your potential will be realized. To put it yet another way: Nature proposes, and nurture disposes.

Still, we may ask: Which of our traits does heredity affect most? And which are most heavily influenced by learning or other environmental factors (such as disease or nutrition)? While more and more information is becoming available to help answer these questions, we must be cautious in our interpretation of these findings. For example, we know that in the genetic disorder known as Down's syndrome, biology has a strong influence. In this condition, the output of abnormal chromosomes leads to mental retardation—and there is no cure. The hazard of knowing about the genetic basis for Down's syndrome is that the parents or teachers of children with such disorders may simply conclude that biology determines the child's destiny and give up hope. By focusing on the genetic side of the disorder, they may overlook effective learning-based treatments that can measurably improve the living skills of these individuals.

Mindful of such dangers, psychologists have nevertheless forged ahead in the study of hereditary and environmental contributions to thought and behavior. To do so, they have invented several clever methods for weighing the effects of nature and nurture. **Twin studies** represent one such method. The work of Thomas Bouchard, for example, with twins separated at birth and then reunited, offers some tantalizing clues about the relative contribution of nature and nurture. This type of twin set, however, is a scarce resource. Far more common are twin sets raised together, and fortunately, psychologists have figured out how to learn from these twins as well. Because *identical twins* have essentially the same genotype and *fraternal twins* have (on the average) 50% of their genes in common,

Harry Potter is a good illustration of the nature–nurture interaction. Born to pure-bloods (parents with magical powers) but raised by muggles (people without magical abilities), his own magic didn't flourish until he entered the magic-supporting environment of Hogwarts School.

Developmental psychology The psychological specialty that studies how organisms grow and change over time as the result of biological and environmental influences.

Nature–nurture issue The long-standing discussion over the relative importance of nature (heredity) and nurture (environment) in their influence on behavior and mental processes.

Twin study A means of separating the effects of nature and nurture by which investigators may compare identical twins to fraternal twins or compare twins separated early in life and raised in different environments.

CONNECTION • CHAPTER 1

The control group in a study serves as a standard against which other groups can be compared.

hereditary effects should show up more strongly in identical twins. (In studies comparing these two twin types, the fraternal twins serve as a sort of control group.) Such studies have given us valuable information on the genetics of mental and behavioral disorders, including alcoholism, Alzheimer's disease, schizophrenia, depression, and panic disorder (Eley, 1997; Plomin et al., 1994).

Yet a third method used to measure the effects of heredity and environment is **adoption studies.** If you adopted a baby, would he or she grow up to resemble you more than the biological parents? Researchers in adoption studies compare the characteristics of adopted children with those of their biological and adoptive family members. Similarities with the biological family point to the effects of nature, while similarities with the adoptive family suggest the influence of nurture. This work, in concert with twin studies, has revealed genetic contributions to a variety of psychological characteristics, such as intelligence, sexual orientation, temperament, and impulsive behavior—all of which we will see in more detail elsewhere in this book (Bouchard, 1994; Dabbs, 2000).

6.1 KEY QUESTION
WHAT INNATE ABILITIES DOES THE INFANT POSSESS?

People used to think that babies began life as a "blank slate"—with an empty brain and no abilities. In modern times, however, that picture has changed. We now see newborns as possessing a remarkable set of abilities acquired through their genes. They are adept at locating food and avoiding potential harm, and their social nature facilitates their survival as well. We focus on these inborn or **innate abilities** in the Core Concept for this section:

core concept

> Newborns have innate abilities for finding nourishment, avoiding harmful situations, and interacting with others—all of which are genetically designed to facilitate survival.

To be sure, the newborn's capabilities are limited, but they are effective enough to promote survival. You arrived in the world already "knowing," for example, how to get nourishment by suckling, how to raise your hands to shield your eyes from bright light, and how to get attention by cooing and crying. Still, it is helpful to think of the newborn's basic abilities as a sort of scaffold to which new and more complex abilities are added as the child grows and develops.

To explain where these abilities come from and how they develop, we will organize our discussion around three important developmental periods: the *prenatal period,* the newborn or *neonatal period,* and *infancy.* You will notice that, in each phase, development builds on the abilities and structures laid down earlier.

Adoption study A method of separating the effect of nature and nurture—by which investigators compare characteristics of adopted children with those of individuals in their biological and adoptive families.

Innate ability Capability of an infant that is inborn or biologically based.

Prenatal period The developmental period before birth.

Zygote A fertilized egg.

Prenatal Development

The **prenatal period** is a time of furious developmental activity between conception and birth that readies the organism for life on its own outside the womb. Development typically occurs over the span of nine months and is divided into three phases: the germinal, embryonic, and fetal stages.

Three Phases of Prenatal Development Shortly after conception, the fertilized egg, also known as a **zygote,** begins to grow through cell division. During this *germinal phase,* one cell becomes two; two become four; and when the number reaches about 150—about a week after conception—the zygote implants itself in the lining of the uterus. At this point, it (along with those cells that will form the *placenta* and other supportive structures) becomes an **embryo.** It is now connected to the mother's body and thus affected by anything she eats, drinks, or to which she is otherwise exposed.

During the *embryonic phase,* the genetic plan determines how all the organs that will later be found in the newborn infant begin to form. In this stage, a process known as differentiation causes the embryo's cells to begin to specialize as components of particular organ systems. (Before differentiation, certain cells in the embryo, known as embryonic stem cells, are capable of forming into any organ of the body.) One example of differentiation is the development of anatomical sex: If the embryo's genetic plan contains two X chromosomes, the child will be a girl, but if it contains an X and a Y chromosome, a boy will develop.

At first, the embryo's cells form distinct layers. Those in the outer layer become the nervous system and the skin. Cells in the middle layer become muscles, bones, blood vessels, and certain internal organs. Those in the inner layer differentiate on a path that will eventually make them into the digestive system, lungs, and glands. By the end of the first month, the initial single cell of the zygote has developed into millions of specialized cells—in an embryo about the size of a grain of sand. Eventually this process of cell division and differentiation, which continues throughout the prenatal period, produces all the tissues and organs of the body.

The first rudimentary "behavior"—a heartbeat—appears in the fifth week and, a few weeks later, the embryo makes reflexive responses to stimulation. These behaviors occur long before the brain has developed to the point where it can think or direct behaviors. Between this time and the tenth week, the major organs and structures of the body will rapidly begin to form, making it especially sensitive to the effects of drugs and other harmful substances.

After the eighth week, the developing embryo is called a **fetus.** In the *fetal stage,* spontaneous movements and basic reflexes begin to appear. For example, as early as 14 weeks, some babies can be seen on ultrasound to curve their hands around something that comes in contact with their palm (Sparling et al., 1999). This is the beginning of the grasping reflex, and it has adaptive significance. By the sixteenth week, the brain is fully formed and the fetus can feel pain (Anand & Hickey, 1987). The baby can hear sounds from outside the womb by the twenty-seventh week, resulting in the ability to recognize certain sounds and rhythms shortly after birth. The brain will continue to develop, growing new neurons at the amazing rate of up to 250,000 per minute. At birth, the newborn's brain contains some 100 billion neurons (Dowling, 1992).

Teratogens: Prenatal Toxins

During prenatal development, the **placenta** is the organ that surrounds the embryo/fetus. It serves as a conduit between mother and child, letting nutrients in and waste out, and can also screen out some—but not all—potentially harmful substances. Some toxic substances, called **teratogens,** still get in and can cause irreparable damage. Teratogens include viruses (such as HIV, the AIDS virus), certain drugs and other chemicals, and even some herbs. Among the most common teratogens are nicotine and alcohol.

Fetal alcohol syndrome (FAS) is one of the more worrisome disorders that can occur in children of mothers who drink alcohol during pregnancy. A leading cause of mental retardation, FAS may also cause babies to have poor motor coordination, impaired attention, and hyperactivity. Mothers who drink one or more drinks per day risk fetal alcohol exposure, which has been found to impair development of language ability, memory, learning, and a host of other cognitive and physical functions (Office of the Surgeon General, 2005). Furthermore, a recent series of studies at the University of Pittsburgh indicates that even minimal exposure—in some cases fewer than five drinks per week—can result in lower IQ and significantly retarded physical development: At age 14, children who had been exposed to even light alcohol consumption in utero weighed on

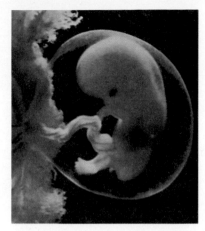

As the brain grows in the developing embryo, it forms as many as 250,000 new neurons per minute.

Embryo In humans, the name for the developing organism during the first eight weeks after conception.

Fetus In humans, the term for the developing organism between the embryonic stage and birth.

Placenta The organ interface between the embryo or fetus and the mother. The placenta separates the bloodstreams, but it allows the exchange of nutrients and waste products.

Teratogen Substance from the environment, including viruses, drugs, and other chemicals, that can damage the developing organism during the prenatal period.

Fetal alcohol syndrome (FAS) A set of physical and mental problems seen in children whose mothers drink exessive amounts of alcohol during pregnancy.

average 16 pounds less than children whose mothers had abstained from alcohol during pregnancy (Day, 2002; Willford, 2006).

Exposure to nicotine, and even to some commonly taken herbs and supplements, can also damage the developing fetus. Women who smoke during pregnancy are more likely to have children with lower birth weight, learning deficits, and ADHD (Button et al., 2005). Maternal smoking is also associated with greater risk of sudden infant death syndrome (SIDS) (Bruin et al., 2007). Even some popular herbal remedies and supplements, such as gingko and ginseng, have been found to have detrimental effects on a developing fetus (Chan et al., 2003; Dugoua et al., 2006).

The Neonatal Period: Abilities of the Newborn Child

By the time a newborn arrives in the world, then, a great deal of neural and sensory development has already taken place. (The term **neonatal period** refers to the first month after birth.) This current understanding of the newborn's sensory awareness is a far cry from the "great blooming, buzzing confusion" that experts once thought characterized the newborn's world (James, 1950/1890). Indeed, more recent research has revealed that newborns have all five senses working, as well as a variety of behavioral reflexes that they use to respond to and manipulate their environment. Together, these many abilities effectively help newborns survive and thrive in their environment.

Sensory Abilities in the Newborn   What exactly can newborns do with their senses? For one thing, they can respond to taste: the sweeter the fluid, the more continuously and forcefully an infant will suck (Lipsitt et al., 1976). For another, they smile when they smell banana essence, and they prefer salted to unsalted cereal (Bernstein, 1990; Harris et al., 1990). They recoil, however, from the taste of lemon or shrimp or the smell of rotten eggs. And, as early as 12 hours after birth, they show distinct signs of pleasure at the taste of sugar water or vanilla. All these responses are part of the newborn's ability to seek healthy nourishment—as the Core Concept for this section suggested.

Just as heredity biases newborns' tastes, it also programs a preference for human faces to most other visual patterns (Fantz, 1963). Even their neonatal nearsightedness helps: Their optimal focus of about 12 inches is ideally suited for looking at faces. By just a few days after birth, they can recognize their mother's face. Their distance vision, however, is poor, with a visual acuity of about 20/500 (which means that they can discriminate at 20 feet stimuli that most older children can see clearly at 500 feet). These immature systems develop very rapidly (Banks & Bennett, 1988), however, and by about seven weeks, the infant has acquired the visual pathways and motor coordination to be able to maintain eye contact with a caregiver—an important element in establishing a relationship.

What else can newborns do with their senses? Although they can see colors, their ability to differentiate colors, such as red from orange from blue, becomes dramatically better a month or two after birth (Teller, 1998). They also prefer to look at objects with a high degree of contrast, such as checkerboards or target shapes. By three months, the baby can perceive depth and is well on the way to enjoying the visual abilities of adults. Moreover, it may surprise you to know that infants seem to possess a rudimentary ability to "count" objects they see. They know, for example, the difference between two dolls and three (Wynn, 1992, 1995). Such core knowledge serves as the foundation for the later development of more complex skills, such as are required for arithmetic (Spelke, 2000).

Newborns also have strong auditory preferences, preferring human voices over other sounds and the sounds and rhythms of their own language to nonnative languages (Goodwyn & Acredolo, 2000). Before assuming these prefer-

Neonatal period   In humans, the neonatal (newborn) period extends through the first month after birth.

CHAPTER 6 ● DEVELOPMENT OVER THE LIFESPAN

ences are genetic, though, we must recall that the developing fetus can hear sounds from outside the womb during the last few months in utero. Thus, an alternate interpretation would be that these auditory preferences are due to prior exposure to human voices and their native language. To distinguish whether these preferences are genetic or environmental, one study had expectant mothers read *The Cat in the Hat* aloud twice a day for the last six weeks of their pregnancy; then, after the babies were born, the researchers played audiotapes of the mothers reading that story as well as a different story. The findings? Babies expressed an overwhelming preference for the sound of the familiar story being read over the sound of a different story. Neonates also display greater attraction to female voices than to those of men, and within a few weeks of birth they begin to recognize their mothers' voice (Carpenter, 1973; DeCasper & Spence, 1986). Thus, nurture—by way of prior experience—may be the driving force behind these newborn auditory preferences.

Social Abilities   Have you ever noticed that if you stick your tongue out at a baby, he will stick his tongue out back at you? This delightful game reveals just one of many behaviors that researchers are finding newborns and infants will mimic. While in the past, some child development experts wondered if this reflected an in-depth cognitive understanding of the other person's behavior, the recent discovery of *mirror neurons* offers a more realistic explanation. Mirror neurons in the motor cortex fire in response to another person's goal-directed behavior and motivate an immediate "mirroring" reponse on the part of the observer. **Mimicry** of a variety of behaviors, like other innate abilities we have discussed, helps the infant survive and thrive in the environment.

CONNECTION • CHAPTER 2
Mirror neurons activate regions in our brains that correspond to actions or mental states we perceive in others.

As the foregoing discussion suggests, infants are built for social interaction. In fact, they not only respond to, but also interact with, their caregivers from the moment of birth. Film studies of this interaction reveal an amazing degree of **synchronicity**: close coordination between the gazing, vocalizing, touching, and smiling of infants and mothers or other caregivers (Martin, 1981). And while babies respond and learn, they also send out their own messages to those willing to listen to and love them. The result of this interaction can be seen in studies showing how the feelings of mothers and infants are coordinated (Fogel, 1991). So, a 3-month-old infant may laugh when her mother laughs and frown or cry in response to her display of negative emotion (Tronick et al., 1980).

Innate reflexes   Aside from their sensory abilities and mimicry, babies are born with a remarkable set of **innate reflexes** that provide a biological platform for later development. Among these reflexes, the *postural reflex* allows babies to sit with support, and the *grasping reflex* enables them to cling to a caregiver. The *rooting reflex* can be seen when newborns turn their heads toward anything that strokes their cheeks—a nipple or a finger—and begin to suck it. And if you have ever noticed that when you hold a baby upright over a solid surface, her legs will lift up as if she were marching, you've witnessed the *stepping reflex,* which helps prepare a baby to walk. There are also a number of reflexes that act as built-in safety features to help them avoid or escape from loud noises, bright lights, and painful stimuli. And in their cooing, smiling, and crying, babies have some effective tools for social interaction. All of this, of course, makes much evolutionary sense because these abilities are highly adaptive and promote survival.

Infancy: Building on the Neonatal Blueprint

Following the neonatal period, the child enters **infancy,** a period that lasts until about 18 months of age—the time when speech begins to become better developed. (The Latin root *infans* means "incapable of speech.") It is a time of rapid, genetically programmed growth and still-heavy reliance on the repertoire of

Mimicry   The imitation of other people's behaviors.

Synchronicity   The close coordination between the gazing, vocalizing, touching, and smiling of infants and caregivers.

Innate reflex   Reflexive response present at birth.

Infancy   In humans, infancy spans the time between the end of the neonatal period and the establishment of language—usually at about 18 months to 2 years.

CONNECTION • CHAPTER 9

"Instinct" is a common but imprecise term that refers to behaviors that have a strong genetic basis.

reflexes and "instinctive" behaviors that we discussed above. All of these abilities arise from a nervous system that continues to develop at a breathtaking pace.

Neural Development   While the prenatal brain was focused on producing new brain cells, many of these neurons are not fully connected to each other at birth. This helps explain why most people have a poor memory for events that occurred before they were about 3½ years of age (Bauer, 2002; Howe & Courage, 1993). To take the next steps in forming the brain's circuitry, stimulation from the environment assumes an important role in creating and consolidating connections. Each time an infant is exposed to a new stimulus, dendrites and axons actually grow and branch out to facilitate connections between the neurons involved in that experience (Kolb, 1989). The more frequently the fledgling neural connections are utilized, the more permanent they become. In other words, "neurons that fire together, wire together" (Courchesne et al., 1994).

Sensitive Periods   The early years are the most fertile time for brain development in many areas, including language and emotional intelligence. In fact, in some domains—such as hearing and vision—stimulation must occur during a specific "window of opportunity," or the ability will not develop normally (Lewis & Maurer, 2005; Trainor, 2005). This is called a **sensitive period** in development. Evidence for sensitive periods comes from, for example, a study of adults who were born profoundly deaf. Some of them learned American Sign Language (ASL) early in life, whereas others didn't learn it until much later. (Parents of the late learners had focused their initial efforts on teaching the children to speak and lip-read, but the children had been unable to acquire spoken language due to their profound deafness.) Those who didn't learn ASL—their first learned language—until adolescence or adulthood never reached the level of competency with the language as did the children who had learned it in early childhood (Mayberry, 1991; Singleton & Newport, 2004). You might feel some connection to this finding if you ever tried to learn a new language as an adult—it was probably far more difficult than it would have been if you'd learned it as a child!

Brain Development   As the dendrites and axons grow and connect, the total mass of neural tissue in the brain increases rapidly—by 50% in the first two years. By 4 years of age, it has nearly doubled its birth size. For the next ten years, the types of experiences the infant is exposed to will largely determine which regions and functions of the brain become most developed. The genetic program (along with the physical limitations imposed by the size of the skull) does not allow the tremendous growth of brain circuitry to continue indefinitely, however. The neural growth rate gradually diminishes; and, by about 11 years of age, the brain attains its ultimate mass. Around that time, unused connections begin to be trimmed away through a process called **synaptic pruning.** Notably, this process does not destroy the neurons themselves but instead returns them to an uncommitted state, awaiting a role in future development (Johnson, 1998).

Maturation and Development   Sitting, crawling, and walking—like the growth of the brain, the growth spurt of puberty, and the onset of menopause—all occur on their own biological time schedules. Psychologists use the term **maturation** for the unfolding of these genetically programmed processes of growth and development over time. When organisms are raised under adequate environmental conditions, their maturation follows a predictable pattern. In humans, maturation generates all of the sequences and patterns of behavior seen in Figure 6.1.

We must, however, keep in mind the role of the environment and how it interacts with our hereditary nature. While maturation dictates the general time frame in which an individual becomes biologically ready for a new phase, the environment can speed up or slow down the exact time of development. Prominent biologist Edward Wilson (1998, 2004) describes this principle as a **genetic leash.** Because of the genetic leash, a child without special training learns to walk fol-

Sensitive period   A span of time during which the organism is especially responsive to stimuli of a particular sort. Organisms may have sensitive periods for exposure to certain hormones or chemicals; similarly, they may have sensitive periods for learning language or receiving the visual stimulation necessary for normal development of vision.

Synaptic pruning   The process of trimming unused brain connections, making neurons available for future development.

Maturation   The process by which the genetic program manifests itself over time.

Genetic leash   Edward Wilson's term for the constraints placed on development by heredity.

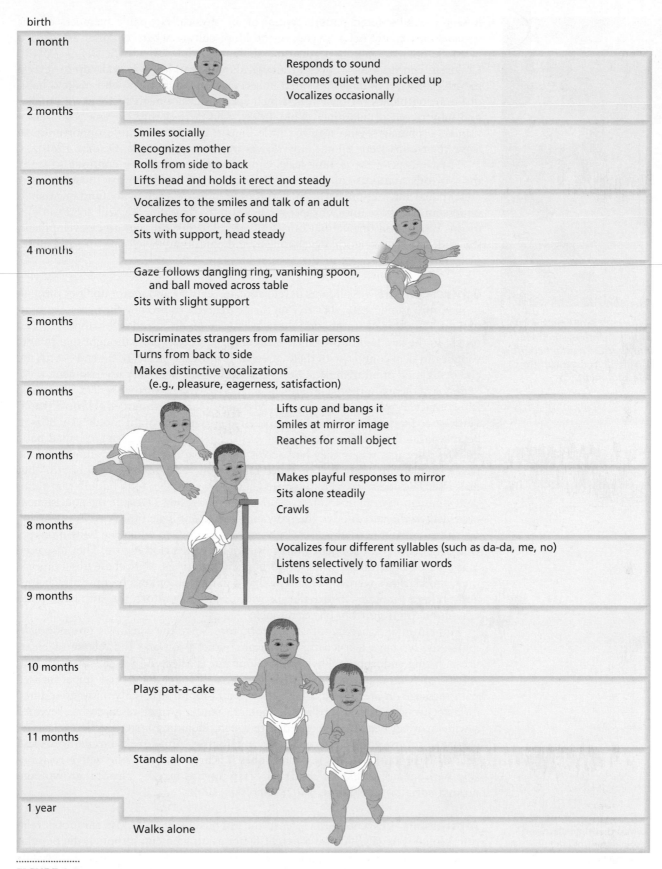

birth

1 month
Responds to sound
Becomes quiet when picked up
Vocalizes occasionally

2 months
Smiles socially
Recognizes mother
Rolls from side to back

3 months
Lifts head and holds it erect and steady
Vocalizes to the smiles and talk of an adult
Searches for source of sound
Sits with support, head steady

4 months
Gaze follows dangling ring, vanishing spoon,
    and ball moved across table
Sits with slight support

5 months
Discriminates strangers from familiar persons
Turns from back to side
Makes distinctive vocalizations
    (e.g., pleasure, eagerness, satisfaction)

6 months
Lifts cup and bangs it
Smiles at mirror image
Reaches for small object

7 months
Makes playful responses to mirror
Sits alone steadily
Crawls

8 months
Vocalizes four different syllables (such as da-da, me, no)
Listens selectively to familiar words
Pulls to stand

9 months

10 months
Plays pat-a-cake

11 months
Stands alone

1 year
Walks alone

FIGURE 6.1
Maturational Timetable for Motor Control

This figure shows average ages at which each behavior is performed. There are considerable individual differences in the *rate* of development, so the time at which each response occurs is variable. Most infants, however, follow the *sequence* of development outlined here.

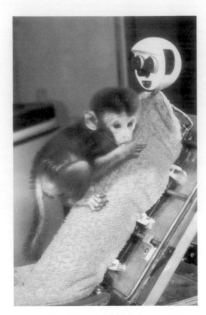

One of Harlow's monkeys and its artificial terry-cloth mother. Harlow found that the contact comfort mothers provide is essential for normal development.

lowing a time-ordered pattern typical of all physically capable members of our species. (See Figure 6.1.) Indeed, in the Hopi culture where children are carried in cradle boards, walking occurs on a similar schedule (Dennis & Dennis, 1940). Children who do receive special training, though, can learn to walk up to several months earlier, a finding illustrated in several African cultures who make a habit of bouncing babies on their feet, which speeds development of their leg muscles and motor control (Gardiner et al., 1998). And at the other extreme, children in Iranian orphanages who received little human contact and little opportunity to leave their cribs were significantly slower in learning to walk (Dennis, 1960).

The concept of the genetic leash can be useful to us as we continue to study the various patterns of human development. It eloquently illustrates the inescapable interaction between nature and nurture that is so fundamental to understanding how and why people develop as they do. We will see examples of this interaction throughout our study of language and cognitive development, social development, moral development, and emotional development—and moreover, in all major stages of the human lifespan.

Contact Comfort   As infants develop greater sensory and motor abilities through both nature and nurture, they rely on their caregivers to provide the necessary stimulation. One type of stimulation that we haven't yet discussed is the importance of touch. In the first half of the nineteenth century, many experts thought that infants sought physical contact with their caregivers only as a means to an end—with the end being food or nourishment. Beyond providing the necessary nourishment, these "cupboard theory" proponents argued, infants derived no further benefit from physical contact. Psychologists Harry and Margaret Harlow disagreed (Harlow, 1965; Harlow & Harlow, 1966) and tested their theory using infant monkeys who had been separated from their mothers at birth. The Harlows placed orphaned baby monkeys in cages where they had access to two artificial surrogate mothers. One was a simple wire figure that provided milk through a nipple—a "cupboard," but little else. The other was a cloth-covered figure providing no milk but offering abundant stimulation from its soft terry-cloth cover. The results? Despite the nourishment provided by the wire model, the baby monkeys spent little time with it, preferring instead to remain nestled to the cloth mother. Moreover, when the baby monkeys were frightened, they sought comfort by clinging to the cloth figure. They also used it as a base of operations when exploring new situations. With these observations, then, the Harlows were able to show that the infant monkeys become attached to and prefer a "mother" figure that provides **contact comfort,** the stimulation and reassurance derived from physical touch.

Human infants need contact comfort, too. Since the Harlow's groundbreaking study, we have learned that physical contact promotes the release of pleasure-inducing endorphins. Physical development is affected by touch as well. University of Miami developmental psychologist Tiffany Field first experimented with massage on premature babies in 1986 and found that daily massage resulted in faster weight gain. Since Field's landmark study, further research has revealed a wide array of benefits associated with touch, including faster intellectual development, improved digestive tract functioning, improved circulation, and decreased production of stress hormones. Clearly, a close, interactive relationship with loving adults is a child's first step toward healthy physical growth and normal socialization (Blum, 2002; Sapolsky, 2002).

Contact comfort Stimulation and reassurance derived from the physical touch of a caregiver.

Attachment The enduring socio-emotional relationship between a child and a parent or other regular caregiver.

Attachment   Psychologists refer to the establishment of a close emotional relationship between a child and a parent figure as **attachment,** although the popular media often refer to it as "bonding." By either name, this relationship is especially important because it lays the foundation for other close relationships that follow.

Attachment appears to occur instinctively in many species, although it is not necessarily limited to the infant's interactions with the biological parents. One striking example occurs in **imprinting**, the powerful attraction of infants of some species (notably in birds) to the first moving object or individual they see. A baby chick hatched by a mother duck will form an attachment to its surrogate mother—even though it is a chicken, not a duck. The imprinted chick will even follow its duck-mother right up to the water's edge when she and her ducklings go for a swim. (This scientific concept was illustrated in Hans Christian Andersen's story "The Ugly Duckling.") Thus, the imprinting tendency is an innate predisposition, although the organism's environment and experience determine what form it will take.

Konrad Lorenz (1903–1989), a researcher who pioneered the study of imprinting, dramatically demonstrated what can happen when young birds become imprinted on an object other than their mother.

In humans, research on contact comfort provides evidence of some physical need for attachment. Building on the Harlows' work with monkeys, psychologist John Bowlby (1969, 1973) suggested that human attachment is innate, begins as early as the first few weeks, and functions as a survival strategy for infants. From an evolutionary perspective, it would stand to reason that infants who stayed close to their caregivers would be less vulnerable to threats from the environment. One study found, for example, that when mothers left the room, their 2- to 4-month-old babies' skin temperature dropped, a sign of emotional distress (Mizukami et al., 1990). In these youngsters, skin temperature dropped even more when a stranger replaced the mother. In contrast, skin temperature remained steady if the mother stayed in the room—even if the stranger was present. Apparently, children only a few months old rely on their caretakers as a "safe base," even before they can indicate attachment by walking or crawling (Bee, 1994).

Attachment Styles   Have you ever noticed, though, that children seem to differ in their types of attachment? Some children seem comfortable with strangers when their primary caregiver is present, while others appear clingy and fearful. Still others seem to care very little who is present. Developmental psychologist Mary Ainsworth not only noticed those patterns but spent a career studying these various forms attachment takes in humans. To do so, she developed an innovative laboratory procedure called the "Strange Situation," which continues to be used today as the standard for measuring attachment.

What is this clever procedure? The Strange Situation involves putting young children and their primary caregiver into a series of interactions—sometimes together, sometimes separated, and sometimes with a stranger. Researchers then observe how the child responds to these various situations (Ainsworth, 1989; Lamb, 1999). Using such methods in a variety of cultures, Ainsworth found that the children's responses fell into two main categories, reflecting either **secure attachment** or insecure attachment. *Securely attached* children were relaxed and comfortable with their caregivers and tolerant of or even interested in strangers and new experiences. When separated from their caregivers, they became upset—which, from 6 to 30 months, is a normal behavior called **separation anxiety**—but calmed down immediately on the caregiver's return and resumed their normal activities. They seemed to perceive their caregivers as a "secure base" from which to explore the world, confident that the caregiver would be available to help if needed.

Insecurely attached children could be divided into two categories: *anxious-ambivalent* and *avoidant*. The **anxious-ambivalent** children wanted contact with their caregivers but cried with fear and anger when separated from their caregivers and proved difficult to console even when reunited. They clung anxiously to their caregivers when a stranger approached and were uncomfortable exploring new situations. Conversely, the **avoidant** children weren't interested in contact, displaying no distress when separated from their caregivers and no particular happiness when

Imprinting   A primitive form of learning in which some young animals follow and form an attachment to the first moving object they see and hear.

Secure attachment   The attachment style of children who are relaxed and comfortable with their caregivers and tolerant of strangers and new experiences—as contrasted with children who are *insecurely attached*.

Separation anxiety   A common pattern of distress seen in young children when separated from their caregivers.

Anxious-ambivalent attachment   One of two primary response patterns seen in insecurely attached children— in which a child wants contact with the caregiver, shows excessive distress when separated from the caregiver, and proves difficult to console even when reunited.

Avoidant attachment   One of two primary response patterns seen in insecurely attached children—in which a child shows no interest in contact with the caregiver and displays neither distress when separated from the caregiver nor happiness when reunited.

reunited. Overall, some 60% of American children develop secure attachment, while about 25% are anxious-ambivalent, and 15% are avoidant.

Attachment has become a very hot topic over the past decade, as research is indicating that patterns established in infancy may influence a variety of childhood and adult behaviors, including aggression, friendships, job satisfaction, relationship choices, and intimacy experiences (Berk, 2004; Gomez & McLaren, 2007). But what causes a child to develop a particular attachment style? For many years, nurture was presumed to be the culprit: Specifically, it was thought that good parents produced securely attached children, while inconsistent parenting produced anxious-ambivalent children, and neglectful parenting led to avoidant attachment.

Today, though, most researchers recognize that nature and nurture interact in the development of attachment style. Infant temperament, for example, which is largely genetic, influences how easy or difficult it is to be responsive to an infant. It is not surprising, then, that one study found that babies who were fussier in the first few days of life were more likely to have an anxious-ambivalent attachment style one year later (Miyake, 1993). This seems quite logical, as most parents would have more difficulty consistently "reading" the signals from a temperamental baby than with an easy baby, thus creating an interaction effect between infant temperament and parenting style.

Culture and Attachment   Before making up your mind about which attachment style is "best," though, consider the important factor of culture. Did you assume, like many Americans do, that secure attachment is the ideal? On the contrary, German families prefer avoidant attachment, as it promotes greater self-sufficiency, while Japanese parents rarely leave their children unattended, fostering greater dependence and an accompanying anxious-ambivalent attachment style (Grossman et al., 1985; Miyake et al., 1985). Like many qualities, then, the judgment of which is "ideal" depends heavily on the prevailing values of the culture.

Long-Term Effects of Attachment   Attachment isn't just for kids. As children grow up and become adults, they no longer restrict their attachment to their primary caregiver: They gradually widen their attachments to include other family members, friends, teachers, coworkers, and others in their community. Some evidence suggests that the primary attachment relationship, though, continues to serve as a working model for later important relationships. In other words, whatever the child learns to expect in that first caregiver relationship becomes the lens through which later relationships are perceived and interpreted. We should emphasize, however, that—powerful as attachment is—individuals who lack healthy attachments in infancy and childhood are not necessarily doomed to failure in life. While attachment problems are good predictors of later problems with social relationships, many people do succeed in overcoming attachment difficulties (Kagan, 1996, 1998). Healthy relationships, later in childhood or even in adulthood, can "reset" the working model. With such caveats in mind, we now invite you to take the quiz in the "Do It Yourself!" box, "What's Your Attachment Style?"

Psychosocial Development: Trust versus Mistrust   The large body of research on attachment dovetails nicely with the first stage in one of the major lifespan theories of development. Erik Erikson (1902–1994) was a prominent psychoanalyst who believed that, on an unconscious level, we form basic beliefs about ourselves and our relationship to our social world as we go through life. These basic beliefs, then, influence our development through the choices we make in our relationships. Furthermore, Erikson thought each of these basic beliefs developed out of a crisis (which could be resolved successfully or remain unresolved) at a critical period in our development. Thus, he characterized each of the eight stages in his developmental theory as a choice between two opposing beliefs, such as *trust versus mistrust,* the first developmental problem of our lives. (See Table 6.1.)

◄ CONNECTION • CHAPTER 1
Erik Erikson was a prominent neo-Freudian theorist.

Identify which one of the following three self-descriptions you most agree with (adapted from Shaver & Hazan, 1994):

1. I am somewhat uncomfortable being close to others; I find it difficult to trust them completely, difficult to allow myself to depend on them. I am nervous when anyone gets too close, and love partners often want me to be more intimate than I feel comfortable being.

2. I find that others are reluctant to get as close as I would like. I often worry that my partner doesn't really love me or won't want to stay with me. I want to get very close to my partner, and this sometimes scares people away.

3. I find it relatively easy to get close to others and am comfortable depending on them. I don't often worry about being abandoned or about someone getting too close to me.

What Your Choice Means We realize that it is probably obvious to you which of the statements above is "best." Nevertheless, just considering the alternatives should help you understand attachment styles—and, perhaps, yourself—a little better. Here's our interpretation: If you selected the first statement, you agreed with the attitude that reflects an avoidant, insecure attachment. This style was chosen by 25% of Shaver and Hazan's respondent sample. The second statement reflects an anxious-ambivalent, insecure attachment style, selected by 20% of the sample. The third statement reflects a secure attachment style, the most common pattern identified, accounting for 55% of respondents (Shaver & Hazan, 1994).

What do these styles signify for later life? Through interviews, observations, and questionnaires, researchers have identified several consequences of attachment style, secure or insecure, in adulthood (see Ainsworth, 1989; Collins & Read, 1990; Hazan & Shaver, 1990; Kirkpatrick & Shaver, 1992; Shaver & Hazan, 1993, 1994; Simpson, 1990):

- Secure individuals have more positive self-concepts and believe that most other people are good natured and well intentioned. They see their personal relationships as trustworthy and satisfying.
- Secure respondents are satisfied with their job security, coworkers, income, and work activity. They put a higher value on relationships than on work and derive their greatest pleasure from connections to others.
- Insecure, anxious-ambivalent persons report emotional extremes and jealousy. They feel unappreciated, insecure, and unlikely to win professional advancement. They make less money than those with other attachment styles, working more for approval and recognition than financial gain. They fantasize about succeeding but often slack off after receiving praise.
- Avoidant people fear intimacy and expect their relationships to fail. They place a higher value on work than on relationships and generally like their work and job security. They follow a workaholic pattern, but (not surprisingly) they are dissatisfied with their coworkers.
- Secure individuals tend to choose as partners others who are secure. After breakups, avoidant individuals claim to be less bothered by the loss of the relationship, although this may be a defensive claim, with distress showing up in other ways (e.g., physical symptoms).

TABLE 6.1 Erikson's Psychosocial Stages

Age/Period (approximate)	Principal challenge	Adequate resolution	Inadequate resolution
0 to 1½ years	Trust vs. mistrust	Basic sense of safety, security; ability to rely on forces outside oneself	Insecurity, anxiety
1½ to 3 years	Autonomy vs. shame or self-doubt	Perception of self as agent; capable of controlling one's own body and making things happen	Feelings of inadequacy about self-control, control of events
3 to 6 years	Initiative vs. guilt	Confidence in oneself as being able to initiate, create	Feelings of guilt over one's limitations or inabilities
6 years to puberty	Industry vs. inferiority	Perceived competence in basic social and intellectual skills; self-acceptance	Lack of self-confidence; feelings of failure
Adolescence	Identity vs. role confusion	Comfortable sense of self as a person, both unique and socially accepted	Sense of self as fragmented, shifting, unclear sense of self
Early adulthood	Intimacy vs. isolation	Capacity for closeness and commitment to another	Feeling of aloneness, loneliness, separation; denial of intimacy needs
Middle adulthood	Generativity vs. stagnation	Focus of concern beyond oneself, to family, society, future generations	Self-indulgent concerns; lack of future orientation
Late adulthood	Ego-integrity vs. despair	Sense of wholeness; basic satisfaction with life	Feelings of futility, disappointment

Erikson theorized that, in the first 18 months of life, the major developmental task facing the infant is to develop a sense of **trust** in the world. As we have seen, infants who develop a secure attachment style see the world as an interesting place, full of new experiences to explore. With the knowledge of a primary caregiver as a "safe base" from which to explore, these infants become prepared to develop into children (and later into adults) who are comfortable in new situations and possess an adventurous and resilient spirit to help them through life. Children who do not develop this will experience difficulties navigating through later developmental challenges, as the issue of trust remains unresolved and acts as a barrier between the individual and the social world. To put it more simply, infants who do not develop a basic sense of trust in their social world will have trouble forming and maintaining satisfactory relationships.

While Erikson's theory has its critics, the criticism revolves primarily around whether his eight stages occur in their prescribed order for everyone or whether they can be experienced at different times for different people (based at least in part on cultural norms). Critics also note that Erikson's work was based primarily on his own clinical observations, rather than rigorous scientific methods. Remarkably, though, many of his observations have since been supported by methodologically sound research. And his was the first theory of human development to encompass the entire lifespan: Previous theories were interested only in the first 12 to 17 years of life, with the misguided assumption that, once you got through adolescence, you were fully and permanently developed! For these reasons, Erikson's theory remains prominent today in the study of human development. We will return to his theory and explore the other seven stages he proposed, in later sections of this chapter.

PSYCHOLOGYMATTERS
Psychological Traits in Your Genes

Eye color and the shape of your earlobes are purely genetic traits. Even some food aversions, such as a distaste for broccoli, can be anchored in the genes. But, as far as we know, heredity by itself determines none of our more complex psychological characteristics (Horgan, 1993). Where personality traits, temperament, interests, and abilities are concerned, heredity always acts in combination with environment. Outgoing people, for example, aren't just born that way; they have also been encouraged to let their tendencies to extraversion show. Still, it's fair for developmental psychologists and biopsychologists to ask which psychological characteristics have strong genetic links.

A genetic contribution to general intelligence, for example, is well established—although psychologists disagree over the magnitude of heredity's role (Plomin et al., 1994). There is also a good possibility that genes contribute to your sexual orientation (Hamer et al., 1993). And it just may be that an interest in skydiving, rock climbing, or other risky behavior has a substantial genetic component (Hamer, 1997). The evidence suggests that genes also contribute to your basic temperament and personality, including all of the "Big Five" personality factors (Bouchard, 1994; Plomin, 1997).

Likewise, some clinical disorders are associated with genetic abnormalities (Eley, 1997; Plomin et al., 1994). One of the first to be discovered was Huntington's disease, a rare problem that causes aggressive behavior and mental deterioration beginning in midlife (Cattaneo et al., 2002). Depression, a far more common problem, can also have genetic roots (although this doesn't mean that everyone who gets depressed has a genetic problem, nor that medication is always the best way to treat it). Similarly, twin studies have revealed a strong genetic contribution to schizophrenia, a major mental disorder. Fear, too, can have a hereditary basis, especially in those who suffer from a condition known as panic disorder. So can anxiety, the basis for repetitive "neurotic" rituals, such

CONNECTION • CHAPTER 1
Clinical observation is a form of the case study method.

CONNECTION • CHAPTER 10
The Big Five are fundamental traits that reliably distinguish different personality patterns among people in all cultures.

Trust The major developmental goal during the first 18 months of life. According to Erikson's theory, the child must choose between trusting or not trusting others.

as compulsively checking and rechecking the alarm-clock setting, seen in obsessive–compulsive disorder. There's also evidence that the violence that may occur in an antisocial personality and the uncontrollable outbursts of Tourette's syndrome stem ultimately from the genes. And, if you are older, you may worry that every instance of forgetting is a sign of Alzheimer's disease, which (in some forms) arises from a genetic flaw that takes first the memory and then the rest of the mind.

Thus, we see that many psychological traits, both desirable and undesirable, have a connection to our genes, as well as our experience. But, at the risk of playing the same tune too often, we must emphasize: Genetics is not everything. While heredity is involved in nearly all we do, human behaviors also are shaped by environment. And by "environment" we mean not only the influence of learning (including the impact of all our experiences) but also physical factors such as nutrition and physical stress (Brown, 1999). In almost all cases, it is the interaction of heredity and environment that drives a behavior, disorder, or trait.

Unfortunately, people sometimes go to extremes by seeing hereditary effects everywhere. A strong hereditarian stance can, for example, lead to unfair labeling of people as having "bad blood," if they come from troubled or abusive families. Just as disturbing, hereditarian expectations can create complacency and self-centeredness in those whose parents have desirable characteristics, such as high intelligence or good looks. Either way, expectations about genetic influences can create a self-fulfilling prophecy, which leads people to live up (or down) to their expectations. If you expect to be smart and successful (or dumb and a failure), chances are you won't be disappointed.

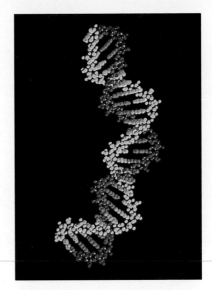

The genetic code, written in DNA, contains our complete hereditary blueprint, grouped into genes and chromosomes.

CheckYourUnderstanding

1. **RECALL:** "Nature" refers to the effects of _____, and "nurture" refers to the effects of _____.

2. **APPLICATION:** You are a psychologist working in a pediatric hospital. What would you recommend as one of the most important things that the staff could do to promote healthy development in the newborns?
   a. Talk to them.
   b. Touch them.
   c. Make eye contact.
   d. Sing to them.

3. **ANALYSIS:** What factors influence the type of attachment style an infant develops?

4. **RECALL:** Teratogens can cause
   a. fetal alcohol syndrome.
   b. impaired cognitive development.
   c. ADHD.
   d. all of the above

5. **UNDERSTANDING THE CORE CONCEPT:** Describe three ways that the infant comes into the world prepared to survive and thrive.

Answers 1. genetics or heredity; the environment **2.** b **3.** infant temperament and the consistency and responsiveness of the caregiver **4.** d **5.** Infants have an array of behavioral reflexes, sensory abilities, and social abilities (such as mimicry) that promote adaptation to their environments.

6.2 KEY QUESTION
WHAT ARE THE DEVELOPMENTAL TASKS OF CHILDHOOD?

Three of the greatest accomplishments of your life include acquiring your native language, forming relationships with the important people in your life, and developing your ability to think and reason. Each of these serves as the basis for further development later in life. And we will see that, as children work through these tasks, they undergo profound psychological changes that are the result of both their genetic code and their environment. Here's how our Core Concept states the main idea of this section:

Nature and nurture work together to help children master important developmental tasks, especially in the areas of language acquisition, cognitive development, and development of social relationships.

As we will see below, the developmental differences between children and adults are huge, but the differences in language, thought, and socialization are not simply the result of adults' greater experience or store of information. The differences between children and adults also involve the unfolding of crucial maturational processes. Let us first observe these processes at work as we examine the development of language in children.

How Children Acquire Language

One of the defining characteristics of humans is the use of complex language—our ability to communicate through spoken and written words and gestures. From a developmental perspective, human language acquisition is awe inspiring: Newborn children know no words at all, yet in only a few years virtually all of them become fluent speakers of any language they hear spoken regularly—or see, in the case of gestural languages such as American Sign Language. What makes them such adept language learners? Developmental specialists believe that human infants possess innate abilities that help them with this task (Pinker, 1994, 2006).

Language Structures in the Brain   According to one prominent theory, children acquire language not merely by imitating but by following an inborn program of steps to acquire the vocabulary and grammar of the language in their environment. Psycholinguist Noam Chomsky (1965, 1975) proposed that children are born with mental structures—built into the brain—that make it possible to comprehend and produce speech. Many experts agree with Chomsky that innate mental machinery orchestrates children's development of language (Hauser et al., 2002). Indeed, research based on the Human Genome Project has provided evidence that the foundations of language are, in part, genetic (Liegeois et al., 2001). One such mechanism, we have seen, lies in Broca's area, the motor speech "controller" in the cerebral cortex. Chomsky refers to these speech-enabling structures collectively as a **language acquisition device,** or **LAD.**

In Chomsky's theory, the LAD—like a computer chip—contains some very basic rules common to all human languages. One such rule might be the distinction between nouns (for names of things) and verbs (for actions). These innate rules, Chomsky argues, make it easier for children to discover patterns in languages to which they are exposed. Additional evidence for Chomsky's theory comes from the fact that children worldwide learn their native languages in very similar stages at very similar times. A logical hypothesis for explaining this pattern would be that children possess inborn "programs" for language development that automatically run at certain times in the child's life.

Despite the widespread agreement that humans possess some kind of innate ability to acquire language, we cannot ignore the role of the environment. Although infants are born with the ability to produce all the sounds in the approximately 4000 languages spoken on our planet, by about 6 months of age they seem to have zeroed in on the dominant language in their environment. The months spent hearing these sounds combine with their own experiments at verbalization to refine their efforts, and they lose the ability to produce the sounds that are not part of their own language. Children being raised in a Japanese-speaking culture, for example, lose the ability to distinguish between the sounds made by the letters *R* and *L,* as the letter *L* is not part of the Japanese language (Iverson et al., 2003).

Such cultural variations in the specifics of children's language development suggest that the built-in capacity for language is not a rigid device but a set of "listening rules" or guidelines for perceiving language (Bee, 1994; Slobin,

Language acquisition device (LAD)
A biologically organized mental structure in the brain that facilitates the learning of language because (according to Chomsky) it is innately programmed with some of the fundamental rules of grammar.

1985a,b). Babies pay attention to the sounds and rhythms of the sound strings they hear others speak (or in sign language, see), especially the beginnings, endings, and stressed syllables. Relying on their built-in "listening guides," young children deduce the patterns and rules for producing their own speech. Such adaptability suggests that the LAD in children is flexible, not rigidly programmed (Goldin-Meadow & Mylander, 1990; Meier, 1991).

Acquiring Vocabulary and Grammar   Clearly, then, inborn language abilities don't tell the whole story, for children must learn the words and the structure of a particular language. Accordingly, learning the basic grammar and vocabulary in the native language represents an important project for children in their first few years of life—and they are excellent language learners. By 4 months of age, babies are **babbling:** making repetitive syllables such as "mamamama." Interestingly, deaf babies being raised in a sign-language environment start babbling at just the same time—but with their hands, mimicking repetitive syllables from ASL (Pettito & Marentette, 1991). By about the time of their first birthday, babies enter the one-word stage, where they are speaking full words, and by 18 months word learning is accelerating rapidly. At this time, you might notice what psychologists call the "naming explosion," when children seem to delight in their efforts to point to objects and name them. By age 2, children are entering the two-word stage, and the range of meanings they can convey increases tremendously. By this time, the average child has a vocabulary of nearly a thousand different words (Huttenlocher et al., 1991). By age 6, that number has burgeoned to an astounding 10,000 words (Anglin, 1993, 1995). And the pace of vocabulary acquisition picks up even more between about ages 6 and 10, as you can see in Figure 6.2.

Practice Makes Perfect   Even though the rapid development of language seems driven largely by a genetic timetable, the role of culture and the environment have an impact on the degree and the pace at which children learn language. Like many learning tasks, the frequency of practice makes a difference. Mothers tend to talk significantly more with their young daughters than with their young sons (Leaper et al., 1998). Even more pronounced is the difference between children raised in low- versus middle-SES households (the term *SES* refers to socioeconomic status, which is a composite indicator of income and education level). Parents in low-SES households read to their children an average of just 25 hours between the ages of 1 and 5—compared to a whopping 1000 hours in the middle-SES group (Neuman, 2003). These differences in early learning are evident in findings that girls and middle-SES children begin kindergarten with more advanced verbal skills than boys and children from low-income SES families (Ready et al., 2005).

Grammar Turns Vocabulary into Language   Even if you have a limited vocabulary, you can combine the same words in different sequences to convey a rich variety of meanings. For example, "I saw him chasing a dog" and "I saw a dog chasing him" both use exactly the same words, but switching the order of the words *him* and *dog* yields completely different meanings. **Grammar** makes this possible: It is a language's set of rules about combining and ordering words to make understandable sentences (Naigles, 1990; Naigles & Kako, 1993). Different languages may use considerably different rules about grammatical combinations. In Japanese, for example, the verb always comes last, while English is much more lax about verb position.

First Sentences   In their early two- and three-word sentences, children produce **telegraphic speech:** short, simple sequences of nouns and verbs without plurals, tenses, or function words like *the* and *of*. For example, "Ball hit Evie cry" is telegraphic speech. To develop the ability to make full sentences, children must learn to use other forms of speech, such as modifiers (adjectives and adverbs) and articles (the, those), and they must learn how to put words together—grammatically.

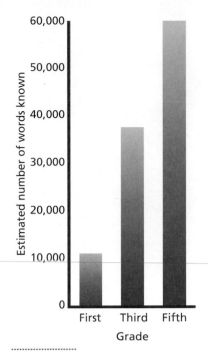

FIGURE 6.2
Growth in Grade-School Children's Vocabulary

The number of words in a child's vocabulary increases rapidly during the grade school years—an even faster rate of increase than during the preschool years. The chart shows total vocabulary, including words that a child can use (production vocabulary) and words that a child can understand (comprehension vocabulary). These data were reported in 1995 by J. M. Anglin of the University of Waterloo, Ontario, Canada.

Babbling   The production of repetitive syllables, characteristic of the early stages of language acquisition.

Grammar   The rules of a language, specifying how to use the elements of language and word order to produce understandable sentences.

Telegraphic speech   Short, simple sequences of nouns and verbs without plurals, tenses, or function words like *the* and *of*—somewhat like the language once used in telegrams.

In English, this means recognizing and producing the familiar subject-verb-object order, as in "The lamb followed Mary."

Finally, as children's language ability develops, they become skilled in using **morphemes**, the meaningful units that make up words. Morphemes mark verbs to show tense (walked, walking) and mark nouns to show possession (Maria's, the people's) and plurality (foxes, children). Often, however, children make mistakes because they do not know the rule or apply an inappropriate one (Marcus, 1996). One common error, known as *overregularization*, applies a rule too widely and creates incorrect forms. For example, after learning to make past tense verb forms by adding *-d* or *-ed*, children may apply this "rule" even to its exceptions, the irregular verbs, creating such nonwords as *hitted* and *breaked*. Learning to add *-s* or *-es* to make plurals, children may apply the rule to irregular nouns, as in *foots* or *mouses*.

Other Language Skills   Words and the grammatical rules for combining them are only some of the ingredients of communication. To communicate well, children also need to learn the *social rules of conversation*. They must learn how to join a discussion, how to take turns talking and listening, and how to make contributions that are relevant. Adult speakers use body language, intonation, and facial expressions to enhance their communication. They also use feedback they get from listeners and are able to take the perspective of the listener. Children must master these skills to become successful communicators—to become part of a human language community.

As they grow older, children also begin to express abstract meanings, especially as their thoughts extend beyond the physical world and into their psychological world. For example, after the age of 2, children begin to use words such as *dream, forget, pretend, believe, guess*, and *hope*, as they talk about internal states (Shatz et al., 1983). They also use words such as *happy, sad*, and *angry* to refer to emotional states. Later, after further cognitive advances that we will explore in the next section, they understand and use highly abstract words such as *truth, justice*, and *idea*.

What is the major point that stands out amidst the complexities of language acquisition? It is part of our Core Concept: *Language is a major developmental task of childhood—for which children are exquisitely prepared.* And the way they acquire and use language suggests that these early steps on the path to adulthood involve a combination of learning and innate processes that unfold on their own developmental timetables.

Cognitive Development: Piaget's Theory

If you have ever known a toddler going through the naming explosion, you have seen that children have an insatiable appetite for labeling things they know. Behind this labeling is their emerging ability for thinking, perceiving, and remembering. The next few pages will focus on the ways that these mental abilities emerge: a process called **cognitive development**, which is the second of the three main developmental tasks of childhood identified in our Core Concept.

Psychologists interested in cognitive development ask such questions as: *When do children realize that objects still exist even when they can't see them? Do they know that it is possible to hold ideas that aren't true? Can they understand that people have desires and dreams, but objects do not?* Developmental psychologists investigate not only what children think but how they think, as illustrated in the pioneering work of Swiss psychologist Jean Piaget. For nearly 50 years, Piaget observed children's intellectual development and formulated his observations into a comprehensive theory.

Piaget began this quest to understand the child's mind by carefully observing the behavior of his own three children. His methods were simple: He would pose problems to them, observe their responses, slightly alter the situations, and once

Morpheme   A meaningful unit of language that makes up words. Some whole words are morphemes (example: *word*); other morphemes include grammatical components that alter a word's meaning (examples: *-ed, -ing,* and *un-*).

Cognitive development   The global term for the development of thought processes from childhood through adulthood.

again observe their responses. Piaget paid special attention to the developmental transitions and changes in his children's thinking, reasoning, and problem solving. This focus led to a **stage theory** of development, which emphasized Piaget's view that people undergo distinctive revolutions in their thought processes, producing four discrete *stages* that emerge as they move through childhood and adolescence. We will see below that three key ideas distinguish Piaget's approach: (1) *schemas,* (2) the interaction of *assimilation* and *accommodation,* and (3) the *stages of cognitive development.*

Schemas   To illustrate the concept of schemas, think of some four-legged animals. Now think of some that are friendly. Then think of one that barks. You might have started by imagining elephants, tigers, cats, and dogs (all four-legged), then narrowed your choices down to cats and dogs (four-legged and friendly), and finally to just dogs (which bark). You could do this easily only because you have developed mental structures that enable you to interpret concepts and events. Piaget termed such mental structures **schemas.** We have schemas for concepts, such as "dog" and "development." We have schemas for actions, such as "eating with chopsticks." We also have schemas for solving problems, such as "finding the area of a circle" or "dealing with a crying baby." In general, schemas are mental frameworks that guide thinking. According to Piaget, they are also the building blocks of development. Schemas form and change as we develop and organize our knowledge to deal with new experiences and predict future events. As you read this, you are building a schema about schemas!

Assimilation and Accommodation   In Piaget's system, two dynamic processes underlie all cognitive growth: assimilation and accommodation. **Assimilation** is a mental process that incorporates new information into existing schemas. So a baby who knows how to grasp a rattle will apply the same strategy to a sparkly piece of jewelry worn by his caregiver. Likewise, an older child whose family has a pet canary might use assimilation during a trip to the zoo when she learns that a large parrot or a flamingo is also a bird. You, too, experience assimilation when you read about a favorite actor's new film or gain skill in using a new program on your computer. Essentially, when we assimilate, we are broadening an existing schema by integrating new information into it.

By contrast, we use **accommodation** when new information does not fit neatly into an existing schema. Accommodation is the process of restructuring or modifying schemas to accommodate the new information. Thus, a child who has learned to grasp rattles and jewelry may have trouble trying to grasp a large ball the same way. Similarly, if the child on her first trip to the zoo later encounters a bat, she will have to create a new schema for "bat," since it is a creature with wings but is not a bird. Adults experience accommodation of their mental schemas, too. For example, the Internet has caused widespread accommodation in the schemas people use to conceptualize shopping and communicating. You, too, may need to modify a schema when the professor in your psychology course says something that surprises you—such as, "Children have innate language abilities," when you had always assumed that language was acquired entirely by learning. As a result, your schema about newborn children may change to accommodate your new knowledge.

For Piaget, cognitive development results from the continual interweaving of assimilation and accommodation. Through these two processes, the individual's behavior and knowledge become less dependent on concrete external reality and increasingly reliant on internal thought. In general, assimilation makes new information fit our existing views of the world, and accommodation changes our views to fit new information.

Piaget's Stages of Cognitive Development   According to Piaget, the way a child thinks about the world progresses through four revolutionary changes. He

CONNECTION • CHAPTER 5
Schemas are knowledge clusters or general conceptual frameworks that provide expectations about topics, events, objects, people, and situations in one's life.

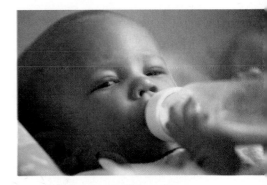

An infant finds that the sucking reflex works just as well with a bottle as with a breast, and thus assimilates when she adds sucking a bottle to her existing schema for sucking.

Stage theory   An explanation of development that emphasizes distinctive or rather abrupt changes. A stage theory of cognitive development, then, emphasizes revolutionary changes in thought processes.

Schema   In Piaget's theory, a mental structure or program that guides a developing child's thought.

Assimilation   A mental process that incorporates new information into existing schemas.

Accommodation   A mental process that modifies schemas in order to include (or accommodate) new information.

A child who knows that small creatures with wings are birds uses accommodation *when he learns that this winged creature is not a bird, but a butterfly.*

Sensorimotor stage   The first stage in Piaget's theory, during which the child relies heavily on innate motor responses to stimuli.

Sensorimotor intelligence   Piaget's term for the infant's approach to the world, relying on relatively simple physical (motor) responses to sensory experience, with very little cognition ("intelligence") involved.

Object permanence   The knowledge that objects exist independently of one's own actions or awareness.

Goal-directed behavior   An ability that emerges during the sensorimotor period by which infants develop the ability to keep a simple goal in mind as they pursue it.

Mental representation   The ability to form internal images of objects and events.

Preoperational stage   The second stage in Piaget's theory, marked by well-developed mental representation and the use of language.

CONNECTION • CHAPTER 3
Observational learning is the process documented in Bandura's famous "Bobo doll" experiment.

described these changes as stages of cognitive growth: the *sensorimotor stage* (infancy), the *preoperational stage* (early childhood), the *concrete operational stage* (middle childhood), and the *formal operational stage* (adolescence). At each stage, distinct thinking styles emerge as the child progresses from sensory reaction to logical thought. It is important to note that the maturation process dictates that all children progress through the four stages in the same sequence. Due to the interaction of heredity and environment, though, some children take longer to pass through a given stage than others.

The Sensorimotor Stage (Birth to about Age 2)   We have seen that children enter the world equipped with many innate sensory abilities and reflexive behaviors, such as recognizing familiar sounds and the grasping and sucking reflexes. None of these require thought—in the sense of the complex mental activity seen later in childhood. Instead, according to Piaget, children in the **sensorimotor stage** explore the world through their senses and motor actions, with very little "thinking" involved. Piaget called this **sensorimotor intelligence.**

During this rapidly evolving stage of development, babies work toward the major achievement of this stage: **object permanence**, which begins at about 8 months. Prior to that time, you might have noticed that babies will not look for a toy or other object that disappears. Piaget interpreted this behavior to mean that they did not understand that the object still existed when they could no longer see it. In other words, it was "out of sight, out of mind." Beginning at around 8 months, though, if you show an infant a toy and then let her see you hide it under, say, a blanket, she will look for it under the blanket. What's more, she will reliably do this even with a delay of a minute or more between the hiding and the seeking. This demonstrates the beginning of the understanding of object permanence. Over the next several months, infants develop the ability to seek something after increasingly longer delays, and they also become more successful at finding objects hidden in different locations than they were the first time (Moore & Meltzoff, 2004).

Concurrently with these accomplishments, infants are learning **goal-directed behavior,** as evidenced by their experiments with various objects. For example, a child who drops a spoon might be very interested in the clatter it makes as it bounces off a tile floor and want to repeat the action over and over again. What may seem annoying to an onlooker with sensitive hearing is really just the infant delighting in exercising some control over her world!

The emergence of object permanence, combined with an infant's increasing experiments with goal-directed behavior, provide substantial evidence that infants are beginning to form **mental representations** of objects and to recognize their own relation to the world. This mental imagery empowers a child's thinking and problem solving. Imitative behaviors that, early in infancy, were confined to the immediate present situation will show up after increasing delays in time, in what is the beginning of *observational learning.* By six months, infants will imitate behaviors they saw the previous day, and during the second year, they can retain and imitate images of previously seen behaviors for as long as a month (Klein & Meltzoff, 1999). These achievements of the sensorimotor stage propel the toddler into the next stage: the preoperational stage.

The Preoperational Stage (from about 2 to 7 Years of Age)   The cognitive advances in the next developmental stage, the **preoperational stage,** grow out of the ability to represent objects mentally. After noting rapid development during the sensorimotor stage, Piaget seems to have seen the preoperational stage as a sort of transition stage between the sensorimotor stage and the third stage (the concrete operational stage). In his observations, this was a period in which symbolic abilities that emerged in the sensorimotor stage were expanded on and consolidated. As such, he described the primary features of this stage as limitations in a child's thinking, rather than advances. Let's consider some of those features.

- **Egocentrism** causes children to see the world only in terms of themselves and their own position. Further, they assume that others see the world in the same way that they do. (We hasten to add that Piaget did not intend egocentrism to be interpreted as selfishness but rather as a limited perspective on the world.) Piaget discovered this through an experiment he called the "three mountains task." (See Figure 6.3.)

  So, when you are talking to a preoperational child on the phone, she may say, "Look at my new dollie!" assuming you can see things on her end of the line. As a result of this egocentrism, Piaget thought that preoperational children were not yet able to fully empathize with others or take others' points of view. This is one aspect of Piaget's theory that has been challenged, a point that we will elaborate on shortly.

- **Animistic thinking** involves the belief that inanimate objects have life and mental processes, just as people do. This is when children display some very charming behaviors, such as having a tea party with their teddy bears, or putting a Band-Aid on a doll that has fallen and hit the ground, or worrying that trimming a tree might hurt it.

- **Centration** is seen when a child focuses attention too narrowly, while ignoring other important information. That is, the child can "center" on only one bit of information at a time. As a result, the child will not understand the "big picture" of an event or problem. So, for example, a thirsty child may insist on drinking a "big glass" of juice, preferring a tall narrow container to a short wide one, mistakenly assuming that the height of the glass ensures that it will hold more juice, while ignoring the other relevant dimension of width (Figure 6.4). (See the nearby "Do It Yourself!" box.)

- **Irreversibility** is the inability to think through a series of events or steps involved in solving a problem and then to reverse course, returning to the mental starting point. In short, preoperational children lack the mental trial-and-error ability of older children to do and then undo an act in their minds. For example, Sam might see Maria spill a box of raisins on the table and—because the raisins are spread out over a large area—think, "Wow! Maria has lots more raisins than I have in my little box." But preoperational Sam cannot mentally reverse the process and think, "If she put them all back in the box, it would look like the same amount I have in mine." This inability—to do a mental "experiment," then undo it and mentally try another approach—represents the biggest obstacle to logical thinking in the preoperational child.

While we might see these as limitations, it is important to recognize what developments are taking place during this time. Children are experimenting with their newly acquired ability to use mental representations, and in the process they are

FIGURE 6.3
Piaget's Three-Mountain Task

In Piaget's Three Mountain task, a child is shown a figure of three mountains. One mountain has a red cross at the top, one has a small house, and the third is snow-capped. On the other side of the figure (across the table from the child) sits a doll. When asked which mountain view the doll has, the preoperational child typically thinks the doll's view is the same as the child's own view. Piaget used this task to illustrate egocentrism, or the inability to understand that others' perspectives may differ from our own.

(*Source:* L. E. Berk, *Development through the Lifespan*, 4th ed. Published by Allyn and Bacon, Boston, MA. Copyright © 2007 by Pearson Education. Reprinted by permission of the publisher.)

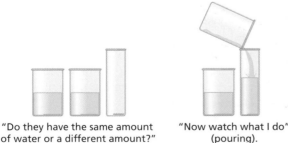

"Do they have the same amount of water or a different amount?"   "Now watch what I do" (pouring).   "Do they have the same amount of water or a different amount?"

FIGURE 6.4
Conservation of Liquid Task

Peoperational thinkers cannot understand that the amount of liquid remains the same when poured into a different-sized container. Mastery of this conservation task marks the transition to the concrete operational stage

Egocentrism   In Piaget's theory, the self-centered inability to realize that there are other viewpoints beside one's own.

Animistic thinking   A preoperational mode of thought in which inanimate objects are imagined to have life and mental processes.

Centration   A preoperational thought pattern involving the inability to take into account more than one factor at a time.

Irreversibility   The inability, in the preoperational child, to think through a series of events or mental operations and then mentally reverse the steps.

often highly creative. We see this creativity in the animism they display and also in their other make-believe games that are a central feature of the preoperational stage. In fact, it can be argued that, when creativity in problem solving declines in the next stage, the decline is not just a gain but in some ways also a loss.

The Concrete Operational Stage (from about 7 to about 11 Years of Age) At the next stage, children break through the barrier of irreversibility to understand, for the first time, that many things may stay essentially the same even when their superficial appearance changes. In this **concrete operational stage,** they can understand that a short, wide glass can hold as much juice as a tall, narrow one or that the spilled raisins must fit back in the box. In mastering **conservation,** the problems that defeated the preoperational child now yield to a new understanding of the way that volume is conserved. Similarly, they now understand that a string of red beads is not longer than an identical string of blue beads, even though the red beads are stretched out in a line while the blue beads lie in a small pile. They realize that the beads look different in their grouping, but this does not mean that they are different in number.

Along with the new ability to understand conservation, children at this stage have a wondrous new ability. They now can solve problems by manipulating concepts entirely in their minds: That is, they can perform **mental operations**. This allows concrete operational children to think things through before taking action. As a result, they may be less impulsive. They are also less gullible, giving up many "magical" notions, such as the belief in Santa Claus, that they now believe to be impossible.

Using their ability for performing mental operations, concrete operational children begin to use simple reasoning to solve problems. The symbols they use in reasoning are, however, still mainly symbols for concrete objects and events, not abstractions. The limitations of their concrete thinking are shown in the familiar game of "20 questions," the goal of which is to determine the identity of an object by asking the fewest possible yes/no questions of the person who thinks up the object. A child in this stage usually makes a series of specific guesses about what the object is ("Is it a bird?" "Is it a cat?"), rather than asking higher-level questions that more efficiently narrow down the possibilities for the correct answer ("Does it fly?" "Does it have fur?").

We will save our discussion of Piaget's final stage of cognitive development—the formal operational stage—for our discussion of adolescence. For now, suffice it to say that this final stage involves the development of abstract thought. Table 6.2 summarizes Piaget's four stages.

Beyond Piaget: Contemporary Perspectives on Cognitive Development

Most psychologists accept the broad picture that Piaget painted of development (Beilin, 1992; Lourenço & Machado, 1996). However, researchers have shown that

Concrete operational stage The third of Piaget's stages, when a child understands conservation but still is incapable of abstract thought.

Conservation The understanding that the physical properties of an object or substance do not change when appearances change but nothing is added or taken away.

Mental operation Solving a problem by manipulating images in one's mind.

TABLE 6.2 Piaget's Stages of Cognitive Development

Stage (Ages)	Characteristics and major accomplishments
Sensorimotor (approximately 0–2 years)	Children explore the world through their senses and motor abilities. Object permanence and goal-directed behavior emerge, along with the beginning of symbolic thought.
Preoperational (approximately 2–7 years)	Childrens' thought is characterized by egocentrism, animistic thinking, centration, and irreversibility. Symbolic thought continues to develop.
Concrete operations (approximately 7–11 years)	Children have mastered conservation and develop the ability to perform mental operations with images of concrete, tangible objects.
Formal operations (approximately 12+ years)	Teens and adults in this stage develop ability for abstract reasoning and hypothetical thought.

children are, in some ways, more intellectually sophisticated at each stage than Piaget had found (Munakata et al., 1997).

Hints of Abilities Appear Earlier Than Piaget Thought   The limitations Piaget observed in the sensorimotor and preoperational stages have all been found to be mastered by children still in these age ranges. Object permanence is one example: The beginning of mental representation occurs as early as 4 months of age, rather than in the second year, as Piaget had thought. Children at that age shown "possible" and "impossible" events do not show surprise when viewing the possible event but do show surprise upon seeing the "impossible" event (Baillargeon & DeVos, 1991). (See Figure 6.5.)

Researchers have also found, in contrast with Piaget's notion of centration, that by age 3 or 4, children understand that the insides of objects (such as an egg, a rubber ball, or a dog), although invisible, are not necessarily identical to their external appearances (Gelman & Wellman, 1991). And in contrast with Piaget's claims about animistic thinking, 3- to 5-year-old children, when pressed to do so, are consistently able to distinguish between real and purely mental (imaginary) entities (Wellman & Estes, 1986). Finally, regarding egocentrism, by age 4, children can often see others' perspectives, as illustrated by the fact that they use simpler language and shorter words when talking with 2-year-olds than they do with older children or adults (Gelman & Shatz, 1978). Overall, Piaget's observations regarding the sequence of stages is accurate, but children today seem to develop some cognitive skills at a more accelerated pace than Piaget believed.

A Theory of Mind   These cognitive advances signal the development of a **theory of mind**, which is an understanding that others may have beliefs, desires, and emotions

Theory of mind   An awareness that other people's behavior may be influenced by beliefs, desires, and emotions that differ from one's own.

Test Events

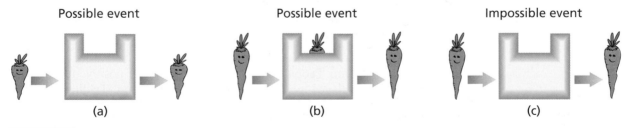

Possible event	Possible event	Impossible event
(a)	(b)	(c)

FIGURE 6.5
Testing Infants for Object Permanence

In this innovative test of object permanence, infants are shown a series of "possible" and "impossible" events. In (a), a short carrot approaches a screen with a window at the top, then moves behind the screen, and finally emerges from the other side of the screen. In (b), a tall carrot does the same thing. The top of the short carrot is *not* visible through the window as it passes (because it is shorter than the window), but the top of the taller carrot *is* visible as it passes the window. Because both of these scenarios are logical, they represent the "possible" events. In (c), a tall carrot approaches and passes behind the screen, but this time the carrot top is *not* visible through the window (as it should be). Three- to four month- old infants gaze longer at this "impossible" scenario than they do at the "possible" events, indicating what may be the beginnings of object permanence. (*Source:* Adapted from L. E. Berk, *Child Development*, 6th ed. Copyright © 2002 by Pearson Education. Reprinted by permission of the publisher.)

different from one's own and that these mental states underlie their behavior (Frith & Frith, 1999). Your theory of mind underlies your expectations about how people will act in certain situations—such as when given a gift or when spoken to angrily. It also includes recognition that expectations about others' actions may have to be adjusted based on what we know about the individual in question. It facilitates empathy for others, enables deception, and increases our chance of making sound judgments about people when it counts.

Recent evidence indicates that these abilities may begin as early as 6 months of age—which dovetails with recent findings on object permanence discussed in the previous section. At that age, one study showed that infants could reliably distinguish between a helpful character and a harmful character and unfailingly chose the helpful character as a playmate (Hamlin et al., 2007). The cognitive milestones of the sensorimotor and preoperational stages facilitate further development of this initial accomplishment; and, by 5 years of age, children cross-culturally seem to understand that others' perceptions of the world may differ from their own (Callaghan et al, 2005).

Stages or Waves? A second criticism of Piaget's theory questions his notion of the stages as abrupt transitions. Newer research suggests that the transitions between one stage and another are more continuous than Piaget's theory implies. Psychologist Robert Siegler suggests that what is needed is a new metaphor for development (Siegler, 1994). Instead of the abrupt changes implied by stage theories, he proposes that we think of "waves." The **wave metaphor,** he says, better fits both the scientific data and our everyday experience, which shows the variability of children's behavior. For example, during a single day, a child may use several different strategies to solve the same linguistic problem: "I ate," "I eated," and "I ated." This is not the pattern we would find if a child were making a sudden leap from one stage to another. Instead, says Siegler, this is a pattern of overlapping developmental waves, where each wave can be thought of as the ebb and flow in the strength of a cognitive strategy (Azar, 1995).

Social and Emotional Development

Our health, happiness, and even our survival depend on forming meaningful, effective relationships, in the family, with peers—and, later in life, on the job. This means that children need to begin the long process of learning the rules their society uses for social and political interactions. They must also learn to monitor their own feelings and behavior and to understand those of others. This process of social and emotional development is one of the most important developmental tasks of childhood.

Smiling is one simple but important way people begin social and emotional interactions. So essential is a smile to human communication that a baby's first smile is probably generated automatically by genetically controlled processes. In fact, smiles occur in babies throughout the world (Gazzaniga, 1998a). The delight parents take in a baby's first smile represents the beginning of lifelong lessons in social behavior. People smile not only as a sign of positive feelings but also because their audience expects such a facial expression (Fridlund, 1990). However, social and emotional development involves much more than a winning smile. On the "nature" side, psychologists have found that our innate disposition or temperament influences our responsiveness to others. And, on the "nurture" side, psychologists have found many environmental factors that influence socialization. Furthermore, children's cognitive advancements are an essential component in their development of effective social relationships. In this section, we will examine how nature and nurture work hand-in-hand in the social and emotional development of children.

Temperament One powerful influence on the way children interact with the world is their **temperament.** Psychologists use the term *temperament* for an individ-

Wave metaphor A way of conceptualizing cognitive development, as occurring more gradually—in "waves"—rather than abruptly, as the stage theory suggests.

Temperament An individual's characteristic manner of behavior or reaction—assumed to have a strong genetic basis.

ual's inherited, "wired-in" pattern of personality and behavior. Harvard researcher Jerome Kagan, who has studied temperament in thousands of children, observed that about 20% of children are born with tendencies toward shyness, while about 40% are born predisposed to boldness (Kagan, 1998). Shy babies, in the face of unfamiliar situations, become upset or subdued and are likely to try to avoid the situation. Bold babies, on the other hand, are more sociable and likely to react with interest to new situations. Brain-imaging studies indicate that these differences are physiological: Shy babies have much more active amygdalas than do bold babies (Schwartz et al., 2003).

While basic temperaments can be recognized almost at birth, they are not written in stone (Kagan, 1996). From very early on, the environment interacts with these genetic tendencies, so that parenting styles and other aspects of a child's experience can modify the way temperament expresses itself. Oftentimes, people are less likely to engage and be playful with a shy baby, which will accentuate the child's initial disposition. On the other hand, if a shy baby's parents recognize the child's withdrawal and gently play with her and encourage her to interact, the child will become more outgoing than her temperament would otherwise have predicted. And a bold child reared by bold parents will certainly experience and respond to the world differently than will a bold child reared by timid or fearful parents.

Thus, family members and friends can teach every individual a variety of responses to the world, all within his or her temperamental range. We must also note that no temperament is ideal for all situations. We should "remember that in a complex society like ours, each temperamental type can find its adaptive niche" (Kagan, quoted in Gallagher, 1994, p. 47).

Socialization   Through interaction with your parents, peers, and others, you learned how to get along with people, a developmental task called **socialization.** Socialization, however, doesn't just happen in childhood. It is the lifelong process of shaping an individual's behavior patterns, values, standards, skills, attitudes, and motives to conform to those regarded as desirable in a particular society (Hetherington & Parke, 1975). Socialization of gender roles is one example. Institutions exert pressure on the child to adopt socially approved values. Among these, the school and leisure-time choices, such as television and peers, have heavy influences. Increasingly, many preschool children are also shaped by their experiences in day care. And one other influence is of supreme importance: parenting styles.

Four Parenting Styles and Their Effects   Most approaches to child rearing fall into one of four distinct parenting styles that developmental psychologists have found in families all over the world (Baumrind, 1967, 1971; Russell et al., 2002). (As you read about these, you might try to imagine how you would have turned out differently if your parents had used one of the other approaches.) **Authoritarian parents** often live by the slogan, "Spare the rod and spoil the child." They demand conformity and obedience, and they tolerate little discussion of rules, which they enforce with punishment or threats of punishment. In an alternative approach, **authoritative parents** can be demanding, too. They have high expectations of their children, which they enforce with consequences. But unlike authoritarian parents, they combine high standards with warmth and respect for the child's views: They are quite willing to listen to a child's ideas and feelings, and they often encourage a democratic family atmosphere. Authoritative parents usually place a heavy emphasis on reasoning and explaining to help their children learn to anticipate the consequences of their behavior.

Taking a third approach, **permissive parents** set few rules and allow the children to make their own decisions. Like authoritative parents, they are caring and communicative, but permissive parents give most decision-making responsibility to their children. Permissive parents believe that children can learn better from the consequences of their own actions than they can from following rules set by

CONNECTION • CHAPTER 2
The amygdala, a part of the limbic system, is especially involved in the emotions of fear and aggression.

Socialization   The lifelong process of shaping an individual's behavior patterns, values, standards, skills, attitudes, and motives to conform to those regarded as desirable in a particular society.

Authoritarian parent   One of the four parenting styles, characterized by demands for conformity and obedience, with little tolerance for discussion of rules, which the parent enforces with punishment or threats of punishment.

Authoritative parent   One of the four parenting styles, characterized by high expectations of the children, which the parent enforces with consequences, rather than punitive actions. Authoritative parents combine high standards with warmth and respect for the child's views.

Permissive parent   One of the four parenting styles, characterized by setting few rules and allowing children to make their own decisions. While they may be caring and communicative, permissive parents give most decision-making responsibility to their children.

TABLE 6.3 Features of the Four Parenting Styles

Style	Emotional involvement	Authority	Autonomy
Authoritative	Parent is warm, attentive, and sensitive to child's needs and interests.	Parent makes reasonable demands for the child's maturity level; explains and enforces rules.	Parent permits child to make decisions in accord with developmental readiness; listens to child's viewpoint.
Authoritarian	Parent is cold and rejecting; frequently degrades the child.	Parent is highly demanding; may use coercion by yelling, commanding, criticizing, and reliance on punishment.	Parent makes most decisions for the child; rarely listens to child's viewpoint.
Permissive	Parent is warm, but may spoil the child.	Parent makes few or no demands—often out of misplaced concern for child's self-esteem.	Parent permits child to make decisions before the child is ready.
Uninvolved	Parent is emotionally detached, withdrawn, and inattentive.	Parent makes few or no demands—often lacking in interest or expectations for the child.	Parent is indifferent to child's decisions and point of view.

Source: From *Development through the Lifespan*, 3rd ed., by L. E. Berk. Copyright © 2004 by Pearson Education. Published and reprinted by permission of Allyn & Bacon, Boston, MA.

their parents. Finally, **uninvolved parents** tend to be either indifferent or rejecting, sometimes to the point of neglect or abuse (Maccoby & Martin, 1983). Typically, parents in this group lead such stress-filled lives that they have little time or energy for their children. (See Table 6.3.)

You can probably guess the usual outcomes of these different parenting styles. Research shows that children with authoritative parents tend to be confident, self-reliant, and enthusiastic. Overall, these children are happier, less troublesome, and more successful. Those with authoritarian parents tend to be anxious and insecure. Children with permissive or uninvolved parents are typically less mature, more impulsive, more dependent, and more demanding. Thinking back to our earlier discussion of attachment, these findings shouldn't be surprising. Generally speaking, authoritative parents take a more involved, interactive role in their children's lives—forming a stronger social–emotional attachment—than do the other three types of parents. This lays a strong foundation for prosocial behavior in the developing child.

Much of the early research on parenting styles was conducted in middle-class Western cultures, however. Can we expect the same findings elsewhere? Recent studies reveal that culture does play a role in parenting styles and parenting effectiveness, but not in the way you might think. Chinese, Hispanic, and Asian Pacific Island parents all tend to engage in stricter parenting than many Western parents, and from a distance may resemble the authoritarian parenting style. A closer look, however, reveals that these same parents typically combine their strict rules and demands for respect with a great deal of warmth—especially from fathers. When this combination is present, their children exhibit the same positive outcomes seen in Western children with authoritative parents (Berk, 2007). And in the United States, low-SES African American families exert high degrees of control over their children with positive results: These children do better in school and with peers than their counterparts who do not receive strict parenting.

Effects of Day Care As working parents make increasing use of day care for their children, we should ask the following question: How necessary is it to have a full-time caregiver? The question is an urgent one in many countries, including the United States, where over 60% of women with 1-year-old children work outside the home, and more children are cared for by paid providers than by relatives (Scarr, 1997, 1998.

Uninvolved parent One of the four parenting styles, characterized by indifference or rejection, sometimes to the point of neglect or abuse.

The research on this issue sends mixed messages. First the good news: Most children thrive in day care. Both intellectually and socially, they do as well as—sometimes better than—children raised at home by a full-time parent. Now the bad news: Poor-quality day care experiences can influence children to be aggressive, depressed, or otherwise maladjusted. Fortunately, a recent nationwide study of child care indicates that the overwhelming majority of day care centers do a fine job (Bower, 1996; NICHD Early Child Care Research Network, 2003).

As important as day care is in our society, it is comforting to note that having alternative caregivers does not in itself cause psychological problems. Rather, difficulties appear most often in poorly staffed centers where large numbers of children get little attention from only a few adults (Howes et al., 1988; NICHD Early Child Care Research Network, 2000). Another source of difficulty results from the unfortunate fact that children who are placed in the poorest-quality day care programs are most often from the poorest, most disorganized, and most highly stressed families. Developmental psychologist Laura Berk (2004) concludes that this volatile combination of inadequate day care and family pressure places some children at high risk for emotional and behavioral problems. Yet, she says, using this evidence to curtail day care services would be mistaken, because forcing a parent on a marginal income to stay home may expose children to an even greater level of risk.

All this means that day care is, in itself, neither good nor bad. It is the quality of care, whether given by a parent or a paid provider, that makes all the difference. Development expert Sandra Scarr (1998) says:

> There is an extraordinary international consensus among child-care researchers and practitioners about what quality child care is: It is warm, supportive interactions with adults in a safe, healthy, and stimulating environment, where early education and trusting relationships combine to support individual children's physical, emotional, social, and intellectual development. . . . (p. 102)

Leisure Influences   Children and adolescents in the United States and other industrialized countries have much more free time than do children elsewhere in the world. In nonindustrialized societies, children average some six hours a day working at some sort of chores or labor. By comparison, the typical American child spends less than one-half hour at such tasks. On the other hand, American children spend more time (on the average) doing schoolwork than did children in years past—although not as much as their foreign counterparts in other industrialized countries. Overall, though, the amount of free time available to U.S. children has increased dramatically over the last several generations (Larson, 2001). On average, American children today spend between 40 and 50% of their waking hours in discretionary activity.

What do children and teens do with all this leisure time? Almost 7 hours per day (averaged to include weekends) is spent with media: A majority of that time is spent watching television, with an additional 2 hours a day on the computer and playing video games (Kaiser Foundation, 2005). Reading for pleasure is moderately popular; it is more so for girls than boys, though, and declines for both sexes as children grow into adolescence (Nippold et al., 2005). Time spent playing decreases as a child ages, becoming replaced largely by media-oriented activities, which are often engaged in with friends as well. Overall, kids and teens spend twice as much time with media as they do with friends and family combined, and six times more than they spend in physical activity, reading, or doing homework.

What impact do these leisure-time activities have on a child's development? Research findings are mixed. Time with friends is associated with well-being at all ages (Rawlins, 1992) and may be especially important in adolescence. Playing sports, which kids and teens do for just over an hour a day on average, has

Time spent in physical activity typically decreases as children get older.

obvious benefits for health, as well as—depending on the sport and the environment—leadership, cooperation, and motivation. The effects of television, a topic of close scrutiny over the past few decades, seem to depend primarily on the type of programming being viewed. Educational television, which accounts for about 25% of children's television viewing, has a positive impact on literacy and cognitive development (Linebarger et. al., 2004). Heavy viewing of entertainment television, on the other hand, is a strong predictor of later deficiency in reading ability for young children (Ennemoser & Schneider, 2007). And the hundreds of studies examining the impact of viewing violent television leave no doubt that it increases aggressive behavior in viewers (Strasburger, 1995). Moreoever, viewing violent or nonviolent entertainment television prior to the age of the 3 is powerfully linked to attention problems later in childhood (Zimmerman & Christakis, 2007). We will examine the mechanics of this association in the next Psychology Matters feature.

Playing video games with violent content affects aggression in a manner similar to that of watching violent television. In addition, research shows that violent video games decrease players' sensitivity to real-world violence (Carnagey et al., 2007) and also decreases prosocial (helping) behavior (Anderson & Bushman, 2001). On the other hand, frequent video-gaming appears to improve visual–spatial processing (Green & Bavelier, 2007). And not all video games are violent. Educational video games have been found to improve critical thinking and learning in a variety of subjects ranging from social studies to math. Once again, the message seems clear: The content matters more than the medium itself.

Gender Differences in Socialization　Anyone who has watched young boys and girls playing has noticed gender differences in their social interaction. The sexes usually prefer to segregate themselves—a pattern that holds across cultures (Maccoby, 1998, 2000). In their play, boys are typically more aggressive than girls, although there are certainly exceptions. Girls tend to organize themselves into small, cooperative groups. By contrast, boys often form larger groups that have a hierarchical structure, or "pecking order." In these groups, individual boys continually compete for higher-ranking positions. They frequently resort to aggressive tactics, such as hitting, shoving, and verbal threats. Gender differences are noticeable in choices of leisure activities as well. Boys are more likely to play sports or computer games with their leisure time than girls are, whereas girls watch more television (Cherney & London, 2006). Evolutionary psychologists believe that these gender differences have an innate basis (Buss, 1999), which may be related, in part, to gender differences in testosterone levels (Dabbs, 2000). This does not mean, of course, that environmental factors, such as parenting styles and peer influences, make no difference. Social-cognitive theorists like Kay Bussey and Albert Bandura (1999) remind us that children also learn gender roles and gender-related behaviors, such as aggressiveness, competitiveness, or cooperation, from their social environments and role models.

Psychosocial Development in Childhood: Erikson's Stages　In the first section of this chapter, we introduced you to Erikson's theory of lifespan development and examined his first stage of trust versus mistrust. In childhood, an individual progresses through three more of Erikson's **psychosocial stages.** In each stage, children encounter a new "crossroad," at which point they develop another key component in their schema regarding themselves and their relation to the world. What do these stages reveal about what the social world looks like through a child's eyes?

Autonomy versus Shame or Self-Doubt　In the second stage, which runs from about 18 months to 3 years of age, toddlers are rapidly learning to walk and talk. This increasing level of interaction with the world is laden with opportunities to directly influence outcomes. To develop a sense of independence, or **autonomy**—the main developmental task in this stage—children need the freedom (and sometimes the encouragement) to try to do things on their own when appropriate. Too much

CONNECTION • CHAPTER 3

Habituation occurs when we become desensitized to a repeated stimulus so that it no longer produces the initial response.

Psychosocial stage　In Erikson's theory, the developmental stages refer to eight major challenges that appear successively across the lifespan, which require an individual to rethink his or her goals, as well as relationships with others.

Autonomy　In Erikson's theory, autonomy is the major developmental task of the second stage in childhood. Achieving autonomy involves developing a sense of independence, as opposed to being plagued by *self-doubt*.

restriction or criticism can lead to self-doubt, whereas harsh demands made too early, such as attempting toilet training before the child is ready, can lead to shame and discourage efforts to persevere in mastering new tasks; hence the name for this stage, *autonomy versus shame or self-doubt.* Children who enter this stage with a general sense of trust in the world are more likely to successfully develop autonomy than children who did not master the first stage.

Although Erikson didn't address the role of temperament in psychosocial development, we should point out its influence: We would expect shy children to need more gentle encouragement than bold children. Thus, although a nurturing and supportive environment is key to development of autonomy, nature plays a role as well.

Initiative versus Guilt   Once a child has developed trust and autonomy, the third challenge is to develop **initiative,** or the ability to initiate activities oneself, rather than merely responding to others. During the preschool years, autonomous children will become more purposeful, wanting to choose what to wear, what to eat, or how to spend their time. The danger at this stage comes from overcontrolling adults, who demand an impossible degree of self-control ("Why can't you sit still?"), which can result in the child feeling overcome by inadequacy and guilt. The term for this stage reflects these two alternatives: *initiative versus guilt.* Caregivers' responses to self-initiated activities either encourage or discourage the freedom and self-confidence needed for the next stage.

Industry versus Inferiority   Children who successfully master Erikson's first three stages enter elementary school ready to develop their skills and competencies in a more systematic way. From ages 6 to 12, school activities and sports offer arenas for learning more complex intellectual and motor skills, while peer interaction offers the chance to develop social skills. Successful efforts in these pursuits lead to feelings of competence, which Erikson called **industry.** Nurturing and supportive parenting at this stage helps children reflect on their experiences, learning from both their successes and failures and also recognizing that some failures are inevitable. On the other hand, children with overly demanding or disengaged parents may have trouble seeing their failures in perspective and ultimately develop a sense of inferiority. Likewise, youngsters who had trouble with one or more of the earlier stages may become discouraged spectators rather than performers, leading also to feelings of inferiority rather than competence. The term for this stage, therefore, is *industry versus inferiority.*

In summary, we have seen how development of language, cognitive skills, and social competencies all interact during the rapid growth and changes of childhood. Individual gains in each of these areas progress on a general biological timetable, but the pace and nature of the gains are heavily influenced by our environment. In the next section, we will see how these achievements of childhood lay the foundation for another period of rapid changes: the world of adolescence.

PSYCHOLOGY**MATTERS**
The Puzzle of ADHD

ADHD, or **attention-deficit hyperactivity disorder,** is a psychological disorder found in 3 to 5% of school-age children in America, with cross-cultural prevalence similar at about 5% (Faraone et al., 2003). Symptoms of ADHD include poor impulse control, difficulty concentrating on a task for a sustained period of time, high distractability, and excessive activity. In boys, these symptoms often manifest themselves in disruptive behavior—such as the boy who frequently jumps out of his seat in class, blurts out answers, or interrupts a conversation. In girls, however—who comprise only about 20% of ADHD diagnoses—the dis-

Initiative   In Erikson's theory, initiative is the major developmental task in the third stage of childhood. Initiative is characterized by the ability to initiate activities oneself, rather than merely responding to others or feeling *guilt* at not measuring up to other's expectations.

Industry   Erikson's term for a sense of confidence that characterizes the main goal of the fourth developmental stage in childhood. Children who do not develop industry (confidence) will slip into a self-perception of *inferiority.*

Attention-deficit hyperactivity disorder (ADHD)   A psychological disorder involving poor impulse control, difficulty concentrating on a task for a sustained period of time, high distractability, and excessive activity.

order more often looks like lack of organization or a tendency to lose things. In both boys and girls, these difficulties bleed over into multiple domains, often resulting in poor academic performance and unstable peer relationships. In fact, the impact of symptoms on multiple domains in life is a key criterion for diagnosis of ADHD and necessary to distinguish true ADHD from commonly occurring symptoms of stressful lives or features of normal childhood development. The disorder seems to follow a predictable developmental path, with symptoms appearing in the early childhood years and, in roughly 50% of cases, spontaneously fading away as the child enters adolescence. Nonetheless, some individuals continue to exhibit symptoms of ADHD throughout adulthood.

CONNECTION • CHAPTER 12

ADHD is classified as one of several developmental disorders—a category that also includes autism and dyslexia.

ADHD has received quite a bit of public attention in recent years, and as a result, most people know something about it. As is often the case, though, the layperson's knowledge of a psychological disorder may rely on media reports, Hollywood portrayals, and the words of a well-meaning (but sometimes misinformed) friend or even teacher—and consequently isn't as factual as he or she thinks it is. And overconfidence in one's knowledge about something medical or psychological sometimes leads to self-diagnosis, which may or may not be accurate. Given the increasing numbers of our students who report having symptoms of ADHD, we think it's important to set the record straight about what ADHD is, what we know about its causes, and what research tells us about effective treatments.

Research to determine the causes of ADHD is in the early stages, although twin studies and other heritability research point to a strong genetic component. From a nurture perspective, prenatal exposure to nicotine and alcohol have been found to increase incidence of ADHD. And while some theories of environmental causes—such as a diet too high in sugar—have been debunked, recent research has revealed some provocative findings. As we know, the first few years of life are a time when the brain is developing synaptic connections at a furious pace. A recent longitudinal study with a nationally representative sample has now provided strong evidence that viewing noneducational television prior to the age of 3 predicts attention deficits later in childhood (Zimmerman & Christakis, 2007). What's more, the culprit wasn't only violent television—even nonviolent entertainment programs and DVDs produced this effect. Researchers suggest that it is the fast-paced movement of entertainment programming driving the finding: In other words, watching programs that quickly and frequently switch from one scene to another—during a time when brain connections are forming—limits the brain's opportunities to create pathways for more extended focus and concentration. This explains why viewing similar amounts of educational television (which moves more slowly) did not increase incidence of attention deficits later in childhood. The study controlled for other factors that may influence development of attention deficits, such as family environment, parenting style, and cognitive stimulation. According to a companion study, 90% of children under 24 months regularly watch television, and half of what they view is entertainment television (Zimmerman et al., 2007).

Physiologically, how does an ADHD brain differ from a "normal" brain? One important difference has to do with the neurotransmitter dopamine, which is active when a person is engaged in an interesting task. People with ADHD seem to receive fewer and/or weaker dopamine bursts, which correlates with less engagement and long-term interest in a task. And while earlier research indicated that ADHD brains were smaller than non-ADHD brains, newer research reveals that ADHD brains develop normally and achieve normal size; they simply take a few years longer to do so in the cortical regions. The prefrontal cortex is slowest to develop in ADHD brains—up to five years later than non-ADHD brains—which fits with ADHD patients' difficulties staying focused on a multistep task requiring planning and follow-through. Interestingly, the motor cortex actually develops faster than normal in ADHD brains, which researchers suggest might explain the hyperactivity feature of ADHD (Shaw et al., 2007). Overall, the finding that ADHD brains develop normally, albeit more slowly, may explain why some children with ADHD seem to "grow out of it" sometime in adolescence—but still leaves a puzzle as to why some do not.

Both medication and psychological treatments can be effective in treating ADHD, but optimal treatment varies considerably among individuals. Some do very well on medication, but careful monitoring and management by a physician with expertise in ADHD is highly recommended to match each patient with the right medication and the right dosage for that individual. Also, recent findings suggest periodic "trial withdrawals" to determine whether a child still needs medication (Swanson et al., 2007)—of course, trial withdrawals must be conducted with the close supervision of the prescribing physician.

Alternatively, behavioral therapy helps children with ADHD learn to control some of their problematic behaviors and replace them with more effective behaviors—for example, learning to recognize an impulse and count to ten before acting on it. Parents and other family members are crucial partners in effective behavioral therapy. Parents can set clear expectations and use principles of operant conditioning to help shape the child's behavior, one step at a time. All members of the family can help provide redirection when the child loses focus and reinforcement for each success. As with any type of behavior modification program, though, consistency is important, which means the family must prioritize the time and attention necessary for treatment to be effective—which can be a challenge when a family is already juggling multiple tasks and priorities.

Behavioral therapy is the treatment of choice for very young children (for whom medication is not recommended). Also, it may be the best initial treatment for someone who has recently developed symptoms of ADHD; then, if it does not improve symptoms, medication may be added to the treatment plan. Indeed, one recent national study found that, for many, a combination of medication and behavior treatment works best (MTA Cooperative Group, 1999).

In closing, we offer a few notes of caution. First, although studies to date do not show any serious long-term effects of ADHD medication, it may be too soon to know for sure. We do know that children not taking ADHD medication grow about an inch taller, on average, than those who have taken medication such as Ritalin (Swanson et al., 2007). Also, families and teachers should keep in mind the power of labeling. When we label someone as having ADHD, especially without a valid diagnosis, we run the risk of the individual developing an identity consistent with the symptoms of ADHD, habits which later may be hard to overcome—even if the individual's brain no longer fits the ADHD profile. Finally, a recent article offers what may be a more balanced perspective on the disorder:

> [We must] remember that ADHD children possess many positive traits. They tend to be free-spirited, inquisitive, energetic and funny, as well as intelligent and creative. Their behavior is often spontaneous, helpful and sensitive. Many ADHD children are talented multitaskers, last-minute specialists and improvisationalists. Parents and educators should encourage these strengths and let their children know whenever possible that these qualities are highly valued (Rothenberger & Banaschewski, 2007).

CONNECTION • CHAPTER 3
Behavioral psychology examines how we learn by association and by reward and punishment.

CheckYourUnderstanding

1. **ANALYSIS:** Is the human ability for language innate or learned?

2. **MATCHING:** Match the ability/limitation with the Piagetian stage at which it becomes an important characteristic of thinking:

a. conservation
b. egocentrism
c. object permanence

1. sensorimotor stage
2. preoperational stage
3. concrete operational stage

3. **APPLICATION:** Imagine that you are a family counselor. What parenting style would you encourage parents to adopt in order to promote confidence and self-reliance in their children?

4. **ANALYSIS:** According to research cited in this section, what is the best advice you can give parents about whether their children should watch television and play video games?

5. **UNDERSTANDING THE CORE CONCEPT:** Which is most important for healthy development in childhood: nature or nurture?

6.3 KEY QUESTION
WHAT CHANGES MARK THE TRANSITION OF ADOLESCENCE?

Were all your developmental tasks finished by the time you entered *adolescence*? Most early theorists thought so. After that, they assumed, the psyche was set for life and would undergo few important changes. Modern research disputes these older views. Today's psychologists agree that we have a remarkable capacity for developmental change throughout our lifespan (Kagan, 1996, 1998). Again in adolescence the big changes lie in three important areas—as our Core Concept says:

core concept

> Adolescence offers new developmental challenges growing out of physical changes, cognitive changes, and socioemotional pressures.

So, when does adolescence begin? Or, to put the question more personally, what event first made you think of yourself as an adolescent? Chances are that it had something to do with your sexual maturation, such as a first menstrual period or a nocturnal ejaculation. Psychologists mark the beginning of **adolescence** at the onset of puberty, when sexual maturity, or the ability to reproduce, is attained. However, they cannot so precisely identify the point at which adolescence ends and adulthood begins.

Adolescence and Culture

Variations among cultures compound the difficulty of specifying the span of adolescence. Although the physical changes that take place at this stage are universal, the social and psychological dimensions of adolescence depend on the cultural context. For example, if you enter your teen years in a society that celebrates puberty as the entry to adulthood and rewards you with the power to make responsible choices, you will have a very different experience from someone whose culture condemns teenagers as confused and potentially dangerous troublemakers.

In fact, most nonindustrial societies do not identify an adolescent stage as we know it. Instead, children in these societies move directly into adulthood with **rites of passage.** These rituals usually take place at about the time of puberty and serve as a public acknowledgment of the transition from childhood to adulthood. Rites of passage vary widely among cultures, from extremely painful rituals to periods of instruction in sexual and cultural practices or periods of seclusion involving survival ordeals. For example, in some tribal groups, the young person may be asked to take a meditative journey alone or to submit to sym-

Adolescence In industrial societies, a developmental period beginning at puberty and ending (less clearly) at adulthood.

Rite of passage Social ritual that marks the transition between developmental stages, especially between childhood and adulthood.

bolic scarring or circumcision surrounded by friends and family. Once individuals have completed the passage, there is no ambiguity about their status: They are adults, and the ties to their childhood have been severed.

Our own culture has some transition rituals, but their meanings are less well defined, and as a result they do not provide clear markers for the beginning of adolescent or adult status. Qualifying for a driver's license is one such rite of passage for many middle-class teenagers in America. Another, as you might recall, is high school graduation. Mexican American girls may celebrate *quinceañeras,* and Jewish American teens may celebrate bat mitzvahs or bar mitzvahs. All provide a young person with an added measure of freedom and independence that is not available to children, but none are necessarily aligned with the transition into or out of adolescence.

Although many issues loom large in adolescence, we will focus on a few of the most important developmental tasks that confront adolescents in the United States and the industrialized Western world: coming to terms with physical maturity, a new level of cognitive development, redefining social roles and emotional issues, dealing with sexual opportunities and pressures, and the development of moral standards. Each of these issues is just one component of the central task of establishing one's identity. We begin with the physical changes that mark the end of childhood and the onset of adolescence.

Physical Maturation in Adolescence

One of the first signs of approaching adolescence is the pubescent growth spurt. Two to three years after the onset of the growth spurt, **puberty,** or sexual maturity, arrives. Puberty for males begins with the production of live sperm (usually at about age 14 in the United States), while for girls it begins at **menarche,** the onset of menstruation (usually between ages 11 and 15). These serve as indicators that the *primary sex characteristics*—the sex organs and genitals—are undergoing dramatic change. Equally dramatic changes are occurring in the *secondary sex characteristics:* the enlargement of breasts and the widening of hips in girls, the deepening of the voice and appearance of facial hair in boys, and the sprouting of pubic hair in both sexes.

During adolescence, you may recall becoming more aware of your own appearance. Boys and girls alike often judge themselves harshly by the standards they think other people may be applying to them. And, unfair as it may be, physical attractiveness does influence the way people think about each other (Hatfield & Rapson, 1993). Thus, one of the most formidable tasks of adolescence involves coming to terms with one's physical self by developing a realistic yet accepting body image (one's personal and subjective view of one's own appearance). This image is dependent not only on measurable features, such as height and weight, but also on perceptions of other people's assessments and on cultural standards of physical beauty. During adolescence, dramatic physical changes and heightened emphasis on peer acceptance—especially acceptance by sexually attractive peers—intensifies concern with one's body image. And the age at which a teen goes through puberty has an impact on his or her body image: boys who mature earlier than their peers generally have a positive body image, whereas early-maturing girls often have a negative body image.

And note other gender differences: Approximately 44% of American adolescent girls and 23% of boys claimed that they have "frequently felt ugly and unattractive"; similar data have been found across many cultures (Offer et al., 1981, 1988). Physical appearance is clearly one of the biggest concerns among adolescents (Perkins & Lerner, 1995). Girls' self-concepts are particularly tied to perceptions of their physical attractiveness, while boys seem more concerned with their physical prowess, athletic ability, and effectiveness in achieving goals (Lerner et al., 1976; Wade, 1991). In general, girls and women

Body image becomes especially important in the teenage years.

Puberty   The onset of sexual maturity.

Menarche   The onset of menstruation.

are more dissatisfied with their weight and shape than are males, and they experience more conflict about food and eating (Rolls et al., 1991). These differences probably mirror a preoccupation with female beauty and male strength—an inevitable source of concern because not all adolescents can embody the cultural ideals of attractiveness. There are also cultural influences on self-concept: Some research indicates that the self-esteem of white adolescents of both sexes is more tied to physical attractiveness than is that of black adolescents (Wade, 1991). Although adolescents seem to become more accepting of their appearances over time, the attainment of acceptable body images can be a difficult task.

Adolescent Sexuality

A new awareness of sexual feelings and impulses accompanies physical maturity. In one large study, a majority of American adolescent males and females reported thinking about sex often (Offer et al., 1981). By age 17, about 40% of teens in the United States and Canada have had their first sexual experience, a figure that rises to about 75% by age 20 (Berk, 2007; Harvey & Spigner, 1995). Many of these teens, however, still lack adequate knowledge or have misconceptions about sex and sexuality.

Masturbation is the most common orgasmic expression of sexual impulses in adolescence (Wilson & Medora, 1990). By age 16, almost 90% of boys and 60% of girls in the United States report that they have masturbated (Janus & Janus, 1993). But the figures we have are only estimates and could well be low. You can imagine the problems scientists face in trying to get good data on such private sexual practices. Sex research typically involves anonymous surveys, which may not give a complete picture of behaviors that are often associated with shame and guilt.

Sexual orientation also begins to emerge in adolescence, with the majority of adolescents having a predominantly heterosexual orientation. Males and females, though, differ in their reports of their first sexual experiences. For the vast majority of females, emotional involvement is an important ingredient of sexual attraction. In contrast, for most males personal relationships appear to be less important than the sex act itself. In fact, the average male reports little emotional involvement with his first sexual partner (Miller & Simon, 1980; Sprecher et al., 1995).

The same cautions that apply to the data on masturbation also apply to the research on adolescents who report they are gay, lesbian, or bisexual. One study involved some 83,000 youth in grades 7 through 12, obtained by combining information from several smaller surveys (Reis & Saewyc, 1999). Overall, the study found that same-sex sexual activity was reported by between 1% and 5.3% of the respondents.

Same-sex sexual behavior does not necessarily mean that the individual considers him- or herself to be homosexual or bisexual. Some experiment with same-sex activity yet think of themselves heterosexual. For others, however, such experiences do fit with a gay, lesbian, or bisexual orientation. And still others remain unsure of their primary sexual orientation. Overall, one sample from the study cited above found that 8.5% of the respondents identified themselves as gay, lesbian, bisexual, or undecided.

Exclusively homosexual feelings are difficult to resolve during adolescence, when individuals are intensely concerned with the conventions and norms of their society. While most gay and lesbian individuals first become aware of their sexual orientation in early adolescence, many may not attain self-acceptance of their sexual identities until their middle or late 20s (Newman & Muzzonigro, 1993). The time lag undoubtedly reflects the relative lack of social support for a homosexual orientation and exemplifies the importance of society's role in all aspects of identity development.

Sexual orientation   The direction of one's sexual interests (usually for individuals of the same sex, the opposite sex, or both sexes).

Cognitive Development in Adolescence

Changes that began in the womb continue to occur in the adolescent brain (Spear, 2000). While early childhood is the most rapid period for development of neural connections, the frontal lobes of the brain are the last to develop. What are the implications of this adolescent change in neurology?

Teens: Guided by Reason or Emotion? The frontal lobes are involved in social and emotional behaviors, as well as rational thinking and judgment. So, during adolescence (when these lobes have not fully developed), the teen brain is more likely to process information through the amygdala rather than through the more rational frontal cortex as they will later in adulthood. As a result, their reactions will be more emotional. In addition, brain-imaging studies indicate that teens' difficulty controlling their impulses is the inevitable consequence of the premature frontal cortex combined with the overactive amygdala. This, along with the increases in estrogen and testosterone levels, probably contributes to adolescents' sensation-seeking and risk-taking behaviors, as well as to increasing preoccupation with body image, sex, and social-emotional issues.

Piaget's Final Stage: Formal Operational Thought Adolescence brings with it Piaget's final stage of cognitive growth, involving the ability for abstract and complex thought. In this **formal operational stage,** the individual begins to ponder introspective problems, such as how to become better accepted by peers. Teens also become capable of dealing with abstract and intangible issues, such as fairness, love, and reasons for existence. Essentially, they learn to deal with hypothetical problems, rather than needing the concrete base of the previous stage. With these formal operational reasoning powers, adolescents and adults can now approach life's problems using more systematic thinking strategies. In the "20 questions" game we mentioned earlier, for example, they impose their own structures on the task, starting with broad categories and then formulating and testing hypotheses in light of their knowledge of categories and relationships. Their questioning moves from general categories ("Is it an animal?") to subcategories ("Does it fly?") and then to specific guesses ("Is it a bird?") (Bruner et al., 1966).

Current research, however, questions Piaget's notion that formal operational thought necessarily develops in adolescence. Some adults, it seems, never develop this capacity; instead, it appears dependent on education and experience. College-educated people are more likely to demonstrate formal operational thought, and in general, people are most skillful with abstractions and hypotheticals in their areas of expertise (Keating, 2004). Overall, development of this type of cognitive ability, more than any of Piaget's other cognitive tasks, appears highly reliant on cultural values and the environment.

Moral Development: Kohlberg's Theory

Is there a pattern in the development of our sense of right and wrong? The best-known psychological approach to moral development comes from the late Lawrence Kohlberg (1964, 1981), who based his theory on Piaget's view of cognitive development. After all, reasoned Kohlberg, moral thinking is just a special form of cognition. Mirroring Piaget's stages, each stage in Kohlberg's theory of moral reasoning is based on a different moral standard. Table 6.4 summarizes these stages.

What interested Kohlberg most were the ways that people reason about moral problems, rather than what they might do when led into temptation (Alper, 1985; Kohlberg, 1968). Accordingly, Kohlberg probed people's moral thinking by presenting people with a series of *moral dilemmas,* such as this one:

In Europe a woman was near death from a very special kind of cancer. There was one drug that the doctors thought might save her. It was a form of

Formal operational stage The last of Piaget's stages, during which abstract thought appears.

TABLE 6.4   Kohlberg's Stages of Moral Reasoning

Levels and stages	Reasons for moral behavior
I. Preconventional morality	
Stage 1: Egocentric pleasure/pain/profit	Avoid pain or avoid getting caught orientation
Stage 2: Cost/benefit orientation; reciprocity	Achieve/receive rewards or mutual benefits ("I'll scratch your back if you'll scratch mine")
II. Conventional morality	
Stage 3: "Good child" orientation	Gain acceptance, avoid disapproval
Stage 4: Law-and-order orientation	Follow rules, avoid penalties
III. Postconventional (principled) morality	
Stage 5: Social contract orientation	Promote the welfare of one's society
Stage 6: Ethical principle orientation (e.g., Gandhi, Jesus, Mohammed)	Achieve justice, be consistent with one's principles, avoid self-condemnation

radium that a druggist in the same town had recently discovered. The drug was expensive to make, but the druggist was charging ten times what the drug cost him to make. He paid $200 for the radium and charged $2000 for a small dose of the drug. The sick woman's husband, Heinz, went to everyone he knew to borrow the money, but he could only get together about $1000, which is half of what it cost. He told the druggist that his wife was dying and asked him to sell it cheaper or let him pay later. But the druggist said, "No, I discovered the drug, and I'm going to make money from it." So Heinz got desperate and broke into the man's store to steal the drug for his wife. Should Heinz have done that? Why? (Colby et al., 1983, p. 77)

Think about your own response to this situation before you read further. Note that it made no difference to Kohlberg whether a person said that Heinz should or should not have stolen the drug. The problem is a genuine dilemma, so a well-reasoned case can be made on either side. For Kohlberg and his colleagues, the interesting part of an individual's answer was the moral thinking behind it. They found that the reasons given fell into six categories, corresponding to the following stages. See if you can tell where your own response to the Heinz problem fits:

- *Stage 1.*   People reasoning at this stage think only of reward and punishment. They show no concern for others. In response to the Heinz dilemma they might say, "He should take the drug because he might get in trouble if he let his wife die." Or, on the other hand, "He shouldn't steal the drug because he might get caught and go to jail."

- *Stage 2.*   The first sign of awareness of other perspectives shows itself at the second stage of moral reasoning. Still concerned about reward and punishment, the stage 2 person may seek personal gain by appealing to another person's self-interest, saying, in effect: "You scratch my back, and I'll scratch yours." Here is a sample stage 2 response to the Heinz case: "He should steal the drug because he is poor and needs his wife to help him make a living."

- *Stage 3.*   The main concerns at this stage are seeking social approval and keeping everyone happy. Decisions are based on personal relationships, rather than on principle. A typical stage 3 response: "They won't blame him for stealing the drug, but everyone would think he is bad if he let his wife die."

- *Stage 4.*   Maintaining social order is paramount at stage 4. In this stage people often emphasize laws, rules, policies, promises, duty, or respect for authority in their responses. Someone at stage 4 might say, "He shouldn't steal the drug because it would violate the Ten Commandments," or "He should steal the drug because his first obligation is to his wife."

- *Stage 5.* Kohlberg called this the "social contract" stage because it emphasized the idea that rules and laws are flexible and can be changed by social consensus and by legislation. Emphasis at this stage is on fairness, rather than on the blind obedience of the previous stage. A possible stage 5 response to the Heinz dilemma: "He should take the drug, and the law should be interpreted to allow an exception under such desperate circumstances."

- *Stage 6.* At this stage the individual bases a decision on universal principles of conscience that he or she would apply to all people in all situations. These are abstract and general principles, which often refer to the dignity and worth of each person, rather than concrete rules, such as the Ten Commandments. A possible stage 6 response: "He should take the drug because, if he doesn't, he is putting a greater value on property than on human life."

You can see how Kohlberg's **stages of moral reasoning** parallel the stages of Piaget's theory, as the individual moves from concrete, egocentric reasons to more other-oriented, abstract ideas of right and wrong. Accordingly, at the first stages, a child may not steal a cookie for fear of punishment, while at a more advanced level, the child may resist stealing for fear of not living up to the parents' expectations. In general, the earliest stages of moral reasoning are based on self-interest, while later, more advanced stages center on others' expectations or on broader standards of social good. Unfortunately, not all people attain the later, least egocentric stages. In fact, Kohlberg found that many adults never even reach stage 4.

Critiques of Kohlberg's Theory Does moral development follow the same developmental sequence everywhere? Yes, said Kohlberg. Cross-cultural work shows that individuals attain the same stages in the same order in all cultures studied, including Turkey, Taiwan, Guatemala, Japan, and the United States (Eckensberger, 1994). However, this research also hints at some limitations of the theory to explain moral development in other cultural contexts: The higher stages, as defined by Kohlberg, have not been found in all cultures. Even in his native United States, Kohlberg found that stages 5 and 6 do not always emerge. Their emergence appears to be associated with high levels of verbal ability and formal education (Rest & Thoma, 1976).

One of the most stinging criticisms of Kohlberg's theory has come from Carol Gilligan (1982), a colleague at Kohlberg's own campus. Gilligan argued that the theory has a male bias and ignores uniquely feminine conceptions of morality. For women, says Gilligan, morality is embedded in social relationships and personal caring, which makes them appear to reach a plateau at stage 3. To his credit, Kohlberg responded by taking a fresh look at his data for stage 3 and stage 4. As a result, he redefined stage 4 by moving militant law-and-order responses (most often given by males) to stage 3. Most subsequent studies have found no significant sex differences in moral reasoning (Walker, 1989, 1991; Walker & de Vries, 1985).

A more telling critique suggests that research on moral reasoning may have limited practical value. Studies have found no close connection between people's moral reasoning and their behavior. Moreover, most moral reasoning comes after people have intuitively decided how to act. Moral reasoning, then, may be little more than rational justification for an emotional decision, claims psychologist Jonathan Haidt (2001). In the arena of morality, says Haidt, it's the "emotional dog" that wags its "rational tail," not the other way around.

Social and Emotional Issues in Adolescence

As teens develop their own identity, the relative importance of others in their spheres of influence shifts. Family ties become stretched as the adolescent spends more time outside the home (Paikoff & Brooks-Gunn, 1991). What adolescents

Stage of moral reasoning Distinctive way of thinking about ethical and moral problems. According to Kohlberg, moral reasoning progresses through a series of developmental stages that are similar to Piaget's stages of cognitive development.

According to Erikson, during the search for identity, adolescents must define their identies as individuals, even as they seek the comfort and feeling of belonging that comes from being with family and friends. One compromise might be to experiment with different norms—such as clothing and hairstyles—within the security of supportive relationships with companions, cliques, or romantic partners.

Identity In Erikson's theory, identity is a sense of who one is—a coherent self. Developing a sense of identity is the main goal of adolescence.

do with that time, however, depends on gender (Buhrmester, 1996). Friendships among girls are built on emotional closeness, with girls often getting together "just to talk." By contrast, friendships among boys emphasize activities, with talk centering on personal achievements or those of others.

Do Parents Still Matter? Some developmental experts argue that the effects of parents, family, and childhood become nearly lost as the adolescent peer group gains influence (Harris, 1995). In American society, the adolescent encounters new values, receives less structure and adult guidance, and feels a strong need for peer acceptance. As a result, adolescents report spending more than four times as much time talking to peers as to adults (Csikszentmihalyi et al., 1977; Larson, 2001). With their peers, adolescents refine their social skills and try out different social behaviors. Gradually, they define their social identities, the kind of people they choose to be, and the sorts of relationships they will pursue.

Are parents still important to the adolescent? The answer is an unequivocal yes. Parents who continue to monitor their teens' activities, and maintain open and healthy communication through these years, are most likely to see their teenagers successfully navigate the challenges of adolescence. A high-quality parent–child relationship remains the strongest predictor of adolescent mental health (Steinberg & Silk, 2002).

Erikson's Psychosocial Development in Adolescence Erik Erikson noted the emergence of an independent self in adolescence and characterized it as the essential dilemma of adolescence. This search for **identity**, Erikson asserted, can be impeded by the confusion of playing many different roles for different audiences in an expanding social world. Thus, he called this stage *identity versus role confusion*. Resolving this *identity crisis* helps the individual develop a sense of a coherent self. While it is normal and healthy for one's identity to change throughout life, failure of the adolescent to find a satisfactory resolution for his or her identity issues may result in a self-concept that lacks a stable core. Resolution of this issue is both a personal process and a social experience (Erikson, 1963).

Is Adolescence a Period of Turmoil? Problems with loneliness, depression, and shyness can also become significant during adolescence, which is one reason for the sharp increase in suicide among teenagers (Berk, 2004; U.S. Bureau of the Census, 2002). Studies of adolescent suicide show that the triggering experience for such a tragedy is often a shaming or humiliating event, such as failure in some achievement or a romantic rejection (Garland & Zigler, 1993). The intensity of a young person's social and personal motives, combined with the overactive emotional brain, can make it hard to keep perspective and recognize that even difficult times will pass and that everyone makes mistakes.

Another factor also has a huge influence on adjustment: the biological changes associated with puberty, for which many teenagers are unprepared. An awakening interest in sexuality is amplified by the hormonal surges of adolescence. High levels of testosterone, particularly in boys, have been associated with risky and antisocial behavior. Again, however, relationships with parents are crucial: Testosterone-related problems are much more likely in teens who lack the stabilizing force of a solid relationship with their parents (Booth et al., 2003).

But is adolescence inevitably a period of turmoil? It is a period in which individuals are likely to have conflicts with their parents, experience extremes of mood, and engage in risky behaviors (Arnett, 1999). For some, adolescence certainly presents overwhelming problems in relationships and in self-esteem. Yet, for most teens these years are not a time of anxiety and despair (Myers & Diener, 1995). While many parents anticipate that the relationship with their children will encounter a rocky road when the children enter adolescence, the more typical experience is relatively tranquil. In fact, the majority of adolescent youth say that they feel close to their parents (Galambos, 1992). In general, those who have the least trouble are adolescents with authoritative parents—who are responsive and, at the same time, hold their children to high standards. Those adolescents who have the most difficulty are most likely to come from homes where parenting is either permissive or authoritarian (Collins et al., 2000).

PSYCHOLOGYMATTERS

Using Psychology to Learn Psychology: Cognitive Development in College Students

Does your arrival at the formal operational stage, in the middle or high school years, signal the end of the cognitive line? Or will your thinking abilities continue to develop as you go on through college? If you are a returning student in your 30s, 40s, or beyond, will your cognitive development continue apace with your younger counterparts? A study by developmental psychologist William Perry suggests that your perspective on learning will change and mature as your college experience unfolds. This prediction is based on a sample of students who Perry followed through their undergraduate years at Harvard and Radcliffe. Specifically, he found that students' views of psychology and their other social science courses changed radically, as did their view of what they were there to learn (Perry, 1970, 1994).

At first, students in Perry's study had the most difficulty coming to grips with the diverse and conflicting viewpoints they encountered in their courses. For example, many confronted, for the first time, the idea that reasonable people can disagree—even about their most cherished "truths" concerning good and evil, God, nature, and human nature:

> A few seemed to find the notion of multiple frames of reference wholly unintelligible. Others responded with violent shock to their confrontation in dormitory chat sessions, or in their academic work, or both. Others experienced a joyful sense of liberation. (Perry, 1970, p. 4)

In dealing with this academic culture shock, Perry's students passed through a series of distinct intellectual stages that were reminiscent of Piaget's stages. And, although they arrived at college at different levels of cognitive maturity and continued to develop at different rates, all progressed through the same intellectual stages in the same sequence. Here are some of the highlights of this intellectual journey:

- Students at first typically see a college or university as a storehouse of information—a place to learn the Right Answers. Thus, they believe it is the professor's job to help students find these answers.

- Sooner or later, students discover an unexpected—perhaps shocking—diversity of opinion, even among the experts. At this stage, college students are likely to attribute conflicting opinions to confusion among poorly qualified experts.

- Eventually, students begin to accept diverse views as legitimate—but only in the fuzzy areas (such as psychology, other social sciences, and humanities) where experts haven't yet found the Right Answers. They decide that, in subjects where the Right Answers haven't been nailed down, professors grade them on "good expression" of their ideas.

- Next, some students (not all) discover that uncertainty and diversity of opinion are everywhere—not just in the social sciences and humanities. They typically solve this problem in their minds by dividing the academic world into two realms: (a) one in which Right Answers exist (even though they haven't all been discovered) and (b) another in which anyone's opinion is as good as anyone else's. Often, at this stage, they perceive math and the "hard" sciences as the realm of Right Answers, leaving the social sciences and humanities in the realm of opinion.

● Finally, the most mature students come to see that multiple perspectives exist in all fields of study.

The students who achieve the final stage begin to see "truth" as tentative. They now realize that knowledge is always building and changing—even in the "hard" sciences. And they realize that a college education is not just learning an endless series of facts. Rather, it is learning to think critically about the important questions and major concepts of a field. In this text we have called them "Key Questions" and "Core Concepts."

At what stage do you find yourself?

CheckYourUnderstanding

1. **RECALL:** What is the major developmental task of adolescence, according to Erikson?
   a. industry
   b. autonomy
   c. identity
   d. intimacy

2. **ANALYSIS:** You are watching a television program and see an interview with a psychologist who has written a new book entitled, "The Teen Years: Face It, Parents—You Don't Matter Anymore!" Is this point of view accurate, according to research?

3. **RECALL:** About what percent of North American teens have had their first sexual experience by age 17?
   a. 20%   c. 60%
   b. 40%   d. 75%

4. **APPLICATION:** Your next-door neighbor is a teenage boy who recently got arrested for shoplifting. In talking about it, he says, "I realize now I shouldn't have done that. My parents are really mad at me, and my teachers think I'm a troublemaker." Which of Kohlberg's stages of moral development does this boy seem to be in?

5. **UNDERSTANDING THE CORE CONCEPT:** What three categories of changes lead to the challenges faced in adolescence?

Answers 1. c **2.** No, it is not accurate. Although peers become more influential in adolescence, parents still play a key role in their teens' healthy development. **3.** b **4.** Kohlberg's Stage 3 **5.** physical changes, cognitive changes, and socioemotional pressures

6.4 KEY QUESTION
WHAT DEVELOPMENTAL CHALLENGES DO ADULTS FACE?

The transition from adolescence to young adulthood is marked by decisions about advanced education, career, and intimate relationships. Making such decisions and adjusting to the consequences are major tasks of adulthood because they shape the course of adult psychological development. But development doesn't stop there. Continuing pressures of careers, families, and friends, along with the relentless physical maturation (and eventual decline) of the body continually present new developmental challenges. In today's world, though, the traditional clock for aging has been set back, essentially "buying more time" for adults in all stages of adulthood. This revolution in aging is a key element in our Core Concept for this section:

core concept | **Nature and nurture continue to interact as we progress through a series of transitions in adulthood, with cultural norms about age combining with new technology to increase both the length and quality of life for many adults.**

A couple of points in our Core Concept should be noted before we examine adulthood in more depth. First, you have probably gathered from reading the earlier sections of this chapter that stage theories—although very popular for describing human development—are often guilty of oversimplification. While the major developmental tasks and categories of the leading stage theories, such as those proposed by Piaget, Kohlberg, and Erikson, are largely holding up to empirical scrutiny, psychologists now agree that development doesn't occur in rigid stages. Rather, it is a more continuous process, occurring in waves or spurts. In other words, then, the stage theories may have gotten the "what" correct, but the "when" is more fluid than they thought it was. At no time in the lifespan is this more true than in adult development. Research on adult development indicates that healthy adults pass through a series of transitions as they progress from early through middle and into late adulthood. Successful passage through these transitions involves some reflection and readjustment, which we will discuss over the next few pages.

A second point worth noting is the changing nature of adulthood in the Western world. Thanks to better health care and technology, people are living longer than ever before and oftentimes enjoying better health during the later years than previous generations. This, in turn, is changing adults' perceptions of the lifespan and the various ages and stages involved in it. Fewer adults feel compelled to marry or settle down in their early 20s, or to retire when they hit 65. We are seeing the beginning of a "revolution" in aging, spawned by both nature (the longer lifespan) and nurture (the ways our culture is adapting to the change).

This **revolution in aging** is prompting renewed attention to the study of adult development in psychological science. Whereas for many years, we relied on theories based on clinical observation, we are now accumulating an increasing body of empirical research. Interestingly, much of the new research supports the traditional clinical theories—but it also sheds new light on the processes of adulthood in the 21st century. To see how these developmental changes unfold, let's begin with personality—where, for once, we find an area of agreement between Freud and psychologists who came after him.

Freud taught that adult development is driven by two basic needs: love and work. Abraham Maslow (1970) described the critical needs as love and belonging, which, when satisfied, allow the emergence of the needs for esteem and fulfillment. Other theorists divide the basic needs of adulthood into affiliation or social acceptance needs, achievement or competence needs, and power needs (McClelland, 1975, 1985; McClelland & Boyatzis, 1982). And in Erikson's theory, the early and middle adult years focus on needs for intimacy and "generativity." Nearly every theorist has proposed some sort of social or affiliative need as a fundamental theme running through adulthood, and this and the other needs they identified play key roles in healthy adulthood. Because Erikson gave the most comprehensive account of adult development, we will use his theory as our framework, into which we will build recent empirical research that illuminates the course of adulthood today.

Early Adulthood: Explorations, Autonomy, and Intimacy

What are the developmental tasks of early adulthood? And perhaps a bigger question for 20-somethings is this: When exactly does adulthood begin? In our teen years, many of us look forward to the "freedom" of turning 18 and becoming a legal adult. But does psychological adulthood arrive at 18 as well?

Intimacy versus Isolation   Early adulthood, said Erikson, poses the challenge of establishing close relationships with other adults (look again at Table 6.1 on page 241). He described **intimacy** as the capacity to make a full commitment—sexual, emotional, and moral—to another person. Making intimate commitments requires compromising personal preferences, accepting responsibilities, and yielding some privacy and independence—but it can also bring great rewards. To achieve intimacy, however, the individual must resolve the conflict between the need for closeness and the fear of the vulnerability and risks such closeness can bring. Failure to successfully resolve this crisis leads to *isolation* and the inability to connect to others in meaningful ways.

Revolution in aging   A change in the way people think about aging in modern industrialized nations. This new perspective grows out of increased longevity, better health care, and more lifestyle choices available to older adults. It has also stimulated the psychological study of adult development.

Intimacy   In Erikson's theory, the main developmental task of early adulthood, involving the capacity to make a full commitment—sexual, emotional, and moral—to another person.

For Erikson, the young adult must consolidate a clear sense of identity (by resolving the crisis of adolescence) before being able to cope successfully with the risks and benefits of adult intimacy. In essence, you must know who and what you are before you can be ready to make a commitment to love and share your life with someone else. However, the sequence from identity to intimacy that Erikson described may not accurately reflect present-day realities. The trend in recent years has been for young adults to live together before marrying and to delay making contractual commitments to lifelong intimacy with one person. In addition, many individuals today must struggle with identity issues (for example, career choices) at the same time they are trying to deal with intimacy issues. Life for young adults today offers more choices and more complications than did the same period of life for the generation described by Erikson.

Emerging Adulthood: The In-Between Stage   Psychologist Jeffrey Arnett (2000, 2001), in recognition of the differences between adulthood today and in previous generations, has proposed a transitional period to adulthood that he calls **emerging adulthood.** This period encompasses the late teens through the 20s, a time during which many individuals in industrialized societies have passed through adolescence but do not yet perceive themselves to be adults. Whereas in earlier historical times, visible events such as marriage, the birth of the first child, and establishment in a career were perceived as the markers of entrance into adulthood, today's young people cite more opaque events such as accepting personal responsibility for themselves and making independent decisions as the most important indicators of adulthood. And most emerging adults today report only partial progress toward these milestones of self-sufficiency (Arnett, 1997).

Emerging adulthood is a time of exploration and experimentation in all areas. Late teens and 20-somethings are trying out different types of work, exploring alternative lifestyles and worldviews, and figuring out what kind of person is right for them romantically. As they do so, they are less predictable in their educational pursuits, choice of residences, and degree of financial responsibility than at any other time in their life. Almost half will move out of their parents' home and back in again during this period, and while 60% start taking college classes within one year after graduating from high school, only half of these students have completed four or more years by their late 20s (Bianchi & Spain, 1996; U.S. Bureau of the Census, 1997). Of those who do graduate from college, though, more are choosing graduate school than in previous generations (Mogelonsky, 1996). They are also more likely to take risks than at any other time of their life—including adolescence. Rates of alcohol and substance abuse, reckless driving, and unprotected sex peak during these years (Arnett, 1992). This latter finding might be explained by the absence of serious role responsibilities combined with freedom from parental supervision.

Did Erikson get it right, then, in his identification of the major tasks of adolescence and early adulthood? In general, he did. Although not widely noted, he observed that, in industrialized societies, young people seemed to enjoy what he called a prolonged period of adolescence during which role experimentation continued. This, indeed, is exactly what empirical research such as that of Arnett is demonstrating today. And current studies indicate that, by about age 30, a majority of Westerners have married and had their first child, have made the transition from school to full-time work, and perceive themselves as having entered adulthood. Presumably, then, at this point they have achieved the intimacy that Erikson described as the major developmental task of early adulthood. Notably, they also name intimacy, or personal relationships, as the key to a happy life (Arnett, 2000b), although many struggle with balancing intimacy with the need for autonomy. As we will see, this pursuit of an optimal balance of the two needs will continue to characterize later phases of adulthood.

Modern Approaches to Intimacy   How, then, do today's adults achieve intimacy? Though 95% still marry, marriage often occurs more than once in an indi-

Emerging adulthood   A transition period between adolescence and adulthood.

vidual's life. The same pattern applies to gay and lesbian long-term relationships—whether they may legally marry in their state or not (Knox & Schact, 2008). In fact, half of all U.S. marriages end in divorce (U.S. Bureau of the Census, 2002). Moreover, an increasing number of couples are cohabitating rather than getting married (Doyle, 2002b). The high divorce rate probably results in part from individuals seeking intimacy before they have resolved their own identities. Unrealistic expectations of each other and of what constitutes an ideal marriage and family structure contribute to divorce as well (Cleek & Pearson, 1985), as does our cultural priority on individual happiness. On the other hand, there is evidence that communication and affection between spouses is now better than it was in earlier times and that those who have learned good communications skills have substantially improved their chances of avoiding divorce (Caplow, 1982; Markman & Notarius, 1993).

This happy couple can expect a successful marriage if they maintain a 5:1 ratio of positive to negative interactions with each other.

Married people are now more likely to see each other as partners and friends and less likely to feel constrained by the stereotype of what society expects of a "husband" or "wife." Partners in **peer marriages** talk with and help each other in ways that work best for their relationship, irrespective of traditional ideas about the man being "boss" or the wife being responsible for "women's work" (Schwartz, 1994). The key to such a fair and satisfying relationship is communication in which both partners feel able to openly express their hopes and fears (Klagsbrun, 1985). A mushrooming of knowledge on how good communication can maintain relationships has helped our culture to view marriage as a worthwhile investment and therapy as a valuable option for supporting such efforts (Gottman, 1994; Notarius, 1996). In brief, relating is no longer viewed as a set of skills that "comes naturally" with the establishment of intimacy. Instead, close relationships are seen as lifelong works in progress, worthwhile investments of time and energy whose quality can be improved with clearer self-understanding, effective conflict resolution, and good communication.

What makes for good communication and effective conflict resolution? Surprisingly, there is no correlation between the frequency of a couple's conflicts and the health of their relationship: Couples who disagree often are no more likely to divorce than couples with less frequent conflict. What does matter is the ratio of positive interactions to negative interactions, with the optimal balance found to be 5:1 (Gottman, 1995). In other words, regardless of how much conflict there is in a marriage, the marriage will be healthy if the couple has five times more positive than negative interactions with each other. And "positive interactions" don't have to be long romantic weekends or elaborate dates: small things such as a smile, a kiss, a compliment, or a thank-you all qualify as positive interactions. (A long romantic weekend or a great date would, then, presumably have quite a few positive interactions.) Negative interactions, on the other hand, can also be small—but pack a powerful punch—and include such behaviors as hostile sarcasm, name calling, a frustrated roll of the eyes, or an angry slam of the door. By maintaining a 5:1 ratio of positive to negative interactions, the couple is creating a supportive foundation that strengthens the relationship's immune system, so to speak. When conflict does arise, then, partners are less likely to take things personally or feel defensive, which allows the focus to remain on problem solving rather than blaming.

The Challenges of Midlife: Complexity and Generativity

For many people, the concept of midlife conjures up thoughts of the dreaded midlife crisis and birthday cards poking fun at being "over the hill." Contrary to stereotypes of middle age, though, research finds middle adulthood to be a peak period of development in many respects. Research in cognitive development reveals that many adults in this age range have developed considerable skill in combining and integrating a variety of thinking styles, including reflection, analysis, and dialectical reasoning (which is the ability to compare and evaluate con-

Peer marriage Marriage in which the couple see each other as partners and friends, as contrasted with the older stereotypic roles of "husband" and "wife."

tradictory viewpoints) (Baltes & Staudinger, 1993; King & Kitchener, 1994). They are also experts at integrating their cognitions and emotions, resulting in more thoughtful, deliberate, and reflective coping responses to stressful events (Diehl et al., 1996).

Taken together, these skills enable the midlife adult to juggle a variety of interests, which often include work, family, community, hobbies, and self-care. And indeed, this busy, complex lifestyle is what characterizes healthy midlife adults today. Psychologists Rosalind Barnett and Janet Hyde (2001) note that dual-career families are now the norm, with women receiving professional training at an unprecedented level. Hand in hand with this trend is the increasing fluidity among roles as worker and family member: Men less often define themselves only as workers and family providers, and women are less likely to define themselves solely as wives and mothers. For most people, these expanded roles provide a greater network of social support and an increased sense of well-being. In addition to greater diversity in roles, midlife adults today enjoy greater variety in their relationships, resources, and lifestyle than ever before (Moen & Wethington, 1999). This *complexity* is related to well-being in that complex individuals see life as a series of challenges, full of variety, that lead to growth (Ryff & Heincke, 1983).

Generativity versus Stagnation   According to Erikson, **generativity** is the major developmental task of middle adulthood. For those who have successfully met the earlier challenges of identity and intimacy, generativity is an opportunity to make a meaningful and lasting contribution to family, work, society, or future generations. Thus, people in this phase of life broaden their focus beyond self and partner, often by raising children, serving as volunteers in community service groups, or nurturing the next generation in some other way. Research confirms that adults who express a strong sense of being generative and productive also report high life satisfaction (McAdams et al., 1993). In contrast, those who have not resolved earlier crises of identity and intimacy may experience a "midlife crisis." Such people may question past choices, becoming cynical and stagnant or, at the other extreme, self-indulgent and reckless. The good news is that—once again contrary to stereotypes of midlife—most people do not undergo a midlife crisis. What's more, the idea that adults become depressed and lose direction when their children "leave the nest" is also a myth (Clay, 2003a,b).

Transitions   What does happen for most adults in midlife is that they progress through a **transition,** which involves redefining, or transformation, of a life role. Indeed, there is evidence that adult life is characterized by a series of transitions, starting with the transition to adulthood and occurring perhaps every 15 to 20 years throughout adulthood (Levinson, 1986; Sugarman, 2001). Successful transitions typically involve a period of heightened self-reflection, which includes a reappraisal of the current role, exploration of new possibilities that offer a renewed sense of meaning, and the decision making involved in letting go of the old role and making a commitment to the new one. Transitions may involve expected events such as getting married, having children, or retiring, or unexpected events such as a sudden illness, breakup, or loss of a job or loved one. In addition, events that were expected but that did not occur—such as a job promotion that never materialized or a person who always wanted children but never had any—can prompt a transition. And finally, transitions can be gradual, as with a relationship or job that over time becomes less and less fulfilling or a person who becomes increasingly self-confident: In any case, at some point the individual becomes aware of a critical difference.

Given that our physical, cognitive, and emotional capabilities—as well as our social contexts—tend to evolve and change throughout our life, transitions are seen as a natural response to these shifts in our internal and external worlds. And there is accumulating evidence that adults who live the longest and health-

Engaging in new challenges is one of the keys to successful passage through the transitions of adulthood.

Generativity   The process of making a commitment beyond oneself to family, work, society, or future generations. In Erikson's theory, generativity is the developmental challenge of midlife.

Transition   An individual's redefinition or transformation of a life role.

iest lives are the ones who successfully navigate through these transitions and emerge from each one with a renewed sense of meaning and passion for life (Levinson, 1978, 1996; Ryff & Heidrich, 1997). Interestingly, transitions may sometimes involve a revisit to one of Erikson's earlier stages, such as a retooling of one's identity or the transformation of an intimate relationship. And, given what we know about complexity, we might predict that complex individuals—with their positive, challenge and growth-oriented outlook—would be more likely to experience successful transitions.

In summary, the reality of middle adulthood in today's Western society is a far cry from the "over-the-hill" stereotype that still persists in some people's minds. Many midlife adults are energetic, forward-moving individuals who are making meaningful contributions to the world and enjoying the many opportunities available to them in love, work, and personal growth. And it appears to be generativity and complexity that fuels achievement of this healthy model of middle adulthood.

Late Adulthood: The Age of Integrity

At the beginning of the 20th century, only 3% of the U.S. population was over 65. One hundred years later that figure is about 13%. As the baby boom generation reaches this age over the next few years, nearly one-fourth of our population will be in this oldest group.

If you are now a 20-something college student, you will be in your 40s by the year 2030, and you will have witnessed a profound demographic shift (change in population characteristics). By that time, more than 80 million Americans will be over 60 years of age. For the first time in history, the number of people in the 60-plus age group will outnumber those under 20 years of age. This will represent a dramatic reversal of all previous demographics and a potentially significant shift away from today's youth-oriented culture (Pifer & Bronte, 1986). Among the effects: Tattoos and body piercings will become common in nursing homes, and there will also be far fewer people to pay the Social Security and Medicare bills.

With drastic changes in our society's age distribution looming, it is more crucial than ever to understand the nature of aging as well as the abilities and needs of the elderly (Roush, 1996). And, on a personal level, it may be helpful to anticipate some of the developmental challenges your parents and grandparents are facing, as well as what you will face in the last phase of your life.

From a biological perspective, aging typically means decline: Energy reserves are reduced, and cell machinery functions less efficiently. From a cognitive perspective, however, aging is no longer synonymous with decline (Qualls & Abeles, 2000). Many abilities, including expert skills and some aspects of memory, may actually improve with age (Azar, 1996; Krampe & Ericsson, 1996). A lifetime's accumulation of experience may finally culminate in wisdom—if the mind remains open and active. Activity, in fact—whether physical, social-emotional, or cognitive—seems to be key to healthy aging: The phrase "Use it or lose it!" applies to many aspects of late adulthood. Thus, we see that theories of aging are models of balance or trade-offs: In old age, a person may lose energy reserves but gain an ability to control emotional experiences and thereby conserve energy (Baltes, 1987). And many of our negative assumptions about aging are related to our cultural values: Cultures that revere their elders have very different perspectives and expectations of aging. What are the tasks of aging, and what resources and limitations must we confront as we look ahead to the autumn of our lives?

Ego-Integrity versus Despair   According to Erikson, an increasing awareness of your own mortality and of the changes in your body, behavior, and social roles will set the stage for late adulthood. Erikson called the crisis he identified at this stage *ego-integrity versus despair.* **Ego-integrity,** the healthy end of this dimension, involves the ability to look back on life without regrets and to enjoy a sense of wholeness. It requires reflection on times both good and bad, with appreciation for what turned out well and acceptance of what did not. By now, you know that Erikson believed that previous crises must have had successful resolutions in order to master new challenges, so you are probably considering how a well-developed identity, meaningful close relationships, and a sense of having contributed to the next generation would probably facilitate this type of reflection and acceptance. For those whose previous crises had unhealthy solutions, however, aspirations may remain unfulfilled, and these individuals may experience futility, despair, and self-deprecation. Sadly, they often then fail to resolve the crisis successfully at this final developmental stage.

Physical Changes   Some of the most obvious changes that occur with age affect people's physical appearances and abilities. As we age, we can expect our skin to wrinkle, our hair to thin and gray, and our height to decrease an inch or two. Our hearts and lungs operate less efficiently, so we can expect decreased physical stamina. We can also expect some of our senses to dull. These changes occur and develop gradually, so we have ample opportunity to gauge them and try to adjust. Successful aging takes into consideration both individual potential and realistic limits (Baltes, 1993). Two of the most noticeable sensory deficiencies occur with vision and hearing.

As we age, the lenses in our eyes become discolored and less flexible, affecting both color vision and distance vision. Most people over 65 experience some loss of visual acuity, and without corrective lenses half of the elderly would be considered legally blind. Glasses do aid in adjusting to these changes in vision, however, especially for night driving or close work such as reading.

Diminished hearing is common among those 60 and older, especially the ability to hear high-frequency sounds. Problems can ensue if the loss is undetected or denied (Maher & Ross, 1984; Manschreck, 1989). Those with a hearing loss might explain others' actions inaccurately because they lack information or blame their misinterpretations on evil intentions instead of simple bad hearing (Zimbardo et al., 1981). The problem can escalate if a person then begins to believe that others are deliberately whispering to avoid being heard, leading to a mild form of paranoia (belief that one is being victimized). Fortunately, early hearing-aid therapy can be more effective than later psychotherapy. Hearing aids can compensate for much of one's hearing loss. Unfortunately, though, hearing aids—though increasingly needed by our population—are rarely covered by medical insurance and often cost several thousand dollars. In addition, those close to someone with a probable hearing loss can help that person by speaking in lower-pitched tones, enunciating clearly, and reducing background noise.

Are declines in other physical capabilities inevitable as well? Not as much as previously thought. Continuing (or even beginning) a consistent program of physical exercise helps older adults ward off some of the physical decline typically associated with aging. Aerobic activity such as walking or swimming improves cardiovascular functioning, and weight training improves blood flow and builds muscle mass, which in turn improves posture, balance, and the ability to physically manage everyday activities (such as grocery shopping or gardening). Even for individuals who have previously been sedentary, beginning an exercise program as late as age 80 results in measurable gains physically, emotionally, and even cognitively. New research indicates that regular exercise provides better blood and oxygen flow to the brain, which in turn reduces deterioration of brain cells and improves attention (Colcombe et al., 2004). There is also evidence that exercise reduces incidence of Alzheimer's and other brain disorders (Marx, 2005).

Another myth about aging in Western culture is that elderly people cannot or should not be sexually active. Belief in such a myth can be a greater obsta-

Ego-integrity   In Erikson's theory, the developmental task of late adulthood—involving the ability to look back on life without regrets and to enjoy a sense of wholeness.

cle than any physical limitations to experiencing satisfying sex in late adulthood. Although frequency and desire may decrease somewhat, there is no age, for either men or women, at which the capability for arousal or orgasm ceases. (This is particularly true now that drugs, such as the well-advertised Viagra, have enhanced erectile ability for millions of older men.) And while sex loses its reproductive functions in late adulthood, it doesn't lose its capacity for providing pleasure. Regular sexual practice also enhances healthy aging because it provides arousal, aerobic exercise, fantasy, and social interaction (Ornstein & Sobel, 1989). Experience and creativity clearly compensate for minor physical changes or losses of physical stamina.

Older adults who pursue higher degrees of environmental stimulation tend to maintain higher levels of cognitive abilities.

Cognitive Changes   Older adults often fear that aging is inevitably accompanied by the loss of mental abilities. But is this fear justified? Certain parts of the brain, particularly the frontal lobes, do lose mass as we age, but there is little evidence that this causes a general mental decline in healthy adults. Performance on tasks requiring imagination, such as vivid imagery strategies for memorizing, does seem to decline with age (Baltes & Kliegl, 1992). And people do acquire information more slowly by the time they are in their 70s and 80s. By that age, many older people—but not all—begin to show some decline in cognitive abilities. The older the group, the more variation we find (Kramer & Willis, 2002). But on the other hand, the decline for the average person may not be as severe as folk wisdom had assumed (Helmuth, 2003c). Brain imaging studies suggest that older people's brains compensate by processing information differently, bringing more regions into play (Cabeza, 2002; Helmuth, 2002). In fact, there is new research showing that moderate physical fitness training improves cognitive abilities in older adults and may forestall or even prevent age-related mental decline (Colcombe et al., 2004). Moreover, some abilities improve with age. Vocabulary, for example, is consistently better in older adults, as are social skills. And, with regard to skilled performance, musicians have been shown to improve well into their 90s (Krampe & Ericsson, 1996). Psychologists are now exploring age-related gains in wisdom, such as expertise in practical knowledge and life experience (Baltes, 1990).

What about memory? A common complaint among older adults is that their ability to remember things is not as good as it used to be. Most of these age-related memory difficulties appear in a part of the memory system that processes and stores new information (Poon, 1985), whereas aging does not seem to diminish access to knowledge or events that occurred long ago. So, an elderly person may have to ask the name of a new acquaintance several times before finally remembering it but have no trouble recalling the names of old friends. A more important concern might be that people explain memory loss differently depending on the age of the forgetful person. Using a double standard, younger adults attribute other young adults' memory failures to lack of effort but those of older adults to loss of ability (Parr & Siegert, 1993).

Particularly worrisome to older people and those who love them is **Alzheimer's disease,** a degenerative disorder of the brain that produces diminished thinking abilities, memory problems, and ultimately, death. Alzheimer's disease is estimated to occur in about 4% of the population over the age of 65, with the incidence increasing with age to over 50% in people beyond age 85 (National Institute on Aging, 2004). One of the early signs involves memory problems, causing many older persons to become anxious when they are unable to remember a name or an event—a difficulty to which they would have given little thought when younger. It is an especially frightening disorder because it can render people helpless, rob them of their ability to make new memories, and make them forget loved ones. New advances in Alzheimer's research, though, are making some promising headway into our understanding and treatment of this serious disorder. Although a cure has not yet been discovered, early diagnosis and treatment can now slow the progress of the disease, thus extending the quality of life of the Alzheimer's patient.

Alzheimer's disease   A degenerative brain disease usually noticed first by its debilitating effects on memory.

Social and Emotional Changes   An unfortunate consequence of living a long life is outliving some friends and family members. In addition, the reduced mobility associated with aging can make people become somewhat less socially active in later adulthood. While older adults reduce the extent of their social contacts, they remain more invested in those ties they choose to keep. Maintaining even a single intimate relationship can markedly improve personal health, as can living with a beloved pet (Siegel, 1990). Research shows that as people age, they tend to engage in **selective social interaction,** maintaining only the most rewarding contacts for the investment of precious physical and emotional energy (Carstensen, 1987, 1991; Lang & Carstensen, 1994).

Emotionally, another stereotype of aging sees old age as a time of depression and restriction of emotions. The evidence, however, doesn't support this view in healthy older adults. Age often improves people's ability to control their emotions—when they want to (Lawton, 2001). Moreover, older individuals report experiencing more positive emotions and fewer negative emotions than do younger adults (Mroczek, 2001).

How do older adults characterize well-being? In a series of interviews with middle-aged and older men and women, Ryff (1989) found that nearly everyone of both sexes defined well-being in terms of relationships with others: They strived to be caring, compassionate people and valued having a good social support network. Respondents also emphasized the value of accepting change, enjoying life, and cultivating a sense of humor.

Keys to Successful Aging   In addition to the information already presented, what other strategies have been found to be effective in coping with aging? Older adults can remain both active and close to people by doing volunteer work in the community, traveling, joining clubs and classes, or spending time with grandchildren. Much research supports this notion of the need for close relationships with others. And it is the basis for one of the most practical applications that you can take with you from this text: *Anything that isolates us from sources of social support—from a reliable network of friends and family—puts us at risk for a host of physical ills, mental problems, and even social pathologies.* We are social creatures, and we need each other's help and support to be effective and healthy (Basic Behavioral Science Task Force, 1996). In addition, we might learn lessons from other cultures where older citizens are respected and venerated for their wisdom. Before this happens, however, people must overcome stereotypes of the elderly as incapable and incompetent (Brewer et al., 1981).

Perhaps successful aging, much like success at any age, consists of making the most of gains while minimizing the impact of losses (Schulz & Heckhausen, 1996). Additionally, it is helpful to realize that losses of specific abilities need not represent threats to one's sense of self. As one's physical and psychological resources change, so do one's goals (Carstensen & Freund, 1994). In this fashion, late adulthood may be a time not of increasing frustration but of increasing fulfillment.

PSYCHOLOGYMATTERS
A Look Back at the Twin Studies
Now that you have learned some key elements of human development over the lifespan, what conclusions can you draw about the similarities of the Jim twins reported at the beginning of this chapter? Are we all simply products of our genes, destined to develop on a preprogrammed path despite environmental influences? By now, you have enough knowledge about the interaction of genes and environment to know that is not the case. How, then, can the remarkable similarities of the "Jim twins" and media reports of others like them be explained?

Selective social interaction
Choosing to restrict the number of one's social contacts to those who are the most gratifying.

To see these twin pairs in a broader perspective, you need to know that they are "outliers"—extreme among the twins studied at Minnesota, even though they have received a lion's share of media coverage. Although Bouchard and his colleagues found many unexpected developmental similarities between individuals in all the twin pairs they studied, most were not nearly so much alike as Oskar and Jack or the Jims. Bouchard acknowledges that many of the similarities are just coincidences (The Mysteries, 1998). It is precisely such coincidences that make the news and catch our eye. But, says twin researcher Richard Rose, "If you bring together strangers who were born on the same day in the same country and ask them to find similarities between them, you may find a lot of seemingly astounding coincidences" (Horgan, 1993). While mere coincidence does not offer a very dazzling explanation, the alternatives seem absurd. No one seriously suggests, for example, that the names of Betty and Linda could have been written into the genes of the two Jims or that heredity really specifies storing rubber bands on one's wrists.

The real story, then, is both less dramatic and more important: Identical twins do show remarkable similarities, but mainly in the characteristics you might expect: intelligence, temperament, gestures, posture, and pace of speech—all of which do make sense as traits that could be genetically influenced. And the fact that fraternal twins and other siblings show fewer similarities also suggests that hereditary forces are at work in all of us, whether we are twins or not. Bouchard (1994) himself takes a rather extreme position, suggesting that heredity accounts for up to 80% of the similarities observed among identical twins (What We Learn, 1998). Critics aren't so sure.

What objections do the critics raise concerning the twin studies Bouchard and his colleagues have been conducting? First, they note that, stunning as the similarities between identical twins may seem, the effect of the environment also shows up in each pair of twins. None of the twin pairs displays behavior that is identical across the board. And the fact that twins reared together typically are more alike than those reared apart provides further testimony to the effect of environment. Furthermore, the personalities of most twin pairs become less alike as they age, providing additional evidence that the environment, as well as heredity, is at work (McCartney et al., 1990). We should note, too, that many of the twin pairs studied by Bouchard had been reunited for some time before he found them—an environmental condition that could easily accentuate, or even create, similarities. This was true, for example, of Oskar Stör and Jack Yufe, the Nazi and Jewish twins, who met five months before Bouchard got to them. In fact, says psychologist Leon Kamin, Bouchard's twins face strong incentives to exaggerate their similarities and minimize their differences to please the research team and to attract media attention (Horgan, 1993). (Since their story broke in the press, Stör and Yufe have hired agents, made paid appearances on TV, and sold their story to a Hollywood film producer.)

A second criticism points out that because identical twins look alike, people often treat them alike. This is an environmental factor that can easily account for many similarities in behavior. For example, some people's faces look good with moustaches, and, if a pair of twins has such faces, people may encourage them to grow moustaches—whether or not they have been raised together. The resulting similarity, then, can be due as much to environment as it is to heredity.

Finally, the critics also remind us that scientists' hopes and expectations can influence their conclusions in this sort of research. Because Bouchard and other investigators of identical twins expect to find some hereditary influences, their attention will be drawn more to similarities than to differences. In fact, this is what most people do when they meet: Their conversation jumps from topic to topic until they discover common interests, attitudes, experiences, or activities.

So, is there any point of consensus about the twin studies and about the effects of heredity and environment? Bouchard and his critics all would say that neither heredity nor environment ever acts alone to produce behavior or mental

CONNECTION • CHAPTER 1

Expectancy bias can distort perceptions and research findings.

processes. They always interact. That is, from a developmental perspective, heredity and environment work together throughout a person's life. In addition, most would agree that the important findings coming out of the Minnesota twin research have nothing to do with unique and amazing similarities between particular twins. Rather, they have to do with the similarities found across all the identical twin pairs they studied: Twins show extraordinary similarities with each other in personality, attitudes, facial expressions, and temperament—almost everything, oddly enough, except their choice of mates: The spouses of identical twins were no more similar to each other than were people who would have been chosen at random (El-Hai, 1999). What the twin studies really did was to remind us that we are products of both heredity and environment—nature and nurture.

CheckYourUnderstanding

1. **ANALYSIS:** How is emerging adulthood different than early adulthood?

2. **APPLICATION:** The couple who lives next door to you has a very successful marriage: They have been together over 25 years, have raised three well-adjusted children, and spend a lot of time together doing things they both enjoy. When a friend of yours visits, though, and notices them arguing in the backyard—which they often seem to do—she asks you how they can have such a good marriage but argue so much. How can you explain that to her?

3. **RECALL:** What are the keys to successful middle adulthood?

4. **RECALL:** Describe at least two ways that the phrase "Use it or lose it!" applies to healthy aging.

5. **UNDERSTANDING THE CORE CONCEPT:** Describe two factors that contribute to the current "revolution" in aging.

Answers 1. Emerging adulthood is a transitional period between adolescence and early adulthood, during which individuals in industrialized societies experiment with different roles, viewpoints, and relationships. **2.** They probably maintain a ratio of 5:1 positive to negative interactions. **3.** Generativity and complexity. **4.** Older adults must keep physically and mentally active in order to keep their bodies and brains healthy. **5.** Technology is helping us stay healthier and live longer, and changing social norms are changing the Western perception of aging.

Critical Thinking Applied: The Mozart Effect

Imagine this: You have just had your first child, and now you are the proud parent of what you are sure is the most amazing baby ever born (we aren't making fun of you—we all feel that way about our kids!). Like many parents, you want to offer your child every opportunity you can to help him (or her) reach full potential. So what would you do if you heard that listening to Mozart would make your baby smarter? In 1993, this provocative finding was announced by a pair of scientific researchers who, indeed, found that listening to Mozart boosted IQ scores (Rauscher et al., 1993). The report received widespread media coverage and gave birth to a host of innovations. Governors in at least two states instituted requirements to provide a Mozart CD to every newborn; websites sprung up that sold all things musical with promises of transforming the listener's "health, education, and well-being" (www.themozarteffect.com); and expectant mothers began to play Mozart to their unborn

children via headphones on their tummies. Before jumping on the bandwagon, though, it might be wise to apply some critical thinking to this remarkable claim.

What Are the Issues?

Could listening to Mozart really improve IQ? If the study appears valid, how does the new finding fit in with other established findings about effects of music and about boosting intelligence? Would other types of music—classical or otherwise—have similar effects? And finally, if listening to a certain type of music really does boost IQ, can we be sure it is the music itself boosting the IQ, or could it be something else about the experience of listening to music that was driving the IQ gain? These are just a few of the questions that a good critical thinker might ask when first hearing this remarkable claim.

What Critical Thinking Questions Should We Ask?

Now that we've identified some of the issues this claim raises, let's apply our critical thinking guidelines to see which ones might help us resolve the issues.

The first thing that might come to mind for you is the extreme nature of this assertion: The original study reported that IQ scores increased by 8 to 9 points after listening to just 10 minutes of Mozart! Is there extraordinary evidence to support this *extraordinary claim?* An inspection of the *source* reveals that the claimants are researchers at a respected university, which lends initial credibility to their assertion. What, then, is the nature of the *evidence?* First, the finding was indeed based on an empirical study, rather than anecdotal evidence, so it passes that test. A second element of the evidence to examine is the sample: Who were the participants, and how well do they represent the population at large? In this case, participants were college students, which might give you pause. But would the findings necessarily apply to babies? Or could the effect be limited to people already at a certain level of cognitive development?

Another critical thinking question to ask concerns the reasoning: Does it avoid *common fallacies?* One common fallacy is the correlation–causation issue. In this study, researchers used an experimental design with random assignment to groups, so the findings do appear causal rather than correlational in nature. Even when the findings of a study are valid, though, another common fallacy can occur when the findings are interpreted in a manner that oversimplifies or exaggerates the meaning of the findings. In this case, is it reasonable to conclude from the findings of this study that listening to Mozart boosts IQ? (Here's where it gets really interesting!) A closer look at the findings reveals that the IQ gain found in the study was only temporary and disappeared after about 15 minutes. And, second, the measure used to assess IQ (which by definition is a global measure) was actually a test of visual–spatial competence (which is just one specific element of IQ tests). To say that Mozart boosts intelligence is clearly an exaggeration of the actual findings.

What Conclusions Can We Draw?

In the years following the original study over 20 similar studies have been conducted and published in recognized scientific journals While a few found evidence of what has become popularly known as "the Mozart effect," most did not (Steele et al., 1999). In fact, in-depth studies of the process reveal that the short-term boost in IQ score is more accurately a result of a slight increase in positive mood that most participants report when listening to the particular Mozart composition used in many of the studies: When mood was measured before and after listening to the music and statistically removed from the equation, the temporary IQ increase disappeared (Thompson et al., 2001). What's more, other mildly positive experiences, such as listening to a story rather than sitting in silence for 10 minutes, produce the same increase in mood and subsequently the same temporary IQ gain (Nantais & Schellenberg, 1999).

A more reasonable conclusion of these studies is that experiences that increase positive mood facilitate better visual–spatial reasoning while the mood remains elevated. This finding, contrary to the "Mozart effect" claim, is corroborated by other psychological research. Some studies, for example, have uncovered a relationship between positive mood and performance on cognitive tasks (Ashby et al., 1999; Kenealy, 1997). And listening to music that promotes happiness has been found to increase speed and productivity on a variety of tasks.

To be fair, it wasn't the original research report that exaggerated the findings or implied that they would apply to babies, but the media reports that proliferated in the wake of the research. Stanford University professor Chip Heath thinks he knows why: His analysis reveals that the original 1993 article received far more attention in newspaper stories than any other research report published around that time, and the greatest coverage in states with the lowest student test scores. "Problems attract solutions," says Heath, and Americans as a culture seem more obsessed with early childhood education than many other cultures worldwide (Krakovsky, 2005).

The anxiety noted by Heath, as we learned in Chapter 1, can breed emotional bias, which in turn can influence people to latch on to solutions that seem simple and promise grand results. Add to that findings from memory research indicating that each time a story is told by one person to another, details become distorted—and can you imagine how many people read a newspaper article (which likely distorted the original finding), then told a friend, who told another friend, and so on? It's no wonder the myth of the Mozart effect took such strong hold in our culture. And finally, the confirmation bias helps us understand why people still persist in believing the Mozart effect to be true, despite research reports and newspaper articles that have debunked it.

Chapter Summary

6.1 What Innate Abilities Does the Infant Possess?

Core Concept 6.1: Newborns have innate abilities for finding nourishment, avoiding harmful situations, and interacting with others—all of which are genetically designed to facilitate survival.

From the moment of conception, genetics and the environment interact to influence early development. During the nine-month **prenatal period,** the fertizilized egg **(zygote)** beomes an **embryo** and then a **fetus. Teratogens** are harmful substances taken in by the mother that can cause damage to the developing fetus. Development of sensory abilities and basic reflexes begins in the prenatal period, and at birth newborns prefer sweet tastes and familiar sounds and have visual abilities ideally suited for looking at faces. **Innate reflexes** such as grasping and sucking help them survive and thrive, as does their ability for **mimicry.** The newborn brain contains some 100 billion neurons.

Infancy spans the first 18 months of life. **Maturation** refers to the genetically programmed events and timeline of normal development, such as crawling before walking and babbling before language development. And while exposure to a rich variety of stimuli in the environment promotes optimal brain development and can speed up the "average" pace of development, the **genetic leash** limits the degree to which the environment plays a role.

Infants need human contact to survive and thrive, and their innate sensory abilities, reflexes, and mimicry promote development of social relationships. During infancy, they establish a close emotional relationship with their primary caregiver that lays the foundation for the way they perceive and interact in close relationships later in their lives. This attachment style is either secure, anxious-ambivalent, or avoidant, and it is influenced by both the child's temperament and the responsiveness and accessibility of the primary caregiver. Erikson referred to this first stage of social development as **trust** versus mistrust. Cultural practices and preferences regarding attachment style vary, illustrating the role of the environment in development.

Adoption study (p. 232)

Anxious-ambivalent (p. 240)

Attachment (p. 238)

Avoidant attachment (p. 240)

Contact comfort (p. 238)

Developmental psychology (p. 231)

Embryo (p. 233)

Fetal alcohol syndrome (FAS) (p. 233)

Fetus (p. 233)

Genetic leash (p. 236)

Imprinting (p. 238)

Infancy (p. 235)

Innate ability (p. 232)

Innate reflex (p. 235)

Maturation (p. 236)

Mimicry (p. 235)

Nature–nurture issue (p. 231)

Neonatal period (p. 234)

Placenta (p. 233)

Prenatal period (p. 232)

Secure attachment (p. 240)

Sensitive period (p. 236)

Separation anxiety (p. 240)

Synaptic pruning (p. 236)

Synchronicity (p. 235)

Teratogen (p. 233)

Trust (p. 242)

Twin study (p. 231)

Zygote (p. 232)

MyPsychLab Resources 6.1:

Watch: Fetal Development

Watch: The Newborn's Reflexes

Watch: Attachment to Infants

6.2 What Are the Developmental Tasks of Childhood?

Core Concept 6.2: Nature and nurture work together to help children master important developmental tasks, especially in the areas of language acquisition, cognitive development, and development of social relationships.

The rapid development of language ability is one of the most amazing developmental feats of early childhood. There is widespread agreement that we are born with innate mental structures that facilitate language development, which Chomsky called **language acquisition devices (LADs).** While all normally developing infants will acquire language on a relatively predictable timeline—as long as they are exposed to language in their environment—the specific language that they develop depends on the language(s) to which they are exposed and can be verbal or sign language. Frequency of exposure can also modify the pace of language development.

Babbling begins about 4 months of age, and is the first step toward language development. **Grammar, telegraphic speech,** and use of **morphemes** follow in just a few years.

Cognitive development refers to the emergence of mental abilities such as thinking, perceiving, and remembering. Jean Piaget proposed the most influential model of cognitive development, which suggests that children progress through four distinct stages, each of which is characterized by identifiable changes in mental abilities. Throughout the stages, **schemas** form the mental frameworks for our understanding of concepts, and these schemas are modified by assimilation and accommodation as we acquire new information. The **sensorimotor stage** is characterized by the emergence of goal-directed behavior and object permanence, while the subsequent **preoperational stage** is marked by egocentrism, animistic thinking, centration, and irreversibility. Progression beyond the limitations of the preoperational stage marks the beginning of the **concrete operations stage,** during which children master conservation. Piaget's fourth stage doesn't begin until adolescence. Although many of Piaget's observations have withstood the test of time, in general today's researchers note that children progress more rapidly and less abruptly through the stages than Piaget believed.

The third developmental task of childhood is development of social relationships. Our basic temperament, present at birth, plays a strong role in our socioemotional development; but, like most other abilities, it can be modified by support or challenges in our environment. **Socialization** refers to the process by which children learn the social rules and norms of their culture, and parenting style plays a significant role in socialization. Overall, the best child outcomes typically result from an **authoritative** parenting style. The influence of day care on development depends entirely on the quality of day care rather than the amount of time spent in day care. The influence of leisure activities, such as television and video games, depends on both the time spent in the activity as well as the type of program or game being viewed or played.

Erikson observed three major developmental stages during childhood. **Autonomy** can be encouraged by an optimal balance of freedom and support. **Initiative,** the goal of the third stage, is marked by increased choices and self-directed behavior. **Industry** can develop in the elementary school years when children are encouraged to develop their skills and abilities and learn to respond effectively to both successes and failures. Optimal development at each stage increases the chances for mastery of each successive stage.

Accommodation (p. 247)	**Language acquisition device (LAD)** (p. 244)
Animistic thinking (p. 249)	
Assimilation (p. 247)	**Mental operation** (p. 250)
Attention-deficit hyperactivity disorder (ADHD) (p. 257)	**Mental representation** (p. 248)
	Morpheme (p. 246)
Authoritarian parent (p. 253)	**Object permanence** (p. 248)
Authoritative parent (p. 253)	**Permissive parent** (p. 253)
Autonomy (p. 256)	**Preoperational stage** (p. 248)
Babbling (p. 245)	**Psychosocial stage** (p. 256)
Centration (p. 249)	**Schema** (p. 247)
Cognitive development (p. 246)	**Sensorimotor intelligence** (p. 248)
Concrete operational stage (p. 250)	**Sensorimotor stage** (p. 248)
Conservation (p. 250)	**Socialization** (p. 253)
Egocentrism (p. 249)	**Stage theory** (p. 247)
Goal-directed behavior (p. 248)	**Telegraphic speech** (p. 245)
Grammar (p. 245)	**Temperament** (p. 252)
Industry (p. 257)	**Theory of mind** (p. 251)
Initiative (p. 257)	**Uninvolved parent** (p. 253)
Irreversibility (p. 249)	**Wave metaphor** (p. 252)

MyPsychLab Resources 6.2:

Explore: Piaget's Stages of Cognitive Development

Watch: Conservation of Liquids

Watch: Early Gender Typing

6.3 What Changes Mark the Transition of Adolescence?

Core Concept 6.3: Adolescence offers new developmental challenges growing out of physical changes, cognitive changes, and socioemotional pressures.

Physically, **adolescence** begin with the onset of **puberty,** marked by the production of live sperm in males and the onset of menstruation in females. Psychologically, the meaning of adolescence varies culturally, as does the

time at which adolescence is thought to end. In Western culture, the physical changes brought on by puberty often promote greater attention to physical appearance, which in some Western cultures is linked to self-esteem. Sexuality and **sexual orientation** begin to develop during adolescence, with almost half of North American teens having their first sexual experience by age 17.

Cognitively, adolescence is characterized by Piaget's **formal operational stage,** during which increasing ability for abstract thought develops—if cultural educational norms support abstract thought. Moral thinking may also progress to higher levels. Risk-taking increases during adolescence for Western teens, and although hormonal surges sometimes increase emotionality, most teens do not experience adolescence as a time of turmoil. While the influence of peers takes on greater importance than in the childhood years, a stable relationship with parents is a crucial factor in the successful transition through adolescence. The primary developmental task of this period, according to Erikson, is the development of a unique **identity**.

MyPsychLab Resources 6.3:

Watch: Adolescent Sexuality: Deborah L. Tolman

Watch: Friends

6.4 What Developmental Challenges Do Adults Face?

Core Concept 6.4: Nature and nurture continue to interact as we progress through a series of transitions in adulthood, and cultural norms about age combine with new technology to increase both the length and quality of life for many adults.

Adult development is a relatively new field of study and is receiving increased attention by psychologists as more adults live longer and healthier lives. Rather than perceiving adulthood as a series of concrete and well-defined stages, research indicates that well-developed adults progress through a series of transitions throughout adulthood, each of which is marked by reflection on past years and growth into new directions.

According to Erikson, the major developmental task of *early adulthood* is the development of **intimacy**, characterized by a long-term commitment to an intimate partner. In previous generations, Westerners expected this to occur in a person's 20s, but in industrialized societies today a transition period called **emerging adulthood** may precede intimacy and early adulthood. After the exploration and experimentation of emerging adulthood, most adults marry. Successful intimate relationships rely on effective communication and conflict resolution and on a 5:1 ratio of positive to negative interactions.

Contrary to popular belief, research indicates that midlife is a peak period of development in many respects. Middle adults' ability to integrate a variety of complex thinking skills facilitates a complex life that includes work, relationships, and healthy coping with stressful life events. Erikson saw the main developmental task of **middle adulthood** as **generativity**, which involves contributing to the next generation. Midlife crises are not experienced by most midlife adults, although those who have not resolved earlier developmental tasks successfully are more at-risk for a midlife crisis.

Late adulthood, according to Erikson, is best navigated by the achievement of **ego-integrity,** or the ability to accept both the successes and failures of one's past and present. While our sensory abilities do typically decline in late adulthood, both cognitive and physical decline can—to some extent—be slowed significantly by regular physical and mental exercise. Moreover, some abilities, such as vocabulary and social skills, actually improve with age. Cultural norms also have an impact on aging and foster expectations of positive or negative changes along with it. Remaining active and engaged on all levels—physically, intellectually, and socially—is the most important key to healthy aging.

Discovering Psychology Viewing Guide

 Watch the following videos by logging into MyPsychLab (www.mypsychlab.com). After you have watched the videos, complete the activities that follow.

 PROGRAM 5:
THE DEVELOPING CHILD

 PROGRAM 6: LANGUAGE
DEVELOPMENT

 PROGRAM 17:
SEX AND GENDER

 PROGRAM 18:
MATURING AND AGING

PROGRAM REVIEW

1. What task of infancy is aided by a baby's ability to recognize his or her mother's voice?
   a. avoiding danger
   b. seeking sustenance
   c. forming social relationships
   d. learning to speak
2. Jean Piaget has studied how children think. According to Piaget, at what age does a child typically master the idea that the amount of a liquid remains the same when it is poured from one container to another container with a different shape?
   a. 2 years old   c. 6 years old
   b. 4 years old   d. 8 years old
3. A baby is shown an orange ball a dozen times in a row. How would you predict the baby would respond?
   a. The baby will make the same interested response each time.
   b. The baby will respond with less and less interest each time.
   c. The baby will respond with more and more interest each time.
   d. The baby will not be interested at any time.
4. Which of the following do newborns appear not to already be equipped with?
   a. a temperament
   b. a preference for novelty
   c. a preference for complexity

   d. the ability to understand reversibility in conservation
5. The Wild Boy of Aveyron represents which important issue in developmental psychology?
   a. ethics in experimentation
   b. the relation of physical development to social development
   c. nature versus nurture
   d. interpretation of experimental data
6. At 1 month of age, babies
   a. are best described as "a blooming, buzzing confusion."
   b. prefer stimuli that are constant and don't vary.
   c. have not yet opened their eyes.
   d. prefer human faces over other visual stimuli.
7. Which of the following is last to emerge in children?
   a. fear of heights
   b. preference for mother's voice over other people's voices
   c. temperament
   d. ability to see analogies between a real situation and a scale model of it
8. Which of the following psychological characteristics appear(s) to have a genetic component?
   a. activity level
   b. tendency to be outgoing
   c. risk for some psychopathologies
   d. all of the above
9. What sounds do very young babies prefer?
   a. ocean sounds   c. other babies
   b. human voices   d. soft music

10. How does the development of language competence compare from culture to culture?
    a. It varies greatly.
    b. It is remarkably similar.
    c. Western cultures are similar to each other, whereas Eastern cultures are very different.
    d. This topic is just beginning to be explored by researchers.

11. Which of the following stages of communication consist of simple sentences that lack plurals, articles, and tenses, but tend to have the constituent words in the order appropriate to the child's native language?
    a. telegraphic speech
    b. babbling
    c. question-asking
    d. ritualistic speech

12. What is the correct progression in the development of communication?
    a. babbling, cooing, crying, two-word phase
    b. crying, babbling, cooing, two-word phase
    c. crying, cooing, babbling, two-word phase
    d. cooing, crying, babbling, two-word phase

13. According to research by Zella Lurin and Jeffrey Rubin, the difference in the language parents use to describe their newborn sons or daughters is primarily a reflection of
    a. actual physical differences in the newborns.
    b. differences in the way the newborns behave.
    c. the way the hospital staff responds to the babies.
    d. the parents' expectations coloring their perceptions.

14. Which difference between the ways in which boys and girls play seems linked to sex hormones?
    a. Girls play with dolls.
    b. Boys engage in rough and tumble play.
    c. Boys play in larger groups than girls do.
    d. Girls build rooms, and boys build towers.

15. The term *androgynous* would best apply to which of the following people?
    a. a macho man who participates in body-building competitions
    b. a dainty woman who belongs to a sewing club
    c. a young boy who never talks in class because he feels shy
    d. a male rock star who wears heavy makeup, long hair, and feminine clothing

16. Because of the way we socialize our children, men tend to experience more freedom to _____, whereas women tend to experience more freedom to _____.
    a. explore; criticize
    b. withdraw; invent
    c. discover; express themselves
    d. express themselves; explore

17. How has research on lifespan development changed our idea of human nature?
    a. We see development as a growth process of early life.
    b. We see that a longer lifespan creates problems for society.
    c. We view people as continuing to develop throughout life.
    d. We regard development as a hormonally based process.

18. According to Erikson, the young adult faces a conflict between
    a. isolation and intimacy.
    b. heterosexuality and homosexuality.
    c. autonomy and shame.
    d. wholeness and futility.

19. Assuming that a person remains healthy, what happens to the ability to derive sexual pleasure as one ages?
    a. It does not change.
    b. It gradually diminishes.
    c. It abruptly ceases.
    d. It depends on the availability of a suitable partner.

20. In which of the following areas do the elderly typically have an advantage over college students?
    a. The elderly are better able to climb stairs.
    b. The elderly generally have higher short-term memory capacity.
    c. The elderly are less lonely.
    d. The elderly have a more developed sense of humor.

QUESTIONS TO CONSIDER

1. How might the knowledge of developmental norms affect a parent's response to a child? How might advanced techniques to detect prenatal perception and cognition inform parents? Speculate on what would happen if parents raised their children following inaccurate or out-of-date theories of child development.

2. Can some of the measures used to determine the cognitive capabilities of preverbal infants be applied to nonhuman animals? What would we be able to conclude from patterns of results that are similar to or different from those found in human infants?

3. How closely tied are language and thought? Is language ability necessary for thought?

4. If you tried to raise a child without exposing him or her to any gender-typing biases, how extensively would you need to change the social and physical environments that the child would normally encounter? How big of a job would this be? Could you ultimately be successful?

5. How do social conditions help create the characteristics of adolescence and adulthood in the human life cycle?

ACTIVITIES

1. Compare yourself to your siblings. What traits, abilities, and interests do you share? Speculate on the roles of genetics and environment in the development of your similarities and differences.
2. Make a list of the labels used to describe people at various stages of life from infancy to old age. Which age group has the most labels? Compare the synonyms and modifiers for childhood to the words that help define adulthood. What might explain the difference?
3. Interview an elderly person to find out what his or her experiences have been of the costs and benefits, both cognitively and socially, of aging in this country. Does the elder ever find that he or she is discriminated against? Does the elder find that people are more generous with him or her than with other people?

Critical Thinking Applied: Subliminal Perception and Subliminal Persuasion

sensation and perception

Can you imagine what your world would be like if you could no longer see colors—but merely black, white, and gray? Such a bizarre sensory loss befell Jonathan I., a 65-year-old New Yorker, following an automobile accident. Details of Jonathan's case appear in neurologist Oliver Sacks's 1995 book *An Anthropologist on Mars*.

Apparently the accident caused damage to a region in Jonathan's brain that processes color information. At first, he also had some amnesia for reading letters of the alphabet, which all seemed like nonsensical markings to him. But, after five days, his inability to read disappeared. His loss of color vision, however, persisted as a permanent condition, known as *cerebral achromatopsia* (pronounced *ay-kroma-TOP-see-a*). Curiously, Jonathan also lost his memory of color and eventually even the names for colors. He could no longer imagine, for instance, what "red" once looked like.

As you might expect, Jonathan became depressed by this turn of events in his life. The problem was aggravated by his occupation: Jonathan was a painter who based his livelihood on representing his visual images of the world in vivid colors. Now this world of colors was all gone, all drab, all "molded in lead." When he looked at his own paintings now, paintings that had seemed bursting with special meaning and emotional associations, all he could see were unfamiliar and meaningless objects on canvas.

Nevertheless, Jonathan's story has a more or less happy ending, one that reveals much about the resilience of the human spirit. First, Jonathan became a "night person," traveling and working at night and socializing with other night people. (As we will see in this chapter, good color vision depends on bright illumination such as daylight; most people's color vision is not as acute in the dark of night.) He also became aware that what remained of his vision was remarkably good, enabling him to read license plates from four blocks away at night. Jonathan began to reinterpret his "loss" as a "gift" in which he was no longer distracted by color, so that he could now focus his work more intensely on shape, form, and content. Finally, he switched to painting only in black and white. Critics acclaimed his "new phase" as a success. He has also become good at sculpting, which he had never attempted before his accident. So, as Jonathan's world of color died, a new world of "pure forms" was born in his perception of the people, objects, and events in his environment.

What lessons can we learn from Jonathan's experience? His unusual sensory loss tells us that our picture of the world around us depends on an elaborate sensory system that processes incoming information. In other words, we don't experience the world directly, but instead through a series of "filters" that we call our *senses*. By examining such cases of sensory loss, psychologists have learned much about how the sensory processing system works. And, on a more personal level, case studies like Jonathan's allow us momentarily to slip outside our own experience to see more clearly how resilient humans can be in the face of catastrophic loss.

But Jonathan's case also raises some deeper issues. Many conditions can produce the inability to see colors: abnormalities in the eyes, the optic nerve, or the brain can interfere with vision and, specifically, with the ability to see colors, as Jonathan's case illustrates. But do colors exist in the world outside us—or is it possible that color is a creation of our brains?

At first, such a question may seem absurd. But by now you have probably learned to expect that we will select a chapter-opening problem that has an unexpected answer. Yes, we will argue that color—and, in fact, all sensation—is a creation of the brain. But perhaps the more profound issue is this:

PROBLEM: How could we tell whether the world we "see" in our minds is the same as the external world—and whether we see the world as others do?

This chapter will show you how psychologists have addressed such questions.

∙ ∙

Sensation The process by which stimulation of a sensory receptor produces neural impulses that the brain interprets as a sound, a visual image, an odor, a taste, a pain, or other sensory image. Sensation represents the first series of steps in processing of incoming information.

Although the very private processes that connect us with the outside world extend deep into the brain, we will begin our chapter at the surface—at the sense organs. This is the territory of *sensory psychology*. We will define **sensation** simply as the process by which a stimulated receptor (such as the eyes or ears) creates a pattern of neural messages that represent the stimulus in the brain, giving rise to our initial experience of the stimulus. An important idea to remember is that sensation involves converting stimulation (such as a pinprick, a sound, or a flash of light) into a form the brain can understand (neural signals)—much as a cell phone converts an electronic signal into sound waves you can hear.

In this chapter you will see how all our sense organs, in some very basic ways, are much alike. They all transform physical stimulation (such as light waves or sound waves) into the neural impulses that give us sensations (such as the experience of light or sound). Along the way, you will learn about the psychological basis for color, odor, sound, texture, and taste. When you have finished the chapter, you will know why tomatoes and limes seem to have different hues, why a pinprick feels different from a caress, and why seeing doesn't always give us an accurate basis for believing.

Happily, under most conditions, our sensory experience is highly reliable. So, when you catch sight of a friend, the sensation usually registers clearly, immediately, and accurately. Yet, we humans do have our sensory limitations— just as other creatures do. In fact, we lack the acute senses so remarkable in many other species: the vision of hawks, the hearing of bats, the sense of smell of rodents, or the sensitivity to magnetic fields found in migratory birds. So, is there a human specialty? Yes. Our species has evolved the sensory equipment that enables us to process a wider range and variety of sensory input than any other creature.

Our ultimate destination in this chapter lies, far beyond mere sensation, in the amazing realm of *perception*. There we will uncover the psychological processes that attach meaning and personal significance to the sensory messages entering our brains. *Perceptual psychology* will help you understand how we assemble a series of tones into a familiar melody or a collage of shapes and shadings into a familiar face. More generally, we will define **perception** as a mental process that elaborates and assigns meaning to the incoming sensory patterns. Thus, *perception creates an interpretation of sensation.* Perception answers questions such as: Is the tomato ripe? Is the sound a church bell or a doorbell? Does the face belong to someone you know?

In this chapter, you will also learn that many complex acts of sensing and perceiving occur behind the scenes, so effortlessly, continuously, and flawlessly that we pay them little conscious mind. Even more fundamentally, you will learn the sobering fact that our minds lack direct access to the outside world. No matter what we do, the information we get about external events must be filtered through our sense organs and then combined with our unique mix of memories, emotions, motives, and expectations. So the inner world of sensation and perception is the only world we can ever know.

As you can see, the boundary of sensation blurs into that of perception. Perception is essentially an interpretation and elaboration of sensation. Seen in these terms, sensation refers just to the initial steps in the processing of a stimulus. It is to these first sensory steps that we now turn our attention.

To hunt small flying objects at night, bats rely on echolocation, a kind of sonar. Bats emit high-frequency sounds that bounce off insects, like the moth in this photo. The returning echo reveals the location of the insect—in much the same fashion that submarines locate objects underwater by listening for the echo of a "ping" they have emitted.

7.1 KEY QUESTION
HOW DOES STIMULATION BECOME SENSATION?

A thunderstorm is approaching, and you feel the electric charge in the air make the hair stand up on your neck. Lightning flashes, and a split second later you hear the thunderclap. It was close by, and you smell the ozone left in the wake of the bolt, as it sizzled through the air. Your senses are warning you of danger.

Our senses have other adaptive functions, too. They aid our survival by directing us toward certain stimuli, such as tasty foods, which provide nourishment. Our senses also help us locate mates, seek shelter, and recognize our friends. Incidentally, our senses also give us the opportunity to find pleasure in music, art, athletics, food, and sex.

How do our senses accomplish all this? The complete answer is complex, but it involves one elegantly simple idea that applies across the sensory landscape:

Perception A process that makes sensory patterns meaningful. It is perception that makes these words meaningful, rather than just a string of visual patterns. To make this happen, perception draws heavily on memory, motivation, emotion, and other psychological processes.

Our sensory impressions of the world involve *neural representations* of stimuli— not the actual stimuli themselves. The Core Concept puts it this way:

The brain senses the world indirectly because the sense organs convert stimulation into the language of the nervous system: neural messages.

As we have noted, the brain never receives stimulation directly from the outside world. Its experience of a tomato is not the same as the tomato itself— although we usually assume that the two are identical. Neither can the brain receive light from a sunset, reach out and touch velvet, or inhale the fragrance of a rose. It must always rely on secondhand information from the go-between sensory system, which delivers only a coded neural message, out of which the brain must create its own experience. (See Figure 7.1.) Just as you cannot receive phone messages without a telephone receiver to convert the electronic energy into sound you can hear, your brain also needs its sensory system to convert the stimuli from the outside world into neural signals that it can comprehend.

To understand more deeply how the world's stimulation becomes the brain's sensation, we need to think about three attributes common to all the senses: *transduction, sensory adaptation,* and *thresholds.* They determine which stimuli will actually become sensation, what the quality and impact of that sensation will be, and whether it grabs our interest. These attributes determine, for example, whether a tomato actually registers in the sensory system strongly enough to enter our awareness, what its color and form appear to be, and how strongly it bids for our attention.

Transduction: Changing Stimulation to Sensation

The idea that basic sensations, such as the redness and flavor of our tomato— or the colors Jonathan could see before his accident—are entirely creations of the sense organs and brain may seem incredible to you. But remember that all sensory communication with the brain flows through neurons in the form of neural signals: Neurons cannot transmit light or sound waves or any other external stimulus. Accordingly, none of the light bouncing off the tomato ever actually reaches the brain. In fact, light only gets as far as the back of the eyes, where the information it contains is converted to neural messages. Likewise, the chemicals that signal taste make their way only as far as the tongue, not all the way to the brain.

In all the sense organs, it is the job of the *sensory receptors* to convert incoming stimulus information into electrochemical signals—neural activity—the only language the brain understands. As Jonathan I.'s case suggests, sensations, such as "red" or "sweet" or "cold," occur only when the neural signal reaches the cerebral cortex. The whole process seems so immediate and direct that it fools us into assuming that the sensation of redness is characteristic of a tomato or

FIGURE 7.1
Stimulation Becomes Perception

For visual stimulation to become meaningful perception, it must undergo several transformations. First, physical stimulation (light waves from the butterfly) is transduced by the eye, where information about the wavelength and intensity of the light is coded into neural signals. Second, the neural messages travel to the sensory cortex of the brain, where they become sensations of color, brightness, form, and movement. Finally, the process of perception interprets these sensations by making connections with memories, expectations, emotions, and motives in other parts of the brain. Similar processes operate on the information taken in by the other senses.

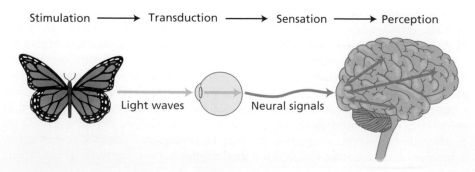

Stimulation ⟶ Transduction ⟶ Sensation ⟶ Perception

Light waves   Neural signals

One of the simplest concepts in perceptual psychology is among the most difficult for most people to grasp: The brain and its sensory systems create the colors, sounds, tastes, odors, textures, and pains that you sense. You can demonstrate this to yourself in the following way.

Close your eyes and press gently with your finger on the inside corner of one eye. On the opposite side of your visual field you will "see" a pattern caused by the pressure of your finger—not by light. These light sensations are *phosphenes*, visual images caused by fooling your visual system with pressure, which stimulates the optic nerve in much the same way light does. Direct electrical stimulation of the occipital lobe, sometimes done during brain surgery, can have

the same effect. This shows that light waves are not absolutely necessary for the sensation of light. The sensory experience of light, therefore, must be a creation of the brain, rather than a property of objects in the external world.

Phosphenes may have some practical value, too. Several laboratories are working on ways to use phosphenes, created by stimulation sent from a TV camera to the occipital cortex, to create visual sensations for people who have lost their sight (Wickelgren, 2006). Another promising approach under development involves replacing a section of the retina with an electronic microchip (Boahen, 2005; Liu et al., 2000). We hasten to add, however, that this technology is in its infancy (Cohen, 2002).

sensation of light

the sensation of cold is a characteristic of ice cream. But they are not! (You can discover how light is not necessary for sensations of light with the demonstration in the "Do It Yourself!" box, "Phosphenes Show That Your Brain Creates Sensations.")

Psychologists use the term **transduction** for the sensory process that converts the information carried by a physical stimulus, such as light or sound waves, into the form of neural messages. Transduction begins with the detection by a sensory neuron of the physical stimulus (such as the sound wave made by a vibrating guitar string). When the appropriate stimulus reaches a sense organ, it activates specialized neurons, called *receptors*, which respond by converting their excitation into a nerve signal. This happens in much the same way that a barcode reader (which is, after all, merely an electronic receptor) converts the series of lines on a frozen pizza box into an electronic signal that a computer can match with a price.

In our own sensory system, neural impulses carry the codes of sensory events in a form that can be further processed by the brain. To get to its destination, this information-carrying signal travels from the receptor cells along a *sensory pathway* by way of the thalamus to specialized sensory processing areas in the brain. From the coded neural impulses arriving from these pathways, the brain then extracts information about the basic qualities of the stimulus, such as its intensity and direction. Please keep in mind, however, that the stimulus itself terminates in the receptor: The only thing that continues on into the nervous system is *information* carried by the neural impulse.

Let's return now to the problem we set out at the beginning of the chapter: How could we tell whether the world we "see" in our minds is the same as the external world—and whether we see the world as others do? The idea of transduction gives us part of the answer. Because we do *not* see (or hear, or smell . . .) the external world directly, what we sense is a rendition of the world created by the sensory receptors and the brain. To give an analogy: Just as digital photography changes a scene first into electronic signals and then into drops of ink on a piece of paper, so the process of sensation changes the world into a pattern of neural impulses realized in the brain.

Transduction Transformation of one form of information into another—especially the transformation of stimulus information into nerve signals by the sense organs. Without transduction, ripe tomatoes would not appear red (or pinkish-gray, in the case of tomatoes purchased in many grocery stores).

Thresholds: The Boundaries of Sensation

What is the weakest stimulus an organism can detect? How dim can a light be and still be visible? How soft can music be and still be heard? These questions refer to the **absolute threshold** for different types of stimulation, which is the minimum amount of physical energy needed to produce a sensory experience. In the laboratory, a psychologist would define this operationally as the intensity at which the stimulus is detected accurately half of the time over many trials. This threshold will also vary from one person to another. So, if you point out a faint star to a friend who says he cannot see it, the star's light is above your absolute threshold (you can see it) but below that of your friend (who cannot).

A faint stimulus does not abruptly become detectable as its intensity increases. Because of the fuzzy boundary between detection and nondetection, a person's absolute threshold is not absolute! In fact, it varies continually with our mental alertness and physical condition. Experiments designed to determine thresholds for various types of stimulation were among the earliest studies done by psychologists—who called this line of inquiry *psychophysics*. Table 7.1 shows some typical absolute threshold levels for several familiar natural stimuli.

We can illustrate another kind of threshold with the following imaginary experiment. Suppose you are relaxing by watching television on the one night you don't need to study, while your roommate busily prepares for an early morning exam. Your roommate asks you to "turn it down a little" to eliminate the distraction. You feel that you should make some effort to comply but really wish to leave the volume as it is. What is the least amount you can lower the volume to prove your good intentions to your roommate while still keeping the sound clearly audible? Your ability to make judgments like this one depends on your **difference threshold** (also called the *just noticeable difference* or *JND*), the smallest physical difference between two stimuli that a person can reliably detect 50% of the time.

If you turn down the volume as little as possible, your roommate might complain, "I don't hear any difference." By this your roommate probably means that the change is volume does not match his or her difference threshold. By gradually lowering the volume until your roommate says "when," you will be able to find his or her difference threshold and keep the peace in your relationship.

Investigation of the difference thresholds across the senses has yielded some interesting insights into how human stimulus detection works. It turns out that *the JND is always large when the stimulus intensity is high, and small when the stimulus intensity is low.* Psychologists refer to this idea—that the size of the JND is proportional to the intensity of the stimulus—as **Weber's law.** And what does Weber's law tell us about adjusting the TV volume? If you have the volume turned up very high, you will have to turn the volume down a lot to make the difference noticeable. On the other hand, if you already have the volume set to a very low level, a small adjustment will probably be noticeable enough for your roommate.

CONNECTION • CHAPTER 1

An *operational definition* describes a concept in terms of the operations required to produce, observe, or measure it.

Absolute threshold   The amount of stimulation necessary for a stimulus to be detected. In practice, this means that the presence or absence of a stimulus is detected correctly half the time over many trials.

Difference threshold   The smallest amount by which a stimulus can be changed and the difference be detected half the time.

Weber's law   The concept that the size of a JND is proportional to the intensity of the stimulus; the JND is large when the stimulus intensity is high and small when the stimulus intensity is low.

TABLE 7.1	Approximate Perceptual Thresholds of Five Senses
Sense	**Detection Threshold**
Vision	A candle flame at 30 miles on a dark, clear night
Hearing	The tick of a mechanical watch under quiet conditions at 20 feet
Taste	One teaspoon of sugar in 2 gallons of water
Smell	One drop of perfume diffused into the entire volume of a three-bedroom apartment
Touch	The wing of a bee falling on your cheek from a distance of one centimeter

Source: From *Encyclopedic Dictionary of Psychology* 3rd ed. by Terry J. Petti. Copyright © 1986. Reprinted by permission of McGraw-Hill Contemporary Learning.

In this simple demonstration, you will see how detection of change in brightness is relative, not absolute. Find a three-way lamp equipped with a bulb having equal wattage increments, such as a 50–100–150-watt bulb. (Wattage is closely related to brightness.) Then, in a dark room, switch the light on to 50 watts, which will seem like a *huge* increase in brightness relative to the dark. Next, turn the switch to change from 50 to 100 watts: This will also seem like a large increase—but not so much as it did when you originally turned on the light in the dark. Finally, switch from 100 to 150 watts. Why does this last 50-watt increase, from 100 to 150 watts, appear only slightly brighter?

Your visual system does not give you an *absolute* sensation of brightness; rather, it provides information about the *relative* change. That is, it compares the stimulus change to the background stimulation, translating the jump from 100 to 150 watts as a mere 50% increase (50 watts added to 100) compared to the earlier 100% increase (50 watts added to 50). This illustrates how your brain computes sensory relationships, rather than absolutes—and it is essentially the same with your other senses.

The same principle operates across all our senses. Knowing this, you might guess that a weight lifter would notice the difference when small amounts are added to light weights, but it would take a much larger addition to be noticeable with heavy weights.

What does all this mean for our understanding of human sensation? The general principle is this: We are built to detect *changes* in stimulation and *relationships* among stimuli. You can see how this works in the box, "Do It Yourself! An Enlightening Demonstration of Sensory Relationships."

Signal Detection Theory

A deeper understanding of absolute and difference thresholds comes from *signal detection theory* (Green & Swets, 1966). Originally developed for engineering electronic sensors, signal detection theory uses the same concepts to explain both the electronic sensing of stimuli by devices, such as your TV set, and by the human senses, such as vision and hearing.

According to **signal detection theory,** sensation depends on the characteristics of the stimulus, the background stimulation, and the detector. Thus, how well you receive a stimulus, such as a professor's lecture, depends on the presence of competing stimuli in the background—the clacking keys of a nearby laptop or intrusive fantasies about a classmate. It will also depend on the condition of your "detector"—your brain—and, perhaps, whether it has been aroused by a strong cup of coffee.

Signal detection theory also helps us understand why thresholds vary—why, for example, you might notice a certain sound one time and not the next. The classical theory of thresholds ignored the effects of the perceiver's physical condition, judgments, or biases. Thus, in classical psychophysics (as the study of stimulation, thresholds, and sensory experience was done before signal-detection theory), if a signal were intense enough to exceed one's absolute threshold, it would be sensed; if below threshold, it would be missed. In the view of modern signal detection theory, sensation is not a simple yes-or-no experience, but a *probability* that the signal will be detected and processed accurately.

So, what does signal detection theory offer psychology that was missing in classical psychophysics? One factor is the variability in human judgment. Another involves the conditions in which the signal occurs. Signal detection theory recognizes that the observer, whose physical and mental status is always in flux, must compare a sensory experience with ever-changing expectations and biological conditions. For example, when something "goes bump in the night" after you have gone to bed, you must decide whether it is the cat, an intruder, or just your imagination. What you decide depends on the keenness of your

Signal detection theory Explains how we detect "signals," consisting of stimulation affecting our eyes, ears, nose, skin, and other sense organs. Signal detection theory says that sensation is a judgment the sensory system makes about incoming stimulation. Often, it occurs out[side] consciousness. In contrast to o[ther] theories from psychophysics[,] detection theory takes obse[rver] characteristics into accou[nt]

hearing and what you expect to hear, as well as other noises in the background. By taking into account the variable conditions that affect detection of a stimulus, signal detection theory provides a more accurate portrayal of sensation than did classical psychophysics.

PSYCHOLOGYMATTERS
Sensory Adaptation

If you have ever jumped into a cool pool on a hot day, you know that sensation is critically influenced by *change*. In fact, a main role of our stimulus detectors is to announce changes in the external world—a flash of light, a splash of water, a clap of thunder, the approach of a lion, the prick of a pin, or the burst of flavor from a dollop of salsa. Thus, our sense organs are *change detectors*. Their receptors specialize in gathering information about new and changing events.

The great quantity of incoming sensation would quickly overwhelm us, if not for the ability of our sensory systems to adapt. Sensory adaptation is the diminishing responsiveness of sensory systems to prolonged stimulation, as when you adapt to the feel of swimming in cool water. To give another example, you probably did not realize, until we called your attention to it, that your sense of touch had adapted to the press of furniture against your body. Thus, any stimulation that persists without changing in some way usually shifts into the background of our awareness, unless it is quite intense or painful. On the other hand, any change in stimulation (as when an air conditioner suddenly becomes louder or higher-pitched) will immediately draw your attention. Incidentally, sensory adaptation accounts for the background music often played in stores being so unmemorable: It has been deliberately selected and filtered to remove any large changes in volume or pitch that might distract attention from the merchandise. (Do you see why it's not a good idea to listen to your favorite music while studying?)

Signal detection theory says that the background stimulation would make it less likely for you to hear someone calling your name on a busy downtown street than in a quiet park.

Sensory adaptation Loss of responsiveness in receptor cells after stimulation has remained unchanged for a while, as when a swimmer becomes adapted to the temperature of the water.

CheckYourUnderstanding

1. **RECALL:** The sensory pathways carry information from _____ to _____.

2. **RECALL:** Why do sensory psychologists use the standard of *the amount of stimulation that your sensory system can detect about half the time* for identifying the absolute threshold?

3. **APPLICATION:** Which one would involve sensory adaptation?
   a. The water in a swimming pool seems warmer after you have been in it for a while than it did when you first jumped in.

   b. The flavor of a spicy salsa on your taco seems hot by comparison with the blandness of the sour cream.
   c. You are unaware of a stimulus flashed on the screen at 1/100 of a second.
   d. You prefer the feel of silk to the feel of velvet.

4. **RECALL:** What is the psychological process that adds *meaning* to information obtained by the sensory system?

5. **UNDERSTANDING THE CORE CONCEPT:** Use the concept of *transduction* to explain why the brain never directly senses the outside world.

Answers 1. From the sense organs to the brain. **2.** The amount of stimulation that we can detect is not fixed. Rather, it varies depending on ever-changing factors such as our level of arousal, distractions, fatigue, and motivation. **3.** a **4.** Perception **5.** The senses transduce stimulation from the external world into the form of neural impulses, which is the only form of information that the brain can use. Therefore, the brain does not deal directly with light, sound, odors, and other stimuli, but only with information that has been changed (transduced) into neural messages.

7.2 KEY QUESTION
HOW ARE THE SENSES ALIKE? AND HOW ARE THEY DIFFERENT?

Vision, hearing, smell, taste, touch, pain, body position: In certain ways, all these senses are the same. They all transduce stimulus energy into neural impulses.

They are all more sensitive to change than to constant stimulation. And they all provide us information about the world—information that has survival value. But how are they different? With the exception of pain, each sense taps a different form of stimulus energy, and each sends the information it extracts to a different part of the brain. These contrasting ideas lead us to the Core Concept of this section:

The senses all operate in much the same way, but each extracts different information and sends it to its own specialized processing region in the brain.

Each sense organ has a different design, and each sends neural messages to its own specialized region in the brain. So, in the end, *different sensations occur because different areas of the brain become activated.* Whether you hear a bell or see a bell depends ultimately on which part of the brain receives stimulation. We will explore how this all works by looking at each of the senses in turn. First, we will explore the visual system—the best understood of the senses—to discover how it transduces light waves into visual sensations of color and brightness.

Vision: How the Nervous System Processes Light

Animals with good vision have an enormous biological advantage. This fact has exerted evolutionary pressure to make vision the most complex, best-developed, and important sense for humans and most other highly mobile creatures. Good vision helps us detect desired targets, threats, and changes in our physical environment and to adapt our behavior accordingly. So, how does the visual system accomplish this?

The Anatomy of Visual Sensation   You might think of the eye as a sort of "camera" the brain uses to make motion pictures of the world. (See Figure 7.2.) Like a

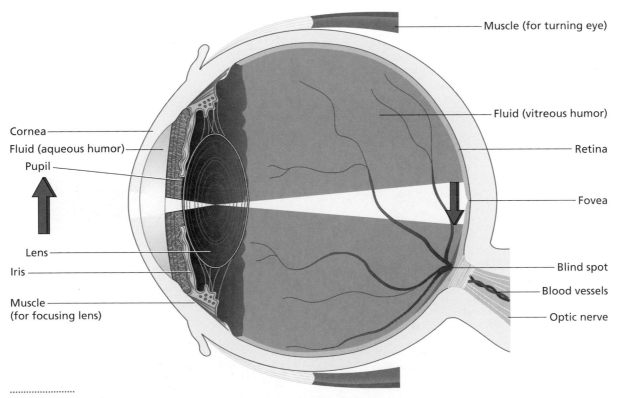

FIGURE 7.2
Structures of the Human Eye

camera, the eye gathers light through a lens, focuses it, and forms an image in the *retina* at the back of the eye. The lens, incidentally, turns the image left-to-right and upside down. (Because vision is so important, this visual reversal may have influenced the very structure of the brain, which, you will remember, tends to maintain this reversal in its sensory processing regions. Thus, most information from the sense organs crosses over to the opposite side of the brain. Likewise, "maps" of the body in the brain's sensory areas are typically inverted.)

But while a digital camera forms an electronic image, the eye forms an image made of neural signals that get further processing in the brain. The unique characteristic of the eye—what makes the eye different from other sense organs—lies in its ability to extract the information from light waves, which are simply a form of electromagnetic energy. The eye, then, *transduces* the characteristics of light into neural signals that the brain can process. This transduction happens in the **retina,** the light-sensitive layer of cells at the back of the eye that acts much like the light-sensitive chip in a digital camera.

And, as with a camera, things can go wrong. In people who are "nearsighted," the lens focuses the image short of (in front of) the retina; in "farsighted" people, the focal point extends behind the retina. Either way, the image is not sharp without a corrective lens.

The real work in the retina is performed by light-sensitive cells known as **photoreceptors,** which operate much like the tiny pixel receptors in a digital camera. These photoreceptors consist of two different types of specialized neurons— the *rods* and *cones* that absorb light energy and respond by creating neural impulses. (See Figure 7.3.) But why are there two sorts of photoreceptors?

Because we function sometimes in near-darkness and sometimes in bright light, we have evolved two types of processors, involving two distinct receptor cell types named for their shapes. The 125 million tiny **rods** "see in the dark"— that is, they detect low intensities of light at night, though they cannot make the fine distinctions that give rise to our sensations of color. Rod cells enable you to find a seat in a darkened movie theater.

Retina   The thin light-sensitive layer at the back of the eyeball. The retina contains millions of photoreceptors and other nerve cells.

Photoreceptors   Light-sensitive cells (neurons) in the retina that convert light energy to neural impulses. The photoreceptors are as far as light gets into the visual system.

Rods   Photoreceptors in the retina that are especially sensitive to dim light but not to colors. Strange as it may seem, they are rod-shaped.

....

FIGURE 7.3
Transduction of Light in the Retina

This simplified diagram shows the pathways that connect three layers of nerve cells in the retina. Incoming light passes through the ganglion cells and bipolar cells first before striking the photoreceptors at the back of the eyeball. Once stimulated, the rods and cones then transmit information to the bipolar cells (note that one bipolar cell combines information from several receptor cells). The bipolar cells then transmit neural impulses to the ganglion cells. Impulses travel from the ganglia to the brain via axons that make up the optic nerve.

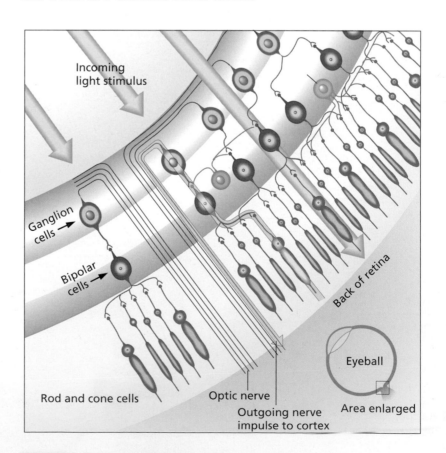

Incoming light stimulus

Ganglion cells →

Bipolar cells →

Back of retina

Rod and cone cells

Optic nerve

Outgoing nerve impulse to cortex

Eyeball

Area enlarged

Making the fine distinctions necessary for color vision is the job of the seven million **cones** that come into play in bright light. Each cone is specialized to detect the light waves we sense either as blue, red, or green. In good light, then, we can use these cones to distinguish ripe tomatoes (sensed as red) from unripe ones (sensed as green). The cones concentrate in the very center of the retina, in a small region called the **fovea**, which gives us our sharpest vision. With movements of our eyeballs, we use the fovea to scan whatever interests us visually—the features of a face or, perhaps, a flower. (You can learn more about the way cones work by trying the accompanying "Do It Yourself!" demonstration.)

There are still other types of cells in the retina, but while they are vital to vision they do not respond directly to light. The *bipolar cells* handle the job of collecting impulses from many photoreceptors (rods and cones) and shuttling them on to the *ganglion cells,* much as an airline hub collects passengers from many regional airports and shuttles them on to other destinations. Recently, vision researchers have found that the retina also contains receptor cells sensitive to edges and boundaries of objects; others respond to light and shadow and motion (Werblin & Roska, 2007).

Bundled together, the axons of the ganglion cells make up the **optic nerve**, which transports visual information from the eye to the brain. (See Figures 7.2 and 7.3.) Again, it is important to understand that your visual system carries no light at all beyond the retina—only patterns of nerve impulses conveying *information* derived from the incoming light.

Just as strangely, there is a small area of the retina in each eye where everyone is blind, because that part of the retina has no photoreceptors. This **blind spot** is located at the point where the optic nerve exits each eye, and the result is a gap in the visual field. You do not experience blindness there because what one eye misses is registered by the other eye, and the brain "fills in" the spot with information that matches the background. You can find your own blind spot by following the instructions in the "Do It Yourself!" box.

It is important to note that the visual impairment we call *blindness* can have many causes—and is usually unrelated to the blind spot. Blindness can result, for example, from damage to the retina, cataracts that make the lens opaque,

Cones Photoreceptors in the retina that are especially sensitive to colors but not to dim light. You may have guessed that the cones are cone-shaped.

Fovea The tiny area of sharpest vision in the retina.

Optic nerve The bundle of neurons that carries visual information from the retina to the brain.

Blind spot The point where the optic nerve exits the eye and where there are no photoreceptors. Any stimulus that falls on this area cannot be seen.

DO IT YOURSELF! Find Your Blind Spot

The "blind spot" occurs at the place on the retina where the neurons from the retina bunch together to exit the eyeball and form the optic nerve. There are no light-sensitive cells at this point on the retina. Consequently, you are "blind" in this small region of your visual field. The following demonstrations will help you determine where this blind spot occurs in your visual field.

Demonstration 1 Hold the text at arm's length, close your right eye, and fix your left eye on the "bank" figure. Keep your right eye closed and bring the book slowly closer. When it is about 10 to 12 inches away and the dollar sign is in your blind spot, the dollar sign will disappear—but you will not see a "hole" in your visual

field. Instead, your visual system "fills in" the missing area with information from the white background. You have "lost" your money!

Demonstration 2 To convince yourself that the brain fills in the missing part of the visual field with appropriate background, close your right eye again and focus on the cross

in the lower part of the figure. Once again, keeping the right eye closed, bring the book closer to you as you focus your left eye on the cross. This time, the gap in the line will disappear and will be filled in with a continuation of the line on either side. This shows that what you see in your blind spot may not really exist!

Bank

FIGURE 7.4
How Visual Stimulation Goes from the Eyes to the Brain

Light from objects in the visual field projects images on the retinas of the eyes. Please note two important things. First, the lens of the eye reverses the image on the retina—so the image of the man falls on the right side of the retina, and the image of the woman falls on the left. Second, the visual system splits the retinal image coming from each eye, so that part of the image coming from each eye crosses over to the opposite side of the brain. (Note how branches of the optic pathway cross at the *optic chiasma*.) As a result, objects appearing in the *left* part of the visual field *of both eyes* (the man, in this diagram) are sent to the *right* hemisphere's visual cortex for processing, while objects in the *right* side of the visual field *of both eyes* (the woman, in this diagram) are sent to the *left* visual cortex. In general, the right hemisphere "sees" the left visual field, while the left hemisphere "sees" the right visual field.

(*Source:* From *SEEING: Illusion, Brain and Mind*, by J. P. Frisby. Copyright © 1979. Reprinted by permission of J. P. Frisby.)

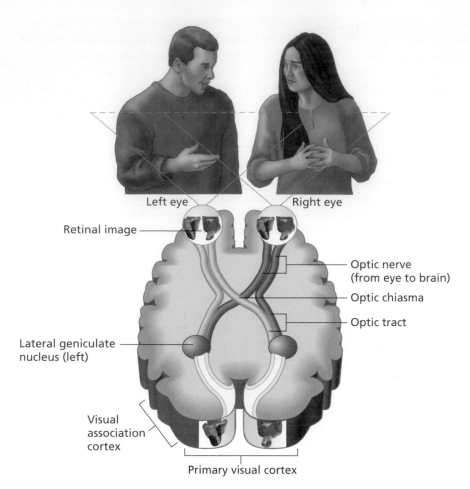

Left eye   Right eye

Retinal image

Optic nerve (from eye to brain)

Optic chiasma

Optic tract

Lateral geniculate nucleus (left)

Visual association cortex

Primary visual cortex

---

damage to the optic nerve, or from damage to the visual processing areas in the brain.

Processing Visual Sensation in the Brain   We *look* with our eyes but we *see* with the brain. To do so, we use a special processing area in the brain to create visual images from the information imported through the optic nerve. (See Figure 7.4.) In the *visual cortex,* the brain begins working its magic by transforming the incoming neural impulses into visual sensations of color, form, boundary, and movement. Amazingly, the visual cortex also manages to take the two-dimensional patterns from each eye and assemble them into a three-dimensional world of depth (Barinaga, 1998; Dobbins et al., 1998). With further processing, the cortex ultimately combines these visual sensations with memories, motives, emotions, and sensations of body position and touch to create a representation of the visual world that fits our current concerns and interests (de Gelder, 2000). Now you know why you can be strongly attracted by the visual appeal of appetizing foods if you go grocery shopping when you are hungry.

Returning for a moment to the chapter problem and to the question of whether we "see" the world as others do: As far as sensation is concerned, the answer is a qualified "yes." That is, most people have essentially the same sensory apparatus (broadly speaking and with the exceptions of a few individuals who, like Jonathan, are "colorblind" or who have other sensory deficits). Therefore, it is reasonable to assume that most people sense colors, sounds, textures, odors, and tastes in at least roughly the same ways.

CONNECTION • CHAPTER 2

Note that part of the visual pathway of each eye crosses over to the cortex on the opposite side of the brain. This produced some of the bizarre responses that we saw in the tests of *split-brain* patients.

How the Visual System Creates Brightness   Sensations of **brightness** come from the intensity or *amplitude* of light, determined by how much light reaches the retina. (See Table 7.2.) Bright light, as from approaching headlights, involves a more intense

Brightness   A psychological sensation caused by the intensity (amplitude) of light waves.

TABLE 7.2 Visual Stimulation Becomes Sensation

Physical Stimulation	Psychological Sensation
Wavelength	Color
Intensity (amplitude)	Brightness

Color and brightness are the psychological counterparts of the wavelength and intensity of a light wave. Wavelength and intensity are physical characteristics of light waves, while color and brightness are psychological characteristics that exist only in the brain.

light wave, which creates much neural activity in the retina, while relatively dim light, from your car's instrument panel, does not. Ultimately, the brain senses brightness by the level of neural activity produced in the retina and passed along through the optic pathways.

How the Visual System Creates Color   You may have been surprised to learn that a flower or a ripe tomato, itself, has no **color,** or *hue.* Physical objects seen in bright light seem to have the marvelous property of being awash with color; but, as we have noted, the red tomatoes, yellow flowers, green trees, blue oceans, and multi-hued rainbows are, in themselves, actually quite colorless. Nor does the light reflected from these objects have color. Despite the way the world appears to us, color does not exist outside the brain because color is a *sensation* that the brain creates based on the wavelength of light striking our eyes. Thus, color exists only in the mind of the viewer—a *psychological* property of our sensory experience. The sensation of color is created when the wavelength in a beam of light is recoded by the photoreceptors in the form of neural impulses and sent to specialized areas of the brain for sensory processing. To understand more fully how this happens, you must first know something of the nature of light.

The eyes detect the special form of energy that we call *visible light.* Physicists tell us that this light is pure energy—fundamentally the same as radio waves, microwaves, infrared light, ultraviolet light, X-rays, and cosmic rays. All are forms of *electromagnetic energy,* consisting of waves that move at light's speed limit of nearly 670 million mph. These waves differ in their wavelength, the distance they travel in making one wave cycle, as they vibrate in space, like ripples on a pond (see Figure 7.5). The light we can see occupies but a tiny segment somewhere near the middle of the vast **electromagnetic spectrum.** Our only access

Color   Also called *hue.* Color is not a property of things in the external world. Rather, it is a *psychological sensation* created in the brain from information obtained by the eyes from the wavelengths of visible light.

Electromagnetic spectrum   The entire range of electromagnetic energy, including radio waves, X-rays, microwaves, and visible light.

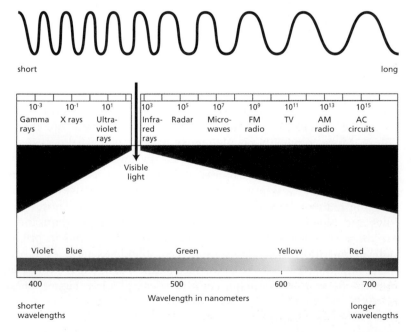

FIGURE 7.5
The Electromagnetic Spectrum

The only difference between visible light and other forms of electromagnetic energy is *wavelength.* The receptors in our eyes are sensitive to only a tiny portion of the electromagnetic spectrum.

(*Source:* From *Perception,* 3rd ed., by Sekuler & Blake. Copyright © 1994. Reprinted by permission of McGraw-Hill.)

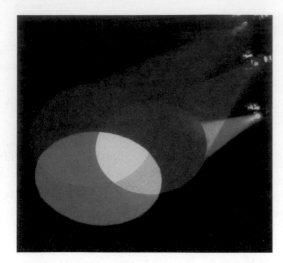

The combination of any two primary colors of light yields the complement of a third color. The combination of all three wavelengths produces white light. (The mixture of pigments, as in print, works differently, because pigments are made to absorb some wavelengths of light falling on them.)

Visible spectrum   The tiny part of the electromagnetic spectrum to which our eyes are sensitive. The visible spectrum of other creatures may be slightly different from our own.

Trichromatic theory   The idea that colors are sensed by three different types of cones sensitive to light in the red, blue, and green wavelengths. The trichromatic (three-color) theory explains the earliest stage of color sensation. In honor of its originators, this is sometimes called the Young-Helmholtz theory.

Opponent-process theory   The idea that cells in the visual system process colors in complementary pairs, such as red or green or as yellow or blue. The opponent-process theory explains color sensation from the bipolar cells onward in the visual system.

Afterimages   Sensations that linger after the stimulus is removed. Most visual afterimages are *negative afterimages,* which appear in reversed colors.

Color blindness   Typically a genetic disorder (although sometimes the result of trauma, as in the case of Jonathan) that prevents an individual from discriminating certain colors. The most common form is red–green color blindness.

to this electromagnetic spectrum lies through a small visual "window" called the **visible spectrum.** Because we have no biological receptors sensitive to the other portions of the electromagnetic spectrum, we must employ special detection instruments, such as radios and TVs, to help us convert energy in the range outside our vision into signals we can use.

Within this narrow visible spectrum, light waves of slightly different wavelengths give rise to different colors. Longer waves make us see a tomato as red, and medium-length waves give rise to the sensations of yellow and green we see in lemons and limes. The shorter waves from a clear sky stimulate sensations of blue. Thus, the eye extracts information from the wavelength of light, and the brain uses that information to construct the sensations we see as colors. (See Table 7.2.)

Remarkably, our visual experiences of color, form, position, and depth are all based on processing the same stream of sensory information in different parts of the visual cortex. Colors themselves are realized in a specialized area, where humans are capable of discriminating among about five million different hues. It was damage in this part of the cortex that shut down Jonathan's ability to see colors. Other nearby cortical areas take responsibility for processing information about boundaries, shapes, and movements.

Two Ways of Sensing Colors   Even though color is realized in the cortex, color processing begins in the retina. There, three different types of cones sense different parts of the visible spectrum—light waves that we sense as red, green, and blue. This three-receptor explanation for color vision is known as the **trichromatic theory,** and for a time it was considered to account for color vision completely. We now know that the trichromatic theory best explains the initial stages of color vision in the cone cells.

Another explanation, called the **opponent–process theory,** better explains negative **afterimages** (see the "Do It Yourself!" box), a phenomenon that involves *opponent,* or complementary, colors. According to the opponent-process theory, from the bipolar cells onward the visual system processes colors in complementary pairs, such as red or green or as yellow or blue. Thus, the sensation of a certain color, such as red, inhibits, or interferes with, the sensation of its complement, green. Taken together, the two theories explain different aspects of color vision involving the retina and visual pathways. Here is the take-home message: The trichromatic theory explains color processing in the cones, while the opponent-process theory explains what happens in the bipolar cells and beyond.

Color Blindness   Not everyone sees colors in the same way, because some people are born with a deficiency in distinguishing colors. The incidence varies among racial groups (highest in whites and lowest in blacks), but overall about 8% of males in the United States are affected. Women rarely have the condition.

At the extreme, complete **color blindness** is the total inability to distinguish colors. More commonly people merely have a color weakness that causes minor problems in distinguishing colors, especially under low-light conditions. People with one form of color weakness can't distinguish pale colors, such as pink or tan. Most color weakness or blindness, however, involves a problem in distinguishing red from green, especially at weak saturations. Those who confuse yellows and blues are rare, about one or two people per thousand. Rarest of all are those who see no color at all and see only variations in brightness. In fact, only about 500 cases of this total color blindness have ever been reported—including Jonathan I., whom we met at the beginning of this chapter. To find out whether you have a major color deficiency, look at Figure 7.6 and note what

After you stare at a colored object for a while, ganglion cells in your retina will become fatigued, causing an interesting visual effect. When you shift your gaze to a blank, white surface, you can "see" the object in complementary colors—as a visual afterimage. The "phantom flag" demonstration will show you how this works.

Stare at the dot in the center of the green, black, and orange flag for at least 30 seconds. Take care to hold your eyes steady and not to let them scan over the image during this time. Then quickly shift your gaze to the center of a sheet of white paper or to a light-colored blank wall. What do you see? Have your friends try this,

too. Do they see the same afterimage? (The effect may not be the same for people who are color-blind.)

Afterimages may be negative or positive. Positive afterimages are caused by a continuation of the receptor and neural processes following stimulation. They are brief. An example of positive afterimages occurs when you see the trail of a sparkler twirled by a Fourth of July reveler. Negative afterimages are the opposite or the reverse of the original experience, as in the flag example. They last longer. Negative afterimages operate according to the *opponent-process*

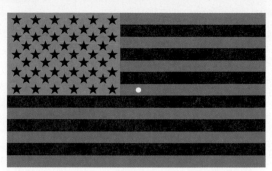

theory of color vision, which involves ganglion cells in the retina and the optic nerve. Apparently, in a negative afterimage, the fatigue in these cells produces sensations of a complementary color when they are exposed to white light.

---

you see. If you see the number 15 in the dot pattern, your color vision is probably normal. If you see something else, you are probably at least partially color blind.

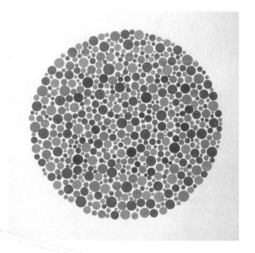

Hearing: If a Tree Falls in the Forest . . .

Imagine how your world would change if your ability to hear were suddenly diminished. You would quickly realize that hearing, like vision, provides you with the ability to locate objects in space, such as the source of a voice calling your name. In fact, hearing may be even more important than vision in orienting us toward distant events. We often hear things, such as footsteps coming up behind us, before we see the source of the sounds. Hearing may also tell us of events that we cannot see, including speech, music, or a car approaching from behind.

But there is more to hearing than its function. Accordingly, we will little deeper to learn *how* we hear. In the next few pages we will review sensory psychologists have discovered about how sound waves are pr how they are sensed, and how these sensations of sound are interprete

The Physics of Sound: How Sound Waves Are Produced
If Hollyw us an honest portrayal of intergalactic battles, those explosions of sp planets would be absolutely silent! On Earth, the vibrational energy objects, such as guitar strings, bells, and vocal cords, transfers to the medium—usually air—as the vibrating objects push the molecules of back and forth. The resulting changes in pressure spread outward sound waves that can travel 1100 feet per second. In space, howevei or other medium to carry the sound wave, so if you were a witnei ing star, the experience would be eerily without sound.

Back here on Earth, the purest tones are made by a tuning 7.7.) When struck, a tuning fork produces an extremely simple has only two characteristics, *frequency* and *amplitude*. These ical properties of any sound wave that determine how it wi

Sound outer ear canal, causing to vibrate. The vibra *anvil and stirrup).* These vibrations pass from the mid to the cochlea, where they set nal fluid in motion. The fluid movemen stimulates tiny hair cells along the basilar membrane, inside the cochlea, to transmit neural impulses from the ear to the brain along the auditory nerve.

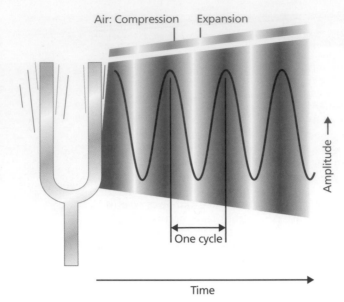

FIGURE 7.7
Sound Waves

Sound waves produced by the vibration of a tuning fork create waves of compressed and expanded air. The pitch that we hear depends on the *frequency* of the wave (the number of cycles per second). High pitches are the result of high-frequency waves. The *amplitude* or strength of a sound wave depends on how strongly the air is affected by the vibrations. In this diagram, amplitude is represented by the height of the graph.

Frequency   The number of cycles completed by a wave in a second.

Amplitude   The physical strength of a wave. This is shown on graphs as the height of the wave.

Tympanic membrane   The eardrum.

Cochlea   The primary organ of hearing; a coiled tube in the inner ear, where sound waves are transduced into nerve messages.

FIGURE 7.8
Structures of the Human Ear

waves are channeled by the (pinna) through the external the tympanic membrane tion activates the le ear (*hammer*, echanical window inter-

brain. **Frequency** refers to the number of vibrations or cycles the wave completes in a given amount of time, which in turn determines the highness or lowness of a sound (the pitch). Frequency is usually expressed in *cycles per second (cps)* or *hertz (Hz)*. **Amplitude** measures the physical strength of the sound wave (shown in graphs as the height of the wave); it is defined in units of sound pressure or energy. When you turn down the volume on your stereo, you are decreasing the amplitude of the sound waves.

Sensing Sounds: How We Hear Sound Waves   Much like vision, the psychological sensation of sound requires that waves be transduced into neural impulses and sent to the brain. This happens in four steps:

1. *Airborne sound waves are relayed to the inner ear.*   In this initial transformation, vibrating waves of air enter the outer ear (also called the *pinna*) and strike the *eardrum,* or **tympanic membrane** (see Figure 7.8). This tightly stretched sheet of tissue transmits the vibrations to three tiny bones in the middle ear: the *hammer, anvil,* and *stirrup,* named for their shapes. These bones immediately pass the vibrations on to the primary organ of hearing, the **cochlea,** located in the inner ear.

2. *The cochlea focuses the vibrations on the basilar membrane.*   Here in the cochlea, the formerly airborne sound wave becomes "seaborne," because the coiled tube of the cochlea is filled with fluid. As the bony stirrup vibrates against the oval window at the base of the cochlea, the vibrations set the fluid

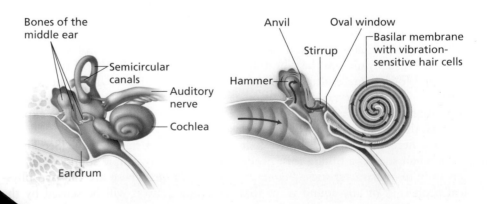

into wave motion, working on the same principle as a submarine sending a sonar "ping" through the water. As the fluid wave spreads through the cochlea, it causes a sympathetic vibration in the **basilar membrane,** a thin strip of tissue running through the cochlea.

3. *The basilar membrane converts the vibrations into neural messages.* The swaying of tiny hair cells on the vibrating basilar membrane stimulates sensory nerve endings connected to the hair cells. The excited neurons, then, transform the mechanical vibrations of the basilar membrane into neural activity.

4. Finally, *the neural messages travel to the auditory cortex in the brain.* Neural signals leave the cochlea in a bundle of neurons called the *auditory nerve.* The neurons from the two ears meet in the brain stem, which passes the auditory information to both sides of the brain. Ultimately, the signals arrive in the *auditory cortex* for higher-order processing.

CONNECTION • CHAPTER 2
The brain's primary auditory cortex lies in the *temporal lobes.*

If the auditory system seems complicated, you might think of it as a sensory "relay team." Sound waves are first funneled in by the outer ear, then handed off from the tissue of the eardrum to bones in the middle ear. Mechanical vibrations of these bones are then passed to the cochlea and basilar membrane in the inner ear, where they finally become neural signals, which are, in turn, passed along to the brain. This series of steps transforms commonplace vibrations into experiences as exquisite and varied as music, doorbells, whispers, shouts, and psychology lectures.

Psychological Qualities of Sound: How We Distinguish One Sound from Another

No matter where they come from, sounds have only three sensory qualities: *pitch*, *loudness*, and *timbre*. In the following discussion, we will show you how the two *physical* characteristics of a sound wave (frequency and amplitude) manage to produce these three *psychological sensations*.

Sensations of Pitch A sound wave's *frequency* determines the highness or lowness of a sound—a quality known as **pitch.** High frequencies produce high-pitched sounds, and low frequencies produce low-pitched sounds, as you see in Table 7.3. As with light, our sensitivity to sound spans only a limited range of the sound waves that occur in nature. The range of human auditory sensitivity extends from frequencies as low as 20 cps (the lowest range of a subwoofer in a good sound system) to

Basilar membrane A thin strip of tissue sensitive to vibrations in the cochlea. The basilar membrane contains hair cells connected to neurons. When a sound wave causes the hair cells to vibrate, the associated neurons become excited. As a result, the sound waves are converted (transduced) into nerve activity.

Pitch A sensory characteristic of sound produced by the *frequency* of the sound wave.

TABLE 7.3 Auditory Stimulation Becomes Sensation

Physical stimulation	Waveform	Psychological sensation
Amplitude (intensity)	Loud Soft	Loudness
Frequency (wavelength)	Low High	Pitch
Complexity	Pure Complex	Timbre

Pitch and loudness are the psychological counterparts of the frequency and amplitude (intensity) of a sound wave. Frequency and amplitude are characteristics of the physical sound wave, while sensations of pitch and loudness exist only in the brain. In addition, sound waves can be complex combinations of simpler waves. Psychologically, we experience this complexity as *timbre*. Compare this table with Table 7.2 for vision.

HOW ARE THE SENSES ALIKE? AND HOW ARE THEY DIFFERENT?

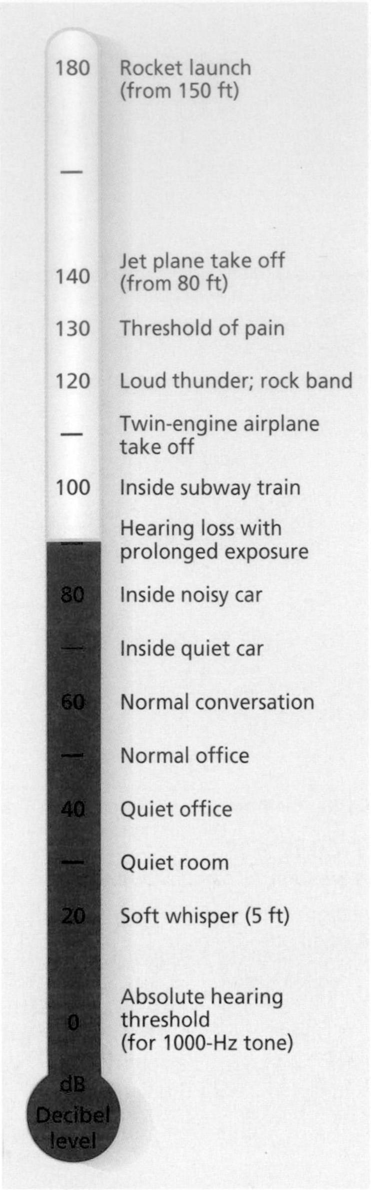

dB Decibel level	
180	Rocket launch (from 150 ft)
—	
140	Jet plane take off (from 80 ft)
130	Threshold of pain
120	Loud thunder; rock band
—	Twin-engine airplane take off
100	Inside subway train
—	Hearing loss with prolonged exposure
80	Inside noisy car
—	Inside quiet car
60	Normal conversation
—	Normal office
40	Quiet office
—	Quiet room
20	Soft whisper (5 ft)
0	Absolute hearing threshold (for 1000-Hz tone)

FIGURE 7.9
Intensities of Familiar Sounds

Loudness   A sensory characteristic of sound produced by the *amplitude* (intensity) of the sound wave.

Timbre   The quality of a sound wave that derives from the wave's complexity (combination of pure tones). *Timbre* comes from the Greek word for "drum," as does the term *tympanic membrane*, or eardrum.

frequencies as high as 20,000 cps (produced by the high-frequency tweeter in your stereo). Other creatures can hear sounds both higher (dogs, for example) and lower (elephants) than we can.

How does the auditory apparatus produce sensations of pitch? Two distinct auditory processes share the task, affording us much greater sensory precision than either could provide alone. Here's what happens:

● When sound waves pass through the inner ear, the basilar membrane vibrates. (See Figure 7.8.) Different frequencies activate different locations on the membrane. Thus, the pitch one hears depends, in part, on which region of the basilar membrane receives the greatest stimulation. This explanation of pitch perception, known as the *place theory,* says that different *places* on the basilar membrane send neural codes for different pitches to the auditory cortex of the brain—much as keys on different places on a piano keyboard can produce different notes. It turns out that the place theory accounts for our ability to hear high tones—above about 1000 Hz (cycles per second).

● Neurons on the basilar membrane respond with different firing rates for different sound wave *frequencies,* much as guitar strings vibrating at different frequencies produce different notes. And so, the rate of firing provides another code for pitch perception in the brain. This *frequency theory* explains how the basilar membrane deals with frequencies below about 5000 Hz. (Between 1000 and 5000 Hz, hearing is based on both place and frequency.)

Why is there overlap in the processes described by these two theories—specifically for sounds within the range of 1000 to 5000 Hz? Simple. This is the range of human speech, and our hearing has evolved two different ways of making sure that we are especially sensitive to sounds in this range. And, just to make sure, the auditory canal is specially shaped to amplify sounds within this speech range.

Sensations of Loudness   The **loudness** of a sound wave is determined by its physical strength or *amplitude* (much as brightness is determined by the intensity of light), as shown in Table 7.3. More intense sound waves (a shout) produce louder sounds, while we experience sound waves with small amplitudes (a whisper) as soft. Amplitude, then, refers to the physical sound wave, and loudness is a psychological sensation.

Because we can hear sound waves across a great range of intensity, the loudness of a sound is usually expressed as a ratio rather than an absolute amount. More specifically, sound intensity is expressed in units called decibels (dB). Figure 7.9 shows the levels of some representative natural sounds in decibel units.

Sensations of Timbre   The bark of a dog, a train whistle, the wail of an oboe, the clink of a spoon in a cup—all sound distinctively different, not just because they have different pitches or loudness but because they are peculiar mixtures of tones. In fact, most natural sound waves are mixtures rather than pure tones, as shown in Figure 7.10. This complex quality of a sound wave is known as **timbre** (pronounced *TAM-b'r*). Timbre is the property that enables you to recognize a friend's voice on the phone or distinguish between the same song sung by different artists.

Hearing Loss   Aging commonly involves loss of hearing acuity, especially for high-frequency sounds so crucial for understanding speech. If you think about the tiny difference between the sounds *b* and *p*, you can see why speech perception depends so heavily on high frequency sounds. But hearing loss is not just the result of aging. It can come from diseases, such as mumps, that may attack the auditory nerves. And it can result from exposure to loud noises (Figure 7.9), such as gunshots, jet engines, or loud music, that damage the hair cells in the cochlea.

How Are Auditory and Visual Sensations Alike?   Earlier we discussed how visual information is carried to the brain by the optic nerve in the form of neural impulses. Now, we find that, in a similar fashion, auditory information is also conveyed to the brain as neural signals—but by a different pathway. Please note the similarity in the ways vision and hearing make use of frequency and amplitude information found in light and sound waves.

But, why do we "see" visual information and "hear" auditory information? As our Core Concept suggested, the answer lies in the region of the cortex receiving the neural message—not on some unique quality of the message itself. In brief, different regions of the brain, when activated, produce different sensations.

How the Other Senses Are Like Vision and Hearing

Of all our senses, vision and hearing have been studied the most. However, our survival and well-being depend on other senses, too. So, to conclude this discussion of sensation, we will briefly review the processes involved in our sense of body position and movement, smell, taste, the skin senses, and pain. (See Table 7.4.) You will note that each gives us information about a different aspect of our internal or external environment. Yet each operates on similar principles. Each transduces physical stimuli into neural activity, and each is more sensitive to change than to constant stimulation. And, as was the case with vision and hearing, each of these senses is distinguished by the type of information it extracts and by the specialized regions of the brain devoted to it. Finally, the senses often act in concert, as when we see a lightning strike and hear the ensuing clap of thunder or when the sensation we call "taste" really encompasses a combination of flavor, odor, sight, and texture of food. Other common sensory combinations occur in sizzling steaks, fizzing colas, and bowls of Rice Krispies®.

Position and Movement To act purposefully and gracefully, we need constant information about the position of our limbs and other body parts in relation to each other and to objects in the environment. Without this information, even our simplest actions would be hopelessly uncoordinated. (You have probably had just this experience when you tried to walk on a leg that had "gone to sleep.") The physical mechanisms that keep track of body position, movement, and balance actually consist of two different systems, the *vestibular sense* and the *kinesthetic sense.*

The **vestibular sense** is the body position sense that orients us with respect to gravity. It tells us the posture of our bodies—whether straight, leaning, reclining, or upside down. The vestibular sense also tells us when we are moving or how our motion is changing. The receptors for this information are tiny hairs (much like those we found in the basilar membrane) in the *semicircular canals* of the inner ear (refer to Figure 7.8). These hairs respond to our movements by detecting corresponding movements in the fluid of the semicircular canals. Disorders of this sense can cause extreme dizziness and disorientation.

The **kinesthetic sense,** the other sense of body position and movement, keeps track of body parts relative to each other. Your kinesthetic sense makes you aware of crossing your legs, for example, and tells you which hand is closer to the telephone when it rings. Kinesthesis provides constant sensory feedback about what the muscles in your body are doing during motor activities, such as whether to continue reaching for your cup of coffee or to stop before you knock it over (Turvey, 1996).

Receptors for kinesthesis reside in the joints, muscles, and tendons. These receptors, as well as those for the vestibular sense, connect to processing regions in the brain's parietal lobes—which help us make a sensory "map" of the spatial relationship among objects and events. This processing usually happens automatically and effortlessly, outside of conscious awareness, except when we are deliberately learning the movements for a new physical skill, such as swinging a golf club or playing a musical instrument.

Smell The sense of smell, or **olfaction,** involves a chain of biochemical events. First, odors (in the form of airborne chemical molecules) interact with receptor

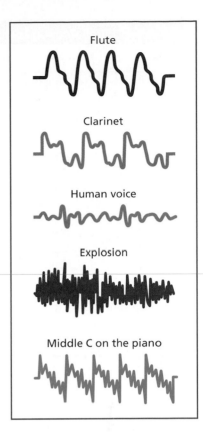

Flute

Clarinet

Human voice

Explosion

Middle C on the piano

FIGURE 7.10
Waveforms of Familiar Sounds

Each sound is a distinctive combination of several pure tones.

(*Source:* From THE SCIENCE OF MUSICAL SOUNDS, by D. C. Miller. Reprinted by permission of Case Western Reserve University.)

Vestibular sense   The sense of body orientation with respect to gravity. The vestibular sense is closely associated with the inner ear and, in fact, is carried to the brain on a branch of the auditory nerve.

Kinesthetic sense   The sense of body position and movement of body parts relative to each other (also called *kinesthesis*).

Olfaction   The sense of smell.

TABLE 7.4 Fundamental Features of the Human Senses

Sense	Stimulus	Sense Organ	Receptor	Sensation
Vision	Light waves	Eye	Rods and cones of retina	Colors, brightness, patterns, motion, textures
Hearing	Sound waves	Ear	Hair cells of the basilar membrane	Pitch, loudness, timbre
Skin senses	External contact	Skin	Nerve endings in skin	Touch, warmth, cold
Smell	Volatile substances	Nose	Hair cells of olfactory epithelium	Odors
Taste	Soluble substances	Tongue	Taste buds of tongue	Flavors
Pain	Many intense or extreme stimuli: temperature, chemicals, mechanical stimuli, etc.	Net of pain fibers all over the body	Specialized pain receptors, overactive or abnormal neurons	Acute pain, chronic pain
Kinesthetic and vestibular senses	Body position, movement, and balance	Semicircular canals, skeletal muscles, joints, tendons	Hair cells in semicircular canals; neurons connected to skeletal muscles, joints, and tendons	Position of body parts in space

proteins associated with specialized cells in the nose (Axel, 1995; Turin, 2006). While the exact mechanism is in dispute, we do know that the stimulated nerve cells convey information about the stimulus to the brain's *olfactory bulbs*, where sensations of smell are realized (Mori et al., 1999). These olfactory bulbs can be found on the underside of the brain just below the frontal lobes. (See Figure 7.11.) Unlike all the other senses, smell signals are not relayed through the thalamus, suggesting that smell evolved earlier than the other senses.

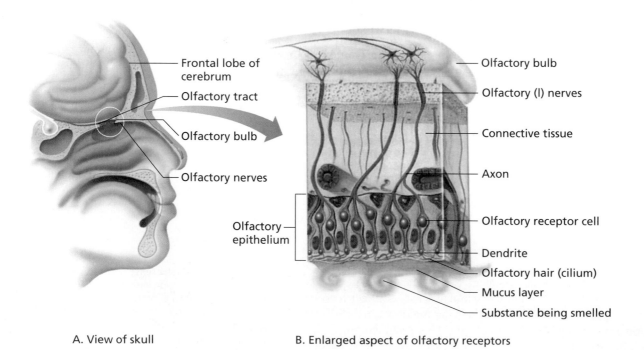

A. View of skull   B. Enlarged aspect of olfactory receptors

FIGURE 7.11
Receptors for Smell

(*Source:* From P. G. Zimbardo and R. J. Gerrig. Copyright, *Psychology and Life,* 15th ed. Published by Allyn and Bacon, Boston, MA © 1999 by Pearson Education. Reprinted by permission of the publisher.)

In humans, olfaction has an intimate connection with memory: Certain smells, such as a favorite perfume, readily evoke emotion-laden memories (Dingfelder, 2004a). Originally, however, smell was probably a system in primitive organisms for detecting and locating food; but even today, smell remains a major factor in survival because it helps us detect and avoid potential sources of danger, such as decaying food.

Many animals exploit the sense of smell for communication. For example, insects such as ants and termites and vertebrates such as dogs and cats communicate with each other by secreting and detecting odorous signals called **pheromones**—especially to signal sexual receptivity, danger, territorial boundaries, and food sources. We humans seem to use the sense of smell primarily in conjunction with taste to seek and sample food, but we may also use pheromones that help us identify family members and potential sex partners by smell (Benson, 2002).

Taste Like smell, taste is a sense based on chemistry. But the similarity doesn't end there: The senses of taste and smell have a cooperative working relationship. Many of the subtle distinctions you may think of as flavors really come from odors. (Much of the "taste" of an onion is odor, not flavor.) You will also notice this when you have a cold, which makes food seem tasteless because your nasal passages are blocked and you can't smell the food.

Isolated in the laboratory, the sense of taste, or **gustation**, has long been known to have four main qualities: sweet, sour, bitter, and salty. Recently, however, researchers have identified a fifth taste quality called *umami* (Chaudhari et al., 2000). Umami is the flavor associated with monosodium glutamate (MSG), often used in Asian cuisine. It also occurs naturally in protein-rich foods, such as meat, seafood, and cheese.

The taste receptor cells, located in the *taste buds* on the top and side of the tongue, easily sample flavors as food and drink pass by on the way to the stomach. These receptors cluster in small mucous-membrane projections called *papillae*, shown in Figure 7.12. Each is especially sensitive to molecules of a particular shape.

Individuals vary in their sensitivity to taste sensations, a function of the density of these papillae on the tongue (Bartoshuk et al., 1994). Those with more taste buds for bitter flavors are "supertasters," who are more sensitive than regular tasters or extreme "nontasters," which accounts for supertasters' distaste for certain foods, such as broccoli or "diet" drinks (Duenwald, 2005). Is there any advantage to being a supertaster? Taste expert Linda Bartoshuk (1993) speculates that, because most poisons are bitter, supertasters have a survival advantage.

Such differences also speak to the problem with which we began the chapter—in particular, the question of whether different people sense the world in the same way. Bartoshuk's research suggests that, to the extent that the sense receptors exhibit some variation from one person to another, so does our sensory experience of the world. We should be clear, however, that nothing in her work suggests any individual variations so bizarre that would make one person's sensation of sweet the same as another person's sensation of sour. The variations observed involve simply the presence or absence of a sensation, such as the bitter detected by "supertasters."

Moving on from the receptors toward the brain, a specialized nerve "hotline" carries nothing but taste messages to specialized regions of cortex. There tastes are realized in the parietal lobe's somatosensory area. Conveniently, this region lies next to the patch of cortex that receives touch stimulation from the face (Gadsby, 2000).

Infants have heightened taste sensitivity, which is why you have probably never met a baby who wouldn't cringe at the bitter taste of lemon. This supersensitivity, however, decreases with age. As a result, many elderly people complain

Gymnasts and dancers rely on their vestibular and kinesthetic senses to give them information about the position and movement of their bodies.

Pheromones Chemical signals released by organisms to communicate with other members of their species. Pheromones are often used by animals as sexual attractants. It is unclear whether or not humans employ pheromones.

Gustation The sense of taste, from the same word root as "gusto"; also called the *gustatory sense*.

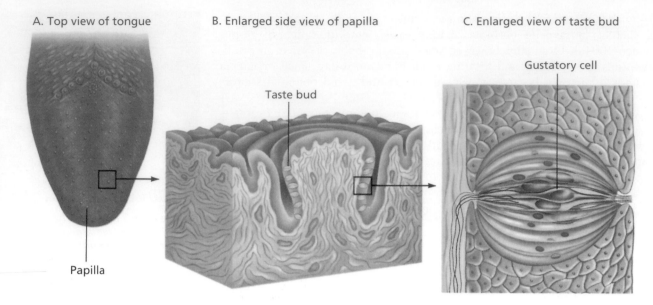

A. Top view of tongue   B. Enlarged side view of papilla   C. Enlarged view of taste bud

Gustatory cell

Taste bud

Papilla

FIGURE 7.12
Receptors for Taste

(A) Distribution of the papillae on the upper side of the tongue; (B) an enlarged view with individual papillae and taste buds visible; (C) one of the taste buds enlarged.

that food has lost its taste—which really means that they have lost much of their sensory ability to detect differences in the taste and smell of food. Compounding this effect, taste receptors can be easily damaged by alcohol, smoke, acids, or hot foods. Fortunately, we frequently replace our gustatory receptors—as we do our smell receptors. Because of this constant renewal, the taste system boasts the most resistance to permanent damage of all our senses, and a total loss of taste is extremely rare (Bartoshuk, 1990).

The Skin Senses Consider the skin's remarkable versatility: It protects us against surface injury, holds in body fluids, and helps regulate body temperature. The skin also contains nerve endings that, when stimulated, produce sensations of touch, pain warmth, and cold. Like several other senses, these **skin senses** are connected to the somatosensory cortex located in the brain's parietal lobes.

The skin's sensitivity to stimulation varies tremendously over the body, depending in part on the number of receptors in each area. For example, we are ten times more accurate in sensing stimulation on our fingertips than stimulation on our backs. In general, our sensitivity is greatest where we need it most—on our faces, tongues, and hands. Precise sensory feedback from these parts of the body permits effective eating, speaking, and grasping.

One important aspect of skin sensitivity—touch—plays a central role in human relationships. Through touch we communicate our desire to give or receive comfort, support, love, and passion (Fisher, 1992; Harlow, 1965). Touch also serves as a primary stimulus for sexual arousal in humans. And it is essential for healthy mental and physical development; the lack of touch stimulation can stunt mental and motor development (Anand & Scalzo, 2000).

Skin senses Sensory systems for processing touch, warmth, cold, texture, and pain.

Synesthesia The mixing of sensations across sensory modalities, as in tasting shapes or seeing colors associated with numbers.

Synesthesia: Sensations across the Senses

A small minority of otherwise "normal" people have a condition called **synesthesia**, which allows them to sense their worlds across sensory domains. Some actually taste shapes—so that pears may taste "round" and grapefruit "pointy" (Cytowic, 1993). Others associate days of the week with colors—so

Most people will not have any trouble seeing the 5 while staring at the cross (left), although the 5 becomes indistinct when surrounded by other numbers (right). If you are a synesthete who associates colors with numbers, however, you may be able to identify the 5 in the figure on the right because it appears as a blotch of the color associated with that number. (Adapted from Ramachandran & Hubbard, 2003.)

+	5

+	3 353 3

that Wednesday may be green and Thursday may be red. Their defining characteristic involves sensory experience that links one sense with another.

By means of some clever experiments, V. S. Ramachandran and his colleagues have shown that these cross-sensory sensations are real, not just metaphors (Ramachandran & Hubbard, 2001). You can take one of their tests in the accompanying Do It Yourself! box. Research shows that this ability runs in families, so it probably has a genetic component.

What causes synesthesia? Apparently it can involve communication between brain areas that lie close to each other but process different sensations. Brain imaging studies implicate an area of cortex called the TPO, lying at the junction of the *t*emporal, *p*arietal, and *o*ccipital lobes (Ramachandran & Hubbard, 2003). This region simultaneously processes information coming from many pathways. We all have some neural connections among these areas, theorizes Ramachandran, but synesthetes seem to have more than most.

The condition occurs slightly more often in highly creative people, Ramachandran notes. And it may account for the "auras" purportedly seen around people by some mystics (Holden, 2004). But perhaps we all have some cross-sensory abilities in us, which may be why we resonate with Shakespeare's famous metaphor in *Romeo and Juliet*, "It is the east, and Juliet is the sun." We know that he was not speaking literally, of course. Rather we understand that, for Romeo—and so for us—Juliet is linked, across our senses, with light, warmth, and sensory pleasure (Ramachandran & Hirstein, 1999).

PSYCHOLOGYMATTERS
The Experience of Pain

If you have severe pain, nothing else matters. A wound or a toothache can dominate all other sensations. And if you are among the one-third of Americans who suffer from persistent or recurring pain, the experience can be debilitating and can sometimes even lead to suicide. Yet pain is also part of your body's adaptive mechanism that makes you respond to conditions that threaten damage to your body.

Unlike other sensations, pain can arise from intense stimulation of various kinds, such as a very loud sound, heavy pressure, a pinprick, or an extremely bright light. But pain is not merely the result of stimulation. It is also affected by our moods and expectations, as you know if you were ever anxious about going to the dentist (Koyama et al., 2005).

One intriguing puzzle about pain concerns the mysterious sensations often experienced by people who have lost an arm, leg—a condition known as a *phantom limb*. In such cases, the amputee feels sensations—sometimes quite painful ones—that seem to come from the missing body part (Ramachandran &

Blakeslee, 1998). Neurological studies show that the phantom sensations do not originate in damaged nerves in the sensory pathways. Nor are they purely imaginary. Rather, the sensations arise in the brain itself—perhaps the result of the brain generating sensation when none comes from the missing limb. The odd phenomenon of phantom limbs teaches us that understanding pain requires understanding not only painful sensations but mechanisms in the brain that both process and inhibit pain.

The Gate-Control Theory No one has yet developed a theory that explains everything about pain, but Melzack and Wall's **gate-control theory** (1965, 1983) explains a lot. In particular it explains why pain can sometimes be blocked by analgesic drugs; competing stimuli, as in acupuncture; and even by the mere expectation of treatment effects. Their proposal asserts that pain depends on the relative amount of traffic in two different sensory pathways that carry information from the sense organs to the brain.

One route, consisting of neurons with a fatty myelin covering on their axons, handles messages quickly; these *fast fibers* deliver most sensory information to the brain. The smaller *slow fibers,* without the fatty sheaths on their axons, send messages more slowly. Very intense stimuli, such as that caused by tissue injury, send strong signals along the slow fibers.

Melzack and Wall hypothesize that competing messages from the fast fibers can block pain messages in the slow fibers. That is, the fast fibers can close a sort of "spinal gate," preventing the slow fibers' messages from reaching the brain. Consequently, the level of pain you experience from a wound results from the combination of information coming through these two pathways. When you hit your finger with a hammer, you automatically try to close the "gate" by vigorously shaking your hand to generate fast-fiber signals that block the pain.

The "gate," itself, probably operates in a brain stem region called the *periaqueductal gray (PAG).* The exact mechanism is unclear, but we do know that pain-blocking opiates and certain opiate-like chemicals called *endorphins,* produced by the brain, act on the PAG. There they cause inhibitory neurons to nullify pain messages ascending in the spinal cord (Basbaum & Fields, 1984; Pinel, 2005). Ultimately, pain signals that pass through the gate are routed to the anterior cingulate cortex, located along the fissure separating the frontal lobes, where we believe pain to be sensed (Craig & Reiman, 1996; Vogel, 1996).

The spinal gate can be opened and closed by top-down psychological factors, as well. As noted above, we have long known that people's interpretations of events affect whether or not stimuli are perceived as painful (Turk, 1994). For example, soldiers and athletes often suffer severe injuries that cause little pain until the excitement of the battle or contest is over. As we will see in a moment, this mind–body effect on pain is also evident in the action of *placebos* or other sham treatments.

Dealing with Pain Wouldn't it be nice to banish the experience of pain altogether? In reality, such a condition can be deadly. People with congenital insensitivity to pain do not feel what is hurting them, and their bodies often become scarred and their limbs deformed from injuries they could have avoided if their brains were able to warn them of danger. Because of their failure to notice and respond to tissue-damaging stimuli, these people tend to die young (Manfredi et al., 1981).

In general, pain serves as an essential defense signal: It warns us of potential harm, and it helps us to survive in hostile environments and to get treatment for sickness and injury. Sometimes, however, chronic pain seems to be a disease in itself, with neurons in the pain pathways becoming hypersensitive, amplifying normal sensory stimulation into pain messages (Watkins & Maier, 2003). Research also suggests that chronic pain may, at least sometimes, arise from genes that get "turned on" in nerve-damaged tissue (Marx, 2004).

What can you do if you are in pain? Analgesic drugs, ranging from over-the-counter remedies such as aspirin and ibuprofen to prescription narcotics such as

CONNECTION • CHAPTER 8

Our brains are sensitive to opium, heroin, and morphine precisely because these drugs mimic the actions of *endorphins,* the brain's natural opiates.

Gate-control theory An explanation for pain control that proposes we have a neural "gate" that can, under some circumstances, block incoming pain signals.

morphine, are widely used and effective. These act in a variety of ways. Morphine, for example, suppresses pain messages in the spinal cord and the brain, while aspirin interferes with a chemical signal produced by damaged tissue (Basbaum & Julius, 2006; Carlson, 2007). Those using such drugs—especially the narcotics—should be aware of unwanted side effects, such as digestive tract or liver damage and even addiction. But studies have shown that if you must use narcotics to control severe pain, the possibility of your becoming addicted is far less than it would be if you were using narcotics recreationally (Melzack, 1990).

Many people can also learn to control pain by psychological techniques, such as hypnosis, relaxation, and thought-distraction procedures (Brown, 1998). For instance, a child receiving a shot at the doctor's office might be asked to take a series of deep breaths and look away. You also may be among those for whom pain can also be modified by *placebos,* mock drugs made to appear as real drugs. For example, a placebo may be an injection of mild saline solution (salt water) or a pill made of sugar. Such fake drugs are routinely given to a control group in tests of new pain drugs. Their effectiveness, of course, involves the people's *belief* that they are getting real medicine (Wager, 2005; Wager et al., 2004). It is important to note, however, that the brain's response to a placebo seems to be much the same as that of pain-relieving drugs. Because this **placebo effect** is common, any drug deemed effective must prove itself stronger than a placebo.

How do placebos produce their effects? Apparently the expectation of pain relief is enough to cause the brain to release painkilling endorphins. We believe this is so because brain scans show that essentially the same pain-suppression areas "light up" when patients take placebos or analgesic drugs (Petrovic et al., 2002). Further, we find that individuals who respond to placebos report that their pain increases when they take the endorphin-blocking drug *naltrexone* (Fields, 1978; Fields & Levine, 1984). It is likely that endorphins are also responsible for the pain-relieving effects of acupuncture (Price et al., 1984; Watkins & Mayer, 1982).

Surprisingly, the placebo effect doesn't necessarily require a placebo! In a controlled experiment, Dr. Fabrizio Benedetti and his colleagues (2005) showed that the physician's bedside manner, even without a painkilling drug, can suppress pain. For psychologists, this is an important discovery, demonstrating that the psychosocial context itself can have a therapeutic effect (Guterman, 2005).

Pain Tolerance The threshold of pain varies enormously from person to person. Some people always demand Novocain from their dentist, while others may prefer dental work without the added hassle of an injection. And in the laboratory, one study found that electric shocks had to be eight times more powerful to produce painful sensations in their least-sensitive subjects as compared with their most-sensitive subjects (Rollman & Harris, 1987). Another experiment found that brain scans of people who are highly sensitive to pain show greater activation of the thalamus and the anterior cingulate cortex than in scans of those with greater pain tolerance (Coghill et al., 2003). At least part of this variation has a genetic basis (Couzin, 2006).

We should be clear on this point: There is no evidence of genetic differences in sensitivity to pain among different ethnic or racial groups, although many reports suggest that culture affects how people interpret pain and respond to painful stimulation. For example, Western women often report that childbirth is an excruciatingly painful experience, while women in some cultures routinely give birth with little indication of distress. Severely wounded soldiers, too, typically need less pain medication than do civilians with comparable injuries—perhaps because of the "culture of bravery" instilled in soldiers or because a soldier knows that a wound represents a ticket out of the combat zone.

Readers should be cautioned, however, that much of the literature on cultural differences in response to pain relies far more on anecdotes than on solid science. Further, the scientific studies that do exist in this area have frequently come

Placebo effect A response to a placebo (a fake drug), caused by the belief that they are real drugs.

to conflicting conclusions (Foster, 2006). Perhaps one of the most important influences on response to pain from medical conditions has to do with socio-economic status and access to health care: Poor people are much less likely to seek medical attention until pain becomes severe.

CheckYourUnderstanding

1. **RECALL:** Name the two types of photoreceptors and indicate what sort of stimulation they detect.

2. **RECALL:** The *wavelength* of light causes sensations of _____, while the *intensity* of light causes sensations of _____.
   a. motion/shape
   b. color/brightness
   c. primary colors/secondary colors
   d. depth/color

3. **RECALL:** The *frequency theory* best explains how we hear _____ sounds, while the *place theory* best explains how we hear _____ sounds.

4. **SYNTHESIS:** What do all of the following senses have in common: vision, hearing, taste, smell, hearing, pain, equilibrium, and body position?

5. **RECALL:** Studies of painful phantom limbs show that the phantom pain originates in _____
   a. the brain.
   b. nerve cells damaged from the amputation.
   c. the imagination.
   d. ascending pathways in the spinal cord.

6. **UNDERSTANDING THE CORE CONCEPT:** Explain why different senses give us different sensations.

7.3 KEY QUESTION
WHAT IS THE RELATIONSHIP BETWEEN SENSATION AND PERCEPTION?

We have described how sensory signals have been transduced and transmitted to specific regions of your brain for further processing as visual images, pain, odors, and other sensations. Then what? You enlist your brain's perceptual machinery to attach *meaning* to the incoming sensory information. Does a bitter taste mean poison? Does a red flag mean danger? Does a smile signify a friendly overture? The Core Concept of this section emphasizes this perceptual elaboration of sensory information:

core concept | Perception brings *meaning* to sensation, so perception produces an interpretation of the world, not a perfect representation of it.

In brief, we might say that the task of perception is to organize sensation into stable, meaningful *percepts.* A **percept,** then, is what we perceive: It is not just a sensation but the associated meaning, as well. Not a simple task, perception must identify features of the world that are invariant (fixed and unchanging) by sorting through a continual flood of information. For example, as you move about the room, the sights in the environment create a rapidly changing, blurred sequence of images—yet you remain sure that it is you who are moving, while the objects around you remain stationary. As we describe this complex process, we will first consider how our perceptual apparatus usually manages to give us an accurate image of the world. Then we will look at some illusions and other instances in which perception apparently fails. Finally, we will examine two theories that attempt to capture the most fundamental principles at work behind the scenes in our perceptual processes.

Percept The meaningful product of perception—often an image that has been associated with concepts, memories of events, emotions, and motives.

Perceptual Processing: Finding Meaning in Sensation

How does the sensory image of a person (such as the individual pictured in Figure 7.13) become the meaningful percept of someone you recognize? That is, how does mere sensation become an elaborate perception? In the following paragraphs, we will explore some of the physical and mental processes involved in forming perceptions. Let's begin with *feature detectors*—brain cells that operate on the front lines of perceptual processing.

Feature Detectors   To help us make perceptual judgments, our brains have specialized groups of cells dedicated to the detection of specific stimulus features, such as length, slant, color, and boundary (Kandel & Squire, 2000). There is even a part of the occipital lobe containing cells that are especially sensitive to features of the human face (Carpenter, 1999). We know this from animal experiments and from cases like Jonathan, in which brain injury or disease selectively robs an individual of the ability to detect certain features, such as colors or shapes. Perceptual psychologists call such highly specialized processing cells **feature detectors.**

Despite our extensive knowledge of feature detectors, we still don't know exactly how the brain manages to combine (or "bind") the multiple features it detects into a single percept of, say, a face. Psychologists call this puzzle the **binding problem,** and it may be the deepest mystery of perceptual psychology (Kandel & Squire, 2000). Yet, a few pieces of this perceptual puzzle may already be in hand: In order to assemble (bind) these pieces into a meaningful percept, the brain apparently synchronizes the firing patterns in different groups of neurons that have each detected different features of the same object—much as an orchestra conductor determines the tempo at which all members of the ensemble will play a musical piece (Buzsáki, 2006).

Bottom-Up and Top-Down Processing   Perception involves two complementary processes that psychologists call *top-down processing* and *bottom-up processing,* both of which may occur simultaneously. In **top-down processing,** the perceiver's goals, past experience, knowledge, expectations, memory, motivations, or cultural background heavily influence the interpretation of an object or event (see Nelson, 1993). For example, searching for the Waldo image in the popular children's books demands top-down processing. So does trying to find your car keys in a cluttered room. Any time you rely primarily on an idea or image in your mind to interpret a stimulus, you are using top-down processing. One more example may clarify what we mean: If you go grocery shopping when you are hungry, top-down processing will probably make you notice ready-to-eat snack foods much more readily than you would have if your brain were not sending top-down hunger signals.

In **bottom-up processing,** the characteristics of the stimulus (rather than a concept in our minds) strongly influence our perceptions. Bottom-up processing relies heavily on stimulus characteristics and the brain's feature detectors: Is it moving? What color is it? Is it loud, sweet, painful, pleasant smelling, wet, hot . . . ? You are doing bottom-up processing when you notice a moving fish in an aquarium or a hot pepper in a stir-fry.

Thus, bottom-up processing involves sending sensory data into the system through receptors and sending it "upward" to the cortex, where a basic analysis, involving the feature detectors, is first performed to determine the characteristics of the stimulus. Psychologists also refer to this as *stimulus-driven processing* because the resulting percept is determined, or "driven," by stimulus features. By contrast, top-down processing flows in the opposite direction, with the percept being driven by some concept in the cortex—at the "top" of the brain. Because this sort of thinking relies heavily on concepts in the perceiver's own mind, it is also known as *conceptually driven processing.*

Perceptual Constancies   We can illustrate another aspect of perception with yet another example of top-down processing. Suppose that you are looking at a door,

FIGURE 7.13
Who Is This?

Perceptual processes help us recognize people and objects by matching the stimulus to images in memory.

Feature detectors   Cells in the cortex that specialize in extracting certain features of a stimulus.

Binding problem   Refers to the process used by the brain to combine (or "bind") the results of many sensory operations into a single percept. This occurs, for example, when sensations of color, shape, boundary, and texture are combined to produce the percept of a person's face. No one knows exactly how the brain does this. Thus, the binding problem is one of the major unsolved mysteries in psychology.

Top-down processing   Perceptual analysis that emphasizes the perceiver's expectations, concept memories, and other cognitive factors, rather than being driven by the characteristics of the stimulus. "Top" refers to a mental set in the brain—which stands at the "top" of the perceptual processing system.

Bottom-up processing   Perceptual analysis that emphasizes characteristics of the stimulus, rather than our concepts and expectations. "Bottom" refers to the stimulus, which occurs at step one of perceptual processing.

(A)

(B)

FIGURE 7.14
A Door by Any Other Shape Is Still a Door

(A) A door seen from an angle presents the eye with a distorted rectangle image. (B) The brain perceives the door as rectangular.

Perceptual constancy   The ability to recognize the same object as remaining "constant" under different conditions, such as changes in illumination, distance, or location.

Change blindness   A perceptual failure to notice changes occurring in one's visual field.

Illusion   You have experienced an illusion when you have a demonstrably incorrect perception of a stimulus pattern, especially one that also fools others who are observing the same stimulus. (If no one else sees it the way you do, you could be having a *hallucination.* We'll take that term up in a later chapter on mental disorder.)

such as the one pictured in Figure 7.14A. You "know" that the door is rectangular, even though your sensory image of it is distorted when you are not looking at it straight-on. Your brain automatically corrects the sensory distortion, so that you perceive the door as being rectangular, as in Figure 7.14B.

This ability to see an object as being the same shape from different angles or distances is just one example of a **perceptual constancy.** In fact, there are many kinds of perceptual constancies. These include *color constancy,* which allows us to see a flower as being the same color in the reddish light of sunset as in the white glare of midday. *Size constancy* allows us to perceive a person as the same size at different distances and also serves as a strong cue for depth perception. *Shape constancy* is responsible for our ability to see the door in Figure 7.14 as remaining rectangular from different angles. Together these constancies help us identify and track objects in a changing world.

Change Blindness   Sometimes we don't notice things that occur right in front of our noses—particularly if they are unexpected and we haven't focused our attention on them. While driving you may not notice a car unexpectedly shifting lanes. Or you may not notice when a friend changes hair color or shaves a mustache. Psychologists call this **change blindness** (Beck et al., 2004; Greer, 2004a).

We *do* notice changes that we anticipate, such as a red light turning to green. But laboratory studies show that many people don't notice when, in a series of photographs of the same scene, a red light is replaced by a stop sign. One way this may cause trouble in the world outside the laboratory is that people underestimate the extent to which they can be affected by change blindness. This probably occurs because our perceptual systems and our attention have limits on the amount of information they can process, so our expectations coming from the "top down" cause us to overlook the unexpected.

Perceptual Ambiguity and Distortion

A primary goal of perception is to get an accurate "fix" on the world—to recognize friends, foes, opportunities, and dangers. Survival sometimes depends on accurately perceiving the environment, but the environment is not always easy to "read." We can illustrate this difficulty with the photo of black and white splotches in Figure 7.15. What is it? When you eventually extract the stimulus figure from the background, you will see it as a Dalmatian dog walking toward the upper left with its head down. The dog is hard to find because it blends so easily with the background. The same problem occurs when you try to single out a voice against the background of a noisy party.

But it is not just the inability to find an image that causes perceptual problems. Sometimes our perceptions can be wildly inaccurate because we misinterpret an image—as happens with sensory and perceptual *illusions.*

What Illusions Tell Us about Sensation and Perception   When your mind deceives you by interpreting a stimulus pattern incorrectly, you are experiencing an **illusion.** Typically, illusions become more likely when the stimulus is unclear, when information is missing, when elements are combined in unusual ways, or when

FIGURE 7.15
An Ambiguous Picture

What is depicted here? The difficulty in seeing the figure lies in its similarity to the background.

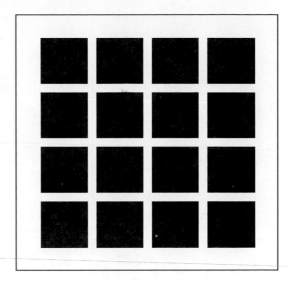

FIGURE 7.16
The Hermann Grid

Why do faint gray dots appear at the intersections of the grid? The illusion, which operates at the sensory level, is explained in the text.

(*Source:* "The Hermann Grid," from *Fundamentals of Sensation & Perception* by M. W. Levine & J. Shefner. Reprinted by permission of Michael W. Levine.)

familiar patterns are not apparent. Such illusions can help us understand some fundamental properties of sensation and perception—particularly the discrepancy between our percepts and external reality (Cohen & Girgus, 1973).

Let's first examine a remarkable illusion that works at the level of sensation: the black-and-white Hermann grid (Figure 7.16). As you stare at the center of the grid, note how dark, fuzzy spots appear at the intersections of the white bars. But when you focus on an intersection, the spot vanishes. Why? The answer lies in the way receptor cells in your visual pathways interact with each other. The firing of certain cells that are sensitive to light–dark boundaries inhibits the activity of adjacent cells that would otherwise detect the white grid lines. This inhibiting process makes you sense darker regions—the grayish areas—at the white intersections just outside your focus. Even though you know the squares in the Hermann grid are black and the lines are white, this knowledge cannot overcome the illusion, which operates at a more basic, sensory level.

To study illusions at the level of perception, psychologists often employ **ambiguous figures**—stimulus patterns that can be interpreted (top-down) in two or more distinct ways, as in Figures 7.17A and B. There you see that both the vase/faces figure and the Necker cube are designed to confound your interpretations, not just your sensations. Each suggests two conflicting meanings: Once you have seen both, your perception will cycle back and forth between them as you look at the figure. Studies suggest that these alternating interpretations may involve the shifting of perceptual control between the left and right hemispheres of the brain (Gibbs, 2001).

Another dramatic illusion, recently discovered, appears in Figure 7.18. Although it is hard to believe, the squares marked A and B are the same shade of gray. Proof appears in the right-hand image, where the vertical bars are also the same gray shade. Why are we fooled by this illusion? Perceptual psychologists respond that the effect derives from color and brightness constancy: our ability to see an object as essentially unchanged under different lighting conditions, from the bright noon sun to near darkness. Under normal conditions, this prevents us from being misled by shadows.

Figure 7.19 shows several other illusions thought to operate primarily at the level of perception. All are compelling, and all are controversial—particularly the

Ambiguous figures Images that are capable of more than one interpretation. There is no "right" way to see an ambiguous figure.

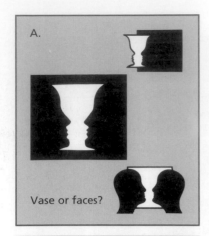

A.

Vase or faces?

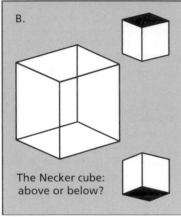

B.

The Necker cube:
above or below?

FIGURE 7.17
Perceptual Illusions

These ambiguous figures are illusions
of perceptual interpretation.

Edward H. Adelson

FIGURE 7.18
The Checkerboard Illusion

Appearances are deceiving: Squares A and B are actually the same shade of gray, as you can see on
the right by comparing the squares with the vertical bars. The text explains why this occurs.
(*Source:* © 1995, Edward H. Adelson)

Müller–Lyer illusion, which has intrigued psychologists for more than 100 years.
Disregarding the arrowheads, which of the two horizontal lines in this figure
appears longer? If you measure them, you will see that the horizontal lines are
exactly the same length. What is the explanation? Answers to that question have
been offered in well over a thousand published studies, and psychologists still
don't know for sure.

One popular theory, combining both top-down and bottom-up factors, has
gathered some support. It suggests that we unconsciously interpret the
Müller–Lyer figures as three-dimensional objects. So, instead of arrowheads, we
see the ends as angles that project toward or away from us like the inside and
outside corners of a building or a room, as in Figure 7.20. The inside corner
seems to recede in the distance, while the outside corner appears to extend
toward us. Therefore, we judge the outside corner to be closer—and shorter.
Why? When two objects make the same size image on the retina and we judge
one to be farther away than the other, then we assume that the more distant one
is larger.

Illusions in the Context of Culture But what if you had grown up in a culture
with no square-cornered buildings? Would you still see one line as longer than the
other in the Müller–Lyer? In other words, do you have to *learn* to see the illusion,
or is it "hard wired" into your brain? One way to answer such questions is through
cross-cultural research. With this in mind, Richard Gregory (1977) went to South
Africa to study a group of Zulus who live in what he called a "circular culture."
Aesthetically, these people prefer curves to lines and square corners: Their round
huts have round doors and windows; they till their fields along curved lines, using
curved plows; the children's toys lack straight lines. And, when confronted with
the Müller–Lyer, the Zulus saw the lines as nearly the same length. This suggests
that the Müller–Lyer illusion is learned. A number of other studies support the conclusion that people who live in "carpentered" environments—where buildings are
built with straight sides and 90-degree angles—are more susceptible to the illusion than those who (like the Zulus) live in "noncarpentered" worlds (Segall et
al., 1999).

Applying the Lessons of Illusions Several prominent modern artists, fascinated
with the visual experiences created by ambiguity, have used perceptual illusion as
a central artistic feature of their work. Consider the two examples of art shown
here. *Gestalt Bleue* by Victor Vasarely (Figure 7.21) produces depth reversals like
those in the Necker cube, with corners that alternately project and recede. In *Sky*

Is the hat taller than the brim is wide?

Top hat illusion

Is the diagonal line straight or broken?

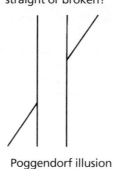

Poggendorf illusion

Turning the tables: Could the table tops be the same size?

Which central circle is bigger?

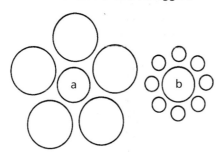

Ebbinghaus illusion

Which horizontal line is longer?

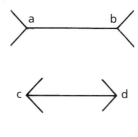

Müller–Lyer illusion

Are the vertical lines parallel?

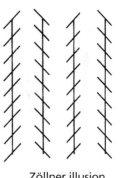

Zöllner illusion

FIGURE 7.19
Six Illusions to Tease Your Brain

Each of these illusions involves a bad "bet" made by your brain. What explanations can you give for the distortion of reality that each of these illusions produces? Are they caused by nature or nurture? The table illusion was originally developed by Roger N. Shepard and presented in his 1990 book *Mind Sights* (Freeman).

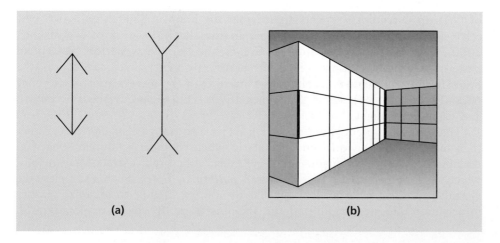

(a)   (b)

FIGURE 7.20
The Müller-Lyer Illusion

One explanation for the Müller–Lyer illusion says that your brain thinks it is seeing the inside and outside corners of a building in perspective.

FIGURE 7.21
Victor Vasarely's *Gestalt Bleue*

FIGURE 7.22
M. C. Escher's *Sky and Water*

◀ **CONNECTION • CHAPTER 2**

The *nature–nurture* issue centers on the relative importance of heredity and environment.

Gestalt psychology From a German word (pronounced *gush-TAWLT*) that means "whole" or "form" or "configuration." (A Gestalt is also a *percept.*) The Gestalt psychologists believed that much of perception is shaped by innate factors built into the brain.

and Water by M. C. Escher (Figure 7.22), you can see birds and fishes only through the process of figure–ground reversal, much like the vase/faces illusion we encountered earlier (in Figure 7.17). The effect of these paintings on us underscores the function of human perception to make sense of the world and to fix on the best interpretation we can make.

To interpret such illusions, we draw on our personal experiences, learning, and motivation. Knowing this, those who understand the principles of perception often can control illusions to achieve desired effects far beyond the world of painting. Architects and interior designers, for example, create illusions that make spaces seem larger or smaller than they really are. They may, for example, make a small apartment appear more spacious when it is painted in light colors and sparsely furnished. Similarly, set and lighting designers in movies and theatrical productions purposely create visual illusions on film and on stage. So, too, do many of us make everyday use of illusion in our choices of cosmetics and clothing (Dackman, 1986). For example, light-colored clothing and horizontal stripes can make our bodies seem larger, while dark-colored clothing and vertical stripes can make our bodies seem slimmer. In these ways, we use illusions to distort "reality" and make our lives more pleasant.

Theoretical Explanations for Perception

The fact that perception is an interpretation and the fact that people perceive most illusions in essentially the same ways suggest that fundamental psychological principles must be at work. Psychologists looking for these fundamental principles have formulated theories that explain how perception works. Below we will examine two of the classic explanations, the *Gestalt theory* of perception and *learning-based inference.* Although these two approaches may seem contradictory at first, they really emphasize complementary influences on perception. The Gestalt theory emphasizes how we organize incoming stimulation into meaningful perceptual patterns—because of the way our brains are innately structured. On the other hand, learning-based inference emphasizes learned influences on perception, including the power of expectations, context, and culture. In other words, Gestalt theory emphasizes *nature,* and learning-based inference emphasizes *nurture.* As you will see, we need both perspectives to understand the complexities of perception.

Perceptual Organization: The Gestalt Theory You may have noticed that a series of blinking lights, perhaps on a theater marquee, can create the illusion of motion, where there really is no motion. Similarly, there appears to be a white triangle in the nearby "Do It Yourself!" box—but there really is no white triangle. And, as we have seen, the Necker cube seems to flip back and forth between two alternative perspectives—but, of course, the flipping is all in your mind.

About 100 years ago, such perceptual tricks captured the interest of a group of German psychologists, who argued that the brain is innately wired to perceive not just stimuli but also *patterns* in stimulation (Sharps & Wertheimer, 2000). They called such a pattern a *Gestalt,* the German word for "perceptual pattern" or "configuration." Thus, from the raw material of stimulation, the brain forms a perceptual whole that is more than the mere sum of its sensory parts (Prinzmetal, 1995; Rock & Palmer, 1990). This perspective became known as **Gestalt psychology.**

The Gestaltists pointed out that we perceive a square as a single figure, rather than merely four individual lines. Similarly, when you hear a familiar song, you do not focus on the individual notes. Rather, your brain extracts the melody, which is your perception of the overall *pattern* of notes. Such examples, the Gestalt psychologists argued, show that we always attempt to organize sensory information into meaningful patterns, the most basic of which are already pres-

318   **CHAPTER 7 •** SENSATION AND PERCEPTION

The tendency to perceive a figure as being in front of a ground is strong. It is so strong, in fact, that you can even get this effect when the perceived figure doesn't actually exist! You can demonstrate this with an examination of the accompanying figure. You probably perceive a fir-tree shape against a ground of red circles on a white surface. But, of course, there is no fir-tree figure printed on the page; the figure consists only of three solid red shapes and a black-line base. You perceive the illusory white triangle in front because the wedge-shaped cuts in the red circles seem to be the corners of a solid white triangle. To see an illusory six-pointed star, look at part B. Here, the nonexistent "top" triangle appears to blot out parts of red circles and a black-lined triangle, when in fact none of these is depicted as such complete figures. Again, this demonstrates that we prefer to see the figure as an object that obscures the ground behind it. (That's why we often call the ground a "*back*ground.")

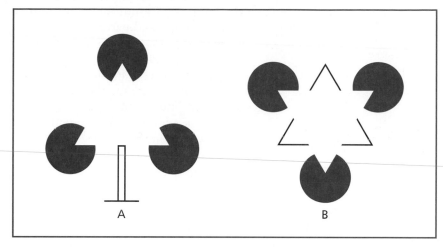

Subjective Contours

(A) A subjective fir tree; (B) a subjective six-pointed star.

ent in our brains at birth. Because this approach has been so influential, we will examine some of the Gestalt discoveries in more detail.

Figure and Ground   One of the most basic of perceptual processes identified by Gestalt psychology divides our perceptual experience into *figure* and *ground*. A **figure** is simply a pattern or image that grabs our attention. As we noted, psychologists sometimes call this a *Gestalt*. Everything else becomes **ground**, the backdrop against which we perceive the figure. A melody becomes a figure heard against a background of complex harmonies, and a spicy chunk of pepperoni becomes the figure against the ground of cheese, sauce, and bread that make up a pizza. Visually, a figure could be a bright flashing sign or a word on the background of a page. And in the ambiguous faces/vase seen in Figure 7.17A, figure and ground reverse when the faces and vase alternately "pop out" as figure.

Closure: Filling in the Blanks   Our minds seem built to abhor a gap, as you saw in the "Do It Yourself!" above. Note especially the illusory white triangle—superimposed on red circles and black lines. Moreover, you will note that you have mentally divided the white area into two regions, the triangle and the background. Where this division occurs you perceive *subjective contours:* boundaries that exist not in the stimulus but only in the subjective experience of your mind.

Your perception of these illusory triangles demonstrates a second powerful organizing process identified by the Gestalt psychologists. **Closure** makes you see incomplete figures as wholes by supplying the missing segments, filling in gaps, and making inferences about potentially hidden objects. So, when you see a face peeking around a corner, your mind automatically fills in the hidden parts of the face and body. In general, humans have a natural tendency to perceive stimuli as complete and balanced even when pieces are missing. (Does this ring a _____ with you?) Closure is also responsible for filling in your "blind spot," as you saw on page 297.

In Weeping Woman, *Picasso challenges our perceptual assumptions by portraying a figure simultaneously from multiple perspectives.*

Figure   The part of a pattern that commands attention. The figure stands out against the ground.

Ground   The part of a pattern that does not command attention; the background.

Closure   The Gestalt principle that identifies the tendency to fill in gaps in figures and to see incomplete figures as complete.

In the foregoing demonstrations we have seen how the perception of subjective contours and closure derives from the brain's ability to create percepts out of incomplete stimulation. Now let us turn to the perceptual laws that explain how we group the stimulus elements that are actually present in Gestalts.

The Gestalt Laws of Perceptual Grouping It's easy to see a school of fish as a single unit—as a Gestalt. But why? And how do we mentally combine hundreds of notes together and perceive them as a single melody? How do we combine the elements of color, shadow, form, texture, and boundary into the percept of a friend's face? And why have thousands of people reported seeing "flying saucers" or the face of Jesus in the scorch marks on a tortilla? That is, how do we pull together in our minds the separate stimulus elements that seem to "belong" together? This is one of the most fundamental problems that the Gestalt psychologists addressed. As we will see, the Gestaltists made great strides in this area, even though the basic processes by which perceptual organization works are still debated today (Palmer, 2002). (This issue is closely related to the *binding problem* that we discussed earlier.)

In the heyday of Gestalt psychology, of course, neuroscience was in its infancy, and there were no MRIs or PET scans. Hence, Gestalt psychologists like Max Wertheimer (1923) had to focus on the problem of perceptual organization in a different way—with arrays of simple figures, such as you see in Figure 7.23. By varying a single factor and observing how it affected the way people perceived the structure of the array, he was able to formulate a set of **laws of perceptual grouping,** which he inferred were built into the neural fabric of the brain.

According to Wertheimer's **law of similarity,** we group things together that have a similar look (or sound, or feel, and so on). So, when you watch a football game, you use the colors of the uniforms to group the players into two teams because of their similarity, even when they are mixed together during a play. Likewise, in Figure 7.23A you see that the Xs and Os form distinct columns, rather than rows, because of similarity. Any such tendency to perceive things as belonging together because they share common features reflects the law of similarity. You can also hear the law of similarity echoed in the old proverb, "Birds of a feather flock together," which is a commentary not only on avian behavior but also on the assumptions we make about perceptual grouping.

Now, suppose that, on one drowsy morning, you mistakenly put on two different-colored socks because they were together in the drawer and you assumed

Laws of perceptual grouping The Gestalt principles of similarity, proximity, continuity, and common fate. These "laws" suggest how our brains prefer to group stimulus elements together to form a percept (Gestalt).

Law of similarity The Gestalt principle that we tend to group similar objects together in our perceptions.

FIGURE 7.23
Gestalt Laws of Perceptual Grouping

(A) Similarity, (B) proximity (nearness), and (C) continuity. In (A) you most easily see the Xs grouped together, while Os form a separate Gestalt. So columns group together more easily than rows. The rows, made up of dissimilar elements, do not form patterns so easily. In (B) dissimilar elements easily group together when they are near each other. In (C), even though the lines cut each other into many discontinuous segments, it is easier to see just two lines—each of which appears to be continuous as a single line cutting through the figure.

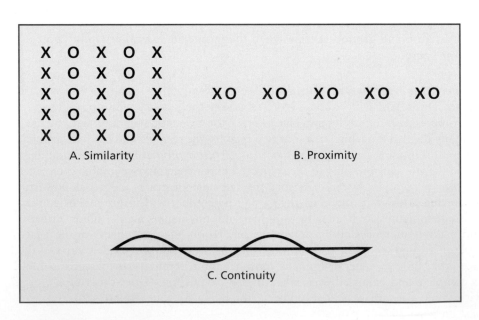

A. Similarity

B. Proximity

C. Continuity

that they were a pair. Your mistake was merely Wertheimer's **law of proximity** (nearness) at work. The proximity principle says that we tend to group things together that are near each other, as you can see in the pairings of the Xs with the Os in Figure 7.23B. On the level of social perception, your parents were invoking the law of proximity when they cautioned you, "You're known by the company you keep."

We can see the Gestalt **law of continuity** in Figure 7.23C, where the straight line appears as a single, continuous line, even though the curved line repeatedly cuts through it. In general, the law of continuity says that we prefer smoothly connected and continuous figures to disjointed ones. Continuity also operates in the realm of social perception, where we commonly make the assumption of continuity in the personality of an individual whom we haven't seen for some time. So, despite interruptions in our contact with that person, we will expect to find continuity—to find him or her to be essentially the same person we knew earlier.

There is yet another form of perceptual grouping—one that we cannot easily illustrate in the pages of a book because it involves motion. But you can easily conjure up your own image that exemplifies the **law of common fate:** Imagine a school of fish, a gaggle of geese, or a uniformed marching band. When visual elements (the individual fish, geese, or band members) are moving together, you perceive them as a single Gestalt.

According to the Gestalt perspective, each of these examples of perceptual grouping illustrates the profound idea that our perceptions are influenced by innate patterns in the brain. These inborn mental processes, in a top-down fashion, determine the organization of the individual parts of the percept, just as mountains and valleys determine the course of a river. Moreover, the Gestalt psychologists suggested, the laws of perceptual grouping exemplify a more general principle known as the **law of Prägnanz** ("meaningfulness"). This principle states that we perceive the simplest pattern possible—the percept requiring the least mental effort. The most general of all the Gestalt principles, Prägnanz (pronounced *PRAYG-nonce*) has also been called the *minimum principle of perception*. The law of Prägnanz is what makes proofreading so hard to do, as you will find when you examine Figure 7.24.

Learning-Based Inference: The *Nurture* of Perception

In 1866, Hermann von Helmholtz pointed out the important role of learning (or nurture) in perception. His theory of **learning-based inference** emphasized how people use prior learning to interpret new sensory information. Based on experience, then, the observer makes *inferences*—guesses or predictions—about what the sensations mean. This theory explains, for example, why you assume a birthday party is in progress when you see lighted candles on a cake.

Ordinarily, such perceptual inferences are fairly accurate. On the other hand, we have seen that confusing sensations and ambiguous arrangements can create perceptual illusions and erroneous conclusions. Our perceptual interpretations are, in effect, hypotheses about our sensations. For example, babies learn to expect that faces will have certain features in fixed arrangements (pair of eyes above nose, mouth below nose). In fact, we so thoroughly learn about faces in their usual configuration that we fail to "see" facial patterns that violate our expectations, particularly when they appear in an unfamiliar orientation. When you look at the two inverted portraits of Beyoncé (Figure 7.25, p. 323), do you detect any important differences between them? Turn the book upside down for a surprise.

What determines how successful we will be in forming an accurate percept? The most important factors include the *context,* our *expectations,* and our *perceptual set.* We will see that each of these involves a way of narrowing our search of the vast store of concepts in long-term memory.

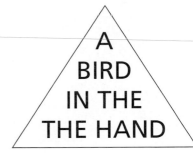

FIGURE 7.24
A Bird in the . . .

We usually see what we expect to see—not what is really there. Look again.

Law of proximity　The Gestalt principle that we tend to group objects together when they are near each other. *Proximity* means "nearness."

Law of continuity　The Gestalt principle that we prefer perceptions of connected and continuous figures to disconnected and disjointed ones.

Law of common fate　The Gestalt principle that we tend to group similar objects together that share a common motion or destination.

Law of Prägnanz　The most general Gestalt principle, which states that the simplest organization, requiring the least cognitive effort, will emerge as the figure. *Prägnanz* shares a common root with *pregnant,* and so it carries the idea of a "fully developed figure." That is, our perceptual system prefers to see a fully developed Gestalt, such as a complete circle—as opposed to a broken circle.

Learning-based inference　The view that perception is primarily shaped by learning (or experience), rather than by innate factors.

Quickly scan this photo. Then look away and describe as much as you recall. Next, turn to page 325 to learn what you may or may not have seen.

Context and Expectations   Once you identify a context, you form expectations about what persons, objects, and events you are likely to experience (Biederman, 1989). To see what we mean, take a look at the following:

$$\boxed{\text{THE CAT}}$$

It says THE CAT, right? Now look again at the middle letter of each word. Physically, these two letters are exactly the same, yet you perceived the first as an *H* and the second as an *A*. Why? Clearly, your perception was affected by what you know about words in English. The context provided by *T__E* makes an *H* highly likely and an *A* unlikely, whereas the reverse is true of the context of *C__T* (Selfridge, 1955).

Here's a more real-world example: You have probably had difficulty recognizing people you know in situations where you didn't expect to see them, such as in a different city or a new social group. The problem, of course, is not that they looked different but that the context was unusual: You didn't *expect* them to be there. Thus, perceptual identification depends on context and expectations as well as on an object's physical properties.

Perceptual Set   Another way learning serves as a platform from which context and expectation exert an influence on perception involves **perceptual set.** Under the influence of perceptual set we have a readiness to notice and respond to certain stimulus cues—like a sprinter anticipating the starter's pistol. In general, perceptual set involves a focused alertness for a particular stimulus in a given context. For example, a new mother is set to hear the cries of her child. Likewise, if you drive a sporty red car, you probably know how the highway patrol has a perceptual set to notice speeding sporty red cars.

Often, a perceptual set leads you to transform an ambiguous stimulus into the one you were expecting. To experience this yourself, read quickly through the series of words that follow in both rows:

FOX; OWL; SNAKE; TURKEY; SWAN; D?CK

BOB; RAY; DAVE; BILL; TOM; D?CK

Notice how the words in the two rows lead you to read D?CK differently in each row. The meanings of the words read prior to the ambiguous stimulus create a perceptual set. Words that refer to animals create a perceptual set that influences you to read D?CK as "DUCK." Names create a perceptual set leading you to see D?CK as DICK. Yet another illustration of perceptual set appears in the "Do It Yourself!" box "You See What You're Set to See."

Cultural Influences on Perception   Which of the following three items go together: chicken, cow, grass? If you are American, you are likely to group chicken and cow, because they are both animals. But if you are Chinese, you are more likely to put the latter two together, because cows eat grass. In general, says cross-cultural psychologist Richard Nisbett, Americans tend to put items in categories by abstract type, rather than by relationship or function (Winerman, 2006d).

Nisbett and his colleagues have also found that East Asians typically perceive in a more holistic fashion than do Americans (Nisbett & Norenzayan, 2002; Nisbett, 2003). That is, the Asians pay more attention to, and can later recall

Perceptual set   Readiness to detect a particular stimulus in a given context—as when a person who is afraid interprets an unfamiliar sound as a threat.

Labels create a context that can impose a perceptual set for an ambiguous figure. Have a friend look carefully at the picture of the "young woman" in part A of the accompanying figure, and have another friend examine the "old woman" in part B. (Cover the other pictures while they do this.) Then, have them look together at part C. What do they see? Each will probably see something different, even though it's the same stimulus pattern. Prior exposure to the picture with a specific label will usually affect a person's perception of the ambiguous figure.

A. A Young Woman | B. An Old Woman | C. Now what do you see?

more detail about, the context than do Americans. (This is true, incidentally, even if the American is of Chinese ancestry.) Specifically, when looking at a scene, Americans spend more time scanning the "figure," while Chinese people usually focus more on details of the "ground" (Chua et al., 2005).

Cross-cultural psychologists have pointed to still other cultural differences in perception (Segall et al., 1999). Consider, for example, the famous Ponzo illusion, based on linear perspective depth cues (see Figure 7.26). In your opinion, which bar is longer: the one on top (marked A) or the one on the bottom (marked B)? In actuality, both bars are the same length. (If you've developed a skeptical scientific attitude, you'll measure them!) Research shows, however, that responses to these figures depend strongly on culture-related experiences. Most readers of this book will report that the top bar appears longer than the bottom bar, yet people from some cultural backgrounds are not so easily fooled.

Why the difference? The world you have grown up in probably included many structures featuring parallel lines that seemed to converge in the distance: railroad tracks, long buildings, highways, and tunnels. Such experiences leave you vulnerable to images, such as the Ponzo illusion, in which cues for size and distance are unreliable.

But what about people from cultures where individuals have had far less experience with this cue for distance? Research on this issue has been carried out on the Pacific island of Guam, where there are no Ponzolike railroad tracks (Brislin, 1974, 1993). There, too, the roads are so winding that people have few opportunities to see roadsides "converge" in the distance. People who have spent their entire lives on Guam, then, presumably have fewer opportunities to learn the strong perceptual cue that converging lines indicate distance.

And, sure enough—just as researchers had predicted—people who had lived all their lives on the island of Guam were less influenced by the Ponzo illusion than were respondents from the mainland United States. That is, they were less likely to report that the top line in the figure was longer. These results strongly support the argument that people's experiences affect their perceptions—as Helmholz had theorized.

Depth Perception: Nature or Nurture? Now that we have looked at two contrasting approaches to perception—Gestalt theory, which emphasizes nature; and learning-based inference, which emphasizes nurture—let's see how each does as an explanation for a classic problem in psychology: depth perception. Are we born with the ability to perceive depth, or must we learn it? Let's look at the evidence.

We know that depth perception appears early in human development, although the idea of being cautious when there is danger of falling seems to develop later in infancy. In a famous demonstration, psychologists Eleanor

FIGURE 7.25
Two Perspectives on Beyoncé

Although one of these photos clearly has been altered, they look similar when viewed this way. However, turn the book upside down and look again.

FIGURE 7.26
The Ponzo Illusion

The two white bars superimposed on the railroad track are actually identical in length. Because A appears farther away than B, we perceive it as longer.

Apprehension about the "visual cliff" shows that infants make use of distance clues. This ability develops at about the same time an infant is learning to crawl.

Binocular cues Information taken in by both eyes that aids in depth perception, including binocular convergence and retinal disparity.

Monocular cues Information about depth that relies on the input of just one eye—includes relative size, light and shadow, interposition, relative motion, and atmospheric perspective.

Gibson and Richard Walk placed infants on a Plexiglas-topped table that appeared to drop off sharply on one end. (See the accompanying photo.) Reactions to the *visual cliff* occurred mainly in infants older than 6 months—old enough to crawl. Most readily crawled across the "shallow" side of the table, but they were reluctant to go over the "edge" of the visual cliff—indicating not only that they could perceive depth but that they associated the drop-off with danger (Gibson & Walk, 1960). Developmental psychologists believe that crawling and depth perception are linked in that crawling helps infants develop their understanding of the three-dimensional world.

Using another technique, Bower (1971) found evidence of depth perception in infants only 2 weeks old. By fitting his subjects with 3-D goggles Bower produced powerful virtual reality images of a ball moving about in space. When the ball image suddenly appeared to move directly toward the infant's face, the reaction was increased heart rate and obvious anxiety. This suggests that some ability for depth perception is probably inborn or heavily influenced by genetic programming that unfolds in the course of early development.

Digging deeper into the problem of depth perception, we find that our sense of depth or distance relies on multiple cues. We can group these depth cues in two categories, either *binocular cues* or *monocular cues*.

Binocular Cues Certain depth cues, the **binocular cues**, depend on the use of two eyes. You can demonstrate this to yourself: Hold one finger about 6 inches from your eyes and look at it. Now move it about a foot farther away. Do you feel the change in your eye muscles as you focus at different distances? This feeling serves as one of the main cues for depth perception when looking at objects that are relatively close. The term for this, *binocular convergence,* suggests how the lines of vision from each eye converge at different angles on objects at different distances.

A related binocular depth cue, *retinal disparity,* arises from the difference in perspectives of the two eyes. To see how this works, again hold a finger about 12 inches from your face and look at it alternately with one eye and then with the other. Notice how you see a different view of your finger with each eye. Because we see greater disparity when looking at nearby objects than we do when viewing distant objects, these image differences coming from each eye provide us with depth information.

We can't say for sure whether the binocular cues are innate or learned. What we can say is that they rely heavily on our biology: a sense of eye muscle movement and the physically different images on the two retinas. The monocular cues, however, present a very different picture.

Monocular Cues for Depth Perception Not all cues for depth perception require both eyes. A one-eyed pilot we know, who manages to perceive depth well enough to maneuver the airplane safely during takeoffs and landings, lives as proof that one-eye cues convey a great deal of depth information. Here are some of the **monocular cues** that a one-eyed pilot (or a two-eyed pilot, for that matter) could learn to use while flying:

- If two objects that are assumed to be the same size cast different-sized images on the retina, observers usually judge them to lie at different distances. So, a pilot flying low can learn to use the *relative size* of familiar objects on the ground as a cue for depth and distance. Because of this cue, automakers who install wide-angle rear-view mirrors always inscribe the warning on them, "Objects in the mirror are closer than they appear."

- If you have ever looked down a long, straight railroad track, you know that the parallel rails seem to come together in the distance. Likewise, a pilot approaching a runway for landing sees the runway as being much wider at the near end than at the far end. Both examples illustrate how *linear perspective,* the apparent convergence of parallel lines, can serve as a depth cue.

- Lighter-colored objects seem closer to us, and darker objects seem farther away. Thus, *light and shadow* work together as a distance cue. You will notice this the next time you drive your car at night, with the headlights on: Objects that reflect the most light appear to be nearer than more dimly lit objects in the distance.

- We assume that closer objects will cut off our vision of more distant objects behind them, a distance cue known as *interposition.* So, we know that partially hidden objects are more distant than the objects that hide them. You can see this effect right in front of you now, as your book partially obscures the background, which you judge to be farther away.

- As you move, objects at different distances appear to move through your field of vision at a different rate or with a different *relative motion.* Look for this one from your car window. Notice how the power poles or fence posts along the roadside appear to move by at great speed, while more distant objects stay in your field of view longer, appearing to move by more slowly. With this cue, student pilots learn to set up a glide path to landing by adjusting their descent so that the end of the runway appears to stay at a fixed spot on the windshield, while more distant points appear to move upward, and nearer objects seems to move downward.

- Haze or fog makes objects in the distance look fuzzy, less distinct, or invisible, creating another learned distance cue called *atmospheric perspective.* In the accompanying photo you can see that more distant buildings lack clarity through the Los Angeles smog. At familiar airports, most pilots have identified a landmark three miles away. If they cannot see the landmark, they know that they must fly on instruments.

So, which of the two theories about perception that we have been discussing—Helmholtz's learning theory or the Gestaltists' innate theory—best accounts for depth perception? Both of them! That is, depth and distance perception—indeed, all our perceptual processes—show the influence of both nature and nurture.

Seeing and Believing

If you assume, as most people do, that your senses give you an accurate and undistorted picture of the outside world, you are mistaken (Segall et al., 1990). Magicians, who base their careers on the difference between appearance and reality, count on fooling people for whom "seeing is believing." And you may have noticed that politicians and marketing experts rely on influencing people's interpretations of events, as well. So we hope that this chapter has shaken your faith in your senses and perceptions . . . just a bit.

Unlike magicians, perceptual psychologists are happy to reveal how sensation and perception play tricks on all of us (Hyman, 1989). They have developed a number of demonstrations that show how your vivid impressions of the world are really highly processed and interpreted images. We have already seen this in many visual illusions presented in the chapter. But, to drive the point home, consider this statement (which, unfortunately, was printed backwards):

.rat eht saw tac ehT

Please turn it around in your mind: What does it say? At first most people see a sensible sentence that says, "The cat saw the rat." But take another look. The difficulty lies in the power of expectations to shape your interpretation of stimulation.

Did you see a woman committing suicide in the photo on page 322? Most people have difficulty identifying the falling woman in the center of the photo because of the confusing background and because they have no perceptual schema that makes them expect to see a person positioned horizontally in midair.

Haze, fog, or air pollution make distant objects less distinct, creating atmospheric perspective, *which acts as a distance cue. Even the air itself provides a cue for distance by giving far-away objects a bluish cast.*

Most of us assume that our senses give us an accurate picture of the world. This helps magicians like Lance Burton fool us with perceptual illusions.

This demonstration illustrates once again that we don't merely sense the world as it is, we perceive it. The goal of the process by which stimulation becomes sensation and, finally, perception is to find meaning in our experience. But it is well to remember that we impose our own meanings on sensory experience.

Differences in the ways we interpret our experiences explain why two people can look at the same sunset, the same presidential candidates, or the same religions and perceive them so differently. Perceptual differences make us unique individuals. An old Spanish proverb makes the point elegantly:

En este mundo traidor	In this treacherous world
No hay verdad ni mentira;	There is neither truth nor lie;
Todo es según el color	All is according to the color
Del cristál con que se mira.	Of the lens through which we spy.

With this proverb in mind, let's return one more time to the problem with which we began the chapter—and in particular to the question of whether the world looks (feels, tastes, smells . . .) the same to different people. We have every reason to suspect that we all (with some variation) *sense* the world in roughly the same way. But, because we attach different *meanings* to our sensations, it is clear that people *perceive* the world in many different ways—with, perhaps, as many differences as there are people.

PSYCHOLOGYMATTERS

Using Psychology to Learn Psychology

One of the most mistaken notions about studying and learning is that students should set aside a certain amount of time for study every day. This is not to suggest that you shouldn't study regularly. Rather, it is to say that you shouldn't focus on merely putting in your time. So where should you place your emphasis? (And, what does this have to do with perceptual psychology?)

Recall the concept of *Gestalt*, the idea of the meaningful pattern, discussed earlier in this chapter. The Gestalt psychologists taught that we have an innate tendency to understand our world in terms of meaningful patterns. Applied to your studying, this means that your emphasis should be on finding meaningful patterns—Gestalts—in your course work.

In this chapter, for example, you will find that your authors have helped you by dividing the material into three major sections. You can think of each section as a conceptual Gestalt, built around a Core Concept that ties it together and gives it meaning. We suggest that you organize your study of psychology around one of these meaningful units of material. That is, identify a major section of your book and study that until it makes sense.

To be more specific, you might spend an hour or two working on the first section of this chapter, where you would not only read the material but also connect each boldfaced term to the Core Concept. For example, what does the *difference threshold* have to do with the idea that the brain senses the world through neural messages? (Sample brief answer: The brain is geared to detect *changes* or *differences* that are conveyed to it in the form of neural impulses.) We suggest that you do the same thing with each of the other boldfaced terms in the chapter. The result will be a deeper understanding of the material. In perceptual terms, you will be constructing a meaningful pattern—a Gestalt— around the Core Concept.

You can do that only by focusing on meaningful units of material, rather than on the clock.

CheckYourUnderstanding

1. **APPLICATION:** Give an example, from your own experience, of top-down processing.

2. **RECALL:** Our brains have specialized cells, known as
_____
dedicated to identifying stimulus properties such as length, slant, color, and boundary.

3. **RECALL:** What do perceptual constancies do for us?

4. **RECALL:** What two basic perceptual properties seem to reverse or alternate in the faces/vase image (in Figure 7.17A)?

5. **APPLICATION:** When two close friends are talking, other people may not be able to follow their conversation because it has many gaps that the friends can mentally fill in from their shared experience. Which Gestalt principle is illustrated by the friends' ability to fill in these conversational gaps?

6. **UNDERSTANDING THE CORE CONCEPT:** Which of the following best illustrates the idea that perception is not an exact internal copy of the world?
   a. the sound of a familiar tune
   b. the Ponzo illusion
   c. a bright light
   d. jumping in response to a pinprick

Answers 1. Your example should involve perception based on expectations, motives, emotions, or mental images—such as seeing a friend's face in a crowd, making sense of an unexpected sound in the house at night. **2.** feature detectors **3.** Perceptual constancies allow us to identify and track objects under a variety of conditions, such as changes in illumination or perspective. **4.** figure and ground **5.** closure **6.** b—because, of all the choices listed, the Ponzo illusion involves the most extensive perceptual interpretation.

Critical Thinking Applied: Subliminal Perception and Subliminal Persuasion

Could extremely weak stimulation—stimulation that you don't even notice—affect your attitudes, opinions, or behavior? We know that the brain does a lot of information processing outside of awareness. So, the notion that your sensory system can operate below the level of awareness is the basis for the industry that sells "subliminal" recordings touted as remedies for obesity, shoplifting, smoking, and low self-esteem. The same notion also feeds the fear that certain musical groups imbed hidden messages in their recordings or that advertisers may be using subliminal messages to influence our buying habits and, perhaps, our votes (Vokey, 2002).

What Is the Issue?

People are always hoping for a bit of "magic." But before you put your money in the mail for that subliminal weight loss CD, let's identify what exactly we're talking about—and what we're *not* talking about. If subliminal persuasion works as claimed, then it works on *groups* of people—a mass audience—rather than just individuals. It also means that a persuasive message can change the behavior of large numbers of people, even though no one is aware of the message. The issue is *not* whether sensory and perceptual processing can occur outside of awareness. The issue is whether subliminal messages can effect a substantial change in people's attitudes, opinions, and behaviors.

What Critical Thinking Questions Should We Ask?

There is always a possibility of fraud when fortune or fame is involved, which is certainly the case with claims of amazing powers—such as subliminal persuasion. This should cue us to ask: What is the source of claims that subliminal persuasion techniques work? That question leads us to an advertising executive, one James Vicary, who dramatically announced to the press some years ago that he had discovered an irresistible sales technique, now known as "subliminal advertising." Vicary said that his method consisted of projecting very brief messages on the screen of a movie theater, urging the audience to "Drink Coke" and "Buy popcorn." He claimed that the ads presented ideas so fleetingly that the conscious mind could not perceive them—yet, he said, the messages would still lodge in the unconscious mind, where they would work on the viewers' desires unnoticed. Vicary also boasted that sales of Coca-Cola and popcorn had soared at a New Jersey theater where he tested the technique.

The public was both fascinated and outraged. Subliminal advertising became the subject of intense debate. People worried that they were being manipulated by powerful psychological forces without their consent. As a result, laws were proposed to quash the practice. But aside from the hysteria, was there any real cause for concern? To answer that question, we must ask: What is the evidence?

Let's first see what the psychological science of perceptual thresholds can tell us. As you will recall, a *threshold* refers to the minimum amount of stimulation necessary to trigger a response. The word *subliminal* means "below the threshold" (*limen* = threshold). In the language of perceptual psychology, *subliminal* more specifically refers to stimuli lying near the absolute threshold. Such stimuli may, in fact, be strong enough to affect the sense organs and to enter the sensory system, without causing conscious awareness of the stimulus. But the real question is this: Can subliminal stimuli in this range influence our thoughts and behavior?

Several studies have found that subliminal words flashed briefly on a screen (for less than 1/100 second) can "prime" a person's later responses (Merikle & Reingold, 1990). For example, can you fill in the following blanks to make a word?

S N _ _ _ E L

If you had been subliminally primed by a brief presentation of the appropriate word or picture, it would be more likely that you would have found the right answer, even though you were not aware of the priming stimulus. So, does the fact that subliminal stimulation can affect our responses on such tasks mean that subliminal persuasion really works?

Of course, priming doesn't *always* work: It merely increases the chances of getting the "right" answer. The answer to the problem, by the way, is "snorkel." And were you aware that we were priming you with the photo of a snorkeler? If you were, it just goes to show that sometimes people *do* realize when they are being primed.

What Conclusions Can We Draw?

Apparently people do perceive stimuli below the absolute threshold, under circumstances such as the demonstration above (Greenwald et al., 1996; Reber, 1993). Under very carefully controlled conditions, **subliminal perception** is a fact. But here is the problem for would-be subliminal advertisers who would attempt to influence us in the uncontrolled world outside the laboratory: Different people have thresholds at different levels. So, what might be *sub*liminal for me could well be *supra*liminal (above the threshold) for you. Consequently, the would-be subliminal advertiser runs the risk that some in the audience will notice—and perhaps be angry about—a stimulus aimed slightly below the average person's threshold. In fact, *no controlled*

research has ever shown that subliminal messages delivered to a mass audience can influence people's buying habits or voting patterns.

And what about those subliminal recordings that some stores play to prevent shoplifting? Again, no reputable study has ever demonstrated their effectiveness. A more likely explanation for any decrease in shoplifting attributed to these messages lies in increased vigilance from employees who know that management is worried about shoplifting. The same goes for the tapes that claim to help you quit smoking, lose weight, become wildly creative, or achieve other dozens of elusive dreams. In a comprehensive study of subliminal self-help techniques, the U.S. Army found all to be without foundation (Druckman & Bjork, 1991). The simplest explanation for reports of success lies in the purchasers' expectations and in the need to prove that they did not spend their money foolishly. And finally, to take the rest of the worry out of subliminal persuasion, you should know one more bit of evidence. James Vicary eventually admitted that his claims for subliminal advertising were a hoax (Druckman & Bjork, 1991).

This photo carries a subliminal message, explained in the text.

Chapter Summary

7.1 How Does Stimulation Become Sensation?

Core Concept 7.1: The brain senses the world indirectly because the sense organs convert stimulation into the language of the nervous system: neural messages.

The most fundamental step in sensation involves the **transduction** by the sense organs of physical stimuli into neural messages, which are sent onward in the sensory pathways to the appropriate part of the brain for further processing. Not all stimuli become sensations because some fall below the **absolute threshold**. Further, changes in stimulation are noticed only if they exceed the **difference threshold**. Classical psychophysics focused on identifying thresholds for sensations and for just-noticeable differences, but a newer approach, called **signal detection theory**, explains sensation as a process involving context, physical sensitivity, and judgment. We should consider our senses to be *change detectors*. But because they accommodate to unchanging stimulation, we become less and less aware of constant stimulation.

Absolute threshold (p. 292) **Sensory adaptation** (p. 294)

Difference threshold (p. 292) **Signal detection theory** (p. 293)

Perception (p. 289) **Transduction** (p. 291)

Sensation (p. 288) **Weber's law** (p. 292)

MyPsychLab Resources 7.1:

Simulation: Methods of Constant Stimuli

Simulation: Weber's Law

7.2 How Are the Senses Alike? And How Are They Different?

Core Concept 7.2: The senses all operate in much the same way, but each extracts different information and sends it to its own specialized sensory processing region in the brain.

All the senses involve transduction of physical stimuli into nerve impulses. In vision, **photoreceptors** in the retina transduce light waves into neural codes, which retain **frequency** and **amplitude** information. This visual information is then transmitted by the optic nerve to the brain's occipital lobes, which converts the neural signals into sensations of **color** and **brightness**. Both the **trichromatic theory** and the **opponent process theory** are required to explain how visual sensations are extracted. Vision makes use of only a tiny "window" in the electromagnetic spectrum.

In the ear, sound waves in the air are transduced into neural energy in the **cochlea** and then sent on to the brain's temporal lobes, where frequency and amplitude information are converted to sensations of **pitch**, **loudness**, and **timbre**. Our sensations of light and sound are not properties of the original stimulus but rather are creations of the brain. Other senses include position and movement (the **vestibular** and **kinesthetic** senses), *smell*, *taste*, the **skin senses** (touch, pressure, and temperature), and *pain*. Like vision and hearing, these other senses are especially attuned to detect changes in stimulation. Further, all sensation is carried to the brain by neural impulses, but we experience different sensations because the impulses are processed by different sensory regions of the brain. In some people, sensations cross sensory domains. Studies suggest that **synesthesia** involves communication between sensory areas of the brain that lie close together. This seems to occur more often in highly creative people.

The experience of pain can be the result of intense stimulation in any of several sensory pathways. While we don't completely understand pain, the **gate-control theory** explains how pain can be suppressed by competing sensations or other mental processes. Similarly, the ideal *analgesic*—one without unwanted side effects—has not been discovered, although the **placebo effect** works exceptionally well for some people.

Afterimages (p. 300) **Color blindness** (p. 300)

Amplitude (p. 302) **Cones** (p. 297)

Basilar membrane (p. 303) **Electromagnetic spectrum** (p. 299)

Blind spot (p. 297)

Brightness (p. 298) **Fovea** (p. 297)

Cochlea (p. 302) **Frequency** (p. 302)

Color (p. 299) **Gate-control theory** (p. 310)

MyPsychLab Resources 7.2:

Explore: Frequency and Amplitude of Sound Waves

Explore: Light and the Optic Nerve

Explore: Major Structures of the Ear

7.3 What Is the Relationship between Sensation and Perception?

Core Concept 7.3: Perception brings meaning to sensation, so perception produces an interpretation of the world, not a perfect representation of it.

Psychologists define perception as the stage at which meaning is attached to sensation. We derive meaning from **bottom-up** stimulus cues picked up by feature detectors and from **top-down** processes, especially those involving expectations. What remains unclear is how the brain manages to combine the output of many sensory circuits into a single percept: This is called the **binding problem.** By studying **illusions** and *constancies*, researchers can learn about the factors that influence and distort the construction of perceptions. Illusions demonstrate that perception does not necessarily form an accurate representation of the outside world.

   Perception has been explained by theories that differ in their emphasis on the role of innate brain processes versus learning—nature versus nurture. **Gestalt psychology** emphasizes innate factors that help us organize stimulation into meaningful patterns. In particular, the Gestaltists have described the processes that help us distinguish **figure** from **ground,** to identify contours and apply **closure,** and to group stimuli according to **similarity, proximity, continuity,** and **common fate.** Some aspects of *depth perception,* such as *retinal disparity* and *convergence,* may be innate as well. The theory of **learning-based inference** also correctly points out that perception is influenced by experience, such as *context,* **perceptual set,** and *culture.*

Many aspects of depth perception, such as *relative motion, linear perspective,* and *atmospheric perspective,* seem to be learned.

   Despite all we know about sensation and perception, many people uncritically accept the evidence of their senses (and perceptions) at face value. This allows magicians, politicians, and marketers an opening through which they can manipulate our perceptions and, ultimately, our behavior.

MyPsychLab Resources 7.3:

Explore: Five Well-Known Illusions

Simulation: Ambiguous Figures

Simulation: Distinguishing Figure-Ground Relationships

Watch the following video by logging into MyPsychLab (www.mypsychlab.com). After you have watched the video, complete the activities that follow.

PROGRAM 7: SENSATION AND PERCEPTION

PROGRAM REVIEW

1. Imagine that a teaspoon of sugar is dissolved in two gallons of water. Rita can detect this level of sweetness at least half the time. This level is called the
   a. distal stimulus.
   b. perceptual constant.
   c. response bias.
   d. absolute threshold.

2. What is the job of a receptor?
   a. to transmit a neural impulse
   b. to connect new information with old information
   c. to detect a type of physical energy
   d. to receive an impulse from the brain

3. In what area of the brain is the visual cortex located?
   a. in the front
   b. in the middle
   c. in the back
   d. under the brain stem

4. What is the function of the thalamus in visual processing?
   a. It relays information to the cortex.
   b. It rotates the retinal image.
   c. It converts light energy to a neural impulse.
   d. It makes sense of the proximal stimulus.

5. David Hubel discusses the visual pathway and the response to a line. The program shows an experiment in which the response to a moving line changed dramatically with changes in the line's
   a. thickness.
   b. color.
   c. speed.
   d. orientation.

6. Misha Pavel used computer graphics to study how
   a. we process visual information.
   b. rods differ from cones in function.
   c. we combine information from different senses.
   d. physical energy is transduced in the visual system.

7. Imagine that a baseball player puts on special glasses that shift his visual field up 10 degrees. When he wears these glasses, the player sees everything higher than it actually is. After some practice, the player can hit with the glasses on. What will happen when the player first tries to hit with the glasses off?
   a. He will think that the ball is lower than it is.
   b. He will think that the ball is higher than it is.
   c. He will accurately perceive the ball's position.
   d. It is impossible to predict an individual's reaction in this situation.

8. Imagine that a small dog is walking toward you. As the dog gets closer, the image it casts on your retina
   a. gets larger.
   b. gets darker.
   c. gets smaller.
   d. stays exactly the same size.

9. Imagine the same small dog walking toward you. You know that the dog's size is unchanged as it draws nearer. A psychologist would attribute this to
   a. perceptual constancy.
   b. visual paradoxes.
   c. contrast effects.
   d. threshold differences.

10. Which of the following best illustrates that perception is an active process?
    a. bottom-up processing
    b. motion parallax
    c. top-down processing
    d. parietal senses

11. The program shows a drawing that can be seen as a rat or as a man. People were more likely to identify the drawing as a man if they
    a. were men themselves.
    b. had just seen pictures of people.
    c. were afraid of rats.
    d. looked at the picture holistically rather than analytically.

12. Where is the proximal stimulus found?
    a. in the outside world
    b. on the retina
    c. in the occipital lobe
    d. in the thalamus

13. How is visual information processed by the brain?
    a. It's processed by the parietal lobe, which relays the information to the temporal lobe.
    b. It's processed entirely within the frontal lobe.
    c. It's processed by the occipital lobe, which projects to the thalamus, which projects to a succession of areas in the cortex.
    d. If the information is abstract, it's processed by the cortex; if it's concrete, it's processed by the thalamus.

14. Which of the following is true about the proximal stimulus in visual perception?
    a. It's identical to the distal stimulus because the retina produces a faithful reproduction of the perceptual world.
    b. It's upside-down, flat, distorted, and obscured by blood vessels.
    c. It's black and white and consists of very sparse information about horizontal and vertical edges.
    d. It contains information about the degree of convergence of the two eyes.

15. Which of the following is an example of pure top-down processing (i.e., requires no bottom-up processing)?
    a. hallucinating
    b. understanding someone else's speech when honking horns are obscuring individual sounds
    c. perceiving a circular color patch that has been painted onto a canvas
    d. enjoying a melody

16. Which sensory information is *not* paired with the cortical lobe that is primarily responsible for processing it?
    a. visual information, occipital lobe
    b. speech, frontal lobe
    c. body senses, parietal lobe
    d. hearing, central sulcus lobe

17. When your eyes are shut, you cannot
    a. hallucinate.
    b. use contextual information from other senses to make inferences about what's there.
    c. transform a distal visual stimulus into a proximal stimulus.
    d. experience perceptual constancy.

18. The researcher David Hubel is best known for
    a. mapping visual receptor cells.
    b. discovering subjective contours.
    c. identifying the neural pathways by which body sensations occur.
    d. realizing that hearing and smell originate from the same brain area.

19. The primary reason why psychologists study illusions is because

a. they help in identifying areas of the cortex that have been damaged.
b. they serve as good "public relations" material for curious novices.
c. they help in categorizing people into good and bad perceivers.
d. they help in understanding how perception normally works.

20. The shrinking-square illusion demonstrated by Misha Pavel relies on processing of which kinds of feature?
    a. edges and corners
    b. color and texture
    c. torque and angular momentum
    d. density gradients and motion

QUESTIONS TO CONSIDER

1. Why do psychologists identify sensation and perception as two different fields of study? Does this reflect the relative youth of psychology as a science, or does it represent a scientific distinction that will still be favored in 50 years?

2. As the population ages, adapting the environment for people with a range of sensory abilities and deficits will become increasingly important. Architects will need to improve access to and safety of buildings, taking into account that older people need about three times as much light as young people in order to distinguish objects. They also need higher visual contrasts to detect potential hazards, such as curbs or steps. How might you identify some changes you could make in and around your home to create a safer, more comfortable environment for a person with disabilities or a person with visual or hearing impairments?

3. Choose a familiar context, such as a grocery store, and describe how the Gestalt principles of perceptual organization are used to help people perceive objects and group them.

4. Describe how film and television directors use sight and sound techniques to create meaning and feeling. As you watch a television commercial, program, or film, notice the way the camera frames the image and how angle and motion create a mood or point of view. Notice the use of sound. Consider how these elements shape viewers' desires, expectations, and feelings.

5. Absolute thresholds seem to differ across species. For example, you are much better at detecting degraded visual stimuli than animals of some other species would be, but at the same time you may be much worse than them at smelling faint odors. Why do you think that humans evolved to favor the visual sense?

ACTIVITIES

1. Blindfold yourself. (Have someone standing by to prevent injury or damage.) Contrast the experience of moving about in a familiar room, such as your bedroom or kitchen, with the experience of moving about a room in which you spend little time. Note the expectations and significant sensory cues you depend on to avoid tripping and bumping into things. How relaxed or tense were you in each room?

2. Listen to a conversation, trying hard to (a) notice all of the other noise going on around you and (b) notice all the instances of imperfect transmission of speech sounds. For example, the speaker might mispronounce something or speak unclearly, or an outside noise may obscure the sound coming from the speaker. Is it hard for you to snap out of top-down mode to do this exercise?

3. If you have access to a virtual reality game, try playing it while also monitoring what is going on in the room around you. While interacting with the virtual objects in the game, think about how you must look to passersby, and think about the layout of the objects in the space that physically surrounds you. How good are you at immersing yourself in two worlds at once? Do you find that you have to switch back and forth, or are you able to consider yourself as being in two very different realities simultaneously?

Key Questions/ Chapter Outline	Core Concepts	Psychology Matters

8.1 How Is Consciousness Related to Other Mental Processes?

Tools for Studying Consciousness

Models of the Conscious and Nonconscious Minds

What Does Consciousness Do for Us?

Levels of Consciousness

- The brain operates on many levels at once—both conscious and unconscious.

Using Psychology to Learn Psychology

The trick is to organize material in preconscious long-term memory so that you can find it when you need it.

8.2 What Cycles Occur in Everyday Consciousness?

Daydreaming

Sleep: The Mysterious Third of Our Lives

Dreaming: The Pageants of the Night

- Consciousness changes in cycles that correspond to our biological rhythms and to the patterns of stimulation in our environment.

Sleep Disorders

Insomnia, sleep apnea, narcolepsy, and daytime sleepiness can be hazardous to your health—and perhaps even to your life.

8.3 What Other Forms Can Consciousness Take?

Hypnosis

Meditation

Psychoactive Drug States

- An altered state of consciousness occurs when some aspect of normal consciousness is modified by mental, behavioral, or chemical means.

Dependence and Addiction

Psychoactive drugs alter brain chemistry, and they can produce physical or psychological addiction. But is addiction a disease or a character flaw?

Critical Thinking Applied: The Unconscious—Reconsidered

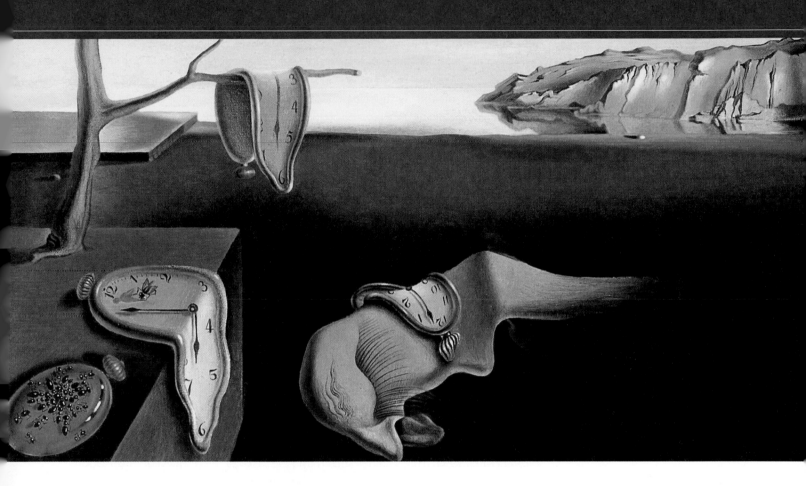

chapter 8
states of consciousness

One rainy Swiss summer day in the early 19th century, a housebound trio of writers eagerly challenged each other to craft ghost stories. Yet, after several days of uninspired effort, Mary Wollstonecraft Shelley feared she would come up empty handed. Then one night, with the problem turning over in her mind, she fell asleep, only to awaken some time later with horrific dream images in her head. She later recalled them clearly:

> My imagination, unbidden, possessed and guided me . . . I saw the pale student of unhallowed arts kneeling beside the thing he had put together. I saw the hideous phantasm of a man stretched out, and then . . . show signs of life, and stir with an uneasy, half vital motion. . . . [The creator] would rush away from his odious handiwork, horror-stricken.

> Early the next day she penned the words: "It was on a dreary night of November . . ." (Shelley, 1831). Thus began the first draft of her "ghost story," *Frankenstein, or The Modern Prometheus.*

Mary Shelley was far from the first to have been inspired by a dream. From ancient times, dreams have been regarded as sources of insight, creativity, and prophecy. We can see this, for example, in the Old Testament story of the Israelite Joseph, who interpreted Pharaoh's dreams of fat and lean cattle as predicting first the years of plenty and then the years of famine that lay in store for the Egyptian kingdom (Genesis, 41:i–vii).

In more modern times, the English poet Samuel Taylor Coleridge attributed the imagery of his poem "Kubla Khan" to a dream (possibly drug-induced) that he experienced after reading a biography of the famed Mongol warrior. Likewise, painters such as surrealist Salvador Dali have found their dreams to be vivid sources of imagery. Composers as varied as Mozart, Beethoven, the Beatles, and Sting have all credited their dreams with inspiring certain works. And in the scientific world, chemist August Kekule's discovery of the structure of the benzene molecule was sparked by his dream of a snake rolled into a loop, grasping its own tail tucked in its mouth. Even the famous horror writer Stephen King claims to have harvested story ideas from his own childhood nightmares.

So why do we dream? Do dreams help us solve problems? Do they reflect the workings of the unconscious mind? Or are dreams just random mental "junk"—perhaps the debris left over from the previous day? The difficulty in studying dreams with the methods of science is that these mental states are private experiences. No one else can experience your dreams directly. These issues, then, frame the problem on which we will focus in this chapter.

PROBLEM: How can psychologists examine objectively the worlds of dreaming and other subjective mental states?

Dreaming represents just one of many states of consciousness that are possible for the human mind. Others include our familiar state of wakefulness and the less-familiar states of dreamless sleep, hypnosis, and meditation, as well as the chemically altered states produced by psychoactive drugs. But that's not all. Behind these conscious states, much of the brain's work occurs off-line—outside of awareness (Wallace & Fisher, 1999). This includes such mundane tasks as the retrieval of information from memory (What is seven times nine?), as well as the primitive operations occurring in the deep regions of the brain that control basic biological functions, such as blood pressure and body temperature. Somewhere between these extremes are parts of the mind that somehow deal with our once-conscious memories and gut-level responses, as varied as the recollection of this morning's breakfast and your most embarrassing moment. As we will see, the nature of this netherworld of nonconscious ideas, feelings, desires, and images has been controversial ever since Freud suggested that dreams may reflect our unrecognized and unconscious fears and desires. In this chapter we will evaluate this claim and others that have been made for the hidden levels of processing in the mind. But to do so, we begin with the more familiar state of consciousness that fills most of our waking hours.

CONNECTION • CHAPTER 2
The *hypothalamus*, for example, unconsciously regulates several biological drives.

8.1 KEY QUESTION
HOW IS CONSCIOUSNESS RELATED TO OTHER MENTAL PROCESSES?

In simplest terms, we can define **consciousness** as the brain process that creates our mental representation of the world and our current thoughts. One of its components is **attention,** a feature that makes one item stand out as *figure* in consciousness—as when someone calls your name—while everything else recedes into *ground*. Attention also makes it possible for you to follow the thread of a conversation against a background of other voices. (Psychologists call this the *cocktail party phenomenon* or *selective attention*.)

We have previously studied another component of consciousness: *working memory,* the part of the mind into which we can combine incoming stimuli with facts, ideas, emotions, and memories of our experiences retrieved from long-term storage. There we stir the conscious stew of information in the processes that we called *thinking* in Chapter 5. In this context, you might think of attention as the ability to focus on a single "chunk" of information in conscious working memory (Engle, 2002; Gaffan, 2005). Everything entering consciousness passes through working memory. Likewise, we are conscious of everything that enters working memory. Therefore, some psychologists have suggested that working memory is actually the long-sought seat of consciousness (Engle; 2002; LeDoux, 1996).

You might also think of consciousness as the part of the mind that helps us combine both reality and fantasy—the "movie" in your head. For example, if you see a doughnut when you are hungry, working memory forms a conscious image of the doughnut (based on external stimulation) and consults long-term memory, which associates the image with food and also allows you to imagine eating it. But exactly *how* the brain does this is perhaps psychology's greatest mystery. How do the patterns in the firing of billions of neurons become the conscious image of a doughnut—or of the words and ideas on this page?

Prescientific Views of Consciousness Folk wisdom merely attributes consciousness to an *anima*, a spirit or inner life force, an explanation that takes us no closer to understanding how consciousness works. A biblical variation on this theme connects consciousness to the soul—although the Bible also suggests that evil spirits or devils sometimes take over consciousness and cause bizarre behavior. (See Mark 5, for example.)

For psychologists, the big difficulty presented by consciousness is that it is so subjective and illusive—like searching for the end of the rainbow (Damasio, 1999, 2000). The problem first presented itself when the structuralists attempted to dissect conscious experience more than a century ago. As you will recall, the structuralists used a simple technique called introspection: People were asked to report on their own conscious experience. The slippery, subjective nature of consciousness quickly became obvious to nearly everyone, and psychologists began to despair that science would never find a way to study objectively something so private as conscious experience. (Think about it: How could you prove that you have consciousness?)

Behaviorism Rejects Consciousness The problem seemed so intractable that, early in the 20th century, the notorious and influential behaviorist John Watson declared that the mind was out of bounds for the young science of psychology. Mental processes were little more than by-products of our actions, he said. (You don't cry because you are sad, you are sad because some event makes you cry.) Under Watson's direction, psychology became simply the science of behavior. And so, psychology not only lost its consciousness but also lost its mind!

The psychology of consciousness remained in limbo until the 1960s, when a coalition of cognitive psychologists, neuroscientists, and computer scientists brought it back to life (Gardner, 1985). They did so for two reasons. First, many

CONNECTION • CHAPTER 7
Similarly, attention accounts for the separation of *figure* from *ground* in perception.

CONNECTION • CHAPTER 4
Working memory imposes a limitation on consciousness, because it holds only about seven "chunks" of information.

CONNECTION • CHAPTER 1
Wundt and the structuralists pioneered the use of *introspection* in their search for "the elements of conscious experience."

Consciousness The process by which the brain creates a mental model of our experience. The most common, or ordinary, consciousness occurs during wakefulness, although there are can be altered states of consciousness.

Attention A process by which consciousness focuses on a single item or "chunk" in working memory.

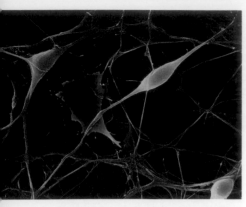

Francis Crick says that our consciousness is "no more than the behavior of a vast assembly of nerve cells and their associated molecules."

psychological issues had come to light that needed a better explanation than behaviorism could deliver: quirks of memory, perceptual illusions, drug-induced states (which were very popular in the 1960s). The second reason for the reemergence of consciousness came from technology. Scientists were acquiring new tools—especially computers, which allowed them to scan the brain. Computers also gave them a model that could be used to explain how the brain processes information.

The Emergence of Cognitive Neuroscience   The combination of new tools and unsolved problems, then, led to a multidisciplinary effort that became known as **cognitive neuroscience.** Attracting scientists from a variety of fields, cognitive neuroscience set out to unravel the mystery of how the brain processes information and creates conscious experience. From the perspective of cognitive neuroscience, the brain acts like a biological computing device with vast resources—among them being 100 billion transistor-like neurons, each with thousands of interconnections—capable of creating the complex universe of imagination and experience we think of as consciousness (Chalmers, 1995).

In this chapter we will see how cognitive neuroscientists have pursued not only ordinary consciousness but the alternative mental states of which we are capable, including sleep, dreaming, hypnosis, and drug-altered awareness. As we travel this path, please keep the following Core Concept readily available to your consciousness:

core concept | **The brain operates on many levels at once—both conscious and unconscious.**

The big picture that emerges is one of a conscious mind that can take on a variety of roles, as we will see, but one that must focus sequentially, first on one thing and then another, like a moving spotlight (see Tononi & Edelman, 1998). Consciousness is not good at multitasking; so, if you try to drive while talking on your cell phone, you must shift your attention back and forth between tasks (Rubenstein et al., 2001; Strayer et al., 2003). Meanwhile, **nonconscious processes** have no such restriction and can work on many jobs at the same time—which is why you can walk, chew gum, and breathe simultaneously. In more technical terms, consciousness must process information *serially,* while nonconscious brain circuits can processes many streams of information *in parallel.* We will begin our exploration of these multifarious mental states and levels with a look at some of the tools and techniques that have opened up this line of research.

Tools for Studying Consciousness

As you will recall from an earlier chapter, high-tech tools, such as the fMRI, PET, and EEG, have opened new windows through which researchers can look into the brain to see which regions are active during various mental tasks—showing us the "what" of consciousness. These imaging devices, of course, do not show the actual contents of conscious experience, but they quite clearly reveal distinct groups of brain structures that "light up," for example, when we read, speak, or shift our attention. (See Figure 8.1.) The resulting images have left no doubt that conscious processing involves simultaneous activity in many brain circuits, especially in the cortex and in the pathways connecting the thalamus to the cortex. But, to glimpse the underlying mental processes—the "how" of consciousness—psychologists have devised other, even more ingenious, techniques. We will see many of these throughout this chapter—in fact, throughout this book. For the moment, though, we will give you just two examples, as previews of coming attractions.

Mental Rotation   A classic experiment by Roger Shepard and Jacqueline Metzler (1971) showed that it's not merely a metaphor when people speak of "turning things

Cognitive neuroscience   An interdisciplinary field involving cognitive psychology, neurology, biology, computer science, linguistics, and specialists from other fields who are interested in the connection between mental processes and the brain.

Nonconscious process   Any brain process that does not involve conscious processing, including both preconscious memories and unconscious processes.

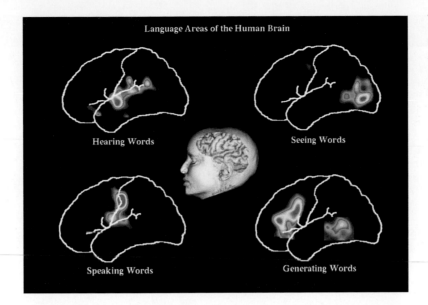

FIGURE 8.1
PET Scans of the Brain at Work

These PET scans show how distinct regions of the brain become active during different conscious tasks.

over" in their minds. Using drawings like those in Figure 8.2, Shepard and Metzler asked volunteers to decide whether the two images in each pair show the same object in different positions. They reasoned that, if the mind actually rotates these images when comparing them, people would take longer to respond when the difference between the angles of the images in each pair is increased. And that is exactly what they found. If you try this experiment on your friends, it is likely that they, too, will respond more quickly to pair A—where the images have been rotated through a smaller angle—than to pairs B and C.

Zooming in with the Mind   Another clever approach to the "how" of consciousness takes a different twist: Stephen Kosslyn found that we can use our conscious minds to "zoom in," camera-like, on the details of our mental images. To demonstrate this, Kosslyn (1976) first asked people to think of objects, such as an elephant or a cat or a chair. Then he asked questions about details of the imagined object (for example, "Is it a black cat?" or "Does it have a long tail?"), recording how long it took for people to answer. He discovered that the smaller the detail he asked for, the longer subjects needed for a response. People required extra time, Kosslyn proposed, to make a closer examination of their mental images.

Both the Shepard and Metzler and the Kosslyn experiments suggest that we consciously manipulate our visual images. And we do so in much the same way that we might manipulate physical objects in the outside world (Kosslyn, 1983). You can try this yourself with the demonstration in the accompanying box, "Do It Yourself! Zooming in on Mental Images." As we progress through the chapter, you will learn about other techniques used by neuroscientists to study consciousness and its allied mental processes. Now, let's see what picture has emerged from this work.

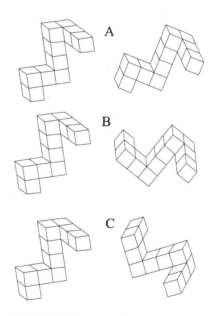

FIGURE 8.2
Figures for the Mental Rotation Experiment

These figures are similar to those used in Shepard and Metzler's mental rotation experiment. Results showed that people took longer to decide whether the images were the same or different, as the images in each pair were rotated through greater angles. You might try your own test to verify their findings.

Models of the Conscious and Nonconscious Minds

William James likened ordinary waking consciousness to a flowing stream that carries ever-changing sensations, perceptions, thoughts, memories, feelings, motives, and desires. This "stream of consciousness" can include awareness both of ourselves and of stimulation from our environment. And, as we have seen, it can also include physical sensations from within, such as hunger, thirst, pain, and pleasure.

Freud used another metaphor that compared consciousness to the tip of an iceberg, which suggests a much larger presence beneath the surface. A large body of evidence now confirms Freud's insight that much of the mind lurks and works

Ask a friend to close his or her eyes and imagine a house. Then ask your friend to describe the color of the roof, the front door, and doorbell button. Using a watch or clock that displays seconds, record the amount of time it takes to get each answer. Based on Kosslyn's research, which item would you predict would require the longest response time? The shortest?

You will probably find that the smaller the detail you ask for, the longer it takes your friend to respond. Kosslyn interpreted this to mean that people need the extra time to "zoom in" on a mental image to resolve smaller features. In other words, we examine our mental images in the same way that we examine physical objects in the external world in order to perceive the "big picture" or the details.

out of sight, beneath the level of awareness. But, as we will see later, the unconscious probably does not work in exactly the way Freud believed it did.

The modern cognitive perspective often uses yet another metaphor for the mind: the *computer metaphor*. This view likens consciousness to what appears on a computer screen, while nonconscious processes are like the electronic activity at work behind the scenes, deep inside the computer. Most of the time this nonconscious machinery quietly operates in parallel with consciousness, but occasionally a nonconscious motive or emotion becomes so strong that it emerges into consciousness—as when a peculiar odor associated with an emotional memory suddenly brings that emotion to awareness or when a growing hunger drive spills into awareness.

To get a better picture of consciousness as psychologists now understand it, we will first consider the major functions of consciousness, asking "What does consciousness do for us?" Then we will review what research and theory can tell us about the layers of mind believed to exist below the level of awareness.

What Does Consciousness Do for Us?

At this very moment, your consciousness is focused on these words, written in black letters on a white page. But the words don't stand alone. They have meaning, which also flows through consciousness as you read. You can, of course, shift the spotlight of your attention to something else—music in the background, perhaps—and, as you do so, the words on the page slip into the fringes of awareness. You may be moving your eyes across the page, but the meaning does not really register. (Every student has had this experience.)

Now, if we can have your attention again, we'd like to remind you that consciousness has many functions. But three especially important ones were illustrated by the scenario in the previous paragraph (Solso, 2001; Tononi & Edelman, 1998):

● *Consciousness restricts our attention.* Because consciousness processes information serially, it limits what you notice and think about. In this way, consciousness keeps your brain from being overwhelmed by stimulation. Unfortunately, the one-thing-at-a-time property of consciousness will not let you concentrate on what you are reading when you shift your attention to music playing in the background.

- *Consciousness also provides a mental "meeting place,"* where sensation can combine with memory, emotions, motives, and a host of other psychological processes in the process we have called *perception*. Consciousness, then, is the canvas on which we customarily create a meaningful picture from the palette of stimulation offered by our internal and external worlds. This is the aspect of consciousness that links meaning to words on a page or connects the emotion of joy to the sight of an old friend's face. Indeed, neuroimaging suggests that the essence of consciousness is to make linkages among different parts of the brain (Massimini et al., 2005). Consciousness, therefore, lies at the very heart of cognition.

CONNECTION • CHAPTER 7

Perception is the process of adding *meaning* to sensation.

- *And consciousness allows us to create a mental model of the world*—a model that we can manipulate in our minds. Unlike simpler organisms, consciousness frees us from being prisoners of the moment: We don't just react reflexively to stimulation. Instead, we can use a conscious model of our world that draws on memory, bringing both the past and the future into awareness. With this model in mind, we can think and plan by manipulating our mental world to evaluate alternative responses and imagine how effective they will be. It is this feature of consciousness that, for example, helps you associate your own experiences with concepts in this text or keeps you from being too brutally honest with a friend wearing clothes you don't like.

These three features—restriction, combination, and manipulation—apply in varying degrees to all states of consciousness, whether dreaming, hypnosis, meditation, a drug state, or our "normal" waking state. On the other hand, nonconscious processes operate in a much different way, as we have said. To show you how this region of the mind works, let's begin by distinguishing two levels of nonconscious processing.

Levels of Consciousness

Sigmund Freud originally proposed that our minds operate on several levels at once. He conceived of the *unconscious* as a reservoir of needs, desires, wishes, and traumatic memories. Moreover, he believed that processing outside awareness could influence our conscious thoughts, feelings, dreams, fantasies, and actions. Today, cognitive psychologists reject much of Freud's theory as prescientific speculation. But they would retain the notion of processing outside of awareness.

The Preconscious   Psychologists often use Freud's term, the **preconscious**, in referring to memories of events (a date last weekend, for example) and facts (Salem is the capital of Oregon) that are not conscious but have once been the focus of attention. These memories can return to consciousness with relative ease when something cues their recall. Otherwise, they lie in the background of the mind, just beyond the boundary of consciousness until needed. Thus, the preconscious, in the modern cognitive sense, is much the same as *long-term memory.*

Preconscious processing isn't restricted to the serial, one-thing-at-a-time limitation of consciousness. That is, it can search for information in many places at once—an ability called *parallel processing*. On the other hand, the preconscious lacks the ability consciousness has for deliberate thinking. You might think of the preconscious as a memory storehouse, where the stock is constantly rotated so that the most recently used and most emotionally loaded information is most easily accessed.

Preconscious   Freud's notion that the mind has a special unconscious storehouse for information not currently in consciousness but available to consciousness. Example: your telephone number is stored in the preconscious.

CONNECTION • CHAPTER 4

Parallel processing involves two or more operations occurring simultaneously, as when preconscious memory is being searched in multiple locations at once.

The Unconscious   A dictionary might define the term *unconscious* as the absence of all consciousness, as in one who has fainted, become comatose, or is under anesthesia. Freud, however, defined the unconscious as a reservoir of primitive motives and threatening memories hidden from awareness. But cognitive psychologists have still another meaning for unconscious that refers to any sort of nonconscious mental process produced in the brain. In this sense, we can define the **unconscious** as a broad term that refers to many levels of processing below the level of awareness, ranging from preconscious memory to brain activity that controls basic body functions to subtle processes that can, without our realization, produce anxiety or depression (Kihlstrom, 1987).

You can get some idea of how these unconscious processes affect us if you think about how you often follow a familiar route to work or school without apparent thought. But unconscious processing can also be studied in the laboratory, as you will see in the following demonstration. Try filling in the blanks to make a word from the following stem:

D E F _ _ _

◀ **CONNECTION • CHAPTER 4**
Psychologists use *priming* to study *implicit memory*.

Using a technique called *priming,* psychologists can have some influence on the answers people give to such problems without their being conscious that they were influenced. In the example just given, there are a number of possible ways to complete the word stem, including *defend, defeat, defect, defile, deform, defray, defuse,* and *define.* We don't know for sure what your answer was, but we have carefully set you up to increase the probability that you would pick the word *define.* To do so, we deliberately "primed" your response by using the word *define* several times in the previous paragraph. (There is no certainty, of course, that you would respond as predicted—merely an increased probability.) With priming methods such as this, psychologists have a powerful tool for probing the interaction of conscious and unconscious processes.

Coma and Related States   The general public profoundly misunderstands what it means to be in a **coma.** This misunderstanding stems, in part, from a few highly publicized and emotion-provoking cases that posed heated discussion about the ethics of discontinuing life support in severely brain-injured patients (Meyers, 2007). The flames have been fanned, too, by reports of "miraculous" recoveries. So what are the facts?

Comas are not stable, long-term states. Rather, they usually last only a few days—up to about two weeks. In a comatose state, patients lack the normal cycles of sleep and wakefulness, their eyes usually remain closed, and they cannot be aroused. Those who improve make a transition to a *minimally conscious state,* during which they may have limited awareness and a functioning brain. Recovery is usually gradual (National Institute of Neurological Disorders and Stroke, 2007).

Those who do not improve soon deteriorate into a *persistent vegetative state.* In this condition, they may open their eyes periodically, but they have only minimal brain activity and basic reflexes. The chances for full recovery from a persistent vegetative state are slim. To be sure, in a few highly publicized cases, persons have made dramatic recoveries from what the press erroneously described as a "coma." In fact, none of these cases has involved a persistent vegetative state.

Unconscious   In classic Freudian theory, a part of the mind that houses emotional memories, desires, and feelings that would be threatening if brought to consciousness. Many modern cognitive psychologists, however, view the unconscious in less sinister terms, as including all nonconscious mental processes.

Coma   An unconscious state, during which a person lacks the normal cycles of sleep and wakefulness, that usually lasts only a few days. The comatose state differs from the *minimally conscious state* and the *persistent vegetative state.*

PSYCHOLOGY**MATTERS**
Using Psychology to Learn Psychology

Want to expand your consciousness? In the strictest sense, it is not really possible, because consciousness has a limited capacity. As we noted at the beginning of the chapter, consciousness can focus on only one thing at a time. What can be expanded, however, is the access your consciousness has to information you have stored in preconscious memory. Learning how to do this can be of tremendous help to students who need to absorb a large amount of information and to prove it on an exam.

You will, of course, have an advantage if you face an exam with your consciousness unimpaired by the massive sleep debt that students sometimes incur in an "all-nighter" study session. No amount of caffeine can bring your sleep-deprived consciousness back to optimum functioning. Just as your teachers have always preached, it is far better to spread your studying over several days or weeks, rather than trying to learn everything at once and losing sleep over it.

Because of its severely limited capacity, you cannot possibly hold in consciousness all the information you need to remember for an exam. The material must be stored, readily accessible but outside of consciousness, in preconscious long-term memory. The trick is to be able to bring it back into consciousness when needed. Here are some strategies that you will find helpful in doing this:

1. *Study for the gist.* Students sometimes think their professors ask "trick questions," although professors almost never do so intentionally. In reality, a good exam question will show whether students understand the meaning of a term—the *gist*—rather than having merely memorized a definition. A twofold study strategy can help you get the gist (pronounced *JIST*) of a concept. First, paraphrase the definition given in the text or in class. Second, think of an example from your own experience that illustrates the concept.

2. *Look for connections among concepts.* Even if you have the gist of the concepts you have studied, you will probably need to know how those concepts are related to each other. The professor may ask you to explain, for example, the relationship between *consciousness* and *preconsciousness*. Therefore a good study strategy is to ask yourself how a new concept (e.g., *preconscious*) is related to other concepts learned previously (e.g., *conscious* or *unconscious*).

3. *Anticipate the most likely cues.* Just because you "know" the material doesn't mean that the exam questions will make the answers spill from long-term memory back into consciousness. It pays, therefore, to spend some of your study time thinking about the kinds of questions your professor might ask. For example, you will learn in this chapter about the effects of various psychoactive drugs, but you could be stumped when the professor asks you to explain why alcohol is more like the barbiturates than the opiates. You can often anticipate such questions by noting what the professor emphasizes in lecture. It also helps to think of the kinds of questions that your professor is known to favor. (A study partner helps a lot with this.) Some of the most common test questions begin with terms such as "Explain," "Evaluate," or "Compare and Contrast."

In general, the relationship between consciousness and memory suggests that learning the kind of material required in your college classes demands that it be actively processed while in consciousness. To do so effectively, the material must be made meaningful. This requires making connections between new information and old information that is already in your memory. It also requires organizing the information so that you see how it is interconnected. And, finally, it requires anticipating the cues that will be used to bring it back to consciousness.

As we noted in the Learning chapter, cognitive learning and behavioral learning seem to involve different brain mechanisms. Most cognitive learning—e.g., your learning of the material in this chapter—involves consciousness. On the other hand, much behavioral learning, particularly classical conditioning—such as the acquisition of a phobic response—relies heavily on processes that can occur outside of consciousness.

CONNECTION • CHAPTER 3

Behavioral learning includes *operant conditioning* and *classical conditioning*.

CheckYourUnderstanding

1. **RECALL:** Why did behaviorist John Watson object to defining psychology as the science of consciousness?

2. **RECALL:** What technology would a cognitive neuroscientist be likely to use in studying consciousness?

3. **APPLICATION:** How would you sample the contents of another person's *preconscious* mind?

4. **UNDERSTANDING THE CORE CONCEPT:** What parts of the mind or mental states occur outside our conscious awareness?

Answers 1. Watson and other behaviorists have argued that consciousness is a subjective mental state, that cannot be studied objectively with the methods of science. **2.** Cognitive neuroscientists commonly use fMRI and other brain scanning techniques. **3.** Ask him or her to recall specific information from memory, such as a phone number or a concept that had been previously learned. **4.** Among the parts of the mind and mental states that occur outside of consciousness, we have discussed the preconscious, unconscious, coma, persistent vegetative state, and the minimally conscious state.

8.2 KEY QUESTION
WHAT CYCLES OCCUR IN EVERYDAY CONSCIOUSNESS?

If you are a "morning person," you are probably at your peak of alertness soon after you awaken. But this mental state doesn't last all day. Like most other people, you probably experience a period of mental lethargy in the afternoon. At this low point in the cycle of wakefulness, you may join much of the Latin world, which wisely takes a siesta. Later, your alertness increases for a time, only to fade again during the evening hours. Punctuating this cycle may be periods of heightened focus and attention and periods of reverie, known as daydreams. Finally, whether you are a "morning" or "night" person, you eventually drift into that third of your life spent asleep, where conscious contact with the outside world nearly ceases.

Psychologists have traced these cyclic changes in consciousness, looking for reliable patterns. Our Core Concept for this section of the chapter summarizes what they have found:

core concept

> Consciousness changes in cycles that correspond to our biological rhythms and to the patterns of stimulation in our environment.

In this section we will devote most of our attention to the cyclic changes in consciousness involved in sleep and nocturnal dreaming. We begin, however, with another sort of "dreaming" that occurs while we are awake.

Daydreaming

In the mildly altered state of consciousness that we call **daydreaming**, attention turns inward to memories, expectations, and desires—often with vivid mental imagery (Roche & McConkey, 1990). Daydreaming occurs most often when people are alone, relaxed, engaged in a boring or routine task, or just about to fall asleep (Singer, 1966, 1975). It can also occur in class, while you are reading or any time the external environment doesn't hold your attention.

But is daydreaming normal? You may be relieved to know that most people daydream every day. In fact, it is abnormal if you do not! Research shows, however, that young adults report the most frequent daydreams, with the amount of daydreaming declining significantly with increasing age (Singer & McCraven, 1961).

Daydreaming as Default   A study by Malia Mason and her colleagues (2007) shows that "mind-wandering" is associated with a "default network" in the brain that remains active during the restful waking state. Thus, daydreaming is what the mind does naturally when there are no external demands placed on it from incoming stimuli. The voices, images, thoughts, and feelings involved in these ruminations apparently arise from the activity in the brain circuits that produce consciousness.

Daydreaming   A common (and quite normal) variation of consciousness in which attention shifts to memories, expectations, desires, or fantasies and away from the immediate situation.

Moreover, daydreams can serve valuable, healthy functions (Klinger, 1987). They often dwell on practical and current concerns in people's lives, such as classes, goals (trivial or significant), and interpersonal relationships. As we ruminate on these concerns, daydreaming can help us make plans and solve problems.

Don't Think about a White Bear   On the other hand, daydreams can feature persistent and unwelcome wishes, worries, or fantasies. What can you do if that happens? Suppose that you decide to stop entertaining a particular thought—fantasies of an old flame, a persistent tune running through your head, or worries about a grade. Studies suggest that deliberate efforts to suppress unwanted thoughts are likely to backfire. In the famous "white bear" experiment (Wegner et al., 1987), students were asked to speak into a tape recorder about anything that came to mind. They were instructed, however, not to think about "a white bear." The results: Despite the instructions, the students mentioned a white bear about once per minute! Obviously, trying to suppress a thought or put something out of your mind can result in an obsession with the very thought you seek to escape. Yet, when you don't try to censor your thoughts but, instead, allow your mind to roam freely, as daydreaming and fantasy naturally do, unwanted or upsetting thoughts usually become less intrusive and finally cease (Wegner, 1989).

And how do daydreams compare with dreams of the night? No matter how realistic our fantasies may be, daydreams are rarely as vivid as our most colorful night dreams. Neither are they as mysterious—because they are more under our control. Nor do they occur, like night dreams, under the influence of biological cycles and the strange world that we call sleep. It is to this nighttime world that we now turn our attention.

Sleep: The Mysterious Third of Our Lives

If you live to be 90, you will have slept for nearly 30 years. Even though this means we "lose" a third of our lives, most of us take this lengthy alteration of daily consciousness for granted. In fact, we often anticipate sleep with pleasure. But what is this mysterious mental state? Once the province of psychoanalysts, prophets, poets, painters, and psychics, the world of sleep has now become a vibrant field of study for scientific researchers, who have shown that sleep must be understood as one of our natural biological cycles (Beardsley, 1996). We begin our exploration of this realm of altered consciousness with an examination of these cycles.

Circadian Rhythms   All creatures fall under the influence of nature's cyclic changes, especially the daily pattern of light and darkness. Among the most important for we humans are those known as **circadian rhythms,** bodily patterns that repeat approximately every 24 hours. (Circadian comes from the Latin *circa* for "about" and *dies* for "a day.") Internal control of these recurring rhythms resides in a "biological clock" that sets the cadence of such functions as metabolism, heart rate, body temperature, and hormonal activity. Although we don't know precisely how this clock works, we know its locus is the hypothalamus—the suprachiasmatic nucleus, to be exact (Pinel, 2005). This group of cells receives input from the eyes, and so is especially sensitive to the light–dark cycles of day and night (Barinaga, 2002). From a biological perspective, then, the cycle of sleep and wakefulness is just another circadian rhythm.

For most of us, the normal sleep–wakefulness pattern is naturally a bit longer than a day in length. When placed for long periods in an environment in which there are no time cues, most people settle into a circadian cycle that is just slightly longer than 24 hours. But under more normal circumstances, the pattern undergoes daily readjustment by our exposure to light and by our habitual routines (Dement & Vaughan, 1999).

Circadian rhythm   Physiological pattern that repeats approximately every 24 hours—such as the sleep–wakefulness cycle.

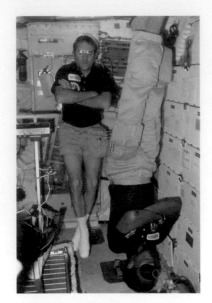

Without the light–dark cycles that continually update their "biological clocks" on Earth, these sleeping astronauts on board the space shuttle face novel problems in synchonizing their work schedule with their circadian rhythms.

You may think of sleep as a process that occurs in an approximately 8-hour period, from the time you go to bed until your alarm wakes you in the morning. But that pattern is rather new in human history and limited mainly to people living in industrialized countries. The more "natural" human tendency is to sleep in a more fluid pattern, whenever one feels like it, in shorter periods during the day or longer stretches during the night (Bosveld, 2007; Warren, 2007). Commonly, in rural villages throughout the world, sleepers will wake up for an hour or two during the middle of the night and converse, play, daydream, have sex, or tend the fire—all of which should show us just how malleable our sleep–wakefulness schedules can be.

Yet, anything that cuts your sleep short or throws your internal clock off its biological schedule can affect how you feel and behave. Work schedules that shift from day to night are notorious for such effects (Dement & Vaughan, 1999; Moore-Ede, 1993). Staying up all night studying for an exam will have similar consequences.

Likewise, flying across several time zones results in *jet lag,* because the internal circadian cycle is disrupted by your new temporal environment. If it is 1:00 A.M. to your body but only 8:00 P.M. to the people around you, you must use energy and resources to adapt to your surroundings. The resulting symptoms of jet lag include fatigue, irresistible sleepiness, and temporary cognitive deficits. Air travelers should note that our biological clocks can adjust more readily to longer days than to shorter ones. Therefore, traveling eastbound (losing hours in your day) creates greater jet lag than traveling westbound (gaining hours).

The Main Events of Sleep   Sleep has been a mystery for most of human history—until late one night in 1952. It was then that graduate student Eugene Aserinsky decided to make recordings of his sleeping son's brain waves and muscle movements of the eyes (Brown, 2003). The session proceeded uneventfully for about an hour and a half, with nothing but the slow rhythms of sleep appearing as tracks on the EEG. Then suddenly, a flurry of eye movements appeared. The recording showed the boy's eyeballs darting back and forth, as though he were watching a fast-changing scene. At the same time, the brain wave patterns told Aserinsky that the boy was alert. Expecting to find that his son had awakened and was looking around, Aserinsky entered the bedroom and was surprised to see him lying quietly, with his eyes closed and fast asleep. What was going on? Wisely, the researcher ran more volunteers through the same procedure, and he found that essentially the same pattern occurred periodically throughout the night in all of them.

About every 90 minutes during sleep, we suddenly enter the state Aserinsky discovered. We now call it **REM sleep,** a stage marked by fast brain waves and rapid eye movements (REM) beneath closed eyelids. These take place for several minutes and then abruptly cease (Aserinsky & Kleitman, 1953). The interim periods, without rapid eye movements, are known as **non-REM (NREM) sleep.**

What happens in the mind and brain during these two different phases of sleep? To find out, researchers awakened sleepers during either REM sleep or NREM sleep and asked them to describe their mental activity (Dement & Kleitman, 1957; McNamara et al., 2005). The NREM reports typically contained either brief descriptions of ordinary daily events or no mental activity at all. By contrast, REM reports were filled with vivid cognitions, featuring fanciful, bizarre scenes, often of an aggressive nature. In other words, rapid eye movements were a sign of dreaming.

Strangely, while the eyes can dance during REM sleep, the voluntary muscles in the rest of the body remain immobile—paralyzed—a condition now known as **sleep paralysis.** From an evolutionary perspective, we can see that this probably kept our ancestors from wandering out of their caves and into trouble while acting out their dreams. (In case you're wondering: Sleepwalking and sleep talking don't occur during REM sleep but in the deepest stage of NREM sleep.)

REM sleep   A stage of sleep that occurs approximately every 90 minutes, marked by bursts of rapid eye movements occurring under closed eyelids. REM sleep periods are associated with dreaming.

Non-REM (NREM) sleep   The recurring periods, mainly associated with the deeper stages of sleep, when a sleeper is not showing rapid eye movements.

Sleep paralysis   A condition in which a sleeper is unable to move any of the voluntary muscles, except those controlling the eyes. Sleep paralysis normally occurs during REM sleep.

We'll have much more to say about dreaming in a moment. For now, let's see how REM sleep fits with the other phases of sleep.

The Sleep Cycle Imagine that you are a volunteer subject in a laboratory sleep experiment. Already connected to EEG recording equipment, you soon become comfortable with the wires linking your body to the machinery, and you are settling in for a night's snooze. While you are still awake and alert, the EEG shows your brain waves pulsing at a rate of about 14 cycles per second (cps). As you begin to relax and become drowsy, they slow to about 8 to 12 cps. When you fall asleep, your brain waves register a cycle of activity much like the pattern you see in Figure 8.3—a cycle that repeats itself over and over through the night. A closer look at the recording of this cycle the next morning will show several distinct stages, each with a characteristic EEG signature (see Figure 8.4):

● In Stage 1 sleep, the EEG displays some slower (theta) activity, along with fast brain (beta) waves similar to those seen in the waking state.

● During the next phase, Stage 2, the generally slower EEG is punctuated by sleep spindles—short bursts of fast electrical activity that reliably signals the end of Stage 1.

● In the following two stages (3 and 4), the sleeper enters a progressively deeper state of relaxed sleep. The heart rate and breathing rate slow down. Brain waves also slow dramatically, with delta waves appearing for the first time. The deepest point in the sleep cycle occurs in Stage 4, about a half hour after sleep onset.

● As Stage 4 ends, the electrical activity of the brain increases, and the sleeper climbs back up through the stages in reverse order.

● Rather than going through Stage 1 again, the sleeper begins to produce fast beta waves on the EEG, along with rapid eye movements—the sign of a new stage called REM sleep, which sleep researchers now recognize as distinct from Stage 1. It is important to note that, in a normal night's sleep, this is the first appearance of REM. After about 10 minutes of REMing, the entire cycle begins to repeat itself, with each succeeding REM period getting longer and longer.

Over the course of an average night's sleep, most people make the circuit up and down through the stages of sleep four to six times. In each successive cycle,

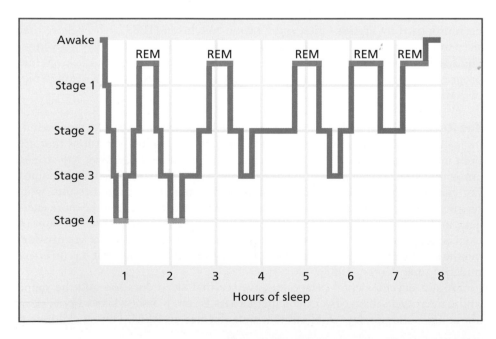

FIGURE 8.3
Stages of Sleep

In a typical night, the deepest sleep (Stages 3 and 4) occurs mainly in the first few hours. As the night progresses, the sleeper spends more and more time in the stages of light sleep and in REM sleep.

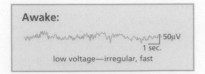

Awake:

~50μV
1 sec.
low voltage—irregular, fast

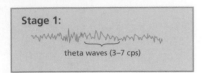

Drowsy:

alpha waves (8–12 cps)

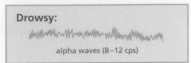

Stage 1:

theta waves (3–7 cps)

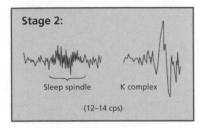

Stage 2:

Sleep spindle   K complex

(12–14 cps)

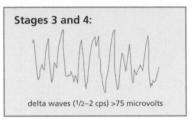

Stages 3 and 4:

delta waves (1/2–2 cps) >75 microvolts

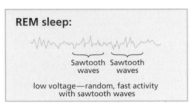

REM sleep:

Sawtooth   Sawtooth
waves   waves

low voltage—random, fast activity
with sawtooth waves

FIGURE 8.4
EEG Patterns in Stages of Sleep

REM rebound A condition of increased REM sleep caused by REM-sleep deprivation.

the amount of time spent in deep sleep (Stages 3 and 4) decreases, and the amount of time spent in REM sleep increases. During the first cycle, the REM period may last only 10 minutes, while in the last cycle, we may spend as much as an hour REMing. A look at Figure 8.3 will show you how this pattern plays out through a typical night's sleep. Studying this pattern will not only help you understand your normal night's sleep but will also provide the framework for understanding the abnormal patterns found in most sleep disorders, which we will consider a little later. Again, please note the three most important features of normal sleep: (a) the 90-minute cycles, (b) the occurrence of deepest sleep near the beginning of the night, and (c) the increase in REM duration as sleep progresses.

What do you suppose would happen if a person were deprived of a substantial amount of REM sleep for a whole night? Laboratory studies show that REM-deprived sleepers feel tired and irritable the next day. Then, during the following night, they spend much more time in REM sleep than usual, a condition known as **REM rebound.** This observation suggests that one function of sleep is to satisfy a biological need for REM. Sleep-deprived college students take note: Because we get most of our REM sleep during the last few cycles of the night, we inevitably suffer some REM deprivation and REM rebound if we cut our night's sleep short.

Why Do We Sleep?   Sleep is so common among animals that it surely must have some essential function, but sleep scientists disagree on what that function is (Maquet, 2001; Rechtschaffen, 1998). There are several possibilities. Evolutionary psychology suggests that sleep may have evolved because it enabled animals to conserve energy and stay out of harm's way at times when there was no need to forage for food or search for mates (Dement & Vaughan, 1999; Miller, 2007). These functions, then, are coordinated by the brain's circadian clock. Some experiments also suggest that sleep aids mental functioning, particularly memory and problem-solving (Wagner et al., 2004).

Another function of sleep was poetically described by William Shakespeare, when he spoke of "sleep that knits up the ravelled sleave of care." Thus, sleep may have a restorative function for the body and mind. But exactly how might sleep restore us? It may be a time when the body replenishes its energy supplies and purges itself of toxins built up during the day. In fact, some studies suggest that damaged brain cells do get repaired during sleep; others suggest that sleep promotes the formation of new neurons in the brain—while sleep deprivation inhibits this process (Siegel, 2003; Winerman, 2006b). Yet another possibility has been proposed by Francis Crick and Graeme Mitchison (1983), who believe that sleep and dreams help the brain to flush out the day's accumulation of unwanted and useless information—much like reformatting a computer disk. While progress has been made in learning how sleep actually restores us, a detailed picture still eludes sleep scientists (Winerman, 2006b).

The Need for Sleep   How much sleep we need depends on several factors, including genetics, which sets the sleep requirements and individual variations that are built into our circadian rhythms (Barinaga, 1997b; Haimov & Lavie, 1996). The amount of sleep we require is also linked to our personal characteristics and habits. For example, those who sleep longer than average tend to be more nervous, worrisome, artistic, creative, and nonconforming. Short sleepers tend to be more energetic and extroverted (Hartmann, 1973). And it is no surprise that the amount of exercise a person gets influences the need for sleep. Strenuous physical activity during the day increases the amount of slow-wave sleep in Stage 4, but it has no effect on REM time (Horne, 1988).

From a developmental perspective, we see that sleep duration and the shape of the sleep cycle change over one's lifetime. As Figure 8.5 shows, newborns sleep about 16 hours per day, with half that time devoted to REM. During childhood,

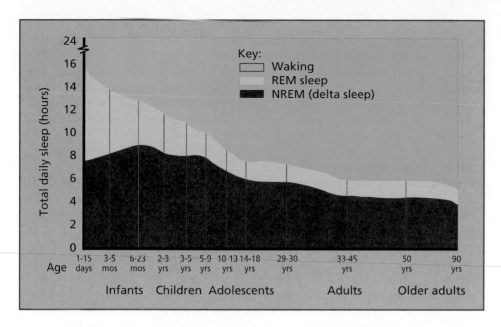

FIGURE 8.5
Patterns of Human Sleep over a Lifetime

The graph shows changes with age in the total amounts of REM and NREM sleep and in the percentage of time spent in REM sleep. Note that, over the years, the amount of REM sleep decreases considerably, while NREM diminishes less sharply.

those numbers gradually decline, probably as a result of the maturing brain. Young adults typically sleep seven to eight hours (although they may need more), with about 20% REM. By old age, we sleep even less, with only 15% of sleep spent in REM. You can find out whether you are getting enough sleep by answering the questions in the accompanying "Do It Yourself!" box.

CONNECTION • CHAPTER 6

The brain continues to develop and also to prune excessive neurons throughout childhood and adolescence.

Sleep Debt versus the Circadian Clock   Your mother was right: Most adults need to sleep about eight hours, or a bit more, to feel good and function efficiently. But that's only an average. For different individuals, the amount of sleep needed ranges from about six to nine hours (although most people need more sleep than they think they do). In the sleep laboratory, when volunteers are placed in a dark room and allowed to sleep without interruption and without reference to clocks, the average adult settles into a pattern that produces about eight and one-half hours of sleep each night. Yet, in their daily lives most Americans get significantly less—night after night (Greer, 2004; Maas, 1999). This creates a sleep shortage that researcher William Dement calls a **sleep debt** (Dement & Vaughan, 1999).

People who pile up a chronic sleep debt usually don't realize it (Dement, 2000; Dement & Vaughan, 1999). They may be groggy and sleepy when the

Sleep debt   A sleep deficiency caused by not getting the amount of sleep that one requires for optimal functioning.

DO IT YOURSELF!   How Much Sleep Do You Need?

Many college students operate in a chronic state of sleep deprivation. Because their schedules are crowded with study, work, and social events, students may convince themselves that they need only a few hours sleep each night. And, in fact, the average college student sleeps only about 6.8 hours a night (Hicks, 1990). Does too little sleep really make a difference in how well you perform in your classes? Psychologist Cheryl Spinweber (1990) has found that sleep-deprived undergraduates get lower grades than their counterparts who get enough sleep.

Recent studies also suggest that sleep deprivation contributes to weight gain: People who sleep less than seven hours a night have high rates of obesity (Harder, 2006).

How can you tell if you need more sleep? Answer the following questions honestly:

1. Do you often feel sleepy in your classes?
2. Do you sleep late on weekends?
3. Do you usually get sleepy when you get bored?
4. Do you often fall asleep while reading or watching TV?

5. Do you usually fall asleep within five minutes of going to bed?
6. Do you awake in the morning feeling that you are not rested?
7. Would you oversleep if you did not use an alarm clock to drive you out of bed?

If you answered "Yes" to any of these questions, chances are that you are shorting yourself on sleep. You may also be paying the price in the quality of your learning and in your grades.

alarm clock rouses them in the morning. But they don't see this as a sign of a sleep debt because their circadian clocks also nudge them into wakefulness over the next few hours. Afternoon drowsiness may be attributed to a big lunch—which, in truth, does not cause sleepiness. (It's the internal clock, again.) They may also rationalize away their struggle to stay awake in a meeting or class by telling themselves that sleepiness is a normal response to boredom (Van Dongen et al., 2003). In fact, the normal response to boredom is restlessness—not sleepiness—unless one is sleep deprived.

The sleep-deprived individual gets caught in a daily tug-of-war between the pulls of a sleep debt, on the one hand, and the combined forces of the environment and circadian rhythms, on the other. In this way your internal clock can fool you: Even when you have not had enough sleep, the clock in the brain can make you feel relatively alert at certain times of the day—usually late morning and late afternoon. But with a chronic sleep debt, you are never as alert and mentally efficient as you could be if the sleep debt were paid with a few good nights of sleep (Van Dongen et al., 2003). Most people don't realize that sleep deprivation is associated with weight gain and even with a shortened lifespan (National Institute of Medicine, 2006). In addition, the sleep debt is sometimes "paid" with a tragedy—as happened dramatically a few years ago, when *Exxon Valdez,* a giant tanker, ran aground, spilling oil across a pristine bay in the Alaskan wilderness. The ensuing investigation revealed that a crew member who was steering the ship at the time had had only six hours of sleep in the previous two days.

Of special interest to students is this fact: Sleep deprivation can have a devastating effect on cognitive and motor functioning (Pilcher & Walters, 1997). In plainer language, William Dement says that a big sleep debt "makes you stupid" (Dement & Vaughan, 1999, p. 231). Evidence of this is found in a study that deprived one group of volunteers of sleep and gave another group enough alcohol to make them legally drunk (their blood alcohol content reached 0.1 percent). After 24 hours of sleep loss—like staying up all night studying for a test—the sleepy volunteers were performing just like the intoxicated group on tests of thinking and coordination (Fletcher et al., 2003). What effects do you suppose chronic sleep deprivation, so common during medical internships and residencies, has on physician performance?[1]

Unfortunately, sleep-deprived people usually don't realize how impaired they actually are. Further, the pressures and opportunities of modern life commonly make us underestimate the amount of sleep we need. We may also believe that we can combat sleepiness and successfully reduce our need for sleep by dint of will power and caffeine. But such measures never give us the clarity of mind that a good night's sleep does. As a result, we may struggle much of our lives with a chronic sleep deficit, never realizing why we must wage a daily battle with drowsiness.

Sleep debt can be dangerous for drivers and others for whom life and limb depend on alertness. Likewise, students who build up a sleep debt jeopardize their mental performance.

Dreaming: The Pageants of the Night

Every night of your life, you experience a spectacular series of events staged only in your dreams. What produces these fantastic cognitive spectacles? And what—if anything—do they mean? As we saw earlier, sleep scientists now know that dreams occur regularly throughout the night, most often in REM sleep. They have also identified the parts of the brain that control dreaming—including, espe-

[1]Further information on the hazards associated with sleep deprivation in physicians is available online from PubMed: www.pubmedcentral.nih.gov/articlerender.fcgi?artid= 1200708

cially, parts of the brain stem. What remains most mysterious about this stage of sleep is *why* we dream.

The ancient Israelites interpreted dreams as messages from God. Their Egyptian contemporaries attempted to influence dreams by sleeping in temples dedicated to the god of dreaming, Serapis. And in India, the sacred Vedas described the religious significance of dreams. Meanwhile, in China dreaming held an element of risk. During a dream, the ancient Chinese believed, the soul wandered about outside the body. For that reason they were reluctant to awaken a sleeper hastily, lest the soul not find its way back to the body (Dement, 1980).

From the perspective of many African and Native American cultures, dreams are an extension of waking reality. Consequently, when traditional Cherokee Indians dreamed of snakebite, they received appropriate emergency treatment upon awakening. Likewise, when an African tribal chieftain dreamed of England, he ordered a set of European clothes; and, when he appeared in the new togs, his friends congratulated him on making the trip (Dement, 1980).

In contrast with such folk theories, sleep scientists have approached dreaming with this question: What biological function do dreams have? Most experts suspect that dreams may be necessary for healthy brain functioning, although the evidence for that is not certain, as you will see in a moment (Siegel, 2003).

A closely related issue concerns the *meaning* of dreams. Evolutionary psychologists have proposed that dreams may offer a safe way to rehearse ways of dealing with dangerous situations, but again the evidence is iffy (Franklin & Zyphur, 2005). From a cognitive perspective, some experts see dreams as meaningful mental events, serving pressing cognitive needs or reflecting important events or fantasies in the dreamer's mental world. But others argue that dreams may have no meaning at all. Rather, they may be merely the brain's random activity during sleep. Let's look at both sides of this debate on the meaningfulness of dreams.

Death-related images appear more often in dreams of Mexican American college students than in those of Anglo-American college students. This probably occurs because death is more prominently a part of Mexican culture, as can be seen in this figure, used in the Day of the Dead celebration.

Dreams as Meaningful Events   At the beginning of the 20th century, Sigmund Freud laid out the most complex and comprehensive theory of dreams and their meanings ever developed—a theory that has since enjoyed enormous influence, despite a lack of scientific evidence to support it (Squier & Domhoff, 1998). In this view, dreams represent "the royal road to the unconscious," paved with clues to an individual's hidden mental life. For this reason, Freud made the analysis of dreams the cornerstone of psychoanalysis, as described in his classic book *The Interpretation of Dreams* (1900).

Freud's Theory of Dreams   In psychoanalytic theory, dreams have two main functions, to guard sleep (by disguising disruptive thoughts with symbols) and to serve as sources of wish fulfillment. Freud believed that dreams play their guardian role by relieving psychic tensions created during the day. They serve their wish-fulfillment function by allowing the dreamer to work harmlessly through unconscious desires.

In his explanation of the meaning of dreams, Freud distinguished between the **manifest content**—the dream's story line—and the **latent content**—the (supposed) symbolic meaning of the dream. Psychoanalytic therapists, therefore, scrutinize the manifest content of their patients' dreams for clues that relate to latent motives and conflicts that may lurk in the unconscious. For example, clues relating to sexual conflicts might take the form of long rigid objects or containers which, in Freudian theory, symbolize the male and female genitals. And for Freud, symbols of death include a departure or a journey.

Must you be a trained psychoanalyst to understand dreams? Not necessarily. The manifest content in many of our dreams has a fairly obvious connection to our waking lives. You have probably noticed that frightening dreams often relate to life stressors that have found their way into your sleeping thoughts. Research has lent support to such observations. For example, one study found that indi-

Manifest content   The story line of a dream, taken at face value without interpretation.

Latent content   The symbolic meaning of objects and events in a dream. Latent content is usually an interpretation based on Freud's psychoanalytic theory or one of its variants. For example, the latent content of a dream involving clocks might involve fear of the menstrual cycle and, hence, of one's sexuality.

viduals depressed about divorce often had dreams that dealt with past relationships (Cartwright, 1984). By analyzing the patterns and content of your own dreams, you may find it is not difficult to assign meaning to many of the images and actions you dream about (Hall, 1953/1966; Van de Castle, 1994). We must emphasize, however, that there is little solid scientific support for Freudian interpretations of latent dream content.

Dreams Vary by Culture, Gender, and Age   Freudian dream analysis has been challenged on the grounds that Freud was not always scrupulous in his research. For example, he asserted that boys frequently dream of strife with their fathers, because boys see their fathers as rivals for the mothers' affections—but he did no careful studies to verify his theoretical suspicions. Rather, on the basis of a few cases, he jumped to the conclusion that such dreams were signs of unconscious sexual jealousy. Many other explanations are possible, however, as anthropologists have shown by studying dreams of the Trobriand Islanders. Boys in that culture don't dream of their fathers so much as their uncles, who act as the disciplinarians in Trobriand society (Malinowski, 1927; Segall et al., 1990). Freud's dream theory, then, may be yet another example of the confirmation bias.

CONNECTION • CHAPTER 1

Confirmation bias leads us to notice evidence that agrees with our views and ignore evidence that does not.

The highly specific effects of culture can also be seen in reports from the West African nation of Ghana, where dreams often feature attacks by cows (Barnouw, 1963). Likewise, Americans frequently find themselves embarrassed by public nakedness in their dreams, although such reports rarely occur in cultures where people customarily wear few clothes. Images of death appear more often in the dreams of Mexican American college students than in the dreams of Anglo American students, probably because concerns about death are more a part of life in Latin American cultures (Roll et al., 1974). In general, the cross-cultural research lends support to Rosalind Cartwright's hypothesis (1977) that dreams merely reflect life events that are important to the dreamer.

Taking a more objective approach to dreams than Freud did, modern sleep scientists now know that the content of dreams also varies by age and gender (see Domhoff, 1996). Children are more likely to dream about animals than adults are, and the animals in their dreams are more likely to be large, threatening, and wild. In contrast, college students dream more usually of small animals, pets, and tame creatures. This may mean that children feel less in control of their world than adults do and so may find that world depicted in scarier imagery while they sleep (Van de Castle, 1983, 1994).

Women everywhere more commonly dream of children, while men more often dream of aggression, weapons, and tools (Murray, 1995). In a sample of over 1800 dreams collected by dream researcher Calvin Hall, American women dreamed about both men and women, while men dreamed about men twice as often as about women. In another sample of over 1300 dreams, Hall found that hostile interactions between characters outnumbered friendly exchanges and that 64% of emotional dreams had a negative complexion, such as anger and sadness (Hall, 1951, 1984).

Dreams and Recent Experience   Sleep research has also found—as we might expect—that dream content frequently connects with recent experience and things we have been thinking about during the previous day. But, strangely, if you deliberately try *not* to think about something, it is even more likely to pop up in your dreams (Wegner et al., 2004). So, if you have been worrying about your job all day—or trying to forget about it—you're likely to dream about work tonight, especially during your first REM period.

Typically, then, the first dream of the night connects with events of the previous day. Dreams in the second REM period (90 minutes later) often build on a theme that emerged during the first REM period. And so it goes through the night, like an evolving rumor passed from one person to another: The final dream that emerges may have a connection—but only a remote one—to events of the previous day. Because the last dream of the night is the one most likely to be remembered, we may not recognize the link with the previous day's events (Cartwright, 1977; Kiester, 1980).

Dreams and Memory The relationship between dreams and recent experience may belie yet another possible function of dreams. Comparisons of individuals who were selectively deprived of REM sleep with those deprived of NREM sleep suggest that REM sleep helps us remember—although we must add that this conclusion is still controversial. Indeed, the brain replenishes neurotransmitters in its memory networks during REM, notes sleep researcher James Maas. It may be that REM sleep is a normal part of weaving new experiences into the fabric of old memories (Greer, 2004b).

Recent research suggests that NREM sleep also selectively reinforces certain kinds of memory (Miller, 2007). Recollection for facts and locations seem to be consolidated in NREM sleep, while REM deals more with motor skills and emotional memories. At this point no one knows why the sleeping brain seems to divide tasks up in this way.

Dreams as Random Activity of the Brain

Not everyone believes that dream content has any special meaning of consequence—certainly not any latent content that warrants "deep" interpretation. In particular, the **activation-synthesis theory** says that dreams result when the sleeping brain tries to make sense of its own spontaneous bursts of activity (Leonard, 1998; Squier & Domhoff, 1998). In this view, dreams have their origin in periodic neural discharges emitted by the sleeping brain stem. As this energy sweeps over the cerebral cortex, the sleeper experiences impressions of sensation, memory, motivation, emotion, and movement. Although the cortical activation is random, and the images it generates may not be logically connected, the brain tries to make sense of the stimulation it receives. To do so, the brain synthesizes or pulls together the "messages" in these random electrical bursts by creating a coherent story. A dream, then, could merely be the brain's way of making sense out of nonsense.

The original proponents of this theory, J. Allan Hobson and Robert McCarley (1977), argued that REM sleep furnishes the brain with an internal source of needed stimulation. This internal activation promotes the growth and development of the brain at the time when the sleeping brain has blocked out external stimulation. Dream content, therefore, results from brain activation, not unconscious wishes or other meaningful mental processes. While Hobson (1988, 2002) claims that the story line in our dreams is added as a "brainstorm afterthought," he does acknowledge that dream content may nevertheless have some psychological meaning in that the dream story is influenced by culture, gender, personality factors, and recent events. Thus, when brain activations are synthesized, dreams seem familiar and meaningful.

Dreams as a Source of Creative Insights

Even if Hobson and McCarley are right—that dreams have no special meaning other than an attempt by the brain to make sense out of nonsense—dreams could still be a source of creative ideas. In fact, it would be astonishing if we did not turn to such wild and sometimes wonderful scenes in the night for inspiration. As we have seen, writers, composers, and scientists have done just that.

"Dream explorer" Robert Moss (1996) cites 19th-century physiologist Herman von Helmholtz, who insisted that creative dreaming would result from doing three things: first, saturating yourself in a problem or issue that interests you; next, letting your creative ideas incubate by not pushing yourself for a solution but by shifting attention to something that is relaxing; and finally, allowing yourself time to experience illumination, a sudden flash of insight into the answer you seek.

Moss himself recommends the following technique, which you may want to try (with your critical thinking skills at the ready) to find creative inspiration in your dreams: First, bring to mind an expert whom you admire in your field of

Sleep and dreaming have inspired many artists, as seen here in Rousseau's Sleeping Gypsy.

Activation-synthesis theory The theory that dreams begin with random electrical activation coming from the brain stem. Dreams, then, are the brain's attempt to make sense of—to synthesize—this random activity.

endeavor. Before you go to sleep, imagine you are asking this person for help in solving your problem; then tell yourself to dream the answer. If you wake from a dream, quickly write or sketch all you can recall—no matter what the dream was about. Later, when you review your notes, you may find that your approach to the problem has been "given a distinct tilt" (Moss, 1996). Your later interpretation of your dream thoughts might surprise you with insights you didn't even know you could achieve. Perhaps, if you take creative control of your dreams, you can create your own "monster," just as Mary Shelley did in *Frankenstein*.

PSYCHOLOGY**MATTERS**
Sleep Disorders

You may be among the more than 100 million Americans who get insufficient sleep or poor-quality sleep. Some of these sleep problems are job related. Among people who work night shifts, for example, more than half nod off at least once a week on the job. And it may be no coincidence that some of the world's most serious accidents—including the disastrous radiation emissions at the Three Mile Island and Chernobyl nuclear plants and the massive toxic chemical discharge at Bhopal—have occurred during late evening hours when people are likely to be programmed for sleep. Sleep experts speculate that many accidents occur because key personnel fail to function optimally as a result of insufficient sleep—as we noted earlier in the catastrophic case of the *Exxon Valdez* oil spill (Dement & Vaughan, 1999).

Along with these job-related sleep problems, there are several clinical sleep disorders that sleep researchers have studied in their laboratories. Some are common, while others are both rare and bizarre. Some are relatively benign, and some are potentially life threatening. The single element that ties them together is a disruption in one or more parts of the normal sleep cycle.

Insomnia is usually the diagnosis when people feel dissatisfied with the amount of sleep they get. Its symptoms include chronic inability to fall asleep quickly, frequent arousals during sleep, or early-morning awakening. Insomnia sufferers number about one-third of all adults, making this the most common of sleep disorders (Dement & Vaughan, 1999).

An occasional bout of sleeplessness is normal, especially when you have exciting or worrisome events on your mind. These incidents pose no special danger in themselves, unless attempts are made to treat the problem with barbiturates or over-the-counter "sleeping pills." These drugs disrupt the normal sleep cycle by cutting short REM sleep periods (Dement, 1980). As a result, they can actually aggravate the effects of insomnia by making the user feel less rested and more sleepy. A new generation of drugs for the treatment of insomnia—the ones you see heavily advertised on TV—seems to avoid most of these problems, although they have not been studied for long-term use (Harder, 2005). An alternative is psychological treatment employing cognitive behavioral therapy, which has had remarkable success in helping people learn effective strategies for avoiding insomnia (Smith, 2001).

Incidentally, counting sheep won't help you break the insomnia barrier. Neither will some other boring mental task. Researchers at Oxford University have shown that it is better to imagine some soothing, but complex, scene, such as a waterfall. Counting one sheep after another apparently isn't interesting enough to keep the sleep-inhibiting worries of the day out of mind (Randerson, 2002).

Sleep apnea, another common disorder, may be apparent only in a person's complaints of daytime sleepiness and a sleep partner's complaints about snoring. But behind the curtain of the night, the cause can be found in an abnormality of breathing. The sleep apnea sufferer actually stops breathing for up to a minute, as often as several hundred times each night! (In case you're concerned,

CONNECTION • CHAPTER 13

Cognitive behavioral therapy combines cognitive and behavioral techniques in treating psychological disorders.

Insomnia The most common of sleep disorders—involving insufficient sleep, the inability to fall asleep quickly, frequent arousals, or early awakenings.

Sleep apnea A respiratory disorder in which the person intermittently stops breathing many times while

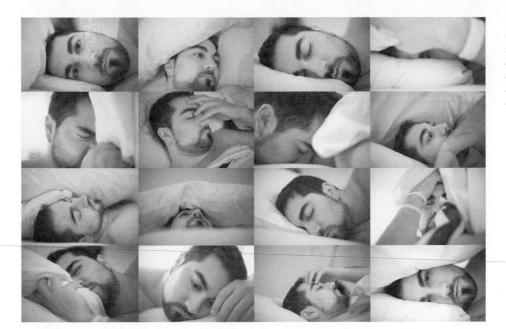

the brief cessation of breathing a few times each hour during the night is normal.) Most commonly, this results from collapse of the airway in the throat when the sleeper's muscle tone relaxes. The result is the second major symptom of sleep apnea: frequent loud snoring, occurring each time the patient runs short of oxygen and tries mightily to get air through the collapsed airway (Seligson, 1994). As breathing stops and the sleeper's blood oxygen level plummets, the body's emergency system kicks into gear, causing distress hormones to course through the body. In the process, the sleeper awakens briefly, begins breathing again, and then falls back to sleep. Because most of this happens in deep sleep, there is usually no memory of the episode.

Failure to recognize the nature of the problem can cause apnea sufferers—and their families and coworkers—to interpret unusual daytime behavior, such as inattention or falling asleep, as laziness or neglect. While this may be disruptive to relationships, sleep apnea can also have harmful biological effects that include damage to brain cells, along with elevated blood pressure that can impose dangerous levels of stress on the blood vessels and heart (Gami et al., 2005).

Occasional episodes of sleep apnea are likely to occur in premature infants, who may need physical stimulation to start breathing again. Further, any tendency toward sleep apnea can be aggravated by putting a young child to bed on its stomach. (Instead, sleep scientists strongly recommend "back to sleep.") Obviously, the problem can be lethal, and it is one possible cause of *sudden infant death syndrome* (SIDS). Until their underdeveloped respiratory systems mature, these infants must remain connected to breathing monitors while they sleep. In contrast, permanent breathing failure is not a strong concern for adults with sleep apnea, for whom treatment focuses on decreasing the hundreds of nightly apnea episodes. This is usually accomplished by using a device that pumps extra air into the lungs and keeps the airway open during sleep.

Night terrors, which occur primarily in children, pose no health threat. Typically, a night terror attack presents itself as the screaming of a terrified-looking child who is actually in Stage 4 sleep and very difficult to awaken. When finally alert, the child may still feel fearful but have no specific memory of what mental events might have caused the night terror. In fact, the whole experience is likely to be more memorable to the beleaguered family members than it is to the child.

Unlike garden-variety nightmares, sleep-terror episodes occur in deep sleep, rather than in REM sleep. In this respect they are like sleepwalking, sleep talking,

Night terrors Deep sleep episodes that seem to produce terror, although any terrifying mental experience (such as a dream) is usually forgotten on awakening. Night terrors occur mainly in children.

The discovery of narcolepsy in dogs showed that the disorder has a biological basis. Here, pioneering sleep researcher William Dement holds one of his sleeping subjects.

Narcolepsy A disorder of REM sleep, involving sleep-onset REM periods and sudden daytime REM-sleep attacks usually accompanied by cataplexy.

and bed-wetting, which also occur in Stage 4. All these conditions seem to have a genetic component. In themselves, they pose no danger, although sleepwalkers can inadvertently climb out of upper-story windows or walk into a busy street—so it pays to take some precautions. (Incidentally, it's just a myth that waking a sleepwalker is dangerous.) In most cases, sleepwalking and night terrors will diminish or disappear in adulthood, but if they pose persistent and chronic problems, the individual should be evaluated by a sleep specialist. Bed-wetting can usually be ameliorated by a simple behavior modification procedure that employs a pad with a built-in alarm that sounds when damp.

Narcolepsy, one of the most unusual of sleep disorders, produces sudden daytime sleep attacks, often without warning. But these are no ordinary waves of drowsiness. So suddenly do these sleep attacks develop that narcolepsy sufferers have reported falling asleep while driving a car, climbing a ladder, or scuba diving under 20 feet of water. Narcoleptic sleep attacks may also be preceded by a sudden loss of muscle control, a condition known as *cataplexy.*

Strangely, anything exciting can trigger a narcoleptic episode. For example, these patients commonly report that they fall asleep while laughing at a joke or even while having sex. Obviously, narcolepsy can be dangerous—and not so good for intimate relationships, either.

Assembling the pieces of this puzzle of symptoms, we find that narcolepsy is a disorder of REM sleep (Marschall, 2007). Specifically, a sleep recording will show that the narcolepsy victim has an abnormal sleep-onset REM period. That is, instead of waiting the usual 90 minutes to begin REMing, the narcoleptic person enters REM as sleep begins. You may have already guessed that the accompanying cataplexy is simply REM sleep paralysis.

Studies of narcoleptic animals show that the disorder stems from a genetic problem affecting the sleep-control circuitry in the brain stem. Recent research implicates a diminished supply of *hypocretin,* a chemical produced in the hypothalamus (Harder, 2004; Marschall, 2007). So far there is no cure, but certain drugs can diminish the frequency of both the sleep attacks and the cataplexy. Now that we know that the cause is biological, narcoleptic patients are no longer sent to psychotherapy aimed at searching for the unconscious conflicts that were once assumed to underlie the disorder.

So, what should you do if you suspect that you have a serious sleep disorder, such as chronic insomnia, sleep apnea, or narcolepsy? An evaluation by a sleep expert is the place to start. Many hospitals have sleep disorder clinics to which your physician or clinical psychologist can refer you.

CheckYourUnderstanding

1. **RECALL:** What do brain scans tell us about the daydreaming brain?

2. **RECALL:** What muscular changes occur during REM sleep?

3. **RECALL:** Suppose that you are working in a sleep laboratory, where you are monitoring a subject's sleep recording during the night. As the night progresses, you would expect to see that
   a. sleep becomes deeper and deeper.
   b. REM periods become longer.
   c. Stage 3 and 4 sleep periods lengthen.

   d. dreaming becomes less frequent.

4. **RECALL:** According to the activation-synthesis theory, what causes our dreams?

5. **APPLICATION:** Which sleep disorder is marked by a REM period at the beginning of sleep?

6. **UNDERSTANDING THE CORE CONCEPT:** Our Core Concept states that consciousness changes in cycles that normally correspond to our biological rhythms and to the patterns of our environment. Give an example of a recurring mental state that illustrates this concept.

Answers 1. Brain scans suggest that daydreaming is generated by activity in a "default network" of circuits in the brain that remains active during the restful waking state. **2.** Sleep paralysis affects all the voluntary muscles except those controlling eye movements. **3.** b **4.** According to the activation-synthesis theory, dreams are an attempt by the brain to make sense of random activity in the brain stem during sleep. **5.** narcolepsy **6.** Sleep and dreaming are among the cyclic changes in consciousness.

8.3 KEY QUESTION
WHAT OTHER FORMS CAN CONSCIOUSNESS TAKE?

Children stand on their heads or spin around to make themselves dizzy. You may seek similar sensations from hair-raising theme-park rides or sky diving. But why do people do these strange things to themselves? One view says that "human beings are born with a drive to experience modes of awareness other than the normal waking one; from very young ages, children experiment with techniques to change consciousness" (Weil, 1977, p. 37). So, sleep, dreams, fantasies, and thrilling experiences offer compelling alternatives to everyday conscious experience.

In this section of the chapter, we will see how certain psychological techniques, such as hypnosis and meditation, can alter consciousness, too. But, for some people, these conventional alternatives may not provide the states of consciousness they seek. Instead, they may turn to drugs that alter ordinary awareness: We will also examine this approach to changing consciousness. Our discussion of drugs will include both legal substances, such as alcohol, tobacco, and caffeine, and illegal drugs, such heroin, PCP, marijuana, meth, ecstasy, and cocaine. So, what is the theme that ties these altered states of consciousness together? The Core Concept of this section says:

> **An altered state of consciousness occurs when some aspect of normal consciousness is modified by mental, behavioral, or chemical means.**

While this notion may, at first, sound simplistic, it carries the important implication that altered states do not involve any mysterious or paranormal phenomena that defy rational explanation. Rather, altered states are modifications of ordinary consciousness that we can study with the tools of science. Let's begin with what is known about hypnosis.

Hypnosis

The cartoon images have it wrong. Neither the hypnotist's eyes nor fingertips emit strange, mesmerizing rays that send subjects into a compliant stupor—nor does a dangling shiny bauble have the power to control people's minds. A more accurate (but much less dramatic) picture would show the hypnotist making suggestions to promote concentration and relaxation (Barber, 1976, 1986). Soon the subject appears to be asleep, although he or she can obviously hear suggestions and carry out requests. In some cases, the individual under hypnosis also seems to have amazing powers to ignore pain, remember long-forgotten details, and create hallucinations. But what mental processes make these things happen? To find out, we will explore several viewpoints on the nature of hypnosis. Then, we will consider some of its valid and practical uses by psychologists.

The term *hypnosis* derives from *Hypnos*, the name of the Greek god of sleep. Yet the EEG record tells us that ordinary sleep plays no role in hypnosis, even though hypnotized individuals may appear to be in a relaxed, sleeplike state. (There is no unique EEG signature for hypnosis.) Most authorities would say **hypnosis** involves a state of awareness characterized by deep relaxation, heightened suggestibility, and focused attention.

When deeply hypnotized, some people will respond to suggestion with dramatic changes in perception, memory, motivation, and sense of self-control (Orne, 1980). And, yes, stage hypnotists can make carefully selected volunteers quack like a duck or seem to like the taste of a bitter lemon. After the experience is over, people often report that they experienced heightened responsiveness to the hypnotist's suggestions and felt that their behavior was performed without intention or any conscious effort.

Hypnotizability Dramatic stage performances of hypnosis give the impression that hypnotic power lies with the hypnotist. However, the real star is the person who

A roller coaster ride is one way to alter your consciousness.

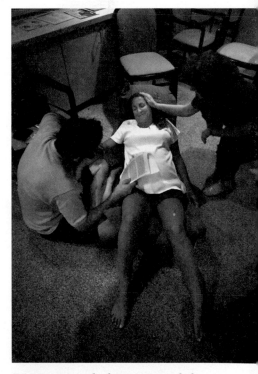

core
concept

For many people, hypnosis can help control pain. Here, a woman is learning hypnotic techniques that she will use in natural childbirth.

Hypnosis An induced state of awareness, usually characterized by heightened suggestibility, deep relaxation, and highly focused attention.

is hypnotized. The hypnotist is more like an experienced guide showing the way. Some individuals can even practice self-hypnosis, or autohypnosis, by inducing the hypnotic state through self-administered suggestions.

The single most important factor in achieving a hypnotic state is a participant's susceptibility. Experts call this *hypnotizability*, and they measure it by a person's responsiveness to standardized suggestions. Individuals differ in this susceptibility, varying from complete unresponsiveness to any suggestion, at one extreme, to total responsiveness to virtually every suggestion, at the other. A highly hypnotizable person may respond to suggestions to move his or her arms, walk about, experience hallucinations, have amnesia for important memories, and become insensitive to painful stimuli. And, we should add, because hypnosis involves heightened suggestibility, any "recovered memories" obtained by this means are highly suspect.

Hypnotizability depends on age. Among adults, 10 to 15% are highly hypnotizable, while up to 85% of children fall into that category (Blakeslee, 2005). Figure 8.6 shows the percentage of college-age people who achieved various levels of hypnotizability the first time they were given a hypnotic induction test. For example, a hypnotist may test a new subject's acceptance of suggestion by saying, "Your right hand is lighter than air," and observing whether the subject allows his or her arm to float upward. High scorers are more likely than low scorers to experience pain relief, or hypnotic analgesia, and to respond to hypnotic suggestions for experiencing perceptual distortions.

Is Hypnosis a Distinct State of Consciousness? The experts disagree about the psychological mechanisms involved in hypnosis (Kirsch & Lynn, 1995, 1998). Some believe that hypnosis is a distinct state of consciousness, quite separate from sleep or our normal waking state (Fromm & Shor, 1979). Other experts propose that hypnosis is simply suggestibility (Barber, 1979; Kirsch & Braffman, 2001). In this latter view, hypnotic subjects are not entranced but merely motivated to focus their attention and respond to suggestion. In yet another view, some experts think that hypnosis is essentially a social process, involving role playing—in which they act as they believe a hypnotized person would, often to please the hypnotist (Sarbin & Coe, 1972). In support of this view, critics of hypnosis as an "altered state" note that people who have *not* been hypnotized can duplicate apparently amazing feats, such as becoming "human planks" suspended between two chairs.

An intriguing perspective, originally proposed by researcher Ernest Hilgard (1992), portrays hypnosis as a dissociated state, involving a "hidden observer" in the person's mind, operating in parallel with normal consciousness. Hilgard has shown that hypnotized individuals who say they feel no pain when their hand is placed in ice water will nevertheless respond affirmatively when told, "If some part of you does feel pain, please raise your right index finger." Hilgard believed that attention to the painful sensation was shifted to the hidden observer, leaving normal consciousness blissfully unaware.

Finally, a cognitive view proposes that hypnosis involves a shift in top-down processing—that is, thinking driven by expectations and mental imagery, rather than by incoming stimulation. Thus, they are hypnotized because they want or expect to be, so they focus on expressing and achieving the responses the hypnotist tries to evoke. To test this idea, neuroscientist Amir Raz and his colleagues altered volunteers' top-down processing by means of hypnotic suggestions that they would "forget" how to read. Brain scans showed that the suggestion temporarily inactivated the part of their brains that decodes words (Blakeslee, 2005; Raz et al., 2002).

In support of the idea that hypnosis creates profound top-down changes in the brain, another study showed that parts of the brain associated with pain perception "lit up" in deeply hypnotized patients who were given suggestions that they were touching uncomfortably warm metal. The same pattern was found in

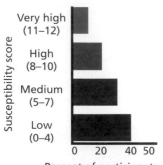

CONNECTION • CHAPTER 4

Studies in which false memories are created call into question 'recovered' memories obtained as the result of any sort of prompting or suggestion.

FIGURE 8.6
Level of Hypnosis Reached at First Induction

This graph shows the results achieved by 533 participants hypnotized for the first time. (Hypnotizability was measured by the 12-item Stanford Hypnotic Susceptibility Scale.)

CONNECTION • CHAPTER 12

In certain clinical disorders, known as *dissociated states*, part of the personality becomes disconnected with rest of the personality. This is the defining feature of dissociative identity disorder—formerly called "multiple personality disorder."

brain scans of a control group who actually touched a 120-degree metal rod (Derbyshire et al., 2004; Winerman, 2006b).

Theorists have attempted to find common ground among these perspectives. And perhaps all have a bit of the truth. It may be that hypnosis, like the normal waking state, can cover a whole range of dissociated states, intensified motives, shifted expectations, and social interactions.

Practical Uses of Hypnosis   Stage tricks aside, what is hypnosis good for? Because it can exert a powerful influence on psychological and physical functions in some people, hypnosis can be a useful tool for researchers studying the mind-body connection (Oakley, 2006). And by using normal volunteers under hypnosis, an experimenter can induce temporary mental conditions, such as anxiety, depression, or hallucinations, instead of having to find individuals who already have these problems. For example, in one study of the psychological issues associated with hearing loss, college students given the hypnotic suggestion to become deaf on cue reported feeling paranoid and excluded because they could not hear what other subjects were saying and assumed they were being deliberately whispered about and excluded (Zimbardo et al., 1981).

Hypnosis has uses in psychological treatment, too. For instance, it can be an effective tool in desensitizing phobic patients who are afraid of heights or spiders. It can also be a part of a relaxation training program designed to combat stress. In addition, therapists find it useful for eliminating unwanted behaviors, such as smoking, where a frequently used technique calls for planting posthypnotic suggestions that can diminish a patient's cravings for nicotine (Barnier & McConkey, 1998; Kihlstrom, 1985). By means of posthypnotic suggestion, a therapist can also induce the patient to forget events that occurred during or before the hypnotic session, an effect called *posthypnotic amnesia*.

Finally, hypnosis has a place in pain management, especially during procedures that would otherswise involve the risks of anesthesia (Nash, 2001; Patterson, 2004). For example, the Lamaze method of natural childbirth uses a hypnosis-like procedure as a primary means of pain control. However, it is important to note that not everyone can be hypnotized deeply enough for effective pain relief (Callahan, 1997). Still, hypnosis alone will allow some patients to undergo treatments that would otherwise cause excruciating pain (Finer, 1980). And for some highly suggestible individuals, hypnosis may actually work better to mask pain than does acupuncture, aspirin, Valium, or even morphine (Stern et al., 1977).

How does hypnosis produce pain relief? Hilgard's hidden-observer explanation is one possibility, although other scientists have taken a more biological approach to the problem. Currently there is no universally accepted explanation, although we can rule out one contender. Experiments have demonstrated that the opiate-like *endorphins*, which account for the pain-relieving property of placebos, are *not* responsible for hypnotic analgesia (Grevert & Goldstein, 1985). As you will recall, we considered another possibility, called the *gate-control theory*, in our discussion of pain (in Chapter 7). For now, we will accept hypnosis as a valuable tool about which much remains to be learned concerning the ways in which it alters consciousness.

Stage hypnotists have given the public a distorted view of hypnosis. Here, The Amazing Kreskin demonstrates the "human plank," which supposedly depends on hypnotic suggestion. In fact, it is a magician's trick. (Don't try this at home—or anywhere else—unless you learn the trick. There is a very real possibility that you could cause serious injury to the "plank.")

CONNECTION • CHAPTER 7
Endorphins are the body's own opiate-like substances.

Meditation

Many religions and traditional psychologies of the Asian and Pacific cultures use forms of **meditation** to direct consciousness away from worldly concerns and temptations. Although the purpose of meditation varies among practitioners, many use it to seek some form of spiritual enlightenment and to increase self-knowledge and well-being. Meditators may use a variety of techniques, but they commonly begin by concentrating on a repetitive behavior (such as breathing), assuming certain body positions (yogic postures), and minimizing external stimulation. You will note the similarities with hypnosis.

Meditation   A state of consciousness often induced by focusing on a repetitive behavior, assuming certain body positions, and minimizing external stimulation. Meditation may be intended to enhance self-knowledge, well-being, and spirituality.

Meditation produces relaxation, changes in brain waves, lower blood pressure, a decrease in stress hormones, and perhaps new insights. Research has not shown meditation to be superior to other relaxation techniques, however.

How is meditation done? There are many techniques, but most involve an attempt to clear the mind, either by focusing on a single process, such as one's breathing or an object, such as a visual icon—or attempting to void one's mind of all thoughts. The meditator typically seeks to remain in this state anywhere from a few minutes to a few hours.

Viewing meditation as an altered state of consciousness may reflect a particularly Western worldview, because Asian beliefs about the mind are typically different from those of Western cultures (Austin, 1998; Rosch, 1999). Buddhism, for example, teaches that the visible universe is an illusion of the senses. To become enlightened, a Buddhist tries to control bodily yearnings, to stop the ordinary experiences of the senses and mind, and to discover how to see things in their truest light. Thus, in the Buddhist view, meditation more accurately captures reality. In contrast, Western cognitive scientists often view meditation as an altered form of consciousness, and they aspire to understand it and to harness it for therapeutic purposes (Barinaga, 2003b).

In contrast with its long history in Asia and the Pacific, meditation has only recently been taken seriously by psychology as a subject for scientific study. Its spiritual aspects aside, studies suggest that meditating is in many ways like resting, because it has been found to reduce various signs of bodily arousal (Morrell, 1986). As for some of the more subjective benefits attributed to meditation, such as its power to bring new understandings and meaning to one's life, such issues lie beyond the limits in which science can operate objectively.

What effects of meditation can be demonstrated objectively? Experienced meditators show changes in their brain-wave patterns, especially in frontal lobe activity, associated with positive emotions (Davidson et al., 2003; Kasamatsu & Hirai, 1966). Other studies have linked meditation with beneficial changes in blood pressure and stress hormones (Seeman et al., 2003). And still other studies have shown that meditation produces relaxation and reduces anxiety, especially in people who live and work in stress-filled environments (Benson, 1975; van Dam, 1996)—although new research with control groups does not show meditation to be superior to other relaxation techniques (Toneatto & Nguyen, 2007). Finally, an intriguing recent study finds that a long-term habit of meditation is associated with an increased thickness of the brain's cortex in regions associated with attention and sensory processing (Lazar et al., 2005).

The overall picture shows meditation to be a method for relaxing, reducing stress, and disengaging from worldly concerns. It also produces health-promoting physical changes. But whether meditation holds an advantage over other techniques—psychological, physical, and spiritual—awaits the finding of future research.

Psychoactive Drug States

For millennia, humans have used alcohol, opium, cannabis, mescaline, coca, caffeine, and other drugs to alter their everyday perceptions of reality. Especially under stress, people throughout the world take drugs for pleasure, for relaxation, or just to avoid the cares of their daily lives. Some drugs, such as LSD, are taken by those seeking the hallucinations they produce. Other drugs (alcohol is an example) can act as "social lubricants," to help people feel comfortable with each other. Still other drugs are used by those seeking a euphoric "rush," a "buzz," a state of tranquility, or even stupor. What, if anything, do all these drugs have in common?

To some extent, all **psychoactive drugs** impair the brain mechanisms that usually help us make decisions (Gazzaniga, 1998a). In addition, the most widely abused drugs, such as cocaine, heroin, PCP, cannabis, and methamphetamines, all stimulate the brain's "reward circuits." From an evolutionary perspective, we know that our brains are built to find pleasure in many substances (such as the taste of sweet or fatty foods) that helped our ancestors survive and reproduce. Cocaine, heroin, and amphetamines trick the brain by exploiting these same

Psychoactive drug Chemical that affects mental processes and behavior by its effect on the brain.

mechanisms with strong, direct, and pleasurable signals that make our bodies "think" that these substances are good for us (Nesse & Berridge, 1997).

Cultural trends influence drug-taking behavior, too. The United States saw this vividly during the 1960s and 1970s, when the country entered a period of casual experimentation with recreational drugs and other mind-altering techniques. Data from several sources, including emergency room visits, drug arrests, and surveys, indicate that overall illicit drug use has declined since the early 1990s. Among teenagers, drug use has shown a modest decline for the last decade—although Figure 8.7 shows that it was somewhat lower in 1990–1991. About half of all high school seniors have used an illegal drug (University of Michigan News Service, 2006). Credit for the decline in illicit drug use is often claimed by proponents of antidrug education programs, although the evidence does not show most of these programs to be especially effective (Murray, 1997).

Let us now have a closer look at the most commonly used and abused psychoactive drugs. We do so by grouping them in categories: *hallucinogens, opiates, depressants,* and *stimulants.* (See Table 8.1.) In general, we will find that all the drugs in each category have similar effects on the mind and brain.

Hallucinogens Drugs known as **hallucinogens** produce changes in consciousness by altering perceptions, creating hallucinations, and blurring the boundary between self and the external world. For example, an individual experiencing hallucinogenic effects might listen to music and suddenly feel that he or she is producing the music or that the music is coming from within. Most hallucinogenic drugs act in the brain at specific receptor sites for the neurotransmitter serotonin (Jacobs, 1987).

Commonly used hallucinogens include *mescaline* (made from a type of cactus), *psilocybin* (from a mushroom), *LSD* or "acid," and *PCP* (also called phencyclidine or "angel dust"). Both LSD and PCP are synthetic drugs made in chemical laboratories. PCP was a favorite of young people who used hallucinogens until the word got around that the intensity and duration of its effects were quite unpredictable. The drug produces a strange dissociative reaction, in which the user feels disembodied or removed from parts of his or her personality. Users may become confused, insensitive to pain, and feel separated (dissociated) from their surroundings.

CONNECTION • CHAPTER 2
Serotonin is a neurotransmitter involved with reward, sleep, memory, and depression.

Hallucinogen A drug that creates hallucinations or alters perceptions of the external environment and inner awareness.

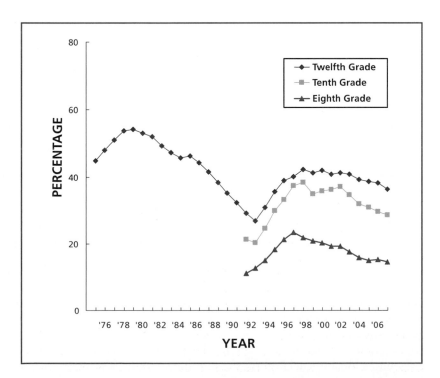

FIGURE 8.7
Trends in an Annual Use of Illicit Drug Use Index

This graph shows the percentage of teens reporting the use of illegal drugs. Note that although teen drug use in the United States has declined over the last decade, it still is not as low as in 1992. The causes of these changes are not clear.

(Source: From the Monitoring the Future Study, University of Michigan. Reprinted by permission of the Inter-University Consortium for Political and Social Research.)

TABLE 8.1 Characteristics of Psychoactive Drugs

Drug	Medical Uses	Common Effects Reported by Users
Opiates		
Morphine	Painkiller, cough suppressant	Euphoria ("rush"), tranquility, drowsiness
Heroin	No medical uses in the United States	Euphoria, tranquility, drowsiness (more powerful than morphine)
Codeine	Painkiller, cough suppressant	Euphoria, drowsiness, "silliness"
Methadone	Treatment of heroin addiction	Slow action prevents heroin craving
Hallucinogens		
Mescaline	None	Hallucinations, sensuality, similar to LSD but fewer reported emotional responses
Psilocybin	None	Well-being, perceptual distortions, less emotionally intense than LSD
LSD	None	Hallucinations, often emotional reactions
PCP	Veterinary anesthetic	Body image distortions, amnesia, unpredicable emotional reactions, dissociation (feeling of being cut off from one's environment)
Cannabis	Reduces nausea from chemotherapy; reduces pressure in the eye	Euphoria, time distortion, intensified sensory experience
Depressants and Antianxiety Drugs		
Barbiturates	Sedative, sleep, anticonvulsant, anesthetic	Relaxation, sedation, euphoria
Benzodiazepines	Antianxiety, sleep, anticonvulsant, sedative	Stress and anxiety reduction ("tranquilizing")
Rohypnol	None in United States (elsewhere: sedation, anxiety, anesthesia, and treatment of insomnia)	Same as other benzodiaepines, but longer lasting; also amnesia (hence its reputation as the "date-rape drug")
Alcohol	Antiseptic	Relaxation, well-being, cognitive and motor impairment
Stimulants		
Amphetamines	Weight control, ADHD, counteract anesthesia	Confidence, mental energy, alertness, hallucinations, paranoia
Methamphetamine	None	Same as other amphetamines, but more intense
MDMA (ecstasy)	None (originally an appetite suppressant)	Euphoria, hot flashes, perceptual distortions, excitement
Cocaine	Local anesthetic	Much the same as amphetamines, sexual arousal (except in chronic users), dramatic mood changes as effects wear off (irritability, depression)
Nicotine	Gum, patch for cessation of smoking	Stimulant effect, relaxation, concentration, reduces nicotine craving
Caffeine	Weight control, stimulant in acute respiratory failure, analgesia	Stimulant effect, increased alertness and concentration

Cannabis, derived from the hemp plant (used to make rope, as well as dope), also acts as a hallucinogen. Its active ingredient is *THC* (tetrahydrocannabinol), found in both the plant's dried leaves and flowers (marijuana) and in its solidified resin (hashish). Most commonly it is smoked, although it can also be eaten.

The experience obtained from ingesting THC depends on its dose. Small doses may create mild, pleasurable highs, and large doses can cause long hallucinogenic reactions. Unlike alcohol, its effects can last for many hours—and long after users feel the drug's influence has ended. The pleasant effects include altered perception, sedation, pain relief, mild euphoria, and distortions of space and time—similar in some respects to the effects of heroin (Wickelgren, 1997). Depending on the social context, and expectations, the effects can also be an unpleasant mixture of fear, anxiety, and confusion. In addition, cannabis often produces temporary failures in memory, as well as impairments in motor coordination. Those who work or drive under its influence suffer a higher risk of accidents—and those who study under its influence are likely to remember little.

Some habitual cannabis users become psychologically addicted to its pleasurable effects. They crave the drug so often that it interferes with other pursuits, including school or work. Nevertheless, the potential for physical dependence on this drug is lower than most other psychoactive substances (Grinspoon et al., 1997; Pinel, 2005). On a more positive note, cannabis has some medical uses, especially in treating nausea associated with chemotherapy and in reducing pressure in the eye associated with glaucoma. Needless to say, its use, even under prescription, is controversial.

What causes the mind-altering effects of this drug? In the brain, THC causes the release of dopamine, which suggests an effect on the brain's reward system (Carlson, 2007). Neuroscientists have discovered cannabis receptors in many parts of the brain, too (Nicoll & Alger, 2004; Wilson & Nicoll, 2002). This strongly suggests that the brain makes its own THC-like chemicals, which it uses to modulate information flow. Thus, marijuana and hashish produce their mind-altering effects by exploiting the natural chemistry of the brain. It is no wonder, then, that they can interfere with cognition, because these receptors are particularly abundant in pathways involving learning, thinking, and memory.

An evolutionary perspective suggests that the brain's own cannabis must also have some beneficial function. Following this lead, a few neuroscientists are exploring just what the brain's "natural marijuana," more properly termed *endocannabinoids*, does for us. The hope, therefore, is for new therapies for a variety of human afflictions linked to the brain loci that respond to THC. These include circuits implicated in the control of appetite, pain, nausea, and addiction. Perhaps this research will lead to new treatments for obesity, chronic pain, the nausea produced by chemotherapy, and addiction to heroin and methamphetamine. Such treatments may not involve ingestion of cannabanoids themselves but drugs that regulate the body's use of its own endocannabinoids (Marx, 2006; Nicoll & Alger, 2004).

Opiates   Another class of drugs, known as **opiates,** includes *morphine, heroin,* and *codeine*—all made from the opium poppy. These are highly addictive drugs that suppress physical sensation and response to stimulation. As a result, some of these drugs have found wide use in medicine, where they have particularly good analgesic (pain-relieving) properties and also serve as cough suppressants. (The only other medical use for opiates is in managing diarrhea.)

Derived from morphine, heroin originally was developed in 19th-century Germany by the Bayer Company (of aspirin fame), but it was abandoned because it is even more highly addictive than morphine. For the intravenous heroin user, however, the drug is attractive because, in the absence of pain, it gives a strong rush of pleasurable sensations. These feelings of euphoria supplant all worries and awareness of bodily needs, although—surprisingly—there are no major changes in cognitive abilities. Under the influence of these drugs, the user is usually able to converse normally and to think clearly. Unfortunately, serious addiction is likely once a person begins to inject heroin for pleasure. To avoid the intense cravings and painful sensations of withdrawal, the addict must take the drug frequently—at least daily—making it a very expensive habit to maintain. Because addicts often steal to support their habit, the use of heroin underlies much of the property crime in cities around the world.

In recent years, several opiate-based drugs have come on the market, under the brand names OxyContin, Vicodin, Darvon, Percodan, and Demerol. Medically, they are effective painkillers, although their potential for addiction is high in chronic users. Unfortunately, because they produce the same feel-good effects as other opiates, they are also widely abused.

Opiate   Highly addictive drug, derived from opium, that can produce a profound sense of well-being and have strong pain-relieving properties.

Like marijuana, the opiates have special receptor sites in the brain. The discovery of these opiate receptors led to the realization that the brain makes its own opiates, the *endorphins,* which act as the body's natural analgesics, or painkillers. This research stimulated a quest for drugs that have the same pain-fighting qualities as opiates but without their addictive properties. The hope is, so far, unfulfilled.

Methadone, a synthetic opiate, can be taken orally and therefore doesn't require injection. It has essentially the same euphoric, analgesic, and addictive effects as heroin, but it doesn't produce the same "rush" because the drug level in the brain increases slowly. This feature makes methadone useful as a substitute for heroin in drug treatment programs, in which the patient is switched to methadone and then gradually weaned from opiates altogether.

Paradoxically, patients who take opiates for pain control under medical supervision rarely become highly addicted. The reason for the difference in effects between the use of opiates for pleasure and for pain is unclear. It appears, however, that the presence of pain causes opiates to affect parts of the brain other than the "reward centers" involved in pleasure. The practical point is this: There is little to fear from the legitimate medical use of these drugs for controlling pain (Melzack, 1990).

Depressants & Antianxiety Drugs   The broad class of drugs that slow the mental and physical activity of the body by inhibiting activity in the central nervous system is collectively known as **depressants.** (Depressants don't necessarily make people feel clinically depressed, in the sense of "sad.") By inhibiting the transmission of messages in the central nervous system, depressants slow down the mental and physical activity of the body. They include *barbiturates* (usually prescribed for sedation), *benzodiazepines* (antianxiety drugs), and *alcohol* (a social stimulant and nervous system depressant). In appropriate dosages, these drugs can relieve symptoms of pain or anxiety, but overuse or abuse is dangerous because they impair reflexes and judgment. They may also be addictive.

Barbiturates, commonly used in sleeping pills, can induce sleep. Unfortunately, they have the side effect of interfering with REM-sleep. This leaves the user feeling unrested, despite a full night's slumber. In addition, withdrawal from barbiturates causes severe REM rebound, filling sleep with unpleasant dreams. Worse yet, overdoses of barbiturates may cause loss of consciousness, sometimes to the point of coma and even death. Fatal reactions to barbiturates are made all the more likely because the lethal dose is relatively close to the dose required for inducing sleep or other desired effects. The chance of accidental overdose can be compounded by alcohol or other depressant drugs, which magnify the depressant action of barbiturates (Maisto et al., 1995).

CONNECTION • CHAPTER 13

Benzodiazepines are used to treat anxiety-related problems, such as *panic disorder* and *obsessive-compulsive disorder.*

Benzodiazepines (pronounced *BEN-zo-dye-AZ-a-peens*), commonly prescribed to treat anxiety, are safer than barbiturates. Physicians frequently prescribe them to calm patients' anxieties, without causing sleepiness or sedation. For this reason, they are often referred to as "minor tranquilizers"—the best-known and most widely prescribed of which include Valium and Xanax. (The tranquilizing drugs used to treat psychotic disorders work differently and are not classified as depressants.)

While most benzodiazepines are relatively safe, compared to barbiturates, they can also be overused and abused. Addiction occurs and is of special concern because these drugs are so commonly prescribed. Overdoses produce poor muscle coordination, slurred speech, weakness, and irritability, while withdrawal symptoms include increased anxiety, muscle twitching, and sensitivity to sound and light. Significantly, the benzodiazepines are almost never taken by recreational drug users because people who are not suffering from anxiety usually do not like their effects (Wesson et al., 1992).

Alcohol, another drug that acts as a brain depressant, was one of the first psychoactive substances used by humankind. Under its influence, people have a

Depressant   Drug that slows down mental and physical activity by inhibiting transmission of nerve impulses in the central nervous system.

variety of reactions that involve loosening of inhibitions. At first, this may seem like a contradiction: How can a depressant make people less inhibited? What actually happens is that the alcohol initially depresses activity in the brain circuits that control self-monitoring of our thoughts and behavior. The result depends on the context and the personality of the imbiber, who may become more talkative or quiet, friendly or abusive, ebullient or, sometimes, psychologically depressed. Alcohol's effects also depend on whether other drugs, such as MDMA ("ecstasy") or Rohypnol (a form of benzodiazepine sometimes known as the "date-rape drug"), are being used simultaneously. Such drugs are believed by users to enhance social interaction and empathy, although their effects can easily spin out of control, especially in combination with alcohol (Gahlinger, 2004).

Physically, alcohol in small doses can induce relaxation and even slightly improve an adult's reaction time. In just slightly larger amounts, it can impair coordination and mental processing—sometimes even when drinkers believe their performance has been improved. Moreover, it is quite easy for alcohol to accumulate in the system because the body may not metabolize it as fast as it is ingested. In general, the body breaks down alcohol at the rate of only one ounce per hour, and greater amounts consumed in short periods stay in the body and depress activity in the central nervous system. When the level of alcohol in the blood reaches a mere 0.1% (1/1000 of the blood), an individual experiences deficits in thinking, memory, and judgment, along with emotional instability and coordination problems. In some parts of the United States, this level of blood alcohol qualifies a driver as being legally drunk. (Most states, in fact, set a somewhat lower limit of 0.08% as the legal threshold for drunkenness.)

Distillers, brewers, and wine makers spend millions of dollars annually promoting the social and personal benefits of alcoholic beverages. And, to be sure, many adults use alcohol prudently. Nevertheless, an estimated 5 to 10% of American adults who use alcohol drink to the extent that it harms their health, career, or family and social relationships. To some extent, the problem is rooted in our genes—but genetics is far from the whole answer (Nurnberger & Bierut, 2007). People also *learn* to abuse alcohol, often in response to social pressure. Eventually, physical dependence, tolerance, and addiction develop with prolonged heavy drinking—of the sort that often begins with binge drinking, common on college campuses. When the amount and frequency of drinking alcohol interferes with job or school performance, impairs social and family relationships, and creates serious health problems, the diagnosis of *alcoholism* is appropriate (see Julien, 2007; Vallee, 1998).

Abuse of alcohol has become a significant problem for more than 17 million Americans (Adelson, 2006; Grant & Dawson, 2006). The effects of the problem are much more widespread, however. For example, alcohol ingested by a pregnant woman can affect the fetus. In fact, alcohol use by expectant mothers is a leading cause of mental retardation (Committee on Substance Abuse, 2000). Alcohol abuse can affect other family members, too. In fact, some 40% of Americans see the effects of alcohol abuse in their families (Vallee, 1998). Among Americans, the problem is especially prevalent among white males and young adults. Too often the problem becomes a lethal one, because alcohol-related automobile accidents are the leading cause of death in the 15-to-25 age group.

Stimulants In contrast with depressants, **stimulants** speed up central nervous system activity. The result is a boost in both mental and physical activity level, which is why long-distance truck drivers sometimes use them to stay awake behind the wheel. Paradoxically, stimulants can also increase concentration and reduce activity level, particularly in hyperactive children with attention-deficit/hyperactivity disorder (ADHD). Physicians also prescribe them for narcoleptic patients, to prevent sleep attacks.

Recreational users of stimulants seek still other effects: intense pleasurable sensations, increased self-confidence, and euphoria. *Cocaine,* in particular, packs

Physical dependence, tolerance, and addiction to alcohol may begin with social pressure and binge drinking—as seen in this student who readies himself to drink from an ice luge at a party.

Stimulant A drug that arouses the central nervous system, speeding up mental and physical responses.

CONNECTION • CHAPTER 13
ADHD is a relatively common disorder of attention span and behavior, usually diagnosed in children but sometimes found in adults.

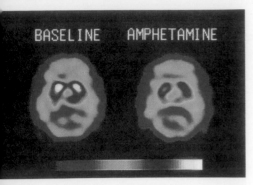

Brain changes during use of drugs can be seen on PET-scan images. Much less activity is seen in the limbic system of the brain under the influence of amphetamines.

When psychologists talk about drugs, they include legal substances, such as tobacco and caffeine, two extremely popular stimulants in most cultures.

General anesthetic Substance that suppresses consciousness and awareness of pain. Most anesthetics also produce sedation and immobility.

what may be the most powerfully rewarding punch of any illegal drug (Landry, 1997). Crack, an especially addictive form of cocaine, produces a swift, pleasurable high that also wears off quickly. Amphetamine (often called "speed") and related drugs have effects comparable to cocaine. Among these, a particularly notorious variant known as *methamphetamine* came into widespread use during the 1990s. Use of "meth" can lead to severe health problems, including physical damage in the brain.

Still another stimulant, known as *MDMA* (often called "ecstasy"), has grown popular in the "rave" culture, where it has a reputation for creating a feeling of euphoria and closeness to others (Thompson et al., 2007; Young, 2007). It is also known for energizing young users to dance for hours, sometimes leading to convulsions, death, and other unpleasant consequences (Gahlinger, 2004; Yacoubian et al., 2004). Ecstasy produces increased blood pressure and heart rate, hyperthermia (elevated temperature), and dehydration. Long-term use is also known to impair attention, learning, and memory, probably through impairment of serotonin-using neurons (Levinthal, 2008; Verbaten, 2003).

Stimulant drugs hold other dangers, as well. Heavy amphetamine and cocaine users may experience frightening hallucinations and paranoid delusions—symptoms also associated with severe mental disorder. And these drugs can send users on an emotional roller coaster of euphoric highs and depressive lows. This leads users to increase the frequency and dosage, quickly making the abuse of such drugs spiral out of control. Yet another danger accrues to "secondhand" users: children who were exposed to cocaine in their mother's blood while in the womb. Studies show that such children are at increased risk for developing cognitive problems, emotional difficulties, and behavior-control disorders (Vogel, 1997).

Two other stimulants that you may not even think of as psychoactive drugs are *caffeine* and *nicotine*—yet their effects on the brain are swift and powerful. Within ten minutes, two cups of strong coffee or tea deliver enough caffeine to have a measurable effect on the heart, blood circulation, and signaling in the brain. Nicotine inhaled in tobacco smoke can have similar effects within just seconds. Both drugs are addictive, and both augment the effects of the natural rewarding chemicals released by the brain. In this way, nicotine and caffeine tease the brain's reward pathways into responding as if using these substances were associated with something beneficial. Fortunately, in the case of caffeine, the negative effects are minor for most people. Further, caffeine has a built-in "braking" action that limits its intake because high dosages also produce uncomfortable anxiety-like feelings.

In contrast to caffeine, nicotine is a much more dangerous drug for two reasons: Nicotine is highly addictive, and it has been associated with a variety of health problems, including cancer, emphysema, and heart disease. In fact, the negative impact of smoking on health is greater than that of all other psychoactive drugs combined—including heroin, cocaine, and alcohol. According to the U.S. Public Health Service, smoking is the leading cause of preventable disease, carrying a human cost of about 438,000 deaths annually (Centers for Disease Control, 2007). As a result, the American Medical Association has formally recommended that the U.S. Food and Drug Administration regard nicotine as a drug to be regulated. Currently, however, nicotine is both legal and actively promoted—with a $2.7 billion budget from the tobacco industry. Although antismoking campaigns have been somewhat effective in reducing the overall level of smoking in the United States, some 45 million adult Americans still smoke. Most worrisome is the fact that more than 3 million teenagers smoke, and their numbers are increasing by about 4000 who start every day (Gardyn & Wellner, 2001; Julien, 2007).

The Altered States of Anesthesia While anesthetics have come a long way in the 160 years since the discoveries of chloroform and ether, science has relatively little knowledge of how **general anesthetics** alter consciousness and suppress awareness of pain (Orser, 2007). Although anesthetized people appear to "go to sleep," general anesthesia is quite different from sleep. Anesthesia involves none of the REM and NREM stages that we associate with sleep, even though it induces these sleep-like components: *sedation* (greatly reduced arousal), *unconsciousness* (lack of awareness and responsiveness), *immobility* (temporary paralysis), and *amnesia* (lack of recall for the period under the influence of the anesthetic). Strangely, these four components of anesthesia seem to be independent of one another. For example, conscious patients often carry on lively conversations as they "go under"—yet they rarely have a memory of these events.

One tentative theory suggests that anesthetics interrupt the process by which different parts of the brain work together, or "synchronize," thereby preventing consciousness. They may do so by mimicking or enhancing the action of GABA, one of the brain's main inhibitory neurotransmitters. In this respect, we can think of anesthetics as just another group of psychoactive drugs that interfere with consciousness.

PSYCHOLOGY MATTERS
Dependence and Addiction

We have seen that psychoactive drugs can alter the functioning of neurons in your brain and, as a consequence, temporarily change your consciousness. Incidentally, the same has recently been suggested about the steroids that some athletes use (Adelson, 2005). Once in your brain, such drugs usually act on synapses to block or stimulate neural messages. In this way, drugs profoundly alter the brain's communication system, affecting perception, memory, mood, and behavior.

CONNECTION • CHAPTER 2

Most *psychoactive drugs* mimic neurotransmitters or enhance or dampen their effects at the synapses.

Significantly, a given dose of many psychoactive drugs begins to have a weaker consciousness-altering effect with continued use. As a result, the user needs larger and larger dosages to achieve the same effect. This reduced effectiveness with repeated use of a drug is called **tolerance.** Hand-in-hand with tolerance goes **physical dependence**—a process in which the body adjusts to and comes to need the substance, in part because the production of neurotransmitters in the brain is affected by the frequent presence of the drug (Wickelgren, 1998c). A person with a physical dependence requires the drug in his or her body and may suffer unpleasant *withdrawal* symptoms if the drug is not present. Some scientists believe that the desire to avoid withdrawal is as important as the pleasurable effects of drugs in producing *addiction* (Everitt, 2006).

A person who develops tolerance to a highly addicting drug such as heroin becomes less sensitive to all sorts of natural reinforcers, including the pleasures of friendship, food, and everyday entertainment: The drug, in increasing dosages, becomes the only thing capable of providing pleasure (Helmuth, 2001a). **Addiction** is said to occur when the person continues to use a drug in the face of adverse effects on his or her health or life—often despite repeated attempts to stop.

Addiction is not all physical, however. When heroin addicts routinely "shoot up" in the same environment—say, in the bathroom—a *learned* response actually anticipates the drug and prepares the body for it. The result is that the addict can tolerate dosages that are larger than when the drugs are injected at a novel location (Dingfelder, 2004b). Overdoses may occur if the user attempts to shoot up with his or her "usual amount" in a novel location.

Withdrawal involves uncomfortable physical and mental symptoms that occur when drug use is discontinued. It can include physical trembling, perspiring, nausea, increased sensitivity to pain, and, in the case of extreme alcohol withdrawal, even death. Although heroin and alcohol are the drugs that most commonly come to mind when we think of withdrawal symptoms, nicotine and caffeine, as well as certain sleeping pills and "tranquilizing" drugs, can also cause unpleasant withdrawal symptoms.

Individuals may find themselves craving or hungering for the drug and its effects, even though they are not physically dependent—a condition known as

Tolerance The reduced effectiveness a drug has after repeated use.

Physical dependence A process by which the body adjusts to, and comes to need, a drug for its everyday functioning.

Addiction A condition in which a person continues to use a drug despite its adverse effects—often despite repeated attempts to discontinue using the drug. Addiction may be based on physical or psychological dependence.

Withdrawal A pattern of uncomfortable or painful physical symptoms and cravings experienced by the user when the level of drug is decreased or the drug is eliminated.

The line between substance use and abuse is easy to cross with addictive drugs, most of which act on the brain's "pleasure centers."

psychological dependence or psychological addiction. This usually results from the powerfully rewarding effects that many psychoactive drugs produce. Psychological dependence can occur with many drugs, including caffeine and nicotine, prescription medications, and over-the-counter drugs.

Addiction, whether biological or psychological, ultimately affects the brain (Nestler & Malenka, 2004). Consequently, in the view of many public health professionals, this makes both forms of addiction brain diseases (Leshner, 1997). On the other hand, the general public has been reluctant to view drug addicts as people who have an illness. Instead, the public often thinks of addicts as weak or bad individuals who should be punished (MacCoun, 1998).

What difference does it make whether or not we label addiction a "disease"? When addicts are seen as persons suffering from a disease, they are most logically placed in treatment programs. By contrast, when they are seen as persons with character defects, addicts are sent to prison for punishment—which does little to break the cycle of drug use, crime, and addiction.

Strange as it may seem, some experts argue that viewing addiction as a disease may also *interfere* with the effective treatment of drug addicts. How could this be? The disease model of addiction, with its emphasis on biological causes and medical treatment, does little to deal with the social and economic context in which addictions develop. This may account for the fact that psychologically based treatment programs that treat alcohol abuse as a behavioral problem may work better than medically based programs (Miller & Brown, 1997).

Treatment programs have an especially poor record with heroin addicts who have picked up their habits on the streets of the United States. In contrast, treatment has been more successful with the thousands of veterans who became addicted to the heroin that was readily available to troops during the war in Vietnam. What made the difference? The addicted veterans did not remain in the environment where they had become addicted—which was the wartime culture of Vietnam. Instead, they returned home to an environment that was not usually so supportive of a heroin habit. On the other hand, heroin users who become addicted at home tend to return, after treatment, to the same environment that originally led to their addiction.

Whether it be physical or psychological, a disease or a character flaw, drug addiction poses many personal and social problems. Clearly, this is a field that has much room for new ideas and new research.

Psychological dependence A desire to obtain or use a drug, even though there is no physical dependence.

CheckYourUnderstanding

1. **RECALL:** What does the evidence show concerning hypnosis as a distinct state of consciousness?

2. **RECALL:** What are the physical changes associated with meditation?

3. **RECALL:** Psychoactive drugs usually create their effects by stimulating _____ in the brain.

4. **RECALL:** Most hallucinogens act on brain sites that involve the neurotransmitter _____.

5. **SYNTHESIS:** In what respect are the opiates like cannabis?

6. **APPLICATION:** Which of the following groups of drugs have the opposite effects on the brain?

   a. hallucinogens and stimulants
   b. opiates and sedatives
   c. stimulants and depressants
   d. depressants and opiates

7. **RECALL:** Why do many psychologists object to the "disease model" of addiction?

8. **UNDERSTANDING THE CORE CONCEPT:** Altered states do not involve any mysterious or paranormal phenomena. Rather they are modifications of ordinary consciousness that we can study with the tools of science, because they are produced by _____.

Answers 1. No solid evidence to date shows that hypnosis is a unique state of consciousness. **2.** Many physical changes occur with meditation, including changes in brain-wave patterns, frontal lobe changes associated with positive emotions, beneficial changes in blood pressure and stress hormones, and, over time, increased thickness of the brain's cortex. **3.** reward circuits (so called "pleasure centers") **4.** serotonin **5.** Both have specific receptor sites in the brain. **6.** c **7.** The disease model tends to emphasize biological causes and medical treatment at the expense of recognizing the social and economic context in which addictions develop. **8.** mental, behavioral, or physical changes in the person

Critical Thinking Applied: The Unconscious— Reconsidered

As we have seen, the term unconscious can have many meanings. In Freud's psychoanalytic theory, for example, powerful unconscious forces actively work to block (or *repress*) traumatic memories and destructive urges (Freud, 1925). If allowed to break through into consciousness, these would cause extreme anxiety, Freud taught. In this view, the unconscious mind, then, serves as a mental dungeon where terrible needs and threatening memories can be kept "locked up" outside of awareness.

Ever since Freud, the art and literature of the Western world have been captivated by the idea of an unconscious mind filled with dark and sinister motives and memories. For example, Joseph Conrad's novel *Heart of Darkness* tells the story of one man's internal and unconscious struggle with the most evil of desires for power, destruction, and death. Unconscious desires can be sexual, as well, said Freud. What else could account for the dubious success of the titillating stories splashed so obviously across the pages of the tabloids and the screens of the "soaps"?

Freud also taught that we "forget" anniversaries because we have unconscious reservations about the relationship. He said that we choose mates who are, on an unconscious level, just substitutes for our fathers and mothers. And he gave us the concept of the "Freudian slip," which one wag defined as "saying one thing when you really mean your mother."

In essence, Freud's view is just a variation on the anima hypothesis mentioned earlier: He placed the *ego*—the rational decision-maker part of the mind—at the center of consciousness. There, said Freud, it assumes the responsibility of keeping the sexual and aggressive forces of the unconscious in check. But was he right? Or were Freud's ideas better as metaphors than as objective science?

What Are the Issues?

Freud's theory can explain almost anything—and in very compelling language. He portrayed a mind perpetually locked in an internal struggle against itself. In fact, we can see evidence all around us of the sexual and aggressive urges that loomed so important in his theory: in advertising, in video games, in movies, in politics, and in the ways people fight and flirt. So the issue is not whether sexual and aggressive urges influence human behavior but whether these urges operate as Freud suggested: primarily at an unconscious level and in a mind that is continually in conflict with itself.

What Critical Thinking Questions Should We Ask?

Without a doubt, Freud was a perceptive observer of people and a creative theorist, and his views have been enormously influential. But his genius and his influence don't necessarily make his views correct. For example, his seeming obsession with sex makes sense in the context of the rigid and "proper" culture of early 20th century Europe, which frowned on public references to sexuality. (In some quarters, the term *leg* was considered inappropriate for mixed company.) Thus, we should consider whether the seething sexual cauldron of desire that was the Freudian unconscious might be the result of biases in Freud's thinking—biases produced not by the unconscious but by the sexually uptight culture of which he was a part. As we noted earlier, Freud may have been guilty of *confirmation bias*.

In fact, Freud seemed to find evidence of the unconscious everywhere: in dreams, forgetting, slips of the tongue and other everyday errors, developmental stages of childhood, and mental disorders. So perhaps he was also guilty of the common logical fallacy, known as *begging the question*: assuming the very thing one is trying to prove. We suggest that Freud begs the question by assuming that unconscious conflict is the cause of all the mental phenomena he describes—from forgetting an anniversary to a fear of dogs to having a dream about flying. Why is this a logical fallacy? Because Freud's argument is also an attempt to prove the existence of a conflicted unconscious. He even suggested that resistance to his arguments is evidence of the unconscious at work! Such arguments are sometimes called *circular reasoning*.

But we can question Freud and still respect his brilliance and his stature. After all, he developed an amazingly comprehensive and appealing theory of mind in the early days of the 20th century—long before brain scans and the other tools of modern psychology were available. Almost certainly, some of his ideas had to be erroneous in light of newer knowledge. The important question, then, is whether Freud's concept of consciousness and the unconscious mind is still reasonable in view of the evidence psychology has accumulated since Freud's time. Let's take a brief look at some of that evidence and see where it leads us.

What Conclusions Can We Draw?

You will recall that the study of dreams in Trobriand Islanders failed to support Freud's contention that young boys see their fathers as rivals for their mothers' affections. Moreover, from the perspective of 21st-century Europe and North America, with sexual content quite common in conversation and in the media, we have no reason to believe that sexual thoughts are mostly unconscious. If anything, many people seem consciously preoccupied with sex. This does not mean, of course, that the unconscious does not exist. But it does raise questions about the unconscious as Freud envisioned it.

As critical thinkers, we must be careful not to commit the fallacy often described as "throwing the baby out with the bath water." That is, we do not need to reject the concept of an unconscious altogether. In fact, as you will see in the next chapter, the unconscious plays a huge role in our motivations and emotions.

In recent years, techniques such as brain scans and priming have made it possible to probe unconscious thought processes in ways never dreamed of by Freud (Kihlstrom, 1990; Kihlstrom et al., 1992). In the resulting picture, the unconscious does not appear so sinister as Freud portrayed it. In fact, it has a much simpler structure than the complicated censoring and repressing system that Freud proposed (Greenwald, 1992).

Brain scans support this newer perspective on unconscious mental activity, suggesting that many parts of the brain can operate outside of consciousness. Most of this activity is devoted to simple background tasks, such as maintaining body temperature and controlling hunger and thirst. In addition, the brain performs a preconscious screening on the incoming stream of sights, sounds, smells, and textures. This screening also provides a quick-and-dirty appraisal of events for their attractiveness or harmfulness (LeDoux, 1996). Such unconscious processing can even save your life, as when you react "without thinking" to a swerving car coming at you.

But this is not the picture of a scheming, and plotting unconscious, full of sinister urges that must be vented (Baumeister, 2005; Wilson, 2002). Rather, the less-than-conscious mind seems to work, for the most part, in concert with consciousness, rather than against it—although, when we discuss mental disorders, we will see that a fearful experience can sometimes leave a lasting mark on the unconscious screening process that is difficult to eradicate.

Ironically, the cognitive view of an unconscious that monitors, sorts, discards, and stores the flood of data we encounter may give the unconscious a larger role than even Freud originally conceived.

Chapter Summary

8.1 How Is Consciousness Related to Other Mental Processes?

Core Concept 8.1: The brain operates on many levels at once—both conscious and unconscious.

Consciousness represents one of the major mysteries of psychology, both in its ordinary waking state and in its many *altered states*. Consciousness involves both **attention** and *working memory*. The behaviorists rejected consciousness as a topic too subjective for scientific study, but cognitive neuroscience has shown that scientific methods can be applied to consciousness, using both psychological techniques and brain scanning technology.

Psychologists have used various metaphors for consciousness. James spoke of a "stream of consciousness"; Freud likened consciousness to an iceberg. The modern cognitive perspective uses a **computer metaphor.**

Consciousness involves at least three important factors: restricted attention, widespread connections among diverse areas of the brain, and an internal mental model of the world that is used in thinking. In addition to consciousness, the mind has many **nonconscious** modes that can operate outside awareness. These include the **preconscious** and various levels of **unconscious** processing. While consciousness is limited to serial processing, the mind can process information nonconsciously in parallel channels. Patients in a **coma** lack consciousness, as well as most unconscious brain processes. Comas are short-term states that transition into either a *minimally conscious state* or a *persistent vegetative state.*

Because consciousness is limited, students using their knowledge of consciousness will employ study methods that facilitate the passage of information from consciousness into long-term memory, so that it remains accessible to consciousness. All such techniques involve making the material meaningful.

Attention (p. 337)

Cognitive neuroscience (p. 338)

Coma (p. 342)

Consciousness (p. 337)

Nonconscious process (p. 338)

Preconscious (p. 341)

Unconscious (p. 342)

MyPsychLab Resources 8.1:

Simulation: Mental Rotation

8.2 What Cycles Occur in Everyday Consciousness?

Core Concept 8.2: Consciousness changes in cycles that correspond to our biological rhythms and to the patterns of stimulation in our environment.

Consciousness shifts and changes in everyday life, commonly taking the form of daydreaming, sleep, and nocturnal dreams. **Daydreaming** is probably the default status of the waking brain and the source of much human creativity. Attempts to keep unwanted ("white bear") thoughts out of daytime reveries may have the unwanted effect of encouraging such thoughts.

Although the function of *sleep* is not altogether clear, everyone agrees that sleep and wakefulness are part of the **circadian rhythms.** Too little sleep incurs a **sleep debt,** which impairs mental functioning. Sleep researchers have revealed the features of the normal *sleep cycle,* including the four *stages of sleep,* as revealed by recordings of brain waves on the EEG. These sleep stages recur in 90-minute cycles, featuring both **REM** and **non-REM** periods. Over the course of the night, each ensuing sleep cycle involves less deep sleep and more REM sleep. The sleep cycle also changes dramatically with age. Most adults need at least eight hours of sleep every night.

The function of *dreams* is also unclear, but they often occur in REM sleep, accompanied by **sleep paralysis.** Dreams have, however, always been a source of inspiration and creativity for humankind in cultures around the world. Among theories of dreams, Freud's has probably been the most influential—although it has little empirical support. Studies show that dreams vary by culture, gender, and age, often in contradiction to Freud. Many theories suggest that dreams are meaningful events, and research shows that they often involve problems of the previous day; **activation-synthesis theory** claims that dreams are essentially meaningless. Recent studies suggest that dreams may help in the consolidation of memory.

Abnormalities in the sleep cycle can produce various sleep disorders. **Narcolepsy** is a disorder of REM sleep, **insomnia** involves shortened sleep, and **sleep apnea** involves abnormalities in deep sleep. Other disorders of a less serious nature include **night terrors,** *sleep talking, bedwetting,* and *sleepwalking.*

MyPsychLab Resources 8.2:

Explore: Theories of Dreaming

Watch: Roberta: Insomnia

8.3 What Other Forms Can Consciousness Take?

Core Concept 8.3: An altered state of consciousness occurs when some aspect of normal consciousness is modified by mental, behavioral, or chemical means.

Altered states of consciousness include hypnosis, meditation, and psychoactive drug states. **Hypnosis** remains especially puzzling as to whether it is a separate state of consciousness. Some scientists view it merely as a suggestible state; others see it as role playing or involving a "hidden observer." Cognitive psychologists have suggested it involves a shift in top-down processing. It is known to block pain, although it does not act like placebos. While hypnosis has many uses in therapy and research, one drawback is that not everyone can be deeply hypnotized.

Meditation has a long history in Asian and Pacific cultures, but has only recently been studied by psychologists. Likewise, experts dispute whether meditation is a distinct state of consciousness, even though it has measurable effects on arousal and anxiety, as well as producing changes in brain waves, blood pressure, and stress hormones.

Most **psychoactive drugs** produce sensations of pleasure and well-being that make these drugs especially attractive and potentially addictive. The **hallucinogens** (such as cannabis, mescaline, psilocybin, LSD, and PCP) generally affect receptor sites for serotonin. Distinct receptor sites for THC and for the **opiates** (including morphine, heroin, codeine, and methadone) suggest that the brain makes its own version of these substances. The **depressants** (including barbiturates, benzodiazepines, and alcohol) act to inhibit communication within the brain; many depressants are among the commonly abused drugs. Medically, the **barbiturates** are often prescribed for their sleep-inducing properties, while the **benzodiazepines** are used to treat anxiety. Most people use alcohol responsibly, although between 5 and 10% of American adults are problem drinkers. **Stimulants** (such as amphetamines, cocaine, and MDMA) are widely abused, although amphetamines are prescribed for ADHD. Caffeine and nicotine also act as stimulants. **General anesthetics** alter consciousness and suppress pain. Their effects are different from sleep. In general, they produce sedation, unconsciousness, immobility, and amnesia for events occurring during anesthesia.

Many psychoactive drugs can lead to **addiction**. One indication of this potential is increased **tolerance**; another is **physical dependence**, marked by **withdrawal symptoms**. Some drugs that are not physically addicting produce **psychological dependence**. Although addiction has been characterized as a *disease*, some psychologists believe that the disease model of addiction is short-sighted.

MyPsychLab Resources 8.3:

Simulation: Hypnosis

Watch: Hypnosis

Watch: Kathy: Substance Abuse

Watch the following videos by logging into MyPsychLab (www.mypsychlab.com). After you have watched the videos, complete the activities that follow.

 PROGRAM 13: THE MIND AWAKE AND ASLEEP

 PROGRAM 14: THE MIND HIDDEN AND DIVIDED

PROGRAM REVIEW

1. Which of the following is an example of a circadian rhythm?
   a. eating three meals a day at approximately the same time
   b. experiencing alternate periods of REM and non-REM sleep
   c. having systematic changes in hormone levels during 24 hours
   d. having changes in fertility levels during a month

2. What is a positive function of daydreaming?
   a. It focuses attention on a task.
   b. It reduces demands made on the brain.
   c. It enables us to be mentally active when we are bored.
   d. It provides delta wave activity normally received only in sleep.

3. According to Freud, dreams are significant because they
   a. permit neurotransmitters to be regenerated.
   b. reveal unconscious fears and desires.
   c. forecast the future.
   d. supply a story line to patterns of electrical charges.

4. According to McCarley and Hobson, what is true about REM sleep?
   a. Adults spend more time in REM sleep than do infants.
   b. REM sleep is an unnecessary physiological function.
   c. The random burst of brain activity occurs first, followed by the dreamer's attempt to make sense of it.
   d. The subconscious expresses its deepest desires during REM sleep.

5. According to Freud, how do we feel when painful memories or unacceptable urges threaten to break into consciousness?
   a. relieved
   b. guilty
   c. sad
   d. anxious

6. What are Freudian slips thought to reveal?
   a. what we have dreamed about
   b. how we really feel
   c. who we would like to be transformed into
   d. why we make certain choices

7. What happens if a hypnotized person who expects to smell cologne actually smells ammonia?
   a. The ammonia smell wakes him from the trance.
   b. He recognizes the ammonia smell, but he remains hypnotized.
   c. He interprets the ammonia smell as a musky cologne.
   d. He overgeneralizes and finds the cologne smells like ammonia.

8. All of the following appear to fluctuate based on circadian rhythm, except
   a. intelligence.
   b. hormone levels.
   c. blood pressure.
   d. body temperature.

9. Consciousness performs all of the following functions, except
   a. filtering sensory data.
   b. enabling us to respond flexibly.
   c. allowing us to have a sense of our own mortality.
   d. guiding performance of highly routinized actions.

10. What occurs about every 90 minutes throughout sleep?
    a. rapid eye movement
    b. rapid irregular changes in brain activity
    c. dreaming
    d. more than one of the above

11. How normal is it to experience alternate states of consciousness?
    a. It happens to most people, mainly in times of stress.
    b. It is something we all experience every day.
    c. It is rare and generally indicates a mental disorder.
    d. It is common in childhood and becomes rarer with age.

12. In the program, the part of the brain that is identified as the "interior decorator" imposing order on experience is the
    a. pons.
    b. hippocampus.
    c. limbic system.
    d. cerebral cortex.

13. Ernest Hartmann points out the logic behind Shakespeare's description of sleep. According to Hartmann, a major function of sleep is that it allows the brain to
    a. process material too threatening to be dealt with consciously.
    b. integrate the day's events with previously learned material.
    c. make plans for the day ahead.
    d. discharge a buildup of electrical activity.

14. Which part of the brain is responsible for conscious awareness?
    a. cerebral cortex
    b. brain stem
    c. limbic system
    d. hypothalamus

15. When societies around the world were studied, what proportion of them practiced some culturally patterned form of altering consciousness?
    a. practically none
    b. about a third
    c. about half
    d. the vast majority

16. Instances in which people believe they have remembered long-forgotten traumatic events are known as
    a. repression.
    b. suppression.
    c. recovered memories.
    d. fugue states.

17. Sigmund Freud is to the unconscious as _____ is to discovered memories.
    a. B. F. Skinner
    b. Jonathan Schooler
    c. Michael Gazzaniga
    d. Stephen LaBerge

18. According to Freud, normal people banish undesirable memories from their conscious minds through
    a. repression.
    b. projection.
    c. anterograde amnesia.
    d. hysteria.

19. Which topic related to human consciousness is conveyed by the story of Dr. Jekyll and Mr. Hyde?
    a. witchcraft
    b. hypnosis
    c. identity transformation
    d. sleep disorders

20. Communication between the two hemispheres of the brain is disrupted when
    a. a person is in deep meditation.
    b. a person is in deep Freudian denial.
    c. a person has just recovered an early memory.
    d. the corpus callosum is severed.

QUESTIONS TO CONSIDER

1. How do you experience REM rebound effects when you have been deprived of sleep? Do you begin dreaming soon after falling asleep? Do you experience vivid visual imagery when you are awake?

2. Changes in perceptions, time sense, memory, feelings of self-control, and suggestibility are aspects of an altered state of consciousness. Would you consider illness, love, or grief to be altered states of consciousness?

3. Psychoactive drugs are only partially responsible for the changes in the drug taker's consciousness. Mental sets, expectations, and the context in which the drugs are taken can also have significant influences. What are the implications for alcohol and drug education and treatment?

4. Do you consider television or other electronic media to have mind-altering influence? What do they have in common with other mind-altering substances or experiences? Are children more susceptible to these effects than adults?

5. Do you think you could benefit from hypnosis or meditation? Do you believe you could easily enter these states? If someone finds it difficult to become hypnotized or to meditate, would you advise the person that it is worth the effort of learning? And how would you suggest he or she learns?

ACTIVITIES

1. Keep a pad and pencil by your bed and start a dream journal. Just before you fall asleep, remind yourself to remember your dreams. Immediately

after awakening, record what you remember: images, actions, characters, emotions, events, and settings. Does your ability to recall your dreams improve over time? Does this change if you set your alarm for different times during the sleep cycle? Does your recall become more vivid or more organized? Can you shape your dreams by telling yourself at bedtime what you want to dream about?

2. Use this visualization technique to achieve a state of relaxation and, perhaps, alter your consciousness. Select a quiet place where you won't be interrupted. Choose a scene in which you have been very relaxed. To help you create a good mental picture, recall all the sensations that enhance in you a feeling of deep calm. Focus on the scene for 15 to 30 minutes. Practice this visualization exercise several times over a period of a few weeks. With practice, calling up the visual image may trigger a sensation of calm whenever you want it to.

3. Go on the Internet and look up various cultures, religions, and communities that practice altered states of consciousness. See if you can develop any insights into what aspects of their art, social interaction, and values appear to be influenced by such practices.

Critical Thinking Applied: Do "Lie Detectors" Really Detect Lies?

emotion and motivation

Elliot presented a puzzle. His life was unraveling, yet he maintained an attitude of composure. Once a model employee, he had let the quality of his work slip to the point that he finally lost his job. If anything, said his supervisors, Elliot had become almost too focused on the details of his work, yet he had trouble setting priorities. He often latched onto a small task, such as sorting a client's paperwork, and spent the whole afternoon on various classification schemes—never quite getting to the real job he had been assigned (Damasio, 1994).

His personal life also fell apart. A divorce was followed by a short marriage and another divorce. Several attempts at starting his own business involved glaringly flawed decisions that finally ate up all his savings.

Yet, surprisingly, in most respects Elliot seemed normal. He had a pleasant personality and an engaging sense of humor. He was obviously smart—well aware of important events, names, and dates. He understood the political and economic affairs of the day. In fact, examinations revealed nothing wrong with his movements, memory, perceptual abilities, language skills, intellect, or ability to learn.

Complaints of headaches led the family doctor to suspect that the changes in Elliot might be the result of a brain lesion. Tests proved the suspicion correct. Brain scans showed a mass the size of a small orange that was pressing on the frontal lobes just above Elliot's eyes.

The tumor was removed, but not before it had done extensive damage. The impact, limited to the frontal lobes, bore a remarkable similarity to that of the notorious Phineas Gage, whom you met in Chapter 2. Like Gage, Elliot had undergone a profound change as the result of frontal lobe damage. But the effects in Elliot were more subtle than in Gage. As a psychologist who examined him said, "We might summarize Elliot's predicament as *to know but not to feel*" (Damasio, 1994, p. 45). His reasoning abilities were intact, but the damage to the circuitry of Elliot's frontal lobes disrupted his ability to use his emotions to establish priorities among the objects, events, and people in his life. In short, Elliot had been emotionally crippled. With a disruption in his ability to connect concepts and emotions, Elliot could not value one course of action over another.

PROBLEM: What does Elliot's case—along with studies of the emotional pathways in the brain—tell us about the role of emotions in our thinking?

One of the most pervasive misunderstandings about the human mind is the idea that emotion is the opposite of reason. But the cases of Elliot, Phineas Gage, and others with similar problems make it clear that emotion is a vital ingredient in making effective personal decisions (Gray, 2004). In this chapter we will explore some discoveries about how the brain processes emotions and what these discoveries mean about the intimate connection between emotion and reason.

- -

CONNECTION • CHAPTER 12

Phobias are one form of *anxiety disorder*.

Emotion A four-part process that involves physiological arousal, subjective feelings, cognitive interpretation, and behavioral expression. Emotions help organisms deal with important events.

So, what is this thing called emotion? In brief, **emotion** has four intersecting components: *physiological arousal, cognitive interpretation, subjective feelings,* and *behavioral expression.* Let's illustrate with a happy example.

Suppose that you win a cool $50 million in the lottery. Chances are that the news will make you jump and shout, your heart race, and a wave of joy wash over your brain. Congratulations: You have just had an emotion, the *physiological arousal* component of which involves an alarm broadcast simultaneously throughout the autonomic nervous system and the endocrine system. The result is an extensive visceral response that includes your racing heart.

The second component of emotion, a *cognitive interpretation* of events and feelings, involves a conscious recognition and interpretation of the situation. Undoubtedly, you would interpret the news about your winning lottery ticket as good fortune. The same processes—both conscious and unconscious—can happen with unpleasant experiences, too. (Think of a hungry bear chasing you.) Such negative experiences, especially those associated with anxiety and fear, can lead to the psychological disorder known as *phobia.*

The *subjective feeling* component of your fear may come from several sources. One involves the brain sensing the body's current state of arousal (Damasio, 1994, 2003). The other comes from memories of the body's state in similar situations in the past. There the brain stores a sort of emotional "body-image" that Antonio Damasio calls a *somatic marker.* (Perhaps you were overjoyed at winning a raffle at school, when you were a child. That association can carry over and attach to the present situation, much as Pavlov's dogs associated a tone with food.) Similarly, in response to the hungry bear, your brain would retrieve a body-image memory of how you felt during past encounters with danger.

The recently discovered "mirror neuron" system is another source of emotional feelings. These brain circuits activate to make you feel an emotion when you see someone else's emotional state, as in a sad movie (Miller, 2006c; Niedenthal, 2007). In our hungry bear example, your mirror neurons may reflect the emotions of a companion who sees the bear before you do. Numerous studies support this conjecture, but one of the more interesting ones looked at the brain scans of romantically involved couples, finding that when one had an unpleasant experience, both showed essentially the same changes in the emotion-related parts of the brain (Singer et al., 2004).

Finally, the fourth component of emotion produces an *expression of emotion in behavior.* So, when you learned of your lottery winnings, you probably smiled, gave a shout of joy, and perhaps danced around the room, as you babbled the news to your companions. Alternatively, the sight of a hungry bear most likely would activate the "fight-or-flight" response, as well as in emotion-laden facial expressions and vocalizations, such as crying, grimacing, or shouting. If a person were angry, the response might also be accompanied by voluntary gestures, such as waving a fist or pointing out one's state of mind with the middle finger.

Because this chapter is titled "Emotion and Motivation," we might ask: How is emotion linked to motivation? Note that both words share a common root, "*mot-,*" from the Latin *motus,* meaning "move." The psychology of motivation and emotion has retained this meaning by viewing emotion and motivation as intimately related processes. We can think of emotions simply as one very important class of motives that help us respond to events of importance to us.

CONNECTION • CHAPTER 2

"Mirror neurons" allow us to understand others' behaviors, emotional states, and intentions.

9.1 KEY QUESTION
WHAT DO OUR EMOTIONS DO FOR US?

The death of a friend, an insult, winning an award, losing a lover to a rival: All induce strong feelings—sorrow, anger, joy, jealousy. But, what do these states have in common? Why do we put them all in the same category called "emotion"? The common thread is this: All emotions involve a state of mental and physical arousal focused on some event of importance to the individual.

And what functions do these emotional responses serve? Surely emotions must do more than just adding variety or "color" to our mental lives. The brief answer to the question is given by our Core Concept:

Emotions help us to attend and respond to important situations and to convey our intentions to others.

core
concept

In this section, we will first consider the adaptive functions of emotions from an evolutionary perspective. Next, we will add a social perspective to see how the language of emotional expression tells others of our emotional state. Finally, at the end of this section, we will consider the issue of gender differences in emotion and how they are shaped by culture.

The Evolution of Emotions

Whether they occur in humans, hyenas, cats, or kangaroos, emotions serve as arousal states that signal important events, such as a threat or the presence of a receptive mate. They also become etched in memory, to help the organism recognize such situations quickly when they recur (Dolan, 2002; LeDoux, 1996). And our ability to connect emotional memories to new situations accounts for emotions as diverse as the fear generated by a hungry bear, the joy produced by a winning lottery ticket, or an A on a term paper.

CONNECTION • CHAPTER 2

The amygdala is a part of the limbic system that is particularly involved in fear.

In general, our emotions are either *positive* or *negative*, and they also involve a tendency for *approach* or *avoidance* (Davidson et al., 2000). The "approach" emotions, such as delight and joy, are generally positive, and they make a person, object, or situation attractive (as when we feel drawn to a friend). Brain scans suggest that these approach emotions involve the dopamine reward system in the brain. In contrast, most of the negative emotions, such as fear and disgust, are associated with rejection or avoidance (as when we fear going to the dentist). These avoidance emotions usually involve the amygdala.

Because our most basic emotions well up in situations that can affect our survival, they have been shaped by natural selection (Gross, 1998; Izard, 2007). Fear, for example, undoubtedly helped individuals in your family tree avoid to situations that could have made them a meal instead of an ancestor. Similarly, the emotion we call "love" may commit us to a family, which helps to continue our genetic line. Likewise, sexual jealousy can be seen as an emotion that evolved to deal with the biologically important problem of mate infidelity, which threatens the individual's chances of producing offspring (Buss & Schmitt, 1993). Humor, too, may have evolved to serve a social purpose, as we can surmise from the "in-jokes" and rampant laughter among people in tightly knit social groups (Provine, 2004; Winerman, 2006d).

We glimpsed yet another important-but-little-known function of emotions in Elliot's story at the beginning of the chapter. As you will recall, his tumor interfered not only with his ability to process emotion but with his judgment. The cases of Elliot and others like him show that our emotions help us make decisions, because they us attach values to the alternatives we are considering (De Martino et al., 2006; Miller, 2006a).

You probably know someone who is "warm hearted" and someone else whom you might call a "cold fish." These extremes represent the important biological fact that people vary tremendously in emotional responsiveness (Davidson, 2000b). We see this, for example, in differing tendencies for depression. Some of these individual differences arise from random genetic variations—genetic "accidents." Others tend to run in families and so are inherited (Gabbay, 1992).

But we should emphasize that emotions are not entirely programmed by genetics. They also involve learning—that is, they arise out of our experiences. Particularly important in setting emotional temperament are experiences that occur early in life, as well as experiences that have evoked strong emotional responses (Barlow, 2000; LeDoux, 1996). Thus, learned emotional responses, along with a biological disposition for emotionality, can be important components of many psychological disorders, including depression, panic attacks, and phobic reactions—to name just a few.

Counting the Emotions

How many emotions are there? A long look in the dictionary turns up more than 500 emotional terms (Averill, 1980). Most experts, however, see a more limited number of *basic emotions*. Carroll Izard (2007) argues for six: interest, joy/happiness, sadness, anger, disgust, and fear. Paul Ekman's list contains seven: anger, disgust, fear, happiness, sadness, contempt, and surprise—based on the universally recognized facial expressions. And Robert Plutchik (1980, 1984) has made a case for eight basic emotions that emerged from a mathematical analysis of people's ratings of a large number of emotional terms. Recent research suggests that Plutchik's list might even be expanded to include pride (Azar, 2006; Tracy & Robins, 2006). Even though different theorists approach the problem in different ways, their differences are relatively minor. Plutchik's list, shown in Figure 9.1, is typical, capturing the essential idea that we have a limited number of basic emotions.

But what about emotions that appear on none of these basic lists? What of envy, regret, or mirth? Those who argue for a simplified list of basic emotions,

Sexual jealousy probably has an evolutionary basis because mate infidelity threatens the individual's chances of producing offspring.

suggest that a larger palette of *secondary emotions* involves blends of the more basic emotions. So, for example, Plutchik's theory describes optimism as a blend of anticipation and joy, as you can see in Figure 9.1.

Cultural Universals in Emotional Expression

You can usually tell when a friend is happy or angry by the look on her face or by her actions. This can be useful in deciding whether to spend Friday evening with her at the movies. More generally, as our Core Concept suggests, communication through emotional expression aids our social interactions. But does raising the eyebrows and rounding the mouth convey the same message in Minneapolis as it does in Madagascar? Much research on emotional expression has centered on such questions.

According to Paul Ekman, the leading authority on facial expression of emotions, people speak and understand the same basic "facial language" the world around (Ekman, 2003). Ekman's group has demonstrated that humans share a built-in set of emotional expressions that testify to the common biological heritage of the human species. Smiles, for example, usually signal happiness, and frowns indicate sadness on the faces of people in such far-flung places as Argentina, Japan, Spain, Hungary, Poland, Sumatra, the United States, Vietnam, the jungles of New Guinea, and the Eskimo villages north of the Arctic Circle (Biehl et al., 1997).

Perhaps it won't surprise you to learn that gender makes a difference in what we read into other people's facial expressions. One study found a bias toward seeing anger in men's faces and happy expressions in women's faces (Becker et al., 2007). This finding makes sense from an evolutionary perspective, of course, because angry men have always been a source of danger, while a happy woman's face may have signaled safety (Azar, 2007).

You can check your own skill at interpreting facial expressions by taking the quiz in the "Do It Yourself!" box on the next page. Ekman and his colleagues claim that people everywhere can recognize at least seven basic emotions: sadness, fear, anger, disgust, contempt, happiness, and surprise. Nevertheless, huge differences exist across cultures in both the context and intensity of emotional displays—because of so-called **display rules**. In many Asian cultures, for example, children are taught to control emotional responses—especially negative ones—while many American children are encouraged to express their feelings more openly (Smith et al., 2006). As a result, people are generally better at judging emotions of people from their own culture than in members of another cultural group (Elfenbein & Ambady, 2003).

Regardless of culture, babies express emotions almost at birth. In fact, a lusty cry is a sign of good health. And from their first days of life, babies display a small repertoire of facial expressions that communicate their feelings (Ganchrow et al., 1983). Likewise, the ability to read facial expressions develops early (but not so early as emotional expression). Very young children pay close attention to facial expressions, and by age 5 they nearly equal adults in their skill at reading emotions in people's faces (Nelson, 1987).

All this work on facial expressions points to a biological underpinning for our abilities to express and interpret a basic set of human emotions. Moreover, as Charles Darwin pointed out over a century ago, some emotional expressions seem to appear across species boundaries. Darwin especially noted the similarity of our own facial expressions of fear and rage to those of chimpanzees and wolves (Darwin, 1998/1862; Ekman, 1984).

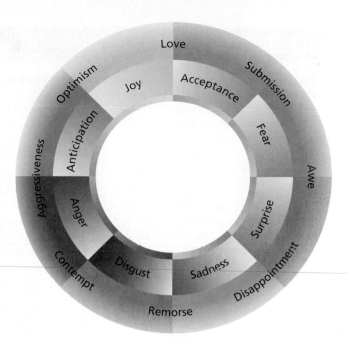

FIGURE 9.1
The Emotion Wheel

Robert Plutchik's emotion wheel arranges eight primary emotions on the inner ring of a circle of opposite emotions. Pairs of adjacent emotions can combine to form more complex emotions noted on the outer ring of the figure. For example, love is portrayed as a combination of joy and acceptance. Still other emotions, such as envy or regret (not shown), emerge from still other combinations of more basic emotions portrayed on the wheel.

(*Source:* From R. Plutchik, "A Language for the Emotions," *Psychology Today*, February 1980. Copyright © 1980. Used with permission of *Psychology Today* © 2008.)

Display rules   The permissible ways of displaying emotions in a particular society.

Take the facial emotion identification test to see how well you can identify each of the seven emotions that Ekman claims are culturally universal. Do not read the answers until you have matched each of the following pictures with one of these emotions: disgust, happiness, anger, sadness, surprise, fear, and contempt. Apparently, people everywhere in the world interpret these expressions in the same way. This tells us that certain facial expressions of emotion are probably rooted in our human genetic heritage.

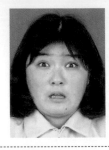

Answers The facial expressions are (top row from left) happiness, surprise, anger, disgust; (bottom row) fear, sadness, contempt.

But are *all* emotional expressions universal? Cross-cultural psychologists tell us that certain emotional responses carry different meanings in different cultures (Ekman, 1992, 1994; Ellsworth, 1994). These, therefore, must be learned rather than innate. For example, what emotion do you suppose might be conveyed by sticking out the tongue? For Americans this might indicate disgust or fatigue, while in China it can signify surprise. Similarly, a grin on an American face may indicate joy, while on a Japanese face it may just as easily mean embarrassment. To give one more example, a somber expression and downcast eyes might indicate unhappiness to someone in a Euro-American culture, whereas it could be a sign of respect to many Asians. Clearly, culture influences emotional expression.

PSYCHOLOGY**MATTERS**

Emotional Differences between Men and Women Depend on Both Biology and Culture

You may have suspected that some emotional differences between males and females have a biological basis. This would explain, for example, why certain emotional disturbances, such as panic disorder and depression, occur more commonly in women. Biological differences may also explain why men show more anger and display more physiological signs of emotional arousal during interpersonal conflicts than do women (Fischer et al., 2004). Anger, of course, can lead to violence—and men commit most of the world's violent acts.

Some gender differences, however, may depend as much on culture as on biology. For instance, in the United States, males and females may learn quite different lessons about emotional control. Display rules dictate that men and boys show their anger (Fischer, 1993). Indeed, they may be rewarded for displays of anger and aggression. On the other hand, they may also be punished for "weak" emotional displays such as crying, depression, and sadness (Gottman, 1994). Meanwhile, the pattern of reinforcement and punishment is reversed for females. Women and girls may receive encouragement for emotions that show vulnerability. But they may be punished for displaying emotions that suggest dominance (Fischer et al., 2004).

Despite these differences, neither sex is more emotionally expressive overall. Rather, cultures differ in emotional expression much more than do the sexes (Brannon, 2008; Wallbott et al., 1986). In Israel and Italy, for example, men more often than women hide their feelings of sadness. The opposite holds true in Britain, Spain, Switzerland, and Germany, where women are more likely than men to hide sadness. In many collectivist cultures, as we have noted, both genders learn display rules to restrain all their emotional expressions. Overall, however, the differences among individuals overshadow the differences of either gender or culture.

CheckYourUnderstanding

1. **RECALL:** What are four main components of emotions?

2. **RECALL:** Name an emotion that is *not* one of the culturally universal emotions identified by Ekman's research.

3. **ANALYSIS:** Give an example that illustrates how *display rules* can modify the universal facial expressions of emotion.

4. **RECALL:** What differences in emotional expression of men and women seem to be heavily influenced by culture?

5. **UNDERSTANDING THE CORE CONCEPT:** According to this section of the chapter, what is the adaptive value of communicating our emotional states?
   a. To help us understand our own needs better
   b. To help us deceive others about our emotional states and get what we want
   c. To help us anticipate each other's responses and so to live more easily in groups
   d. To help us get rid of strong negative emotions, such as fear and anger

Answers 1. Four main components of emotions: physiological arousal, cognitive interpretation, subjective feelings, and behavioral expression **2.** Pride, optimism, jealousy, envy, anxiety—in fact, any emotion other than Ekman's seven universal emotions: sadness, fear, anger, disgust, contempt, happiness, and surprise **3.** Smiles may indicate happiness in some cultures and embarrassment in others. Other examples are mentioned in the section on display rules. **4.** Cultures often encourage men to show emotions related to anger, aggression and dominance, while they encourage women to show emotions related to compliance and submission. **5.** c; our emotions convey our intentions to others.

9.2 KEY QUESTION
WHERE DO OUR EMOTIONS COME FROM?

Suppose that you are touring a "haunted house" at Halloween, when a filmy figure startles you with ghostly "Boo!" Your emotional response is immediate. It may involve an outward reaction, such as jumping, gasping, or screaming. At the same time, you respond internally, with changes in your body chemistry, the function of your internal organs, and arousal in certain parts of your brain and autonomic nervous system. Moreover, these gut-level responses, such as an accelerated heart beat, can persist long after the you realize that you were really in no danger—after you realize that you were fooled by someone dressed in a sheet.

This suggests that emotion operates on both the conscious and unconscious levels. And that idea connects to one of the great recent discoveries in psychology: the existence of two emotion pathways in the brain. These dual pathways are the focus of the Core Concept for this section:

> The discovery of two distinct brain pathways for emotional arousal has clarified how emotion works and has suggested solutions to long-standing issues in the psychology of emotion.

core concept

In the following pages we will see how the young neuroscience of emotion has begun to identify the machinery that produces our emotions. The details have not yet become entirely clear, but we do have a broad-brush picture of the emotion pathways in the brain and their connections throughout the body. In this section we will first see how the two emotion pathways work. Then we will see how they have helped resolve some long-standing disputes in the field. Finally, at the end of this section, we will turn to a practical application, to learn how emotional arousal can affect our performance—say, on an examination or in an important athletic contest.

The Neuroscience of Emotion

People who suffer from phobias, such as an intense fear of snakes, usually know that their responses are irrational. But what causes a person to hold two such conflicting mind sets? The answer lies in the brain's two distinct emotion processing systems (LeDoux, 1996, 2000).

Emotions in the Unconscious   One emotion system—a *fast response system*—operates mainly at an unconscious level, where it quickly screens incoming stimuli and helps us respond quickly to cues of potentially important events, even before they reach consciousness. This system, linked to *implicit memory,* acts as an early-warning defense that produces, for example, a near-instantaneous fright response to an unexpected loud noise (Helmuth, 2003b). It relies primarily on deep-brain circuitry that operates automatically, without requiring deliberate conscious control. (See Figure 9.2.)

Thanks to natural selection, these unconscious emotion circuits seem to have a built-in sensitivity to certain cues—which explains why fears of spiders and snakes are more common than fears of, say, electricity (which actually causes more deaths than do spiders and snakes but has only recently in human history has become a common cause of death). In addition, this quick-response system can easily learn emotional responses through classical conditioning—but it can also be slow to forget. Thus, a person may quickly learn to fear dogs

CONNECTION • CHAPTER 4

Implicit memories involve material of which we are unaware—but that can affect behavior.

FIGURE 9.2
Two Emotion-Processing Pathways

Two emotion systems are at work when the hiker sees a snake. One is fast and unconscious; the other operates more slowly and consciously. The fast system routes incoming visual information through the visual thalamus to the amygdala (dotted pathway), which quickly initiates fear and avoidance responses—all occurring unconsciously. The slower pathway involves the visual cortex, which makes a more complete appraisal of the stimulus and also sends an emotional message to the amygdala and other lower brain structures. The result of this is a conscious perception of the situation and a conscious feeling of fear.

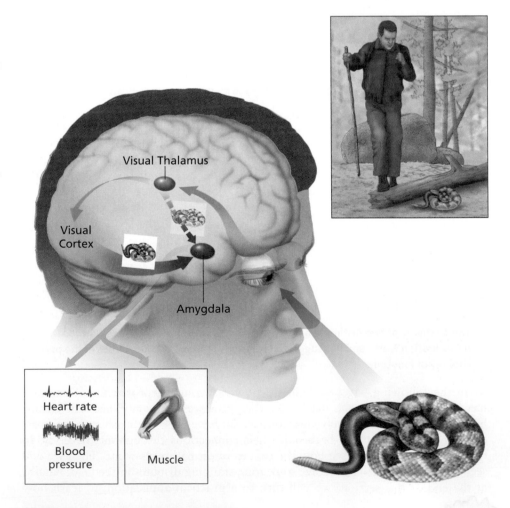

Visual Thalamus

Visual Cortex

Amygdala

Heart rate

Blood pressure

Muscle

after being bitten, yet the emotional memory of the incident may be quite difficult to extinguish.

Conscious Emotional Processing   The other emotional system—the one that involves conscious processing—is linked to *explicit memory* (LeDoux, 1996; Mather, 2007). Its circuitry can create, for example, the fear that grows in your mind when you anticipate giving a speech. This conscious system generates emotions more slowly than the unconscious pathways, but it is more thorough and deliberate. Relying heavily on the cerebral cortex, your conscious view of events can differ significantly from that of your unconscious processing system. Thus, if you have a phobia, you can feel fear, despite "knowing" that there is no sensible basis for the feeling.

The Interaction of Conscious and Unconscious Emotions   As you can see, then, the brain has no "emotion center" (Davidson, 2000a). Rather, it has many emotion-related circuits that serve the two distinct emotion systems. And, to complicate matters, these two systems also interact. As a result, the feelings that we associate with an emotion such as fear can well up into consciousness from the unconscious system. This process may produce the feelings that we call "intuition" (Myers, 2002). Alternatively, the conscious emotional system can signal fear to the unconscious circuits, which might produce the knot in your stomach just before giving a speech.

Let us take a more detailed look at these biological mechanisms at work behind our emotions.

The Limbic System's Role in Emotion   Both emotion pathways rely on circuits in the brain's limbic system, as you can see in Figure 9.2. Situated in the layer above the brain stem, the limbic structures undoubtedly evolved as control systems for behaviors used in attack, defense, and retreat: the "fight-or-flight" response (Caldwell, 1995; LeDoux, 1994, 1996). Evidence for this comes from lesioning (cutting) or electrically stimulating parts of the limbic system, which can produce dramatic changes in emotional responding. Depending on which part of the limbic system is affected, tame animals may become killers, whereas prey and predators may become peaceful companions (Delgado, 1969).

Particularly well documented is the importance of the amygdala in the emotion of fear (LeDoux, 1996; Whalen, 1998). Like a guard dog, the amygdala stands alert for threats, and it may have a role in positive emotions, too (Hamann et al., 2002; Helmuth, 2003a). As you can see in the figure, the amygdala receives messages from the quick-and-unconscious emotion-processing pathway, as well as the longer-and-slower conscious pathway.

The Cerebral Cortex's Role in Emotion   The cerebral cortex—the outermost layer of brain tissue and our "thinking cap"—plays the starring role in the conscious emotion pathway, where it both interprets events and associates them with memories and feelings. This connection, as we have seen, helps us make decisions by attaching emotional values to alternative choices we face, such as: Do I want chocolate or strawberry? or, Do I want to save my money or buy a new stereo?

Neuroscientists now think they know where emotion and reason meet in the brain. It's a small patch of brain with a big name: the *ventromedial prefrontal cortex (VMPFC)*. Located on the floor of the brain's frontal lobes, just behind the eyes, the VMPFC has extensive connections with both the amygdala and the hippocampus, at the heart of the brain's emotion circuitry (Wagar & Thagard, 2006). There, like a recording technician combining inputs for a sound track, the VMPFC mixes external stimulation with the body's "gut" reaction and converts the result into an emotional memory: Was it positive or negative? Did it make your skin creep? Did you feel a lump in your throat? A knot in your stomach? Thanks to your VMPC most of your memories probably have such visceral associations attached.

When faced with a decision—perhaps between Italian or Chinese take-out or between spending a vacation in the mountains or at the shore—positive or negative associations spring to mind as you mull each alternative. When we "weigh" our choices, we are actually balancing the positives and negatives of these associations. You will recall, in our opening vignette, that is exactly what Elliot was not able to do as the result of the tumor in his frontal lobes.

One other cortical quirk deserves mention: The two frontal lobes have complementary roles in controlling our emotions. Just as distinct patches of cortex produce different sensations, positive and negative emotions are associated with opposite hemispheres, an effect called **lateralization of emotion**. The evidence comes from EEG recordings of normal people's emotional reactions, along with EEGs of people with damage to the right or left hemisphere (Davidson et al., 2000). In general, the right hemisphere specializes in negative emotions, such as anger and depression, while the left processes more positive, joyful emotions (Kosslyn et al., 2002).

The Autonomic Nervous System's Role in Emotion   When you become emotionally aroused, the messages that you "take to heart" (and to your other internal organs) are routed through the autonomic nervous system (Levenson, 1992). The parasympathetic division usually dominates in pleasant emotions. But when you are startled or when you experience some unpleasant emotion, the sympathetic division becomes more active. (See Table 9.1.)

Suppose an emergency—or merely the memory of an emergency—occurs (A speeding car is coming directly at you!). The brain alerts the body by means of messages carried along pathways of the sympathetic system. Some signals direct the adrenal glands to release stress hormones. Others make the heart race and blood pressure rise. At the same time, the sympathetic system directs certain blood vessels to constrict, diverting energy to the voluntary muscles and away from the stomach and intestines. (This causes the feeling of a "knot" in your stomach.) Then, when the emergency has passed, the parasympathetic division takes over, carrying instructions that counteract the emergency orders of a few moments earlier. You may, however, remain aroused for some time after experiencing a strong emotional activation because hormones continue to circulate in the bloodstream. If the emotion-provoking situation is prolonged (as when you work every day for a boss whom you detest), the emergency response can sap your energy and cause both physical and mental deterioration.

The Hormones' Role in Emotion   Your body produces dozens of hormones, but among the most important for your emotions are serotonin, epinephrine (adrenalin), and norepinephrine. Serotonin is associated with feelings of depression. Epinephrine is the hormone produced in fear. Norepinephrine is more abundant in anger.

CONNECTION • CHAPTER 2
The autonomic nervous system controls the internal organs, along with many signs of emotional arousal.

Lateralization of emotion   Different influences of the two brain hemispheres on various emotions. The left hemisphere apparently influences positive emotions (for example, happiness), and the right hemisphere influences negative emotions (anger, for example).

CONNECTION • CHAPTER 13
Drugs that inhibit the reuptake of serotonin are often used to treat depression.

TABLE 9.1   Responses Associated with Emotion

Component of emotion	Type of response	Example
Physiological arousal	Neural, hormonal, visceral, and muscular changes	Increased heart rate, blushing, becoming pale, sweating, rapid breathing
Subjective feelings	The private experience of one's internal affective state	Feelings of rage, sadness, happiness
Cognitive interpretation	Attaching meaning to the emotional experience by drawing on memory and perceptual processes	Blaming someone, perceiving a threat
Social/behavioral reactions	Expressing emotion through gestures, facial expressions, or other actions	Smiling, crying, screaming for help

Steroid hormones (the same ones abused by some bodybuilders and other athletes) exert an especially powerful influence on our emotions. In addition to their effects on muscles, steroids act on nerve cells, causing them to change their excitability. This is a normal part of the body's response to emergency situations. But when steroid drugs are ingested over extended periods, these potent chemicals have the effect of keeping the body (including the brain) in a continual emergency state. Brain circuits, especially those associated with arousal, threat, stress, and strong emotions may remain in a state of heightened alert. One of the results may be tendencies to "roid" rage or depression (Daly et al., 2003; Miller et al., 2002). You will learn more about the effects of steroid hormones in our discussion of stress in Chapter 14.

Psychological Theories of Emotion: Resolving Some Old Issues

Borrowing an illustration from the late great William James, let's suppose that you have the unlikely misfortune to encounter a hungry bear while on your way to class one morning. We will bet that you will experience the emotion of fear. But what internal process actually produces your fearful sensation? Does it come from the thought, "Uh-oh. I'm in danger"? Or does it come from sensing your racing heart and wrenching gut? And, you may be wondering, why would anyone care where emotions come from?

In response to the last question: Psychologists have long argued over the relationship between emotion, cognition, and physical responses—not only out of intellectual curiosity but because an understanding of emotion is a key to finding effective treatments for certain emotional problems, such as panic attacks and depression, as well as the everyday problems of anger, envy, and jealousy. Should we try to treat anger, for example, by targeting thoughts, visceral reactions, or angry behaviors? Or should we treat the brain itself with chemicals?

Recent discoveries in neuroscience have helped psychologists resolve some long-disputed issues surrounding the interaction of biology, cognition, and behavior in emotion. Let's look briefly at these controversies and how new insights have begun to resolve them.

Do Our Physical Responses Produce Our Emotions?

In the early days of psychology, just over a century ago, William James taught that our physical responses underlie our emotions. "We feel sorry because we cry, angry because we strike, afraid because we tremble," James said (1890/1950, p. 1006). As for the bear we mentioned earlier, James argued that you would not run from the bear because you afraid, but you feel afraid because you run. While this statement may appear absurd on its face, James is really saying something quite sensible—that emotions require a *combination* of cognitions and physical sensations:

> Without the bodily states following on the perception [of the bear], the latter would be purely cognitive in form, pale, colourless, destitute of emotional warmth. We might then see the bear, and judge it best to run, receive the insult and deem it right to strike, but we could not actually *feel* afraid or angry.

This view, simultaneously proposed by the Danish psychologist Carl Lange, became known as the **James–Lange theory**.

Other scientists, notably Walter Cannon and Philip Bard, objected that physical changes in our behavior or our internal organs occur too slowly to account for split-second emotional reactions, such as those we feel in the face of danger. They also objected that our physical responses are not varied enough to account for the whole palate of human emotion. In their view, referred to as the **Cannon–Bard theory**, the emotional feeling and the internal physical response occurred simultaneously.

James–Lange theory The proposal that an emotion-provoking stimulus produces a physical response that, in turn, produces an emotion.

Cannon–Bard theory The counterproposal that an emotional feeling and an internal physiological response occur at the same time: One is not the cause of the other. Both were believed to be the result of cognitive appraisal of the situation.

The two-factor theory would predict that decaffeinated-coffee drinkers who accidentally drank coffee with caffeine could mistake the resulting physical arousal for an emotion. Could that be happening here?

During a break at the Western Psychological Association convention near Vancouver, British Columbia, psychologists Susan Horton and Bob Johnson (one of your authors) reenact the Dutton study of attraction on the Capilano Bridge, where the original study was performed.

Two-factor theory   The idea that emotion results from the cognitive appraisal of both physical arousal (Factor #1) and an emotion-provoking stimulus (Factor #2).

Which side was right? It turns out that both had part of the truth. On the one hand, modern neuroscience has confirmed that our physical state can influence our emotions—much as the James–Lange theory argued (LeDoux, 1996). In fact, you may have noted how your own physical state affects your emotions, as when you get edgy feelings after drinking too much coffee or grumpy when hungry. Similarly, psychoactive drugs, such as alcohol or nicotine, can influence the physical condition of our brains and hence alter our moods. These emotional responses arise from circuits deep in the brain responding unconsciously to our physical condition.

Another important new insight comes from the discovery that the brain maintains memories of physical states that are associated with events. These are the "somatic markers" we mentioned earlier (Damasio, 1994; Niedenthal, 2007). When you see the bear on the path in front of you, your brain can quickly conjure a body-memory of the physical response it had previously in a threatening situation. This somatic-marker idea, then, effectively counters Walter Cannon's objection that physical changes in the body occur too slowly to cause our feelings—because the somatic marker of emotion resides in the brain itself.

On the other hand—and in support of Cannon—emotions can also be aroused by external cues detected either by the conscious or the unconscious emotional system. Thus, emotion can result from conscious thought (as when you fret over an exam) or from unconscious memories (as when you feel disgust at the sight of a food that had once made you sick). Incidentally, cognitive psychologists now believe that depression and phobic reactions can result from conditioned responses of the unconscious emotional system.

What's the Role of Cognition in Emotion?   As we noted, you can make yourself emotional just by thinking, as any student with "test anxiety" will testify. The more you think about the dire consequences of failing a test, the more the anxiety builds. "Method" actors, like the late Marlon Brando, have long exploited this fact to make themselves feel real emotions on stage. They do so by recalling an incident from their own experience that produced the emotion they want to portray, such as grief, joy, or anger.

Stanley Schachter's (1971) **two-factor theory** adds an interesting twist to the role of cognition in emotion. His theory suggests that the emotions we feel depend on our appraisal of both (a) our internal *physical state* and (b) the *external situation* in which we find ourselves. Strange effects occur when these two factors conflict—as they did in the following classic study of emotion, which enterprising students may want to adapt in order to spice up their romantic lives.

An attractive female researcher positioned herself at the end of a footbridge and interviewed unsuspecting males who had just crossed. On one occasion she selected a safe, sturdy bridge; another time, a wobbly suspension bridge across a deep canyon—deliberately selected to elicit physical arousal. The researcher, pretending to be interested in the effects of scenery on creativity, asked the men to write brief stories about a picture. She also invited them to call her if they wanted more information about the study. As predicted, those men who had just crossed the wobbly bridge (and were, presumably, more physically aroused by the experience) wrote stories containing more sexual imagery than those who used the safer structure. And four times as many of them called the female researcher "to get more information"! Apparently, the men who had crossed the shaky bridge interpreted their increased arousal as emotional attraction to the female interviewer (Dutton & Aron, 1974).

Before you rush out to find the love of your life on a wobbly bridge, we must caution you, numerous attempts to test the two-factor theory have produced conflicting results (Leventhal & Tomarken, 1986; Sinclair et al., 1994). So, under what conditions are we most likely to confound physical arousal with emotion? Normally, external events confirm what our biology tells us, without much need for elaborate interpretation—as when you feel disgust at smelling an unpleasant odor or joy at seeing an old friend. But what happens when we experience physical arousal from not-so-obvious sources, such as exercise, heat, or drugs? Misattribution, it seems, is most likely in a complex environment where many stimuli are competing for our attention, as in the bridge study, above. It is also likely in an environment where we have faulty information about our physical arousal, as when unsuspected caffeine in a soft drink makes us edgy. (See Figure 9.3.)

Can We Separate Cognition and Emotion? Some theorists have argued that emotion and cognition are separate and independent brain processes (Izard, 1989, 1993; Zajonc, 1980, 1984). In panic disorder, for example, panic attacks can occur suddenly and without warning—in the absence of a threatening situation and without emotion-provoking thoughts.

An opposing view has been set forth by those who specialize in cognitive psychotherapy. This perspective asserts that cognition and emotion have an intimate connection. Richard Lazarus (1984, 1991a), for example, argues that we can conquer negative emotional responses by changing the way we think about events. In this view, cognition and emotion are components of a single mental system.

Again, insights from neuroscience can help us resolve this conflict. And again, both sides have part of the truth (LeDoux, 1996). Whether emotion and cognition are separate or intertwined depends on which of the two main emotion circuits in the brain is involved. The emotion-and-cognition-are-separate view emphasizes emotions arising in the unconscious emotion systems. In contrast, the emotion-and-cognition-are-connected view emphasizes emotions originating in the conscious emotion pathways.

Most recently, Carroll Izard (2007) has proposed a resolution of the issue along similar lines but with different terminology that makes a distinction

Theories of Emotion Compared

James–Lange Theory: Every emotion corresponds to a distinctive pattern of psychological arousal.

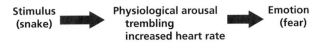

Cannon–Bard Theory: Emotions arise from a cognitive appraisal of the stimulus. (Offered as an alternative to the James–Lang theory because Canon & Bard believed that emotions often occur too quickly to be the result of psychological arousal, as the James–Lang theory asserted.)

Schachter's Two-Factor Theory: Emotions arise from a cognitive interpretation of the stimulus *and* psychological arousal. (But the arousal state is not necessarily a reaction to the stimulus (the snake) to which the person attributes the arousal.)

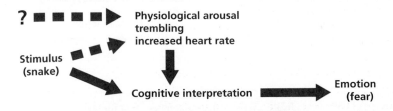

FIGURE 9.3
Theories of Emotion Compared

between *basic emotions* and *emotional schemas*. He suggests that the *basic emotions* (such as fear, joy, and anger) are driven by deep structures in the primitive brain, while *emotional schemas* (such as, the attachment you feel to your favorite team or your dislike for a certain type of music) involve the cortex. In this view, then, basic emotions are essentially automatic, reflexive responses that rely on brain circuits operating outside of consciousness. By contrast, emotional schemas rely heavily on conscious cognitions.

PSYCHOLOGY**MATTERS**
Arousal, Performance, and the Inverted U

Athletes always want to be "up" for a game—but how far up should they be? Cheering sports fans might think that increased arousal will always improve performance—but that is not necessarily true. Too much arousal can make an athlete "choke" and performance falter. The same is true for you when you take an examination. Up to a point, increasing levels of arousal can motivate you to study, but only slightly higher levels can cause test anxiety and poor performance.

This complex relationship between arousal and behavior has been studied both in laboratory animals and in humans under all sorts of conditions. For example, in experiments on learning, the curve plotting the performance of hungry rats working to get a food reward first rises and then later declines with increasing arousal. The same pattern holds for humans in a variety of circumstances, including athletes under pressure. Psychologists call this the **inverted U function** (so named because the graph resembles an upside-down letter U, as you can see in Figure 9.4). It suggests that either too little or too much arousal can impair performance. Think about it: How much pressure would you want your dentist or surgeon to feel?—which brings us to a second important point.

The optimum amount of arousal varies with the task. As you can see in the figure, it takes more arousal to achieve peak performance on simple tasks or tasks in which responses have been thoroughly rehearsed in advance (as in most sports) than it does on complex tasks or those that require much thinking and planning as the situation develops. So it is not surprising that cheers and high levels of arousal are more likely to boost performance in basketball games than in brain surgery.

Finally, the amount of stimulation needed to produce optimal arousal also varies with the individual. In fact, some people seem to thrive on the thrill of dangerous sports, such as rock climbing and skydiving—activities that would produce immobilizing levels of arousal in most of us. Marvin Zuckerman (2004), who has studied people he calls **sensation seekers**, believes that such individuals

Inverted U function A term that describes the relationship between arousal and performance. Both low and high levels of arousal produce lower performance than does a moderate level of arousal.

Sensation seekers In Zuckerman's theory, individuals who have a biological need for higher levels of stimulation than do most other people.

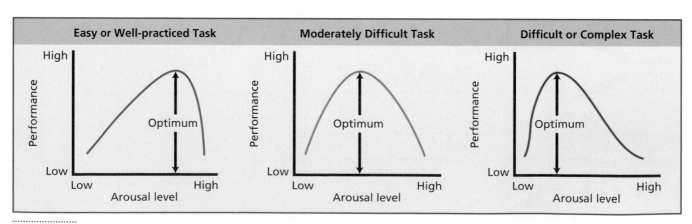

FIGURE 9.4
The Inverted U

Performance varies with arousal level and task difficulty. For easy or well-practiced tasks, a higher level of arousal increases performance effectiveness. However, for difficult or complex tasks, a lower level or arousal is optimal. A moderate level of arousal is generally best for tasks of moderate

have a biological need for high levels of stimulation. Research suggests that the underlying biology involves the brain's dopamine pathways (Bevins, 2001). You can test your own sensation-seeking tendencies with Zuckerman's scale, found in the "Do It Yourself!" box.

DO IT YOURSELF! Are You a Sensation Seeker?

Different people seem to need different levels of emotional arousal. Marvin Zuckerman argues that "sensation seekers" have an unusually high need for stimulation that produces arousal. In addition to the need for thrills, sensation seekers may be impulsive, engage in risky behaviors, prefer new experiences, and be easily bored (Kohn et al., 1979; Malatesta et al., 1981; Zuckerman, 1974).

From your score on the Sensation Seeking Scale below, you can get a rough idea of your own level of sensation seeking. You may also want to give this scale to some of your friends. Do you suppose that most people choose friends who have sensation-seeking tendencies similar to their own? Wide differences in sensation-seeking tendencies may account for strain on close relationships, when one person is reluctant to take the risks that the other actively seeks.

The Sensation-Seeking Scale

Choose A or B for each item, depending on which response better describes your preferences. The scoring key appears at the end.

1. A I would like a job that requires a lot of traveling.
   B I would prefer a job in one location.
2. A I am invigorated by a brisk, cold day.
   B I can't wait to get indoors on a cold day.
3. A I get bored seeing the same old faces.

B I like the comfortable familiarity of everyday friends.
4. A I would prefer living in an ideal society in which everyone is safe, secure, and happy.
   B I would have preferred living in the unsettled days of our history
5. A I sometimes like to do things that are a little frightening.
   B A sensible person avoids activities that are dangerous.
6. A I would not like to be hypnotized.
   B I would like to have the experience of being hypnotized.
7. A The most important goal of life is to live it to the fullest and experience as much as possible.
   B The most important goal of life is to find peace and happiness.
8. A I would like to try parachute jumping.
   B I would never want to try jumping out of a plane, with or without a parachute.
9. A I enter cold water gradually, giving myself time to get used to it.
   B I like to dive or jump right into the ocean or a cold pool.
10.A When I go on a vacation, I prefer the comfort of a good room and bed.
   B When I go on a vacation, I prefer the change of camping out.
11.A I prefer people who are emotionally expressive even if they are a bit unstable.
   B I prefer people who are calm and even tempered.

12.A A good painting should shock or jolt the senses.
   B A good painting should give one a feeling of peace and security.
13.A People who ride motorcycles must have some kind of unconscious need to hurt themselves.
   B I would like to drive or ride a motorcycle.

Key Each of the following answers earns one point: 1A, 2A, 3A, 4B, 5A, 6B, 7A, 8A, 9B, 10B, 11A, 12A, 13B. Compare your point total with the following norms for sensation seeking: **0–3:** Very low, **4–5:** Low, **6–9:** Average, **10–11:** High, **12–13:** Very high

Source: From "The Search for High Sensation" by M. Zuckerman, *Psychology Today,* February 1978. Copyright © 1978 by Sussex Publishers, Inc. Reprinted by permission of Sussex Publishers, Inc.

Sensation seekers thrive on stimulation that might terrify others.

Check Your Understanding

1. **RECALL:** During emotional arousal, the _____ nervous system sends messages to the internal organs.

2. **APPLICATION:** Give an example of a situation in which a person would be likely to misattribute the source of arousal.

3. **RECALL:** Briefly describe two issues that have raised controversy among psychologists interested in emotion.

4. **UNDERSTANDING THE CORE CONCEPT:** Briefly describe the two emotion pathways that neuroscientists have discovered.

Answers 1. autonomic **2.** The "swinging bridge" study is the classic example, but others include unexpected physical changes that might occur when you are getting sick, becoming overheated or dehydrated, or mistakenly drinking a caffeinated beverage instead of one without caffeine. **3.** One issue centers on whether physical arousal is the cause or the effect of emotion. Another is whether we can separate cognition and emotion. **4.** The fast pathway produces a near-immediate response and operates mainly at an unconscious level. The slower pathway involves the cerebral cortex and operates largely at the conscious level.

HOW MUCH CONTROL DO WE HAVE OVER OUR EMOTIONS?

An Army squad leader needs emotional intelligence to lead people under stressful conditions.

The ability to deal with emotions is important in many professions. Physicians, nurses, firefighters, and police officers, for example, must be able to comfort others, yet maintain a "professional distance" when dealing with disability and death. But is such emotional control something you are born with—or without? Or can it be learned? Richard Lazarus (1991a,b) has shown that training can help people not only to modify and control their private feelings but also to control the expression of them.

In many situations, aside from work, it can be desirable to mask or modify what you are feeling. If you dislike a professor, you might be wise not to show your true emotions. And if you have strong romantic feelings toward someone—more than he or she realizes—it might be safest to reveal the depth of your feelings gradually, lest you frighten the person away with too much too soon. Similarly, in business negotiations, you will do better if you can prevent yourself from signaling too much emotional arousal. Even in leisure activities like playing poker or planning your next move in chess, you will be most successful if you keep your real feelings, beliefs, and intentions guarded. All of these examples testify that emotional control has an important role in our ability to interact with other people.

In this section, then, we look at the issues involved in emotional control. We begin with the concept of "emotional intelligence," the ability to modulate your own emotions and to understand and react appropriately to those of others. Then we will look at the other side of emotional control: the detection of deception—which is really a problem in detecting emotional responses that someone is trying to hide. Then, in Psychology Matters, we will examine the control of anger. Here is the Core Concept that ties these topics together:

core concept | Although emotional responses are not always consciously regulated, we can learn to control them.

The practical, takeaway message from this section is that, while emotions do sometimes slip out of control, we are not simply at their mercy. Emotional understanding and control are skills that can be acquired (Clifton & Myers, 2005).

Developing Emotional Intelligence

Peter Salovey and John Mayer (1990) have suggested that it takes a certain sort of "smarts" to understand and control one's emotions. They called it **emotional intelligence**. More recently, Salovey and his colleague Daisy Grewal (2005) have emphasized four components of emotional intelligence:

- *Perceiving emotions.* The ability to detect and decipher emotions in oneself and others
- *Using emotions.* The ability to harness one's emotions in the service of thinking and problem-solving
- *Understanding emotions.* The ability to comprehend the complex relationships among emotions, such as the relationship between grief and anger or how two people can have different emotional reactions to the same event
- *Managing emotions.* The ability to regulate one's own emotions and influence those of others

Emotional intelligence The ability to understand and control emotional responses.

The Predictive Power of Emotional Intelligence Those with high emotional intelligence are not only tuned in to their own emotions and those of others, but they can manage their negative feelings and curtail inappropriate expression of their impulses. The power of this ability can be seen in the results of the "marshmallow test," says Daniel Goleman (1995):

> Just imagine you're four years old, and someone makes the following proposal: If you'll wait until after he runs an errand, you can have two marshmallows for a treat. If you can't wait until then, you can have only one—but you can have it right now.

How did the children in this experiment respond to the temptation of the single marshmallow that sat before them, within reach? Goleman continues:

> Some four-year-olds were able to wait what must surely have seemed an endless fifteen to twenty minutes for the experimenter to return. To sustain themselves in their struggle they covered their eyes so they wouldn't have to stare at temptation, or rested their heads in their arms, talked to themselves, sang, played games with their hands and feet, even tried to go to sleep. These plucky preschoolers got the two-marshmallow reward. But others, more impulsive, grabbed the one marshmallow, almost always within seconds of the experimenter's leaving the room on his "errand." (pp. 80–81)

When these same children were tracked down in adolescence, the amazing predictive power of the marshmallow test was revealed. As a group, those who had curbed their impulse to grab the single marshmallow were, as adolescents, better off on all counts. They had become more self-reliant, more effective in interpersonal relationships, better students, and better able to handle frustration and stress. By contrast, the children who had given in to temptation had adolescent lives marked by troubled relationships, shyness, stubbornness, and indecisiveness. They also were much more likely to hold low opinions of themselves, to mistrust others, and to be easily provoked by frustrations. In the academic sphere, they were more likely to be uninterested in school. Goleman notes that the marshmallow test also correlated clearly with SAT scores: Those who, as 4-year-olds, were able to delay gratification scored, on the average, 210 points higher than did their counterparts who had grabbed the single marshmallow years earlier.

The usefulness of marshmallow test, of course, is limited to young children. But other, more sophisticated measures have been developed for use with older children and adults. (See Figure 9.5.) The Mayer-Salovey-Caruso Emotional Intelligence Test (MSCEIT), for example, predicts satisfaction with social relationships among college students, deviant behavior in male adolescents, marital satisfaction, and success on the job (Salovey & Grewal, 2005).

But, cautions John Mayer (1999), emotional intelligence is not a perfect predictor of success, happiness, and good relationships. Nor should we think of it as a replacement for traditional IQ scores. Rather, says Mayer, emotional intelligence is merely another variable that can help us refine our understanding of behavior.

FIGURE 9.5
Sample Item from a Test of Emotional Intelligence

Shown is an item similar to those found on the Mayer-Salovey-Caruso Emotional Intelligence Test. Respondents are asked to click on the number on each scale that corresponds to the emotional state of the person shown in the photo.

(*Source:* From Salovey & Grewel, "The Science of Emotional Intelligence," *Current Directions in Psychological Science, 14,* p. 283 © 2005. Reprinted by permission of Blackwell Publishing.)

The Nature and Nurture of Emotional Intelligence   Is emotional intelligence a characteristic fixed by heredity, or is it influenced by early experience? Goleman (1995) believes that emotional intelligence, like academic intelligence, can be learned. Based on programs already in place in visionary schools across the country, Goleman has a plan for adding emotional training to the curriculum. The result, he predicts, will bring improved relationships, increased self-respect, and even, perhaps, gains in academic achievement. Not so fast, say Matthew Lieberman and Robert Rosenthal (2001) in an article titled "Why Introverts Can't Always Tell Who Likes Them." Lieberman and Rosenthal suggest that emotional intelligence may be just another name for *extraversion,* a personality characteristic that has roots in biology as well as learning. *Introverts,* according to their study, are just not as good at sensing other people's emotions, especially in settings that require multitasking—and, Lieberman and Rosenthal suggest, perhaps they can never learn to be as sensitive as extraverts. The resolution of this issue remains uncertain at the moment.

CONNECTION • CHAPTER 10
Extraversion-Introversion is one of the basic Big Five personality dimensions that seem to apply to people all over the world.

Critics also point out that emotional control has a dark side. Just as some people get into trouble when they let their emotions—particular negative emotions—go unchecked, others take emotional control to the opposite extreme. They become so guarded that they never convey affection, humor, or honest displeasure. Studies also show that overcontrolling emotions interferes with memory for emotionally charged events (Carpenter, 2000; Richards & Gross, 2000). Before we launch a program of encouraging emotional control, perhaps we should consider what such training may do to people who already overcontrol their emotions. In fact, research shows that emotionally healthy people know how both to control and to express their emotions—and when it is appropriate to do so (Bonanno et al., 2004).

Finally, we should note that some people have learned to control their emotions for devious purposes. This is the skill practiced by con artists. Their victims are likely to be people who believe that physical or behavioral cues are reliable indicators of people's private feelings. Let's turn now to the branch of psychology that studies these deceptive tactics of emotional control.

Detecting Deception

You might think you can spot deception when someone fails to "look you in the eye" or fidgets nervously. If so, you could be setting yourself up to be duped. Most of us are poor lie detectors—or truth detectors, for that matter. One reason is that social interactions often occur in familiar situations, with people we know and trust, and where we pay little attention to nonverbal cues.

Experts who study deception find that these nonverbal cues are the best signs of deceit: A person who deliberately tries to hoodwink us may "leak" uncontrolled nonverbal signals of deception. Knowing how to read these cues could help you decide whether a huckster is lying to you, your physician might be holding back some bad news, or a politician is shading the truth.

Deception Cues   The real key to effective deception detection, say the experts, lies in perceiving a person's behavior over time. Without the chance for repeated observations, you are much less able to judge a person's honesty (Marsh, 1988). Still, we can offer some pointers for situations in which even a little help in deception detection might be better than none at all (Adelson, 2004; DePaulo et al., 2003):

- Some lies involve giving false information, as when a used-car salesperson is telling you that a junker is in good working order. At such times, the effort to hide the truth requires some cognitive effort. This may result in heightened attention (evident in dilation of the pupils), longer pauses in speech (to choose words carefully), and more constrained movement and gesturing (in an attempt to avoid "giving away" the truth).

- Criminals sometimes confess to crimes for which there is other specific evidence showing that they are lying to minimize the extent of their involvement in the crime. Analysis of such taped confessions shows that the liar tends to repeat the distorted details of the story (Dingfelder, 2004c).

- When a lie involves hiding one's true feelings of anger or exuberance—as a good poker player does when holding a straight flush—the liar may become physically and behaviorally more aroused. This becomes evident in postural shifts, speech errors, nervous gestures (such as preening by touching or stroking the hair or face), and shrugging (as if to dismiss the lie).

- The face is easier to control than the body, so a deceiver may work on keeping a "poker face" but forget to restrain bodily clues. A smart deception detective might therefore concentrate on a speaker's body movements: Are they rhythmic? Are they calculated? Do the hands move freely or nervously?

- The eyes can sometimes give deceivers away—especially when they're using the common social deception of trying to look happy or amused, when they are not. While our attention may more naturally focus on a smile as an indicator of happiness or amusement, the mouth can be manipulated much more easily than the muscles around the eyes. Only in genuine grins do the eye muscles crinkle up the skin on either side of the eyes. You can test your ability to tell a real from a fake smile in the "Do It Yourself!" box below.

- Speaking of eyes, the ability to "look you straight in the eye" is, in fact, a reasonably good indicator of truth telling—but only when dealing with people who usually tell the truth. When they do lie, their amateurish efforts to deceive often show up in averted gaze, reduced blinking (indicating concentration of attention elsewhere), and less smiling. But you may be fooled by a practiced liar who can look straight at you while telling complete fiction.

- Culture affects the way we distinguish truth from lies. Thus, people are more accurate in telling truth-tellers from liars among people in their own culture. For example, one study found that Jordanians are generally more animated than Americans when talking and that Americans may incorrectly perceive this as "nervousness" and judge the Jordanian to be lying (Bond & Atoum, 2000; Dingfelder, 2004c).

And what about *polygraph* machines—so-called "lie detectors" that are sometimes used by police interrogators and government security agencies? We will take a closer look at these devices in our "Critical Thinking Applied" section at the end of the chapter.

DO IT YOURSELF! The Eyes Have It

Can you tell if people are sincere when they smile at you? Smiles aren't made just with the mouth, but with the whole face, especially the eyes. A real smile is different from a fake one, primarily around the eyes. Specifically, when we feel genuine joy or mirth, the orbicularis occuli muscles wrinkle up the skin around the eyes.

With this in mind, take a look at these two pictures of smiling faces and see if you can tell which one is the real smile and which one is forced.

PSYCHOLOGYMATTERS
Controlling Anger

Anger has a bad reputation because of its association with aggression and violence. But, says anger expert Howard Kassinove, aggression accompanies anger only about 10% of the time (DeAngelis, 2003). And, say psychologists, anger can—if properly controlled—have a positive effect by communicating feelings, helping people stand up for their rights, and clarifying problems in a relationship. Says social psychologist Carol Tavris (1989), "Imagine what the women's suffrage movement would have been like if women had said, 'Guys, it's really so unfair, we're nice people and we're human beings too. Won't you listen to us and give us the vote?'"

Most people feel angry a few times a week and manage to keep their anger in bounds, so the results are usually positive (Kassinove et al., 1997). On the other hand, a small minority go much too far, say anger researchers Raymond Tafrate and his colleagues (2002). Episodes of rage that occur frequently—to the point of being a personality trait—are pathological and need treatment. Likewise, violence that causes harm to someone is never normal or acceptable. That said, however, there is no clinically recognized category for abnormal levels of anger—which can be a problem for clinicians who are trying to bill insurance for helping patients learn to manage their anger.

Anger Management Therapy So, what happens in therapy for anger? According to Colorado State University's Jerry Deffenbacher, the best treatment strategies involve some combination of relaxation training, cognitive therapy, and skill development (J. D. Holloway, 2003a). During therapy, patients practice relaxation techniques until they can quickly put themselves in a relaxed mood during a situation that presses their "anger button," such as being cut off by another driver on the freeway.

The cognitive component of anger management therapy teaches alternative ways of interpreting situations that would otherwise cause anger. So, the anger-prone motorist might learn to think of rude or dangerous behavior by another driver this way: "There's an accident waiting to happen, and I don't want to be part of it."

The third part of anger therapy—skill development—involves practical applications. For the angry driver, this might mean practicing safe driving techniques, as an alternative to aggressive driving. In this phase, the therapist might shift the treatment setting out of the office and on the road.

"Anger has long been a problem for me," writes anger management trainer Melvyn Fein. "Over the years it has cost me a great deal of pain and denied me much happiness" (1993, p. ix). Failing at various efforts to control and constructively express his anger, Fein himself became a clinician and developed an approach to anger disorders. Fein's program, Integrated Anger Management (I.A.M.), adds three more components to Deffenbacher's list:

1. Learning to express anger safely, so that it will not spin out of control

2. Identifying the underlying source of one's anger, such as frustration with injustice or the inability to achieve a valued goal

3. Letting go of unrealistic goals that feed the anger, such as the naive belief that expressing anger will motivate others to "do the right thing"

Dangerous Myths All the experts agree that the public holds some dangerous myths about anger. On television shows, for example, you can see people attacking and humiliating others, as if the public venting of feelings and the act of revenge will eliminate their anger. In fact, retaliation for a real or imagined wrong is likely to bring only the most fleeting feeling of satisfaction.

While many people believe that "bottling up" emotions risks an uncontrollable emotional outburst, this belief is at odds with the truth. It is far more likely that venting one's anger will increase the tendency to become enraged at ever smaller provocations. Solid psychological research indicates that, when you are angry with someone, "getting it off your chest" by aggressively confronting or hurting that individual will not neutralize your bad feelings. Instead it will almost certainly intensify them. It also makes an angry response more likely the next time you face a similar situation. And it invites retaliation by the other party—which is more likely to fuel a feud than to end it. A saner and safer strategy is to keep your feelings to yourself, at least until the passion of your anger has subsided and you can be more rational about the nature of your real complaint and what might be done to solve the problem (Tavris, 1989, 1995). Often, all it takes to defuse a tense and angry situation is to communicate the facts and your feelings to the person toward whom you feel anger.

CheckYourUnderstanding

1. **RECALL:** What are the four components of emotional intelligence?

2. **APPLICATION:** What telltale behavioral signs might signal that your auto mechanic might be trying to sell you an unnecessary engine overhaul?

3. **ANALYSIS:** Why is it *not* a good idea to deal with anger by "venting" it, as by yelling, throwing things, or hitting the wall?

4. **UNDERSTANDING THE CORE CONCEPT:** Is the ability to control one's emotional responses the result of nature or nurture?

Answers 1. perceiving, using, understanding, and managing emotions **2.** Among the signs mentioned in this section: longer pauses in speech, constrained movements, and nervous gestures. **3.** Venting actually intensifies feelings of anger. Also, it typically does nothing to solve the problem, but instead makes an angry response more likely the next time one faces a threat to pride, status, or honor. **4.** It is always both, but the important point made in this section is that emotional control can be learned (which is the influence of nurture). Evidence for this comes from studies of emotional intelligence, deception, and anger management therapy.

9.4 KEY QUESTION
MOTIVATION: WHAT MAKES US ACT AS WE DO?

Why are some people obsessed with food or sex, while others' passion is to rob banks or go into politics? What drives individuals with anorexia to starve themselves—sometimes to their deaths? Why do some of us feel a need to achieve, while others seek security? Such questions lie in the domain of the psychology of motivation, which deals with the internal processes that cause us to move toward a goal or away from a situation we judge to be unpleasant. As you will remember, we can think of motivation as involving arousal to action. We saw that motivation includes emotions, a special class of motives that are usually aroused by external situations of special importance to us. Other motives, however, are likely to be more focused on internal physical states, as in hunger or thirst, or on mental states, as in the need for achievement or power.

Motivation, then, is the general term for all the processes involved in initiating, directing, and maintaining physical and psychological activities. Motivation involves arousal. It also determines which of many possible responses you will select at any moment—although the selection is not always a deliberate, conscious one. Will it be laughing or crying? Fight or flight? Studying or partying? The motivational menu always offers multiple choices. Our Core Concept for this section puts it this way:

Motivation Refers to all the processes involved in initiating, directing, and maintaining physical and psychological activities.

Motivation takes many forms, but all involve mental processes that arouse us and then select and direct our behavior.

core concept

We begin our study of this topic with a look at the many different ways in which we use the concept of motivation.

How Psychologists Use the Concept of Motivation

Professors may think that students who do poorly on exams are "not well motivated." Sports commentators speculate that winning teams were "hungrier" or "more motivated" than their opponents. Detectives seek to establish a motive in building a case against a criminal suspect. That is, the public uses the term *motivation* in everyday conversation to refer to a variety of responses that seem to arise from a person's internal state rather than from the external situation.

Psychologists, too, find the concept of motivation useful in explaining behaviors that cannot be explained by the external situation alone:

CONNECTION • CHAPTER 10

However, Americans are biased toward ignoring the pressures of the situation. This tendency of attributing behavior to internal motives, is known as the *fundamental attribution error*.

- *Motivation connects observable behavior to internal states.* When we see someone eating, we may infer that a hunger drive is at work. We must be careful about drawing such inferences too quickly, though, because eating might be caused by something else that we have overlooked (e.g., social pressure, the availability of a favorite food, or a desire to gain weight).

- *Motivation accounts for variability in behavior.* Psychologists use motivational explanations when the variations in people's performances are not obviously due to differences in physical or mental abilities or to differing environmental demands. For example, the intensity of motivation may help explain why a basketball player scores well one day but poorly another.

- *Motivation explains perseverance despite adversity.* Motivation helps us understand why organisms continue to perform reliably even under difficult or variable conditions. Motivation gets you to work on time, even when you had a sleepless night or a long commute in the rain.

- *Motives relate biology to behavior.* We are biological organisms with complex internal mechanisms that automatically regulate bodily functions to promote survival. States of deprivation (such as needing nutrients) automatically trigger these mechanisms, which then influence bodily functioning (such as feeling hungry) and create motivational states.

In each of these cases, an internal motivational process channels the organism's energies into a particular pattern of behavior.

Types of Motivation

A cat may stalk and kill a mouse because it is hungry, or it may do the same thing purely as feline play (Burghardt, 2006). What is the difference? None, from the mouse's perspective—but for psychologists it is the difference between a *drive* and a *motive*. Psychologists prefer the term **drive** for motivation that is assumed to respond to a biological need and therefore assumes an important role in survival or reproduction. Hunger and thirst are examples of biological drives. In contrast, many psychologists reserve the term **motive** for urges that, like play, serve no immediate biological need or are strongly rooted in learning, such as the human need for achievement. Obviously, however, many motivated behaviors in humans—such as eating, drinking, and sexual behavior—can stem from both biology and learning.

Psychologists also distinguish between *intrinsic* and *extrinsic* motivation. It's the difference between reading a book for pleasure and reading a book because you will be tested on it. **Intrinsic motivation** comes from within: That is, the individual engages in an activity for its own sake, in the absence of an external reward. Leisure activities, such as cycling, kayaking, or playing the guitar, are usually intrinsically motivated. Intrinsic motivation arises from inner qual-

Drive Biologically instigated motivation.

Motive An internal mechanism that arouses the organism and then selects and directs behavior. The term *motive* is often used in the narrower sense of a motivational process that is learned, rather than biologically based (as are drives).

Intrinsic motivation The desire to engage in an activity for its own sake, rather than for some external consequence, such as a reward.

ities, such as personality traits or special interests. In contrast, **extrinsic motivation** comes from the *outside* in the form of rewards and punishments. It involves behavior aimed at some external consequence, such as money, grades, or praise, rather than at satisfying an internal need.

A final distinction contrasts motives and drives that arise from **conscious motivation** with those stemming from **unconscious motivation**. That is, motivated individuals may or may not be aware of the drives or motives underlying their behavior—much as emotional arousal can occur on a conscious or unconscious level. As we will see in a moment, Freud took this idea a step further, suggesting that the unconscious mind harbors complex motives arising from traumatic experiences and sexual conflicts.

The fact that some people do better in competition than others can be explained in part by different degrees of motivation. These men are participating in the International Games for the Disabled.

Theories of Motivation

Unfortunately, psychology has no comprehensive theory that successfully accounts for the whole gamut of human motives and drives. Sex, for example, seems to obey rather different motivational rules from those regulating hunger or thirst or regulation of body temperature, even though all are rooted in biology: You can die from lack of food or warmth but not from lack of sex. Much of the difficulty in explaining diverse types of motivation arises because of our dual nature: We are simultaneously creatures driven by our biology (as when you are ravenous because you haven't eaten all day) and by learning (as when you associate the lunch bell with food).

In the following pages, we will look at several theories of motivation, beginning with *instinct theory,* the grandparent of all modern motivational theories. As we do, please keep in mind the limited domain of each.

Instinct Theory   According to **instinct theory**, organisms are born with a set of biologically based behaviors, called *instincts,* that generally promote survival. The concept of "instinct" accounts reasonably well for regular cycles of animal activity, seen in essentially the same form across a species, as in salmon that travel thousands of miles to spawn and die in the stream where they were hatched. Although such instinctive behavior patterns do not depend heavily on learning, experience can modify them. We see a combination of instinctive behavior and learning when, for example, bees communicate the location of food to each other, when young salmon learn to distinguish the scent of their native stream, or when birds remember landmarks to guide them in their annual migrations. Such examples, then, show that instincts involve both a lot of nature and a little nurture.

Because it seemed to explain so much, the term *instinct* migrated from the scientific vocabulary to the speech of everyday life. So we speak casually of "maternal instincts," of an athlete who "instinctively catches the ball," and of an agent who has an "instinct" for picking new talent. In fact, we use the term in so many ways that its meaning has become vague and imprecise—a mere label, rather than an explanation for behavior. As a result, the term *instinct* has dropped out of favor among scientists (Deckers, 2001). Ethologists, who study animal behavior in natural habitats, now prefer the term **fixed-action patterns**, more narrowly defined as unlearned behavior patterns that occur throughout a species and are triggered by identifiable stimuli. Examples of fixed-action patterns include not only the "instinctive" behaviors described earlier but also such diverse behaviors as nest-building in birds, suckling responses in newborn mammals, and dominance displays in baboons.

Do instincts—perhaps in their new guise as fixed-action patterns—explain any part of human behavior? The question raises the nature–nurture controversy under a new name. Biology *does* seem to account for some human behaviors, such as nursing, that we see in newborns. But it is not clear how useful instinct is in explaining the array of more complex behaviors found in people at work

Extrinsic motivation   The desire to engage in an activity to achieve an external consequence, such as a reward.

Conscious motivation   A motive of which one is aware.

Unconscious motivation   A motive of which one is consciously unaware. Freud's psychoanalytic theory emphasized unconscious motivation.

Instinct theory   The now-outmoded view that certain behaviors are completely determined by innate factors. The instinct theory was flawed because it overlooked the effects of learning and because it employed instincts merely as labels, rather than as explanations for behavior.

Fixed-action patterns   Genetically based behaviors, seen across a species, that can be set off by a specific stimulus. The concept of fixed-action patterns has replaced the older notion of instinct.

and play. For example, while we might speculate that the motivation of a hard-driving executive could involve some basic "killer" instinct, such an explanation is weak at best.

Drive Theory   The concept of *drive* originated as an alternative to instinct for explaining behavior with a strong biological basis, as in eating, drinking, and mating. A drive was defined as the hypothetical state of energy or tension that moves an organism to meet a biological need (Woodworth, 1918). Thus, an animal that needs water is driven to drink. Likewise, a need for food drives organisms to eat. So, in **drive theory**, a biological **need** produces a drive state that channels behavior toward meeting the need. The drive, then, motivates the animal to act to reduce the drive level, a process called *drive reduction*. You have felt such a buildup and release of tension if you have been extremely cold and then felt driven to find shelter.

According to drive theory, the desirable state that organisms seek is a balanced condition known as **homeostasis** (Hull, 1943, 1952). Organisms that have a biological imbalance (caused, say, by lack of fluids) are driven to seek a homeostatic balance (by drinking). Similarly, we can understand hunger as an imbalance in the body's energy supply. This imbalance drives an animal that has been deprived of food to eat in order to restore a condition of equilibrium.

Unfortunately for drive theory, the story of motivation has proved not to be that simple—in part because cognitive, social, and cultural forces are at work, as well, as we will see later in our discussion of hunger. In addition, drive theory cannot explain why, in the absence of any apparent deprivation or drives, organisms sometimes act merely to *increase* stimulation. It is hard to imagine a basic need or a biological drive that, for example, could prompt people to jump out of airplanes or propel them up the granite face of Yosemite's El Capitán. We can even see this issue in the laboratory, where rats will cross an electrified grid merely to reach a novel environment to explore. Apparently, both for people and animals, exploring and taking an interest in the world are rewarding experiences in themselves.

For these reasons, psychologists have concluded that drive theory does not hold all the answers to motivation. Still, they have been reluctant to abandon the concept of drive, which has come to mean a biologically based motive that plays an important role in survival or reproduction. We now look on drive theory as a useful, but incomplete, theory of motivation.

Cognitive Theory and Locus of Control   Watching TV, reading a book, listening to music, climbing a mountain all owe their motivational push to cognitive processes, rather than to basic drives or instincts. In fact, much of human behavior is motivated by our cognitions—among the most important of which are our *expectations*—which brings us to Julian Rotter's important concept of *locus of control*.

In his cognitive *social-learning theory* (1954), Rotter (pronounced *ROE-ter*) asserted that the likelihood of a certain behavior (Should I study tonight?) is determined by two factors: (1) the *expectation* of attaining a goal (Will studying get me a good grade?) and (2) the *personal value* of the goal (How much do I care about grades?). But what determines our expectations? Rotter says that they depend largely on our **locus of control**, our beliefs about our ability to control the events in our lives. If, for example, you believe that you can get good grades by studying, you have an *internal locus of control*, and you will behave differently from those students who have an *external locus of control* based on the belief that grades depend on luck or on the teacher's whims. Rotter's theory would also predict that people who exercise, save money, or use seat belts have an internal locus of control. On the other hand, the theory also predicts that those who buy lottery tickets or smoke cigarettes have an external locus of control. Such predictions have been supported by thousands of studies that you can find simply by typing "locus of control" into Google or PsychInfo.

According to drive theory, a need for fluids motivates (drives) us to drink. A homeostatic balance is reached when the need is satisfied.

Drive theory   Developed as an alternative to instinct theory, drive theory explains motivation as a process in which a biological *need* produces a *drive*, a state of tension or energy that moves an organism to meet the need. For most drives this process returns the organism to a balanced condition, known as *homeostasis*.

Need   In drive theory, a need is a biological imbalance (such as dehydration) that threatens survival, if the need is left unmet. Biological needs are believed to produce drives.

Homeostasis   The body's tendency to maintain a biologically balanced condition, especially with regard to nutrients, water, and temperature.

Locus of control   An individual's sense of whether control over his or her life is internal or external.

Freud's Psychodynamic Theory   In contrast to all the other views we have considered, Sigmund Freud taught that motivation comes mainly from the murky depths of the unconscious mind, which he called the *id*. There, he said, lurked two basic desires: *eros*, the erotic desire; and *thanatos*, the aggressive or destructive impulse. Virtually everything we do, said Freud, is based on one of these urges or on the maneuvers that the mind uses to keep these desires in check. To avoid mental problems, we must continually seek acceptable outlets for our sexual and aggressive needs. Freud believed that work, especially creative work, indirectly satisfied the sex drive, while aggressive acts like swearing and shouting or playing aggressive games serve as a psychologically safe outlet for our destructive tendencies.

Freud developed his ideas in the heyday of instinct theory, so eros and thanatos are often thought of as instincts. But it would oversimplify Freud's theory to think of it as just another instinct theory. He wasn't trying to explain the everyday, biologically based behaviors that we find in eating, drinking, mating, nursing, and sleeping. Rather, he was trying to explain the symptoms we find in mental disorders such as phobias or depression.

Modern-day psychologists stand divided on Freud's view of unconscious motivation, a thread that will continue in the next chapter (Bornstein, 2001; Westen, 1998). Aside from introducing you here to Freud's views on motivation, we would like to make one other point. Among the principal theories of motivation discussed in this chapter, Freud's is the only one that takes a *developmental* approach to motivation. That is, Freud theorized about the ways our motives undergo change as we move from childhood to adulthood. With maturity, our sexual and aggressive desires become less conscious. We also develop more and more subtle and sophisticated ways of letting off Freud's two kinds of motivational "steam"—ways that are usually both socially acceptable and acceptable to our conscious minds. (See Table 9.2.)

Maslow's Humanistic Theory   What happens when you must choose between meeting a biological need and fulfilling a desire based on learning, as when you choose between sleeping and staying up all night to study for an exam? Abraham Maslow (1970) said that you act on your most pressing needs, which occur in a natural *hierarchy* or priority order, with biological needs taking precedence. Unlike the other theories of motivation we have considered, Maslow's perspective attempts to span a wide range of human motivation from biological drives to social motives to creativity (Nicholson, 2007).

Maslow's great innovation was a **hierarchy of needs**: six classes of needs listed in priority order (Figure 9.6). The "higher" needs exert their influence on behavior when the more basic need are satisfied:

Hierarchy of needs   In Maslow's theory, the notion that needs occur in priority order, with the biological needs as the most basic.

- *Biological needs*, such as hunger and thirst, lie at the base of the hierarchy and must be satisfied before higher needs take over.

TABLE 9.2	Theories of Motivation Compared	
Theories	**Emphasis**	**Examples**
Instinct Theory	Biological processes that motivate behavior patterns specific to a species	bird migration, fish schooling
Drive Theory	Needs produce drives that motivate behavior until drives are reduced	hunger, thirst
Cognitive Theories	Many motives are the result of perception and learning, rather than biology	locus of control, *n Ach*
Maslow's Theory	Motives result from needs, which occur in a priority order (a needs hierarchy)	esteem needs, self-actualization
Freud's Theory	Motivation arises from unconscious desires; developmental changes in these urges appear as we mature	sex, aggression

- *Safety needs* motivate us to avoid danger, but only when biological needs are reasonably well satisfied. Thus, a hungry animal may risk its physical safety for food until it gets its belly full, and then the safety needs take over.

- *Attachment and affiliation needs* energize us when we are no longer concerned about the more basic drives such as hunger, thirst, and safety. These higher needs make us want to feel we belong, to affiliate with others, to love, and to be loved.

- *Esteem needs,* following next in the hierarchy, include the needs to like oneself, to see oneself as competent and effective, and to do what is necessary to earn the respect of oneself and others.

- *Self-actualization* motivates us to seek the fullest development of our creative human potential. Self-actualizing persons are self-aware, self-accepting, socially responsive, spontaneous, and open to novelty and challenge.

- In his original formulation, Maslow put self-actualization at the peak of the needs hierarchy. But late in his life, Maslow suggested yet another need that he called *self-transcendence*. This he conceptualized as going beyond self-actualization, seeking to further some cause beyond the self (Koltko-Rivera, 2006). Satisfying this need could involve anything from volunteer work to absorption in religion, politics, music, or an intellectual pursuit. What distinguishes self-transcendence from self-actualization is its shift beyond personal pleasure or other egocentric benefits. (You may have noticed the parallel between transcendence and *generativity*, Erikson's mid-life stage of development.)

CONNECTION • CHAPTER 6

In Erikson's theory, *generativity* involves making a contribution to family, work, society, or future generations.

How does Maslow's theory square with observation? It explains why we may neglect our friends or our career goals in favor of meeting pressing biological needs signaled by pain, thirst, sleepiness, or sexual desire. Yet—in contradiction to Maslow's theory—people may sometimes neglect their basic biological needs in favor of higher ones, as we saw in rescue workers during the 9/11 attack on New York. But to Maslow's credit, he called our attention to the important role of social motivation in our lives at a time when these motives were being neglected by psychology (Nicholson, 2007). As a result, a great body of work now demonstrates this need we have for relationships with others.

Critics point out that Maslow's theory also fails to explain other important human behaviors: why you might miss a meal when you are absorbed in an interesting book or why sensation seekers would pursue risky interests (such as jumping out of airplanes) that override their safety needs. It also fails to explain the behavior of people who deliberately take their own lives.

Exceptions to Maslow's theory and other "self theories" have also been pointed out by cross-cultural psychologists. They note that an emphasis on self applies primarily to individualistic cultures, which emphasize individual achievement (Gambrel & Cianci, 2003). In contrast, group-oriented (collectivistic) cultures emphasize success of the group (Shiraev & Levy, 2007). In fairness to Maslow, however, we should note that he recognized that there could be cultural differences in motivation (1943). And even the severest critics will acknowledge that, with all its flaws, Maslow's theory was an important step toward a comprehensive theory of motivation.

Overall, Maslow's influence has been greater in the spheres of psychotherapy and education than in motivational research. Business, too, has been especially receptive to Maslow's ideas. Many dollars have been made by consultants using this theory as the basis for seminars on motivating employees. The main idea they

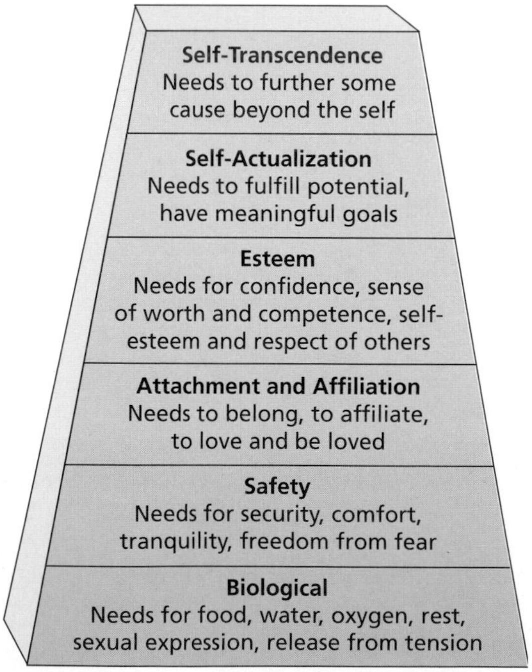

FIGURE 9.6
Maslow's Hierarchy of Needs

According to Maslow, needs at the lower level of the hierarchy dominate an individual's motivation as long as those needs are unsatisfied. Once the lower-level needs are adequately satisfied, the higher needs occupy an individual's attention.

have promoted is that humans have an innate need to grow and actualize their highest potentials. Such an upbeat approach was also welcomed by psychologists who had wearied of the negative emphasis on hunger, thirst, anxiety, and fear in the psychology of motivation (Nicholson, 2007).

The Unexpected Effects of Rewards on Motivation

It's likely that, at some time or another, you have had to take a test in a subject that didn't interest you. If you were a conscientious student, you learned the material anyway, to get a good grade or, perhaps, to avoid disappointing your parents. As we have noted, psychologists say that such behavior is *extrinsically* motivated because it aims at getting an external reward (or avoiding aversive consequences). Teachers often use grades as extrinsic motivators, hoping to get students more involved in their studies. Extrinsic motivation also explains why people take vitamins, marry for money, pay their taxes, and use deodorant.

But what do you suppose would happen if people were given extrinsic rewards (praise, money, or other incentives) for *intrinsically* motivated behavior—doing things that they already find enjoyable? Would the reward make the activity even more enjoyable? Or less?

Overjustification   To find out, Mark Lepper and his colleagues (1973) performed a classic experiment, using two groups of school children who enjoyed drawing pictures. One group agreed to draw pictures for a reward certificate, while a control group made drawings without the expectation of reward. Both groups made their drawings enthusiastically. Some days later, however, when given the opportunity to draw pictures again, without a reward, the previously rewarded children were much less enthusiastic about drawing than those who had not been rewarded. In fact, the group that had received no rewards were actually *more* interested in drawing than they had been the first time!

Lepper's group concluded that external reinforcement had squelched the internal motivation in the reward group, an effect they called **overjustification**. As a result of overjustification, they reasoned, the children's motivation had changed from intrinsic to extrinsic. Consequently, the children were less interested in making pictures in the absence of reward.

A Justification for Rewards   But do rewards *always* have this overjustification effect? If they did, how could we explain the fact that many professionals both love their work and get paid for it? Many subsequent experiments make it clear that rewards interfere with intrinsic motivation only under certain conditions (Covington, 2000; Eisenberger & Cameron, 1996). Specifically, the newer research shows that overjustification occurs when the reward is given *without regard for quality of performance*. In fact, this is just what happened to the children who were all given certificates for their drawings. The same thing can happen in the business world, when employees are given year-end bonuses regardless of the quality of their work.

The lesson is this: Rewards can be used effectively to motivate people—if the rewards are given, not as a bribe, but for a job well done. So, if your child doesn't like to practice the piano, wash the dishes, or do homework, no amount of reward is going to change her attitude. On the other hand, if she enjoys piano practice, you can feel free to give praise, or a special treat, for a job well done. Such rewards can make a motivated person even more motivated. Similarly, if you have disinterested employees, don't bother trying to motivate them with pay raises (unless, of course, the reason they're unmotivated is that you are paying them poorly). But when it is deserved, impromptu praise, an unexpected certificate, or some other small reward may make good employees even better. The danger of rewards seems to occur when the rewards are extrinsic and they are given without regard to the level of performance.

So, how do you think professors should reward their students?

Overjustification occurs when extrinsic rewards for doing something enjoyable take the intrinsic fun out of the activity. It is likely that this person would not enjoy video games as much if he were paid for playing.

Overjustification   The process by which extrinsic (external) rewards can sometimes displace internal motivation, as when a child receives money for playing video games.

PSYCHOLOGY**MATTERS**
Using Psychology to Learn Psychology

The world's greatest achievements in music, art, science, business, and countless other pursuits usually arise from intrinsically motivated people pursuing ideas in which they are deeply interested. People achieve this state of mind when focusing intently on some problem or activity that makes them lose track of time and become oblivious to events around them. Psychologist Mihaly Csikszentmihalyi calls this **flow** (1990, 1998). And although some people turn to drugs or alcohol to experience an artificial flow feeling, he finds that meaningful work produces far more satisfying and more sustained flow experiences.

What is the link with studying and learning? If you find yourself lacking in motivation to learn the material for a particular class, the extrinsic promise of grades may not be enough to prod you to study effectively. You may, however, be able to trick yourself into developing intrinsic motivation and flow by posing this question: What do people who are specialists in this field find interesting? Among other things, the experts are fascinated by an unsolved mystery, a theoretical dispute, or the possibility of an exciting practical application. A psychologist, for example, might wonder: What motivates violent behavior? Or, how can we increase people's motivation to achieve? Once you find such an issue, try to find out what solutions have been proposed. In this way, you will share the mind set of those who are leaders in the field. And—who knows?—perhaps you will become fascinated, too.

CheckYourUnderstanding

1. **RECALL:** Give four reasons why psychologists find the concept of *motivation* useful.

2. **RECALL:** Why has the term *instinct* has dropped out of favor with psychologists?

3. **ANALYSIS:** What is the role of *homeostasis* in drive theory?

4. **UNDERSTANDING THE CORE CONCEPT:** Motivation takes many forms, but all involve inferred mental processes that select and direct our
   a. cognitions.
   b. behaviors.
   c. sensations.
   d. emotions.

Answers **1.** The concept of motivation (a) connects observable behavior to internal states, (b) accounts for variability in behavior, (c) explains perseverance despite adversity, and (d) relates biology to behavior. **2.** Instinct has become an imprecise term that merely labels behavior, rather than explaining it. **3.** Homeostasis refers to the equilibrium condition to which an organism tends to return after reducing a biological drive. **4.** b

9.5 KEY QUESTION
HOW ARE ACHIEVEMENT, HUNGER, AND SEX ALIKE? DIFFERENT?

Now that we have reviewed some essential motivational concepts and theories, we will shift our focus to three diverse and important motives: *achievement, hunger,* and *sex*. We will see how each of these motives differs from the others, not just in the behavior it produces, but in deeper ways as well. The Core Concept expresses the point:

core concept

> No single theory accounts for all forms of motivation because each motive involves its own mix of biological, mental, behavioral, and social/cultural influences.

Flow In Csikszentmihalyi's theory, an intense focus on an activity, accompanied by increased creativity and near-ecstatic feelings. Flow involves intrinsic motivation.

Each of the motives to be discussed in this section differs in its blend of nature and nurture. They also differ in their sensitivity to internal and environmental cues, in the reinforcers that satisfy them, and in the social/cultural influences to which they respond. So far, no one—not even Maslow—has been clever enough to devise a theory that encompasses the whole range of motivations, takes all these factors into account, and still fits the facts.

Recent developments in evolutionary psychology, however, show promise in explaining diverse drives heavily rooted in biology, such as hunger and the sex drive (Buss, 2008, 2001). Evolutionary theory suggests that each motivational mechanism evolved in response to different environmental pressures. Thus, we can think of each motive as a mechanism that adapted to help humans survive and reproduce. We will see, however, that this evolutionary perspective suggests some particularly controversial proposals to explain gender differences.

But even with these tools, we still have no complete and comprehensive theory of motivation. For the moment, then, psychologists must be content with an array of specific theories, each of which explains a different motive. The contrasts between hunger, sex, and achievement will make this point clear.

Achievement Motivation

Before you read the caption for Figure 9.7, just look at the picture and imagine what might be happening there. The story you tell yourself about the boy and his violin may reveal some of your dominant motives, especially your *need for achievement,* a psychological motive that accounts for a wide range of behaviors in our culture. Achievement, of course, can be motivated by a desire for recognition, fame, praise, money, or other extrinsic incentives. But, for most of us, there is an intrinsic satisfaction that comes with meeting a challenge and attaining a goal of personal significance. Whatever its source, the need for achievement is an important source of human motivation.

Measuring the Need for Achievement
Psychologists Henry Murray and David McClelland pioneered the measurement of achievement motivation with an instrument called the *Thematic Apperception Test (TAT).* On this test, people are asked to tell stories in response to a series of ambiguous pictures, like the one of the boy with the violin in Figure 9.7. Each story, Murray and McClelland theorized, represents a *projection* of the respondent's psychological needs. That is, they assumed that the stories would reflect the themes that were psychologically important for the storyteller. From responses to several of these *TAT* pictures, Murray and McClelland worked out measures of the **need for achievement** *(n Ach)*, which they saw as the desire to attain a difficult, but desired, goal.

If you haven't already done so, read the caption for Figure 9.7: It gives examples of how a high *n Ach* individual and a low *n Ach* individual might interpret the picture. With these examples in mind, you can judge where your own story fits on a scale from low to high *n Ach.*

What characteristics distinguish people with a high need for achievement? Numerous studies show that those high in *n Ach* work harder and become more successful at their work than those lower in achievement motivation (Schultz & Schultz, 2006). More specifically, people high in *n Ach* show more persistence on difficult tasks than do people with low achievement needs (McClelland, 1987b). In school, those with high *n Ach* tend to get better grades (Raynor, 1970); they also tend to have higher IQ scores (Harris, 2004). In their career paths, they take more competitive jobs (McClelland, 1965), assume more leadership roles, and earn more rapid promotions (Andrews, 1967). If they become entrepreneurs, those with high *n Ach* become more successful than individuals with low *n Ach* (McClelland, 1987a, 1993).

Research also suggests that people can satisfy their need for achievement in two main ways: through *mastery* or *performance* (Barron & Harackiewicz, 2001). We can illustrate these two pathways by imagining two students: The one seeking mastery focuses on acquiring knowledge and developing expert-level skills—getting satisfaction from mastering the material. In contrast, the

FIGURE 9.7
Alternative Interpretations of a TAT Picture

Story Showing High *n Ach:* The boy has just finished his violin lesson. He's happy at his progress and is beginning to believe that all his sacrifices have been worthwhile. To become a concert violinist, he will have to give up much of his social life and practice for many hours each day. Although he knows he could make more money by going into his father's business, he is more interested in being a great violinist and giving people joy with his music. He renews his personal commitment to do all it takes to make it.

Story Showing Low *n Ach:* The boy is holding his brother's violin and wishing he could play it. But he knows it isn't worth the time, energy, and money for lessons. He feels sorry for his brother, who has given up all the fun things in life to practice, practice, practice. It would be great to wake up one day and be a top-notch musician, but it doesn't happen that way. The reality is boring practice, no fun, and the likelihood that he'll become just another guy playing a musical instrument in a small-town band.

Need for achievement *(n Ach)* In Murray and McClelland's theory, a mental state that produces a psychological motive to excel or to reach some goal.

According to McClelland, people have different patterns of motivation for work. Some are motivated by affiliation, some by power, and some by the need for achievement (n Ach). A good leader knows how to capitalize on each of these.

performance-oriented student has a competitive focus, satisfying the achievement need by attempting to out-perform other students.

Organizational Psychology: Putting Achievement Motivation in Perspective   Anyone who has ever held a job knows that not everyone is motivated to work by the need for achievement. People work for money, of course. But beyond that, Industrial/Organizational (I/O) psychologists seek to understand what motivates people to work and to advise managers on ways of encouraging employees to be productive.

David McClelland (1985) identified three distinct motivational patterns, based on people's needs. Some of us are motivated primarily by the *need for affiliation,* some by the *need for power,* and others by the *need for achievement.* The job of the manager (who is probably motivated by achievement or power) is to find ways of structuring work so that people simultaneously meet their dominant needs and the "need" of the employer for productivity.

Should you find yourself in a management position, here are some need-specific pointers:

● Give those high in *n Ach* tasks that challenge them, but with achievable goals. Even though they are not primarily motivated by external rewards, bonuses, praise, and recognition can serve effectively as feedback on performance.

● For those high in power, give them the opportunity to manage projects or work teams. You can encourage power-oriented workers to become leaders who help their subordinates satisfy their own needs. Although power motivation can be purely self-serving, don't fall into the trap of thinking that the need for power is necessarily bad.

● A cooperative, rather than competitive, environment is best for those high in the need for affiliation. Find opportunities for them to work with others in teams, rather than at socially isolated work stations.

Satisfying people's needs should make them happier and more motivated to work. But does job satisfaction actually lead to increased productivity? Indeed, job satisfaction is the most frequently studied variable by I/O psychologists. And the result is as we might expect: Higher job satisfaction correlates with lower absenteeism, lower employee turnover, better performance, and increased productivity—all of which are reflected in increased profits (Schultz & Schultz, 2006).

A Cross-Cultural Perspective on Achievement   When she won the Olympic gold medal in the women's 200-meter butterfly, American swimmer Misty Hyman said:

I think I just stayed focused. It was time to show the world what I could do. I am just glad I was able to do it. I knew I could beat Suzy O'Neil, deep down in my heart I believed it, and I know this whole week the doubts kept creeping in, they were with me on the blocks, but I just said, "No, this is my night." (Neal, 2000)

Contrast that with Naoko Takahashi's explanation of why she won the women's marathon:

Here is the best coach in the world, the best manager in the world, and all of the people who support me—all of these things were getting together and became a gold medal. So I think I didn't get it alone, not only by myself. (Yamamoto, 2000)

As you can see from these distinctively different quotes, the American perspective on achievement motivation reflects a distinctively Western bias. We

Americans tend to see achievement as the result of individual talent, determination, intelligence, or attitude. Much of the world, however, sees achievement differently—in a broader context, as a combination of personal, social, and emotional factors (Markus et al., 2006).

This observation is consistent with Harry Triandis's distinction between cultures that emphasize *individualism* or *collectivism* (1990). Western cultures, including the United States, Canada, Britain, and Western Europe, emphasize **individualism**. People growing up in these cultures learn to place a high premium on individual performance. By contrast, says Triandis, the cultures of Latin America, Asia, Africa, and the Middle East often emphasize **collectivism**, which values group loyalty and subordination of self to the group. Even in the collectivist cultures of Japan, Hong Kong, and South Korea, where very high values are placed on doing well in school and business, the overarching goal is not of achieving individual honors but of bringing honor to the family, team, or other group.

Without a cross-cultural perspective, it would be easy for Americans to jump to the erroneous conclusion that motivation for individual achievement is a "natural" part of the human makeup. But Triandis's insight suggests that this is not true in many parts of the world. (See Table 9.3.) Instead, in collectivist cultures the social context is just as important for achievement as are talent, intelligence, or other personal characteristics in individualistic cultures.

Hunger Motivation

You will probably survive if you don't care about achievement, but you will die if you don't eat. Unlike achievement motivation, hunger is one of our biological maintenance and survival mechanisms (Rozin, 1996). And if eating were a behavior that had to be entirely learned, many people would starve to death before they mastered its complexities. Instead, when food is available and we are hungry, eating seems to come naturally. But biology isn't the whole story: Hunger motivation and eating behavior have turned out to be far more complex than had originally been thought. So psychologists now incorporate the complexities of hunger and eating into a view we will call the *multiple-systems approach*. (See Figure 9.8.)

The Multiple-Systems Approach to Hunger Your brain combines hunger-related information of many kinds: your body's energy requirements and nutritional state, your food preferences, food cues in your environment, and cultural demands. For example, your readiness to eat a slice of bacon depends on factors such as your blood sugar level, how long it has been since you last ate, whether

Individualism The view, common in the Euro-American world, that places a high value on individual achievement and distinction.

Collectivism The view, common in Asia, Africa, Latin America, and the Middle East, that values group loyalty and pride over individual distinction.

TABLE 9.3 A Comparison of Three Motives	
Motive	**Distinguishing features**
Achievement	A psychological motive; operates mainly at a conscious level
	Affected by learning, especially the culture's emphasis on individualism or collectivism
Hunger	A homeostatic biological drive, but also influenced by learning
	A deficiency motive; aroused by deprivation
	May involve unconscious processes
Sex	A biological drive, but not homeostatic; also influenced by learning
	Not primarily a deficiency motive
	May involve unconscious processes

FIGURE 9.8
Multiple-Systems Model of Hunger and Eating

Hunger isn't just a matter of an empty stomach. The multiple-systems model combines all the known influences on hunger and eating.

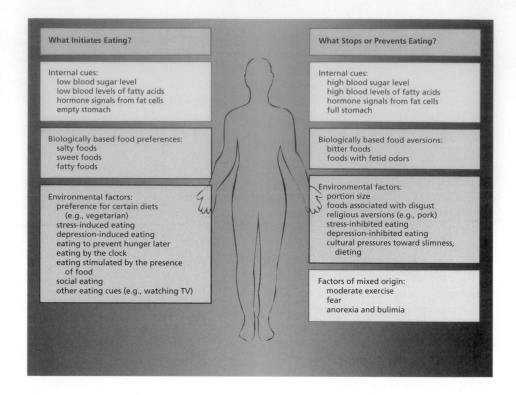

you like bacon, what time of day it is (breakfast?), whether a friend might be offering you a slice, and whether bacon is an acceptable food in your culture. Assembling all these data, the brain sends signals to neural, hormonal, organ, and muscle systems to start or stop food-seeking and eating (DeAngelis, 2004b; Flier & Maratos-Flier, 2007).

Biological Factors Affecting Hunger and Eating   In the brain, the stomach, the blood, and in fat cells stored all over the body a host of biological factors is at work to regulate hunger and eating behavior. Among the most important are these:

- *Brain mechanisms controlling hunger.*   For nearly 70 years, physiologists thought they had the brain mechanisms of hunger figured out: One part of the hypothalamus produced hunger, while another dampened hunger. Gradually, however, research has shown that the picture is much more complicated—which explains why hunger and obesity are so difficult to control. True, the hypothalamus has a central role in hunger, but so do other brain regions, particularly in the brain stem. These circuits monitor the status of blood sugar, fat and other energy stores, and nutrients in the gut, using a suite of hormones and other chemical messengers (Flier, 2006).

- *Set point (homeostatic) mechanisms.*   An internal biological "scale" continually weighs the body's fat stores and informs the central nervous system of the result. Whenever deposits stored in specialized fat cells fall below a certain level, or **set point**, signals trigger eating behavior—a homeostatic process. In fact, research suggests that one cause of obesity may involve problems with certain chemicals (e.g., the hormone *ghrelin*) that signal hunger and others (e.g., *leptin*) that signal when the set point has been reached. Animals lacking leptin, for example, continue to eat even when not hungry (Grimm, 2007).

- *Sensors in the stomach.*   Pressure detectors in the stomach signal fullness or a feeling of emptiness. These messages are sent to the brain, where they combine with information about blood nutrients and the status of the body's fat cells.

- *Reward system preferences.*   The brain's reward system gives us preferences for sweet and high-fat foods. These preferences have a biological basis that

Set point   Refers to the tendency of the body to maintain a certain level of body fat and body weight.

evolved to steer our ancestors toward the calorie-dense foods that enabled them to survive when food supplies were unpredictable. This tendency has been exploited in modern times by the manufacturers of sweet and fatty snack foods.

- *Exercise.* Physical activity also contributes to hunger and satiation. Extreme exercise provokes hunger, but studies show that moderate exercise actually suppresses appetite (Hill & Peters, 1998).

These hunger mechanisms usually work in concert to keep fat stores and body weight within a narrow range, specified by the biological set point. Still, the set point doesn't always keep weight in a desirable range, as we shall see.

Psychological Factors Affecting Hunger and Eating In addition to the biological mechanisms that regulate eating, our emotional state can encourage or discourage eating. For example, both humans and animals refrain from eating when they are fearful. Stress and depression can also affect appetite, although the effects are variable: Some people respond by eating more, and some by eating less.

Learning plays a role, too. Because we also associate certain situations with eating, we can feel hungry regardless of our biological needs. This explains why you may suddenly want to eat when you notice that the clock says lunch time. It also explains why you snack while watching TV or dish up a second helping at Thanksgiving dinner.

Likewise, culture can influence hunger and eating. This can be seen in societies, such as the United States, where social norms among teenage girls promote thinness. On the other hand, in Oceania, where larger figures are often considered more attractive, the social norms promote heftier bodies (Newman, 2004).

While the ideal promoted in movies, magazines, and on TV is one of thinness, Americans receive a different message from commercials that encourage eating. The result is a growing obesity problem in a population obsessed with weight. Moreover, as the influence of U.S. culture becomes more global, American eating habits have become more universal, with the result that calorie-dense snacks and fast foods are making people fatter all over the world (Hébert, 2005; Popkin, 2007).

Recently, the media splashed across the front pages and TV screens of the nation the news that obesity is "socially contagious." But, contrary to the ensuing hype, you can't "catch" obesity from a friend or relative or coworker. What the report by Nicholas Christakis and James Fowler (2007) actually said was that people influence each other with their eating habits. So people align their expectations about food and eating to those of their friends and family members. It just goes to show that eating is based on culture as much as it is on biology.

In the global economy, calorie-dense fast foods have become readily available, changing dietary habits and contributing to a worldwide epidemic of obesity.

Eating Disorders When a person weighs less than 85% of the desirable weight and still worries about being fat, the likely diagnosis is *anorexia nervosa*. This condition may also be accompanied by *bulimia nervosa,* characterized by periods of binge eating followed by purging measures, which may include vomiting, fasting, or using laxatives. In the United States, these disorders are estimated to occur about ten times as often in females as in males, with the greatest risk being in adolescent girls and young women.

Significantly, such eating disorders seem to be most prevalent in Western cultures in which hunger is not uncommon. They are especially likely to develop among middle- and upper-middle-class young women.

Anorexia Nervosa Technically, the condition called *anorexia* (persistent lack of appetite) may develop as a consequence of certain physical diseases or conditions, such as shock, nausea, or allergic reactions. However, when loss of appetite that endangers an individual's health stems from emotional or psychological causes, the syndrome is called **anorexia nervosa** ("nervous anorexia"). A person suffering from anorexia nervosa may act as though she is unconcerned with her condition, although she is emaciated. Anorexia nervosa sufferers not only become dangerously thin, their health suffers in other ways, including cessation of menstruation, osteoporosis, bone fractures, and shrinkage of brain tissue. Over time, "purging" (vomiting to rid oneself of food one has eaten) results in stomach acid damaging the esophagus and throat, as well as the teeth. Psychologically, anorexia nervosa victims may be clinically depressed or show signs of obsessive–compulsive disorder. The condition is associated with extreme dieting—so extreme, in fact, that anorexia nervosa posts the highest mortality rate of any recognized mental disorder (Agras et al., 2004).

What causes anorexia? (We will shorten the term in conformity with common usage.) A strong hint comes from the finding that most persons with anorexia are young females. They may have backgrounds of good behavior and academic success, but they starve themselves, hoping to become acceptably thin and attractive (Keel & Klump, 2003). While cultural ideals of feminine beauty change over time, in recent decades the mass media—including fashion magazines and MTV—have promoted extremely slim models and celebrities. Especially during adolescence, when people tend to evaluate themselves in terms of physical attractiveness, they judge themselves harshly for failing to live up to cultural ideals. A victim of anorexia typically holds a distorted body image, believing herself to be unattractively fat, and rejects others' reassurances that she is not overweight (Bruch, 1978; Fallon & Rozin, 1985). In an effort to lose imagined "excess" weight, the person with anorexia rigidly suppresses her appetite, feeling rewarded for such self-control when she does lose pounds and inches— but never feeling quite thin enough. (See Figure 9.9.)

Recent work on anorexia and bulimia has questioned the assumption that social pressures play the dominant role—focusing instead on possible genetic factors (Grice et al., 2002; Kaye et al., 2004). This makes sense from an evolutionary standpoint, says clinical psychologist Shan Guisinger (2003). She points out the hyperactivity often seen in individuals with anorexia—as opposed to the lethargy common in most starving persons—suggesting that hyperactivity under conditions of starvation may have been an advantage that motivated the ancestors of modern-day individuals with anorexia to leave famine-impoverished environments.

Bulimia In the "binge-and-purge" syndrome known as **bulimia nervosa** (usually just called *bulimia*), the sufferer overeats (binges) and then attempts to lose weight (purges) by means of self-induced vomiting, laxative use, or fasting (Rand & Kuldau, 1992). Those who suffer from bulimia usually keep their disorder inconspicuous and may even be supported in their behavior patterns by peers and by competitive norms in their academic, social, and athletic lives (Polivy & Herman, 1993).

Eating disorders are commonly associated with other forms of psychopathology. For example, bulimia nervosa is a predictor of depression (Walters et al., 1992). Further, individuals with anorexia and bulimia apparently take little joy in their thinner profiles, even though their original rationale might have been to lose weight. And, while hungry normal people look forward to eating and enjoying a good meal, individuals who have eating disorders do not associate pleasure with food and may even dread having to eat. Corroborating this observation, patients with bulimia in one study took longer to begin eating a scheduled meal, ate more slowly, and reported significantly more negative moods during eating than did individuals without bulimia (Hetherington et al., 1993).

Cognitive explanations for eating disorders analyze how the individual sees herself and thinks about food, eating, and weight. Accordingly, many treatments for eating disorders employ strategies that alter self-perception and boost feelings of self-efficacy (Baell & Wertheim, 1992).

CONNECTION • CHAPTER 12

People with obsessive compulsive disorder have persistent and intrusive thoughts and also feel compelled to act out ritual behaviors.

Anorexia nervosa An eating disorder involving persistent loss of appetite that endangers an individual's health and stemming from emotional or psychological reasons rather than from organic causes.

Bulimia nervosa An eating disorder characterized by eating binges followed by "purges," induced by vomiting or laxatives; typically initiated as a weight-control measure.

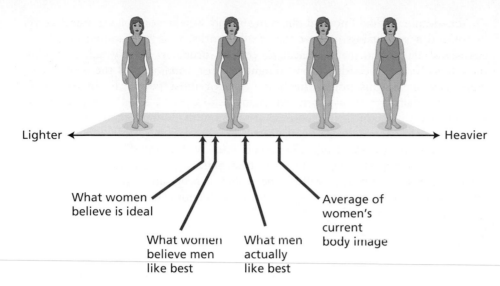

Lighter ←——————————————————→ Heavier

What women
believe is ideal

What women
believe men
like best

What men
actually
like best

Average of
women's
current
body image

FIGURE 9.9
Women's Body Images

April Fallon and Paul Rozin (1985) asked
female college students to give their
current weight, their ideal weight, and
the weight they believed men would
consider ideal. The results show that
the average woman felt that her current weight was significantly higher
than her ideal weight—and higher than
the weight she thought men would like.
To make matters worse, women also
see their bodies as looking larger than
they actually are (Thompson, 1986).
When men were asked to rate themselves on a similar questionnaire, Fallon
and Rozin found no such discrepancies
between ideal and actual weights. But,
when asked what they saw as the ideal
weight for women, they chose a higher
weight than women did. No wonder
women go on diets more often than
men and are more likely to have a major
eating disorder (Mintz & Betz, 1986;
Striegel-Moore et al., 1993).

Obesity and Weight Control At the other extreme of weight control, the problem of obesity has grown at an alarming rate since the early 1980s, with the result
that 65% of Americans are overweight, and 30% are now classified as obese (DeAngelis, 2004b). The real problem, of course, is not obesity but the associated health
risks for such problems as heart disease, stroke, and diabetes—although experts
disagree on just how much of a problem this is among the merely overweight
(Couzin, 2005; Gibbs, 2005). Unfortunately, the fundamental causes of this obesity
epidemic are complex and poorly understood (Doyle, 2006).

No one in the field of obesity research believes that the condition results from
the lack of "will power"—a simplistic and scientifically useless concept (Friedman, 2003). Rather, most experts believe that obesity results from such factors
as poor diet (including super-size portions and an increasing amount of "junk
food") and a spate of biological factors, including genetics (DeAngelis, 2004a;
Flier & Maratos-Flier, 2007). Research also shows that lack of exercise plays a
major part. For example, the long-term Nurses' Health Study showed that every
two-hour increase in daily TV-watching translated into a 23% increase in obesity (Hu et al., 2003). Other research has shown that lean individuals are not
only more active than obese individuals, they also fidget more when they are sitting (Levine et al., 2005; Ravussin, 2005). Finally, one study suggests that running a sleep debt may trigger eating and a resulting weight gain, perhaps because
the body mistakes sleepiness for hunger (Hasler et al., 2004).

From an evolutionary viewpoint, humans are Stone Age creatures biologically
adapted to deal with periods of feast and famine. So, we tend to eat more than
we need when food is abundant, as a hedge against future periods of starvation.
Unfortunately, this Stone-Age strategy is not well suited to life in a modern
world—where most people in developed countries also have no need to expend
energy running down game or digging roots. Nor are we well suited for a world
of French fries, milkshakes, candy bars, and nachos, which appeal to our deeply
ingrained tastes for salty, fatty, and sweet foods—which just happen to be rich
in calories (Pinel et al., 2000). In many respects, the typical school or office bears
far less resemblance to the environment in which humans evolved than it does
to feedlots, where animals are fattened with abundant food and little opportunity for exercise.

The problem is not lack of concern. Americans, especially, seem obsessed by
weight and weight loss, as a glance at the magazine headlines on the newsstand
will show. At any given time, one-third of adult Americans say that they are on
some sort of weight-control diet (Gibbs, 1996).

Yet, despite all we know about hunger and weight control, no one has yet discovered a weight-loss scheme that really works. Notwithstanding nationally advertised claims, no diet, surgical procedure, drug, or other weight-loss gimmick has ever produced long-term weight loss for a majority of the people who have tried it. At this point, the best odds for most people lie in cognitive-behavioral therapies (Institute of Medicine, 2002; Rich, 2004). And for those struggling with weight, it is encouraging to know that some potentially effective weight-control chemicals are being tested as you read this, although it may be several years before any come to market (Flier & Maratos-Flier, 2007). In the meantime, the experts suggest that the best pathway to long-term weight control involves maintaining a well-balanced diet, a program of moderate exercise, and, if you want some extra help, cognitive-behavioral therapy.

Sexual Motivation

Our cultural lessons and life experiences influence the meaning of sex in our lives.

You may have noticed that sex is a most unusual biological drive. Unlike hunger or thirst, arousal of the sex drive can be pleasurable. Even so, sexually aroused individuals typically seek to reduce the tension with sexual activity. And again unlike hunger and thirst, sex is not homeostatic, because it does not return the body to an equilibrium condition. Moreover, sexual motivation can serve diverse goals, including pleasure, reproduction, and social bonding.

In one respect, sexual motivation does have a kinship with hunger and thirst: It has its roots in survival. But even in this respect, sex is unique among biological drives because lack of sex poses no threat to the individual's survival. We can't live for long without food or water, but some people live their lives without sexual activity (although some would say that that's not really living!). Sexual motivation involves the survival of the species, not the individual.

All the biological drives—sex included—exert such powerful influences on behavior that they have led to numerous social constraints and taboos, such as prohibitions on eating certain meats or drinking alcohol. In the realm of sexuality, we find extensive culture-specific rules and sanctions involving a wide variety of sexual practices. In fact, all societies regulate sexual activity, but the restrictions vary widely. For example, homosexuality has been historically suppressed in American and Arab cultures, but it is widely accepted in Polynesian societies. Rules about marriage among relatives also varies from culture to culture.

Even the discussion of sex can become mired in taboo, misinformation, and embarrassment. Scientists who study human sexuality have felt intense social and political pressures, which show no signs of abating in the present. The result is that the scientific understanding of sexuality, which we will survey below, has been hard won.

The Scientific Study of Sexuality   The first major scientific study of human sexuality was initiated by Alfred Kinsey and his colleagues (1948, 1953) in the mid-20th century, with interviews of some 17,000 Americans concerning their sexual behavior. To a generally shocked public, these researchers revealed that certain behaviors (oral sex, for example) previously considered rare, and even abnormal, were actually quite widespread. While Kinsey's data are now over 50 years old, his interviews continue to be considered an important source of information about human sexual behavior, especially since no one else has interviewed such a large and varied sample.

In the 1990s, another large survey of American sexuality was described in *The Social Organization of Sexuality: Sexual Practices in the United States* (Laumann et al., 1994) and in a smaller, more readable companion volume called *Sex in America* (Michael et al., 1994). (See Table 9.4.) This project, known as the National Health and Social Life Survey (NHSLS), involved interviews of 3432 adults, ages 18 to 59. While there were some built-in sources of bias (for

TABLE 9.4 Sexual Preferences and Behaviors of Adult Americans

Frequency of intercourse	Not at all	A few times per year		A few times per month	Two or more times per week	
Percentage of men	14	16		37	34	
Percentage of women	10	18		36	37	

Number of sexual partners since age 18	0	1	2–4	5–10	10–20	21+
Percentage of men	3	20	21	23	16	17
Percentage of women	3	31	31	20	6	3

Infidelity while married						
Men	15.1%					
Women	2.7%					

Sexual orientation	Males	Females				
Heterosexual	96.9	98.6				
Homosexual	2.0	.9				
Bisexual	.8	.5				

Source. Adapted from Michael et al., 1994. Table based on survey of 3432 scientifically selected adult respondents.

example, only English-speaking persons were interviewed), the NHSLS managed to get a remarkable response rate: Of those recruited for the survey, 79% agreed to participate. When melded with other surveys taken since Kinsey's time, this study showed, among other things, a marked increase in the percentage of youth who are sexually active, along with a declining age at first intercourse (Wells & Twenge, 2005). A smaller but more recent survey, however, shows that the percentage of teens who say they are virgins has increased slightly in the last decade (Doyle, 2007).

But virginity is not controlled solely by social pressures. In a study comparing identical twins with fraternal twins, researchers have found that the age at which individuals first have sex is strongly influenced by genetics (Weiss, 2007). Because the same work also showed a genetic influence on the tendency to get in trouble with the law, the scientists speculate that the underlying factor may be a risk-taking tendency—which could be the same one that we saw earlier in Zuckerman's research on sensation seeking.

Masters and Johnson: Gender Similarities and the Physiology of Sex   While it was Kinsey who first shocked the nation's sensibilities with sexual science, it was William Masters and Virginia Johnson (1966, 1970, 1979) who really broke with tradition and taboo by bringing sex into their laboratory. There they studied sex by directly observing and recording the physiological patterns of people engaging in sexual activity of various types, including masturbation and intercourse. By doing observational studies, they discovered not what people *said* about sex (which carries obvious problems of response bias: People are not always willing to give completely honest answers to very personal questions), but Masters and Johnson discovered how people actually *reacted physically* during sex. In the wake of their daring departure from tradition, the study of human sexual behavior has become much more accepted as a legitimate field of scientific inquiry.

FIGURE 9.10

The Sexual Response Cycle

Note that the phases of sexual response in males and females have similar patterns. The primary differences are in the time it takes for males and females to reach each phase and in the greater likelihood that females will achieve multiple orgasms.

(*Source:* From J. H. Gagnon, *Human Sexualities,* © 1977. Reprinted by permission of J. H. Gagnon.)

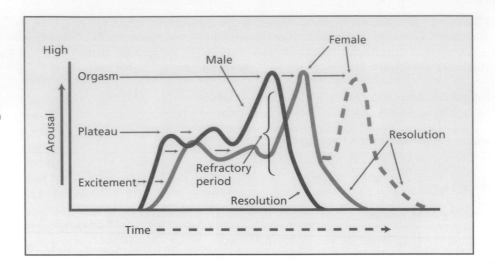

Based on their observations, Masters and Johnson identified four phases of human sexual responding, which they collectively called the **sexual response cycle.** (See Figure 9.10.) These are the distinguishing events of each phase:

- In the *excitement phase,* blood vessel changes in the pelvic region cause the clitoris to swell and the penis to become erect. Blood and other fluids also become congested in the testicles and vagina.

- During the *plateau phase,* a maximal level of arousal is reached. Rapid increases occur in heartbeat, respiration, blood pressure, glandular secretions, and muscle tension.

- When they reach the *orgasm phase,* males and females experience a very intense and pleasurable sense of release from the cumulative sexual tension. Orgasm, characterized by rhythmic genital contractions, culminates in ejaculation of semen in men and clitoral and vaginal sensations in women.

- During the *resolution phase,* the body gradually returns to its preexcitement state, as fluids dissipate from the sex organs. At the same time, blood pressure and heart rate, which had increased dramatically, drop to their customary levels. Note how similar men's and women's physical responses are at each phase of the cycle.

Note also that Masters and Johnson focused on physiological arousal and responses. Accordingly, they paid relatively little attention to psychological aspects of sexuality—for example, emotional responses, sexual desire, or the motivation to seek out a partner or make oneself available for sexual experience. Still, from their biological observations of subjects' sexual behavior, Masters and Johnson drew several newsworthy conclusions:

- Men and women have remarkably similar patterns of biological response, regardless of the source of sexual arousal—whether it be intercourse or masturbation. This is clearly seen in the four phases of the sexual response cycle.

- Although the phases of the sexual response cycle are similar in the two sexes, women tend to respond more slowly but often remain aroused longer.

- Many women can have multiple orgasms in a short time period, while men rarely do.

- Size of the genitals or other physical sex characteristics (such as vagina, breasts, penis) is generally unrelated to any aspect of sexual performance (except, perhaps, attitudes about one's sexual capability).

Sexual response cycle   The four-stage sequence of arousal, plateau, orgasm, and resolution occurring in both men and women.

Most important, perhaps, Masters and Johnson used their discoveries about sexual behavior to develop effective behavioral therapies for a variety of sexual disorders, including male erectile disorder (inability to achieve or maintain an erection), premature ejaculation, and female orgasmic disorder.

But How Do Men and Women Differ in Their Sexuality?   While Masters and Johnson called our attention to the similarities between men and women in the sexual response cycle, Ann Peplau (2003) points out four crucial differences. First, she notes, *men show more interest in sex than do women*—on the average, of course. Men not only think about sex more often, but they are more likely to attend to visual sexual stimuli; they also prefer to have sex more frequently than do women.

Second, *women are more likely than men to view sex in the context of a committed relationship*. That is, says Peplau, women are more likely to "romanticize" sexual desire as a longing for emotional intimacy, while men tend to see sex more as physical pleasure. As a result, women (both heterosexual and lesbian women, incidentally) generally have a less permissive attitude toward casual sex than do men (including both gay and straight men).

Third, *sex is more likely to be linked with aggression for males than for females*. As you probably know, rape is almost exclusively an act committed by males. But even in milder forms, aggression is more a male than a female characteristic. For example, men are more likely to be domineering or abusive in a sexual relationship. (We should add that, even though these gender differences seem to have a biological basis, nothing in this fact excuses hurtful or forced sexual behavior.)

Fourth, Pleplau argues that *women's sexuality has greater "plasticity."* By that she means that women's behaviors and beliefs are more readily shaped by cultural and social factors, as well as by the immediate situation. For example, women's sexual activity over time is far more variable in its frequency than men's. This is especially true when circumstances change, as in a divorce. Cultural factors, such as religion and cultural norms, also influence women's sexuality more than men's. Especially interesting is the fact that higher education is, for both men and women, correlated with more liberal sexual attitudes—but the effect is much stronger for women.

Sexual Cues   What turns you on depends not only on your gender but also on learning. While the sequence of sexual activities that may lead to orgasm can begin with a single unconditioned stimulus—often a touch—it most likely will be accompanied by a variety of conditioned stimuli, such as sights, sounds, and smells. In the form of genital caresses, touch is a universal component of sexual foreplay (Ford & Beach, 1951). Virtually any stimulus that becomes associated with genital touch and orgasm can become a conditioned stimulus that motivates sexual activity—whether the stimulus is present physically or only in memory or fantasy.

Visual stimuli can also be arousing to both men and women (Murnen & Stockton, 1997). Exactly what a person finds sexually stimulating, however, is often determined by stimuli associated with sex (such as chocolate, perfume, or erotic pictures) and sexual fantasies experienced during masturbation (Storms, 1980, 1981). Inanimate objects, textures, sounds, visual images, odors—any tangible or imagined stimulus—can become the focus of arousal through this conditioned association. For reasons that are poorly understood, some people learn to become aroused only by specific stimuli, such as pain or the sight of undergarments.

Sexual Scripts   Generalized sexual arousal can be channeled into specific behaviors (such as kissing or masturbation) that depend on how the individual has been conditioned to think about sexual matters—particularly about **sexual scripts**, which are socially learned programs of sexual interpretation and responsiveness.

How do you know how you are "supposed" to feel when aroused? What do you do when you feel that way? Your culture provides you with many clues from which you develop the sexual scripts for your own behavior, and these scripts differ from one culture to another. For example, in some cultures,

CONNECTION • CHAPTER 13

The behavior therapies focus on what people do, rather than on what they think or feel. Such treatments are effective for a variety of problems, including phobias and other anxiety disorders.

Sexual scripts   Socially learned ways of responding in sexual situations.

CONNECTION • CHAPTER 8

In general, scripts are the expectations we have for events in various situations, such as classrooms, restaurants, traffic jams, and picnics. Scripts often involve social situations—including sexual relation-

foreplay is associated with fondling of the breasts; in others, breasts are regarded merely as appendages for nursing children.

Within our own culture, images from movies and television suggest the importance of kissing and touching and how to engage in these activities—or at least how beautiful actors and actresses (with many hours of "method" rehearsal) manage to engage in these displays. Advertisements, music videos, and conversations with friends also contribute to many young people's sexual scripts. Unfortunately, while these scripts suggest images and goals, they can provide unreliable and unrealistic information. We assemble aspects of these scripts through social interaction over a lifetime. The attitudes and values embodied in one's sexual scripts define one's general approach to sexuality.

Problems can develop when people have different scripts for the same interaction. For example, a casual comment or a touch on the arm can mean something quite different for men and women—or even different persons of the same sex. Even when they are mates, one person's merely friendly gesture may be perceived by the other as a sexual invitation. To avoid misunderstandings, it pays to rely on good communication rather than the assumption that both parties are following the same script.

An Evolutionary Perspective on Sexuality   While the theory of sexual scripts emphasizes learned sexual behavior patterns, the evolutionary perspective looks for the origins of sexual motivation in our genes. Some observers (Buss, 2008) argue that genetic pressures have resulted in different mating strategies and, therefore, different gender roles, for males and females. (These views are a matter of emphasis: All theorists recognize that both learning and genetics affect our sexual behaviors.)

Biologically speaking, the goal of both sexes is to leave as many offspring as possible. Yet the potential physical costs of mating differ for males and females (Bjorklund & Shackelford, 1999). As a result, the sexes have evolved different—and sometimes conflicting—mating strategies, say evolutionary psychologists.

Females can produce only a few children over a lifetime, and they make a huge biological investment in pregnancy and a substantial commitment of time and energy in child rearing. Therefore, the best sexual strategy for females involves caution in mate selection. For males, however, the costs and benefits are much different because they cannot become pregnant—nor do they usually spend as much time with children as women do. For males, the theory says, the biggest payoff results from copulating as often as possible with mates who are in prime breeding condition. As a result, men tend to seek young and physically well-developed partners, while females may seek somewhat older mates who can offer resources, status, and protection for offspring. Not incidentally, these agendas often produce conflict, promiscuity, and sexual jealousy.

Although the evolutionary perspective may seem harsh in its view of sexual motivation, it does account for many gender differences in mating behaviors, such as the larger number of sexual partners typically reported by men than women. (See Table 9.4 on page 413.) Even so, biology does not prohibit the learning of alternative sex roles and scripts, nor does it explain the social and cultural pressures that cast men and women in different roles, as in religious groups that allow only men into the priesthood (Eagly & Wood, 1999). Moreover, it does not explain why most people remain with their mates over extended periods of time (Hazan & Diamond, 2000). A complete understanding of sexual motivation must include both its evolutionary roots and, especially in humans, the many variations that occur through learning.

The What and Why of Sexual Orientation   Ever since Alfred Kinsey's first reports, we have known that human **sexual orientation** is a complex issue. *Heterosexuality* and *homosexuality* represent two forms of sexual orientation, which refers to the direction or object of one's sexual interests, either to the opposite sex or to the same sex. Another variation is *bisexuality,* which refers to attrac-

Sexual orientation   One's erotic attraction toward members of the same sex (a homosexual orientation), the opposite sex (heterosexual orientation), or both sexes (a bisexual orientation).

tion to both males and females. But to complicate matters, cross-cultural studies reveal considerable variability in sexual orientation. In parts of New Guinea, for example, the culture dictates that homosexual behavior is universal among young males, who then switch to a heterosexual orientation when they marry (Money, 1987). Among Americans, various estimates put the percentage of homosexuality at 1 to 4%, more or less, depending on whether homosexuality is defined as one's primary orientation or, more broadly, as any same-sex erotic behavior during one's lifetime (Diamond, 2007). As Table 9.4 (page 413) indicates, the incidence of homosexuality among females is about half that of males.

Incidentally, *transsexualism* refers to people who view themselves as persons of the sex opposite to their biological sex. They should not be confused with cross-dressers who indulge in a sexual fetish known as *transvestism*. (Those who cross-dress for nonsexual reasons are not classified under transvestism.) It is also important to realize that none of these variations predicts sexual orientation. That is, knowing that a person is transsexual or a cross-dresser does not tell us whether he or she is gay, lesbian, bisexual, or straight.

Origins of Sexual Orientation   So, what does the available evidence tell us about the factors that determine sexual orientation? We know several things that are *not* involved. Speaking biologically, we know that sexual orientation in adults is *not* related to testosterone levels—although the issue of testosterone or estrogen influences in the fetus is still an open question (McAnulty & Burnette, 2004). From a social perspective, we also know that parenting styles or family configurations do *not* cause children to turn either toward heterosexuality or homosexuality (Golombok & Tasker, 1996). Similarly, researchers have come up empty handed in their attempts to link human sexual orientation to early sexual experiences.

A controversial theory proposed by Daryl Bem asserts that we become attracted to the sex that we, as young children, consider most unlike us. Bem has amassed considerable evidence in support of this "exotic becomes erotic" theory (Bem, 1996, 2001). (For an opposing viewpoint, however, see Peplau et al., 1998, who dispute Bem's interpretation of the evidence and argue that his theory does not take women's experiences into account.)

Attempts to identify biological origins of sexual feelings in the genes and the brain have also provoked controversy—and have shown some promise. For example, Richard Pillard and Michael Bailey (1991) studied sexual orientation of male identical twins. They discovered that when one twin is homosexual the chance of the other being homosexual is about 50%—as compared with an incidence of roughly 5 or 6% in the general population. This study also found that the rate drops to 22% for fraternal twins and 11% for adoptive brothers of homosexuals. A later study of female twin pairs produced essentially the same results (Bower, 1992).

One of the more puzzling findings links sexual orientation in males (but not females) to birth order, specifically how many older brothers one has (Abrams, 2007; Blanchard & Bogaert, 1996). The more older brothers a boy has, the more likely he is to have a same-sex orientation. This effect occurs whether or not boys are raised with their biological brothers, according to a study of adopted versus biological brothers—a finding that apparently rules out environmental influences (Bogaert, 2006). While no one knows what the causative factor is, some scientists believe that some aspect of the prenatal environment tips the balance one way or another (Bower, 2006a).

Research in this area remains controversial because of the strong feelings, political issues, and prejudices involved (Herek, 2000). Further, it has attracted scientific criticism because much of it is correlational—rather than experimental—so the data cannot establish cause and effect with certainty. Moreover, some observers object to this whole line of research, saying that gay men and lesbians should not feel pressured to justify their behavior by seeking a biological basis for it (Byne, 1995).

The origins of sexual orientation are unclear, although some evidence points to biological factors. What is clear is that research on sexual orientation often generates controversy.

Not a Disorder   We should also note that, until the 1970s, the diagnostic manual of the American Psychiatric Association listed homosexuality as a mental disorder—a classification that has since been removed and repudiated by both psychologists and psychiatrists (Greenberg, 1997). But what does the evidence say about sexual orientation and mental health? The message coming through numerous recent studies show that mental problems and problem relationships occur in about the same proportion in heterosexuals and homosexuals (DeAngelis, 2002c; Kurdek, 2005). The exception involves stress-related problems (e.g., anxiety and depression) associated with discrimination against homosexuals.

So, where does this leave us in our understanding of sexual orientation? Attitudes toward minority forms of sexual orientation, such as homosexuality, differ sharply among cultures around the world, with Americans among the most divided on issues such as gay marriage. Most experts—but not all—would say that the research strongly supports some biological influence on sexual orientation. Just how biology might influence our behavior in the bedroom, however, remains a major puzzle and a topic for continuing research.

PSYCHOLOGY**MATTERS**
A Question of Will Power, Laughter, and Chocolate Cookies

Psychologists don't talk much about "will power," although the term can be heard in everyday conversation, where it usually refers to resisting food, drink, or some other temptation. In particular, psychologists don't like the archaic assumption of the "will" as a special faculty of the mind—a throwback to 19th-century phrenology. Thus "will power" is like the term "instinct"—merely a label rather than an explanation. For example, we may say that people who are thin have "will power" but this label may simply obscure a difference in body chemistry. Psychologists also object to the term "will power" because it is often used as a put-down, to suggest that a person has a deficiency in character—a "weak will."

Alternatives to Will Power   Modern psychologists usually prefer terms such as *self-control* or *impulse control*—terms that have somewhat less baggage and can be related to environmental influences and to known brain mechanisms. For example, we know that controlling one's eating is more difficult during the holiday season, with its abundance of food. Similarly, damage to parts of the limbic system is known to make emotional control more difficult.

Psychologists have also contrived devilish tests to measure impulse control. (Recall the "marshmallow test" in our discussion of emotional intelligence.) What have they found? To nobody's surprise, the ability to control one's impulses correlates with to all sorts of positive outcomes, including better mental health, more effective coping skills, better relationships, and higher academic achievement. But the problem has been that such research still leaves the big question unanswered: What *is* self-control—or "will power"?

The Biology of Self-Control   A team of researchers at Florida State University seems to have placed the ability to resist temptation on a solid scientific footing (Gailliot et al., 2007). What they found is that self-control has a biological basis. And it also has a price.

The Florida group first placed undergraduate psychology students in one of several onerous situations in which they were asked to exercise self-control—such as resisting a tempting plate of freshly baked chocolate cookies or watching a funny video clip without laughing. Then the researchers gave the students a second task, such as a scrambled-word problem or a hand-eye coordination test. A control group also performed the second task, but they were not first asked to stifle their laughter nor were they exposed to plates of tempting cookies.

CONNECTION • CHAPTER 2

The 19th-Century phrenologists erroneously believed that the brain contains specialized "organs" corresponding to various mental faculties, including courage, pride, religion, perseverance, and sagacity.

Before we go any further, see if you can predict who did better on the second task. Was it the ones who had successfully resisted their impulses? Or the control group, who had been allowed to indulge themselves?

You were right if you guessed that those who had faced down temptation (resisting the cookies or soberly watching the funny video) were *less* successful on the subsequent task. Apparently self-control is a cognitive resource that, like physical stamina, can become temporarily depleted—and, surprisingly, it seems to have a physical presence in the blood, as well as in behavior. The study found that those who had been asked to control their urges had lower blood-sugar levels than those who had not restrained themselves. Because sugar (glucose) is an energy source for the body, the researchers speculate that exerting will power used up some of that energy, making people less efficient on the second task (Baumeister et al., 1998).

But there is hope for those weak of will! A sugared drink not only brought blood glucose back up to its original level, but it brought the performance of the self-controllers back to the level of the indulgers. Apparently, what we call "will power" is based, at least in part, on the body's ready energy reserves.

So, should you have a cola and a candy bar to boost your "will" before the next psychology test? Probably not such a good idea, says Matthew Gaillot, leader of the Florida study—especially if you are trying to control your weight. Better, he says to keep your energy level up with longer-lasting proteins or complex carbohydrates (Cynkar, 2007).

And some additional advice from a cognitive perspective: If you want to insure that you are mentally sharp, moderation is a better strategy than denial.

CheckYourUnderstanding

1. **RECALL:** Describe the *multiple systems approach* to understanding hunger.

2. **RECALL:** Explain, from an evolutionary perspective, why obesity is becoming more prevalent in industrialized nations.

3. **RECALL:** From a biological perspective, in what respect is sex different from other biological drives, such as hunger and thirst?

4. **RECALL:** What are the four major differences between men's and women's sexuality, according to Peplau?

5. **ANALYSIS:** Why do psychologists avoid the term *will power*? What terms do they prefer instead?

6. **UNDERSTANDING THE CORE CONCEPT:** For which of the motives discussed in this section would biological factors be *least* important in accounting for the differences between one person and another?
   a. hunger
   b. thirst
   c. a *n Ach*
   d. sex

Answers **1.** Because hunger has not only biological components but also cognitive, social, and cultural aspects, it must be understood as involving a complex interaction of factors. The multiple systems approach recognizes such factors as blood sugar and fat levels monitored by the hypothalamus, homeostatic feedback from fat cells, pressure and nutrient detectors in the stomach, reward systems in the brain, physical activity, emotional state, food-related stimuli, and social-cultural pressures. **2.** From an evolutionary standpoint, the human body evolved in an environment that required much more physical exertion than is required of most people in industrialized countries. This decrease in activity, along with an abundance of calorie-dense foods, has led to obesity. **3.** Sex is not a homeostatic drive. **4.** Peplau says that (a) men show more interest in sex than do women, (b) women are more likely to view sex in the context of a committed relationship, (c) males are more likely to associate sex with aggression, and (d) women's sexuality has more plasticity than men's. **5.** The term *will power* suggests that it is a separate faculty of the mind, yet there is no evidence of a "will" that cannot be explained in more conventional terms that do not carry the baggage of a defect in character. Psychologists prefer to speak of "self-control" or "impulse control." **6.** c (because all the others involve biological drives)

The **polygraph**, often called a "lie detector," relies on the assumption that people will display physical signs of arousal when lying; so most polygraph machines make a record of the suspect's heart rate, breathing rate, perspiration, and blood pressure. Occasionally, voice-print analysis is also employed. Thus, the device really acts as an emotional arousal detector, rather than a direct indicator of truth or lies. But does it work?

What Are the Issues?

Who is telling the truth, and who is lying? It's a question that poker players, the police, and ordinary citizens on jury duty confront routinely. It's also a problem for U.S. embassy personnel around the world because people claiming to have information about bomb threats and other acts of terrorism show up in their offices every day (Dingfelder, 2004c). It is no wonder, then, that the polygraph has found wide use. Even if it doesn't always work perfectly, it does seem better to have *some* way of distinguishing truth-tellers from liars than none at all. Or does it?

What Critical Thinking Questions Should We Ask?

If you are unfamiliar with the issues—as most people are with the controversy surrounding the use of "lie detectors"—it may be impossible to know what critical thinking questions to ask. In that event, the best course of action is to look at the arguments on all sides (not a bad approach to any issue, in fact!). Having done so with the polygraph issue, your authors believe that the following issues are most important:

- *Is there a possibility of bias?* We think there is, and it comes in two forms. One comes from a formidable polygraph industry that has a vested interest in convincing the public that polygraph tests can, indeed, distinguish truth-tellers from liars. A second form of bias comes from those obsessed by fear of crime and terrorism and who see humanity in stark black-and-white terms—as consisting of good people and evil people. We should be especially wary in weighing claims presented by either of these groups.

- *Are there errors of logic involved?* We believe that proponents of the polygraph commit two types of

Polygraph A device that records or graphs many ("poly") measures of physical arousal, such as heart rate, breathing, perspiration, and blood pressure. A polygraph is often called a "lie detector," even though it is really an arousal detector.

logical error. The first involves pointing to individual cases in which they claim a "lie detector" test either revealed a liar or forced a confession from a reluctant suspect. This is nothing more than "proof by testimonial," as we see all the time in ads for "miracle" weight-loss products or engine-oil additives. The fact is that testimonials are no substitute for a controlled scientific test.

- The other main logical error is *oversimplification*. By focusing on apparent successes, they may gloss over the failures—which, in the case of the polygraph, can be quite serious. As we will see, the polygraph failures can lead to a surprisingly large number of honest people being identified as liars.

To see what we mean, we need to ask a third question: *What is the evidence?*

Evidence or Intimidation? Without a doubt, wrongdoers sometimes confess when confronted with polygraph evidence against them. Yet, critics have pointed out several problems with the polygraphic procedure that could easily land innocent people in prison and let the guilty walk free (Aftergood, 2000). For example, polygraph subjects know when they are suspects, so some will give heightened responses to the critical questions, even when they are innocent. On the other hand, some people can give deceptive responses because they have learned to control or distort their emotional responses. To do so they may employ simple physical movements, drugs, or biofeedback training—a procedure in which people are given moment-to-moment information on certain biological responses, such as perspiration or heart rate (Saxe et al., 1985). Either way, a polygraph examiner risks incorrectly identifying innocent people as guilty and failing to spot the liars.

To help you judge whether "lie detectors" can reliably discriminate truth from falsehood, let's sit in on a polygraph session.

How Is a Polygraph Examination Conducted? Polygraphers typically employ several tricks of their trade. They may start the interview by persuading the subject that the machine is highly accurate. A common ploy is to ask a series of loaded questions designed to provoke obvious emotional reactions. For example, "Did you ever, in your life, take anything that did not belong to you?" In another favorite technique, the examiner uses a deceptive stimulation procedure, or "stim test," in which the subject draws a card from a "stacked" deck. Then, the examiner pretends to identify the card from the subject's polygraph responses (Kleinmuntz & Szucko, 1984).

When the actual interrogation begins, it will consist of an artistic mix of *critical questions, irrelevant questions,* and *control questions.* The irrelevant questions ("Are you sitting down right now?") are designed to elicit truthful answers accompanied by a physical response consistent with truth telling. The control questions ("Did you ever lie to your parents?") are designed to elicit an anxious, emotionally aroused response pattern. Then, the examiner can compare the subject's responses to these two types of questions with responses to the critical questions ("Did you steal the jewels?"). It is assumed that a guilty suspect will give a stronger response to the critical questions than to the irrelevant and control questions.

What Conclusions Can We Draw?

Sensible as the procedure may seem, statistical issues call the polygraph procedure into question. Consider, for example, the problem of accuracy. Even if the examination were 95% accurate, the 5% error rate could lead to the misidentification of many innocent people as being guilty. To illustrate, imagine that your company arranges for all 500 of your employees to take a polygraph test to find out who has been stealing office supplies. Imagine also that only about 4% (20 out of 500 people) are really stealing, which is not an unreasonable estimate. If the lie detector test is 95% accurate, it will correctly spot 19 of these 20 thieves. But the polygrapher will still have a big problem. The test will also give 5% **false positives**, falsely fingering 5% of the innocent people. Of the 480 innocent employees, the polygraph will inaccurately implicate 24 as liars. That is, *you could end up with more people falsely accused of lying than people correctly accused of lying.* This was borne out in a field study of suspected criminals, who were later either convicted or declared innocent. The polygraph results were no better than a random coin flip (Brett et al., 1986).

An equally serious concern with polygraphy is that there are no generally accepted standards either for administering a polygraph examination or for interpreting its results. Different examiners could conceivably come to different conclusions based on the same polygraph record.

For these reasons, the U.S. Congress has outlawed most uses of polygraph tests in job screening and in most areas of the government, except for high security risk positions. Laws on the admissibility of polygraph evidence vary greatly among the states, with a few imposing complete bans and 20 more allowing such evidence only on agreement of both sides—although, in a few states, polygraph results are still routinely admissible in court (Gruben & Madsen, 2005). The National Academies of Science (2003) has recently released a report saying that the polygraph is too crude to be useful for screening people to identify possible terrorists or other national security risks.

Alternative Approaches to Deception Detection

The reining-in of polygraph testing has spurred the development of alternative means of detecting dishonesty (Capps & Ryan, 2005; Lane, 2006). Much of this work has been devoted to paper-and-pencil instruments that are often called "integrity tests." How well do these instruments work? Not very well, according to reports by the American Psychological Association and by the U.S. government's Office of Technology Assessment. In general, like the polygraph, these instruments seem to be more accurate than mere interviews, but they also suffer from a high false-positive rate.

More recently, researchers have turned to brain scanning techniques to see if they can catch liars (Ross, 2003). A certain brain wave pattern known as P300 has been linked with a variety of attention-getting cues, such as hearing one's name, but studies show it can also be evoked by fibbing. In addition, fMRI images show that lying activates all the brain areas involved in telling the truth, plus several more (Langleben et al., 2002). This suggests that lying is not something completely separate from the truth but an operation the liar must perform on the truth, says psychiatrist Daniel Langleben. All of which raises the concern that there is too much hype and too little solid evidence behind brain-scan based lie detection. In addition, some neuroscientists worry about the ethics of peering directly into people's brains to "read" the neural traces of their private thoughts (Pearson, 2006).

The potential advantage of these newer brain-scan techniques is that they bypass the anxiety-response pathway used by polygraphy. By registering neural activity, they get much closer to the person's actual thoughts. But how well do these alternative methods work? Not well enough for the police and the courts—yet.

Finally, Paul Ekman—the same one who studies universal facial expressions of emotion—has found that liars often display fleeting "microexpressions" and other nonverbal cues. In one study, Ekman and his colleague Maureen O'Sullivan found that some people are especially good at detecting deception, but they are a small minority. In their tests, most people perform at about the chance level. Still, Ekman and O'Sullivan hope to learn what the most perceptive look for and teach that to police officers and other concerned with crime and security issues (Adelson, 2004).

For more information on polygraphy, see "The Truth About Lie Detectors (aka Polygraph Tests)" on the *Psychology Matters* website: *www.psychologymatters .org/polygraphs.html.*

False positives Mistaken identification of a person as having a particular characteristic. In polygraphy, a false positive is an erroneous identification of a truthful person as being a liar.

Chapter Summary

9.1 What Do Our Emotions Do for Us?

Core Concept 9.1: Emotions help us to attend and respond to important situations and to convey our intentions to others.

Emotion is a process involving physiological arousal, cognitive interpretation, subjective feelings, and behavioral expression. Emotions can also act as motives. From an evolutionary standpoint, they help us approach or avoid recurring stimuli that are important for survival and reproduction. Socially, emotional expressions serve to communicate feelings and intentions.

At least seven basic facial expressions of emotion are universally understood across cultures, although these can be modified by culture-specific **display rules**. There is no consensus on the number of emotions humans can experience; most experts believe that there is a small number of basic emotions, which can mix to produce more complex emotions.

Some emotional differences between males and females have biological roots. This is seen in differential rates of certain emotional disorders, as well as more frequent displays of anger in men. On the other hand, cultural differences demonstrate that some gender differences in emotion are learned. Specifically, different cultures teach men and women different display rules about controlling emotional expression. Despite the differences, neither sex can be said to be more emotional than the other.

Display rules (p. 381)   **Emotion** (p. 378)

MyPsychLab Resources 9.1:

Watch: Humor and Brains

Simulation: Survey on Happiness

Watch: Michael Cohn

9.2 Where Do Our Emotions Come From?

Core Concept 9.2: The discovery of two distinct brain pathways for emotional arousal has clarified how emotion works and has suggested solutions to long-standing issues in the psychology of emotion.

Neuroscience has revealed two distinct emotion systems in the brain. One, a fast-response system, operates mainly at an unconscious level and relies on deep limbic structures, especially the amygdala. The other involves conscious processing in the cortex. Emotions also involve visceral changes in response to messages transmitted by the autonomic nervous system and the hormone system. Understanding how the two emotion systems work has begun to resolve some controversies involving the roles of physical responses and cognition in emotion—particularly the interplay among physical responses, cognitions, and feelings of emotion.

The inverted U theory describes the complex relationship between arousal and performance: Increasing arousal produces improved performance, but only up to a certain level of optimum arousal, which depends on the complexity of the task. **Sensation seekers** seem to have an especially high need for arousal.

Cannon–Bard theory (p. 387)   **Lateralization of emotion** (p. 386)
Inverted U function (p. 391)
James–Lange theory (p. 387)   **Sensation seekers** (p. 391)
Two-factor theory (p. 388)

MyPsychLab Resources 9.2:

Explore: Physiological, Evolutionary, and Cognitive Theories of Emotion

Watch: Emotion Regulation: James Coan

Watch: Interaction of Cognition and Emotion: Jutta Joormann

9.3 How Much Control Do We Have over Our Emotions?

Core Concept 9.3: Although emotional responses are not always consciously regulated, we can learn to control them.

Emotional intelligence, the ability to keep one's emotions from getting out of control, is vital for maintaining good social relationships. It is distinct from the abilities measured by traditional IQ tests. Increased emotional control can be achieved by learning, as demonstrated in anger management programs. Tests of emotional intelligence show that those who score highly tend to succeed in social situations.

On the negative side of emotional control, some people have learned to control their emotions for purposes of deception. Psychologists have sought, with some success, to discover cues, both verbal and nonverbal, associated with lying. Most people, however, cannot detect liars at much better than a chance level.

While aggression can be the result of anger, people usually hold aggression in check. Under some circumstances, however, the expression of anger without aggression can have positive results—although the commonsense view that it is always good to vent anger and aggression is a dangerous myth. People who have trouble managing anger and aggression may benefit from cognitive therapy.

Emotional intelligence (p. 392)

MyPsychLab Resources 9.3:

Watch: Lie Spy

9.4 Motivation: What Makes Us Act As We Do?

Core Concept 9.4: Motivation takes many forms, but all involve inferred mental processes that arouse us and then select and direct our behavior.

The concept of **motivation** refers to inferred internal processes that select and direct behavior, and it helps explain behavior that cannot be explained by the circumstances alone. Psychologists find it useful to distinguish psychological **motives** from biological **drives**, **intrinsic motivation** from **extrinsic motivation**, and **conscious motivation** from **unconscious motivation**.

Psychology has no successful theory that accounts for all of human motivation. Psychologists explain biologically based motivation in terms of **instinct theory** (and **fixed-action patterns**) and **drive theory.** They use cognitive theories to explain psychological motives, as in Rotter's **locus of control** theory. Freud called attention to **unconscious motivation** and taught that all our motives derive from unconscious sexual and aggressive desires. Maslow attempted to tie together a wide range of human motivation—from biological drives to psychological motives—into a **hierarchy of needs.** Critics have pointed out problems with all of these approaches.

Psychologists find that extrinsic rewards can produce **overjustification,** especially when rewards are given without regard for the quality of performance.

Great achievements usually come from people in a state of **flow.** Those in a flow state are intrinsically motivated by some problem or activity. The use of drugs or alcohol to achieve an artificial flow feeling is not usually effective.

Conscious motivation (p. 399)	**Instinct theory** (p. 399)
Drive (p. 398)	**Intrinsic motivation** (p. 398)
Drive theory (p. 400)	**Locus of control** (p. 400)
Extrinsic motivation (p. 399)	**Motivation** (p. 397)
Fixed-action patterns (p. 399)	**Motive** (p. 398)
Flow (p. 404)	**Need** (p. 400)
Hierarchy of needs (p. 401)	**Overjustification** (p. 403)
Homeostasis (p. 400)	**Unconscious motivation** (p. 399)

MyPsychLab Resources 9.4:

Explore: Theories of Motivation and Job Performance

Explore: Maslow's Hierarchy of Needs

9.5 How Are Achievement, Hunger, And Sex Alike? Different?

Core Concept 9.5 No single theory accounts for all forms of motivation because each motive involves its own mix of biological, mental, behavioral, and social/cultural influences.

Some motives rely heavily on learning, while others depend more heavily on biological factors. Moreover, motives differ in their sensitivity to environmental cues, reinforcers, and social/cultural influences.

Achievement is a psychological motive that accounts for an important segment of human behavior, both in school and on the job, although McClelland has argued that the needs for power and affiliation are just as important as *n Ach*. Studies also show that societies vary in the intensity of their need for achievement, depending on their tendencies toward **individualism** or **collectivism.**

In contrast, hunger and eating are motivated at many levels—by biological processes, external cues, social influences, and learning, for example—and are best understood by a multiple-systems approach. Americans receive mixed messages from the media, promoting both thinness and calorie-dense foods. The causes of the eating disorders **anorexia nervosa** and **bulimia nervosa** are not known, but both cultural and genetic factors have been implicated. The problem of obesity has become epidemic in America and is rapidly being exported throughout the world. Many people seek to control their appetite and body weight, although no weight-loss scheme is effective for most people over the long run.

Unlike hunger and weight control, the sex drive is not homeostatic, even though sexual motivation is heavily influenced by biology. Sexual behavior in humans also depends on learning—of various sexual scripts. Particularly since Kinsey's surveys, the scientific study of sexuality has long caused controversy in America, even though survey research shows that, over the last half century, Americans have become more liberal in their sexual practices. Masters and Johnson were the first to do extensive studies of sexual behavior in the laboratory, finding that the **sexual response cycles** of men and women are similar. More recently, Peplau has emphasized differences in male and female sexuality. Those adhering to the controversial evolutionary perspective argue that differences in male and female sexuality arise from conflicting mating strategies and from the large biological investment women have in pregnancy—both of which encourage more promiscuity in men. Despite its roots in biology, sexuality is affected by learning, as seen in sexual cues and **sexual scripts.** The greatest puzzle about sexuality, however, centers on the origins of **sexual orientation,** although there is good evidence that biological factors play a role.

Will power is a common term in everyday language, although psychologists avoid it because it suggests a separate faculty of the mind. They prefer *impulse control* or *self-control,* terms that can be explained in terms of brain mechanisms and environmental influences. Recently, researchers have found that impulse control takes a cognitive toll and is reflected in blood sugar levels.

Anorexia nervosa (p. 410)	**Polygraph** (p. 420)
Bulimia nervosa (p. 410)	**Set point** (p. 408)
Collectivism (p. 407)	**Sexual orientation** (p. 416)
Individualism (p. 407)	**Sexual response cycle** (p. 414)
False positive (p. 422)	**Sexual scripts** (p. 415)
Need for achievement *(n Ach)* (p. 405)	

MyPsychLab Resources 9.5:

Watch: Cognition, Emotion, and Motivation Across Cultures: Shinoby Kitayama

Watch: Food and the Brain

Watch: Eating Disorders

Discovering Psychology Viewing Guide

Watch the following video by logging into MyPsychLab (www.mypsychlab.com). After you have watched the video, complete the activities that follow.

PROGRAM 12: MOTIVATION AND EMOTION

PROGRAM REVIEW

1. What is the general term for all the physical and psychological processes that start behavior, maintain it, and stop it?
   a. explanatory style
   b. repression
   c. addiction
   d. motivation

2. Phoebe has a phobia regarding cats. What is her motivation?
   a. environmental arousal
   b. overwhelming fear
   c. repressed sexual satisfaction
   d. a need for attachment to others

3. What is the role of the pleasure-pain principle in motivation?
   a. We repress our pleasure in others' pain.
   b. We seek pleasure and avoid pain.
   c. We persist in doing things, even when they are painful.
   d. We are more intensely motivated by pain than by pleasure.

4. Which activity most clearly involves a "reframing" of the tension between desire and restraint?
   a. eating before you feel hungry
   b. seeking pleasurable physical contact with others
   c. working long hours for an eventual goal
   d. getting angry at someone who interferes with your plans

5. Sigmund Freud thought there were two primary motivations. One of these is
   a. expressing aggression.
   b. seeking transcendence.
   c. fulfilling creativity.
   d. feeling secure.

6. Compared with Freud's view of human motivation, that of Abraham Maslow could be characterized as being more
   a. negative.
   b. hormonally based.
   c. optimistic.
   d. pathologically based.

7. Behaviors, such as male peacocks displaying their feathers or male rams fighting, are related to which part of sexual reproduction?
   a. providing a safe place for mating
   b. focusing the male's attention on mating
   c. selecting a partner with good genes
   d. mating at the correct time of year

8. In Norman Adler's research on mating behavior in rats, what is the function of the ten or so mountings?
   a. to trigger hormone production and uterine contractions in the female
   b. to warn off rival males
   c. to cause fertilization
   d. to impress the female

9. What kinds of emotions tend to be involved in romantic love?
   a. mainly intense, positive emotions
   b. mainly intense, negative emotions
   c. a mixture of intense and weak emotions that are mainly positive
   d. a mixture of positive and negative emotions that are intense

10. Charles Darwin cited the similarity of certain expressions of emotions as evidence that
    a. all species learn emotions.
    b. emotions are innate.
    c. emotions promote survival of the fittest.
    d. genetic variability is advantageous.

11. Pictures of happy and sad American workers are shown to U.S. college students and to Italian workers. Based on your knowledge of Paul Ekman's research, what would you predict about how well the groups would identify the emotions?
    a. Both groups will identify the emotions correctly.
    b. Only the Americans will identify the emotions correctly.

c. Only the Italians will identify the emotions correctly.

d. Neither group will identify the emotions correctly.

12. Theodore has an explanatory style that emphasizes the external, the unstable, and the specific. He makes a mistake at work that causes his boss to become very angry. Which statement is Theodore most likely to make to himself?

a. "I always make such stupid mistakes."

b. "I was just distracted by the noise outside."

c. "All my life, people have always gotten so mad at me."

d. "If I were a better person, this wouldn't have happened."

13. Why does Martin Seligman believe that it might be appropriate to help children who develop a pessimistic explanatory style?

a. These children are unpleasant to be around.

b. These children lack contact with reality.

c. These children are at risk for depression.

d. Other children who live with these children are likely to develop the same style.

14. What other outcome will a pessimistic explanatory style likely affect, according to Seligman?

a. health

b. artistic ability

c. reasoning skills

d. language competence

15. All of the following are possible origins of a pessimistic explanatory style, *except*

a. assessments by important adults in our lives.

b. the reality of our first major negative life event.

c. our mother's pessimism level.

d. our level of introversion/extraversion.

16. Which theorist is best known for positing a hierarchy of needs that humans strive to meet?

a. Freud

b. Rogers

c. Maslow

d. Seligman

17. Although motivation can lead to unpleasant states (e.g., hunger, frustration), it seems to have evolved because of its benefits to

a. survival.

b. propagation of the species.

c. health.

d. all of the above.

18. What has Robert Plutchik argued about emotions?

a. There are three basic types of emotions: happiness, sadness, and anger.

b. There are eight basic emotions, consisting of four pairs of opposites.

c. Love is not a universal emotion; some cultures do not show signs of having it.

d. Emotional experience is determined by physiology alone.

19. Four people have been obese for as long as they can remember. Their doctors tell all of them that their obesity is putting them at risk for several illnesses. Who is most likely to join a gym, go on a diet, and get in shape?

a. Al, whose explanatory style includes an internal locus of control

b. Bob, who has a pessimistic explanatory style

c. Chuck, whose explanatory style includes an unstable locus of control

d. Dwayne, who is depressed about his obesity

20. Wolves and squirrels are most likely to show which of the following in their mating patterns?

a. romantic love

b. competition by females for males

c. competition by males for females

d. a preference for mating in the autumn so that the offspring will be born during the winter

QUESTIONS TO CONSIDER

1. Human sexual motivation expresses itself in sexual scripts that include attitudes, values, social norms, and expectations about patterns of behavior. Consider how males and females might develop different sexual scripts. How might lack of synchronization affect a couple? How might sexual scripts change as the bad news about sexually transmitted diseases and AIDS increases?

2. If you could choose between taking this course and receiving a pass/fail (credit only) or getting a letter grade, which would you choose? How would your decision affect your study time, motivation, and test-taking behavior?

3. Imagine you are moving to a country whose culture you aren't familiar with. Describe some of the social problems you might encounter because you don't know the cultural norms regarding expression of emotion.

ACTIVITIES

1. Are people sad because they cry, or do people cry because they are sad? Can making a sad face make someone feel sad? Does going through the motions trigger the emotion? Try this: Set aside 10 to 15 minutes for this experiment. Write down the words *happy, sad, angry,* and *fearful* on slips of paper. In

front of a mirror, select one of the slips and watch yourself as you create the facial expression for it. Hold the expression for at least a minute. Note the thoughts and physical reactions that seem to accompany your facial expression. Then relax your face and repeat the exercise with another slip of paper. Which theories does your experience support or challenge?

2. Observe the activities on which you need to concentrate when your hunger has been satisfied, compared with when you are very hungry. How well can you focus on more abstract motivations when your biological motivations have been left unmet?

Key Questions/ Chapter Outline	Core Concepts	Psychology Matters

10.1 What Forces Shape Our Personalities?

Biology, Human Nature, and Personality

The Effects of Nurture: Personality and the Environment

The Effects of Nature: Dispositions and Mental Processes

Social and Cultural Contributions to Personality

- Personality is shaped by the combined forces of biological, situational, and mental processes—all embedded in a sociocultural and developmental context.

Explaining Unusual People and Unusual Behavior

You don't need a theory of personality to explain why people do the expected.

10.2 What Persistent Patterns, or *Dispositions*, Make Up Our Personalities?

Personality and Temperament

Personality as a Composite of Traits

Personality Disorders

- The *dispositional* theories all suggest a small set of personality characteristics, known as temperaments, traits, or types, that provide consistency to the individual's personality over time.

Finding Your Type

When it comes to classifying personality according to types, a little caution may be in order.

10.3 What Mental *Processes* Are at Work within Our Personalities?

Psychodynamic Theories: Emphasis on Motivation and Mental Disorder

Humanistic Theories: Emphasis on Human Potential and Mental Health

Social-Cognitive Theories: Emphasis on Social Learning

Current Trends: The Person in a Social System

- While each of the *process* theories sees different forces at work in personality, all portray personality as the result of both internal mental processes and social interactions.

Using Psychology to Learn Psychology

An external locus of control about grades poses danger for students.

10.4 What "Theories" Do People Use to Understand Themselves and Others?

Implicit Personality Theories

Self-Narratives: The Stories of Our Lives

The Effects of Culture on Our Views of Personality

- Our understanding of ourselves and others is based on implicit theories of personality and our own self-narratives—both of which are influenced by culture.

Developing Your Own Theory of Personality

You'll probably want to be eclectic.

Critical Thinking Applied: **The Person–Situation Controversy**

personality: theories of the whole person

The idea that you are a distinct individual, with a *self* that makes you different from everyone else, is an assumption that people growing up in Europe or America rarely question. Nor do most psychologists realize that the concept of the self took root in psychology in no small part because of a woman who struggled all her life to be recognized as a competent scholar by an academic world that dismissed her because of her gender (Calkins, 1906, 1930; DiFebo, 2002).

Mary Calkins came into psychology through the back door. Wellesley College, where she had been teaching languages, recognized her as an outstanding teacher and offered her a job in the emerging new discipline of psychology, provided she could get some training—a practice not unusual at women's colleges at the time, in the late 1800s. But finding a graduate school that would take a woman was not easy. Harvard was an attractive possibility, especially because the legendary William James wanted her to be his student.

There was only one obstacle: Harvard did not accept women students. Its president, Charles Eliot, strongly believed in separate education for men and women, but

Mary Whiton Calkins, the first woman to become president of the American Psychological Association, never received her PhD, although she earned it.

he relented under pressure from James and other members of the psychology department—only under the condition that Calkins attend classes informally and not be eligible for a degree. (Harvard refused to award doctorates to women until 1963.)

By the spring of 1895, Calkins had finished her course work and had completed ground-breaking research on memory, which became her doctoral dissertation, *Association: An Essay Analytic and Experimental.* The rebellious psychology faculty at Harvard held an unauthorized oral defense of her dissertation and petitioned the board of directors to award her a PhD James praised her performance as "the most brilliant examination for the PhD that we have had at Harvard." But the directors refused. An incensed William James told Calkins that Harvard's action was "enough to make dynamiters of you and all women" (Furumoto, 1979, p. 350).

Despite being denied the doctoral degree she had earned, Mary Calkins returned to Wellesley where, as promised, she was welcomed as a teacher of psychology. A productive scholar as well as a teacher, she eventually published over 100 articles and books, including her best-selling text, *An Introduction to Psychology.* In 1902, she pointedly refused the consolation prize of a PhD from Radcliffe College, a women's institution associated with Harvard. And in 1905, she became the first woman president of the American Psychological Association.

The pattern of persistence and dogged determination seen in Calkins across the 40 years of her professional life illustrates the central idea of this chapter: **Personality** consists of all the psychological qualities and processes that bring continuity to an individual in different situations and at different times. It's a broad concept that we might also describe as the thread of consistency that runs through our lives (Cervone & Shoda, 1999). And should this thread of personality break, it may leave a personality fraught with the inconsistencies that we see, for example, in bipolar disorder, schizophrenia, and so-called "multiple personality" disorder.

CONNECTION • CHAPTER 12

Multiple personality and *split personality* are older terms for dissociative identity disorder.

The puzzle facing the psychologist interested in personality requires fitting together all the diverse pieces that make up the individual. It requires an integration of everything we have studied up till now—learning, perception, development, motivation, emotion, and all the rest—in the attempt to understand the individual as a unified whole. In Chapter 1 we named this the *whole-person perspective.*

In some respects, personality is pretty simple because we are all somewhat alike. We generally prefer pleasure to pain, we seek meaning in our lives, and we often judge ourselves by the standards set by the behavior of others. But beyond such obvious similarities, we are also unique individuals—each unlike anyone else. So personality is also the psychology of *individual differences.*

How does a psychologist go about making sense of personality? Let us illustrate using Mary Calkins as the subject of the problem around which this chapter is organized.

PROBLEM: What influences were at work to produce the unique pattern and consistency that we see in the personality of Mary Calkins?

Was her personality shaped primarily by the people and events in her life? Those events were so often beyond her control that we must consider another possibility—that her strength and determination arose from internal traits—from her basic makeup. You may recognize these two broad alternatives as another variation on the nature–nurture question. The answer, of course, lies with both:

Personality The psychological qualities that bring continuity to an individual's behavior in different situations and at different times.

Experience *and* innate factors shaped Mary Calkins's personality, just as they shape our own.

In this chapter we will examine several theoretical explanations for personality. As we do so, you will find that some theories place more emphasis on nature and others on nurture. You will also find that particular theories are suited to dealing with particular kinds of issues. For example:

- If what you need is a snapshot of a person's current personality characteristics—as you might want if you were screening job applicants for your company—a theory of *temperaments, traits,* or *types* may be your best bet.

- If your goal is to understand someone as a developing, changing being—a friend who asks you for advice, perhaps—you will probably find one of the *psychodynamic, humanistic,* or *social-cognitive theories* of personality most helpful.

- If you are most interested in how people understand each other—as you might be if you were doing marriage counseling or conflict management—you will want to know the assumptions people make about each other. That is, you will want to know their *implicit theories of personality.*

- And, if you are wondering whether people understand each other in the same ways the world around, you will want to know about the *cross-cultural* work in personality, infused throughout the chapter.

We begin our exploration of personality now with an overview of the forces that have shaped us all.

10.1 KEY QUESTION
WHAT FORCES SHAPE OUR PERSONALITIES?

Personality makes us not only human but different from everyone else. Thus, we might think of personality as the "default settings" for our individually unique patterns of motives, emotions, and perceptions, along with our learned schemas for understanding ourselves and our world (see McAdams & Pals, 2006). Personality is also the collective term for the qualities that make us who we are. All of this, in turn, is embedded in the context of our culture, social relationships, and developmental level. In other words, virtually every aspect of our being comes together to form our personality. (See Figure 10.1.) We can capture this idea in our Core Concept for this section.

Personality is shaped by the combined forces of biological, situational, and mental processes—all embedded in a sociocultural and developmental context.

core concept

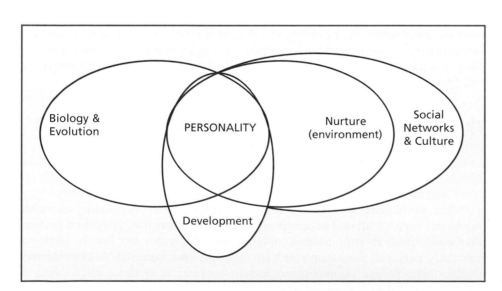

....
FIGURE 10.1
Personality as the Psychology of the Whole Person

We can think of personality as the intersection of all the psychological characteristics and processes that make us both human and, at the same time, different from everyone else.

William James studied conscious-ness and was interested in how the mind functions to guide behavior.

Let's look at each of these elements of personality, beginning with an overview of the forces of biology and evolution.

Biology, Human Nature, and Personality

Put two laboratory rats in a cage and electrify the floor with repeated shocks, and the rats will attack each other. We can see much the same thing in humans, who lash out at any convenient target when they feel threatened. Thus, in the early 20th century, the number of lynchings of blacks in the Southern United States rose and fell in a mirror-image response to the state of the economy—particularly the price of cotton. And more recently in the African nation of Rwanda, two groups of Earth's most unhappy people turned on each other in an astounding bloodbath that left perhaps three-quarters of a million people dead.

These are all examples of what Sigmund Freud called *displacement of aggression.* Sometimes we call it *scapegoating,* after the ancient Hebrew ritual of symbolically transferring the sins of the tribe to a goat that was then driven out into the desert to die. Displacement was also what William James was talking about when he suggested that Harvard's refusal to give Mary Calkins the degree she earned was "enough to make dynamiters of you and all women."

Nothing, of course, can justify mayhem, murder, or genocide—but perhaps we can explain them. According to David Barash (2007), human history is the story of those who responded to painful or threatening situations by striking at the nearest target. Those who did had a clear evolutionary advantage over those who just sat and "took it" because they were less likely to be victims the next time around. They were also more likely to breed and pass along this tendency for aggression and displacement to their descendants.

Displacement of aggression is not the only human characteristic that seems to be built into our biology. As we noted above, most people prefer pleasure to pain—often sexual pleasure. The obvious human propensity for sex and aggression fits with Darwin's idea that we come from a long line of ancestors who were driven to survive and reproduce. Sigmund Freud, picking up this "survival of the fittest" notion, argued that everything we do arises from a sex-based survival "instinct" and an "instinct" for defense and aggression. Other great theorists have proposed that personality is based on still other motives that undoubtedly have some basis in biology—particularly social motives. Much like ants and bees, they have pointed out, we humans are "social animals," too.

Which view is right? Modern neuroscience and evolutionary psychology suggest that the search for only a few basic urges behind all human behavior is wrong-headed (McAdams & Pals, 2006). The emerging picture is a far messier one. We (that is, our brains) seem to be collections of "modules," each adapted to a different purpose—which is the reason that we have so many different motives, each operating by different rules, as we saw in the previous chapter. Sex, aggression, hunger, affiliation, thirst, and achievement: Each is simultaneously a separate module in the brain but also a part of the collective entity we call "personality."

The Effects of Nurture: Personality and the Environment

Biology and evolution can't explain everything. Even the geneticists grudgingly admit that heredity accounts for only roughly half our characteristics (Robins, 2005). The rest, broadly speaking, comes from environment, which molds us according to the principles of behavioral conditioning and cognitive learning.

What environments make the most difference? Many personality theorists emphasize early childhood experiences: From this perspective, your own personality owes much to your parents, not just for their genes but for the environment they gave you (assuming you were raised by your parents). At the extreme, children who receive essentially no human contact, as in those abandoned to

CONNECTION • CHAPTER 3

Environment often affects us through *operant conditioning* and *classical conditioning.*

custodial care in the worst of orphanages, emerge as stunted on virtually every measure of physical and mental well-being (Nelson et al., 2007; Spitz, 1946).

There is some dispute over just how persistent the family environment is as we come under the sway of adolescent peer pressures (Harris, 1995). Yet even birth order seems to influence personality throughout our lives, because the environment for each successive child in a family—from the oldest to the youngest—is different. Were you the first child? If so, you are more likely than your later-born siblings to end up in a career that requires use of your intellect, says development theorist J. Frank Sulloway (1996). Or are you the youngest? Chances are that you are more likely to make people laugh than your more sober older siblings. Incidentally, the high-achieving Mary Calkins, as the first-born of five children in her family, fits the pattern. (We should add that no one believes these patterns *always* hold true; they are merely statistical probabilities.)

So important are environmental influences that Walter Michel has suggested that they usually overwhelm all other effects—including any inborn traits. Just think how often during the day you simply respond to environmental dictates, from the ringing of your alarm clock, to the commands of red traffic lights, to the inquiry, "How are you?" So, is Michel right? We will examine this issue, better known as the *person–situation controversy*, in the Critical Thinking section at the end of the chapter.

The Effects of Nature: Dispositions and Mental Processes

Important as the environment is, we still must pass our experiences through a series of internal mental "filters" that represent core elements of personality. Suppose, for example, that you are an outgoing person—an *extravert*—who loves to be with other people. You will interpret your experiences from your extraverted point of view. The introvert–extravert dimension exemplifies the *descriptive* approach to personality, focusing on an individual's relatively stable *personality characteristics* or **dispositions.** Others that we might call *process theories* go beyond description to explain personality in terms of the internal **personality processes** we have been studying throughout this book: motivation, perception, learning, and development, as well as conscious and unconscious processes. For a complete explanation of personality we seem to need both the *dispositional theories* and *process theories* that we will encounter later in the chapter.

Social and Cultural Contributions to Personality

The very concept of personality theory is a Western (Euro-American) invention, said cross-cultural psychologist Juris Draguns (1979). So it is not surprising that the most comprehensive and influential theories of personality were created by people trained in the framework of the Western social sciences, with a built-in bias toward individualism and a unique "self" (Guisinger & Blatt, 1994; Segall et al., 1999). Other cultures, however, address the problem of differences among people in their own ways. Most of these non-Western perspectives have originated in religion (Walsh, 1984). Hindus, for example, see personality as a union of opposing characteristics (Murphy & Murphy, 1968). The Chinese concept of complementary opposite forces, *yin* and *yang*, provides another variation on this same theme.

But what about the inverse problem? What influence does culture have on personality? We will see that, in a few respects, personality is much the same across cultures. That is, we can describe people all over the world in terms of just a few basic personality traits. For instance, people everywhere vary in their level of anxiety and in their tendency to be outgoing or introverted. But there are also components of personality on which cultures themselves have huge differences. One example involves *individualism* (highly prized in the United States

Disposition Relatively stable personality pattern, including temperaments, traits, and personality types.

Personality process The internal working of the personality, involving motivation, emotion, perception, and learning, as well as unconscious processes.

and other Western countries) versus *collectivism* (a group orientation more valued in Asian societies). People in the United States and other Western countries tend to emphasize **individualism,** which rewards those who stand out from the crowd because of such characteristics as talent, intelligence, or athletic ability. In contrast, people in the more group-oriented cultures of Asia, Africa, Latin America, and the Middle East emphasize **collectivism,** which rewards people for fitting in with the group and promoting social harmony.

And *within* any culture, be it individualistic or collectivistic, social relationships have an enormous impact on personality—as we have noted in neglected children and in those forced to grow up in "tough" neighborhoods. To a large extent, who you are is determined by those with whom you interacted while growing up, including not just your parents but your siblings, classmates, teachers, and perhaps the butcher and baker. Thus, your personality is, in part, a creation of other people—so, in the final section of the chapter, we will look more closely at just how these social and cultural factors shape our personalities.

PSYCHOLOGY**MATTERS**

Explaining Unusual People and Unusual Behavior

You don't need a theory of personality to explain why people generally get to work on time, sing along at concerts, or spend weekends with their family and friends. That is, you don't need a theory of personality to explain why people do what you would expect them to do. But, when they behave in odd and unexpected ways, a personality theory comes in very handy. A good theory can help you understand interesting and unusual people, such as Mary Calkins, or those whom you read about in the newspaper—perhaps a serial killer, a politician embroiled in scandal, or the antics of your favorite movie star.

But which approach to personality is best? Unfortunately, we will see that none has the whole truth. Each theory we cover in this chapter can help you see people from a different angle, so you may need to use several perspectives to get the whole-person picture. To give you a preview of coming attractions, let's suppose that you are a counseling psychologist, working at a college counseling center, and a client, a young woman, tells you that she is contemplating suicide. How can your knowledge of personality help you understand her?

From a purely descriptive point of view, you might assess her personality *traits* and *temperament.* Is she conscientious? Is she outgoing or shy? Anxious? To find out, you might give her one of several personality "tests" that we will talk about in the next section of the chapter. Her profile of traits and temperament may suggest some form of psychological treatment or, perhaps, drug therapy.

If you decide on a psychological therapy, you will be working with the internal *processes* in her personality and, perhaps, social forces at work in her environment and culture. This is the territory originally staked out by Sigmund Freud and his disciples and, more recently, by experimental psychologists.

A *psychodynamic theory* would direct your focus toward her motives and emotions, some of which may be unconscious. Is she a hostile person who has turned her hostility on herself? Does she have some unfinished emotional business from an earlier developmental stage, such as guilt for angry feelings toward her parents? Does she have "neurotic" goals? What is the nature of her social relationships?

In contrast, a *humanistic theory* would emphasize the exploration of her potentialities rather than of her deficiencies. What are her talents? Her hopes and desires? And what obstacles stand between her and her goals? A humanistic theory would also help you explore her unmet needs. Do her suicidal thoughts result from conscious feelings that she is alone, unloved, or not respected?

A *social-cognitive theory,* with its emphasis on perception and learning, might suggest that her difficulty lies in the way she interprets events. Does she always assume that her best efforts are not good enough? Does she believe that she can

A theory of personality is helpful in understanding unusual personalities.

Individualism The view, common in the Euro-American world, that places a high value on individual achievement and distinction.

Collectivism The view, common in Asia, Africa, Latin America, and the Middle East, that values group loyalty and pride over individual distinction.

control the events in her life, or do events control her? A cognitive approach might also alert you to the possibility that her suicidal thoughts reflect a suicidal role model—perhaps a friend or a family member.

All of these approaches to personality will be explored in detail later in the chapter. For now, here is the take-away message: No one theory has a complete answer to the problem of understanding why people do what they do. The trait and temperament theories can provide a descriptive snapshot of a person's characteristics, while the "process" theories describe the forces that underlie those characteristics. In the case of the suicidal young woman we described, some combination of both is in order.

CheckYourUnderstanding

1. RECALL: The fact that displacement of aggression is found in humans everywhere, as well as in animals, suggests that it is rooted in _____.

2. APPLICATION: Give an example that shows the influence of nurture on personality.

3. ANALYSIS: What is the distinction between the *dispositional* theories and the *process* theories of personality?

4. RECALL: A person from a collectivist culture is more likely than one from an individualist culture to emphasize _____.

5. UNDERSTANDING THE CORE CONCEPT: What are the major factors that affect the formation of the personality?

10.2 KEY QUESTION
WHAT PERSISTENT PATTERNS, OR *DISPOSITIONS*, MAKE UP OUR PERSONALITIES?

Two thousand years before academic psychology appeared, people were classifying each other according to four *temperaments*, based on a theory proposed by the Greek physician Hippocrates *(Hip-POCK-rah-tees)*. A person's temperament, he suggested, resulted from the balance of the four **humors,** or fluids, secreted by the body. (See Figure 10.2.) A *sanguine*, or cheerful, person was characterized by strong, warm blood. A *choleric* temperament, marked by anger, came from yellow bile (called *choler*), believed to flow from the liver. Hippocrates thought that the liver also produced black bile, from which arose a *melancholic*, or depressed, temperament. Finally, if the body's dominant fluid is phlegm, or mucus, the person will have a *phlegmatic* temperament: cool, aloof, slow, and unemotional. Hippocrates' biology may have been a little off the mark, but his notion of temperaments established itself as "common sense." Even today you will occasionally encounter his terms used to describe people's personalities.

In modern times, other personality classification systems have appeared. The most simplistic ones are just stereotypes: If fat, then jolly; if an engineer, then conservative; if female, then sympathetic. Obviously, these beliefs oversimplify the very complicated problem of understanding the patterns found in personality. Even you may be guilty of such oversimplifications, if you think of people strictly according to categories and stereotypes: college major, gender, ethnicity, and qualities such as honesty, shyness, or sense of humor.

Still, something in human nature seems to encourage us to group people in categories. So, some personality theorists have sought to describe people in terms

Hippocrates was an early contributor to the idea of a mind–body connection. One of his beliefs was that our individual temperament is driven by our predominant body fluid, or humor, *and could be either* sanguine, choleric, melancholic, *or* phlegmatic.

Humors Four body fluids—blood, phlegm, black bile, and yellow bile—that, according to an ancient theory, control personality by their relative abundance.

FIGURE 10.2
The Humor Theory

The Humor Theory		
Humors	**Source**	**Temperament**
blood	heart	sanguine (cheerful)
choler (yellow bile)	liver	choleric (angry)
melancholer (black bile)	spleen	melancholy (depressed)
phlegm	brain	phlegmatic (sluggish)

of just a few basic *temperaments:* global dispositions of personality, such as "outgoing" or "shy," that have a strong biological basis. Others prefer to look for combinations of *traits,* which are generally thought of as multiple dimensions of personality, such as cautious versus reckless or friendly versus unfriendly, which are usually considered more influenced by experience (learning) than are temperaments. Still others classify people according to personality *types,* which are categories, rather than dimensions: You either fit the pattern for a type, or you do not. For example, if introversion is a *trait dimension,* then people can have degrees of introversion. On the other hand, if introversion is a *type,* then people are classified as either being introverted or not.

While each of these approaches is a bit different, our Core Concept indicates that they also have a common meeting ground:

core
concept

> The *dispositional* theories all suggest a small set of personality characteristics, known as temperaments, traits, or types, that provide consistency to the individual's personality over time.

Because the terms *temperament, trait,* and *type* overlap, we will follow the custom of placing them all under the generic heading of a **dispositional theories.** But what makes such theories different from mere stereotypes—the conservative engineer, the macho male, or the dismal economics professor? It's all in the science. A good temperament, trait, or type theory must have a solid scientific base. In that light, let's evaluate each of these approaches to personality, beginning with *temperament.*

Personality and Temperament

Psychologists define *temperament* as the biologically based personality dispositions that are usually apparent in early childhood and that establish the foundation of the personality and the mood of an individual's approach to life (Hogan et al., 1996; Mischel, 1993). When speaking of temperaments, psychologists are usually referring to one or two dominant and long-standing themes, such as shyness or moodiness, that characterize a person's personality, perhaps from birth. Modern psychology has, of course, abandoned the four humors theory of temperament, but it has retained its most basic concept: *Biological dispositions do affect our basic personalities.* In support of this view, psychologists can now point to structures in the brain that are known to regulate fundamental aspects of personality (LeDoux, 2002). You will recall, for example, the case of Phineas Gage, who received an accidental "lobotomy" and thereby demonstrated the role of the frontal lobes in regulating one's basic disposition—an observation confirmed by modern neuroscience.

Dispositional theory   A general term that includes the temperament, trait, and type approaches to personality.

Temperament from Transmitters?   Biological psychologists now suspect that some individual differences in temperament also arise from the balance of chemicals in the brain, which may, in turn, have a genetic basis (Azar, 2002b; Sapolsky, 1992). In this sense, the theory of humors still lives but in a different guise: Modern biological psychology has replaced the humors with neurotransmitters. So, depression—which characterizes most suicidal people—may result from an imbalance of certain transmitters. Likewise, anxiety, anger, and euphoria may each arise from other neurochemical patterns. As developmental psychologist Jerome Kagan says (in Stavish, 1994), "We all have the same neurotransmitters, but each of us has a slightly different mix" (p. 7). That, says Kagan, is what accounts for many of the temperamental differences among people.

In fact, Kagan runs a fascinating research program focusing on the inherited basis of shyness (Kagan, 2005; Kagan et al., 1994). This program has clearly demonstrated that, on their very first day, newborns already differ in the degree to which they are responsive to stimulation. About 20% of all children are highly responsive and excitable, while approximately twice as many (35 to 40%) remain calm in response to new stimulation. Over their first few months of life, these initial differences manifest themselves in temperamental differences: Most of the excitable children become shy and introverted, while the less excitable ones become extraverted. Although these tendencies change in some children, for most they persist over time, with the majority of children being classified with the same temperament in measurements taken over an 11-year interval.

Some shyness is inherited, and some is learned through experience.

Tempered with a Bit of Learning?

On the other hand, we know that the percentage of shy college-age students—40% or more—is much higher than the percentage of shy children (Zimbardo, 1990). It is thus reasonable to assume that some shyness is inherited, while even more is learned through negative experiences in one's social life. It is also the case that if a child is withdrawn, startles easily, is unlikely to smile, and is fearful of both strangers and novelty, then that child will create an environment that is not friendly, playful, or supportive. In this way, heredity and environment interact, with initially inherited characteristics becoming amplified—or perhaps muted—over time, because they produce social signals telling others to either approach or stay away.

So does biology determine your destiny? An inherited temperament may set the *range* of your responses to some life situations. However, temperament by itself does not fully determine your life experiences (Kagan & Snidman, 1998). Even among your biological relatives, your unique family position, experiences, and sense of self guarantee that your personality pattern is unlike that of anyone else (Bouchard et al., 1990).

Personality as a Composite of Traits

If you were to describe a friend, you will probably use the language of *traits:* moody, cheerful, melancholy, enthusiastic, volatile, friendly, or smart. **Traits** are multiple, stable personality characteristics that are presumed to exist within the individual and guide his or her thoughts and actions under various conditions. We might think of traits as the product of hidden psychological processes—the way our motives, emotions, and cognitions are customarily expressed in behavior (Winter et al., 1998).

How do traits differ from temperament? Think of temperament as the foundation of personality, deeply rooted in our individual biological nature. Then think of traits as a multidimensional structure built on the foundation of temperament but also influenced by experience.

The "Big Five" Traits: The Five-Factor Theory

Trait theorists focus primarily on the motivational and emotional components of personality, excluding other attributes such as IQ and creativity. With the mathematical tool of *factor analysis* (which helps them look for relationships, or clusters, among personality test items), investigators have identified five dominant personality factors. Personality theorists

Traits Multiple stable personality characteristics that are presumed to exist within the individual and guide his or her thoughts and actions under various conditions.

often call these the *Big Five* (Carver & Scheier, 2008; John & Srivastava, 1999). As yet, we have no universally accepted names for these five factors, although the italicized term in the list below are widely used.

You will note that, although we give each trait a single label, the Big Five traits are really *bipolar dimensions*. That is, they exist on a continuum, with most people falling somewhere between the extremes—near the middle of the continuum—on most of these dimensions. (In parenthesis below, we list the name of the opposite end of the dimension for each trait.)

● *Openness to experience*, also called inquiring intellect, curiosity, independence (at the opposite pole: closed-mindedness, low curiosity, unimaginative).

● *Conscientiousness*, also called dependability, goal-directedness, perseverance, superego strength, prudence, or constraint (at the opposite pole: impulsiveness, carelessness, or irresponsibility).

● *Extraversion*, also called social adaptability, assertiveness, sociability, boldness, or self-confidence (at the opposite pole: introversion, shyness).

● *Agreeableness*, also called warmth and likeability, with those on this end of the continuum taking a prosocial approach to others (at the opposite pole: coldness, negativity, or antagonism).

● *Neuroticism*, also called anxiety or emotionality (at the opposite pole: emotional stability or emotional control).

Here's an aid to remembering these five trait dimensions: Think of the acronym *OCEAN*, standing for Openness, Conscientiousness, Extraversion, Agreeableness, and Neuroticism.

As you ponder this **five-factor theory,** it is important to realize that no score is necessarily "good" or "bad." While our culture tends to value extroversion over introversion, either one can be adaptive, depending on the social and cultural situation. Thus, introversion may be a desirable trait for a writer, while extraversion may be preferred in a sales manager. Similarly, we value conscientiousness, openness, agreeableness, and emotional stability, but scoring on the "lower" end of each of these isn't necessarily a bad thing. For example, for a creative person, the tendency to follow one's own beliefs and not be unduly swayed by others (lower agreeableness) is beneficial. Similarly, too much conscientiousness probably limits one's ability to take advantage of unexpected opportunities, and too much openness could lead a person to be a "Jack (or Jill) of all trades," and master of none. Rather than making judgments about what traits we "should" possess, it is better to capitalize on the traits we have and find an environment that offers a good fit.

The five-factor theory greatly simplifies a formerly confusing picture. Although debate still continues about the details, a broad coalition of theorists has now concluded that we can describe people with reasonable accuracy on just these five dimensions—quite an achievement, in view of the several hundred trait terms one can find listed in the dictionary (Allport & Odbert, 1936)! Significantly, the five-factor model also seems to have validity across cultures, with several large studies demonstrating that the five-factor model works in more than 50 cultures in Europe, Asia, Africa, and the Americas (McCrae et al., 2005; Schmitt et al., 2007).

Assessing Traits with Personality Inventories   If you were a clinical or counseling psychologist, you might want to assess a client's personality on the five factors, using a paper-and-pencil instrument such as the *NEO Personality Inventory* (or *NEO-PI*).[1] This simple but highly respected measure has been used to study

Five-factor theory   A trait perspective suggesting that personality is composed of five fundamental personality dimensions (also known as the Big Five): openness to experience, conscientiousness, extraversion, agreeableness, and neuroticism.

---

[1]NEO stands for neuroticism, extraversion, and openness. Conscientiousness and agreeableness were added later, but the name, *NEO Personality Inventory,* was not changed.

	Strongly disagree	Disagree somewhat	Neither agree nor disagree	Agree somewhat	Strongly agree
1. I am a talkative person.	O	O	O	O	O
2. I often feel shy.	O	O	O	O	O
3. I am usually full of energy.	O	O	O	O	O
4. I worry a lot.	O	O	O	O	O
5. I am inventive.	O	O	O	O	O
6. I have no artistic interests.	O	O	O	O	O
7. I like new challenges and experiences.	O	O	O	O	O
8. I see myself as reliable.	O	O	O	O	O
9. I like to be with people.	O	O	O	O	O
10. I can remain calm in difficult situations.	O	O	O	O	O

FIGURE 10.3

Sample Five-Factor Personality Inventory Items

An instrument measuring the Big Five personality traits might ask you to indicate how much you agree or disagree with each statement by checking the circle under the appropriate point on the scale. There are no right or wrong answers.

personality stability across the lifespan and also the relationship of personality characteristics to physical health and various life events. (See Figure 10.3.)

If, however, you want an instrument that measures clinical traits—that is, signs of mental disorder—the *Minnesota Multiphasic Personality Inventory,* usually referred to as the **MMPI-2,** is a good bet. (The "2" means it is a revised form of the original *MMPI.*) Unlike the *NEO-PI,* the *MMPI-2* does not measure the Big Five personality dimensions. Rather, its ten clinical scales (shown in Table 10.1) were developed to assess serious mental problems, such as depression, schizophrenia, and paranoia (Helmes & Reddon, 1993). Its 567 items deal with a variety of attitudes, habits, fears, preferences, physical health, beliefs, and general outlook. We won't compromise the actual test items, but here are some true-false statements, similar to those on the *MMPI-2:*

● I am often bothered by thoughts about sex.

● Sometimes I like to stir up some excitement.

● If people had not judged me unfairly, I would have been far more successful.

Respondents are asked to indicate whether each statement describes them, and their answers are compared against responses of people clinical populations with known mental disorders. Thus, the scoring is *empirically* based—that is, it is based on scientific data, rather than just opinion.

TABLE 10.1 *MMPI-2* Clinical Scales

Hypochondriasis (Hs): Abnormal concern with bodily functions

Depression (D): Pessimism; hopelessness; slowing of action and thought

Conversion hysteria (Hy): Unconscious use of mental problems to avoid conflicts or responsibility

Psychopathic deviate (Pd): Disregard for social custom; shallow emotions; inability to profit from experience

Masculinity–femininity (Mf): Differences between men and women

Paranoia (Pa): Suspiciousness; delusions of grandeur or persecution

Psychasthenia (Pt): Obsessions; compulsions; fears; low self-esteem; guilt; indecisiveness

Schizophrenia (Sc): Bizarre, unusual thoughts or behavior; withdrawal; hallucinations; delusions

Hypomania (Ma): Emotional excitement; flight of ideas; overactivity

Social introversion (Si): Shyness; disinterest in others; insecurity

MMPI-2 A widely used personality assessment instrument that gives scores on ten important clinical traits. Also called the *Minnesota Multiphasic Personality Inventory.*

People who take personality inventories such as the *MMPI-2* often agonize over their answers to particular questions, concerned that a "wrong" answer might lead to being diagnosed as mentally disturbed. Not to worry! Personality profiles derived from *MMPI-2* responses are *never* based on a single item—or even two or three. Rather, each item merely makes a weighted contribution to one or more of the scales.

Could you fake a good or bad score on the *MMPI-2?* Probably not. The test has four cleverly designed "lie" scales that signal something amiss when they pick up too many unusual responses. Here are some items similar to those on the lie scales:

- Sometimes I put off doing things I know I ought to do.
- On occasion I have passed on some gossip.
- Once in a while, I find a dirty joke amusing.

Too many attempts to make yourself look good or bad will elevate your lie scale scores into the questionable range.

From a scientific standpoint, the *MMPI-2* and the *NEO-PI* are exemplary instruments—for two reasons. First, they have excellent **reliability.** This means that they provide consistent and stable scores. So, when a person takes the same test on two different occasions, the scores are likely to be much the same. In fact, any usable test must have good reliability; otherwise the scores would be erratic and undependable.

Second, the *MMPI-2* and the *NEO-PI* have good **validity**—which means that they actually measure what they were designed to measure—e.g., personality traits or signs of mental disturbance. The *MMPI-2* does a credible job, for example, of identifying depressed or psychotic persons (Greene, 1991)—although it must be used with care in non-Western cultures because it is not clear that its validity holds when the instrument has been translated into other languages (Dana, 1993). Moreover, some observers suggest that some items may have culture-specific content (Golden & Figueroa, 2007). Clinicians should also exercise caution when giving personality inventories to members of ethnic minorities in the United States, because minority groups are not always well represented in the samples used in developing the test (Butcher & Williams, 1992; Graham, 1990).

Evaluating the Temperament and Trait Theories   Several criticisms have been leveled at the temperament and trait theories and the tests they have spawned. For one, these theories give us a "snapshot" of personality—a picture that portrays personality as fixed and static, rather than as a dynamic process that can undergo developmental changes, depending on our experience. Another criticism says that they oversimplify our complex natures by describing personality on just a few dimensions. What would we gain, for example, by finding that Mary Calkins scored high on traits such as conscientiousness or and dominance but low on agreeableness? While such judgments might validate our observations, labels leave out important detail.

On the positive side, trait theories give us some ability to *predict* behavior in common situations, such as work settings—to select employees who are well suited to the job and to screen out those who might cause problems. Moreover, the Big Five traits really do predict most of the things that truly matter to most of us, including health, academic success, and success in our interpersonal relationships—and with accuracy comparable to that of many diagnostic tests used in medicine (Robins, 2005).

But in the end, trait theories suffer from one of the same problems as the old instinct theories. Both *describe* behavior with a label but do not *explain* it. For example, we can attribute depression to a depressive trait or an outgoing personality to extraversion without really understanding the behavior. In short, trait theories identify common traits, but they do not tell us much about their source

Reliability   An attribute of a psychological test that gives consistent results.

Validity   An attribute of a psychological test that actually measures what it is being used to measure.

or how traits interact (McAdams, 1992; Pervin, 1985). Moreover, because most people display a trait only to a moderate degree, we must ask how useful traits are for understanding all but the extreme cases.

Finally, with trait theory we again encounter the problem of the *self-fulfilling prophecy*. When given trait labels, people may be influenced by the expectations implied by those labels, making it difficult for them to change undesirable behavior. A child labeled "shy," for example, may have to struggle against both the label and the trait.

CONNECTION • CHAPTER 5
The original *self-fulfilling prophecy* in psychology involved an experiment in which students' academic performance was altered by manipulating teachers' expectations.

Personality Disorders

Disorders of personality account for the quirkiness of many historical and public figures, including the much-married King Henry VIII; the late Enron executive Ken Lay, perpetrator of massive financial shenanigans; and the fatal femme Lizzie Borden, who famously dispatched her parents with a hatchet. The **personality disorders** show themselves in chronic patterns of poor judgment, disordered thinking, emotional disturbances, disrupted social relationships, or lack of impulse control. The key element is a maladaptive personality pattern of long standing. Here we consider three of the better known such conditions: *narcissistic personality disorder, antisocial personality disorder,* and *borderline personality disorder.*

Narcissistic Personality Disorder
If one believes the entertainment tabloids, narcisstic personalities are common in the film and recording industries. People with *narcissistic personality disorder* display an exaggerated sense of self-importance, a need for constant attention or admiration, and often a preoccupation with fantasies of success or power. They may respond inappropriately to criticism or minor defeat, either by acting indifferent or by overreacting. They usually have problems in interpersonal relationships, feel entitled to favors without obligations, exploit others selfishly, and have difficulty understanding how others feel.

Antisocial Personality Disorder
Everyone from ruthless executives to serial killers is a candidate for this category, which includes those with a long-standing pattern of irresponsible or harmful behavior. Persons with *antisocial personality disorder* seem to lack conscience or a sense of responsibility to others. Characteristically, their violations of social norms begin early in their lives—disrupting class, getting into fights, and running away from home. This pattern may progress to acts of cruelty and wanton disregard for others, such as abusing animals or setting fires. Other common signs of antisocial personality disorder include chronic lying and stealing. And, even though people with antisocial personalities may frequently find themselves in trouble, they may not experience anxiety, shame, or any other sort of intense emotion. Often, in fact, they can "keep cool" in situations that would arouse and upset normal people. Those who show a violent or criminal pattern of antisocial personality disorder, such as committing murders and other serious crimes, are popularly referred to as "psychopaths" or "sociopaths."

Although we may expect to find antisocial personalities among street criminals and con artists, they are also well represented among successful politicians and businesspeople who put career, money, and power above everything and everyone (Babiak & Hare, 2006). People with antisocial personalities are often charming and intelligent, and they use these characteristics to their advantage by manipulating others and taking advantage of people's tendency to be trusting. These same characteristics also help them avoid getting caught for long periods of time—and when they do get caught, they are often able to charm, lie, or manipulate their way out of trouble. As many as 3% of the population in the United States may exhibit this pattern, with men being four times more likely to be so diagnosed than women (Regier et al., 1988, 1993).

Borderline Personality Disorder
A third form of personality disorder, *borderline personality disorder* manifests itself as instability and impulsivity

Personality disorder Condition involving a chronic, pervasive, inflexible, and maladaptive pattern of thinking, emotion, social relationships, or impulse control.

(Carson et al., 2000; Holmes, 2001). People with this diagnosis have unpredictable moods and stormy interpersonal relationships, often becoming upset and abusive in response to perceived slights. They also have little tolerance for frustration. Their impulsivity may be seen in a tendency for substance abuse, gambling, sexual promiscuity, binge eating, reckless driving, self-mutilation, or suicide attempts. As with the other personality disorders, the treatment outlook for borderline personality disorder is guarded.

PSYCHOLOGYMATTERS
Finding Your Type

Do you fancy yourself an introvert or an extravert? Emotionally stable or excitable? Dependable or irresponsible? Modern trait theory assumes that you could fall anywhere between these extremes, while the older notion of **personality types** puts people in distinct categories. Which view—trait or type—more accurately captures human nature? To find out, let's perform a critical examination of the most widely used instrument for assessing personality types, the *Myers–Briggs Type Indicator (MBTI)*. Because the *Myers–Briggs* derives from the personality types found in Carl Jung's theory, this discussion will also serve as a bridge to the next section of the chapter, where we will study Jung's theory, as well as other classical theories of personality, in detail.

Uses of the *MBTI* Chances are you have taken the *Myers–Briggs Type Indicator,* because it is given to some two million people each year, often at self-awareness workshops and team-building business seminars (Druckman & Bjork, 1991). In the business world, consultants commonly use the *MBTI* in management training sessions to convey the message that people have distinct personality patterns that suit them for specific kinds of jobs. In college counseling centers, students may be advised to select a career that fits with their personality type, as revealed on the *MBTI*. It also finds a use in relationship counseling, where couples are taught to accommodate to each other's personality types.

On the Myers–Briggs test, examinees answer a series of questions about how they make judgments, perceive the world, and relate to others (Myers & Myers, 1995). Based on these responses, a scoring system assigns an individual to a four-dimensional personality type, derived from the Jungian dimensions of Introversion–Extraversion, Thinking–Feeling, Sensation–Intuition, and Judgment–Perception.

What Does Research on the *MBTI* Tell Us about Personality Types?
Remember that a *reliable* test gives consistent results, as when a person takes the same test repeatedly. Unfortunately, the reliability of the *MBTI* is questionable. One study, for example, found that fewer than half of those tested on the *MBTI* had the same type when retested five weeks later (McCarley & Carskadon, 1983). Another study found a change in at least one of the four type categories in about 75% of respondents (see Druckman & Bjork, 1991). Such results certainly raise questions about the fundamental concept of "type."

A second issue concerns the *validity* of the *Myers–Briggs* test. We have said that a valid test actually measures what it is being used to measure. And again the research on the *MBTI* gives a mixed picture (Druckman & Bjork, 1991). The data fail to show that the *MBTI* truly identifies distinct personality *types* (Furnham et al., 2003). In fact, it is much more consistent with the concept of *traits*—that is, the idea that different people have different degrees of a characteristic—rather than the *type* notion of either having it or not. Thus, the idea that people are distributed all along the introversion–extraversion continuum fits the evidence better than the approach, encouraged by the *Myers–Briggs,* of simply lumping people in one category or the other.

Personality type Similar to a trait, but instead of being a *dimension,* a type is a *category* that is believed to represent a common cluster of personality characteristics.

Myers–Briggs Type Indicator (MBTI) A widely used personality test based on Jungian types.

As for identifying personality patterns associated with particular occupations, the evidence is also shaky. True enough, people who work with people—entertainers, counselors, managers, and sellers—tend to score higher on extraversion. By comparison, librarians, computer specialists, and physicians number many introverts in their ranks. The danger lies, however, in turning averages into stereotypes. In fact, the data show a diversity of types within occupations. Further, we find a conspicuous lack of evidence documenting a relationship between personality type and occupational success: There is no basis for the idea that having a particular personality type makes you better suited for a particular career. Although proponents of the *MBTI* claim it to be useful in vocational counseling, a review of the literature by a team from the National Academy of Sciences found no relationship between personality type, as revealed by the *MBTI*, and performance on a particular job (Druckman & Bjork, 1991). This report has, however, been hotly disputed by users of the instrument (Pearman, 1991). But overall, we can say that the *Myers–Briggs Type Indicator* has not proved to have the validity or reliability needed as the basis for making important life decisions. Says the National Academy of Sciences Report (Druckman & Bjork, 1991), "Lacking such evidence, it is a curiosity why the instrument is used so widely" (p. 99).

So, what can we conclude on the issue of traits versus types? The fact that people commonly score all along each dimension strongly favors the concept of *traits* that people have in varying amounts, rather than the discrete yes/no categories of *type*. As evolution scholar Stephen Jay Gould remarked, "The world does not come to us in neat little packages" (1996, p. 188).

CheckYourUnderstanding

1. **RECALL:** Jerome Kagan has suggested that the biological basis for different temperaments may come from each person's unique mix of _____.

2. **APPLICATION:** A friend of yours always seems agitated and anxious, even when nothing in the circumstances would provoke such a response. Which one of the Big Five traits seems to describe this characteristic of your friend?

3. **RECALL:** The *MMPI-2* does not assess conventional traits. Instead, its ten clinical scales assess _____.

4. **RECALL:** A pattern of stormy relationships and impulsive behavior is characteristic of which personality disorder?

5. **ANALYSIS:** If you were using a *trait theory*, you would

assess people _____; but if you were using a *type theory*, you would assess people _____.
   a. clinically / experimentally
   b. according to their behavior / according to their mental processes
   c. on their positive characteristics / on their negative characteristics
   d. on dimensions / in categories

6. **UNDERSTANDING THE CORE CONCEPT:** Temperament, trait, and type theories describe the differences among people in terms of _____ but not _____.
   a. personality characteristics/personality processes
   b. mental disorders/mental health
   c. nature/nurture
   d. conscious processes/unconscious processes

Answers 1. neurotransmitters 2. neuroticism 3. tendencies toward serious mental problems 4. borderline personality disorder 5. d 6. a

10.3 KEY QUESTION
WHAT MENTAL *PROCESSES* ARE AT WORK WITHIN OUR PERSONALITIES?

On January 31, 2006, Ken Lay and his cohort Jeffrey Skilling were convicted on massive securities fraud charges that involved billions of dollars in illegal "insider" stock trading and the bankruptcy of a company known as Enron. Not only was Enron's financial meltdown the biggest bankruptcy case in U.S. history, it cost about 20,000 Enron employees their jobs. Many lost their life savings in company stock that Lay encouraged them to buy, even as he was dumping his own.

Why did Lay do it? Greed is the obvious answer, along with egotism and not a little ruthlessness. But these traits do little to explain the *why* of Ken Lay. What was going on within the man that channeled his brilliance (he had a PhD in economics and a highly successful career both in government and in the boardroom) into such nasty actions? We will use Lay's case, along with that of Mary Calkins, to illustrate various theories of personality throughout the rest of the chapter.

To understand the psychological forces underlying both Lay's and Calkins's traits, we turn to theories that look at the *processes* that shape people's personalities. Specifically, we will consider three kinds of "process" theories: the *psychodynamic,* the *humanistic,* and the *cognitive theories.* What do they have in common? Our Core Concept says:

core concept

While each of the *process* theories sees different forces at work in personality, all portray personality as the result of both internal mental processes and social interactions.

Although the three viewpoints we will consider in this section of the chapter—the *psychodynamic, humanistic,* and *social-cognitive* theories—share some common ground, each emphasizes a different combination of factors. The **psychodynamic theories** call attention to motivation, especially unconscious motives, and the influence of past experiences on our mental health. **Humanistic theories** emphasize consciousness and our present, subjective reality: what we believe is important now and how we think of ourselves in relation to others. And the **social-cognitive theories** describe the influence of learning, perception, and social interaction on behavior.

Psychodynamic Theories: Emphasis on Motivation and Mental Disorder

The psychodynamic approach originated in the late 1800s with a medical puzzle called *hysteria,* now known as *conversion disorder.* In patients with this condition, the physician sees physical symptoms, such as a muscle weakness, loss of sensation in a part of the body, or even a paralysis—but no apparent physical cause, such as nerve damage. The psychological nature of hysteria finally became

Psychodynamic theory A group of theories that originated with Freud. All emphasize motivation—often unconscious motivation—and the influence of the past on the development of mental disorders.

Humanistic theories A group of personality theories that focus on human growth and potential, rather than on mental disorder. All emphasize the functioning of the individual in the present, rather than on the influence of past events.

Social-cognitive theories A group of theories that involve explanations of limited, but important, aspects of personality (e.g., locus of control). All grew out of experimental psychology.

French physician Jean Charcot showed that he could temporarily eliminate symptoms of hysteria in patients who were hypnotized. Young Sigmund Freud found inspiration in Charcot's demonstrations.

apparent when the French physician Jean Charcot (pronounced *Shar-COE*) demonstrated that he could make hysterical symptoms disappear by suggestion—while his patients were in a hypnotic trance.

Freud and Psychoanalysis   Hearing of Charcot's work, the young and curious doctor Sigmund Freud (1856–1939) traveled to Paris to observe Charcot's renowned hypnotic demonstrations for himself. Inspired by what he saw, Freud returned to Vienna, resolving to try the hypnotic cure on his own patients. But to his dismay, Dr. Freud found that he could not hypnotize many of them deeply enough to duplicate Charcot's results. Moreover, even the ones who lost their symptoms under hypnosis usually regained them after the trance was lifted. Finally, a frustrated Freud resolved to find another way to understand and treat the mysterious illness. The result was the first comprehensive theory of personality—and still a standard by which all others are compared.

The new approach Freud created became known as **psychoanalysis** or **psychoanalytic theory**. Technically, *psychoanalytic theory* is the term for Freud's explanation of personality and mental disorder, while *psychoanalysis* refers to his system of treatment for mental disorder. In practice, however, it has always been difficult to separate Freud's theory from his therapeutic procedures. Thus the term *psychoanalysis* is often used to refer to both (Carver & Scheier, 2008).

As you study Freud's theory, you may find some points on which you agree and others on which you disagree. We recommend bringing all your critical thinking skills to bear, but at the same time you should maintain a respect for Freud and the task he faced, over 100 years ago, as the first great explainer of human personality.

The Freudian Unconscious   At center stage in personality, Freud placed the **unconscious**, the mind's hidden, seething cauldron of powerful impulses, instincts, motives, and conflicts that energize the personality. We normally have no awareness of this hidden psychic territory, said Freud, because its contents are so threatening and anxiety provoking that the conscious mind refuses to acknowledge its existence, even in the healthiest of us. Only by using the special techniques of psychoanalysis can a therapist find, for example, that a person who had been sexually molested in childhood still holds these festering memories in the unconscious. We glimpse such memories when they attempt to escape from the unconscious, disguised perhaps as a dream or as a symptom of mental disorder, such as depression or a phobia. So, mentally healthy or not, we go about our daily business without knowing the real motives behind our behavior.

Unconscious Drives and Instincts   Freud taught that the turbulent processes in the unconscious mind are fueled by psychological energy from our most basic and secret motives, drives, and desires—the mental equivalent of steam in a boiler. Psychoanalytic theory, then, explains how this mental "steam" is transformed and expressed in disguised form in our conscious thoughts and behavior.

The unconscious sex drive, which Freud named *Eros*, after the Greek god of passionate love, could be expressed either directly through sexual activity or indirectly through such releases as joking, work, or creative pursuits. (Perhaps you had never thought of activities like dancing, drawing, cooking, studying, or body building as sexual acts—but Freud did!) The energy produced by Eros he termed **libido**, from the Latin word for "lust." Libidinal energy, in turn, fuels the rest of the personality.

But Eros and its libidinal energy did not explain everything that fascinated Freud. Specifically, it did not explain acts of human aggression and destruction. Nor did it explain the symptoms of the war veterans who continued to relive their wartime traumas in nightmares and hallucinations. Such misery could only be accounted for by another drive, which he named *Thanatos* (from the Greek word for "death"). Freud conceived of Thanatos as the unconscious "death instinct"

Psychoanalysis   A method of treating mental disorders that is based on Sigmund Freud's psychoanalytic theory. The goal of psychoanalysis is to release unacknowledged conflicts, urges, and memories from the unconscious. (In common usage, the term often refers broadly both to Freud's psychoanalytic theory and to his psychoanalytic treatment method.)

Psychoanalytic theory   Freud's theory of personality and mental disorder.

Unconscious   In Freudian theory, this is the psychic domain of which the individual is not aware but that is the storehouse of repressed impulses, drives, and conflicts unavailable to consciousness.

Libido   The Freudian concept of psychic energy that drives individuals to experience sensual pleasure.

CONNECTION • CHAPTER 4
False memory experiments by Elizabeth Loftus and others have raised serious questions about memories of abuse recovered during therapy.

Sigmund Freud is seen here walking with his daughter Anna Freud, who later became a psychoanalyst in her own right.

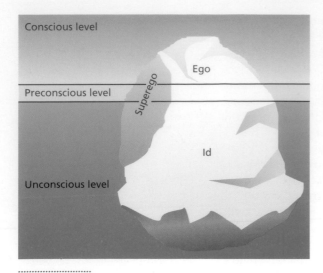

Conscious level

Preconscious level

Unconscious level

Ego

Superego

Id

FIGURE 10.4
Freud's Model of the Mind

In another famous metaphor, Freud likened the mind to an iceberg because only a small portion appears "above the surface"—in consciousness. Meanwhile, the vast unconscious mind lurks "beneath the surface" of our awareness.

Id The primitive, unconscious portion of the personality that houses the most basic drives and stores repressed memories.

Superego The mind's storehouse of values, including moral attitudes learned from parents and from society; roughly the same as the common notion of the conscience.

Ego The conscious, rational part of the personality, charged with keeping peace between the superego and the id.

Psychosexual stages Successive, instinctive developmental phases in which pleasure is associated with stimulation of different bodily areas at different times of life.

During the phallic stage, said Freud, a child must resolve feelings of conflict and anxiety by identifying more closely with the same-sex parent.

that drives the aggressive and destructive acts that humans commit against each other and even against themselves. (Think of smoking, compulsive gambling, reckless driving, or drug abuse.) We can guess that Freud would have attributed the unexpected death of Enron executive Ken Lay, shortly after his conviction for fraud and perjury, to a Thanatos that Lay could no longer control.

The Structure of the Personality Freud pictured the personality as a trinity composed of the *ego,* the *id,* and the *superego,* which together form a mind continually at war within itself. He believed that the sexual and aggressive forces of the id wage a continuing battle against the moralistic forces of the superego. The ever-practical ego serves as the moderator of this conflict. (Figure 10.4 represents the three parts of the personality pictorially.)

The Id: Source of Energy for the Personality Freud conceived of the **id** as the primitive, unconscious reservoir that contains the basic motives, drives, and instinctive desires—including Eros and Thanatos—that energize all three parts of the personality. Like a child, the id always acts on impulse and pushes for immediate gratification—especially sexual, physical, and emotional pleasures—to be experienced here and now without concern for consequences.

The Superego: Conscience and the Ego Ideal By contrast, the superego serves as the mind's parental avatars—virtual "parents" living in the mind—in charge of values and morals learned from parents, teachers, other authority figures, and from society. The **superego** corresponds roughly to our common notion of "conscience." It develops as the child forms an internal set of rules based on the external rules imposed by parents and other adults. And it is the inner voice of "shoulds" and "should nots." The superego also includes the *ego ideal,* an individual's view of the kind of person he or she should strive to become. Understandably, the superego frequently opposes id's desires, because the id wants to do only what feels good, while the superego insists on doing only what is right and moral.

The Ego: The Rational Mind Former President Jimmy Carter once famously remarked, "I've looked on a lot of women with lust. I've committed adultery in my heart many times." In Freudian parlance, that was his *ego,* the conscious, rational portion of the mind, describing how it must resolve conflicts between desires of the id and moral ideals of the superego. The **ego,** like a referee, often must make decisions that satisfy no part of the personality completely, but it keeps the whole out of trouble. Even so, pressures can escalate to the point where the ego cannot find workable compromises. The result can be mental disorder.

The Influence of Early Experience on Personality Development As Freud talked with his patients about their past, he began to understand that personality follows a developmental pattern through childhood and into adulthood. The emerging sexual and aggressive drives propel the child through a series of **psychosexual stages.** In each stage, stimulation of specific body regions is associated with erotic pleasure.

In the *oral stage,* pleasure is associated with the mouth: suckling, crying, spewing. In the *anal stage,* pleasure comes from stimulating parts of the body associated with elimination. Next, in the *phallic stage,* pleasure comes from "immature" sexual expression, such as masturbation. (This also explains the humor popular with the prepubescent set.) Finally, after a quiet period of *latency,* the adult *genital stage* brings maturity and mental well-being to those fortunate enough to resolve the conflicts of earlier stages. (See Table 10.2 on page 448.)

Why such a seemingly bizarre theory of child development? Among the issues that Freud was trying to resolve with his theory of psychosexual development were those of gender identity and gender roles. Why, he wondered, do boys usually develop a masculine identity, even though most boys are raised primarily by their mothers? Why do boys and girls, as they become adults, most often develop a sexual attraction to the opposite sex? And why do some *not* follow this pattern?

Freud's answers to these questions were convoluted and, many psychologists would say, contrived. His psychodynamic perspective ignored the external influence of the different ways that boys and girls are socialized; it also ignored the possibility of differences in genetic programming, about which almost nothing was known in Freud's day. For boys his solution was the **Oedipus complex,** an unconscious conflict that initially drives young males to feel an immature erotic attraction toward their mothers. (You may have heard a little boy say that he wants to marry his mother when he grows up.) As the boy goes through the stages of psychosexual development, resolution of the Oedipal conflict requires him to *displace* (shift) his emerging sexual desires away from his mother, directing them instead to females of his own age. At the same time, he develops an **identification** with his father. In a parallel fashion, Freud theorized that girls develop an attraction to their fathers and so become competitive with their mothers for his affections.

Most psychologists today reject these Freudian assumptions about psychosexual development because they lack scientific support. Yet it is important, however, to remember three things: First, we still don't fully understand how sexual attraction works. Second, Freudian concepts about psychosexual development—strange as they may seem—continue to have a wide impact outside psychology, particularly in literature. And finally: While Freud may have been wrong about the details of psychosexual development, he may have been right about the overall pattern and about the idea of *stages of development* (Bower, 1998b).

For example, Freud may have been right in his assertion that certain difficulties early in life lead to **fixation,** or arrested psychological development. An *oral stage* fixation, caused by a failure to throw off the dependency of the first year of life, may lead to dependency on others in later childhood and adulthood. We may also see an oral fixation, he said, in certain behaviors involving "oral tendencies," such as overeating, alcoholism, smoking, and talkativeness. Among these diverse problems we find a common theme: using the mouth as the way to connect with what one needs or wants. Similarly, Freud presumed that fixation in the *anal stage* came from problems associated with the second year of life when toilet training is a big issue. Anal fixations, he said, can result in a stubborn, compulsive, stingy, or excessively neat pattern of behavior—all related to the theme of controlling one's body or life. People who swear, especially with "dirty" language, also have anal fixations. In Table 10.2 you will find examples of fixation at other developmental stages.

Ego Defenses
In dealing with conflict between the id's impulses and the superego's demand to deny them, Freud said that the ego calls upon a suite of **ego defense mechanisms.** All operate, he said, at the *preconscious level*—just beneath the surface of consciousness. So, under mild pressure from the id we may rely, as President Carter did, on simple ego defenses, such as *fantasy* or *rationalization*. But if unconscious desires become too insistent, the ego may solve the problem by "putting a lid on the id"—that is, by sequestering extreme desires and threatening memories deep in the unconscious mind. Freud called this **repression.** It is this ego defense mechanism, then, that makes people in unhappy relationships "forget" their anniversaries. It makes unhappy employees "forget" important duties. And it makes anxious students "forget" to hand in assignments.

Freud also taught that repression can block access to feelings, as well as memories. So, a child might repress strong feelings of anger toward her father—

"All right, deep down it's a cry for psychiatric help—but at one level it's a stick-up."

Oedipus complex According to Freud, a largely unconscious process whereby boys displace an erotic attraction toward their mother to females of their own age and, at the same time, identify with their fathers.

Identification The mental process by which an individual tries to become like another person, especially the same-sex parent.

Fixation Occurs when psychosexual development is arrested at an immature stage.

Ego defense mechanism A largely unconscious mental strategy employed to reduce the experience of conflict or anxiety.

Repression An unconscious process that excludes unacceptable thoughts and feelings from awareness and memory.

TABLE 10.2 Freud's Stages of Psychosexual Development

Psychosexual Stage	Later Signs of Problems Beginning at This Stage	
Oral Stage (1st year)	Smoking	Obesity
Desires: Oral stimulation by sucking, eating, crying, babbling	Nail-biting	Talkativeness
	Chewing	Dependency
Challenge: Overcoming dependency	Gluttony	Gullibility
Anal Stage (approximately 1–3 years)	Messiness	Excessive cleanliness
Desires: Anal stimulation by bladder and bowel function	Temper tantrums	Stinginess
Challenge: Toilet training	Destructiveness	Coldness, distance, aloofness
Self-control	Cruelty	
Phallic Stage (approximately 3–6 years)	Masturbation (not considered abnormal by modern psychology and psychiatry; see Chapter 9)	
Desires: Stimulation of genitals	Jealousy	
Challenge: Resolving Oedipus complex, involving erotic attraction to parent of opposite sex and hostility to parent of same sex	Egocentric sex	
	Sexual conquests	
	Problems with parents	
Latency (approximately 6 years to puberty)	Excessive modesty	
	Preference for company of same sex	
Desires: Repression of sexual and aggressive desires, including those involved in the Oedipus complex	Homosexuality (considered by Freud to be a disorder, but not by modern psychology and psychiatry; see Chapter 9)	
Challenge: Consciously: learning modesty and shame		
Unconsciously: dealing with repressed Oedipal conflict		
Genital Stage (puberty and adulthood)	(none)	
Desires: Mature sexual relationships		
Challenge: Displacing energy into healthy activities		
Establishing new relationship with parents		

which, if acted on, might incur severe punishment. Likewise, boys repress the erotic Oedipal feelings they have for their mothers. Once repressed, a feeling or a desire can no longer operate consciously. But, said Freud, it is not gone. At an unconscious level, repressed feelings, desires, and memories continue to influence behavior, but in less direct ways, perhaps disguised, as we have seen, in dreams, fantasies, or symptoms of mental disorder.

Always the keen observer of human behavior, Freud proposed many other ego defense mechanisms besides fantasy, rationalization, and repression. Here are some of the most important:

CONNECTION • CHAPTER 8
Freud developed an elaborate system of dream interpretation.

● *Denial.* "I don't have a problem." This defense avoids a difficult situation by simply denying that it exists. Denial is a defense frequently seen, for example, in alcoholics, child abusers, people who have problems managing anger, and people who engage in risky behavior, such as casual, unprotected sex.

- *Rationalization.* A student who feels stressed by academic pressures may decide to cheat on a test, rationalizing it by saying that "everyone does it." People using this defense mechanism give socially acceptable reasons for actions that are really based on motives that they believe to be unacceptable.

- *Reaction formation.* We see reaction formation in people who, troubled by their own sexual desires, rail against "dirty books" in the city library or seek laws regulating other people's sexual behavior. This ego defense mechanism occurs whenever people act exactly in opposition to their unconscious desires.

- *Displacement.* When your boss makes you angry, you may later displace your anger by yelling at your friend or pounding on the wall. More generally, displacement involves shifting your reaction from the real source of your distress to a safer individual or object. Freud would have agreed that Enron executive Ken Lay displaced any feelings of guilt he may have had (along with the blame for the economic collapse he himself had engineered) onto what he characterized as a conspiracy of rogue executives, stock traders, and the hostile media.

- *Regression.* Under stress, some people hide; others cry, throw things, or even wet their pants. That is, they regress back to an earlier developmental stage by adopting immature, juvenile behaviors that were effective ways of dealing with stress when they were younger.

- *Sublimation.* This ego defense mechanism may account for the glory of Rome, the genius of Mozart, and the triumph of the Microsoft empire. In other words, sublimation involves channeling the gratification of sexual or aggressive desires in ways that are acceptable in one's culture. Freud conjectured that sublimation was responsible for civilization's major advances.

- *Projection.* We may see projection when two people argue, each accusing the other of causing the problem. Similarly, the neighborhood gossip may call someone a "busybody"; an insecure business executive may see an innocent coworker as a threat; or a person in a committed relationship who is feeling attracted to someone else accuses his or her partner of cheating. More generally, people may use the defense of projection to attribute their own unconscious desires and fears to other people or objects.

This latter concept—projection—led to the development of projective tests, which have found extensive use in clinical psychology for evaluating personality and mental disorders. We take a brief detour at this point to introduce you to these projective techniques.

Projective Tests: Diagnosis by Defense Mechanism What do you see in Figure 10.5? The head of an insect? An MRI scan of the brain? Something else? Ambiguous images such as these are the basis for **projective tests** that psychodynamic clinicians employ to probe their patients' innermost feelings, motives, conflicts and desires. The assumption is that troubled people will *project* their hidden motives and conflicts onto such images, much as people gazing at the clouds may see objects in them that fit their fantasies.

In the most famous of projective techniques, the ***Rorschach Inkblot Technique*** (pronounced *ROAR-shock*), the stimuli are merely symmetrical inkblots. The technique calls for showing the images one at a time and asking the respondent, "What do you see? What does this seem to be?" The examiner usually interprets responses psychoanalytically by noting how they might reflect unconscious sexual and aggressive impulses or repressed conflicts (Erdberg, 1990).

How well does the *Rorschach* work? It gets low marks from many psychologists because objective studies of its use in measuring individual differences in

Projective test Personality assessment instrument, such as the Rorschach and TAT, which is based on Freud's ego defense mechanism of projection.

Rorschach Inkblot Technique A projective test requiring subjects to describe what they see in a series of ten inkblots.

FIGURE 10.5
An Inkblot Similar to Those Used in the Rorschach Test

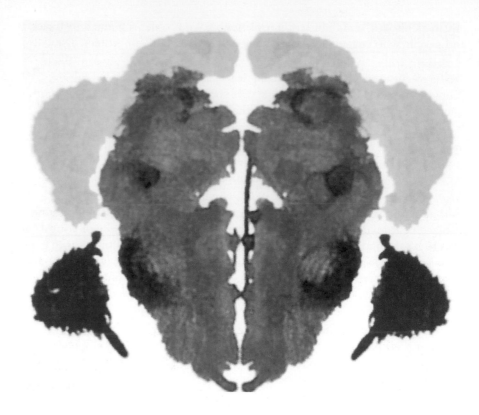

FIGURE 10.6
Sample Card from the *TAT*

Thematic Apperception Test (TAT) A projective test requiring subjects to make up stories that explain ambiguous pictures.

Psychic determinism Freud's assumption that all our mental and behavioral responses are caused by unconscious traumas, desires, or conflicts.

personality with consistency and accuracy have been disappointing (Lilienfeld et al., 2000a,b). Moreover, critics claim that the test is based on concepts such as unconscious motivation that are impossible to demonstrate objectively. Despite these criticisms, many clinicians have continued to champion the *Rorschach*, arguing that it can provide unique insights as part of a broader personality assessment (Hibbard, 2003).

By comparison, the ***Thematic Apperception Test (TAT)***, developed by Henry Murray, is a projective test that stands on somewhat firmer scientific ground, especially for assessing achievement motivation, as we saw in Chapter 9. The test consists of ambiguous pictures, like the one in Figure 10.6, for which respondents are instructed to generate a story, telling what the characters in the scenes are doing and thinking, what led up to each event, and how each situation might end. According to the projection hypothesis underlying the *TAT*, the respondent first perceives the elements in the picture and then *apperceives* (fills in) personal interpretations and explanations, based on his or her own thoughts, feelings, and needs. The examiner then interprets the responses by looking for psychological themes, such as aggression, sexual needs, and relationships among people mentioned in the stories.

Psychic Determinism Psychoanalysis literally leaves nothing to accident. According to the principle of **psychic determinism,** all our acts are determined by unconscious memories, desires, and conflicts. So, Freud would have said that being consistently late for a class is intentional (on an unconscious level, of course). Inevitably, the way you feel unconsciously leaks out in your behavior. You just can't help it.

Accordingly, everything a person does potentially has a deep psychological meaning to the Freudian analyst. In therapy, mental symptoms such as fears and phobias are signs of unconscious difficulties. Similarly, the analyst may catch a glimpse of the unconscious at work in a so-called *Freudian slip*—when "accidental" speech or behavior belies an unconscious conflict or desire. Former President George W. Bush was famous for slips of the tongue, as when intending to emphasize how strongly his party felt about the family, he said instead, "Republicans understand the importance of bondage between a mother and child." (We hasten to add, in defense of anyone who has committed a speech blunder, that cognitive psychologists today believe that most slips of the tongue are mix-ups in the brain mechanisms we use to produce language and so have no relationship to unconscious intentions.)

The idea of psychic determinism originated in Freud's work with hysterical patients, when he observed that their physical symptoms often seemed connected to a traumatic event that had been long "forgotten" (repressed). During therapy, a patient who was hysterically "blind" might suddenly recall with horror having seen her parents having intercourse when she was a small child. How could this have produced blindness? Freud would conjecture that, as she became an adult, she anticipated her first sexual encounter, which aroused powerful feelings associated with the upsetting memory of her parents. Thus, the young woman's blindness could represent an unconscious attempt to "blind" herself both to her parents' sexuality and to her own erotic feelings.

Evaluating Freud's Work Whatever your reaction to Freud, you must give him credit for developing the first and still, perhaps, the most comprehensive theory of personality, mental disorder, and psychotherapy. He did so at a time when we had no understanding of genetics and neurotransmitters, no particularly effective treatments for most mental disorders, and no understanding of the influences on gender identity or sexual development. His writing was so incisive and his arguments so compelling that he has had a greater impact than any other theorist on the way all of us think about personality and mental abnormality, whether we realize it or not. He gave us the unconscious, the concept of developmental stages, the notion of defense mechanisms, and the idea that behavior—and even our dreams—may have hidden meanings. And not the least of his contributions was freeing us from the shackles of Victorian sexuality. Even among psychologists, who had largely rejected his ideas in recent years, Freud is enjoying renewed support as one of the keenest observers of human behavior who has ever lived (Solms, 2004). Again and again he saw things that others missed, even if his explanations were sometimes contrived. Nearly everyone would agree that people *do* displace aggression, rationalize their behavior, and see their own shortcomings more easily in others than in themselves.

Freud as Unscientific Nevertheless, Freud still plays to mixed reviews (Azar, 1997; McCullough, 2001). The biggest problem is that many of his concepts, such as "libido," "anal stage," or "repression," are vague, lacking clear operational definitions. In an earlier chapter, we saw this problem in the controversy over recovery of repressed memories. Without credible supporting evidence (which rarely exists), how could one ever determine whether a recovered memory was truly repressed or merely implanted by suggestion? Such difficulties make psychoanalytic theory devilishly difficult evaluate scientifically.[2]

CONNECTION • CHAPTER 1

Operational definitions are stated in objective, observable, and measurable terms.

---

[2]Because many of Freud's ideas are not testable, his psychoanalytic theory is not truly a *scientific* theory, as we defined the term in Chapter 1. Here we follow common usage, which nevertheless calls it a theory because it is such a comprehensive explanation for personality and mental disorder. It should be noted, however, that valiant efforts are being made to put Freud's concepts on a scientific footing (Cramer, 2000).

Retrospective but Not Prospective A second criticism says that Freudian theory is a seductive explanation for the past but a poor predictor of future responses. That is, it may be merely a clever example of *hindsight bias,* in which we have the illusion of seeing things more clearly in retrospect. And by overemphasizing the origins of behavior in childhood, psychoanalysis may compound the problem by directing attention away from the stressors of the present that may be the real causes of mental and behavioral disorders.

Gender Issues A third criticism faults Freud for giving short shrift to women. Particularly aggravating is his portrayal of women as inevitably suffering from "penis envy." (He thought that women spent their lives unconsciously trying to make up for their biological deficit in this department.) A better explanation is that Freud's theory simply projects onto women his own attitudes and those of the male-centered world of his time.

Newer Views of the Unconscious A final criticism claims that the unconscious mind is not as smart or purposeful as Freud believed (Loftus & Klinger, 1992). In this newer view, coming out of neuroscience research in emotion, the brain has parallel conscious and unconscious processing pathways, with the unconscious quick to detect emotion-provoking stimuli (think of your "gut" reaction to a shadowy figure approaching you on a dark street), while consciousness acts more deliberately and logically ("OK," you say to yourself. "Remain calm and act naturally, and maybe he won't sense that you are scared.") This new view of an unconscious emotional processing system is much less malign than the unconscious filled with sexual desires and death wishes that Freud had imagined (LeDoux, 1996).

CONNECTION • CHAPTER 9
Emotion-provoking stimuli are processed in two parallel pathways in the brain.

Freud's Appeal beyond Psychology Despite these objections, Freud's ideas have found a receptive audience with the public at large (Adler, 2006). Much of his appeal may be explained by his graceful writing and by his emphasis on sexuality, a topic that grabs everyone's interest—as Freud well knew! As a result, Freudian images and symbols abound in the art and literature of the 20th century. His ideas have had an enormous influence on marketing, as well. For example, advertisers make billions by associating products with sexy models, hinting that the products will bring sexual satisfaction to their owners. They also capitalize on Freud's destructive instinct by reminding us of threats to our happiness (social rejection, irregularity, untimely death) and then offering products and services to reduce our anxiety and restore hope. Perhaps Freud was right, after all!

How Would Freud Have Seen Mary Calkins? Let us end our discussion of Freud by seeing whether his explanation of personality can give us a useful perspective on Mary Calkins. A psychoanalyst interpreting her sense of purpose and willingness to fight the system might look first to her childhood for experiences that may have shaped her personality.

The Calkins family was especially close (Furumoto, 1979). Mary's mother, Charlotte Calkins, suffered from deteriorating health, so Mary, as the eldest child, took over many of the duties of running the household—an especially interesting development in view of Freud's suggestion that girls compete with their mothers for their fathers' attention. For his part, Mary's father, the Reverend Wolcott Calkins, was Congregationalist minister who placed a high value on education and personally tutored Mary at a time when education for women was not fashionable.

Another decisive event, which caused Mary great distress, was the death of her younger sister. From a Freudian viewpoint, the sister's death may have produced a conflict, based on unconscious feelings of *sibling rivalry* for the parents' affections. A Freudian analyst might suggest that, in her work, Calkins sublimated her sadness or, perhaps, her anger at the necessity of taking on mother's role and at the prejudices she endured. As is usual with psychoanalysis, of course, these guesses are guided by hindsight—and cannot be either proved or disproved.

The Neo-Freudians Freud was always a controversial and charismatic figure—an image he liked to promote (Sulloway, 1992). And although he attracted many followers, Freud brooked no criticism from any of them concerning the basic principles of psychoanalysis. So, like rebellious children, several of Freud's equally strong-willed disciples broke away to establish their own systems of personality, mental disorder, and treatment. While these **neo-Freudians** (literally, "new Freudians") sometimes departed from Freud's theory, they always retained his *psychodynamic* emphasis. That is, they kept Freud's idea of personality as a process driven by motivational energy—even as they disagreed about the specific motives that energize personality. And you may disagree, too: Are our motives primarily sexual or social? Conscious or unconscious? Is personality determined by events in the past or by our goals for the future? The next few pages will give you a sense for the divergent paths followed by these neo-Freudians.

Carl Jung: Extending the Unconscious
Freud attracted many disciples but none more famous than Carl Jung (pronounced *YOONG*), a member of the inner circle of colleagues who helped Freud develop and refine psychoanalytic theory during the first decade of the 1900s. For a time, Freud viewed the somewhat younger Jung as his "crown prince" and probable successor. But Freud's paternal attitude increasingly vexed Jung, who was developing radical theoretical ideas of his own (Carver & Scheier, 2008). Eventually this personality conflict—which Freud interpreted as Jung's unconscious wish to usurp his fatherly authority—caused a split in their relationship.

For Jung, the break with Freud centered on two issues. First, Jung thought that his mentor had overemphasized sexuality at the expense of other unconscious needs and desires that Jung saw at the heart of personality. In particular, he believed spirituality to be a fundamental human motive, coequal with sexuality. Moreover, he disputed the very structure of the unconscious mind. Jung's new and expanded vision of the unconscious is Jung's most famous innovation.

The Collective Unconscious In place of the Freudian id, Jung installed a two-part unconscious, consisting of both a *personal unconscious* and a *collective unconscious*. While the Jungian **personal unconscious** spanned essentially the same territory as the Freudian id, its collective twin was another matter—and wholly a Jungian creation. He saw in the **collective unconscious** a reservoir for instinctive "memories" shared by people everywhere—in much the same way that humans share a common genetic code. These collective memories tie together countless generations of human history and give us the ancient images, called **archetypes,** that appear and reappear in art, literature, and folktales around the world (Jung, 1936/1959). For Jung, the causes of mental disorder include not only repressed traumas and conflicts in the personal unconscious but failure to acknowledge the archetypes we find unacceptable in our collective unconscious.

Among these archetypal memories, Jung identified the *animus* and the *anima*, which represent the masculine and feminine sides of our personalities. Other archetypes give us the universal concepts of *mother, father, birth, death,* the *hero,* the *trickster, God,* and the *self.* On the darker side of the self lurks the *shadow* archetype, representing the destructive and aggressive tendencies (similar to Freud's Thanatos) that we don't want to acknowledge in our personalities. You can recognize your own shadow archetype at work the next time you feel angry or hostile.

From a Jungian perspective, Enron bad boy Ken Lay let his trickster archetype range out of control. One might also wonder whether he was rebelling against his father, a Baptist minister, whose rules may have felt like a moral straitjacket to the young Ken. And finally, by denying his guilt up to the time of his death, we might wonder whether Lay was denying, even to himself, the shadow in his personality.

Neo-Freudian Literally "new Freudian"; refers to theorists who broke with Freud but whose theories retain a psychodynamic aspect, especially a focus on motivation as the source of energy for the personality.

Personal unconscious Jung's term for that portion of the unconscious corresponding roughly to the Freudian id.

Collective unconscious Jung's addition to the unconscious, involving a reservoir for instinctive "memories," including the archetypes, which exist in all people.

Archetype One of the ancient memory images in the collective unconscious. Archetypes appear and reappear in art, literature, and folktales around the world.

Jungian archetypes abound in art, literature, and film. This photo, from The Lord of the Rings, *shows Gandalf, who embodies the archetype of magician or trickster. The same archetype is evoked by the coyote in Native American legends and by Merlin in the King Arthur legends.*

Personality Types Revisited Jung's *principle of opposites* portrays each personality as a balance between opposing pairs of tendencies or dispositions, which you see in Table 10.3. Jung taught that most people tend to favor one or the other in each pair. The overall pattern of such tendencies, then, was termed a *personality type,* which Jung believed to be a stable and enduring aspect of the individual's personality.

The most famous of these pairs is **introversion** and **extraversion.** Extraverts turn attention outward, on external experience. As a result, extraverts are more in tune with people and things in the world around them than they are with their own inner needs. They tend to be outgoing and unaffected by self-consciousness. Introverts, by contrast, focus on inner experience—their own thoughts and feelings—which makes them seem more shy and less sociable. Jung believed that few people have all pairs of forces in perfect balance. Instead, one or another dominates, giving rise to personality types (Fadiman & Frager, 2001).

Evaluating Jung's Work Like Freud, Jung's influence is now most evident outside of psychology, particularly in literature and the popular press—again because they do not lend themselves to objective observation and testing. In two respects, however, Jung has had a big impact on psychological thinking. First, he challenged Freud and thereby opened the door to a spate of alternative personality theories. Second, his notion of *personality types,* and especially the concepts of *introversion* and *extraversion,* makes Jung not only a psychodynamic theorist but a pillar of the temperament/trait/type approach. And, as we noted earlier, his theory of types underlies the widely used Myers-Briggs test.

Could Jung's theory give us a new perspective on Mary Calkins? He might have suspected that her determination to succeed in the male-dominated world of her day was energized by conflicts between the masculine and feminine sides of her nature, the animus and anima. Another Jungian possibility is that her mother's ill health, which caused her to relinquish much of the maternal role, made Mary deny her own maternal archetype—which may have been why she never married.

Karen Horney: A Feminist Voice in Psychodynamic Psychology
Karen Horney *(HORN-eye)* and Anna Freud, Sigmund Freud's daughter, represent virtually the only feminine voices within the early decades of the psychoanalytic movement. In this role Horney disputed the elder Freud's notion of the Oedipus complex and especially his assertion that women must suffer from *penis envy* (Horney, 1939). Instead, said Horney, women want the same opportunities and rights that men enjoy, and many personality differences between males and females result from social roles, not from unconscious urges. She also disputed Freud's contention that personality is determined mainly by early childhood experiences. For Horney, normal growth involves the full development of social relationships and of one's potential. This development, however, may be blocked by a sense of uncertainty and isolation that she called **basic anxiety.** It is this basic anxiety that can lead to adjustment problems and mental disorder.

Neurotic Needs When basic anxiety gets out of control, people become *neurotic.* The neurotic person, said Horney, suffers from "unconscious strivings developed in

Introversion The Jungian dimension that focuses on inner experience—one's own thoughts and feelings—making the introvert less outgoing and sociable than the extravert.

Extraversion The Jungian personality dimension that involves turning one's attention outward, toward others.

Basic anxiety An emotion, proposed by Karen Horney, that gives a sense of uncertainty and loneliness in a hostile world and can lead to maladjustment.

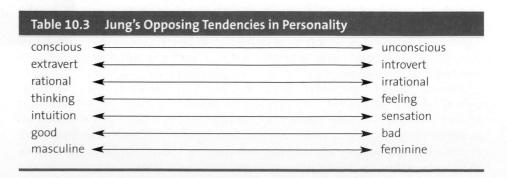

Table 10.3	Jung's Opposing Tendencies in Personality
conscious	⟷ unconscious
extravert	⟷ introvert
rational	⟷ irrational
thinking	⟷ feeling
intuition	⟷ sensation
good	⟷ bad
masculine	⟷ feminine

| Table 10.4 | Horney's Ten Neurotic Needs |

Table 10.4	Horney's Ten Neurotic Needs

1. Need for affection and approval
2. Need for a partner and dread of being left alone
3. Need to restrict one's life and remain inconspicuous
4. Need for power and control over others
5. Need to exploit others
6. Need for recognition or prestige
7. Need for personal admiration
8. Need for personal achievement
9. Need for self-sufficiency and independence
10. Need for perfection and unassailability

Psychoanalyst Karen Horney asserted that personality differences betweeen men and women are largely the result of different social roles, rather than unconscious urges or early childhood experiences. She believed that people are driven more by social motives than sexual motives.

order to cope with life despite fears, helplessness, and isolation" (1942, p. 40). These unconscious strivings manifest themselves in one or more **neurotic needs**, which are normal desires taken to extremes. You can see these neurotic needs listed in Table 10.4.

Horney also identified three common patterns of attitudes and behavior that people use to deal with basic anxiety: They move either *toward others, against others,* or *away from others.* Those who neurotically move *toward others* have a pathological need for constant reminders of love and approval. Such persons may need someone to help, to take care of, or for whom to "sacrifice" themselves. Alternatively, they may seek someone on whom they can become dependent. They may end up behaving passively and feeling victimized. In contrast, those who move *against others* earn power and respect by competing or attacking successfully, but they risk being feared and ending up "lonely at the top." Those who take the third route, moving *away from others* to protect themselves from imagined hurt and rejection, are likely to close themselves off from intimacy and support.

What analysis would Horney have made of Mary Calkins? We suspect that she would have focused on Calkins's achievements, attempting to determine whether they were the result of a healthy drive to fulfill her potential or a neurotic need for power. Undoubtedly, Horney would have reminded us that society often praises these needs in men and punishes them in women. She would also have pointed out that much of Calkins's professional identity was shaped by having to deal with the male-centered academic world of her time. In that context, Calkins not only drew on the strength of a supportive family of her childhood but the support of the all-female Wellesley faculty that became the "family" of her adulthood. From this point of view, it is likely that Horney may have seen in Calkins a robust and healthy personality caught in a difficult web of social constraints and contradictions.

Evaluating Horney's Work   Neglect engulfed Karen Horney's ideas during the midcentury (Monte, 1980). Then her 1967 book, *Feminine Psychology,* appeared at just the right time to elevate her among those seeking a feminist perspective within psychology and psychiatry (Horney, 1967). But, having attracted renewed interest, will Horney eventually slip again into oblivion? Her ideas suffer from the same flaw that plagues the other psychodynamic theories: a weak scientific foundation. It awaits someone to translate her concepts into operational terms that can be put to a scientific test.

Other Neo-Freudian Theorists
Sigmund Freud's revolutionary ideas attracted many others to the psychoanalytic movement—many of whom, like Karl Jung, Karen Horney, Erik Erikson, and Alfred Adler, also broke from Freud to develop their own ideas. For the most part, the post-Freudian theorists accepted the notions

Neurotic needs   Signs of neurosis in Horney's theory, the ten needs are normal desires carried to a neurotic extreme.

of psychic determinism and unconscious motivation. But they did not always agree with Freud on the details, especially about the sex and death instincts or the indelible nature of early life experiences. Broadly speaking, the neo-Freudians made several significant changes in the course of psychoanalysis:

- They put greater emphasis on ego functions, including ego defenses, development of the self, and conscious thought as the major components of the personality—whereas Freud focused primarily on the unconscious.

- They gave social variables (culture, family, and peers) an important role in shaping personality—whereas Freud focused mainly on instinctive urges and unconscious conflicts.

- They extended personality development beyond childhood to include the lifespan—whereas Freud focused mainly on early childhood experiences.

CONNECTION • CHAPTER 6

Erikson's theory described the development of personality across the life span.

As we saw in Chapter 6, neo-Freudian Erik Erikson proposed an elaborate theory of personality development that unfolded in stages throughout the life span, a conjecture that has recently received support from Sanjay Srivastava and his team (2003) at the University of Oregon. Their data show that personality continues to change well into adulthood, with people in their 20s growing more conscientious and those in their 30s and beyond gaining as they age on measures of agreeableness, warmth, generosity, and helpfulness.

In such ways, then, the post-Freudians broke Freud's monopoly on personality theory and paved the way for the new ideas developed by the humanistic and cognitive theorists.

Humanistic Theories: Emphasis on Human Potential and Mental Health

Neither Freud nor the neo-Freudians had much to say about those of us who are "normal." With an emphasis on internal conflict and mental disorder, they offered compelling explanations for mental disorders, but they largely failed to provide a usable theory of the healthy personality. And so the humanistic approach stepped in to fill that need.

Humanistic psychologists are an optimistic lot. For them, personality is not driven by unconscious conflicts and defenses against anxiety but rather by needs to adapt, learn, grow, and excel. They have retained the idea of motivation as a central component of personality, but they have accentuated the positive motives, such as love, esteem, and self-actualization. They see mental disorders as stemming from unhealthy *situations,* rather than from unhealthy *individuals.* Once people are freed from negative situations, such as negative self-evaluations ("I'm not smart") and abusive relationships, the tendency to be healthy should actively guide them to life-enhancing choices.

Maslow considered Eleanor Roosevelt to be a self-actualizing person.

Abraham Maslow and the Healthy Personality Abraham Maslow referred to the humanistic view as psychology's "third force," to contrast his ideas with the psychoanalytic and behaviorist movements that had dominated psychology during most of his lifetime. He was especially concerned by the Freudian fixation on mental disturbance and maladjustment. Instead, Maslow argued, we need a theory that describes mental health as something more than just the absence of illness. That theoretical need became his life's quest. He sought the ingredients of the healthy personality where no one had ever looked for them before: in people who had lived especially full and productive lives (Maslow, 1968, 1970, 1971).

Self-Actualizers Maslow's subjects included the historical figures Abraham Lincoln and Thomas Jefferson, plus several persons of stature during his own lifetime: Albert Einstein, Albert Schweitzer, and Eleanor Roosevelt. In these individuals Maslow found healthy personalities focused on goals beyond their own basic needs. Some, like Lincoln and Roosevelt, were oriented toward the needs of humanity. Others, like Einstein, were oriented toward understanding the natural world. Most became engaged them in causes about which they felt deeply. Maslow called them all **self-actualizing personalities.** He characterized his self-actualizers as creative, full of good humor, and given to spontaneity—but, at the same time, accepting of their own limitations and those of others. In brief, self-actualizers are those who feel free to fulfill their potentialities.

Needs in a Hierarchy Although Maslow was most interested in the healthy, self-actualizing personality, his theory of a *hierarchy of needs* also offers an explanation of maladjustment. As you will recall, Maslow proposed that our needs are arranged in a priority order, from the biological needs to needs for safety, love, esteem, and self-actualization. An unfulfilled "deficiency" need, such as a need for love or esteem, can produce maladjustment, while satisfaction of such needs allows the person to pursue interests that promote growth and fulfillment. Indeed, research shows that people who have low self-esteem may go through life feeling fearful, angry, or depressed, while those who are self-accepting lead far happier lives (Baumeister, 1993; Brown, 1991).

CONNECTION • CHAPTER 9
Maslow's *hierarchy of needs* claims that motives occur in a priority order.

Carl Rogers's Fully Functioning Person

Unlike Maslow, Carl Rogers (1961) was a therapist who often worked with dysfunctional people rather than self-actualizers. Yet he did not overlook the healthy personality, which he called the **fully functioning person.** He described such an individual as having a self-concept that is both *positive* and *congruent* with reality. That is, the fully functioning person has high self-esteem, which is consistent (congruent) with the messages he or she receives from others, who express their approval, friendship, and love. Negative experiences, such as loss of a job or rejection by a lover, can produce *incongruence*, a threat to one's self-esteem.

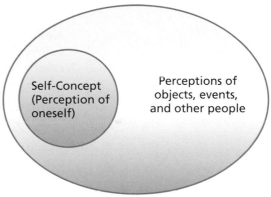

The Phenomenal Field: The Person's Reality Rogers insisted that psychology recognize the importance of perceptions and feelings, which he called the **phenomenal field.** We respond only to this subjective experience, not to an objective reality. That is why a student's reaction to a grade depends entirely on the student's perception. Receiving a C may shock a student who is used to receiving As but thrill one who has been failing: Both are reacting to their own subjective phenomenal fields. In Rogers's system, then, the phenomenal field is part of the personality, as a sort of filter for our experience (see Figure 10.7). It contains our interpretations of both the external and internal worlds, and it also contains the *self*, the humanists' version of the Freudian ego.

FIGURE 10.7
Rogers's Phenomenal Field

For Carl Rogers, what we perceive and feel is the only reality. The totality of all our feelings and perceptions he dubbed the *phenomenal field*. Note that the *self-concept* is a perception of oneself and therefore a part of the phenomenal field. In the *fully functioning person*, the self-concept is both positive and *congruent* with the feedback received from others.

Conditional versus Unconditional Relationships Perhaps it won't surprise you to hear that Rogers himself had an unhappy and dysfunctional childhood, dominated by the rigid rules of his parents' strict religious beliefs. So restrictive was this environment that he once remarked that he felt "wicked" when he first tasted a bottle of pop without his parents' knowledge (Rogers, 1961). Later, from an adult perspective, Rogers concluded that children from homes like his, where parental love is *conditional* (dependent) on good behavior, may grow up with anxiety and a strong sense of guilt that leads to low self-esteem and mental disorder. Instead of guilt-mongers, he believed, we need people who can give us *unconditional positive regard*—love without conditions attached.

Unlike the psychodynamic theorists who focused on sinister motives, Rogers, Maslow, and other humanistic personality theorists believe that our most basic motives are for positive growth. In its healthiest form, self-actualization is a striving to realize one's potential—to develop fully one's capacities and talents. (Examples might include Einstein or even Freud.) According to the humanistic

Self-actualizing personality A healthy individual who has met his or her basic needs and is free to be creative and fulfill his or her potentialities.

Fully functioning person Carl Rogers's term for a healthy, self-actualizing individual, who has a self-concept that is both positive and congruent with reality.

Phenomenal field Our psychological reality, composed of one's perceptions and feelings.

theorists, this innate quest is a constructive, guiding force that moves each person toward positive behaviors and the enhancement of the self.

A Humanistic Perspective on Mary Calkins A humanist trying to understand what drove Mary Calkins would probably begin by asking: How did she see her world—and herself? And what mattered to her? They would be especially interested in her strengths: her intelligence, her nurturing family background, and her supportive circle of colleagues at Wellesley and in the psychology group at Harvard. They would also note that Calkins worked all her life to make psychology the science of the self (by which she meant the whole person, not the fragmented and narrow approach of the structuralists or the "mindless" approach of the behaviorists). In this respect, Mary Calkins might be considered one of the pioneers of humanistic psychology.

CONNECTION • CHAPTER 1
Structuralism sought the "elements" of conscious experience.

Evaluating the Humanistic Theories
The upbeat humanistic view of personality brought a welcome change for therapists who had wearied of the dark, pessimistic Freudian perspective, with its emphasis on unspeakable desires and repressed traumas. They liked the humanistic focus on making one's present and future life more palatable, rather than dredging up painful memories of an unalterable past. They also liked its attention to mental health rather than mental disorder.

Are Humanistic Theories "Self"-Centered? But not everyone jumped on the humanists' bandwagon. Many critics chided the humanists for their fuzzy concepts: What exactly is "self-actualization," they asked? Is it an inborn tendency or is it created by one's culture? And, added the psychoanalysts, the humanistic emphasis on conscious experience does not recognize the power of the unconscious. Finally, cross-cultural psychologists criticized the humanists' emphasis on the self—as in *self*-concept, *self*-esteem, and *self*-actualization. This "self-centered" picture of personality, they noted, may merely be the viewpoint of observers looking through the lens of an individualistic Western culture (Heine et al., 1999).

We should be clear: No one denies the existence of a self within the personality—that is, some sort of process that distinguishes the individual from everything else. We all distinguish "me" from "thee." In fact, MRI and PET scans demonstrate the existence of specialized brain modules related to processing thoughts about the self (Heatherton et al., 2004). And even in the collectivistic cultures, the self exists, although the emphasis is on a self embedded in a social context. The real issue, then, is whether the self should be the centerpiece of personality.

Self-Esteem: Cause or Effect? Recently, the whole popular notion of self-esteem as the essential ingredient for mental health has been brought under the lens of research and critical thinking . . . and found questionable. Why is this important? Many programs designed to improve education, combat drug abuse, and discourage teen sex and violence are based on boosting self-esteem. Yet, after a review of the research, psychologist Roy Baumeister and his colleagues (2003) report that low self-esteem causes none of these problems. In fact, studies show that bullies and drug users often have *high* self-esteem. So, rather than focusing on high self-esteem as an end in itself, Baumeister and his colleagues urge promoting positive achievements and prosocial behaviors, with the expectation that self-esteem will follow in their wake.

Positive Psychology: The New Humanism? Recently, a movement known as **positive psychology** has formed to pursue essentially the same goals established by the humanists. The difference is that those allied with positive psychology are more concerned than were most humanists about laying a scientific foundation for their theories, and their effort has produced important work that we will see on happiness, social support, health, and well-being in Chapter 14. Even so, the positive psychology movement itself is limited as an explanation of personality by its restricted focus on desirable aspects of human functioning.

Positive psychology A recent movement within psychology, focusing on desirable aspects of human functioning, as opposed to an emphasis on psychopathology.

So, is there an alternative view that overcomes the problems we have seen in the psychodynamic, humanistic, and the new positive psychology theories? Let's consider the cognitive approach.

Social-Cognitive Theories: Emphasis on Social Learning

To understand why we must put up with those tamper-proof seals on pill bottles, we need to go back a few years to 1982, when someone (the case is still unsolved) slipped cyanide into a batch of Tylenol capsules. The result was seven deaths. And before manufacturers could get those pesky seals in place, several copy-cat attempts to contaminate other drugs occurred. Sales of those drugs plummeted, so observers speculated that the motive was to bankrupt the drug companies.

The personality-related question is this: Can we explain these despicable acts entirely by looking at motives? Social-cognitive theorists answer with a resounding, "No!" We must take learning into account—*social learning* to be more precise. In fact we must take into account the full range of psychological processes, including cognition, motivation, and emotion, as well as the environment (Cervone, 2004). Here we will sample two of these approaches.

Observational Learning and Personality: Bandura's Theory
You don't have to yell "Fire!" in a crowded theater to know what would happen if you did. In Albert Bandura's view, we are driven not just by motivational forces or even by rewards and punishments but by our *expectations* of how our actions might gain us rewards or punishments. And many of those expectations, he notes, don't come from direct experience but from observing what happens to others (Bandura, 1986). Thus, a distinctive feature of the human personality is the ability to foresee the consequences of actions, particularly in what happens to others.

Perhaps this is the most important contribution of Bandura's theory: the idea that we can learn *vicariously*—that is, from others. This *social learning*, or **observational learning**, is the process by which people learn new responses by watching each others' behavior and noting the consequences. That is, others act as *role models* that we either accept or reject, depending on whether they are rewarded or punished for their behavior. So, when Ramon sees Billy hit his brother and get punished for it, Ramon learns through observation that hitting is not a good strategy to adopt. Thus, through observational learning Ramon can see what works and what does not work, without having to go through trial-and-error for himself. In Bandura's view, then, personality is a collection of *learned* behavior patterns, many of which we have borrowed by observational learning.

Through observational learning, children and adults acquire information about their social environment. Likewise, skills, attitudes, and beliefs may be acquired simply by noting what others do and the consequences that follow. In this way, children may learn to say "please" and "thank you," to be quiet in libraries, and to refrain from public nose picking. The down side, of course, is that bad habits can be acquired by observing poor role models, such as a relative with a fear of spiders, or by exposure to TV shows that seem to reward antisocial behaviors, like shooting people, abusing drugs, or putting poison in Tylenol capsules. The point is that people don't always have to try out behaviors themselves in order to learn from experience.

But, says Bandura, personality is not just a repertoire of learned behavior. Understanding the whole person means understanding the continued interaction among behavior, cognition, and the environment. He calls this **reciprocal determinism** (Bandura, 1981, 1999).

As Bandura's theory suggests, children develop a clearer sense of identity by observing how men and women behave in their culture.

Observational learning A form of cognitive learning in which new responses are acquired after watching others' behavior and the consequences of their behavior.

Reciprocal determinism The process in which cognitions, behavior, and the environment mutually influence each other.

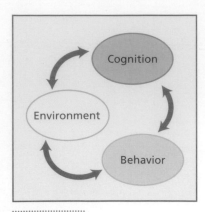

FIGURE 10.8
Reciprocal Determinism

In reciprocal determinism, the individual's cognitions, behavior, and the environment all interact.

Locus of control An individual's sense of whether control over his or her life is maternal or external.

How does reciprocal determinism work in real life? If, for example, you like psychology, your interest (a cognition) will probably lead you to spend time in the psychology department on campus (an environment) interacting with students and faculty (social behavior) who share your interest. To the extent that you find this stimulating and rewarding, this activity will reciprocally strengthen your interest in psychology and encourage you to spend more time in the psychology department. Each of the three elements—behavior, cognition, and the environment—reinforces the others. You can see the simple but powerful relationship among these variables in Figure 10.8.

Locus of Control: Rotter's Theory Another cognitive psychologist, Julian Rotter (rhymes with *voter*) has a hybrid theory that we first introduced to you in connection with motivation in Chapter 9. Rotter tells us that our behavior depends on our sense of personal power or **locus of control.** Perceived locus of control, then, acts as a sort of filter through which we see our experiences and as a motive for action or inaction. Thus, Rotter's theory is both a trait theory and a "process" theory that focuses on a single but important dimension of personality.

To illustrate, we ask you this question: When you ride in a car, do you always use a seat belt, or do you think that being hurt or killed in an accident depends on when your "number comes up"? If you always use the belt, you probably have an *internal locus of control* because by doing so you are exerting some control over your fate. On the other hand, if you have the feeling that you have no control over the events in your life, you probably don't buckle up. In that case, you have an *external locus of control.*

Scores on Rotter's *Internal–External Locus of Control Scale* correlate with people's emotions and behavior in many situations (Rotter, 1990). For example, those with an internal locus of control are not only more likely to get good grades, but they also are more likely to exercise and watch their diets than are externals (Balch & Ross, 1975; Findley & Cooper, 1983). As you might expect, externals are more likely to be depressed (Benassi et al., 1988).

Many studies suggest that locus of control is an important characteristic of our personalities. That is, an internal or external disposition seems to be a reliable personality characteristic—although Rotter resists calling this a *trait* because he believes the term conveys the erroneous idea that internality–externality could be fixed and unchangeable. You can capture the flavor of Rotter's *Locus of Control Scale* by following the instructions in the "Do It Yourself!" box.

DO IT YOURSELF! Finding Your Locus of Control

Julian Rotter (1966) has developed a test that assesses a person's sense of internal or external control over events. The test items consist of pairs of contrasting statements, and subjects must choose one statement with which they most agree from each pair. This format is called a forced choice test. Unlike many other personality tests, the scoring for each item on Rotter's Internal–External Scale is transparent: The test-taker can easily tell in which direction most items are scored. Here are some items from a preliminary version of the test (Rotter, 1971).

You can see which direction you lean by counting up the number of statements with which you agreed in each column. Agreement with those in the left column suggests an internal locus of control.

1a. Promotions are earned through hard work and persistence.

2a. In my experience I have noticed that there is usually a direct connection between how hard I study and the grades I get.

3a. If one knows how to deal with people, they are really quite easily led.

4a. People like me can change the course of world affairs if we make ourselves heard.

5a. I am the master of my fate.

1b. Making a lot of money is largely a matter of getting the right breaks.

2b. Many times the reactions of teachers seem haphazard to me.

3b. I have little influence over the way other people behave.

4b. It is only wishful thinking to believe that one can really influence what happens in society at large.

5b. A great deal that happens to me is probably a matter of chance.

Evaluating the Social-Cognitive Approach to Personality   Critics argue that the cognitive theories generally overemphasize rational information processing and overlook both emotion and unconscious processes as important components of personality. So, for those who feel that emotions and motives are central to the functioning of human personality, the cognitive approaches to personality have a blind spot. However, because emotion and associated unconscious processes have assumed a greater role in cognitive psychology recently, we can anticipate a new generation of cognitive theories of personality that do take these aspects of personality into account (Mischel & Shoda, 1995).

The real strength of the social-cognitive theories is their foundation of solid psychological research—unlike most of the ideas proposed by the Freudians, neo-Freudians, and humanists. You will recall, for example, Bandura's famous Bobo doll experiment in observational learning, which we discussed in Chapter 6. The price paid for the social-cognitive theories, however, is that they are much less comprehensive than the old and grand theories of personality proposed by Freud and his successors. The payoff, however, has come in the form of both explanations and treatments for a number of mental disorders that often seem to involve observational learning, particularly anxiety-based disorders, such as phobias, and behavior disorders in children.

CONNECTION • CHAPTER 12
Other *anxiety disorders* include *panic disorder* and *obsessive–compulsive disorder*.

Finally, we might ask how cognitive psychologist would explain Mary Calkins. One focus would be on how she interpreted the rewards and punishments she experienced in trying to complete her graduate work in psychology and how these interpretations shaped her behavior. A cognitive theorist might note that Calkins obviously had an internal locus of control that was part of a reciprocal interaction with the social support she received at home, at Wellesley, and from the her mentors at Harvard—which, in turn, reinforced her determination and hard work. And, they might add, Mary Calkins became a role model for the women who came after her to study psychology.

Current Trends: The Person in a Social System

Gone are the days when Freud, Jung, Horney, and others were building the grand, sweeping theories of personality that attempted to explain everything we humans do. First the humanistic and later the cognitive theorists arose to point out blind spots in the older psychodynamic theories. Now the emphasis has shifted again, as psychologists have brought elements of the psychodynamic, humanistic, and cognitive perspectives together with new knowledge about the impact of culture, gender, and family dynamics. You should be especially aware of three important new trends in our thinking about personality.

In **family systems theory,** for example, the basic unit of analysis is not the individual but the family (Gilbert, 1992; Mones et al., 2007). This perspective says that personality is shaped by the ways people interacted first in the family and, later, in the peer group. While Freud and others did recognize that parents influence children, the new emphasis is on *interaction*—on the ways that members of the family or the peer group influence each other. This has led to viewing people with psychological problems as individuals embedded in dysfunctional groups, rather than as "sick" persons. This emphasis has also given us a new interpersonal language for personality. We often speak now of *codependence* (instead of *dependent* personalities) and *communication* (instead of mere talk). We also have a heightened awareness of relationships and process (the changes that occur as relationships develop).

A second trend comes from psychology's increasing awareness of cultural differences, as more and more publications on personality come from psychologists around the world—not just from Europe and America (Quiñones-Vidal et al., 2004). Psychologist Stanley Sue (1991) also reminds us that our own society is becoming ethnically more diverse. No longer can we assume that everyone we meet shares the same cultural experience or the same values.

Family systems theory   A perspective on personality and treatment that emphasizes the family, rather than the individual, as the basic unit of analysis.

A third trend comes from an increasing appreciation of gender influences. While we do not know the weights to assign nature and nurture in our attempts to understand gender differences, we do know that males and females often perceive situations differently (Tavris, 1991). We have also seen that males tend to be more physically aggressive than females. And females tend to form close relationships in small, equal-status groups, while males tend to connect in larger groups (teams) organized hierarchically with leaders and followers.

Together these three trends have enlarged our understanding of the forces that shape personality. The new emphasis is on diversity and group processes, rather than on the traits and mental processes of individuals. As a result, the picture of personality has become much more complex—but it is becoming far more realistic.

PSYCHOLOGYMATTERS
Using Psychology to Learn Psychology

Although an internal or external locus of control can be a central feature of your personality, your perceived locus of control can also change from situation to situation. When you are speaking in front of a group you may feel that the situation is beyond your control, yet when you are behind the wheel or on skis you may feel that your are fully the master. And what about your education? Do you have a sense of internal or external control with regard to—say—your grade in psychology?

An external locus of control about grades poses a danger for the college student because college life is so full of distractions and temptations. If you believe that your grades are largely beyond your control, you can easily be driven by the enticements of the moment and let your studies slide. This attitude can, of course, become a self-fulfilling prophecy that ruins your grades not only in psychology but across the board.

The following questions will help you assess your own academic locus of control:

- On a test do you often find that, even when you know the material, anxiety wipes the information from your memory?

- Do you often know the material well but perceive that the test is unfair or covers material that the professor did not indicate would be on the test?

- Are you so easily distracted that you can never quite get around to studying?

- Do you believe that some people are born to be good students, and some are not?

- Do you feel that you have no control over the grades you receive?

- Do you feel that you are not smart enough to cope with college-level work?

- Do you feel that success in college is largely a matter of playing up to the professors?

If you answered "yes" to several of these questions, then you probably have an external locus of control with respect to your college work—an attitude that can hamper your chances of college success. What can be done? Nothing—if you are completely convinced that your success in college is beyond your control. If, however, you are open to the idea of establishing more control over your college experience, here are a few suggestions:

- If you suffer from test anxiety, get help from your counseling center or learning resources center.

- Form a study group among friends taking the same classes or find a tutor at your learning resources center.

- Talk to your professors individually: Ask them to give you some pointers on what they consider to be especially important in their classes. (But don't ask, "What's going to be on the test?")

- Go to your college's learning resources center and get an assessment of your strengths and weaknesses and of your interest patterns. Then make a plan to correct your weaknesses (e.g., with tutoring or with remedial classes in your weak areas). At the same time, build on your strengths by selecting a major that capitalizes on your aptitudes and interests.

We would wish you good luck—but only an externalizer would want that!

Check Your Understanding

1. **RECALL:** What was Sigmund Freud's greatest discovery— and the concept that distinguishes psychoanalysis from the humanistic and social-cognitive theories?

2. **APPLICATION:** Name a type of behavior that, according to the Freudians, is driven by Thanatos?

3. **RECALL:** What is the ego defense mechanism on which the *Rorschach* and *TAT* are based?

4. **APPLICATION:** If you react strongly to angry outbursts in others, you may be struggling with which Jungian archetype?

5. **RECALL:** In contrast with Freud, Karen Horney believed that the forces behind our behaviors are _____.

6. **RECALL:** The humanistic theorists were very different

from the psychodynamic theorists because of their emphasis on _____.

7. **APPLICATION:** You try to understand people based on the role models they follow. Which kind of personality theorist are you?

8. **UNDERSTANDING THE CORE CONCEPT:** What do the psychodynamic, humanistic, and cognitive theories of personality have in common?
   a. They all view personality as largely unconscious.
   b. They all acknowledge the importance of internal mental processes.
   c. They all say that men and women have entirely different motives underlying their behaviors.
   d. They all have a strong basis in psychological research.

Answers 1. Most psychologists would say that it was Freud's discovery of unconscious mind. **2.** Any aggressive or destructive behavior would be correct. **3.** projection **4.** the shadow archetype **5.** social **6.** the healthy personality and human potential **7.** a social-cognitive theorist **8.** b

10.4 KEY QUESTION
WHAT "THEORIES" DO PEOPLE USE TO UNDERSTAND THEMSELVES AND OTHERS?

We have seen how psychologists view personality. But how do ordinary people go about understanding each other? And how do they understand themselves? All of us regularly make assumptions—right or wrong—about other people's personalities, as well as our own. You do so when you go on a date, apply for a job, or form your first impression of a professor or classmate. We might also wonder whether people in other cultures make the same assumptions about personality that we do. These issues are significant because the "folk theories," or *implicit personality theories,* that people use to understand people can support or undermine relationships among individuals—or even among nations. Our Core Concept says:

> Our understanding of ourselves and others is based on implicit theories of personality and our own self-narratives—both of which are influenced by culture.

core concept

Let's look first at the implicit theories we use to understand others, before moving on to consider how we understand ourselves.

Implicit Personality Theories

Think of someone who has been a role model for you. Now think of someone you can't stand to be around. In both cases, you associate those individuals with personal traits: honesty, reliability, sense of humor, generosity, outgoing attitude, aggressiveness, moodiness, pessimism, and so on. Even as a child, you had a rudimentary system for appraising personality. You tried to determine whether new acquaintances would be friend or foe; you worked out ways of dealing with your parents or teachers based on how you read their personalities.

In each case, your judgments were personality assessments reflecting your **implicit personality theory**, your personal explanation of personality that almost certainly relied on connecting people's behavior with the traits you attributed to them. Like the *implicit memories* we studied in Chapter 4, *implicit theories of personality* operate in the background, largely outside of our awareness, where they simplify the task of understanding other people (Fiske & Neuberg, 1990; Macrae et al., 1994).

Most of the time, implicit theories work well enough to make social relationships run smoothly—at least in familiar environments. While our expectations can easily miss the mark in unfamiliar cultures, in more familiar territory our implicit theories of personality help us anticipate people's motives and behavior, allowing us to perform our work, buy our morning mochas, pass our courses, and interact with our friends. In some respects, our implicit theories may not be all that different from the five-factor theory. According to a study in which college students rated the personalities of other students they had observed but didn't know, their impressions agreed remarkably well with scores derived from the *Big Five Inventory* (Mehl et al., 2006). There was one interesting exception: Assertive or argumentative behavior was seen by the raters as a sign of emotional stability in men but as indicating emotional *instability* in women!

Implicit theories can have other blind spots, too. They may err by relying on naive assumptions and stereotypes about traits and physical characteristics (Hochwalder, 1995). So, hefty people may be assumed to be jolly or blondes a little short on intellect. Similarly, we may erroneously assume certain traits always go together—creativity and emotional instability, for example. So, what implicit assumptions would you make about the personality of Ken Lay, knowing only that he was a rich entrepreneur who bilked thousands of their life savings?

Implicit theories may also give bad predictions when people's motives and feelings influence their judgment of others' personalities, as Freud suggested with his concept of *projection*. Accordingly, a person who is feeling angry, happy, or depressed may naïvely assume that other people are feeling the same way, too.

Finally, people's implicit theories may conflict on the issue of whether personality traits are fixed or changeable. As you might expect, those believing in fixed traits are more likely to see others as stereotypes (e.g., "all Italians are alike") than are those whose implicit theories assumed the malleability of personality (Molden & Dweck, 2006; Levy et al., 1998). And consider the impact that either assumption—personality as fixed or changeable—could have on a teacher's evaluation of a child or a supervisor's performance review of an employee.

Self-Narratives: The Stories of Our Lives

How do you respond when someone says, "Tell me about yourself"? You probably reply with a few sentences about where you are from, what you like to do with your leisure time, and what your occupational goals are. But what do you say when you ask yourself the same question? The "story" that you tell yourself about yourself is what psychologist Dan McAdams calls a **self-narrative**. He claims that the self-narrative is just as important a component of personality as are motives, emotions, or social relationships.

The self-narrative is really a broader conception of the self-concept: It is the story of the self-concept over time: The self-narrative serves as the common

Implicit personality theory A person's set of unquestioned assumptions about personality, used to simplify the task of understanding others.

Self-narrative The "stories" one tells about oneself. Self-narratives help people sense a thread of consistency through their personality over time.

thread that holds the elements of personality together, like beads on a necklace. And, says McAdams, our identity depends on keeping this narrative going throughout our lives, to give us a sense of unity and purpose.

Culture, of course, has a big effect on the self-narrative stories we *want* to tell ourselves. While McAdams hasn't yet done extensive cross-cultural research, he has identified a peculiarly important self-narrative in the American culture. He calls it the **redemptive self.** See if you recognize yourself in some elements of the redemptive self-narrative:

- You have always felt fortunate—not necessarily because of an economic advantage but perhaps because you have a special talent or were singled out for special treatment by a teacher or other nurturing adult.

- At some point you realized that other people are not so fortunate. Through no fault of their own, they experience suffering or disadvantage.

- Because you are advantaged and others are not, you feel a responsibility or a challenge to improve the lives of others in some way.

- Probably in childhood or adolescence, you developed a belief system, perhaps rooted in religion, although not necessarily so, that has since guided your actions, particularly in your efforts to help others.

- You meet unexpected obstacles and overcome them. You have negative experiences but learn and grow from them, and you see a future of continued growth and progress, despite the near-certainty of daunting obstacles ahead.

It's a narrative of hope and "redemption," because good triumphs over evil; hard work and good intentions succeed despite all obstacles.

Not everyone's self-narrative follows exactly this pattern, of course. But McAdams often finds a pattern like this in *generative* adults, a term originally used by developmental psychologist Erik Erikson to describe healthy, productive adults. More specifically, **generativity** refers to adults who are committed to something outside themselves—to the community and to the welfare of future generations. It remains to be seen what narratives characterize healthy adults in other cultures.

Redemptive self A common self-narrative identified by McAdams in generative Americans. The redemptive self involves a sense of being called to overcome obstacles in the effort to help others.

Generativity The process of making a commitment beyond oneself to family, work, society, or future generations. In Erikson's theory, generativity is the developmental challenge of midlife.

The Effects of Culture on Our Views of Personality

As we have seen, Westerners tend to put the *individual* or the *self* at the center of personality. While people the world over do make the assumption of a distinct self, much of the world—especially those in collectivist cultures—assumes that the self is embedded in a larger social network. They further assume that the individual cannot be understood in isolation from others with whom they have some sort of relationship—which brings us to Harry Triandis.

Individualism, Collectivism, and Personality According to Dr. Triandis (1995), cultures differ most fundamentally on the dimension of *individualism* versus *collectivism*. For those raised in the Euro-American tradition, the individual is the basic unit of society, while those raised in many Asian and African cultures emphasize the family or other social groups. In collectivistic cultures people tend to form identities that blend harmoniously with the group, and they expect that others are motivated to do the same. In individualistic cultures, people think of themselves as having a unique identity, independent of their social relationships (Pedersen, 1979). Thus, for Euro-Americans, the self is a whole, while for many Asians and Africans the self is only a part (Cohen & Gunz, 2002).

Let us be clear: Neither the individualistic nor the collectivistic approach is "better." Each has advantages. The collectivist cultures encourage group effort,

Most Asian cultures have a collectivist tradition that affirms the group, rather than the individual, as the fundamental social unit.

typically for the benefit and glory of the group—often a work group or a family group. On the other hand, a person such as Mary Calkins, who challenged society's norms, would be more likely to thrive in an individualistic culture.

Many aspects of peoples' personalities and behavior derive from their culture's position on the individualism versus collectivism spectrum. So, in judging people, Americans and Europeans tend to make the **fundamental attribution error.** This misperception stems from the assumption that other people's actions, especially annoying, clumsy, inappropriate, or otherwise undesirable behaviors, result from their personalities, rather than from the situation. If you come to your psychology class late, other students are likely to assume that you are a "late" or disorganized person—if you are at an American college or university. But, if you arrived late to a psychology class in China or Japan, the students there would be more likely to assume that your behavior had some external cause, such as traffic problems. In general, the fundamental attribution error is less common in group-oriented, *collectivistic* cultures, such as are found in Latin American and Asia (Church et al., 2005; Lillard, 1997).

Cultures also differ on other dimensions, too. For example, when given the choice of competition or cooperation, individualistic Americans characteristically choose to compete (Aronson, 2004; Gallo & McClintock, 1965). And as we saw in Chapter 9, Americans, on the average, also score higher on measures of need for achievement than do people in collectivist cultures.

Other Cultural Differences   Here is a short list of other personality-related dimensions on which people differ around the world:

- *Status of different age groups and sexes.* The status of the elderly is higher in many Asian and Native American cultures than in the United States; women have second-class status in many non-Western societies (Segall et al., 1999).

- *Romantic love.* While love and affection occur in all cultures, the assumption that romantic love should be the basis for marriage is a historically recent European invention and is most often found in individualistic cultures (Hatfield & Rapson, 1998; Rosenblatt, 1966).

- *Expression of feelings.* Asian cultures teach people to suppress the expression of intense feelings (Tsai & Uemura, 1988), while Euro-Americans are much more likely to express strong emotions (although there can be pronounced gender differences).

- *Locus of control.* Persons in industrialized nations, such as the United States and Canada, more often have an internal locus of control than do those in developing countries, such as Mexico or China (Berry et al., 1992; Draguns, 1979; Shiraev & Levy, 2004).

- *Thinking versus feeling.* Many cultures (e.g., in Latin America) do not make the strong distinction between thoughts and emotions that Americans do (Fajans, 1985; Lutz, 1988).

Cultures also differ in their views of the ideal personality (Matsumoto, 1996). In the Western psychological tradition, mental health consists of integrating opposite and conflicting parts of the personality. This can be seen especially clearly in Freudian and Jungian theory. By contrast, some Asian psychologies, particularly those associated with Buddhism, seek the opposite: to dissociate consciousness from sensation and from memories of worldly experience (Gardiner et al., 1998; Pedersen, 1979).

Despite these differences, can we say that people are fundamentally the same the world over? On the level of neurons and brain circuits, the answer is certainly "yes." But personality is also locked in the embrace of culture, so a more comprehensive answer would be "no—but perhaps they can be described on some of the same dimensions." In the words of Erika Bourguignon (1979), "It

CONNECTION • CHAPTER 11
To avoid the fundamental attribution error, social psychologists recommend first looking for a situational explanation for unusual behavior.

CONNECTION • CHAPTER 9
McClelland has found the *need for achievement* to be an important variable predicting employee performance.

Fundamental attribution error   The dual tendency to overemphasize internal, dispositional causes and minimize external, situational pressures. The FAE is more common in individualistic cultures than in collectivistic cultures.

is one of the major intellectual developments of the twentieth century to call into question the concept of a universal human nature."

Even though personality and culture are partners in a perpetual dance, we can make this distinction between them:

> "Culture" refers to those aspects of a society that all its members share, are familiar with, and pass on to the next generation. "Personality" refers to unique combinations of traits (which all people in a culture know about, even though a given trait does not describe a given person) which differentiate individuals within a culture. (Brislin, 1981, pp. 51–52)

But don't forget that culture and personality interact. A culture shapes the personalities of the individuals within it, just as individuals can influence a culture. So, your personality is, to a certain extent, a product of your society's values, attitudes, beliefs, and customs about morality, work, child rearing, aggression, achievement, competition, death, and dozens of other matters important to humans everywhere. In the broadest sense, then, a culture is the "personality" of a society (Benedict, 1934).

PSYCHOLOGYMATTERS
Developing Your Own Theory of Personality

Each of the theories we have examined has its limitations and strengths. Consequently, most psychologists become **eclectic.** That is, they either apply elements of different theories to best fit each situation or person or construct a hybrid theory of personality by borrowing ideas from many perspectives. While an eclectic approach may appear to offer the easiest route, it presents difficulties that arise from fundamental conflicts among theories. To give one example: How could we reconcile Freud's concept of our behavior being driven by primitive and frightening instincts with humanism's assumption of the innate goodness of our nature?

It may help to think of a personality theory as a map showing the major pathways through a person's psychological landscape. As you formulate your own theory, you must decide how to weight the forces that determine which paths we select—the forces of conditioning, motivation and emotion, heredity and environment, individualism and collectivism, cognition, traits, culture, self-concept, and potential. We propose the following questions, which will help you sort out the assumptions in your own theory of personality:

- In your opinion, are people more rational and logical (as the cognitive theories contend), or do they more often act on the basis of feelings and emotions (as the psychodynamic theories argue)?

- Are people usually conscious of the reasons for their behavior, as many of the neo-Freudians claimed? Or, are their actions mainly caused by unconscious needs, desires, and urges (as Freud suggested)?

- What do you see as the basic motives behind human behavior: sex, aggression, power, love, spirituality . . . ?

- Are human motives essentially egocentric and self-serving? Or are they altruistic, unmotivated by the desire for personal gain (as the humanists suggest)?

- When you try to understand another person's actions, which of the following do you consider to be most important: the person's inner needs, drives, motives, and emotions (as the psychodynamic theories say); the person's basic personality characteristics (as the trait and type theories say); or simply the demands of the situation in which the person is embedded?

- Is our basic, inner nature essentially healthy and good (as the humanists see it) or composed of primitive and self-serving desires (as Freud saw it)?

No one has yet found the "right" answers, but the answers you give say a great deal about your own personality.

Eclectic Either switching theories to explain different situations or building one's own theory of personality from pieces borrowed from many perspectives.

CheckYourUnderstanding

1. **APPLICATION:** Name a country that generally values the achievement of a team or group over that of the individual.

2. **RECALL:** In what important respect have people's implicit theories of personality been found to differ?

3. **RECALL:** McAdams's idea of the redemptive self-narrative is characteristic of American adults who share a characteristic that Erikson called _____.

4. **APPLICATION:** Give an example of the *fundamental attribution error*. In what cultures would you be likely to

find people committing the fundamental attribution error?

5. **UNDERSTANDING THE CORE CONCEPT:** People's implicit personality theories involve
   a. negative, but not positive, characteristics.
   b. the assumptions that they make about each other's motives, intentions, and behaviors.
   c. assumptions about themselves that they want to hide from others.
   d. opinions that they privately hold about others but will not say openly.

Critical Thinking Applied: The Person-Situation Controversy

Cognitive theorist Walter Mischel dropped a scientific bombshell on the personality theorists with evidence suggesting that we behave far less consistently from one situation to another than most had assumed (1968, 1973, 2003). A person who is extraverted at a party can become shy and retiring in class; your "neurotic" friend may become a pillar of strength in a crisis. Like Rosalind, in Shakespeare's *As You Like It*, one person can present different personalities in different situations and to different people. So, Mischel argued, knowledge of the *situation* is more important in predicting behavior than knowing a person's traits. The ensuing tumult within the field has become known as the **person–situation controversy** (Pervin, 1985).

Mischel's argument challenged the very foundations of most personality theories. After all, if people do act inconsistently in different situations, then what good is a theory of personality? Is there no continuity in personality? Critics mounted withering attacks on Mischel's thesis, pointing out that his methods underestimated a thread of consistency across situations (Epstein, 1980). Bem and Allen (1974) have also pointed out that some people behave more consistently than others. Moreover, people are most consistent when others are watching (Kenrick & Stringfield, 1980) and when in familiar situations (Funder, 1983a,b; Funder & Ozer, 1983).

Person–situation controversy A theoretical dispute concerning the relative contribution of personality factors and situational factors in controlling behavior.

While the foundations of personality psychology were shuddering, the person–situation controversy gave a boost to social psychology, where psychologists had always argued the *power of the situation*. As we will see in the next chapter, situations can turn normal college students into liars, lovers, or even cruel tormentors. But where does all this leave us in dealing with the person–situation controversy?

What Is the Issue?

This is *not* an either-or dispute: It's not a question of whether traits *or* situations control behavior. Rather it is a question of which has more influence. All sides of the person–situation debate agree that both the person and the situation have an effect. It's the weighting of the person and the situation that is at issue.

There is a second issue, too. How much does the power of personality traits vary from one situation to another? At the extreme, for a prisoner in solitary confinement, the situation obviously has overwhelming importance. But the more important focus is on ordinary people in their everyday lives: How much power does the situation have vis-à-vis traits? It's not an easy question to answer.

What Critical Thinking Questions Should We Ask?

In defining the issue, we tried to make clear that neither side was making unreasonable or extreme claims, even though Mischel's position came as a shock to the field of personality. So the critical thinking questions that we must ask are, first, "What does the evidence tell us?" And second, "How we can interpret the evidence?"

People Are Inconsistent   Across a wide range of studies, personality traits, as measured by personality tests, typically account for fewer than 10% of all the factors that affect behavior (Digman, 1990)—a small number, indeed! But don't make the mistake of assuming that the situation accounts for the remaining 90%. Correlations between situations and behaviors can be weak, too, as you can plainly see in different people's reactions to a joke or events on the evening news.

Moreover, if we look at the same person over time, we may find him or her reacting very differently to the same situation on different occasions. Consider: Do you *always* order the same thing when you go to your favorite restaurant? Or, are you *always* cheerful with your friends? Psychologist William Fleeson urges us to think of personality traits as a sort of average of how the person customarily behaves. (Perhaps you are *usually* cheerful—on the average.)

Even more surprising was what researchers found when they monitored people as they moved from one situation to another. One study had volunteers carry small personal data assistant (PDA) devices and, several times a day, record their situation, their behavior, and their self-assessment on the Big Five traits. The discovery: People's self-described personality traits change as radically as their behavior when they move from one situation to another (Fleeson, 2004).

The lesson to be learned here is that the majority of factors affecting behavior simply cannot be assigned to the person *or* the situation. Behavior seems to result from an *interaction* of trait and situational variables (Kenrick & Funder, 1988). In fact, Mischel has never suggested that we abandon theories of personality. Rather, he sees behavior as a function of the situation, the individual's *interpretation* of the situation, and the personality (Mischel, 1990, 2003; Mischel & Shoda, 1995).

It Also Depends on *What Kind of* Situation   Suppose that you are walking leisurely through campus, and you see a crowd gathered around a student who has collapsed on the sidewalk. Will you go for help? Because the cues are not clear, this is a "weak" situation, and your actions are likely to depend more strongly on your past experience and on such personality variables as independence and extraversion. Walter Mischel has argued that personality variables have their greatest impact on behavior when cues in the situation are *weak* or *ambiguous.*

Now suppose that, one day when you are in your psychology class, a student collapses, apparently unconscious, onto the floor. After a stunned silence, the instructor asks the class to keep their seats and then points at you, demanding loudly, "Use your cell phone to call 911, and get an ambulance here—Now!" What do you do? This is a "strong" situation: Someone is in control, an instructor you already see as an authority figure; that person has told you unambiguously what to do. You are likely to comply—as would most people in that situation. But when situations are strong and clear, there will be less individual variation in response.

What Conclusions Can We Draw?

Which side of the person-situation debate is right? Both are. The difficulty was that that they were right about different things. According to personality psychologist William Fleeson (2004), traits help us understand behavior over long periods of time, when a thread of consistency can be seen in personality—as an individual's behavior converges on a personal average. Over shorter intervals, and especially in particular situations, a person's behavior can be highly variable, as we have seen. So, by taking a long view, the trait perspective is right, while on a moment-to-moment basis, the situation perspective wins.

But which side gets the most weight also depends on whether the situation is strong or weak, as Michel has said. And to further complicate matters, we have to figure culture into the equation as part of the situation: Evidence has emerged that an individual's personality traits have more influence on behavior in individualistic cultures than in collectivistic cultures (Church et al., 2006). That makes sense, of course, when we think that an individualistic culture places high values on certain traits, such as intelligence (as opposed to hard work). And it also makes sense in light of the finding that people in collectivist cultures are less susceptible to the fundamental attribution error—because they emphasize the power of the situation.

Chapter Summary

10.1 What Forces Shape Our Personalities?

Core Concept 10.1: Personality is shaped by the combined forces of biological, situational, and mental processes—all embedded in a sociocultural and developmental context.

We can think of **personality** as the "default settings" for our unique pattern of motives, emotions, and perceptions, along with our learned schemas for understanding ourselves and our world. Personality also has deep evolutionary roots, as seen in displacement of aggression. Neuroscience suggests that the biology of personality comprises a collection of brain modules, each adapted to a different purpose.

But personality also involves nurture—that is learning driven by the environment, as seen in the effect of family position on personality. The person–situation controversy centers on the relative importance of situations (the environment) as compared with internal traits and mental processes.

The chapter makes an important distinction between personality characteristics, or **dispositions**, and **personality processes**. We need both dispositional theories and process theories for a complete understanding of personality.

Cross-cultural psychologists have complicated the problem of personality by suggesting that personality may not be a universal concept and that Western cultures have a bias toward individualism and a unique self. In fact, all cultures have a tendency either to **individualism** or **collectivism**, both of which leave their imprint on personality. In any culture, however, an individual's personality is, in part, a creation of interactions with other people.

One does not need a theory of personality for explaining ordinary behavior. A good theory, however, is helpful for explaining unusual behavior and eccentric people. The most common theories can be grouped as follows: *dispositional theories* (trait and temperament theories), and *process theories* (psychodynamic theories, humanistic theories, and social-cognitive theories).

Collectivism (p. 434)   **Personality** (p. 430)

Dispositions (p. 433)   **Personality processes** (p. 433)

Individualism (p. 434)

MyPsychLab Resources 10.1:

Explore: Psychodynamic, Behavioral, Trait and Type, Humanistic, and Cognitive Approaches to Personality

- -

10.2 What Persistent Patterns, Or *Dispositions,* Make Up Our Personalities?

Core Concept 10.2: The *dispositional* theories all suggest a small set of personality characteristics, known as temperaments, traits, or types, that provide consistency to the individual's personality over time.

Temperament, trait, and type theories are descriptive approaches to personality with a long history stretching back to the humor theory of the ancient Greeks. Modern theories speak of types, traits, and temperaments. In this chapter, we group all three under the heading of **dispositional theories perspectives.**

Temperament refers to innate personality dispositions, which may be tied to factors in the brain and in the genes. Kagan's work has focused on the inhibited versus uninhibited dimension of temperament. By contrast, traits are thought of as multiple dimensions existing to some degree in each person's personality. Traits give personality consistency across situations and may be influenced by both heredity and learning. Many psychologists now agree on the Big Five traits, which seem to have validity across cultures. Trait assessment is the basis for many psychological tests: Some assess common traits, such as the Big Five, while others, such as the *MMPI-2*, assess clinical characteristics. Both the trait and temperament theories do a reasonably good job of describing and predicting behavior, but they offer no explanations for the underlying processes.

Personality disorders involve long-term defects in personality, such as poor judgment, lack of impulse control, and disturbances in thoughts, emotions, or social relationships.

The person–situation controversy, however, has raised questions about the relative contribution of personality traits and situations to behavior. Narcissistic personality disorder involves egocentric needs. Antisocial personality disorder involves irresponsible or harmful behavior. Borderline personality disorder involves impulsivity and instability.

Type theory is exemplified in the controversial and widely used *MBTI,* based on Jung's personality typology. Research suggests that people's characteristics, as measured by the *MBTI* or other personality tests, do not fall into neat type categories but are more accurately conceived of on trait dimensions.

MyPsychLab Resources 10.2:

Explore: The Five Factor Model

Explore: Personality Assessment

10.3 What Mental *Processes* Are At Work Within Our Personalities?

Core Concept 10.3 While each of the *process* theories sees different forces at work in personality, all portray personality as the result of both internal mental processes and social interactions.

The **psychodynamic, humanistic,** and **social-cognitive theories** all seek to explain the internal processes and social interactions that shape our personalities. Freud's **psychoanalytic theory** states that the personality arises out of **unconscious** desires, conflicts, and memories. None of our thoughts or behaviors happens by accident, according to the principle of **psychic determinism.** Early childhood experiences also have a strong influence on personality, as the child goes through predictable **psychosexual stages** in which conflicts are dealt with unconsciously. Freud believed that the personality consisted of three main structures, the **id** (the reservoir of unconscious desires), the **ego** (the largely conscious part of the mind), and the **superego** (which contains the conscience and the ego ideal). Part of the ego, involving the **ego defense mechanisms,** operates outside of consciousness. One of these defense mechanisms, projection, is the basis for widely used **projective tests,** including the *Rorschach* and the *TAT.*

Freud's theory has been extremely influential. Still, critics fault Freud's work for being scientifically unsound, a poor basis for prediction, and unfair to women. Modern psychology also suggests that the unconscious mind is less clever and purposeful than Freud believed.

Other psychodynamic theories, such as those proposed by Jung and Horney, also assume that personality is a dynamic process that involves strong and often-conflicting motives and emotions. Each of these **neo-Freudians,** however, emphasizes different aspects of personality. Jung proposed a **collective unconscious,** populated by **archetypes.** He also proposed that people fall into certain personality types, characterized especially by tendencies to **introversion** and **extraversion.** Horney, on the other hand, emphasized conscious processes, **basic anxiety, neurotic needs,** and feminist issues in personality theory. Some other neo-Freudians,

such as Erikson, also emphasized consciousness, as well as life-long personality development.

The humanistic theories, such as those of Maslow and Rogers, argue that people are naturally driven toward **self-actualization,** but this tendency can be suppressed by unhealthy conditions and perceptions. Maslow proposed a hierarchy of needs, suggesting that when the deficiency needs are met, a person is more likely to pursue self-actualization. Rogers taught that the **fully functioning person** has a positive self-concept that is congruent with reality, while mental disorder arises from incongruence. High self-esteem is more likely which a child comes from a family that provides unconditional positive regard.

The humanistic theories have had considerable impact on psychotherapy, but they have been criticized for being "self"-centered and lacking a strong scientific base. The social-cognitive theories, by contrast, do have a scientific basis, although they are much more limited in scope than are the psychodynamic and humanistic theories. Bandura's social-cognitive theory suggests that personality is shaped by **observational learning.** This occurs in an interaction of cognition, behavior, and the environment known as **reciprocal determinism.** According to Rotter's **locus-of-control theory,** those with an internal locus are more likely to feel they can control events in their lives than those who have an external locus of control.

Modern theories of personality, unlike those of Freud, Jung, Horney, and the other psychodynamic theorists, have not attempted to provide comprehensive explanations for all aspects of personality. In **family systems theory,** for example, emphasis has turned to the individual acting in a social environment. Other emphases include cultural influences on personality, as well as an awareness of gender differences.

MyPsychLab Resources 10.3:

Explore: The Id, Ego, and Superego

Explore: Freud's Five Psychosexual Stages of Personality
Development

10.4 What "Theories" Do People Use to Understand Themselves And Others?

Core Concept 10.4: Our understanding of ourselves and others is based on implicit theories of personality and our own self-narratives—both of which are influenced by culture.

People everywhere deal with each other on the basis of their **implicit personality theories,** which simplify the task of understanding others. Implicit theories often use the same traits that the five-factor theory does, although some gender biases have been reported. Implicit theories also may rely on naïve assumptions, and they often differ on whether personality is fixed or changeable.

People also have theories about themselves, found in the stories, called **self-narratives,** that they tell about themselves. These stories provide a sense of consistency and purpose in their lives. McAdams finds that **generative** American adults often use a **redemptive self** narrative that involves feeling a need to help others, despite facing daunting obstacles that are finally overcome.

Moreover, cross-cultural psychologists have found that the assumptions people make about personality and behavior vary widely across cultures—depending especially on whether the culture emphasizes individualism or collectivism. Those in individualistic cultures are more prone to the **fundamental attribution error.** There are many other dimensions impinging on personality on which cultures differ, including social status, romantic love, expression of feelings, locus of control, and thinking versus feeling.

Because no single personality theory can describe and explain the whole personality, most psychologists develop their own **eclectic** theories of personality by combining ideas from various perspectives.

Discovering Psychology Viewing Guide

 Watch the following video by logging into MyPsychLab (www.mypsychlab.com). After you have watched the video, complete the activities that follow.

 PROGRAM 15: THE SELF

PROGRAM REVIEW

1. What name did William James give to the part of the self that focuses on the images we create in the mind of others?
   a. the material self
   b. the spiritual self
   c. the social self
   d. the outer self

2. Gail is a toddler who is gradually separating from her mother. This process is called
   a. identification.
   b. individuation.
   c. self-presentation.
   d. self-consciousness.

3. In Freudian theory, the part of the person that acts as a police officer restraining drives and passions is called the
   a. superego.
   b. ego.
   c. id.
   d. libido.

4. Which statement reflects the humanistic view of the self, according to Carl Rogers?
   a. Our impulses are in constant conflict with society's demands.
   b. We have a capacity for self-direction and self-understanding.
   c. We form an image of ourselves that determines what we can do.
   d. Our views of ourselves are created by how people react to us.

5. When we characterize self-image as a schema, we mean that
   a. we use it to organize information about ourselves.
   b. other people see us in terms of the image we project.

   c. it is a good predictor of performance in specific situations.
   d. we rationalize our behavior to fit into an image.

6. In Albert Bandura's research, people were given the task of improving production at a model furniture factory. They performed best when they believed that performance
   a. depended on their intelligence.
   b. related mainly to how confident they felt.
   c. would be given a material reward.
   d. was based on learning an acquirable skill.

7. Which of the following behaviors signal low status in a status transaction?
   a. maintaining eye contact
   b. using complete sentences
   c. moving in slow, smooth way
   d. touching one's face or hair

8. According to the principles of behavioral confirmation, what reaction do people generally have to a person who is depressed?
   a. People sympathetically offer help to the person.
   b. People regard the person as inadequate.
   c. People act falsely cheerful to make the person happy.
   d. People treat a depressed person the same as anybody else.

9. What was referred to in the film as a type of psychological genocide?
   a. drugs
   b. falling emphasis on education
   c. prejudice
   d. immigration

10. What is the relevance of schemas to the self?
    a. We try to avoid schemas in constructing our sense of self.

b. We organize our beliefs about ourselves in terms of schemas.

c. Schemas are what makes us individuals.

d. Schemas are always negative, since they underlie prejudice.

11. In Teresa Amabile's work on creativity, how did being in a competitive situation affect creativity?

a. It reduced creativity.

b. It increased creativity.

c. Its effects varied depending on the person's innate creativity.

d. There was no effect.

12. According to Hazel Markus, culture is what you

a. think.

b. see.

c. do.

d. hate.

13. The phrase "mutual constitution" refers to which two components, according to Hazel Markus?

a. parent and child

b. art and scholarship

c. religion and society

d. self and culture

14. In which culture are you most likely to find a definition of the person as a part of the group?

a. Japanese

b. American

c. Portugese

d. Russian

15. The high rate of alcoholism among Native Americans was cited as an example of

a. individualism.

b. the psychological effects of prejudice.

c. mutual constitution.

d. striving for superiority.

16. According to William James, which part of the self serves as our inner witness to outside events?

a. the material self

b. the spiritual self

c. the social self

d. the outer self

17. Of the following psychologists, who is considered to be the least optimistic about the human condition?

a. Freud

b. Adler

c. Rogers

d. Maslow

18. Which of the following refers to how capable we believe we are of mastering challenges?

a. self-efficacy

b. self-handicapping

c. confirmatory behavior

d. status transaction

19. Teresa Amabile is to creativity as _____ is to behavioral confirmation.

a. Alfred Adler

b. Patricia Ryan

c. Mark Snyder

d. Albert Bandura

20. Who is credited as being responsible for psychology's return to the self?

a. William James

b. B. F. Skinner

c. Patricia Ryan

d. Carl Rogers

QUESTIONS TO CONSIDER

1. What are some of the positive and negative aspects of the id, according to Freud?

2. Compare the social skills of your friends and yourself to people who did not grow up with computers and the Internet playing a central role in their lives. Do you see systematic differences in sociability, shyness, and apparent self-concept?

ACTIVITIES

1. How do you recognize extroverts and introverts? Observe people on television, in a public place, or at home. Rate their behavior on a continuum between the opposites of extrovert and introvert. How helpful is the distinction? Do these qualities seem to be a primary dimension of personality?

2. Describe yourself by highlighting your special abilities, admirable qualities, and accomplishments. Write a brief description of your parents, spouse, children, or a close friend. Consider how often you appreciate the positive aspects of your own or another's personality and how often you focus on the negatives. How does your

focus affect your own self-esteem and your relationships?

3. Take some characteristic about yourself that you have never liked (e.g., the tendency to interrupt, or the tendency to become tongue-tied around people of higher status than you). Spend the next month seeing if you can completely rid yourself of that characteristic. If you are successful, how would you describe the shift? Was it a change in your personality, or was it a change in behavior despite the underlying traits that used to produce it?

Critical Thinking Applied: Is Terrorism "a Senseless Act of Violence, Perpetrated by Crazy Fanatics"?

 امروز
عراق

W hile reading the Sunday newspaper, Bill notices that a prestigious university is recruiting people to participate in a psychological study designed to help people improve their memory. He decides to volunteer for what seems like an interesting and worthwhile experiment, for which he will also get paid a fee. On his arrival at the university's laboratory, Bill is greeted by the researcher and introduced to a second applicant named Douglas. The experimenter explains that the research study will test a new method of improving people's learning and memory—by punishing them for their errors. "We know," he says, "from earlier research by psychologist B. F. Skinner and other behaviorists that positive reinforcement for correct responding is a key to developing animal and human memory. We now want to test whether punishing someone for incorrect responses will have a similar effect."

The task is straightforward: Bill will play the role of the "Teacher" and give Douglas, the "Learner," a set of word pairings to memorize in a given time period. Every time that the Learner provides the correct answer, the Teacher gives him a verbal reward, "Good" or "That's right." When wrong, the Teacher is to press a lever on the impressive-looking shock apparatus that delivers an immediate shock to punish the error.

The shock generator has 30 switches, starting from a low level of only 15 volts and increasing in intensity all the way up to 450 volts. The control panel indicates both the voltage level of each of the switches and a corresponding description of that level. For instance, the 25th level (375 volts) is labeled "Danger, Severe Shock," and at the 29th and 30th levels (435 and 450 volts) the control panel is simply marked with an ominous XXX. The experimenter goes on to note that every time the Learner makes a mistake, the Teacher must press the next higher level voltage switch.

The Learner is escorted into an adjacent room, where his arms are strapped down and an electrode is attached to his right wrist. The shock generator in the next room will deliver the shocks to the Learner—if and when he makes any errors. Doug mentions that he has a slight heart condition and hopes the shocks will not hurt him much. He is reassured not to worry, that the shocks may become strong but will not cause any permanent damage. Bill administers the test material and communicates over the intercom to Doug, while the Experimenter stands near him.

Initially, Doug performs well, getting rewarding praise from Bill. However, he soon starts making errors, for which Bill immediately starts pressing those shock switches. As Doug messes up more and more, the shock levels are going up, and he complains that the shocks are starting to hurt. At 75 volts, he moans and groans; at 150 volts, the tenth level, Doug has had enough and demands to be released from the experiment. Bill looks anxiously at the Experimenter, who nods that he must continue. As the shock levels increase in intensity, so do the Learner's screams, as well as his reminder that he has a heart condition. Bill is now really distressed: "Sir, who will be responsible if anything happens to that man?" The Experimenter dismisses his concern about personal responsibility by declaring, "I will be fully responsible, now continue your task, Teacher." More trials, more shocks, more screams from the next room. Bill hesitates, questioning whether he should go on, but the Experimenter insists that he has no choice but to do so.

At 300 volts, the Learner demands to be freed and complains louder about his heart condition. Bill has had enough, he verbally dissents, "I can't continue to hurt him, sir, I refuse to go on." The Experimenter calmly insists that Bill must continue because he has a contract to complete the experimental procedure.

Reluctantly, Bill goes on punishing Doug for his errors until he reaches the level of 330 volts. Bill hears screams, a thud, and then silence from the shock chamber. "He is not responding; someone should go in there to see if he is all right." But the Experimenter is impassive and tells Bill, "If the learner doesn't answer in a reasonable time, about 5 seconds, consider it wrong," because errors of omission (failing to respond) must be punished in the same way as errors of commission—that is The Rule you must obey.

As Bill continues to give the next test stimulus, there is no response from his pupil, Doug. Bill complains louder that it doesn't make sense for him to continue under these circumstances. However, nothing he says gets the Experimenter to allow him to exit from this unexpectedly distressing situation. Instead, he is told to mind his business, to simply follow the rules because Bill's job as Teacher is to keep posing the test items and shocking the Learner's errors—even if it means going all the way up the scale to the full and final 450 volts.

How do you think you would act if you were in Bill's seat as the Teacher in this memory experiment? At what shock level would you absolutely refuse to continue?

Most of us believe that we would have verbally dissented, then disobeyed behaviorally, and just walked out. You would never sell out your morality for few dollars!

This experiment was actually conducted by a young social psychologist named Stanley Milgram back in 1963, at Yale University in New Haven, Connecticut, where he was a new assistant professor. He tested more than 500 ordinary citizens from all walks of life (none were students) and discovered that two out of every three Teachers (65%) went all the way up to the maximum shock level of 450 volts. You will read more about Milgram's experiment later in this chapter, but for now let's examine what this experiment tells us about human nature.

PROBLEM: What makes ordinary people harm other people, as they did in this shocking experiment?

It is equally important to realize that although the majority obeyed fully, there was a minority who did refuse to give into this unjust authority. We then want to consider what makes people help others, come to the aid of the distressed, volunteer their time and services, and even act heroically?

• •

Welcome to **social psychology**, the field that investigates how individuals affect each other. It may be a relief to hear that not all of social psychology brings such bad news about ourselves as does this experiment on obedience to authority. The exciting field of psychology also explores the forces that bring people together for friendships and loving relationships, as well for cooperation and conflict resolution. As you study social psychology in this chapter, you will learn how people's thoughts, feelings, perceptions, motives, and behavior are influenced by interactions with others. Social psychologists try to understand behavior within its social context. Defined broadly, the **social context** includes the real, imagined, or symbolic presence of other people; the activities and interactions that take place among people; the settings in which behavior occurs; and the expectations and social norms governing behavior in a given setting (Sherif, 1981). Simply put, social psychologists study the person in her or his behavioral context. They are curious to discover the interrelationships between the person and the situation, how individual personality and character may affect behavior in social settings, and also how they are in turn influenced by factors in the social situation. Of course, such a focus includes investigating group behavior, such as teamwork and conformity, as well as group prejudice and terrorism.

Most of all, the obedience research underscores *the power of social situations to control human behavior*. This is a major theme to emerge from social psychological research of the past 50 years. In the first part of this chapter, you will see how seemingly minor features of social settings can have a huge impact on what we think and how we feel and act. In these studies you will see how the situation can produce conformity to group standards—even when the group is clearly "wrong."

Yet, as powerful as any situation can be, psychologists know that it is not only objective reality to which we respond. It is not just the physical size and shape and color of a room that might affect how we act when in it; rather, we respond to our subjective interpretation of the situation—to our personal *perception*—of what it means to us. Thus, the same physical setting can differ significantly from person to person, and it can change over time as we experience it differently. You know this intuitively from how you came to like or dislike your homeroom in grade school, your dorm room, or even the psychology classroom from day one to now. This, then, is the second important theme in social psychology: *the personal construction of a subjective social reality*. We

Social psychology The branch of psychology that studies the effects of social variables and cognitions on individual behavior and social interactions.

Social context The combination of (a) people, (b) the activities and interactions among people, (c) the setting in which behavior occurs, and (d) the expectations and social norms governing behavior in that setting.

SOCIAL PSYCHOLOGY   **479**

must grasp this world of expectations and perceptions to understand the attractive forces at work in building friendships and romantic relationships as well as the repulsive forces underlying violence, prejudice, and discrimination.

In the third part of this chapter, we inquire *who or what creates various situations and maintains them*, such as prisons, gangs, cults, torture centers, and other settings that have an impact on human behavior. Initially, we will focus on research that highlights the ways that *situations* matter in influencing how we think, feel, and act. Next, we expand our perspective to highlight the ways that *systems* matter in creating, maintaining, and justifying various life situations, for better or for worse. A classroom where bullying is taking place would be a *situation*, a behavioral context, whereas the *system* would be the school administration and its policies and procedures. We will also see how social psychologists have experimented with altering the situation to change subjective social reality that, in turn, helps to promote the human condition. Sometimes that also involves ways to change systems from destructive or unproductive to constructive and engaging. That is a lofty goal of many social psychologists who are hard at work to help realize it in many domains.

We begin now with the first of these three themes, the power of the situation, and we are delighted to share with you what we consider to be some of the most interesting research in all of psychology.

11.1 KEY QUESTION
HOW DOES THE SOCIAL SITUATION AFFECT OUR BEHAVIOR?

Imagine you find yourself in an interview for great summer job, with the possibility of being hired as an intern at Google.com. During the interview, the interviewer tries to break the ice by telling an off-color sexual joke that you personally find a bit offensive. Do you let him know what you are feeling, or do you laugh? Afterward, he suggests that you go to lunch together in the company cafeteria. Because the lunch is free, do you go all out and order a full-course meal with some good wine, or a simpler healthier one? Do you start the conversation or wait for him to direct it? Do you gulp down your favorite dessert before the soup that is less appealing to you? After you cut the meat, will you shift your fork from your left hand to your right hand as you put the food you cut into your mouth, or do you stick with it in your left hand? Even in this simple social situation, there are many social and cultural rules governing what is appropriate and acceptable behavior. If you are like most people in an unfamiliar situation such as this, you will take your cues of what is the "right" thing to do from those around you. The interviewer essentially sets the table for the conversation, and you follow suit, as well as order the kind of meal he is having, and pretend to like his off-color joke. You want the job and therefore are more compliant than you might be otherwise. Europeans do not switch hands, as Americans do, when eating, a habit learned in family settings by observing others, rarely being told to do so. Desserts, however desirable, come last in the eating sequence.

The power of situations to dominate our personalities and override our past history of learning, values, and beliefs is greatest when we are enmeshed in new settings. The more novel the situation, the less we rely on our past habitual ways of responding and call into action our usually automatic cognitive biases. We look to others to define for us what is necessary to behave in ways others will find acceptable and appropriate. But what is acceptable in your first visit to a church service or a funeral will be quite different from your first experience with fraternity hazing or at a rock concert "mosh pit." We will see that the pressures of these social situations can have powerful psychological effects, getting us to do things we might never do ordinarily—even immoral, unethical, and illegal actions. Those pressures were operating on Bill when he was acting the role of

"Teacher" in Milgram's obedience experiment leading him to deliver extremely painful shocks to an innocent, likeable "Learner." Social roles, situational rules, how we are dressed, whether we are anonymous or highly visible, if we are in a competition, or the mere presence of others can all profoundly influence how we behave. Often, these subtle situational variables affect us in many ways even without our awareness. They may guide our actions in mindless ways. Our Core Concept emphasizes this point:

In this section, we will review some research that explores this concept, called *situationism*. **Situationism** assumes that the external environment, or the behavioral context, can have both subtle and forceful effects on people's thoughts, feelings, and behaviors. Situationism is contrasted with *dispositionism*, the tendency to attribute behavior to internal factors, such as genes, personality traits, and character qualities. **Dispositionism** is the tendency to look within the individual actor for explanations of why someone acted in a particular way. Social psychologists argue that such a tendency has limited our appreciation of the extent to which social situations offer the better explanation for that behavior. Of course, it is not a matter of either-or, but usually there is an interaction between dispositional tendencies and situational forces to shape the final behavior that we observe and want to understand. Here we will look particularly at the power of the situation to create conformity, obedience, mindless groupthink, and the failure to help others in distress.

Social Standards of Behavior

A job interview, such as the one described above, provides an example of a situational influence on your behavior as you try to do "what is right" in front of your prospective employer, sometimes to do anything to get that prized job. You will also notice the power of the situation when you compare the way students talk to their friends versus their professors or how you act at family dinners versus watching favorite TV programs with your pals. Most people learn to size up their social circumstances and conform their behavior to situational demands. The responses most people make depend heavily on two factors, the *social roles* they play and *social norms* of the group. Let us look at both of these closely.

Social Roles and Social Norms   How do you go about answering the basic question: Who are you? One answer might be: I am a student, work part-time at a store, firstborn in a big family, religious, patriotic, a cyclist, musician, good friend, and occasional spammer. Each of those descriptors become a *social role* you play in your personal life drama. People from a culture that is more focused on collective values than individual values might answer the "Who am I?" question with: I am a sister, a part of family X, of member or tribe Y. A **social role** is one of several socially defined patterns of behavior that are expected of persons in a given setting or group. The roles you assume may result from your interests, abilities, and goals— or they may be imposed on you by the group or by cultural, economic, or biological conditions beyond your control. In any case, social roles prescribe your behavior by making obvious what you should do, how you should do it, when, where, and why. Some roles are organized around our gender, such as women being more likely to be caregivers for children and the elderly. Other key roles are organized around family activities, such as plans vacations, takes out trash, cooks, sets table, repairs broken things. Occupations are filled with many roles, such as receptionist, union organizer, manager, claims agent, and more.

The situations in which you live and function also determine the roles that are available to you and the behaviors others expect of you. Being a college stu-

Situationism   The view that environmental conditions may influence people's behavior as much or more than their personal dispositions do, under some circumstances.

Dispositionism   A psychological orientation that focuses primarily on the inner characteristics of individuals, such as personality dispositions, values, character, and genetic makeup. Contrasted with situationism, the focus is on external causes of behavior.

Social role   A socially defined pattern of behavior that is expected of persons in a given setting or group.

dent, for example, is a social role that carries certain implicit assumptions about attending classes, studying, and handing in papers before deadline. It also implies a certain degree of privilege, of usually not having to work full time, and of being interested in improving how your mind works and also your career options. In addition, the adoption of this role makes other roles less likely. Thus, your role as college student diminishes the chances that you will assume the role of homeless person, drug pusher, or witch doctor, for example. But more mature students might head their own family, hold full-time jobs, be returning veterans, and be social-political activists.

In addition to specific social roles that individuals enact, groups develop many "unwritten rules" for the ways that all members should act. Gangs may demand unquestioned obedience to their leader and a willingness to fight or kill anyone designated as the enemy. Male executives in technology businesses usually do not wear ties and often wear jeans to work, which would be the wrong attire in other business settings. Muslim women students may wear veils to class (as a religious statement). People from some cultures greet each other by kissing on the cheek in a fixed order, right then left, and in Poland add a third kiss for good measure. These expectations, called **social norms,** dictate socially appropriate attitudes and behaviors in particular behavioral settings. Social norms can be broad guidelines, such as ideas about which political or religious attitudes are considered acceptable. Social norms can also be quite specific, embodying standards of conduct such as being quiet in the library or shining your shoes for a job interview. Norms can guide conversation, as when they restrict discussion of sensitive or taboo subjects in the presence of certain company. And norms can define dress codes, whether requiring uniforms or business suits or prohibiting shorts and tank tops. Some norms exist in unwritten rules that are built into various situations, such as when teachers are lecturing, students are expected to listen and not talk simultaneously. However, what about the norms governing your behavior in elevators? We bet you always face the front of the elevator and either stop talking to a friend or talk lower when others are there as well. Why? Where are those rules written? How did you learn them? What will happen the next time when you enter an elevator filled with other people and you face the rear? Try that little experiment and see how others react. Or try sitting down when everyone stands up for the national anthem. To know if a social norm is operating, just try to violate it and check out the reactions of others in that same setting. If they express distress of some kind, you broke the norm.

When a person joins a new group, such as a work group or a group of friends, there is always an adjustment period during which the individual tries to discover how best to fit in. Adjustment to a group typically involves discovering its social norms. Individuals experience this adjustment in two ways: by first noticing the *uniformities* and *regularities* in certain behaviors, and then by observing the *negative consequences* when someone violates a social norm.

For example, a new student in your school who carries books and notes in an attaché case will be seen as "out of it" if backpacks are in, and vice versa in other schools. The same is true of dress codes, which are rarely explicit but can guide how almost everyone dresses. Guys wearing baseball caps backward or sideways would have been laughed at a generation ago, before they were "in." The same is now true with athletes wearing diamond earrings or flashy body tattoos. Also, elaborate handshake rituals among some guys have replaced the "old-fashioned" simple hand-in-hand.

Schemas and Scripts Recall the way in which we form schemas to help organize lots of information and for guiding our actions. A *schema* is a cluster of related concepts that provides a general conceptual framework for thinking about a topic, an event, an object, a person, or a situation in one's life. Once a schema is formed, it enables us to make predictions about what to expect in various settings. It is often upsetting when one of our schemas is violated and fails to predict the

CONNECTION • CHAPTER 3
Bandura demonstrated that we acquire many social behaviors through observational learning.

Social norms A group's expectations regarding what is appropriate and acceptable for its members' attitudes and behaviors.

CONNECTION • CHAPTER 5
Schemas are cognitive structures that integrate knowledge and expectations about a topic or concept.

expected. Imagine going into a (non–fast food) restaurant, ordering your meal, and getting the bill before any food appears. Imagine that the waitperson brings the dessert first, then the main course, then the appetizer. Violation of expectation! Schemas become "shoulds" about how people ought to behave in certain settings; and when they do not, this provokes negative reactions, when we assume that person must be sharing our schema. The restaurant example involved a violation of an event schema or script. A **script** involves a person's knowledge about the *sequence* of events and actions that is expected of a particular social role in a given setting.

Social Norms Influence Students' Political Views   Can the political views of faculty influence those of their students? Social psychologist Theodore Newcomb posed this question. The college: Vermont's Bennington College. The time: the 1930s. The students: women from wealthy, conservative homes with decidedly conservative values. The faculty: young, dynamic, and liberal. Bennington's campus culture had a prevailing norm of political and economic liberalism. The researcher wondered: Which forces most shape the attitudes of these students, their family's or their faculty's? His data showed that the immediately present norms of the campus won the war of influence against the remote norms of the family. In most women, their initial attitude of conservatism was transformed as they progressed through their college years, so that by their senior year they had clearly converted to liberal thinking and causes (Newcomb, 1943). But was that shift in attitudes enduring?

Twenty years later, the social influence of the Bennington experience was still evident. Women who had graduated as liberals were still liberals; the minority who had resisted the prevailing liberal norm had remained conservative. This was accomplished in part by each of them marrying their "own kind" politically. Most of the women had married husbands with values similar to their own—either liberal or conservative—and created supportive new home environments that sustained those different ideologies. The liberal Bennington allegiance was evident in the 1960 presidential election, when 60% of the class Newcomb had investigated voted for liberal John Kennedy, rather than conservative Richard Nixon—in contrast to less than 30% support for Kennedy among graduates of comparable colleges at that time (Newcomb et al., 1967).

Campus culture is not the only source of norms and group pressure, of course. One's workplace, neighborhood, religious group, and family all communicate standards for behavior—and threaten sanctions (such as firing, social rejection, or excommunication) for violating those norms. But a high school, college, or university environment can have a powerful impact on young people. This is especially true if they have had narrow life experiences and had not previously encountered attitudes radically different from their own. For example, new college students commonly adopt classmates' political opinions, as in the Bennington study, and also frequently take on religious beliefs of classmates, as well as attitudes about sex and alcohol (see Prentice & Miller, 1993; Schroeder & Prentice, 1995).

Conformity

How powerful are these social pressures? We can see the effects of social pressure in people's moods, clothing styles, and leisure activities (Totterdell, 2000; Totterdell et al., 1998). This tendency to mimic other people is called the **chameleon effect,** after the animal that changes its skin color to fit into its varied environments (Chartrand & Bargh, 1999). We have seen how social pressure in political attitudes influenced Bennington College students. But can social influence be strong enough to make people follow a group norm that is clearly and objectively wrong? Could the power of that situation prove stronger than the evidence of your own eyes? Could a group of strangers get you to see the world through their distorted eyes?

Script   Knowledge about the sequence of events and actions that is expected in a particular setting.

Chameleon effect   The tendency to mimic other people, named after the animal that changes its skin color to fit into its varied environments.

FIGURE 11.1
Conformity in the Asch experiments

In this photo from Asch's study, the naive individual, number 6, displays obvious concern about the majority's erroneous judgment. At top right, you see a typical stimulus array. At top left, the graph illustrates conformity across 12 critical trials, when individuals were grouped with a unanimous majority or had the support of a single dissenting partner. (A lower percentage of correct estimates indicates a greater degree of conformity with the group's false judgment.)

The Asch Effect

Solomon Asch (1940, 1956) set out to answer just such questions by having a group of his confederates challenge the perception of individual students by making them think that their eyes were deceiving them. (Some researchers use confederates as their assistants who act as regular participants to either model some behavior or try to influence the behavior of the actual participant.) In Asch's study, male college students were told they would be participating in a study of visual perception. They were shown cards with three lines of differing lengths and asked to indicate which of the three lines was the same length as a separate, standard line. (See Figure 11.1.) The problem was simple: The lines were different enough so that mistakes were rare when volunteers responded alone. But when those same individuals were put in a group of other students who had been coached to give wrong answers, then everything changed.

Here's how the experiment worked. On the first three trials, everyone agreed on the correct answer. But the first person to respond on the fourth trial reported an obviously incorrect judgment, reporting as equal two lines that were clearly different. So did the next person and so on, until all members of the group but the remaining one (the only real subject in the experiment) had unanimously agreed on an erroneous judgment. That person then had to decide whether to go along with everyone else's view of the situation and conform or remain independent, standing by the objective evidence of his own eyes. This group pressure was imposed on 12 of the 18 trials.

What did he and other participants in his position finally do? As you might expect, nearly everyone showed signs of disbelief and discomfort when faced with a majority who saw the world so differently from the way he did. But despite his distress, the group pressure usually prevailed. Three-quarters of those subjected to group pressure conformed to the false judgment of the group one or more times, while only one-fourth remained completely independent on all trials. In various related studies, between 50 and 80% conformed with the majority's false estimate at least once; a third yielded to the majority's wrong judgments on half or more of the critical trials. Pressure to conform to the group standard won over pressure to believe what one's eyes and brain were reporting to the mind.

Social psychologists call this the **Asch effect:** the influence of a group majority on the judgments of an individual. The Asch effect has become the classic illustration of **conformity**—the tendency for people to adopt the behavior and opinions presented by other group members. Even though individuals were judging matters of fact, not merely personal opinions, most caved in to conformity pressures.

At the same time, we should recognize that the Asch effect, powerful as it is, still does not make everyone conform. Conformity researchers do regularly find "independents," individuals who are bothered and even dismayed to find themselves in disagreement with the majority but who nonetheless stand their ground and "call 'em as they see 'em"—even to the point of deliberately giving a wrong answer when the group gives a correct one (Friend et al., 1990). As we will see in a host of other studies in this chapter, more often than not the majority conforms, complies, and gives up personal standards for group standards.

Group Characteristics That Produce Conformity   In further experiments, Asch identified three factors that influence whether a person will yield to group pressure: (1) the size of the majority, (2) the presence of a partner who dissented from the majority, and (3) the size of the discrepancy between the correct answer and the majority's position. He found that individuals tended to conform with a unanimous majority of as few as three people but not if they faced only one or two. However, even in a large group, giving the person one ally who dissented from the majority opinion sharply reduced conformity (as shown in Figure 11.1). With such a "partner," nearly all subjects resisted the pressures to conform. Remarkably, however, some individuals continued to yield to the group even with a partner present. All who yielded later underestimated the influence of the social pressure and the frequency of their conformity; a few even claimed that they really had seen the lines as the majority had claimed so were not conforming, but were only reporting accurately what they were seeing (Asch, 1955, 1956). The Asch effect is the demonstration of a group's conformity impact on an individual's perception and judgments. Numerous studies have revealed additional factors that influence conformity. (These experiments have included both females and males.) Specifically, a person is more likely to conform under the following circumstances:

- When a judgment task is difficult or ambiguous (Saltzstein & Sandberg, 1979).
- When the group members are perceived as especially competent.
- When their responses are given publicly rather than privately.
- When the group majority is unanimous—but once that unanimity is broken, the rate of conformity drops dramatically (Allen & Levine, 1969; Morris & Miller, 1975).

So now imagine you are about to vote openly in a group, as is common in clubs or on boards of directors. You will probably conform to the group majority if: (a) the issue being decided is complex or confusing, (b) others in the group seem to know what they are talking about, (c) you must vote by raising your hand instead of casting an anonymous ballot, (d) the entire group casting their votes before you all vote in a certain way, and especially if (e) the leader votes first.

Being informed about such conformity pressures should make you wiser about how you might go along with the group even when they are heading in a wrong or even immoral direction. Resisting such influence requires critical thinking and being mindful of what you have learned about the power of social forces.

Asch effect   A form of conformity in which a group majority influences individual judgments of unambiguous stimuli, as with line judgments.

Conformity   The tendency for people to adopt the behaviors, attitudes, and opinions of other members of a group.

In the Asch effect, people conform because of *normative influences,* wanting to be accepted, approved, liked, and not to be rejected by others. Another reason for conformity comes from *informational influences,* wanting to be correct and to understand the correct way to act in any given situation.

The Autokinetic Effect   A classic experiment, conducted by Muzafer Sherif (1935), demonstrated how informational influence can lead to norm formation and internalization of that new norm. Participants were asked to judge the amount of movement of a spot of light, which was actually stationary but that appeared to move when viewed in total darkness with no reference points. This is a perceptual illusion known as the **autokinetic effect.** Originally, individual judgments varied widely. However, when the participants were brought together in a group consisting of strangers and stated their judgments aloud, their estimates began to converge. They began to see the light move in the same direction and in similar amounts. Even more interesting was the final part of Sherif's study—when alone in the same darkened room after the group viewing, these participants continued to follow the group norm that had emerged when they were together.

Once norms are established in a group, they tend to perpetuate themselves. In later research, these autokinetic group norms persisted even when tested a year later when the former participants were retested alone—without former group members witnessing the judgments (Rohrer et al., 1954). Norms can be transmitted from one generation of group members to the next and can continue to influence people's behavior long after the original group that created the norm no longer exists (Insko et al., 1980). How do we know that norms can have transgenerational influence? In autokinetic effect studies, researchers replaced one group member with a new one after each set of autokinetic trials until all the members of the group were new to the situation. The group's autokinetic norm remained true to the one handed down to them across several successive generations (Jacobs & Campbell, 1961). Do you see how this experiment captures the processes that allow real-life norms to be passed down across generations?

Conformity and Independence Light Up the Brain Differently   New technology, not available in Asch's day, offers intriguing insights into the role of the brain in social conformity. When people conform, are they rationally deciding to go along with the group out of normative needs, or are they actually changing their perceptions and accepting the validity of the new, though erroneous, information provided by the group? A recent study used advanced brain-scanning technology to answer this question. It also answers the question of whether the old Asch effect could work with the current generation of more sophisticated students. (A peek ahead says, "Yes.")

Using functional magnetic resonance imaging (fMRI), researchers can now peer into the active brain as a person engages in various tasks and detect which specific brain regions are energized as they carry out these tasks. Understanding what mental functions those brain regions control tells us what it means when they are activated by any given experimental task.

Here's how the study worked. Imagine that you are one of 32 volunteers recruited for a study of perception. You have to mentally rotate images of three-dimensional objects to determine if the objects are the same or different from a standard object. In the waiting room, you meet four other volunteers, with whom you begin to bond by practicing games on laptop computers, taking photos of one another, and chatting. They are really actors, "confederates" who will soon be faking their answers on the test trials so that they are in agreement with each other, but not with the correct responses that you generate. You are selected as the one to go into the scanner while the others outside look at the objects first as a group and then decide if they are same or different. As in Asch's original experiment, the actors unanimously give wrong answers on some trials, correct answers on others, with occasional mixed-group answers thrown in to make the test more believable. On each round, when it is your turn at bat, you are shown

CONNECTION • CHAPTER 2

Neuroscientists use *brain scanning* as a technique for studying specific brain areas activated by different mental tasks.

Autokinetic effect   The perceived motion of a stationary dot of light in a totally dark room. Used by Muzafir Sherif to study the formation of group norms.

the answers given by the others. You have to decide if the objects are the same or different—as the group assessed them or as you saw them.

As in Asch's experiments, you (as the typical subject) would have caved in to group pressure, on average giving the group's wrong answers 41% of the time. When you yielded to the group's erroneous judgment, your conformity would have been seen in the brain scan as changes in selected regions of the brain's cortex dedicated to vision and spatial awareness (specifically, activity increases in the right intraparietal sulcus). Surprisingly, there would be no changes in areas of the forebrain that deal with monitoring conflicts, planning, and other higher-order mental activities. On the other hand, if you made independent judgments that went against the group, then your brain lit up in the areas that are associated with emotional salience (the right amygdala and right caudate nucleus regions). This means that resistance creates an emotional burden for those who maintain their independence—autonomy comes at a psychic cost.

The lead author of this research, neuroscientist Gregory Berns (2005), concludes that "We like to think that seeing is believing, but the study's findings show that seeing is believing what the group tells you to believe." This means that other people's views, when crystallized into a group consensus, can actually affect how we perceive important aspects of the external world, thus calling into question the nature of truth itself. It is only by becoming aware of our vulnerability to social pressure that we can begin to build resistance to conformity when it is not in our best interest to yield to the mentality of the herd.

It is also important to mention that this research using neurobiology techniques to study social psychological processes is becoming widespread in the field of social psychology, and is known as **social neuroscience.** Social neuroscience is a new area of research that uses methodologies from brain sciences to investigate various types of social behavior, such as stereotyping in prejudice, attitudes, self-control, and emotional regulation (Azar, 2002a; Cacioppo & Brentson, 2005).

Groupthink   Groups themselves can also be pressured to conform. This important social psychological process that encourages conformity in the thinking and decision making of individuals when they are in groups, like committees, has been termed **groupthink** by psychologist Irving Janis (1972; Janis & Mann, 1977). In groupthink, members of the group attempt to conform their opinions to what each believes to be the consensus of the group. This conformity bias leads the group to take actions on which each member might normally consider to be unwise. Five conditions likely to promote groupthink are:

- Directive leadership, a dominant leader.
- High group **cohesiveness,** with absence of dissenting views.
- Lack of norms requiring methodical procedures for evidence collection/evaluation.
- Homogeneity of members' social background and ideology.
- High stress from external threats with low hope of a better solution than that of the group leader.

This concept was first developed to help understand bad decisions made by the U.S. government regarding the bombing of Pearl Harbor in 1941, the Vietnam War, and especially the disastrous invasion of Cuba's Bay of Pigs. In that case, really smart members of President John Kennedy's cabinet made a foolish decision to start an invasion against Cuba based on faulty reports by anti-Castro Cuban refugees. Later, others have cited groupthink as a factor that contributed to the faulty decisions in the space shuttle disasters, the bankruptcy of Enron Corporation, and, more recently, the 2003 decision to wage preemptive war against Iraq (see Schwartz & Wald, 2003). The U.S. Senate Intelligence Committee investigating the justifications for the Iraq War cited groupthink as

CONNECTION • CHAPTER 5
Our judgments and decisions are often affected by personal biases.

Social neuroscience   An area of research that uses methodologies from brain sciences to investigate various types of social behavior, such as stereotyping in prejudice, attitudes, self-control, and emotional regulation.

Groupthink   The term for the poor judgments and bad decisions made by members of groups that are overly influenced by perceived group consensus or the leader's point of view.

Cohesiveness   Solidarity, loyalty, and a sense of group membership.

one of the processes involved in that decision. It is interesting to note the use of this social psychological concept in an official report of that government committee:

> The Intelligence Community (IC) has long struggled with the need for analysts to overcome analytic biases. . . . This bias that pervaded both the IC's analytic and collection communities represents "group think," a term coined by psychologist Irving Janis in the 1970's to describe a process in which a group can make bad or irrational decisions as each member of the group attempts to conform their opinions to what they believe to be the consensus of the group. IC personnel involved in the Iraq WMD issue demonstrated several aspects of groupthink: examining few alternatives, selective gathering of information, pressure to conform within the group or withhold criticism, and collective rationalization. (U.S. Senate, 2004, p. 4)

Recently, the U.S. Directorate of Intelligence has found a way of minimizing the risk of groupthink by developing "Red Teams" whose task is to challenge all decisions with more reliable evidence. They insist on convergence of multiple sources of independent evidence to support all action-based decisions by government agencies. Former CIA Director Porter Goss has encouraged innovation and creativity in how the CIA approaches its mission. In a report outlining the new defenses against mindless groupthink, Gross has said:

> The primary criticism was that our analysts were "too wedded to their assumptions" and that our tradecraft—the way we analyze a subject and communicate our findings—needed strengthening. . . . Above all, we seek to foster in each analyst a sense of individual initiative, responsibility and ownership, as well as the recognition that providing analysis vital to our national security requires challenging orthodoxy and constantly testing our assumptions. Mastering the fundamentals of tradecraft and building expertise are critical, but we also must aspire to a level of creativity and insight that allows us to look beyond the obvious and flag the unexpected. Only then can we truly fulfill our obligation to help protect the American people. (See Kringen, 2006)

Obedience to Authority

So far, we have seen how groups influence individuals. But the arrow of influence also points the other way: Certain individuals, such as charismatic leaders and authorities, can command the obedience of groups—even large masses of people. The ultimate demonstration of this effect was seen in the World War II era, with the emergence of Adolph Hitler in Germany and Benito Mussolini in Italy. These dictators transformed the rational citizens of whole nations into mindlessly loyal followers of a fascist ideology bent on world conquest. But the same was true in Cambodia in the 1970s where Pol Pot, the brutal dictator and leader of the Khmer Rouge, decided to eliminate social classes by forcing everyone to work on farms. Those likely to resist—the educated, intellectuals, and foreigners—were tortured, starved to death, and murdered. In a four-year reign of terror, known as the Killing Fields of Cambodia, nearly 2 million people were killed.

Modern social psychology had its origins in this World War II wartime crucible of fear and prejudice. It was natural, then, that many of the early social psychologists focused on the personalities of people drawn into fascist groups. Specifically, they looked for an authoritarian personality behind the fascist group mentality (Adorno et al., 1950). But that dispositional analysis failed to recognize the social, economic, historical, and political realities operating on those populations at that time. To clarify this point, let us reflect for a moment on some more recent examples of unquestioning obedience to authority.

In 1978, a group of American citizens left California to relocate their Protestant religious order, called "Peoples Temple," in the South American jungle of Guyana. There, following the orders of their charismatic leader, the Reverend Jim Jones, over 900 members of the Peoples Temple willingly administered lethal doses of cyanide to hundreds of their children, then to their parents, and then to themselves. Those who refused were murdered by other members of this cult.

Then, in 1993, 100 members of a religious sect in Waco, Texas, joined their leader, David Koresh, in defying federal agents who had surrounded their compound. After a standoff of several weeks, the Branch Davidians set fire to their quarters rather than surrender. In the resulting conflagration, scores of men, women, and children perished. Four years later, the college-educated members of another group calling itself "Heaven's Gate" followed their leader's command to commit mass suicide in order to achieve a "higher plane" of being. And, on September 11, 2001, followers of Osama bin Laden weaponized American commercial airliners and piloted them into the Pentagon and the World Trade Center. In addition to murdering thousands of people on those planes and working at those sites, they knowingly committed suicide. And even more recently, scores of suicide bombers, both men and women, have blown themselves apart as "revolutionary martyrs" in the Palestinian campaign against Israel. Were these people mentally deranged, stupid, and totally strange creatures—unlike us? Are there any conditions under which you would blindly obey an order from a person you love and respect (or fear) to do such extreme deeds? Would

Unquestioning obedience to authority led more than 900 members of a cult community in Jonestown to commit mass suicide, under orders from their leader, the Reverend Jim Jones.

you, for example, obey an authority figure that told you to electrocute a stranger? Of course, you are saying to yourself, "No way," "Not me," "I am not that kind of person." But think about what each of the people we have described above must have been thinking before they were caught up in their obedience trap—the same thing as you, probably.

Let's return to our opening story of Bill trapped in the experiment created by social psychologist Stanley Milgram (1965, 1974). His research revealed that the willingness of people to follow the orders of an authority, even potentially lethal ones, is not confined to a few extreme personalities or deranged individuals. This finding, along with certain ethical issues that the experiment raises, places Milgram's work at the center of one of the biggest controversies in psychology (Blass, 1996). We will look at more of the findings generated by that program of research on *obedience* and visit a series of follow up studies that expand its relevance and applicability to everyday life settings.

Milgram's Research Revisited   Milgram described his experimental procedure to each of 40 psychiatrists and then asked them to estimate the percentage of American citizens who would go to each of the 30 levels in the experiment. On average, they predicted that fewer than 1% would go all the way to the end, that only sadists would engage in such sadistic behavior, and that most people would drop out at the tenth level of 150 volts. They could not have been more wrong! These experts on human behavior were totally wrong for two reasons. (This dual tendency of overestimating person power and underestimating situation power is known as the *fundamental attribution error*.) First, they ignored all the situational determinants of behavior in the procedural description of the experiment. They failed to recognize the significance of the authority power, the roles of Teacher and Learner, the rules, the diffusion of personal responsibility (when the experimenter claimed to the "Teacher" that he would be responsible for anything that might happen to the "Learner"), the definition of what were appropriate

CONNECTION • CHAPTER 10
In contrast to most personality theories focusing on *internal* processes as determinants of behavior, social psychology emphasizes the importance of the *external* social situation.

The Milgram Obedience Experiment
The "shock generator" looked ominous, but didn't actually deliver shocks to the
"learner" (middle photo), who was a confederate of the experimenter. The last photo
shows the experimenter giving instructions to the "teacher" who is seated in front of the
shock generator.

and expected behaviors by the Teacher, and the other social pressures toward obedience.

Second, their training in traditional psychiatry led them to rely too heavily on the dispositional perspective to understand unusual behavior, to look for explanations within the individual's personality makeup and not in the external behavioral context. Thus, their estimate of only 1% as blindly obedient to authority, as going all the way up to the maximum shock level of 450 volts, is a base rate against which we can assess what actually happened in this research.

Before examining the actual results we need to add that Milgram wanted to show that his results were not due to the authority power of Yale University—which is what New Haven is all about. So he transplanted his laboratory to a rundown office building in downtown Bridgeport, Connecticut, and repeated the experiment as a project of a fictitious, private research firm with no apparent connection to Yale. There he tested another 500 ordinary citizens and added female participants as Teachers to the experimental mix. So what was the actual level of blind obedience to authority?

As we've seen, two out of every three (65%) of the volunteers went all the way up the maximum shock level of 450 volts! These "Teachers" shocked their "Learner-victim" over and over again despite his increasingly desperate pleas to stop. This was as true of the young and old, men and women, well educated and less so, and across many occupations and careers.

Variations on an Obedience Theme   Over the course of a year, Milgram carried out 19 different experiments—each one a different variation of the basic paradigm of: Experimenter/-Teacher/-Learner/-Memory Testing/-Errors Shocked. In each of these studies he varied one social-psychological variable and observed its impact on the extent of obedience to the authority's pressure to continue to shock the "Learner-Victim." He added women in one study, varied the physical proximity or remoteness of either the Experimenter-Teacher link or the Teacher-Learner link, had peers model rebellion or full obedience before the Teacher had his chance to begin, and added more social variations in each experiment.

As can be seen in Figure 11.2, the data for 16 variations clearly reveal the extreme pliability of human nature: Almost everyone could be totally obedient or almost everyone could resist authority pressures. It all depends on how the social situation was constructed by the researcher and experienced by the participants. Milgram was able to demonstrate that compliance rates could soar to over 90% of people administering the 450-volt maximum, or the obedience rate could be reduced to less than 10% by introducing just one crucial social variable into the compliance recipe.

Want maximum obedience? Allow the new Teacher to first observe someone else administering the final shock level. Want people to resist authority

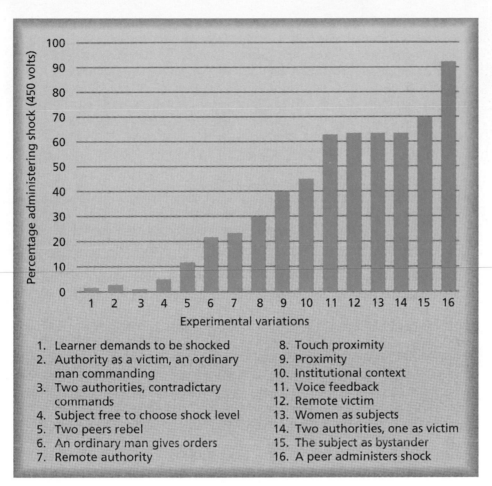

FIGURE 11.2
Obedience in Milgram's Experiments

The graph shows a profile of weak or strong obedience effects across situational variations of Milgram's study of obedience to authority.

(*Source:* From *The Obedience Experiments: A Case Study of Controversy in the Social Sciences,* by A. G. Miller. Copyright © 1986 by Praeger Publishers, Inc. Reproduced with permission of Greenwood Publishing Group, Inc., Westport, CT.)

1. Learner demands to be shocked
2. Authority as a victim, an ordinary man commanding
3. Two authorities, contradictary commands
4. Subject free to choose shock level
5. Two peers rebel
6. An ordinary man gives orders
7. Remote authority
8. Touch proximity
9. Proximity
10. Institutional context
11. Voice feedback
12. Remote victim
13. Women as subjects
14. Two authorities, one as victim
15. The subject as bystander
16. A peer administers shock

pressures? Provide social models of peers who rebel. Participants also refused to deliver the shocks if the Learner said he wanted to be shocked; that's masochistic, and they are not sadists! They also were reluctant to give high levels of shock when the Experimenter filled in as the Learner, and they were supposed to shock him. They were more likely to shock when the Learner was remote than nearby. In each of the other variations on this diverse range of ordinary American citizens, of widely varying ages, occupations, and of both sexes, it was possible to elicit low, medium, or high levels of compliant obedience with a flick of the Situational Switch—as if one were simply turning a Human Nature Dial within their psyches. This large sample of a thousand ordinary citizens from such varied backgrounds makes the results of *Milgram's Obedience to Authority* studies among the most generalizable in all the social sciences.

Of course, no shocks were ever delivered to the learner. The "victim" of the "shocks" was an accomplished actor who congenially chatted with his "teacher" after the experiment and assured him he was fine and had never felt any shocks. All of his comments during the study had been tape recorded to standardize the procedure across the many trials and variations of the study. Moreover, the powerful authority figure in the gray lab coat was not a "real" authority, not Milgram himself, but a high school biology teacher. And, for all the "Teachers" knew, when once the learner fell silent after the 350 volt shock, he may have been unconscious or dead—but in any case his memory could not be improved by further shocks. Nevertheless, hundreds of people mindlessly obeyed and continued doing as ordered even though it made no sense—had they thought rationally about what they were doing.

CONNECTION • CHAPTER 6

Moral judgments depend both on the person's *stage of moral development* and the *situational influences* acting on him or her.

British author C. P. Snow reminds us, "When you think of the long and gloomy history of man, you will find more hideous crimes have been committed in the name of obedience than have been committed in the name of rebellion."

Such research, and the many replications that followed in countries around the world, challenge our conception that "good people" cannot be seduced into becoming perpetrators of evil. It suggests that the line between good and evil is not fixed and permanent but rather is sufficiently permeable to allow almost anyone to move across from one behavioral realm to the other. It all depends on the power of the new, unfamiliar situation that they face and with which they most cope.

Heroic Defiance   This concept of situational power faces one challenge, that of individual heroic defiance. **Heroes** are people who are able to resist situational forces that overwhelm their peers and remain true to their personal values. They are the "whistle-blowers" who challenge corrupt or immoral systems by not going along with the company norm.

Would you risk your life to defy authority in defense of your beliefs, as this Chinese student did, defying a tank force coming to crush the student rebellion at Tiananmen Square?

An Army Reservist, Joe Darby, exposed the horrendous abuses of prisoners by his buddies at Iraq's Abu Ghraib Prison in 2004. He showed a CD with the images taken by other MPs on the night shift to a senior investigating officer, who then initiated the investigation that stopped those abuses, which had been going on for months.

But such "heroes" are often despised by their former colleagues and made to pay a high price for not being a silent "team player." Darby, for example, had to go into hiding under protective custody for three years, along with his wife and mother, because of death threats against him by soldiers in his battalion and by people in their hometown for humiliating the American military in exposing those photos of sadistic abuse of prisoners. After being released in 2007, Darby did finally receive a hero award at the Kennedy Center in Washington, DC.

Cross-Cultural Tests of Milgram's Research

Because of its structural design and its detailed protocol, the basic Milgram obedience experiment encouraged replication by independent investigators in many countries. A recent comparative analysis was made of the rates of obedience across eight studies conducted in the United States and of nine replications in European, African, and Asian countries. There were comparably high levels of compliance by research volunteers in these different studies and nations. The majority obedience effect of a mean 61% found in the U.S. replications was matched by the 66% obedience found across all the other national samples. The range of obedience went from a low of 31 to a high of 91% in the U.S. studies, and from a low of 28% (Australia) to a high of 88% (South Africa) in the cross-national replications. There was also stability of obedience over decades of time as well as over place. There was no association between when a study was done (between 1963 and 1985) and degree of obedience (Blass, 2004).

Using a variation of the Milgram paradigm, researchers in Utrecht University, Holland, and in Palermo University, Sicily, found obedience rates comparable to those in some of Milgram's experimental variations. The situation they created was that of a coach who had to deliver increasingly critical feedback to his performer when he did poorly, allegedly to build resilience in performers. They had to deliver a series of graded hostile comments, as if they were their own, for each error. Critical feedback given to the Performer consisted of a graded series of increasingly negative comments on his performance and rude remarks about his lack of ability. For example, a mild criticism was "You are going bad . . ." a moderately negative feedback was "You are really ridiculous!" and an extremely negative feedback was "You are really the most stupid person I have ever seen!" Obedience to authority was determined as delivering the full set of 15 hostile comments. In one of the Utrecht studies, more than 90%

Heroes   People whose actions help others in emergencies or challenge unjust or corrupt systems, doing so without concern for reward or likely negative consequences for them by acting in deviant ways.

of the students playing the role of coach went all the way (Meeus & Raaijmakers, 1986). In the Sicilian study using that same procedure, obedience was only 30%, but that was in a condition where coach and performer were in close proximity and the experimenter was in an adjacent room. That is exactly what Milgram found for those experimental variations (Bocchiaro & Zimbardo, 2008).

Why Do We Obey Authority?   From the many variations Milgram conducted on his original study, we can conclude that people tended to be obedient under the following conditions (Milgram, 1965, 1974; Rosenhan, 1969):

- When a peer modeled obedience by complying with the authority figure's commands.
- When the victim was remote from the Teacher and could not be seen or heard, thereby promoting a sense of anonymity.
- When the Teacher was under direct surveillance of the authority figure so that he was aware of the authority's presence.
- When the authority figure had higher relative status to the Teacher.

What are the lessons to be learned? If you carefully review these conditions (Figure 11.2), you can see that the obedience effect results from situational variables and not personality variables. In fact, personality tests administered to the subjects did not reveal any traits that differentiated those who obeyed from those who refused, nor did they identify any psychological disturbance or abnormality in the obedient punishers. These findings enable us to rule out individual personality as a variable in obedient behavior. Going beyond the experimental findings to applying them to real world settings, we can outline ten basic steps or processes that can seduce ordinary, even good, people to go down the slippery slope of evil, as seen in Table 11.1.

Some Real-World Extensions of the Milgram Obedience to Authority Paradigm

If the relationship between teachers and students is one of power-based authority, how much more so is that between physicians and nurses? To find out, a team of doctors and nurses tested obedience in their authority system by determining whether nurses would follow or disobey an illegitimate request by an unknown physician in a real hospital setting (Hofling et al., 1966). Each of 22 nurses individually received a call from an unknown staff doctor who told her

TABLE 11.1   Ten Steps toward Evil—Getting Good People to Harm Others
• Provide people with an ideology to justify beliefs for actions.
• Make people take a small first step toward a harmful act with a minor, trivial action and then gradually increase those small actions.
• Slowly transform a once compassionate leader into a dictatorial figure.
• Provide people with vague and ever-changing rules.
• Relabel the situation's actors and their actions to legitimize the ideology.
• Provide people with social models of compliance.
• Allow verbal dissent but only if people continue to comply behaviorally with orders.
• Encourage dehumanizing the victim.
• Diffuse responsibiiity
• Make exiting the situation difficult.

One of the innocent victims of the Authority Hoax, on the witness stand. She received a large settlement from the fast-food company where she worked and had been abused.

to administer a medication to his patient immediately, before he got to the hospital. His order doubled the maximum amount indicated as a high dose. When this dilemma was presented as a hypothetical scenario, 10 of 12 nurses in that hospital said they would refuse to obey because it violated hospital procedures (Krackow & Blass, 1995). However, the power of the situation took over on the hospital ward: Twenty-one of 22 nurses put to the test started to pour the medication (actually a harmless drug) to administer to the patient—before the researcher stopped them from doing so. That solitary disobedient nurse should have been given a raise and a hero's medal.

Another remarkable real-world illustration of the Milgram effect in action comes from a telephone hoax perpetrated in 68 fast-food restaurants across 32 states. Assistant store managers blindly followed the orders of a phone caller, pretending to be a police officer, who insisted that they strip search a young female employee he said had stolen property on her.

The alleged officer instructs the assistant manager to detain the employee in the back room, strip her naked, and search her extensively for the stolen goods. The caller insists on being told in graphic detail what is happening, and all the while the video surveillance cameras are recording these remarkable events as they unfold. In some cases, the abuse escalates to having her masturbate and perform sexual acts on a male assistant who is supposed to guarding her (Wolfson, 2005).

This bizarre authority-influence-in-absentia has seduced dozens of ordinary people in that situation to violate store policy, and presumably their own ethical and moral principles, to molest and humiliate honest young employees. In 2007, the perpetrator was uncovered—a former corrections officer—but freed for lack of direct evidence.

One reasonable reaction to learning about this hoax is to focus on the dispositions of the victim and her assailants, as naïve, ignorant, gullible, weird individuals. However, when we learn that this scam has been carried out successfully in a great many similar settings across many states, in a half dozen different restaurant chains, then our analysis must shift away from simply blaming the victims to recognizing the power of situational forces involved in this scenario.

The Bystander Problem: The Evil of Inaction

The only thing necessary for evil to triumph is for good men to do nothing.
—British Statesman, Edmund Burke

Harm doesn't always come from a hurtful act. It can also come from inaction when someone needs help. We can illustrate this fact with an event that stunned the nation and became a legend about the callousness of human nature. On March 13, 1964, the *New York Times* reported that 38 citizens of Queens watched for more than half an hour as a man with a knife stalked and killed Kitty Genovese, one of their neighbors, in three separate attacks. The article said that the sound of the bystanders' voices and the sudden glow of their bedroom lights twice interrupted the assault, but each time the assailant returned and stabbed her again. Again according to the report, only one witness called the police—after the woman was finally raped and murdered.

The story of Kitty Genovese's murder dominated the news for days, as a shocked nation was served up media commentary that played on the angles of bystander apathy and the indefference of New Yorkers. Why didn't they help? Was it something about New York—or could the same thing happen anywhere?

A recent investigation of police records and other archival materials has found that the real story was different from the original *Times* report (Manning, Levine, & Collins, 2007). For one thing, there was no basis for the claim that 38 people witnessed the event. Further, most of the assault took place in an entry hall, out of view of neighbors. And, in fact, phone calls to the police *were* made during the attack. It was still a tragedy, of course, but not one that proved the people of New York to be the indefferent bystanders the original story made them out to be.

For psychology, the important result of this misreported incident was that it led to some important research on bystander intervention that focused on the *power of the situation*. Under what circumstances will people help—or not?

Contrived Emergencies Soon after learning of the Kitty Genovese murder and the analysis in the press, two young social psychologists, Bibb Latané and John Darley, began a series of studies on the **bystander intervention problem.** These studies all ingeniously created laboratory analogues of the difficulties faced by bystanders in real emergency situations. In one such experiment, a college student, placed alone in a room with an intercom, was led to believe that he was communicating with one or more students in adjacent rooms. During a discussion about personal problems, this individual heard what sounded like another student having a seizure and gasping for help. During the "seizure," the bystander couldn't talk to the other students or find out what, if anything, they were doing about the emergency. The dependent variable was the speed with which he reported the emergency to the experimenter. The independent variable was the number of people he believed were in the discussion group with him.

It turned out that the speed of response by those in this situation depended on the number of bystanders they thought were present. The more other people they believed to be listening in on the situation in other rooms, the slower they were to report the seizure, if they did so at all. As you can see in Figure 11.3, all those in a two-person situation intervened within 160 seconds, but only 60% of those who believed they were part of a large group ever informed the experimenter that another student was seriously ill (Latané & Darley, 1968).

Was it the person or the situation? Personality tests showed no significant relationship between particular personality characteristics of the participants and their speed or likelihood of intervening. The best predictor of bystander intervention was the situational variable of group size present. By way of explana-

Kitty Genovese, victim of brutality and bystander apathy.

CONNECTION • CHAPTER 1

The *independent variable* refers to the stimulus conditions or experimenter varied conditions for different groups in an experiment, while the *dependent variable* is the measured outcome.

Bystander intervention problem
Laboratory and field study analogues of the difficulties faced by bystanders in real emergency situations.

FIGURE 11.3
Bystander Intervention in an Emergency

The more people present in a crisis, the less likely it is that any one bystander will intervene. As this summary of research findings shows, bystanders act most quickly in two-person groupings.

(*Source:* From "Bystander Intervention in Emergencies: Diffusion of Responsibilities," by S. M. Darley and B. Latané, *Journal of Personality & Social Psychology*, 1968, Vol. 8, No. 4, pp. 377–384. Copyright © 1968 by the American Psychological Association.)

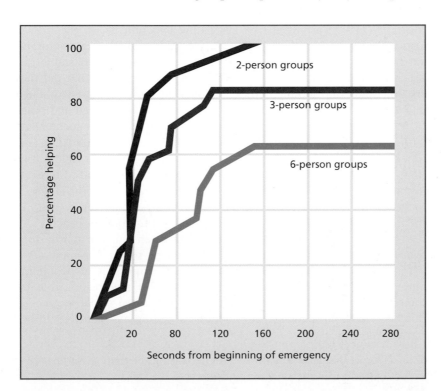

tion, Darley and Latané proposed that the likelihood of intervention decreases as the group increases in size because each person assumes that others will help, so he or she does not have to make that commitment. Individuals who perceive themselves as part of a large group of potential interveners experience a **diffusion of responsibility**: a dilution or weakening of each group member's obligation to help, to become personally involved. You may have experienced moments of diffused responsibility if you have driven past a disabled car beside a busy highway because you believed "surely someone else" would stop and help—as you went on your way.

Another factor was undoubtedly also at work: *conformity.* As you will remember from our Core Concept and from Asch's studies of conformity, when people don't know what to do, they take their cues from others. The same thing occurred in the bystander studies, where those who failed to intervene were observing and conforming to the behavior of other people who were doing nothing. They allowed the absence of helping by others to define the situation for them as one in which the norm was that it was OK to be passively indifferent.

Does Training Encourage Helping?   Two studies suggest that the bystander problem can be countered with appropriate training. Ted Huston and his colleagues (1981) found no personality traits that distinguished people who had helped in actual emergency situations from those who had not. But they did find that helpers more often had had some medical, police, first-aid, or CPR training in dealing with emergency situations. And another study shows that even a psychology class lecture on the bystander problem can help (Beaman et al., 1978). Students had an opportunity to help a "victim" slumped in a doorway while walking by with a nonresponsive confederate of the experimenter. Those who had attended a lecture on bystander intervention were twice as likely to stop and attempt to help as those who had not received the lecture on helping. Education apparently can make a difference; we hope you will also use the lessons of this chapter in constructive ways.

Need Help? Ask for It!

To demonstrate the positive effects of situational power, social psychologist Tom Moriarity (1975) arranged two fascinating experiments. In the first study, New Yorkers watched as a thief snatched a woman's suitcase in a restaurant when she left her table. In the second, they watched a thief grab a portable radio from a beach blanket when the owner left it for a few minutes. What did these onlookers do? Some did nothing, letting the thief go on his merry way. But others did intervene. What were the conditions under which some helped and others did not?

In each experiment, the would-be theft victim (the experimenter's accomplice) had first asked the soon-to-be observer of the crime either "Do you have the time?" or "Will you please keep an eye on my bag (radio) while I'm gone?" The first interaction elicited no personal responsibility, and almost all of the bystanders stood by idly as the theft unfolded. However, of those who had agreed to watch the victim's property, almost every bystander intervened. They called for help, and some even tackled the runaway thief on the beach.

The encouraging message is that we can often convert apathy to action and transform callousness to kindness just by asking for it. The mere act of requesting a favor forges a special human bond that involves other people in ways that materially change the situation. It makes them feel responsible to you and thereby responsible for what happens in your shared social world. You can use this knowledge to increase your chances of getting aid from would-be helpers in several ways (Schroeder et al., 1995):

- *Ask for help.* Let others know you need it rather than assuming they realize your need or know what is required.

Diffusion of responsibility   Dilution or weakening of each group member's obligation to act when responsibility is perceived to be shared with all group members or accepted by the leader.

- *Reduce the ambiguity of the situation* by clearly explaining the problem and what should be done: "She's fainted! Call an ambulance right away," or "Someone broke into my house—call the police and give them this address!"
- *Identify specific individuals* so they do not diffuse responsibility with others present: "You, in the red shirt: Call 911!" or "Will the person in the blue Toyota please call for a tow truck right away?"

None of these tactics guarantees the safety of your person or possessions, of course. Nevertheless they probably represent your best hope if you find yourself, alone in a crowd, facing a real emergency.

DO IT YOURSELF! What Makes a Samaritan Good or Bad?

Now that you know something about bystander intervention, let's see how good you are at picking the crucial variable out of a bystander situation inspired by the biblical tale of the Good Samaritan (see Luke 10:30–37). In the biblical account, several important people are too busy to help a stranger in distress. He is finally assisted by an outsider, a Samaritan, who takes the time to offer aid. Could the failure of the distressed individual's countrymen to help be due to character flaws or personal dispositions? Or was it determined by the situation?

Social psychologists decided to put students at the Princeton Theological Seminary into a similar situation. It was made all the more ironic because they thought that they were being evaluated on the quality of the sermons they were about to deliver on the parable of the Good Samaritan. Let's see what happened when these seminarians were given an opportunity to help someone in distress.

With sermon in hand, each was directed to a nearby building where the sermon was to be recorded. But as the student walked down an alley between the two buildings, he came on a man slumped in a doorway, in obvious need of help. The student now had the chance to practice what he was about to preach. What would you guess was the crucial variable that predicted how likely a seminarian—ready to preach about the Good Samaritan—was to help a person in distress? Choose one:

- How religious the seminarian was (as rated by his classmates).
- How "neurotic" the seminarian was (as rated on the "Big Five" personality traits).

- How much of a hurry the seminarian was in.
- How old the seminarian was.

All of the dispositional variables (personal characteristics) of the seminarians were controlled by random assignment of subjects to three different conditions. Thus, we know that personality was not the determining factor. Rather, it was a situational variable: time. Before the seminarians left the briefing room to have their sermons recorded in a nearby building, each was told how much time he had to get to the studio. Some were assigned to a late condition, in which they had to hurry to make the next session; others to an on-time condition, in which they would make the next session just on time; and a third

group to an early condition, in which they had a few spare minutes before they would be recorded.

What were the results? Of those who were in a hurry, only 10% helped. Ninety percent failed to act as Good Samaritans! If they were on time, 45% helped the stranger. The greatest bystander intervention came from 63% of those who were not in any time bind. (See Figure 11.4.)

Remarkably, the manipulation of time urgency made those in the "late" condition six times less likely to help than those in the "early" condition. While fulfilling their obligation to hurry, these individuals appeared to have a single-minded purpose that blinded them to other events around them. Again, it was the power of the situation.

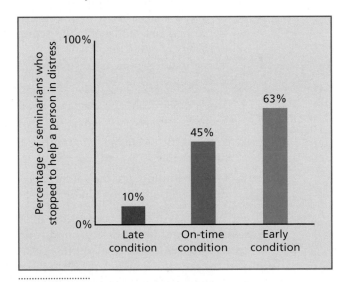

FIGURE 11.4
Results of the "Good Samaritan" Study

Even on their way to deliver the Good Samaritan Sermon, the vast majority of seminary students did not stop to help a distressed victim.

PSYCHOLOGY**MATTERS**

On Being "Shoe" at Yale U

When I (PGZ) arrived at Yale University to start my graduate career in the mid-1950s, I was dressed in all my South Bronx splendor—blue suede shoes, peg pants, long dangling key chain, big rolled collar, and other cool clothes. A month or two later, I was wearing chino pants, button-down shirt, and loafer-type shoes. I was not fully aware of the subtle social pressures to change my "taste" in apparel but knew that I felt more "in" in those weird Yalie clothes than I had in my good old Bronx duds. But as a budding psychologist, I used my personal case study to motivate me to find out more about that unwritten dress code, one that everyone around the campus at that time was following as if a Marine drill instructor was ordering our total mindless compliance.

My interviews with seniors revealed that indeed there was a powerful dress code that the **in-group** formulated regularly to distinguish them from the mass of **out-group** pretenders. Every single item of clothing could be identified by those in the know as socially appropriate at that time for real Yale men to wear (it was all male at that time). I was informed that the underlying concept was termed "shoe." (Yale men of that era and earlier could be identified as wearing white buck shoes.) To be "shoe" was to be in, to be cool, to be with it, to be right on, and so forth. Not only was every bit of clothing indexed as to its degree of "shoeness," but so was everything else in that universe. Tennis, golf, and crew were shoe; basketball was not. Asking questions in lecture classes was not shoe; tailgating before football games was shoe, but only if done with the right style, or panache. Of equal interest to me was the fact that shoe ratings changed periodically to keep outsiders from being mistaken as really true blue shoe. One year the Yale senior ring was shoe to wear, the next year it might be unshoe; or handmade bow ties would become unshoe and clip-on bow ties would vault from low-shoe to high-shoe rating.

My team of informants helped me to form an index of the shoe strengths of every conceivable item of clothing that a Yale student might wear that year. With the help of my introductory psychology students, we went into the dormitories and found out what students from each college class actually had in their wardrobes. We then multiplied each of those items of clothing by their Shoe Index and averaged those ratings across each class from frosh to senior. Next, we separated out students' shoe scores by whether they had come from prep schools versus public high schools.

Three major significant results were obvious from our graphs of the quantification of shoeness at Yale:

1. Student wardrobes become ever more shoe as they progress from lowly frosh up to high-powered seniors.

2. Preppy frosh were much more shoe than were their classmates from public high schools.

3. Over the four years, the gap between prep schoolers and high schoolers diminished, so that by senior year they were almost equally shoe.

When Yale became coed in the next decade, this kind of "shoeness" became less apparent, went underground, and now may exist only in very modified forms. But let this be a lesson to you whatever school you are in: Much of what you think is the You in Your Taste, is really the Them in social conformity pressures subtly imposed on you to be like Them and to liked by Them (Zimbardo, 2008).

In-group The group with which an individual identifies.

Out-group Those outside the group with which an individual identifies.

CheckYourUnderstanding

1. **RECALL:** Which of the following would be a social role?
   a. prisoner
   b. student
   c. professor
   d. all of the above

2. **RECALL:** In the Asch studies, which of the following produced a *decrease* in conformity?
   a. The task was seen as difficult or ambiguous.
   b. The subject had to respond publicly, rather than privately.
   c. The majority was not unanimous in its judgment.
   d. The group was very large.

3. **RECALL:** In Milgram's original study, about what proportion of the teachers gave the maximum shock?
   a. about two-thirds
   b. about 50%
   c. about 25%
   d. nearly all

4. **RECALL:** Although conformity is a social phenomenon, brain regions that are activated when someone con-

forms are different from those brain regions activated by resisting and being independent.
   True
   False

5. **APPLICATION:** If you were a victim in an emergency, what lessons from social psychology would you apply to get the help you need?
   a. Ask for it.
   b. Make your request specific.
   c. Engage particular individual observers.
   d. Do all of the above.

6. **UNDERSTANDING THE CORE CONCEPT:** What consequences does attempting to understand human behavior in terms of situational causes have for the personal responsibility of the actors involved?
   a. excuses them entirely
   b. limits their guilt if they murdered someone
   c. does not change personal responsibility and guilt, only severity of sentence
   d. forces the situation to be put on trial as well

Answers 1. d **2.** c **3.** a **4.** True **5.** d **6.** d

11.2 KEY QUESTION
CONSTRUCTING SOCIAL REALITY: WHAT INFLUENCES OUR JUDGMENTS OF OTHERS?

Powerful as a social situation is, it doesn't account for everything that people do. For example, it does not account for the individual differences we see in people's choices of friends and romantic partners, nor does it account for their prejudices. To explain the patterns we find in social interaction, we must also look at cognitive processes. In the language of social psychology, we need to understand how we construct our **social reality** —our subjective interpretations of other people and of our relationships. Thus, the social reality that we construct determines whom we find attractive, whom we find threatening, whom we seek out, and whom we avoid. This, then, leads us to the second lesson of social psychology, captured in our next Core Concept:

> **The judgments we make about others depend not only on their behavior but also on our interpretation of their actions within a social context.**

core concept

We will illustrate how these cognitive factors operate by analyzing how they affect our attitudes toward other people. Let's start out by asking a simple question: What makes people like each other? That is, what produces interpersonal attraction?

Interpersonal Attraction

It is no surprise that we are attracted to people who have something to offer us (Brehm et al., 2002; Simpson & Harris, 1994). We tend to like those who give us gifts, agree with us, act friendly toward us, share our interests, entertain us, and help us in times of need—unless, of course, we suspect that their behavior

Social reality An individual's subjective interpretation of other people and of one's relationships with them.

is self-serving or hypocritical. Although we don't necessarily mind giving something back in the form of a social exchange, we shrink from relationships that merely take from us and offer nothing in return. In the best of relationships, as in a friendship, partnership, marriage, or business relationship, both parties receive rewards. You might consider whether this is true in your own relationships as we look at the reward theory of attraction next.

Reward Theory: We (Usually) Prefer Rewarding Relationships   Most good relationships can be seen as an exchange of benefits (Batson, 1987; Clark et al., 1989). The benefits could be some combination of money and material possessions. Or the exchange might involve something intangible like praise, status, information, sex, or emotional support.

Social psychologist Elliot Aronson (2004) summarizes this in a **reward theory of attraction,** which says that attraction is a form of social learning. By looking at the social costs and benefits, claims Aronson, we can usually understand why people are attracted to each other. In brief, reward theory says that we like best those who give us maximum rewards at minimum cost. After we look at the evidence, we think you will agree that this theory explains (almost) everything about interpersonal attraction. Social psychologists have found four especially powerful sources of reward that predict interpersonal attraction: proximity, similarity, self-disclosure, and physical attractiveness. Most of us choose our friends, associates, and lovers because they offer some combination of these factors at a relatively low social cost.

Proximity   An old saying advises, "Absence makes the heart grow fonder." Another contradicts with "Out of sight, out of mind." Which one is correct? Studies show that frequent sightings best predict our closest relationships and the people we see most often are the people who live and work nearest us (Simpson & Harris, 1994). In college dormitories, residents more often become close friends with the person who lives in the next room than they do with the person who lives two doors down (Priest & Sawyer, 1967). Residents of apartments make more friendships among people who live on the same floor than among those who live on other floors (Nahemow & Lawton, 1975). Those who live in neighborhoods more often become friends with the occupants of the house next door than with people living two houses away (Festinger et al., 1950). This **principle of proximity** (nearness) also accounts for the fact that many people end up married to the boy or girl next door (Ineichen, 1979). And it correctly predicts that people at work will make more friends among those with whom they have the most contact (Segal, 1974).

Although you don't have to like your neighbors, the proximity rule says that when two individuals are equally attractive, you are more likely to make friends with the nearest one: The rewards are equal, but the cost is less in time and inconvenience (Gilbertson et al., 1998). Apparently, another old saying, that familiarity breeds contempt, should be revised in light of social psychological research: In fact, familiarity more often breeds friendship. Increased contact, itself, often increases peoples' liking for each other (Bornstein, 1989).

Similarity   Do birds of a feather flock together, or do opposites attract? Which of these proverbs has the best research evidence to support it? People usually find it more rewarding to strike up a friendship with someone who shares their attitudes, interests, values, and experiences than to bother with people who are disagreeable or merely different (Simpson & Harris, 1994). If two people have just discovered that they share tastes in music, politics, and attitudes toward education, they will probably hit it off because they have, in effect, exchanged compliments that reward each other for their tastes and attitudes (Byrne, 1969). The **similarity principle** also explains why teenagers are most likely to make friends among those who share their political and religious views, educational aspirations, and attitudes toward music, alcohol, and drugs (Kandel, 1978). Likewise, similarity accounts for

CONNECTION • CHAPTER 3

Social learning involves expectations of rewards and punishments learned through social interactions and observation of others.

Reward theory of attraction   A social learning view that predicts we like best those who give us maximum rewards at minimum cost.

Principle of proximity   The notion that people at work will make more friends among those who are nearby—with whom they have the most contact. *Proximity* means "nearness."

Similarity principle   The notion that people are attracted to those who are most similar to themselves on significant dimensions.

CONNECTION • CHAPTER 7

The Gestalt principal of *similarity* refers to grouping stimulus objects that shared common perceptual features.

the fact that most people find marriage partners of the same age, race, social status, attitudes, and values (Brehm, 1992; Hendrick & Hendrick, 1992). In general, similarity, like proximity, makes the heart grow fonder.

Self-Disclosure   Good friends and lovers share intimate details about themselves (Sternberg, 1998). This practice of **self-disclosure** not only allows people to know each other more deeply, but it sends signals of trust. It is as if I say, "Here is a piece of information that I want you to know about me, and I trust you not to hurt me with it." Friends and lovers usually find such exchanges highly rewarding. When you observe people exchanging confidences and details about their lives, you can predict that they are becoming more and more attracted to each other. Given that sharing personal disclosures comes after a sense of trust has been created in a relationship, it both takes time to reach this level of intimacy and is an index of that trust which the disclosing person has in the other. Think about the people with whom you share secrets and those you never would. What underlies these acts of sharing or withholding secrets?

Physical Attractiveness   Yet another old saying tells us that beauty is only skin deep. Nevertheless, people usually find it more rewarding to associate with people they consider physically attractive than with those they consider to be plain or homely (Patzer, 1985). Fair or not, good looks are a real social asset. Potential employers, for example, prefer good-looking job candidates to plainer applicants (Cash & Janda, 1984). Looks also affect people's judgments of children. Attractive children are judged as happier and more competent than their peers (Eagly et al., 1991). Even babies judge people by their appearances. We know this because babies gaze longer at pictures of normal faces than at those of distorted faces (Langlois et al., 1987).

Most people are repelled by the idea that they might make judgments based only on looks. Indeed, when asked what they look for in a dating partner, college students rank physical attractiveness down the middle of the list. But what people say does not match what they do—at least as far as their first impressions go. Across many studies, involving a variety of characteristics, including intelligence, sincerity, masculinity, femininity, and independence, it was *physical attractiveness* that overwhelmed everything else as the best predictor of how well a person would be liked after a first meeting (Aronson, 2004).

Other research shows that the principle of attractiveness applies equally to same-sex and opposite-sex relationships (Maruyama & Miller, 1975). Gender differences do exist, however. While both males and females are strongly influenced by physical attractiveness, men seem to be more influenced by looks than are women (Feingold, 1990).

These findings may come as bad news for the majority of us, who consider ourselves rather average-looking at best. But we can take some comfort in a study that suggests that people actually consider a composite of "average" features to be the most attractive. Investigators fed images of many students' faces into a computer program that manipulated the facial features to be more or less of an average combination of all features from the many different student portraits. Surprisingly, they found that people usually liked best the images having features closest to the average size and shape (Rhodes et al., 1999).

Now some bad news for you exceptionally attractive readers: While we usually associate positive qualities with attractive individuals (Calvert, 1988), extreme attractiveness can also be a liability. Although physically attractive people are seen as more poised, interesting, sociable, independent, exciting, sexual, intelligent, well adjusted, and successful, they are also perceived as more vain and materialistic (Hassebrauck, 1988). A "double standard" also comes into play. For example, the public favors good-looking male politicians but disparages their attractive female counterparts (Sigelman et al., 1986). It is also double trouble to be shy and handsome or beautiful because others mistake those with a reserved demeanor as being cold, indifferent, or feeling superior.

Self-disclosure   The sharing of personal information and feelngs to another person as part of the process of developing trust.

These effects of physical attractiveness hint that reward, as powerful as it is, does not account for everything. We will see this more clearly below, as we explore some important exceptions to the reward theory of attraction.

Exceptions to the Reward Theory of Attraction While the rules of proximity, similarity, self-disclosure, and physical attractiveness may explain a lot about interpersonal attraction, a casual look around reveals lots of relationships that don't seem especially rewarding. Why, for example, might a woman be attracted to a man who abuses her? Or, why would a person want to join an organization that requires a difficult or degrading initiation ritual? Such relationships pose most interesting puzzles (Aronson, 2004). Could some people actually feel more attraction when they find that another person has less to offer them? Let's try to uncover the principles of social cognition operating behind some interesting exceptions to a reward theory of attraction.

Expectations and the Influence of Self-Esteem We have seen that reward theory predicts our attraction to smart, good-looking, nearby, self-disclosing, like-minded, and powerful people. Yet, you have probably observed that most people end up with friends and mates whom you would judge to be of about their same level of attractiveness—the so-called **matching hypothesis** (Feingold, 1988; Harvey & Pauwels, 1999). How does this happen? Is our selection of associates the result of a sort of bargaining for the best we can get in the interpersonal marketplace?

Yes, says **expectancy-value theory.** People usually decide whether to pursue a relationship by weighing the value they see in another person (including such qualities as physical attractiveness, wit, interests, and intelligence) against their expectation of success in the relationship (Will the other person be attracted to me?). Most of us don't waste too much time on interpersonal causes we think are lost. Rather, we initiate relationships with the most attractive people we think will probably like us in return. In this sense, expectancy-value theory is not so much a competitor of reward theory as it is a refinement of it.

One noteworthy exception to this argument involves people who suffer from low self-esteem. Sadly, people with low opinions of themselves tend to establish relationships with people who share their views, often with people who devalue them. Such individuals generally feel a stronger commitment to a relationship when their partner thinks poorly of them than they do when the partner thinks well of them (Swann et al., 1992).

Those individuals who appear to be extremely competent can also be losers in the expectancy-value game. Why? Most of us keep such people at a distance probably because we fear that they will be quick to reject our approaches. But, if you happen to be one of these stunningly superior people, do not despair: Social psychologists have found hope! When highly competent individuals commit minor blunders—spilling a drink or dropping a sheaf of papers—other people actually like them better, probably because blunders bring them down to everyone else's level and "normalize" them (Aronson et al., 1966, 1970). Don't count on this, however, unless you are so awesomely competent as to be unapproachable. The latté-in-the-lap trick only makes most of us look like klutzes whom people like less.

Attraction and Dissonance *Semper fidelis,* says the Marine Corps motto: "Always faithful." Considering the discomforting experiences that people must go through to become Marines (grueling physical conditioning, loss of sleep, lack of privacy, being yelled at, suffering punishment for small infractions of rules), it may seem remarkable that recruits routinely develop so much loyalty to their organization. The same is true of more enduring loyalty to fraternities that practice hazing compared to college house plans that do not. Obviously, some powerfully attractive and interesting forces are at work.

Cognitive dissonance theory offers a compelling explanation for the mental adjustments that occur in people who voluntarily undergo unpleasant experi-

---

Matching hypothesis The prediction that most people will find friends and mates that are perceived to be of about their same level of attractiveness.

Expectancy-value theory A social psychology theory that states how people decide whether to pursue a relationship by weighing the potential value of the relationship against their expectation of success in establishing the relationship.

Cognitive dissonance A highly motivating state in which people have conflicting cognitions, especially when their voluntary actions conflict with their attitudes or values. Leon Festinger was its originator.

ences (Festinger, 1957). The theory says that when people voluntarily act in ways that produce discomfort or otherwise clash with their attitudes and values, they develop a highly motivating mental state called cognitive dissonance. Those who continue to smoke yet know the negative consequences of cigarette addiction experience dissonance, as do gamblers who continually lose but keep playing. The same holds true for people who find themselves acting in ways that cause them to experience physical discomfort. Thus, our Marine recruits may feel cognitive dissonance when they find that they have volunteered for an experience that is far more punishing than they had imagined from the recruiting ads. And what is the psychological result?

According to cognitive dissonance theory, people are motivated to avoid the uncomfortable state of dissonance. If they find themselves experiencing cognitive dissonance, they attempt to reduce it in ways that are predictable, even if not always entirely logical. The two main ways of reducing dissonance are to change either one's behavior or one's cognitions. So, in civilian life, if the boss is abusive, you might avoid dissonance by simply finding another job. But in the case of a Marine recruit, changing jobs is not an option: It is too late to turn back once basic training has started. A recruit experiencing cognitive dissonance therefore is motivated to adjust his or her thinking. Most likely the recruit will resolve the dissonance by rationalizing the experience ("It's tough, but it builds character!") and by developing a stronger loyalty to the organization ("Being a member of such an elite group is worth all the suffering!").

In general, cognitive dissonance theory says that when people's cognitions and actions are in conflict (a state of *dissonance*), they often reduce the conflict by changing their thinking to fit their behavior. Why? People don't like to see themselves as being foolish or inconsistent. So, to explain their own behavior to themselves, people are motivated to change their attitudes. Otherwise, it would threaten their self-esteem.

One qualification on this theory has recently come to light. In Japan, and, perhaps, in other parts of Asia, studies show that people have a lesser need to maintain high self-esteem than do North Americans (Bower, 1997a; Heine et al., 1999). As a result, cognitive dissonance was found to have less power to change attitudes among Japanese. Apparently, cognitive dissonance is yet another psychological process that operates differently in collectivist and individualistic cultures.

The Explanatory Power of Dissonance   Despite cultural variations, cognitive dissonance theory explains many things that people do to justify their behavior and thereby avoid dissonance. For example, it explains why smokers so often rationalize their habit. It explains why people who have put their efforts into a project, whether it be volunteering for the Red Cross or writing a letter of recommendation, become more committed to the cause as time goes on—to justify their effort. It also explains why, if you have just decided to buy a Toyota Prius, you will attend to new information supporting your choice (such as Prius commercials on TV), but you will tend to ignore dissonance-producing information (such as its higher price or a Prius broken down alongside the freeway).

Cognitive dissonance theory also helps us understand certain puzzling social relationships, such as a woman who is attracted to a man who abuses her. Her dissonance might be summed up in this thought: "Why am I staying with someone who hurts me?" Her powerful drive for self-justification may make her reduce the dissonance by focusing on his good points and minimizing the abuse. And, if she has low self-esteem, she may also tell herself that she deserved his abuse. To put the matter in more general terms: Cognitive dissonance theory predicts that people are attracted to those for whom they have agreed to suffer. A general reward theory, by contrast, would never have predicted that outcome. Another vital contribution made by dissonance theorists is providing a theoretical framework for understanding why we all come to justify our foolish beliefs,

CONNECTION • CHAPTER 9
Social psychologists view cognitive dissonance as a powerful *psychological motive*.

Cognitive dissonance theory predicts that these recruits will increase their loyalty to the Marine Corps as a result of their basic training ordeal.

CONNECTION • CHAPTER 6
Collectivist cultures socialize people to value the needs of the group before the desires of the individual.

bad decisions, and even hurtful acts against others—by justification and disowning personal responsibility for dissonance-generating decisions (Tavris & Aronson, 2007).

To sum up our discussion on interpersonal attraction: You will not usually go far wrong if you use a reward theory to understand why people are attracted to each other. People initiate social relationships because they expect some sort of benefit. It may be an outright reward, such as money or status or sex, or it may be an avoidance of some feared consequence, such as pain. But social psychology also shows that a simple reward theory cannot, by itself, account for all the subtlety of human social interaction. A more sophisticated and useful understanding of attraction must take into account such cognitive factors as expectations, self-esteem, and cognitive dissonance. That is, a complete theory must take into account the ways that we interpret our social environment. This notion of interpretation also underlies other judgments that we make about people, as we shall see next in our discussion of attributions.

Making Cognitive Attributions

We are always trying to explain to ourselves why people do what they do. Suppose you are riding on a bus when a middle-aged woman with an armload of packages gets on. In the process of finding a seat, she drops everything on the floor as the bus starts up. How do you explain her behavior? Do you think of her as the victim of circumstances, or is she incompetent, or eliciting sympathy so someone will give up a seat to her?

Social psychologists have found that we tend to attribute other people's actions and misfortunes to their personal traits, rather than to situational forces, such as the unpredictable lurching of the bus. This helps explain why we often hear attributions of laziness or low intelligence to the poor or homeless, rather than an externally imposed lack of opportunity (Zucker & Weiner, 1993). It also helps us understand why most commentators on the Kitty Genovese murder attributed the inaction of the bystanders to defects in character of those who did not help, rather than to social influences on them (emergency 911 was not in effect at that time, so it was not clear who to call in emergencies; it was difficult to view the crime scene from high story apartments, and so on).

On the other side of the attributional coin, we find that people use the same process to explain each other's successes. So, you may ascribe the success of a favorite singer, athlete, or family member to personal traits, such as exceptional talent or intense motivation. In doing so, we tend to ignore the effects of situational forces, such as the influence of family, coaches, a marketing blitz, long practice, sacrifices, or just a "lucky break."

The Fundamental Attribution Error Psychologists refer to the **fundamental attribution error** (FAE) as the dual tendency to overemphasize personal traits (the rush to the dispositional) while minimizing situational influences. Recall our use of the FAE to explain the low estimates of psychiatrists when predicting the typical shock level of most American citizens in the Milgram obedience experiment. The FAE is not always an "error," of course. If the causes really are dispositional, the observer's guess is correct. So the FAE is best thought of as a bias rather than a mistake. However, the FAE is an error in the sense that an observer may overlook legitimate, situational explanations for another's actions. For example, if the car in front of you brakes suddenly so that you almost collide, your first impression may be that the other driver is at fault, a dispositional judgment. But what if the driver slowed down to avoid hitting a dog that ran into the road? Then the explanation for the near-accident would be situational, not dispositional. By reminding ourselves that circumstances may account for seemingly inexplicable actions, we are less likely to commit the FAE. As a general principle, your authors encourage you to practice "attributional charity," which involves always trying first to find a situa-

Fundamental attribution error (FAE) The dual tendency to overemphasize internal, dispositional causes and minimize external, situational pressures. The FAE is more common in individualistic cultures than in collectivistic cultures.

tional explanation for strange or unusual behavior of others before blaming them with dispositional explanations.

Despite its name, however, the fundamental attribution error is not as fundamental as psychologists at first thought. Cross-cultural research has suggested that it is more pervasive in individualistic cultures, as found in the United States or Canada, than in collectivist cultures, as found in Japan or China (Norenzayan & Nisbett, 2000). Even within the United States, urban children are more susceptible to the fundamental attribution error than are their country cousins (Lillard, 1999).

Biased Thinking about Yourself   Oddly, you probably judge yourself by two different standards, depending on whether you experience success or failure. When things go well, most people attribute their own success to internal factors, such as motivation, talent, or skill ("I am good at taking multiple-choice tests"). But when things go poorly, they attribute failure to external factors beyond their control ("The professor asked trick questions") (Smith & Ellsworth, 1987). Psychologists have dubbed this tendency the **self-serving bias** (Bradley, 1978; Fletcher & Ward, 1988). Self-serving biases are probably rooted in the need for self-esteem, a preference for interpretations that save face and cast our actions in the best possible light (Schlenker et al., 1990).

Social pressures to excel as an individual make the self-serving bias, like the fundamental attribution error, more common in individualist cultures than in collectivist cultures (Markus & Kitayama, 1994). In addition, when trying to understand the behavior of others we tend often to use dispositional explanations, finding things "in them" that might explain why they did this or that. However, when we are trying to figure out the reasons for our own actions, we tend to look to the situational factors acting on us, because we are more aware of them than in our judgments of others. If you believed that you would have defied the authority in the Milgram study and quit long before the 450-volt shock level, despite the evidence that the majority went all the way, a self-serving bias was at work to make you think of yourself as able to resist situational forces that overwhelmed others.

Universal Dimensions of Social Cognition: Warmth and Competence
Among the most basic social perceptions anyone makes are those of "others" as friend or foe, intending to do us good or ill, and able to enact those intentions or not. A large body of new research has established that perceived *warmth* and *competence* of others are the two universal dimensions of human social cognition, at both individual and group levels. People in all cultures differentiate each other by liking (warmth and trustworthiness) and by respecting (competence, efficiency). The warmth dimension is captured in traits that are related to perceived intent, including friendliness, helpfulness, sincerity, trustworthiness, and morality. By contrast, the competence dimension reflects those traits that are related to perceived ability, intelligence, skill, creativity, and efficacy (Fiske et al., 2007).

When these two dimensions are plotted on a graph, as in Figure 11.5, we see that four quadrants emerge: I. high warmth and low competence; II. high warmth and high competence; III. low warmth and low competence; and IV. low warmth and high competence. A large body of research reveals distinct emotions and behaviors associated with each of the social perceptions typical of the four quadrants (Fiske et al., 2007).

Those who are perceived to be high in warmth fall into quadrants I and II. But, as you will see, even though we are drawn to those in both groups because of their perceived warmth, we react to these them quite differently. For people that we view as fitting in quadrant I, we tend to feel pity and may actively seek to help them. (People frequently perceive the elderly and those with disabilities as falling in to quadrant I.) The added perception of competence, however, produces quadrant II, containing those we like or admire—and with whom we want

Can you think of at least three factors discussed so far in this chapter that might be motivating the helping behavior shown in this situation?

Self-serving bias   An attributional pattern in which one takes credit for success but denies responsibility for failure. (Compare with *fundamental attribution error*.)

FIGURE 11.5

The Dimensions of Warmth and Competence

The dimensions of warmth and competence generate four quadrants of action and emotion toward others.

(*Source:* Based on data from Fiske, S. T., Cuddy, A. J. C., & Glick, P. [2007]. Universal dimensions of social cognition: warmth and competence. *Trends in Cognitive Science, 11*, 77–83.)

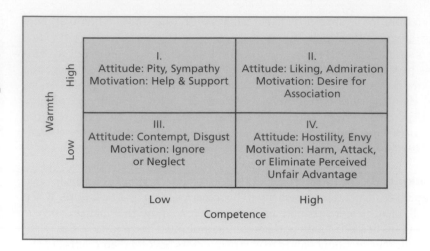

to associate. (This quadrant includes those with whom we identify or aspire to associate—perhaps pastors or rabbis, movie stars, sports heroes, or Bill Gates.)

Now consider how we react to those we perceive as low in warmth. For those we pigeonhole in quadrant III—whom we perceive as being low in both warmth and competence—we feel disdain and a desire to avoid, ignore, or neglect them. (For many people these would include members of some minority groups or welfare recipients.) But our most negative feelings are reserved for those we place in quadrant IV: people whom we perceive as privileged but somehow undeserving. For us, the occupants of quadrant IV provoke feelings of envy and the wish to "bring them down a notch or two"—perhaps even the desire to cause them harm. (Common examples might include politicians, lawyers, and the very rich.)

The authors of this research argue that group-based prejudices and stereotypes appear high on one of these two dimensions and low on the other, thereby creating ambivalent affect and volatile behavior that has the potential to endanger constructive intergroup relationships.

Loving Relationships

Although people often do terrible things to one another, the complexity and beauty of the human mind also enable people to be caring and loving. Liking and loving are essential for happiness (Kim & Hatfield, 2004). Further, the pleasure of attraction and love appear to be part of the very circuitry and chemistry of our brains (Bartels & Zeki, 2004).

How do we know when attraction becomes love? To a large extent, our culture tells us how. Each culture has certain common themes defining love—such as sexual arousal, attachment, concern for the other's welfare, and a willingness to make a commitment. But the idea of "love" can vary greatly from culture to culture (Sternberg, 1998).

There are also many kinds of love. The love that a parent has for a child differs from the love that longtime friends have for each other. Both differ from the commitment found, say, in a loving couple who have been married for 40 years. Yet, for many Americans, the term *love* brings to mind yet another form of attraction based on infatuation and sexual desire: **romantic love,** a temporary and highly emotional condition that generally fades after a few months (Hatfield et al., 1995; Hatfield & Rapson, 1998). But the American assumption that romantic love is the basis for a long-term intimate commitment is not universal. In many other cultures marriage is seen as an economic bond or, perhaps, as a political relationship linking families.

Psychologist Robert Sternberg (1998) has proposed an interesting view in his **triangular theory of love.** He says that love can have three components: passion (erotic attraction), intimacy (sharing feelings and confidences), and commitment

Romantic love A temporary and highly emotional condition based on infatuation and sexual desire.

Triangular theory of love A theory that describes various kinds of love in terms of three components: passion (erotic attraction), intimacy (sharing feelings and confidences), and commitment (dedication to putting this relationship first in one's life). Developed by Robert Sternberg.

(dedication to putting this relationship first in one's life). Various forms of love can be understood in terms of different combinations of these three components. Thus, Sternberg suggests that:

- Romantic love is high on passion and intimacy but low on commitment.
- Liking and friendship are characterized by intimacy but not by passion and commitment.
- Infatuation has a high level of passion, but it has not developed into intimacy or a committed relationship.
- Complete love (consummate love) involves all three: passion, intimacy, and commitment. Companionate love often follows the consummate kind with a dimming of the passion but often with greater intimacy and commitment.

Is it love? Social psychologists have been exploring the psychology of the human heart, collecting and interpreting data about how people fall in love and strengthen their bonds of intimacy. Most recently the emphasis has shifted to the factors that keep relationships together.

The need to understand what strengthens and weakens loving relationships in our own culture has acquired some urgency because of the "divorce epidemic" in the United States (Brehm, 1992; Harvey & Pauwels, 1999). If current rates hold, approximately half of all today's first marriages—and up to 60% of second marriages—will end in divorce. Much research stimulated by concern about high divorce rates has focused on the effects of divorce on children (Ahrons, 1994). The negative effects are lessened when the divorce is amicable and former spouses coparent and do not denigrate each other to the children. Sometimes removing children from a conflict-ridden family setting, or one with an abusive parent, is clearly better for them.

In the past decade or so, however, research emphasis has shifted to the processes by which couples maintain loving relationships and the environments that challenge relationships (Berscheid, 1999). We now know, for example, that for a relationship to stay healthy and to thrive both partners must see it as rewarding and equitable. As we saw in our discussion of reward theory, both must, over the long run, feel that they are getting something out of the relationship, not just giving. What they get—the rewards of the relationship—can involve many things, including adventure, status, laughter, mental stimulation, and material goods, as well as nurturance, love, and social support.

In addition, for a relationship to thrive, communication between partners must be open, ongoing, and mutually validating (Monaghan, 1999). Research shows that couples in lasting relationships have five times more positive interactions than negative ones—including exchanges of smiles, loving touches, laughter, and compliments (Gottman, 1994). Yet, because every relationship experiences an occasional communication breakdown, the partners must know how to deal with conflicts effectively. Conflicts must be faced early and resolved fairly and effectively. Ultimately, each partner must take responsibility for his or her own identity, self-esteem, and commitment to the relationship—rather than expect the partner to engage in mind reading or self-sacrifice.

This has been the briefest sampling from the growing social psychology of relationships. Such research has practical applications. Teachers familiar with research findings can now inform their students about the basic principles of healthy relationships. Therapists apply these principles in advising clients on how to communicate with partners, negotiate the terms of their relationships, and resolve inevitable conflicts. More immediately, as you yourself learn about the factors that influence how you perceive and relate to others, you should gain a greater sense of self-control and well-being in your own intimate connections with others (Harvey, 1996; Harvey et al., 1990).

Cross-Cultural Research on the Need for Positive Self-Regard

Before moving on to the final section in our exploration of social psychology, it is important to consider a rather profound question about the self in relationship to others. Is it true that all people seek positive self-regard—that is, are all people motivated to possess, enhance, and maintain a positive self-concept? Is this a basic attribute of humankind? It would seem so if we consider what people around us do to enhance their self-esteem, the efforts made to be special, even through self-serving biases and personal affirmations. If we look around in North America, the answer might be different than if we look around in Japan.

Researchers have carefully examined both cultural contexts to identify how specific social environmental arrangements of their practices and institutions can promote and sustain the mentalities associated with self-regard. They have found that many aspects of life in North America lead both to an excessive focus on the self as an individual entity as well as encouraging motivation to regard one's self in positive ways, as special, unique, and entitled. This can be seen in ads, movies, songs, diaries, and many aspects of contemporary American culture. By contrast, what is more typical in Japanese culture is the development of a self-critical focus. Personal evaluation usually begins with a critique of the individual's performance or even lifestyle. That critical orientation is both self-effacing and humbling, thereby minimizing any tendency toward arrogance. However, its goal is to seek ways to improve one's attitudes and behaviors in constructive fashion, which satisfies both the individual's needs as well as that of the family, team, business, and the larger community. Such research is important in qualifying what appear to be universal aspects of human nature, but are actually culturally specific (Heine et al., 1999)

Prejudice and Discrimination

While our attributions about others can be positive or negative, prejudice, as social psychologists use the term, is always a negative judgment some people hold about other people. *Prejudice* can make an employer discriminate against women (or men) for a management job. It can make a teacher expect poor work from a minority student. And, in some places in the world, it has led to genocide, the systematic extermination of a group of people because of their racial or ethnic origins. We will define **prejudice** as negative attitudes, beliefs, and feelings toward an individual based solely on his or her membership in a particular group or category. That category may be real, like gender or ethnicity, but it can also be created in the mind of the prejudiced person, such as considering some people as "poor white trash," or others as "left-wing liberals." Prejudice may be expressed as negative emotions (such as dislike or fear), negative attributions or stereotypes that justify the attitude, and/or the behavioral attempt to avoid, control, dominate, or eliminate those in the target group. Prejudiced attitudes serve as extreme biasing filters that influence the way others are perceived and treated. Thus, prejudice exerts a powerful force for selectively processing, organizing, and remembering pertinent information about particular people. It is also pervasive; most people in most nations harbor prejudices of varying kinds, some conscious, and some nonconscious (as new research is uncovering, to be treated later in this section).

Let's distinguish prejudice from *discrimination*, a related concept. While prejudice is an attitude, discrimination is a behavior. **Discrimination** can be defined as a negative action taken against an individual because of his or her group membership. Racial profiling, for example, is often considered a discriminatory procedure because it singles out individual people based solely on racial features. It can result in more arrests of minority members because police are more likely to confront them than majority members for their "suspicious behavior." But, while discrimination can arise from prejudice, we will see soon that this is not always the case. In this section we will review the causes of prejudice, the role of dehumanization as a basic process in prejudice, and combating prejudice, and we will end with new research on stereotype threat.

Prejudice A negative attitude toward an individual based solely on his or her membership in a particular group or category, often without any direct evidence.

Discrimination A negative action taken against an individual as a result of his or her group or categorical membership. It is the behavior that prejudice generates.

Causes of Prejudice   Prejudices can emerge from many sources (Allport, 1954; Aronson, 2004). Some we acquire at an early age. Some are defensive reactions when we feel threatened. Some are the result of conformity to social customs. And some help us distinguish strangers (and possible foes) from friends (Whitley, 1999). An understanding of these sources of prejudice will provide us with the foundation necessary for thinking about possible "cures," ways to combat these antisocial reactions. Here, we present five causes of prejudice that have been studied by social psychologists: *dissimilarity and social distance, economic competition, scapegoating, conformity to social norms,* and *media stereotyping.*

Schoolchildren in Nazi Germany (1930s and 1940s) read textbooks describing Jews as inferior to the "Aryan race." Illustrations in those books also depicted Jewish children excluded from schools.

Dissimilarity and Social Distance   If similarity breeds liking, then *dissimilarity* can breed disdain—and prejudice. So, if you wear baggy shorts, a baseball cap backwards, and a nose ring, it's a good bet that some middle-aged people from a traditional background would feel uncomfortable around you. They are likely to perceive you as a part of a social group that flaunts values and encourages "radical" behaviors quite distinct from those of their own group. Even small perceived differences in appearance can easily become fertile ground for the growth of prejudice.

What psychological principles are at work? When you perceive someone to be unlike the people in your in-group, you mentally place that person at a greater **social distance** than members of your own group. You are then less likely to view that individual as a social equal (Turner & Oakes, 1989). This inequality easily translates into inferiority, making it easier for you to treat members of an out-group with contempt. Historically, more powerful groups have discriminated against out-groups by withholding privileges, sending members of out-groups to different schools, making them sit in the back of the bus, forcing them into low-wage jobs, sending them to jail and into restrictive neighborhood ghettos, and otherwise violating their personal dignity.

Economic Competition   A second cause of prejudice occurs in highly competitive situations, where one group wins economic benefits or jobs at the other group's expense, which can easily fan the flames of prejudice. For example, in the Pacific Northwest, where competition over old-growth forests threatens jobs and wildlife habitat, prejudice sets timber workers and environmentalists against each other. Likewise, surveys have found, for example, prejudice against black Americans to be greatest among white groups poised at an economic level just above the black American average—precisely the ones who would feel their jobs most threatened by black Americans (Greeley & Sheatsley, 1971). It is often true that much prejudice exists not only down from those in privileged positions to those in minority positions but across minority groups, between recent immigrants from different countries, or when new immigrants threaten the financial security of established minorities.

This was the case in New York City's South Bronx area when, after World War II, thousands of migrants from Puerto Rico emigrated to that neighborhood (after a massive sugar crop failure and given free government airfare to the United States). They competed with blacks living there and others coming back from war service for housing and low-level jobs. Researchers discovered high levels of antagonism and prejudice between these two minority groups, each struggling "to make it" in America and also coping with top-down prejudice against both of them by the majority white population (Zimbardo, 1953).

Scapegoating   To understand a third cause of prejudice, consider how the Hebrew priests of olden times performed a ritual that symbolically transferred the sins of the people to a goat—the *scapegoat.* The animal was then driven into the desert to

Social distance   The perceived difference or similarity between oneself and another person.

carry its burden of guilt away from the community. The term *scapegoat* has been applied in modern times to an innocent person or group who receives blame when others feel threatened. On a large and horrifying scale, German Jews served as scapegoats for the Nazis in World War II. Hitler's propaganda program encouraged this by creating visual images of German Jews as totally different from the rest of the German population; such terrible images set them apart as the "faces of the enemy" (Keen, 1991). **Scapegoating** works most readily when the object of scorn is readily identifiable by skin color or some distinctive physical features or when media propaganda can create such differences in the minds of the dominant group (Sax, 2002). It also becomes more probable when conditions worsen in a neighborhood or a country, and people are seeking to blame someone for that change from the good old days to bad times.

Conformity to Social Norms   The source of discrimination and prejudice that is perhaps the most pervasive is an unthinking tendency to maintain conditions the way they are, even when those conditions involve unfair assumptions, prejudices, and customs. For example, in many offices it is the norm for secretaries to be female and executives to be male. Only 18% of private corporations have women on their boards in the United States. That low percentage drops to 2% in Italy and less than 1% in Japan in 2008. Because of this norm, it may be difficult for highly qualified women to break into the executive ranks, to breach the "glass ceiling" above them. We may find the same process where the norm says that nurses and lab technicians should be females and that engineers and mathematicians should be males. When we see that most people in a given profession are of a particular gender or race we assume that is the way of the world, the way the social order meant it to be, rather than to consider the social and economic conditions that have made it that way. So when women note that most computer workers are males, they are likely to avoid taking computer science courses or going into such careers, which then become for "men only." The opposite is now true in psychology. The majority of students taking psychology courses, majoring in it, and going on in psychology careers are now women, a major gender reversal in the past decade. As our field becomes identified as "women only," males are less likely to enter it, and salaries in all such fields decrease substantially.

So we see, then, that a social norm develops for various reasons and it becomes the accepted standard of what is perceived as appropriate and "right." When that happens, behavioral discrimination itself can cause or reinforce prejudiced attitudes. Imagine that you were the male executive who discriminated against a woman applying for an executive position. Or imagine that you were the white bus driver in the 1950s South who routinely sent black passengers to a special section in the back of the bus. In both cases, you were simply following the social norm of what others like you were all doing. However, you would have had to justify your own behavior to yourself. And if you have just treated people as second-class citizens because of their gender or ethnicity, it will be difficult, perhaps impossible, for you to think of them as anything other than inferior beings (without having a severe attack of cognitive dissonance). In this way, your discriminatory behavior can cause or strengthen prejudices. Because we are rationalizing creatures as much as rational ones, we endlessly justify our decisions and behavior to make them appear reasonable by generating "good reasons" for our bad behaviors.

Media Stereotypes   Our fifth cause of prejudice occurs when stereotyped images used to depict groups of people in film, in print, and on television reinforce prejudicial social norms. Such images are far from harmless, because people have learned many of their prejudices from the stereotypes they saw on TV and in books, movies, and magazines (Greenberg, 1986). On the other hand, images in the media can also change those norms. Until the Black Power movement gained media attention, Africans and African Americans were most often portrayed in movies and on TV

Scapegoating   Blaming an innocent person or a group for one's own troubles and then discriminating against or abusing them.

as simple, slow, comic characters, perpetuating the "Sambo" image that many whites held. Fortunately, the most blatant racial stereotypes have disappeared from the national media in the past few decades. Media distortions still occur, of course, but they are subtler. Prime time features three times as many male as female characters (Aronson, 2004). Most are shown in professional and managerial positions, even though two-thirds of the U.S. workforce is employed in blue-collar and service jobs. The proportion of nonwhites and older persons who appear on TV is also much smaller than in the general population. For viewers, the result is a biased picture of the world. This is where it becomes critical to have a variety of role models in the media that portray positions of influence and credibility to young people from those subgroups, such as woman and ethnic/racial minority members as TV news anchors.

Dehumanization   The most powerful psychological process underlying prejudice, discrimination, and intergroup violence is *dehumanization*. It does so by causing some people to view others as less than human, even subhuman. **Dehumanization** can be defined as a psychological process that biases perception and cognitions of others in ways that deprive them of their humanity, rendering them as totally dissimilar and worthless. It is the mechanism behind thinking of particular disliked other people as objects, as the enemy, as animals and insects. Just as a retinal cataract blurs one's visual field, dehumanization is like a "cortical cataract" that blinds the mind to any perceived similarity between Us and Them. Thinking about others as less than human means that one can suspend moral reasoning, empathy, compassion, and other processes that constrain hate and violence. It enables ordinary, even good, people to do bad, even evil deeds (Zimbardo, 2007).

A recent case in point of dehumanization in action occurred in 1994 in Rwanda, Africa. The Hutu government spread propaganda that the Tutsi people living there were the enemy of the Hutus; that they were insects, cockroaches, and had to be destroyed. Men armed with government-supplied machetes and women with clubs massacred 800,000 of their neighbors in 100 days (see Hatzfeld, 2005). A powerful documentary of this dehumanization leading to genocide can be seen at www.pbs.org/wgbh/pages/frontline/shows/evil/.

Can such a complex psychological process be studied experimentally? Yes, indeed, and with a remarkably simple manipulation used by researcher Albert Bandura and his students (Bandura et al., 1975).

A small group of students from one college were supposed to be helping another group of students from a different local college to improve their decision-making skills. They were to provide standard problems to be solved collectively and then reward good solutions and punish bad ones. Punishment was via increasing levels of electric shock administered to the entire working group (no shocks were actually given; they only believed they were). The experimental manipulation consisted of the research assistant telling the experimenter that the students from the other school were ready to begin as the working group. Those who would do the shocking were randomly assigned to one of three conditions: Neutral, hearing only that the other students were ready; Dehumanizing, hearing that the other students seemed like "Animals," and Humanizing, hearing that the other students seemed like "Nice Guys." Simply hearing others labeled "Animals" by a stranger and believing they were also college students was sufficient to induce the students in that condition to administer significantly more shock than in the Neutral condition, and increasingly so over the ten trials. The good news: Humanizing others resulted in significantly less punishment than in the control condition, where students had no information about those others. So sticks and stones may break your bones, but bad names and dehumanization might kill you.

Combating Prejudice   During the civil rights struggles of the 1950s and 1960s, educators believed that prejudice could be overcome through a gradual process of

CONNECTION • CHAPTER 10

Bandura pioneered the study of social models and observational learning.

Dehumanization   The psychological process of thinking about certain other people or groups as less than human, as like feared or hated animals. A basic process in much prejudice and mass violence.

Golfer Tiger Woods is a role model in a sport that has traditionally had few representatives of minority groups.

information campaigns and education. But experience provided no encouragement for this hope. In fact, these informational approaches are among the least effective tools for combating prejudice. The reason? Selective exposure! Prejudiced people (like everyone else) usually avoid information that conflicts with their view of the world, so they never watched or listened to those messages. Even for those who want to change their prejudiced attitudes, erasing the strong emotions and motivational foundations associated with long-standing prejudices is difficult with merely cognitively based informational messages (Devine & Zuwerink, 1994). The process is even more difficult for those who cherish their prejudices because their sense of self-worth is boosted by perceiving others as less worthy than them.

So, how can one attack the prejudices of people who do not want to listen to another viewpoint? Research in social psychology suggests several possibilities. Among them are the use of new role models, equal status contact, and (surprisingly) new legislation.

New Role Models   Golfer Tiger Woods, Secretary of State Condoleezza Rice, Hillary Clinton, Barack Obama, and many others serve as new role models in prestigious jobs and leadership positions where few of their race or gender have appeared before. These role models encourage people in these groups who might never have considered such careers. What we do not know much about, however, is the ability of role models to change the minds of people who are already prejudiced. It is likely that they are perceived as "exceptions to the rule"; but, as the exceptions increase, maybe the rule bends or changes. Role models may serve better to prevent prejudice than to cure it.

Equal Status Contact   Slave owners always had plenty of contact with their slaves, but they always managed to hang onto their prejudices. Obviously, mere contact with people from an out-group is not enough to erase in-group prejudices against them. Evidence, however, from integrated public housing (where the economic threat of lowered property values is not an issue) suggests that when people are placed together under conditions of equal status, where neither wields power over the other, the chances of developing understanding increase (Deutsch & Collins, 1951; Wilner et al., 1955). In an extensive review of all available literature, Tom Pettigrew (1998) found strong support for the power of equal status contact to prevent and reduce prejudice among many different kinds of groups.

Legislation   You can't legislate morality. Right? Wrong! The evidence of several studies suggests that the old cliché may be wrong. One of the most convincing of these studies was an experiment, done in the late 1940s, comparing the attitudes of white tenants toward black tenants in public housing projects. In one project, white and black occupants were assigned to different buildings, that is, the project was racially segregated. A second project mixed or integrated the two racial groups by assigning housing in the same buildings. Only in the racially integrated project did prejudicial attitudes sharply decrease (Deutsch & Collins, 1951). This result strongly suggests that rules requiring equal status contact can diminish prejudice.

This notion is reinforced by a larger social "experiment" that was done under far less controlled conditions. During the past half century, the United States has adopted laws abolishing racial discrimination. The consequences were sometimes violent, but prejudice and discrimination have gradually diminished. Evidence for this shift comes from polls showing that, in the 1940s, fewer than 30% of white Americans favored desegregation. That percentage has steadily climbed to well above 90% today (Aronson, 2004).

Because these changes in public opinion were not part of a carefully controlled experiment, we cannot say that the data prove that legislation has caused peoples' prejudices to diminish. Nevertheless, we can argue that the increased number of white Americans favoring desegregation is exactly what one might predict from cognitive dissonance theory: When the law requires people to act in a less discriminatory fashion, people have to justify their new behavior by softening their prejudiced attitudes. From this vantage point, it appears that legislation—when enforced—can affect prejudiced attitudes, after all. We now see that with dramatic changes in attitudes toward smoking and smokers following legal bans on smoking in many public venues.

Stereotype Threat   Who we think we are may determine how we perform on various tests of ability. That principle emerges from a large body of research in this new area of social psychology, started by researcher Claude Steele, his colleagues and students (Steele et al., 2002). **Stereotype threat** refers to the negative effect on performance that arises when an individual becomes aware that members of his or her group are expected to perform poorly in that domain. This research reveals that performance on both intellectual and athletic tasks is shaped by awareness of existing stereotypes about the groups to which one belongs. It happens even if the person does not believe the stereotype is true; what matters is that others do, and the performer becomes aware that such a negative stereotype threaten his or her self-identity (Haslam et al., 2008).

College women in a math course take a special math test and do as well as male students, except when they first check off the gender box: Female. When reminded of their gender, then their performance becomes significantly poorer, confirming the stereotype about woman and math. The same was found with high-achieving African American students from Stanford University who were taking a test of verbal ability. When told it was a test of intelligence they performed worse than when the same test was supposedly not diagnostic of any intellectual ability. The stereotype of blacks having lower IQ than whites subconsciously creates anxiety that their performance will risk confirming this stereotype. That anxiety interferes with optimal cognitive processing and their positive self-identity, and they end up doing more poorly.

This effect extends to sports performance as well. Expert golfers who are exposed to the stereotype that members of their sex are worse at putting than are those of the opposite sex, hit their putts further away from the hole than those not given this false stereotype threat. In other research white golfers told that their performance will be compared with that of black golfers perform worse if they are led to believe it is a test of "natural athletic ability," which blacks are supposed to have more of, according to the stereotype. However, when told it is a test of "sport strategic intelligence," then they do much better. This enhanced performance of a reverse stereotype that makes you believe you are superior to another group on any dimension is known as "stereotype lift." If Asian women taking a math test are required to focus on the fact that they are either woman or Asian, they do worse when reminded of their female status but better than the control condition of no identity focus when they are reminded of their Asian status (and the implicit stereotype of Asian math superiority). Again, here is stereotype lift at work. Thus, we can make stereotypes work for us as well as against our performance (Shih et al., 1999).

PSYCHOLOGY**MATTERS**

The Sweet Smells of Attraction

The perfume industry spends millions annually to discover scents that will make the wearer more alluring. Pleasant body scents are assumed to enhance human attractiveness, as animal pheromones are known to be vital in sexual attraction within many species. Research reveals that certain odors can regulate mood, cognition, and even mate selection (Herz & Schooler, 2002; Jacob et al., 2002). We know that information presented subliminally, not consciously detectable, can influence social judgments (Fazio, 2001). Can subliminal smells similarly guide our social preferences? A team of researchers recently set out to answer that provocative question.

Stereotype threat   The negative effect on performance that arises when an individual becomes aware that members of his or her group are expected to perform poorly in that domain.

Undergraduates of both sexes underwent a procedure to determine their individual thresholds for detecting a set of odors, first above threshold for odors that were pleasant, neutral, and unpleasant, then below their thresholds for awareness of any odor. Next, they sniffed a bottle that contained a pleasant, neutral, or unpleasant odorant in low concentrations below their individual awareness threshold. After each sniff, a face was briefly flashed on a screen, which had been premeasured to be "neutral-average." Each student then rated the degree of likeability of each of a variety of these neutral faces over many trials, pairing subliminal scents with the faces.

The results clearly demonstrate that likeability was influenced by faces paired with odors that elicited different affective reactions. Students liked most the faces they viewed after smelling a pleasant odor and liked least those accompanied by an unpleasant odor—even though they were totally unaware of having smelled either scent. Heart rates of the students examining the faces were also altered by these same scents, increasing with the unpleasant ones significantly more than the pleasant or neutral odors. The researchers conclude that, "the time-honored belief that scents play an important role in human social interaction appears to withstand scientific scrutiny." (Li et al., 2007, p. 1048). This research also highlights the importance of the olfactory system in influencing social judgments and makes us hope that the subtle scents we emit will make pleasant impressions on those we want to like us.

CheckYourUnderstanding

1. RECALL: According to Aronson, we can explain almost everything about interpersonal attraction with a theory of
   a. love.
   b. rewards.
   c. genetic predispositions.
   d. gender.

2. RECALL: Which of the following does the research say is most important in predicting initial attraction?
   a. physical attractiveness
   b. money
   c. personality
   d. nurturing qualities

3. RECALL: In trying to understand why Bill was late for an appointment, Jane blamed his lack of conscientiousness and ignored the facts of rush hour traffic and a major storm that hit town. Jane is guilty of
   a. the chamelon effect.
   b. the expectancy-value violation.
   c. scapegoating.
   d. fundamental attribution error.

4. APPLICATION: According to cognitive dissonance theory, which of the following would be the best strategy for getting people to like you?
   a. Give them presents.
   b. Show interest in their interests.
   c. Tell them that you like them.
   d. Persuade them to perform a difficult or unpleasant task for you.

5. RECALL: Prejudice is a(n) _____, while discrimination is a(n) _____.
   a. behavior/attitude
   b. instinct/choice
   c. attitude/behavior
   d. stimulus/response

6. RECALL: The evidence suggests that one of the most effective techniques for eliminating racial prejudice has been
   a. education.
   b. threat and force.
   c. legislation.
   d. tax incentives.

7. UNDERSTANDING THE CORE CONCEPT: Reward theory, expectancy-value theory, cognitive dissonance theory, and attribution theory all tell us that we respond not just to situations but to
   a. our cognitive interpretations.
   b. our social instincts.
   c. the intensity of the stimuli.
   d. our biological needs and drives.

Answers 1. b **2.** a **3.** d **4.** d **5.** c **6.** d **7.** a

11.3 KEY QUESTION
HOW DO SYSTEMS CREATE SITUATIONS THAT INFLUENCE BEHAVIOR?

We spend most of our lives in various institutions—family, schools, hospitals, jobs, military, prison, elderly homes—and may end in a hospice. Each of these settings involve *systems* of management and control, explicit and implicit rules of conduct, and reward and punishment structures, and they come with a history, a culture, and a legal status. In many cases it is **system power** that creates, maintains, and gives meaning and justification to a situation. Although social psychologists have highlighted the power of situations on behavior, as you have seen in this chapter, they have tended not to acknowledge the greater power that systems have to make those situations work as they do, sometimes for the better, but sometimes for the worse. This then leads us to the third lesson of social psychology, captured in our final Core Concept:

> Understanding how systems function increases both our understanding of why situations work as they do to influence human behavior and is also the most effective way to plan behavior change from the top down; systems change situations, which in turn change behavior.

CONNECTION • CHAPTER 13
Marriage counselors and family therapists often use a *systems* approach to understanding and resolving family conflicts.

core concept

We will illustrate how **system power** can create a remarkably powerful social situation that in turn affected the behavior of all within its behavioral context in research known as the **Stanford Prison Experiment**. Then we will briefly examine other systems that have also generated abusive behavior, such as that in the Abu Ghraib prison in Iraq. We do not have the space to also illustrate how network systems are involved in most nonviolent movements that train citizens in passive resistance, such as Gandhi in India, Martin Luther King Jr. in the American South, and Nelson Mandela in opposing apartheid in South Africa. Similar system networks were critical to develop by Christians who helped Jews escape the Holocaust.

The Stanford Prison Experiment

On a summer Sunday in California, a siren shattered the serenity of college student Tommy Whitlow's morning. A city police car screeched to a halt in front of his home. Within minutes, Tommy was charged with a felony, informed of his constitutional rights, frisked, and handcuffed. After he was booked and fingerprinted at the city jail, Tommy was blindfolded and transported to the Stanford County Prison, where he was stripped and issued a smock-type uniform with an I.D. number on the front and back. Tommy became "Prisoner 8612." Eight other college students were also arrested and assigned numbers during that mass arrest by the local police.

The prison guards were anonymous in their khaki military uniforms, reflector sunglasses, and nameless identity as "Mr. Correctional Officer," but with symbols of power shown off in their big nightsticks, whistles, and handcuffs. To them, the powerless prisoners were nothing more than their worthless numbers.

The guards insisted that prisoners obey all of their many arbitrary rules without question or hesitation. Failure to do so led to losses of privileges. At first, privileges included opportunities to read, write, or talk to other inmates. Later, the slightest protest resulted in the loss of "privileges" of eating, sleeping, washing, or having visitors during visiting nights. Failure to obey rules also resulted in a variety of unpleasant tasks such as endless push-ups, jumping jacks, and number count-offs that lasted for hours on end. Each day saw an escalation of the level of hostile abuse by the guards against their prisoners: making them clean toilets with bare hands, doing push-ups while a guard stepped on the prisoner's back, spending long hours naked in solitary confinement, and finally engaging in degrading forms of sexual humiliation.

System power Influences on behavior that come from top-down sources in the form of creating and maintaining various situations that in turn have an impact on actions of individuals in those behavioral contexts.

Stanford Prison Experiment Classic study of institutional power in directing normal, healthy college student volunteers playing randomly assigned roles of prisoners and guards to behave contrary to their dispositional tendencies, as cruel guards or pathological prisoners.

"Prisoner 8612" encountered some guards whose behavior toward him and the other prisoners was sadistic, taking apparent pleasure in cruelty; others were just tough and demanding; a few were not abusive. However, none of the few "good" guards ever challenged the extremely demeaning actions of the "perpetrators of evil."

Less than 36 hours after the mass arrest, "Prisoner 8612," who had become the ringleader of an aborted prisoner rebellion that morning, had to be released because of an extreme stress reaction of screaming, crying, rage, and depression. On successive days, three more prisoners developed similar stress-related symptoms. A fifth prisoner developed a psychosomatic rash all over his body when the parole board rejected his appeal, and he too was released from the Stanford County Jail.

Everyone in the prison, guard and prisoner alike, had been selected from a large pool of student volunteers. On the basis of extensive psychological tests and interviews, the volunteers had been judged as law-abiding, emotionally stable, physically healthy, and "normal-average" on all personality trait measures. In this mock prison experiment, assignment of participants to the independent variable treatment of "guard" or "prisoner" roles had been determined by random assignment. Thus, in the beginning, there were no systematic differences between the "ordinary" college males who were in the two different conditions. By the end of the study, there were no similarities between these two alien groups. The prisoners lived in the jail around the clock, and the guards worked standard eight-hour shifts.

As guards, students who had been pacifists and "nice guys" in their usual life settings behaved aggressively—sometimes even sadistically. As prisoners, psychologically stable students soon behaved pathologically, passively resigning themselves to their unexpected fate of learned helplessness. The power of the simulated prison situation had created a new social reality—a functionally real prison—in the minds of both the jailers and their captives. The situation became so powerfully disturbing that the researchers were forced to terminate the two-week study after only six days.

Although Tommy Whitlow said he wouldn't want to go through it again, he valued the personal experience because he learned so much about himself and about human nature. Fortunately, he and the other students were basically healthy, and extensive debriefing showed that they readily bounced back from the prison experience. Follow-ups over many years revealed no lasting negative effects on these students. The participants had all learned an important lesson: Never underestimate the power of a bad situation to overwhelm the personalities and good upbringing of even the best and brightest among us and of a system to create such situations (Zimbardo, 2007).

The basic results of this study were replicated in cross-cultural research in Australia (Lovibond et al., 1979). However, there was never the same degree of violence exhibited by the guards, perhaps because this study followed the cultural norm of everyone having afternoon teatime. For detailed information about this study see www.prisonexp.org.

Suppose you had been a subject in the Stanford prison experiment. Would you have been a good guard—or a sadist? A model compliant prisoner—or a rebel? Could you have resisted the pressures and stresses of these circumstances? It is a similar question raised about how you think you might have behaved if you were the "Teacher" in the Milgram obedience research—obey or defy? We'd all like to believe we would be good guards and heroic prisoners; we would never step across that line between good and evil. And, of course, we all believe that we would be able to keep things in perspective, knowing that it was "just an experiment," only role-playing and not real. But the best bet is that most of us would react the same way as these participants did. This disturbing study raises many questions about how well we really know ourselves, our inner dispositional qualities, and how much we appreciate the subtle powers of external

Scenes from the Stanford prison experiment.

forces on us, the situational qualities. Obviously, it also raises ethical issues about whether such research should have ever been done or allowed to continue.

By the conclusion of the Stanford Prison Experiment, guards' and prisoners' behavior differed from each other in virtually every observable way. (See Figure 11.6.) Yet it was only chance, in the form of random assignment, that had decided their roles—roles that had created status and power differences that were validated in the prison situation and supported by the system of prison authorities. No one taught the participants to play their roles. Without ever visiting real prisons, all the participants learned something about the interaction between the powerful and the powerless. A guard type is someone who limits the freedom of prisoner types to manage their behavior and make them behave more predictably. This task is aided by the use of coercive rules, which include explicit punishment for violations. Prisoners can only react to the social structure of a prisonlike setting created by those with power. Rebellion and compliance are the only options of the prisoners; the first choice results in punishment, while the second results in a loss of autonomy and dignity.

The student participants had already experienced such power differences in many of their previous social interactions in various systems of control: parent–child, teacher–student, doctor–patient, boss–worker, male–female. They merely refined and intensified their prior patterns of behavior for this particular setting. Each student could have played either role. Many students in the guard role reported being surprised at how easily they enjoyed controlling other people. Just putting on the uniform was enough to transform them from passive college students into aggressive prison guards.

Milgram's obedience research and the Stanford Prison Experiment form bookends of much research illustrating the power of situations over behavior. However, the obedience studies were about individual authority power, while the prison experiment is about the power of an institution, a system of domination. The guards maintained the situation of abuse, but so did the research team of psychologists; the police contributed to its reality, as did many others who visited the prison setting—a prison chaplain, a public defender, parents and friends on visiting nights, and civilians on the parole board.

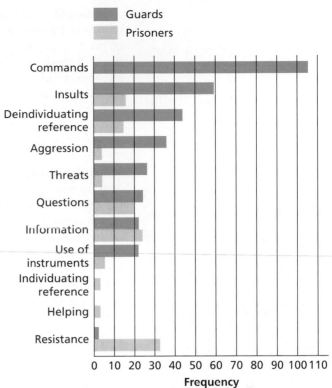

FIGURE 11.6
Guard and Prisoner Behavior

(*Source:* From R. J. Gerrig and P. G. Zimbardo, *Psychology and Life*, 18th ed. Published by Allyn and Bacon, Boston, MA. Copyright © 2008 by Pearson Education. Reprinted by permission of the publisher.

Chains of System Command

Psychologists seek to understand behavior in order to promote prosocial forms and alter for the better antisocial aspects of behavior. Understanding why some people engage in "bad behaviors" does not excuse them; rather it leads to new ideas about changing the causal influences on those behaviors. A full understanding of most complex human behavior should include an appreciation of the ways in which situational conditions are created and shaped by higher-order factors—*systems of power*. Systems, not just dispositions and situations, must be taken into account in order to understand complex behavior patterns.

Aberrant, illegal, or immoral behavior by individuals in service professions, such as policemen, corrections officers, or soldiers, or even in business settings, is typically labeled the misdeeds of "a few bad apples." The implication is they are a rare exception and must be set on one side of the impermeable line between evil and good, with the majority of good apples set on the other side. But who is making that distinction? Usually it is the guardians of the system—who want to isolate the problem to deflect attention and blame away from those at the top who may be responsible for creating impossible working conditions or for a lack of their oversight or supervision. Again the bad apple-dispositional view ignores the bad apple barrel-situational view and its potentially corrupting situational impact on those within it. A systems analysis focuses on the next step higher, on the "bad barrel makers," on those with the power to design the barrel. It is the "power elite," the barrel makers, often working behind the scene, who arrange many of the conditions of life for the rest of us who must spend time in the variety of institutional settings they have constructed.

What Happened at Abu Ghraib Prison?   The world became aware of the abuses of Iraqi prisoners by American Military Police guards in **Abu Ghraib Prison** with the April 2004 televised exposure of horrific images that they had taken (see one such image on this page).

Immediately, the military chain of command dismissed it all as the work of a few rogue soldiers, while the president's chain of command likewise blamed it on a few bad apples. Both systems were quick to assert that it was not systemic, not occurring in other military prisons. However, investigative reporter Seymour Hersh (2004a) exposed the lie in that attribution with his analysis of the culpability of both of those systems of power, those chains of "irresponsible" command. The title of his May 5, 2004, article in *The New Yorker*, was "Torture at Abu Ghraib. American soldiers brutalize Iraqis: How far up does the responsibility go?" His answer: all the way to the top of the military and civilian system of command (see also Hersh, 2004b).

A review of the dozen reports investigating these abuses, most by generals and government officials, clearly highlights the distorting influences on those American Army Reserve soldiers from their impossible working conditions in that dungeon coupled with total failures of military leadership and surveillance. Of the many factors responsible for those abuses, these reports point to many situational and system failures in addition to the personal moral failures of the soldiers (see Zimbardo, 2007). In fact, similar abuses in military prisons and other war zones had occurred before, during, and after this revelation of unthinkable behavior by American men and women soldiers at Abu Ghraib. So there were dispositional, situational, and systemic processes all interacting in this instance.

The Systems Lesson   The most important lesson to be learned from the Core Concept for this section is that *situations are created by systems*. Systems provide the institutional support, authority, and resources that allow situations to operate as they do. System power involves authorization or institutionalized permission to behave in prescribed ways or to forbid and punish actions that are disapproved. It provides the "higher authority" that gives validation to playing new roles, following new rules, and taking actions that would ordinarily be constrained by preexistent laws, norms, morals, and ethics. Such validation usually comes cloaked in the mantle of ideology. Ideology is a slogan or proposition that usually legitimizes whatever means are necessary to attain an ultimate goal. The programs, policies, and standard operating procedures that are developed to support an ideology become an essential component of the system. The system's procedures are considered reasonable and appropriate as the ideology comes to be accepted as sacred.

However, although all systems involve individuals at varying levels of power and status, most systems are not transparent, concealing much of their operation from outsiders. So even when a system is failing to meet its objectives and goals, as many failing educational or correctional systems are, or in mega corporations that engage in corrupt practices, higher-ups are hidden from public scrutiny.

Nevertheless, to change undesirable behavior and promote more socially desirable behavior, it is not sufficient to continue to rely on the individualistic medical model of treating people for problem behavior, when the situation might

One of the photos taken by American Military Police at Abu Ghraib.

Abu Ghraib Prison   Prison in Iraq made famous by revelation of photos taken by Army Reserve MP guards in the acts of humiliating and torturing prisoners.

be a fault. And plans to improve situations must involve understanding and modifying the systems that create and maintain them. Instead, the call is for using a public health model that recognizes individual affliction and illness as the consequence of a vector of disease in society. Prevention rather than just treatment becomes the goal; inoculating against a virus prevents the spread of an epidemic. This should be as true for the evils of prejudice, violence, and bullying in our society as it is for viral infections.

Using Psychology to Understand the Abuses at Abu Ghraib   Over a three-month period, Military Police, Army Reservists, working the night shift at Tier 1-A in that dungeon, used some of the 1000 prisoners detained there as their "playthings"—piling them naked in pyramids, hanging them upside down with women's panties over their heads, dragging them around the ground on dog leashes, and sexually degrading them in various ways. Tier 1-A was the interrogation center run by Military Intelligence, the CIA, and civilian interrogator companies. When the unexpected insurgency against the U.S. forces suddenly escalated, the chain of command needed "actionable intelligence" from these detainees. So the MPs were given permission by higher-ups "to soften up" the prisoners, to prepare them for interrogation, to "take the gloves off." Given that official permission for abuse, and with no senior officer ever providing oversight or surveillance of that night shift, all hell broke loose. However, the soldiers did not think what they were doing was wrong; one said it was only "fun and games." They also documented these games with candid photographs of themselves with their abused prisoners in hundreds of horrific images.

One investigating committee was headed by James Schlesinger, former Secretary of Defense, and included generals and other high-ranking officials. The report notes the relevance of social psychological research and theory to the understanding of these abuses:

> The potential for abusive treatment of detainees during the Global War on Terrorism was entirely predictable based on a fundamental understanding of the principles of social psychology coupled with an awareness of numerous known environmental risk factors. . . . Findings from the field of social psychology suggest that the conditions of war and the dynamics of detainee operations carry inherent risks for human mistreatment, and therefore must be approached with great caution and careful planning and training.
>
> Such conditions neither excuse nor absolve the individuals who engaged in deliberate immoral or illegal behaviors [even though] certain conditions heightened the possibility of abusive treatment.

The *Schlesinger Report* boldly proclaims that the "landmark Stanford study provides a cautionary tale for all military detention operations." In contrasting the relatively benign environment of the Stanford Prison Experiment, the report makes evident that "in military detention operations, soldiers work under stressful combat conditions that are far from benign." The implication is that those combat conditions might be expected to generate even more extreme abuses of power by military police than were observed in our mock prison experiment. The *Schlesinger Report* concludes with a statement that underscores much of what we have presented in this chapter: "Psychologists have attempted to understand how and why individuals and groups who usually act humanely can sometimes act otherwise in certain circumstances." Among the concepts this reports outlines to help explain why abusive behaviors occur among ordinarily humane individuals are deindividuation, dehumanization, enemy image, groupthink, moral disengagement, social facilitation, and other environmental factors.

There are fewer more direct statements that your authors are aware of that highlight the value of psychological theories and social psychological research than this official government report. The full report, and especially Appendix G,

Schlesinger Report   Report issued by one of the official investigations of the Abu Ghraib Prison abuses, headed by James Schlesinger, former Secretary of Defense. It highlighted the social psychological factors that contributed to creating an abusive environment.

which is notable for students of psychology, can be found at www.prisonexp.org/pdf/SchlesingerReport.pdf.

Preventing Bullying by Systemic Changes

Bullying in school and in the workplace is about some students and workers making life miserable for others by extreme teasing, threatening, physically abusing, and damaging personal reputations through lies and gossip. Most other students and coworkers who are neither bully nor victim are aware of the problem but usually ignore it or passively accept it. The traditional method for dealing with bullies is to identify the culprits and punish them in various ways, moving them to other classes or schools, or jobs. This is likely to move the abusers and their abuse to different venues but not change them; often it makes them even angrier and vengeful. **Bullying** is defined as systematically and chronically inflicting physical hurt and/or psychological distress on one or more others, students in school and workers in the workplace.

Statistics on the prevalence of bullying vary from a conservative estimate of 15% of all Swedish school children being bullied or bullies themselves (Olweus, 1993) to 73% of a British sample who reported being bullied, being the bully perpetrator, or having witnessed bullying directly (McLeod, 2008). This large-scale study included nearly 2000 students, aged 12 through 19, across 14 schools. Girls are more like to be the target of bullying than boys, and they are more emotionally affected by it. While male bullies use direct physical abuse, females tend toward indirect verbal abuse, exclusion, group rejection, and rumors.

Prevention of bullying requires switching from the usual punishment model of bullies to a systemwide set of practices that give zero tolerance for bullying. The impetus for change must come top-down from school superintendents and principles, involving teachers and parents, and then enabling students themselves as agents of change. Researcher Dan Olweus (1993) has used such a system change model in Sweden and other Scandinavian countries with considerable success. In the United States, students are bullied who seem "different," the more shy, those with physical handicaps or alternative sexual orientations. "Actual or perceived sexual orientation is one of the most common reasons that students are harassed by their peers, second only to physical appearance," according to psychologist Peter Goldbaum (cited in Novotney, 2008). At the core of new programs to combat and prevent bullying is developing curricula and practices from elementary school throughout all grades that promote respect for the dignity of individuals and for acceptance and tolerance of human diversity.

PSYCHOLOGYMATTERS
Using Psychology to Learn Psychology

You may associate persuasion with advertising and politics, but persuasion does not stop there. It is woven into all human interaction—including the exchanges of ideas that occur in the classroom. There, your professors and fellow students will attempt to persuade you with reasoned arguments, and they will expect you to set out your points of view in the same fashion. But, aside from the open exchange of ideas and opinions, there are other, more subtle persuasive pressures of which you should be aware, says social psychologist Robert Cialdini (2001). If you don't know about these, you run the risk of letting other people make up your mind for you. We will discuss three such subtle forms of influence that you will encounter in your college or university experience.

Social Validation   Although you may see a popular movie because your friends like it, going along with the crowd is a poor basis for judging the theories you encounter in your classes. Many of the world's discarded ideas were once accepted

Bullying   The act of tormenting others, in school classrooms or work settings, by one or more others, for personal, sadistic pleasure. It qualifies as a form of ordinary or everyday evil.

by nearly everyone. In psychology, these include the false notions that we use only 10% of our brain, that personality is determined by the first two years of life, and that IQ tests are a good measure of innate abilities. So, rather than accepting what you hear and read, questioning even the most widely held concepts is a good habit. In fact, most famous scientists have built their careers on challenging ideas that everyone else accepted.

Authority   The lectures you hear and the textbooks you read are full of authority figures. Every parenthetical reference in this book, for example, cites an authority. Most are given, in part, to persuade you that the argument being offered is credible. The problem, of course, is that ideas are not true merely because some authority says so. For example, just a few years ago, every introductory psychology text in print taught that no new neurons were created in the brain after birth. Now we know that the textbooks and the experts they cited were wrong. Real proof of such assertions, however, requires more objective evidence obtained by the scientific method—not just the declaration of an authority.

The Poison Parasite Argument   In advertising, a good way to undermine a competitor, says Cialdini, is with a message that calls into question the opponent's credibility. Then, to get people to remember what you have said, you can infect your opponent with a "parasite"—a mnemonic link that reminds people of your message every time they hear your opponent's pitch (Brookhart, 2001). A classic example involved antismoking ads that looked like Marlboro commercials, except that they featured a coughing, sickly "Marlboro Man." You may encounter the same sort of poison parasite argument in a lecture or a textbook that attempts to hold someone's ideas up to ridicule. That's not necessarily bad: In the academic world, weak ideas should perish. The sneaky, dishonest form of this technique, however, involves a misrepresentation or oversimplification of the opponent's arguments. The antidote is to be alert for ridicule and to check out the other side of the argument yourself.

The social psychology of persuasion, of course, involves much more than we have discussed here. A good place to look for more information is Cialdini's book *Influence: The Psychology of Persuasion* (2007). Perhaps the most important idea is that some knowledge of persuasion can forearm you against the persuasive techniques you will encounter, both in and out of the classroom. When you know how effective persuaders operate, you are less likely to donate money to causes you don't care about, buy a car you don't really like, or accept a theory without examining the evidence critically.

CheckYourUnderstanding

1. **RECALL:** The Stanford prison experiment illustrates the power of _____ to influence people's behavior.
   a. personality
   b. heredity
   c. childhood experiences
   d. the situation

2. **RECALL:** What was the independent variable in the Stanford Prison Experiment?
   a. random assignment to prisoner or guard roles
   b. IQ level differences of those in the two roles
   c. cultural backgrounds of the volunteers
   d. all of the above

3. **RECALL:** The abuses perpetrated by the MPs at Abu Ghraib Prison were blamed entirely on the soldiers as symptoms of their being "bad apples." Who is *least* likely to make such a negative dispositional attribution?
   a. a social psychologist
   b. a trial lawyer for the prosecution
   c. military leaders
   d. civilian chain of command leaders

4. **UNDERSTANDING THE CORE CONCEPT:** If you wanted to stop bullying in your school, what would be most likely to be an effective strategy to follow?
   a. Punish the bully publicly.
   b. Teach the victim to fight back.
   c. Reward the bully for not bullying any victims.
   d. Change the entire school system to have zero tolerance for bullying.

Answers 1. d **2.** a **3.** a **4.** d

Critical Thinking Applied: Is Terrorism "A Senseless Act of Violence, Perpetrated by Crazy Fanatics"?

The terrorist attacks of September 11, 2001, and suicide bombings in Israel, Iraq, London, Madrid, and elsewhere around the world raise questions for which there are no easy answers. *Terrorism* is really about psychology. It typically involves a relatively small group of people working as a network who take dramatic, violent actions against a larger group with the intention of spreading fear among them and inducing anxiety and uncertainty about their government's ability to protect them. Terrorists do not want to conquer other nations' land, as in traditional wars, but to conquer the minds of their enemies by making them feel victimized and fearful of random attacks.

What Are the Issues?

Global terrorism is an escalating threat that many nations must face in the coming years. Terrorists operate in networks that vary in their degree of organization, but they are not national states. A war against terrorism is an *asymmetrical war,* of nations against collectives of individuals, without uniforms or designated sovereign territories. Their tactics are hit and run, attacking at random times, amplifying the surprise value of their destructive power.

Some of the critical issues for you to consider include the following. How can a war against terrorism ever be "won"? What would winning actually look like if there were no one leader to surrender? Why is the best strategy for meeting this global challenge international cooperation and intelligence resource sharing rather than dominant nations acting unilaterally? What is the pipeline that is generating so many terrorists? In what sense can the threat of terrorism be reduced by "winning the hearts and minds" of young people who might be recruited by elders to join terrorist cells or be trained to become suicide bombers?

What Critical Thinking Questions Should We Ask?

The reasons for terrorist violence are many and complex. However, media sources of such claims try to simplify complexity and reduce ambiguity to simple frameworks. They often exaggerate fears for viewers and listeners. "If it bleeds, it leads," is a classic statement about what it takes to be the lead TV news item (See Breckenridge & Zimbardo, 2006, about mass-mediated fear). When they or the general public do not understand something, there is a readiness to label it "senseless." That only means it does not make sense to them or that there is no solid evidence for the motivations behind it. For example, vandalism has been called senseless, until it becomes apparent that it is often done by have-nots who are trying to make an impact on society, a destructive, dramatic one when they are not able to make a more constructive one. As citizens and critical thinkers, we need to call for better information from our politicians, educators, journalists, and others who may try to assign easy answers to complex problems.

Is the Claim Reasonable or Extreme? Obviously this is an extreme generalization and simplification of a complex social-political-cultural issue. Unfortunately, the easiest and most simplistic response is to demonize those who perpetrate evil deeds—but that is merely name calling, and we should resist it. This tactic blinds us to the power of the situation to create aggression in ordinary people, as we have seen in the Milgram and Stanford Prison research. More important, it prevents us from dealing with the situations that nurture violence. Labeling others as "evil" or "pathological" usually prevents any attempt to understand the reasons for their actions, instead making them into objects of scorn or disdain. Again, it is a related mistake to think of violence and terrorism as "senseless." On the contrary, destructive deeds always make sense from the perpetrator's frame of reference. As Shakespeare's Hamlet said, there is "method" in madness: We must understand the method in the minds of potential terrorists if we are to deter them.

What Is the Evidence? Research has shown that aggressive behavior can be induced by situations that create prejudice, conformity, frustration, threat, or wounded pride (Aronson, 2004; Baumeister et al., 1996). There is no evidence that terrorists, even suicide bombers, are pathological, rather that they are filled with anger and feelings of revenge against what they perceive as injustice. They are often well educated, in stable relationships, and now likely to be from both sexes. In many cases, they become part of systematic training program to learn the skills necessary to effectively destroy one's perceived enemy and accept being a martyr for a cause they believe is just (Merari, 2006).

The flammable combination of poverty, powerlessness, and hopelessness are the tinder that the September 11 attacks were intended to ignite, says Jonathan

Lash, president of the World Resources Institute in Washington, D.C. (2001). Much of the world lives in poverty and hunger and sees no way out. Ethnic hatred and wars aggravate their plight. Moreover, the number of people living in these miserable conditions is increasing, as most of the world's population explosion is occurring in poorer countries. And, to make matters more volatile, says Lash, a large proportion of these desperate people depend directly on resources that are rapidly being depleted: fisheries, forests, soils, and water resources. As a result, every day thousands flee their traditional homelands and stream into the largest and poorest cities. Most are young—a result of the high birth rates in the Third World. Mr. Lash warns that urban slums, filled with restless, jobless young men, are "tinderboxes of anger and despair; easy recruiting grounds for bin Laden or those who may come after him" (p. 1789). We have seen this in recent violent riots in the slums outside Paris by young immigrants without jobs and educational opportunities.

Could Bias Contaminate This Conclusion?

Indeed, several biases are at work here: first, the dispositional bias of focusing on individual perpetrators and ignoring their behavioral context, the situation and the system that gives shape and purpose to their actions; second, a simplification bias that reduces difficult complex issues into simple terms that give an illusion of simple, easy solutions.

Does the Reasoning Avoid Common Fallacies?

The reasoning behind making and accepting this assertion about terrorism and terrorists includes giving into common fallacies as we have seen. Combating it involves understanding the immediate causal contributions leading to becoming a terrorist as well as the broader systemic influences on such extreme decisions.

Does the Issue Require Multiple Perspectives?

Understanding terrorism requires the combined insights of many perspectives—and not just those from psychology. Issues of money, power, resources, and ancient grudges must be considered as well. But—like it or not—many people in the world perceive the United States as the enemy. Understanding this perception—and dealing constructively with it—demands that Americans see the conflict from someone else's point of view: those who consider the United States to be the enemy.

What Conclusions Can We Draw?

We must also realize that terrorism does not always involve international conflict. The student shootings at Columbine High, Virginia Tech University, and many other schools were terrorist acts, along with thousands of racial/ethnic hate crimes, attacks against gays, and violence directed at abortion providers that have made news in recent years (Doyle, 2001). It would be a mistake to believe that terrorism is always an outside threat from foreigners: Even though some cultures are more violent than others, every culture can breed violent people who terrorize others (Moghaddam et al., 1993; Shiraev & Levy, 2001). Just remember that the bomber who blew up the Oklahoma City federal building and killed hundreds of innocent people was an American terrorist named Timothy McVeigh. The Ku Klux Klan was (is) a uniquely American terrorist organization acting in violent ways to instill fear and terror in blacks and others they considered their enemy.

The Need for a Cross-Cultural and Historical Perspective

A complete picture, however, necessitates taking perspectives that extend beyond psychology (Segall et al., 1999). When we expand our view of terrorism, we can see that long-standing hostilities arise from religious, ethnic, and racial prejudices and from poverty, powerlessness, and hopelessness. To arrive at this understanding, however, we must view terrorism from historical, economic, and political perspectives—again, not to excuse violent acts but to understand their origins. We cannot understand, for example, the tensions between Christianity and Islam without knowing about the 200-year-war that the Western world calls the Crusades (1095–1291) or the fall of the six-centuries-old Ottoman Empire (1300–1922) at the end of World War I. Although such events may seem remote, they changed the trajectory of history, and their religious significance continues to fuel conflict in the Middle East today.

A Positive Endnote

We can think of no better way to end a chapter that focused mostly on the way good people go bad than to leave you with a wonderful statement about the unity of humankind, and the need to respect our kinship with one another. It is from poet, preacher John Donne (*Meditations XV11*):

All mankind is of one author, and is one volume; when one man dies, one chapter is not torn out of the book, but translated into a better language; and every chapter must be so translated. . . . As therefore the bell that rings to a sermon, calls not upon the preacher only, but upon the congregation to come: so this bell calls us all. . . . No man is an island, entire of itself . . . any man's death diminishes me, because I am involved in mankind; and therefore never send to know for whom the bell tolls; it tolls for thee.

Chapter Summary

11.1 How Does the Social Situation Affect Our Behavior?

Core Concept 11.1: We usually adapt our behavior to the demands of the social situation, and in new or ambiguous situations we take our cues from the behavior of others in that setting.

Social psychologists study the behavior of individuals or groups in the context of particular situations. Much research in this area reveals how norms and social roles can be major sources of situational influence. The Asch studies demonstrated the powerful effect of the group to produce conformity, even when the group is clearly wrong. Another shocking demonstration of situational power came from Stanley Milgram's controversial experiments on obedience to authority. Situational influence can also lead to inaction: The bystander studies showed that individuals are inhibited by the number of bystanders, the ambiguity of the situation, and their resultant perception of their social role and responsibility. Groupthink occurs even in the highest level of government decision making, whereby smart people advocate actions that may be disastrous by mindlessly following the consensus of the group or its leader's opinion. Heroes are often ordinary people who take extraordinary action to help others or oppose evil activities. We usually adapt our behavior to the demands of the social situation, and in ambiguous situations we take our cues from the behavior of others.

Asch effect (p. 485)

Autokinetic effect (p. 486)

Bystander intervention problem (p. 495)

Chameleon effect (p. 483)

Cohesiveness (p. 487)

Conformity (p. 485)

Diffusion of responsibility (p. 496)

Dispositionism (p. 481)

Groupthink (p. 487)

Heroes (p. 492)

In-group (p. 498)

Out-group (p. 498)

Script (p. 483)

Situationism (p. 481)

Social neuroscience (p. 487)

Social context (p. 479)

Social norms (p. 482)

Social psychology (p. 479)

Social role (p. 481)

MyPsychLab Resources 11.1:

Watch: Conformity and Influence in Groups

Watch: Social Influence: Robert Cialdini

Watch: Milgram Obedience Study Today

11.2 Constructing Social Reality: What Influences Our Judgments of Others?

Core Concept 11.2: The judgments we make about others depend not only on their behavior but also on our interpretation of their actions within a social context.

The situation, by itself, does not determine behavior. Rather, it is our personal interpretation of the situation—our constructed social reality—that regulates behavior, including our social interactions. Usually we are attracted to relationships that we find rewarding, although there are exceptions, predicted by **expectancy-value theory** and **cognitive dissonance theory**. Attribution theory predicts that we will attribute other people's blunders to their traits or character (the **fundamental attribution error**) and our own to the situation (the **self-serving bias**), although this tendency depends on one's culture. Healthy loving relationships also demonstrate the social construction of reality, because there are many kinds of love and many cultural variations in the understanding and practice of love.

Prejudice and **discrimination** also demonstrate how we construct our own social reality through such cognitive processes as the perception of social distance and threats, the influence of media stereotypes, **scapegoating**, and **dehumanization**. We are all vulnerable to stereotype threat that can have a negative impact on our performance when we are made aware that we belong to a group that does poorly on certain tasks and tests.

The judgments we make about others depend not only on their behavior but also on our interpretation of their actions within a social context.

Cognitive dissonance theory (p. 502)

Dehumanization (p. 511)

Discrimination (p. 508)

Expectancy-value theory (p. 502)

Fundamental attribution error (FAE) (p. 504)

Matching hypothesis (p. 502)

Prejudice (p. 508)

Principle of proximity (p. 500)

Reward theory of attraction (p. 500)

Romantic love (p. 506)

Scapegoating (p. 510)

Self-disclosure (p. 501)

Self-serving bias (p. 505)

11.3 How Do Systems Create Situations That Influence Behavior?

Core Concept 11.3: Understanding how systems function increases both our understanding of why situations work as they do to influence human behavior and is also the most effective way to plan behavior change from the top down; systems change situations, which in turn change behavior.

Many studies in social psychology—particularly those dealing with obedience and conformity—show that the power of the situation can pressure ordinary people to commit horrible acts, such as those of soldiers in Iraq's **Abu Ghraib prison.** Understanding such complex behavior involves three levels of analysis: the individual's dispositions, the situation's forces, and the power of the system that creates and maintains specific situations.

The **Stanford Prison Experiment** put "good apples" in a "bad barrel" for nearly a week to test the dispositional versus situational explanations for the adverse outcomes. However, what has been ignored is the system that generates such bad barrels. Changing unac-

ceptable behavior, such as **bullying,** discrimination, or terrorism requires understanding how to modify systems of power and the situations they create and sustain, not just behavior modification of the individual actors.

Systems are complex structures embedded in a matrix of cultural, historical, economic, political and legal subsystems that must be identified and changed if they generate illegal, immoral, or unethical behavior.

Discovering Psychology Viewing Guide

Watch the following videos by logging into MyPsychLab (www.mypsychlab.com). After you have watched the videos, complete the activities that follow.

PROGRAM 19: THE POWER OF THE SITUATION

PROGRAM REVIEW

1. What do social psychologists study?
   a. how people are influenced by other people
   b. how people act in different societies

PROGRAM 20: CONSTRUCTING SOCIAL REALITY

   c. why some people are more socially successful than others
   d. what happens to isolated individuals

2. What precipitated Kurt Lewin's interest in leadership roles?
   a. the rise of social psychology
   b. the trial of Adolf Eichmann
   c. Hitler's ascent to power
   d. the creation of the United Nations after World War II

3. In Lewin's study, how did the boys behave when they had autocratic leaders?
   a. They had fun but got little accomplished.
   b. They were playful and did motivated, original work.
   c. They were hostile toward each other and got nothing done.
   d. They worked hard but acted aggressively toward each other.

4. In Solomon Asch's experiments, about what percent of participants went along with the group's obviously mistaken judgment at least once?
   a. 70%   b. 50%   c. 30%   d. 90%

5. Before Stanley Milgram did his experiments on obedience, experts were asked to predict the results. The experts
   a. overestimated people's willingness to administer shocks.
   b. underestimated people's willingness to administer shocks.
   c. gave accurate estimates of people's behavior.
   d. believed most people would refuse to continue with the experiment.

6. Which light did Milgram's experiment shed on the behavior of citizens in Nazi Germany?
   a. Situational forces can bring about blind obedience.
   b. Personal traits of individuals are most important in determining behavior.
   c. Cultural factors unique to Germany account for the rise of the Nazis.
   d. Human beings enjoy being cruel when they have the opportunity.

7. Which statement most clearly reflects the fundamental attribution error?
   a. Everyone is entitled to good medical care.
   b. Ethical guidelines are essential to conducting responsible research.
   c. People who are unemployed are too lazy to work.
   d. Everyone who reads about the Milgram experiment is shocked by the results.

8. Why did the prison study conducted by Philip Zimbardo and his colleagues have to be called off?
   a. A review committee felt that it violated ethical guidelines.
   b. It consumed too much of the students' time.
   c. The main hypothesis was supported, so there was no need to continue.

   d. The situation that had been created was too dangerous to maintain.

9. How did Tom Moriarity get people on a beach to intervene during a robbery?
   a. by creating a human bond through a simple request
   b. by reminding people of their civic duty to turn in criminals
   c. by making the thief look less threatening
   d. by providing a model of responsible behavior

10. Which leadership style tends to produce hard work when the leader is watching but much less cooperation when the leader is absent?
    a. authoritative   c. democratic
    b. autocratic   d. laissez-faire

11. Typically, people who participated in Milgram's study
    a. appeared to relish the opportunity to hurt someone else.
    b. objected but still obeyed.
    c. refused to continue and successfully stopped the experiment.
    d. came to recruit others into shocking the learner.

12. Psychologists refer to the power to create subjective realities as the power of
    a. social reinforcement.   c. cognitive control.
    b. prejudice.   d. the Pygmalion effect.

13. When Jane Elliot divided her classroom of third-graders into the inferior brown-eyed people and the superior blue-eyed students, what did she observe?
    a. The students were too young to understand what was expected.
    b. The students refused to behave badly toward their friends and classmates.
    c. The boys tended to go along with the categorization, but the girls did not.
    d. The blue-eyed students acted superior and were cruel to the brown-eyed students, who acted inferior.

14. In the research carried out by Robert Rosenthal and Lenore Jacobson, what caused the performance of some students to improve dramatically?
    a. Teachers were led to expect such improvement and so changed the way they treated these students.
    b. These students performed exceptionally well on a special test designed to predict improved performance.
    c. Teachers gave these students higher grades because they knew the researchers were expecting the improvement.
    d. The students felt honored to be included in the experiment and therefore were motivated to improve.

15. Robert Rosenthal demonstrated the Pygmalion effect in the classroom by showing that teachers

behave differently toward students for whom they have high expectations in all of the following ways, *except*

    a. by punishing them more for goofing off.

    b. by providing them with a warmer learning climate.

    c. by teaching more to them than to the other students.

    d. by providing more specific feedback when the student gives a wrong answer.

16. What happens to low-achieving students in the "Jigsaw classroom"?

    a. They tend to fall further behind.

    b. They are given an opportunity to work at a lower level, thus increasing the chance of success.

    c. By becoming "experts," they improve their performance and their self-respect.

    d. By learning to compete more aggressively, they become more actively involved in their own learning.

17. When Robert Cialdini cites the example of the Hare Krishnas' behavior in giving people at airports a flower or other small gift, he is illustrating the principle of

    a. commitment.   c. scarcity.

    b. reciprocity.   d. consensus.

18. Salespeople might make use of the principle of scarcity by

    a. filling shelves up with a product and encouraging consumers to stock up.

    b. claiming they have a hard time ordering the product.

    c. imposing a deadline by which the consumer must make a decision.

    d. being difficult to get in touch with over the phone.

19. Nancy is participating in a bike-a-thon next month and is having a large group of friends over to her house in order to drum up sponsorships for the event. She is capitalizing on the principle of

    a. liking.   c. commitment.

    b. consensus.   d. authority.

20. An appropriate motto for the principle of consensus would be

    a. "I've reasoned it through."

    b. "I am doing it of my own free will."

    c. "It will be over quickly."

    d. "Everyone else is doing it."

QUESTIONS TO CONSIDER

1. Some psychologists have suggested that participants in Milgram's research must have suffered guilt and loss of dignity and self-esteem, although they were told later that they hadn't actually harmed the learner. Follow-up studies to the prison experiment revealed that the participants had not suffered long-term ill effects. What psychological principle might explain these outcomes? Did the value of the research outweigh the risks for participants? Was Milgram in a position to weigh the relative value and risks ahead of time? Would you participate in such experiments?

2. What is the difference between respect for authority and blind obedience? How do you tell the difference? How would you explain the difference to a child?

3. Imagine that you are on vacation in New York City and you have dropped your keys in the pond in Central Park. What could you do to counteract people's tendencies toward diffusion of responsibility? Using what you know about social psychology, how might you increase the odds of actually getting people to help you?

4. How can personal factors interact with social influences to affect behavior?

5. Many of the socially undesirable aspects of human behavior (e.g., violent crime, rudeness, apathy, etc.) seem to be more likely in urban than in suburban or rural environments. How can social psychology help to explain this phenomenon?

ACTIVITIES

1. Norms of social behavior include "social distances" that we place between ourselves and friends, acquaintances, and strangers. Observe and compare the social distance you maintain between yourself and family members, friends, and strangers. Purposely change how close to them you would normally stand. Observe their responses. Does anyone mention it? Do others adjust their positions to achieve normal distances?

2. Look for editorials, news stories, or political cartoons that portray an international situation. Which words, labels, and images promote "us versus them" thinking? How might someone with opposite views have written the articles or drawn the cartoons differently? Do you find that the tendency to present an "us versus them" view changes over time or that it differs across cultures?

3. Think of norms of proper dress or social behavior that you can violate. For example, what would happen if you wore shorts to a formal gathering? Or asked a stranger an extremely personal question? Or arrived at work in your bedroom slippers? Pay attention to your feelings as you think about carrying out these activities. What fears or inhibitions do you have? How likely is it that you could actually carry out these activities?

Critical Thinking Applied Insane Places Revisited—Another Look at the Rosenhan Study

chapter *chapter* 12

psychological disorders

T he volunteers knew they were on their own. If they managed to get into the hospital, the five men and three women knew that they would be treated as mental patients, not observers. None had ever been diagnosed with a mental illness, but perhaps they were not so "normal" after all: Would a normal person lie to get into such a place? In fact, all were collaborators in an experiment designed to find out whether normality would be recognized in a mental hospital.

The experimenter, David Rosenhan—himself one of the pseudopatients—suspected that terms such as *sanity, insanity, schizophrenia, mental illness,* and *abnormal* might have fuzzier boundaries than the psychiatric community thought. He also suspected that some strange behaviors seen in mental patients might originate in the abnormal atmosphere of the mental hospital rather than in the patients themselves. To test these ideas, Rosenhan and his collaborators decided to see how mental hospital personnel would deal with patients who were, in fact, not mentally ill.

Individually, they applied for admission at different hospitals, complaining that they had recently heard voices that seemed to say "empty," "hollow," and "thud." Aside from this, they claimed no other symptoms. All used false names, and the four who were mental health professionals gave false occupations—but, apart from these fibs, the subjects answered all questions truthfully. They tried to act normally, although the prospect of entering the alien hospital environment made them feel anxious; they also worried about not being admitted and—worse yet—being exposed as frauds. Their concerns about fraud vanished quickly, for all readily gained admittance at 12 different hospitals (some did it twice). All but one were diagnosed with "schizophrenia," a major psychological disorder often accompanied by hearing imaginary voices.

After admission, the pseudopatients made no further claims of hearing voices or any other abnormal symptoms. Indeed, all wanted to be on their best behavior to gain release. Their only apparent "deviance" involved taking notes on the experience—at first privately and later publicly, when they found that the staff paid little attention. The nursing records indicated that, when the staff did notice, they interpreted the note taking as part of the patient's illness. (One comment: "Patient engages in writing behavior.") But for the most part, the patients found themselves ignored by the staff—even when they asked for help or advice. When the staff did interact with the patients it was as though the patients were simply "patients," not persons. Consequently, it took an average of 19 days for the pseudopatients to convince the hospital staff that they were ready for discharge, despite the absence of abnormal symptoms. One unfortunate volunteer wasn't released for almost two months.

Two main findings from this classic study jarred the psychiatric community to its core. First, *no professional staff member at any of the hospitals ever realized that any of Rosenhan's pseudopatients was a fraud*. Of course, the staff may have assumed that the patients had been ill at the time of admission and had improved during their hospitalization. But that possibility did not let the professionals off Rosenhan's hook: Despite apparently normal behavior, not one pseudopatient was ever labeled as "normal" or "well" while in the hospital. And, on discharge, they were still seen as having schizophrenia—but "in remission."

The mistaken diagnosis does not suggest that the hospital staff members were unskilled or unfeeling. The fact that they did not detect the pseudopatients' normal behavior is probably because, busy with other duties, they spent little time observing and interacting with the patients. Most of the time they kept to themselves in a glassed-in central office that patients called "the cage." As Rosenhan (1973a) said:

> It could be a mistake, and a very unfortunate one, to consider that what happened to us derived from malice or stupidity on the part of the staff. Quite the contrary, our overwhelming impression of them was of people who really cared, who were committed and who were uncommonly intelligent. Where they failed, as they sometimes did painfully, it would be more accurate to attribute those failures to the environment in which they, too, found themselves than to personal callousness. Their perceptions and behavior were controlled by the situation. (p. 257)

The mental hospital, then, may become another example of a "sick" system that we discussed in the last chapter.

A second finding tells us volumes about the patients and the nature of psychological disorder itself: *To everyone's surprise, the hospital patients readily detected the ruse, even though the professional staff did not*. The pseudopatients reported that the

CONNECTION • CHAPTER 11
Social psychology has also emphasized the power of the situation on behavior.

other patients regularly voiced their suspicions: "You're not crazy. You're a journalist or a professor. . . . You're checking up on the hospital." In his report of this experience, entitled "On Being Sane in Insane Places," Rosenhan (1973a) noted dryly: "The fact that the patients often recognized normality when staff did not raises important questions" (p. 252). You will hear the echo of these "important questions" as we critically examine the medical view of mental disorder in this chapter.

Here's the problem that the Rosenhan study raises for us:

PROBLEM: Can we reliably distinguish mental disorder from merely unusual behavior?

This is the issue around which this chapter is organized. Please note that Rosenhan did not deny the existence of psychological disorders. Rather, he called into question the *reliability* of psychiatric diagnoses. People *do* suffer the anguish of **psychopathology** (also called *mental disorder* or *mental illness*). According to the National Institute of Mental Health (NIMH), over 26% of the U.S. population—more than one in four Americans—suffer from diagnosable mental health problems in a given year (2008d). For one in 17 it will be a mental illness of serious proportions, such as major depression, schizophrenia, or another debilitating disorder. Over the lifespan, an estimated 46% of Americans will suffer from some psychological disorder (Butcher et al., 2008). Again, Rosenhan was not suggesting that these conditions do not exist or do not exact a horrendous toll in human suffering—just that it can be difficult to distinguish normality from abnormality.

Rosenhan's pseudopatient study caused a tremendous flap, and many psychiatrists and clinical psychologists cried foul. Several ensuing responses in *Science*, the journal in which the study had been published, accused Rosenhan of slipshod research and of damaging the reputation of the mental health professions. Did they have a point? Was Rosenhan's study flawed? Or was it simply the cries of those who perceived Rosenhan's study as a personal attack? We will take a close look at these issues in the Critical Thinking section at the end of the chapter. In the meantime, let's explore the problem of determining what mental disorder is and how it might be diagnosed.

● ●

12.1 KEY QUESTION
WHAT IS PSYCHOLOGICAL DISORDER?

On the world stage, the picture of mental disorder is arresting. According to the World Health Organization, some 450 million people around the world suffer from mental disorders, with a large proportion living in poor countries that have no mental health care system (Miller, 2006d). Depression, for example, caused more disability among people aged 15 to 44 than any other cause except HIV/AIDS.

Yet, as Rosenhan's study suggests, distinguishing "normal" from "abnormal" is not always a simple task. Consider, for example, how you would classify such eccentric personalities as Michael Jackson or Britney Spears. And what about a soldier who risks his or her life in combat: Is that "normal"? Or consider a grief-stricken woman who is unable to return to her normal routine three months after her husband died: Does she have a psychological disorder?

Psychopathology Any pattern of emotions, behaviors, or thoughts inappropriate to the situation and leading to personal distress or the inability to achieve important goals. Other terms having essentially the same meaning include *mental illness, mental disorder,* and *psychological disorder.*

Advertisements like the one shown here have gone a long way toward correcting our views of mental illness and creating sympathy for its sufferers.

core concept

| The medical model takes a "disease" view, while psychology sees psychological disorder as an interaction of biological, mental, social, and behavioral factors.

Some disorders may be more easily detected. Clinicians (specialists in the treatment of psychological problems) look for three classic symptoms of severe psychopathology: *hallucinations, delusions,* and *extreme affective disturbances.* Hallucinations are false sensory experiences, such as hearing nonexistent voices. (Rosenhan's pseudopatients claimed they were hallucinating.) Delusions are extreme disorders of thinking that involve persistent false beliefs. For example, if you think you are the president of the United States (and you are not), you have a symptom of psychopathology. Or if you think people are out to "get" you, you may also have a delusional disorder. Similarly, those whose **affect** (emotion) is characteristically depressed, anxious, or manic—or those who seem to have no emotional response at all—have affective disturbances.

Beyond such extreme signs of distress, the experts do not always agree, however. What is abnormal and what is not becomes a judgment call, a judgment made more difficult because no sharp boundary separates normal from abnormal thought and behavior. It may be helpful to think of psychological disorder as part of a continuum ranging from the absence of disorder to severe disorder, as shown in Table 12.1. The big idea here is that people with psychological disorders are not in a class by themselves. Rather, their disorders are an exaggeration of normal responses.

In this section of the chapter, we will focus on two contrasting views of psychological disorder. One, coming to us from medicine, is sometimes called the "medical model." It portrays mental problems much as it does physical disorders: as sickness or disease. The other view, a psychological view, sees psychological disorders as the result of multiple factors that can involve both nature and nurture. As our Core Concept puts it:

No matter how we conceptualize psychopathology, nearly everyone agrees that psychological disorder is common. It touches the daily lives of millions. It can be insidious, working its way into thoughts and feelings, diminishing its victims' emotional and physical well-being, along with their personal and family relationships. And it can create an enormous financial burden through lost productivity, lost wages, and the high costs of prolonged treatment. Yet the way people think of psychopathology does have a consequence: As we will see, it determines how they attempt to treat it—whether with drugs, charms, rituals, talk, torture, brain surgery, hospitalization, or commitment to an "insane asylum."

In this section of the chapter, we will find that the two main ways of looking at psychopathology, the medical model and the psychological view, are often at odds. Some of this conflict is territorial, resulting from professional infighting. But some of the conflict has historical roots, as we shall see next.

Changing Concepts of Psychological Disorder

Before December 10, 1973, homosexuality was considered an illness. But on that day the Board of Directors of the American Psychiatric Association voted to drop homosexuality from its list of officially recognized disorders. After a year of rancorous debate, the membership voted to remove homosexuality from the *Diagnostic and Statistical Manual of Mental Disorders (DSM)*. The decision—that homosexuality is not associated with any evidence of mental disorder, with the understandable exception of problems related to the stress of discrimination—has since been repeatedly verified (Cochran et al., 2003; Meyer, 2003). This change in the perception of homosexuality, however, was only one of the

Hallucination A false sensory experience that may suggest mental disorder. Hallucinations can have other causes, such as drugs or sensory isolation.

Delusion An extreme disorder of thinking, involving persistent false beliefs. Delusions are the hallmark of paranoid disorders.

Affect Emotion or mood.

TABLE 12.1 The Spectrum of Mental Disorder

Mental disorder occurs on a spectrum that ranges from the absence of signs of pathology to severe disturbances, such as are found in major depression or schizophrenia. The important point is that there is no sharp distinction that divides those with mental disorders from those who are "normal."

No disorder	Mild disorder	Moderate disorder	Severe disorder
Absence of signs of psychological disorder	Few signs of distress or other indicators of psychological disorder	Indicators of disorder are more pronounced and occur more frequently	Clear signs of psychological disorder, which dominate the person's life
Absence of behavior problems	Few behavior problems; responses usually appropriate to the situation	More distinct behavior problems; behavior is often inappropriate to the situation	Severe and frequent behavior problems; behavior is usually inappropriate to the situation
No problems with interpersonal relationships	Few difficulties with relationships	More frequent difficulties with relationships	Many poor relationships or lack of relationships with others

most recent in a continuously evolving concept of mental disturbance that stretches back thousands of years.

Historical Roots   In the ancient world, people assumed that supernatural powers were everywhere, accounting for good fortune, disease, and disaster. In this context, psychopathology was believed to be caused by demons and spirits that had taken possession of the person's mind and body (Sprock & Blashfield, 1991). If you had been living in the ancient world, your daily routine would have included rituals aimed at outwitting or placating these supernatural beings.

In about 400 B.C., the Greek physician Hippocrates took humanity's first step toward a scientific view of mental disorder when he declared that abnormal behavior has physical causes. As we saw in the Personality chapter, Hippocrates taught his disciples to interpret the symptoms of psychopathology as an imbalance among four body fluids called "humors": blood, phlegm (mucus), black bile, and yellow bile. Those with an excess of black bile, for example, were inclined to melancholy or depression, while those who had an abundance of blood were sanguine, or warmhearted. With this simple but revolutionary idea, Hippocrates incorporated mental disorder into medicine, and his view—that mental problem had natural, not supernatural, causes—influenced educated people in the Western world until the end of the Roman Empire.

Then, in the Middle Ages, superstition eclipsed the Hippocratic model of mental disorder. Under the influence of the medieval Church, physicians and clergy reverted to the old ways of explaining abnormality in terms of demons and witchcraft. In these harsh times, the Inquisition was driven by the belief that unusual behavior was the work of Satan. The "cure" involved attempts to drive out the demons that possessed the unfortunate victim's soul. As a result, thousands of mentally disturbed people were tortured and executed all across the European continent. Even in 1692, the same view of mental disorder led the young American colony in Salem, Massachusetts, to convict and execute a group of its residents for witchcraft (Karlsen, 1998). A group of young girls had frightened the community with a rash of convulsions and reports of sensory disturbances that were interpreted as signs of demonic possession. A modern analysis of the Salem witch trials has concluded that the girls were probably suffering from poisoning by a fungus growing on rye grain—the same fungus that produces the hallucinogenic drug LSD (Caporeal, 1976; Matossian, 1982, 1989).

The Medical Model   In the latter part of the 18th century, the "disease" view that originated with Hippocrates reemerged with the rise of science. The resulting **medical model** held that mental disorders are *diseases* of the mind that, like ordi-

> **CONNECTION • CHAPTER 10**
> Hippocrates' humor theory was a theory of temperaments.

Medical model   The view that mental disorders are diseases that, like ordinary physical diseases, have objective physical causes and require specific treatments.

A painting of the witchcraft trials held in Salem, Massachusetts, in 1692. Twenty people were executed before the hysteria subsided.

◀ **CONNECTION • CHAPTER 1**

Psychiatrists, but not psychologists, are trained in medicine.

nary physical diseases, have objective causes and require specific treatments. People began to perceive individuals with psychological problems as sick (suffering from illness), rather than as demon possessed or immoral. And what a difference a new theory made! Treating mental disorders by torture and abuse no longer made sense. The new view of mental illness brought sweeping reforms that were implemented in "asylums" for the "insane." In this supportive atmosphere, many patients actually improved—even thrived—on rest, contemplation, and simple but useful work (Maher & Maher, 1985). Unfortunately, political pressures eventually turned the initially therapeutic asylums into overcrowded warehouses of neglect.

Despite such problems, however, the revived medical model was unquestionably an improvement over the old demon model. Yet modern psychologists think that we are ready for another revolutionary change in perspective. The medical model has its own weaknesses, they say, pointing out that the assumption of "disease" leads to a doctor-knows-best approach in which the therapist takes all the responsibility for diagnosing the illness and prescribing treatment. Under this "disease" assumption, the patient may become a passive recipient of medication and advice, rather than an active participant in treatment—as we see in so many mental patients today who are treated simply by the dispensing of pills. Psychologists believe that this attitude wrongly encourages dependency on the doctor, encourages unnecessary drug therapy, and does little to help the patient develop good coping skills.

Not incidentally, a doctor-knows-best approach also takes responsibility away from psychologists and gives it to psychiatrists. Psychologists bristle at the medical model's implication that their treatment of mental "diseases" should be done under the supervision of a physician. In effect, the medical model assigns psychologists to second-class professional status. As you can see, ownership of the whole territory of psychological disorder is hotly contested.

Psychological Models   What does psychology have to offer in place of the medical model? Most clinical psychologists have now turned to a combination of psychological perspectives that derive from *behaviorism, cognitive psychology, social learning,* and *biological psychology.* We will look at these more closely.

The Social–Cognitive–Behavioral Approach   Modern psychologists often combine ideas from perspectives that were once considered incompatible: cognitive psychology and behaviorism. In brief, cognitive psychology looks inward, emphasizing mental processes, while behaviorism looks outward, emphasizing the influence of the environment. As we saw in the chapter on learning, bridges between these perspectives were built by social-learning theorists and others. As a result, a major shift in psychological thinking in recent years now views these traditions as complementary, rather than competitive. Moreover, both sides now acknowledge that cognition and behavior usually occur in a social context, requiring a *social perspective.*

In addition, the *behavioral perspective* tells us that abnormal behaviors can be acquired in the same fashion as healthy behaviors—through behavioral learning. This view focuses on our behavior and the environmental conditions, such as rewards, punishments, and social pressures, that maintain it. For example, the behavioral perspective would suggest that a fear of public speaking could result from a humiliating public speaking experience and subsequent avoidance of any opportunity to develop public speaking skills.

Finally, the *cognitive perspective* suggests that we must also consider how people *perceive* or *think about* themselves and their relations with other people.

Among the important cognitive variables are these: whether people believe they have control over events in their lives (an *internal* or *external locus of control*), how they cope with threat and stress, and whether they attribute behavior to situational or personal factors (Bandura, 1986).

The **social–cognitive–behavioral approach**, then, is a psychological alterative to the medical model, combining three of psychology's major perspectives. Typical of this approach is Albert Bandura's theory of *reciprocal determinism,* which proposes that behavior, cognition, and social/environmental factors all influence each other. From this viewpoint, if you have a fear of public speaking, for example, it can be understood as a product of social learning, behavioral learning, and cognitive learning. Thus, your fear of public speaking could have its origins in *social learning:* hearing people talk about "stage fright" and their anxiety about public speaking. Against that backdrop, then, you may have had an unpleasant *behavioral conditioning* experience in which people laughed at you while you were making a speech. That experience, in turn, could easily make you view yourself as "a poor public speaker"—as a result of *cognitive learning.* The result of this chain of social learning, behavioral learning, and cognitive learning—in which each step *reciprocally* reinforces the others—is the idea that public speaking is fear-producing experience.

CONNECTION • CHAPTER 10

Reciprocal determinism is a part of Bandura's social learning theory.

The Biopsychology of Mental Disorder Although most psychologists have reservations about the medical model, they do not deny the influence of biology on thought and behavior. Modern biopsychology assumes that some mental disturbances involve the brain or nervous system in some way, and this view is taking an increasingly prominent position. An explosion of recent research in neuroscience confirms the role of the brain as a complex organ whose mental functions depend on a delicate balance of chemicals and ever-changing circuits. Subtle alterations in the brain's tissue or in its chemical messengers—the neurotransmitters—can profoundly alter thoughts and behaviors. Genetic influences, brain injury, infection, and learning are a few factors that can tip the balance toward psychopathology.

On the heredity front, the Human Genome Project has specified the complete human genetic package. Many psychologists see this accomplishment as a ripe opportunity for specialists in behavioral genetics who are searching for genes associated with specific psychological disorders (National Institute of Mental Health, 2003b). It won't be easy, however. So far, suspicious genetic abnormalities have been linked to schizophrenia, bipolar disorder, anxiety disorders, and autism, although their exact roles in these conditions remain unclear. Most experts believe that such disorders are likely to result from multiple genes interacting with forces in the environment (See National Institute of Mental Health, 2008c). Watch the news for further developments.

Indicators of Abnormality

While clinicians sometimes disagree about the *etiology* (causes) of psychological disorders, they usually agree broadly on the indicators of abnormality (Rosenhan & Seligman, 1995). What are these indicators? Earlier we noted that hallucinations, delusions, and extreme affective changes are signs of severe mental disorder. But many psychological problems don't reveal themselves in such stark ways. Accordingly, clinicians also look for the following more subtle signs that may also indicate psychological disturbances, ranging from mild to severe (see Table 12.1):

- *Distress.* Does the individual show unusual or prolonged levels of unease or anxiety? Almost anyone will get nervous before an important test, but feeling so overwhelmed with unpleasant emotions that concentration becomes impossible for long periods is a sign of abnormality.

- *Maladaptiveness.* Does the person act in ways that make others fearful or interfere with his or her well-being? We can see this in someone who drinks so

Social–cognitive–behavioral approach A psychological alternative to the medical model that views psychological disorder through a combination of the social, cognitive, and behavioral perspectives.

Behaviors that make other people feel uncomfortable or threatened may be a sign of abnormality.

heavily that she or he cannot hold down a job or drive a car without endangering others.

●   *Irrationality.* Does the person act or talk in ways that are irrational or incomprehensible to others? A woman who converses with her long-dead sister, whose voice she hears in her head, is behaving irrationally. Likewise, behavior or emotional responses that are inappropriate to the situation, such as laughing at the scene of a tragedy, show irrational loss of contact with one's social environment.

●   *Unpredictability.* Does the individual behave erratically and inconsistently at different times or from one situation to another, as if experiencing a loss of control? For example, a child who suddenly smashes a fragile toy with his fist for no apparent reason is behaving unpredictably. Similarly, a manager who treats employees compassionately one day and abusively the next is acting unpredictably.

●   *Unconventionality and undesirable behavior.* Does the person behave in ways that are statistically rare and violate social norms of what is legally or morally acceptable or desirable? Being merely "unusual" is not a sign of abnormality—so feel free to dye your hair red and green at Christmastime. But if you decide to act beyond the bounds of social acceptability by strolling naked in the mall, that would be considered abnormal.

Is the presence of just one indicator enough to demonstrate abnormality? It's a judgment call. Clinicians are more confident in labeling behavior as "abnormal" when two or more of the indicators are present. (You will remember that the pseudopatients in Rosenhan's study presented only one symptom: hearing voices.) And the more extreme and prevalent the indicators are, the more confident psychologists can be about identifying an abnormal condition. Moreover, none of these criteria is a condition shared by all forms of disorder that we will describe later in this chapter. Different diagnoses, we shall see, include different combinations from the above list.

While these indicators may suggest a disorder, the clinician still must decide which disorder it is. This can be difficult, because psychopathology takes many forms. Some diagnoses may have a familiar ring: *depression, phobias,* and *panic disorder.* You may be less well acquainted with others, such as *conversion disorder* or *catatonic schizophrenia.* In all, 300-plus specific varieties of psychopathology are described in the *Diagnostic and Statistical Manual of Mental Disorders* (4th edition), known by clinicians and researchers as the *DSM-IV* ("DSM-four") and used by mental health professionals of all backgrounds to describe and diagnose psychopathology. So influential is this system that we will devote the entire middle section of this chapter to an explanation of it.

A Caution to Readers

As you read about the symptoms of psychological disorder, you are likely to wonder about your own mental health. All students studying abnormal psychology face this hazard. To see what we mean, you might answer the following questions, which are based on the indicators of abnormality discussed earlier:

1. Have you had periods of time when you felt "blue" for no apparent reason? (distress)

2. Have you ever gone to a party on a night when you knew you should be studying? (maladaptiveness)

3. Have you had an experience in which you thought you heard or saw something that wasn't really there? (irrationality)

4. Have you had a flash of temper in which you said something that you later regretted? (unpredictability)

5. Have you had unusual thoughts that you told no one about? (unconventionality)

How often is the plea of insanity used? Before you read about the insanity defense in the next part of the chapter, try to guess the approximate percentage of accused crimi- nals in the United States who use a plea of insanity in court: _____%. You will find the correct answer in the "Psychology Matters" section below. (An answer within 10% indicates that you have an exceptionally clear grasp of reality!)

Hint: Research shows that the public has an exaggerated impression of the problem.

6. Have you made someone fearful or distressed because of something you said or did? (maladaptiveness)

The fact is that almost everyone will answer "yes" to at least one—and perhaps all—of these questions. This does not necessarily mean abnormality. Whether you, or anyone else, is normal or abnormal is a matter of degree and frequency—and clinical judgment.

So, as we take a close look at specific psychological disorders in the next section of the chapter, you will most likely find some symptoms that you have experienced. So will your classmates. Even though they may not say so, most other students will find themselves in one or more of the disorders that we will be studying. (A similar problem is common among medical students, who begin to notice that they, too, have symptoms of the physical diseases they learn about.) You should realize that *this is normal.* Another reason, of course, that you may see yourself in this chapter arises from the fact that no sharp line separates psychopathology from normalcy. All psychological disorders involve exaggerations of normal tendencies. Moreover, people who are basically healthy may occasionally become depressed, for example—although they do not *stay* depressed or develop the depths of despair that persons with clinical depression do. We are not suggesting that concerns about psychological disorder should be taken lightly, however. If, after reading this chapter, you suspect that you may have a problem, you should discuss it with a professional.

"It's a little early for a definitive diagnosis—although we can certainly rule out normalcy."

(*Source:* That's Life © 2003 Mike Twohy. All rights reserved. Used with permission of Mike Twohy and the Cartoonist Group.)

PSYCHOLOGYMATTERS
The Plea of Insanity

Now let's look at a closely related issue: the *plea of insanity.* What is your opinion: Does the insanity plea really excuse criminal behavior and put thousands of dangerous people back on the streets? Let's take a critical look at the facts.

In 1843, Daniel M'Naughten, a deranged woodcutter from Glasgow, thought he had received "instructions from God" to kill the British Prime Minister, Robert Peel. Fortunately for Peel, this would-be assassin struck down his secretary by mistake. Apprehended and tried, M'Naughten was found "not guilty by reason of insanity." The court reasoned that M'Naughten's mental condition prevented him from knowing right from wrong. The public responded with outrage. Fast-forwarding 138 years, a similarly outraged public decried the modern-day insanity ruling involving John Hinckley, the young man who shot and wounded then-President Ronald Reagan.

Such infamous cases have molded a low public opinion of the insanity defense. The citizenry blames psychologists and psychiatrists for clogging the courts with insanity pleas, allowing homicidal maniacs back on the streets, and letting criminals go to hospitals for "treatment" instead of prisons for punishment. But this public image of insanity stems from several erroneous assumptions.

For one thing, "insanity" appears nowhere among the *DSM-IV* listing of disorders recognized by psychologists and psychiatrists. Technically, **insanity** is

Insanity A legal term, not a psychological or psychiatric one, referring to a person who is unable, because of a mental disorder or defect, to conform his or her behavior to the law.

The plea of insanity is rare—and it is usually unsuccessful.

neither a psychological nor psychiatric term. Rather, it is a *legal* term, which only a court—not psychologists or psychiatrists—can officially apply. By law, insanity can include not only psychosis, but jealous rage, mental retardation, and a wide variety of other conditions in which a person might not be able to control his or her behavior or distinguish right from wrong (Thio, 1995).

So, why can we not simply abolish the laws that allow this technicality? The answer to that question turns on the definition of a crime. Legally, a crime requires two elements: (a) an *illegal act* (just wanting to commit a crime is not enough) and (b) the *intent* to commit the act. Merely wishing your boss dead is no crime (because you committed no illegal act). Neither is flattening the boss who accidentally steps in front of your moving car in the parking lot (assuming you had not planned the deed). But, if you plot and plan and then lie in wait to willfully run over the dastardly dude, you have committed an intentional and illegal act—and the courts can convict you of murder. From this example, you can see why no one wants to give up the legal requirement of intent. But you can also see why this safeguard leaves the door open for the controversial plea of insanity.

With these things in mind, take a moment to recall your estimate of the percentage of accused criminals who use the insanity plea. (See the "Do It Yourself!" box above.) In reality, accused criminals use the insanity defense far less often than the public realizes. In actuality, it occurs in less than 1% of criminal cases, and of this tiny number, only a fraction are successful (Chiaccia, 2007), although we would note that it has been tried *unsuccessfully* in several famous murder cases, including those of David Birkowitz, Ted Bundy, Charles Manson, John Wayne Gacey, and Jeffrey Dahmer. Still, public concern about abuses of the insanity plea has led several states to experiment with alternatives. Some now require separate verdicts on the act and the intent, allowing a jury to reach a verdict of "guilty but mentally ill" (Savitsky & Lindblom, 1986).

CheckYourUnderstanding

1. **RECALL:** How did Rosenhan go about studying the way psychiatrists diagnose mental disorders?

2. **RECALL:** What are the three classic symptoms of severe mental disorder?

3. **ANALYSIS:** Consider the symptoms presented by the pseudopatients in Rosenhan's study. To what would their hallucinations have probably been attributed by (a) Hippocrates, (b) a physician or priest in the Middle Ages, and (c) a physician in the 1800s?

4. **RECALL:** Approximately how often do psychologists diagnose criminals as being insane? How often is the plea of insanity used in criminal cases in the United States?

5. **UNDERSTANDING THE CORE CONCEPT:** Give an example of what a psychologist might look for in attempting to understand a person's mental disorder (but that a psychiatrist using the "medical model" would probably *not* explore).

Answers 1. He arranged for mentally healthy volunteers to request admission to mental hospitals, based on the assertion that they had been hearing voices. Rosenhan interpreted their success (all were admitted) as an indicator that psychiatric diagnoses are not reliable. **2.** Hallucinations, delusions, and severe affective disturbances are the classic symptoms of severe mental disorder. **3. a.** Hippocrates would have said that the hallucinations stemmed from a physical cause, most likely an imbalance in the four humors. **b.** A medieval physician or priest would probably have attributed hallucinations to demon position. **c.** A physician in the 1800s would have attributed the symptoms to a disease—much as Hippocrates would have done. **4.** Psychologists do not diagnose people as sane or insane: Those are legal terms. In U.S. courts, the plea of insanity is used in less than 1% of criminal cases—most often unsuccessfully. **5.** A psychologist might look for many social, cognitive, and behavioral factors, such as the family environment (social), attention for disturbing behavior (behavioral), or locus of control (cognitive).

12.2 KEY QUESTION
HOW ARE PSYCHOLOGICAL DISORDERS CLASSIFIED IN THE *DSM-IV*?

Imagine that you have entered a music store looking for a particular CD. Anything you could possibly want is there, but the employees do not bother grouping albums by musical category: They just dump everything randomly into the bins. With so many selections, but no organization, shopping there would be impossible—which is why music stores never operate this way. Instead, they organize selections into categories, such as rock, blues, classical, rap, country, and jazz. In much the same way, the *Diagnostic and Statistical Manual of Mental Disorders* (4th ed.) brings order to the more than 300 recognized mental disorders. Usually called simply the *DSM-IV,* this manual represents the most widely used system for classifying such disorders. We will use it as the scheme for organizing the disorders we have selected for discussion in this chapter.

What is the organizing pattern employed by the *DSM-IV?* It groups nearly all recognized forms of psychopathology into categories, *according to mental and behavioral symptoms,* such as anxiety, depression, sexual problems, and substance abuse. Our Core Concept states:

> **The *DSM-IV,* the most widely used system, classifies disorders by their mental and behavioral symptoms.**

core
concept

With over 300 disorders described in the *DSM-IV,* it would be impossible to cover all of them in this chapter. Therefore we must focus on those that you are most likely to encounter either in daily life or in the study of psychopathology in more advanced courses.

Overview of the *DSM-IV* Classification System

The fourth edition of the *Diagnostic and Statistical Manual of Mental Disorders,* the *DSM-IV,* was published in 1994 by the American Psychiatric Association. Then, in 2000, that volume was given a mid-edition update, called the *DSM-IV-TR*[1] (*TR* means *Text Revision*). It offers practitioners a common and concise language for the description of psychopathology. It also contains criteria for diagnosing each of the disorders it covers. Even though the manual was developed primarily by psychiatrists, its terminology has been adopted by clinicians of all stripes, including psychiatrists, psychologists, and social workers. In addition, most health insurance companies use *DSM-IV-TR* standards in determining what treatments they will pay for—a fact that gives this manual enormous economic clout.

The fourth edition of the *DSM* brought with it some big changes. For example, it banished the term *neurosis* from the official language of psychiatry (although you will frequently hear the term used in more casual conversation). Originally, a **neurosis** or *neurotic disorder* was conceived of as a relatively common pattern of subjective distress or self-defeating behavior that did not show signs of brain abnormalities or grossly irrational thinking. In short, a "neurotic" was someone who might be unhappy or dissatisfied but not considered dangerously ill or out of touch with reality. In the *DSM-IV,* the term *neurosis* has been dropped or replaced by the term *disorder* (Carson et al., 2000; Holmes, 2001). So, for example, "obsessive–compulsive neurosis" is now simply *obsessive–compulsive disorder.*

Similarly, a **psychosis** was thought to differ from neurosis in both the quality and severity of symptoms. A condition was frequently designated as *psychotic* if it involved profound disturbances in perception, rational thinking, or affect (emotion)—the three classic signs we discussed earlier. As a result, a clinician using previous editions of the *DSM* would have been more likely to diagnose severe depression, for example, as "psychotic." In the *DSM-IV,* the term *psychotic* is restricted mainly to a loss of contact with reality, as is found in the *schizophrenic disorders,* which we shall discuss later.

DSM-IV   The fourth edition of the *Diagnostic and Statistical Manual of Mental Disorders,* published by the American Psychiatric Association; the most widely accepted psychiatric classification system in the United States.

Neurosis   Before the *DSM-IV,* this term was used as a label for subjective distress or self-defeating behavior that did not show signs of brain abnormalities or grossly irrational thinking.

Psychosis   A disorder involving profound disturbances in perception, rational thinking, or affect.

---

[1]For our purposes, both versions of the *DSM*'s fourth edition are essentially the same, so we will refer to them here simply as the *DSM-IV.*

As you may have surmised from its origins in psychiatry, the *DSM-IV* has close ties to the medical model of mental illness. Its language is the language of medicine—symptoms, syndromes, diagnoses, and diseases—and its final form is a curious mixture of science and tradition. (Note: It contains no diagnosis of "normal.") Yet, in contrast with early versions of the manual, which had a distinctly Freudian flavor, the *DSM-IV* manages, for the most part, to avoid endorsing theories of cause or treatment. It also differs from early versions of the *DSM* by giving extensive and specific descriptions of the symptoms of each disorder. So, while the *DSM-IV* has its critics, the need for a common language of psychological disorder has brought it wide acceptance.

Let us turn now to a sampling of disorders described in the *DSM-IV*. A look at the chart in the margin will give you an overview of the scheme the manual uses to classify these disorders. We begin with those that involve sustained extremes of emotion: the *mood disorders*, also known as *affective disorders*.

Mood Disorders

Everyone, of course, experiences occasional strong or unpleasant emotional reactions. Emotionality, including the everyday highs and lows, is a normal part of our ability to interpret and adapt to our world. However, when moods careen out of control, soaring to extreme elation or plunging to deep depression, the diagnosis will probably be one of the **mood disorders**. The clinician will also suspect an affective disorder when an individual's moods are consistently inappropriate to the situation. Here we will discuss the two best-known of these affective disturbances, *major depression* and *bipolar disorder*.

Major Depression   If you fail an important examination, lose a job, or lose a love, it is normal to feel depressed for a while. If a close friend dies, it is also normal to feel depressed. But if you remain depressed for weeks or months, long after the depressing event has passed, then you may have the clinically significant condition called **major depression** or *major depressive disorder*, among the commonest of all major mental disturbances.

Novelist William Styron (1990) writes movingly about his own experience with severe depression. The pain he endured convinced him that clinical depression is much more than a bad mood: He characterized it as "a daily presence, blowing over me in cold gusts" and "a veritable howling tempest in the brain" that can begin with a "gray drizzle of horror." Major depression lingers; it does not give way to manic periods.

Incidence   Psychologist Martin Seligman (1973, 1975) has called depression the "common cold" of psychological problems. Nearly everyone has, at some time, suffered either major depression or a milder form that clinicians call *dysthymia*. In the United States, depression accounts for the majority of all mental hospital admissions, but clinicians still believe it to be underdiagnosed and undertreated (Kessler et al., 2003; Robins et al., 1991). The National Institute of Mental Health (2006) estimates that depression costs Americans about $83 billion each year, including the costs of hospitalization, therapy, and lost productivity. But the human cost cannot be measured in dollars. Countless people in the throes of depression may feel worthless, lack appetite, withdraw from friends and family, have difficulty sleeping, lose their jobs, and become agitated or lethargic. In severe cases, they may also have psychotic distortions of reality. You can give yourself a quick evaluation for signs of depression in the box, "Do It Yourself! A Depression Check."

Most worrisome of all, suicide claims one in 50 depression sufferers (Bostwick & Pankratz, 2000). Significantly, a person with depression faces a greater risk of suicide on the way down in a depressive episode or on the mend than during the deepest phase of the depressive cycle. Why? Because, in the depths of

Mood Disorders: Extremes of mood, from mania to depression

- Major depression
- Bipolar disorder

Dutch artist Vincent Van Gogh showed signs of bipolar disorder. This problem seems to have a high incidence among very creative people.

Mood disorder Abnormal disturbance in emotion or mood, including bipolar disorder and unipolar disorder. Mood disorders are also called affective disorders.

Major depression A form of depression that does not alternate with mania.

Most people think that depression is marked by outward signs of sadness, such as weeping. But depression affects other aspects of thought and behavior, as well. For a quick check on your own tendencies to depression, please answer "yes" or "no" to each of the following questions, all adapted from the signs of depression listed in the *DSM-IV*:

1. Do you feel deeply depressed, sad, or hopeless most of the day?
2. Do you feel you have lost interest in most or all activities?
3. Have you experienced any major change in appetite or body weight, though not from dieting?
4. Have you experienced a significant change in your sleeping patterns?
5. Do you feel more restless than usual—or more sluggish than usual?
6. Do you feel more fatigued than you ought to?
7. Do you feel persistently hopeless or inappropriately guilty?
8. Have you been finding it increasingly difficult to think or concentrate?
9. Do you have recurrent thoughts of death or suicide?

Your answers to these items do not constitute any proof that you are, or are not, depressed. While there is no "magic number" of items to which you must answer "yes" to qualify as depressed, if you answered "yes" to some of them and if you are concerned, you might want to seek a professional opinion. Remember that a diagnosis of depression is a clinical judgment call, based on the signs listed in the *DSM-IV*: Essentially, it is the pattern and the quality of your life, your feelings, and your behavior that determine whether or not you are depressed. Remember also that self-report is always subject to some bias. If you are concerned after considering the signs of depression in your life, we recommend an examination by a competent mental health professional, who will take into account not only your self-descriptions but also your behavior, your social context, and the rewards and aversive circumstances in your life.

depressive despair, a person may have no energy or will to do *anything*, much less carry out a plan for suicide.

Incidentally, your authors advise that a suicide threat always be taken seriously, even though you may think it is just a bid for attention—and even if you see no other signs of depression. Other factors may be at work. Abuse of alcohol or other drugs, for example, multiplies the likelihood of suicide, as do chronic physical diseases or brain abnormalities (Ezzell, 2003). You should direct any person who suggests he or she is thinking about suicide to a competent professional for help.

Cross-cultural studies indicate that depression is the single most prevalent form of disability around the globe (Holden, 2000a), although the incidence of major depression varies widely throughout the world, as Table 12.2 shows. While some of the variation may be the result of differences in reporting and in readiness or reluctance to seek help for depression, other factors seem to be at work, too. In Taiwan and Korea, for example, these factors may include relatively low rates of marital separation and divorce—factors known to be associated with high risk of depression in virtually all cultures. In contrast, the stresses of war have undoubtedly inflated the rate of depression in the Middle East (e.g., Thabet, 2004).

Causes of Depression   We have many pieces for the puzzle of depression, but no one has managed to put them all together into a coherent picture yet. Some cases almost certainly have a genetic predisposition: Severe bouts with depression often run in families (Plomin et al., 1994). Further indication of a biological basis for depression comes from the favorable response that many patients with depression have to drugs that affect the brain's neurotransmitters norepinephrine, serotonin, and dopamine (Ezzell, 2003). These drugs also stimulate growth of new neurons in the hippocampus—although no one has yet figured out whether this is a key to depression or just a by-product (Insel, 2007).

Evidence also connects depression with lower brain wave activity in the left frontal lobe (Davidson, 1992a,b, 2000; Robbins, 2000). And, in a few cases, depression may be caused by viral infection (Bower, 1995b; Neimark, 2005). Such evidence leads some observers to view depression as a collection

TABLE 12.2	Lifetime Risk of a Depressive Episode Lasting a Year or More
Taiwan	1.5%
Korea	2.9%
Puerto Rico	4.3%
United States	5.2%
Germany	9.2%
Canada	9.6%
New Zealand	11.6%
France	16.4%
Lebanon	19%

of disorders having a variety of causes and involving many parts of the brain (Kendler & Gardner, 1998).

Most recently, neuroimaging has suggested a link between a part of the cerebral cortex called *area 25,* located at the base of the frontal cortex, just over the roof of the mouth. In depressed brains, where many functions seem to slow down, area 25 shows up on scans as "hot," says neuroscientist Helen Mayberg (Dobbs, 2006b). Moreover, when therapies for depression work—either drugs or psychotherapy—area 25 calms down. No one is sure exactly what area 25 is or exactly how it works, although Mayberg suspects that it acts as a sort of "switch" that controls the brain's "alarm system." Whatever it does, area 25 does not act alone but rather as a whole suite of brain modules that, together, produce depression.

SAD   Adding to this rather confusing picture, it seems that lack of sunlight can also initiate a special form of depression that most commonly appears during the long, dark winter months among people who live in high latitudes (Lewy et al., 2006). (See Figure 12.1.) Aptly named, **seasonal affective disorder,** or **SAD,** is related to levels of the light-sensitive hormone melatonin, which regulates our internal biological clocks (Campbell & Murphy, 1998; Oren & Terman, 1998). Based on this knowledge, researchers have developed an effective therapy that regulates melatonin by exposing SAD sufferers daily to bright artificial light. Some therapists report that combining light therapy with cognitive-behavioral therapy or antidepressants works even better in treating SAD (DeAngelis, 2006).

Psychological Factors   Biology alone cannot entirely explain depression. We must also understand it as a mental, social, and behavioral condition. Initially, a negative event, such as losing a job, can make anyone feel depressed, but low self-esteem and a pessimistic attitude can fuel a cycle of depressive thought patterns that psychologists call *rumination* (Law, 2005; Nolen-Hoeksema & Davis, 1999). Those

CONNECTION • CHAPTER 8

The "biological clock," located in the hypothalamus, regulates our circadian rhythms.

Seasonal affective disorder (SAD)

A form of depression believed to be caused by deprivation of sunlight.

....

FIGURE 12.1

Relationship between Light and SAD

People who suffer from seasonal affective disorder are most likely to experience symptoms of depression during months with shortened periods of sunlight.

(*Source:* Adaptation of Fig. 1, p. 74, from "Seasonal Affective Disorder: A Description of the Syndrome and Preliminary Findings with Light Therapy," by N. E. Rosenthal et al., *Archives of General Psychiatry, 41*(1984), pp. 72–80. American Medical Association.)

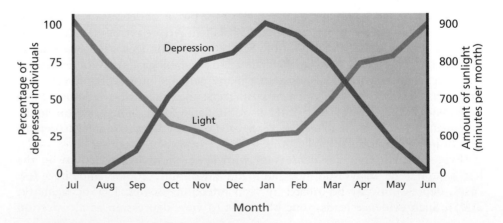

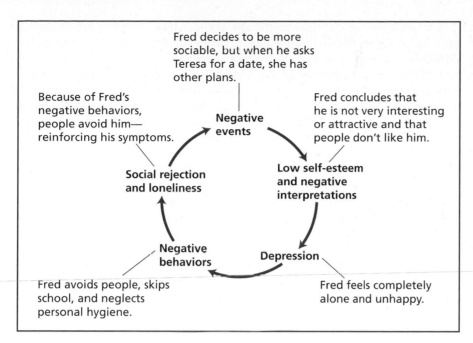

FIGURE 12.2
The Cognitive–Behavioral Cycle of Depression

As you follow Fred around the cycle, note how his depression feeds on itself.

Fred decides to be more sociable, but when he asks Teresa for a date, she has other plans.

Because of Fred's negative behaviors, people avoid him—reinforcing his symptoms.

Negative events

Fred concludes that he is not very interesting or attractive and that people don't like him.

Social rejection and loneliness

Low self-esteem and negative interpretations

Negative behaviors

Depression

Fred avoids people, skips school, and neglects personal hygiene.

Fred feels completely alone and unhappy.

who ruminate will dwell on depressive thoughts, going over and over them again. While this may initially garner sympathy, it soon turns other people away, leaving the individual with depression isolated and even more depressed. (See Figure 12.2.)

Probably because of low self-esteem, depression-prone people are more likely to perpetuate the depression cycle by attributing negative events to their own personal flaws or external conditions that they feel helpless to change (Azar, 1994). Martin Seligman calls this **learned helplessness.** The resulting negative self-evaluation generates a depressed mode, which leads in turn to negative behaviors such as crying. These behaviors encourage others to avoid those suffering from depression. Consequently, they feel rejected and lonely, which also feeds the cycle of their despair (Coyne et al., 1991).

The cognitive approach to depression points out that negative thinking styles are learned—and therefore modifiable. So, if you are depressed, working to change the way you *think*—perhaps blaming yourself less and focusing more on constructive plans for doing better—can ultimately change how you feel and how you act. Indeed, Peter Lewinsohn and his colleagues have found that they can treat many cases of depression effectively with cognitive–behavioral techniques. (Lewinsohn et al., 1980, 1990; Lewinsohn & Gottlib, 1995) Their approach intervenes at several points in the cycle of depression to teach people how to change their helpless thinking, to cope adaptively with unpleasant situations, and to build more rewards into their lives.

Who Becomes Depressed? Clinicians have noted that women have higher depression rates than do men (Holden, 2005). According to Susan Nolen-Hoeksema (2001), the difference may lie in the differing response styles of men and women. When women experience sadness, she says, they tend to think about the possible causes and implications of their feelings. In contrast, men attempt to distract themselves from depressed feelings, either by shifting their attention to something else or by doing something physical that will take their minds off their mood. This model suggests that the more *ruminative* response of women—characterized by a tendency to concentrate on problems—increases women's vulnerability to depression (Shea, 1998). Another possible source of the gender discrepancy in depression may involve norms that encourage women to seek help but discourage men from doing so. Thus, the difference may be, at least in part, due to differences in reporting depressive feelings.

Learned helplessness A condition in which depressed individuals learn to attribute negative events to their own personal flaws or external conditions that the person feels helpless to change. People with learned helplessness can be thought of as having an extreme form of *external locus of control.*

The incidence of depression and the age at which it strikes are changing—at least in the United States. According to Seligman, depression is between 10 and 20 times as common as it was 50 years ago (National Press Club, 1999). In the mid-1900s, most casualties of depression were middle-aged women, but now depression is more often a teenage problem—still more prevalent in females than in males (National Institute of Mental Health, 2000). Seligman, who has studied depression extensively, blames this increase in occurrence and decrease in age to three factors: (1) an out-of-control individualism and self-centeredness that focuses on individual success and failure, rather than group accomplishments; (2) the self-esteem movement, which has taught a generation of schoolchildren that they should always feel good about themselves, irrespective of their efforts and achievements; and (3) a culture of *victimology*, which reflexively points the finger of blame for one's own mistakes at someone else, causing people to think of themselves as victims.

Bipolar Disorder   The other mood disorder we will consider also involves periods of depression—but, in addition, alternating periods of extreme elation. Formerly known as *manic–depressive disorder,* the condition is now listed in the *DSM-IV* as **bipolar disorder.** The alternating periods of *mania* (excessive elation or manic excitement) and the profound sadness of depression represent the two "poles."

During the *manic phase,* the individual becomes euphoric, energetic, hyperactive, talkative, and emotionally wound tight like a spring. It is not unusual for people, swept up in mania, to spend their life savings on extravagant purchases or to engage promiscuously in a number of sexual liaisons or other potentially high-risk actions. When the mania diminishes, they are left to deal with the damage they have created during their frenetic period. Soon, in the *depressive phase,* a dark wave of melancholy sweeps over the mind, producing symptoms indistinguishable from the "unipolar" form of depression we discussed earlier. Biologically speaking, however, these two forms of depression differ: We know this because the antidepressant drugs that work well on major depression are not usually effective for bipolar disorder—sometimes even making it worse.

Research has established a genetic component in bipolar disorder, although the exact genes involved have not been pinpointed (Bradbury, 2001). While only 1% of the general population has bipolar attacks, having an identical twin afflicted with the problem inflates one's chances to about 70% (Allen, 1976; Tsuang & Faraone, 1990). The fact that bipolar disorder usually responds well to medication also suggests biological factors at work.

Anxiety Disorders

Would you pick up a snake or let a tarantula rest on your shoulder? For some people the mere thought of snakes or spiders is enough to send chills of fear down their spines. Everyone, of course, has experienced anxiety or fear in threatening or dangerous situations. But pathological anxiety is far more severe than the normal anxiety associated with life's challenges. It is also relatively common—even more common than major depression (Barlow, 2000). One estimate says that over our lifetimes 30% of us—more women than men—will experience symptoms that are serious enough to qualify as one of the **anxiety disorders** recognized in the DSM (Hébert, 2006; Holden, 2005).

Here we will review four major disorders that have anxiety as their main feature: (1) *generalized anxiety disorder,* (2) *panic disorder,* (3) *phobic disorder,* and (4) *obsessive–compulsive disorder* (shown in the chart in the margin). You will note that the major differences among them have to do with the focus and duration of anxiety: Is anxiety present most of the time or only occasionally? Does the anxiety seem to come from nowhere—unrelated to the individual's environment? Does it come from an external object or situation, such as the sight of

Anxiety Disorders: Fear, anxiety, panic attacks

- Generalized anxiety disorder
- Panic disorder
- Agoraphobia
- Specific phobias
- Obsessive–compulsive disorder

Bipolar disorder   A mental abnormality involving swings of mood from mania to depression.

Anxiety disorder   Mental problem characterized mainly by anxiety. Anxiety disorders include panic disorder, specific phobias, and obsessive–compulsive disorder.

CHAPTER 12 ● PSYCHOLOGICAL DISORDERS

blood or a snake? Does it involve the victim's own ritualistic behavior, as in a person who compulsively avoids stepping on cracks in the sidewalk?

Generalized Anxiety Disorder   Some people spend months or years of their lives coping with anxiety. Charles, a heavy-equipment operator, says he has dizzy spells, headaches, cold sweats, and frequent feelings of anxiety. But he has no clue why he feels anxious. It is "free-floating" anxiety, as clinicians sometimes call it, and they would diagnose his condition as **generalized anxiety disorder.** People with this problem have a pervasive and persistent sense of anxiety. They are not just worried or fearful about specific situations or objects, such as heights or spiders. Nor does the anxiety come in waves, punctuated by periods of relative calm. Instead, they feel anxious much of the time, without knowing why.

How common is this condition? According to the National Institute of Mental Health (2008a), about 6.8 million adult Americans suffer from generalized anxiety disorder, affecting about twice as many women as men. It comes on gradually, with the highest risk during the first half of life.

Panic Disorder   While calmly eating lunch, an unexpected wave of panic sweeps over you, seemingly from nowhere. Your heart races, your body shakes, you feel dizzy, your hands become clammy and sweaty, you are afraid that you might be dying. You are having a *panic attack*.

The distinguishing feature of **panic disorder** is a recurring strong feeling of anxiety that occurs "out of the blue," has no connection with present events (Barlow, 2001). As in generalized anxiety disorder, the feeling is one of "free-floating anxiety." Attacks usually last for only a few minutes and then subside (McNally, 1994). Because of the unexpected nature of these "hit-and-run" attacks, *anticipatory anxiety* often develops as an added complication. The dread of the next attack and of being helpless and suddenly out of control can lead a person to avoid public places, yet fear being left alone. Cognitive–behavioral theorists view panic attacks as conditioned responses to physical sensations that may have initially been learned during a period of stress (Antony et al., 1992).

Biologically, we have evidence of a genetic influence in panic disorder (Hettema et al., 2001). The brain mechanism responsible for this condition apparently lies in the limbic system—especially in the amygdala (Hébert, 2006; Mobbs et al., 2007). Significantly, it is part of the brain's notorious unconscious arousal pathway, described by Joseph LeDoux (1996). Overstimulation of these circuits can produce lasting physical changes that make the individual more susceptible to anxiety attacks in the future (Rosen & Schulkin, 1998).

CONNECTION • CHAPTER 9
The brain has two main emotional pathways; one operates mainly at an unconscious level.

To complicate matters, many victims of panic disorder suffer additional symptoms of **agoraphobia.** This condition involves panic that develops when they find themselves in situations from which they cannot easily escape, such as crowded public places or open spaces (Antony et al., 1992; Magee et al., 1996). The term *agoraphobia* can be literally translated from the ancient Greek as "fear of the marketplace." Victims of agoraphobia often fear that, if they experience an attack in one of these locations, help might not be available or the situation will be embarrassing to them. These fears deprive afflicted persons of their freedom, and some become prisoners in their own homes. If the disorder becomes extreme, they cannot hold a job or carry on normal daily activities.

It's entirely possible that you may know someone who has panic disorder or agoraphobia, because these disorders occur in nearly 4% of the population in a given year, much more commonly in women than in men (Kessler et al., 2005). Fortunately, the treatment outlook is good. Medical therapy involves antianxiety drugs to relieve the panic attacks. Purely psychological treatment is also effective: Studies have shown that cognitive–behavioral therapy may equal or outperform drug therapy in combating panic attacks ("Cognitive–Behavior Therapy," 1991; Craske et al., 1991).

Generalized anxiety disorder   A psychological problem characterized by persistent and pervasive feelings of anxiety, without any external cause.

Panic disorder   A disturbance marked by panic attacks that have no obvious connection with events in the person's present experience. Unlike generalized anxiety disorder, the victim is usually free of anxiety between panic attacks.

Agoraphobia   A fear of public places and open spaces, commonly accompanying panic disorder.

TABLE 12.3	Phobias	
DSM-IV category	Object/Situation	Incidence
Agoraphobia	Crowds, open spaces	Common (3.5–7% of adults)
Social phobias	Fear of being observed or doing something humiliating	common (11–15%)
Specific phobias	Varies by category	(up to 16% of adults)
Animals	Cats (ailurophobia)	
	Dogs (cynophobia)	
	Insects (insectophobia)	
	Spiders (arachnophobia)	
	Birds (avisophobia)	
	Horses (equinophobia)	
	Snakes (ophidiophobia)	
	Rodents (rodentophobia)	
Inanimate objects or situations	Closed spaces (claustrophobia)	
	Dirt (mysophobia)	
	Thunder (brontophobia)	
	Lightning (astraphobia)	
	Heights (acrophobia)	
	Darkness (nyctophobia)	
	Fire (pyrophobia)	
Bodily conditions	Illness or injury (nosophobia)	
	Sight of blood (hematophobia)	
	Cancer (cancerophobia)	
	Venereal disease (venerophobia)	
	Death (thanatophobia)	
Other specific phobias	Numbers (numerophobia)	rare
	The number 13 (triskaidekaphobia)	rare
	Strangers, foreigners (xenophobia)	rare
	String (linonophobia)	rare
	Books (bibliophobia)	rare
	Work (ergophobia)	rare

Note: Hundreds of phobias have been described and given scientific names; this table provides only a sample. Some of the rare and strange-sounding phobias may have been observed in a single patient.

Phobic Disorders In contrast with panic disorder, **phobias** involve a persistent and irrational fear of a specific object, activity, or situation—a response all out of proportion to the circumstances. (These are sometimes called *specific phobias,* as contrasted with the broader fears found in agoraphobia.) Many of us respond fearfully to certain stimuli, such as spiders or snakes—or perhaps to multiple-choice tests! But such emotional responses only qualify as full-fledged phobic disorders when they cause substantial disruption to our lives.

And they do cause substantial disruption for lots of people, affecting more than 10 million Americans each year (Winerman, 2005b). While some specific phobias are quite rare, as in a fear of a certain type of insect, others, such as an extreme fear of public speaking, are quite common—so common that they seem almost the norm (Stein et al., 1996). Other common phobic disorders include *social phobias,* which are irrational fears of normal social situations, and fear of heights (acrophobia), snakes (ophidiophobia), and closed-in spaces (claustrophobia). Still other phobias, some quite rare, appear in Table 12.3.

Phobia One of a group of anxiety disorders involving a pathological fear of a specific object or situation.

What causes phobias? Long ago, John Watson and Rosalie Rayner demonstrated that fears can be learned. And we also have good evidence that fears and phobias can be *un*learned through cognitive–behavioral therapy based on conditioning (Mineka & Zinbarg, 2006). But learning may not tell the whole story, says Martin Seligman (1971), who has argued that humans are biologically predisposed to learn some kinds of fears more easily than others. This **preparedness hypothesis** suggests that we carry an innate biological tendency, acquired through natural selection, to respond quickly and automatically to stimuli that posed a survival threat to our ancestors (Öhman & Mineka, 2001). This explains why we develop phobias for snakes and lightning much more easily than we develop fears for automobiles and electrical outlets—objects that have posed a danger only in recent times. Again, the underlying brain mechanism includes the amygdala and the quick-and-dirty emotion pathway mapped by Joseph LeDoux and his colleagues (Schafe et al., 2005; Wilensky et al., 2007).

CONNECTION • CHAPTER 3
Watson and Rayner's infamous experiment with Little Albert showed that fears could be learned by classical conditioning.

Obsessive–Compulsive Disorder   Seventeen-year-old Jim seemed to be a normal adolescent with many talents and interests. Then, almost overnight, he was transformed into a lonely outsider, excluded from social life by his psychological disabilities. Specifically, he developed an obsession with washing. Haunted by the notion that he was dirty—in spite of what his senses told him—Jim began to spend more and more time cleansing himself. At first his ritual ablutions were confined to weekends and evenings, but soon they consumed all his time, forcing him to drop out of school (Rapoport, 1989).

Jim had developed **obsessive–compulsive disorder,** or OCD, a condition characterized by patterns of persistent, unwanted thoughts and behaviors. Obsessive–compulsive disorder affects about 1% of us in any given year, regardless of culture (Steketee & Barlow, 2002). And, to put your mind at ease: Nearly everyone occasionally has had some OCD symptoms in a mild form.

The *obsession* component of OCD consists of thoughts, images, or impulses that recur or persist despite a person's efforts to suppress them. For example, a person with an obsessive fear of germs may avoid using bathrooms outside his or her home or refuse to shake hands with strangers. And because sufferers realize that their obsessive thoughts and compulsive rituals are senseless they often go to great lengths to hide their compulsive behavior from other people. This, of course, places restrictions on their domestic, social, and work lives. Not surprisingly, OCD patients have extremely high divorce rates.

You probably have had some sort of mild obsessional experience, such as petty worries ("Did I remember to lock the door?") or a haunting phrase or melody that kept running through your mind. Such thoughts are normal if they occur only occasionally and have not caused significant disruptions of your life. As we have noted in other disorders, it is a matter of degree.

Compulsions, the other half of obsessive–compulsive disorder, are repetitive, purposeful acts performed according to certain private "rules," in response to an obsession. OCD victims feel that their compulsive behavior will, somehow, reduce the tension associated with their obsessions. These urges may include irresistible urges to clean, to check that lights or appliances have been turned off, and to count objects or possessions. When they are calm, people with obsessive–compulsive disorder view the compulsion as senseless, but when their anxiety rises, they can't resist performing the compulsive behavior ritual to relieve tension. Part of the pain experienced by people with OCD comes from realizing the utter irrationality of their obsessions and their powerlessness to eliminate them.

The tendency for OCD to run in families suggests a genetic link. Another hint comes from the finding that many people with OCD also display tics, unwanted involuntary movements, such as exaggerated eye blinks. In these patients, brain imaging often shows oddities in the deep motor control areas, suggesting something amiss in the brain (Resnick, 1992). OCD expert Judith

A common form of social phobia involves an extreme fear of public speaking.

Preparedness hypothesis   The notion that we have an innate tendency, acquired through natural selection, to respond quickly and automatically to stimuli that posed a survival threat to our ancestors.

Obsessive–compulsive disorder (OCD)   A condition characterized by patterns of persistent, unwanted thoughts and behaviors.

Obsessive–compulsive disorder makes people engage in sensless, ritualistic behaviors, such as repetitive hand washing.

◀ **CONNECTION • CHAPTER 3**

In classical and operant conditioning, extinction involves the suppression of a response as the result of learning a competing response.

Somatoform Disorders:
Physical symptoms or overconcern with one's health

- Conversion disorder
- Hypochondriasis

Somatoform disorders Psychological problem appearing in the form of bodily symptoms or physical complaints, such as weakness or excessive worry about disease. The somatoform disorders include conversion disorder and hypochondriasis.

Conversion disorder A type of somatoform disorder, marked by paralysis, weakness, or loss of sensation but with no discernible physical cause.

Rapoport tells us to think of compulsions as "fixed software packages" programmed in the brain. Once activated, she theorizes, the patient gets caught in a behavioral "loop" that cannot be switched off (Rapoport, 1989).

Studies show a biological contribution, evidenced in the tendency of this disorder to run in families. Adding weight to the biological argument, certain drugs that are commonly prescribed for depression can alleviate both the obsessions and the compulsive rituals (Poling et al., 1991). In further support of a biological basis for OCD, investigators have found that these drugs can reverse compulsive behavior in animals, such as dogs, that display a preoccupation with grooming themselves (Ross, 1992).

Again, however, we must note that biology cannot explain everything. Some victims of OCD have clearly *learned* that their anxiety-provoking thoughts are connected to harmful consequences (Barlow, 2000). Further evidence that learning plays a role can be seen in the results of behavioral therapy, which is effective in reducing compulsive actions. The behavioral strategy for treating compulsive hand washing, for example, calls for a form of *extinction*, in which the therapist soils the patient's hands and prevents him or her from washing for progressively longer periods. Indeed, behavioral therapy can produce changes that show up in PET scans of OCD sufferers' brains (Schwartz et al., 1996). The general principle is this: When we change behavior, we inevitably change the brain, demonstrating once again that biology and behavior are inseparable.

Somatoform Disorders

"Soma" means *body*. Thus, we use the term **somatoform disorders** for psychological problems appearing in the form of bodily symptoms or physical complaints, such as weakness or excessive worry about disease, as in the person who constantly frets about getting cancer. While the somatoform disorders are not especially common—occurring in about 2% of the population—they have captured the popular imagination under their more common names: "hysteria" and "hypochondria" (Holmes, 2001).

The *DSM-IV* recognizes several types of somatoform disorders, but we will cover only two: *conversion disorder* and *hypochondriasis*, shown in the chart in the margin. And, while we're talking about somatoform disorders, please note their potential for confusion with *psychosomatic disorders*, in which mental conditions—especially stress—lead to actual physical disease. The *DSM-IV* places psychosomatic disorders under a separate heading, "Psychological Factors Affecting Medical Condition."

Conversion Disorder Paralysis, weakness, or loss of sensation—with no discernible physical cause—distinguishes **conversion disorder** (formerly called "hysteria"). Patients with this diagnosis may, for example, be blind, deaf, unable to walk, or insensitive to touch in part of their bodies. ("Glove anesthesia," shown in Figure 12.3, is a classic form of sensory loss in conversion disorder.) Significantly, individuals with this condition have no organic disease that shows up on neurological examinations, laboratory tests, or X-rays. In conversion disorder, the problem really seems to be "all in the mind."

The term *conversion disorder* carries with it some baggage from the Freudian past. Originally, the term implied an unconscious displacement (or *conversion*) of anxiety into physical symptoms—although most clinicians no longer subscribe to that explanation. The diagnosis, however, has a reputation for being used as a "dumping ground" for patients—especially female patients—who present physical symptoms but no obvious medical abnormality (Kinetz, 2006).

Some cases of conversion disorder are now thought to stem from physical stress responses. Another possibility, suggested by David Oakley (1999) of the University College in London, is that a common brain mechanism underlies conversion disorder and hypnosis. Accordingly, he suggests that conversion disorder and related mental problems be reclassified as *auto-suggestive disorders*.

No one knows why, but conversion disorder was much commoner a century ago in Europe and the United States. The problem has declined in industrialized countries, probably due to increased public understanding of physical and mental disorders (American Psychiatric Association, 1994; Nietzel et al., 1998). Meanwhile, it is still relatively common in economically undeveloped regions, such as parts of China (Spitzer et al., 1989) and Africa (Binitie, 1975) and among poorly educated persons in the U.S. (Barlow & Durand, 2005).

Hypochondriasis   "Hypochondriacs" worry about getting sick. Every ache and pain signals a disease. Because of their exaggerated concern about illness, patients with **hypochondriasis** often bounce from physician to physician until they find one who will listen to their complaints and prescribe some sort of treatment—often minor tranquilizers or placebos. Naturally, these individuals represent easy marks for health fads and scams. They also find their way to the fringes of the medical community, where disreputable practitioners may encourage them to buy extensive treatments.

On the other side of the problem we find the clinician who is too eager to conclude that the patient's concerns are imaginary—much as we found with conversion disorder. That is, some physicians seem to have a mental set to see hypochondria when they find no physical evidence of disease. This, of course, can have disastrous consequences, as when a mistaken impression of hypochondriasis blinds the physician to a very real and very serious physical disease, such as cancer.

Dissociative Disorders

The common denominator for all the **dissociative disorders** is "fragmentation" of the personality—a sense that parts of the personality have detached (dissociated) from others. Among the dissociative disorders, we find some of the most fascinating forms of mental pathology, including *dissociative fugue, depersonalization disorder,* and the controversial *dissociative identity disorder* (formerly called "multiple personality"), made famous by the fictional Dr. Jekyll and Mr. Hyde. (See the chart in the margin on the next page.) Unfortunately, the underlying causes of dissociative disorders remain unclear.

Dissociative Amnesia   You may know an *amnesia* victim who has suffered a memory loss as the result of a severe blow to the head, perhaps in an auto accident. In many cases, memory loss is selective, with memories for the immediate and remote unaffected. That is, the amnesia victim may be able to repeat back what you have just said and also recall childhood events. What's missing are specific categories of memory, such as recollections of yesterday's events.

The cause is not always physical trauma. Sometimes, people may develop a purely psychological form of amnesia, known as **dissociative amnesia,** as the result of a psychologically traumatic or highly stressful experience. In this disorder, the memory loss typically involves a specific event or series of events. It may also involve the inability to remember aspects of one's own identity.

Dissociative amnesia has a close kinship with *posttraumatic stress disorder,* which we will discuss more extensively in Chapter 14. In both conditions, memory loss is related to a stressful incident or period in the person's life. We should note, however, that dissociative amnesia can be a controversial diagnosis when it is associated with recovered memories of childhood abuse. As we discussed in connection with memory, some psychologists have raised important questions about the accuracy of such recovered memories. And, as the *DSM-IV* states, dissociative amnesia may have "been overdiagnosed in individuals who are highly suggestible" (p. 479).

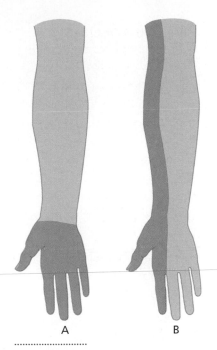

FIGURE 12.3
Glove Anesthesia

The form of conversion disorder known as "glove anesthesia" (A) involves a loss of sensation in the hand, as though the patient were wearing a thick glove. This cannot be a neurological disorder because the pattern of "anesthesia" does not correspond to the actual pattern of nerves in the hand, shown in (B).

Hypochondriasis   A somatoform disorder involving excessive concern about health and disease; also called hypochondria.

Dissociative disorders   One of a group of pathologies involving "fragmentation" of the personality, in which some parts of the personality have become detached, or dissociated, from other parts.

Dissociative amnesia   A psychologically induced loss of memory for personal information, such as one's identity or residence.

This is "Jane Doe," a victim of dissociative fugue who has never recovered the memory of her identity or her past.

Dissociative fugue Essentially the same as dissociative amnesia but with the addition of "flight" from one's home, family, and job. *Fugue* (pronounced *FEWG*) means "flight."

Depersonalization disorder An abnormality involving the sensation that mind and body have separated, as in an "out-of-body" experience.

Dissociative identity disorder A condition in which an individual displays multiple identities, or personalities; formerly called "multiple personality disorder."

Dissociative Fugue   Now consider the very real story of "Jane Doe," a woman with *dissociative fugue*, who was found near death in a Florida park, where she was incoherent and suffering the effects of exposure. In contrast with victims of dissociative amnesia, Jane Doe had a pervasive memory loss: no memory of her identity or any ability to read or write. Therapy revealed general information about the kind of past she must have had, but no good clues to her origins. After a nation-wide television appeal, Jane Doe and her doctors were flooded with calls from possible relatives, the most promising of which was an Illinois couple, certain she was their daughter. They had not heard from her for over four years, since she had moved from Illinois to Florida. Despite their confidence that they had found her, she was never able to remember her past or what had happened to her (Carson et al., 2000).

Jane Doe's **dissociative fugue** was a combination of *amnesia* and *fugue*, or "flight." In such persons amnesia takes the form of a lost sense of identity, while fugue may cause them to flee their homes, families, and jobs. Some victims appear disoriented and perplexed. Others may travel to distant locations and take up new lives, appearing unconcerned about the unremembered past. Usually the fugue state lasts only hours or days, followed by complete and rapid recovery. A few cases may continue for months—or, as with Jane Doe, for years.

Heavy alcohol use may predispose a person to dissociative fugue. This suggests that it may involve some brain impairment—although no certain cause has been established. Like dissociative amnesia, fugue occurs more often in those under prolonged high stress, especially in times of war and other calamities. Some psychologists also suspect memory dissociation and repression accompany instances of sexual and physical childhood abuse (Spiegel & Cardeña, 1991). As with dissociative amnesia, this conjecture, however, is disputed.

Depersonalization Disorder   Yet another form of dissociation involves a sensation that mind and body have separated. Patients with **depersonalization disorder** commonly report "out-of-body experiences" or feelings of being external observers of their own bodies. Some patients feel as if they are in a dream. (Fleeting, mild forms of this are common, so there is no cause for alarm!) A study of 30 such cases found that obsessive–compulsive disorder and certain personality disorders often accompany this condition (Simeon et al., 1997). The causes are unknown.

People undergoing severe physical trauma, such as a life-threatening injury in an auto accident, may also report symptoms of depersonalization. So do some patients who have had near-death experiences. The effect is also common with recreational drugs. Usually the sensation passes rather quickly, although it can recur. In such individuals, investigators have attributed the disorder to hallucinations and to natural changes in the brain that occur during shock (Siegel, 1980), and one study has found patients with depersonalization disorder to have abnormalities in the visual, auditory, and somatosensory cortex (Simeon et al., 2000).

Dissociative Identity Disorder   Robert Louis Stevenson's famous story of Dr. Jekyll and Mr. Hyde has become a misleading stereotype of **dissociative identity disorder**. In reality, most such cases occur in women, and most display more than two identities (Ross et al., 1989). Unlike the homicidal Mr. Hyde in Stevenson's yarn, seldom do people with dissociative identity disorder pose a danger to others.

Although it was once thought to be rare, some specialists now believe that this controversial condition has always been common but hidden or misdiagnosed. Others believe that it is primarily the result of suggestion by the therapist (Piper & Mersky, 2004a,b). Proponents of the diagnosis say that dissociative identity disorder usually first appears in childhood (Vincent & Pickering, 1988). Its victims frequently report having been sexually abused (Putnam et al., 1986; Ross et al., 1990). If so, the formation of multiple identities or selves (sometimes referred to as *alters*) may be a form of defense by the dominant self to protect itself from terrifying events.

Dissociative identity disorder (DID) has now become a familiar diagnosis because of its portrayal in books such as *Sybil* (Schreiber, 1973) and *The Flock* (Cascy & Wilson, 1991) and films such as the 1996 production *Primal Fear*. Each emerging "personality" contrasts in some significant way with the original self. For example, the new alter might be outgoing if the original personality is shy, tough if the original is weak, and sexually assertive if the other is fearful and sexually naive. These alternate identities, each apparently with its own consciousness, emerge suddenly—usually under stress.

What lies behind this mysterious disturbance? Psychodynamic theories explain it as a fracturing of the ego as a result of ego defense mechanisms that do not allow energy from conflicts and traumas to escape from the unconscious mind. Cognitive theories see it as a form of role playing or mood-state dependency, a form of memory bias in which events experienced in a given mood are more easily recalled when the individual is again in that mood state (Eich et al., 1997). Others suggest that at least some cases are frauds (as in the case of a student, charged with plagiarizing a term paper, who claimed that he had multiple personalities and that one of them copied the paper without the knowledge of his dominant personality). Some observers have even suggested that the disorder exists only in the minds of a few therapists (Piper, 1998). In this view, espoused by memory expert Elizabeth Loftus, patients may initially be led by the suggestive questioning of their therapists, who seek to uncover what they suspect are repressed memories of trauma and molestation (Loftus & Ketcham, 1994).

CONNECTION • CHAPTER 4

Loftus is a leading critic of "recovered" memories of sexual abuse.

In an unfortunate choice of terms, dissociative identity disorder is sometimes called "split personality." This causes confusion because schizophrenia (which literally means "split mind") has *no* relationship to dissociative identity disorder at all. In schizophrenia, the "split" refers to a psychotic split from reality, not to a fracturing of one personality into many personalities. Nor is dissociative identity disorder a psychotic disorder. We suggest that the reader avoid confusion by avoiding the term "split personality."

Schizophrenia

Schizophrenia is the disorder that people have in mind when they use the terms "madness," "psychosis," or "insanity." In psychological terms, **schizophrenia** is a severe form of psychopathology in which personality seems to disintegrate, emotional life becomes disrupted, and cognitive processes distorted. (It was also the diagnosis given to all but one of Rosenhan's pseudopatients.)

The schizophrenic world may grow bleak and devoid of meaning, or it may become so filled with sensation that everything appears in a confusion of multiple realities layered with hallucinations and delusions. In schizophrenia, emotions often become blunted, thoughts turn bizarre, language may take strange twists, and memory becomes fragmented (Danion et al., 1999). The disorder breaks the unity of the mind, often sending its victims on meaningless mental detours, sometimes spouting sequences of "clang" associations (associations involving similar-sounding words) and producing confused verbalizations that clinicians call "word salads." Here is an example of schizophrenic speech:

> The lion will have to change from dogs into cats until I can meet my father and mother and we dispart some rats. I live on the front of Whitton's head. You have to work hard if you don't get into bed. . . . It's all over for a squab true tray and there ain't no squabs, there ain't no men, there ain't no music, there ain't no nothing besides my mother and my father who stand alone upon the Island of Capri where is no ice. Well it's my suitcase sir. (Rogers, 1982)

In a lifetime, more than one of every 100 Americans—more than 2 million over the age of 18—will become afflicted. For as yet unknown reasons, men are

Schizophrenia (pronounced *skits-o-FRENNY-a*) A psychotic disorder involving distortions in thoughts, perceptions, and/or emotions.

Schizophrenia: Psychotic deterioration of the personality, including disturbances in affect, thinking, and socialization

- Disorganized type
- Catatonic type
- Paranoid type
- Undifferentiated type
- Residual type

more often afflicted, with the first appearance of schizophrenia typically occurring in men before they are 25 and for women between 25 and 45 years of age (Holden, 2005; National Institute of Mental Health, 2008b).

Major Types of Schizophrenia   Many investigators consider schizophrenia a constellation of separate disorders. Here are the five most common forms:

- *Disorganized type* represents everyone's image of mental illness, featuring incoherent speech, hallucinations, delusions, and bizarre behavior. A patient who talks to imaginary people most likely has this diagnosis.

- *Catatonic type,* involving a spectrum of motor dysfunctions, appears in two forms. Persons with the more common catatonic stupor may remain motionless for hours—even days—sometimes holding rigid, statuelike postures. In the other form, called catatonic excitement, patients become agitated and hyperactive.

- *Paranoid type* features delusions and hallucinations but no catatonic symptoms and none of the incoherence of disorganized schizophrenia. The paranoid delusions of persecution or of grandiosity (highly exaggerated self-importance) found in this type of schizophrenia are less well organized—more illogical—than those of the patient with a purely delusional disorder.

- *Undifferentiated type* serves as a catchall category for schizophrenic symptoms that do not clearly meet the requirements for any of the other categories above.

- *Residual type* is the diagnosis for individuals who have suffered from a schizophrenic episode in the past but currently have no major symptoms such as hallucinations or delusional thinking. Instead, their thinking is mildly disturbed, or their emotional lives are impoverished. The diagnosis of residual type may indicate that the disease is entering remission, or becoming dormant. (This diagnosis was assumed in most of Rosenhan's pseudopatients, whom we met at the beginning of the chapter.)

In Table 12.4, you can see what would be required for a diagnosis of schizophrenia, according to criteria in the *DSM-IV.* See whether you think the symptoms presented by the Rosenhan's pseudopatients would warrant such a diagnosis under today's standards.

The fact that most such patients display a hodgepodge of symptoms places them into the "undifferentiated" category, further clouding our picture of schiz-

---

TABLE 12.4   Criteria for a Diagnosis of Schizophrenia

- Two or more of the following symptoms, present for a significant portion of time during a one-month period (less if successfully treated):
  1. Delusions
  2. Hallucinations
  3. Disorganized speech
  4. Grossly disorganized or catatonic behavior
  5. Negative symptoms

  (Only one symptom is required if the delusions are bizarre, or if the hallucinations consist of a voice keeping up a running commentary on the person's behavior or thoughts, or if two or more voices are conversing with each other.)
- Dysfunction in work, interpersonal relations, or self-care
- Signs of disturbance for at least six months, with at least two months of symptoms listed above

---

Source: Adapted from the *Diagnostic and Statistical Manual of Mental Disorders,* 4th ed., 1994, pp. 285–286.

ophrenia. Trying to make more sense of the problem, many investigators now merely divide the symptoms of schizophrenia into *positive* and *negative* categories (Javitt & Coyle, 2004; Sawa & Snyder, 2002). *Positive symptoms* refer to active processes, such as delusions and hallucinations, while *negative symptoms* refer to passive processes and deficiencies, such as social withdrawal, "flat" affect (lack of emotional expression), lack of pleasure in life, and poverty of thinking.

Patient responses to drug therapy support the positive–negative division: Those with positive symptoms usually respond to antipsychotic drugs, while those with negative symptoms do not (Andreasen et al., 1995; Heinrichs, 1993). But even this distinction has its problems. The negative form of schizophrenia often looks like major depression. In addition, both positive and negative symptoms may occur in a single patient. All these difficulties have led some researchers to conclude that schizophrenia is a name for many separate disturbances.

CONNECTION • CHAPTER 13

Many antipsychotic drugs work by reducing the activity of the neuro-transmitter dopamine in the brain.

Possible Causes of Schizophrenia   No longer do most theorists look through the Freudian lens to see schizophrenia as the result of defective parenting or repressed childhood trauma (Johnson, 1989). Studies show that adopted children with no family history of the disorder run no increased risk of developing schizophrenia when placed in a home with a parent who has schizophrenia (Gottesman, 1991). Thus, an emerging consensus among psychiatrists and psychologists views schizophrenia as fundamentally a brain disorder—or a group of disorders (Sawa & Snyder, 2002).

Support for this brain-disorder view comes from many quarters. As we have noted, the antipsychotic drugs (sometimes called *major tranquilizers*)—which interfere with the brain's dopamine receptors—can suppress the symptoms of positive schizophrenic symptoms (Carlsson, 1978; Snyder, 1986). On the other hand, drugs that stimulate dopamine production (e.g., the amphetamines) can actually produce schizophrenic reactions. Recently, attention has turned to deficiencies in the neurotransmitter glutamate (Javitt & Coyle, 2004). Other evidence of a biological basis for schizophrenia comes in the form of brain abnormalities shown by brain scans (Conklin & Iacono, 2004; National Institute of Mental Health, 2005). (See Figure 12.4.) In that vein, an especially provocative

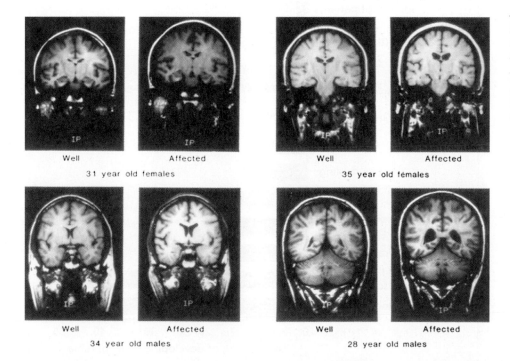

FIGURE 12.4
MRI Scans of a Twin with Schizophrenia and a Twin without Schizophrenia

The normal twin is on the left. Note the enlarged ventricles (fluid-filled spaces) in the brain of the schizophrenic twin on the right.

new finding from MRI studies suggests that the schizophrenic brain fails to synchronize its neural firing across the cortex (Bower, 2005; Symond et al., 2005).

Yet another line of evidence for the biological basis of schizophrenia comes from family studies (Conklin & Iacono, 2004; Holden, 2003a). While no gene has been linked to schizophrenia with certainty, we do know that the closer one's relationship to a person with the disorder, the greater one's chances of developing it (Gottesman, 1991, 2001). This conclusion comes from impressive studies of identical twins reared apart and from adoption studies of children having blood relatives who have been diagnosed with schizophrenia. While only about 1% of us in the general population develop schizophrenia, the child of a parent with schizophrenia incurs a risk about 14 times higher than normal. The worst case would be to have an identical twin who has developed the condition. In that event, the other twin's chances of developing schizophrenia jump to nearly 50%.

As with the mood disorders, biology does not tell the whole story of schizophrenia. We can see the effect of the environment, for example, in the fact that 90% of the relatives of patients who have schizophrenia do not develop the disorder themselves (Barnes, 1987). Even in identical twins who share exactly the same genes, the *concordance rate* (the rate at which the disorder is shared by both) for schizophrenia is only about 50%. That is, in half the cases in which schizophrenia strikes identical twins, it leaves one twin untouched. (See Figure 12.5.)

A hopeful Finnish study found that being raised in a healthy family environment can actually lower the risk of schizophrenia in adopted children who have a genetic predisposition to the disease (Tienari et al., 1987). Apparently, schizophrenia requires a biological predisposition plus some unknown environmental agent to "turn on" the hereditary tendency (Cromwell, 1993; Iacono & Grove, 1993). This agent could be a chemical toxin, stress, or some factor we have not yet dreamed of. Taken as a whole, this research suggests that genetic factors may

....
FIGURE 12.5
Genetic Risk of Developing Schizophrenia

The graph shows average risks for developing schizophrenia in persons with a schizophrenic relative. Data were compiled from family and twin studies conducted in European populations between 1920 and 1987; the degree of risk correlates highly with the degree of genetic relatedness.

(*Source:* Fig. 10, p. 96, "Genetic Risk of Developing Schizophrenia," from SCHIZOPHRENIA GENESIS: The Origins of Madness, by Irving Gottesman. Copyright © 1991. Reprinted by permission of W. H. Freeman and Company/Worth Publishers.)

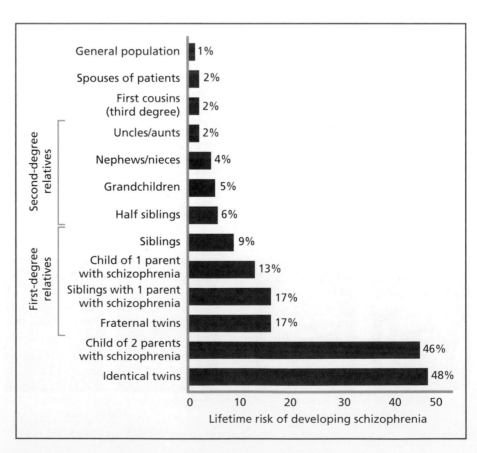

not themselves be sufficient for the disorder to develop (Nicol & Gottesman, 1983). In view of all the evidence, we must remember that psychological disorder is always an interaction of biological, cognitive, and environmental factors, as our first Core Concept of the chapter suggested.

This broader perspective is often called the **diathesis–stress hypothesis.** It says that biological factors may place the individual at risk for schizophrenia (as well as many other disorders), but environmental stressors transform this potential into an actual disorder (Walker & Diforio, 1997). (The word *diathesis* refers to a predisposition or physical condition that makes one susceptible to disease.) Thus, schizophrenia can be seen as a stress response by one who is predisposed to the disorder. In this view, then, susceptible individuals may never develop schizophrenia if they are spared certain damaging conditions or stressors that might push them "over the edge."

Developmental Disorders

Developmental problems can appear at any age, but several common ones are first seen in childhood, including *autism, attention-deficit hyperactivity disorder (ADHD),* and *dyslexia.* Here we will give you a brief description of these disorders, because you have already encountered them in earlier chapters. (See the chart in the margin.)

Autism A complex and mysterious disorder, **autism** involves an impoverished ability to "read" other people, use language, and interact socially. To illustrate, imagine the following situation: Sally and Shania are playing together, when Sally puts a piece of candy in a box and then leaves the room. While Sally is gone, Shania opens the box, removes the candy, and stashes it in her purse. When Sally comes back, where will she look for the candy? Normal children will say that Sally will look in the box. Children with autism are most likely to say (if they communicate at all) that Sally will look in the purse. Thus, the child has a poorly developed *theory of mind* (Frith, 1993). Children with severe autism cannot imagine themselves in Sally's place, believing something they know is not the case. As a result of this deficit, the child has difficulty in social relationships, usually existing in a world of extreme social isolation.

Besides the theory-of-mind deficiencies and social isolation, most persons with autism also have language difficulties. In fact, many never achieve functional language at all. Perhaps because of all these difficulties, many are classified as mentally retarded (although most mentally retarded persons are not autistic). In severe cases, such children may engage in destructive self-stimulation, such as head-banging. Often they will also display repetitive behavior, such as rocking, for extended periods. Typically a physician or the parents first suspect the disorder at about 1½ to 2 years of age, when the child fails to develop language (Kabot et al., 2003).

Recently, neuroscience and epidemiology have produced some other leads in the puzzle of autism. Some evidence suggests a link between autism and toxic materials in the environment (Neimark, 2007). But creating the most excitement is the discovery of "mirror neurons" and a possible link to autism. Studies show that autistic children have either fewer mirror neurons in their brains, or else the mirror neurons they do have are defective (Miller, 2005; Ramachandran & Oberman, 2006). The interesting thing about this finding is that the mirror neurons are supposed to do exactly what persons with autism cannot do: sense what other people's intentions are (Dobbs, 2006a; Rizzolatti et al., 2006). It remains to be seen whether these developments can be translated into effective therapies.

How prevalent is autism? The numbers are disputed. The National Institute of Health estimates that some form of the disorder occurs in about 1 in 500 children. Although you may have seen news reports of a rising incidence of autism in recent decades, experts attribute this primarily to an expanded defini-

Developmental Disorders: Disorders usually first diagnosed in infancy, childhood, or adolescence
- Autism
- Dyslexia
- Attention-deficit hyperactivity disorder (ADHD)

CONNECTION • CHAPTER 13
A *theory of mind* involves the understanding that others may have different beliefs, desires, and emotions that underlie their behavior.

Diathesis–stress hypothesis In reference to schizophrenia, the proposal that says that genetic factors place the individual at risk while environmental stress factors transform this potential into an actual schizophrenic disorder.

Autism A developmental disorder marked by disabilities in language, social interaction, and the ability to understand another person's state of mind.

CONNECTION • CHAPTER 2
"Mirror neurons" in the brain "reflect" other people's responses.

tion of the disorder that came into wide use in the 1990s (Gernsbacher et al., 2005). Most experts believe that autism is fundamentally a brain disorder. At present there is no cure, although there are treatment programs that can improve socialization and speech—but they are intensive and relatively expensive.

Dyslexia Reading is a key that opens many doors in a modern, information-driven society. But those doors can remain closed for people who have difficulty in reading—people with **dyslexia.** The disorder affects about one of five children to some degree, often leading to poor school performance. And because school is so important in our society, it often leads to diminished self-esteem and eventually to lost career opportunities (Shaywitz, 1996).

Contrary to popular presumption, dyslexia is not a visual disorder. It doesn't cause letters and words to "jump around" or reverse themselves. Research over the last 15 years suggests, instead, that the disorder involves the abnormalities in the brain's language processing circuits (Breier et al., 2003). Ironically, another "cause" may be language itself: Speakers of English—with its bizarre ways of spelling, including some 1120 ways to spell only 40 different sounds—are much more likely to develop dyslexia than are Italian speakers, who must contend with only 33 combinations of letters for 25 sounds (Helmuth, 2001c; Paulesu et al., 2001).

In a sense, dyslexia may not even be a distinct disorder. Researcher Sally Shaywitz and her colleagues have made a case that there is no marker that sets individuals with dyslexia entirely apart from others who are merely average readers. She argues that dyslexia is simply the diagnosis we give to an arbitrarily defined group of people occupying the lower end of the reading-abilities spectrum (Shaywitz et al., 1990).

Everyone does agree that dyslexia involves reading difficulties. Everyone also agrees that recent years have seen great strides made in understanding the neurological basis of the disorder, developing treatments, and debunking some of the myths surrounding dyslexia (smart people *can* have dyslexia: Einstein apparently did!). Currently, the most effective treatments include special reading programs that emphasize the matching of sounds to letter combinations.

Attention-Deficit Hyperactivity Disorder (ADHD) Some children have more trouble than others sitting still and focusing attention on a task, such as solving a math problem or listening to directions from the teacher. Many things can cause these symptoms, including distracting problems at home, abuse from peers, or merely a cultural tradition that places low value on the tasks that demand quiet attention. Besides those, there seems to be a brain-based condition, known as **attention-deficit hyperactivity disorder** (ADHD), that can interfere with even the best of intentions to focus attention and sit quietly (Barkley, 1998). The disorder is estimated to affect some 3 to 5% of school-age children (Brown, 2003b).

ADHD is a controversial diagnosis, and its treatment is even more controversial (Sax & Kautz, 2003). Critics have claimed that ADHD is overdiagnosed, often being used to describe normal rambunctiousness or to blame children for the mistakes made by unskilled parents and teachers. In addition, drug treatment consisting of stimulant drugs strikes many people as being wrongheaded. On the other hand, many careful studies have demonstrated that properly administered drug therapy, along with behavioral therapy, can improve attention and diminish hyperactivity in a majority (about 70%) of individuals diagnosed with ADHD (Daley, 2004; MTA Cooperative Treatment Group, 2004).

Adjustment Disorders and Other Conditions

Although the large majority of everyday psychological problems involve making choices and dealing with confusion, frustration, and loss, the *DSM-IV* gives these problems short shrift under *adjustment disorders* and under the awkwardly

CONNECTION • CHAPTER 1
Hyperactivity is not caused by eating sugar.

Dyslexia A reading disability, thought by some experts to involve a brain disorder.

Attention-deficit hyperactivity disorder (ADHD) A developmental disability involving short attention span, distractibility, and extreme difficulty in remaining inactive for any period.

named category, *other conditions that may be a focus of clinical attention.* Together, these categories represent a catch basin for relatively mild problems that do not fit well under other headings. They span a diverse range of conditions that include mild depression, physical complaints, marital problems, academic problems, job problems, parent–child problems, bereavement, and even *malingering* (faking an illness). Consequently, the largest group of people suffering from mental problems may fit these headings—even though the *DSM-IV* devotes disproportionately little space to them. Ironically, because these adjustment difficulties are so prevalent, sufferers who turn to psychologists and psychiatrists account for a large proportion of the patient load seen by professionals in private practice.

Gender Differences in Mental Disorders

No one knows exactly why, but the data show large gender differences in susceptibility to various mental disorders (Holden, 2005). We have seen, for example, that women more often suffer from mood disorders, especially depression. Women also are diagnosed more often with anxiety disorders and eating disorders. In contrast, men are overwhelmingly more likely to have personality disorders that involve aggressive or control-related disorders, such as drug and alcohol abuse and violence. Thus men, far more often than women, are diagnosed as having antisocial personality disorder. As we have noted, one possibility is that social norms encourage more women than men to report feelings of depression. At the same time, social norms may encourage men to "act out" their feelings in a more physical manner.

Another possibility is that the differences originate in biology. For example, men's brains seem to be more strongly *lateralized* (that is, they tend to have specific cortical functions more localized on one side of the brain or the other). This may explain why men are less likely than women to recover language after a left-side stroke. Some neuroscientists also suspect that the "one-sidedness" of the male brain may contribute to the much higher incidence of schizophrenia and most developmental disorders, such as autism, dyslexia, and attention deficit hyperactivity disorder (ADHD) in males (Holden, 2005). Similarly, there may be some, as yet undiscovered, biological difference that underlies women's greater susceptibility to depression. Unfortunately, deciding between the social and biological explanations for gender differences in mental disorders awaits further research. Don't be surprised, however, if the final answer reflects the nature–nurture interaction: It probably involves both.

CONNECTION • CHAPTER 10
Personality disorders are generally conditions of long standing that affect fundamental personality traits.

PSYCHOLOGY**MATTERS**
Shyness

Being shy is a common problem, but it is not a *DSM-IV* disorder. Rather, **shyness** is a distressing pattern of avoiding or withdrawing from social contact. At the extreme, shy behavior may become a social phobia or an avoidant personality disorder, as afflicted individuals seek to limit or escape from social interactions. As we have seen many times before, it is a matter of degree. The tragedy of shyness is that such people may suffer from loneliness and from lost opportunities to pursue interests and relationships.

What are the origins of this often-painful problem? For some people it may begin at birth: Shyness is one of three basic temperaments that have been observed among infants and traced through adult life (Kagan et al., 1988, 1994). Jerome Kagan has also recently proposed that shyness may have its origin in an overly excitable amygdala (Kagan, 2001). But shyness and other forms of social anxiety are also *learned* responses, so that even those who are not "born shy" can acquire shy behavior patterns.

Shyness may be painful, but it is not a DSM-IV disorder.

Shyness A common temperamental condition but not a disorder recognized by the *DSM-IV.*

On a hopeful note, shyness does not have to be a permanent condition. Many people overcome it on their own. Organizations such as Toastmasters help people build verbal skills and confidence in social situations. And many others have found the help they need in cognitive–behavioral therapy groups.

CheckYourUnderstanding

1. **ANALYSIS:** What are the main differences between the medical model and the psychological model of mental disorder?

2. **RECALL:** Describe one kind of evidence suggesting that depression has a biological basis.

3. **APPLICATION:** According to the *preparedness hypothesis,* which one of the following phobias would you expect to be most common?
   a. fear of snakes (ophidiophobia)
   b. fear of books (bibliophobia)
   c. fear of horses (equinophobia)
   d. fear of the number 13 (triskaidekaphobia)

4. **RECALL:** Which of the following is most common: schizo-

phrenia, depression, phobias, dissociative identity disorder?

5. **RECALL:** What mental processes may be disrupted by schizophrenia?

6. **RECALL:** In which type of anxiety disorder is the anxiety focused on a particular object or situation?

7. **UNDERSTANDING THE CORE CONCEPT:** The *DSM-IV* groups most mental disorders by their
   a. treatments.
   b. causes.
   c. symptoms.
   d. theoretical basis.

Answers 1. The medical model views mental disorders as diseases—as something wrong with the individual—while the psychological model encompasses biology, the environment, and mental processes. The medical model also tends to emphasize the patient receiving treatment, while the psychological model involves patients as partners in the treatment process. **2.** Depression runs in families; the disorder often responds favorably to drugs; people with depression tend to have distinctive patterns on the EEG and on brain scans. **3.** a—Fear of snakes: All the others are relatively modern objects that have not existed long enough to be incorporated into our biological natures. **4.** Depression **5.** Schizophrenia may disrupt virtually all mental processes, including thinking, perception, motivation, and emotion. **6.** Phobias **7.** c

12.3 KEY QUESTION
WHAT ARE THE CONSEQUENCES OF LABELING PEOPLE?

"Mad." "Maniac." "Mentally ill." "Crazy." "Insane." "Disturbed." "Neurotic." These, along with all the official diagnostic terms that appear in the *DSM-IV,* are labels used by the public, the courts, and mental health professionals to describe people who display mental disturbances. Ideally, of course, an accurate diagnostic label leads to good communication among mental health professionals and an effective treatment program for the afflicted individual. Sometimes, however, labels create confusion and hurt. **Labeling** can turn people into stereotypes, masking their personal characteristics and the unique circumstances that contribute to their disorders. And, if that is not enough, labels can provoke prejudices and social rejection.

In this section we will begin with the problem of labeling as it affects the individual. Then we will pursue the issue of labeling in a larger context: Does *psychological disorder* mean the same thing in all cultures? Finally, we will bring the topic home with a critical look at the dangers of applying diagnostic labels to your friends and family. The Core Concept that organizes all this says:

Labeling Refers to the undesirable practice of attaching diagnoses of mental disorders to people and then using them as stereotypes—treating the afflicted individuals as if the labels explained their whole personalities. Psychiatric labels can also stigmatize people.

core concept | Ideally, accurate diagnoses lead to proper treatments, but diagnoses may also become labels that depersonalize individuals and ignore the social and cultural contexts in which their problems arise.

Diagnostic Labels, Labeling, and Depersonalization

Labeling a person as mentally disturbed can have both serious and long-lasting consequences, aside from the mental disturbance itself. Not so with a physical illness. A person may suffer a broken leg or an attack of appendicitis, but when the illness is over, the diagnosis moves into the past. Not so with mental disorders. A label of "depression" or "mania" or "schizophrenia" can be a stigma that follows a person forever (Farina et al., 1996; Wright et al., 2000). But what about a mistaken diagnosis? As Rosenhan pointed out, a mistaken diagnosis of cancer is cause for celebration, but almost never is a diagnosis of mental disorder retracted. As you will recall in the "pseudopatient" study, discussed at the beginning of the chapter, the glaring fact of normalcy never emerged—a fact that Rosenhan attributed to being labeled as schizophrenic.

The diagnostic label may also become part of a cycle of neglect resulting from the inferior status accorded people with mental disorders. Sadly, in our society, to have severe mental problems is to be stigmatized and devalued. And, as seen in the Rosenhan study, the mentally ill also suffer depersonalization— that is, robbing people of their individuality and identity by treating them impersonally, as objects rather than as individuals. Depersonalization can easily result from labeling, but, as in Rosenhan's study, it can also result from an impersonal environment, as in some mental hospitals. All of this, of course, lowers self-esteem and reinforces disordered behavior. Thus, society extracts costly penalties from those who deviate from its norms—and in the process it perpetuates the problem of mental disorder.

Perhaps the most extreme reaction against labeling has come from radical psychiatrist Thomas Szasz, who claimed that mental illness is a "myth" (1961, 1977). Szasz argued that the symptoms used as evidence of mental illness are merely medical labels that give professionals an excuse to intervene in what are really social problems: deviant people violating social norms. Once labeled, these people can be treated simply for their "problem of being different."

We must keep in mind, therefore, that the goal of diagnosis is not just to fit a person into a neat diagnostic box or to identify those who are "different." Instead, a diagnosis should initiate a process that leads to a greater understanding of a person and to the development of a plan to help. A diagnosis should be a beginning, not an end.

The Cultural Context of Psychological Disorder

Few other clinicians would go as far as Thomas Szasz, but many advocate an **ecological model** that takes the individual's external world into account (Levine & Perkins, 1987). In this view, abnormality is seen as an interaction between individuals and the social and cultural context. Disorder results from a mismatch between a person's behavior and the needs of the situation. If you are a private investigator, for example, it might pay to have a slightly suspicious, or "paranoid," complexion to your personality, but if you are a nurse or a teacher, this same characteristic might be called "deviant."

In support of an ecological model, studies show beyond doubt that culture influences both the prevalence of psychological disorders and the symptoms that disturbed people display (Jenkins & Barrett, 2004; Matsumoto, 1996). For example, work done by the World Health Organization (1973, 1979) in Colombia, Czechoslovakia, Denmark, India, Nigeria, Taiwan, Britain, the United States, and the former USSR established that the incidence of schizophrenia varies from culture to culture. More recent studies also support this conclusion (Jablensky, 2000).

Even within a culture, there can be huge generational differences. As Seligman points out, if you live in the United States, your lifetime chance of being

Depersonalization Depriving people of their identity and individuality by treating them as objects rather than as individuals. Depersonalization can be a result of labeling.

Ecological model Similar to the social-cognitive-behavioral model but with an emphasis on the social and cultural context.

diagnosed with depression depends on your age (Barber, 2008). For those born early in the 20th century, the chances are about 1%. The rate rises to 5% for those born in midcentury, and for those born in the 1960s or later the lifetime incidence of depression rises to 10 to 15%.

Psychiatry, too, is beginning to note the effects of culture on psychopathology. The *DSM-IV,* in fact, has a section devoted to culture-specific disorders (although this section recognizes no disorders that are found specifically in the United States). According to psychiatrists Arthur Kleinman and Alex Cohen (1997), psychiatry has clung too long to three persistent myths:

1. The myth that mental disorders have a similar prevalence in all cultures.
2. The myth that biology creates mental disorder, while culture merely shapes the way a person experiences it.
3. The myth that culture-specific disorders occur only in exotic places, rather than here at home.

But are cultural differences so great that a person who hallucinates might be labeled schizophrenic in our culture but visionary or shaman (a healer or seer) in another? Jane Murphy (1976) set out to answer this question in a study of two non-Western groups, the Eskimos of northwest Alaska and the Yorubas of rural tropical Nigeria, societies selected because of their wide geographic separation and cultural dissimilarity. In both groups she found separate terms and distinct social roles for the shaman and for the psychotic individual. Similar findings have since come from studies of cultures all over the world (Draguns, 1980). If mental illness is a socially defined myth, as Szasz asserts, it is a myth nurtured by cultures everywhere.

PSYCHOLOGYMATTERS
Using Psychology to Learn Psychology

Don't do it! Don't use your new knowledge of psychological disorders to diagnose your family and friends. Violating this caveat causes grief for many a psychology student.

We realize how tempting it is to apply what you are learning to the people in your life. Some of the disorders that we have considered here are common. So, as you go through this chapter, you will almost certainly notice signs of anxiety, paranoia, depression, mania, and various other impairments of perception, memory, or emotion that remind you of your friends and relatives. It is a variation on the tendency, discussed earlier, to see signs of psychological disorder in oneself. You should recognize this as a sign that you are acquiring some new knowledge about psychological disorder. But we suggest that you keep these thoughts to yourself.

Remember that reading one chapter does not make you an expert on psychopathology; so you should be cautious about making amateur diagnoses. What you especially should not do is to tell someone that you think he or she has schizophrenia, bipolar disorder, obsessive–compulsive disorder—or any other mental condition.

Having said that, we should also note that erring too far in the opposite direction by ignoring signs of pathology could also be hazardous. If someone you know is struggling with significant mental problems—and even if he or she asks for your opinion—you should refrain from putting a label on the problem. But you can and should encourage that person to see a competent professional for diagnosis and possible treatment.

We will discuss more about how treatment is done—in the next chapter.

CheckYourUnderstanding

1. **RECALL:** Which one of the following statements is true?
    a. Mental disorders have a similar prevalence in all cultures.
    b. In general, biology creates mental disorder, while culture merely shapes the way a person experiences it.
    c. Culture-specific stressors occur primarily in developing countries.

    d. Cultures around the world seem to distinguish between people with mental disorders and people who are visionaries or prophets.

2. **ANALYSIS:** Why did Roenhan claim that mental patients are *depersonalized?*

3. **UNDERSTANDING THE CORE CONCEPT:** What are the positive and negative consequences of diagnostic labeling?

Critical Thinking Applied: Insane Places Revisited—Another Look at the Rosenhan Study

Probably no other experiment in the history of psychology has caused such a furor as did Rosenhan's "pseudopatient" study. And no wonder: By raising questions about the reliability of psychiatric diagnosis, it threatened the very foundations of psychiatry and clinical psychology. Rosenhan summarized his study by saying, "It is clear that we cannot distinguish the sane from the insane in psychiatric hospitals." If Rosenhan was right, the whole mental health enterprise might be built on nothing but opinion. But was this the correct conclusion?

What Are the Issues?

Our first task in evaluating Rosenhan is to identify the issues at the heart of the controversy. For Rosenhan, the issue was the reliability of psychiatric diagnosis and the question of whether mental disorder can be distinguished from normalcy. But his critics claim that the experiment wasn't even designed to answer the question Rosenhan had posed, and so his conclusions were fatally flawed. Perhaps it shouldn't surprise us that the two sides in such a heated dispute have focused on different issues.

What Critical Thinking Questions Should We Ask?

From a critical thinking standpoint, then, the central question involves the extent to which the reasoning on both sides is accurate or flawed. To what extent do the arguments of Rosenhan and his critics avoid common errors and fallacies? Let's look at the specifics.

Insanity Is Not a Diagnosis Robert Spitzer (1973), the leader of the charge against Rosenhan, pointed out that *sanity* and *insanity* are legal terms, as we have seen. Because these terms have no meaning in psychology or psychiatry, says Spitzer, Rosenhan's argument is essentially meaningless. While we can agree that Rosenhan was indeed sloppy with his terminology, your authors suggest that his conclusion has the effect of tossing the baby out with the bath water. In fact, Spitzer admits that Rosenhan apparently uses *insanity* to mean *psychosis.* Score one point for the critics.

Unfair! Rosenhan's critics also claimed that the study was unfair because people don't usually lie about their symptoms so that they can be admitted to mental hospitals. So, we should not fault a psychiatrist for assuming that a person asking for help is sincere. Moreover, doctors and hospitals can be held liable if they don't admit people who might pose a danger to themselves or the community (Ostow, 1973). Rosenhan countered that, even if the doctors were erring on the side of caution, the fact that the patients were "sane" should have been detected, if not at admission, then at some time during their hospitalization. Again, we score a tie.

Not Enough Data A third criticism targets the narrative approach Rosenhan used in his report of the pseudopatient study. The article tells a vivid story, but it is, in fact, sparse in data. Rosenhan's conclusions are mostly driven by his impressions, rather than by facts—an irony, in view of his criticism of psychiatric diagnosis as contaminated by unreliable "impressions." We award this one to Rosenhan's critics.

Conclusions Applied to the Wrong Group
A fourth and most telling criticism accuses Rosenhan of a beginner's mistake. The failure of psychiatrists to detect "sanity" in the pseudopatients, said Spitzer (1973), tells us nothing about their ability to diagnose real patients—who aren't lying about their symptoms. True enough. But Rosenhan (1973b) replied that his study is only one small part of a vast literature attesting to the unreliability of psychiatric diagnosis: Different psychiatrists quite commonly give different diagnoses to the same patient. We give Rosenhan the edge on this point.

Basis
We can see the dispute as one between two camps that each perceived themselves under siege by the other. Psychiatrists thought the original study was a frontal assault on the integrity of their profession, so they responded in kind. The counterattack on Rosenhan impugned his integrity as a researcher. The relevant critical thinking question: Could each side's stance be contaminated by bias? The answer is a resounding yes.

So, where does that leave us?

What Conclusions Can We Draw?

Without doubt, Rosenhan is guilty of using the terms *sane* and *insane* inappropriately. He is also guilty of overstatement and sensationalism, as when he says:

> The facts of the matter are that we have known for a long time that [psychiatric] diagnoses are often not useful or reliable, but we have nevertheless continued to use them. We now know that we cannot distinguish insanity from sanity.

Even so, the fact that not one of the pseudopatients was ever discovered to be mentally sound is a startling finding.

Power of the Situation in Mental Hospitals
Even more important, in our opinion, is a point to which the critics did not respond: Mental hospitals, said Rosenhan, are not primarily places of treatment. Rather, they are places in which patients are labeled, medicated, and ignored by the staff. Most of the time, Rosenhan found, ward attendants and nurses sequestered themselves in a small staff cubicle that patients called "the cage." Psychiatrists were even less available, making only rare appearances on the wards. When patients approached staff members with questions, they were often given curt replies or ignored.

Rosenhan was not the first person to decry mental hospitals as impersonal places, but he did offer some ideas as to why this is so. One factor rests on society's attitudes toward the mentally ill, attitudes that are colored by fear, distrust, and misunderstanding. These attitudes, said Rosenhan, have an effect on mental health workers.

A second factor involves *labeling:* the pernicious effect of a psychiatric diagnosis. Once a diagnosis is made, doctors are extremely reluctant to change their minds. Part of the reason has to do with pride, but an even bigger problem stems from the lack of contact the staff—and especially the doctors—have with patients. Therapy in mental hospitals, then, is largely a matter of medications. And time.

As we noted at the beginning of the chapter, Rosenhan does not fault the doctors, nurses, ward attendants, or other staff members. He suggested that the problem lay in "the situation"—the whole hospital environment, which depersonalizes patients and discourages staff from interacting with patients. But that was 1973. What about now? Do these problems still plague mental hospitals?

A New Controversy Erupts
A brand new controversy erupted in 2005, with the publication of a book entitled *Opening Skinner's Box.* In it, author Lauren Slater describes her own reenactment of Rosenhan's classic experiment. In nine visits to different mental hospitals, Slater told doctors that she heard a voice saying, "Thud." Although she was never hospitalized, she claims that she was "prescribed a total of 25 antipsychotics and 60 antidepressants." In most cases she was diagnosed as having "depression with psychotic features." Slater asserts that her experience supports Rosenhan.

Slater's assertion did not go unnoticed by Robert Spitzer, who still sees the Rosenhan experiment as "an embarrassment" (Jaffe, 2006). Spitzer and two of his colleagues were provoked to write a critique of Slater published in the *Journal of Nervous and Mental Disease* (2005). In that piece, they fired back a salvo consisting of their own study in which they provided 74 psychiatrists with a written vignette based on Slater's "experiment." They claim that only three gave a diagnosis of psychotic depression. (We would note, however, that Slater's experiment has its own biases: We would guess that virtually every psychiatrist in the world is intimately familiar with the Rosenhan study, and Slater's study would immediately bring it to mind for most of the participants.)

The bottom line? Rosenhan put his finger on some important problems with mental hospitals and psychiatric diagnoses. But he did *not* prove that diagnoses of most mental patients are useless or completely unreliable. And, for our purposes, that conclusion makes the perfect transition to the next chapter, where we will study the treatment of mental disorders.

Chapter Summary

12.1 What Is Psychological Disorder?

Core Concept 12.1: The medical model takes a "disease" view, while psychology sees psychological disorder as an interaction of biological, mental, social, and behavioral factors.

Psychopathology is common in America. Three classic signs suggest severe psychological disorder: **hallucinations, delusions,** and *extreme affective disturbances.* But beyond these, the signs of disorder are more subtle, and a diagnosis depends heavily on clinical judgment.

Our modern conception of abnormality has evolved from attributing disorders to demon possession or imbalances of humors to the current **medical model,** which sees psychopathology as "illness" or "disease"—a perspective with which many psychologists disagree. The broader psychological model, the **social-cognitive-behavioral approach,** includes social, mental, and behavioral factors, as well as biological ones. Aside from the three classic signs of disorder, psychopathology is usually judged by the degree to which a person exhibits distress, maladaptiveness, irrationality, unpredictability, and unconventionality.

It is normal to experience symptoms of psychological disorders on occasion, so psychology students are often unjustifiably concerned that they have a mental disorder. Frequent signs of abnormality, however, should prompt a consult with a mental health professional.

The plea of **insanity** is often misunderstood by the public, because it is infrequently used and even more infrequently successful. The term *insanity* is a legal term, not a psychological or psychiatric diagnosis.

Affect (p. 532)

Delusions (p. 532)

Hallucinations (p. 532)

Insanity (p. 537)

Medical model (p. 533)

Psychopathology (p. 531)

Social–cognitive–behavioral approach (p. 535)

MyPsychLab Resources 12.1:

Watch: Current Diagnostic Models: Sue Mineka

12.2 How Are Psychological Disorders Classified in the *DSM-IV*?

Core Concept 12.2: The *DSM-IV,* the most widely used system, classifies disorders by their mental and behavioral symptoms.

The most widely used system for classifying mental disorders is the *DSM-IV,* which derives from psychiatry and has a bias toward the medical model. The *DSM-IV* recognizes more than 300 specific disorders, categorized by symptoms rather than by cause. It has no category for "normal" functioning. Unlike its predecessor, it does not use the term **neurosis;** the term **psychosis** is restricted to a loss of contact with reality.

Among the *DSM-IV* categories are the **mood disorders** *(affective disorders),* which involve emotional disturbances. **Major depression** is the most common affective disorder, while **bipolar disorder** occurs less commonly. Strong gender differences have also been noted. All mental disorders are believed to have some biological basis.

The *anxiety disorders* include **generalized anxiety disorder, panic disorder, phobias,** and **obsessive–compulsive disorder.** Although they may have some basis in temperament, they are also affected by experience. The **somatoform disorders** involve the mind–body relationship in various ways. Persons with **conversion disorder** have physical symptoms but no organic disease, while those with **hypochondriasis** suffer from exaggerated concern about illness.

The controversial **dissociative disorders** include **dissociative amnesia, dissociative fugue, depersonalization disorder,** and **dissociative identity disorder.** All disrupt the integrated functioning of memory, consciousness, or personal identity. Among the psychotic disorders, **schizophrenia** is the most common. It is characterized by extreme distortions in perception, thinking, emotion, behavior, and language. It has five forms: *disorganized, catatonic, paranoid, undifferentiated,* and *residual.* Evidence for the causes of schizophrenia has been found in a variety of factors including genetics, abnormal brain structure, and biochemistry.

The *DSM-IV* also lists a variety of *developmental disorders,* including **autism, dyslexia,** and **attention-deficit hyperactivity disorder.** There are significant gender differences across the spectrum of mental disorder, especially in depression and antisocial personality disorder.

The most common disorders of all are classified in the *DSM-IV* as the *adjustment disorders* and "other conditions that may be a focus of clinical attention." These include a wide range of problems in living. **Shyness** is a widespread problem—and a treatable one—but it is not officially a disorder, unless it goes to the extreme of a *social phobia* or *avoidant personality disorder.*

Agoraphobia (p. 545)

Anxiety disorders (p. 544)

Attention-deficit hyperactivity disorder (ADHD) (p. 556)

Autism (p. 555)

Bipolar disorder (p. 544)

Conversion disorder (p. 548)

Depersonalization disorder (p. 550)

Diathesis–stress hypothesis (p. 555)

Dissociative amnesia (p. 549)

Dissociative disorders (p. 549)

Dissociative fugue (p. 550)

Dissociative identity disorder (p. 550)

DSM-IV (p. 539)

Dyslexia (p. 556)

Generalized anxiety disorder (p. 545)

Hypochondriasis (p. 549)

Learned helplessness (p. 543)

Major depression (p. 540)

Mood disorders (p. 540)

Neurosis (p. 539)

Obsessive–compulsive disorder (p. 547)

Panic disorder (p. 545)

Phobias (p. 546)

Preparedness hypothesis (p. 547)

Psychosis (p. 539)

Schizophrenia (p. 551)

Seasonal affective disorder (SAD) (p. 542)

Shyness (p. 557)

Somatoform disorders (p. 547)

MyPsychLab Resources 12.2:

Watch: Bipolar Disorder: Craig

Watch: Donald: Panic Disorder

Watch: Panic Disorder: Jerry

Watch: Anxiety Disorders

Watch: Schizophrenia: Larry

Watch: Depression: Helen

● ●

12.3 What Are the Consequences of Labeling People?

Core Concept 12.3: Ideally, accurate diagnoses lead to proper treatments, but diagnoses may also become labels that depersonalize individuals and ignore the social and cultural contexts in which their problems arise.

Labeling someone as psychologically or mentally disordered is ultimately a matter of human judgment. Yet even professional judgments can be biased by prejudices. Those labeled with psychological disorders may suffer **depersonalization** in ways that most physically ill people do not.

Culture has an effect on whether a behavior is called normal, abnormal, or merely unusual, although cross-cultural research suggests that people everywhere distinguish between psychotic individuals and those whom they label shamans, prophets, or visionaries.

Ideally, accurate diagnoses lead to proper treatments, but diagnoses may also become labels that depersonalize individuals and ignore the social and cultural contexts in which their problems arise. Readers are cautioned not to apply diagnostic labels to people.

Depersonalization (p. 559)

Ecological model (p. 559)

Labeling (p. 558)

Watch the following video by logging into MyPsychLab (www.mypsychlab.com). After you have watched the videos, complete the activities that follow.

PROGRAM 21: PSYCHOPATHOLOGY

PROGRAM REVIEW

1. Psychopathology is defined as the study of
   a. organic brain disease.
   b. perceptual and cognitive illusions.
   c. clinical measures of abnormal functioning.
   d. mental disorders.

2. What is the key criterion for identifying a person as having a mental disorder?
   a. The person has problems.
   b. The person's functioning is clearly abnormal.
   c. The person's ideas challenge the status quo.
   d. The person makes other people feel uncomfortable.

3. Which is true about mental disorders?
   a. They are extremely rare, with less than one-tenth of 1% of Americans suffering from any form of mental illness.
   b. They are not that uncommon, with about one-fifth of Americans suffering from some form of recently diagnosed mental disorder.
   c. The number of Americans with psychotic disorders fluctuates with the calendar, with more cases of psychosis during the weekends than during weekdays.
   d. The actions of people with mental disorders are unpredictable.

4. Fran is a mental health specialist who has a Ph.D. in psychology. She would be classified as a
   a. psychiatrist.
   b. clinical psychologist.
   c. social psychologist.
   d. psychoanalyst.

5. What happened after David Rosenhan and his colleagues were admitted to mental hospitals by pretending to have hallucinations and then behaved normally?
   a. Their sanity was quickly observed by the staff.
   b. It took several days for their deception to be realized.

   c. In most cases, the staff disagreed with each other about these "patients."
   d. Nobody ever detected their sanity.

6. Olivia is experiencing dizziness, muscle tightness, shaking, and tremors. She is feeling apprehensive. These symptoms most resemble those found in cases of
   a. anxiety disorders.
   b. affective disorders.
   c. psychoses.
   d. schizophrenia.

7. Prior to the eighteenth century, people with psychological problems were most likely to be
   a. placed in a mental hospital.
   b. tortured, trained, or displayed for public amusement.
   c. encouraged to pursue the arts.
   d. treated through psychotherapy only.

8. When Sigmund Freud studied patients with anxiety, he determined that their symptoms were caused by
   a. actual childhood abuse, both physical and sexual.
   b. imbalances in body chemistry.
   c. childhood conflicts that had been repressed.
   d. cognitive errors in the way patients viewed the world.

9. Which of the following statements about clinical depression is true?
   a. Most depressed people commit suicide.
   b. Depression is characterized by excessive elation of mood.
   c. Depression is often called the cancer of mental illness.
   d. In its milder forms, depression is experienced by almost everyone.

10. People lose touch with reality in cases of
    a. neurosis but not psychosis.
    b. psychosis but not neurosis.

c. both psychosis and neurosis.

d. all psychoses and some neuroses.

11. The term *neurosis* is no longer used by psychologists and psychiatrists as a diagnostic category because

a. it has been replaced by the term *psychosis*.

b. it is generally understood by everyone in our society.

c. it does not include chronic anxiety.

d. it is considered too general and imprecise.

12. Irving Gottesman and Fuller Torrey have been studying twins to learn more about schizophrenia. If the brain of a twin with schizophrenia is compared with the brain of a normal twin, the former has

a. less cerebrospinal fluid.

b. larger ventricles.

c. a larger left hemisphere.

d. exactly the same configuration as the latter.

13. For Teresa LaFromboise, the major issue influencing mental disorders among Native Americans is

a. the prevalence of genetic disorders.

b. alcohol's impact on family structure.

c. the effect of imposing white American culture.

d. isolation due to rural settings.

14. According to experts, what proportion of Americans suffer from some form of mental illness?

a. about one-fifth

b. less than one in ten thousand

c. about two-thirds

d. about one in a thousand

15. Which of the following people would argue that psychopathology is a myth?

a. Philippe Pinel

b. Thomas Szasz

c. Teresa LaFromboise

d. Sigmund Freud

16. What might a severe viral infection do to a woman who has a genetic predisposition toward schizophrenia?

a. make her schizophrenic

b. destroy the genetic marker and make her mentally more stable

c. redirect the predisposition toward a different class of mental illness

d. kill her with greater likelihood than if she did not have a predisposition toward mental illness

17. Which of the following has been nicknamed "the common cold of psychopathology" because of its frequency?

a. phobia

b. personality disorder

c. schizophrenia

d. depression

18. All of the following are typically true about schizophrenia, *except* that

a. less than one-third improve with treatment.

b. the people who have it are aware that they are mentally ill.

c. about 1% of the world's total population is schizophrenic.

d. it is associated with impaired thinking, emotion, and perception.

19. Who is credited as being the first to introduce the idea that insane people are ill?

a. Sigmund Freud

b. Jean Charcot

c. Emil Kraepelin

d. Philippe Pinel

20. Which of the following is characterized by boundless energy, optimism, and risk-taking behavior?

a. a manic episode

b. paranoid schizophrenia

c. anxiety disorders

d. depression

QUESTIONS TO CONSIDER

1. If a person is mentally ill and has violated the law, under what circumstances should he or she be considered responsible for the criminal actions? Under what circumstances should we consider the person to be rehabilitatable?

2. Why has the *DSM* been criticized?

3. Is homosexuality a deviant behavior?

4. Are standards for psychological health the same for men and women? Why are most patients women?

5. How can you tell whether your own behavior, anxieties, and moods are within normal limits or whether they signal mental illness?

ACTIVITIES

1. Collect the advice columns in the daily papers for a week or two (such as "Ann Landers" or "Dear Abby"). What kinds of problems do people write about? How often does the columnist refer people to a psychologist, psychiatrist, or other professional

for counseling? Why do people write to an anonymous person for advice about their problems?

2. Ask several people (who are not psychology professionals) to define the terms *emotionally ill, mentally ill,* and *insane.* Ask them to describe behaviors that characterize each term. Do some terms indicate more extreme behavior than others? How do their definitions compare with the ones in your text? What can you conclude about the attitudes and understanding of mental illness shown by the people you interviewed?

3. Read through the *DSM-IV-TR* with an eye toward seeing that it is a statistically based manual. The behaviors that define mental illness fall on the same continuum as those that define mental health. Notice whether there are any classifications within the *DSM-IV-TR* for which some of the criteria are a partial match to you.

Key Questions/ Chapter Outline	Core Concepts	Psychology Matters

13.1 **What Is Therapy?**

Entering Therapy

The Therapeutic Alliance and the Goals of Therapy

Therapy in Historical and Cultural Context

● Therapy for psychological disorders takes a variety of forms, but all involve some relationship focused on improving a person's mental, behavioral, or social functioning.

Paraprofessionals Do Therapy, Too

Some studies show that the therapist's level of training is not the main factor in therapeutic effectiveness.

13.2 **How Do Psychologists Treat Psychological Disorders?**

Insight Therapies

Behavior Therapies

Cognitive–Behavioral Therapy: A Synthesis

Evaluating the Psychological Therapies

● Psychologists employ two main forms of treatment, the insight therapies (focused on developing understanding of the problem) and the behavior therapies (focused on changing behavior through conditioning).

Where Do Most People Get Help?

A lot of therapy is done by friends, hairdressers, and bartenders.

13.3 **How Is the Biomedical Approach Used to Treat Psychological Disorders?**

Drug Therapy

Other Medical Therapies for Psychological Disorders

Hospitalization and the Alternatives

● Biomedical therapies seek to treat psychological disorders by changing the brain's chemistry with drugs, its circuitry with surgery, or its patterns of activity with pulses of electricity or powerful magnetic fields.

What Sort of Therapy Would You Recommend?

There is a wide range of therapeutic possibilities to discuss with a friend who asks for your recommendation.

13.4 **How Do the Psychological Therapies and Biomedical Therapies Compare?**

Depression: Psychological versus Medical Treatment

Anxiety Disorders: Psychological versus Medical Treatment

Schizophrenia: Psychological versus Medical Treatment

"The Worried Well": Not Everyone Needs Drugs

● While a combination of psychological and medical therapies is better than either one alone for treating some (but not all) mental disorders, most people who suffer from unspecified "problems in living" are best served by psychological treatment alone.

Using Psychology to Learn Psychology

Consider the ways in which therapy is like your college experience.

Critical Thinking Applied: **Evidence-Based Practice**

chapter *chapter* 13

therapies for psychological disorders

O ff and on, Derek had felt tired and unhappy for months, and he knew it was affecting not only his work but the relationship with his partner. Michele, a coworker and friend, tactfully suggested he seek professional help, but Derek was unsure where to turn. As many people do, he asked for a recommendation from another friend, who he knew had sought therapy three years ago. And that is how he ended up, a little apprehensively, at Dr. Sturm's office.

She was easy to talk to, it turned out, and it didn't take long for both of them to agree that Derek was depressed. After some more conversation about the nature of depression, Dr. Sturm said, "We have several treatment alternatives." She added, "The one in which I am trained is cognitive-behavioral therapy, which approaches depression as a learned problem to be treated by changing the way a person thinks about life events and interpersonal relationships. If we take that route, we will explore what is happening at work and at home that might trigger depressive episodes. I would also give you 'homework' every week—assignments designed to help you build on your strengths, rather than focusing on your weaknesses." "Just like school," she added with a little laugh.

569

"As a second option," she said, "I could refer you to a colleague who does psycho-dynamic therapy. If you choose that approach, you and Dr. Ewing would explore your past, looking for events that may have pushed you down the path to the feelings you are experiencing now. Essentially it would be a treatment aimed at bringing some unpleasant parts of your unconscious mind into the light of day.

"The other thing I could do is to arrange to get you some medication that has been proven effective in treating depression. It would probably be one of those anti-depressants, like Prozac, that you have seen advertised in magazines and on TV. The problem there is that it takes several weeks for them to have an effect. And, besides, I'm not sure they really treat the problems that keep making you feel depressed."

"Oh, yes," she added, "There are some additional medical options, such as electro-convulsive therapy—people often call it 'shock treatment,' but I don't think it is indicated in your case."

"Just hearing that makes me feel better," Derek sighed. "So, the choice is between drugs and psychological therapy?"

"Or perhaps a combination of the two," replied Dr. Sturm.

"How do I decide?"

PROBLEM: **What is the best treatment for Derek's depression: psychological therapy, drug therapy, or both? More broadly, the problem is this: How do we decide among the available therapies for any of the mental disorders?**

Despite the diversity of approaches that Dr. Sturm and her colleagues bring to their work, the overwhelming majority of people who enter **therapy** receive significant help. Not everyone becomes a success case, of course. Some people wait too long, until their problems become intractable. Some do not end up with the right sort of therapy for their problems. And, unfortunately, many people who could benefit from therapy do not have access to it because of financial constraints. Still, the development of a wide range of effective therapies is one of the success stories in modern psychology.

In this next-to-last chapter of our journey together through psychology, we begin an overview of therapy by considering what therapy is, who seeks it, what sorts of problems they bring to it, and who administers it. Here we will also see how therapeutic practices have been influenced by history and culture. In the second section of the chapter, we will consider the major types of psychological treatments currently used and how well they work. Then we will look at medical treatments for mental disorders, including drug therapy, hospitalization, psychosurgery, and "shock treatment." In the final parts of the chapter, we will take a critical look at two of the major unresolved issues in the field of therapy, the question of drugs versus psychotherapy and the divisive problem of restricting therapy to demonstrably effective techniques.

As you read through this chapter, we hope you will weigh the advantages and disadvantages of each therapy. Keep in mind, too, that you may sometime be asked by a friend or relative to use what you, like Derek, have learned here to recommend an appropriate therapy. It's even possible that you may sometime need to select a therapist for yourself.

Therapy   A general term for any treatment process; in psychology and psychiatry, therapy refers to a variety of psychological and biomedical techniques aimed at dealing with mental disorders or coping with problems of living.

13.1 KEY QUESTION
WHAT IS THERAPY?

When you think of "therapy," chances are that a stereotype pops into mind, absorbed from countless cartoons and movies: a "neurotic" patient lying on the analyst's couch, with a bearded therapist sitting by the patient's head, scribbling notes and making interpretations. In fact, this is a scene from classic Freudian psychoanalysis, which is a rarity today, although it dominated the first half of the 20th century.

The reality of modern therapy differs from the old stereotype on several counts. First, most therapists don't have their patients (or *clients*) lie on a couch. Second, people now seek therapeutic help for a wide range of problems besides the serious *DSM-IV* disorders. People also go to counselors or therapists for help in making difficult choices, dealing with academic problems, and coping with losses or unhappy relationships. And here's a third way in which the popular image of therapy is mistaken: Some forms of therapy now involve as much action as they do talk and interpretation—as you will see shortly.

At first, the therapeutic menu may appear to offer a bewildering list of choices, involving talk and interpretation, behavior modification, drugs, and, in some cases, even "shock treatment," or brain surgery. No matter what form therapy takes, however, there is one constant, as our Core Concept suggests:

> **Therapy for psychological disorders takes a variety of forms, but all involve some relationship focused on improving a person's mental, behavioral, or social functioning.**

core concept

In this chapter, as we examine a sample from the therapeutic universe, we will see that each form of therapy is based on different assumptions about mental disorder. Yet all involve relationships designed to change a person's functioning in some way. Let's begin our exploration of therapy by looking at the variety of people who enter treatment and the problems they bring with them to the therapeutic relationship.

Entering Therapy

Why would you go into therapy? Why would anyone? Most often, people enter therapy when they have a problem that they are unable to resolve by themselves. They may seek therapy on their own initiative, or they may be advised to do so by family, friends, a physician, or a coworker.

Obviously, you don't have to be declared "crazy" to enter therapy. But you may be called either a "patient" or a "client." Practitioners who take a biological or medical-model approach to treatment commonly use the term *patient*, while the term *client* is usually used by professionals who think of psychological disorders not as mental *illnesses* but as *problems in living* (Rogers, 1951; Szasz, 1961).

CONNECTION • CHAPTER 12
The *medical model* assumes that mental disorders are similar to physical diseases.

Access to therapy can be affected by several factors. People who have money or adequate health insurance can get therapy easily. For the poor, especially poor ethnic minorities, economic obstacles block access to professional mental health care (Bower, 1998d; Nemecek, 1999). Another problem can be lack of qualified therapists. In many communities, it is still much easier to get help for physical health problems than for psychological problems. Even the nature of a person's psychological problems can interfere with getting help. An individual with agoraphobia, for example, finds it hard, even impossible, to leave home to seek therapy. Similarly, paranoid persons may not seek help because they don't trust mental health professionals. Obviously, many problems remain to be solved before all those who need therapy can get it.

The Therapeutic Alliance and the Goals of Therapy

Sometimes you only need to talk out a problem with a sympathetic friend or family member, perhaps to "hear yourself think" or to receive reassurance that you are still worthwhile or likeable. But friends and family not only lack the training to deal with difficult mental problems; they also have needs and agendas of their own that can interfere with helping you. In fact, they may sometimes be part of the problem. For many reasons, then, it may be appropriate to seek the help of a professionally trained therapist. You might also want professional help if you wish to keep your problems and concerns confidential. In all these ways, a professional relationship with a therapist differs from friendship or kinship.

What Are the Components of Therapy?   In nearly all forms of therapy there is some sort of *relationship*, or **therapeutic alliance**, between the therapist and the patient/client seeking assistance—as our Core Concept indicates. (We must admit that there are computer-therapy programs, where the idea of a "relationship" is stretching the point.) Trust is one of the essential ingredients of a good therapeutic alliance. You and your therapist must be able to work together as allies, on the same side and toward the same goals, joining forces to cope with and solve the problems that have brought you to therapy (Horvath & Luborsky, 1993). And, as clinicians have become more aware of gender and ethnic diversity among their clientele, research has shown that the most effective therapists are those who can connect with people in the context of their own culture and native language (Griner & Smith, 2006).

In addition to the relationship between therapist and client, the therapy process typically involves the following steps:

1. *Identifying the problem.* This may mean merely agreeing on a simple description of circumstances or feelings to be changed, or, in the case of a *DSM-IV* disorder, this step may lead to a formal diagnosis about what is wrong.

2. *Identifying the cause of the problem or the conditions that maintain the problem.* In some forms of therapy, this involves searching the past, especially childhood, for the source of the patient's or client's discomfort. Alternatively, other forms of therapy emphasize the present causes—that is, the conditions that are keeping the problem alive.

3. *Deciding on and carrying out some form of treatment.* This step requires selecting a specific type of therapy designed to minimize or eliminate the troublesome symptoms. The exact treatment will depend on the problem and on the therapist's orientation and training.

Who Does Therapy?   Although more people seek out therapy now than in the past, they usually turn to trained mental health professionals only when their psychological problems become severe or persist for extended periods. And when they do, they usually turn to one of seven main types of professional helpers: counseling psychologists, clinical psychologists, psychiatrists, psychoanalysts, psychiatric nurse practitioners, clinical (psychiatric) social workers, or pastoral counselors. The differences among these specialties are detailed in Table 13.1. As you examine that table, note that each specialty has its own area of expertise. For example, in most states the only therapists who are licensed to prescribe drugs are physicians (including psychiatrists) and psychiatric nurse practitioners.

Currently, through their professional organizations, clinical psychologists are seeking to obtain prescription privileges. Past APA President Robert Sternberg (2003) made the following argument:

Psychologists, like other professionals, once viewed physical and psychological disorders as relatively distinct. No longer. We now know that physical and psychological symptoms are highly interactive. Some practicing psychol-

Therapeutic alliance   The relationship between the therapist and the client, with both parties working together to help the client deal with psychological or behavioral issues.

TABLE 13.1	Types of Mental Health Care Professionals	
Professional title	**Specialty and common work settings**	**Credentials and qualifications**
Counseling psychologist	Provides help in dealing with the common problems of normal living, such as relationship problems, child rearing, occupational choice, and school problems. Typically counselors work in schools, clinics, or other institutions.	Depends on the state: typically at least a master's in counseling, but more commonly a PhD (Doctor of Philosophy), EdD (Doctor of Education), or PsyD (Doctor of Psychology)
Clinical psychologist	Trained primarily to work with those who have more severe disorders, but may also work with clients having less severe problems. Usually in private practice or employed by mental health agencies or by hospitals. Not typically licensed to prescribe drugs.	Usually required to hold PhD or PsyD; often an internship and state certification required.
Psychiatrist	A specialty of medicine; deals with severe mental problems—most often by prescribing drugs. May be in private practice or employed by clinics or mental hospitals.	MD (Doctor of Medicine); may be required to be certified by medical specialty board
Psychoanalyst	Practitioners of Freudian therapy. Usually in private practice.	MD (some practitioners have doctorates in psychology, but most are psychiatrists who have taken additional training in psychoanalysis).
Psychiatric nurse practitioner	A nursing specialty; licensed to prescribe drugs for mental disorders. May work in private practice or in clinics and hospitals	Requires RN (Registered Nurse) credential, plus special training in treating mental disorders and prescribing drugs.
Clinical or psychiatric social worker	Social workers with a specialty in dealing with mental disorders, especially from the viewpoint of the social and environmental context of the problem.	MSW (Master of Social Work)
Pastoral counselor	A member of a religious order or ministry who specializes in treatment of psychological disorders. Combines spiritual guidance with practical counseling.	Varies

ogists may believe, therefore, that to treat the whole person, they need to supplement psychotherapy with medications. Indeed, the biopsychosocial model adopted by many psychologists is consistent with an integration of kinds of treatments. (p. 5)

Already, a few military psychologists have undergone training that allows them to prescribe drugs for mental disorders to military personnel (Dittmann, 2004). And in 2002, New Mexico became the first state to grant prescription privileges to civilian psychologists who have completed a rigorous training program, including 850 hours of course work and supervised internship (Dittmann, 2003). Similar legislation has been introduced in more than a dozen other states. Nevertheless, prescription privileges for psychologists remain a highly political issue, hotly contested by the medical profession (Clay, 1998). Surprising, even some clinical psychologists oppose prescription privileges, fearing that psychology will "sell its soul" to serve a public that demands drug therapy. Said former APA President, George Albee (2006):

The current drive for people who are in practice to become drug prescribers is a matter of survival. Society has been sold the fallacy that mental/emotional disorders are all brain diseases that must be treated with drugs. The only way for psychology practitioners to survive is to embrace this invalid nonsense. (p. 3)

In this painting from the 1730s, we see the chaos of a cell in the London hospital St. Mary of Bethlehem. Here, the upper classes have paid to see the horrors, the fiddler who entertains, and the mental patients chained, tortured, and dehumanized. The chaos of Bethlehem eventually became synonymous with the corruption of its name—Bedlam.

Whether you agree with Sternberg or Albee, it appears that the era of prescription privileges for properly trained psychologists is coming. It remains to be seen how that will change the face of psychology.

Therapy in Historical and Cultural Context

How you deal with mental disorder depends on how you *think* about mental disorder. If you believe, for example, that mental problems are *diseases,* you will treat them differently from another person who believes they indicate a flaw in one's character or a sign of influence by evil spirits. The way society has treated people with mental disorders has always depended on its prevailing beliefs.

History of Therapy   As we saw in the previous chapter, people in medieval Europe interpreted mental disorder as the work of devils and demons. In that context, then, the job of the "therapist" was to perform an exorcism or to "beat the devil" out of the disordered person—to make the body an inhospitable place for a spirit or demon. In more recent times, however, reformers have urged that the mentally ill be placed in institutions called asylums, where they could be shielded from the stresses of the world—and from the brutal "therapies" that had been all too customary. Unfortunately, the ideal of the insane asylums was not often realized.

One of the most infamous of the asylums was also one of the first: Bethlehem Hospital in London, where for a few pence on the weekend sightseers could go to observe the inmates, who often put on a wild and noisy "show" for the curious audience. As a result, "Bedlam," the shortened term Londoners used for "Bethlehem," became a word used to describe any noisy, chaotic place.

In most asylums, inmates received, at best, only custodial care. At worst, they were neglected or put in cruel restraints, such as cages and straightjackets. Some even continued to receive beatings, cold showers, and other forms of abuse. It's not hard to guess that such treatment rarely produced improvement in people suffering from psychological disorders.

Modern Approaches to Therapy   Modern mental health professionals have abandoned the old demon model and frankly abusive treatments in favor of therapies based on psychological and biological theories of mind and behavior. Yet, as we will see, even modern professionals disagree on the exact causes and the most appropriate treatments—a state of the art that gives us a wide variety of therapies from which to choose. To help you get an overview of this cluttered therapeutic landscape, here is a preview of things to come.

The **psychological therapies** are often collectively called simply *psychotherapy.*[1] They focus on changing disordered thoughts, feelings, and behavior

---

Psychological therapy   Therapy based on psychological principles (rather than on the biomedical approach); often called "psychotherapy."

[1]No sharp distinction exists between counseling and psychotherapy, although in practice *counseling* usually refers to a shorter process, more likely to be focused on a specific problem, while *psychotherapy* generally involves a longer-term and wider-ranging exploration of issues.

using psychological techniques (rather than biomedical interventions). And they come in two main forms. One, called *insight therapy*, focuses on helping people understand their problems and change their thoughts, motives, or feelings. The other, known as *behavior therapy*, focuses primarily on behavior change. More recently, a combination of the two, *cognitive–behavioral therapy*, has been developed.

In contrast with psychotherapy, the **biomedical therapies** focus on treating mental problems by changing the underlying biology of the brain, using a variety of drugs, including antidepressants, tranquilizers, and stimulants. Occasionally the brain may be treated directly with electromagnetic stimulation or even surgery. Sometimes, therapists use a combination approach, involving both drugs and psychotherapy.

Disorder and Therapy in a Cultural Context

Ways of thinking about and treating mental disorder vary widely across cultures (Matsumoto, 1996). People in individualistic Western cultures (that is, from Europe and North America) generally regard psychological disorders to be the result of disease processes, abnormal genetics, distorted thinking, unhealthy environments, or stressors. But collectivist cultures often have quite different perspectives (Triandis, 1990; Zaman, 1992). Asian societies may regard mental disorder as a disconnect between the person and the group. Likewise, many Africans believe that mental disorder results when an individual becomes estranged from nature and from the community, including the community of ancestral spirits (Nobles, 1976; Sow, 1977). In such cultures, treating mentally disturbed individuals by removing them from society is unthinkable. Instead, healing takes place in a social context, emphasizing a distressed person's beliefs, family, work, and life environment. An African use of group support in therapy has developed into a procedure called "network therapy," where a patient's entire network of relatives, coworkers, and friends becomes involved in the treatment (Lambo, 1978).

In many places around the world, the treatments of both mental and physical problems are also bound up with religion and the supernatural—much as in medieval Europe—although their treatments are not usually so harsh. Had Derek been in such a culture, he would undoubtedly have received treatment from a sorcerer or *shaman* who was assumed to have special mystical powers. His therapy would have involved ceremonies and rituals that bring emotional intensity and meaning into the healing process. Combined with the use of symbols, these rituals connect the individual sufferer, the shaman, and the society to supernatural forces to be won over in the battle against madness (Devereux, 1981; Wallace, 1959).

PSYCHOLOGYMATTERS
Paraprofessionals Do Therapy, Too

Does the best therapy always require a highly trained (and expensive) professional? Or can **paraprofessionals**— persons who may have received on-the-job training, in place of graduate training and certification—be effective therapists? If you are seeking treatment, these questions are important because hospitals, clinics, and agencies are increasingly turning to paraprofessionals as a cost-cutting measure: Those who lack full professional credentials can be hired at a fraction of the cost of those with professional degrees. They are often called "aides" or "counselors" (although many counselors do have professional credentials).

Surprisingly, a review of the literature has found no substantial differences in the effectiveness of the two groups across a wide spectrum of psychological problems (Christensen & Jacobson, 1994). This is good news in the sense that the need for mental health services is far greater than the number of professional therapists can possibly provide. And, because paraprofessional therapists can be

Biomedical therapy Treatment that focuses on altering the brain, especially with drugs, psychosurgery, or electroconvulsive therapy.

Paraprofessional Individual who has received on-the-job training (and, in some cases, undergraduate training) in mental health treatment in lieu of graduate education and full professional certification.

effective, highly trained professionals may be freed for other roles, including prevention and community education programs, assessment of patients, training and supervision of paraprofessionals, and research. The reader should be cautioned about overinterpreting this finding, however. Professionals and paraprofessionals have been found to be equivalent only in the realm of the insight therapies, which we will discuss in a moment (Zilbergeld, 1986). Such differences have not yet been demonstrated in the areas of behavior therapies, which require extensive knowledge of operant and classical conditioning and of social learning theory.

CheckYourUnderstanding

1. **RECALL:** People in individualistic cultures often view mental disorder as a problem originating in a person's mind. In contrast, people in collectivist cultures are more likely to see mental disorder as a symptom of a disconnect between the person and _____.

2. **RECALL:** How is a therapist different from a friend?

3. **APPLICATION:** Which type of therapist would be most likely to treat depression by searching for the cause in the unconscious mind?

4. **UNDERSTANDING THE CORE CONCEPT:** In what respect are all therapies alike?
   a. All may be legally administered only by licensed, trained professionals.
   b. All make use of insight into a patient's problems.
   c. All involve the aim of altering the mind, behavior, or social relationships.
   d. All focus on discovering the underlying cause of the patient's problem, which is often hidden in the unconscious mind.

13.2 KEY QUESTION
HOW DO PSYCHOLOGISTS TREAT PSYCHOLOGICAL DISORDERS?

In the United States and most other Western nations, the sort of therapy Derek receives would depend on whether he had gone to a medical or psychological therapist. By choosing a psychologist like Dr. Sturm, he would almost certainly receive one of two main types of therapy described by our Core Concept:

core concept | **Psychologists employ two main forms of treatment, the insight therapies (focused on developing understanding of the problem) and the behavior therapies (focused on changing behavior through conditioning).**

The insight therapies, we shall see, were the first truly psychological treatments developed, and for a long time they were the only psychological therapies available. In recent years they have been joined by the behavior therapies, which are now among the most effective tools we have. But it is with the insight therapies that we begin.

Insight Therapies

The **insight therapies** attempt to change people on the *inside*—changing the way they think and feel. Sometimes called *talk therapies,* these methods share the assumption that distressed persons need to develop an understanding of the disordered thoughts, emotions, and motives that underlie their mental difficulties.

The insight therapies come in dozens of different "brands," but all aim at revealing and changing a patient's disturbed mental processes through discussion and interpretation. Some, like Freudian *psychoanalysis,* assume that problems lie hidden deep in the unconscious, so they employ elaborate and time-consuming techniques to draw them out. Others, like Carl Rogers's *nondirective therapy,*

Insight therapy Psychotherapy in which the therapist helps the patient/client understand (gain insight into) his or her problems.

minimize the importance of the unconscious and look for problems in the ways people consciously think and interact with each other. We have space here to sample only a few of the most influential ones, beginning with the legendary methods developed by Sigmund Freud himself.

Freudian Psychoanalysis   In the classic Freudian view, psychological problems arise from tension created in the unconscious mind by forbidden impulses and threatening memories. Therefore, Freudian therapy, known as **psychoanalysis,** probes the unconscious in the attempt to bring these issues into the "light of day"—that is, into consciousness, where they can be rendered harmless. The major goal of psychoanalysis, then, is to reveal and interpret the unconscious mind's contents.

To get at unconscious material, Freud sought ways to get around the defenses the ego has erected to protect itself. One ingenious method called for *free association,* by which the patient would relax and talk about whatever came to mind, while the therapist would listen, ever alert for veiled references to unconscious needs and conflicts. Another method involved *dream interpretation,* which you may recall from Chapter 3.

With these and other techniques, the psychoanalyst gradually develops a clinical picture of the problem and proceeds to help the patient understand the unconscious causes for symptoms. To give you the flavor of this process, we offer Freud's interpretation of a fascinating case involving a 19-year-old girl diagnosed with "obsessional neurosis" (now listed in the *DSM-IV* as *obsessive–compulsive disorder*). Please bear in mind that Freud's ideas no longer represent the mainstream of either psychology or psychiatry, but they remain important because many of Freud's techniques have carried over into newer forms of therapy. They are also important because many of Freud's concepts, such as *ego, repression, the unconscious, identification,* and *the Oedipus complex,* have become part of our everyday vocabulary. The following case, then—in which you may find Freud's interpretations shocking—will give you a sense of the way psychotherapy began about a century ago.

When Freud's patient entered psychoanalysis, she was causing her parents distress with a strange bedtime ritual that she performed each night. As part of this obsessional ritual, she first stopped the large clock in her room and removed other smaller clocks, including her wrist watch. Then, she placed all vases and flower pots together on her writing table, so—in her "neurotic" way of thinking—they could not fall and break during the night. Next, she assured that the door of her room would remain half open by placing various objects in the doorway. After these precautions, she turned her attention to the bed, where she was careful to assure that the bolster did not touch the headboard and a pillow must lie diagonally in the center of the bolster. Then, she shook the eiderdown in the quilt until all the feathers sank to the foot-end, after which she meticulously redistributed them evenly again. And, finally, she would crawl into bed and attempt to sleep with her head precisely in the center of the diagonal pillow.

The ritual did not proceed smoothly, however. She would do and then redo first one and then another aspect of the ritual, anxious that she had not performed everything properly—although she acknowledged to Freud that all aspects of her nightly precautions were irrational. The result was that it took the girl about two hours to get ready for bed each night.

Before you read Freud's interpretation, you might think about how you would make sense of such strange behaviors. Now then, in Freud's own words (1965/1920), here is the psychoanalytic interpretation of the case:

> The patient gradually learnt to understand that she banished clocks and watches from her room at night because they were symbols of the female genitals. Clocks, which we know may have other symbolic meanings besides this, acquire this significance of a genital organ by their relation to periodical processes and regular intervals. A woman may be heard to boast that

Insight Therapies: Freudian psychoanalysis
- Neo-Freudian therapies
- Humanistic therapies
- Cognitive therapies
- Group therapies

CONNECTION • CHAPTER 12

The *ego defense mechanisms* include repression, regression, projection, denial, rationalization, reaction formation, displacement, and sublimation.

Sigmund Freud's study, including the famous couch (right), is housed in London's Freud Museum. The 82-year-old Freud fled to London in 1938 upon the Nazi occupation of Austria and died there the following year.

Psychoanalysis   The form of psychodynamic therapy developed by Sigmund Freud. The goal of psychoanalysis is to release conflicts and memories from the unconscious.

menstruation occurs in her as regularly as clockwork. Now this patient's special fear was that the ticking of the clocks would disturb her during sleep. The ticking of a clock is comparable to the throbbing of the clitoris in sexual excitation. This sensation, which was distressing to her, had actually on several occasions wakened her from sleep; now her fear of an erection of the clitoris expressed itself by the imposition of a rule to remove all going clocks and watches far away from her during the night. Flower-pots and vases are, like all receptacles, also symbols of the female genitals. Precautions to prevent them from falling and breaking during the night are therefore not lacking in meaning. . . . Her precautions against the vases breaking signified a rejection of the whole complex concerned with virginity. . . .

One day she divined the central idea of her ritual when she suddenly understood her rule not to let the bolster touch the back of the bed. The bolster had always seemed a woman to her, she said, and the upright back of the bedstead a man. She wished therefore, by a magic ceremony, as it were, to keep man and woman apart; that is to say, to separate the parents and prevent intercourse from occurring. . . .

If the bolster was a woman, then the shaking of the eiderdown till all the feathers were at the bottom, making a protuberance there, also had a meaning. It meant impregnating a woman; she did not neglect, though to obliterate the pregnancy again, for she had for years been terrified that intercourse between her parents might result in another child and present her with a rival. On the other hand, if the large bolster meant the mother then the small pillow could only represent the daughter. . . . The part of the man (the father) she thus played herself and replaced the male organ by her own head.

Horrible thoughts, you will say, to run in the mind of a virgin girl. I admit that; but do not forget that I have not invented these ideas, only exposed them. . . . (pp. 277–279)

This case shows how Freud used the patient's symptoms as symbolic signposts pointing to underlying and unconscious conflicts, desires, and memories. In the course of treatment, then, he would help the patient understand how her unconscious problems have been changed into her obsessive rituals by her ego defense mechanisms, such as *displacement* (by which the girl's fears about losing virginity were displaced into the ritual of protecting the vases in her bedroom). But whatever a patient's symptoms might be, the ego struggles to keep the "real" problem blocked from consciousness by means of the defense mechanism of *repression*. A psychoanalyst's main task, then, is to help a patient break through the barriers of repression and bring threatening thoughts to awareness. By doing so, the patient gains insight into the relationship between the current symptoms and the repressed conflicts. In the final stage of psychoanalysis, patients learn how the relationship they have established with the therapist reflects unresolved conflicts, especially problems they had with their parents. This projection of parental attributes onto the therapist is called *transference,* and so the final phase of therapy is known as the **analysis of transference.** According to psychoanalytic theory, the last step in recovery occurs when patients are finally released from the unconscious troubles established long ago in the relationship with their parents during early childhood (Munroe, 1955).

Neo-Freudian Psychodynamic Therapies
Please pardon us for doing a bit of analysis on Freud: He obviously had a flair for the dramatic, and he also possessed a powerful, charismatic personality—or, as he himself might have said, a strong ego. Accordingly, Freud encouraged his disciples to debate the principles of psychoanalysis, but he would tolerate no fundamental changes in his doctrines. This inevitably led to conflicts with some of his equally strong-willed followers, such as Alfred Adler, Carl Jung, and Karen Horney, who eventually broke with Freud to establish their own schools of therapy.

CONNECTION • CHAPTER 10
Repression is Freud's ego defense mechanism that causes forgetting by blocking off threatening memories in the unconscious.

Analysis of transference The Freudian technique of analyzing and interpreting the patient's relationship with the therapist, based on the assumption that this relationship mirrors unresolved conflicts in the patient's past.

In general the neo-Freudian renegades retained many of Freud's basic ideas and techniques, while adding some and modifying others. In the true psychodynamic tradition, the **neo-Freudian psychodynamic therapies** have retained Freud's emphasis on motivation. Most now have abandoned the psychoanalyst's couch and treat patients face-to-face. Most also see patients once a week for a few months, rather than several times a week for several years, as in classical psychoanalysis.

So how do the neo-Freudian therapists get the job done in a shorter time? Most have shifted their emphasis to *conscious* motivation—so they don't spend so much time probing for hidden conflicts and repressed memories. Most have also made a break with Freud on one or more of the following points:

- The significance of the self or ego (rather than the id)
- The influence of life experiences occurring after childhood (as opposed to Freud's emphasis on early-childhood experience)
- The role of social needs and interpersonal relationships (rather than sexual and aggressive desires)

And, as we saw in Chapter 10, each constructed a theory of disorder and therapy that had different emphases. We do not have space here to go into these approaches in greater detail, but let's briefly consider how a neo-Freudian therapist might have approached the case of the obsessive girl that Freud described. Most likely a modern psychodynamic therapist would focus on the current relationship between the girl and her parents, perhaps on whether she has feelings of inadequacy for which she is compensating by becoming the center of her parents' attention for two hours each night. And, instead of working so intensively with the girl, the therapist might well work with the parents on changing the way they deal with the problem. And what about Derek, whom we met at the beginning of the chapter? Again, a Freudian analyst would probe his early childhood memories for clues as to his depression. On the other hand, a modern psychodynamic therapist would be more likely to look for clues in his current relationships, assuming the cause to be social rather than sexual.

Humanistic Therapies In contrast with the psychodynamic emphasis on conflicting motives, the *humanistic* therapists believe that mental problems arise from low self-esteem, misguided goals, and unfulfilling relationships. Indeed, the primary symptoms for which college students seek therapy include feelings of alienation, failure to achieve all they feel they should, difficult relationships, and general dissatisfaction with their lives. Therapists often refer to these problems in everyday existence as *existential crises,* a term emphasizing how many human problems deal with questions about the meaning and purpose of one's existence. The humanistic psychologists have developed therapies aimed specifically at such problems.

Again, in contrast with the psychodynamic view, humanistic therapists believe that people are generally motivated by *healthy* needs for growth and psychological well-being. Thus, they dispute Freud's assumption of a personality divided into conflicting parts, dominated by a selfish id, and driven by hedonistic instincts and repressed conflicts. Instead, the humanists emphasize the concept of a whole person engaged in a continual process of growth and change. Thus, mental disorder occurs only when conditions interfere with normal development and produce low self-esteem. **Humanistic therapies,** therefore, attempt to help clients confront their problems by recognizing their own freedom, enhancing their self-esteem, and realizing their fullest potential (see Schneider & May, 1995). A humanistic therapist (if there had been one around a century ago) would probably have worked with Freud's patient to explore her self-concept and her feelings about her parents. As for Derek, a humanistic therapist might guess that his depression arose either from unsatisfying relationships or from a sense of personal inadequacy.

Neo-Freudian psychodynamic therapy Therapy for a mental disorder that was developed by psychodynamic theorists who embraced some of Freud's ideas but disagreed with others.

Humanistic therapy Treatment technique based on the assumption that people have a tendency for positive growth and self-actualization, which may be blocked by an unhealthy environment that can include negative self-evaluation and criticism from others.

Humanistic therapist Carl Rogers (right center) facilitates a therapy group.

Client-centered therapy, developed by Carl Rogers (1951, 1977), assumes that healthy development can be derailed by a conflict between one's desire for a positive self-image and criticism by self and others. This conflict creates anxiety and unhappiness. The task of Rogerian therapy, then, is to create a nurturing environment in which clients can work through their concerns and finally achieve self-respect and self-actualization.

One of the main techniques used by Rogerian therapists involves **reflection of feeling** (also called *reflective listening*) to help clients understand their emotions. With this technique, therapists paraphrase their clients' words, attempting to capture the emotional tone expressed and acting as a sort of psychological "mirror" in which clients can see themselves. Notice how the Rogerian therapist uses this technique in the following excerpt from a therapy session with a young woman (Rogers, 1951, p. 152):

CLIENT: It probably goes all the way back into my childhood. . . . My mother told me that I was the pet of my father. Although I never realized it—I mean, they never treated me as a pet at all. And other people always seemed to think I was sort of a privileged one in the family. . . . And as far as I can see looking back on it now, it's just that the family let the other kids get away with more than they usually did me. And it seems for some reason to have held me to a more rigid standard than they did the other children.

THERAPIST: You're not so sure you were a pet in any sense, but more that the family situation seemed to hold you to pretty high standards.

CLIENT: M-hm. That's just what has occurred to me; and that the other people could sorta make mistakes, or do things as children that were naughty . . . but Alice wasn't supposed to do those things.

THERAPIST: M-hm. With somebody else it would be just—oh, be a little naughtiness; but as far as you were concerned, it shouldn't be done.

CLIENT: That's really the idea I've had. I think the whole business of my standards . . . is one that I need to think about rather carefully, since I've been doubting for a long time whether I even have any sincere ones.

THERAPIST: M-hm. Not sure whether you really have any deep values which you are sure of.

CLIENT: M-hm. M-hm.

Note how most of the therapist's statements in this example paraphrased, or "reflected," what the client has just said.

To summarize, the Rogerian therapist assumes that people have basically healthy motives. These motives, however, can be stifled or perverted by social pressures and low self-esteem. The therapist's task is mainly to help the client clarify feelings that stand in the way of personal growth. This is accomplished within a non-threatening atmosphere of *genuineness, empathy,* and *unconditional positive regard*—that is, nonjudgmental acceptance and respect for the client.

Is such an approach effective, or is it merely a naive hope? In fact, it has scientific support. An American Psychological Association task force, charged with finding research-based practices that contribute to the effectiveness of therapy, found that the common factor in therapies that work were precisely the Rogerian qualities of *empathy, positive regard, genuineness,* and *feedback* (Ackerman et al., 2001).

Cognitive Therapies The insight therapies we have discussed so far focus primarily on people's emotions or motives. (See Figure 13.1.) **Cognitive therapy,** on the other hand, assumes that psychological problems arise from erroneous thinking and sees rational thinking as the key to positive therapeutic change (Butler et al., 2006). Cognitive therapy takes multiple forms, but we can give you some of its flavor with one example: Aaron Beck's cognitive therapy for depression.

Client-centered therapy A humanistic approach to treatment developed by Carl Rogers, emphasizing an individual's tendency for healthy psychological growth through self-actualization.

Reflection of feeling Carl Rogers's technique of paraphrasing the clients' words, attempting to capture the emotional tone expressed.

Cognitive therapy Emphasizes rational thinking (as opposed to subjective emotion, motivation, or repressed conflicts) as the key to treating mental disorder.

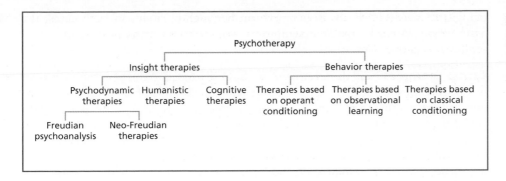

FIGURE 13.1
Types of Psychotherapy

Each of the two major branches of psychotherapy has many variations.

Beck, who was originally trained in classical psychoanalysis, broke with the Freudian tradition when he began noticing that the dreams and free associations of his depressed patients were filled with negative thoughts (Beck, 1976; Bowles, 2004). Commonly they would make such self-deprecating statements as, "Nobody would like me if they really knew me" and "I'm not smart enough to make it in this competitive school." Gradually Beck came to believe that depression occurs because of this negative self-talk. The therapist's job, then, is to help the client learn more positive ways of thinking.

Here's a sample of Beck's approach, taken from a therapy session with a college student of about Derek's age (Beck et al., 1979, pp. 145–146):

CLIENT: I get depressed when things go wrong. Like when I fail a test.

THERAPIST: How can failing a test make you depressed?

CLIENT: Well, if I fail, I'll never get into law school.

THERAPIST: Do you agree that the way you interpret the results of the test will affect you? You might feel depressed, you might have trouble sleeping, not feel like eating, and you might even wonder if you should drop out of the course.

CLIENT: I have been thinking that I wasn't going to make it. Yes, I agree.

THERAPIST: Now what did failing mean?

CLIENT: (tearful) That I couldn't get into law school.

THERAPIST: And what does that mean to you?

CLIENT: That I'm just not smart enough.

THERAPIST: Anything else?

CLIENT: That I can never be happy.

THERAPIST: And how do these thoughts make you feel?

CLIENT: Very unhappy.

THERAPIST: So it is the meaning of failing a test that makes you very unhappy. In fact, believing that you can never be happy is a powerful factor in producing unhappiness. So, you get yourself into a trap—by definition, failure to get into law school equals "I can never be happy."

As you can see from this exchange, the cognitive therapist helps the individual confront the destructive thoughts that support depression. Studies have shown that Beck's approach can be at least as effective in the treatment of depression as is medication (Antonuccio, 1995; Beck, 2005).

In Derek's case, a cognitive therapist would probably probe for negative self-talk that might be feeding the depression. And how might a cognitive therapist have approached Freud's 19-year-old obsessive patient? The focus would have been on irrational beliefs, such as the idea that flowerpots and vases could, by themselves, fall down in the night and break. A cognitive therapist would also challenge the assumption that something catastrophic might happen (such as not being able to sleep!) if she didn't perform her nightly ritual. In both cases, the assumption would be that the symptoms would disappear as positive thoughts replaced negative ones.

Group Therapies   All the treatments we have discussed to this point involve one-to-one relationships between a patient or client and therapist. However, **group therapy** can have value in treating a variety of concerns, particularly problems with social behavior and relationships. This can be done in many ways—with couples, families, or groups of people who have similar problems, such as depression or drug addiction. Usually they meet together once a week, but some innovative therapy groups are even available on the Internet (Davison et al., 2000). Most typically, group approaches employ a humanistic perspective, although psychodynamic groups are also common. Among the benefits of group therapy, clients have opportunities to observe and imitate new social behaviors in a forgiving, supportive atmosphere. We will touch on only a small sample of group therapies below: self-help groups and marital and family therapy.

Self-Help Support Groups   Perhaps the most noteworthy development in group therapy has been the surge of interest in **self-help support groups.** Thousands of such groups exist. Many are free, especially those that are not directed by a paid health care professional. Such groups give people a chance to meet under nonthreatening conditions to exchange ideas with others having similar problems and who are surviving and sometimes even thriving (Schiff & Bargal, 2000).

One of the oldest, Alcoholics Anonymous (AA), pioneered the self-help concept, beginning in the mid-1930s. Central to the original AA process is the concept of "12 steps" to recovery from alcohol addiction, based not on psychological theory but on the trial-and-error experience of early AA members. The first step begins with recognizing that one has become powerless over alcohol; the second affirms that faith in a "greater power" is necessary for recovery. In the remaining steps the individual seeks help from God and sets goals for making amends to those who have been hurt by his or her actions. Members are urged and helped by the group to accept as many of the steps as possible to maintain recovery.

The feminist consciousness-raising movement of the 1960s brought the self-help concept to a wider audience. As a result, self-help support groups now exist for an enormous range of problems, including:

- Managing life transition or other crises, such as divorce or death of a child
- Coping with physical and mental disorders, such as depression or heart attack
- Dealing with addictions and other uncontrolled behaviors, such as alcoholism, gambling, overeating, sexual excess, and drug dependency
- Handling the stress felt by relatives or friends of those who are dealing with addictions

Group therapy also makes valuable contributions to the treatment of terminally ill patients. The goals of such therapy are to help patients and their families live their lives as fully as possible, to cope realistically with impending death, and to adjust to the terminal illness (Adams, 1979; Yalom & Greaves, 1977). One general focus of such support groups for the terminally ill is to help them learn "how to live fully until you say goodbye" (Nungesser, 1990).

Couples and Family Therapy   Perhaps the best setting in which to learn about relationships is in a group of people struggling with relationships. *Couples therapy* (or counseling), for example, may involve one or more couples who are learning to clarify their communication patterns and improve the quality of their interaction (Napier, 2000). By seeing couples together, a therapist can help the partners identify the verbal and nonverbal styles they use to dominate, control, or confuse each other. The therapist then helps them to reinforce more desirable responses in the other and with-

Group therapy   Any form of psychotherapy done with more than one client/patient at a time. Group therapy is often done from a humanistic perspective.

Self-help support groups   Groups, such as Alcoholics Anonymous, that provide social support and an opportunity for sharing ideas about dealing with common problems. Such groups are typically organized and run by laypersons, rather than professional therapists.

draw from conflicts. Couples are also taught nondirective listening skills that help clarify and express feelings and ideas (Jacobson et al., 2000; Wheeler et al., 2001).

Couples therapy typically focuses not on personalities but on the *processes* of the relationship, particularly on patterns of conflict and communication (Gottman, 1994; Christensen & Heavey, 1999). Difficult as this may be, changing a couple's interaction patterns can be more effective than individual therapy with one individual at a time (Gottman, 1994, 1999).

In *family therapy*, the "client" is an entire family group, with each family member being treated as part of a *system of relationships* (Fishman, 1993). A family therapist helps troubled family members perceive the issues or patterns that are creating problems for them. The aim is on altering the interpersonal dynamics (interactions) among people (Foley, 1979; Schwebel & Fine, 1994). Family therapy can not only reduce tensions within a family, but it can also improve the functioning of individual members by helping them recognize their roles in the group. It has proved to be especially effective in the treatment of anorexia nervosa, depression, and other mood disorders, and even as a boon to families struggling with schizophrenia (Miklowitz, 2007).

Virginia Satir, a pioneer of family therapy, noted that the therapist, too, has roles to play during therapy. Among them, the therapist acts as an interpreter and clarifier of the interactions that take place in the therapy session, as well as an advisor, mediator, and referee (Satir, 1983; Satir et al., 1991). As in couples therapy, family therapy focuses on the *situational* rather than the *dispositional* aspects of a problem. That is, the therapist helps family members look at how they interact. So, the therapist might point out how one family member's unhappiness affects everyone's feelings and relationships—rather than seeking to blame someone as "the problem." The goal of a family therapy meeting, then, is not to have a "gripe session," but to develop the family's ability to come together for constructive problem solving.

In couples therapy, the therapist can help people work together to improve the communication patterns that have developed in their relationship.

Behavior Therapies

If the problem is overeating, bed-wetting, shyness, antisocial behavior, or anything else that can be described in purely behavioral terms, the chances are good that it can be modified by one of the behavior therapies (also known as **behavior modification**). Based on the assumption that these undesirable behaviors have been learned and therefore can be *un*learned, **behavior therapy** relies on the principles of operant and classical conditioning. In addition to those difficulties listed above, behavior therapists report success in dealing with fears, compulsions, depression, addictions, aggression, and delinquent behaviors.

As the label suggests, behavior therapists focus on problem *behaviors*, rather than inner thoughts, motives, or emotions. They seek to understand how the problem behaviors might have been learned and, even more important, how they can be eliminated and replaced by more effective patterns. To see how this is done, we will look first at the therapy techniques borrowed from *classical conditioning.*

Classical Conditioning Therapies The first example of behavior therapy, reported by psychologist Mary Cover Jones (1924), treated a fearful little boy named Peter, who was afraid of furry objects. Jones was able to desensitize the boy's fear, over a period of weeks, by gradually bringing a rabbit closer and closer to the boy while he was eating. Eventually, Peter was able to allow the rabbit to sit on his lap while he petted it. (You may notice the similarity to John Watson's experiments on Little Albert. Indeed, Jones was an associate of Watson and knew of the Little Albert study. Unlike Albert, however, Peter came to treatment already possessing an intense fear of rabbits and other furry objects.)

Surprisingly, it was another 14 years before behavior therapy reappeared, this time as a treatment for bed-wetting (Mowrer & Mowrer, 1938). The method

Behavior Therapies
- Systematic desensitization
- Aversion therapy
- Contingency management
- Token economies
- Participant modeling

CONNECTION • CHAPTER 3

In *classical conditioning,* a CS comes to produce essentially the same response as the UCS.

Behavior modification   Another term for behavior therapy.

Behavior therapy   Any form of psychotherapy based on the principles of behavioral learning, especially operant conditioning and classical conditioning.

involved a fluid-sensitive pad placed under the patient. When moisture set off an alarm, the patient would awaken. The treatment was effective in 75% of cases—an amazing success rate, in view of the dismal failure of psychodynamic therapy to prevent bed-wetting by talking about the "meaning" of the symptom. And it took yet another 20 years before behavior therapy entered the mainstream of psychological treatment. Why the delay? The old Freudian idea—that every symptom has an underlying, unconscious cause that must be discovered and eradicated—was extremely well rooted in clinical lore. Therapists dared not attack symptoms (behaviors) directly for fear of *symptom substitution:* the idea that by eliminating one symptom another, which could be much worse, could take its place.

Systematic Desensitization   It took the psychiatrist Joseph Wolpe to challenge the entrenched notion of symptom substitution. Wolpe reasoned that the development of irrational fear responses and other undesirable emotionally based behaviors might follow the classical conditioning model, rather than the Freudian model. As you will recall, *classical conditioning* involves the association of a new stimulus with an unconditioned stimulus, so that the person responds the same way to both. Thus, a fear response might be associated with, say, crowds or spiders or lightning. Wolpe also realized another simple truth: The nervous system cannot be relaxed and agitated at the same time because these two incompatible processes cannot be activated simultaneously. Putting these two ideas together formed the foundation for Wolpe's method, called **systematic desensitization** (Wolpe, 1958, 1973).

Systematic desensitization begins with a training program, teaching patients to relax their muscles and their minds (Rachman, 2000). With the patient in this deeply relaxed state, the therapist begins the process of *extinction* by having the patient imagine progressively more fearful situations. This is done in gradual steps, called an *anxiety hierarchy,* that move from remote associations to imagining an intensely feared situation.

To develop the anxiety hierarchy, the therapist and client first identify all the situations that provoke the patient's anxiety and then arrange them in levels, ranked from weakest to strongest (Shapiro, 1995). For example, a patient suffering from severe fear of public speaking constructed the hierarchy of unconditioned stimuli seen in Table 13.2.

Later, during desensitization, the relaxed client vividly imagines the weakest anxiety stimulus on the list. If it can be visualized without discomfort, the client goes on to the next stronger one. After a number of sessions, the client can imagine the most distressing situations on the list without anxiety (Lang & Lazovik,

---

TABLE 13.2   A Sample Anxiety Hierarchy

The following is typical of anxiety hierarchies that a therapist and a patient might develop to desensitize a fear of public speaking. The therapist guides the deeply relaxed patient in imagining the following situations:

1. Seeing a picture of another person giving a speech
2. Watching another person give a speech
3. Preparing a speech that I will give
4. Having to introduce myself to a large group
5. Waiting to be called on to speak in a meeting
6. Being introduced as a speaker to a group
7. Walking to the podium to make a speech
8. Making a speech to a large group

Systematic desensitization   A behavioral therapy technique in which anxiety is extinguished by exposing the patient to an anxiety-provoking stimulus.

1963)—hence the term *systematic* desensitization. In some forms of systematic desensitization, called **exposure therapy,** the therapist may actually have the patient confront the feared object or situation, such as a spider or a snake, rather than just imagining it. You will recall that Sabra, whom you met at the beginning of Chapter 3, went through a form of desensitization to deal with her fear of flying. The technique has been used successfully with a multitude of patients with phobias, including many whose fears of blood, injections, and germs stand in the way of getting needed medical or dental treatment (Dittmann, 2005b).

A number of studies have shown that desensitization works especially well for the specific phobias (Smith & Glass, 1977). Desensitization has also been successfully applied to a variety of anxiety-related problems that include stage fright, social phobias, agoraphobia and anxiety about sexual performance (Dittman, 2005a). In the last few years, some cognitive–behavioral therapists have added a high-tech twist by using computer-generated images that expose phobic patients to fearful situations in a safe virtual-reality environment. To enter the virtual-reality environment, patients don a helmet containing a video screen, on which are projected images to which they will be desensitized: spiders, snakes, high places, closed-in spaces—all the common phobia-producing objects or images (Winerman, 2005e).

In "virtual reality," phobic patients can confront their fears safely and conveniently in the behavior therapist's office. On a screen inside the headset, the patient sees computer-generated images of feared situations, such as seeing a snake, flying in an airplane, or looking down from the top of a tall building.

Aversion Therapy So, desensitization therapy helps clients deal with stimuli that they want to avoid. But what about the reverse? What can be done to help those who are attracted to stimuli that are harmful or illegal? Examples include drug addiction, certain sexual attractions, and tendencies to violence—all problems in which undesirable behavior is elicited by some specific stimulus. **Aversion therapy** tackles these problems with a conditioning procedure designed to make tempting stimuli repulsive by pairing them with unpleasant (aversive) stimuli. For example, the therapist might use electric shocks or nausea-producing drugs, whose effects are highly unpleasant but not in themselves dangerous to the client. In time, the negative reactions (unconditioned responses) to the aversive stimuli come to be associated with the conditioned stimuli (such as an addictive drug), and so the client develops an aversion that replaces the desire.

To give another example, if you were to elect aversion therapy to help you quit smoking, you might be required to chain-smoke cigarettes while having a foul odor blown in your face—until you develop a strong association between smoking and nausea. (See Figure 13.2.) A similar conditioning effect occurs in alcoholics who drink while taking Antabuse, a drug often prescribed to encourage sobriety.

In some ways, aversion therapy resembles nothing so much as torture. So why would anyone submit voluntarily to it? Sometimes the courts may assign a probationer to aversion therapy. Usually, however, people submit to this type of treatment because they have a troublesome addiction that has resisted other treatments.

Operant Conditioning Therapies

Four-year-old Tyler has a screaming fit when he goes to the grocery store with his parents and they refuse to buy him candy. He acquired this annoying behavior through operant conditioning, by being rewarded when his parents have given in to his demands. In fact, most behavior problems found in both children and adults have been shaped by rewards and punishments. Consider, for example, the similarities between Tyler's case and the employee who chronically arrives late for work or the student who waits until the last minute to study for a test. Changing such behaviors requires operant conditioning techniques. Let's look at two therapeutic variations on this operant theme.

Contingency Management Tyler's parents may learn to extinguish his fits at the grocery store by simply withdrawing their attention—no easy task, by the way. In addition, the therapist may coach them to "catch Tyler being good" and give him the

Exposure therapy A form of desensitization therapy in which the patient directly confronts the anxiety-provoking stimulus (as opposed to imagining the stimulus).

Aversion therapy As a classical conditioning procedure, aversive counterconditioning involves presenting the individual with an attractive stimulus paired with unpleasant (aversive) stimulation to condition a repulsive reaction.

> **CONNECTION • CHAPTER 3**
> In *operant conditioning*, behavior changes because of consequences, such as rewards and punishments.

Is there a behavioral habit that you would like to acquire—studying, initiating conversations with others, exercising to keep fit? Write this activity in behavioral terms on the line below. (Don't use mentalistic words, such as "feeling" or "wanting." Behaviorists require that you keep things objective by specifying only an observable behavior.)

The desired new behavior: _____

_____

When or under what conditions would you like to engage in this new behavior? On the line below, write in the time or stimulus conditions when you want to initiate the behavior (for example: in class, when relaxing with friends, or at a certain time every morning).

The time or conditions for the new behavior: _____

_____

To increase your likelihood of producing the desired response, apply some positive reinforcement therapy to yourself. Choose an appropriate reward that you will give yourself when you have produced the desired behavior at the appropriate time. Write the reward that you will give yourself on the line below.

Your reward: _____

Give yourself feedback on your progress by keeping a daily record of the occurrence of your new behavior. This could be done, for example, on a calendar or a graph. In time, you will discover that the desired behavior has increased in frequency. You will also find that your new habit carries its own rewards, such as better grades or more satisfying social interactions (Kazdin, 1994).

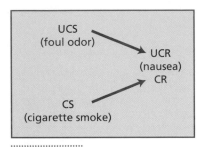

FIGURE 13.2

Conditioning an Aversion for Cigarette Smoke

Aversion therapy for smoking might simultaneously pair a foul odor with cigarette smoke blown in the smoker's face. The foul odor (such as rotten eggs) produces nausea. This response then becomes the conditioned response associated with cigarette smoke.

(*Source:* From J. Wolpe, *The Practice of Behavior Therapy,* 4th ed. Published by Allyn & Bacon, Boston, MA. Copyright © 1991 by Pearson Education. Reprinted by permission of the publisher.)

Contingency management An operant conditioning approach to changing behavior by altering the consequences, especially rewards and punishments, of behavior.

Token economy An operant technique applied to groups, such as classrooms or mental hospital wards, involving the distribution of "tokens" or other indicators of reinforcement contingent on desired behaviors. The tokens can later be exchanged for privileges, food, or other reinforcers.

attention he needs then. Over time, the changing contingencies will work to extinguish the old, undesirable behaviors and help to keep the new ones in place. This approach is an example of **contingency management:** changing behavior by modifying its consequences. It has proved effective in managing behavior problems found in such diverse settings as families, schools, work, prisons, the military, and mental hospitals. The careful application of reward and punishment can also reduce the self-destructive behaviors in autistic children (Frith, 1997). And, if you would like to change some undesirable habit or acquire a new one, you can even apply contingency management techniques to yourself: See the accompanying box, "Do It Yourself! Behavior Self-Modification."

Token Economies   The special form of therapy called a **token economy,** commonly used in group settings such as classrooms and institutions, is the behavioral version of group therapy (Ayllon & Azrin, 1968; Martin & Pear, 1999). The method takes its name from the plastic tokens sometimes awarded by therapists or teachers as immediate reinforcers for desirable behaviors. In a classroom, earning a token might mean sitting quietly for several minutes, participating in a class discussion, or turning in an assignment. Later, recipients may redeem the tokens for food, merchandise, or privileges. Often, "points" or play money are used in place of tokens. The important thing is that the individual receive something as a reinforcer immediately after giving desired responses. With the appropriate modifications, the token economy also works well with children having developmental disabilities, with mental patients, and with correctional populations (Higgins et al., 2001).

Participant Modeling: An Observational-Learning Therapy   "Monkey see—monkey do," we say. And sure enough, monkeys learn fears by observation and imitation. One study showed that laboratory monkeys with no previous aversion to snakes could acquire a simian version of *ophidiophobia* by observing their parents reacting fearfully to real snakes and toy snakes. (You don't remember that phobia? Look back at Table 12.3 on page 546.) The more disturbed the monkey parents were at the sight of the snakes, the greater the resulting fear in their offspring (Mineka et al., 1984). A follow-up study showed that such fears were not just a family matter. When other monkeys that had previously shown no fear of snakes were given the opportunity to observe unrelated adults responding to snakes fearfully, they quickly acquired the same response, as you can see in Figure 13.3 (Cook et al., 1985).

Like monkeys, people also learn fears by observing the behavior of others. But for therapeutic purposes, observational learning in the form of *participant modeling* can also be used to encourage *healthy* behaviors. In **participant modeling,** then, the client, or *participant,* observes and imitates someone *modeling* desirable behaviors. Athletic coaches, of course, have used participant modeling for years. Similarly, a behavior therapist treating a snake phobia might model the desired behavior by first approaching a caged snake, then touching the snake, and so on. The client then imitates the modeled behavior but at no time is forced to perform. If the therapist senses resistance, the client may return to a previously successful level. As you can see, the procedure is similar to systematic desensitization, with the important addition of observational learning. In fact, participant modeling draws on concepts from both operant and classical conditioning.

The power of participant modeling in eliminating snake phobias can be seen in a study that compared the participant modeling technique with several other approaches: (1) *symbolic modeling,* a technique in which subjects receive indirect exposure by watching a film or video in which models deal with a feared situation; (2) desensitization therapy, which, as you will remember, involves exposure to an imagined fearful stimulus; and (3) no therapeutic intervention (the control condition). As you can see in Figure 13.4, participant modeling was the most successful. The snake phobia was virtually eliminated in 11 of the 12 subjects in the participant modeling group (Bandura, 1970).

Cognitive–Behavioral Therapy: A Synthesis

Suppose you are having difficulty controlling feelings of jealousy every time the person you love is friendly with someone else. Chances are that the problem originates in your cognitions about yourself and the others involved ("Marty is stealing Terry away from me!") These thoughts may also affect your behavior, making you act in ways that could drive Terry away from you. A dose of therapy aimed at *both* your cognitions and your behaviors may be a better bet than either one alone.

In brief, **cognitive–behavioral therapy** combines a cognitive emphasis on thoughts and attitudes with the behavioral strategies that we have just discussed. This dual approach assumes that an irrational self-statement often underlies maladaptive behavior. For example, an addicted smoker might automatically tell himself, "One more cigarette won't hurt me" or "I'll go crazy if I don't have a smoke now." These irrational self-statements must be changed or replaced with rational, constructive coping statements before the unacceptable behavior pattern can be modified. Here is an example of healthier thinking: "I can get through this craving if I distract myself with something else I like to do, like going to a movie."

So, in cognitive–behavioral treatment, the therapist and client work together to modify irrational self-talk, set attainable behavioral goals, develop realistic strategies for attaining them, and evaluate the results. In this way, people change the way they approach problems and gradually develop new skills and a sense of self-efficacy (Bandura, 1986, 1992; Schwarzer, 1992).

Rational–Emotive Behavior Therapy: Challenging the "Shoulds" and "Oughts"
One of the most famous forms of cognitive–behavioral therapy was developed by the colorful and notorious Albert Ellis (1987, 1990, 1996) to help people eliminate self-defeating thought patterns. Ellis has dubbed his treatment **rational–emotive behavior therapy (REBT),** a name derived from its method of challenging certain "irrational" beliefs and behaviors.

What are the irrational beliefs challenged in REBT, and how do they lead to maladaptive feelings and actions? According to Ellis, maladjusted individuals base their lives on a set of unrealistic values and unachievable goals. These

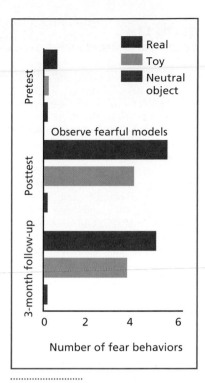

FIGURE 13.3
Fear Reactions in Monkeys

In a pretest, young monkeys raised in laboratories show little fear of snakes (top bars). But after observing other monkeys showing a strong fear of snakes, they are conditioned to fear both real snakes and toy snakes (middle bars). A follow-up test shows that the fear persists over a 3-month interval (bottom bars).

(*Source:* From "Observational Conditioning of Snake Fear in Unrelated Rhesus Monkeys," by M. Cook, S. Mineka, B. Wokenstein, and K. Laitsch, *Journal of Abnormal Psychology, 94,* pp. 591–610. Copyright © 1985 by American Psychological Association. Reprinted by per-

Participant modeling A social learning technique in which a therapist demonstrates and encourages a client to imitate a desired behavior.

Cognitive–behavioral therapy A newer form of psychotherapy that combines the techniques of cognitive therapy with those of behavioral therapy.

Rational–emotive behavior therapy (REBT) Albert Ellis's brand of cognitive therapy, based on the idea that irrational thoughts and behaviors are the cause of mental disorders.

FIGURE 13.4
Participant Modeling Therapy

The client shown in the photo first watches a model make a graduated series of snake-approach responses and then repeats them herself. Eventually, she can pick up the snake and let it move about on her. The graph compares the number of approach responses clients made before and after receiving participant modeling therapy with the responses of those exposed to two other therapeutic techniques and a control group. The graph shows that participant modeling was far more effective in the posttest.

(*Source:* From "Modeling Therapy," by D. Albert Bandura. Reprinted by permission of the author.)

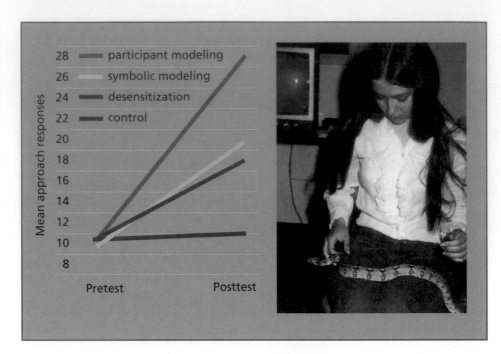

CONNECTION • CHAPTER 10

Compare Ellis's "neurotic" goals with Karen Horney's neurotic trends.

"neurotic" goals and values lead people to hold unrealistic expectations that they should always succeed, that they should always receive approval, that they should *always* be treated fairly, and that their experiences should always be pleasant. (You can see the most common irrational beliefs in the accompanying box, "Do It Yourself! Examining Your Own Beliefs.") For example, in your own daily life, you may frequently tell yourself that you "should" get an A in math or that you "ought to" spend an hour exercising every day. Further, he says, if you are unable to meet your goals and seldom question this neurotic self-talk, it may come to control your actions or even prevent you from choosing the life you want. If you were to enter REBT, your therapist would teach you to recognize such assumptions, question how rational they are, and replace faulty ideas with more valid ones. Don't "should" on yourself, warned Ellis.

DO IT YOURSELF! Examining Your Own Beliefs

It may be obvious that the following are not healthy beliefs, but Albert Ellis found that many people hold them. Do you? Be honest: Put a check mark beside each of the following statements that accurately describes how you feel about yourself.

1. _____ I must be loved and approved by everyone.
2. _____ I must be thoroughly competent, adequate, and achieving.
3. _____ It is catastrophic when things do not go the way I want them to go.
4. _____ Unhappiness results from forces over which I have no control.
5. _____ People must always treat each other fairly and justly; those who don't are nasty and terrible people.
6. _____ I must constantly be on my guard against dangers and things that could go wrong.
7. _____ Life is full of problems, and I must always find quick solutions to them.
8. _____ It is easier to evade my problems and responsibilities than to face them.
9. _____ Unpleasant experiences in my past have had a profound influence on me. Therefore, they must continue to influence my current feelings and actions.
10. _____ I can achieve happiness by just enjoying myself each day. The future will take care of itself.

In Ellis's view, all these statements were irrational beliefs that can cause mental problems. The more items you have checked, the more "irrational" your beliefs. His cognitive approach to therapy, known as rational–emotive behavior therapy, concentrates on helping people see that they can "drive themselves crazy" with such irrational beliefs. For example, a student who parties rather than studying for a test holds belief #8. A person who is depressed about not landing a certain job holds irrational belief #3. You can obtain more information on Ellis's system from his books.

So, how might a cognitive–behavioral therapist have dealt with Freud's obsessive patient? First, taking a cognitive approach, the therapist would challenge the girl's irrational beliefs, as we suggested earlier. Then, switching to a behavioral mode, the therapist might teach the girl relaxation techniques to use when she began to get ready for bed each evening. These techniques then would substitute for the obsessive ritual. It is also likely that the therapist would work with the parents, focusing on helping them learn not to reward the girl with attention for her ritual behavior.

Positive Psychotherapy (PPT)   Our depressed client Derek might be an especially good candidate for a new form of cognitive-behavioral treatment called **positive psychotherapy** (PPT), developed by Martin Seligman. Like the humanists, Seligman and his fellow *positive psychologists* see their mission as balancing psychology's negative emphasis on mental disorders with their own positive emphasis on growth, health, and happiness. So it was a "natural" for Seligman to tackle the problem of depression by accentuating the positive (Seligman et al., 2006). Unlike the humanists, however, the PPT approach is largely cognitive–behavioral, with an emphasis on research.

In PPT Derek might find himself treated more like a student than a patient. For example, the therapist might give him a "homework" assignment, such as the "three good things" exercise: "Before you go to sleep, write down three things that went well today and why they went well." Derek would also learn to focus on positive emotions, respond constructively to others, and otherwise to seek more pleasure in his work and home life. How well does this work? Seligman and his group have applied this approach to dozens of clients and report preliminary results showing that PPT relieved depression far more effectively than did conventional therapy or antidepressant medication (Seligman et al., 2006).

Changing the Brain by Changing the Mind   Brain scans now show that cognitive–behavioral therapy not only helps people change their minds, but it can change the brain itself (Dobbs, 2006b). In one study, patients who suffered from obsessions, such as worrying that they had not turned off their stoves or locked their doors, were given cognitive behavior modification (Schwartz et al., 1996). When they felt an urge to run home and check on themselves, they were trained to relabel their experience as an obsession or compulsion—not a rational concern. They then focused on waiting out this "urge" rather than giving in to it, by distracting themselves with other activities for about 15 minutes. Positron emission tomography (PET) scans of the brains of subjects who were trained in this technique indicated that, over time, the part of the brain responsible for that nagging fear or urge gradually became less active.

As that study shows, psychology has come a long way since the days when we wondered whether thoughts and behavior were the product of nature *or* nurture. With cognitive–behavioral therapy we now know that experience can change the biology behind behavior.

Evaluating the Psychological Therapies

Now that we have looked at a variety of psychological therapies (see Figure 13.5), let us step back and ask how effective therapy is. Think about it: How could you tell objectively whether therapy really works? The answer to this question hasn't always been clear (Kopta et al., 1999; Shadish et al., 2000).

Lots of evidence says that most people who have undergone therapy *like* it. This was shown, for example, by surveying thousands of subscribers to *Consumer Reports* (1995). Respondents indicated how much their treatment helped, how satisfied they were with the therapist's treatment of their problems, how much their "overall emotional state" changed following therapy, as well as what kind of therapy they had undergone. For about 3000 of the 7000 who

Positive psychotherapy (PPT)   A relatively new form of cognitive-behavioral treatment that seeks to emphasize growth, health, and happiness.

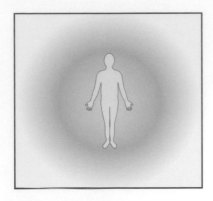

Behavior therapies
aim to change things *outside the individual*: rewards, punishments, and cues in the environment in order to change the person's external behaviors.

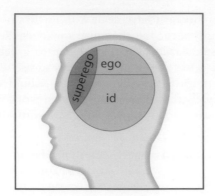

Psychodynamic therapies
aim to make changes *inside the person's mind*, especially the unconscious.

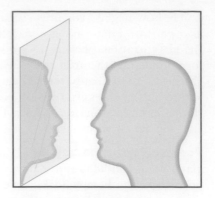

Humanistic therapies
aim to change the way people *see themselves*.

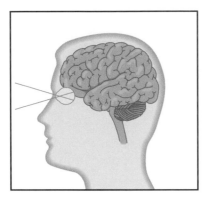

Cognitive therapies
aim to change the way people *think and perceive*.

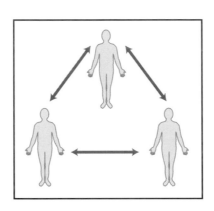

Group therapies
aim to change the way people *interact*.

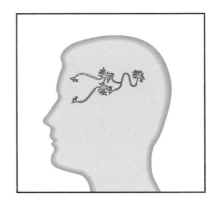

Biomedical therapies
aim to change the structure or function of the brain.

FIGURE 13.5
A Comparison of Different Types of Therapy

answered the questionnaire, "therapy" merely meant talking to a friend, a relative, or to clergy (as might be expected from our discussion earlier in this chapter). Another 2900 saw a mental health professional; the rest saw family doctors or attended support groups. Among the results: (a) Therapy works—that is, it was perceived to have helped clients diminish or eliminate their psychological problems; (b) long-term therapy is better than short-term therapy; and (c) all forms of therapy are about equally effective for improving clients' problems (see Jacobson & Christensen, 1996).

We can't give a thumbs-up to therapy, however, merely because people say they like it or that it helped them (Hollon, 1996). Testimonials don't make for good science—which is why psychologists now demand that therapy be judged by studies having a *comparison group* or *control group*. Let's turn, therefore, to the controlled studies of therapy's effectiveness, beginning with a report that nearly upset the therapeutic applecart.

> **CONNECTION • CHAPTER 1**
> A *control group* is treated exactly as the experimental group, except for the crucial independent variable.

Eysenck's Controversial Proclamation   The issue of therapy's effectiveness came to a head in 1952, when British psychologist Hans Eysenck proclaimed that roughly two-thirds of all people who develop nonpsychotic mental disorders would recover within two years, *whether they get therapy or not*. Eysenck's evidence came from a review of several outcome studies of various kinds of insight therapy, all of which compared patients who received therapy to those who were on waiting lists, awaiting their turn in treatment. What he noted was that just as many people on the waiting lists recovered as those in therapy. If taken at face value, this meant that psychotherapy was essentially worthless—no better than having no treatment at all! To say the least, this wasn't received happily by therapists. But Eysenck's challenge had an immensely productive result: It stimulated therapists to do a great deal of research on the effectiveness of their craft.

In Response to Eysenck   Major reviews of the accumulating evidence on therapy began to be reported in 1970 (by Meltzoff & Kornreich), in 1975 (by Luborsky et al.), and in 1977 (by Smith and Glass). Overall, this literature—numbering some 375 studies—supported two major conclusions. First, therapy is, after all, more effective than no therapy—much to everyone's relief! And second, Eysenck had overestimated the improvement rate in no-therapy control groups.

Gradually, then, a scientific consensus supporting the value of psychotherapy emerged (Meredith, 1986; VandenBos, 1986). In fact, for a broad range of disorders, psychotherapy has been demonstrated to have an effect comparable or superior to many established medical practices (Wampold, 2007). Moreover, the research began to show that therapy was effective not only in Western industrialized countries (in the United States, Canada, and Europe) but also in a variety of cultural settings throughout the world (Beutler & Machado, 1992; Lipsey & Wilson, 1993). A number of writers have cautioned, however, that therapists must be sensitive to cultural differences and adapt their techniques appropriately (Matsumoto, 1996; Shiraev & Levy, 2001).

New Questions   But the new studies have raised new questions. Are some therapies better than others? Can we identify therapies that are best suited for treating specific disorders? The Smith and Glass survey (1977) hinted that the answers to those questions were "Yes" and "Yes." Smith and Glass found that the behavior therapies seemed to have an advantage over insight therapies for the treatment of many anxiety disorders. More recent evaluations have found insight therapies can also be used effectively to treat certain problems, such as marital discord and depression. Indeed, there is now a clear trend toward matching specific therapies to specific conditions. It is important to realize, however, that these therapeutic techniques do not necessarily "cure" psychological disorders. In the treatment of schizophrenia, mental retardation, or autism, for example, psychological therapies may be deemed effective when people suffering from these afflictions learn more adaptive behaviors (Hogarty et al., 1997).

PSYCHOLOGYMATTERS
Where Do Most People Get Help?

The effectiveness of psychotherapy for a variety of problems seems to be established beyond doubt. Having said that, we should again acknowledge that *most people experiencing mental distress do not turn to professional therapists for help*. Rather they turn to "just people" in the community (Wills & DePaulo, 1991). Those suffering from mental problems often look to friends, clergy, hairdressers, bartenders, and others with whom they have a trusting relationship. In fact, for some types of problems—perhaps the most common problems of everyday living—a sympathetic friend may be just as effective as a trained professional therapist (Berman & Norton, 1985; Christensen & Jacobson, 1994).

To put the matter in a different way: Most mental problems are not the crippling disorders that took center stage in the previous chapter. Rather, the psychological difficulties most of us face result from lost jobs, difficult marriages, misbehaving children, friendships gone sour, loved ones dying. . . . In brief, the most familiar problems involve chaos, confusion, choice, frustration, stress, and loss. People who find themselves in the throes of these adjustment difficulties may not need extensive psychotherapy, medication, or some other special treatment. They need someone to help them sort through the pieces of their problems. Usually this means that they turn to someone like you.

So, what can you do when someone asks you for help? First, you should realize that some problems do indeed require immediate professional attention. These include a suicide threat or an indication of intent to harm others. You should not delay finding competent help for someone with such tendencies. Second, you should remember that most therapy methods require special training, especially those calling for cognitive–behavioral therapy techniques or psychodynamic interpretations. We urge you to learn as much as you can about these methods—but we strongly recommend that you leave them to the professionals. Some other techniques, however, are simply extensions of good human relationships, and they fall well within the layperson's abilities for mental "first aid." Briefly, we will consider three of these:

- *Listening.* You will rarely go wrong if you just listen. Sometimes listening is all the therapy a person in distress needs. It works by encouraging the speaker to organize a problem well enough to communicate it. Consequently, those who talk out their problems frequently arrive at their own solutions. As an **active listener,** you take the role a step farther by giving the speaker feedback: nodding, maintaining an expression that shows interest, paraphrasing, and asking for clarification when you don't understand. As we saw in the client-centered therapy excerpts on pages 580 and 581, active listening lets the speaker know that the listener is interested and *empathetic* (in tune with the other person's feelings). At the same time, you will do well to avoid the temptation of giving advice. Advice robs the recipient of the opportunity to work out his or her own solutions.

- *Acceptance.* Nondirective therapists call this a *nonjudgmental attitude.* It means accepting the person and the problem as they are. It also means suppressing shock, disgust, or condemnation that would create a hostile climate for problem solving.

- *Exploration of alternatives.* People under stress may see only one course of action, so you can help by identifying other potential choices and exploring the consequences of each. (You can point out that *doing nothing* is also a choice.) Remember that, in the end, the choice of action is not up to you but to the individual who owns the problem.

Beyond these basic helping techniques lies the territory of the trained therapist. Again, we strongly advise you against trying out the therapy techniques discussed in this chapter for any of the serious psychological disorders discussed in the previous chapter or listed in the *DSM-IV.*

Active listener   A person who gives the speaker feedback in such forms as nodding, paraphrasing, maintaining an expression that shows interest, and asking questions for clarification.

CheckYourUnderstanding

1. **RECALL:** On what form of behavioral learning is the behavioral technique of counterconditioning based?

2. **APPLICATION:** You could use contingency management to change the behavior of a child who comes home late for dinner by
   a. pairing food with punishment.
   b. having the child observe someone else coming home on time and being rewarded.
   c. refusing to let the child have dinner when he comes home late.
   d. having the child relax and imagine being home on time for dinner.

3. **RECALL:** What is the primary goal of psychoanalytic therapy? That is, what makes psychoanalytic therapy different from behavioral therapy or the cognitive therapies?

4. **RECALL:** Carl Rogers invented a technique to help people see their own thinking more clearly. Using this technique, the therapist paraphrases the client's statements. Rogers called this _____.

5. **RECALL:** Which form of therapy directly confronts a client's self-defeating and irrational thought patterns?

6. **RECALL:** Eysenck caused a furor with his claim that people who receive psychotherapy _____.

7. **UNDERSTANDING THE CORE CONCEPT:** A phobia would be best treated by _____, while a problem of choosing a major would be better suited for _____.
   a. behavioral therapy/insight therapy

b. cognitive therapy/psychoanalysis
c. insight therapy/behavioral therapy
d. humanistic therapy/behavioral therapy

13.3 KEY QUESTION
HOW IS THE BIOMEDICAL APPROACH USED TO TREAT PSYCHOLOGICAL DISORDERS?

The mind exists in a delicate biological balance. It can be upset by irregularities in our genes, hormones, enzymes, and metabolism, as well as by damage from accidents and disease. When something goes wrong with the brain, we can see the consequences in abnormal patterns of behavior or peculiar cognitive and emotional reactions. The biomedical therapies, therefore, attempt to treat these mental disorders by intervening directly in the brain. Our Core Concept specifies the targets of these therapies:

Biomedical therapies seek to treat psychological disorders by changing the brain's chemistry with drugs, its circuitry with surgery, or its patterns of activity with pulses of electricity or powerful magnetic fields.

core concept

Each of the biomedical therapies emerges from the medical model of abnormal mental functioning, which assumes an organic basis for mental illnesses and treats them as diseases—as we saw in Chapter 12. We begin our examination of these biomedical therapies with medicine's arsenal of prescription psychoactive drugs.

Drug Therapy

In the history of the treatment of mental disorder, nothing has ever rivaled the revolution created by the discovery of drugs that could calm anxious patients, elevate the mood of depressed patients, and suppress hallucinations in psychotic patients. This brave new therapeutic era began in 1953 with the introduction of the first antipsychotic drugs (often called "tranquilizers"). As these drugs found wide application, many unruly, assaultive patients almost miraculously became cooperative, calm, and sociable. In addition, many thought-disordered patients, who had previously been absorbed in their delusions and hallucinations, began to respond to the physical and social environment around them.

The effectiveness of drug therapy had a pronounced effect on the census of the nation's mental hospitals. In 1955, over half a million Americans were living in mental institutions, each staying an average of several years. Then, with the introduction of tranquilizers, the numbers began a steady decline. In just over 10 years, fewer than half that number actually resided in mental hospitals, and those who did were usually kept for only a few months.

Drug therapy has long since steamrolled out of the mental hospital and into our everyday lives. Currently, millions of people take drugs for anxiety, stress, depression, hyperactivity, insomnia, fears and phobias, obsessions and compulsions, addictions, and numerous other problems. Clearly, a drug-induced revolution has occurred. But what are these miraculous drugs?

You have probably heard of Prozac and Valium, but those are just two of scores of psychoactive drugs that can alter your mood, your perceptions, your desires, and perhaps your basic personality. Here we will consider four major

Drug Therapies
- Antipsychotic drugs
- Antidepressants and mood stabilizers
- Antianxiety drugs
- Stimulants

categories of drugs used today: *antipsychotics, antidepressants and mood stabilizers, antianxiety drugs,* and *stimulants.*

Antipsychotic Drugs

As their name says, the **antipsychotics** treat the symptoms of psychosis: delusions, hallucinations, social withdrawal, and agitation (Dawkins et al., 1999). Most work by reducing the activity of the neurotransmitter dopamine in the brain—although the precise reason why this may has an antipsychotic effect is not known. For example, *chlorpromazine* (sold under the brand name Thorazine) and *haloperidol* (brand name: Haldol) are known to block dopamine receptors in the synapse between nerve cells. A newer antipsychotic drug, *clozapine* (Clozaril), both decreases dopamine activity and increases the activity of another neurotransmitter, serotonin, which also inhibits the dopamine system (Javitt & Coyle, 2004; Sawa & Snyder, 2002). While these drugs reduce overall brain activity, they do not merely "tranquilize" the patient. Rather, they reduce schizophrenia's "positive" symptoms (hallucinations, delusions, emotional disturbances, and agitated behavior), although they do little for the "negative" symptoms of social distance, jumbled thoughts, and poor attention spans seen in many patients (Wickelgren, 1998a). A recent study suggests that, for reducing psychotic symptoms, the newer "second generation" antipsychotic drugs being promoted by the drug companies may be no more effective than the older ones (Lieberman et al., 2005; Rosenheck et al., 2006).

Unfortunately, long-term administration of any antipsychotic drug can have unwanted side effects. Physical changes in the brain have been noted (Gur & Maany, 1998). But most worrisome is **tardive dyskinesia,** which produces an incurable disturbance of motor control, especially of the facial muscles. Although some of the newer drugs, like clozapine, have reduced motor side effects because of their more selective dopamine blocking, they also can cause serious problems, too. Are antipsychotic drugs worth the risk? There is no easy answer. The risks must be weighed against the severity of the patient's current suffering.

Antidepressants and Mood Stabilizers

The drug therapy arsenal also includes several compounds that have revolutionized the treatment of depression and bipolar disorder. As with other psychoactive drugs, neither the *antidepressants* nor *mood stabilizers* can provide a "cure." Their use, however, has made a big difference in the lives of many people suffering from mood disorders.

Antidepressant Drugs

All three major classes of **antidepressants** work by "turning up the volume" on messages transmitted over certain brain pathways, especially those using norepinephrine and serotonin (Holmes, 2001). *Tricyclic* compounds such as Tofranil and Elavil reduce the neuron's reabsorption of neurotransmitters after they have been released in the synapse between brain cells—a process called *reuptake.* A second group includes the famous antidepressant Prozac (fluoxetine). These drugs, known as SSRIs (selective serotonin reuptake inhibitors), interfere with the reuptake of serotonin in the synapse. As a result, the SSRIs keep serotonin available in the synapse longer. For many people, this prolonged serotonin effect lifts depressed moods (Hirschfeld, 1999; Kramer, 1993). The third group of antidepressant drugs, the *monoamine oxidase (MAO) inhibitors,* limits the activity of the enzyme MAO, a chemical that breaks down norepinephrine in the synapse. When MAO is inhibited, more norepinephrine is available to carry neural messages across the synapse.

Strangely, most patients report that it takes at least a couple of weeks before antidepressants begin to lift the veil of depression. And recent research seems to suggest why. In animal studies, antidepressants stimulate the growth of neurons in this brain's hippocampus. No one is sure why the hippocampus seems to be involved in depression, but the animal studies offer another tantalizing clue: Stress slows the growth of new neurons in this part of the brain—and depression is believed to be a stress response (Santarelli et al., 2003).

CONNECTION • CHAPTER 12

Positive symptoms of schizophrenia include active hallucinations, delusions, and extreme emotions; negative symptoms include withdrawal and "flat" emotions.

Antipsychotics Medicines that diminish psychotic symptoms, usually by effects on the dopamine pathways in the brain.

Tardive dyskinesia An incurable disorder of motor control, especially involving muscles of the face and head, resulting from long-term use of antipsychotic drugs.

Antidepressants Medicines that treat depression, usually by their effects on the serotonin and/or norepinephrine pathways in the brain.

CONNECTION • CHAPTER 2

Reuptake is a process by which neurotransmitters are taken intact from the synapse and cycled back into the terminal buttons of the axon. Reuptake, therefore, "tones down" the message being sent from one neuron to another.

The possibility of suicide poses a special concern in the treatment of depression. And now it seems that the very drugs used for treating depression may provoke or amplify suicidal thoughts, particularly during the first few weeks of therapy and especially in children (Bower, 2004b). One recent study revived hopes by showing that the increased short-term risk is small—less than 1% (Bridge et al., 2007). And another study shows that patients taking antidepressants have a somewhat *lower* risk of suicide over the long haul (Bower, 2007). Obviously, the picture is confusing at the moment and the Food and Drug Administration is advising prescribers to use caution. (Bower, 2006b; Jick et al., 2004).

Controversy over SSRIs In his book *Listening to Prozac*, psychiatrist and Prozac advocate Peter Kramer (1993) encourages the use of the drug to deal not only with depression but with general feelings of social unease and fear of rejection. Such claims have brought heated replies from therapists who fear that drugs may merely mask the psychological problems that people need to face and resolve. Some worry that the wide use of antidepressants may produce changes in the personality structure of a huge segment of our population—changes that could bring unanticipated social consequences (Breggin & Breggin, 1994; Sleek, 1994). In fact, more prescriptions are being written for antidepressants than there are people who have been diagnosed as clinically depressed (Coyne, 2001). The problem seems to be especially acute on college and university campuses, where increasing numbers of students are taking antidepressants (Young, 2003). At present, no one knows what the potential dangers might be of altering the brain chemistry of large numbers of people over long periods.

Just as worrisome for the medical model, another report suggests that antidepressants may owe nearly as much to their hype as to their effects on the brain. According to data mined from the Food and Drug Administration files, studies showing positive results find their way into print far more often than do studies showing no effects for these medicines. While these drugs do better overall than placebos, reports of their effects seem to be exaggerated by selective publication of positive results (Turner et al., 2008).

Mood Stabilizers A simple chemical, *lithium* (in the form of *lithium carbonate*), has proved highly effective as a mood stabilizer in the treatment of bipolar disorder (Paulus, 2007; Schou, 1997). Not just an antidepressant, lithium affects both ends of the emotional spectrum, dampening swings of mood that would otherwise range from uncontrollable periods of hyperexcitement to the lethargy and despair of depression. Unfortunately, lithium also has a serious drawback: In high concentrations, it is toxic. Physicians have learned that safe therapy requires that small doses be given to build up therapeutic concentrations in the blood over a period of a week or two. Then, as a precaution, patients must have periodic blood analyses to ensure that lithium concentrations have not risen to dangerous levels. In a welcome development, scientists have found a promising alternative to lithium for the treatment of bipolar disorder (Azar, 1994; Walden et al., 1998). *Divalproex sodium* (brand name: Depakote), originally developed to treat epilepsy, seems to be even more effective than lithium for most patients but with fewer dangerous side effects (Bowden et al., 2000).

Antianxiety Drugs To reduce stress and suppress anxiety associated with everyday hassles, untold millions of Americans take **antianxiety drugs,** either *barbiturates* or *benzodiazepines*. Barbiturates act as central nervous system depressants, so they have a relaxing effect. But barbiturates can be dangerous if taken in excess or in combination with alcohol. By contrast, the benzodiazepines, such as Valium and Xanax, work by increasing the activity of the neurotransmitter GABA, thereby decreasing activity in brain regions more specifically involved in feelings of anxiety. The benzodiazepines are sometimes called "minor tranquilizers."

Many psychologists believe that these antianxiety drugs—like the antidepressants—are too often prescribed for problems that people should face rather than

Antianxiety drugs A category of medicines that includes the barbiturates and benzodiazepines, drugs that diminish feelings of anxiety.

◄ **CONNECTION • CHAPTER 2**
GABA is the major inhibitory neurotransmitter in the brain.

mask with chemicals. Nevertheless, antianxiety compounds can be useful in helping people deal with specific situations, such as anxiety prior to surgery. Here are some cautions to bear in mind about these compounds (Hecht, 1986):

- If used over long periods, barbiturates and benzodiazepines can be physically and psychologically addicting (Holmes, 2001; Schatzberg, 1991).

- Because of their powerful effects on the brain, these medicines should not be taken to relieve anxieties that are part of the ordinary stresses of everyday life.

- When used for extreme anxiety, antianxiety drugs should not normally be taken for more than a few days at a time. If used longer than this, their dosage should be gradually reduced by a physician. Abrupt cessation after prolonged use can lead to withdrawal symptoms, such as convulsions, tremors, and abdominal and muscle cramps.

- Because antianxiety drugs depress parts of the central nervous system, they can impair one's ability to drive, operate machinery, or perform other tasks that require alertness (such as studying or taking exams).

- In combination with alcohol (also a central nervous system depressant) or with sleeping pills, antianxiety drugs can lead to unconsciousness and even death.

Finally, we should mention that some antidepressant drugs have also been found useful for reducing the symptoms of certain anxiety disorders such as panic disorders, agoraphobia, and obsessive–compulsive disorder. (A modern psychiatrist might well have prescribed antidepressants for Freud's obsessive patient.) But because these problems may arise from low levels of serotonin, they may respond even better to drugs like Prozac that specifically affect serotonin function.

Stimulants   Ranging from caffeine to nicotine to amphetamines to cocaine—any drug that produces excitement or hyperactivity falls into the category of **stimulants.** We have seen that stimulants find some use in the treatment of narcolepsy. They also have an accepted niche in treating *attention-deficit/hyperactivity disorder (ADHD)*. While it may seem strange to prescribe stimulants (a common one is Ritalin) for hyperactive children, studies comparing stimulant therapy with behavior therapy and with placebos have shown a clear role for stimulants (American Academy of Pediatrics, 2001). Although the exact mechanism is unknown, stimulants may work in hyperactive children by increasing the availability of dopamine, glutamate, and/or serotonin in their brains (Gainetdinov et al., 1999).

As you can imagine, the use of stimulants to treat ADHD has generated controversy (O'Connor, 2001). Some objections, of course, stem from ignorance of the well-established calming effect these drugs have in children with this condition. Other worries have more substance. For some patients, the drug will interfere with normal sleep patterns. Additionally, there is evidence that stimulant therapy can slow a child's growth (National Institute of Mental Health, 2004). Legitimate concerns also center on the potential for abuse that lurks in the temptation to see every child's behavior problem as a symptom of ADHD (Smith, 2002a). And finally, critics suggest that the prescription of stimulants to children might encourage later drug abuse (Daw, 2001). Happily, recent studies have found cognitive-behavioral therapy (CBT) to be comparable to stimulants as a treatment for ADHD (Sinha, 2005). Even better, say many experts, is a *combination therapy* regimen that employs both CBT and stimulants.

Evaluating the Drug Therapies   The drug therapies have caused a revolution in the treatment of severe mental disorders, starting in the 1950s, when virtually the only treatments available were talk therapies, hospitalization, restraints, "shock treatment," and lobotomies. Of course, none of the drugs discovered so far can "cure" any mental disorder. Yet, in many cases they can alter the brain's chemistry to suppress symptoms.

Stimulants   Drugs that normally increases activity level by encouraging communication among neurons in the brain. Stimulants, however, have been found to suppress activity level in persons with attention-deficit/hyperactivity disorder.

But is all the enthusiasm warranted? According to neuroscientist Elliot Valenstein, a close look behind the scenes of drug therapy raises important questions (Rolnick, 1998; Valenstein, 1998). Valenstein believes that much of the faith in drug therapy for mental disorders rests on hype. He credits the wide acceptance of drug therapy to the huge investment drug companies have made in marketing their products. Particularly distressing are concerns raised recently about the willingness of physicians to prescribe drugs for children—even though the safety and effectiveness of many drugs has not been established in young people (K. Brown, 2003a).

Few question that drugs are the proper first line of treatment for certain conditions, such as bipolar disorder and schizophrenia. In many other cases, however, the apparent advantages of drug therapy are quick results and low cost. Yet some research raises doubts about simplistic time-and-money assumptions. Studies show, for example, that treating depression, anxiety disorders, and eating disorders with cognitive–behavioral therapy—alone or in combination with drugs—may be both more effective and economical in the long run than reliance on drugs alone (Clay, 2000).

Psychosurgery The general term for surgical intervention in the brain to treat psychological disorders.

Other Medical Therapies for Psychological Disorders

Describing a modern-day counterpart to Phineas Gage, the headline in the *Los Angeles Times* read, ".22-Caliber Surgery Suicide Bid Cures Psychological Disorder" (February 23, 1988). The article revealed that a 19-year-old man suffering from severe obsessive–compulsive disorder had shot a .22 caliber bullet through the front of his brain in a suicide attempt. Remarkably, he survived, his pathological symptoms were gone, and his intellectual capacity was not affected.

CONNECTION • CHAPTER 2
Phineas Gage survived—with a changed personality—after a steel rod was blasted through his frontal lobe.

We don't recommend this form of therapy, but the case does illustrate the potential effects of physical intervention in the brain. In this vein, we will look briefly at two medical alternatives to drug therapy that were conceived to alter the brain's structure and function, psychosurgery and direct stimulation of the brain.

Psychosurgery With scalpels in place of bullets, surgeons have long aspired to treat mental disorders by severing connections between parts of the brain or by removing small sections of brain. In modern times, **psychosurgery** is usually considered a method of last resort. Nevertheless, psychosurgery has a history dating back at least to medieval times, when surgeons might open the skull to remove "the stone of folly" from an unfortunate madman. (There is, of course, no such "stone"—and there was no anesthetic except alcohol for these procedures.)

In modern times, the best-known form of psychosurgery involved the now-discredited *prefrontal lobotomy.* This operation, developed by Portuguese psychiatrist Egas Moñiz,[2] severed certain nerve fibers connecting the frontal lobes with deep brain structures, especially those of the thalamus and hypothalamus—much as happened accidentally to Phineas Gage. The original candidates for Moñiz's scalpel were agitated schizophrenic patients and patients who were compulsive and anxiety ridden. Surprisingly, this rather crude operation often produced a dramatic reduction in agitation and anxiety. On the down side, the operation permanently destroyed basic aspects of the

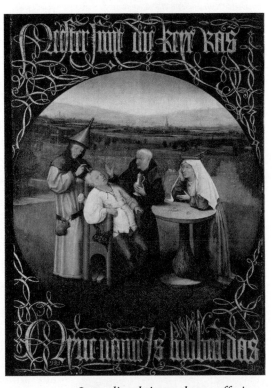

In medieval times, those suffering from madness might be treated by trephenation, *or making a hole in the skull. This painting portrays the operation as the removal of the "stone of folly."*

---

[2]In an ironic footnote to the history of psychosurgery, Moñiz was shot by one of his disgruntled patients, who apparently had not become as pacified as Moñiz had expected. This fact, however, did not prevent Moñiz from receiving the Nobel Prize for Medicine in 1949.

patients' personalities. Frequently, they emerged from the procedure crippled by a loss of interest in their personal well-being and their surroundings. As experience with lobotomy accumulated, doctors saw that it destroyed patients' ability to plan ahead, made them indifferent to the opinions of others, rendered their behavior childlike, and gave them the intellectual and emotional flatness of a person without a coherent sense of self. Not surprisingly, when the antipsychotic drug therapies came on the scene in the 1950s, with a promise to control psychotic symptoms with no obvious risk of permanent brain damage, the era of lobotomy came to a close (Valenstein, 1980).

Psychosurgery is still occasionally done, but it is now much more limited to precise and proven procedures for very specific brain disorders. In the "split-brain" operation, for example, severing the fibers of the corpus callosum can reduce life-threatening seizures in certain cases of epilepsy, with relatively few side effects. Psychosurgery is also done on portions of the brain involved in pain perception in cases of otherwise intractable pain. Today, however, no *DSM-IV* diagnoses are routinely treated with psychosurgery.

Brain-Stimulation Therapies   Electrical stimulation of the brain, also known as **electroconvulsive therapy (ECT)**, is still widely used, especially in severely depressed patients who have not responded to drugs or psychotherapy for depression. (You will recall that the therapist said that Derek was not a good candidate for ECT.) The treatment induces a convulsion by applying an electric current (75 to 100 volts) to a patient's temples briefly—from one-tenth to a full second. The convulsion usually runs its course in less than a minute. Patients are prepared for this traumatic intervention by putting them to "sleep" with a short-acting barbiturate, plus a muscle relaxant. This not only renders them unconscious but minimizes any violent physical spasms during the seizure (Abrams, 1992; Malitz & Sackheim, 1984). Within half an hour the patient awakens but has no memory of the seizure or of the events preparatory to treatment.

Does it work? Crude as it may seem to send an electric current through a person's skull and brain, studies have shown ECT to be a useful tool in treating depression, especially those in whom suicidal tendencies demand an intervention that works far more quickly than medication or psychotherapy (Shorter & Healy, 2007). Typically the symptoms of depression often yield in a three- or four-day course of treatment, in contrast with the one- to two-week period required for drug therapy.

Although most clinicians regard ECT, properly done, as safe and effective, some critics fear that it also could be abused to silence dissent or punish patients who are uncooperative (Butcher et al., 2008; Holmes, 2001). Other worries about ECT stem from the fact that its effects are not well understood. To date no definitive theory explains why inducing a mild convulsion should alleviate disordered symptoms, although there are some hints that it may also stimulate neuron growth in parts of the brain, particularly the hippocampus.

Most worrisome, perhaps, are the memory deficits sometimes caused by electroconvulsive therapy (Breggin, 1979, 1991). Proponents claim, however, that patients generally recover full memory functions within months of the treatment (Calev et al., 1991). In the face of such concerns, the National Institute of Mental Health investigated the use of ECT and, in 1985, gave it a cautious endorsement for treating a narrow range of disorders, especially severe depression. Then, in 1990, the American Psychiatric Association also proclaimed ECT to be a valid treatment option. To minimize even short-term side effects, however, ECT is usually administered "unilaterally"—only to the right temple—to reduce the possibility of speech impairment.

Another promising new therapeutic tool for stimulating the brain with magnetic fields may offer all the benefits of ECT without the risk of memory loss. Still in the experimental stages, **transcranial magnetic stimulation (TMS)** involves directing high-powered magnetic stimulation to specific parts of the brain. Stud-

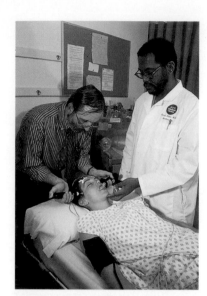

A sedated patient about to receive ECT. Electroconvulsive therapy involves a weak electrical current to a patient's temples, causing a convulsion. Some psychiatrists have found ECT successful in alleviating symptoms of severe depression, but it remains a treatment of last resort for most therapists.

Electroconvulsive therapy (ECT)   A treatment used primarily for depression and involving the application of an electric current to the head, producing a generalized seizure. Sometimes called "shock treatment."

Transcranial magnetic stimulation (TMS)   A treatment that involves magnetic stimulation of specific regions of the brain. Unlike ECT, TMS does not produce a seizure.

CONNECTION • CHAPTER 2

In most people, speech is controlled in the brain's left hemisphere.

ies indicate that TMS may be useful for treating not only depression but schizophrenia and bipolar disorder (George, 2003). Because most applications of TMS therapy do not require the induction of a seizure, researchers hope also that it offers a safer alternative to ECT.

Most recently, neurologist Helen Mayberg has reported using *deep brain stimulation,* which requires the surgical implantation of a microelectrode through a small hole in the skull and directly into the brain, where it delivers a continual trickle of electric current. Dr. Mayberg likens the treatment to a "pacemaker" for an area of cortex that seems to range out of control in depression (Gutman, 2006). Although the treatment at present is still highly experimental and has been used on only a few patients, Mayberg reports many positive outcomes, with little risk to her patients (Mayberg et al., 2005). She views the treatment not as an alternative to other therapies but as a promising last-resort for severely depressed patients who have not responded to other approaches.

Hospitalization and the Alternatives

We have seen that mental hospitals were originally conceived as places of refuge—"asylums"—where disturbed people could escape the pressures of normal living. In fact, they often worked very well (Maher & Maher, 1985). But by the 20th century these hospitals had become overcrowded and, at best, little more than warehouses for the disturbed with nowhere else to go. Rarely were people of means committed to mental hospitals; instead, they were given private care, including individual psychotherapy (Doyle, 2002a). By contrast, in the large public mental hospitals, a feeble form of "group therapy" was often done with a whole ward—perhaps 50 patients—at a time. But too many patients and too few therapists meant that little, if any, real therapy occurred. The drugs that so profoundly altered treatment in mental hospitals did not appear until the 1950s, so prior to that time institutionalized patients often found themselves controlled by straitjackets, locked rooms, and, sometimes, lobotomies. It's too bad that Maxwell Jones didn't come to the rescue a half-century earlier, with his frontal attack on the mental hospital system.

The Therapeutic Community   In 1953—at about the time antipsychotic drugs were introduced—psychiatrist Maxwell Jones proposed replacing traditional hospital "treatment" for mental disorders with a **therapeutic community** designed to bring meaning to patients' lives. He envisioned the daily hospital routine itself structured as a therapy that would help patients learn to cope with the world outside. With these goals in mind, he abolished the dormitory accommodations that had been typical of mental hospitals and gave patients more private living quarters. He required that they make decisions about meals and daily activities. Then, as they were able to take more responsibilities, patients assumed the tasks of everyday living, including laundry, housekeeping, and maintenance. Further, Jones involved them in helping to plan their own treatment, which included not only group psychotherapy but occupational therapy and recreational therapy (Jones, 1953).

Eventually, variations on the therapeutic community concept were adopted across the United States, Canada, Britain, and Europe—sometimes more on paper than in reality, as we saw in Rosenhan's "pseudopatient" study in Chapter 12. But the changes did not come cheaply. The newer approach obviously required more staff and more costly facilities. The high costs led to a search for still another alternative, which came in the form of community-based treatment—which began to look more and more attractive with the increasing availability of drug therapies.

Deinstitutionalization and Community Mental Health   For mental health professionals of all stripes, the goal of **deinstitutionalization** was to remove patients from mental hospitals and return them to their communities for treatment in a

Therapeutic community   Jones's term for a program of treating mental disorder by making the institutional environment supportive and humane for patients.

Deinstitutionalization   The policy of removing patients, whenever possible, from mental hospitals.

Deinstitutionalization put mental patients back in the community—but often without adequate resources for continued treatment.

Community mental health movement An effort to deinstitutionalize mental patients and to provide therapy from outpatient clinics. Proponents of community mental health envisioned that recovering patients could live with their families, in foster homes, or in group homes.

more familiar and supportive environment. The concept of deinstitutionalization also gained popularity with politicians, who saw large sums of money being poured into mental hospitals (filled, incidentally, with nonvoting patients). Thus, by the 1970s, a consensus formed among politicians and the mental health community that the major locus of treatment should shift from mental hospitals back to the community. There both psychological and drug therapies would be dispensed from outpatient clinics, and recovering patients could live with their families, in foster homes, or in group homes. This vision became known as the **community mental health movement.**

Unfortunately, the reality did not match the vision (Doyle, 2002a; Torrey, 1996, 1997). Community mental health clinics—the centerpieces of the community mental health movement—rarely received the full funding they needed. Chronic patients were released from mental hospitals, but they often returned to communities that could offer them few therapeutic resources and to families ill-equipped to cope with them (Smith et al., 1993). Then, as patients returned to the community and needed care, they entered psychiatric wards at local general hospitals—rather than mental hospitals. As a result, hospital care has continued to consume a large share of mental health expenditures in the United States (Kiesler, 1993; U.S. Department of Health and Human Services, 2002).

Some disturbed individuals, who would have been hospitalized in an earlier time, have now all but disappeared from view within their communities. Among them, an estimated 150,000 persons, especially those with chronic schizophrenia, have ended up homeless, with no network of support (Torrey, 1997). Although estimates vary widely, up to 52% of homeless men and 71% of homeless women in the United States probably suffer from psychological disorders, and many of them are former mental hospital patients (Lamb, 1998). Many also have problems with alcohol or other drugs. Under these conditions, they survive by shuttling from agency to agency. With no one to monitor their behavior, they usually stop taking their medication, and so their condition deteriorates until they require a period of rehospitalization.

Despite the dismal picture we have painted, community treatment has not proved altogether unsuccessful. After a review of ten studies in which mental patients were randomly assigned to hospital treatment or to various community-based programs, Kiesler (1982) reported that patients more often improved in the community treatment programs. Further, those given community-based treatment were less likely to be hospitalized at a later date. When community health programs have adequate resources, they can be highly effective (McGuire, 2000).

Unfortunately, some 60 million Americans live in rural areas where they have no easy access to mental health services. But, thanks to the Internet and the telephone, some of them can now get help through remote "telehealth" sessions (Winerman, 2006c). Using the telehealth approach, psychologists and other professionals can quickly establish a link with their rural clients, to answer questions, make referrals, and even provide therapy. Besides the convenience, the cost savings in commuting time for therapists is huge.

Most recently, a daring new community mental health approach is being tried in five communities across the nation. Leader of this effort is psychiatrist William McFarlane, who believes—and has evidence to support his belief—that psychosis can be prevented if the early symptoms are recognized and treated aggressively (Schmidt, 2007). To do so, McFarlane's group identifies at-risk youth through such symptoms as declining schoolwork, confused thoughts, difficulty in speaking clearly, and hearing nonexistent sounds: About one-third of such individuals actually become psychotic. After enrollment in their program (which is optional), the youths receive counseling aimed at helping them cope with stress, and those with the highest risk factors also get a low dose of antipsychotic medication. Critics object to the program because of its high false-positive identification rate (two-thirds of untreated individuals with these symptoms do *not* develop psychosis) and because antipsychotic medications can have

CHAPTER 13 ● THERAPIES FOR PSYCHOLOGICAL DISORDERS

serious side effects. Nevertheless, the program is in progress: Stay tuned for the results.

The "telehealth" approach to therapy brings mental health services to clients in rural areas, where help might not otherwise be available.

PSYCHOLOGY**MATTERS**

What Sort of Therapy Would You Recommend?

Now that we have looked at both the psychological and biomedical therapies, consider the following situation. A friend tells you about some personal problems he or she is having and requests your help in finding a therapist. Because you are studying psychology, your friend reasons, you might know what kind of treatment would be best. How do you respond?

First, you can lend a friendly ear, using the techniques of active listening, acceptance, and exploration of alternatives, which we discussed earlier in the chapter. In fact, this may be all that your troubled friend needs. But if your friend wants to see a therapist or if the situation looks in any way like one that requires professional assistance, you can use your knowledge of mental disorders and therapies to help your friend decide what sort of therapist might be most appropriate. To take some of the burden off your shoulders, both of you should understand that any competent therapist will always refer the client elsewhere if the required therapy lies outside the therapist's specialty.

A Therapy Checklist Here, then, are some questions you will want to consider before you recommend a particular type of therapist:

- *Is medical treatment needed?* While you should not try to make a diagnosis, you should encourage your friend to see a medical specialist, such as a psychiatrist or nurse practitioner if you suspect that the problem involves a major mental disorder, such as psychosis, mania, or bipolar disorder. Medical evaluation is also indicated if you suspect narcolepsy, sleep apnea, epilepsy, Alzheimer's disease, or other problems recognized to have a biological basis. If your suspicion is confirmed, the treatment may include a combination of drug therapy and psychotherapy.

- *Is there a specific behavior problem?* For example, does your friend want to eliminate a fear of spiders or a fear of flying? Is the problem a rebellious child? A sexual problem? Is she or he depressed—but not psychotic? If so, behavior therapy or cognitive–behavioral therapy with a counseling or clinical psychologist is probably the best bet. (Most psychiatrists and other medical practitioners are not usually trained in these procedures.) You can call the prospective therapist's office and ask for information on specific areas of training and specialization.

- *Would group therapy be helpful?* Many people find valuable help and support in a group setting, where they can learn not only from the therapist but also from other group members. Groups can be especially effective in dealing with shyness, lack of assertiveness, and addictions, and with complex problems of interpersonal relationships. (As a bonus, group therapy is often less expensive than individual therapy.) Professionals with training in several disciplines, including psychology, psychiatry, and social work, run therapy groups. Again, your best bet is a therapist who has had special training in this method and about whom you have heard good things from former clients.

- *Is the problem one of stress, confusion, or choice?* Most troubled people don't fall neatly into one of the categories that we have discussed in the previous points. More typically, they need help sorting through the chaos of their lives, finding a pattern, and developing a plan to cope. This is the territory of the insight therapies.

Some Cautions We now know enough about human biology, behavior, and mental processes to know some treatments to avoid. Here are some particularly important examples:

- *Drug therapies to avoid.* The minor tranquilizers (antianxiety drugs) are too frequently prescribed for patients leading chronically stressful lives. As we have said, because of their addicting and sedating effects, these drugs should only be taken for short periods—if at all. Similarly, some physicians ignore the dangers of sleep-inducing medications for their patients who suffer from insomnia. While these drugs have legitimate uses, many such prescriptions carry the possibility of drug dependence and of interfering with the person's ability to alter the conditions that may have caused the original problem.

- *Advice and interpretations to avoid.* Although psychodynamic therapy can be helpful, patients should also be cautioned that some such therapists may give ill-advised counsel in problems of anger management. Traditionally, Freudians have believed that individuals who are prone to angry or violent outbursts harbor deep-seated aggression that needs to be vented. But, as we have seen, research shows that trying to empty one's aggressions through aggressive behavior, such as shouting or punching a pillow, may actually increase the likelihood of later aggressive behavior.

With these cautions in mind, then, your friend can contact several therapists to see which has the combination of skills and manner that offer the best fit for her problem and her personality.

CheckYourUnderstanding

1. **APPLICATION:** Imagine that you are a psychiatrist. Which type of drug would you prescribe for a patient diagnosed with attention-deficit/hyperactivity disorder (ADHD)?

2. **RECALL:** Which class of drugs blocks dopamine receptors in the brain? Which type magnifies the effects of serotonin?

3. **RECALL:** Name three types of medical therapies for mental disorder, including one that has now been largely abandoned as ineffective and dangerous.

4. **RECALL:** The community mental health movement followed a deliberate plan of _____ for mental patients.

5. **UNDERSTANDING THE CORE CONCEPT:** _____, _____, and _____ all are medical techniques for treating mental disorders by directly altering the function of the brain.

Answers **1.** a stimulant **2.** Antipsychotic drugs block dopamine receptors in the brain. Antidepressants, particularly the selective serotonin reuptake inhibitors (SSRIs), amplify the effects of serotonin. **3.** Electroconvulsive therapy, drug therapy, and prefrontal lobotomy; the latter is no longer done as a treatment for mental disorders. **4.** deinstitutionalization. **5.** Any three of the following would be correct: drug therapies, psychosurgery, ECT, and transcranial magnetic stimulation.

13.4 KEY QUESTION
HOW DO THE PSYCHOLOGICAL THERAPIES AND BIOMEDICAL THERAPIES COMPARE?

Now that we have looked at both the psychological and medical therapies, can we say which approach is best? In this section, we will see that the answer to that question depends on the disorder. But before we look at the treatment choices for several major conditions, we should acknowledge some other influences that cloud the issue of medical versus psychological treatments.

We have seen that psychologists and psychiatrists have long been at odds over the best forms of treatment for mental disorders. In part, the dispute is over territory and money: Who gets to treat people with mental problems—and bill their insurance? The big pharmaceutical companies, with billions of dollars at stake, play a huge role in this dispute, too. You can glimpse the sort of hardball game Big Pharma plays by noting the advertising for prescription drugs that is directed at the general public. Because of these conflicting interests and pressures, research on medical and psychological therapies has been done largely in parallel, with

Drug companies now do a hard sell on psychotropic drugs through advertisements like this one aimed at the general public. Here, the not-so-subtle message is that unhappy people can be treated with medication.

each side promoting its own approach and ignoring the other's. Unfortunately, this has meant that comparatively little research has C focused on the effectiveness of **combination therapies**, involving both medication and psychotherapy used in concert.

That said, let's take a look at how we might weigh the options of medical and psychological treatment in some specific disorders with which you are now familiar. Here's the Core Concept:

> While a combination of psychological and medical therapies is better than either one alone for treating some (but not all) mental disorders, most people who suffer from unspecified "problems in living" are best served by psychological treatment alone.

Combination therapy A therapeutic approach that involves both psychological and medical techniques—most often a drug therapy with a behavioral or cognitive-behavioral therapy.

core
concept

More specifically, what we will find is that a very large numbers of people with psychological problems do not have a *DSM-IV* disorder but need psychological counseling or therapy to help them work through difficult periods in their lives.

On the other hand, many of the well-known *DSM-IV* disorders, including the mood disorders, most of the anxiety disorders, and schizophrenia, are best treated by a combination of medical and psychological therapies. Let's begin with the latter.

Depression: Psychological versus Medical Treatment

Fluoxetine (Prozac) is the planet's most widely prescribed drug. Together with other SSRI medications, it represents a $10 billion, worldwide industry (Bower, 2006b). But it may be worth every penny, if it is effective in treating depression, thought to be the world's most common disorder. But how effective is it? And how effective is it in comparison with psychological therapies?

CBT versus Drugs   Studies show that antidepressant drugs and cognitive–behavioral therapy (CBT)—the psychological treatment for which we have the most evidence of efficacy—are equally effective ways of treating depression, at least in the short run (DeRubeis et al., 1999; Hollon 1996; Hollon et al., 2002). A recent study, however, found that CBT may have the edge over drug therapy over the long term. While 58 percent of patients improved under either treatment regimen, at the end of a two-year follow-up, only one-quarter of those in CBT had a recurrence of their depression, while half of the medication group had experienced a relapse (DeRubeis et al., 2005).

But what happens if depressed patients get antidepressants *and* CBT? The research shows that they generally do even better than with either treatment alone (Keller et al., 2000; Thase et al., 1997). Advances in understanding the brain substrates of depression now suggest why such a combination therapy approach seems to be best. Neuroscientist Helen Mayberg has shown that CBT and the antidepressants work their wonders by targeting different parts of the brain. Antidepressants seem to act through the limbic system—which contains the brain's main emotion pathways. In contrast, CBT affects a part the frontal cortex associated with reasoning. The common factor in both approaches is an "alarm switch" that gets turned off, either by the effect of drugs on the "fast" emotion pathway in the limbic system or by the effect of CBT on the brain's "slow" emotional circuitry in the cortex (Goldapple et al., 2004). Thus, as research from the clinic and the lab come together, many clinicians have come to favor a *combination therapy* approach for depression, using both drugs and CBT. A recent study supports a combined drug-and-medicine approach for bipolar patients, as well (Miklowitz et al., 2007).

ECT   And what about electroconvulsive therapy (ECT)? Although clinicians commonly assert that ECT is the most effective treatment for psychotic depression (Hollon et al., 2002), only one study, done in Sweden, has compared ECT head-to-head with antidepressants. The principal finding: Suicide attempts were less common among those patients receiving ECT than among those taking antidepressants (Brådvik & Berglund, 2006). As for transcranial magnetic stimulation, it is too early to tell. As of this writing, no studies have reported a one-on-one comparison of TMS with other therapies for depression.

Anxiety Disorders: Psychological versus Medical Treatment

The evidence points to a similar conclusion in the anxiety disorders—with one important exception. Again, many studies show that, for most anxiety disorders, either cognitive–behavioral therapy or drug therapy can be effective. Among the relatively few studies that have included a comparison of medicine and psychotherapy in combination, two have found that the most effective way of treating panic disorder is a combination of cognitive-behavioral therapy and antidepressants (Barlow et al., 2000; Roy-Byrne et al., 2005). Similarly, psychologist Richard Heimberg, who studies *social phobia,* a condition that affects more than

5 million Americans, reports that CBT and antidepressants relieve the anxieties of about 80 percent of his patients (Dittman, 2005a; Heimberg et al., 1998).

We said that there is an important exception to the rule of combination therapy for anxiety disorders. It is this: Medication is *not* effective for treating the *specific phobias*. In fact, studies suggest that drugs may even interfere with *exposure therapy*, which is the treatment of choice (Antony & Barlow, 2002).

Schizophrenia: Psychological versus Medical Treatment

Ever since the discovery of antipsychotics more than 50 years ago, these drugs have represented the front line of treatment for schizophrenia. Supplemental treatment, in the form of family therapy, social skills training (often in community residental treatment centers), and occupational therapy (through sheltered workshops, such as Goodwill Industries) has brought schizophrenic patients back into contact with their communities. But until recently, conventional psychological therapies were little used. In the last few years, however, advocates of cognitive-behavioral therapy have been trying their hands at treating schizophrenia, with encouraging results, even with patients who have not responded to medication (McGurk et al., 2007; Rector & Beck, 2001).

"The Worried Well": Not Everyone Needs Drugs

While a combination of psychological therapy and drugs may be best for some disorders, we have seen that drugs are *not* useful for treating specific phobias. Likewise, medication has little value as a therapy for most learning disabilities, sexual dysfunctions, most personality disorders, and most developmental disorders (with the exception of ADHD). In addition, we should remember that many people who have psychological problems do not have a diagnosed mental disorder, such as depression, a phobia, or schizophrenia. These are the people that clinicians sometimes call "the worried well." That's not to say that their problems are not real and genuinely troubling. But they do not have one of the "brand name" disorders specifically listed in the *DSM-IV*. Technically, they are classified under the heading of "other conditions that may be a focus of clinical attention," but they suffer from what we might term generic "problems in living"—often problems involving difficult choices (e.g., "Should I stay in this marriage?" or "What career should I pursue?"). Again, these are problems that, by themselves, do not require drugs or other medical intervention. The difficulty is that people with such problems-in-living too often persuade a physician to prescribe antidepressants or antianxiety medications. What they really need is a referral to a mental health professional who could help them sort through their problems and choices.

PSYCHOLOGYMATTERS
Using Psychology to Learn Psychology

Consider the ways in which psychotherapy is like your educational experiences in college:

- Most therapists, like most professors, are professionals with special training in what they do.
- Most patients/clients are like students in that they are seeking professional help to change their lives in some way.
- Much of what happens in therapy and in the classroom involves learning: new ideas, new behaviors, new insights, and new connections.

Learning as Therapy It may help you learn psychology (and other subjects, as well) to think of your college education in therapeutic terms. As we have seen, therapy seems to work best when therapist and client have a good working relationship and when the client believes in the value of the experience—and the same is almost certainly true for the student–professor relationship. You can take the initiative in establishing a personal-but-professional relationship with your psychology professor by doing the following two things: (a) asking questions or otherwise participating in class (at appropriate times and without dominating, of course) and (b) seeking your instructor's help on points you don't understand or on course-related topics you would like to pursue in more detail (doing so during regular office hours). The result will be learning more about psychology because you will be taking a more active part in the learning process. Incidentally, an active approach to the course will also help you stand out from the crowd in the professor's mind, which could be helpful if you later need a faculty recommendation.

Now consider a parallel between group therapy and education. In group therapy, patients learn from each other, as well as from the therapist. Much the same can occur in your psychology course, if you consider other students as learning resources. As we noted earlier in this book, the most successful students often spend part of their study time sharing information in groups.

Change Behavior, Not Just Thinking   One other tip for learning psychology we can borrow from the success of behavior therapies: the importance of changing behavior, as well as thinking. It is easy to "intellectualize" a fact or an idea passively when you read about it or hear about it in class. But you are likely to find that the idea makes little impact on you ("I know I *read* about it, but I can't *remember* it!") if you don't use it. The remedy is to do something with your new knowledge: Tell someone about it, come up with illustrations from your own experience, or try acting in a different way. For example, after reading about active listening in this chapter, try it the next time you talk to a friend. Educators sometimes speak of this as "active learning."

And, we suggest, it's one of those psychological therapies that works best without drugs!

Critical Thinking Applied: Evidence-Based Practice

The field of therapy for mental disorders is awash in controversy. Psychologists and psychiatrists dispute the value of drugs versus psychological therapies. Arguments rage over the advantages and disadvantages of electroconvulsive therapy for treating depression. And, as we saw in the pervious chapter, debates still echo the issues Rosenhan raised over three decades ago about the effectiveness of mental hospitals and the reliability of psychiatric diagnoses. But there is no dispute more acrimonious than the one over *evidence-based practice,* a dispute that is particularly bitter among clinical psychologists (Bower, 2005a).

What Is the Issue?

A decade ago, the American Psychological Association established a special task force charged with evaluating the effectiveness of various psychological therapies (Chambless et al., 1996). The thrust of their findings is

that literally dozens of specific disorders can be treated successfully by therapies that have been validated in well-designed experiments (Barlow, 1996). Here are a few examples of therapies pronounced effective by the APA task force:

● Behavior therapy for specific phobias, enuresis (bedwetting), autism, and alcoholism

● Cognitive–behavioral therapy for chronic pain, anorexia, bulimia, agoraphobia, and depression

● Insight therapy for couples relationship problems

More recently, a report by the American Psychological Society focused specifically on evidence-based treatments for depression (Hollon et al., 2002). That document asserts that several varieties of psychotherapy can be effective. These include cognitive, behavioral, and family therapy. (The APS report also acknowledged that there is a legitimate role for both drug and electroconvulsive therapies in the treatment of depression.) As we have seen, some studies now suggest that, for depression, a combination of cognitive–behavioral therapy and drug therapy can have a greater effect than either treatment alone (Keller et al., 2000).

So, what's all the fuss about? At issue is whether counselors and therapists should be *limited* to the use of therapy methods known as **empirically supported treatments (EST),** that is, to treatments that have been validated by research evidence showing that they actually work (Westen et al., 2005). So how could anyone possibly object to that, you might ask? It may surprise you to learn that psychologists line up on both sides of this issue (Johnson, 2006). Those in opposition say that the devil is in the details: They say that they are not antiscience, but they believe "empirically supported treatments" is a fuzzy concept (Westen & Bradley, 2005). They also worry about an overly strict interpretation that might inhibit a practitioner's freedom to meet the needs of an individual client. Let's take a critical look at these details.

What Critical Thinking Questions Should We Ask?

No one doubts that the people on both sides of the evidence-based practice issue are decent and honorable and that among them are genuine experts on therapy. So we won't question their credibility. But it might be a good idea to ask: What biases does each side have that might make them weigh the options differently?

The Evidence-Based Practice Movement Those pushing the idea of evidence-based practice point to a long history of misguided, and even harmful therapies— from beatings to lobotomies—to which people with mental problems have been subjected. Even in modern times, some practitioners continue to advocate techniques that can potentially harm their clients (Lilienfeld, 2007). These include "scared straight" interventions for juvenile offenders, facilitated communication for autism, recovered-memory therapies, induction of "alter" personalities in cases diagnosed as dissociative identity disorder, DARE (antidrug education) programs in the schools, boot-camp programs for conduct disorder in prisoner populations, sexual reorientation for homosexuality, and catharsis ("get-it-out-of-your-system") treatment for anger disorders. An even longer list (based on a survey of clinical psychologists), ranging from the merely ineffective to the crackpot, would include: angel therapy, past lives therapy, treatments for PTSD caused by alien abduction, aromatherapy, therapeutic touch, Neuro-Linguistic Programming, primal scream therapy, and handwriting analysis (Norcross et al, 2006).

Empirically supported treatment (EST) Treatment regimen that has been demonstrated to be effective through research.

On a more positive note, those who favor evidence-based practice argue that, if psychology is a science, then its practitioners must follow the science wherever it leads, even if that means giving up favored treatments that don't work. But what would that leave in the therapeutic tool kit? As we have seen, abundant evidence supports the use of behavioral therapy for phobias, obsessive–compulsive disorder, certain sexual dysfunctions, autism, and enuresis (bed-wetting). In addition, cognitive–behavioral therapy has been demonstrated to be effective for depression, the anxiety disorders, and the treatment of chronic pain, while the insight therapies have a superlative record for dealing with relationship problems.

Those Favoring Caution While acknowledging that we have made great strides in developing highly effective treatments for a number of disorders, those urging caution point out that we are light-years from having the tools to treat all mental disorders—even with the use of drugs. Consequently, they fear that insurance companies and HMOs will be unwilling to pay for treatments not on the official list or for any deviations from "approved" treatments, no matter what the needs of the individual patient. They also worry that the managed care companies will force therapists into a one-size-fits-all approach that would ignore both the clinician's judgment and the client's individual needs (Shedler, 2006). Because therapy is such a time-consuming process, they also fear that nonmedical therapists will be squeezed out of the picture by drug prescribers who may take only a few minutes with each patient.

Those with reservations about evidence-based practice have several other, more subtle, concerns (Westen & Bradley, 2005). For example, they point out that therapy is more than the application of specific *techniques:* Researchers find that a common element in successful therapy is a caring, hopeful relationship and a new way of looking at oneself and the world (Wampold et al., 2007). This conclusion has been supported by studies that find the effectiveness of therapy to depend less on the *type of therapy* used and more on the *quality of the relationship* (also called the *therapeutic alliance*) between therapist and client (Wampold & Brown, 2005). Therapy also involves a host of *individual client factors,* such as motivation, intelligence, and the nature of the problem itself. We can represent these three aspects of therapy graphically, as in Figure 13.6. For some problems (such as a relationship issue or a vocational choice problem—the "problems in living" that we discussed earlier), no specific ESTs exist. Moreover, the specific type of therapy used in such cases may be less important than a supportive therapeutic relationship (DeAngelis, 2005; Martin et al., 2000).

Finally, the critics of evidence-based practice also point out that most patients/clients present themselves with multiple problems, such as an anxiety disorder *and* a per-

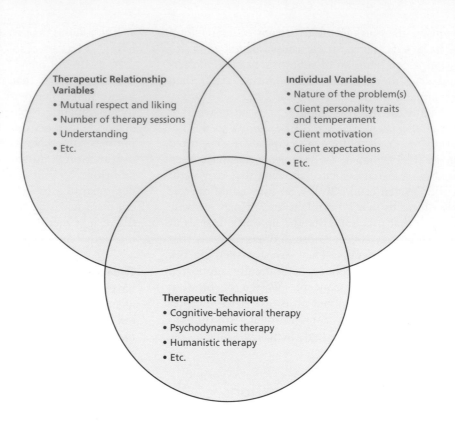

FIGURE 13.6

Three Aspects of Therapy

Therapy is more than a set of techniques. It also involves a number of individual variables (including the nature of the problem) and the relationship between the client and therapist—the *therapeutic alliance*. All must come together for therapy to be successful.

Therapeutic Relationship Variables
• Mutual respect and liking
• Number of therapy sessions
• Understanding
• Etc.

Individual Variables
• Nature of the problem(s)
• Client personality traits and temperament
• Client motivation
• Client expectations
• Etc.

Therapeutic Techniques
• Cognitive-behavioral therapy
• Psychodynamic therapy
• Humanistic therapy
• Etc.

sonality disorder. Yet most ESTs have been validated on an unusually "pure" sample of individuals presenting single problems. Moreover, most research aimed at validating therapeutic techniques is severely restricted to just a few sessions—usually no more than a dozen—after which most patients still have some residual problems. But little evidence exists to validate what sort of therapy is required over the long term to finish the process.

To end this discussion on a more encouraging note: A recent study of 200 practitioners found that they all tended to modify their approach to treatment to fit the needs of their clients, as the situation unfolds during counseling or psychotherapy (Holloway, 2003b). That is, despite our emphasis in this chapter on conflicting opinions about treatment of psychological disorders, most practitioners are quite willing to adapt their methods to the individual client, rather than holding rigidly to a particular theoretical orientation. And that is good news, indeed, coming from a field that has traditionally had strongly divided allegiances. It appears that the emphasis on science-based practice is finally breaking down the old therapeutic boundaries.

What Conclusions Can We Draw?

Both sides make good points. (See Table 13.3.) On the one hand, practitioners should favor empirically validated treatments, when they are clearly appropriate and effective. And they certainly should eschew treatments that are ineffective or harmful. But who is going to make that determination: the individual practitioners, the

insurance companies, legislators, or professional organizations? Your authors think that the professional psychology associations, such as the APA, must take stands against putting the therapist into a straightjacket by limiting him or her to a cast-in-stone list of treatments and disorders for which those treatments may be applied.

In fact, the American Psychological Association has a proposed policy under consideration (APA Presidential Task Force, 2006). The policy would define *evidence-based practice in psychology* as "the integration of the best available research with clinical expertise in the context of patient characteristics, culture, and preferences." Who wouldn't agree with that? Many people, it turns out. In particular, the evidence-based practice advocates are concerned that "clinical expertise" could trump "research," with the result that clinicians could ignore the science and do as they please (Stuart & Lilienfeld, 2007). It is a knotty issue that doesn't lend itself to easy answers.

Is there a solution in sight? A partial solution may lie in a proposal made by David Barlow (2004), who suggested that psychologists make a distinction between *psychological treatments* and what he calls "generic psychotherapy." The empirically validated therapies for specific disorders listed in the *DSM-IV* would fall under the heading of *psychological treatments,* while reserving the term *psychotherapy* for work with the nonspecific "problems-in-living" that make up a large proportion of the caseloads of many counselors and clinicians. Barlow's proposal would, at least, shrink the disputed territory.

TABLE 13.3	Summary of the Evidence-Based Practice (EBP) Debate	

Arguments Favoring EBP	Arguments opposing EBP
• Some treatments are clearly harmful, and practitioners should not be allowed to use them.	• Empirically supported therapies (ESTs) is a poorly defined, even meaningless, concept.
• Specific empirically supported therapies (ESTs) have been demonstrated to be effective in dealing with certain disorders.	• EBP is a "one-size-fits-all" approach that would limit the flexibility of clinicians to deal with individual client's problems, particularly those who have multiple problems or do not fit a *DSM-IV* category.
• Psychology is a science, and psychological practitioners should follow what the research shows to be best.	• Insurance companies would not pay for therapy that was not on an approved list of empirically validated treatments.
• Giving clinical judgment equal weight with science would lead to anarchy, in which clinicians could ignore the evidence and do what they please.	• EBP would prevent practitioners from trying new ideas and developing even more effective therapies.
	• Scientists have not yet validated treatments for many disorders, so under an EBP approach many people might have to go without treatment.
	• Evidence suggests that certain common factors (e.g., the therapeutic alliance) are just as important as the specific type of treatment.

Chapter Summary

13.1 What Is Therapy?

Core Concept 13.1: Therapy for psychological disorders takes a variety of forms, but all involve some relationship focused on improving a person's mental, behavioral, or social functioning.

People seek **therapy** for a variety of problems, including *DSM-IV* disorders and problems of everyday living. Treatment comes in many forms, both psychological and biomedical, but most involve diagnosing the problem, finding the source of the problem, making a prognosis, and carrying out treatment. In earlier times, treatments for those with mental problems were usually harsh and dehumanizing, often based on the assumption of demonic possession. Only recently have people with emotional problems been treated as individuals with "illnesses," which has led to more humane treatment.

Currently in the United States, there are two main approaches to therapy: the **psychological** and the **biomedical therapies.** Other cultures often have different ways of understanding and treating mental disorders, often making use of the family and community. In the United States there is a trend toward increasing use of **paraprofessionals** as mental health care providers, and the literature generally supports their effectiveness.

Biomedical therapy (p. 575)   **Therapeutic alliance** (p. 572)

Paraprofessional (p. 575)   **Therapy** (p. 570)

Psychological therapy (p. 574)

MyPsychLab Resources 13.1:

Watch: Asylum: History of Mental Institutions in America

Explore: Psychotherapy Practitioners and Their Activities

13.2 How Do Psychologists Treat Psychological Disorders?

Core Concept 13.2: Psychologists employ two main forms of treatment, the insight therapies (focused on developing understanding of the problem) and the behavior therapies (focused on changing behavior through conditioning).

Psychoanalysis, the first of the *insight therapies,* grew out of Sigmund Freud's theory of personality. Using such techniques as *free association* and dream interpretation, its goal is to bring repressed material out of the unconscious into consciousness, where it can be interpreted and neutralized, particularly in the **analysis of transference. Neo-Freudian psychodynamic therapies** typically emphasize the patient's current social situation, interpersonal relationships, and self-concept.

Among other insight therapies, **humanistic therapy** focuses on individuals becoming more fully self-actualized. In one form, **client-centered therapy,** practitioners strive to be *nondirective* in helping their clients establish a positive self-image.

Another form of insight therapy, **cognitive therapy** concentrates on changing negative or irrational thought patterns about oneself and one's social relationships. The client must learn more constructive thought patterns and learn to apply the new technique to other situations. This has been particularly effective for depression.

Group therapy can take many approaches. **Self-help support groups,** such as AA, serve millions, even though they are not usually run by professional therapists. *Family therapy* and *couples therapy* usually concentrate on situational difficulties and interpersonal dynamics as a total system in need of improvement, rather than on internal motives.

The **behavior therapies** apply the principles of learning—especially operant and classical conditioning—to problem behaviors. Among the classical conditioning techniques, **systematic desensitization** is commonly employed to treat fears. **Aversion therapy** may also be used for eliminating unwanted responses. Operant techniques include **contingency management,** which especially involves positive reinforcement and extinction strategies. And, on a larger scale, behavior therapy may be used to treat or manage groups in the form of a **token economy. Participant modeling,** based on research in observational learning, may make use of both classical and operant principles, involving the use of models and social skills training to help individuals practice and gain confidence about their abilities.

In recent years a synthesis of cognitive and behavioral therapies has emerged, combining the techniques of insight therapy with methods based on behavioral learning theory. **Rational–emotive behavior therapy** helps clients recognize that their irrational beliefs about themselves interfere with life and helps them learn how to change those thought patterns. **Positive psychotherapy (PPT)** is a similar approach coming out of the positive psychology movement. Brain scans suggest that **cognitive–behavioral therapy** produces physical changes in brain functioning.

The effectiveness of therapy was challenged in the 1950s by Eysenck. Since that time, however, research has shown that psychotherapy can be effective for a variety of psychological problems. Often it is more effective than drug therapy. As the research on mental disorders becomes more refined, we are learning to match specific psychotherapies to specific disorders.

Most people do not get psychological help from professionals. Rather, they get help from teachers, friends, clergy, and others in their community who seem sympathetic. Friends can often help through **active listening,** acceptance, and exploration of alternatives, but serious problems require professional assistance.

Active listener (p. 592)

Analysis of transference (p. 578)

Aversion therapy (p. 585)

Behavior modification (p. 583)

Behavior therapy (p. 583)

Client-centered therapy (p. 580)

Cognitive therapy (p. 580)

Cognitive–behavioral therapy (p. 587)

Contingency management (p. 586)

Exposure therapy (p. 585)

Group therapy (p. 582)

Humanistic therapy (p. 579)

Insight therapy (p. 576)

Neo-Freudian psychodynamic therapy (p. 579)

Participant modeling (p. 587)

Positive psychotherapy (PPT) (p. 589)

Psychoanalysis (p. 577)

Rational–emotive behavior therapy (REBT) (p. 587)

Reflection of feeling (p. 580)

Self-help support groups (p. 582)

Systematic desensitization (p. 584)

Token economy (p. 586)

MyPsychLab Resources 13.2:

Watch: Cognitive Behavioral Therapy

Explore: Key Components of Psychoanalytic, Humanistic, Behavior, and Cognitive Therapies

13.3 How Is the Biomedical Approach Used to Treat Psychological Disorders?

Core Concept 13.3: Biomedical therapies seek to treat psychological disorders by changing the brain's chemistry with drugs, its circuitry with surgery, or its patterns of activity with pulses of electricity or powerful magnetic fields.

Biomedical therapies concentrate on changing the physiological aspects of mental illness. Drug therapy includes **antipsychotic, antidepressant,** *mood stabilizing,* **antianxiety drugs,** and **stimulants.** Most affect the function of neurotransmitters, but the precise mode of action is not known for any of them. Nevertheless, such drugs have caused a revolution in the medical treatment of mental disorder, such as schizophrenia, depression, bipolar disorder, anxiety disorders, and ADHD. Critics, however, warn of their abuse, particularly in treating the ordinary stress of daily living.

Psychosurgery is rarely done anymore because of its radical, irreversible side effects. **Electroconvulsive therapy,** however, is still widely used—primarily with depressed patients—although it, too, remains controversial. A new and potential less harmful alternative involves **transcranial magnetic stimulation** of specific brain areas. Meanwhile, hospitalization has been a mainstay of medical treatment, although the trend is away from mental hospitals to community-based treatment. The policy of **deinstitutionalization** was based on the best intentions, but many mental patients have been turned back into their communities with few resources and little treatment. When the resources are available, however, community treatment is often successful.

If someone asks your advice on finding a therapist, you can refer him or her to any competent mental health professional. While you should avoid trying to make a diagnosis or attempting therapy for mental disorders, you may use your knowledge of psychology to steer the person toward a medical specialist, a behavior therapist, group therapy, or some other psychological treatment that you believe might be appropriate. There are, however, some specific therapies and therapeutic techniques to avoid.

Antianxiety drugs (p. 595)

Antidepressants (p. 594)

Antipsychotics (p. 594)

Community mental health movement (p. 600)

Deinstitutionalization (p. 599)

Electroconvulsive therapy (ECT) (p. 598)

Psychosurgery (p. 597)

Stimulants (p. 596)

Tardive dyskinesia (p. 594)

Therapeutic community (p. 599)

Transcranial magnetic stimulation (TMS) (p. 598)

MyPsychLab Resources 13.3:

Explore: Drugs Commonly Used to Treat Psychiatric Disorders

Watch: Alternative Approaches to Treating ADHD

13.4 How Do the Psychological Therapies And Biomedical Therapies Compare?

Core Concept 13.4: While a combination of psychological and medical therapies is better than either one alone for treating some (but not all) mental disorders, most people who suffer from unspecified "problems in living" are best served by psychological treatment alone.

Both medical and biological therapies can point to their successes, but until recently, few studies have compared medical and psychological therapies directly. New studies show that for depression, a **combination therapy,** consisting of CBT and medication, is often best. Comparative data for ECT and the new transcranial magnetic stimulation are sparse. As for the anxiety disorders, some studies have shown a combination of drugs and CBT to be effective. A clear exception involves the specific phobias, for which behavioral therapy is superior to drug therapy—which may actually aggravate the problem. For schizophrenia, medications are the front line of treatment, although they do not cure the disorder. Until recently, conventional psychotherapies were not often used with schizophrenia, but new research suggests that combination therapy may be effective.

Medication is not useful for treating many psychological problems, such as learning disabilities, many sexual dysfunctions, most personality disorders, and most developmental disorders. In addition, most people who have psychological problems do not have a *DSM-IV* disorder but rather suffer from "problems in living."

Education and psychotherapy have many points in common. In particular, both involve learning and the ultimate goal of changes in behavior. The authors suggest that both education and psychotherapy are more likely to be successful when the client takes an active role.

Combination therapy (p. 603)

Empirically supported treatment (EST) (p. 607)

Watch the following video by logging into MyPsychLab (www.mypsychlab.com). After you have watched the video, complete the activities that follow.

PROGRAM 22: PSYCHOTHERAPY

PROGRAM REVIEW

1. What are the two main approaches to therapies for mental disorders?
   a. the Freudian and the behavioral
   b. the client-centered and the patient-centered
   c. the biomedical and the psychological
   d. the chemical and the psychosomatic

2. The prefrontal lobotomy is a form of psychosurgery. Although no longer widely used, it was at one time used in cases in which a patient
   a. was an agitated schizophrenic.
   b. had committed a violent crime.
   c. showed little emotional response.
   d. had a disease of the thalamus.

3. Leti had electroconvulsive shock therapy a number of years ago. She is now suffering a side effect of that therapy. What is she most likely to be suffering from?
   a. tardive dyskinesia
   b. the loss of her ability to plan ahead
   c. depression
   d. memory loss

4. Vinnie suffers from manic-depressive disorder, but his mood swings are kept under control because he takes the drug
   a. chlorpromazine.
   b. lithium.
   c. Valium.
   d. tetracycline.

5. The Silverman family is receiving genetic counseling because a particular kind of mental retardation runs in their family. What is the purpose of such counseling?
   a. to explain the probability of passing on defective genes
   b. to help eliminate the attitudes of biological biasing
   c. to repair specific chromosomes
   d. to prescribe drugs that will keep problems from developing

6. In psychodynamic theory, what is the source of mental disorders?
   a. biochemical imbalances in the brain
   b. unresolved conflicts in childhood experiences

   c. the learning and reinforcement of nonproductive behaviors
   d. unreasonable attitudes, false beliefs, and unrealistic expectations

7. Imagine you are observing a therapy session in which a patient is lying on a couch, talking. The therapist is listening and asking occasional questions. What is most likely to be the therapist's goal?
   a. to determine which drug the patient should be given
   b. to change the symptoms that cause distress
   c. to explain how to change false ideas
   d. to help the patient develop insight

8. Rinaldo is a patient in psychotherapy. The therapist asks him to free associate. What would Rinaldo do?
   a. describe a dream
   b. release his feelings
   c. talk about anything that comes to mind
   d. understand the origin of his present guilt feelings

9. According to Hans Strupp, in what major way have psychodynamic therapies changed?
   a. Less emphasis is now placed on the ego.
   b. Patients no longer need to develop a relationship with the therapist.
   c. Shorter courses of treatment can be used.
   d. The concept of aggression has become more important.

10. In the program, a therapist helped a girl learn to control her epileptic seizures. What use did the therapist make of the pen?
    a. to record data
    b. to signal the onset of an attack
    c. to reduce the girl's fear
    d. to reinforce the correct reaction

11. When Albert Ellis discusses with the young woman her fear of hurting others, what point is he making?
    a. It is the belief system that creates the "hurt."
    b. Every normal person strives to achieve fulfillment.
    c. Developing a fear-reduction strategy will reduce the problem.
    d. It is the use of self-fulfilling prophecies that cause others to be hurt.

12. What point does Enrico Jones make about investigating the effectiveness of different therapies in treating depression?
    a. All therapies are equally effective.
    b. It is impossible to assess how effective any one therapy is.
    c. The job is complicated by the different types of depression.
    d. The most important variable is individual versus group therapy.
13. What is the most powerful antidepressant available for patients who cannot tolerate drugs?
    a. genetic counseling
    b. electroconvulsive therapy
    c. psychoanalysis
    d. family therapy
14. All of the following appear to be true about the relation between depression and genetics, *except* that
    a. depression has been linked to a defect in chromosome #11.
    b. depression appears to cause genetic mutation.
    c. most people who show the genetic marker for depression do not exhibit depressive symptoms.
    d. genetic counseling allows families to plan and make choices based on their risk of mental illness.
15. For which class of mental illness would Chlorpromazine be prescribed?
    a. mood disorder
    b. psychosis
    c. personality disorder
    d. anxiety disorder
16. Which approach to psychotherapy emphasizes developing the ego?
    a. behavioral
    b. desensitization
    c. humanistic
    d. psychodynamic
17. In behavior modification therapies, the goal is to
    a. understand unconscious motivations.
    b. learn to love oneself unconditionally.
    c. change the symptoms of mental illness through reinforcement.
    d. modify the interpretations that one gives to life's events.
18. Which style of therapy has as its primary goal to make the client feel as fulfilled as possible?
    a. humanistic
    b. cognitive-behavioral
    c. Freudian
    d. social learning
19. Which psychologist introduced rational-emotive therapy?
    a. Carl Rogers
    b. Hans Strupp

c. Albert Ellis
d. Rollo May

20. Which type of client would be ideal for modern psychoanalytic therapy?
    a. someone who is smart, wealthy, and highly verbal
    b. someone who is reserved and violent
    c. someone who has a good sense of humor but takes herself seriously
    d. someone who grew up under stressful and economically deprived conditions

QUESTIONS TO CONSIDER

1. Why might it be that behavioral and medical approaches to the same psychological problem can result in similar effects on the brain? Does this imply that in the future, effective behavioral treatments can be developed for cases that had been successful only through medical intervention?

2. How does someone decide on an appropriate therapy?

3. Can everyone benefit from psychotherapy, or do you think it is only for people with serious problems?

4. Why is there a stigma sometimes associated with seeking professional help for psychological problems? What might be some effective ways to change that?

5. If you found that you had a specific phobia, would you be willing to undergo exposure therapy?

ACTIVITIES

1. Identify the services and resources available in your community in case you ever need emotional support in a crisis, want to seek therapy, or know someone who needs this information. How much do these services cost? Look for names of accredited professional therapists and counselors, support groups, hotlines, medical and educational services, and in church and community programs. Is it difficult to find information?

2. Do you have any self-defeating expectations? Do you feel that you might benefit from cognitive therapy? Write out statements of positive self-expectations. Then try to use them in situations in which you feel anxious or insecure. Do they have any effect?

3. Run an Internet search with the goal of finding social support groups for various psychological disorders. In what ways do they serve a therapeutic role? How are they helpful, and how might they potentially be counterproductive?

Key Questions/ Chapter Outline	Core Concepts	Psychology Matters

14.1 What Causes Stress?
Traumatic Stressors
Chronic Stressors

- Traumatic events, chronic lifestyle conditions, major life changes, and even minor hassles can all cause stress.

Student Stress

College students face some unique stressors, in addition to typical developmental stressors.

14.2 How Does Stress Affect Us Physically?
Physiological Responses to Stress
Stress and the Immune System

- The physical stress response begins with arousal, which stimulates a series of physiological responses that in the short term are adaptive but that can turn harmful after prolonged stress.

Using Drugs for Stress Relief: A Costly Defense

Smoking is one of the most common defenses for stress, but causes more health problems than it solves.

14.3 Who Is Most Vulnerable to Stress?
Type A Personality and Hostility
Locus of Control
Hardiness
Optimism
Resilience

- Personality characteristics affect our individual responses to stressful situations and, consequently, on the degree to which we feel stress when exposed to potential stressors.

Using Psychology to Learn Psychology

Anyone—even people who don't think of themselves as "good writers"—can use writing as a valuable tool in the "coping strategies" toolbox.

14.4 How Can We Reduce the Impact of Stress on Our Health?
Psychological Coping Strategies
Positive Lifestyle Choices: A "Two-for-One" Benefit to Your Health
Putting It All Together: Developing Happiness and Subjective Well-Being

- Coping strategies reduce the impact of stress on our health, and positive lifestyle choices reduce both our perceived stress and its impact on our health.

Health Psychology and Behavioral Medicine

These exciting new fields focus on how psychological and social factors influence health, and also on how these same factors can be applied to successful prevention of illness.

Critical Thinking Applied   Is Change Really Hazardous to Your Health?

chapter 14
stress, health, and well-being

On September 11, 2001, at 8:46 A.M., retired firefighter Dennis Smith sat outside a New York clinic, waiting for his annual physical, when a nurse rushed in and announced that a plane had just crashed into the North tower of the World Trade Center in lower Manhattan (Smith, 2003b). The engine and ladder companies of New York's fire department (FDNY) were already responding to the alarms—trucks racing to the scene and firefighters running into the same buildings that hordes of people desperately sought to escape. Smith asked himself what conditions his coworkers were facing: the heat of the fire, the best access to the buildings, the stairwells' integrity. How many were already trapped inside and facing death?

One firefighter later described the chaos: "It looked like a movie scene, where the monster was coming . . . [W]e got showered with debris. . . . Things were hitting—bing, bang, boom—over your head" (Smith, 2003b, pp. 70–71). He had climbed high into the North Tower when the South Tower was hit, and "suddenly, there was this

Firefighters and other emergency workers responding to the September 11 terrrorist attacks needed to quickly determine the conditions they faced and the resources they had to meet those demands.

loud, loud noise overhead." He recalled huddling inside a stairwell, inventorying his resources: "I was thinking of my situation—what should I do, what can I do? What do I have that is positive? What tools do I have? . . . The main thing I had was my helmet. I remember thinking how important it was to have had that helmet. That was the biggie: the helmet, and holding on to my helmet . . . " (p. 75).

But the critical need for the helmet was forgotten in one ironic moment by Smith's fellow firefighter, Father Mychael Judge. The FDNY chaplain was among the first to arrive and, after hearing that firefighters were trapped inside, rushed into the smoke. While performing last rites, he removed his helmet out of respectful habit—just as a shower of debris fell, killing him instantly (Downey, 2004).

In the weeks and months after the terrorist attacks, firefighters continued to search for bodies. They buried, memorialized, and mourned their brothers and sisters. Few of the 343 missing were ever recovered. Those who had made it—while others died just a few feet away—endured survivor's guilt, ambivalent and uncertain why they deserved to live, asking themselves, "Why me?" Some developed symptoms of posttraumatic stress disorder (PTSD), reliving the terrifying moments of the disaster again and again. And the aftereffects of that day weren't limited to those individuals personally involved: Millions of people around the world remained glued to their televisions for days, repeatedly watching the towers as they fell and hearing firsthand accounts from survivors.

The surviving firefighters continued to grieve. Many of them rejected false reverence or gloom in remembering their friends, preferring instead to laugh and joke about their fallen comrades' quirks and screwups. Manhattan's Engine 40/Ladder 35 lost 12 firefighters, more than any other firehouse, and like everyone else, wondered what really happened to the missing victims. Then, five months after 9/11, the members of 40/35 learned of a news tape that appeared to show their 12 lost partners entering the tower minutes before it collapsed on them. The video had been shot at a distance, but the moving figures gradually became recognizable. Staring intently at the screen, the surviving firefighters gazed once more on friends who had not returned. They played the video over and over again (Halberstam, 2002).

PROBLEM: Were the reactions and experiences of the 9/11 firefighters and others at the World Trade Center attacks typical of people in stressful situations? And what factors explain individual differences in our physical and psychological responses to stress?

Of course, running into a falling building is not a typical human response; rather, it is a learned response of trained rescue workers. But what about the survivor's guilt and PTSD, or the repeated viewing of the disaster on websites and televisions around the world—are these "normal" stress responses? What connections can we make between these reactions and our own reactions to stress? In considering these questions, several related issues emerge:

● Stress isn't limited to major tragedies, traumas, and disasters. All of us encounter potentially stressful situations in our everyday lives—at our jobs, in our relationships, at school, in traffic, or as the result of illness. Have you ever noticed, though, that some people seem to get "stressed out" at even minor annoyances, while others appear calm, cool, and collected even in a crisis situation? In addition, some people bounce back quickly after major stress, in contrast to others who have trouble regaining their equilibrium. How can we explain these individual differences in our reactions to stress?

- We must also consider how our stress responses have evolved over the years and millenia and how they aid our survival. Many cultures today live much faster-paced lives than those of previous generations. Are the stresses we face today similar to those faced by our ancient ancestors? What impact might the differences in our environments have on the effectiveness of our stress response?

- Multiple perspectives are necessary to understand our human response to stress. What goes on in the body and the brain that influence our reactions to stress? And how are these physiological responses mediated by our thought processes, our prior learning, our personality, our stage in life, and our social context? (See Figure 14.1.)

- Finally, to what extent do we have control over our own reactions to stress and to the potential toll that stress is taking on our physical and our mental health? Are we "stuck" with our current stress level, or are there specific changes we can make that are guaranteed to help us meet the challenges of stress more effectively?

As we explore these questions in this chapter, keep in mind the stresses you have faced and consider how this information can help you understand the sources of stress in your life—and improve the way you perceive and manage that stress.

14.1 KEY QUESTION
WHAT CAUSES STRESS?

What images come to mind when you hear the word *stress?* Most people think of the pressures in their lives: difficult jobs, unhappy relationships, financial woes, health problems, and final exams. You may have some visceral associations with stress, too: a churning stomach, perspiration, headache, or tension in your neck or upper back. We use the word *stress* loosely in everyday conversation, referring to a situation that confronts us (Lazarus et al., 1985). For example, if your employer or professor has been giving you a difficult time, you may say that you are "under stress," as though you were being squashed by a heavy object. You may also say you are "feeling stress" as a result. Thus, in everyday conversation, we use the word *stress* to refer both to an external threat and to the response we feel when exposed to it.

Psychologists, however, make a distinction between the pressure or event that causes stress and its impact on us as individuals. External events or situations that cause stress are referred to as **stressors.** The word **stress** denotes the physical and mental changes that occur in response to the stressor (Krantz et al., 1985). Thus, a stressor is the large, angry man climbing out of the car you just bashed into; stress is your response to that large, angry man—your racing heart, shaky hands, and sudden perspiration.

What are the common stressors faced by humans today? We begin this chapter with a review of the stressors that research has found to have the most impact on us. These include everything from petty hassles to relationship problems to terrorist attacks, as noted in our Core Concept for this section:

Traumatic events, chronic lifestyle conditions, major life changes, and even minor hassles can all cause stress.

core
concept

Before embarking on our discussion of stressors, we should first recall the concept of cognitive interpretation from our study of emotion in Chapter 9. There, we learned that a key component in our emotional response to a situation is the interpretation we make of that situation. Stress is a type of emotional response—

Stressor   A stressful event or situation.

Stress   The physical and mental response to a stressor.

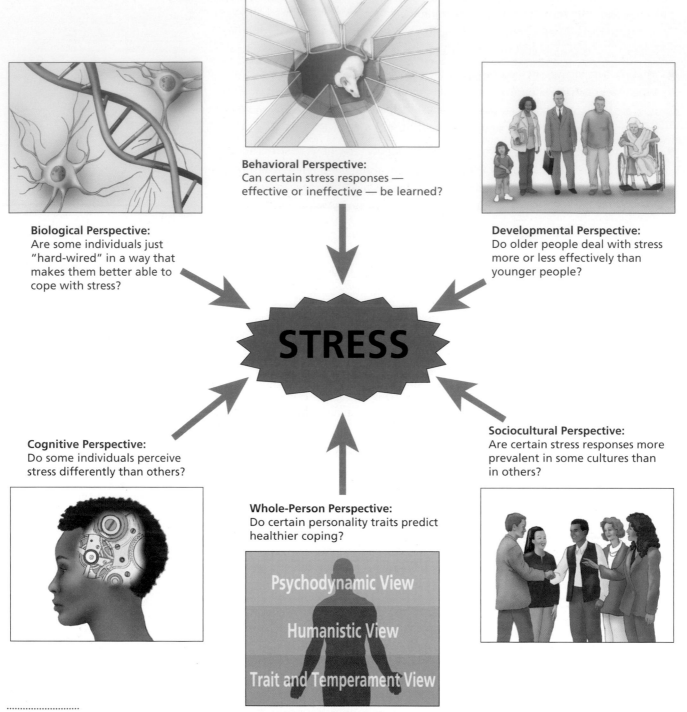

Biological Perspective:
Are some individuals just "hard-wired" in a way that makes them better able to cope with stress?

Behavioral Perspective:
Can certain stress responses — effective or ineffective — be learned?

Developmental Perspective:
Do older people deal with stress more or less effectively than younger people?

STRESS

Cognitive Perspective:
Do some individuals perceive stress differently than others?

Whole-Person Perspective:
Do certain personality traits predict healthier coping?

Psychodynamic View

Humanistic View

Trait and Temperament View

Sociocultural Perspective:
Are certain stress responses more prevalent in some cultures than in others?

FIGURE 14.1
The Multiple Perspectives Applied to Stress

This figure suggests just a few examples of the many ways that multiple perspectives are necessary to understand the complex nature of stress.

CONNECTION • CHAPTER 13

Cognitive reappraisal is at the heart of cognitive behavioral therapy.

Cognitive appraisal Our interpretation of a stressor and our resources for dealing with it.

consequently, **cognitive appraisal** or interpretation plays an important role in the degree of stress we feel when faced with a stressor. As we will see later in this chapter, cognitive appraisal accounts for some of the individual differences we see in how people respond to stressors. In the previous paragraph, for example, a person who felt entirely capable of defending himself against a large angry man may interpret that situation as less stressful (and thus feel less stress) than a person who felt defenseless.

To make an effective appraisal of the situation, we must have a concrete understanding of the nature of the threat. For example, the victims of the 9/11 terrorist attacks indisputably experienced stress, recognizing the specific dangers in which they were immersed. But much later, any person might also feel some stress when the Homeland Security Advisory System announces an increase from Yellow to Orange Alert. These color-coded warnings cannot in themselves harm anyone, but each successive color symbolizes an increasing level of threat. If you know and accept the psychological meaning of the color alerts, you experience stress, although it may not be clear how you should behave or what you should do differently under Orange as opposed to Yellow conditions (Zimbardo, 2004a). This uncertainty can add to the perceived stress of the situation. The key role of interpretation, and its dependence on the context of the world we live in, suggests how both severe trauma and vague threats can evoke the same human stress response

Traumatic Stressors

Catastrophic events, such as natural disasters and terrorist attacks, qualify as **traumatic stressors**—situations that threaten your own or others' physical safety, arousing feelings of fear, horror, or helplessness. On a more personal level, a sudden major life change, such as the loss of a loved one, constitutes a trauma as well—despite the fact that death and separation are likely to affect everyone at some time. We will examine traumatic stress by first considering natural and human-made catastrophes, then personal loss, and finally posttraumatic stress.

Catastrophe   In August 2005, Hurricane Katrina devasted the city of New Orleans and the surrounding areas. In May 2008, a massive earthquake in China killed more than 67,000 people. Natural disasters such as this, as well as human-made tragedies like terrorist attacks and warfare, comprise the category of traumatic stressors known as **catastrophic events.** These sudden, violent calamities are inevitably accompanied by extreme stress and loss: Anyone caught up in such a catastrophic event can lose loved ones or possessions. Less obvious is the fact that one's response to a catastrophe can have devastating effects on physical and mental health, which creates additional stress. Moreover, the consequences can last far longer than the original event, as in the weeks after 9/11, when firefighters and emergency workers sometimes found themselves reliving the events in nightmares and in daytime flashbacks.

Studies of catastrophe survivors provide some insight into the various ways individuals respond to these ordeals (Asarnow et al., 1999; Sprang, 1999). It's worth noting here that research of this type is difficult: Ethics prevent psychologists from creating disastrous events to study their effects on volunteer subjects. Instead, researchers must get to the scene immediately after the catastrophe, hearing the story from survivors while it is fresh in their minds.

Traumatic stressor   A situation that threatens one's physical safety, arousing feelings of fear, horror, or helplessness.

Catastrophic event   A sudden, violent calamity, either natural or man-made, that causes trauma.

A Laboratory for Disaster   One opportunity to understand disaster response presented itself in San Francisco in the early fall of 1989, just as the baseball World Series was about to begin at Candlestick Park. Spectators were settling into their seats when the entire stadium began to shake violently, the lights went out, and the scoreboard turned black. Sixty thousand fans fell silent. They were experiencing a major earthquake. Elsewhere in the city, fires erupted, a bridge collapsed, highways were crushed—and people were dying.

One week after the quake, a team of research psychologists began a series of follow-up surveys with about 800 regional residents. Survey responses revealed a pattern: The lives of respondents who experienced the earthquake continued to revolve heavily around the disaster for about a month. After this period, they ceased obsessing about the quake, but at the same time reported an increase in other stress-related symptoms including sleep disruption and relationship

Survivors of catastrophic events, such as the May 2008 earthquake in China, often suffer long-term psychological effects.

problems. Some survivors relived the trauma in frequent nightmares about earthquakes (Wood et al., 1992). Over the next two months, most symptoms diminished, although one year later as many as 20% of San Francisco area residents remained distressed about the quake (Pennebaker & Harber, 1991).

Both natural disasters and human-made catastrophes are violent, destroying life and property in the affected area. But human-made catastrophes such as massive crime and terrorism have an added dimension of threat because they are produced intentionally by other people. **Terrorism** has been defined as a type of disaster caused by "human malevolence" with the goal of disrupting society by creating fear and danger (Hall et al., 2002). Like survivors of natural disasters, terrorism survivors report elevated symptoms of distress that substantially subside after several months (Galea et al., 2003). What appears to be different about the experience of surviving a terror attack, however, is the long-term change in perception of threat. Studies of individuals affected—both directly and indirectly—by the 9/11 attacks in America or by the 2005 bombings at the underground train station in London found that 50 to 75% continued to worry about the safety of themselves and their family for a year or more following the attack (Rubin et al., 2005; Torabi & Seo, 2004; Weissman et al., 2005).

Psychological Response to Catastrophe   Psychological responses to extreme natural and human-caused disasters have been theorized to occur in stages, as victims experience shock, feel intense emotion, and struggle to reorganize their lives (Beigel & Berren, 1985; Horowitz, 1997). Cohen and Ahearn (1980) identified five stages that we pass through:

1. Immediately after the event, victims experience *psychic numbness,* including shock and confusion, and for moments to days cannot comprehend what has happened.

2. During a phase of *automatic action,* victims have little awareness of their own experiences and later show poor recall for what occurred. This phase is worsened by a lack of preparedness, delaying rescue and costing lives.

3. In the third stage of *communal effort,* people pool resources and collaborate, proud of their accomplishments but also weary and aware they are using up precious energy reserves. Without better planning, many survivors lose hope and initiative for rebuilding their lives.

4. In the fourth phase, survivors may experience a *letdown* as, depleted of energy, they comprehend and feel the tragedy's impact. Public interest and media attention fade, and survivors feel abandoned although the state of emergency continues.

5. An extended final period of *recovery* follows as survivors adapt to the changes created by the disaster. The fabric of the community will change as the natural and business environment are altered. After both 9/11 and Hurricane Katrina, survivors demanded to know how the catastrophes could have happened in the first place—reflecting a basic need to know "why?" and to find meaning in loss.

Keep in mind, however, that stage theories don't necessarily apply to the entire population, but attempt to summarize commonalities among experiences. In this instance, stage theories of stress response are useful because they help us to anticipate what survivors may go through and what kinds of assistance they may need.

Research also indicates the importance of **narratives** in working through catastrophic experiences. To learn from and make sense of catastrophic loss, we formulate accounts that describe what happened and why. These stories help us to explain ourselves to each other; and, in fact, sharing them may reflect a basic human need to be understood by those close to us (Harvey, 1996; Harvey et al., 1990). We are especially likely to develop narratives when an event is surpris-

Terrorism   A type of disaster caused by human malevolence with the goal of disrupting society by creating fear and danger.

Narrative   A personal account of a stressful event that describes our interpretation of what happened and why.

CONNECTION • CHAPTER 6

Stage theories emphasize distinctive changes that occur as one develops or progresses through a life stage or event.

ing or unpleasant (Holtzworth-Munroe & Jacobson, 1985). By confiding our stories to others, we begin to work through the pain of loss (Harvey, 2000; Weber & Harvey, 1994b). And, as we'll see later in this chapter, narratives help us find meaning in loss, which facilitates healing.

Catastrophic events merit extended news coverage, and in this Internet Age the sounds and images of others' pain are broadcast and viewed repeatedly. Viewers are not immune to such programs, however, and may experience a sort of "secondhand" traumatization.

Trauma in the Media Media news coverage expands the experience of catastrophe, so all viewers can experience it. How many times did you watch the towers collapsing on 9/11? Recall that, in our opening story, surviving members of the Manhattan firefighters' crew repeatedly viewed a videotape showing their now-dead comrades rushing into the World Trade Center just before the building collapsed. At last they knew for certain the fate of their friends. But was repeated viewing really therapeutic for them? Conventional wisdom suggests that identifying the figures on the tape as their friends might give them some closure, and their friends' heroism could help them find meaning in tragedy.

But there is a dark side to the "instant replay" of catastrophe. While New York firefighters were responding to the terrorist attacks, a research team in Washington state was conducting a longitudinal (long-term) study of firefighters in their region. Though safely distant from the dangers in the East, firefighters in the study could still experience the events of the eastern United States via the media, especially the extended television coverage of the Twin Towers' collapse. Counselors and therapists had already found that secondhand experiences of catastrophe could create severe stress for emergency rescue and medical workers who merely heard or watched others' trauma (McCann & Pearlman, 1990; Pearlman & Mac Ian, 1995). The Washington researchers found that, one week after 9/11, firefighters in their study were significantly stressed by constant news of the terrorist attacks. What were the signs of stress? They perceived greater personal risk and threat from their jobs than they had before. They questioned their own competence in handling mass casualties, and they felt dissatisfied with the level of social support available on the job (Murphy et al., 2004). Thus, just being exposed to media coverage of such intense, relevant news had brought the catastrophe home to these firefighters 3000 miles away from Ground Zero.

This research dovetails with findings about the impact of media coverage on Americans all over the country. Even those who had no direct connection to the attack felt the effects, even though they didn't live in or near New York, they didn't have friends or loved ones in that area, and their jobs and lives weren't affected by the situation. In a nationwide survey conducted one week after the catastrophe, a whopping 90% reported experiencing at least one symptom of stress (Schuster et al., 2001). Moreoever, a team of prominent dream researchers found that people who watched more television coverage were more likely to have dreams containing images of the tragedy. Significantly, participants in that same dream study who spent time talking with others about the tragedy—presumably working through it, similar to the process of narratives—did not experience increased dreams about the attack (Propper et al., 2007). It is possible that repeated media viewing of catastrophe increases arousal, while talking about it with others may provide an opportunity to share feelings and thus ameliorate the effects to some degree.

> **CONNECTION • CHAPTER 8**
> One prominent theory of dreams asserts that dreams reflect current concerns.

Vicarious Traumatization Clearly, then, revisiting and reliving catastrophe causes its own stress. **Vicarious traumatization** is severe stress caused when one is exposed to others' accounts of trauma and the observer becomes captivated by it (McCann & Pearlman, 1990). Whether it be plane crashes, riots in a far-off country, or natural disasters, what matters is the amount of exposure: Schuster and colleagues (2001) found that the more hours viewers had spent watching television coverage of the

Vicarious traumatization Severe stress caused by exposure to traumatic images or stories that cause the observer to become engaged with the stressful material.

9/11 attacks, the more likely they were to report stress symptoms later. By reliving the disaster, heavy viewers of media coverage, including those who lived safely distant from the actual disaster site, nonetheless became engaged with the victims' suffering and experienced measurable stress as a result.

Repeated exposure to bad news can do more harm than good. One way to reduce vicarious stress in your own life is to go on a "news diet": Stop reading and watching news for a while. Bestselling author-physician Andrew Weil recommends that, after only a few days without (mostly bad) news, you will feel healthier, happier, and more in control of your life (Weil, 1998). A useful lesson is to be choosy about news and about where you get it: Some "news" channels present more emotion than information.

Statistically, if you live in the United States, your chances of experiencing catastrophic trauma remain low. However, other traumatic stressors are not so uncommon. For example, at some point in our lives, we are all likely to experience the loss of someone close to us. Loss is one of the great levelers of human experience, similarly affecting individuals in every part of the world, of every circumstance. Let us now turn to an examination of the effects of such loss on our stress and health.

Personal Loss   Like many other species, humans are social creatures: We depend on each other for survival. The loss of a loved one is severely stressful, even if it is anticipated (such as after a long illness). A sudden, unexpected loss is traumatic: In a rated listing of life changes at the end of this section, you will see "death of spouse" listed as the most stressful of all life changes (Holmes & Rahe, 1967; Scully et al., 2000). **Grief** is the emotional response to loss, a painful complex of feelings including sadness, anger, helplessness, guilt, and despair (Raphael, 1984). Whether you are grieving the death of a loved one, the breakup of a romantic relationship, or the betrayal of a trusted friend, you experience the pain of separation and loneliness and have a number of difficult questions to ponder. We seek to come to terms with the loss, make sense of it and understand what it means (Davis & Nolen-Hoeksema, 2001; Neimeyer et al., 2002). Some of our core assumptions about life may be challenged, and we may be forced to adapt to a different reality (Parkes, 2001). As a result, our identities and future plans may be permanently altered (Davis et al., 1998; Janoff-Bulman, 1992).

Psychologists view grieving as a normal, healthy process of adapting to a major life change, with no "right" method or time period (Gilbert, 1996; Neimeyer, 1995, 1999). Some experts recommend achieving closure, a Gestalt term for perceiving an incomplete stimulus as complete. But grief psychologists oppose the goal of closing off the pain and memories of loss and instead recommend **integration**. To understand this, think for a moment about someone you have lost: Perhaps you have "gotten over" it and don't think about it much any more—yet it is still there in your memory, with some images, emotions, and thoughts still vivid and accessible and still part of who you are (Harvey, 1996; Harvey et al., 1990). Thus, the final phase of grieving is more accurately thought of as an ongoing process of integration, in which each life loss becomes a part of the self (Murray, 2002).

Everyone will experience loss at some time, but we never get used to it: Personal loss is a serious stressor, creating change and triggering the stress response. The mourning process also requires you to interact socially at a time when you feel especially vulnerable and socially withdrawn. Ironically, friends' offers of help or sympathy can sometimes add to the stress of the loss. Hollander (2004) writes of losing first her husband and then, a few months later, her mother. "Am I all right? Everyone seems to be asking me that. . . . Often I find I don't know how to respond to the question" (pp. 201–202). Her friends feel uncomfortable when she weeps openly, and they encourage her to cheer up, to be herself again. Hollander concludes that her pain cannot and must not be rushed: "Closure is not my goal. . . . I am all right exactly because I weep" (p. 204).

CONNECTION • CHAPTER 1
Gestalt psychologists study how we construct perceptual wholes.

Grief   The emotional response to loss, which includes sadness, anger, helplessness, guilt, and despair.

Integration   A final phase of grieving, in which the loss becomes incorporated into the self.

CHAPTER 14 ● STRESS, HEALTH, AND WELL-BEING

Humiliation as Loss   Which would be more stressful: losing your romantic partner when he or she dies, or having that person leave you? Both tragedies involve losing your partner, but in addition, being rejected and left by someone involves not only grief but humiliation. One study interviewed thousands of adults, categorizing their experiences of loss and other life event stressors and diagnosing symptoms of major depression or anxiety. Results indicated that rejected respondents were more likely to suffer from depression than those whose partners had died (Kendler et al., 2003). In discussing their findings, researchers observed that the death of one's partner is a "pure loss event," which does not represent a failure or deficiency on the part of the grieving person. In contrast, being left by your spouse "raises issues . . . [such] as humiliation, which is usually seen as the loss of status, the loss of a sense of self-esteem and the loss of a sense of your own worth" (National Public Radio, 2003a). Such humiliation, rather than the loss itself, they conclude, is a key cause of depression.

Why do we feel so bad about humiliation? Animal studies reveal that in primate colonies, individuals who lose status withdraw, lose their appetite, and become more submissive. In evolutionary terms, the loss of social status threatens survival and has serious consequences. By taking action to prevent such losses, humans and other primates who suffer because of humiliation can increase their chances of adaptation and survival. Perhaps rejection makes us feel bad because we *need* to feel bad; in other words, perhaps the depression or loss of self-esteem that comes with rejection keeps us from entering into unwise or insecure partnerships, thus protecting us from further rejection or humiliation.

Disenfranchised Grief   Grief is also especially stressful when others minimize your loss and fail to sympathize. Experiences such as death, divorce, and trauma are recognized with formal condolences, such as funerals or hospital visits, and professional attention from undertakers, attorneys, and physicians (Lensing, 2001). But other painful losses, with no official "status"—such as a nonmarital breakup or the death of a beloved pet—may be ignored or dismissed by the community. These marginalized losses can leave you feeling alone and bereft of social support (Harrist, 2003). For example, adults who grieve after a miscarriage, young adults who have lost friends, and children saddened by the death of a favorite TV or movie star may find themselves alone in their sorrow, getting little sympathy or understanding from others. Their **disenfranchised grief** cannot be mourned through public rituals like memorials or funerals. Fearing others' reactions and unsure whom they might talk to, disenfranchised grievers may try to hide their sorrow—but continue to suffer (Doka, 1989, 1995; Rickgarn, 1996).

Experiencing such pain while feeling unable to confide in others can create additional feelings of mistrust, betrayal, and withdrawal. Confiding in others has been found to help enormously in coping with loss and trauma (Harvey, 1996; Pennebaker, 1990). During these times, it is important to keep in mind the role of professional counselors or psychotherapists, who might be counted on to take your pain seriously. Also, it is also therapeutically worthwhile to "confide" in other ways, such as by keeping a written journal of your feelings (see the "Psychology Matters," later in this chapter).

Posttraumatic Stress   Individuals who have undergone severe ordeals—rape, combat, beatings, or torture, for example—may experience a belated pattern of stress symptoms that can appear months, or even years, after their trauma. In **posttraumatic stress disorder (PTSD)**, the individual reexperiences mental and physical responses that accompanied the trauma. Nearly one adult in 12 in the United States will experience PTSD at some time in his or her life, with symptoms lasting more than ten years in over one-third of cases. Traumas described by PTSD victims most frequently include having witnessed another person being killed or badly injured, having lived through a natural disaster, and having survived a life-threatening accident. Men cite more experiences of physical attack, military combat,

Disenfranchised grief   The emotion surrounding a loss that others do not support, share, or understand.

Posttraumatic stress disorder (PTSD)   A delayed stress reaction in which an individual involuntarily reexperiences emotional, cognitive, and behavioral aspects of past trauma.

disaster or fire, or being held captive or hostage, whereas women cite more experiences of rape, sexual molestation, physical abuse, and neglect during childhood (Bower, 1995a). Women are more likely than men to develop symptoms of PTSD after experiencing a traumatic event (Tolin & Foa, 2006), and Hispanic Americans are more at risk than non-Hispanic Caucasian or black Americans (Pole et al., 2005).

What Are the Symptoms of PTSD? Victims of posttraumatic stress disorder typically become distracted, disorganized, and experience memory difficulties (Arnsten, 1998). They become emotionally numb and are less likely to feel pleasure from positive events. They may also feel alienated from other people. The emotional pain of this reaction can result in various symptoms, such as problems with sleeping, guilt about surviving, difficulty concentrating, and an exaggerated "startle response" (wide-eyed, gasping, surprised behavior displayed when one perceives a sudden threat). Rape survivors, for example, may experience a barrage of psychological aftereffects, including feelings of betrayal by people close to them, anger about having been victimized, and fear of being alone (Baron & Straus, 1985; Cann et al., 1981).

Posttraumatic stress disorder can also have lasting biological consequences (Crowell, 2002; Sapolsky, 1998). The brain may undergo physical changes when the stress is extreme in intensity or duration. Specifically, the brain's hormone-regulating system may develop hair-trigger responsiveness, making the victim of posttraumatic stress overreact to mild stressors or even harmless but surprising stimulation.

PTSD in Combat Personnel While the term *posttraumatic stress disorder* was coined fairly recently, historical accounts have noted similar symptoms referred to as "combat fatigue," "shell-shock," or "soldier's heart" in soldiers for centuries. In the wake of the Vietnam War, where early estimates noted symptoms of PTSD in 30% of combat veterans, public attention on the disorder grew. Military psychologists now provide at least some minimal treatment for combat-related stress at deployment sites in Iraq, for instance, and a variety of educational programs aim to help soldiers and their families prepare more effectively for deployment and to cope better with the aftermath of war once the soldiers have returned home. And even though the military cultural norm has historically taught soldiers not to talk about combat experiences, which contributed to the stigma most veterans felt about asking for help with psychological symptoms, these new programs are helping participants slowly overcome that barrier to effective coping. A program entitled Battlemind, for example, was developed to help soldiers develop realistic expectations of deployment prior to combat and also to help them readjust to life at home when they return from deployment. Initial research indicates that soldiers who participate in Battlemind report fewer symptoms of PTSD than their comrades who receive more traditional training (Munsey, 2007).

The increased scrutiny on PTSD in combat personnel has also unearthed a fascinating new finding about the brain's role in certain PTSD symptoms. Prompted by the groundbreaking research of neurologist Ibolja Cernak, U.S. military doctors now recognize that soldiers who were exposed to an explosion often develop cognitive symptoms such as memory loss, reduced ability to concentrate, slowed reaction time, and difficulty performing simple math tasks—even if the soldier wasn't hit by the blast. While researchers are still unsure exactly how the brain is affected by the blast, there is general agreement that the force of the explosion causes damage to brain functioning. Up to 20% of soldiers returning from Iraq and Afghanistan are estimated to suffer from some type of traumatic brain injury such as this, and researchers now think that neurological effects of blast exposure may account for the cognitive deficits seen in some veterans diagnosed with PTSD (Bhattacharjee, 2008).

Chronic Stressors

The traumatic stressors reviewed in the previous section—catastrophe, personal loss, and posttraumatic stress—involve an event that, like the 9/11 attack, occurs abruptly, intensely, and is typically short-lived in nature. In contrast, **chronic stressors** are stressful conditions that may have a gradual onset and lower intensity but are long-lasting. They may involve a major life change such as a divorce, long-term living conditions like poverty or a demanding job, or minor recurrent problems that accumulate over a long period—like the proverbial straws on the camel's back. Here we examine five chronic stressors: societal stressors, burnout, compassion fatigue, major life changes, and daily hassles.

Societal stressors include unemployment, homelessness, and discrimination. Such conditions can exact a toll on both mental and physical health.

Societal Stressors   For most of us, stress comes not from sudden catastrophic events but from **societal stressors,** which are pressures in our social, cultural, and economic environment. These societal stressors often involve difficulties at home, work, or school that are chronic (recurring or continuing over time). Societal stressors also include unemployment, poverty, racism, and other conditions and conflicts that handicap or oppress individuals because of their social group or status.

For example, a study of unemployed men revealed more depression, anxiety, and worries about health than men who had jobs. Almost miraculously, these symptoms usually disappeared when the unemployed individuals found work (Liem & Rayman, 1982). Prejudice and discrimination, too, can be significant sources of stress (Contrada et al., 2000). For example, high blood pressure among African Americans—long thought to be primarily genetic—is correlated with the chronic stress caused by menial jobs, limited education, and low socioeconomic status (Klag et al., 1991). And people living in poverty have less access to good health care; they are also more likely to live in areas containing greater health hazards such as environmental pollutants and even noise—which affects cognitive development in children as well as a variety of physical and emotional factors in adults (Evans et al., 1998; Staples, 1996).

Burnout   Having a job, however—even a high-paying one—does not innoculate one against stress. On the contrary, it can create stress of its own both emotionally and physically. In fact, for many people, the greatest source of chronic stress involves the pressures of work. Continually stressful work can lead to **burnout,** a syndrome of emotional exhaustion, physical fatigue, and cognitive weariness (Shirom, 2003). Christina Maslach (1998, 2003; Maslach et al., 2001), a leading researcher on this widespread problem, notes that burnout was first recognized in professions demanding high-intensity interpersonal contact, such as physicians with patients, teachers with students, and social workers with clients. And we now know that burnout can occur anywhere—even among college students, stay-at-home parents, or volunteer workers. People experiencing burnout report feelings of detachment, failure, and cynicism about coworkers and clients. They seek escape and avoid their work, leading to decreased personal accomplishment. Burnout has been found to correlate with absenteeism, job turnover, impaired performance, poor coworker relations, family problems, and decreased personal health (Maslach & Leiter, 1997; Schaufeli et al., 1993).

Is burnout inevitable in human service professions? It appears to arise from conditions ranging from long hours and heavy workloads to abusive coworkers, manager, and clients. Nearly three-quarters of all employees identify the worst aspect of their job as their immediate supervisor (Hogan et al., 1994).

Burnout is often misunderstood as a personal problem—almost a weakness in character—when in reality it more likely signifies a weakness in the organization rather than the individual employee (Leiter & Maslach, 2000; Maslach et al., 2001). Faced with stiff competition and corporate downsizing, employers may use "Band-Aid" measures, such as stress-management workshops for employees, rather than addressing real sources of burnout, such as poor working conditions. But effective burnout prevention requires both managers and

Chronic stressor   Long-lasting stressful condition.

Societal stressor   A chronic stressor resulting from pressure in one's social, cultural, or economic environment.

Burnout   A syndrome of emotional exhaustion, physical fatigue, and cognitive weariness, often related to work.

workers to take responsibility for developing conditions that improve engagement with the job and create a better "fit" between employee and job, and by making decisions that focus on the long-term health of the employees and the organization (Berglas, 2001; Maslach & Goldberg, 1998).

Compassion Fatigue   After 9/11, New York Ladder Company 5's Lieutenant O'Neill joined others in day after day of fruitless rescue searches. One day, instead of going home, O'Neill checked into a hospital and asked for help with the stress-related symptoms he was experiencing. He met with a doctor to whom he poured out the story of the horrors he had seen. Contrary to O'Neill's assumption that, as a doctor, "He . . . could handle this," the doctor himself went to the hospital psychologist after treating O'Neill. "[H]e kind of lost it," O'Neill learned. "He had become freaked out from the story I told him, because he lost a friend from the tragedy. . . . He didn't show up for work for a couple of days" (Smith, 2003b, p. 259). Even medical professionals and therapists, though trained to be objective, are still very much at risk for the stress of vicarious traumatization (Sabin-Farrell & Turpin, 2003).

You, as a student of psychology, might well imagine the work of psychotherapists and counselors working with victims of trauma and abuse. If merely watching bad news on television can cause vicarious trauma, what are the effects of jobs that require a person to deal with bad news every day? When medical professionals, caregivers, and therapists are overexposed to trauma and its victims, they are at risk for **compassion fatigue,** a state of exhaustion that leaves caregivers feeling stressed, numb, or indifferent to those in need (Figley, 2002).

Compassion fatigue is also called *secondary traumatic stress* because it afflicts the helpers, who "catch" the stress suffered by the victims. The consequences are similar to those of burnout in that it leaves people unhappy with their work and resistant to contact with the people they are supposed to help. Fatigued helpers develop symptoms of stress and illness, and withdraw emotionally from their clients. Dreading further stories of trauma, they overuse the "silencing response," distracting, minimizing, or redirecting what their clients are saying to reduce their own discomfort and pain (Baranowsky, 2002). When therapists feel they are unable to listen to their clients, they can no longer function as therapists. Compassion fatigue and burnout harm not only the providers and receivers of care and attention but entire professions as well. Fortunately, healers can learn the warning signs in time to take action—and researchers have been able to suggest what kinds of action to take:

● First, caregivers must focus on supporting their sense of **compassion satisfaction,** an appreciation of the work they do as helpers that drew them to their professions in the first place. Compassion satisfaction can be increased by creating and maintaining a sense of team spirit with coworkers. Also, whenever possible, caregivers and rescue workers should be able to see clients recover so they realize their work is effective (Collins & Long, 2003).

● While it is important to care for those one is helping, helpers must monitor and avoid becoming overinvolved, or their lack of control over most of their clients' experiences will facilitate a sense of defeat (Keidel, 2002).

● When new at their work, trauma counselors may simply distance themselves from stressful exchanges; more experienced workers are better able to cope directly with their own stress (Pinto, 2003).

● Caregivers should resist overvolunteering. Volunteers who worked with more than one agency or effort after 9/11 were at greater risk for compassion fatigue than those who volunteered with only one organization, such as the American Red Cross (Roberts et al., 2003).

● Finally, professional helpers and emergency workers should use humor—but use it carefully! While tasteless jokes and black humor with fellow workers

Compassion fatigue   A state of exhaustion experienced by medical and psychological professionals, as well as caregivers, which leaves the individual feeling stressed, numb, or indifferent.

Compassion satisfaction   A sense of appreciation felt by a caregiver, medical or psychological professional, of the work he or she does.

can relieve some anxiety and establish a sense of sharing and teamwork among coworkers, workers must be cautious in their use of these types of humor. Because it is not publicly acceptable to laugh in the face of tragedy, humor should be expressed selectively, with sensitivity to the environment, so as not to offend or further hurt those already suffering (Moran, 2002).

Major Life Events   The beginning or end of a relationship is always a time of adjustment, accompanied by emotional ups and downs, tension, and turmoil. Earlier in this section, for example, we discussed the impact of sudden loss on stress. Other changes can cause stress, too: a new job, starting or finishing college, or—ironically—even taking a vacation! Even events that we welcome, such as the birth of a child, often require major changes in our routines and adaptations to new demands and lifestyles. Especially when the events are considered positive events (such as an exciting new job or getting married), we may not recognize their potential impact on our stress level.

What if there were a simple questionnaire you could complete that would assess your current stress level? Several decades ago, psychologists Thomas Holmes and Richard Rahe (pronounced "Ray") developed just such a tool. They first identified a variety of common stressful events and had a large number of respondents rate the events in terms of how stressful each one was in their own lives. After analyzing all the results, they created the **Social Readjustment Rating Scale (SRRS)**, which lists 43 life events—ranging from death of a spouse at the high end, to pregnancy or a new job in the middle, to getting a traffic ticket at the low end. Each life event is assigned a particular number of life-change units (LCUs), so you can calculate your current stress level by adding up the LCUs for each life change you have recently experienced.

Research has indeed found relationships between life changes and stress. The birth of a child, for example, is often associated with lower marital satisfaction (Cowan & Cowan, 1988). Since it was developed, the SRRS has been used in thousands of studies worldwide and has been found to apply cross-culturally. We must be cautious in interpreting our scores, though, in light of what we know about the role of cognitive appraisal in stress. We will examine the SRRS more closely at the end of this chapter, but for now you can assess yourself in the "Do It Yourself!" box on the next page. You may want to compare your scores with those of your classmates and consider how your individual interpretations of your recent life changes may be mediating the link between the changes and your own stress level.

Daily Hassles   After a difficult workday, you get stuck in a traffic jam on your way to the grocery store. Finally arriving, you find they don't have the very item or brand you wanted. After selecting a substitute, you proceed to the checkout, only to be snapped at by an impatient clerk when you don't have exact change. Taken individually, such minor irritations and frustrations, known as **hassles,** don't seem like much in comparison to a natural disaster. But psychologists confirm that hassles can accumulate, especially when they are frequent and involve interpersonal conflicts (Bolger et al., 1989).

Any annoying incident can be a hassle, but some of the most common hassles involve frustrations—the blocking of some desired goal—at home, work, or school. In a diary study, a group of men and women kept track of their daily hassles over a one-year period, also recording major life changes and physical symptoms. A clear relationship emerged between hassles and health problems: The more frequent and intense the hassles people reported, the poorer their health, both physical and mental (Lazarus, 1981; 1984; 1999). The opposite was also true: As daily hassles diminish, people's sense of well-being increases (Chamberlain & Zika, 1990). Thus, a life filled with hassles can exact as great a price as that of a single, more intense, stressor (Weinberger et al., 1987).

Social Readjustment Rating Scale (SRRS)   Psychological rating scale designed to measure stress levels by attaching numerical values to common life changes.

Hassle   Situation that causes minor irritation or frustration.

For each of the following events, multiply the life-change units rating times the number of times that event occurred in your life in the past year. Add your scores for all items completed to compute your total.

Event	Life-change units	Your score
Death of spouse	100	
Divorce	73	___
Marital separation	65	___
Jail term	63	___
Death of close family member	63	___
Personal injury or illness	53	___
Marriage	50	___
Being fired	47	___
Marital reconciliation	45	___
Retirement	45	___
Change in health of family member	44	___
Pregnancy	40	___
Sex difficulties	39	___
Gain of new family member	39	___
Business readjustment	39	___
Change in financial state	38	___
Death of close friend	37	___
Change to different line of work	36	___
Change in number of arguments with spouse	35	___
*Home mortgage over $100,000	31	___
Foreclosure of mortgage or loan	30	___
Change in responsibilities at work	29	___
Son or daughter leaving home	29	___
Trouble with in-laws	29	___
Outstanding personal achievement	28	___
*Spouse beginning/stopping work	26	___

Event	Life-change units	Your score
Beginning or ending school	26	___
Change in living conditions	25	___
Revision of personal habits	24	___
Trouble with one's boss	23	___
Change in work hours/conditions	20	___
Change in residence	20	___
Change in schools	20	___
Change in recreation	19	___
Change in church activities	19	___
Change in social activities	18	___
*Mortgage/loan less than $100,000	17	___
Change in sleeping habits	16	___
Change in number of family get-togethers	15	___
Change in eating habits	15	___
Vacation	13	___
Celebrated Christmas	13	___
Minor violations of the law	11	___
YOUR TOTAL		___

INTERPRET YOUR TOTAL CAUTIOUSLY!

A total of less than 150 is good, suggesting a low level of stress and a low probability of developing a stress-related disorder. For people scoring from 150 to 200, Holmes and Masuda (1974) found a 50% chance of problems: Half their respondents in this range developed a significant mental or physical disorder in the next few months. Those scoring 200 to 299 have a moderate risk of stress illness. About 70% of those scoring over 300 became ill, so such scores may indicate high risk. Before drawing any conclusions about your score, though, be sure to read the "Critical Thinking Applied" feature at the end of this chapter for more information!

(*Source:* Adapted from Holmes & Rahe (1967). *Starred items have been updated.)

Cognitive appraisal plays a role in the impact of hassles as well. If you interpret a frustrating situation as "too much" to deal with, or as a major threat to well-being, it will affect you more than if you dismiss it as less important (Lazarus, 1984). Some people may be especially prone to see the world as hassle filled. One study showed that college students with a more pessimistic outlook experienced both more hassles and poorer health (Dykema et al., 1995). This finding serves as a good reminder that correlation does not imply causation: In other words, we know a correlation exists between hassles and health but do not know what causes the link. On one hand, experiencing many hassles may have a negative impact on health—but on the other hand, having more health problems to begin with might increase a person's perception of minor annoyances as hassles. It is also possible that a third variable—something other than hassles or health—might be driving the correlation: For example, pessimists (as noted above) might be more likely to perceive minor annoyances as hassles and also more likely to have health problems.

One way to destress your life is to reconsider your own daily hassles. Look back on recent frustrations with a sense of humor, put problems in perspective, and consider just how unimportant such difficulties and delays really turned out to be. By reappraising everyday difficulties as minor, you enable yourself to remain good natured and productive and even to have a good laugh. Shake your head, put on the brakes, let the vending machine keep your dollar—and move along. Daily hassles are idiosyncratic: They are interpreted uniquely by each person experiencing them. What is a hassle or an annoyance to you may be unnoticed or even amusing to someone else. One person's agonizing traffic jam is another person's opportunity to listen to the radio or engage in people watching. If your life seems hassle filled, some reappraisal of regularly irritating situations can save you psychological wear and tear. Later we will see how cognitive reappraisal can play a central role in one's general strategies for coping with stress.

Traffic can be a hassle, and consequently contribute to your stress— if you choose to interpret it that way.

PSYCHOLOGYMATTERS
Student Stress

It's timely for you to be studying stress and well-being right now, because merely being a college student qualifies as a stressor. College freshmen in particular have been found to undergo major challenges in making the transition to college life. One study found that freshman stress unfolds in three phases. First, new students experience the shock and excitement of new roles, environments, and social relationships. Next comes a protracted period of disillusionment and struggle as students face both the serious work and mundane chores of academic life. Finally, as roles gel and mastery is developed in at least some efforts, a sense of improved well-being and possibilities emerges (Rambo-Chroniak, 1999). But stress isn't limited to first-year students. Whatever their year in college, students experience a specific pattern of stress during the school year, with stress peaks at the beginning, middle, and end of each term (Bolger, 1997). Two points in time are particularly difficult, the "midwinter crash" and the final exam period, when studying competes with regular sleep and healthy eating and when flu and cold viruses afflict those with low resistance.

Some causes of student stress are obvious, with academic pressure topping the list (Bolger, 1997). Also, new social interactions increase the possibility of problems in interpersonal relationships, such as having friends lose their temper, being taken advantage of, or having one's privacy invaded (Edwards et al., 2001). Romantic love, often considered a souce of joy, can also be a source of stress and illness, especially among college women (Riessman et al., 1991). Students complain, too, of stress caused by their families, particularly interactions involving difficult emotions, control, and manipulation (Anderson, 1987). Perhaps the essential source of stress for traditional-aged college students is freedom—specifically, the lack of structure or monitoring student experience in a college environment as contrasted with the structure of home and high school curriculum (*USA Today*, 1996). For students returning to college after years in the workforce or raising children, stress often involves the challenge of "retraining the brain" to process and retain massive amounts of new information.

Solutions for student stress, fortunately, may be within arm's reach—the distance needed to reach for the phone and call a friend for support or the college health center, counseling office, or tutoring center for professional advice. Most students express a reluctance to seek help (Rambo-Chroniak, 1999), so simply overcoming this ambivalence—especially as an enlightened student of the many uses of psychology—can be a step toward feeling better. Young-adult freshmen in particular do better if they have positive attitudes about becoming independent individuals on a course of normal separation from their parents (Smith, 1995).

In terms of self-help, students report better results when taking specific action to resolve the problem, rather than simply dwelling on their emotional response (Smith, 1995). Cultivating more hopeful attitudes and better self-esteem—for example, by setting and meeting realistic goals—also leads to lower stress and better adjustment. Students appear to be more adaptive if they report better social support and a greater sense of control in their lives (Rambo-Chroniak, 1999). Involvement in student organizations can offer both structure and social contact, but beware of the stress of excessive commitment (Bolger, 1997). Two qualities in particular characterize students who are most effective in preventing and coping with stress: resilience, based in part in self-acceptance, effective communication, and coping skills; and cognitive hardiness, an ability to interpret potential stressors as challenging rather than threatening (Nowack, 1983; Yeaman, 1995). We will examine these two characteristics in greater detail a little later in this chapter.

CheckYourUnderstanding

1. **RECALL:** External events or situations which cause stress are called _____, whereas the term _____ denotes the physical and mental changes that occur as a result.

2. **APPLICATION:** An example of a chronic societal stressor is _____.
   a. an earthquake
   b. vicarious trauma
   c. being stuck in traffic
   d. widespread unemployment

3. **ANALYSIS:** Which of the following statements about daily hassles is true?
   a. Some of the most common hassles involve threats to survival.

b. As daily hassles diminish, people's sense of well-being increases.
c. More frequent and intense hassles are associated with better health.
d. The effects of hassles do not accumulate: Many hassles are no worse than a few.

4. **SYNTHESIS:** Your friend Rob has recently lost his wife to cancer. Devon, another friend, recently found out his partner was cheating on him, and she left him for someone else. What difference would you predict between Rob and Devon in terms of the impact of these two different types of losses on their well-being?

5. **UNDERSTANDING THE CORE CONCEPT:** Name four categories of common stressors, along with an example of each.

Answers 1. stressors; stress **2.** d **3.** b **4.** Both Rob and Devon have suffered a personal loss, which involves grief, stress, and mourning. Devon, however, is more at risk for depression due to the accompanying humiliation of being rejected, whereas Rob's loss is a "pure loss event." **5.** traumatic events, such as catastrophe and personal loss; chronic stressors, such as societal stressors, burnout, and compassion fatigue; major life events, such as a new job or the birth of a child; and daily hassles, such as traffic jams or computer crashes.

14.2 KEY QUESTION
HOW DOES STRESS AFFECT US PHYSICALLY?

Since our earliest days on Earth, humans have survived by responding quickly and decisively to potentially lethal attacks by predators or hostile tribes. Our ancestors adapted to an enormous variety of environmental conditions worldwide, confronting climate extremes, scarce resources, and hostile neighbors. Faced with these challenges, quick action was necessary to obtain shelter and protection, to find food, and to defend themselves. The faster an individual was to feel fear or anger, appraise the situation accurately, and take appropriate action, the better his or her chances of success and survival. Those who responded most quickly and effectively to danger survived and passed those responsive genes to their offspring, whereas slower or less clever individuals were less likely to survive and bear children in the course of human evolution.

Some of the serious stressors confronting our ancestors, such as catastrophe or combat, continue to face us today. Modern life, of course, adds some new dangers: demanding jobs, financial worries, and computer crashes. More often chronic in nature, these new threats aren't necessarily solved effectively with the same responses that suited our ancestors and their more immediate challenges. Yet our stress response system remains the result of our ancestors' evolutionary legacy, because human physiology cannot evolve and change nearly as fast as our societies have. This ancient biological script is retained in our body's automatic responses to frightening or enraging conditions. If someone insults you, your face feels hot and your fists seem to clench by themselves, readying you for a physical contest. Or imagine a very different sort of "threat": Your instructor calls on you in a class discussion for which you are unprepared. Your heart races, your knees feel wobbly, and you feel the urge to run away.

These examples illustrate the two poles of the **fight-or-flight response**, a sequence of internal and behavioral processes triggered when a threat is perceived, preparing the organism for either struggle or escape. This response worked very well for our predecessors, but doesn't always suit us as well today. After all, is running out of the classroom really an effective response to being called on in class? Our Core Concept summarizes this point:

The physical stress response begins with arousal, which stimulates a series of physiological responses that in the short term are adaptive, but that can turn harmful after prolonged stress.

Amazingly, we deal with stress effectively most of the time, managing to be not only healthy but even happy. But, as you will see in this section, there can be serious consequences when we don't deal effectively with stress—no matter what its source. On the positive side, we should emphasize that the emotional arousal we call stress usually works to our advantage. It brings threatening events into focus and readies us to respond. On the negative side, extreme or prolonged emotional arousal threatens our health. The results can include physical conditions such as heart disease, stroke, high blood pressure, and ulcers. Our mental health can also suffer. Some of us are prone to "worrying ourselves sick" by anticipating what might go wrong, from minor irritants to major traumas (Sapolsky, 1994). Depression, as well as PTSD and other anxiety disorders, has direct linkages to stress. We see these consequences not only in emergency response workers and air traffic controllers, but in public- and private-sector employees at all status levels and in people of all ages and all walks of life. Let's take a closer look at the physiology of our stress response, which will lay the foundation for a clear understanding of exactly how this adaptive response triggers negative health consequences when chronic stress strains the limits of our resources.

Physiological Responses to Stress

Firefighters usually report that they love their work, and for some the job is a family tradition. But these individuals' camaraderie and commitment cannot lessen the threat, the risk of injury and death—the stress they experience—when they must answer the alarm and race into harm's way. How does the body of an experienced firefighter respond to the perception of that stressor? And what about your own physical responses to stress?

The Fight-or-Flight Response   When a stressful situation begins suddenly—as when a professional firefighter first hears the alarm—the stress response begins with abrupt and intense physiological arousal, produced by the autonomic nervous system (ANS). Signs of this arousal include accelerated heart rate, quickened breathing, increased blood pressure, and profuse perspiration. This scenario illustrates a case of **acute stress,** a temporary pattern of stressor-activated arousal with a distinct onset and limited duration first described by physiologist Walter Cannon almost a century ago (Cannon, 1914).

Almost instantaneously, reactions in our nervous system, endocrine system, and muscles equip us to make an efficient and effective response—supplying, for example, extra strength if needed. Figure 14.2 provides a detailed illustration of the many ways that the body prepares for an emergency response.

The fight-or-flight response can be a lifesaver when you need to escape from a fire, confront a hostile rival, or protect your children from a hurricane. When

In cases of acute stress, such as this woman faces as a fire races through her house, the stressor arises suddenly, and the stress response begins with abrupt and intense physiological arousal.

CONNECTION • CHAPTER 2
The *Autonomic Nervous System* regulates our most basic vital functions.

Fight-or-flight response   Sequence of internal responses preparing an organism for struggle or escape.

Acute stress   A temporary state of arousal, caused by a stressor, with a distinct onset and limited duration.

FIGURE 14.2
Bodily Reactions to Stress

An amazing array of physiological reactions prepare us to fight or flee in acute stressful situations.

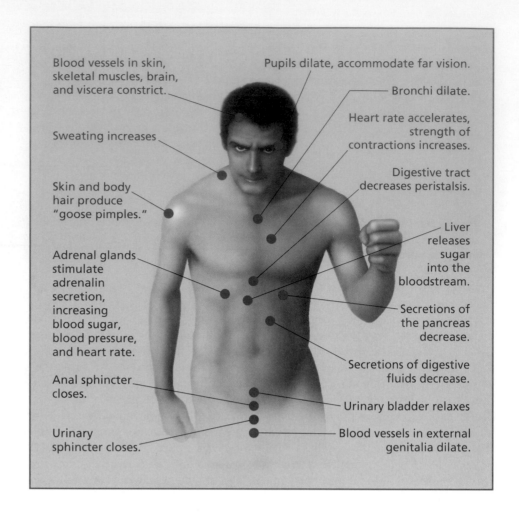

Blood vessels in skin, skeletal muscles, brain, and viscera constrict.

Sweating increases

Skin and body hair produce "goose pimples."

Adrenal glands stimulate adrenalin secretion, increasing blood sugar, blood pressure, and heart rate.

Anal sphincter closes.

Urinary sphincter closes.

Pupils dilate, accommodate far vision.

Bronchi dilate.

Heart rate accelerates, strength of contractions increases.

Digestive tract decreases peristalsis.

Liver releases sugar into the bloodstream.

Secretions of the pancreas decrease.

Secretions of digestive fluids decrease.

Urinary bladder relaxes

Blood vessels in external genitalia dilate.

faced with a chronic stressor, though, it has a cost: Staying physiologically "on guard" against a threat eventually wears down the body's natural defenses. In this way, suffering from frequent stress—or frequently interpreting experiences as stressful—can create a serious health risk: An essentially healthy stress response can become a health hazard. In the next section, we will explore exactly how and why this occurs.

The General Adaptation Syndrome   How do victims of stress and persistent negative emotions become candidates for disease? Our understanding of how stress causes illness began in the mid-20th century with the work of Canadian endocrinologist Hans Selye (pronounced *SELL-yeh*). In brief, Selye discovered that different stressors trigger essentially the same systemic reaction, or general physical response, which mobilizes the body's resources to deal with the threat. Moreover, he found, all stressors provoke some attempt at adaptation, or adjustment of the body to the stressor. Because the bodily response was a general rather than a specific adaptation effort, Selye dubbed it the **general adaptation syndrome (GAS).** (See Figure 14.3.)

Normally, these responses are helpful, but under chronically stressful conditions, they can lead to heart disease, asthma, headache, gastric ulcers, arthritis, and a variety of other disorders (Carlson, 2007; Salovey et al., 2000).

Selye's model of the GAS describes a three-phase response to any threat, consisting of an *alarm phase*, a *resistance phase*, and an *exhaustion phase* (Johnson, 1991; Selye, 1956, 1991).

The Alarm Phase   In the first stage of stress, the body's warning system activates and begins to mobilize its resources against the stressor. Selye called this first stage the

General adaptation syndrome (GAS)   A three-phase pattern of physical responses to a chronic stressor.

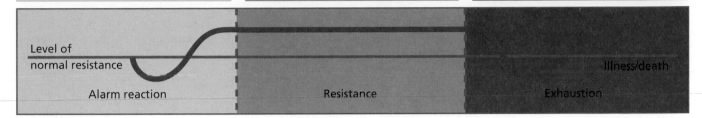

Stage 1: Alarm reaction	Stage 2: Resistance	Stage 3: Exhaustion
General arousal caused by: • increase of adrenal hormones. • reaction of sympathetic nervous system. If stressor is not removed, organism moves to Stage 2.	Arousal subsides because of: • decrease in adrenal output. • counter reaction of parasympathetic nervous system. If stressor is not removed, the organism moves to Stage 3.	General arousal of Stage 1 reappears. Powerful parasympathetic response opposes arousal. If stressor is not removed in time, death occurs.

Level of normal resistance

Illness/death

Alarm reaction | Resistance | Exhaustion

FIGURE 14.3
The General Adaptation Syndrome

In Stage 1, the body produces an emergency arousal response to a stressor. Then, in Stage 2, the body adapts to the continuous presence of the stressor. In Stage 3, if the stressor is not reduced, an arousal response begins again, although the body's defenses are depleted—with dangerous results.

alarm phase—but it is similar to the pattern of reactions Cannon called the fight-or-flight response. The hypothalamus sets off two parallel emergency messages. One message signals the hormone system, especially the adrenal glands, through the pathway shown in Figure 14.4. The result is a flood of steroid hormones into the bloodstream—chemicals that support strength and endurance (the reason why some

Alarm phase First phase of the GAS, during which body resources are mobilized to cope with the stressor.

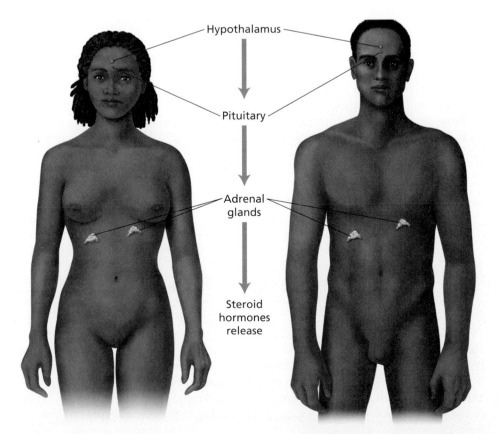

Hypothalamus

Pituitary

Adrenal glands

Steroid hormones release

FIGURE 14.4
Hormonal Response in the Alarm Phase

In the alarm phase of the GAS, the hormone system response shown here is one of the two parallel response pathways set off by the hypothalamus.

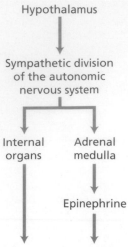

Hypothalamus

↓

Sympathetic division of the autonomic nervous system

↓

Internal organs   **Adrenal medulla**

↓

Epinephrine

↓   ↓

- Heart rate increases.
- Blood pressure increases.
- Blood sugar rises.
- Blood flow to gut decreases.
- Blood flow to heart, brain, and muscles increases.
- Perspiration increases.
- Pupils dilate.

FIGURE 14.5
Sympathetic Nervous System Response in the Alarm Phase

This diagram shows the path of the sympathetic nervous system's response to acute stress, which occurs simultaneously with the parallel response of the hormone system.

Resistance phase Second phase of the GAS, during which the body adapts to and maintains resources to cope with the stressor.

Exhaustion phase Third phase of the GAS, during which the body's resources become depleted.

athletes might risk dangerous side effects by abusing steroids). Endorphins are also released, which reduce the body's awareness of pain signals. A concurrent message is relayed through the sympathetic division of the autonomic nervous system to internal organs and glands, arousing the body for action.

It's the cascade of messages through these two pathways—the sympathetic nervous system and the endocrine system—that readies us for action. Blood flow to the heart, brain, and muscles increases, enabling us to think and react better and faster. Blood flow to the digestive system, conversely, decreases—presumably so our bodies are not expending precious energy on nonessential functions during an emergency. Pupils dilate, enhancing peripheral vision, and perspiration helps keep the body from overheating. Available blood sugar increases as well, to provide an additional energy boost. All in all, our body is amazingly responsive to immediate danger! Figure 14.5 details this autonomic series of responses.

The function of the alarm phase is to enable the organism to fight or to flee, which usually didn't take very long for our ancestors. Given the chronic nature of modern stresses, though, we often progress into the second stage—resistance.

The Resistance Phase   If the stressor persists—but is not so strong that it overwhelms us during the first stage—we enter the **resistance phase,** during which all the physiological changes of the alarm phase remain in effect. During this stage, the body is attempting to fight off the effects of the stressor. The immune system is in high gear as well, and white blood cell count increases to help the body fight off infection.

Surprisingly, the resistance displayed during this stage applies only to the original stressor. In his research, Selye found that if an experimental animal had adapted to one stressor (e.g., electric shock), but a second stressor was introduced (e.g., extreme cold), the animal soon died. The animal's resources were apparently so depleted that it could not mobilize a defense against the new stressor. A tragic human example is found in a soldier who collapses and dies in response to the new stress of a prison camp after surviving months of stressful combat.

Thus, we see that our alarm and resistance defenses use physical energy. They reduce the levels of resources available in case of additional stressors. Imagine yourself as the star of an action movie, pursued by an evil archenemy. You race your old car a long distance to escape your pursuer. But the engine oil was low to begin with, and now it's worse. Just when it seems you have a good lead and can safely pull over to add some oil, another evildoer's vehicle appears in your rear view mirror! You must go on—but how long can you run like this before you burn out your engine?

Now imagine your body responding to a stressful scenario: You've just completed final exams; you got minimal sleep, studying day and night, surviving on junk food and caffeine for a week. Now it's over. You can relax and rest at last. But the phone rings: It's the welcome voice of the love of your life, with an unwelcome note of some negative emotion. Before you can announce the good news that you survived your exams, the voice says, "I don't know how to say this, but—look, we have to talk. . . . " This is probably not good news, but may signal serious trouble, even a breakup—definitely a stressor. Already exhausted by the stresses of finals week, how will you handle this important conversation? You feel stricken, frightened, and even angry: Why this threat? Why now? Because your system is depleted, you may overreact and find yourself without the cognitive and emotional resources to handle the situation effectively.

The Exhaustion Phase   The resistance phase is the body's last-ditch effort to combat the stressor, and if the stressful situation is not ameliorated during that phase, the body can no longer keep up the intense physiological battle. In this third stage, the **exhaustion phase,** body functions drop back into normal range—and then fall below normal. At this point, the body requires rest and rejuvenation to bring our physiological functioning back up to acceptable levels. If it does not get that much-needed respite, as is often the case in today's world of chronic stressors, the very responses that were so adaptive in the first two phases put the body at risk for illness in the third phase.

Several processes may contribute to the physical and mental deterioration seen in the exhaustion phase. For example, increased blood pressure can cause headaches in the short term, and over an extended period of time it contributes to stroke and coronary heart disease (CHD), which are two leading causes of death today. Meanwhile, the compromised digestive system contributes to formation of certain types of ulcers and, over the long term, obesity. Chronic stress is also linked to increased fatty deposits in the bloodstream, which increases risk of stroke. Still other dangers lurk in the depleted immune system, making the stressed person a prime candidate for infections or other diseases. In addition, studies suggest that prolonged or repeated stress may produce long-term changes in the brain that provoke depression (Sapolsky, 1998; Schulkin, 1994). Stress hormones also act on the brain, interfering with its ability to regenerate neurons, especially in the hippocampus (Gould et al., 1998; Sapolsky, 1998). This helps explain why prolonged use of steroids—which are really stress hormones— is dangerous (except under certain medical conditions): They effectively put the body into a state of exhaustion, producing perilous deterioration.

So, we see that Selye's GAS model offers a useful explanation of how stress can lead not only to the initial fight-or-flight reaction but to chronic and debilitating conditions. In particular, it has enlightened medical and psychological researchers about the connections between stressful experiences and physical ailments. And while new research is beginning to reveal that not all stresses produce exactly the same response from the endocrine system (Kemeny, 2003), the model remains widely viewed as the key to understanding the link between stress and illness. Before we look more closely at the details of the chronic stress response, let's first consider an intriguing alternative to fight-or-flight: nurturance.

After responding to one stressor, such as finishing a difficult test, you may find your bodily resources somewhat depleted, leaving you less able to deal with another, unexpected stressor.

Tend and Befriend   Psychologist Shelley Taylor noticed that the fight-or-flight model was developed by male theorists doing research with male subjects—male rats, mice, and humans. The fear and aggression so prominent in fight-or-flight may, noted Taylor, characterize the responses of males more than females (Taylor, 2003; Taylor et al., 2000b). A **tend-and-befriend** model may better explain the behavior of females in response to threats to themselves and their offspring. Taylor's theory argues that, because females are the primary caretakers of offspring, priority must be given to protecting the survival of the young. Aggression ("fight") can cause injury to oneself or one's children; escape ("flight") leaves children defenseless. Neither response promotes adaptation and survival from the female caretaker's point of view (Volpe, 2004).

This tend-and-befriend model proposes that females are biologically predisposed—through brain and hormonal activity—to respond to threat by nurturing and protecting their offspring. Seeking social support creates networks that increase an individual's ability to protect and nurture (Eisler & Levine, 2002; Taylor et al., 2000b). One study in support of the tend-and-befriend model examined men's and women's hormonal changes and self-reports prior to an important examination. While reported anxiety levels did not differ, men had significantly higher levels of **cortisol** production—an important steroid in the fight-or-flight response—than did women (Ennis et al., 2001). Additional research reveals that **oxytocin**, another stress hormone released on exposure to a stressor, may combine with estrogen in females to prompt affiliation-seeking behavior (Taylor, 2006). Higher oxytocin levels are also associated with greater calmness and decreased anxiety, which are important components of effective nurturing.

It might surprise you to know that both men and women show some signs of social support seeking as a stress response, although evidence at this point

Tend-and-befriend   Stress response model proposing that females are biologically predisposed to respond to threat by nurturing and protecting offspring and seeking social support.

Cortisol   A steroid produced by the fight-or-flight response.

Oxytocin   A hormone produced (by both women and men) in response to a stressor.

indicates that women respond this way much more frequently and consistently than men (Tamres et al., 2002). Research also reveals that providers of social support benefit, too, as seen in a lower mortality rate for older adults who give help and emotional support to friends, relatives, and neighbors (Brown et al., 2003).

The picture emerging from these complementary responses to stressful situations—fight-or-flight and tend-and-befriend—is of a more complex stress response than previously thought. We now see a response system that works both to defend and to nurture, promoting the survival not only of the individual but also of offspring, family, and community. Thus, we can see that the hormonal systems and brain processes have evolved to enable both self-protection and reaching out to others in times of danger (Pitman, 2003). Tending-and-befriending powerfully complements the fight-or-flight pattern, together accounting for the survival of not only individuals but of relationships and communities.

Stress and the Immune System

Earlier in this section, we noted that the immune system becomes compromised in the face of chronic stress—specifically, when we enter the exhaustion phase of the GAS. Research has shown, for example, that individuals coping with the death of a spouse or the end of an important long-term relationship are frequently subject to both depression and **immunosuppression** (impairment in the function of the immune system), leaving them more vulnerable to disease (Cohen & Syme, 1985; Kiecolt-Glaser & Glaser, 1987, 2001).

Psychoneuroimmunology   In recent years, with the help of tremendous leaps forward in biotechnology, an exciting new field of study has emerged to examine precisely what mechanisms are involved in this stress–illness relationship. **Psychoneuroimmunology** pulls together psychologists with expertise in psychological factors of stress, such as cognition and emotion; neurologists, who are experts in brain functioning; and immunologists, who offer special knowledge of the immune system. And while the field has an impressive multisyllabic title, this interest in the mind–body connection is nothing new: What we are seeing now is simply a 21st-century approach to the same question pondered by ancient civilizations such as the Greeks and Chinese over two thousand years ago.

How Do Mental Processes Affect the Immune System?   While the field of psychoneuroimmunology is in its relative infancy, we know that the central nervous system and immune systems maintain a communication "loop" in response to stress, injury, or infection (Maier & Watkins, 1999). When a stressor is perceived, the brain sends messages to the autonomic nervous system and endocrine system, which have links to organs that produce the immune response. (Components of the immune system include the blood, lymphatic system, bone marrow, the liver, and the thymus gland.) The brain then receives feedback from the immune system via neural and endocrine pathways (Maier & Watkins, 2000). Among the chemical messengers shuttling between the brain and the immune system are proteins known as **cytokines,** released by immune cells to fight infection. Cytokines cause symptoms like fever, inflammation, and listlessness—responses that usually help fight disease but can sometimes get out of control (DeAngelis, 2002a). In addition to tiredness, cytokines may produce feelings of depression, involving a spiral of negative emotion and thought. Such a response can prolong stress and illness (National Public Radio, 2004).

One factor that determines whether an immune reaction will harm rather than support health is the nature of the stressor (Pert, 1997), particularly whether it is acute or chronic. Many physical stressors, such as strenuous exercise or an attack by an aggressive animal, begin and end abruptly. These acute stressors trigger natural immunity responses, which help reduce the risk of injury. Production of **natural killer cells,** a type of immune cell that attacks foreign cells

Immunosuppression   Impairment in the function of the immune system.

Psychoneuroimmunology   Multidisciplinary field that studies the influence of mental states on the immune system.

Cytokine   Hormonelike chemical that fights infection and facilitates communicaton between the brain and immune system.

Natural killer cell   Cell produced by the immune system that attacks foreign cells.

such as tumors and infectious agents, increases during acute stress (Segerstrom and Miller, 2004). Production of these cells is accomplished by cell devision, and each time a cell divides, the lifespan of the cell is reduced. In contrast, chronic psychological stressors—a difficult marriage, unemployment, or caring for a spouse with Alzheimer's disease—emerge gradually, last a long time, and are not readily solved with fight or flight or with an immune response. Thus, prolonged increased production of the natural killer cells deteriorates the immune system and indeed, research has found compromised immune systems in both men and women coping with these three chronic conditions, regardless of age (Segerstrom & Miller, 2004).

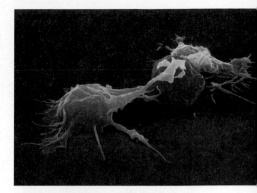

This natural killer cell helps fight off infectious cells, but overproduction of these cells during prolonged stress actually deteriorates the immune system.

One important study compared the immune systems of women with healthy children to those of mothers whose children had serious chronic diseases. The results were sobering: Mothers of the sick children had immune systems that appeared fully *ten years older* than the women's actual chronological age (Epel et al., 2004). In these situations, there is no physical enemy to battle, no safe haven to seek—no quick fix. Bodily responses become maladaptive, the body becomes more vulnerable to infection and injury, and eventually immune disorders can develop. This immunosuppression, a diminished effectiveness of immune response, entails serious health risks.

Another major factor that plays a role in the stress–illness relationship is the role of perception. At the beginning of this chapter we introduced the concept of cognitive appraisal, and research in psychoneuroimmunology indeed finds that individuals who commonly perceive events in a negative light suffer greater immunosuppression than those who habitually see the brighter side. This may explain the differences we see among individuals who are faced with similar stressors: Studies indicate that some suffer little or no immune suppression, while the immune systems of others become seriously compromised.

Stressful conditions, then, can cause physical disease just as surely as can viruses, bacteria, and physical trauma. We have seen what some of our most common stressors are, as well as how our bodies respond to these stressors. Thus, we have a basic understanding of the relationship between stressors, stress, and illness. We know, however, that not everyone becomes stressed when faced with a stressor and also that not everyone who feels stress eventually becomes ill. Why not? We devote the second half of this chapter to answering that very question.

PSYCHOLOGY**MATTERS**
Using Drugs for Stress Relief: A Costly Defense

For millennia, people have used substances to cope with—or escape from—the stresses of their lives. Illicit drugs, such as methamphetamine, cocaine, heroin, and ecstasy, can serve the same purpose. And it's no wonder: Many of these substances tickle the pleasure centers in our brains. The problem, as we saw in Chapter 8, is that the use of alcohol and other drugs can create new and even more stressful problems through their potential for addiction and distortion of thought processes, not to mention their interpersonal and economic impact. Relying on certain substances to "escape" the stress of life's problems is more of a defense than a coping strategy. Such habits are more likely to delay effective coping or allow the stress to worsen.

Drugs and alcohol, while pleasurable, risk becoming defensive "escape routes" from stress or worry. Smoking, too, is a favored habit among those who feel anxious and stressed. Nicotine, the major drug in tobacco products, is a special problem because of the large number of people who smoke cigarettes to alleviate feelings of stress, mild anxiety, or boredom in the short term. In the long run, however, smoking is one of the drugs most frequently blamed for serious health problems. In the United States, 400,000 people die annually from their

CONNECTION • CHAPTER 2
The *limbic system* contains several pleasure centers that create good feelings when aroused by electrical stimulation, drugs, chocolate, or exciting activities.

Smoking is often used as a temporary stress reliever, but it has dangerous long-term consequences.

own smoking; 38,000 people die from others' (secondhand) smoke. On average, the life expectancy for smokers is 14 years less than for nonsmokers (U.S. Department of Health and Human Services, 2006). Smoking kills, harms, and costs billions in health care, insurance expenses, and lost work productivity.

So why do people smoke? And why don't they quit? The tenacity of the smoking habit is maintained by multiple factors. Nicotine is a legal drug, and even though recent legislation has put restraints on advertising, smoking is still considered by many to be relatively "safe." Second, tobacco use is associated through advertising with promises of popularity, sex, friendship, status, and pleasure—so nicotine ingestion becomes a classically conditioned response. Third, nicotine is a highly addictive drug, so smokers periodically need a dose of nicotine to reduce their cravings (Schachter, 1977). When nicotine levels drop, smokers feel nervous, light-headed, and dizzy. They may develop cramps, tremors, heart palpitations, and cold sweats. The nicotine in a cigarette reverses these symptoms and makes them temporarily feel better. (We should note that this process is similar to what occurs in coffee drinkers and is what keeps us reliant on the "wake-up juice.") Stress, however, increases the rate at which the body uses and excretes nicotine. Therefore, stressed individuals who are addicted to nicotine must smoke more to maintain their accustomed level of this drug.

Nicotine has a psychological side, too. As a habit, smoking can also become associated, through classical conditioning, with many aspects of a smoker's life that have nothing to do with stress. So, when a smoker attempts to quit, the world seems to come alive with stimulus cues that suggest smoking. Smoking becomes associated with finishing a meal, driving to work, taking a coffee break, going to a bar, watching television—with almost everything but showering and sleeping. Quitting, then, becomes both a matter of building new nonsmoking associations to all the situations in which the person once smoked and at the same time going through the biological discomfort of withdrawal.

Despite the difficulties, an estimated 35 million smokers have kicked the habit, and about 1.3 million smokers quit every year (U.S. Department of Health and Human Services, 2000). Most quit on their own, without formal stop-smoking programs. In recent years, the use of nicotine gum or a nicotine patch as part of a plan for quitting has made it much easier for smokers to endure the withdrawal process. Antianxiety medications can also be effective. But most quitters find that withdrawal from the stimulant dependency is not enough: The smoker must also make lasting changes in his or her behavior, from the tiniest rituals, gestures, and habits to larger issues of how to reduce risk but still maintain relationships with others who continue to smoke.

CheckYourUnderstanding

1. RECALL: The first stage in Selye's GAS is_____.
   a. attention
   b. alertness
   c. alarm
   d. activity

2. SYNTHESIS: According to researcher Shelley Taylor, how might the responses of a man and a woman differ in the face of the same stressor?

3. APPLICATION: Which of the following stressors would be the most likely to cause the immune system to malfunction and even cause harm?

   a. accidentally slipping and falling on an icy surface
   b. caring for a dying family member for a prolonged period
   c. being rejected by someone you are romantically interested in
   d. receiving a bad grade on an important test

4. UNDERSTANDING THE CORE CONCEPT: Describe how our stress response system is well suited to acute stress, but less effective in the face of chronic stress.

Answers 1. c **2.** Taylor's tend-and-befriend model would predict that the woman would be more likely to respond with the aggression characteristic of the fight-or-flight response. **3.** b **4.** The short-lived alarm phase of the GAS sets off a host of physiological changes that help us combat stressors. We can maintain these high levels of "combat-readiness" during the resistance phase, but if the stressor is chronic, the exhaustion phase kicks in and our immune system suffers the effects of depleted resources.

638   **CHAPTER 14 ● STRESS, HEALTH, AND WELL-BEING**

14.3 KEY QUESTION
WHO IS MOST VULNERABLE TO STRESS?

Why do some people seem to bounce back after severely traumatic experiences such as 9/11 or the death of a loved one, while others are derailed by seemingly minor hassles? We can see a snapshot of the individual differences in response to stress in the way people handle being caught in a traffic jam. Some drivers calmly daydream or listen to their radios, while others frantically hit their horns or "rubberneck," straining to see what the obstruction is. To a large extent, the stressful effects of an unpleasant event are a personal matter. How much stress we experience is determined not only by the quality and intensity of the stressful situation but by how we interpret the stressor. In this section we will focus our attention on the personality characteristics that influence our responses to stressors. A summary of what we will learn is captured in our Core Concept:

Personality characteristics affect our individual responses to stressful situations and, consequently, the degree to which we feel stress when exposed to potential stressors.

core concept

Before we delve into this fascinating field of study, we want to introduce to you a model of the stress–illness relationship that will serve as our guide for the remainder of this chapter.

Figure 14.6 gives you a visual picture of this model, showing how stressors can lead to stress, which in turn can cause physical and mental illness. Note that there are two opportunities for intervention: One lies between stressors and stress, and the other occurs between stress and illness. To put it another way, one set of factors can prevent stressors from causing us to feel stress; similarly,

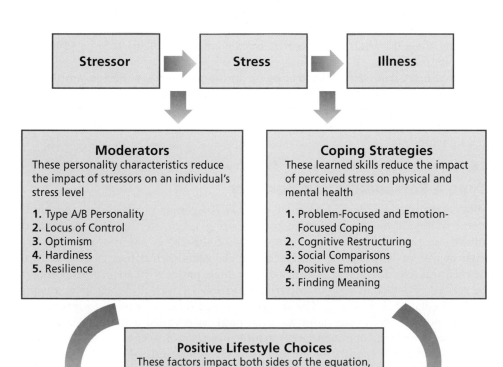

FIGURE 14.6
How Individual Factors Influence Our Stress Response

Oftentimes, stressors cause stress, which in turn can cause illness. However, three categories of psychological responses can intervene in the stress–illness relationship. *Moderators* can help keep stressors from causing stress, *coping strategies* can help prevent stress from leading to illness, and *positive lifestyle choices* can intervene in both places.

Stressor → **Stress** → **Illness**

Moderators
These personality characteristics reduce the impact of stressors on an individual's stress level

1. Type A/B Personality
2. Locus of Control
3. Optimism
4. Hardiness
5. Resilience

Coping Strategies
These learned skills reduce the impact of perceived stress on physical and mental health

1. Problem-Focused and Emotion-Focused Coping
2. Cognitive Restructuring
3. Social Comparisons
4. Positive Emotions
5. Finding Meaning

Positive Lifestyle Choices
These factors impact both sides of the equation, acting as moderators *and* as coping strategies

1. Social Support
2. Exercise
3. Nutrition and Diet
4. Sleep and Meditation

a second set of factors can prevent stress from escalating into physical or mental illness. The first set of factors—those that can intervene in the relationship between stressors and stress—we call **moderators** because they moderate or regulate the impact of stressors on our perceived level of stress. Most of them are variations on the concept of cognitive appraisal: In other words, these moderators influence the judgments and interpretations we make of the stressor. It is this set of possible interventions that we explore in this section, beginning with a couple of examples.

First, let's illustrate how moderators work by looking at the contrasting cases of Anya and Ben. Anya is a conscientious student who never takes a lunch break, preferring to grab a bite while keeping ahead on assigned reading. She says she is "dead set on getting a 4.0." She carries her course texts in her backpack though they aren't required in class and is never without her cell phone. Hurrying to and from classes to be sure she is never late, she feels anxious about delays and angry when traffic slows. She eats while checking her e-mail, reads assignments in bed, and often needs medication to help her relax and get some sleep. In contrast, Ben's approach to school is very different. He usually stops for conversations or lunch with friends. He doesn't lug books to campus unless he needs them, doesn't drive in a hurry, and arrives at class on time most of the time. Though not a perfectionist like Anya, Ben somehow earns grades as good or better than hers in most courses. They both have similarly demanding schedules, but they respond to them very differently.

Or consider this scenario: Demetria and Cory are newlyweds who are trying to plan their life together. They want to buy a home as soon as possible and hope to start a family. They have recently begun to argue about these issues, however, as their outlooks toward their goals differ markedly. Demetria is optimistic that they'll be able to afford the downpayment on a home within a year and strongly believes they can achieve this goal as long as they carefully manage their money. Cory is less positive. In his mind, it seems as though every time he gets close to reaching a goal, something gets in the way, and he's sure this will be no different. To him, "what's gonna happen will just happen," and he is afraid they risk disappointment if they get their hopes up about getting the house in a year.

Do you see yourself or someone you know in either of these examples? If the different styles of approaching and perceiving events are long standing, consistent across situations, and similar to those of others, they could be called personality characteristics. Let's examine their impact on the stressor-stress relationship.

◀ **CONNECTION** · **CHAPTER 12**

Personality is the pattern of characteristics unique to an individual that persists over time and across situations.

Type A Personality and Hostility

When cardiologists Meyer Friedman and Ray Rosenman (1974) hired an upholsterer to repair the furnishings in their waiting room, the upholsterer noticed something that the doctors had not: Most of the chairs showed an unusually high degree of wear on the front edges of the seats. When they became aware of this, the two doctors wondered whether their patients' heart problems might be related to a certain style of coping with stress—it was as if they were always "on the edge of their seats." The doctors began a series of studies to investigate their hypothesis, and interviews with the patients revealed a striking pattern of common behaviors. Impatience, competitiveness, aggressiveness, and hostility— all stress-related responses—were noted again and again. Many also admitted they were notorious workaholics. Friedman and Rosenman ultimately found this collection of attitudes and behaviors not just correlated with heart disease but actually predictive of it. They dubbed it the Type A pattern: Type A men and women were found to have twice as much risk of heart disease as the Type B individual who takes a relaxed approach to life (Matthews, 1982).

Moderator   Factor that helps prevent stressors from causing stress.

Since the initial identification of the **Type A** personality, careful research has revealed that it is specifically the anger and hostility common in Type A people that increases risk of heart disease. Time urgency, perfectionism, and competitiveness, without the anger and hostility, are not risk factors. Hostile individuals are less trusting, quicker to anger, and more antagonostic than their nonhostile counterparts. If you're noticing a connection to cognitive appraisal, you are right: Hostile people would be more likely than most to perceive threat in a situation. This interpersonal style makes it more difficult to maintain relationships, which in turn reduces availability of social support. Hostility is also associated with a variety of risky health behaviors—such as smoking, drinking alcohol, and overeating—that themselves increase risk of heart disease (Taylor, 2006).

This basketball coach displays some Type A behaviors.

From a physiological perspective, those high in hostility become aroused more quickly in the face of a potential stressor, exhibit greater levels of arousal, and take more time for their arousal level to return to normal once the stressor has passed (Guyll & Contrada, 1998; Fredrickson et al., 2000). Hostility is also associated with higher levels of cytokines, which can prolong the stress response (Niaura et al., 2002). Researchers aren't yet sure, though, whether these biological differences are entirely genetic in nature or partially a result of early childhood environment: Boys who grow up in families rife with conflict, and low in acceptance and support, are at greater risk to develop hostility (Matthews et al., 1996). At this time, both nature and nurture are thought to play roles in development of hostility and later heart disease. Clearly, though, there are multiple channels through which hostility promotes heart disease.

At this point, you may be starting to suspect that someone you know (or perhaps even yourself) fits the description of hostile, with all its associated health risks. Let us reassure you that, while many people may sometimes feel angry, there are important differences between normal anger and a truly hostile personality style. We all feel angry at times in response to a negative situation—in these instances, anger can be healthy and even adaptive: It signals us that something is wrong and provides the energy to take measures to correct the situation. That type of normal anger stands in marked contrast to the hostile personality style, which reflects a long-term pattern of hostile behavior that manifests frequently across a variety of situations. The level of arousal is a distinguishing factor as well: It is reasonable to feel irritated when a slow-moving vehicle blocks you in traffic, but feeling enraged is irrational and dangerous, especially if this becomes a common pattern in your life.

Besides cardiovascular diseases, other illnesses have been linked with Type A habits: allergies, head colds, headaches, stomach disorders, and mononucleosis (Suls & Marco, 1990; Suls & Sanders, 1988). Likewise, the perfectionism characteristic of Type A has been linked to anxiety (about reaching impossible goals) and to depression (from failing to reach them) (Joiner & Schmidt, 1995).

Understanding the link between Type A behavior and heart disease, as well as other health risks, can help in developing more effective disease prevention. Regular aerobic exercise, relaxation training, and even a program aimed at teaching hostile individuals to speak more slowly and quietly have proven effective at reducing risk of heart disease (Taylor, 2006). Comprehensive stress management training may offer some of the most promising benefits, however. One study in particular showed heart attack survivors given stress-management training had half as many heart attacks in the next three years as a control group who received no such training (Friedman & Ulmer, 1984). The researchers concluded: "No drug, food, or exercise program ever devised, not even a coronary bypass surgical program, could match the protection against recurrent heart attacks" afforded by learning to manage stress (p. 141). Thus, even though Type A behavior seems to show up early in life and persist into adulthood, well-designed interventions can be effective in helping Type As who are committed to change.

Type A Behavior pattern characterized by intense, angry, competitive, or hostile responses to challenging situations.

Locus of Control

How confident are you that you can make your life turn out pretty much the way you want it to? In our example at the beginning of this section, newlyweds Cory and Demetria were struggling with their differences on this dimension of personality known as **locus of control** (from the Greek *loci,* meaning place). You probably remember our discussion of this concept in Chapter 9 on motivation and Chapter 10 on personality, so you already understand it is a relatively stable pattern of behavior that characterizes individuals' expectations about our ability to influence the outcomes in our life. **Internals** (those with an internal locus of control) generally believe that if they take certain action, they are likely to gain the outcome they desire—diligent studying, for example, will result in good grades. **Externals,** on the other hand, see an unpredictable relationship between their efforts and their outcomes. They are more likely to believe that factors outside their control, such as the fairness of the test or how much the professor likes them, will have a decisive effect on their grades—regardless of how much they study. In the face of a stressful event, internals are more likely to perceive the stressor as manageable than are externals, which leads to lower stress, and ultimately to a variety of health benefits. And perception of control can, at least to some extent, be learned: Firefighters and other 9/11 personnel who were trained for such disasters suffered lower rates of PTSD in the years following the attacks (Perrin et al., 2007)

Locus of Control, Health, and Longevity   A landmark study illuminating the importance of perceived control on health took place in a Connecticut nursing home 30 years ago. Elderly residents on one floor were offered a variety of choices about their daily lives. For example, they were allowed to choose whether and when to watch available movies, how they wanted the funiture and personal items in their rooms arranged, and whether or not to have a plant in their room—which they were responsible for watering. In communications with this group, nursing home staff emphasized the residents' personal responsibility for their own satisfaction; the nursing home staff was happy to help in any way (for example, moving the furniture) on request of a resident. Residents on a different floor, matched on important characteristics such as health and age, acted as the control group. Here the staff took full charge of the residents' care, watering all the plants, assigning movie times, and arranging furniture as per administrative decisions.

The results? After 18 months, the "more responsible" residents were more active, more alert, and happier than the controls. What's more—in an entirely unexpected outcome—locus of control actually affected the residents' lifespans. By the end of the study, the mortality rate of the control group was 67% higher than that of the group with increased personal responsibility (Rodin, 1986).

Consistency in control is important to health as well. A second nursing-home study arranged for college students to make regular visits to the residents. Some residents were allowed to choose when a student would visit and how long he or she would stay, while others received visits on a prearranged schedule. As expected, residents who chose the time and duration of the visits had better health outcomes than those who did not. What surprised researchers was that, once the study was completed and college students no longer visited the residents, the "choice" group suffered more negative health effects than the "non-choice" group (Schulz, 1976). Predictability, it seems, is an important element of control.

Locus of control has been found to impact a wide range of health-related outcomes. In addition to being more likely to wear seat belts, exercise regularly, and pay attention to their diets—all of which have obvious health benefits—internals have better immune systems than do externals (Chen et al., 2003). They get sick less often and recover more quickly from illnesses and surgeries alike (Skinner, 1996). What's more, a strong sense of internal control actually dissolves the well-documented relationship between social class and health: Low-income

Locus of control   A relatively stable pattern of behavior that characterizes individual expectations about the ability to influence the outcomes in life.

Internals   People with an internal locus of control who believe they can do much to influence their life outcomes.

Externals   People with an external locus of control who believe they can do little to influence thier life outcomes.

CHAPTER 14 ● STRESS, HEALTH, AND WELL-BEING

individuals who have an internal locus of control are just as healthy as those with higher incomes (Lachman & Weaver, 1998).

Culture Affects Locus of Control   Cultural studies have identified an interesting distinction between perceptions of control in Western and Eastern cultures. **Primary control,** prevalent in the West, is the type of control discussed above: taking action aimed at controlling external events. Eastern cultures are more likely to engage in **secondary control,** which emphasizes controlling one's reactions to events (Rothbaum et al., 1982). A culture's general value system, such as the individualist and collectivist perspectives discussed in Chapter 10, influences the type of control most highly prized and promoted in that culture. In Japan, for example, which has traditionally been a collectivist culture, child-rearing practices encourage development of secondary control. Children are taught to adjust their reactions to a situation, to help maintain social harmony. This stands in direct contrast to the individualistic approach to child rearing, which fosters efforts to control the situation itself. Research indicates that both strategies work well in the context of their respective cultures (Weisz et al., 1984). Furthermore, when efforts at primary control fail or are not possible for an individualist, engaging in secondary control improves health—a topic we will explore a little later in this chapter.

CONNECTION • CHAPTER 10

Individualistic cultures value the individual over the group, whereas *collectivistic cultures* prioritize group needs over individual needs.

Is Locus of Control Innate, or Learned?   While locus of control does tend to appear early and run in families—factors that often indicate a genetic component— our experiences also impact our expectations. Individuals who repeatedly experience failure when they attempt to escape threatening conditions may simply stop trying, a concept called **learned helplessness.** Evidence of learned helplessness originally came from animal studies performed by Martin Seligman and his colleagues. Dogs receiving inescapable electric shocks soon gave up their attempts to avoid the punishment and passively resigned themselves to their fate (Seligman, 1975, 1991; Seligman & Maier, 1967). Later, when given the opportunity to escape the shocks, the dogs typically did nothing but whimper and accept them. In contrast, a control group of dogs that had not been subjected to previous punishment was quick to escape. Seligman concluded that the experimental group of animals had already learned that nothing they did mattered or altered the consequences, so they passively accepted their fate (Seligman & Maier, 1967).

An experiment by Donald Hiroto (1974) employed human participants in a variation of Seligman's dog research. One at a time, students were placed in a very noisy room; some found a way to turn off the noise, but for others the noise controls did not work. When the students were sent to a new room and exposed to a different irritating noise, those who had successfully turned off the noise in the previous room quickly found the simple solution in the second room. In contrast, those who had failed in their efforts to shut off the noise earlier just sat in the new room, making no effort to stop the latest stressor. They had already learned to be helpless. Seligman and other scholars see symptoms of the same learned helplessness syndrome in a variety of human populations, including abused and discouraged children, battered wives, and prisoners of war (Overmier, 2002; Yee et al., 2003). Conversely, workers at all skill levels in a variety of professions report greater well-being when given some measure of control over their environment and working conditions (Faulkner, 2001; Zarit & Pearlin, 2003).

Thus, although we may be born with an individual predisposition to an internal or external locus of control, our experiences play a role as well. Research with 9/11 rescue personnel and regarding learned helplessness are just two areas in which this important fact has been illustrated.

Hardiness

One of the most effective stress moderators is **hardiness,** an outlook based on distinctive attitudes toward stress and how to manage it. In contrast with risky Type A behavior, hardiness is a personality pattern that promotes healthy cop-

In hospitals and nursing homes, patients may learn to feel helpless because they are not given opportunities to make decisions or exert control over their own lives.

Primary control   Efforts aimed at controlling external events.

Secondary control   Efforts aimed at controlling one's reactions to external events.

Learned helplessness   Pattern of failure to respond to threatening stimuli after an organism experiences a series of ineffective responses.

Hardiness   Attitude of resistance to stress, based on a sense of challenge (welcoming change), commitment (engagement), and control (maintaining an internal guide for action).

ing. Hardiness first emerged in a large-scale study of managers working for Illinois Bell Telephone (IBT) in the 1970s and 1980s. Salvatore Maddi and a team of researchers from the University of Chicago gathered extensive data from the managers over a period of years, during which federal deregulation of public utilities resulted in massive layoffs and downsizing of IBT. Working conditions, positions, and expectations changed frequently, creating a highly stressful work environment. Two-thirds of the managers suffered negative health consequences, including heart attacks, strokes, depression, and anxiety disorders. The other third—who were exposed to the same conditions—not only suffered no ill effects but actually appeared to thrive (Kobasa et al., 1979). The distinguishing factor, it turned out, came to be known as hardiness, a concept comprised of three specific characteristics:

- *Challenge*. Hardy people perceive change as a challenge to be overcome and an opportunity to learn and grow, rather than a threat.
- *Commitment*. Hardy individuals became highly engaged in their lives, demonstrating a focused commitment to involvement in purposeful activity.
- *Control*. Hardy persons have an internal locus of control and are good at problem-solving—that is, they have not become victims of learned helplessness.

Let's apply these three factors—known as "the three Cs" of hardiness—to the life of a college student. Suppose that on the day you must prepare for a major test, a friend confides in you about a terrible problem and begs for your help. These two stressors—an important test and a needy friend—could be overwhelming, especially if you are already stretching some of your resources to the limit. But a hardy individual would employ the "three Cs" to reduce the stress of the situation: commitment ("I'm committed to my friend and to preparing for this test; I'm not going to let either one down"); challenge ("Now I have two important things I need to do—what are my options for meeting both needs?"); and control ("I'll study all afternoon, talk to my friend over dinner—after all, I have to eat to keep my brain functioning—then review more before bed").

Hardiness has been shown to reduce the effects of stressful situations across a wide variety of populations: in businesspeople, children, couples, Olympic athletes, military, and law enforcement (Maddi, 2002). And—like locus of control—although some indications of a hardy personality show up early in life, hardiness can also be learned. Researchers have successfully developed hardiness training programs that help individuals learn more adaptive ways of reacting to stressors in their life (Maddi, 1987; Beasley et al., 2003).

Optimism

When you think about your future, do you generally expect good things to happen, or do you tend to worry about all the things that could go wrong? Optimists see a future of bright possibilities; for them, "the glass is half full," whereas pessimists are far less positive, instead "seeing the glass as half-empty." And pessimism isn't simply a case of learned helplessness. "Life inflicts the same setbacks and tragedies on the optimist as on the pessimist," says psychologist Martin Seligman (1991), "but the optimist weathers them better." In general, optimistic people have fewer physical symptoms of illness, recover more quickly from certain disorders, are healthier, and live longer than pessimists do (Bennett & Elliott, 2002; Taylor et al., 2000a). What accounts for the differences? **Optimism** has a direct impact on health in that optimists feel more positive emotions, which in turn boosts their immune systems (Cohen et al., 2003). In addition, optimism aids in coping with stress via more active coping strategies, which we will discuss in the last section of this chapter.

Optimism   An attitude that interprets stressors as external in origin, temporary, and specific in their effects.

A long-term research program by Seligman (2002) and associates indicates that an optimistic style of thinking makes three particular assumptions, or attributions, about negative events:

● They are the result of specific causes rather than global problems: *"I got a low grade on my last psychology test,"* instead of *"I'm doing badly in school."*

● They are situational rather than personal problems: *"It probably happened because I missed class the day before the exam when the professor gave a review session,"* rather than *"I'm not smart enough to do well."*

● They are temporary, rather than permanent: *"If I'm careful not to miss class anymore, I'll do better on the next test,"* rather than *"I won't be able to recover from this low score."*

Seligman, one of the founders of the International Positive Psychology Association, believes that an optimistic thinking style can be learned. One way to do so, he advises, is by talking to yourself in a particular way when feeling depressed or helpless. Positive self-talk, says Seligman, should concentrate on the meaning and causes of personal setbacks. For example, if a dieter splurges on a piece of dessert, instead of thinking, "Because I've ruined my whole diet, I might as well eat the whole cake!" she or he should think, "Well, I enjoyed that, but I know I'm strong enough to stick to this diet most of the time." In essence, Seligman argues that optimism is learned by adopting a constructive style of thinking, self-assessment, and behavioral planning.

In considering this, you might be reminded of the importance of cognitive appraisal in our stress response, and of our problem for this chapter concerning individual variations in the stress response. Learning to think more optimistically, or to respond with greater hardiness, changes our interpretation of a potential stressor and thus, lowers our perceived stress.

Resilience

Born in 1971, Lance Armstrong was raised as an only child by a working mother and was an enthusiastic athlete from a young age. A competitive swimmer, runner, and cyclist, Armstrong focused in high school on bicycling, his favorite event. He was invited to spend his senior year training for the U.S. Olympic team and later took private classes to earn his high school diploma. The following year he became the U.S. national amateur champion bicyclist and won two major races; the year after that he won the Tour DuPont, over 1000 miles in 11 days. Armstrong had ups and downs but always rebounded. Then, in 1993 he won three major races in cycling's "Triple Crown." His popularity grew as he persisted through adversity: pouring rain, bicycle crashes, and bronchitis that prevented completion of a race. In 1995 he won his first Tour de France, the world's premier cycling race at over 2200 miles. Autumn of 1996, however, brought what would surely be the final setback: a diagnosis of testicular cancer. He characteristically tackled this challenge too, however, with surgery, chemotherapy, and a change in diet. His chances for recovery seemed good—then plummeted when tumors were found on his brain. His sponsor canceled his professional contract. What did he do?

In brief, he bounced back (Armstrong, 2001). He found a new sponsor, and by 2005 he had placed or won in several events, before going on to win the Tour de France—seven times! Along the way he survived unsupported rumors of drug use and a car collision while biking. He is founder of a cancer research foundation, author of a best-selling autobiography, and an inspiration to people worldwide. With his life of successes and setbacks, you couldn't call him "lucky." Instead, psychologists recognize in Lance Armstrong something more precious to well-being than talent or genius: **resilience.**

Resilience The capacity to adapt, achieve well-being, and cope with stress, in spite of serious threats to development.

Resilience is the capacity to adapt and achieve well-being in spite of serious threats to development (Masten, 2001). In fact, the word *resilience* comes from a Latin root meaning "buoyant"—literally bouncing amid waves. For over two decades, most resilience research has focused on this quality in children and adolescents who have dealt with stressful life conditions, including parental neglect or abuse, parental mental illness, and other serious risk factors. How could some at-risk children survive and even thrive, when others became ill and failed *because* of the same types of risks?

Even at young ages, resilient children are distinguished by an assortment of qualities. They tend to have higher cognitive abilities, greater conscientiousness, better social skills, greater competence, and access to better caretaking or parenting resources (Masten, 2001; Riolli, 2002). Identifying resilient qualities so early in life supports the inference that one is either born resilient or not. More recently, however, attention has been focused on the quality of resilience among adult populations, and also on whether resilience can be learned. One study of resilience among adults examined survivors of the 1999 conflict in Kosovo in the former Yugoslavia. Resilience was related to a combination of personality traits, including extraversion, conscientiousness, and optimism (Riolli, 2002). Of these, optimism in particular holds promise for helping people to become more resilient and less vulnerable or brittle. Also, you may have noticed that resilience seems to overlap somewhat with hardiness, and indeed the two concepts are related. While hardiness is focused on three specific characteristics, though, resilience encompasses a broader range of qualities. And, because hardiness can be developed with the help of specific training programs, perhaps the future will bring similar findings to resilience.

Lance Armstrong's story may be extraordinary, but his resilience need not be rare. In fact, many everyday heroes and "unknown celebrities" overcome terrible difficulties without our awareness. Their ability to deal with pain and challenge is actually the result not of extraordinary forces but of "ordinary magic," resilience researcher Ann Masten's (2001) term for normal adaptation processes which she argues are capable of greater outcomes than we might expect. By expecting more, perhaps we take a step toward greater optimism and resilience in our own lives.

PSYCHOLOGY**MATTERS**

Using Psychology to Learn Psychology

Imagine that you have just suffered a loss: a friend picked a fight and insulted you, violating your sense of trust; the one you love doesn't return your feelings and has rejected you; or your family pet has died, leaving you grief stricken though friends insist you should "get over it." Whatever the stress, you aren't sure where to go or to whom you can talk—yet you feel a strong need to express your thoughts and feelings. What can you do? Here's a place to start: Write it out. In the process, you'll learn more about your own psychology.

Why write? Why not just rant and rave and get it out of your system? For one thing, aggressively venting emotions is not enough to relieve stress or support your health; on the contrary, it can even have aggravating or harmful effects (Gross & Psaki, 2004; Smythe, 1998). Conversely, writing about your fears and losses has therapeutic emotional effects (Pennebaker, 1990, 1997; Zimmerman, 2002), and writing about feelings and worries has been found to support the health of patients with immune disorders (Pennebaker, 1997). When you write out your thoughts and feelings, you talk only to and for yourself. With no audience to perform for and no patient listener to please, you can use frank language, tell all, and rest assured you don't have to "explain" anything. All you need is a place, a time, the materials you need, and commitment to maintain the habit. There are several ways to make the practice easier and more effective:

- Write in any medium that is efficient or comforting to you—it's OK to type at your keyboard, but you may not always have convenient access to your computer. Handwriting is more personally expressive, and you don't have to make it legible—it's for your eyes only. By using a pen and paper, you can not only write but draw or doodle, expressing yourself nonverbally. And a small notebook is inexpensive and easy to keep handy.

- Choose a topic or theme to get you started. If a loss or fear has prompted your writing exercise, start with that. If not, choose an "assignment" that prompts emotions and ideas about important challenges in your life. One professor asks students in a class on psychology of loss to develop a journal of loss, referring either to personal losses or to memorable events such as a terrorist attack or the death of a celebrity and what that has meant to the writer (Harvey & Hofmann, 2001).

- Write out your thoughts as well as your feelings. Focus on finding the meaning in difficult experiences. You may not know the answers ("Why didn't our relationship last?"), but you can reason and fantasize ("Maybe this is a good time for me to be on my own anyway"). An important purpose in therapeutic writing or talking is to achieve insight, growth, and change. It may also help to write out memories as if telling a story: with a beginning, middle, and end; descriptions of characters and events; and your own conclusions about the "moral of the story" and lessons you have learned (Harvey et al., 1990; Murray, 2002).

- Write in spare moments, setting a goal such as a few pages every week. Write as if you were a reporter, including whatever details seem important (DeSalvo, 2000). Experiment with various forms, such as writing love or hate letters. Identify blessings-in-disguise or categorize various things you do (e.g., things you do for others versus things you do for yourself) (Zimmerman, 2002).

- Stick with it. Make writing a habit, not just a release for the bad times. One researcher found that writing only about trauma intensified the pain and left subjects less able to open up or work it through. So even at times when you don't "need" to write, write a few lines anyway—*because* you feel fine—so you can later remember that you have felt good and remind yourself how you got that way!

Your goal in using writing is not to become a great writer (though it's possible!) but to work through your stress, learn about your responses and coping patterns, and heal. You set the goals, you make the rules. In doing so, you might consider how to incorporate some of what you have learned in this section about perceptions and hardiness. Perhaps, through writing, we can focus on improving our abilities to perceive stressors in an adaptive manner. In addition, remember our discussion in the first Core Concept of this chapter about the importance of narratives. But don't let it stress you out! You issue these writing "assignments" to yourself, so you can relax knowing there is no deadline pressure and no grade to worry about.

CheckYourUnderstanding

1. **RECALL:** In terms of health, the riskiest component of Type A behavior is_____.
   a. hostility
   b. perfectionism
   c. competitiveness
   d. time urgency

2. **ANALYSIS:** People who believe they can take action to affect their life outcomes have an _____ locus of control and are more likely to _____.

   a. internal; suffer more frequent frustrations
   b. external; suffer more frequent frustrations
   c. internal; live longer
   d. external; live longer

3. **APPLICATION:** Roz recently got a new assignment at work that she didn't really want. In responding to this change, she decided to see it as an opportunity for growth and to fully commit to doing whatever was necessary to do a good job with it. Which personality

characteristic discussed in this section best describes Roz's response?

4. APPLICATION: Think of a recent negative event or situation in your own life. According to Martin Seligman, what three attributions should you make in perceiving the event/situation?

5. UNDERSTANDING THE CORE CONCEPT: Describe how personality characteristics fit into the stress–illness relationship.

14.4 KEY QUESTION
HOW CAN WE REDUCE THE IMPACT OF STRESS ON OUR HEALTH?

Is it possible to choose to live a long and healthy life? Or will your health be determined by factors out of your hands, such as your genetic background or simply your access to health care? After exposure to a traumatic stressor such as 9/11, or a chronic stressor such as the ones we have discussed in this chapter, is there something we can do to reduce its impact on our health?

By now, you've probably gathered that taking a hardy approach to these questions, with an internal locus of control and an optimistic attitude, will increase your odds of success! And there is more good news: Illness and mortality can also be affected by the coping strategies we employ and the lifestyle choices we make (Elliott & Eisdorfer, 1982; Taylor, 2006). As you can see by "reading between the lines" in Table 14.1, many early deaths result from behaviors over which we have control. Stress, of course, is part of the lifestyle equation, too. In this section of the chapter, we will explore effective ways of coping with stress, as well as lifestyle choices that can help us ward off the devastating effects of stress through better health. As our Core Concept puts it:

core concept

Healthy coping strategies reduce the impact of stress on our health, and positive lifestyle choices reduce both our perceived stress and its impact on our health.

Coping strategy Action that reduces or eliminates the impact of stress.

Revisiting the model we introduced in the previous section (Figure 14.6), **coping strategies** work by reducing the impact of stress—once we're feeling it—on our

Table 14.1	Leading Causes of Death in the United States						
Rank	Females, all races	Contributors	Percentage	Rank	Males, all races	Contributors	Percentage
1.	Heart disease	DS	29.3	1.	Heart disease	DS	28.7
2.	Cancer	DS	21.6	2.	Cancer	DS	24.3
3.	Stroke	DS	8.1	3.	Stroke	A	5.6
4.	Chronic lower respiratory disease	S	5.1	4.	Chronic lower respiratory disease	DS	5.3
5.	Diabetes	D	3.1	5.	Diabetes	S	5.0
6.	Alzheimer's disease		3.1	6.	Alzheimer's disease	D	2.8
7.	Unintentional injuries	A	2.9	7.	Unintentional injuries	A	2.3
8.	Influenza and pneumonia		2.8	8.	Influenza and pneumonia	A	2.1
9.	Kidney disease		1.7	9.	Kidney disease		1.6
10.	Septicemia		1.5	10.	Septicemia	A	1.5

Contributors to causes of death: D = Diet, A = Alcohol, S = Smoking.

(*Source:* Centers for Disease Control and Prevention, U.S. Department of Health and Human Services, 2004. Retrieved on November 19, 2004, from www.cdc.gov/od/spotlight/nwhw/lcod.htm)

health. In other words, they decrease the effects of stress on our bodies. **Positive lifestyle choices** have the same power to help us cope effectively with stress and have an added benefit: They also act as stress moderators, diminishing the stress we perceive when exposed to stressors. That is, positive lifestyle choices increase our resistance to stress, as well as our resistance to illness. We begin this section of the chapter by examining coping strategies that are most useful in combating stress. Then, we examine the lifestyle choices associated with stress reduction and disease prevention. Finally, we will look at the characteristics of people who say they have found happiness and a sense of well-being.

Psychological Coping Strategies

Earlier in the chapter we saw how the Type A personality, pessimism, and learned helplessness can aggravate the stress response, just as hardiness, optimism, an internal locus of control, and resilience can moderate it. Certainly, we advise that for serious stressors and difficulties, you seek out professional advice and help. (If you don't know a psychotherapist or licensed counselor, ask a trusted instructor or health care provider for a referral.) What can you do on your own, however, to cope effectively with stress? And what exactly is meant by coping?

Defending versus Coping   There are two broad categories of stress management behaviors: defending and coping. **Defending** involves reducing the *symptoms* of stress or reducing one's awareness of them. For example, if you feel stress over an important psychology exam for which you feel unprepared, you might simply defend against that anxious feeling by distracting yourself with some activity that is fun—going to a party or visiting friends. Your defense won't make the problem go away—there will still be an exam, and now you'll be even less prepared for it! But for a brief period, you might feel less stress. Defending has the advantage of alleviating some symptoms like worry, discomfort, or pain; but it has the serious drawback of failing to deal with the stressor. Inevitably stress returns, only now it may be more difficult to alleviate.

In contrast with merely defending against stress, **coping** involves taking action that reduces or eliminates the causes of stress, not merely its symptoms. To cope, you must confront the stress, identify the stressor, and develop a way of solving the problem or reducing the harm it causes you. This means not just feeling better but improving the entire stressful situation. To cope with stress over a looming psychology exam, you must (a) realize that you feel unprepared for the exam, (b) identify effective strategies to study for the test, (c) implement the strategies in a timely manner, and (d) take the test. This way you will not only feel prepared, you will be prepared and feel less anxious. Of course, you may have to postpone having fun until after the exam, but you'll enjoy yourself more without the test anxiety. (Remember the Premack principle?)

Problem-Focused and Emotion-Focused Coping   In general, there are two basic approaches to healthy coping: emotion-focused coping and problem-focused coping. **Problem-focused coping** involves clarifying the stressor and taking action to resolve it. This may involve some advance planning, such as when you are nervous about starting a new school. Problem-focused coping in that situation could involve a visit to the school to figure out where your classes are and to talk with an academic advisor to get some tips for success, thus reducing your anxiety about knowing your way around and about being able to do well. **Emotion-focused coping,** on the other hand, involves efforts to regulate your emotional response to the stressor by identifying your feelings, focusing on them, and working through them. Effective emotion-focused coping must be distinguished from **rumination,** which is dwelling on negative thoughts (rather than emotions); not surprisingly, rumination has been found to compromise our immune systems (Thomsen et al., 2004)—and it doesn't help us feel better, either!

Positive lifestyle choices   Deliberate decisions about long-term behavior patterns that increase resistance to both stress and illness.

Defending   Efforts taken to reduce the symptoms of stress or one's awareness of them.

Coping   Taking action that reduces or eliminates the causes of stress, not merely its symptoms

Problem-focused coping   Action taken to clarify and resolve a stressor.

Emotion-focused coping   Regulating one's emotional response to a stressor.

Rumination   Dwelling on negative thoughts in response to stress, a behavior which compromises the immune system.

CONNECTION • CHAPTER 3

The *Premack principle* notes the strategy of using a preferred activity as a reward for completing a less-preferred activity.

Both types of coping can be useful. In general, problem-focused coping is best when there is some concrete action that can be taken to reduce the stressor. In contrast, emotion-focused coping can help at times when you must simply accept a situation or when you need to work through your emotions before you can think clearly enough to act rationally (Folkman & Lazarus, 1980; Zakowski et al., 2001).

Sometimes the two coping styles work best together. For example, if you get fired from your job, you might try to start looking for another job (problem-focused) but find that you can't focus on the task because you are too angry and confused about being fired. In that type of situation, it can be helpful to do some emotion-focused coping to help yourself calm down and be able to think more clearly. You might go for a run or to the gym, talk to a trusted friend, write in your journal, or engage in some other task that helps you work through your feelings. Alternatively, you might take a hot bath, get some rest, or eat something nourishing. Such emotion-focused coping is not merely a defense (as in distracting yourself completely from the problem). Rather, it focuses on processing your emotional responses before they careen out of control and become hazardous to your health. Then, when you feel calm and prepared, you can concentrate on what it takes to address the stressor and solve the problem.

Cognitive Restructuring   Throughout this chapter, we have recognized the role of cognitive appraisal in the stress-illness relationship. And while the personality factors that make us less vulnerable to stress—such as hardiness and locus of control—are deeply ingrained in our general outlook, with a little conscious effort we can apply their basic principles to our coping efforts (Kohn & Smith, 2003). **Cognitive restructuring** involves just that: cognitively reappraising stressors with the goal of seeing them from a less-stressful perspective (Meichenbaum & Cameron, 1974; Swets & Bjork, 1990). The approach involves recognizing the thoughts you have about the stressor that are causing anxiety, then challenging yourself to see the situation in a more positive light. Getting fired, for example, offers the opportunity to find a new job that is more enjoyable, offers better pay, or has more potential for advancement. Cognitive restructuring is especially suitable for people suffering from chronic stress. Indeed, it is one of the cornerstones of cognitive–behavioral therapy, which we discussed in the previous chapter.

Making **social comparisons** is a type of cognitive restructuring that specifically compares your own situation to others in similar situations. Health psychologist Shelley Taylor (1983) first noted the use of social comparision in a study of breast cancer patients. Some of them engaged in **downward social comparison,** in which they compared their own situations to those of women worse off than they were, which in turn helped them see their illness in a more positive light. (Please note that, in making these downward comparisons, no one is taking any pleasure in others' pain; the strategy is simply noticing and acknowledging the existence of grimmer possibilities.) Others engaged in **upward social comparison** and used breast cancer patients who were doing better than they were as models and inspiration for improvement. Corroborating research has demonstrated that both types are effective coping strategies. In a sense, downward social comparisons represent a type of emotion-focused coping—in that the comparison ultimately makes you feel less worried—whereas upward comparisons are a type of problem-focused coping because the models serve as a guide for specific action (Wills, 1991).

Positive Emotions   If negative thinking and negative emotions such as hostility are stress inducing, then is the opposite true as well: Are positive emotions health inducing? Several areas of study indicate that they may be.

One study investigated this question in a group of Catholic nuns who ranged in age from 75 to 95 years old. The researchers gained access to autobiographies the nuns had written just prior to entering the convent (when most were in their

Cognitive restructuring   Reappraising a stressor with the goal of seeing it from a more positive perspective.

Social comparison   A type of cognitive restructuring involving comparisons between oneself and others in similar situations.

Downward social comparison   Comparison between one's own stressful situation and others in a similar situation who are worse off, with the goal of gaining a more positive perspective on one's own situation.

Upward social comparison   Comparison between one's own stressful situation and others in a similar situation who are coping more effectively, with the goal of learning from others' examples.

CHAPTER 14 ● STRESS, HEALTH, AND WELL-BEING

early twenties) and measured the emotional content of the writings. Each one-page autobiography was rated for the number of positive, negative, and neutral emotional words used. Clear differences emerged: Nuns who used the most positive-emotion words lived an average of 9.4 years longer than those who expressed the fewest positive emotions! Moreover, expressing a wider variety of positive emotions in their autobiographies increased lifespan by an additional year (Danner et al., 2001).

Cultivating and expressing a sense of humor has also been found to buffer the effects of stress. The ability to find something to laugh about during exposure to a stressor not only improves mood, but decreases the physiological impact of the stressor as well (Dillard, 2007). Having a good sense of humor, as a personality characteristic, has also been found to reduce an individual's cognitive appraisal of a stressor (Lefcourt, 2000; Kulper et al., 1993). These findings dovetail with work by Harvard psychologist George Vaillant, whose lifespan study of men noted joy in living as one of the key predictors of health and long life (Vaillant, 1990).

Feeling and expressing positive emotions can lengthen your lifespan.

If you don't possess a naturally good sense of humor or don't characteristically experience a lot of positive emotions, you can still benefit from these tools in your coping efforts. Making a conscious effort to note positive moments in your life and to seek out situations in which you find humor and joy can and will improve your life, says positive psychology proponent Martin Seligman in his book *Authentic Happiness* (2002). A poignant expression of this was noted by an AIDS patient, who said this:

> Everyone dies sooner or later. I have been appreciating how beautiful the Earth is, flowers, and the things I like. I used to go around ignoring all those things. Now I stop to try and smell the roses more often, and just do pleasurable things. (G. M. Reed, cited in Taylor, 2006)

Finding Meaning Viktor Frankl was a well-respected neurologist in Austria when Nazi forces deported him and his family to a concentration camp. They, along with thousands of other Jews, were subjected to various forms of deprivation, torture, and unspeakable atrocities, and many—including Frankl's wife and parents—died in the camps. Frankl, however, survived, and after the war ended he made a significant contribution to the field of psychology with his work on the importance of finding meaning in seemingly inexplicable events such as what he had experienced in the camps. In his seminal work *Man's Search for Meaning (1959)*, he says, "When we are no longer able to change a situation—just think of an incurable disease such as inoperable cancer—we are challenged to change ourselves."

Frankl's hypthesis has spawned research investigating the benefit of finding meaning in loss, which has identified two specific types of meaning, **sense-making** and **benefit-finding.** Following a significant negative life event, people try to make sense of the event in some way so that it fits with our perception of the world as predictable, controllable, and nonrandom (Tait & Silver, 1989; Tedeschi & Calhoun, 1996). For example, a death might be explained as inevitable if the person had been battling a long illness or if he or she had a history of heavy smoking. In the wake of Hurricane Katrina, discussions of the long-standing problems with New Orleans' levees reflected a similar attempt for sense-making. Individuals with strong religious beliefs may make sense of loss by attributing it to God's will. A second path to finding meaning lies in recognizing some benefit that ultimately came from the loss, such as a renewed sense of appreciation for life or other loved ones, or discovery of a new path in life.

Successful coping appears to involve both sense-making and benefit-finding, although at different times. Sense-making is the first task people struggle with, but ultimately working through the loss and regaining momentum in life seems to hinge on resolving this first question and moving on to the second (Janoff-Bulman & Frantz, 1997). This may explain why people who have lost a child,

Sense-making One aspect of finding meaning in a stressful situation, which involves perceiving the stressor in a manner consistent with our expectations of the world as predictable, controllable, and nonrandom.

Benefit-finding The second phase of finding meaning in a stressful situation, which involves seeing some ultimate benefit from the stressor.

individuals coping with an accidental or violent death of a loved one, and others dealing with a loss that defies our perception of the natural order of life often have a harder time recovering from the loss (Davis et al., 1998).

Finding meaning in tragedy, then, is not an easy task. Is there anything that can help? Not surprisingly, perhaps, optimists have an easier time of it than do pessimists, especially with regards to benefit-finding (Park et al., 1996). Strong religious beliefs appear to facilitate sense-making, particularly with the loss of a child, as evidenced in a study of parents who had lost a child to sudden infant death syndrome (SIDS) (McIntosh et al., 1993). And the benefits of social support—which we will explore shortly—are not limited to a particular personality type or to the religious but can play an important role in finding meaning of both types.

Psychological Debriefing: Help or Hindrance?

On April 20, 1999, two heavily armed students at Columbine High School in Littleton, Colorado, carried out a preplanned massacre, fatally gunning down 12 students and a teacher before turning their guns on themselves. Those who survived needed assistance in coping, but so did their horrified loved ones and the larger community. Although the vast majority of trauma survivors recover from early trauma without professional help, community leaders and mental health professionals may initiate counseling sessions—seeking out individuals or gathering groups in meeting spaces—in hopes of reducing posttraumatic stress. After the Columbine massacre, counselors visited all classes regardless of whether individual students had reported problems. Similarly, after the World Trade Center attacks, a program was funded to offer free counseling for New Yorkers—but only a fraction of the predicted number sought help, leaving $90 million in therapy funds unspent (Gittrich, 2003). Don't survivors want help—or isn't such help very effective?

This form of crisis intervention, called **psychological debriefing,** is a brief, immediate type of treatment focusing on venting emotions and discussing reactions to the trauma (McNally et al., 2003). This practice is based on the assumption that it is psychologically healthier to express negative feelings than to keep them inside. This belief, in turn, is based on the ancient concept of **catharsis,** which involves relieving emotional "pressure" by expressing feelings either directly (as by hitting a punching bag) or indirectly (as by watching a violent play or movie). Unfortunately, the theory of catharsis doesn't hold up to empirical scrutiny—rather than reducing arousal and feelings of distress, studies show it often prolongs them.

Critical Incident Stress Debriefing (CISD)

Recently, a specific type of psychological debriefing known as **critical incident stress debriefing** (CISD) has emerged and taken center stage in the field of psychological debriefing. CISD programs typically offer group sessions to trauma survivors within 72 hours of the traumatic event; these sessions are two to three hours long and are often mandated by organizations (such as by Columbine High School in the aftermath of the shooting). CISD programs follow a strict agenda that requires participants to first describe the facts of the traumatic event, then recount the immediate cognitive reactions they had to it, followed by their feelings, and disclose any symptoms of psychological distress they have begun to notice as a result. Next, program leaders offer information about frequently occurring symptoms and provide referrals for follow-up treatment.

Is CISD Effective?

As we have learned, extraordinary claims require extraordinary evidence. Also, remember that we are biased when it comes to emotionally charged topics—our strong desire to find a "cure" can interfere with our ability to think critically about the evidence. In cases like this, it is all too easy to jump on the bandwagon of an exciting new treatment before it has been soundly tested. And while proponents of CISD argue for its effectiveness, very few studies have followed sound methodological procedures to accurately measure the outcomes

Psychological debriefing Brief, immediate strategy focusing on venting emotions and discussing reactions to a trauma.

Catharsis A theory suggesting that emotional pressure can be relieved by expressing feelings directly or indirectly.

Critical incident stress debriefing (CISD) A specific type of psychological debriefing that follows a strict, step-by-step agenda.

CHAPTER 14 ● STRESS, HEALTH, AND WELL-BEING

(Devilly et al., 2006). On the contrary, caution some trauma experts, the procedures of CISD can actually strengthen the memory of a traumatic experience—the opposite of helpful intervention. Moreover, the procedures involved in CISD run contrary to some long-established findings regarding the ineffectiveness of catharsis, which casts further doubt on the true efficacy of the program. At this point in time, research suggests that we should be skeptical of the value of CISD in helping trauma survivors.

In the short term, talking to others may help—if the individual wants and seeks out this opportunity. Organizations that require survivors of a traumatic event to participate in CISD whether they want to or not, however—with the assumption that "it couldn't hurt"—may be doing more harm than good. Sadly, many emergency-response workers are unaware of research questioning the value of debriefing, and, as a result, debriefing is still used widely and indiscriminately (Holden, 2003d; McNally et al., 2003). Cognitive and behavioral therapies that focus on cognitive reappraisal and use well-established procedures to reduce emotional arousal associated with the event may be more effective than CISD, especially when therapy is delivered not immediately but many weeks after the traumatic event (McNally et al., 2003).

These, then, are the coping strategies found to be effective in keeping stress from taking a toll on our health—problem-focused and emotion-focused coping, cognitive restructuring, upward and downward social comparisons, positive emotions, and finding meaning. Each of these factors offers an additional piece of the puzzle to help us understand individual differences in how stress affects us. As you consider your own use of these tools, please remember two things. First, people facing chronic stressors often rely on a combination of strategies. Second, there are also a number of lifestyle choices we can make that can be added to our "coping strategies toolbox" and have the added benefit of moderating stress as well. We turn our attention next to a review of those factors.

◀ **CONNECTION • CHAPTER 13**
Cognitive-behavioral therapies treat maladaptive behavior by helping to change both unwanted cognitions and unwanted behaviors.

Positive Lifestyle Choices: A "Two-for-One" Benefit to Your Health

If you are like most people, you like a bargain! We want the most for our money, the most for our time, and the most for our efforts. The positive lifestyle choices we will discuss in this section are bargains for your health, in that each investment you make in this category gives you not one, but two benefits: They act both as moderators and as coping strategies. (See Figure 14.6.) The more of these you integrate into your life, the better health you will enjoy. Let's start with a little help from our friends.

Social Support One of the best antidotes for stress is **social support**: the psychological and physical resources that others provide to help an individual cope with adversity. Research shows that people who encounter major life stresses, such as the loss of a spouse or job, suffer fewer physical and psychological ailments if they have an effective network of friends or family for social support (Billings & Moos, 1985). They are less likely to contract colds and have less risk of depression or anxiety. Similarly, social support has demonstrable health benefits for those suffering from physical disease (Davison et al., 2000; Kelley et al., 1997): Individuals diagnosed with conditions including heart disease, cancer, arthritis, and diabetes all recover more quickly with a good social support network (Taylor, 2006). By contrast, people with few close relationships die younger, on the average, than people with good social support networks (Berkman & Syme, 1979; Pilisuk & Parks, 1986)—even when other factors known to affect lifespan, such as health and socioeconomic status, are controlled for. Remarkably, the lack of a reliable support network increases the risk of dying from disease, suicide, or accidents by about the same percentage as does smoking (House et al., 1988).

Social support Resources others provide to help an individual cope with stress.

These women are doing two things for their health: spending time with friends, and laughing.

Benefits of Social Support   What is it about social support that gives it such power to enhance our health? Research has revealed three specific benefits. *Emotional support* may be what immediately comes to mind when you think of social support, and this indeed is one of its benefits. Having trusted friends and loved ones we can count on to be there with us through difficult times lends immeasurable relief. *Tangible assistance* comes in the form of specific, task-oriented help, such as rides to the doctor's office or hospital, help with housecleaning, or cooking meals. Finally, *informational support* aims to help an individual better understand the nature of the stressor as well as available resources to cope with it. In the aftermath of a serious auto accident, for example, someone with spinal cord injuries might benefit from information regarding typical timeline and strategies for recovery but not be mobile enough to get to a computer to research it. A friend can help. And even though social support networks often consist of family and close friends, support groups or other community resources can provide these benefits as well.

Physiologically, social support reduces the intensity and the duration of the arousal associated with the fight-or-flight response. This finding has emerged from experimental studies that first expose participants to a stressor, then measure such responses as their heart rate, blood pressure, and levels of stress hormones either in the presence of social support or alone (Christenfeld et al., 1997). Social support in the form of a friend or loved one provides optimal benefits, but arousal is also reduced when the support comes from a stranger, a video (Thorsteinsson et al., 1998), or even a pet—although dogs somewhat outperform cats in this regard (Allen et al., 2002). And when social support is not present, simply thinking about loved ones even provides some benefit (Broadwell & Light, 1999).

Physical affection, such as hugs, hand holding, and touch, helps combat stress as well. Several studies note lower arousal in women exposed to a stressor when their partners held their hand or gave them a hug—and, recently, this effect was found in men as well (Coan et al., 2006; Light et al., 2005;). For both sexes, as in animals, physical contact with a trusted partner raises oxytocin levels, which decreases anxiety and stress. These findings fit nicely with the tend-and-befriend model we introduced earlier in this chapter.

Supporters Reap What They Sow   What impact does social support have on the supporter? People in need of social support sometimes worry that they might raise their loved ones' stress levels by asking for help. And while this does sometimes occur—caregivers of Alzheimer's patients, for example, show greater risk of depression and disease—overall, support-givers benefit from helping. In fact, one study of married couples measured amounts of support giving and receiving over a five-year period and found that those who provided more support lived longer (Brown et al., 2003). It is important to note, however, that supporters need support as well.

Exercise   For better or worse, our bodies are still better adapted to the strenuous, Stone-Age demands of hunting and gathering than to sedentary life in a digital, urban world. Spending our days in relative inactivity behind a desk or computer terminal is not a formula for physical or mental health. Unfortunately, while many of us may know this, few are taking it seriously—two-thirds of Americans aren't getting enough exercise, according to the Center for the Advancement of Health (2004).

Just 30 minutes of aerobic exercise per day lowers risk of heart disease, stroke, and breast cancer, among others (Taylor, 2006). It can increase muscle tone and eliminate fat—changes that produce a variety of health benefits. Most importantly, perhaps, it can prolong your life. A long-term study of 17,000 middle-aged men showed that those who were on an exercise regimen (the equivalent of walking five hours a week) had mortality rates that were almost one-third lower than their couch-potato counterparts (Paffenbarger et al., 1986). Even smokers who exercised reduced their death rate by about 30%.

Regular exercise has not only physical but psychological benefits, including stress reduction (McDonald, 1998) and mental health. For example, a regular aerobic exercise program improved the emotional health of female college students who were mildly depressed (McCann & Holmes, 1984). Another study found that a 20-week physical fitness course could produce measurably lower levels of anxiety in sedentary women (Popejoy, 1967). Exercise programs have also been shown to have a positive effect on self-concept (Folkins & Sime, 1981). And a recent study of depressed patients found that, compared to a group receiving antidepressant medication, those assigned to an exercise-only regimen had a similar decline in symptoms. Even better, the exercisers maintained their improvement longer and were less likely to become diagnosed again as depressed than were nonexercisers (Babyak et al., 2000).

Exercise is a good way to reduce stress and improve your general health.

An exercise-for-health program has several big pluses. Exercise usually requires a change of environment, removing people from their daily hassles and other sources of stress. It also it has a physical training effect by putting short-term physical stress on the body, which causes the body to rebound and become physically stronger. Third, when we exercise we get a boost of endorphins and other pleasure chemicals such as serotonin, which improves our mood and makes us better able to respond effectively to potentially stressful situations. In this way, it moderates stress. The benefit of exercise as a coping strategy lies in its use as a healthy outlet for anger, as well as a facilitator of the cognitive functioning required for good problem solving. These benefits apply to all ages, from preschoolers to the elderly (Alpert et al., 1990).

Despite these advantages, most resolutions to increase exercise are short lived; people often find it difficult to maintain their motivation. Nevertheless, studies show that people can learn to make exercise a regular part of their lives (Myers & Roth, 1997). The keys are (a) finding an activity you like to do and (b) fitting exercise sessions into your schedule several times a week. Having an exercise partner often provides the extra social support people need to stick with their program.

Nutrition and Diet   Good health and the ability to cope effectively with stress require a brain that has the nutrients it needs to function well. Fortunately, a balanced diet can provide all the nutrients necessary to accurately appraise potential stressors from a cognitive perspective. When we fuel ourselves with complex carbohydrates instead of simple sugars, for example, we metabolize the nutrients at a more stable pace, which may help keep us from overreacting. Many people, however, grab a fast-food meal or a candy bar instead of taking time for good nutrition. For example, a survey of students in 21 European countries revealed that only about half attempt to follow healthy eating practices. The same study found that women were more likely than men to be conscious of good nutrition (Wardle et al., 1997).

When chronic nutritional deficiencies occur in childhood—when the brain is growing fastest—development can be retarded (Stock & Smythe, 1963; Wurtman, 1982). Poor nutrition can have adverse affects on adults, too. A diet high in saturated fat increases risk of heart disease and some types of cancer. Excessive salt intake increases risk of high blood pressure. Potassium deficiency can cause listlessness and exhaustion. One should be cautious, however, about going to the other extreme by ingesting large quantities of vitamins and minerals. Overdoses of certain vitamins (especially vitamin A) and minerals (such as iron) are easy to achieve and can cause problems that are even more severe than deficiencies.

What can you do to nurture your health through nutrition? The categories in Table 14.2 are good places to start. We suggest, also, that you beware of nutritional fads, including dietary supplements that come with miraculous promises that seem almost too good to be true. Nutrition is a science in its infancy, and much remains to be discovered about its connections to physical and mental health.

TABLE 14.2	Ten Steps to Personal Wellness

1. Exercise regularly.
2. Eat nutritious, balanced meals (high in vegetables, fruits, and grains, low in fat and cholesterol).
3. Maintain a sensible weight.
4. Sleep 7 to 8 hours nightly; rest/relax daily.
5. Wear seat belts and bike helmets.
6. Do not smoke or use drugs.
7. Use alcohol in moderation, if at all.
8. Engage only in protected, safe sex.
9. Get regular medical/dental checkups; adhere to medical regimens.
10. Develop an optimistic perspective and supportive friendships.

Sleep and Meditation   In Chapter 8, you learned about the benefits of good sleep. Sleep affects our health and stress in a variety of ways. First, given the link between REM sleep and cognitive functioning, we are reminded that to deal effectively with the cognitive demands of potential stressors, we must get enough sleep to enjoy the long REM periods that come only after about six hours of sleep. In addition to the increased risk of accidents we discussed in Chapter 8, chronic sleep deprivation has been linked to diabetes and heart disease, as well as decreased immune system functioning.

Meditation, which for many years was viewed with skepticism by Westerners, has earned increased consideration recently due to provocative findings from a spate of studies. The ancient Buddhist practice of "mindful meditation" originated 2500 years ago and, translated, means "to see with discernment" (Shapiro et al., 2005). Mindfulness-based stress reduction (MBSR), a modern variation on the Buddhist tradition, aims to increase awareness of one's reactions to stress, become at ease with them, and develop healthier responses. These goals are achieved in part through meditation that teaches the participant first to focus on body sensations and cognitions involved in stress reactions, and then to let them go by fully accepting (rather than judging or resisting) them. Research on MBSR indicates that participation in an eight-week training program reduces stress; decreases risk of anxiety, depression, and burnout; and increases immune system functioning (Shapiro et al., 2005; Carlson et al., 2007). This fascinating work is just one example of how, in the 21st century, the pursuit of health is relying increasingly on East–West collaborations.

Putting It All Together: Developing Happiness and Subjective Well-Being

Making changes to live a healthier life can lead to a feeling-good state that researchers call **subjective well-being** (**SWB**), a psychologically more precise term for what you might call "happiness." Do you usually have that feeling?

We cannot observe happiness directly. Instead, in SWB studies, researchers rely on respondents' own ratings of their experiences, answers to questions about what they find satisfying, and assessments of their well-being, mood, or success (Diener, 1984, 2000). To avoid confusion about what words like *well-being* mean, researchers also use nonverbal scales like the one in the smiley-faces in Figure 14.7 (Andrews & Withey, 1976).

Happiness, or SWB, is an increasingly popular subject of study with psychologists, evident in the emerging field of positive psychology. Accumulating research (Myers, 2000; Myers & Diener, 1995) shows that, despite many individual differences, SWB is defined by three central components:

Subjective well-being (SWB) An individual's evaluative response to life, commonly called happiness, which includes cognitive and emotional reactions.

| 20% | 46% | 27% | 4% | 2% | 1% | 0% |

FIGURE 14.7
The Faces Scale

"Which face comes closest to expressing how you feel about your life as a whole?" Researchers often use this simple scale to obtain people's ratings of their level of well-being. As the percentages indicate, most people select one of the happy faces.

(*Source:* "The Faces Scale," pp. 207, 306, from *Social Indicators of Well-Being: Americans' Perception of Life Quality* by F. M. Andrews and S. B. Withey. Copyright © 1976 by Plenum Publishers. Reprinted by permission of Springer Science and Business Media.)

1. *Satisfaction with present life.* People who are high in SWB like their work and are satisfied with their current personal relationships. They are sociable and outgoing, and they open up to others (Pavot et al., 1990). High SWB people enjoy good health and high self-esteem (Baumeister et al., 2003; Janoff-Bulman, 1989, 1992).

2. *Relative presence of positive emotions.* High SWBs more frequently feel pleasant emotions, mainly because they evaluate the world around them in a generally positive way. They are typically optimistic and expect success (Seligman, 1991). They have an internal locus of control, and are able to enjoy the "flow" of engaging work (Crohan et al., 1989; Csikszentmihalyi, 1990).

3. *Relative absence of negative emotions.* Individuals with a strong sense of subjective well-being experience fewer and less severe episodes of negative emotions such as anxiety, depression, and anger. Very happy people are not emotionally extreme. They are positive (but not ecstatic) most of the time, and they do report occasional negative moods (Diener & Seligman, 2002).

What underlies a healthy response on these dimensions? Twin studies show that feelings of well-being are influenced by genetics (Lykken & Tellegen, 1996), but biology is not destiny: Environmental effects are revealed in studies showing that people feel unhappy if they lack social support, are pressured to pursue goals set by others, and infrequently receive positive feedback on their achievements. Accordingly, experts in this field suggest that feelings of well-being require the satisfaction of (a) a need to feel competent, (b) a need for social connection or relatedness, and (c) a need for autonomy or a sense of self-control (Baumeister et al., 2003; Ryan & Deci, 2000).

So who are the happy people? What characteristics and experiences are linked with feelings of subjective well-being and happiness? Before reading further, take a moment to consider whether you think some groups of people are happier than others. If so, which ones? A review of the SWB evidence by Myers and Diener (1995) shows that:

● *Younger (or older, or middle-aged) people are not happier than other age groups.* SWB cannot be predicted from someone's age. Although the causes of their happiness may change with age (Inglehart, 1990), an individual's SWB tends to remain relatively stable over a lifetime.

● *Happiness has no "gender gap."* While women are more likely than men to suffer from anxiety and depression, and men are more at risk for alcoholism and certain personality disorders, approximately equal numbers of men and women report being fairly satisfied with life (Fujita et al., 1991; Inglehart, 1990).

● *There are minimal racial differences in happiness.* African Americans and European Americans report nearly the same levels of happiness, with African

Americans being slightly less vulnerable to depression (Diener et al., 1993). Despite racism and discrimination, members of disadvantaged minority groups generally seem to think optimistically—by making realistic self-comparisons and by attributing problems more to unfair circumstances than to themselves (Crocker & Major, 1989).

- *Money does not buy happiness.* It is true that people in wealthier societies report greater well-being. However, except for extremely poor nations like Bangladesh, once the necessities of food, shelter, and safety are provided, happiness is only weakly correlated with income. Poverty may be miserable, but wealth itself cannot guarantee happiness (Diener & Diener, 1996; Diener et al., 1993). The happiest people are not those who get what they want, but rather those who want what they have (Myers & Diener, 1995).

- *Those who have a spiritual dimension in their lives most often report being happy* (Myers & Diener, 1995). This may result from many factors, including a healthier lifestyle, social support, and optimistic thinking. Whatever the reasons, spiritually involved people enjoy, on average, better mental and physical health (Seybold & Hill, 2001).

These findings tell us that life circumstances—one's age, sex, race, nationality, or income—do not predict happiness. The key factors in subjective well-being appear to be psychological traits and processes, many of which you have learned about in this chapter or elsewhere in this book. It is impressive to see how well people can adapt to major changes in their lives and still feel happy. For example, while the moods of victims of spinal cord injuries were extremely negative shortly after their accidents, several weeks later they reported feeling even happier than they had been before sustaining their injuries (Silver, 1983).

Overall, studies of happiness and well-being show that people are exceedingly resilient. Those who undergo severe stress usually manage to adapt. Typically they return to a mood and level of well-being similar to—or even better than—that prior to the traumatic event (Headey & Wearing, 1992). Using effective coping strategies and making smart lifestyle choices both increase the likelihood of positive outcomes. These, then, are the final components in our search to understand individual differences in the impact of stress on our health.

PSYCHOLOGY**MATTERS**
Behavioral Medicine and Health Psychology

Amazingly, 93% of patients don't follow the treatment plans prescribed by their doctors (Taylor, 1990). Obviously, this can have terrible consequences. Accordingly, the need to understand why people fail to take their medicine, get little exercise, eat too much fat, and cope poorly with stress has stimulated the development of two new fields: *behavioral medicine* and *health psychology*. **Behavioral medicine** is the medical field that links lifestyle and disease. **Health psychology** is the comparable psychological specialty. Practitioners in both fields are devoted to understanding the psychosocial factors influencing health and illness (Taylor, 1990, 2006). Among their many concerns are health promotion and maintenance; prevention and treatment of illness; causes and correlates of health, illness, and dysfunction; and improvement of the health care system and health policy (Matarazzo, 1980).

Both behavioral medicine and health psychology are actively involved in the prevention and treatment of trauma and disease that result from stressful or dangerous environments and from poor choices with regard to nutrition, exercise, and drug use. Both are emerging disciplines in countries all over the world (Holtzman, 1992). The two fields overlap, and the differences between them are ones of emphasis. Psychologists have brought increased awareness of emotions and cognitive factors into behavioral medicine, making it an interdisciplinary

Behavioral medicine Medical field specializing in the link between lifestyle and disease.

Health psychology Psychological specialty devoted to understanding how people stay healthy, why they become ill, and how they respond when ill.

field rather than an exclusively medical specialty (Miller, 1983; Rodin & Salovey, 1989). Both fields also recognize the interaction of mind and body and place emphasis on preventing illness, as well as changing unhealthy life styles after illness strikes (Taylor, 1990, 2006).

But—as the saying goes—old habits die hard. To help patients change long-held habits that are harmful to their health, social psychologists have identified the specific persuasive strategies that are most effective (Zimbardo & Leippe, 1991). For example, research shows that people are more likely to comply with requests when they feel they have freedom of choice. Therefore, instead of demanding that a patient strictly adhere to one course of treatment, a physician could offer the patient several options and ask him or her to choose one. Studies also suggest that patients are most likely to adhere to physicians' requests when they get active social support from friends and family (Gottlieb, 1987; Patterson, 1985). And, one landmark study of heart disease prevention (see Figure 14.8) found that specific skills training, such as workshops designed to help participants implement positive changes to their health habits, was the key that resulted in greatest change (Maccoby et al., 1977).

Overall, the field of psychology has contributed numerous findings and strategies—based on solid scientific evidence—that can be applied to our efforts to improve our health, both physically and mentally. For example, behavioral principles discussed in Chapter 3 can be combined with what we know about good thinking strategies (from Chapter 5) and indeed often are combined in cognitive–behavioral therapy. Principles of emotion and motivation—the topics of Chapter 9—provide additional insight into factors affecting our emotional health and the behaviors that support our basic needs for food, social support, and other basic needs. You can apply many of these same principles on your own as you work towards maximizing your health and wellness—and we wish you well on your journey!

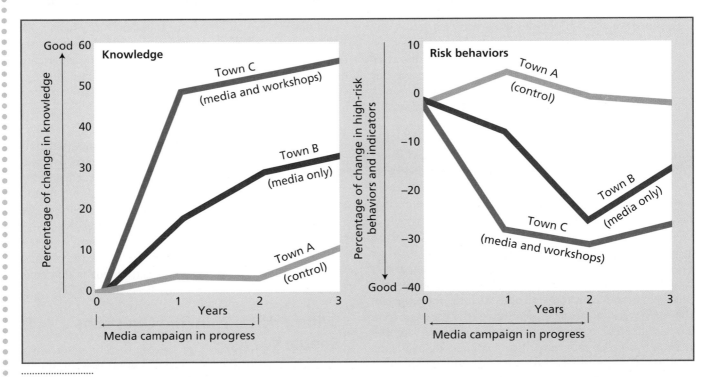

FIGURE 14.8
Response to Campaign for Healthy Change

Town A, whose residents received no mass media campaign for heart-healthy behavior, showed the least knowledge gain over two years. Town B residents, exposed to a media campaign, showed significant improvement. Knowledge gain was greatest for residents of Town C, whose residents participated in intense workshops and instruction sessions for several months prior to the media blitz. As knowledge increased, risk behaviors

CheckYourUnderstanding

1. **ANALYSIS:** Mai was recently in a car accident. In coping with the situation, she has focused on getting estimates for her car repair, seeking medical treatment, and working with her insurance agent to obtain compensation for the expenses of the car repair and her medical needs. What type of coping strategy is Mai employing?

2. **RECALL:** In coping with a loss, efforts to make sense of what happened or to find some ultimate benefit from the loss are examples of _____, which is an _____ coping strategy.
   a. finding meaning; effective
   b. finding meaning; ineffective
   c. emotion-focused coping; effective
   d. emotion-focused coping; ineffective

3. **APPLICATION:** Think of a recent stressor in your own life.

Now identify at least two ways that you can use cognitive restructuring to reduce the impact of the stressor on your health.

4. **RECALL:** Name at least four lifestyle choices you can make that will reduce the impact of stress on your health.

5. **UNDERSTANDING THE CORE CONCEPT:** _____ reduce the effects of stress on our health, while _____ decrease our vulnerability to both stress and to stress-related illness.
   a. Stress moderators; coping strategies
   b. Positive lifestyle choices; stress moderators
   c. Positive lifestyle choices; coping strategies
   d. Coping strategies; positive lifestyle choices

Critical Thinking Applied: Is Change Really Hazardous to Your Health?

The more we hear about the links between stress and illness, the more we might wonder if our own stress levels put us at risk. In this chapter, we have discussed a variety of factors that have an impact on the stress–illness relationship. At least one issue, however, remains in question: To what extent do major life changes impact our vulnerability to illness?

Recall the Social Readjustment Rating Scale (SRRS) introduced in the first section of this chapter. Like many students, you probably calculated your own score in the "Do It Yourself!" box on page 628. But how should you interpret your score? If you scored high, does that mean you are at greater risk for illness?

In the first 15 years after it was published, the SRRS was used in more than 1000 studies worldwide (Holmes, 1979), and research consistently found correlations between scores on the SRRS and both physical and behavioral symptoms. People with higher scores on the scale were more at risk for heart attacks, bone fractures, diabetes, multiple sclerosis, tuberculosis, complications of pregnancy and birth, decline in academic performance, employee absenteeism, and many other difficulties (Holmes & Masuda, 1974). High SRRS scores among federal prisoners were even associated with the length of their prison sentences. And the test was effective across cultural boundaries, too: Both male and female respondents were found to rate events with similar scores (Holmes & Masuda, 1974), and ratings were also validated with Japanese, Latin American, European, and Malaysian samples. Do these findings indicate that higher scores lead to greater stress?

What Are the Issues?

Recall, first, that the SRRS lists 43 life events that purport to be stressful. Given what we've learned about the importance of cognitive appraisal in determining how stressful a situation is to an individual, we should probably take a close look at the list of events to see if each one really would qualify as a stressor in our own lives.

Second, proponents of the SRRS claim that higher scores predict later illness. To what extent is this true, and how have the associations been measured?

What Critical Thinking Questions Should We Ask?

The SRRS can allegedly predict your risk of illness based on the events of the past year of your life. In other words, it presents a cause–effect hypothesis that the number of LCUs you have experienced in the last year will cause a particular risk of illness. Are the research findings in support of the LCU–illness relationship really causal, or are they merely correlational?

Second, if the claim that a quick and simple self-administered test can determine your risk for illness strikes you as extraordinary, you might be right. As we have learned, answers to questions psychological are rarely simple—humans are complex, and so are the explanations for our thoughts, feelings, and behaviors. At the very least, we might wonder if the SRRS oversimplifies the relationship between life events and illness. And finally, we must ask what other perspectives might help explain the relationship between stress and illness?

What Conclusions Can We Draw?

Research has shown that the number of LCUs accumulated during the previous year are a modest predictor of changes in a person's health (Johnson & Sarason, 1979; Rahe & Arthur, 1978). The implication that stressful events cause illness, however, is misleading (Dohrenwend & Shrout, 1985; Rabkin & Struening, 1976). The correlational data merely show a relationship between certain life changes and health; the research does not show that life changes are the cause of illness. The reverse could also be true: Illness can sometimes be the cause of life changes—someone who frequently gets colds or the flu is more likely to have problems at school, work and in relationships, for example. And remember the possibility of a third variable driving the relationship: Several other factors we've studied, such as economic status or Type-A hostility, could also be affecting both the frequency of life changes and the risk of illness.

The importance of multiple perspectives is critical to a thorough and accurate understanding of the stress–illness relationship. Let's review what we know about stress and health from the major perspectives we used to learn about psychology in this book:

- The *biological perspective* clearly plays a role in an individual's vulnerability to stress-related illness. We have seen that our hereditary makeup predisposes us to certain illnesses, such as heart disease, diabetes, obesity, and many forms of cancer. In addition, genetics probably gives some of us a better chance of being optimistic, hardy, or resilient—just as others of us are more at risk for hostility and other negative emotions.

- The *behavioral perspective* influences stress and illness in the health habits we learn as children growing up, in situations of learned helplessness, and in the coping strategies we see modeled by our parents and others in our immediate social environment. Likewise, the *sociocultural context*—the culture in which we live—creates social norms that influence these learned habits and strategies. Currently, for example, in Western culture we receive mixed messages about health. On one hand, we hear a lot about the importance of a healthy diet and regular exercise. On the other hand, however, the fast-paced nature of our culture—combined with a barrage of ads for fast food—encourage us to grab a burger and fries, then sit on the couch and watch television instead of working out and preparing a healthy meal.

- The *cognitive perspective* helps us undertand why, in a particular culture, individual health habits and perspectives vary. Someone with an internal locus of control, for example, would be more likely than an external to pay attention to diet and exercise in pursuit of a healthy life. Likewise, an optimistic thinker or someone high in hardiness would be more likely to perceive certain life events as possibilities rather than as threats. In general, people's chances of incurring an illness may be more related to their interpretations and responses to life changes than to the changes themselves (Lazarus et al., 1985).

- The *developmental perspective* illuminates certain aspects of stress and health as well. College students, for example—who are primarily in early adulthood—are at change points in their lives and tend to get high scores; it is not clear, however, if they are more at risk for illness. Youth may offer some protection. Similarly, as our bodies age and our cells become less effective at regeneration, we develop greater susceptibility to illness in late adulthood. It is possible, though, that older adults who have mastered the challenges of generativity and integrity may offset their physical vulnerability with a better system of stress moderators and coping strategies. Much research remains to be done at the intersection of developmental and health psychology.

- The *whole-person perspective* explains many of the personal qualities that have an impact on an individual's vulnerability to stress. Locus of control, optimism, hardiness, resilience, and Type A behavior all originated in the study of personality psychology, and we have seen how these factors moderate an individual's response to stressors. Likewise, traits such as openness to experience and conscientiousness probably affect the degree to which individuals are willing to try new coping strategies or lifestyle habits, as well as their likelihood of sticking to the changes once they've made them.

Clearly, then, there is much more to the relationship between stress and illness than the particular life events you experience. A high score does not mean that illness is certain, nor does a low score guarantee health. People differ in their abilities to deal with change because of genetic differences, general physical condition, personality and outlook, lifestyles, and coping skills. The SRRS takes none of these factors into account, but it remains the most widely used measure of stress-related risk for illness.

Should you, then, pay attention to your SRRS score? We offer it as one source of information about your own possible vulnerability—and we trust that you will interpret your score with caution. Overall, we hope you will keep in mind the many tools you have accumulated that, together, can help you respond more effectively to potential stressors—and ultimately live a longer and healthier life.

Chapter Summary

14.1 What Causes Stress?

Core Concept 14.1: Traumatic events, chronic lifestyle conditions, major life changes, and even minor hassles can all cause stress.

Stressors are external events that cause **stress,** while the term *stress* refers to the physical and emotional changes that occur in response to the stressor. And while **cognitive appraisal** influences our individual responses to stressors, there are several major categories of events that typically cause stress.

Traumatic stressors include natural disasters, acts of **terrorism,** or sudden personal loss such as the death of a loved one or an unforeseen breakup. All of these situations occur with little or no warning, and almost always cause extreme stress in the immediate aftermath of the event. Research indicates that about 20% of survivors of natural disaster remain distressed after one year, while as many as 75% of those exposed to a terrorist attack report continued worry at the one-year mark. Repeated media coverage of the event often exacerbates and prolongs the effects, and can also cause stress in people who were not directly exposed to the event in a phenomenon known as **vicarious traumatization. Grief** is a normal, healthy process in response to a personal loss, and the humiliation of rejection can put an individual at greater risk for depression.

Posttraumatic stress disorder (PTSD) can occur in individuals who have been exposed to severe circumstances such as combat, rape, or other violent attack. Symptoms of PTSD can be cognitive, behavioral, and emotional, as evidenced (for example) by difficulty concentrating, an exaggerated "startle response," and survivor's guilt. About 8% of Americans will experience PTSD at some time in their life, with symptoms lasting more than ten years in over one-third of the cases. Combat personnel may be especially at risk for PTSD, and military psychologists are working increasingly to develop and provide more effective education and treatment for combat veterans and their families.

Chronic stressors have a more gradual onset and are longer-lasting than traumatic events. **Societal stressors** such as poverty and unemployment, as well as difficulties at home, school, or work, are one type of chronic stressor. Another is **burnout,** which is a syndrome of emotional exhaustion, physical fatigue, and cognitive weariness that results from demanding and unceasing pressures at work, at home, or in relationships. **Compassion fatigue** is found in medical and psychological professionals, as well as caregivers and other individuals who spend a great deal of time caring for others. Research in this area offers at least five steps caregivers and service providers can take to reduce their risk of compassion fatigue.

Major life changes—whether positive or negative—can be a source of stress as well, in that they involve changes in our daily routines and adaptation to new situations and environments. Finally, minor **hassles** such as computer crashes or an incessantly barking dog can accumulate and cause stress that adds up over time.

Burnout (p. 625)

Catastrophic event (p. 619)

Chronic stressor (p. 625)

Cognitive appraisal (p. 618)

Compassion fatigue (p. 626)

Compassion satisfaction (p. 626)

Disenfranchised grief (p. 623)

Grief (p. 622)

Hassle (p. 627)

Integration (p. 622)

Narrative (p. 620)

Posttraumatic stress disorder (PTSD) (p. 623)

Social Readjustment Rating Scale (SRRS) (p. 627)

Societal stressor (p. 625)

Stress (p. 617)

Stressor (p. 617)

Terrorism (p. 620)

Traumatic stressor (p. 619)

Vicarious traumatization (p. 621)

MyPsychLab Resources 14.1:

Watch: 9/11 Post-Traumatic Stress Disorder

Simulation: How Stressed Are You?

14.2 How Does Stress Affect Us Physically?

Core Concept 14.2: The physical stress response begins with arousal, which stimulates a series of physiological responses that in the short term are adaptive, but that can turn harmful after prolonged stress.

When faced with **acute stressors**, our bodies are equipped with amazing abilities to meet the challenges effectively. The **fight-or-flight response** is produced by the autonomic nervous system, and includes such immediate changes as accelerated heart rate, increased respiration and blood pressure, perspiration, and pupil dilation. A more comprehensive explanation of our response to stress is offered by Hans Selye's **GAS**. A three-phase system, the GAS begins with the **alarm phase**, then progresses into the **resistance phase** and finally the **exhaustion phase** if the stressor is chronic in nature. Under such circumstances, the resources that so effectively helped us combat an acute stressor become depleted, resulting in a host of physical and emotional symptoms. Consequently, we become more vulnerable to illness. While the fight-or-flight response has been well documented in both animals and humans, psychologist Shelley Taylor notes an alternative pattern of response to stress. Her **tend-and-befriend** theory suggests that social support-seeking can be a more effective response to stress when protection or survival of offspring is involved. These models complement each other, rather than competing with each other, in helping us understand the complex human stress response.

The emerging field of **psychoneuroimmunology** studies the relationship between stress and illness. Research in this area has revealed that the central nervous system and the immune system remain in constant communication with each other in response to stress. **Cytokines** are proteins that fight infection, but under prolonged stress produce feelings of listlessness and depression. **Natural killer cells,** also released by the immune system to fight infection, also become depleted by chronic stress, resulting in compromised immune systems and greater health risk. These are two of the ways in which our bodies are well-equipped to fight acute stress but less well suited to deal with more modern chronic stressors.

Acute stress (p. 631)	**Immunosuppression** (p. 636)
Alarm phase (p. 633)	**Natural killer cell** (p. 636)
Cortisol (p. 635)	**Oxytocin** (p. 635)
Cytokine (p. 636)	**Psychoneuroimmunology** (p. 636)
Exhaustion phase (p. 634)	
Fight-or-flight response (p. 631)	**Resistance phase** (p. 634)
General adaptation syndrome (GAS) (p. 632)	**Tend-and-befriend** (p. 635)

MyPsychLab Resources 14.2:

Watch: Stress and Wellness

Watch: Women, Health and Stress: Florence Denmark

14.3 Who Is Most Vulnerable to Stress?

Core Concept 14.3: Personality characteristics affect our individual responses to stressful situations and, consequently, the degree to which we feel stress when exposed to potential stressors.

Stress moderators reduce the impact of stressors on our perceived level of stress. Most of them function as variations of cognitive appraisal (although often on a nonconscious level). Hostile individuals are more likely to perceive stress in the face of a stressful situation and consequently have twice the risk of heart disease. Fortunately, stress-management programs have proven effective at reducing these individuals' response to stress and their resulting health vulnerability.

Locus of control is a second personality characteristic that has an impact on the stressor–stress relationship. People with an **internal** locus of control have greater resistance to stress than do **externals,** probably as a result of their perceived capability to take some

action to ameliorate it. Locus of control has been found to affect not only stress but also health and longevity. While locus of control may have some genetic underpinnings, our experiences also influence it, as evidenced by research on **learned helplessness**. From a cultural perspective, **secondary control** involves controlling one's reactions to events, rather than controlling the events themselves, and is more prevalent in Eastern cultures. Research has found both types of control to be effective in the cultures in which they operate.

Hardiness is an outlook based on three "Cs"— a perception of internal control, of change as a challenge rather than a threat, and of commitment to life activities rather than alienation or withdrawal. Individuals with a hardy attitude exhibit greater resistance to stress. Similarly, optimistic people feel less stressed in the face of stressful situations, as they are more likely to focus on the positives rather than the negatives of the situation. **Optimism** is also characterized by specific, situational, and temporary attributions about negative situations. Both hardiness and optimism, like locus of control, appear to have some biological underpinnings but can be improved with well-designed training programs. **Resilience** is the ability to rebound and adapt to challenging circumstances and is related to optimism and hardiness, as well as social skills, cognitive abilities, and resources such as caring parents or support providers.

External (p. 642) **Internal** (p. 642)

Hardiness (p. 643) **Learned helplessness** (p. 643)

Locus of control (p. 642) **Resilience** (p. 645)

Moderator (p. 640) **Secondary control** (p. 643)

Optimism (p. 644) **Type A** (p. 641)

Primary control (p. 643)

MyPsychLab Resources 14.3:

Watch: Optimism and Resilience

Watch: Applying Positive Psychology

· ·

14.4 How Can We Reduce the Impact Of Stress On Our Health?

Core Concept 14.4: Healthy coping strategies reduce the impact of stress on our health, and positive lifestyle choices reduce both our perceived stress and its impact on our health.

Coping involves taking action that reduces or eliminates the causes of stress, rather than just the symptoms of stress. **Problem-focused coping** is accomplished by specific actions aimed at resolving a problem or stressor, whereas **emotion-focused coping** relies on efforts to regulate our emotional response to stress. Both types of coping can be useful and sometimes best work together. **Cognitive restructuring** is another type of effective **coping strategy,** and involves modifying our perceptions of the stressor or our reactions to it. Cognitive restructuring can include **upward** and **downward social comparisons.**

Cultivating positive emotions, including humor, also helps reduce the effects of stress on our health, as can efforts to find meaning in the stressful situation. In finding meaning, making sense of the event appears to be the first step, but those who ultimately succeed in finding meaning in tragedy must also identify some benefit of the event or situation. **Psychological debriefing,** which in some cases takes the form of **critical incident stress debriefing (CISD),** is probably not very effective in reducing the link between stress and illness.

A variety of **positive lifestyle choices** carry a two-for-one benefit to the stress–illness puzzle: They can increase our resistance to stress and also decrease our vulnerabilty to stress-related illness. **Social support** may be the most important of these lifestyle factors, as people with stronger social support live longer and healthier lives than those with little or no support. Social support is helpful in that it carries emotional, tangible, and informational benefits. Regular aerobic exercise has both physical and psychological benefits, and has been found to reduce the impact of stress on our health. Similarly, a healthy diet, adequate sleep, and even meditation have been found to decrease our vulnerability to stress and illness.

Subjective well-being (SWB) includes satisfaction with life, prevalence of positive emotions, and absence of negative emotions. Like many of the concepts we have studied, an individual's SWB is influenced both by heredity and by environment. Neither age nor wealth predict happiness—happy people can be found in the youngest and the oldest, the richest and the poorest, and even in victims of serious illness or life-changing injury.

Behavioral medicine (p. 658) **Health psychology** (p. 658)

Benefit-finding (p. 651) **Positive lifestyle choice** (p. 649)

Catharsis (p. 652) **Problem-focused coping** (p. 649)

Cognitive restructuring (p. 650) **Psychological debriefing** (p. 652)

Coping (p. 649) **Rumination** (p. 649)

Coping strategy (p. 648) **Sense-making** (p. 651)

Critical incident stress debriefing (CISD) (p. 652) **Social comparison** (p. 650)

 Social support (p. 653)

Defending (p. 649) **Subjective well-being (SWB)**

Downward social comparison (p. 656)

 (p. 650) **Upward social comparison**

Emotion-focused coping (p. 649) (p. 650)

MyPsychLab Resources 14.4:

Explore: Coping Strategies and Their Effects

Watch: Flow

Watch: Gender Differences in Stress Vulnerability

Watch the following video by logging into MyPsychLab (www.mypsychlab.com). After you have watched the video, complete the activities that follow.

PROGRAM 23: HEALTH, MIND, AND BEHAVIOR

PROGRAM REVIEW

1. How are the biopsychosocial model and the Navajo concept of *hozho* alike?
   a. Both are dualistic.
   b. Both assume individual responsibility for illness.
   c. Both represent holistic approaches to health.
   d. Both are several centuries old.
2. Dr. Wizanski told Thad that his illness was psychogenic. This means that
   a. Thad is not really sick.
   b. Thad's illness was caused by his psychological state.
   c. Thad has a psychological disorder, not a physical one.
   d. Thad's lifestyle puts him at risk.
3. Headaches, exhaustion, and weakness
   a. are not considered to be in the realm of health psychology.
   b. are considered to be psychological factors that lead to unhealthful behaviors.
   c. are usually unrelated to psychological factors.
   d. are considered to be symptoms of underlying tension and personal problems.
4. When Judith Rodin talks about "wet" connections to the immune system, she is referring to connections with the
   a. individual nerve cells.
   b. endocrine system.
   c. sensory receptors.
   d. skin.
5. What mind-body question is Judith Rodin investigating in her work with infertile couples?
   a. How do psychological factors affect fertility?
   b. Can infertility be cured by psychological counseling?
   c. What effect does infertility have on marital relationships?
   d. Can stress cause rejection of in vitro fertilization?
6. When Professor Zimbardo lowers his heart rate, he is demonstrating the process of
   a. mental relaxation.
   b. stress reduction.
   c. biofeedback.
   d. the general adaptation syndrome.
7. Psychologist Neal Miller uses the example of the blindfolded basketball player to explain
   a. the need for information to improve performance.
   b. how chance variations lead to evolutionary advantage.
   c. the correlation between life-changing events and illness.
   d. how successive approximations can shape behavior.
8. In which area of health psychology has the most research been done?
   a. the definition of health
   b. stress
   c. biofeedback
   d. changes in lifestyle
9. Imagine a family is moving to a new and larger home in a safer neighborhood with better schools. Will this situation be a source of stress for the family?
   a. No, because the change is a positive one.
   b. No, because moving is not really stressful.
   c. Yes, because any change requires adjustment.
   d. Yes, because it provokes guilt that the family does not really deserve this good fortune.
10. Which response shows the stages of the general adaptation syndrome in the correct order?
    a. alarm reaction, exhaustion, resistance
    b. resistance, alarm reaction, exhaustion
    c. exhaustion, resistance, alarm reaction
    d. alarm reaction, resistance, exhaustion
11. What important factor in stress did Hans Selye *not* consider?
    a. the role of hormones in mobilizing the body's defenses
    b. the subjective interpretation of a stressor
    c. the length of exposure to a stressor
    d. the body's vulnerability to new stressors during the resistance stage

12. Today, the major causes of death in the United States are
    a. accidents.
    b. infectious diseases.
    c. sexually transmitted diseases.
    d. diseases related to lifestyle.

13. When Thomas Coates and his colleagues, in their study of AIDS, conduct interview studies, they want to gain information that will help them
    a. design interventions at a variety of levels.
    b. determine how effective mass media advertisements are.
    c. motivate AIDS victims to take good care of themselves.
    d. stop people from using intravenous drugs.

14. The body's best external defense against illness is the skin, whereas its best internal defense is
    a. the stomach.
    b. the heart.
    c. T-cells.
    d. the spinal cord.

15. In which stage of the general adaptation syndrome are the pituitary and adrenals stimulated?
    a. exhaustion
    b. alarm
    c. reaction
    d. resistance

16. Which stage of the general adaptation syndrome is associated with the outcome of disease?
    a. alarm
    b. reaction
    c. exhaustion
    d. resistance

17. What claim is Richard Lazarus most closely associated with?
    a. The individual's cognitive appraisal of a stressor is critical.
    b. The biopsychosocial model is an oversimplified view.
    c. Peptic ulcers can be healed through biofeedback.
    d. The general adaptation syndrome can account for 80% of heart attacks in middle-aged men.

18. Thomas Coates and Neal Miller are similar in their desire to
    a. eradicate AIDS.
    b. outlaw intravenous drug use.
    c. institute stress management courses as part of standard insurance coverage.
    d. teach basic skills for protecting one's health.

19. How should an advertising campaign ideally be designed in order to get people to use condoms and avoid high-risk sexual activities?
    a. It should be friendly, optimistic, and completely nonthreatening.
    b. It should have enough threat to arouse emotion but not so much that viewers will go into denial.
    c. It should contain a lot of humor.
    d. It should feature an older, white, male doctor and a lot of scientific terminology.

20. Neal Miller is to biofeedback as Judith Rodin is to
    a. analgesics.
    b. meditation.
    c. a sense of control.
    d. social support.

QUESTIONS TO CONSIDER

1. How can you help another person cope with stress?

2. How can self-deprecating thoughts and behavior increase stress?

3. How might perfectionism lead to stress?

4. What common lifestyle differences might make men or women more susceptible to different kinds of health problems?

ACTIVITIES

1. Sort the following behaviors into two categories: Category A, Stress Warning Signals, and Category B, Signs of Successful Coping. (You may add others from your own experience.)

Indigestion	Ability to sleep
Fatigue	Tolerance for frustration
Loss of appetite	Constipation
Indecision	Overeating
Sense of belonging	Overuse of drugs or alcohol
Sense of humor	Adaptability to change
Irritability	Optimism
Reliability	Cold hands
Sexual problems	Ulcers
Frequent urination	Sleep problems
Migraine headaches	Difficulty concentrating
Boredom	Free-floating anxiety
Temper tantrums	Frequent colds

2. Consider three periods in history: Prehistoric cultures, 0 B.C., and twenty-first–century America. Compare these three moments in history for the impact on health of (a) the reigning understanding of illness and health and (b) the demands of everyday living. What trade-offs do you see?

Glossary

Absent-mindedness Forgetting caused by lapses in attention.

Absolute threshold The amount of stimulation necessary for a stimulus to be detected. In practice, this means that the presence or absence of a stimulus is detected correctly half the time over many trials.

Abu Ghraib Prison Prison in Iraq made famous by revelation of photos taken by Army Reserve MP guards in the acts of humiliating and torturing prisoners.

Accommodation A mental process that modifies schemas in order to include (or accommodate) new information.

Acoustic encoding The conversion of information, especially semantic information, to sound patterns in working memory.

Acquisition The initial learning stage in classical conditioning, during which the conditioned response comes to be elicited by the conditioned stimulus.

Action potential The nerve impulse caused by a change in the electrical charge across the cell membrane of the axon. When the neuron "fires," this charge travels down the axon and causes neurotransmitters to be released by the terminal buttons.

Activation-synthesis theory The theory that dreams begin with random electrical activation coming from the brain stem. Dreams, then, are the brain's attempt to make sense of—to synthesize—this random activity.

Active listener A person who gives the speaker feedback in such forms as nodding, paraphrasing, maintaining an expression that shows interest, and asking questions for clarification.

Acute stress A temporary state of arousal, caused by a stressor, with a distinct onset and limited duration.

Addiction A condition in which a person continues to use a drug despite its adverse effects—often despite repeated attempts to discontinue using the drug. Addiction may be based on physical or psychological dependence.

Adolescence In industrial societies, a developmental period beginning at puberty and ending (less clearly) at adulthood.

Adoption study A method of separating the effect of nature and nurture—by which investigators compare characteristics of adopted children with those of individuals in their biological and adoptive families.

Affect Emotion or mood.

Afterimages Sensations that linger after the stimulus is removed. Most visual afterimages are *negative afterimages,* which appear in reversed colors.

Agonists Drugs or other chemicals that enhance or mimic the effects of neurotransmitters.

Agoraphobia A fear of public places and open spaces, commonly accompanying panic disorder.

Alarm phase First phase of the GAS, during which body resources are mobilized to cope with the stressor.

Algorithms Problem-solving procedures or formulas that guarantee a correct outcome, if correctly applied.

All-or-none principle Refers to the fact that the action potential in the axon occurs either completely or not at all.

Alzheimer's disease A degenerative brain disease usually noticed first by its debilitating effects on memory of the elderly.

Ambiguous figures Images that are capable of more than one interpretation. There is no "right" way to see an ambiguous figure.

Amplitude The physical strength of a wave. This is shown on graphs as the height of the wave.

Amygdala A limbic system structure involved in memory and emotion, particularly fear and aggression. Pronounced *a-MIG-da-la.*

Analysis of transference The Freudian technique of analyzing and interpreting the patient's relationship with the therapist, based on the assumption that this relationship mirrors unresolved conflicts in the patient's past.

Analytical intelligence According to Sternberg, the ability measured by most

IQ tests; includes the ability to analyze problems and find correct answers.

Anchoring bias A faulty heuristic caused by basing (anchoring) an estimate on a completely irrelevant quantity.

Animistic thinking A preoperational mode of thought in which inanimate objects are imagined to have life and mental processes.

Anorexia nervosa An eating disorder involving persistent loss of appetite that endangers an individual's health and stemming from emotional or psychological reasons rather than from organic causes.

Antagonists Drugs or other chemicals that inhibit the effects of neurotransmitters.

Anterograde amnesia The inability to form new memories (as opposed to retrograde amnesia, which involves the inability to remember information previously stored in memory).

Antianxiety drugs A category of medicines that includes the barbiturates and benzodiazepines, drugs that diminish feelings of anxiety.

Antidepressants Medicines that treat depression, usually by their effects on the serotonin and/or norepinephrine pathways in the brain.

Antipsychotics Medicinea that diminish psychotic symptoms, usually by their effects on the dopamine pathways in the brain.

Anxious-ambivalent attachment One of two primary response patterns seen in insecurely attached children—in which a child wants contact with the caregiver, shows excessive distress when separated from the caregiver, and proves difficult to console even when reunited.

Anxiety disorder Mental problem characterized mainly by anxiety. Anxiety disorders include panic disorder, specific phobias, and obsessive–compulsive disorder.

Applied psychologists Psychologists who use the knowledge developed by experimental psychologists to solve human problems.

Aptitudes Innate potentialities (as contrasted with abilities acquired by learning).

Archetype   One of the ancient memory images in the collective unconscious. Archetypes appear and reappear in art, literature, and folktales around the world. Emphasized by Carl Jung.

Artificial concepts   Concepts defined by rules, such as word definitions and mathematical formulas.

Asch effect   A form of conformity in which a group majority influences individual judgments of unambiguous stimuli, as with line judgments.

Assimilation   A mental process that incorporates new information into existing schemas.

Association cortex   Cortical regions throughout the brain that combine information from various other parts of the brain.

Attachment   The enduring socio-emotional relationship between a child and a parent or other regular caregiver.

Attention   A process by which consciousness focuses on a single item or "chunk" in working memory.

Attention-deficit hyperactivity disorder or **ADHD**   A psychological disorder involving poor impulse control, difficulty concentrating on a task for a sustained period of time, high distractability, and excessive activity.

Authoritarian parent   One of the four parenting styles, characterized by demands for conformity and obedience, with little tolerance for discussion of rules, which the parent enforces with punishment or threats of punishment.

Authoritative parent   One of the four parenting styles, characterized by high expectations of the children, which the parent enforces with consequences, rather than punitive actions. Authoritative parents combine high standards with warmth and respect for the child's views.

Autism   A developmental disorder marked by disabilities in language, social interaction, and the ability to understand another person's state of mind.

Autokinetic effect   The perceived motion of a stationary dot of light in a totally dark room. Used by Muzafir Sherif to study the formation of group norms.

Autonomic nervous system (ANS)   The portion of the peripheral nervous system that sends communications between the central nervous system and the internal organs and glands.

Autonomy   In Erikson's theory, autonomy is the major developmental task of the second stage in childhood. Achieving autonomy involves developing a sense of independence, as opposed to being plagued by *self-doubt*.

Availability bias   A faulty heuristic strategy that estimates probabilities based on information that can be recalled (made readily available) from personal experience.

Aversion therapy   As a classical conditioning procedure, aversive counterconditioning involves presenting the individual with an attractive stimulus paired with unpleasant (aversive) stimulation to condition a repulsive reaction.

Avoidant attachment   One of two primary response patterns seen in insecurely attached children—in which a child shows no interest in contact with the caregiver and displays neither distress when separated from the caregiver nor happiness when reunited.

Axon   In a nerve cell, an extended fiber that conducts information from the soma to the terminal buttons. Information travels along the axon in the form of an electric charge, called the *action potential*.

Babbling   The production of repetitive syllables, characteristic of the early stages of language acquisition.

Basic anxiety   An emotion, proposed by Karen Horney, that gives a sense of uncertainty and loneliness in a hostile world and can lead to maladjustment.

Basilar membrane   A thin strip of tissue sensitive to vibrations in the ear's cochlea. The basilar membrane contains hair cells connected to neurons. When a sound wave causes the hair cells to vibrate, the associated neurons become excited. As a result, the sound waves are converted (transduced) into nerve activity.

Behavior modification   Another term for behavior therapy.

Behavior therapy   Any form of psychotherapy based on the principles of behavioral learning, especially operant conditioning and classical conditioning.

Behavioral learning   Forms of learning, such as classical conditioning and operant conditioning, that can be described in terms of stimuli and responses.

Behavioral medicine   Medical field specializing in the link between lifestyle and disease.

Behavioral perspective   A psychological viewpoint that finds the source of our actions in environmental stimuli, rather than in inner mental processes.

Behaviorism   A historical school (as well as a modern perspective) that has sought to make psychology an objective science that focused only on behavior—to the exclusion of mental processes.

Benefit-finding   The second phase of finding meaning in a stressful situation, which involves seeing some ultimate benefit from the stressor.

Binding problem   Refers to the process used by the brain to combine (or "bind") the results of many sensory operations into a single percept. This occurs, for example, when sensations of color, shape, boundary, and texture are combined to produce the percept of a person's face. No one knows exactly how the brain does this. Thus, the binding problem is one of the major unsolved mysteries in psychology.

Binocular cues   Information taken in by both eyes that aids in depth perception, including binocular convergence and retinal disparity.

Biological perspective   The psychological perspective that searches for the causes of behavior in the functioning of genes, the brain and nervous system, and the endocrine (hormone) system.

Biomedical therapy   Treatment that focuses on altering the brain, especially with drugs, psychosurgery, or electroconvulsive therapy.

Biopsychology   The specialty in psychology that studies the interaction of biology, behavior, and mental processes.

Bipolar disorder   A mental abnormality involving swings of mood from mania to depression.

Blind spot   The point where the optic nerve exits the eye and where there are no photoreceptors. Any stimulus that falls on this area cannot be seen.

Blocking   Forgetting that occurs when an item in memory cannot be accessed or retrieved. Blocking is caused by interference.

Bottom-up processing   Perceptual analysis that emphasizes characteristics of the stimulus, rather than our concepts and expectations. "Bottom" refers to the stimulus, which occurs at step one of perceptual processing.

Brain stem The most primitive of the brain's three major layers. It includes the medulla, pons, and the reticular formation.

Brightness A psychological sensation caused by the intensity (amplitude) of light waves.

Bulimia nervosa An eating disorder characterized by eating binges followed by "purges," induced by vomiting or laxatives; typically initiated as a weight-control measure.

Bullying The act of tormenting others, in school classrooms or work settings, by one or more others, for personal, sadistic pleasure. It qualifies as a form of ordinary or everyday evil.

Burnout A syndrome of emotional exhaustion, physical fatigue, and cognitive weariness, often related to job stress.

Bystander intervention problem Laboratory and field study analogues of the difficulties faced by bystanders in real emergency situations.

Cannon–Bard theory The counterproposal that an emotional feeling and an internal physiological response occur at the same time: One is not the cause of the other. Both were believed to be the result of cognitive appraisal of the situation.

Case study Research involving a single individual (or, at most, a few individuals).

Catastrophic event A sudden, violent calamity, either natural or man-made, that causes trauma.

Catharsis A theory suggesting that emotional pressure can be relieved by expressing feelings directly or indirectly.

Central nervous system The brain and the spinal cord.

Centration A preoperational thought pattern involving the inability to take into account more than one factor at a time.

Cerebellum The "little brain" attached to the brain stem. The cerebellum is responsible for coordinated movements.

Cerebral cortex The thin gray matter covering the cerebral hemispheres, consisting of a 1/4-inch layer dense with cell bodies of neurons. The cerebral cortex carries on the major portion of our "higher" mental processing, including thinking and perceiving.

Cerebral dominance The tendency of each brain hemisphere to exert control over different functions, such as language or perception of spatial relationships.

Cerebral hemispheres The large symmetrical halves of the brain located atop the brain stem.

Chameleon effect The tendency to mimic other people, named after the animal that changes its skin color to fit into its varied environments.

Change blindness A perceptual failure to notice changes occurring in one's visual field.

Childhood amnesia The inability to remember events during the first two or three years of life.

Chromosome Tightly coiled threadlike structure along which the genes are organized, like beads on a necklace. Chromosomes consist primarily of DNA.

Chronic stressor Long-lasting stressful condition.

Chronological age (CA) The number of years since the individual's birth.

Chunking Organizing pieces of information into a smaller number of meaningful units (or chunks)—a process that frees up space in working memory.

Circadian rhythm Physiological pattern that repeats approximately every 24 hours—such as the sleep–wakefulness cycle.

Classical conditioning A form of behavioral learning in which a previously neutral stimulus acquires the power to elicit the same innate reflex produced by another stimulus.

Client-centered therapy A humanistic approach to treatment developed by Carl Rogers, emphasizing an individual's tendency for healthy psychological growth through self-actualization.

Closure The Gestalt principle that identifies the tendency to fill in gaps in figures and to see incomplete figures as complete.

Cochlea The primary organ of hearing; a coiled tube in the inner ear, where sound waves are transduced into nerve messages.

Cognitive appraisal Our interpretation of a stressor and our resources for dealing with it.

Cognitive–behavioral therapy A newer form of psychotherapy that combines the techniques of cognitive therapy with those of behavioral therapy.

Cognitive development The global term for the development of thought processes from childhood through adulthood.

Cognitive dissonance A highly motivating state in which people have conflicting cognitions, especially when their voluntary actions conflict with their attitudes or values. Leon Festinger was its originator.

Cognitive map In Tolman's work a cognitive map was a mental representation of a maze or other physical space. Psychologists often use the term *cognitive map* more broadly to include an understanding of connections among concepts. (Note that your *Grade Aid* study guide uses the related term *concept map* for the diagrams showing the relationships among concepts in every chapter.) Thus, a cognitive map can represent either a physical or a mental "space."

Cognitive neuroscience An interdisciplinary field involving cognitive psychology, neurology, biology, computer science, linguistics, and specialists from other fields who are interested in the connection between mental processes and the brain.

Cognitive perspective Another of the main psychological viewpoints distinguished by an emphasis on mental processes, such as learning, memory, perception, and thinking, as forms of information processing.

Cognitive restructuring Reappraising a stressor with the goal of seeing it from a more positive perspective.

Cognitive therapy Emphasizes rational thinking (as opposed to subjective emotion, motivation, or repressed conflicts) as the key to treating mental disorder.

Cohesiveness Solidarity, loyalty, and a sense of group membership.

Collective unconscious Jung's addition to the unconscious, involving a reservoir for instinctive "memories," including the archetypes, which exist in all people.

Collectivism The view, common in Asia, Africa, Latin America, and the Middle East, that values group loyalty and pride over individual distinction.

Collectivism The view, common in Asia, Africa, Latin America, and the Middle East, that values group loyalty and pride over individual distinction.

Color Also called *hue*. Color is not a property of things in the external world. Rather, it is a *psychological sensation* created in the brain from information obtained by the eyes from the wavelengths of visible light.

Color blindness Typically a genetic disorder (although sometimes the result of trauma, as in the case of Jonathan) that prevents an individual from discriminating certain colors. The most common form is red–green color blindness.

Coma An unconscious state, during which a person lacks the normal cycles of sleep and wakefulness, that usually lasts only a few days. The comatose state differs from the *minimally conscious state* and the *persistent vegetative state*.

Combination therapy A therapeutic approach that involves both psychological and medical techniques—most often a drug therapy with a behavioral or cognitive-behavioral therapy.

Community mental health movement An effort to deinstitutionalize mental patients and to provide therapy from outpatient clinics. Proponents of community mental health envisioned that recovering patients could live with their families, in foster homes, or in group homes.

Compassion fatigue A state of exhaustion experienced by medical and psychological professionals, as well as caregivers, which leaves the individual feeling stressed, numb, or indifferent.

Compassion satisfaction A sense of appreciation felt by a caregiver, medical or psychological professional, of the work he or she does.

Computer metaphor The idea that the brain is an information-processing organ that operates, in some ways, like a computer.

Concept hierarchies Levels of concepts, from most general to most specific, in which a more general level includes more specific concepts—as the concept of "animal" includes "dog," "giraffe," and "butterfly."

Concepts Mental groupings of similar objects, ideas, or experiences.

Concrete operational stage The third of Piaget's stages, when a child understands conservation but still is incapable of abstract thought.

Conditioned reinforcer or **secondary reinforcer** SA simulus, such as money or tokens, that acquires its reinforcing power by a learned association with primary reinforcers.

Conditioned response (CR) In classical conditioning, a response elicited by a previously neutral stimulus that has become associated with the unconditioned stimulus.

Conditioned stimulus (CS) In classical conditioning, a previously neutral stimulus that comes to elicit the conditioned response. Customarily, in a conditioning experiment, the neutral stimulus is called a conditioned stimulus when it is first paired with an unconditioned stimulus (UCS).

Cones Photoreceptors in the retina that are especially sensitive to colors but not to dim light. You may have guessed that the cones are cone-shaped.

Confirmation bias The tendency to attend to evidence that complements and confirms our beliefs or expectations, while ignoring evidence that does not.

Conformity The tendency for people to adopt the behaviors, attitudes, and opinions of other members of a group.

Conscious motivation A motive of which one is aware.

Consciousness The process by which the brain creates a mental model of our experience. The most common, or ordinary, consciousness occurs during wakefulness, although there are can be altered states of consciousness.

Conservation The understanding that the physical properties of an object or substance do not change when appearances change but nothing is added or taken away.

Consolidation The process by which short-term memories are changed to long-term memories over a period of time.

Contact comfort Stimulation and reassurance derived from the physical touch of a caregiver.

Contingency management An operant conditioning approach to changing behavior by altering the consequences, especially rewards and punishments, of behavior.

Continuous reinforcement A type of reinforcement schedule by which all correct responses are reinforced.

Control group Participants who are used as a comparison for the experimental group. The control group is not given the special treatment of interest.

Conversion disorder A type of somatoform disorder, marked by paralysis, weak-

ness, or loss of sensation but with no discernible physical cause.

Coping Taking action that reduces or eliminates the causes of stress, not merely its symptoms.

Coping strategy Action that reduces or eliminates the impact of stress.

Corpus callosum The band of nerve cells that connects the two cerebral hemispheres.

Correlational study A form of research in which the relationship between variables is studied, but without the experimental manipulation of an independent variable. Correlational studies cannot determine cause-and-effect relationships.

Cortisol A steroid produced by the fight-or-flight response.

Creative intelligence According to Sternberg, the form of intelligence that helps people see new relationships among concepts; involves insight and creativity.

Creativity A mental process that produces novel responses that contribute to the solutions of problems.

Critical incident stress debriefing (CISD) A specific type of psychological debriefing that follows a strict, step-by-step agenda, but is without any empirical support.

Critical thinking skills This book emphasizes six critical thinking skills, based on the following questions: What is the source? Is the claim reasonable or extreme? What's the evidence? Could bias contaminate the conclusion? Does the reasoning avoid common fallacies? Does the issue require multiple perspectives?

Cross-cultural psychologists Those who work in this specialty are interested in how psychological processes may differ among people of different cultures.

Crystallized intelligence The knowledge a person has acquired, plus the ability to access that knowledge.

CT scanning or **computerized tomography** A computerized imaging technique that uses X-rays passed through the brain at various angles and then combined into an image.

Culture A complex blend of language, beliefs, customs, values, and traditions developed by a group of people and shared with others in the same environment.

Cytokine Hormonelike chemical that fights infection and facilitates communicaton between the brain and immune system.

Data Pieces of information, especially information gathered by a researcher to be used in testing a hypothesis. (Singular: datum.)

Daydreaming A common (and quite normal) variation of consciousness in which attention shifts to memories, expectations, desires, or fantasies and away from the immediate situation.

Declarative memory A division of LTM that stores explicit information; also known as *fact memory*. Declarative memory has two subdivisions, episodic memory and semantic memory.

Defending Efforts taken to reduce the symptoms of stress or one's awareness of them.

Dehumanization The psychological process of thinking about certain other people or groups as less than human, as like feared or hated animals. A basic process in much prejudice and mass violence.

Deinstitutionalization The policy of removing patients, whenever possible, from mental hospitals.

Delusion An extreme disorder of thinking, involving persistent false beliefs. Delusions are the hallmark of paranoid disorders.

Dendrite Branched fiber that extends outward from the cell body and carries information into the neuron.

Dependent variable The measured outcome of a study; the responses of the participants in a study.

Depersonalization Depriving people of their identity and individuality by treating them as objects rather than as individuals. Depersonalization can be a result of labeling.

Depersonalization disorder An abnormality involving the sensation that mind and body have separated, as in an "out-of-body" experience.

Depressant Drug that slows down mental and physical activity by inhibiting transmission of nerve impulses in the central nervous system.

Developmental perspective One of the six main psychological viewpoints, distinguished by its emphasis on nature and nurture and on predictable changes that occur across the lifespan.

Developmental psychology The psychological specialty that studies how organisms grow and change over time as the result of biological and environmental influences.

Diathesis–stress hypothesis In reference to schizophrenia, the proposal that says that genetic factors place the individual at risk while environmental stress factors transform this potential into an actual schizophrenic disorder.

Difference threshold The smallest amount by which a stimulus can be changed and the difference be detected half the time.

Diffusion of responsibility Dilution or weakening of each group member's obligation to act when responsibility is perceived to be shared with all group members or accepted by the leader.

Discrimination A negative action taken against an individual as a result of his or her group or categorical membership. It is the behavior that prejudice generates.

Disenfranchised grief The emotion surrounding a loss that others do not support, share, or understand.

Display rules The permissible ways of displaying emotions in a particular society.

Disposition Relatively stable personality pattern, including temperaments, traits, and personality types.

Dispositional theory A general term that includes the temperament, trait, and type approaches to personality.

Dispositionism A psychological orientation that focuses primarily on the inner characteristics of individuals, such as personality dispositions, values, character, and genetic makeup. Contrasted with situationism, the focus is on external causes of behavior.

Dissociative amnesia A psychologically induced loss of memory for personal information, such as one's identity or residence.

Dissociative disorders A group of pathologies involving "fragmentation" of the personality, in which some parts of the personality have become detached, or dissociated, from other parts.

Dissociative fugue Essentially the same as dissociative amnesia but with the addition of "flight" from one's home, family, and job. *Fugue* (pronounced *FEWG*) means "flight."

Dissociative identity disorder A condition in which an individual displays multiple identities, or personalities; formerly called "multiple personality disorder."

Distributed learning A technique whereby the learner spaces learning sessions over time, rather than trying to learn the material all in one study period.

DNA A long, complex molecule that encodes genetic characteristics. DNA is an abbreviation for deoxyribonucleic acid.

Double-blind study An experimental procedure in which both researchers and participants are uninformed about the nature of the independent variable being administered.

Downward social comparison Comparison between one's own stressful situation and others in a similar situation who are worse off, with the goal of gaining a more positive perspective on one's own situation.

Drive Biologically instigated motivation.

Drive theory Developed as an alternative to instinct theory, drive theory explains motivation as a process in which a biological *need* produces a *drive*, a state of tension or energy that moves an organism to meet the need. For most drives this process returns the organism to a balanced condition, known as *homeostasis*.

DSM-IV The fourth edition of the *Diagnostic and Statistical Manual of Mental Disorders*, published by the American Psychiatric Association; the most widely accepted psychiatric classification system in the United States.

Dyslexia A reading disability, thought by some experts to involve a brain disorder.

Eclectic Either switching theories to explain different situations or building one's own theory of personality from pieces borrowed from many perspectives.

Ecological model Similar to the social-cognitive-behavioral model but with an emphasis on the social and cultural context.

Ego The conscious, rational part of the personality, charged with keeping peace between the superego and the id.

Ego defense mechanism A largely unconscious mental strategy employed to reduce the experience of conflict or anxiety.

Egocentrism In Piaget's theory, the self-centered inability to realize that there are other viewpoints beside one's own.

Ego-integrity   In Erikson's theory, the developmental task of late adulthood—involving the ability to look back on life without regrets and to enjoy a sense of wholeness.

Eidetic imagery   An especially clear and persistent form of memory that is quite rare; sometimes known as "photographic memory."

Elaborative rehearsal   A working-memory process in which information is actively reviewed and related to information already in LTM.

Electroconvulsive therapy (ECT)   A treatment used primarily for depression and involving the application of an electric current to the head, producing a generalized seizure. Sometimes called "shock treatment."

Electroencephalograph(EEG)   A device for recording brain waves, typically by electrodes placed on the scalp. The record produced is known as an electroencephalogram (also called an EEG).

Electromagnetic spectrum   The entire range of electromagnetic energy, including radio waves, X-rays, microwaves, and visible light.

Embryo   In humans, the name for the developing organism during the first eight weeks after conception.

Emerging adulthood   A transition period between adolescence and adulthood.

Emotion   A four-part process that involves physiological arousal, subjective feelings, cognitive interpretation, and behavioral expression. Emotions help organisms deal with important events.

Emotional bias   The tendency to make judgments based on attitudes and feelings, rather than on the basis of a rational analysis of the evidence.

Emotional intelligence   Contrasted (by Dan Goleman) with IQ, as a broader social-emotional form of understanding and responding.

Emotion-focused coping   Regulating one's emotional response to a stressor.

Empirical investigation   An approach to research that relies on sensory experience and observation as research data.

Encoding   The first of the three basic tasks of memory, involving the modification of information to fit the preferred format for the memory system.

Encoding specificity principle   The doctrine that memory is encoded and stored with specific cues related to the context in which it was formed. The more closely the retrieval cues match the form in which the information was encoded, the better it will be remembered.

Endocrine system   The hormone system—the body's chemical messenger system, including the endocrine glands: pituitary, thyroid, parathyroid, adrenals, pancreas, ovaries, and testes.

Engram   The physical changes in the brain associated with a memory. It is also known as the *memory trace*.

Episodic memory   A subdivision of declarative memory that stores memory for personal events, or "episodes."

Event-related potentials   Brain waves shown on the EEG in response to stimulation.

Evolution   The gradual process of biological change that occurs in a species as it adapts to its environment.

Evolutionary psychology   A relatively new specialty in psychology that sees behavior and mental processes in terms of their genetic adaptations for survival and reproduction.

Exhaustion phase   Third phase of the GAS, during which the body's resources become depleted.

Expectancy bias   The researcher unknowingly allows his or her expectations to affect the outcome of a study.

Expectancy-value theory   A social psychology theory that states how people decide whether to pursue a relationship by weighing the potential value of the relationship against their expectation of success in establishing the relationship.

Experiment   A kind of research in which the researcher controls all the conditions and directly manipulates the conditions, including the independent variables, and measures the dependent outcomes.

Experimental group   Participants in an experiment who are exposed to the treatment of interest.

Experimental neurosis   A pattern of erratic behavior resulting from a demanding discrimination learning task, typically one that involves aversive stimuli.

Experimental psychologists   Psychologists who do research on basic psychological processes—as contrasted with applied psychologists; also called research psychologists.

Experts   Individuals who possess well-organized funds of knowledge, including the effective problem-solving strategies, in a field.

Explicit memory   A memory that has been processed with attention and can be consciously recalled.

Exposure therapy   A form of desensitization therapy in which the patient directly confronts the anxiety-provoking stimulus (as opposed to imagining the stimulus).

Externals   People with an external locus of control who believe they can do little to influence their life outcomes.

Extinction (in classical conditioning) The weakening of a conditioned response in the absence of an unconditioned stimulus.

Extinction (in operant conditioning)   A process by which a response that has been learned is weakened by the absence or removal of reinforcement. (Compare with *extinction in classical conditioning*.)

Extraversion   The Jungian personality dimension that involves turning one's attention outward, toward others.

Extrinsic motivation   The desire to engage in an activity to achieve an external consequence, such as a reward.

Family systems theory   A perspective on personality and treatment that emphasizes the family, rather than the individual, as the basic unit of analysis.

Feature detectors   Cells in the cortex that specialize in extracting certain features of a stimulus.

Fetal alcohol syndrome (FAS)   A set of physical and mental problems seen in children whose mothers drink exessive amounts of alcohol during pregnancy.

Fetus   In humans, the term for the developing organism between the embryonic stage and birth.

Fight-or-flight response   Sequence of internal responses preparing an organism for struggle or escape.

Figure   The part of a pattern that commands attention. The figure stands out against the ground.

Five-factor theory   A trait perspective suggesting that personality is composed of five fundamental personality dimensions (also known as the Big Five): openness to

experience, conscientiousness, extraversion, agreeableness, and neuroticism.

Fixation   Occurs when psychosexual development is arrested at an immature stage.

Fixed-action patterns   Genetically based behaviors, seen across a species, that can be set off by a specific stimulus. The concept of fixed-action patterns has replaced the older notion of instinct.

Fixed interval (FI) schedule   A program by which reinforcement is contingent upon a certain, fixed time period.

Fixed ratio (FR) schedule   A program by which reinforcement is contingent on a certain, unvarying number of responses.

Flashbulb memory   A clear and vivid long-term memory of an especially meaningful and emotional event.

Flow   In Csikszentmihalyi's theory, an intense focus on an activity, accompanied by increased creativity and near-ecstatic feelings. Flow involves intrinsic motivation.

Fluid intelligence   The ability to see complex relationships and solve problems.

fMRI or functional magnetic resonance imaging   A newer form of magnetic resonance imaging that reveals different activity levels in different parts of the brain.

Forgetting curve   A graph plotting the amount of retention and forgetting over time for a certain batch of material, such as a list of nonsense syllables. The typical forgetting curve is steep at first, becoming flatter as time goes on.

Formal operational stage   The last of Piaget's stages, during which abstract thought appears.

Fovea   The tiny area of sharpest vision in the retina.

Frequency   The number of cycles completed by a wave in a second.

Frontal lobes   Cortical regions at the front of the brain that are especially involved in movement and in thinking.

Fully functioning person   Carl Rogers's term for a healthy, self-actualizing individual, who has a self-concept that is both positive and congruent with reality.

Functional fixedness   The inability to perceive a new use for an object associated with a different purpose; a form of constrained mental set.

Functionalism   A historical school of psychology that believed mental processes could best be understood in terms of their adaptive purpose and function.

Fundamental attribution error (FAE)   The dual tendency to overemphasize internal, dispositional causes and minimize external, situational pressures. The FAE is more common in individualistic cultures than in collectivistic cultures.

g factor   A general ability, proposed by Spearman, as the main factor underlying all intelligent mental activity.

Gate-control theory   An explanation for pain control that proposes we have a neural "gate" that can, under some circumstances, block incoming pain signals.

Gender similarities hypothesis   Hyde's notion that males and females are similar on most, but not all, psychological variables.

Gene   Segment of a chromosome that encodes the directions for the inherited physical and mental characteristics of an organism. Genes are the functional units of a chromosome.

General adaptation syndrome (GAS)   A three-phase pattern of physical responses to a chronic stressor.

General anesthetic   Substance that suppresses consciousness and awareness of pain. Most anesthetics also produce sedation and immobility.

Generalized anxiety disorder   A psychological problem characterized by persistent and pervasive feelings of anxiety, without any external cause.

Generativity   The process of making a commitment beyond oneself to family, work, society, or future generations. In Erikson's theory, generativity is the developmental challenge of midlife.

Genetic leash   Edward Wilson's term for the constraints placed on development by heredity.

Genotype   An organism's genetic makeup.

Gestalt psychology   From a German word (pronounced *gush-TAWLT*) that means "whole" or "form" or "configuration." (A Gestalt is also a *percept*.) The Gestalt psychologists believed that much of perception is shaped by innate factors built into the brain.

Giftedness   Often conceived as representing the upper 2% of the IQ range, commencing about 30 points above average (at about 130 IQ points).

Gist (pronounced *JIST*)   The sense or meaning, as contrasted with the exact details.

Glial cell   One of the cells that bind the neurons together. Glial cells also provide an insulating covering (the myelin sheath) of the axon for some neurons, which facilitates the electrical impulse.

Goal-directed behavior   An ability that emerges during the sensorimotor period by which infants develop the ability to keep a simple goal in mind as they pursue it.

Grammar   The rules of a language, specifying how to use the elements of language and word order to produce understandable sentences.

Grief   The emotional response to loss, which includes sadness, anger, helplessness, guilt, and despair.

Ground   The part of a pattern that does not command attention; the background.

Group therapy   Any form of psychotherapy done with more than one client/patient at a time. Group therapy is often done from a humanistic perspective.

Groupthink   The term for the poor judgments and bad decisions made by members of groups that are overly influenced by perceived group consensus or the leader's point of view.

Gustation   The sense of taste, from the same word root as "gusto"; also called the *gustatory sense.*

Habituation   Learning not to respond or adapt to the repeated presentation of a stimulus.

Hallucination   A false sensory experience that may suggest mental disorder. Hallucinations can have other causes, such as drugs or sensory isolation.

Hallucinogen   A drug that creates hallucinations or alters perceptions of the external environment and inner awareness.

Hardiness   Attitude of resistance to stress, based on a sense of challenge (welcoming change), commitment (engagement), and control (maintaining an internal guide for action).

Hassle   Situation that causes minor irritation or frustration.

Health psychology   Psychological specialty devoted to understanding how people stay healthy, why they become ill, and how they respond when ill.

Heritability The amount of trait variation within a group, raised under the same conditions, that can be attributed to genetic differences. Heritability tells us nothing about between-group differences.

Heroes People whose actions help others in emergencies or challenge unjust or corrupt systems, doing so without concern for reward or likely negative consequences for them by acting in deviant ways.

Heuristics Cognitive strategies or "rules of thumb" used as shortcuts to solve complex mental tasks. Unlike algorithms, heuristics do not guarantee a correct solution.

Hierarchy of needs In Maslow's theory, the notion that needs occur in priority order, with the biological needs as the most basic.

Hindsight bias The tendency, after learning about an event, to "second guess" or believe that one could have predicted the event in advance.

Hippocampus A component of the limbic system, involved in establishing long-term memories.

Homeostasis The body's tendency to maintain a biologically balanced condition, especially with regard to nutrients, water, and temperature.

Hormones Chemical messengers used by the endocrine system. Many hormones also serve as neurotransmitters in the nervous system.

Humanistic psychology A clinical approach emphasizing human ability, growth, potential, and free will.

Humanistic theories Personality theories that focus on human growth and potential, rather than on mental disorder. All emphasize the functioning of the individual in the present, rather than on the influence of past events.

Humanistic therapy Treatment technique based on the assumption that people have a tendency for positive growth and self-actualization, which may be blocked by an unhealthy environment that can include negative self-evaluation and criticism from others.

Humors Four body fluids—blood, phlegm, black bile, and yellow bile—that, according to an ancient theory, control personality by their relative abundance.

Hypnosis An induced state of altered awareness, usually characterized by heightened suggestibility, deep relaxation, and highly focused attention.

Hypochondriasis A somatoform disorder involving excessive concern about health and disease; also called hypochondria.

Hypothalamus That part of the brain that links the nervous system to the endocrine system via the pituitary gland. Its main function is maintaining the body's status quo.

Hypothesis A statement predicting the outcome of a scientific study; a statement describing the expected relation among variables in a study.

Id The primitive, unconscious portion of the personality that houses the most basic drives and stores repressed memories.

Identification The mental process by which an individual tries to become like another person, especially the same-sex parent.

Identity In Erikson's theory, identity is a sense of who one is—a coherent self. Developing a sense of identity is the main goal of adolescence.

Illusion You have experienced an illusion when you have a demonstrably incorrect perception of a stimulus pattern, especially one that also fools others who are observing the same stimulus. (If no one else sees it the way you do, you could be having a *hallucination*.

Immunosuppression Impairment in the function of the immune system.

Implicit memory A memory that was not deliberately learned or of which you have no conscious awareness.

Implicit personality theory A person's set of unquestioned assumptions about personality, used to simplify the task of understanding others.

Imprinting A primitive form of learning in which some young animals follow and form an attachment to the first moving object they see and hear.

Independent variable A stimulus condition so named because the experimenter changes it independently of all the other carefully controlled experimental conditions.

Individualism The view, common in the Euro-American world, that places a high value on individual achievement and distinction.

Individualism The view, common in the Euro-American world, that places a high value on individual achievement and distinction.

Industry Erikson's term for a sense of confidence that characterizes the main goal of the fourth developmental stage in childhood. Children who do not develop industry (confidence) will slip into a self-perception of *inferiority*.

Infancy In humans, infancy spans the time between the end of the neonatal period and the establishment of language—usually at about 18 months to 2 years.

Information-processing model A cognitive understanding of memory, emphasizing how information is changed when it is encoded, stored, and retrieved.

In-group The group with which an individual identifies.

Initiative In Erikson's theory, initiative is the major developmental task in the third stage of childhood. Initiative is characterized by the ability to initiate activities oneself, rather than merely responding to others or feeling *guilt* at not measuring up to other's expectations.

Innate ability Capability of an infant that is inborn or biologically based.

Innate reflex Reflexive response present at birth.

Insanity A legal term, not a psychological or psychiatric one, referring to a person who is unable, because of a mental disorder or defect, to conform his or her behavior to the law.

Insight learning A form of cognitive learning, originally described by the Gestalt psychologists, in which problem solving occurs by means of a sudden reorganization of perceptions.

Insight therapy Psychotherapy in which the therapist helps the patient/client understand (gain insight into) his or her problems.

Insomnia The most common of sleep disorders—involving insufficient sleep, the inability to fall asleep quickly, frequent arousals, or early awakenings.

Instinct theory The now-outmoded view that certain behaviors are completely determined by innate factors. The instinct theory was flawed because it overlooked the effects of learning and because it employed instincts merely as labels, rather than as explanations for behavior.

Instinctive drift   The tendency of an organism's innate (instinctive) responses to interfere with learned behavior.

Integration   A final phase of grieving, in which the loss becomes incorporated into the self.

Intelligence   The mental capacity to acquire knowledge, reason, and solve problems effectively.

Intelligence quotient (IQ)   A numerical score on an intelligence test, originally computed by dividing the person's mental age by chronological age and multiplying by 100.

Intermittent reinforcement   A type of reinforcement schedule by which some, but not all, correct responses are reinforced; also called *partial reinforcement*.

Internals   People with an internal locus of control who believe they can do much to influence their life outcomes.

Interneuron   A nerve cell that relays messages between nerve cells, especially in the brain and spinal cord.

Interval schedule   A program by which reinforcement depends on the time interval elapsed since the last reinforcement.

Intimacy   In Erikson's theory, the main developmental task of early adulthood, involving the capacity to make a full commitment—sexual, emotional, and moral—to another person.

Intrinsic motivation   The desire to engage in an activity for its own sake, rather than for some external consequence, such as a reward.

Introspection   The process of reporting on one's own conscious mental experiences.

Introversion   The Jungian dimension that focuses on inner experience—one's own thoughts and feelings—making the introvert less outgoing and sociable than the extravert.

Intuition   The ability to make judgments without consciously reasoning.

Inverted U function   A term that describes the relationship between arousal and performance. Both low and high levels of arousal produce lower performance than does a moderate level of arousal.

Irreversibility   The inability, in the preoperational child, to think through a series of events or mental operations and then mentally reverse the steps.

James–Lange theory   The proposal that an emotion-provoking stimulus produces a physical response that, in turn, produces an emotion.

Kinesthetic sense   The sense of body position and movement of body parts relative to each other (also called *kinesthesis*).

Labeling   Refers to the undesirable practice of attaching diagnoses of mental disorders to people and then using them as stereotypes—treating the afflicted individuals as if the labels explained their whole personalities. Psychiatric labels can also stigmatize people.

Language acquisition device (LAD)   A biologically organized mental structure in the brain that facilitates the learning of language because (according to Chomsky) it is innately programmed with some of the fundamental rules of grammar.

Latent content   The symbolic meaning of objects and events in a dream. Latent content is usually an interpretation based on Freud's psychoanalytic theory or one of its variants.

Lateralization of emotion   Different influences of the two brain hemispheres on various emotions. The left hemisphere apparently influences positive emotions (for example, happiness), and the right hemisphere influences negative emotions (anger, for example).

Law of common fate   The Gestalt principle that we tend to group similar objects together that share a common motion or destination.

Law of continuity   The Gestalt principle that we prefer perceptions of connected and continuous figures to disconnected and disjointed ones.

Law of effect   The idea that responses that produced desirable results would be learned, or "stamped" into the organism.

Law of Prägnanz   The most general Gestalt principle, which states that the simplest organization, requiring the least cognitive effort, will emerge as the figure. *Prägnanz* shares a common root with *pregnant*, and so it carries the idea of a "fully developed figure."

Law of proximity   The Gestalt principle that we tend to group objects together when they are near each other. *Proximity* means "nearness."

Law of similarity   The Gestalt principle that we tend to group similar objects together in our perceptions.

Laws of perceptual grouping   The Gestalt principles of similarity, proximity, continuity, and common fate. These "laws" suggest how our brains prefer to group stimulus elements together to form a percept (Gestalt).

Learned helplessness   A condition in which depressed individuals learn to attribute negative events to their own personal flaws or external conditions that the person feels helpless to change. People with learned helplessness can be thought of as having an extreme form of *external locus of control*.

Learning   A lasting change in behavior or mental processes that results from experience.

Learning-based inference   The view that perception is primarily shaped by learning (or experience), rather than by innate factors.

Levels-of-processing theory   The explanation for the fact that information that is more thoroughly connected to meaningful items in long-term memory (more "deeply" processed) will be remembered better.

Libido   The Freudian concept of psychic energy that drives individuals to experience sensual pleasure.

Limbic system   The middle layer of the brain, involved in emotion and memory. The limbic system includes the hippocampus, amygdala, hypothalamus, and other structures.

Locus of control   An individual's sense of whether control over his or her life is internal or external.

Long-term memory (LTM)   The third of three memory stages, with the largest capacity and longest duration; LTM stores material organized according to meaning.

Long-term potentiation   A biological process involving physical changes that strengthen the synapses in groups of nerve cells that is believed to be the neural basis of learning.

Loudness   A sensory characteristic of sound produced by the *amplitude* (intensity) of the sound wave.

Maintenance rehearsal   A working-memory process in which information is merely repeated or reviewed to keep it from fading while in working memory. Maintenance rehearsal involves no active elaboration.

Major depression A form of depression that does not alternate with mania.

Manifest content The story line of a dream, taken at face value without interpretation.

Matching hypothesis The prediction that most people will find friends and mates that are perceived to be of about their same level of attractiveness.

Maturation The process by which the genetic program manifests itself over time.

Medical model The view that mental disorders are diseases that, like ordinary physical diseases, have objective physical causes and require specific treatments.

Meditation A state of consciousness often induced by focusing on a repetitive behavior, assuming certain body positions, and minimizing external stimulation. Meditation may be intended to enhance self-knowledge, well-being, and spirituality.

Medulla A brain-stem structure that controls breathing and heart rate. The sensory and motor pathways connecting the brain to the body cross in the medulla.

Memory Any system—human, animal, or machine—that encodes, stores, and retrieves information.

Menarche The onset of menstruation.

Mental age (MA) The average age at which normal (average) individuals achieve a particular score.

Mental operation Solving a problem by manipulating images in one's mind.

Mental representation The ability to form internal images of objects and events.

Mental retardation Often conceived as representing the lower 2% of the IQ range, commencing about 30 points below average (below about 70 points). More sophisticated definitions also take into account an individual's level of social functioning and other abilities.

Mental set The tendency to respond to a new problem in the manner used for a previous problem.

Mere exposure effect A nonconscious preference for stimuli to which we have been previously exposed.

Method of loci A mnemonic technique that involves associating items on a list with a sequence of familiar physical locations.

Mimicry The imitation of other people's behaviors.

Mirror neuron A recently discovered class of neuron that fires in response to ("mirroring") observation of another person's actions or emotions.

Misattribution A memory fault that occurs when memories are retrieved but are associated with the wrong time, place, or person.

Misinformation effect The distortion of memory by suggestion or misinformation.

MMPI-2 A widely used personality assessment instrument that gives scores on ten important clinical traits. Also called the *Minnesota Multiphasic Personality Inventory*.

Mnemonic strategy Technique for improving memory, especially by making connections between new material and information already in long-term memory, often by imagery and sounds.

Moderator Factor that helps prevent stressors from causing stress.

Monocular cues Information about depth that relies on the input of just one eye—includes relative size, light and shadow, interposition, relative motion, and atmospheric perspective.

Mood-congruent memory A memory process that selectively retrieves memories that match (are congruent with) one's mood.

Mood disorder Abnormal disturbance in emotion or mood, including bipolar disorder and unipolar disorder. Mood disorders are also called affective disorders.

Morpheme A meaningful unit of language that makes up words. Some whole words are morphemes (example: *word*); other morphemes include grammatical components that alter a word's meaning (examples: *-ed*, *-ing*, and *un-*).

Motivation Refers to all the processes involved in initiating, directing, and maintaining physical and psychological activities.

Motive An internal mechanism that arouses the organism and then selects and directs behavior. The term *motive* is often used in the narrower sense of a motivational process that is learned, rather than biologically based (as are drives).

Motor cortex A narrow vertical strip of cortex in the frontal lobes, lying just in front of the central fissure; controls voluntary movement.

Motor neuron A nerve cell that carries messages *away* from the central nervous system toward the muscles and glands. Also called *efferent neurons*.

MRI or **magnetic resonance imaging** An imaging technique that relies on cells' responses in a high-intensity magnetic field.

Multiple intelligences A term used to refer to Gardner's theory, which proposes that there are seven (or more) forms of intelligence.

Myers–Briggs Type Indicator (MBTI) A widely used personality test based on Jungian types.

Narcolepsy A disorder of REM sleep, involving sleep-onset REM periods and sudden daytime REM-sleep attacks usually accompanied by cataplexy.

Narrative A personal account of a stressful event that describes our interpretation of what happened and why.

Natural concepts Mental representations of objects and events drawn from our direct experience.

Natural killer cell Cell produced by the immune system that attacks foreign cells.

Natural language mediator Word associated with new information to be remembered.

Natural selection The driving force behind evolution, by which the environment "selects" the fittest organisms.

Naturalistic observation A form of descriptive research involving behavioral assessment of people or animals in their home surroundings.

Nature–nurture issue The long-standing discussion over the relative importance of nature (heredity) and nurture (environment) in their influence on behavior and mental processes.

Necker cube An ambiguous two-dimensional figure of a cube that can be seen from different perspectives.

Need In drive theory, a need is a biological imbalance (such as dehydration) that threatens survival, if the need is left unmet. Biological needs are believed to produce drives.

Need for achievement *(n Ach)* In Murray and McClelland's theory, a mental state that produces a psychological motive to excel or to reach some goal.

Negative correlation A correlation coefficient indicating that the variables change simultaneously in opposite directions: As one becomes larger, the other gets smaller.

Negative punishment The removal of an attractive stimulus after a response.

Negative reinforcement The removal of an unpleasant or aversive stimulus, contingent on a particular behavior. Compare with *punishment*.

Neo-Freudian Literally "new Freudian"; refers to theorists who broke with Freud but whose theories retain a psychodynamic aspect, especially a focus on motivation as the source of energy for the personality.

Neo-Freudian psychodynamic therapy Therapy for a mental disorder that was developed by psychodynamic theorists who embraced some of Freud's ideas but disagreed with others.

Neonatal period In humans, the neonatal (newborn) period extends through the first month after birth.

Nervous system The entire network of neurons in the body, including the central nervous system, the peripheral nervous system, and their subdivisions.

Neural pathways Bundles of nerve cells that follow generally the same route and employ the same neurotransmitter.

Neuron Cell specialized to receive and transmit information to other cells in the body—also called a *nerve cell*. Bundles of many neurons are called *nerves*.

Neuroscience The field devoted to understanding how the brain creates thoughts, feelings, motives, consciousness, memories, and other mental processes.

Neurosis Before the *DSM-IV*, this term was used as a label for subjective distress or self-defeating behavior that did not show signs of brain abnormalities or grossly irrational thinking.

Neurotic needs Signs of neurosis in Horney's theory, the ten needs are normal desires carried to a neurotic extreme.

Neurotransmitter Chemical messenger that relays neural messages across the synapse. Many neurotransmitters are also hormones.

Neutral stimulus Any stimulus that produces no conditioned response prior to learning. When it is brought into a conditioning experiment, the researcher will call it a conditioned stimulus (CS). The assumption is that some conditioning occurs after even one pairing of the CS and UCS.

Night terrors Deep sleep episodes that seem to produce terror, although any terrifying mental experience (such as a dream) is usually forgotten on awakening. Night terrors occur mainly in children.

Nonconscious process Any brain process that does not involve conscious processing, including both preconscious memories and unconscious processes.

Non-REM (NREM) sleep The recurring periods, mainly associated with the deeper stages of sleep, when a sleeper is not showing rapid eye movements.

Normal distribution (normal curve) A bell-shaped curve, describing the spread of a characteristic throughout a population.

Normal range Scores falling near the middle of a normal distribution.

Object permanence The knowledge that objects exist independently of one's own actions or awareness.

Observational learning A form of cognitive learning in which new responses are acquired after watching others' behavior and the consequences of their behavior.

Observational learning A form of cognitive learning in which new responses are acquired after watching others' behavior and the consequences of their behavior.

Obsessive–compulsive disorder (CCD) A condition characterized by patterns of persistent, unwanted thoughts and behaviors.

Occipital lobes The cortical regions at the back of the brain, housing the visual cortex.

Oedipus complex According to Freud, a largely unconscious process whereby boys displace an erotic attraction toward their mother to females of their own age and, at the same time, identify with their fathers.

Olfaction The sense of smell.

Operant chamber A boxlike apparatus that can be programmed to deliver reinforcers and punishers contingent on an animal's behavior. The operant chamber is often called a "Skinner box."

Operant conditioning A form of behavioral learning in which the probability of a response is changed by its consequences—that is, by the stimuli that follow the response.

Operational definitions Objective descriptions of concepts involved in a scientific study. Operational definitions may restate concepts to be studied in behavioral terms (e.g., fear may be operationally defined as moving away from a stimulus).

Operational definitions also specify the procedures used to produce and measure important variables under investigation (e.g., "attraction" may be measured by the amount of time one person spends looking at another).

Opiate Highly addictive drug, derived from opium, that can produce a profound sense of well-being and have strong pain-relieving properties.

Opponent-process theory The idea that cells in the visual system process colors in complementary pairs, such as red or green or as yellow or blue. The opponent-process theory explains color sensation from the bipolar cells onward in the visual system.

Optic nerve The bundle of neurons that carries visual information from the retina to the brain.

Optimism An attitude that interprets stressors as external in origin, temporary, and specific in their effects. Also a generally positive world view.

Out-group Those outside the group with which an individual identifies.

Overjustification The process by which extrinsic (external) rewards can sometimes displace internal motivation, as when a child receives money for playing video games.

Oxytocin A hormone produced (by both women and men) in response to a stressor.

Panic disorder A disturbance marked by panic attacks that have no obvious connection with events in the person's present experience. Unlike generalized anxiety disorder, the victim is usually free of anxiety between panic attacks.

Paraprofessional Individual who has received on-the-job training (and, in some cases, undergraduate training) in mental health treatment in lieu of graduate education and full professional certification.

Parasympathetic division The part of the autonomic nervous system that monitors the routine operations of the internal organs and returns the body to calmer functioning after arousal by the sympathetic division.

Parietal lobes Cortical areas lying toward the back and top of the brain; involved in touch sensation and in perceiving spatial relationships (the relationships of objects in space).

Participant modeling A social learning technique in which a therapist demonstrates and encourages a client to imitate a desired behavior.

Peer marriage Marriage in which the couple see each other as partners and friends, as contrasted with the older stereotypic roles of "husband" and "wife."

Percept The meaningful product of perception—often an image that has been associated with concepts, memories of events, emotions, and motives.

Perception A process that makes sensory patterns meaningful. It is perception that makes these words meaningful, rather than just a string of visual patterns. To make this happen, perception draws heavily on memory, motivation, emotion, and other psychological processes.

Perceptual constancy The ability to recognize the same object as remaining "constant" under different conditions, such as changes in illumination, distance, or location.

Perceptual set Readiness to detect a particular stimulus in a given context—as when a person who is afraid interprets an unfamiliar sound as a threat.

Peripheral nervous system All parts of the nervous system lying outside the central nervous system. The peripheral nervous system includes the autonomic and somatic nervous systems.

Permissive parent One of the four parenting styles, characterized by setting few rules and allowing children to make their own decisions. While they may be caring and communicative, permissive parents give most decision-making responsibility to their children.

Persistence A memory problem in which unwanted memories cannot be put out of mind.

Personal unconscious Jung's term for that portion of the unconscious corresponding roughly to the Freudian id.

Personality The psychological qualities that bring continuity to an individual's behavior in different situations and at different times.

Personality disorder Condition involving a chronic, pervasive, inflexible, and maladaptive pattern of thinking, emotion, social relationships, or impulse control.

Personality process The internal working of the personality, involving motivation, emotion, perception, and learning, as well as unconscious processes.

Personality type Similar to a trait, but instead of being a *dimension,* a type is a *category* that is believed to represent a common cluster of personality characteristics.

PET scanning or **positron emission tomography** An imaging technique that relies on the detection of radioactive sugar consumed by active brain cells.

Phenomenal field Our psychological reality, composed of one's perceptions and feelings.

Phenotype An organism's observable physical and behavioral characteristics.

Pheromones Chemical signals released by organisms to communicate with other members of their species. Pheromones are often used by animals as sexual attractants. It is unclear whether or not humans employ pheromones.

Phobia One of a group of anxiety disorders involving a pathological fear of a specific object or situation.

Photoreceptors Light-sensitive cells (neurons) in the retina that convert light energy to neural impulses. The photoreceptors are as far as light gets into the visual system.

Physical dependence A process by which the body adjusts to, and comes to need, a drug for its everyday functioning.

Pitch A sensory characteristic of sound produced by the *frequency* of the sound wave.

Pituitary gland The "master gland" that produces hormones influencing the secretions of all other endocrine glands, as well as a hormone that influences growth. The pituitary is attached to the brain's hypothalamus, from which it takes its orders.

Placebo *(pla-SEE-bo)* Substance that appears to be a drug but is not. Placebos are often referred to as "sugar pills" because they might contain only sugar, rather than a real drug.

Placebo effect A response to a placebo (a fake drug), caused by the belief that they are real drugs. Also when beliefs are about reality change functioning to fit those beliefs.

Placenta The organ interface between the embryo or fetus and the mother. The placenta separates the bloodstreams, but it allows the exchange of nutrients and waste products.

Plasticity The nervous system's ability to adapt or change as the result of experi-ence. Plasticity may also help the nervous system adapt to physical damage.

Pons A brain-stem structure that regulates brain activity during sleep and dreaming. The name pons derives from the Latin word for "bridge."

Positive correlation A correlation coefficient indicating that the variables change simultaneously in the same direction: As one grows larger or smaller, the other grows or shrinks in a parallel way.

Positive lifestyle choices Deliberate decisions about long-term behavior patterns that increase resistance to both stress and illness.

Positive psychology A recent movement within psychology, focusing on desirable aspects of human functioning, as opposed to an emphasis on psychopathology. Emphasizes strengths and virtues.

Positive psychotherapy (PPT) A relatively new form of cognitive-behavioral treatment that seeks to emphasize growth, health, and happiness.

Positive punishment The application of an aversive stimulus after a response.

Positive reinforcement A stimulus presented after a response and increasing the probability of that response happening again.

Posttraumatic stress disorder (PTSD) A delayed stress reaction in which an individual involuntarily reexperiences emotional, cognitive, and behavioral aspects of past trauma.

Practical intelligence According to Sternberg, the ability to cope with the environment; sometimes called "street smarts."

Preconscious Freud's notion that the mind has a special unconscious storehouse for information not currently in consciousness but available to consciousness. Example: your telephone number is stored in the preconscious.

Prejudice A negative attitude toward an individual based solely on his or her membership in a particular group or category, often without any direct evidence.

Premack principle The concept, developed by David Premack, that a more-preferred activity can be used to reinforce a less-preferred activity.

Prenatal period The developmental period before birth.

Preoperational stage The second stage in Piaget's theory, marked by well-developed mental representation and the use of language.

Preparedness hypothesis The notion that we have an innate tendency, acquired through natural selection, to respond quickly and automatically to stimuli that posed a survival threat to our ancestors.

Primary control Efforts aimed at controlling external events.

Primary reinforcer A reinforcer, such as food or sex, that has an innate basis because of its biological value to an organism.

Priming A technique for cuing implicit memories by providing cues that stimulate a memory without awareness of the connection between the cue and the retrieved memory.

Principle of proximity The notion that people at work will make more friends among those who are nearby—with whom they have the most contact. *Proximity* means "nearness."

Proactive interference A cause of forgetting by which previously stored information prevents learning and remembering new information.

Problem-focused coping Action taken to clarify and resolve a stressor.

Procedural memory A division of LTM that stores memories for how things are done.

Projective test Personality assessment instrument, such as the Rorschach and TAT, which is based on Freud's ego defense mechanism of projection.

Prospective memory The aspect of memory that enables one to remember to take some action in the future—as remembering a doctor's appointment.

Prototype An ideal or most representative example of a conceptual category.

Pseudopsychology Erroneous assertions or practices set forth as being scientific psychology.

Psychiatry A medical specialty dealing with the diagnosis and treatment of mental disorders.

Psychic determinism Freud's assumption that all our mental and behavioral responses are caused by unconscious traumas, desires, or conflicts.

Psychoactive drug Chemical that affects mental processes and behavior by its effect on the brain.

Psychoanalysis An approach to psychology based on Sigmund Freud's assertions, which emphasize unconscious processes. The term is used to refer broadly both to Freud's psychoanalytic theory and to his psychoanalytic treatment method.

Psychoanalysis The form of psychodynamic therapy developed by Sigmund Freud. The goal of psychoanalysis is to release conflicts and memories from the unconscious.

Psychoanalytic theory Freud's theory of personality and mental disorder.

Psychodynamic psychology A clinical approach emphasizing the understanding of mental disorders in terms of unconscious needs, desires, memories, and conflicts.

Psychodynamic theories A group of theories that originated with Freud. All emphasize motivation—often unconscious motivation—and the influence of the past on the development of mental disorders.

Psychological debriefing Brief, immediate strategy focusing on venting emotions and discussing reactions to a trauma.

Psychological dependence A desire to obtain or use a drug, even though there is no physical dependence.

Psychological therapy Therapy based on psychological principles (rather than on the biomedical approach); often called "psychotherapy."

Psychology The science of behavior and mental processes.

Psychoneuroimmunology Multidisciplinary field that studies the influence of mental states on the immune system.

Psychopathology Any pattern of emotions, behaviors, or thoughts inappropriate to the situation and leading to personal distress or the inability to achieve important goals. Other terms having essentially the same meaning include *mental illness, mental disorder,* and *psychological disorder.*

Psychosexual stages Successive, instinctive developmental phases in which pleasure is associated with stimulation of different bodily areas at different times of life.

Psychosis A disorder involving profound disturbances in perception, rational thinking, or affect.

Psychosocial stage In Erikson's theory, the developmental stages refer to eight major challenges that appear successively across the lifespan, which require an individual to rethink his or her goals, as well as relationships with others.

Psychosurgery The general term for surgical intervention in the brain to treat psychological disorders.

Puberty The onset of sexual maturity.

Punishment An aversive consequence which, occurring after a response, diminishes the strength of that response. (Compare with *negative reinforcement.*)

Random assignment A process used to assign individuals to various experimental conditions by chance alone.

Ratio schedule A program by which reinforcement depends on the number of prior correct responses.

Rational–emotive behavior therapy (REBT) Albert Ellis's brand of cognitive therapy, based on the idea that irrational thoughts and negative emotions are the cause of mental disorders.

Recall A retrieval method in which one must reproduce previously presented information.

Reciprocal determinism The process in which cognitions, behavior, and the environment mutually influence each other.

Recognition A retrieval method in which one must identify present stimuli as having been previously presented.

Redemptive self A common self-narrative identified by McAdams in generative Americans. The redemptive self involves a sense of being called to overcome obstacles in the effort to help others.

Reflection of feeling Carl Rogers's technique of paraphrasing the clients' words, attempting to capture the emotional tone expressed.

Reflex Simple unlearned response triggered by stimuli—such as the knee-jerk reflex set off by tapping the tendon just below your kneecap.

Reinforcement contingencies Relationships between a response and the changes in stimulation that follow the response.

Reinforcer A condition (involving either the presentation or removal of a stimulus) that occurs after a response and strengthens that response.

Reliability An attribute of a psychological test that gives consistent results.

REM rebound A condition of increased REM sleep following REM-sleep deprivation.

REM sleep   A stage of sleep that occurs approximately every 90 minutes, marked by bursts of rapid eye movements occurring under closed eyelids. REM sleep periods are associated with dreaming.

Replication   In research, this refers to doing a study over to see whether the same results are obtained. As a control for bias, replication is often done by someone other than the researcher who performed the original study.

Representativeness bias   A faulty heuristic strategy based on the presumption that, once people or events are categorized, they share all the features of other members in that category.

Repression   An unconscious process that excludes unacceptable thoughts and feelings from awareness and memory.

Resilience   The capacity to adapt, achieve well-being, and cope with stress, in spite of serious threats to development.

Resistance phase   Second phase of the GAS, during which the body adapts to and maintains resources to cope with the stressor.

Resting potential   The electrical charge of the axon in its inactive state, when the neuron is ready to "fire."

Reticular formation   A pencil-shaped structure forming the core of the brain stem. The reticular formation arouses the cortex to keep the brain alert and attentive to new stimulation.

Retina   The thin light-sensitive layer at the back of the eyeball. The retina contains millions of photoreceptors and other nerve cells.

Retrieval   The third basic task of memory, involving the location and recovery of information from memory.

Retrieval cue   Stimulus that is used to bring a memory to consciousness or to cue a behavior.

Retroactive interference   A cause of forgetting by which newly learned information prevents retrieval of previously stored material.

Retrograde amnesia   The inability to remember information previously stored in memory. (Compare with anterograde amnesia.)

Revolution in aging   A change in the way people think about aging in modern industrialized nations. This new perspective grows out of increased longevity, better health care, and more lifestyle choices available to older adults. It has also stimulated the psychological study of adult development.

Reward theory of attraction   A social learning view that predicts we like best those who give us maximum rewards at minimum cost.

Rite of passage   Social ritual that marks the transition between developmental stages, especially between childhood and adulthood.

Rods   Photoreceptors in the retina that are especially sensitive to dim light but not to colors. They are rod-shaped.

Romantic love   A temporary and highly emotional condition based on infatuation and sexual desire.

Rorschach Inkblot Technique   A projective test requiring subjects to describe what they see in a series of ten inkblots.

Rumination   Dwelling on negative thoughts in response to stress, a behavior which compromises the immune system.

Savant syndrome   Found in individuals having a remarkable talent (such as the ability to determine the day of the week for any given date) even though they are mentally slow in other domains.

Scapegoating   Blaming an innocent person or a group for one's own troubles and then discriminating against or abusing them.

Schedule of reinforcement   A program specifying the frequency and timing of reinforcements.

Schema   Cluster of related information that represents ideas or concepts in semantic memory. Schemas provide a context for understanding objects and events.

Schizophrenia   (pronounced *skits-o-FRENNY-a*)   A psychotic disorder involving distortions in thoughts, perceptions, and/or emotions. Biologically based.

Schlesinger Report   Report issued by one of the official investigations of the Abu Ghraib Prison abuses, headed by James Schlesinger, former Secretary of Defense. It highlighted the social psychological factors that contributed to creating an abusive environment.

Scientific method   A five-step process for empirical investigation of a hypothesis under conditions designed to control biases and subjective judgments.

Script   A cluster of knowledge about sequences of events and actions expected to occur in particular settings.

Seasonal affective disorder (SAD)   A form of depression believed to be caused by deprivation of sunlight.

Secondary control   Efforts aimed at controlling one's reactions to external events.

Secure attachment   The attachment style of children who are relaxed and comfortable with their caregivers and tolerant of strangers and new experiences—as contrasted with children who are *insecurely attached*.

Selective social interaction   Choosing to restrict the number of one's social contacts to those who are the most gratifying.

Self-actualizing personality   A healthy individual who has met his or her basic needs and is free to be creative and fulfill his or her potentialities.

Self-consistency bias   The commonly held idea that we are more consistent in our attitudes, opinions, and beliefs than we actually are.

Self-disclosure   The sharing of personal information and feelings to another person as part of the process of developing trust.

Self-fulfilling prophecy   Observations or behaviors that result primarily from expectations.

Self-help support groups   Groups, such as Alcoholics Anonymous, that provide social support and an opportunity for sharing ideas about dealing with common problems. Such groups are typically organized and run by laypersons, rather than professional therapists.

Self-narrative   The "stories" one tells about oneself. Self-narratives help people sense a thread of consistency through their personality over time.

Self-serving bias   An attributional pattern in which one takes credit for success but denies responsibility for failure. (Compare with *fundamental attribution error*.)

Semantic memory   A subdivision of declarative memory that stores general knowledge, including the meanings of words and concepts.

Sensation seekers   In Zuckerman's theory, individuals who have a biological need for higher levels of stimulation than do most other people.

Sensation   The process by which stimulation of a sensory receptor produces neural impulses that the brain interprets as a sound, a visual image, an odor, a taste, a pain, or other sensory image. Sensation represents the first series of steps in processing of incoming information.

Sense-making   One aspect of finding meaning in a stressful situation, which involves perceiving the stressor in a manner consistent with our expectations of the world as predictable, controllable, and nonrandom.

Sensitive period   A span of time during which the organism is especially responsive to stimuli of a particular sort. Organisms may have sensitive or "critical" periods for exposure to certain hormones or chemicals; similarly, they may have sensitive or "critical" periods for learning language or receiving the visual stimulation necessary for normal development of vision.

Sensorimotor intelligence   Piaget's term for the infant's approach to the world, relying on relatively simple physical (motor) responses to sensory experience, with very little cognition ("intelligence") involved.

Sensorimotor stage   The first stage in Piaget's theory, during which the child relies heavily on innate motor responses to stimuli.

Sensory adaptation   Loss of responsiveness in receptor cells after stimulation has remained unchanged for a while, as when a swimmer becomes adapted to the temperature of the water.

Sensory memory   The first of three memory stages, preserving brief sensory impressions of stimuli.

Sensory neuron   A nerve cell that carries messages *toward* the central nervous system from sense receptors. Also called *afferent neurons.*

Separation anxiety   A common pattern of distress seen in young children when separated from their caregivers.

Serial position effect   A form of interference related to the sequence in which information is presented. Generally, items in the middle of the sequence are less well remembered than items presented first or last.

Set point   Refers to the tendency of the body to maintain a certain level of body fat and body weight.

Sex chromosomes   The X and Y chromosomes that determine our physical sex characteristics.

Sexual orientation   One's erotic attraction toward members of the same sex (a homosexual orientation), the opposite sex (heterosexual orientation), or both sexes (a bisexual orientation).

Sexual orientation   The direction of one's sexual interests (usually for individuals of the same sex, the opposite sex, or both sexes).

Sexual response cycle   The four-stage sequence of arousal, plateau, orgasm, and resolution occurring in both men and women.

Sexual scripts   Socially learned ways of responding in sexual situations.

Shaping   An operant learning technique in which a new behavior is gradually produced by reinforcing responses that are similar to the desired response.

Shyness   A common temperamental condition marked by social inhibition, introversion, and social skills deficits.

Signal detection theory   Explains how we detect "signals," consisting of stimulation affecting our eyes, ears, nose, skin, and other sense organs. Signal detection theory says that sensation is a judgment the sensory system makes about incoming stimulation. Often, it occurs outside of consciousness. In contrast to older theories from psychophysics, signal detection theory takes observer characteristics into account.

Similarity principle   The notion that people are attracted to those who are most similar to themselves on significant dimensions.

Situationism   The view that environmental conditions may influence people's behavior as much or more than their personal dispositions do, under some circumstances.

Skin senses   Sensory systems for processing touch, warmth, cold, texture, and pain.

Sleep apnea   A respiratory disorder in which the person intermittently stops breathing many times while asleep.

Sleep debt   A sleep deficiency caused by not getting the amount of sleep that one requires for optimal functioning.

Sleep paralysis   A condition in which a sleeper is unable to move any of the voluntary muscles, except those controlling the eyes. Sleep paralysis normally occurs during REM sleep.

Social–cognitive–behavioral approach   A psychological alternative to the medical model that views psychological disorder through a combination of the social, cognitive, and behavioral perspectives.

Social-cognitive theories   A group of theories that involve explanations of limited, but important, aspects of personality (e.g., locus of control). All grew out of experimental psychology. **Social comparison**   A type of cognitive restructuring involving comparisons between oneself and others in similar situations.

Social context   The combination of (a) people, (b) the activities and interactions among people, (c) the setting in which behavior occurs, and (d) the expectations and social norms governing behavior in that setting.

Social distance   The perceived difference or similarity between oneself and another person or group.

Social neuroscience   An area of research that uses methodologies from brain sciences to investigate various types of social behavior, such as stereotyping in prejudice, attitudes, self-control, and emotional regulation.

Social norms   A group's expectations regarding what is appropriate and acceptable for its members' attitudes and behaviors.

Social psychology   The branch of psychology that studies the effects of social variables and cognitions on individual behavior and social interactions.

Social Readjustment Rating Scale (SRRS)   Psychological rating scale designed to measure stress levels by attaching numerical values to common life changes.

Social reality   An individual's subjective interpretation of other people and of one's relationships with them.

Social role   A socially defined pattern of behavior that is expected of persons in a given setting or group.

Social support   Resources others provide to help an individual cope with stress.

Socialization   The lifelong process of shaping an individual's behavior patterns, values, standards, skills, attitudes, and motives to conform to those regarded as desirable in a particular society.

Societal stressor A chronic stressor resulting from pressure in one's social, cultural, or economic environment.

Sociocultural perspective A main psychological viewpoint emphasizing the importance of social interaction, social learning, and a cultural perspective.

Soma The part of a cell (such as a neuron) containing the nucleus, which includes the chromosomes. Also called the *cell body*.

Somatic nervous system A division of the peripheral nervous system that carries sensory information to the central nervous system and also sends voluntary messages to the body's skeletal muscles.

Somatoform disorders Psychological problem appearing in the form of bodily symptoms or physical complaints, such as weakness or excessive worry about disease. The somatoform disorders include conversion disorder and hypochondriasis.

Somatosensory cortex A strip of the parietal lobe lying just behind the central fissure. The somatosensory cortex is involved with sensations of touch.

Spontaneous recovery The reappearance of an extinguished conditioned response after a time delay.

Stages of moral reasoning Distinctive way of thinking about ethical and moral problems. According to Kohlberg, moral reasoning progresses through a series of developmental stages that are similar to Piaget's stages of cognitive development.

Stage theory An explanation of development that emphasizes distinctive or rather abrupt changes. A stage theory of cognitive development, then, emphasizes revolutionary changes in thought processes.

Stanford Prison Experiment Classic study of institutional power in directing normal, healthy college student volunteers playing randomly assigned roles of prisoners and guards to behave contrary to their dispositional tendencies, as cruel guards or pathological prisoners.

Stereotype threat The negative effect on performance that arises when an individual becomes aware that members of his or her group are expected to perform poorly in that domain.

Stimulant A drug that arouses the central nervous system, speeding up mental and physical responses.

Stimulus discrimination Learning to respond to a particular stimulus but not to stimuli that are similar.

Stimulus generalization The extension of a learned response to stimuli that are similar to the conditioned stimulus.

Storage The second of the three basic tasks of memory, involving the retention of encoded material over time.

Stress The physical and mental response to a stressor.

Stressor A stressful event or situation.

Structuralism A historical school of psychology devoted to uncovering the basic structures that make up mind and thought. Structuralists sought the "elements" of conscious experience.

Subjective well-being (SWB) An individual's evaluative response to life, commonly called happiness, which includes cognitive and emotional reactions.

Suggestibility The process of memory distortion as the result of deliberate or inadvertent suggestion. Occurs in hypnosis.

Superego The mind's storehouse of values, including moral attitudes learned from parents and from society; roughly the same as the common notion of the conscience.

Survey A technique used in descriptive research, typically involving seeking people's responses to a prepared set of verbal items.

Sympathetic division The part of the autonomic nervous system that sends messages to internal organs and glands that help us respond to stressful and emergency situations.

Synapse The microscopic gap that serves as a communications link between neurons. Synapses also occur between neurons and the muscles or glands they serve.

Synaptic pruning The process of trimming unused brain connections, making neurons available for future development.

Synaptic transmission The relaying of information across the synapse by means of chemical neurotransmitters.

Synchronicity The close coordination between the gazing, vocalizing, touching, and smiling of infants and caregivers.

Synesthesia The mixing of sensations across sensory modalities, as in tasting shapes or seeing colors associated with numbers.

System power Influences on behavior that come from top-down sources in the form of creating and maintaining various situations that in turn have an impact on actions of individuals in those behavioral contexts.

Systematic desensitization A behavioral therapy technique in which anxiety is extinguished by exposing the patient to an anxiety-provoking stimulus.

Tardive dyskinesia An incurable disorder of motor control, especially involving muscles of the face and head, resulting from long-term use of antipsychotic drugs.

Teachers of psychology Psychologists whose primary job is teaching, typically in high schools, colleges, and universities.

Telegraphic speech Short, simple sequences of nouns and verbs without plurals, tenses, or function words like *the* and *of*—somewhat like the language once used in telegrams.

Temperament An individual's characteristic manner of behavior or reaction—assumed to have a strong genetic basis.

Temporal lobes Cortical lobes that process sounds, including speech. The temporal lobes are probably involved in storing long-term memories.

Tend-and-befriend Stress response model proposing that females are biologically predisposed to respond to threat by nurturing and protecting offspring and seeking social support.

Teratogen Substance from the environment, including viruses, drugs, and other chemicals, that can damage the developing organism during the prenatal period.

Terminal buttons Tiny bulblike structures at the end of the axon that contain neurotransmitters that carry the neuron's message into the synapse.

Terrorism A type of disaster caused by human malevolence with the goal of disrupting society by creating fear and danger.

Thalamus The brain's central "relay station," situated just atop the brain stem. Nearly all the messages going into or out of the brain go through the thalamus.

Thematic Apperception Test (TAT) A projective test requiring subjects to make up stories that explain ambiguous pictures.

Theory A testable explanation for a set of facts or observations. In science, a theory is not just speculation or a guess.

Theory of mind An awareness that other people's behavior may be influenced by beliefs, desires, and emotions that differ from one's own.

Therapeutic alliance The relationship between the therapist and the client, with both parties working together to help the client deal with psychological or behavioral issues.

Therapeutic community Jones's term for a program of treating mental disorder by making the institutional environment supportive and humane for patients.

Therapy A general term for any treatment process; in psychology and psychiatry, therapy refers to a variety of psychological and biomedical techniques aimed at dealing with mental disorders or coping with problems of living.

Timbre The quality of a sound wave that derives from the wave's complexity (combination of pure tones). *Timbre* comes from the Greek word for "drum," as does the term *tympanic membrane,* or eardrum.

Token economy A therapeutic method, based on operant conditioning, by which individuals are rewarded with tokens, which act as secondary reinforcers. The tokens can be redeemed for a variety of rewards and privileges.

Tolerance The reduced effectiveness a drug has after repeated use.

Top-down processing Perceptual analysis that emphasizes the perceiver's expectations, concept memories, and other cognitive factors, rather than being driven by the characteristics of the stimulus. "Top" refers to a mental set in the brain—which stands at the "top" of the perceptual processing system.

TOT phenomenon The inability to recall a word, while knowing that it is in memory. People often describe this frustrating experience as having the word "on the tip of the tongue."

Trait and temperament psychology A psychological perspective that views behavior and personality as the products of enduring psychological characteristics.

Traits Multiple, stable personality characteristics that are presumed to exist within the individual and guide his or her thoughts and actions under various conditions.

Transcranial magnetic stimulation (TMS) A treatment that involves magnetic stimulation of specific regions of the brain.

Unlike ECT, TMS does not produce a seizure.

Transduction Transformation of one form of information into another—especially the transformation of stimulus information into nerve signals by the sense organs.

Transience The impermanence of a long-term memory. Transience is based on the idea that long-term memories gradually fade in strength over time.

Transition An individual's redefinition or transformation of a life role.

Traumatic stressor A situation that threatens one's physical safety, arousing feelings of fear, horror, or helplessness.

Triangular theory of love A theory that describes various kinds of love in terms of three components: passion (erotic attraction), intimacy (sharing feelings and confidences), and commitment (dedication to putting this relationship first in one's life). Developed by Robert Sternberg.

Triarchic theory The term for Sternberg's theory of intelligence; so called because it combines three ("tri-") main forms of intelligence.

Trichromatic theory The idea that colors are sensed by three different types of cones sensitive to light in the red, blue, and green wavelengths. The trichromatic (three-color) theory explains the earliest stage of color sensation. In honor of its originators, this is sometimes called the Young-Helmholtz theory.

Trust The major developmental goal during the first 18 months of life. According to Erikson's theory, the child must choose between trusting or not trusting others.

Twin study A means of separating the effects of nature and nurture by which investigators may compare identical twins to fraternal twins or compare twins separated early in life and raised in different environments.

Two-factor theory The idea that emotion results from the cognitive appraisal of both physical arousal (Factor #1) and an emotion-provoking stimulus (Factor #2).

Tympanic membrane The eardrum.

Type A Behavior pattern characterized by intense, angry, competitive, or hostile responses to challenging situations.

Tyranny of choice The impairment of effective decision making, when con-

fronted with an overwhelming number of choices.

Unconditioned response (UCR) In classical conditioning, the response elicited by an unconditioned stimulus without prior learning.

Unconditioned stimulus (UCS) In classical conditioning, UCS is the stimulus that elicits an unconditioned response.

Unconscious In Freudian theory, this is the psychic domain of which the individual is not aware but that is the storehouse of repressed impulses, drives, and conflicts unavailable to consciousness.

Unconscious motivation A motive of which one is consciously unaware. Freud's psychoanalytic theory emphasized unconscious motivation.

Uninvolved parent One of the four parenting styles, characterized by indifference or rejection, sometimes to the point of neglect or abuse.

Upward social comparison Comparison between one's own stressful situation and others in a similar situation who are coping more effectively, with the goal of learning from others' examples.

Validity An attribute of a psychological test that actually measures what it is being used to measure.

Variable interval (VI) schedule A reinforcement program by which the time period between reinforcements varies from trial to trial.

Variable ratio (VR) schedule A reinforcement program by which the number of responses required for a reinforcement varies from trial to trial.

Vestibular sense The sense of body orientation with respect to gravity. The vestibular sense is closely associated with the inner ear and, in fact, is carried to the brain on a branch of the auditory nerve.

Vicarious traumatization Severe stress caused by exposure to traumatic images or stories that cause the observer to become engaged with the stressful material.

Visible spectrum The tiny part of the electromagnetic spectrum to which our eyes are sensitive. The visible spectrum of other creatures may be slightly different from our own.

Visual cortex The visual processing areas of cortex in the occipital and temporal lobes.

Wave metaphor   A way of conceptualizing cognitive development, as occurring more gradually—in "waves"—rather than abruptly, as the stage theory suggests.

Weber's law   The concept that the size of a JND is proportional to the intensity of the stimulus; the JND is large when the stimulus intensity is high and small when the stimulus intensity is low.

Whole method   The mnemonic strategy of first approaching the material to be learned "as a whole," forming an impression of the overall meaning of the material. The details are later associated with this overall impression.

Whole-person perspectives   A group of psychological perspectives that take a global view of the person: Included are *psychodynamic psychology, humanistic psychology,* and *trait and temperament psychology.*

Withdrawal   A pattern of uncomfortable or painful physical symptoms and cravings experienced by the user when the level of drug is decreased or the drug is eliminated.

Working memory   The second of three memory stages, and the one most limited in capacity. It preserves recently perceived events or experiences for less than a minute without rehearsal.

Zygote   A fertilized egg.

references

ABC News. (1995). "My Family, Forgive Me." *20/20*, Transcript #1526, June 30, pp. 6–10. New York: American Broadcasting Companies, Inc.

Abelson, P., & Kennedy, D. (2004, June 4). Editorial: The obesity epidemic. *Science, 304,* 1413.

Abelson, R. P. (1981). Psychological status of the script concept. *American Psychologist, 36,* 715–729.

Abrams, A. R. (1992). *Electroconvulsive therapy.* New York: Oxford University Press.

Abrams, M. (2007, June). Born gay? *Discover, 28*(6), 58–83.

Abramson, L. Y., Metalsky, G. I., & Alloy, L. B. (1989). Hopelessness depression: A theory-based subtype. *Psychological Review, 96,* 358–372.

Ackerman, P. L. (2007). New developments in understanding skilled performance. *Current Directions in Psychological Science, 16,* 235–239.

Ackerman, S. J., Benjamin, L. S., Beutler, L. E., Gelso, C. J., Goldfried, M. R., Hill, C., Lambert, M. J., Norcross, J. C., Orlinsky, D. E., & Rainer, J. (2001). Empirically supported therapy relationships: Conclusions and recommendations of the Division 29 task force. *Psychotherapy, 38,* 495–497.

Adams, J. (1979). Mutual-help groups: Enhancing the coping ability of oncology clients. *Cancer Nursing, 2,* 95–98.

Adelson, R. (2003, December). Conquering fear: Kick-starting extinction through massed exposure helps mice overcome conditioned fear faster. *Monitor on Psychology,* 20–21.

Adelson, R. (2004, July/August). Detecting deception. *Monitor on Psychology, 35*(7), 70–71.

Adelson, R. (2005, July/August). The power of potent steroids. *Monitor on Psychology, 36*(7), 20–22.

Adelson, R. (2006, January). Nationwide survey spotlights U.S. alcohol abuse. *Monitor on Psychology, 37*(1), 30–32.

Ader, R., & Cohen, N. (1993). Psychoneuroimmunology: Conditioning and stress. *Annual Review of Psychology, 44,* 53–85.

Adler, J. (2006, March 27). Freud in our midst. *Newsweek, 157*(13), 43–49.

Adolphs, R., Jansari, A., & Tranel, D. (2001). Hemispheric perception of emotional valence from facial expressions. *Neuropsychology, 15,* 516–524.

Adorno, T. W., Frenkel-Brunswick, E., Levinson, D. J., & Sanford, R. N. (1950). *The authoritarian personality.* New York: Harper.

Aftergood, S. (2000, November 3). Polygraph testing and the DOE National Laboratories. *Science, 290,* 939–940. [See also: Holden, 2001b; Saxe, 1991, 1994]

Agras, W. S., Brandt, H. A., Bulik, C. M., Dolan-Sewell, R., Fairburn, C. G., Halmi, K. A., Herzog, D. B., Jimerson, D. C., Kaplan, A. S., Kaye, W. H., le Grange, D., Lock, J., Mitchell, J., Rudorfer, M. V., Street, L. L., Striegel-Moore, R., Vitousek, K. M., Walsh, B. T., & Wilfley, D. E. (2004). Report of the National Institutes of Health workshop on overcoming barriers to treatment research in anorexia nervosa. *International Journal of Eating Disorders, 35,* 509–521.

Ahern, G. L., & Schwartz, G. E. (1985). Differential lateralization for positive and negative emotion in the human brain: EEG spectral analysis. *Neuropsychologia, 23,* 744–755.

Ahrons, C. R. (1994). *The good divorce: Keeping your family together when your marriage comes apart.* New York: HarperCollins.

Aiken, L. R. (1987). *Assessment of intellectual functioning.* Boston, MA: Allyn & Bacon.

Ainsworth, M. D. S. (1973). The development of infant–mother attachment. In B. M. Caldwell & H. N. Ricciuti (Eds.), *Review of child development research (Vol. 3).* Chicago: University of Chicago Press.

Ainsworth, M. D. S. (1989). Attachments beyond infancy. *American Psychologist, 44,* 709–716.

Ainsworth, M. D. S., Blehar, M., Water, E., & Wall, S. (1978). *Patterns of attachment.* Hillsdale, NJ: Erlbaum.

Ainsworth, M. D. S., & Wittig, B. A. (1969). Attachment and exploratory behavior of one-year-olds in a strange situation. In B. M. Foss (Ed.), *Determinants of infant behavior (Vol. 4).* London, U.K.: Methuen.

Albee, G. W. (2006, Fall) Is it time for the Third Force in American psychology? *The General Psychologist, 41*(2), 1-3. Retrieved February 16, 2008, from www.apa.org/divisions/div1/archive.html.

Alferink, L. (2005, Spring). Behaviorism died today, again! *The General Psychologist, 40*(1), 7–8. [Electronic version available at www.apa.org/divisions/div1/newspub.html]

Alford, G. S., & Bishop, A. C. (1991). Psychopharmacology. In M. Hersen, A. E. Kazdin, & A. S. Bellack (Eds.), *The clinical psychology handbook* (2nd ed., pp. 667–694). New York: Pergamon Press.

Allen, K., Blascovich, J., & Mendes, W. B. (2002). Cardiovascular reactivity and the presence of pets, friends, and spouses: The truth about cats and dogs. *Psychosomatic Medicine, 64,* 727–739.

Allen, M. G. (1976). Twin studies of affective illness. *Archives of General Psychiatry, 33,* 1476–1478.

Allen, M. J. (1995). *Introduction to psychological research.* Itasca, IL: Peacock.

Allen, V. S., & Levine, J. M. (1969). Consensus and conformity. *Journal of Experimental Social Psychology, 5,* 389–399.

Allport, G. W. (1954). *The nature of prejudice.* Cambridge, MA: Addison-Wesley.

Allport, G. W., & Odbert, H. S. (1936). Trait-names, a psycho-lexical study. *Psychological Monographs, 47*(1, Whole No. 211).

Alper, J. (1985, March). The roots of morality. *Science, 85,* 70–76.

Alper, J. (1993). Echo-planar MRI: Learning to read minds. *Science, 261,* 556.

Amabile, T. M. (1983). *The social psychology of creativity.* New York: Springer-Verlag.

Amabile, T. M. (1987). The motivation to be creative. In S. Isaksen (Ed.), *Frontiers in creativity: Beyond the basics.* Buffalo, NY: Bearly Limited.

Amabile, T. M. (2001). Beyond talent: John Irving and the passionate craft of creativity. *American Psychologist, 56,* 333–336.

Amabile, T. M., Hadley, C. N., & Kramer, S. J. (2002, August). Creativity under the gun. *Harvard Business Review, 80*(8), 52–60.

Ambady, N., & Rosenthal, R. (1993). Half a minute: Predicting teacher evaluations from thin slices of nonverbal behavior and physical attractiveness. *Journal of Personality and Social Psychology, 64,* 431–441.

Amedi, A., Merabet, L. B., Bermpohl, F., & Pascual-Leone, A. (2005, December). The occipital cortex in the blind. *Current Directions in Psychological Science, 14,* 306–311.

American Academy of Pediatrics, Subcommittee on Attention Deficit Hyperactivity Disorder, Committee on Quality Improvement. (2001). Clinical practice guideline: Treatment of the school-aged child with attention-deficit/hyperactivity disorder. *Pediatrics, 108,* 1033–1044. [See also: Henker & Whalen, 1989; Poling et al., 1991; Welsh et al., 1993]

American Psychiatric Association. (1994). *Diagnostic and statistical manual of mental disorders* (4th ed.). Washington, DC: American Psychiatric Association.

American Psychiatric Association. (2000). *Diagnostic and statistical manual of mental disorders, 4th edition, text revision.* Washington, DC: American Psychiatric Association.

American Psychological Association. (2002a). Ethical principles of psychologists and code of conduct. *American Psychologist, 57,* 1060–1073.

American Psychological Association. (2002b, June 26). Is corporal punishment an effective means of discipline? Retrieved July 2, 2007, from www.apa.org/releases/spanking.html.

American Psychological Association. (2003a). *Careers in psychology for the twenty-first century.* Retrieved on October 14, 2004, from www.apa.org/students/brochure/brochurenew.pdf.

American Psychological Association. (2003b). *Council policy manual.* Retrieved on October 14, 2004, from www.apa.org/about/division/cpmscientific.html.

American Psychological Association. (2003c). Degree Fields of Psychology PhDs Awarded in 1981–2001. Retrieved on October 14, 2004, from http://research.apa.org/doctoraled05.html.

American Psychological Association. (2003d). Facilitated communication: Sifting the psychological wheat from the chaff. Retrieved April 16, 2007, from www.psychologymatters.org/facilitated.html. [See also Cabay, 1994; Wheeler et al., 1993]

American Psychological Association. (2004). *About APA.* Retrieved on October 14, 2004, from www.apa.org/about/.

APA Presidential Task Force on Evidence-Based Practice. (2006). Evidence-based practice in psychology. *American Psychologist, 61,* 271–285.

American Psychological Association. (2007a). About the American Psychological Association. Retrieved April 13, 2007, from www.apa.org/about/.

American Psychological Association. (2007b). Frequently asked questions about teaching high school psychology. Retrieved, April 17, 2007, from www.apa.org/ed/topss/topss_faqs.html.

Anand, K. J. S., & Hickey, P. R. (1987). Pain and its effects in the human neonate and fetus. *The New England Journal of Medicine, 317,* 1321–1329.

Anand, K. J. S., & Scalzo, F. M. (2000). Can adverse neonatal experiences alter brain development and subsequent behavior? *Biology of the Neonate, 77,* 69–82.

Anastasi, A. (1988). *Psychological testing* (6th ed.). New York: Macmillan.

Anch, A. M., Browman, C. P., Mitler, M. M., & Walsh, J. K. (1988). *Sleep: A scientific perspective.* Englewood Cliffs, NJ: Prentice Hall.

Anderson, A. E., & DiDomenico, L. (1992). Diet vs. shape content of popular male and female magazines: A dose-response relationship to the incidence of eating disorders? *International Journal of Eating Disorders, 11,* 283–287.

Anderson, C. A., & Bushman, B. J. (2001). Effects of violent video games on aggressive behavior, aggressive cognition, aggressive affect, physiological arousal, and prosocial behavior: A meta-analytic review of the scientific literature. *Psychological Science, 12,* 353–359.

Anderson, C. A., & Bushman, B. J. (2002). Media violence and the American public revisited. *American Psychologist, 57,* 448–450. [See also: Bloom, 2002; Ferguson, 2002; Freedman, 1984, 1996]

Anderson, J. R. (1982). Acquisition of cognitive skill. *Psychological Review, 89,* 369–406.

Anderson, W. (1987). Parents as a source of stress for college students. *College Student Journal, 21,* 317–323.

Andreasen, N. C., Arndt, S., Alliger, R., Miller, D., et al. (1995). Symptoms of schizophrenia: Methods, meanings, and mechanisms. *Archives of General Psychiatry, 52,* 341–351.

Andreasen, N. C., Rice, J., Endicott, J., Coryell, W., Grove, W. W., & Reich, T. (1987). Familial rates of affective disorder. *Archives of General Psychiatry, 44,* 461–472.

Andrews, F. M., & Withey, S. B. (1976). *Social indicators of well-being: Americans' perceptions of life quality.* New York: Plenum.

Andrews, J. D. W. (1967). The achievement motive and advancement in two types of organization. *Journal of Personality and Social Psychology, 6,* 163–168.

Angerer, J. M. (2003). Job burnout. *Journal of Employment Counseling, 40,* 98–107.

Anglin, J. M. (1993). Vocabulary development: A morphological analysis. *Monographs of the Society for Research in Child Development, 58*(Serial No. 238).

Anglin, J. M. (1995, March). Word learning and the growth of potentially knowable vocabulary. Paper presented at the biennial meetings of the Society for Research in Child Development, Indianapolis, IN.

Angold, A., Erkanli, A., Egger, H. L., & Costello, E. J. (2000). Stimulant treatment for children: A community perspective. *Journal of the American Academy of Child and Adolescent Psychiatry, 39,* 975–984.

Anthony, E. J. (Ed.). (1987). *The invulnerable child.* New York: Guilford Press.

Antonova, I., Arancio, O., Trillat, A-C., Hong-Gang W., Zablow, L., Udo, H., Kandel, E. R., & Hawkins, R. D. (2001, November 16). Rapid increase in clusters of presynaptic proteins at onset of long-lasting potentiation, *Science, 294,* 1547–1550.

Antonuccio, D. (1995). Psychotherapy for depression: No stronger medicine. *American Psychologist, 50,* 450–452.

Antony, M. M., & Barlow, D. H. (2002). Specific phobias. In D. H. Barlow (Ed.), *Anxiety and its disorders* (2nd ed., pp. 380-417). New York: Guilford.

Antony, M. M., Brown, T. A., & Barlow, D. H. (1992). Current perspectives on panic and panic disorder. *Current Directions in Psychological Science, 1,* 79–82.

APA Online. (2004). *Empirical studies on lesbian and gay parenting.* Retrieved on November 8, 2004, from www.apa.org/pi/l&gbib.html.

Archer, J. (1996). Sex differences in social behavior: Are the social role and evolutionary explanations compatible? *American Psychologist, 51,* 909–917.

Armstrong, L. (2001). *It's not about the bike: My journey back to life.* Madison, WI: Turtleback Books.

Arnett, J. J. (1992). Reckless behavior in adolescence: A developmental perspective. *Developmental Review, 12,* 339–373.

Arnett, J. J. (1997). Young people's conceptions of the transition to adulthood. *Youth & Society, 29,* 1–23.

Arnett, J. J. (1999). Adolescent storm and stress, reconsidered. *American Psychologist, 54,* 317–326.

Arnett, J. J. (2000a). Emerging adulthood: A theory of development from the late teens through the twenties. *American Psychologist, 55*(5), 469–480.

Arnett, J. J. (2000b). High hopes in a grim world: Emerging adults' view of their futures and "Generation X." *Youth & Society, 31,* 267–286.

Arnett, J. J. (2001). Conceptions of the transition to adulthood: Perspectives from adolescence through midlife. *Journal of Adult Development, 8,* 133–144.

Arnhoff, F. N. (1975). Social consequences of policy toward mental illness. *Science, 188,* 1277–1281.

Arnsten, A. F. T. (1998, June 12). The biology of being frazzled. *Science, 280,* 1711–1712. [See also Caldwell, 1995; Mukerjee, 1995; Sapolsky, 1990]

Aron, A., & Aron, E. (1994). Love. In A. L. Weber & J. H. Harvey (Eds.), *Perspectives on close relationships* (Chapter 7, pp. 131–152). Boston: Allyn & Bacon.

Aronson, E. (2000). *Nobody left to hate: Teaching compassion after Columbine.* New York: W. H. Freeman & Company.

Aronson, E. (2004). *The social animal* (9th ed.). New York: Worth. [See also: Feingold, 1990; Langlois et al., 1998; Tesser & Brodie, 1971]

Aronson, E., Helmreich, R., & LeFan, J. (1970). To err is humanizing—sometimes: Effects of self-esteem, competence, and a pratfall on interpersonal attraction. *Journal of Personality and Social Psychology, 16,* 259–264.

Aronson, E., Willerman, B., & Floyd, J. (1966). The effect of a pratfall on increasing interpersonal attractiveness. *Psychonomic Science, 4,* 227–228.

Aronson, J., Fried, C. B., & Good, C. (2001). Reducing the effects of stereotype threat on African American college students by shaping theories of intelligence. *Journal of Experimental Social Psychology, 38,* 1–13.

Asarnow, J., Glynn, S., Pynoos, R. S., Nahum, J., Guthrie, D., Cantwell, D. P., & Franklin, B. (1999). When the earth stops shaking: Earthquake sequelae among children diagnosed for pre-earthquake psychopathology. *Journal of the American Academy of Child and Adolescent Psychiatry, 38,* 1016–1025.

Asbell, B. (1995). *The Pill: A biography of the drug that changed the world.* New York: Random House.

Asch, S. E. (1940). Studies in the principles of judgments and attitudes: 11. Determination of judgments by group and by ego standards. *Journal of Social Psychology, 12,* 433–465.

Asch, S. E. (1955). Opinions and social pressure. *Scientific American, 193*(5), 31–35.

Asch, S. E. (1956). Studies of independence and conformity: A minority of one against a unanimous majority. *Psychological Monographs, 70*(9, Whole No. 416).

Aserinsky, E., & Kleitman, N. (1953). Regularly occurring periods of eye mobility and concomitant phenomena during sleep. *Science, 118,* 273–274.

Ashby, F. Isen, A., & Turken, A. (1999). A neuropsychological theory of positive affect and its influence on cognition. *Psychological Review, 106,* 529–550.

Ashby, F. G., & Waldron, E. M. (2000). The neuropsychological bases of category learning. *Current Directions in Psychological Science, 9,* 10–14. [See also: Beardsley, 1997a; Behrmann, 2000; Freedman et al., 2001; Thorpe & Fabre-Thorpe, 2001]

Atkinson, R. C., & Schiffrin, R. M. (1968). Human memory: A control system and its control processes. In K. Spence (Ed.), *The psychology of learning and motivation* (Vol. 2). New York: Academic Press.

Attig, T. (1996). *How we grieve: Relearning the world.* New York: Oxford University Press.

Austin, J. H. (1998). *Zen and the brain: Toward an understanding of meditation and consciousness.* Cambridge, MA: MIT Press.

Averill, J. A. (1980). A constructivist view of emotion. In R. Plutchik & H. Kellerman (Eds.), *Emotion: Theory, research, and experience: Vol. 1. Theories of emotion.* New York: Academic Press.

Axel, R. (1995, October). The molecular logic of smell. *Scientific American, 273,* 154–159.

Ayllon, T., & Azrin, N. H. (1965). The measurement and reinforcement of behavior of psychotics. *Journal of Experimental Analysis of Behavior, 8,* 357–383.

Ayllon, T., & Azrin, N. H. (1968). *The token economy: A motivational system for therapy and rehabilitation.* New York: Appleton-Century-Crofts.

Azar, B. (1994, October). Seligman recommends a depression "vaccine." *APA Monitor, 4.* [See also: Robins, 1988; Seligman, 1991; Seligman et al., 1979]

Azar, B. (1995, June). New cognitive research makes waves. *APA Monitor, 16.*

Azar, B. (1996, November). Some forms of memory improve as people age. *APA Monitor, 27.*

Azar, B. (1997, October). Was Freud right? Maybe, maybe not. *American Psychological Association Monitor, 28,* 30.

Azar, B. (1998a, January). Certain smells evoke stronger memories. *APA Monitor, 10.*

Azar, B. (1998b, January). Communicating through pheromones. *APA Monitor, 1,* 12.

Azar, B. (2002a, January). At the frontier of science. *Monitor on Psychology,* 40–43.

Azar, B. (2002b, September). Searching for genes that explain our personalities. *Monitor on Psychology, 33*(8), 44–45.

Azar, B. (2006, March). The faces of pride. *Monitor on Psychology, 37*(3). Retrieved March 30, 2008, from www.apa.org/monitor/mar06/pride.html.

Azar, B. (2007, April). A case for angry men and happy women. *Monitor on Psychology, 38*(4), 18–19.

Babiak, P., & Hare, R. D. (2006). *Snakes in suits: When psychopaths go to work.* New York: Harper Collins.

Babyak, M., Blumenthall, J. A., Herman, S., Khatri, P., Doraiswamy, M., Moore, K., Craighead, W. E., Baldewicz, T. T., & Krishnan, K. R. (2000). Exercise treatment for major depression: Maintenance of therapeutic benefit at 10 months. *Psychosomatic Medicine, 62,* 633–638.

Baddeley, A. (1998). *Human memory: Theory and practice.* Boston: Allyn & Bacon.

Baddeley, A., Gathercole, S., & Papagno, C. (1998). The phonological loop as a language learning device. *Psychological Review, 105,* 158–173.

Baddeley, A. D. (2000). The episodic buffer: A new component of working memory? *Trends in Cognitive Sciences, 4,* 417–423.

Baddeley, A. D. (2001). Is working memory still working? *American Psychologist, 56,* 851–864.

Baddeley, A. D., & Hitch, G. (1974). Working memory. In G. A. Bower (Ed.), *Recent advances in learning and motivation, Vol. 8.* New York: Academic Press.

Baell, W. K., & Wertheim, E. H. (1992). Predictors of outcome in the treatment of bulimia nervosa. *British Journal of Clinical Psychology, 31*(3), 330–332.

Bahrick, H. P., Bahrick, L. E., Bahrick, A. S., & Bahrick, P. E. (1993). Maintenance of foreign language vocabulary and the spacing effect. *Psychology Science, 4,* 316–321.

Bailey, J. M., Bobrow, D., Wolfe, M., & Mikach, S. (1995). Sexual orientation of adult sons of gay fathers. *Developmental Psychology, 31,* 124–129.

Baillargeon, R., & DeVos, J. (1991). Object permanence in young infants: Further evidence. *Child Development, 62,* 1227–1246.

Balch, P., & Ross, A. W. (1975). Predicting success in weight reduction as a function of locus of control: A uni-dimensional and multi-dimensional approach. *Journal of Consulting and Clinical Psychology, 43,* 119.

Baldwin, D. A. (2000). Interpersonal understanding fuels knowledge acquisition. *Current Directions in Psychological Science, 9,* 40–45.

Baldwin, M. W. (1992). Relational schemas and the processing of social information. *Psychological Bulletin, 112,* 461–484.

Balter, M. (2000, October 20). Celebrating the synapse. *Science, 290,* 424.

Baltes, M. M. (1995). Dependency in old age: Gains and losses. *Current Directions in Psychological Science, 4,* 14–19.

Baltes, P. B. (1987). Theoretical propositions on lifespan developmental psychology: On the dynamics between growth and decline. *Developmental Psychology, 23,* 611–626.

Baltes, P. B. (1990, November). Toward a psychology of wisdom. Invited address presented at the annual convention of the Gerontological Society of America, Boston, MA.

Baltes, P. B. (1993). The aging mind: Potential and limits. *The Gerontologist, 33,* 580–594.

Baltes, P. B., & Kliegl, R. (1992). Further testing of limits of cognitive plasticity: Negative age differences in a mnemonic skill are robust. *Developmental Psychology, 28,* 121–125.

Baltes, P. B., & Staudinger, U. M. (1993). The search for a psychology of wisdom. *Current Directions in Psychological Science, 2,* 75–80.

Bamshad, M. J., & Olson, S. E. (2003, December). Does race exist? *Scientific American, 289*(6), 78–85. [See also: Gould, 1996; Zuckerman, 1990]

Bandura, A. (1970). Modeling therapy. In W. S. Sahakian (Ed.), *Psychopathology today: Experimentation, theory and research.* Itasca, IL: Peacock.

Bandura, A. (1981). In search of pure unidirectional determinants. *Behavior Therapy, 12,* 30–40.

Bandura, A. (1986). *Social foundations of thought and action: A social cognitive theory.* Englewood Cliffs, NJ: Prentice-Hall.

Bandura, A. (1992). Exercise of personal agency through the self-efficacy mechanism. In R. Schwarzer (Ed.), *Self-efficacy: Thought control of action* (pp. 3–38). Washington, DC: Hemisphere.

Bandura, A. (1999). Social cognitive theory of personality. In L. A. Pervin & O. P. John (Eds.), *Handbook of personality: Theory and research* (2nd ed., pp. 154–196). New York: Guilford Press.

Bandura, A., Ross, D., & Ross, S. A. (1963). Imitation of film-mediated aggressive models. *Journal of Abnormal and Social Psychology, 66,* 3–11.

Bandura, A., Underwood, B., & Fromson, M. E. (1975). Disinhibition of aggression through diffusion of responsibility and dehumanization of victims. *Journal of Personality and Social Psychology, 9,* 253–269.

Banich, M. T. (1998). Integration of information between the cerebral hemispheres. *Current Directions in Psychological Science, 7,* 32–37.

Banks, M. S., & Bennet, P. J. (1988). Optical and photoreceptor immaturities limit the spatial and chromatic vision of human neonates. *Journal of the Optical Society of America, 5,* 2059–2079.

Barab, S. A., & Plucker, J. A. (2002). Smart people or smart contexts? Cognition, ability, and talent development in an age of situated approaches to knowing and learning. *Educational Psychologist, 37,* 165–182.

Barach, J. (2003). Reorganization of the brain may provide blind with superior verbal memory. Retrieved May 16, 2007, from www.bioisrael.com/upload/research/blind_research.doc.

Baranowsky, A. B. (2002). The silencing response in clinical practice: On the road to dialogue. In C. R. Figley (Ed.), *Treating compassion fatigue* (pp. 155–170). New York: Brunner-Routledge.

Barash, D. P. (2007, October 5). The targets of aggression. *The Chronicle of Higher Education,* B6–B9.

Barber, C. (2008, February/March). The medicated Americans. *Scientific American Mind, 19*(1), 44–51.

Barber, T. X. (1976). *Hypnosis: A scientific approach.* New York: Psychological Dimensions.

Barber, T. X. (1979). Suggested ("hypnotic") behavior: The trance paradigm versus an alternative paradigm. In E. Fromm & R. E. Shor (Eds.), *Hypnosis: Developments in research and new perspectives.* New York: Aldine.

Barber, T. X. (1986). Realities of stage hypnosis. In B. Zilbergeld, M. G. Edelstein, & D. L. Araoz (Eds.), *Hypnosis: Questions and answers.* New York: Norton.

Barinaga, M. (1994, July 29). To sleep, perchance to . . . learn? New studies say yes. *Science, 265,* 603–604.

Barinaga, M. (1995, December 1). Brain researchers speak a common language. *Science, 270,* 1437–1438.

Barinaga, M. (1996, January 19). Social status sculpts activity of crayfish neurons. *Science, 271,* 290–291.

Barinaga, M. (1997a, July 25). How jet-lag hormone does double duty in the brain. *Science, 277,* 480.

Barinaga, M. (1997b, June 27). New imaging methods provide a better view into the brain. *Science, 276,* 1974–1976.

Barinaga, M. (1998, April 17). Listening in on the brain. *Science, 280,* 376–377.

Barinaga, M. (1999, July 9). The mapmaking mind. *Science, 285,* 189, 191–192.

Barinaga, M. (2000, October 27). Synapses call the shots. *Science, 290,* 736–738.

Barinaga, M. (2002, February 8). How the brain's clock gets daily enlightenment. *Science, 295,* 955–957.

Barinaga, M. (2003a, January 3). Newborn neurons search for meaning. *Science, 299,* 32–34. [See also Kennedy, 2000; Matus, 2000]

Barinaga, M. (2003b, October 3). Studying the well-trained mind. *Science, 302,* 44–46.

Barker, L. M., Best, M. R., & Domjan, M. (Eds.). (1978). *Learning mechanisms in food selection.* Houston: Baylor University Press.

Barkley, R. A. (1998, September). Attention-deficit hyperactivity disorder. *Scientific American, 279*(9), 66–71.

Barlow, D. H. (1996). Health care policy, psychotherapy research, and the future of psychotherapy. *American Psychologist, 51,* 1050–1058.

Barlow, D. H. (2000). Unraveling the mysteries of anxiety and its disorders from the perspective of emotion theory. *American Psychologist, 55,* 1247–1263.

Barlow, D. H. (2001). A modern learning theory perspective on the etiology of panic disorder. *Psychological Review, 108,* 4–32.

Barlow, D. H. (2004). Psychological treatments. *American Psychologist, 59,* 869–878.

Barlow, D. H., & Durand, V. M. (2005). *Abnormal psychology: An integrative approach.* Belmont, CA: Wadsworth.

Barlow, D. H., Gorman, J. M., Shear, M. K., & Woods, S. W. (2000, May). Cognitive-behavioral therapy, imipramine, or their combination for panic disorder: A randomized controlled trial. *JAMA: Journal of the American Medical Association, 283,* 2529–2536.

Barlow, J. (2008, February 15). *Parental intervention boosts education of kids at high risk of failure.* Retrieved March 16, 2008, from http://pmr.uoregon.edu/science-and-innovation/uo-research-news/research-news-2008/february-2008/parental-intervention-boosts-education-of-kids-at-high-risk-of-failure.

Barnes, D. M. (1987). Biological issues in schizophrenia. *Science, 235,* 430–433.

Barnett, R. C., & Hyde, J. S. (2001). Women, men, work, and family: An expansionist theory. *American Psychologist, 56,* 781–796.

Barnier, A. J., & McConkey, K. M. (1998). Posthypnotic responding away from the hypnotic setting. *Psychological Science, 9,* 256–262.

Barnouw, V. (1963). *Culture and personality.* Homewood, IL: Dorsey Press.

Baron, L., & Straus, M. A. (1985). *Four theories of rape in American society: A state-level analysis.* New Haven, CT: Yale University Press.

Barron, F., & Harrington, D. M. (1981). Creativity, intelligence and personality. *Annual Review of Psychology, 32,* 439–476.

Barron, K., & Harackiewicz, J. (2001). Achievement goals and optimal motivation: Testing multiple goal models. *Journal of Personality and Social Psychology, 80,* 706–722.

Bartels, A., & Zeki, S. (2004). The neural correlates of maternal and romantic love. *NeuroImage, 22,* 419–433.

Bartoshuk, L. M. (1990, August–September). Psychophysiological insights on taste. *Science Agenda,* 12–13.

Bartoshuk, L. M. (1993). The biological basis of food perception and acceptance. *Food Quality and Preference, 4,* 21–32.

Bartoshuk, L. M., Duffy, V. B., & Miller, I. J. (1994). PCT/PROP tasting: Anatomy, psychophysics and sex effects. *Physiology and Behavior, 56,* 1165–1171.

Basbaum, A. I., Clanton, C. H., & Fields, H. L. (1976). Opiate and stimulus-produced analgesia: Functional anatomy of a medullospinal pathway. *Proceedings of the National Academy of Sciences, 73,* 4685–4688.

Basbaum, A. I., & Fields, H. L. (1984). Endogenous pain control systems: Brainstem spinal pathways and endorphin circuitry. *Annual Review of Neuroscience, 7,* 309–338.

Basbaum, A. I., & Julius, D. (2006, June). Toward better pain control. *Scientific American, 294*(6), 60–67.

Basic Behavioral Science Task Force of the National Advisory Mental Health Council. (1996). Basic behavioral science research for mental health: Family processes and social networks. *American Psychologist, 51,* 622–630.

Bass, E., & Davis, L. (1988). *The courage to heal.* New York: HarperCollins.

Batista, A. P., Buneo, C. A., Snyder, L. H., & Andersen, R. A. (1999, July 9). Reach plans in eye-centered coordinates. *Science, 285,* 257–260.

Batson, C. D. (1987). Prosocial motivation: Is it ever truly altruistic? In L. Berkowitz (Ed.), *Advances in experimental social psychology* (Vol. 20). Orlando, FL: Academic Press.

Bauer, P. J. (2002). Long-term recall memory: Behavioral and neuro-developmental changes in the first 2 years of life. *Current Directions in Psychological Science, 11,* 137–141.

Bauer, P. J., Wiebe, S. A., Carver, L. J., Waters, J. M., & Nelson, C. A. (2003). Developments in long-term explicit memory late in the first year of life: Behavioral and electrophysiological indices. *Psychological Science, 14,* 629–635.

Baum, A. (1990). Stress, intrusive imagery, and chronic distress. *Health Psychology, 9,* 653–675.

Baum, D. (2004, July 12, 19). The price of valor. *The New Yorker, 80,* 44–52.

Baum, W. M. (1994). *Understanding behaviorism: Science, behavior, and culture.* New York: HarperCollins.

Baumeister, A. A. (1987). Mental retardation: Some conceptions and dilemmas. *American Psychologist, 42,* 796–800.

Baumeister, R. F. (Ed.). (1993). *Self-esteem: The puzzle of low self-regard.* New York: Plenum.

Baumeister, R. F. (2005). The unconscious is alive and well, and friendly too. *Journal of Social & Clinical Psychology, 24,* 293–295.

Baumeister, R. F. (2007, August). *Is there anything good about men?* Invited address given at the 2007 APA convention in San Francisco, CA. Retrieved November 16, 2007, from http://www.psy.fsu.edu/~baumeistertice/goodaboutmen.htm.

Baumeister, R. F., Bratslavsky, E., Muraven, M., & Tice, D. M. (1998). Ego depletion: Is the active self a limited resource? *Journal of Personality and Social Psychology, 74,* 1252–1265.

Baumeister, R. F., Campbell, J. D., Krueger, J. I., & Vohs, K. D. (2003). Does high self-esteem cause better performance, interpersonal success, happiness, or healthier lifestyles? *Psychological Science in the Public Interest, 4,* 1–44.

Baumeister, R. F., & Leary, M. R. (1995). The need to belong: Desire for interpersonal attachments as a fundamental human motivation. *Psychological Bulletin, 117,* 427–529.

Baumeister, R. F., Smart, L., & Boden, J. M. (1996). Relation of threatened egotism to violence and aggression: The dark side of high self-esteem. *Psychological Review, 103,* 5–33.

Baumeister, R. F., Stillwell, A. M., & Wotman, S. R. (1990). Victim and perpetrator accounts of interpersonal conflict: Autobiographical narratives about anger. *Journal of Personality and Social Psychology, 59,* 994–1005.

Baumrind, D. (1967). Child care practices anteceding three patterns of preschool behavior. *Genetic Psychology Monographs, 75,* 43–88.

Baumrind, D. (1971). Current patterns of parental authority. *Developmental Psychology Monograph, 4*(1, Part 2).

Baumrind, D. (1985). Research using intentional deception: Ethical issues revisited. *American Psychologist, 40,* 165–174.

Baynes, K., Eliassen, J. C., Lutsep, H. L., & Gazzaniga, M. S. (1998). Modular organization of cognitive systems masked by interhemispheric integration. *Science, 280,* 902–905.

Beall, A. E., & Sternberg, R. J. (1995). The social construction of love. *Journal of Social and Personal Relationships, 12*(3), 417–438.

Beaman, A. L., Barnes, P. J., Klentz, B., & McQuirk, B. (1978). Increasing helping rates through information dissemination: Teaching pays. *Personality and Social Psychology Bulletin, 4,* 406–411.

Beardsley, T. (1996, July). Waking up. *Scientific American, 14,* 18.

Beardsley, T. (1997a, August). The machinery of thought. *Scientific American, 277,* 78–83.

Beardsley, T. (1997b, March). Memories are made of . . . *Scientific American*, 32–33.

Beasley, M., Thompson, T., & Davidson, J. (2003). Resilience in response to life stress: The effects of coping style and cognitive hardiness. *Personality and Individual Differences, 34*, 77–95.

Bechara, A., Damasio, H., Tranel, D., & Damasio, A. R. (1997, February 28). Deciding advantageously before knowing the advantageous strategy. *Science, 275*, 1293–1295.

Bechara, A., Tranel, D., Damasio, H., Adolphs, R., Rockland, C., & Damasio, A. R. (1995, August 25). Double dissociation of conditioning and declarative knowledge relative to the amygdala and hippocampus in humans. *Science, 269*, 1115–1118.

Beck, A., Kline, S., & Greenfeld, L. (1988). *Survey of youth in custody, 1987*. Washington, DC: Bureau of Justice Statistics.

Beck, A. T. (1976). *Cognitive therapy and emotional disorders*. New York: International Universities Press.

Beck, A. T. (2005). The current state of cognitive therapy: A 40-year retrospective. *Archives of General Psychiatry, 62*, 953–959.

Beck, A. T., Rush, A. J., Shaw, B. F., & Emery, G. (1979). *Cognitive therapy of depression*. New York: Guilford Press.

Beck, M. R., Angelone, B. L., & Levin, D. T. (2004). Knowledge about the probability of change affects change detection performance. *Journal of Experimental Psychology: Human Perception and Performance, 30*, 778–791.

Becker, D. V., Kenrick, D. T., Neuberg, S. L., Blackwell, K. C.; Smith, D. M. (2007). The confounded nature of angry men and happy women. *Journal of Personality and Social Psychology, 92*, 179–190.

Bédard, J., & Chi, M. T. H. (1992). Expertise. *Current Directions in Psychological Science, 1*, 135–139.

Bee, H. (1994). *Lifespan development*. New York: HarperCollins.

Beeman, M. J., & Chiarello, C. (1998). Complementary right- and left-hemisphere language comprehension. *Current Directions in Psychological Science, 7*, 2–8.

Begley, S. (1995, November 20). Lights of madness. *Newsweek*, 76–77.

Behrmann, M. (2000). The mind's eye mapped onto the brain's matter. *Current Directions in Psychological Science, 9*, 50–54.

Beigel, A., & Berren, M. R. (1985). Human-induced disasters. *Psychiatric Annals, 15*, 143–150.

Beilin, H. (1992). Piaget's enduring contribution to developmental psychology. *Developmental Psychology, 28*, 191–204.

Bell, A. P., Weinberg, M. S., & Hammersmith, S. K. (1981). *Sexual preference*. Bloomington: Indiana University Press.

Bem, D. J. (1996). Exotic becomes erotic: A developmental theory of sexual orientation. *Psychological Review, 103*, 320–335.

Bem, D. J. (2001). Interplay of theory and politics in explaining the enigma of sexual orientation. Address given at the annual convention of the American Psychological Association in San Francisco, CA.

Bem, D. J., & Allen, A. (1974). On predicting some of the people some of the time: The search for cross-situational consistencies in behavior. *Psychological Review, 81*(6), 506–520.

Benassi, V. A., Sweeney, P. D., & Dufour, C. L. (1988). Is there a relation between locus of control orientation and depression? *Journal of Abnormal Psychology, 97*, 357–367.

Benedetti, F., Mayberg, H. S., Wager, T. D., Stohler, C. S., & Zubieta, J. (2005, November 9). Neurobiological mechanisms of the placebo effect. *The Journal of Neuroscience, 25*, 10390–10402.

Benedict, R. (1934). *Patterns of culture*. Boston: Houghton Mifflin.

Benjamin, L. T., Jr., & Nielsen-Gammon, E. (1999). B. F. Skinner and psychotechnology: The case of the heir conditioner. *Review of General Psychology, 3*, 155–167.

Bennett, K. K., & Elliott, M. (2002). Explanatory style and health: Mechanisms linking pessimism to illness. *Journal of Applied Social Psychology, 32*, 1508–1526.

Benson, E. (2002, October). Pheromones, in context. *Monitor on Psychology, 33*(9), 46–49. [See also: Azar, 1998b; Holden, 1996b]

Benson, E. (2003a, February) Intelligent intelligence testing. *Monitor on Psychology, 34*(2), 48–51.

Benson, E. (2003b, July/August). Rehabilitate or punish? *Monitor on Psychology, 34*(7), 46–47.

Benson, E. (2003c, February). Sleep apnea linked to brain damage. *Monitor on Psychology, 34*(2), 15.

Benson, H. (1975). *The relaxation response*. New York: Morrow.

Berglas, S. (2001). *Reclaiming the fire: How successful people overcome burnout*. New York: Random House.

Berk, L. E. (2004). *Development through the lifespan* (4th ed.). Boston: Allyn & Bacon.

Berk, L. E. (2007). *Development through the lifespan*, (4th ed.) Boston: Allyn & Bacon.

Berkman, L. F., & Syme, S. L. (1979). Social networks, host resistance, and mortality: A nine-year follow-up study of Alameda County residents. *American Journal of Epidemiology, 109*, 186–204.

Berlyne, D. E. (1960). *Conflict, arousal, and curiosity*. New York: McGraw-Hill.

Berman, B. (2003, September). Fooled by the full moon. *Discover, 24*(9), 30.

Berman, J. S., & Norton, N. C. (1985). Does professional training make a therapist more effective? *Psychological Bulletin, 98*, 401–407.

Berndt, T. J. (1992). Friendship and friends' influence in adolescence. *Current Directions in Psychological Science, 1*, 156–159.

Berns, G. S., et al. (2005). Neurobiological correlates of social conformity and independence during mental rotation. *Biological Psychiatry, 58*, 245–253. [See also: www.nytimes.com/2005/06/28/science/28brai.html.]

Bernstein, I. L. (1988). What does learning have to do with weight loss and cancer? *Proceedings of the Science and Public Policy Seminar of the Federation of Behavioral, Psychological and Cognitive Sciences*. Washington, DC.

Bernstein, I. L. (1990). Salt preference and development. *Developmental Psychology, 26*, 552–554.

Bernstein, I. L. (1991). Aversion conditioning in response to cancer and cancer treatment. *Clinical Psychology Review, 11*, 185–191.

Berntsen, D., Rubin, D. C. (2007). When a trauma becomes a key to identity: Enhanced integration of trauma memories predicts posttraumatic stress disorder symptoms. *Applied Cognitive Psychology, 21*, 417–431.

Berry, J. (1992). Cree conceptions of cognitive competence. *International Journal of Psychology, 27*, 73–88.

Berry, J. W., Poortinga, Y. H., Segall, M. H., & Dasen, P. R. (1992). *Cross-cultural psychology: Research and applications*. New York: Cambridge University Press.

Berscheid, E. (1988). Some comments on love's anatomy: Or, Whatever happened to old-fashioned lust? In R. J. Sternberg & M. L. Barnes (Eds.), *The psychology of love*. New Haven, CT: Yale University Press.

Berscheid, E. (1999). The greening of relationship science. *American Psychologist, 54*, 260–266.

Beutler, L. E., Brown, M. T., Crothers, L., Booker, K., & Seabrook, M. K. (1996). The dilemma of factitious demographic distinctions in psychological research. *Journal of Consulting and Clinical Psychology, 64*, 892–902.

Beutler, L. E., & Machado, P. P. (1992). Research on psychotherapy. In M. R. Rosenzweig (Ed.), *International psychological science: Progress, problems, and prospects* (pp. 227–252). Washington, DC: American Psychological Association.

Bevins, R. A. (2001). Novelty seeking and reward: Implications for the study of high-risk behaviors. *Current Directions in Psychological Science, 10*, 189–193.

Bhattacharjee, Y. (2008, January 25). Shell shock revisited: Solving the puzzle of blast trauma. *Science, 319*, 406–408.

Bianchi, S. M., & Spain, D. (1996). Women, work, and family in America. *Population Bulletin, 51*, 1–48.

Bicklen, D. (1990). Communication unbound: Autism and praxis. *Harvard Educational Review, 60*(3), 291–314.

Biederman, I. (1989). Higher-level vision. In D. N. Osherson, H. Sasnik, S. Kosslyn, K. Hollerbach, E. Smith, & N. Block (Eds.), *An invitation to cognitive science*. Cambridge, MA: MIT Press.

Biehl, M., Matsumoto, D., Ekman, P., Hearn, V., Heider, K., Kudoh, T., & Ton, V. (1997). Matsumoto and Ekman's Japanese and Caucasian facial expressions of emotion (JACFEE): Reliability data and cross-national differences. *Journal of Nonverbal Behavior, 21*, 3–21. [See also: Ekman et al., 1987; Izard, 1994]

Bilkey, D. K. (2004, August 27). In the place space. *Science, 305*, 1245–1246.

Billings, A. G., & Moos, R. H. (1985). Life stressors and social resources affect posttreatment outcomes among depressed patients. *Journal of Abnormal Psychology, 94*, 140–153.

Binet, A. (1911). *Les idées modernes sur les enfants*. Paris: Flammarion.

Binitie, A. (1975). A factor-analytical study of depression across cultures (African and European). *British Journal of Psychiatry, 127*, 559–563.

Bink, M. L., & Marsh, R. L. (2000). Cognitive regularities in creative activity. *Review of General Psychology, 4*, 59–78.

Bird, S. J. (2005). The ethics of using animals in research. Case Western Reserve University. Retrieved April 14, 2007, from http://onlineethics.org/reseth/mod/animalres.html.

Birenbaum, M., & Montag, I. (1986). On the location of the sensation seeking construct in the personality domain. *Multivariate Behavioral Research, 21*, 357–373.

Bjork, R. (1991, November). How do you improve human performance? *APS Observer*, 13–15.

Bjork, R. A. (2000). Creating desirable difficulties for the learner. Implications for theory and practice. Address given at the American Psychological Society's annual convention, Miami Beach, FL.

Bjork, R. A., & Richardson-Klavehn, A. (1989). On the puzzling relationship between environmental context and human memory. In C. Izawa (Ed.), *Current issues in cognitive processes: The Tulane-Floweree symposium on cognition*. Hillsdale, NJ: Erlbaum.

Bjorklund, D. F., & Shackelford, T. K. (1999). Differences in parental investment contribute to important differences between men and women. *Current Directions in Psychological Science, 8*, 86–89.

Blakeslee, S. (2005, November 22). This is your brain under hypnosis. *New York Times*. Retrieved December 4, 2007, from www.nytimes.com/2005/11/22/science/22hypno.html [See also: Kirsch & Lynn, 1995; Woody & Sadler, 1998]

Blanchard, R., & Bogaert, A. F. (1996). Homosexuality in men and number of older brothers. *American Journal of Psychiatry, 153*, 27–31.

Blaney, P. H. (1986). Affect and memory: A review. *Psychological Bulletin, 99*, 229–246.

Blass, E. M. (1990). Suckling: Determinants, changes, mechanisms, and lasting impressions. *Developmental Psychology, 26*, 520–533.

Blass, T. (1996). Experimental invention and controversy: The life and work of Stanley Milgram. *The General Psychologist, 32*, 47–55.

Blass, T. (2004). *The man who shocked the world: The life and legacy of Stanley Milgram*. New York: Basic Books.

Blatt, S. J., Sanislow, C. A. III, & Pilkonis, P. A. (1996). Characteristics of effective therapists: Further analyses of data from the National Institute of Mental Health treatment of depression collaborative research program. *Journal of Consulting and Clinical Psychology, 64,* 1276–1284.

Bloom, R. W. (2002). On media violence: Whose facts? Whose misinformation? *American Psychologist, 57,* 447–448.

Blum, D. (2002). *Love at Goon Park: Harry Harlow and the science of affection.* New York: Perseus Publishing.

Boahen, K. (2005, May). Neuromorphic microchips. *Scientific American, 292*(5), 56–63.

Bocchiaro, P., & Zimbardo, P. G. (2008). Deciding to resist unjust authority. (Submitted for publication).

Bodmer, W. F., & Cavalli-Sforza, L. L. (1970, October). Intelligence and race. *Scientific American,* 19–29.

Bogaert, A. F. (2006, July 11). Biological versus non-biological older brothers and men's sexual orientation. *Proceedings of the National Academy of Sciences, 103,* 10,771–10,774.

Bolger, M. A. (1997). An exploration of college student stress. *Dissertation Abstracts International, 58,* 5-A, 1597.

Bolger, N., DeLongis, A., Kessler, R. C., & Schilling, E. A. (1989). Effects of daily stress on negative mood. *Journal of Personality and Social Psychology, 57,* 808–818.

Bonanno, G. A., Papa, A., Lalande, K., Westphal, M., & Coifman, K. (2004). The importance of being flexible: The ability to both enhance and suppress emotional experession predicts long-term adjustment. *Psychological Science, 15,* 482–487.

Bond, C. F. Jr., & Atoum, A. O. (2000). International deception. *Personality and Social Psychology Bulletin, 26,* 385–395.

Bond, M. H., Nakazato, H. S., & Shiraishi, D. (1975). Universality and distinctiveness in dimensions of Japanese person perception. *Journal of Cross-Cultural Psychology, 6,* 346–355.

Boomsma, D., Anokhin, A., & de Geus, E. (1997, August). Genetics of electrophysiology: Linking genes, brain, and behavior. *Current Directions in Psychological Science, 6,* 106–110.

Booth, A., Johnson, D. R., Granger, D. A., Crouter, A. C., & McHale, S. (2003). Testosterone and child and adolescent adjustment: The moderating role of parent–child relationships. *Developmental Psychology, 39,* 85–98.

Bornstein, R. F. (1989). Exposure and affect: Overview and meta-analysis of research, 1968–1987. *Psychological Bulletin, 106,* 265–289.

Bornstein, R. F. (2001). The impending death of psychoanalysis. *Psychoanalytic Psychology, 18,* 3–20. [See also: Bruner, 1992; Erdelyi, 1992; Greenwald, 1992; Jacoby et al., 1992; Kihlstrom et al., 1992; Loftus & Klinger, 1992]

Borod, C., Koff, E., Lorch, M. P., Nicholas, M., & Welkowitz, J. (1988). Emotional and non-emotional facial behavior in patients with unilateral brain damage. *Journal of Neurological and Neurosurgical Psychiatry, 5,* 826–832.

Bostwick, J. M., & Pankratz, V. S. (2000). Affective disorders and suicide risk: A reexamination. *American Journal of Psychiatry, 157,* 1925–1932.

Bosveld, J. (2007, December). Sleeping like a hunter-gatherer. *Discover, 28*(12), 66–67.

Botvinick, M. (2004, August 6). Probing the neural basis of body ownership. *Science, 305,* 782–783.

Bouchard, T. J. Jr. (1994, June 17). Genes, environment, and personality. *Science, 264,* 1700–1701.

Bouchard, T. J., Lykken, D. T., McGue, M., Segal, N. L., & Tellegen, A. (1990). Sources of human psychological differences: The Minnesota study of twins reared apart. *Science, 250,* 223–228.

Bourguignon, E. (1979). *Psychological anthropology: An introduction to human nature and cultural differences.* New York: Holt, Rinehart and Winston.

Bowden, C. L., Calabrese, J. R., McElroy, S. L., Gyulai, L. Wassef, A., Petty, F., Pope, H. G. Jr., Chou, J. C., Keck, P. E. Jr., Rhodes, L. J., Swann, A. C., Hirschfeld, R. M., & Wozniak, P. J. (2000). A randomized, placebo-controlled 12-month trial of divalproex and lithium in treatment of outpatients with bipolar I disorder. Divalproex Maintenance Study Group. *Archives of General Psychiatry, 57,* 481–489.

Bower, B. (1992, August 22). Genetic clues to female homosexuality. *Science News, 142,* 117.

Bower, B. (1995a, December 23 & 30). Trauma disorder high, new survey finds. *Science News, 148,* 422.

Bower, B. (1995b, March 4). Virus may trigger some mood disorders. *Science News, 147,* 132.

Bower, B. (1996, April 27). Mom–child relations withstand day care. *Science News, 149,* 261.

Bower, B. (1997a, October 18). My culture, my self: Western notions of the mind may not translate to other cultures. *Science News, 152,* 248–249.

Bower, B. (1997b, August 2). Preschoolers get grip on hidden emotions. *Science News, 152,* 70.

Bower, B. (1997c, August 9). The ties that bond: Adult romantic and sexual styles may grow out of parent–child affiliations. *Science News, 152,* 94–95.

Bower, B. (1998a, February 21). All fired up: Perception may dance to the beat of collective neuronal rhythms. *Science News, 153,* 120–121.

Bower, B. (1998b, November 28). Dr. Freud goes to Washington. *Science News, 154,* 347–349.

Bower, B. (1998c, April 25). The name game: Young kids grasp new words with intriguing dexterity. *Science News, 153,* 268–269.

Bower, B. (1998d, June 20). Psychology's tangled web. *Science News, 153,* 394–395.

Bower, B. (1999, March 6). Learning may unify distant brain regions. *Science News, 155,* 149.

Bower, B. (2000a, January 22). Cultures of reason: Thinking styles may take Eastern and Western routes. *Science News, 157,* 56–58.

Bower, B. (2000b, September, 30). Memory echoes in brain's sensory terrain. *Science News, 158,* 213.

Bower, B. (2003, April 19). Words get in the way: Talk is cheap, but it can tax your memory. *Science News, 163,* 250–251. [See also Dodson et al., 1997]

Bower, B. (2004a, July 17). Neuroscience: Female brains know how to fold 'em. *Science News, 166*(3), 46.

Bower, B. (2004b, July 24). Suicide watch: Antidepressants get large-scale inspection. *Science News, 166,* 51.

Bower, B. (2005a, November 5). Questions on the couch: Researchers spar over how best to evaluate psychotherapy. *Science News, 168,* 299–301.

Bower, B. (2005b, March 19). Schizophrenia syncs fast: Disconnected brain may lie at heart of disorder. *Science News, 167,* 180.

Bower, B. (2006a, July 1). Gay males' sibling link: Men's homosexuality tied to having older brothers. *Science News, 170*(1), 3.

Bower, B. (2006b, March 18). Prescription for controversy: Medications for depressed kids spark scientific dispute. *Science News, 169,* 168–172.

Bower, B. (2006c, February 11). Self-serve brains: Personal identity veers to the right hemisphere. *Science News, 169,* 90–92. [See also: Botvinick, 2004; Zimmer, 2005]

Bower, B. (2007, July 28). Antidepressants trim suicide tries. *Science News, 172,* 61. [See also: Gibbons et al., 2007; Simon & Savarino, 2007]

Bower, G. H. (1972). A selective review of organizational factors in memory. In E. Tulving & W. Donaldson (Eds.), *Organization of memory.* New York: Academic Press.

Bower, G. H. (1981). Mood and memory. *American Psychologist, 36,* 129–148.

Bower, J. M., & Parsons, L. M. (2003, August). Rethinking the "lesser brain." *Scientific American,* 50–57.

Bower, T. G. R. (1971, October). The object in the world of the infant. *Scientific American, 225*(4), 30–39.

Bowers, K. S. (1983). *Hypnosis for the seriously curious* (2nd ed.) New York: Norton.

Bowlby, J. (1969). *Attachment and loss: Vol. 1. Attachment.* New York: Basic Books.

Bowlby, J. (1973). *Attachment and loss: Vol. 2. Separation, anxiety and anger.* London: Hogarth.

Bowles, A. (2004). Beck in action: Grawemeyer-winning psychiatrist influential in psychology. *APS Observer, 17*(3), 7–8.

Bradbury, J. (2001, May 19). Teasing out the genetics of bipolar disorder. *Lancet, 357,* 1596.

Bradley, G. W. (1978). Self-serving biases in the attribution process: A re-examination of the fact or fiction question. *Journal of Personality and Social Psychology, 35,* 56–71.

Bradshaw, G. (1992). The airplane and the logic of invention. In R. N. Giere (Ed.). *Minnesota studies in the philosophy of science* (pp. 2239–2250). Minneapolis: University of Minnesota Press.

Brådvik, L., & Berglund, M. (2006). Long-term treatment and suicidal behavior in severe depression: ECT and antidepressant pharmacotherapy may have different effects on the occurrence and seriousness of suicide attempts. *Depression and Anxiety, 23,* 34–41.

Braine, M. D. S. (1976). Children's first word combinations. *Monographs of the Society for Research in Child Development, 41* (Serial No. 164).

Brannon, L. (2008). *Gender: Psychological perspectives* (5th ed.). Boston: Allyn & Bacon.

Bransford, J., Sherwood, R., Vye, N., & Rieser, J. (1986). Teaching thinking and problem solving: Research foundations. *American Psychologist, 41,* 1078–1089.

Bransford, J. D., & Franks, J. J. (1971). The abstraction of linguistic ideas. *Cognitive Psychology, 2,* 331–350.

Braun, K. A., Ellis, R., & Loftus, E. F. (2002). Make my memory: How advertising can change our memories of the past. *Psychology and Marketing, 19,* 1–23.

Breckenridge, J. N., & Zimbardo, P. G. (2006). The strategy of terrorism and the psychology of mass-mediated fear. In B. Bongar, L. M. Brown, L. Beutler, J. N. Breckenridge, & P. G. Zimbardo (Eds.), *Psychology and Terrorism* (pp. 116–133). New York: Oxford University Press.

Breggin, P. R. (1979). *Electroshock: Its brain-disabling effects.* New York: Springer.

Breggin, P. R. (1991). *Toxic psychiatry.* New York: St. Martin's Press.

Breggin, P. R., & Breggin, G. R. (1994). *Talking back to Prozac.* New York: St. Martin's Press.

Brehm, S. S. (1992). *Intimate relationships* (2nd ed.). Boston: McGraw-Hill.

Brehm, S. S., Miller, R., Perlman, D., & Campbell, S. M. (2002). *Intimate relationships* (3rd ed.). New York: McGraw-Hill.

Breier, J. I., Simos, P. G., Fletcher, J. M., Castillo, E. M., Zhang, W., & Papanicolaou, A. C. (2003). Abnormal activation of temporoparietal language areas during phonetic analysis in children with dyslexia. *Neuropsychology, 17,* 610–621.

Breland, K., & Breland, M. (1961). The misbehavior of organisms. *American Psychologist, 16,* 681–684.

Brett, A. S., Phillips, M., & Beary, J. F. III. (1986, March 8). Predictive power of the polygraph: Can the "lie detector" really detect liars? *Lancet, 1*(8480), 544–547.

Brewer, C. L. (1991). Perspectives on John B. Watson. In G. A. Kimble, M. Wertheimer, & C. L. White (Eds.), *Portraits of pioneers in psychology* (pp. 170–186). Washington, DC: American Psychological Association.

Brewer, M. B., Dull, V., and Lui, L. (1981). Perceptions of the elderly: Stereotypes and prototypes. *Journal of Personality and Social Psychology, 41,* 656–670.

Bridge, J. A., Satish, I., Salary, C. B., Barbe, R. P., Birmaher, B., Pincus, H. A., Ren, L., & Brent, D. A. (2007, April 18). Clinical response and risk for reported suicidal ideation and suicide attempts in pediatric antidepressant treatment: A meta-analysis of randomized controlled trials. *JAMA: Journal of the American Medical Association, 297,* 1683–1696.

Brigham, J. C. (1980). Limiting conditions of the "physical attractiveness stereotype": Attributions about divorce. *Journal of Research in Personality, 14,* 365–375.

Brislin, R. (1974). The Ponzo illusion: Additional cues, age, orientation, and culture. *Journal of Cross-Cultural Psychology, 5,* 139–161.

Brislin, R. (1993). *Understanding culture's influence on behavior.* Fort Worth, TX: Harcourt Brace Jovanovich.

Brislin, R. W. (1981). *Cross-cultural encounters: Face-to-face interaction.* Boston: Allyn & Bacon.

Broadwell, S. D., & Light, K. C. (1999). Family support and cardiovascular responses in married couples during conflict and other interactions. *International Journal of Behavioral Medicine, 6,* 40–63.

Broman, S. H., Nichols, P. I., & Kennedy, W. A. (1975). *Preschool IQ: Prenatal and early developmental correlates.* Hillsdale, NJ: Erlbaum.

Bronfenbrenner, U., & Ceci, S. J. (1994). Nature–nurture reconceptualized in developmental perspective: A bioecological model. *Psychological Review, 101,* 568–586.

Bronheim, S. (2000, January/February). The impact of the Human Genome Project on the science and practice of psychology. *Psychological Science Agenda, 13*(1), 12.

Brookhart, S. (2001). Persuasion and the "poison parasite." *APS Observer, 14*(8), 7.

Brooks, R., & Goldstein, S. (2004). *The power of resilience: Achieving balance, confidence, and personal strength in your life.* New York: Contemporary Books.

Brown, A. M. (1990). Human universals. Unpublished manuscript, University of California, Santa Barbara.

Brown, B. (1999). Optimizing expression of the common human genome for child development. *Current Directions in Psychological Science, 8,* 37–41.

Brown, C. (2003, October). The stubborn scientist who unraveled a mystery of the night. *Smithsonian,* 92–99.

Brown, J. D. (1991). Accuracy and bias in self-knowledge. In C. R. Snyder & D. F. Forsyth (Eds.), *Handbook of social and clinical psychology: The health perspective.* New York: Pergamon.

Brown, J. L., & Pollitt, E. (1996, February). Malnutrition, poverty and intellectual development. *Scientific American, 274*(2), 38–43.

Brown, K. (2003a, March 14). The medication merry-go-round. *Science, 299,* 1646–1649.

Brown, K. (2003b, July 11). New attention to ADHD genes. *Science, 301,* 160–161.

Brown, R., & Kulik, J. (1977). Flashbulb memories. *Cognition, 5,* 73–99.

Brown, R., & McNeill, D. (1966). The "tip of the tongue" phenomenon. *Journal of Verbal Learning and Verbal Behavior, 5,* 325–337.

Brown, S. L., Nesse, R. M., Vinokur, A. D., & Smith, D. M. (2003). Providing social support may be more beneficial than receiving it: Results from a prospective study of mortality. *Psychological Science, 14,* 320–327.

Brown, W. A. (1998, January). The placebo effect. *Scientific American,* 90–95.

Bruce, D. (1991). Integrations of Lashley. In G. A. Kimble, M. Wertheimer, & C. L. White (Eds.), *Portraits of pioneers in psychology* (pp. 306–323). Washington, DC: American Psychological Association.

Bruch, H. (1978). *The golden cage: The enigma of anorexia nervosa.* Cambridge, MA: Harvard University Press.

Bruck, M., & Ceci, S. (1997). The suggestibility of young children. *Current Directions in Psychological Science, 6,* 75–79.

Bruck, M., & Ceci, S. (2004). Forensic developmental psychology: Unveiling four common misconceptions. *Current Directions in Psychological Science, 13,* 229–232. [See also: Loftus, 2004; Neimark, 2004]

Bruin, J. E., Kellenberger, L. D., Gerstein, H. C., Morrison, K. M., & Holloway, A C. (2007). Fetal and neonatal nicotine exposure and postnatal glucose homeostasis: identifying critical windows of exposure. *Journal of Endocrinology, 194,* 171–178.

Bruner, J. (1992). Another look at new look 1. *American Psychologist, 47,* 780–783.

Bruner, J. S., Olver, R. R., & Greenfield, P. M. (1966). *Studies in cognitive growth.* New York: Wiley.

Brunner, H. G., Nelen, M., Breakefield, X. O., Ropers, H. H., & van Oost, B. A. (1993). Abnormal behavior associated with a point mutation in the structural gene for monoamine oxidase A. *Science, 262,* 578.

Büchel, C., Coull, J. T., & Friston, K. J. (1999). The predictive value of changes in effective connectivity for human learning. *Science, 283,* 1538–1541. [See also: Bower, 1999]

Buck, L., & Axel, R. (1991). A novel multigene family may encode odorant receptors: A molecular basis for odor recognition. *Cell, 65,* 175–187.

Buhrmester, D. (1996). Need fulfillment, interpersonal competence, and the developmental contexts of early adolescent friendship. In W. M. Bukowski, A. F. Newcomb, & W. W. Hartup (Eds.), *The company they keep: Friendship during childhood and adolescence* (pp. 158–185). New York: Cambridge University Press.

Buie, J. (1988, July). "Control" studies bode better health in aging. *APA Monitor,* 20.

Bullock, T. H., Bennett, M. V. L., Johnston, D., Josephson, R., Marder, E., & Fields, R. D. (2005, November 4). The neuron doctrine, redux. *Science, 310,* 791–793.

Bureau of Justice Statistics. (2007). *Corrections statistics.* Retrieved July, 2007, from www.ojp.usdoj.gov/bjs/correct.htm.

Burghardt, G. M. (2006). *The genesis of animal play: Testing the limits.* Cambridge, MA: MIT Press.

Bushman, B. J., & Anderson, C. A. (2001). Media violence and the American public: Scientific facts versus media misinformation. *American Psychologist, 56,* 477–489.

Buss, D. M. (2000). The evolution of happiness. *American Psychologist, 55,* 15–23.

Buss, D. M. (2001). Human mating strategies and human nature. Address given at the annual convention of the American Psychological Association, San Francisco, CA.

Buss, D. M. (2004). *Evolutionary psychology: The new science of the mind* (2nd ed.). Boston: Allyn & Bacon.

Buss, D. M. (2008). *Evolutionary psychology: The new science of the mind* (3rd ed.). Boston: Allyn & Bacon. [See also: Archer, 1996; Buss & Schmitt, 1993]

Buss, D. M., Haselton, M. G., Shackelford, T. K., Bleske, A. L., & Wakefield, J. C. (1998). Adaptations, exaptations, and spandrels. *American Psychologist, 53,* 533–548.

Buss, D. M., & Schmitt, D. P. (1993). Sexual strategies theory: An evolutionary perspective on human mating. *Psychological Review, 100,* 204–232.

Bussey, K., & Bandura, A. (1999). Social cognitive theory of gender development and differentiation. *Psychological Review, 106,* 676–713.

Butler, A. C., Chapman, J. E., Forman, E. M. & Beck, A. T. (2006). The empirical status of cognitive-behavioral therapy: A review of meta-analyses. *Clinical Psychology Review, 26,* 17–31.

Buzsáki, G. (2006). *Rhythms of the brain.* Oxford, U.K.: Oxford University Press.

Butcher, J. N., Graham, J. R., Williams, C. L., & Ben-Porath, Y. (1989). *Development and use of the MMPI-2 content scales.* Minneapolis: University of Minnesota Press.

Butcher, J. N., Mineka, S., & Hooley, J. M. (2008). *Abnormal psychology: Core concepts.* Boston, MA: Allyn & Bacon.

Butcher, J. N., & Williams, C. L. (1992). *Essentials of MMPI-2 and MMPI-A interpretation.* Minneapolis: University of Minnesota Press.

Button, T. M. M., Thapar, A., & McGuffin, P. (2005). Relationship between antisocial behavior, attention-deficit hyperactivity disorder, and maternal prenatal smoking. *British Journal of Psychiatry, 187,* 155–160.

Byne, W. (1995). The biological evidence challenged. *Scientific American, 270*(5), 50–55.

Byrne, D. (1969). Attitudes and attraction. In L. Berkowitz (Ed.), *Advances in experimental social psychology (Vol. 4).* New York: Academic Press.

Cabay, M. (1994). A controlled evaluation of facilitated communication using open-ended and fill-in questions. *Journal of Autism and Developmental Disorders, 24*(4), 517–527.

Cabeza, R. (2002). Hemispheric asymmetry reduction in older adults: The HAROLD model. *Psychology & Aging, 17*(1), 85–100.

Cacioppo, J. T., & Brentson, G. G. (2005). *Essays in neuroscience.* Cambridge, MA: MIT Press.

Cahill, L., Prins, B., Weber, M., & McGaugh, J. L. (1994). b-Adrenergic activation and memory for emotional events. *Nature, 371,* 702–704.

Cain, C. K., Blouin, A. M., & Barad, M. (2003). Temporally massed CS presentations generate more fear extinction than spaced presentations. *Journal of Experimental Psychology: Animal Behavior Processes, 29,* 323–333.

Caldwell, M. (1995, June). Kernel of fear. *Discover, 16,* 96–102.

Calev, A., Nigal, D., Shapira, B., Tubi, N., Chazan, S., Ben-Yehuda, Y., Kugelmass, S., & Lerer, B. (1991). Early and long-term effects of electroconvulsive therapy and depression on memory and other cognitive functions. *Journal of Nervous and Mental Disorders, 179,* 526–533.

Calkins, M. W. (1906). A reconciliation between structural and functional psychology. *Psychological Review, 13,* 61–81. Archived at the Classics in the History of Psychology site: http://psychclassics.yorku.ca/Calkins/reconciliation.htm.

Calkins, M. W. (1930). Autobiography of Mary Whiton Calkins. In C. Murchison (Ed.), *History of psychology in autobiography (Vol. 1),* pp. 31–61. Archived at the Classics in the History of Psychology site: http://psychclassics.yorku.ca/Calkins/murchison.htm.

Callaghan, E., Rochat, P., Lillard, A., Claux, M. L., Odden, H., Itakura, S., Tapanya, S., & Singh, S. (2005). Synchrony in the onset of mental-state reasoning: Evidence from five futures. *Psychological Science, 16,* 378–384.

Callahan, J. (1997, May/June). Hypnosis: Trick or treatment? *Health, 11*(1), 52–55. [See also: Miller & Bowers, 1993; Orne, 1980]

Callaway, C. W. (1987). Obesity. *Public Health Reports Supplement, 102,* 26–29.

Calvert, J. D. (1988). Physical attractiveness: A review and reevaluation of its role in social skill research. *Behavioral Assessment, 10,* 29–42.

Camara, W. J., & Schneider, D. L. (1994). Integrity tests: Facts and unresolved issues. *American Psychologist, 49,* 112–119.

Campbell, S. S., & Murphy, P. J. (1998, January 16). Extraocular circadian phototransduction in humans. *Science, 279,* 396–399.

Campfield, L. A., Smith, F. J., & Burn, P. (1998, May 29). Strategies and potential molecular targets for obesity treatment. *Science, 280,* 1383–1387.

Campos, J. J., Barrett, K. C., Lamb, M. E., Goldsmith, H. H., & Stenberg, C. (1983). *Socioemotional development (Vol. 2).* New York: Wiley.

Canli, T., Sivers, H., Whitfield, S. L., Gotlib, I. H., & Gabreli, J. D. E. (2002, June 21). Amygdala response to happy faces as a function of extraversion. *Science, 296,* 2191.

Cann, A., Calhoun, L. G., Selby, J. W., & Kin, H. E. (Eds.). (1981). Rape. *Journal of Social Issues, 37* (Whole No. 4).

Cannon, W. B. (1914). The interrelations of emotions as suggested by recent physiological researchers. *American Journal of Psychology, 25,* 256.

Caplow, T. (1982). *Middletown families: Fifty years of change and continuity.* Minneapolis: University of Minnesota Press.

Caporeal, L. R. (1976). Ergotism: The Satan loosed in Salem? *Science, 192,* 21–26.

Capps, J. G., & Ryan, R. (2005). It's not just polygraph anymore. *APA Online: Psychological Science Agenda.* Retrieved December 21, 2007, from www.apa.org/science/psa/polygraph_prnt.html.

Caprara, G. V., Barbaranelli, C., Borgoni, L., & Perugini, M. (1993). The Big Five Questionnaire: A new questionnaire for the measurement of the five-factor model. *Personality and Individual Differences, 15,* 281–288.

Carey, S. (1978). The child as word learner. In M. Halle, J. Bresnan, & G. A. Miller (Eds.), *Linguistic theory and psychological reality* (pp. 265–293). Cambridge, MA: MIT Press.

Carlsmith, K.M. (2006). The roles of retribution and utility in determining punishment. *Journal of Experimental Social Psychology, 42,* 437–451.

Carlson, L. E., Speca, M., Faris, P., & Patel, K.D. (2007). One year pre-post intervention follow-up of psychological, immune, endocrine and blood pressure outcomes of mindfulness-based stress reduction (MBSR) in breast and prostate cancer outpatients. *Brain, Behavior, and Immunity, 21,* 1038–1049.

Carlson, N. R. (2007). *Physiology of behavior* (9th ed.). Boston: Allyn & Bacon.

Carlsson, A. (1978). Antipsychotic drugs, neurotransmitters, and schizophrenia. *American Journal of Psychiatry, 135,* 164–173.

Carmichael, L. (1970). The onset and early development of behavior. In P. H. Mussen (Ed.), *Carmichael's manual of child psychology* (3rd ed., Vol. 1). New York: Wiley.

Carnagey, N. L., Anderson, C. A., & Bushman, B. J. (2007). The effect of video game violence on physiological desensitization to real-life violence. *Journal of Experimental Social Psychology, 43,* 489–496.

Carpenter, G. C. (1973). Differential response to mother and stranger within the first month of life. *Bulletin of the British Psychological Society, 16,* 138.

Carpenter, S. (1999, August 14). A new look at recognizing what people see. *Science News, 156,* 102.

Carpenter, S. (2000, September). Stoicism reconsidered. *Monitor on Psychology, 31*(8), 58–61.

Carpenter, S. (2001a, February). Different dispositions, different brains. *Monitor on Psychology, 32*(2), 66–68.

Carpenter, S. (2001b, January). When at last you don't succeed . . . *Monitor on Psychology, 32*(1), 70–71.

Carson, R. C., Butcher, J. N., & Mineka, S. (2000). *Abnormal psychology and modern life* (11th ed.). Boston: Allyn & Bacon.

Carstensen, L. L. (1987). Age-related changes in social activity. In L. L. Carstensen & B. A. Edelstein (Eds.), *Handbook of clinical gerontology* (pp. 222–237). New York: Pergamon Press.

Carstensen, L. L. (1991). Selectivity theory: Social activity in life-span context. In K. W. Schaie (Ed.), *Annual Review of Geriatrics and Gerontology (Vol. 11)*. New York: Springer.

Carstensen, L. L., and Freund, A. M. (1994). Commentary: The resilience of the aging self. *Developmental Review, 14,* 81–92.

Cartwright, R. D. (1977). *Night life: Explorations in dreaming.* Englewood Cliffs, NJ: Prentice Hall.

Cartwright, R. D. (1978). *A primer on sleep and dreaming.* Reading, MA: Addison-Wesley.

Cartwright, R. D. (1984). Broken dreams: A study of the effects of divorce and depression on dream content. *Psychiatry, 47,* 251–259.

Carver, C. S., & Scheier, M. F. (2008). *Perspectives on personality* (6th ed.). Boston: Allyn & Bacon. [See also: Digman, 1990; Goldberg, 1981, 1993]

Casey, J. F., & Wilson, L. (1991). *The flock.* New York: Fawcett Columbine.

Cash, T. F., & Duncan, N. C. (1984). Physical attractiveness stereotyping among black American college students. *Journal of Social Psychology, 122,* 71–77.

Cash, T. F., & Janda, L. H. (1984, December). The eye of the beholder. *Psychology Today, 18,* 46–52.

Cash, T. F., & Kilcullen, R. N. (1985). The aye of the beholder: Susceptibility to sexism and beautyism in the evaluation of managerial applicants. *Journal of Applied Social Psychology, 15,* 591–605.

Caspi, A., McClay, J., Moffitt, T. E., Mill, J., Martin, J., Craig, I. W., Taylor, A., & Poulton, R. (2002, August 2). Role of genotype in the cycle of violence in maltreated children. *Science, 297,* 851–852.

Cattaneo, E., Rigamonti, D., & Zuccato, C. (2002, December). The enigma of Huntington's disease. *Scientific American,* 92–97.

Cattell, R. B. (1963). Theory of fluid and crystallized intelligence: A critical experiment. *Journal of Educational Psychology, 54,* 1–22.

Ceci, S. J., & Bruck, M. (1993). Suggestibility of the child witness: A historical review and synthesis. *Psychological Bulletin, 113,* 403–439.

Ceci, S. J., & Liker, J. K. (1986). A day at the races: A study of IQ, expertise, and cognitive complexity. *Journal of Experimental Psychology: General, 115,* 255–266.

Ceci, S. J., & Williams, W. M. (1997). Schooling, intelligence, and income. *American Psychologist, 52,* 1051–1058.

Centers for Disease Control and Prevention. (2000). *Health, United States, 2000: Adolescent Health Chartbook.* Retrieved on November 8, 2004, from www.cdc.gov/nchs/hus.htm.

Centers for Disease Control and Prevention. (2007). Smoking and tobacco use. Retrieved March 28, 2008, from www.cdc.gov/tobacco/data_statistics/Factsheets/adult_cig_smoking.htm.

Cervone, D. (2004). The architecture of personality. *Psychological Review, 111,* 183–204.

Cervone, D., & Shoda, Y. (1999). Beyond traits in the study of personality coherence. *Current Directions in Psychological Science, 8,* 27–32.

Chalmers, D. J. (1995, December). The puzzle of conscious experience. *Scientific American, 273*(6), 80–86. [See also: Churchland, 1995; Crick, 1994]

Chamberlain, K., & Zika, S. (1990). The minor events approach to stress: Support for the use of daily hassles. *British Journal of Psychology, 81,* 469–481.

Chambless, D. L., Sanderson, W. C., Shoham, V., Johnson, S. B., Pope, K. S., Crits-Christoph, P., Baker, M., Johnson, B., Woody, S. R., Sue, S., Beutler, L., Williams, D. A., & McCurry, S. (1996). An update on empirically validated therapies. *The Clinical Psychologist, 49,* 5–18.

Chan, L., et al. (2003). An in-vitro study of ginsenoside Rb1–induced teratogenicity using a whole rat embryo culture model. *Human Reproduction, 18,* 2166–2168.

Chapman, P. D. (1988). *Schools as sorters: Lewis M. Terman, applied psychology, and the intelligence testing movement, 1890–1930.* New York: New York University Press.

Chartrand, T. L., & Bargh, J. A. (1999). The chameleon effect: The perception–behavior link and social interaction. *Journal of Personality & Social Psychology, 76,* 893–910.

Chase, W. G., & Simon, H. A. (1973). The mind's eye in chess. In W. G. Chase (Ed.), *Visual information processing* (pp. 215–281). New York: Academic Press.

Chaudhari, N., Landin, A. M., & Roper, S. D. (2000). A metabotropic glutamate receptor variant functions as a taste receptor. *Nature Neuroscience, 3,* 113–119.

Chen, E., Fisher, E. B., Bacharier, L. B., & Strunk, R. C. (2003). Socioeconomic status, stress, and immune markers in adolescents with asthma. *Psychosomatic Medicine, 65,* 984–992.

Cherney, E. D., & London, K. (2006). Gender-linked differences in the toys, television shows, computer games, and outdoor activities of 5- to 13-year-old children. *Sex Roles, 54,* 717–726.

Chi, M., Glaser, R., & Rees, E. (1982). Expertise in problem solving. In R. Sternberg (Ed.), *Advances in the psychology of human intelligence* (Vol. 1). Hillsdale, NJ: Erlbaum.

Chiaccia, K. B. (2007). Insanity defense. *Encyclopedia of Psychology.* Retrieved February 9, 2008, from http://findarticles.com/p/articles/mi_g2699/is_0005/ai_2699000509. [See also: Consensus Project (n. d.)]

Chilman, C. S. (1983). *Adolescent sexuality in a changing American society* (2nd ed.). New York: Wiley.

Chomsky, N. (1965). *Aspects of a theory of syntax.* Cambridge, MA: MIT Press.

Chomsky, N. (1975). *Reflections on language.* New York: Pantheon Books.

Chorney, M. J., Chorney, N. S., Owen, M. J., Daniels, J., McGuffin, P., Thompson, L. A., Detterman, D. K., Benbow, C., Lubinski, D., Eley, T., & Plomin, R. (1998). A quantitative trait locus associated with cognitive ability in children. *Psychological Science, 9,* 159–166.

Christakis, N. A., & Fowler J. H. (2007, July 26). The spread of obesity in a large social network over 32 years. *New England Journal of Medicine, 357,* 370–379.

Christenfeld, N., Gerin, W., Linden, W., Sanders, M., Mathus, J., & Deich, J. D., et al. (1997). Social support effects on cardiovascular reactivity: Is a stranger as effective as a friend? *Psychosomatic Medicine, 59,* 388–398.

Christensen, A., & Heavey, C. L. (1999). Interventions for couples. *Annual Review of Psychology, 50,* 165–190.

Christensen, A., & Jacobson, N. S. (1994). Who (or what) can do psychotherapy: The status and challenge of nonprofessional therapies. *Psychological Science, 5,* 8–14.

The Chronicle of Higher Education. (2004, August 27). *2001–2002 Almanac, 51*(1), 19.

Chua, H. F., Boland, J. E. and Nisbett, R. E. (2005, August 30). Cultural variation in eye movements during scene perception. *Proceedings of the National Academy of Sciences, 102,* 12629–12633.

Church, A. T., Katigbak, M. S., Del Prado, A. M., Ortiz, F. A., Mastor, K. A., Harumi, Y., Tanaka-Matsumi, J., De Jesús Vargas-Flores, J., Ibáñez-reyes, J., White, F. A., Miramontes, L. G., Reyes, J. A. S., & Cabrera, H. F. (2006). Implicit theories and self-perceptions of traitedness across cultures: Toward integration of cultural and trait psychology perspectives. *Journal of Cross-Cultural Psychology, 37,* 694–716.

Church, A. T., Katigbak, M. S., Ortiz, F. A., Del Prado, A. M., De Jesús Vargas-Flores, J., Ibáñez-Reyes, J., Pe-Pua, R., & Cabrera, H. F. (2005). Investigating implicit trait theories across cultures. *Journal of Cross-Cultural Psychology, 36,* 476–496.

Church, R. M. (2001). A turning test for computational and associative theories of learning. *Current Directions in Psychological Science, 10,* 132–136.

Churchland, P. M. (1995). *The engine of reason, the seat of the soul: A philosophical journey into the brain.* Cambridge, MA: MIT Press.

Cialdini, R. B. (2001a). *Influence: Science and practice* (4th ed.). Boston: Allyn & Bacon.

Cialdini, R. B. (2001b, February). The science of persuasion. *Scientific American, 284,* 76–81.

Cialdini, R. B. (2007). *Influence: The psychology of persuasion.* New York: HarperCollins.

Clark, H. H., & Clark, E. V. (1977). *Psychology and language: An introduction to psycholinguistics.* New York: Harcourt Brace Jovanovich.

Clark, M. S., Mills, J. R., & Corcoran, D. M. (1989). Keeping track of needs and inputs of friends and strangers. *Personality and Social Psychology Bulletin, 15,* 533–542.

Clark, R. E., & Squire, L. R. (1998, April 3). Classical conditioning and brain systems: The role of awareness. *Science, 280,* 77–81.

Clarke-Stewart, K. A. (1989). Infant day care: Maligned or malignant? *American Psychologist, 44,* 266–273.

Clay, R. A. (1998, November). Preparing for the future: Practitioners seek training for prescribing medication. *APA Monitor,* 22–23.

Clay, R. A. (2000, January). Psychotherapy is cost-effective. *Monitor on Psychology, 31*(1) 40–41.

Clay, R. A. (2001, January). Research to the heart of the matter. *Monitor on Psychology, 32*(1), 42–49.

Clay, R. A. (2003a, April). An empty nest can promote freedom, improved relationships. *Monitor on Psychology,* 40–41.

Clay, R. A. (2003b, April). Researchers replace midlife myths with facts. *Monitor on Psychology*, 38–39.

Cleek, M. B., & Pearson, T. A. (1985). Perceived causes of divorce: An analysis of interrelationships. *Journal of Marriage and the Family, 47*, 179–191.

Clifton, S., & Myers, K. K. (2005). The socialization of emotion: Learning emotion management at the fire station. *Journal of Applied Communication Research, 33*, 67–92.

Coan, J. A., Schaefer, H., & Davidson, R. J. (2006). Lending a hand: Social regulation of the neural responses to threat. *Psychological Science, 17*, 1032–1039.

Cobb, S. (1976). Social support as a moderator of stress. *Psychosomatic Medicine, 35*, 375–389.

Cochran, S. D., Sullivan, J. G., & Mays, V. M. (2003). Prevalence of mental disorders, psychological distress, and mental health services use among lesbian, gay, and bisexual adults in the United States. *Journal of Consulting and Clinical Psychology, 71*, 53–61.

Coghill, R. C., McHaffie, J. G., & Yen, Y. (2003, July 8). Neural correlates of interindividual differences in the subjective experience of pain. *Proceedings of the National Academy of Sciences, 14*, 8538–8542.

Cognitive–behavior therapy effective for panic disorder. (1991, November). *APS Observer*, 8.

Cohen, D., & Gunz, A. (2002). As seen by the other . . . : Perspectives on the self in the memories and emotional perceptions of Easterners and Westerners. *Psychological Science, 55*–59. [See also: Gardiner et al., 1998; Markus & Kitayama, 1994]

Cohen, J. (2002, February 8). The confusing mix of hype and hope. *Science, 295*, 1026.

Cohen, J. D., & Tong, F. (2001, 28 September). The face of controversy. *Science, 293*, 2405–2407.

Cohen, M. N. (1998). *Culture of intolerance: Chauvinism, class, and racism in the United States*. New Haven, CT: Yale University Press.

Cohen, R. E., & Ahearn, F. L. Jr. (1980). *Handbook for mental health care of disaster victims*. Baltimore: Johns Hopkins University Press.

Cohen, S. (1988). Psychosocial models of the role of social support in the etiology of physical disease. *Health Psychology, 7*, 269–297.

Cohen, S., Doyle, W. J., Turner, R. B., Alper, C. M., & Skoner, D. P. (2003). Emotional style and susceptibility to the common cold. *Psychosomatic Medicine, 63*, 652–657.

Cohen, S., & Girgus, J. S. (1973). Visual spatial illusions: Many explanations. *Science, 179*, 503–504.

Cohen, S., & McKay, G. (1983). Social support, stress, and the buffering hypotheses: A theoretical analysis. In A. Baum, S. E. Taylor, & J. Singer (Eds.), *Handbook of psychology and health (Vol. 4)*. Hillsdale, NJ: Erlbaum.

Cohen, S., & Syme, S. L. (Eds.). (1985). *Social support and health*. Orlando, FL: Academic Press.

Colby, A., Kohlberg, L., Gibbs, J., & Lieberman, M. (1983). A longitudinal study of moral judgment. *Monographs of the Society for Research in Child Development, 481*(1–2, Serial No. 200).

Colcombe, S. J., Kramer, A. F., Erickson, K. I., Scalf, P., McAuley, E., Cohen, N. J., Webb, A., Jerome, G. J., Marquez, D. X., & Elavsky, S. (2004). Cardiovascular fitness, cortical plasticity, and aging. *Proceedings of the National Academy of Sciences, 101*, 3316–3321.

Cole, M. (2006). Internationalism in psychology: We need it now more than ever. *American Psychologist, 61*, 904–917. [See also Fowers & Richardson, 1996; Gergen et al., 1996; Segall et al., 1998; Triandis, 1994, 1995]

Collins, A. W., Maccoby, E. E., Steinberg, L., Hetherington, E. M., & Bornstein, M. H. (2000). Contemporary research on parenting: The case for nature and nurture. *American Psychologist, 55*, 218–232.

Collins, G. P. (2001, October). Magnetic revelations: Functional MRI highlights neurons receiving signals. *Scientific American*, 21.

Collins, N. L., & Read, S. J. (1990). Adult attachment, working models, and relationship quality in dating

couples. *Journal of Personality and Social Psychology, 58*, 644–663.

Collins, S., & Long, A. (2003). Too tired to care? The psychological effects of working with trauma. *Journal of Psychiatric and Mental Health Nursing, 10*, 17–27.

Committee on Substance Abuse and Committee on Children with Disabilities. (2000). Fetal alcohol syndrome and alcohol-related neurodevelopmental disorders. *Pediatrics, 106*, 358–361.

Comuzzie, A. G., & Allison, D. B. (1998, May 29). The search for human obesity genes. *Science, 280*, 1374–1377.

Conger, J. J., & Peterson, A. C. (1984). *Adolescence and youth* (3rd ed.) New York: Harper & Row.

Conklin, H. M., & Iacono, W. G. (2004). Schizophrenia: A neurodevelopmental perspective. In T. F. Oltmans & R. E. Emery (Eds.), *Current Directions in Abnormal Psychology* (pp. 122–129). Upper Saddle River, NJ: Prentice Hall.

Conrad, R. (1964). Acoustic confusions in immediate memory. *British Journal of Psychology, 55*, 75–84.

Consensus Project. (n.d.). The advocacy handbook. Retrieved February 9, 2008, from http://consensus-project.org/advocacy/step2_main

Consumer Reports. (1995, November). Mental health: Does therapy help? 734–739.

Contrada, R. J., Ashmore, R. D., Gary, M. L., Coups, E., Egeth, J. D., Sewell, A., Ewell, K., Goyal, T. M., & Chasse, V. (2000). Ethnicity-related sources of stress and their effects on well-being. *Current Directions in Psychological Science, 9*, 136–139.

Conway, J. K. (1992). *Written by herself: Autobiographies of American women: An anthology*. New York: Vintage.

Cook, M., Mineka, S., Wolkenstein, B. & Laitsch, K. (1985). Observational conditioning of snake fear in unrelated rhesus monkeys. *Journal of Abnormal Psychology, 94*, 591–610.

Coon, D. J. (1992). Testing the limits of sense and science: American experimental psychologists combat spiritualism, 1880–1920. *American Psychologist, 47*, 143–151.

Cooper, R. S. (2005). Race and IQ: Molecular genetics as deus ex machina. *American Psychologist, 60*, 71–76.

Cooper, W. H. (1983). An achievement motivation normological network. *Journal of Personality and Social Psychology, 44*, 841–861.

Corkin, S. (2002). What's new with the amnesic patient H. M.? *Nature Reviews Neuroscience, 3*, 153–160. Retrieved March 10, 2008, from http://homepage.mac.com/sanagnos/corkin2002.pdf.

Corrigan, P. W. (1995). Use of token economy with seriously mentally ill patients: Criticisms and misconceptions. *Psychiatric Services, 46*, 1258–1263.

Costa, P. T., Jr., & McCrae, R. R. (1992a). Four ways five factors are basic. *Personality and Individual Differences, 13*, 653–665.

Costa, P. T., Jr., & McCrae, R. R. (1992b). *Revised NEO Personality Inventory (NEO-PI-R) and NEO Five-Factor Inventory (NEO-FFI) professional manual*. Odessa, FL: Psychological Assessment Resources.

Coughlin, E. K. (1994, October 26). Class, IQ, and heredity. *The Chronicle of Higher Education*, A12, A20.

Courchesne, E., Chisum, H., & Townsend, J. (1994). Neural activity-dependent brain cells in development: Implications for psychopathology. *Development and Psychopathology, 6*, 697–722.

Couzin, J. (2005, May 6). A heavyweight battle over CDC's obesity forecasts. *Science, 308*, 770–771.

Couzin, J. (2006, October 27). Unraveling pain's DNA. *Science, 314*, 585–586.

Covington, M. V. (2000). Intrinsic versus extrinsic motivation in schools: A reconciliation. *Current Direction in Psychology Science, 9*, 22–25.

Cowan, N. (2001). The magical number 4 in short-term memory: A reconsideration of mental storage capacity. *Behavioral and Brain Sciences, 24*, 87–185.

Cowan, P., & Cowan, P. A. (1988). Changes in marriage during the transition to parenthood. In G. Y. Michaels & W. A. Goldberg (Eds.), *The transition to parenthood: Current theory and research*. Cambridge, U.K.: Cambridge University Press.

Coyne, J. C., Burchill, S. A. L., & Stiles, W. B. (1991). An interactional perspective on depression. In C. R. Snyder & D. O. Forsyth (Eds.), *Handbook of social and clinical psychology: The health perspective* (pp. 327–349). New York: Pergamon Press.

Coyne, K. J. C. (2001, February). Depression in primary care: Depressing news, exciting research opportunities. *APS Observer, 14*(2), 1, 18.

Craig, A. D., & Reiman, E. M. (1996, November 21). Functional imaging of an illusion of pain. *Nature, 384*, 258–260.

Craik, F. I. M. (1979). Human memory. *Annual Review of Psychology, 30*, 63–102.

Craik, F. I. M., & Lockhart, R. S. (1972). Levels of processing: A framework for memory research. *Journal of Verbal Learning and Verbal Behavior, 11*, 671–684.

Craik, F. I. M., Moroz, T. M., Moscovitch, M., Stuss, D. T., Winocur, G., Tulving, E., & Shitij, K. (1999). In search of the self: A positron emission tomography study. *Psychological Science, 10*, 26–34.

Craik, F. I. M., & Tulving, E. (1975). Depth of processing and the retention of words in episodic memory. *Journal of Experimental Psychology: General, 104*, 268–294.

Cramer, P. (2000). Defense mechanisms in psychology today. *American Psychologist, 55*, 637–646.

Craske, M. G., Brown, T. A., & Barlow, D. H. (1991). Behavioral treatment of panic disorder: A two year follow-up. *Behavior Therapy, 19*, 577–592.

Cree, G. S., & McRae, K. (2003). Analyzing the factors underlying the structure and computation of the meaning of chipmunk, cherry, cheese, and cello (and many other such concrete nouns). *Journal of Experimental Psychology: General, 132*, 163–201. [See also: Posner & McCandliss, 1993; Raichle, 1994; Solso, 2001]

Crick, F. (1994). *The astonishing hypothesis: The scientific search for the soul*. New York: Charles Scribner's Sons.

Crick, F., & Mitchison, G. (1983). The function of dream sleep. *Nature, 304*, 111–114.

Crocker, J., & Major, B. (1989). Social stigma and self-esteem: The self-protective properties of stigma. *Psychological Review, 96*, 608–630.

Crohan, S. E., Antonucci, T. C., Adelmann, P. K., & Coleman, L. M. (1989). Job characteristics and well-being at mid-life. *Psychology of Women Quarterly, 13*, 223–235.

Cromwell, R. L. (1993). Searching for the origins of schizophrenia. *Psychological Science, 4*, 276–279.

Crowder, R. G. (1992). Eidetic images. In L. R. Squire (Ed.), *The encyclopedia of learning and memory* (pp. 154–156). New York: Macmillan.

Crowell, T. A. (2002). Neuropsychological findings in combat-related posttraumatic stress disorder. *Clinical Neuropsychologist, 16*, 310–321.

Crowley, B. J., Hayslip, B., Jr., & Hobdy, J. (2003). Psychological hardiness and adjustment to life events in adulthood. *Journal of Adult Development, 10*, 237–248.

Csikszentmihalyi, M. (1990). *Flow: The psychology of optimal experience*. New York: Harper & Row.

Csikszentmihalyi, M. (1996, July/August). The creative personality. *Psychology Today, 29*(4), 34–40.

Csikszentmihalyi, M. (1998). *Finding flow*. New York: Basic Books.

Csikszentmihalyi, M., Larson, R., & Prescott, S. (1977). The ecology of adolescent activity and experience. *Journal of Youth and Adolescence, 6*, 281–294.

Csikszentmihalyi, M., Rathunde, K. R., Whalen, S., & Wong, M. (1993). *Talented teenagers: The roots of success and failure*. New York: Cambridge University Press.

Cushman, P. (1990). Why the self is empty: Toward a

historically situated psychology. *American Psychologist, 45,* 599–611.

Cynkar, A. (2007, April). Low glucose levels compromise self-control. *Monitor on Psychology, 38*(4), 13.

Cytowic, R. E. (1993). *The man who tasted shapes.* Cambridge, MA: MIT Press.

Dabbs, J. M. (2000). *Heroes, rogues, and lovers: Testosterone and behavior.* New York: McGraw-Hill.

Dackman, L. (1986). Everyday illusions. *Exploratorium Quarterly, 10,* 5–7.

Daily, D. K., Ardinger, H. H., & Holmes, G. E. (2000). Identification and evaluation of mental retardation. *American Family Physician, 61,* 1059–1067.

Daley, K. C. (2004). Update on attention-deficit/hyperactivity disorder. *Current Opinion in Pediatrics, 16,* 217–226.

Dally, J. M., Emery, N. J., & Clayton, N. S. 2005. Cache protection strategies by western scrub-jays (*Aphelocoma californica*): Implications for social cognition. *Animal Behaviour, 70,* 1251–1263.

Daly, R. C., Su, T.-P., Schmidt, P. J., Pagliaro, M., Pickar, D., & Rubinow, D. R. (2003). Neuroendocrine and behavioral effects of high-dose anabolic steroid administration in male normal volunteers. *Psychoneuroendocrinology, 28,* 317–331.

Damasio, A. R. (2003). *Looking for Spinoza: Joy, sorrow, and the feeling brain.* Orlando, FL: Harcourt. [See also LeDoux, 1996; Whalen, 1998]

Damasio, A. R. (1994). *Descartes' error: Emotion, reason, and the human brain.* New York: Avon Books.

Damasio, A. R. (1999, December). How the brain creates the mind. *Scientific American,* 112–117.

Damasio, A. R. (2000). *The feeling of what happens: Body and emotion in the making of consciousness.* New York: Harcourt Brace.

Dana, R. H. (1993). *Multicultural assessment perspectives for professional psychology.* Boston: Allyn & Bacon.

Danion, J., Rizzo, L., & Bruant, A. (1999). Functional mechanisms underlying im paired recognition memory and conscious awareness in patients with schizophrenia. *Archives of General Psychiatry, 56,* 639–644.

Dannefer, D., & Perlmutter, M. (1990). Developmental as a multidimensional process: Individual and social constit uents. *Human Development, 33,* 108–137.

Danner, D. D., Snowdon, D. A., & Friesen, W. V. (2001). Positive emotions in early life and longevity: Findings from the nun study. *Journal of Personality and Social Psychology, 80,* 804–813.

Darley, J. M., & Batson, C. D. (1973). From Jerusalem to Jericho: A study of situational and dispositional variables in helping behavior. *Journal of Personality and Social Psychology, 27,* 100–108.

Darley, J. M., & Latané, B. (1968) Bystander intervention in emergencies: Diffusion of responsibility. *Journal of Personality and Social Psychology, 8,* 377–383.

Darling, N., & Steinberg, L. (1993). Parenting style as context: An integrative model. *Psychological Bulletin, 113,* 487–496.

Darwin, C. (1963). *On the origin of species.* London: Oxford University Press. (Original work published in 1859.)

Darwin, C. (1998). *The expression of the emotions in man and animals* (3rd ed., with Introduction, Afterword, and Commentaries by P. Ekman). New York: Oxford University Press. (Original work published in 1862.)

Darwin, C. J., Turvey, M. T., & Crowder, R. G. (1972). The auditory analogue of the Sperling partial report procedure: Evidence for brief auditory stage. *Cognitive Psychology, 3,* 255–267.

Dattilio, F. M., & Padesky, C. A. (1990). *Cognitive therapy with couples.* Sarasota, FL: Professional Resource Exchange.

Davidson, R. J. (1992a). Anterior cerebral asymmetry and the nature of emotion. *Brain and Cognition, 20,* 125–151.

Davidson, R. J. (1992b). Emotion and affective style: Hemispheric substrates. *Psychological Science, 3,* 39–43.

Davidson, R. J. (2000a). Affective neuroscience. Address given at the American Psychological Association's annual convention, Washington, DC.

Davidson, R. J. (2000b). Affective style, psychopathology, and resilience: Brain mechanisms and plasticity. *American Psychologist, 55,* 1196–1214.

Davidson, R. J. (2002, April). Synaptic substrates of the implicit and explicit self. *Science, 296,* 268.

Davidson, R. J., Jackson, D. C., & Kalin, N. H. (2000). Emotion, plasticity, context, and regulation: Perspectives from affective neuroscience. *Psychological Bulletin, 126,* 890–909. [See also: Adolphs et al., 2001; Ahern & Schwartz, 1985; Borod et al., 1988]

Davidson, R. J., Kabat-Zinn, J., Schumacher, J., Rosenkranz, M., Muller, D., Santorelli, S. F., Urbanowski, F., Harrington, A., Bonus, K., & Sheridan, J. F. (2003). Alternations in brain and immune function produced by mindfulness meditation. *Psychosomatic Medicine, 65,* 564–570.

Davidson, R. J., Putnam, K. M., & Larson, C. L. (2000, July 28). Dysfunction in the neural circuitry of emotion regulation—a possible prelude to violence. *Science, 289,* 591–594.

Davis, C. G., & Nolen-Hoeksema, S. (2001). Loss and meaning: How do people make sense of loss? *American Behavioral Scientist, 44,* 726–743.

Davis, C. G., Nolen-Hoeksema, S., & Larson, J. (1998). Making sense of loss and benefiting from the experience: Two construals of meaning. *Journal of Personality and Social Psychology, 75,* 561–574.

Davison, K. P., Pennebaker, J. W., & Dickerson, S. S. (2000). Who talks? The social psychology of illness support groups. *American Psychologist, 55,* 205–217.

Daw, J. (2001, June). The Ritalin debate. Monitor on Psychology, 32(6), 64–65.

Daw, J. (2002a). New Mexico becomes first state to gain Rx privileges. *Monitor on Psychology, 33*(3), 24–25.

Daw, J. (2002b, March). Steady and strong progress in the push for Rx privileges. *Monitor on Psychology, 33*(3), 56 58.

Daw, J. (2002c, November). Why and how normal people go mad. *Monitor on Psychology,* 20–21.

Dawes, R. M. (2001). *Everyday irrationality: How pseudoscientists, lunatics, and the rest of us fail to think rationally.* Boulder, CO: Westview Press.

Dawkins, K., Lieberman, J. A., Lebowitz, B. D., & Hsiao, J. K. (1999). Antipsychotics: Past and future. *Schizophrenia Bulletin, 25,* 395–405. [See also: Gitlin, 1990; Holmes, 2001; Kane & Marder, 1993]

Day, N. L. (2002). Prenatal alcohol exposure predicts continued deficits in offspring size at 14 years of age. *Alcoholism: Clinical and Experimental Research, 26,* 1584–1591.

Deadwyler, S. A., & Hampson, R. E. (1995, November 24). Ensemble activity and behavior: What's the code? *Science, 270,* 1316–1318.

DeAngelis, T. (1997, January). Chromosomes contain clues on schizophrenia. *APA Monitor,* 26.

DeAngelis, T. (2002a, June). A bright future for PNI. *Monitor on Psychology,* 46–50.

DeAngelis, T. (2002b, July–August). If you do just on thing, make it exercise. *Monitor on Psychology,* 4–51.

DeAngelis, T. (2002c, February). New data on lesbian, gay, and bisexual mental health. *Monitor on Psychology, 33*(2), 46–47.

DeAngelis, T. (2003, March). When anger's a plus. *Monitor on Psychology, 34,* 44–45.

DeAngelis, T. (2004a, January). Family-size portions for one. *Monitor on Psychology, 35*(1), 50–51.

DeAngelis, T. (2004b, January). What's to blame for the surge in super-size Americans? *Monitor on Psychology, 35*(1), 46–49. [See also: Abelson & Kennedy, 2004; Marx, 2003; Newman, 2004; Taubes, 1998; Wickelgren, 1998c]

DeAngelis, T. (2005, November). Where psychotherapy meets neuroscience. *Monitor on Psychology, 36*(11), 72–73.

DeAngelis, T. (2006, February). Promising new treatments for SAD. *Monitor on Psychology, 37*(2), 18–20.

DeCasper, A. J., & Fifer, W. P. (1980). Of human bonding: Newborns prefer their mothers' voices. *Science, 208,* 1174–1176.

DeCasper, A. J., & Spence, M. J. (1986). Prenatal maternal speech influences newborns' perception of speech sounds. *Infant Behavior and Development, 9,* 133–150.

Deckers, L. (2001). *Motivation: Biological, psychological, and environmental.* Boston: Allyn & Bacon.

de Gelder, B. (2000, August 18). More to seeing than meets the eye. *Science, 289,* 1148–1149. [See also: Barinaga, 1999; Batista et al., 1999; Maunsell, 1995]

DeGrandpre, R. J. (2000). A science of meaning: Can behaviorism bring meaning to psychological science? *American Psychologist, 55,* 721–739.

de Groot, A. D. (1965). *Thought and choice in chess.* The Hague: Mouton.

Delgado, J. M. R. (1969). *Physical control of the mind: Toward a psychocivilized society.* New York: Harper & Row.

De Martino, B., Kumaran, D., Seymour, B., & Dolan, R. J. (2006, August 4). Frames, biases, and rational decision-making in the human brain. *Science, 313,* 684–687.

Dembroski, T. M., & Costa, P. T., Jr. (1987). Coronary prone behavior: Components of the Type A pattern and hostility. *Journal of Personality, 55,* 211–235.

Dembroski, T. M., Weiss, S. M., Shields, J. L., et al. (1978). *Coronary-prone behavior.* New York: Springer-Verlag.

Dement, W. (1999, March 10). Sleep apnea information and resources (Stanford University). Retrieved December 4, 2007, from www.stanford.edu/~dement/apnea.html.

Dement, W. C. (1980). *Some watch while some must sleep.* San Francisco: San Francisco Book Company.

Dement, W. C. (2000, September 25). Sleep debt. Retrieved March 9, 2004, from SleepQuest website: www.sleepquest.com/d_column_archive6.html.

Dement, W. C., & Kleitman, N. (1957). Cyclic variations in EEG during sleep and their relations to eye movement, body mobility and dreaming. *Electroencephalography and Clinical Neurophysiology, 9,* 673–690.

Dement, W. C., & Vaughan, C. (1999). *The promise of sleep.* New York: Delacorte Press.

Dennis, W. (1960). Causes of retardation among institutionalized children: Iran. *Journal of Genetic Psychology, 96,* 47–59.

Dennis, W., & Dennis, M. G. (1940). The effect of cradling practices upon the onset of walking in Hopi children. *Journal of Genetic Psychology, 56,* 77–86.

DePaulo, B. M., Lindsay, J. J., Malone, B. E., Muhlenbruck, L., Charlton, K, & Cooper, H. (2003). Cues to deception. *Psychological Bulletin, 129,* 74–118.

Derbyshire, S. W. G., Whalley, M. G., Stenger, V. A., & Oakley, D. A. (2004). Cerebral activation during hypnotically induced and imagined pain. *Neuroimage, 23,* 392–401.

Deregowski, J. B. (1980). *Illusions, patterns and pictures: A cross-cultural perspective* (pp. 966–977). London, U.K.: Academic Press.

Dermietzel, R. (2006, October/November). The electrical brain. *Scientific American Mind, 17*(5), 56–61.

DeRubeis, R. J., Gelfand, L. A., Tang, T. Z., & Simons, A. D. (1999). Medications versus cognitive behavior therapy for severely depressed outpatients: Megaanalysis of four randomized comparisons. *American Journal of Psychiatry, 156,* 1007–1013.

DeSalvo, L. (2000). *Writing as a way of healing: How telling our stories transforms our lives.* Boston: Beacon Press.

Detterman, D. K. (1999). The psychology of mental retardation. *International Review of Psychiatry, 11,* 26–33.

Deutsch, M., & Collins, M. E. (1951). *Interracial housing: A psychological evaluation of a social ex-*

periment. Minneapolis: University of Minnesota Press.

Deutsch, M., & Gerard, H. B. (1955). A study of normative and informational social influence upon individual judgment. *Journal of Abnormal and Social Psychology, 51,* 629–636.

Devereux, G. (1981). Mohave ethnopsychiatry and suicide: The psychiatric knowledge and psychic disturbances of an Indian tribe. *Bureau of American Ethology Bulletin 175.* Washington, DC: Smithsonian Institution.

Devilly, G. J., Gist, R., & Cotton, P. (2006). Ready! Fire! Aim! The status of psychological debriefing and therapeutic interventions: In the work place and after disasters. *Review of General Psychology, 10,* 318–345.

Devine, P. G., & Zuwerink, J. R. (1994). Prejudice and guilt: The internal struggle to overcome prejudice. In W. J. Lonner & R. Malpass (Eds.), *Psychology and culture* (pp. 203–207). Boston: Allyn & Bacon.

de Waal, F. B. M. (1999, December). The end of nature versus nurture. *Scientific American,* 94–99.

Dewsbury, D. A. (1990). Early interactions between animal psychologists and animal activists and the founding of the APA Committee on Precautions in Animal Experimentation. *American Psychologist, 45,* 315–327.

Dewsbury, D. A. (1997). In celebration of the centennial of Ivan P. Pavlov's (1897/1902) *The work of the digestive glands. American Psychologist, 52,* 933–935.

Diamond, M. (2007). Psychosexual development—male or female? Address given at the 2007 convention of the American Psychological Association in San Francisco.

Dickens, W. T., & Flynn, J. R. (2001). Heritability estimates versus large environmental effects: The IQ paradox resolved. *Psychological Review, 108,* 346–369.

Dickens, W. T., & Flynn, J. R. (2006). Black Americans reduce the racial IQ gap: Evidence from standardization samples. *Psychological Science 17,* 913–920.

Dickinson, A. (2001). Causal learning: Association versus computation. *Current Directions in Psychological Science, 10,* 127–132.

Diehl, M., Coyle, N., & Labouvie-Vief, G. (1996). Age and sex differences in strategies of coping and defense across the life span. *Psychology and Aging, 11,* 127–139.

Diener, E. (1984). Subjective well-being. *Psychological Bulletin, 95,* 542–575.

Diener, E. (2000). Subjective well-being: The science of happiness and a proposal for a national index. *American Psychologist, 55,* 34–43.

Diener, E., & Diener, C. (1996). Most people are happy. *Psychological Science, 7,* 181–189.

Diener, E., Sandvik, E., Seidlitz, L., & Diener, M. (1993). The relationship between income and subjective well-being: Relative or absolute? *Social Indicators Research, 28,* 195–223.

Diener, E., & Seligman, M. E. P. (2002). Very happy people. *Psychological Science, 13,* 81–84.

DiFebo, H. (2002). *Psyography: Mary Whiton Calkins.* Retrieved January 11, 2008, from http://faculty.frostburg.edu/mbradley/psyography/marywhiton-calkins.html.

Digman, J. M. (1990). Personality structure: Emergence of the five-factor model. *Annual Review of Psychology, 41,* 417–440.

Dillard, A. J. (2007). Humor, laughter, and recovery from stressful experiences. *Dissertation Abstracts International: Section B: The Sciences and Engineering, 68(5-B),* 3432.

Dillbeck, M. C., & Orme-Johnson, D. W. (1987). Physiological differences between transcendental meditation and rest. *American Psychologist, 42(9),* 879–881.

Dingfelder, S. F. (2004a, July/August). Gateways to memory. *Monitor on Psychology, 35(7),* 22-23. [See also: Azar, 1998a; Holloway, 1999]

Dingfelder, S. F. (2004b, March). Pavlovian psychopharmacology. *Monitor on Psychology, 35(3),* 18–19.

Dingfelder, S. F. (2004c, March). To tell the truth. *Monitor on Psychology, 35(3),* 22–23. [See also: Aftergood, 2000; Holden, 2001b; Saxe, 1991, 1994]

Dingfelder, S. F. (2005, September). Feelings' sway over memory. *Monitor on Psychology, 36(8),* 54–55.

Dingfelder, S. F. (2006, June). The formula for funny. *Monitor on Psychology, 37(6),* 54–56.

Dion, K. K. (1986). Stereotyping based on physical attractiveness: Issues and conceptual perspectives. In C. P. Herman, M. P. Zanna, & E. T. Higgins (Eds.), *Physical appearance, stigma, and social behavior: The Ontario symposium on personality and social psychology (Vol. 3).* Hillsdale, NJ: Erlbaum.

Dittmann, M. (2003). Psychology's first prescribers. *Monitor on Psychology, 34(2),* 36.

Dittmann, M. (2004). Prescriptive authority. *Monitor on Psychology, 35(5),* 34–35.

Dittmann, M. (2005a, July/August). Stemming social phobia. *Monitor on Psychology, 36(7),* 92–94. [See also: Kazdin, 1994; Kazdin & Wilcoxin, 1976]

Dittmann, M. (2005b, July/August). When health fears hurt health. *Monitor on Psychology, 36(7),* 100–103.

Dixon, R. A., Kramer, D. A., & Baltes, P. B. (1985). Intelligence: A life-span developmental perspective. In B. B. Wolman (Ed.), *Handbook of intelligence* (pp. 301–352). New York: Wiley.

Dobbins, A. C., Jeo, R. M., Fiser, J., & Allman, J. M. (1998, July 24). Distance modulation of neural activity in the visual cortex. *Science, 281,* 552–555.

Dobbs, D. (2006a). A revealing reflection. *Scientific American Mind, 17(2),* 22–27.

Dobbs, D. (2006b, August/September). Turning off depression. *Scientific American, 17(4),* 26–31.

Dobelle, W. (1977). Current status of research on providing sight to the blind by electrical stimulation of the brain. *Journal of Visual Impairment and Blindness, 71,* 290–297.

Dodson, C. S., Johnson, M. K., & Schooler, J. W. (1997). The verbal overshadowing effect: Why descriptions impair face recognition. *Memory & Cognition, 25,* 129–139.

Doetsch, F. (2002). Genetics of childhood disorders: XXXVIII. Stem cell research, part 2: Reconstructing the brain. *Journal of the American Academy of Child & Adolescent Psychiatry, 41,* 622–624.

Dohrenwend, B. P., & Shrout, P. E. (1985). "Hassles" in the conceptualization and measurement of life stress variables. *American Psychologist, 40,* 780–785.

Dohrenwend, B. S., & Dohrenwend, B. P. (1974). *Stressful life events: Their nature and effects.* New York: Wiley.

Doka, K. J. (1989). *Disenfranchised grief: Recognizing hidden sorrows.* Lexington, MA: Lexington Books.

Doka, K. J. (1995). Friends, teachers, movie stars: The disenfranchised grief of children: Friends, teachers, movie stars. In E. A. Grollman (Ed.), *Bereaved children and teens: A support guide for parents and professionals* (pp. 37–45). Boston: Beacon Press.

Dolan, R. J. (2002). Emotion, cognition, and behavior. *Science, 298,* 1191–1194.

Domhoff, G. W. (1996). *Finding meaning in dreams: A quantitative approach.* New York: Plenum Press.

Doob, L. W. (1964). Eidetic images among the Ibo. *Ethnology, 3,* 357–363.

Dowling, J. E. (1992). *Neurons and networks: An introduction to neuroscience.* Cambridge, MA: Harvard University Press.

Downey, T. (2004). *The last men out: Life on the edge at Rescue 2 Firehouse.* New York: Henry Holt and Co.

Downing, P. E., Jiang, Y., Shuman, M., & Kanwisher, N. (2001, 28 September). A cortical area selective for visual processing of the human body. *Science, 293,* 2470–2473.

Doyère, V., Débiec, J., Monfils, M-H, Schafe, G. E., & LeDoux, J. E. (2007, November 1). Synapse-specific reconsolidation of distinct fear memories in the lateral amygdala. *Nature Neuroscience, 10,* 414–416. [See also: Riccio et al., 2003; Wixted, 2005]

Doyle, R. (2001, June). The American terrorist. *Scientific American, 285(6),* 28.

Doyle, R. (2002a). Deinstitutionalization: Why a much maligned program still has life. *Scientific American, 287,* 38.

Doyle, R. (2002b, January). Going solo: Unwed motherhood in industrial nations rises. *Scientific American,* 24.

Doyle, R. (2006, February). Sizing up: Roots of obesity epidemic lie in the mid-20th century. *Scientific American, 294(2),* 32.

Doyle, R. (2007, January). Teen sex in America: Virginity into the third millennium takes an uptick. *Scientific American, 296(1),* 30.

Dracheva, S., Marras, S. A. E., Elhakem, S. L., Kramer, F. R., Davis, K. L., & Haroutunian, V. (2001). N-methyl-d-aspartic acid receptor expression in the dorsolateral prefrontal cortex of elderly patients with schizophrenia. *American Journal of Psychiatry, 158,* 1400–1410.

Draguns, J. (1980). Psychological disorders of clinical severity. In H. Triandis & J. Draguns (Eds.), *Handbook of cross-cultural psychology, Vol. 6: Psychopathology* (pp. 99–174). Boston: Allyn & Bacon.

Draguns, J. G. (1979). Culture and personality. In A. J. Marsella, R. G. Tharp, & T. J. Ciborowski (Eds.), *Perspectives on cross-cultural psychology* (pp. 179–207). New York: Academic Press.

Drake, R. E., Osher, F. C., & Wallach, M. A. (1991). Homelessness and dual diagnosis. *American Psychologist, 46,* 1149–1158.

Druckman, D., & Bjork, R. A. (1991). *In the mind's eye: Enhancing human performance.* Washington, DC: National Academy Press.

Dubuc, B. (2002). Antidepressants and the growth of new neurons. McGill University, Canada. Retrieved February 14, 2008, from http://thebrain.mcgill.ca/flash/a/a_08/a_08_cl/a_08_cl_dep/a_08_cl_dep.html.

Duck, S. (1992). *Human relationships* (2nd ed.). Newbury Park, CA: Sage.

Duenwald, M. (2005, March). Building a better grapefruit. *Discover, 26(3),* 26–27.

Dugoua, J., Mills, E., Perri, D., & Koren, G. (2006). Safety and efficacy of ginkgo (*Ginkgo biloba*) during pregnancy and lactation. *Canadian Journal of Clinical Pharmacology, 13,* e277–e284.

Duncan, J., Seitz, R. J., Kolodny, J., Bor, D., Herzog, H., Ahmed, A., Newell, F. N., & Emslie, H. (2000, July 21). A neural basis for general intelligence. *Science, 289,* 457–460.

Dunn, K. (2006, December). Runners-up: John Donoghue, neuroscientist at Brown University. *Discover, 27(2),* 39.

Dutton, D. G., & Aron, A. P. (1974). Some evidence for heightened sexual attraction under conditions of high anxiety. *Journal of Personality and Social Psychology, 30,* 510–517.

Dweck, C. S. (December 2007/January 2008). The secret to raising smart kids. *Scientific American Mind, 18(6),* 37–43.

Dykema, J., Bergbower, K., & Peterson, C. (1995). Pessimistic explanatory style, stress, and illness. *Journal of Social and Clinical Psychology, 14,* 357–371.

Eaddy, S. L. (2001). An exploration of the relationship between hardiness and resilience for people impacted by HIV. *Dissertation Abstracts International, Section A: Humanities and Social Sciences, 61,* 4301.

Eagly, A. H., Ashmore, R. D., Makhijani, M. G., & Kennedy, L. C. (1991). What is beautiful is good, but . . . : A meta-analytic review of the social psychological literature. *Psychological Bulletin, 100,* 283–308. [See also: Dion, 1986; Hatfield & Sprecher, 1986]

Eagly, A. H., & Wood, W. (1999). The origins of sex differences in human behavior: Evolved dispositions versus social roles. *American Psychologist, 54,* 408–423.

Ebbinghaus, H., (1973). *Psychology: An elementary textbook.* New York: Arno Press. (Original work published 1908.)

Eberhardt, J. L., & Randall, J. L. (1997). The essential notion of race. *Psychological Science, 8,* 198–203.

Eccles, J. S., Midgley, C., Wigfield, A., Buchanan, C. M., Reuman, D., Flanagan, C., & Mac Iver, D. (1993). Development during adolescence: The impact of stage-environment fit on young adolescents' experiences in schools and in families. *American Psychologist, 48,* 90–101.

Eckensberger, L. H. (1994). Moral development and its measurement across cultures. In W. J. Lonner & R. Malpass (Eds.), *Psychology and culture* (pp. 71–78). Boston, MA: Allyn & Bacon.

Edwards, A. E., & Acker, L. E. (1962). A demonstration of the long-term retention of a conditioned galvanic skin response. *Psychosomatic Medicine, 24,* 459–463.

Edwards, K. J., Hershberger, P. J., Russell, R. K., & Markert, R. J. (2001). Stress, negative social exchange, and health symptoms in university students. *Journal of American College Health, 50,* 75–86.

Ehrlich, P. R. (2000a). *Genes, cultures and the human prospect.* Washington, DC: Island Press.

Ehrlich, P. R. (2000b, September 22). The tangled skeins of nature and nurture in human evolution. *The Chronicle of Higher Education,* B7–B11.

Eich, E., Macaulay, D., Loewenstein, R. J., & Dihle, P. H. (1997). Memory, amnesia, and dissociative identity disorder. *Psychological Science, 8,* 417–422.

Eichenbaum, H. (1997, July 18). How does the brain organize memories? *Science, 277,* 330–332.

Eichorn, D. H., & VandenBos, G. R. (1985). Dissemination of scientific and professional knowledge: Journal publication within the APA. *American Psychologist, 40,* 1309–1316.

Einstein, G. O., & McDaniel, M. A. (2005) Prospective memory: Multiple retrieval processes. *Current Directions in Psychological Science 14 ,* 286–290.

Eisenberger, R., & Cameron, J. (1996). Detrimental effects of reward: Reality or myth? *American Psychologist, 51,* 1153–1166.

Eisler, R., & Levine, D. S. (2002). Nurture, nature, and caring: We are not prisoners of our genes. *Brain and Mind, 3,* 9–52.

Ekman, P. (1984). Expression and the nature of emotion. In K. R. Scherer & P. Ekman (Eds.), *Approaches to emotion.* Hillsdale, NJ: Erlbaum.

Ekman, P. (1992). Facial expressions of emotion: New findings, new questions. *Psychological Science, 3,* 34–38.

Ekman, P. (1993). Facial expression and emotion. *American Psychologist, 48,* 384–392.

Ekman, P. (1994). Strong evidence for universals in facial expressions: A reply to Russell's mistaken critique. *Psychological Bulletin, 115,* 268–287.

Ekman, P. (2003). *Emotions revealed: Recognizing faces and feelings to improve communication and emotional life.* New York: Times Books, Henry Holt and Company. [See also: Ekman, 1984, 1992, 1993; Ekman & Friesen, 1971, 1986; Ekman & Rosenberg, 1997; Ekman et al., 1969, 1987; Keating, 1994]

Ekman, P., & Friesen, W. V. (1971). Constants across cultures in the face and emotion. *Journal of Personality and Social Psychology, 17,* 124–129.

Ekman, P., & Friesen, W. V. (1986). A new pan-cultural facial expression of emotion. *Motivation and Emotion, 10,* 159–168.

Ekman, P., Friesen, W. V., O'Sullivan, M., Chan, A., Diacoyanni-Tarlatzis, I., Heider, K., Krause, R., LeCompte, W. A., Pitcairn, T., Ricci-Bitti, P. E., Scherer, K., Tomita, M., & Tzavaras, A. (1987). Universal and cultural differences in the judgments of facial expressions of emotion. *Journal of Personality and Social Psychology, 53,* 712–717.

Ekman, P., & Rosenberg, E. (1997). *What the face reveals.* New York: Oxford University Press.

Ekman, P., Sorenson, E. R., & Friesen, W. V. (1969). Pan-cultural elements in facial displays in emotion. *Science, 764,* 86–88.

Elbert, T., Pantev, C., Wienbruch, C., Rockstroh, B., & Taub, E. (1995, October 13). Increased cortical representation of the fingers of the left hand in string players. *Science, 270,* 305–307.

Eley, T. C. (1997). General genes: A new theme in developmental psychopathology. *Current Directions in Psychological Science, 6,* 90–95.

Elfenbein, H. A., & Ambady, N. (2003). Universals and cultural differences in recognizing emotions. *Current Directions in Psychological Science, 12,* 159–164.

El-Hai, J. (1999). Uniquely twins. *Minnesota Medicine.* Retrieved on November 8, 2004, from www.mnmed.org/Protected/99MNMED/9903/El-Hai .html.

Elliott, G. R., & Eisdorfer, C. (Eds.). (1982). *Stress and human health: Analysis and implications of research (A study by the Institute of Medicine/National Academy of Sciences).* New York: Springer.

Ellis, A. (1987). *The practice of rational emotive therapy (RET).* New York: Springer.

Ellis A. (1990). *The essential Albert Ellis: Seminal writings on psychotherapy.* New York: Springer.

Ellis, A. (1996). *Better, deeper, and more enduring brief therapy: The rational emotive behavior therapy approach.* New York: Brunner/Mazel.

Ellison, J. (1984, June). The seven frames of mind. *Psychology Today, 18,* 21–24, 26.

Ellsworth, P. C. (1994). William James and emotion: Is a century of fame worth a century of misunderstanding? *Psychological Review, 101,* 222–229.

Engle, R. W. (2002). Working memory capacity as executive attention. *Current Directions in Psychological Science, 11,* 19–23.

Ennemoser, M., & Schneider, W. (2007). Relations of television viewing and reading: Findings from a 4-Year longitudinal study. *Journal of Educational Psychology, 99,* 349–368.

Ennis, M., Kelly, K. S., & Lambert, P. L. (2001). Sex differences in cortisol excretion during anticipation of a psychological stressor: Possible support for the tend-and-befriend hypothesis. *Stress and Health, 17,* 253–261.

Enserink, M. (2000, July 28). Searching for the mark of Cain. *Science, 289,* 575–579.

Epel, E. S., Blackburn, E. H., Lin, J., Dhabhar, F. S., Adler, N. E., Morrow, J. D., & Cawthon, R. M. (2004, December 7). Accerated telomere shortening in response to life stress. *Proceedings of the National Academy of Science, 101,* 17, 312–17, 315.

Epstein, S. (1980). The stability of confusion: A reply to Mischel and Peake. *Psychological Review, 90,* 179–184.

Epstein, S., & Feist, G. J. (1988). Relation between self- and other-acceptance and its moderation by identification. *Journal of Personality and Social Psychology, 54,* 309–315.

Erdberg, P. (1990). Rorschach assessment. In G. Goldstein & M. Hersen (Eds.), *Psychological assessment* (2nd ed.). New York: Pergamon.

Erdelyi, M. H. (1992). Psychodymanics and the unconscious. *American Psychologist, 47,* 784–787.

Ericsson, K. A., & Charness, N. (1994). Expert performance: Its structure and acquisition. *American Psychologist, 49,* 725–747.

Ericsson, K. A., Charness, N., Feltovich, P. J., & Hoffman, R. R. (Eds.). (2006). *The Cambridge handbook of expertise and expert performance.* New York: Cambridge University Press. [See also: Bransford et al., 1986; Gardner, 1993; Glaser, 1984; Greeno, 1989; Klahr & Simon, 2001; Mayer, 1983; Who Wants to Be a Genius?, 2001]

Ericsson, K. A., Krampe, R. T., & Tesch-Römer, C. (1993). The role of deliberate practice in the acquisition of expert performance. *Psychological Review, 100,* 363–406.

Erikson, E. H. (1963). *Childhood and society* (2nd ed.). New York: Norton.

Evans, G. W., Bullinger, M., & Hygge, S. (1998). Chronic noise exposure and physiological response: A prospective study of children living under environmental stress. *Psychological Science, 9,* 75–77.

Exner, J. E. Jr. (1974). *The Rorschach: A comprehensive system: Vol. 1.* New York: Wiley.

Exner, J. E. Jr. (1978). *The Rorschach: A comprehensive system: Vol. 2: Current research and interpretation.* New York: Wiley.

Exner, J. E. Jr., & Weiner, I. B. (1982). *The Rorschach: A comprehensive system: Vol. 3: Assessment of children and adolescents.* New York: Wiley.

Eysenck, H. J. (1952). The effects of psychotherapy: An evaluation. *Journal of Consulting Psychology, 16,* 319–324.

Ezzell, C. (2003, February). Why??? The neuroscience of suicide. *Scientific American, 288,* 45–51. [See also: Hirschfeld & Goodwin, 1988; Nemeroff, 1998]

Fackelmann, K. (1998, November 28). It's a girl! Is sex selection the first step to designer children? *Science News, 154,* 350–351.

Fadiman, J., & Frager, R. (2001). *Personality and personal growth.* Upper Saddle River, NJ: Prentice-Hall.

Fajans, J. (1985). The person in social context: The social character of Baining "psychology." In G. M. White & J. Kirkpatrick (Eds.), *Person, self, and experience* (pp. 367–400). Berkeley: University of California Press.

Fallon, A., & Rozin, P. (1985). Sex differences in perceptions of desirable body states. *Journal of Abnormal Psychology, 94,* 102–105.

Fancher, R. E. (1979). *Pioneers of psychology.* New York: W. W. Norton.

Fantz, R. L. (1963). Pattern vision in newborn infants. *Science, 140,* 296–297.

Farah, M. J. (2008, February). Stimulation, stress and brain development. Paper delivered at the American Association for the Advancement of Science Annual Meeting in Boston, MA.

Faraone, S. V., Sergeant, J., Gillberg, C., & Biederman, J. (2003). The worldwide prevalence of ADHD: is it an American condition? *World Psychiatry, 2,* 104–113.

Farina, A., Fischer, E. H., Boudreau, L. A., & Belt, W. E. (1996). Mode of target presentation in measuring the stigma of mental disorder. *Journal of Applied Social Psychology, 26,* 2147–2156.

Farquhar, J. W., Maccoby, N., & Solomon, D. S. (1984). Community applications of behavioral medicine. In W. D. Gentry (Ed.), *Handbook of behavioral medicine* (pp. 437–478). New York: Guilford Press.

Faulkner, M. (2001). The onset and alleviation of learned helplessness in older hospitalized people. *Aging and Mental Health, 5,* 379–386.

Fazio, R. H. (2001). On the automatic activation of associated evaluations: An overview. *Cognition & Emotion, 15,* 115–141.

Fehr, B. (1988). How do I love thee? Let me consult my prototype. *Journal of Personality and Social Psychology, 55*(4), 557–579.

Fein, M. L. (1993). *I.A.M.: A common sense guide to coping with anger.* Westport, CT: Praeger/Greenwood.

Feingold, A. (1988). Matching for attractiveness in romantic partners and same-sex friends: A meta-analysis and theoretical critique. *Psychological Bulletin, 104,* 226–235. [See also: Cash & Killcullen, 1985; Folkes, 1982; Hatfield & Sprecher, 1986]

Feingold, A. (1990). Gender differences in effects of physical attractiveness on ro mantic attraction: A comparison across five research paradigms. *Journal of Personality and Social Psychology, 59,* 981–993.

Ferguson, C. J. (2002). Media violence: Miscast causality. *American Psychologist, 57,* 446–447.

Fernandez, A., & Glenberg, A. M. (1985). Changing environmental context does not reliably affect memory. *Memory and Cognition, 13,* 333–345.

Ferster, D., & Spruston, N. (1995, November 3). Cracking the neuronal code. *Science, 270,* 756–757.

Festinger, L. (1957). *A theory of cognitive dissonance.* Stanford, CA: Stanford University Press.

Festinger, L., Schachter, S., & Back, K. (1950). *Social pressures in informal groups: A study of a housing community.* New York: Harper & Row.

Field, T. F., & Schanberg, S. M. (1990). Massage alters growth and catecholamine production in preterm newborns. In N. Gunzenhauser (Ed.), *Advances in touch* (pp. 96–104). Skillman, NJ: Johnson & Johnson Co.

Fields, H. L. (1978, November). Secrets of the placebo. *Psychology Today*, 172.

Fields, H. L., & Levine, J. D. (1984). Placebo analgesia: A role for endorphins. *Trends in Neuroscience, 7*, 271–273.

Fields, R. D. (2004, April). The other half of the brain. *Scientific American, 290*(4), 54–61.

Figley, C. R. (2002). *Treating compassion fatigue.* New York: Brunner-Routledge.

Filsinger, E. E., & Fabes, R. A. (1985). Odor communication, pheromones, and human families. *Journal of Marriage and the Family, 47*, 349–359.

Finamore, D. C. (2000). The relationship of learned helplessness, hardiness, and depression in married, abused women. Doctoral dissertation, University of Sarasota.

Finckenauer, J. O., Gavin, P. W., Hovland, A., Storvoll, E. (1999). *Scared straight: The panacea phenomenon revisited.* Prospect Heights, IL: Waveland Press.

Findley, M. J., & Cooper, H. M. (1983). Locus of control and academic achievement: A literature review. *Journal of Personality and Social Psychology, 44*, 419–427.

Finer, B. (1980). Hypnosis and anaesthesia. In G. D. Burrows & L. Donnerstein (Eds.), *Handbook of hypnosis and psychosomatic medicine.* Amsterdam: Elsevier/North Holland Biomedical Press.

Fiorillo, C. D., Tobler, P. N., & Schultz, W. (2003, March 21). Discrete coding of reward probability and uncertainty by dopamine neurons. *Science, 299*, 1898–1902.

Fiorito, G., & Scotto, P. (1992). Observational learning in Octopus vulgaris. *Science, 256*, 545–547.

Fischer, A. H. (1993). Sex differences in emotionality: Fact or stereotype? *Feminism & Psychology, 3*, 303–318.

Fischer, A. H., Rodriguez Mosquera, P. M., van Vianen, A. E. M., & Manstead, A. S. R. (2004). Gender and culture differences in emotion. *Emotion, 4*, 87–94. [See also: Baumeister et al., 1990; Fischer et al., 1993; Gottman, 1994; Gottman & Krokoff, 1989; Gottman & Levenson, 1986; Oatley & Duncan, 1994; Polefrone & Manuck, 1987; Rusting & Nolen-Hoeksema, 1998; Shaver & Hazan, 1987; Shields, 1991]

Fischer, P. C., Smith, R. J., Leonard, E., Fuqua, D. R., Campbell, J. L., & Masters, M. A. (1993). Sex differences on affective dimensions: Continuing examination. *Journal of Counseling and Development, 71*, 440–443.

Fischer, P. J., & Breakey, W. R. (1991). The epidemiology of alcohol, drug, and mental disorders among homeless persons. *American Psychologist, 46*, 1115–1128.

Fischhoff, B. (1975). Hindsight AD foresight: The effect of outcome knowledge on judgment under uncertainty. *Journal of Experimental Psychology: Human Perception and Performance, 1*, 288–299.

Fisher, H. E. (1992). *Anatomy of love: The natural history of monogamy, adultery, and divorce.* New York: W. W. Norton and Company.

Fisher, S., & Greenberg, R. P. (1985). *The scientific credibility of Freud's theories and therapy.* New York: Columbia University Press.

Fishman, H. C. (1993). *Intensive structural therapy: Treating families in their social context.* New York: Basic Books.

Fiske, D. W., & Fogg, L. (1990). But the reviewers are making different criticisms of my paper! Diversity and uniqueness in reviewer comments. *American Psychologist, 45*, 591–598.

Fiske, S. T., Cuddy, A. J. C., & Glick, P. (2007). Universal dimensions of social cognition: Warmth and competence. *Trends in Cognitive Science, 11*, 77–83.

Fiske, S. T., & Neuberg, S. L. (1990). A continuum of impression formation, from category-based to individuating processes: Influences of information and motivation on attention and interpretation. In M. P.

Zanna (Ed.), *Advances in experimental social psychology (Vol. 23).* San Diego, CA: Academic Press.

Flavell, J. H. (1985). *Cognitive development* (2nd ed.). Englewood Cliffs, NJ: Prentice-Hall.

Flavell, J. H. (1996). Piaget's legacy. *Psychological Science, 7*, 200–203.

Fleeson, W. (2004). Moving personality beyond the person-situation debate: The challenge and the opportunity of within-person variability. *Current Directions in Psychological Science, 13*, 83–87.

Fleischman, J. (2002). *Phineas Gage: A gruesome but true story about brain science.* Boston: Houghton Mifflin.

Fletcher, A., Lamond, N., van den Heuvel, C. J., & Dawson, D. (2003). Prediction of performance during sleep deprivation and alcohol intoxication using a quantitative model of work-related fatigue. *SleepResearch Online, 5*, 67–75. Retrieved on November 6, 2004, from www.sro.org/2003/Fletcher/67/.

Fletcher, G. J. O., & Ward, C. (1988). Attribution theory and processes: A cross-cultural perspective. In M. H. Bond (Ed.), *The cross-cultural challenge to social psychology* (pp. 230–244). Newbury Park, CA: Sage.

Flier, J. S. (2006, May 12). Regulating energy balance: The substrate strikes back. *Science, 312*, 861–864.

Flier, J. S., & Maratos-Flier, E. (2007, September). What fuels fat. *Scientific American, 297*(3), 72–81. [See also: Campfield et al., 1998; Comuzzie & Allison, 1998; Gura, 1998, 2003; Hill & Peters, 1998; Levine et al., 1999; Ravussin & Danforth, 1999]

Flynn, J. R. (1987). Massive IQ gains in 14 nations: What IQ tests really measure. *Psychological Bulletin, 101*, 171–191.

Flynn, J. R. (2003, June). Movies about intelligence: The limitations of g. *Current Directions in Psychological Science, 12*, 95–99.

Flynn, J. R. (2007, October/November). Solving the IQ puzzle. *Scientific American Mind, 18*(5), 25–31.

Fogel, A. (1991). Movement and communication in human infancy: The social dynamics of development. *Human Movement Science, 11*, 387–423.

Foley, V. D. (1979). Family therapy. In R. J. Corsini (Ed.), *Current psychotherapies* (2nd ed., pp. 460–469). Itasca, IL: Peacock.

Folkes, V. S. (1982). Forming relationships and the matching hypothesis. *Journal of Personality and Social Psychology, 8*, 631–636.

Folkins, C. H., & Sime, W. (1981). Physical fitness training and mental health. *American Psychologist, 36*, 373–389.

Folkman, S. & Lazarus, R. S. (1980). An analysis of coping in a middle-aged community sample. *Journal of Health and Social Behavior, 21*, 219–239.

Ford, C. S., & Beach, F. A. (1951). *Patterns of sexual behavior.* New York: Harper & Row.

Forgatch, M. S., Patterson, G. R., & Ray, J. A. (1994). Divorce and boys' adjustment problems: Two paths with a single model. In E. M. Hetherington, D. Reiss, & R. Plomin (Eds.), *Stress, coping, and resiliency in children and the family* (pp. 96–110). Hillsdale, NJ: Erlbaum.

Foster, J. B. (2006, November 1). Racial, ethnic variables shape the experience of chronic pain. *Applied Neurology.* Retrieved November 26, 2007, from http://appneurology.com/showArticle.jhtml?articleId=196604178.

Fowers, B. J., & Richardson, F. C. (1996). Why is multiculturalism good? *American Psychologist, 31*, 609–621.

Fowler, H. (1965). *Curiosity and exploratory behavior.* New York: Macmillan.

Franklin, M. S., & Zyphur, M. J. (2005). The role of dreams in the evolution of the human mind. *Evolutionary Psychology, 3*, 59–78.

Fraser, S. (Ed.). (1995). *The bell curve wars: Race, intelligence, and the future of America.* New York: Basic Books.

Fredrickson, B. L., Maynard, K. E., Helms, M. J., Haney, T. L., Siegler, I. C., & Barefoot, J. C. (2000). Hostility predicts magnitude and duration of blood pressure response to anger. *Journal of Behavioral Medicine, 23*, 229–243.

Freedman, D. J., Riesenhuber, M., Poggio, T., & Miller, E. K. (2001, January 12). Categorical representation of visual stimuli in the primate prefrontal cortex. *Science, 291*, 312–316.

Freedman, J. L. (1984) Effect of television violence on aggression. *Psychological Bulletin, 96*, 227–246.

Freedman, J. L. (1996, May). Violence in the mass media and violence in society: The link is unproven. *Harvard Mental Health Letter, 12*(11), 4–6.

French, E. G. & Thomas, F. H. (1958). The relation of achievement motivation to problem-solving effectiveness. *Journal of Abnormal and Social Psychology, 56*, 46–48.

Freud, S. (1915). *The collected papers.* New York: Collier.

Freud, S. (1925). The unconscious. In S. Freud, *The collected papers (Vol. 4).* London: Hogarth.

Freud, S. (1953). *The interpretation of dreams.* New York: Basic Books. (Original edition published in 1900).

Fridlund, A. J. (1990). Evolution and facial action in reflex, social motive, and paralanguage. In P. K. Ackles, J. R. Jennings, & M. G. H. Coles (Eds.), *Advances in psychophysiology.* Greenwich, CT: JAI Press.

Friedman, H. S., & Booth-Kewley, S. (1988). Validity of the Type A construct: A reprise. *Psychological Bulletin, 104*, 381–384.

Friedman, H. S., Hawley, P. H., & Tucker, J. S. (1994). Personality, health, and longevity. *Current Directions in Psychological Science, 3*, 37–41.

Friedman, H. S., Tucker, J. S., Schwartz, J. E., Tomlinson-Keasey, C., Martin, L. R., Wingard, D. L., & Criqui, M. H. (1995). Psychosocial and behavioral predictors of longevity: The aging and death of the "termites." *American Psychologist, 50*, 69–78.

Friedman, J. M. (2003, February 7). A war on obesity, not the obese. *Science, 299*, 856–858.

Friedman, M., & Rosenman, R. F. (1974). *Type A behavior and your heart.* New York: Knopf.

Friedman, M., & Ulmer, D. (1984). *Treating Type A behavior—and your heart.* New York: Knopf.

Friedman, M. J. (2004). Acknowledging the psychiatric cost of war. *New England Journal of Medicine, 351*, 75–77.

Friend, R., Rafferty, Y., & Bramel, D. (1990). A puzzling misinterpretation of the Asch "conformity" study. *European Journal of Social Psychology, 20*, 29–44.

Frincke, J. L., & Pate, W. E. II (2004). Yesterday, today, and tomorrow. Careers in psychology: 2004. What students need to know. Retrieved on October 14, 2004, from http://research.apa.org.

Frith, C. D., & Frith, U. (1999, November 26). Interacting minds—A biological basis. *Science, 286*, 1692–1695.

Frith, U. (1993, June). Autism. *Scientific American, 268*, 108–114.

Frith, U. (1997). Autism. *Scientific American (Special Issue: The Mind), 7*(1), 92–98.

Fromm, E., & Shor, R. E. (Eds.). (1979). *Hypnosis: Developments in research and new perspectives* (2nd ed.). Hawthorne, NY: Aldine.

Fujita, F., Diener, E., & Sandvik, E. (1991). Gender differences in dysphoria and well-being: The case for emotional intensity. *Journal of Personality and Social Psychology, 61*, 427–434.

Funder, D. C. (1983a). Three issues in predicting more of the people: A reply to Mischel & Peake. *Psychological Review, 90*, 283–289.

Funder, D. C. (1983b). The "consistency" controversy and the accuracy of personality judgments. *Journal of Personality, 51*, 346–359.

Funder, D. C., & Ozer, D. J. (1983). Behavior as a function of the situation. *Journal of Personality and Social Psychology, 44*, 107–112.

Furnham, A. (1982). Explanations for unemployment in Britain. *European Journal of Social Psychology, 12*, 335–352.

Furnham, A., Moutafi, J., & Crump, J. (2003). The relationship between the revised NEO-Personality Inventory and the Myers-Briggs Type Indicator. *Social Behavior and Personality, 31,* 577–584. [See also: McCrae & Costa, 1989; Pittenger, 1993]

Furumoto, L. (1979). Mary Whiton Calkins (1863–1930), fourteenth president of the American Psychological Association. *Journal of the History of the Behavioral Sciences, 15,* 346–356. [Cited in Milar, K. S. (n.d.). An historical view of some early women psychologists and the psychology of women. Archived at the Classics in the History of Psychology site: http://psychclassics.yorku.ca/Special/Women/variability.htm.]

Furumoto, L. (1991). From "paired associates" to a psychology of self: The intellectual odyssey of Mary Whiton Calkins. In G. A. Kimble, M. Wertheimer, & C. White (Eds.), *Portraits of pioneers in psychology* (pp. 57–72). Washington, DC: American Psychological Association; and Hillsdale, NJ: Erlbaum.

Furumoto, L., & Scarborough, E. (1986). Placing women in the history of psychology: The first American women psychologists. *American Psychologist, 41,* 35–42.

Fyhn, M., Molden, S., Witter, M. P., Moser, E. L., & Moser, M. B. (2004, August 27). Spatial representation in the entorhinal cortex. *Science, 305,* 1258–1264.

Gabbay, F. H. (January, 1992). Behavior-genetic strategies in the study of emotion. *Psychological Science, 3*(1), 50–54.

Gadsby, P. (2000, July). Tourist in a taste lab. *Discover, 21,* 70–75.

Gaffan, D. (2005, September 30). Widespread cortical networks underlie memory and attention. *Science, 309,* 2172–2173.

Gage, F. H. (2003, September). Brain, repair yourself. *Scientific American, 289*(3), 46–53. [See also Baringa, 2003a; Kempermann & Gage, 1999]

Gahlinger, P. M. (2004). Club drugs: MDMA, gamma-hydroxybutyrate (GHB), rohypnol, and ketamine. *American Family Physician, 69,* 2619–2626.

Gailliot, M. T., Baumeister, R. F., DeWall, C. N., Maner, J. K., Plant, E. A., Tice, D. M., Brewer, L. E., & Schmeichel, B. J. (2007). Self-control relies on glucose as a limited energy source: Willpower is more than a metaphor. *Journal of Personality and Social Psychology, 92,* 325–336.

Gainetdinov, R. R., Wetsel, W. C., Jones, S. R., Levin, E. D., Jaber, M., & Caron, M. G. (1999). Role of serotonin in the paradoxical calming effect of psychostimulants on hyperactivity. *Science, 283,* 397–401. [See also: Barkley, 1998; Wu, 1998]

Galambos, N. L. (1992). Parent–adolescent relations. *Current Directions in Psychological Science, 1,* 146–149.

Galea, S., Vlahov, D., Resnick, H., Ahern, J., Susser, E., & Gold, J., Bucuvalas, M., & Kilpatrick, D. (2003). Trends of probable post-traumatic stress disorder in New York City after the September 11th terrorist attacks. *American Journal of Epidemiology, 158,* 514–524.

Gallagher, W. (1994, September). How we become what we are. *The Atlantic Monthly,* 39–55.

Gallo, P. S., & McClintock, C. G. (1965). Cooperative and competitive behavior in mixed-motive games. *Journal of Conflict Resolution, 9,* 68–78.

Gallo, V., & Chittajallu, R. (2001, May 4). Unwrapping glial cells from the synapse: What lies inside? *Science, 292,* 872–873.

Gambrel, P. A., & Cianci, R. (2003). Maslow's hierarch of needs: Does it apply in a collectivist culture? *Journal of Applied Management and Entrepreneurship, 8,* 143–161. Retrieved April 4, 2008, from www3.tjcu.edu.cn/wangshangketang/lyxgl/yuedu/21.pdf

Gami, A. S., Howard, D. E., Olson, E. J., & Somers, V. K. (2005, March 24). Day-night pattern of sudden death in obstructive sleep apnea. *New England Journal of Medicine, 352,* 1206–1214. [See also Dement, 1999; Benson, 2003c]

Ganchrow, J. R., Steiner, J. E., & Daher, M. (1983). Neonatal facial expressions in response to different qualities and intensities of gustatory stimuli. *Infant Behavior and Development, 6,* 189–200.

Garcia, J. (1981). The logic and limits of mental aptitude testing. *American Psychologist, 36,* 1172–1180.

Garcia, J. (1990). Learning without memory. *Journal of Cognitive Neuroscience, 2,* 287–305.

Garcia, J. (1993). Misrepresentations of my criticisms of Skinner. *American Psychologist, 48,* 1158.

Garcia, J., & Koelling, R. A. (1966). The relation of cue to consequence in avoidance learning. *Psychonomic Science, 4,* 123–124.

Gardiner, H. W., Mutter, J. D., & Kosmitzki, C. (1998). *Lives across cultures: Cross-cultural human development.* Boston: Allyn & Bacon.

Gardner, H. (1983). *Frames of mind.* New York: Basic Books.

Gardner, H. (1985). *The mind's new science: A history of the cognitive revolution.* New York: Basic Books.

Gardner, H. (1993). *Creating minds: An anatomy of creativity seen through the lives of Freud, Einstein, Picasso, Stravinsky, Eliot, Graham, and Gandhi.* New York: Basic Books.

Gardner, H. (1999a). *Intelligence reframed.* New York: Basic Books.

Gardner, H. (1999b, February). Who owns intelligence? *The Atlantic Monthly,* 67–76

Gardner, R. A., & Gardner, B. T. (1969). Teaching language to a chimpanzee. *Science, 165,* 664–672.

Gardyn, R., & Wellner, A. S. (2001, February). Blowin' smoke. *American Demographics, 23*(2), 20–22.

Garland, A., & Zigler, E. (1993). Adolescent suicide prevention: Current research and social policy implications. *American Psychologist, 48,* 169–182.

Garmezy, N. (1991). Resilience in children's adaptation to negative life events and stressed environments. *Pediatrics, 20,* 459–466.

Garnsey, S. M. (1993). Event-related brain potentials in the study of language: An introduction. *Language and Cognitive Processes, 8,* 337–356.

Gazzaniga, M. S. (1970). *The bisected brain.* New York: Appleton-Century-Crofts.

Gazzaniga, M. S. (1998a). *The mind's past.* Berkeley: University of California Press.

Gazzaniga, M. S. (1998b, July). The split brain revisited. Scientific American, 279, 50–55.

Gazzaniga, M. S. (2005). Forty-five years of split-brain research and still going strong. *Nature Reviews Neuroscience, 6,* 653–659.

Gehring, W. J., & Willoughby, A. R. (2002, March 22). The medial frontal cortex and the rapid processing of monetary gains and losses. *Science, 295,* 2279–2282.

Gelernter, J. (1994, June 17). Behavioral genetics in transition. *Science, 264,* 1684–1689.

Gelman, R., & Shatz, M. (1978). Appropriate speech adjustments: The operation of conversational constraints on talk to two-year-olds. In M. Lewis & L. A. Rosenblum (Eds.), *Interaction, conversation, and the development of language* (pp. 27–61). New York: Wiley.

Gelman, S. A., & Wellman, H. M. (1991). Insides and essences: Early understandings of the non-obvious. *Cognition, 38,* 213–244.

Gentner, D., & Stevens, A. L. (1983). *Mental models.* Hillsdale, NJ: Erlbaum.

George, M. S. (2003, September). Stimulating the brain. *Scientific American, 289*(3), 67–73. [See also: George et al., 1999; Helmuth, 2001b; Travis, 2000b; Wassermann & Lisanby, 2001]

George, M. S., Nahas, Z., Kozel, F. A., Goldman, J., Molloy, M., & Oliver, N. (1999). Improvement of depression following transcranial magnetic stimulation. *Current Psychiatry Reports, 1,* 114–124.

Gergen, K. J., Gulerce, A., Lock, A., & Misra, G. (1996). Psychological science in cultural context. *American Psychologist, 51,* 496–503.

Gernsbacher, M. A., Dawson, M., & Goldsmith, H. H. (2005). Three reasons not to believe in an autism epidemic. *Current Directions in Psychological Science, 14,* 55–58.

Getzels, J. W., & Csikszentmihalyi, M. (1976). *The creative vision.* New York: Wiley.

Gibbons, A. (1998, September 4). Which of our genes make us human? *Science, 281,* 1432–1434.

Gibbons, R. D., Brown, C. H., Hur, K., Marcus, S. M., Bhaumik, D. K., & Mann, J. J. (2007) Relationship between antidepressants and suicide attempts: an analysis of the veterans health administration data sets. *American Journal of Psychiatry, 164,* 1044–1049.

Gibbs, W. W. (1995, March). Seeking the criminal element. *Scientific American,* 100–107.

Gibbs, W. W. (1996, August). Gaining on fat. *Scientific American, 275*(2), 88–94. [See also: Callaway, 1987; Jeffery, 1987]

Gibbs, W. W. (2001). Side splitting. *Scientific American, 284,* 24–25.

Gibbs, W. W. (2003, December). The unseen genome: Beyond DNA. *Scientific American, 289*(6), 106–113.

Gibbs, W. W. (2005, June). Obesity: An overblown epidemic. *Scientific American, 292*(6), 70–77.

Gibson, E. J., & Walk, R. D. (1960, April). The "visual cliff." *Scientific American,* 64–71.

Gilbert, K. R. (1996). "We've had the same loss, why don't we have the same grief?" Loss and differential grief in families. *Death Studies, 20,* 269–283.

Gilbert, P., & Gilbert, J. (2003). Entrapment and arrested fight and flight in depression: An exploration using focus groups. *Psychology and Psychotherapy: Theory, Research, and Practice, 76,* 173–188.

Gilbert, R. M. (1992). *Extraordinary relationships: A new way of thinking about human interactions.* New York: Wiley.

Gilbertson, J., Dindia, K., & Allen, M. (1998). Relational continuity, constructional units, and the maintenance of relationships. *Journal of Social and Personal Relationships, 15,* 774–790.

Gilligan, C. (1982). *In a different voice: Psychological theory and women's development.* Cambridge, MA: Harvard University Press.

Gilligan, S. G., & Bower, G. H. (1984). Cognitive consequences of emotional arousal. In C. Izard, J. Kagan, & R. Zajonc (Eds.), *Emotions, cognitions and behavior.* New York: Cambridge University Press.

Gitlin, M. J. (1990). *The psychotherapist's guide to psychopharmacology.* New York: The Free Press.

Gittrich, G. (2003, May 27). Trauma aid in limbo: Millions unspent as relative few seek counseling. *New York Daily News,* 8.

Givens, D. B. (1983). *Love signals: How to attract a mate.* New York: Crown.

Gladwell, M. (2005). *Blink.* New York: Little Brown and Company. [See also: Bechara et al., 1997; Gehring & Willoughby, 2002; Vogel, 1997a]

Glanz, J. (1998, April 3). Magnetic brain imaging traces a stairway to memory. *Science, 280,* 37.

Glaser, R. (1984). Education and thinking: The role of knowledge. *American Psychologist, 39,* 93–104.

Glaser, R. (1990). The reemergence of learning theory within instructional research. *American Psychologist, 45,* 29–39.

Glass, R. M. (2001, March). Electroconvulsive therapy: Time to bring it out of the shadows. *JAMA: Journal of the American Medical Association, 285,* 1346–1348.

Gleitman, H. (1991). Edward Chace Tolman: A life of scientific and social purpose. In G. A. Kimble, M. Wertheimer, & C. L. White (Eds.), *Portraits of pioneers in psychology* (pp. 226–241). Washington, DC: American Psychological Association. [See also: Kesner & Olton, 1990; Olton, 1992; Tolman, 1932]

Glenn, D. (2003, October 24). Nightmare scenarios. *The Chronicle of Higher Education,* A-14–A-16.

Goel, V., & Dolan, R. J. (2001). The functional anatomy of humor: Segregating cognitive and affective components. *Nature Neuroscience, 4,* 237–238. [See also: Winerman, 2006]

Goldapple, K., Segal, Z., Garson, C., Lau, M., Bieling, P., Kennedy, S., & Mayberg, H. (2004). Modulation of cortical-limbic pathways in major depression:

Treatment-specific effects of cognitive behavior therapy. *Archives of General Psychiatry, 61,* 34–41.

Goldberg, L. R. (1981). Language and individual differences: The search for universals in personality lexicons. In L. Wheeler (Ed.), *Review of personality and social psychology* (Vol. 2, pp. 141–165). Beverly Hills, CA: Sage.

Goldberg, L. R. (1993). The structure of phenotypic personality traits. *American Psychologist, 48,* 26–34.

Golden, C., & Figueroa, M. (2007). Facing cultural challenges in personality testing: A review of *Assessing hispanic clients using the MMPI-2 and MMPI-A*. Retrieved April 16, 2008, from PsycCritiques at http://content.apa.org/critiques/52/41/1.html?sid=7903CA01-0711-4940-886C-9E3D3DB7D4AA.

Golden, O. (2000). The federal response to child abuse and neglect. *American Psychologist, 55,* 1050–1053.

Goldin-Meadow, S., & Mylander, C. (1990). Beyond the input given: The child's role in the acquisition of language. *Language, 66,* 323–355.

Goldman-Rakic, P. S. (1992, September). Working memory and the mind. *Scientific American, 267,* 110–117.

Goleman, D. (1980, February). 1528 little geniuses and how they grew. *Psychology Today, 14,* 28–53.

Goleman, D. (1995). *Emotional intelligence.* New York: Bantam Books.

Golombok, S., & Tasker, F. (1996). Do parents influence the sexual orientation of their children? Findings from a longitudinal study of lesbian families. *Developmental Psychology, 32,* 3–11. [See also: Bailey et al., 1995; Bell et al., 1981; Isay, 1990]

Gomez, R., & McLaren, S. (2007). The inter-relations of mother and father attachment, self-esteem and aggression during late adolescence. *Aggressive Behavior, 33,* 160–169.

Gonzalvo, P., Cañas, J. J., & Bajo, M. (1994). Structural representations in knowledge acquisition. *Journal of Educational Psychology, 86,* 601–616.

Goodall, J. (1986). *The chimpanzees of Gombe: Patterns of behavior.* Cambridge, MA: Harvard University Press.

Goodwin, A. H., Sher, K. J. (1993). Effects of induced mood on diagnostic interviewing: Evidence for a mood and memory effect. *Psychological Assessment, 5,* 197–202.

Goodwyn, S. W., & Acredolo, L. P. (2000). *Baby minds.* New York: Bantum Books.

Gorman, J. (1999, January). The 11-year-old debunker. *Discover, 20*(1), 62–63.

Gottesman, I. I. (1991). *Schizophrenia genesis: The origins of madness.* New York: Freeman.

Gottesman, I. I. (1997, June 6). Twins: En route to QTLs for cognition. *Science, 276,* 1522–1523.

Gottesman, I. I. (2001). Psychopathology through a life span–genetic prism. *American Psychologist, 56,* 867–878.

Gottlieb, B. H. (Ed.). (1981). *Social networks and social support.* Beverly Hills, CA: Sage.

Gottlieb, B. H. (1987). Marshalling social support for medical patients and their families. *Canadian Psychology, 28,* 201–217.

Gottman, J., Coan, J., Carrere, S., & Swanson, C. (1998). Predicting marital happiness and stability from newlywed interactions. *Journal of Marriage and the Family, 60,* 5–22.

Gottman, J., & Silver, N. (1994). *Why marriages succeed or fail.* New York: Simon and Schuster.

Gottman, J. M. (1994). *What predicts divorce?* Hillsdale, NJ: Erlbaum.

Gottman, J. M. (1995). *Why marriages succeed or fail.* New York: Fireside.

Gottman, J. M. (1999). *Seven principles for making marriages work.* New York: Crown.

Gottman, J. M., & Krokoff, L. J. (1989). Marital interaction and satisfaction: A longitudinal view. *Journal of Consulting & Clinical Psychology, 57,* 47–52.

Gottman, J. M., & Levenson, R. W. (1986). Assessing the role of emotion in marriage. *Behavioral Assessment, 8,* 31–48.

Gould, E., Tanapat, P., McEwen, B. S., Flüge, G., & Fuchs, E. (1998). Proliferation of granule cell precursors in the dentate gyrus of adult monkeys is diminished by stress. *Proceedings of the National Academy of Science, 99,* 3168–3171.

Gould, S. J. (1996). *The mismeasure of man* (2nd ed.). New York: Norton.

Graham, J. R. (1990). *MMPI-2: Assessing personality and psychopathology.* New York: Oxford University Press.

Grant, B. F., & Dawson, D. A. (2006). Introduction to the national epidemiologic survey on alcohol and related conditions. *National Epidemiologic Survey on Alcohol and Related Conditions: Selected Findings.* Special issue: *Alcohol Research & Health, 29,* 74–78.

Gray, C. R., & Gummerman, K. (1975). The enigmatic eidetic image: A critical examination of methods, data, and theories. *Psychological Bulletin, 82,* 383–407.

Gray, J. R. (2004). Integration of emotion and cognitive control. *Current Directions in Psychological Science, 13,* 46–48.

Gray, P. (1993, November 29). The assault on Freud. *Time, 142*(23), 46–51.

Graziano, M. S. A., Cooke, D. F., & Taylor, C. S. R. (2000, December 1). Coding the location of the arm by sight. *Science, 290,* 1782–1786.

Greeley, A., & Sheatsley, P. (1971). The acceptance of desegregation continues to advance. *Scientific American, 225*(6), 13–19.

Green, C. S., & Bavelier, D. (2007). Action-video-game experience alters the spatial resolution of vision. *Psychological Science, 18,* 88–94.

Green, D. M. & Swets, J. A. (1966). *Signal detection theory and psychophysics.* New York: Wiley.

Greenberg, B. S. (1986). Minorities and the mass media. In J. Bryant & D. Zillman (Eds.), *Perspectives in media effects* (pp. 17–40). Hillsdale, NJ: Erlbaum.

Greenberg, G. (1997). Right answers, wrong reasons: Revisiting the deletion of homosexuality from the DSM. *Review of General Psychology, 1,* 256–270.

Greenberg, L. S., & Johnson, S. (1988). *Emotionally focused therapy for couples.* New York: Guilford.

Greene, R. L. (1991). *The MMPI-2/MMPI: An interpretive manual.* Boston: Allyn & Bacon.

Greeno, J. G. (1989). A perspective on thinking. *American Psychologist, 44,* 134–141.

Greenspan, S. (1999, February). What is meant by mental retardation? *International Review of Psychiatry, 11,* 6–18.

Greenwald, A. G. (1992). New Look 3: Unconscious cognition reclaimed. *American Psychologist, 47*(6), 766–779.

Greenwald, A. G., Draine, S. C., & Abrams, R. L. (1996, September 20). Three cognitive markers of unconscious semantic activation. *Science, 273,* 1699–1702.

Greer, M. (2004a, September). People don't notice unexpected visual changes—though they predict they will. *Monitor on Psychology, 35*(8), 10.

Greer, M. (2004b, July/August). Strengthen your brain by resting it. *Monitor on Psychology, 35*(7), 60–62. [See also: Maquet, 2001; Siegel, 2001; Stickgold et al., 2001]

Greer, M. (2005, March). When intuition misfires. *Monitor on Psychology, 36*(3), 58–60.

Gregory, R. (1997). *Mirrors in mind.* New York: W. H. Freeman.

Gregory, R. L. (1977). *Eye and brain: The psychology of seeing* (3rd ed.). New York: World University Library.

Grevert, P., & Goldstein, A. (1985). Placebo analgesia, naloxone, and the role of en dogenous opioids. In L. White, B. Turks, & G. E. Schwartz (Eds.), *Placebo* (pp. 332– 351). New York: Guilford. [See also: Mayer, 1979; Watkins & Mayer, 1982]

Grice, D. E., Halmi, K. A., Fichter, M. M., Strober, M., Woodside, D. B., Treasure, J. T., Kaplan, A. S., Magistretti, P. J., Goldman, D., Bulik, C. M., Kaye, W. H., & Berrettini, W. H. (2002). Evidence for a susceptibility gene for anorexia nervosa on chromo-

some 1. *American Journal of Human Genetics, 70,* 787–792.

Grimm, O. (2007, April/May). Addicted to food? *Scientific American Mind, 18*(2), 36–39. [See also: Gura, 2000; Woods et al., 1998]

Griner, D., & Smith, T. B. (2006). Culturally adapted mental health intervention: A meta-analytic review. *Psychotherapy: Theory, Research, Practice, Training, 43,* 531–548.

Grinspoon, L., Bakalar, J. B., Zimmer, L., & Morgan, J. P. (1997, August 8). Marijuana addiction. *Science, 752,* 748.

Gross, A. E., & Psaki, J. (2004, June 25). Venting: Its role in mediation. Annual Conference, Association for Conflict Resolution of Greater New York, Columbia Law School.

Gross, J. J. (1998). The emerging field of emotion regulation: An integrative review. *Review of General Psychology, 2,* 271–299.

Grossman, D. (1996). *On killing: The psychological cost of learning to kill in war and society.* New York: Brown & Co.

Grossmann, K., Grossmann, K. E., Spangler, S., Suess, G., & Unzner, L. (1985). Maternal sensitivity and newborn attachment orientation responses as related to quality of attachment in northern Germany. In I. Bretherton and E. Waters (Eds.), *Growing points of attachment theory: Monographs of the Society of Research in Child Development, 50* (1–2, Serial No. 209).

Gruben, D., & Madsen, L. (2005, June). Lie detection and the polygraph: A historical review. *The Journal of Forensic Psychiatry & Psychology, 16,* 357–369.

Guisinger, S. (2003). Adapted to flee famine: Adding an evolutionary perspective on anorexia nervosa. *Psychological Review, 110,* 745–761.

Guisinger, S., & Blatt, S. J. (1994). Individuality and relatedness: Evolution of a fundamental dialectic. *American Psychologist, 49,* 104–111.

Gulya, M., Rovee-Collier, C., Galluccio, L., & Wilk, A. (1998). Memory processing of a serial list by young infants. *Psychological Science, 9,* 303–307.

Gur, R. E., & Maany, V. (1998). Subcortical MRI volumes in neuroleptic-naive and treated patients with schizophrenia. *American Journal of Psychiatry, 155,* 1711–1718.

Gura, T. (1998, May 29). Uncoupling proteins provide new clue to obesity's causes. *Science, 280,* 1369–1370.

Gura, T. (2000, March 10). Tracing leptin's partners in regulating body weight. *Science,* 1738–1741.

Gura, T. (2003, February 7). Obesity drug pipeline not so fat. *Science, 299,* 849–852.

Guterman, L. (2005, December 2). Duping the brain into healing the body. *The Chronicle of Higher Education,* A12–A14.

Guthrie, G. M., & Bennett, A. B. (1970). Cultural differences in implicit personality theory. *International Journal of Psychology, 6,* 305–312.

Guthrie, R. V. (1998). *Even the rat was white.* Boston: Allyn & Bacon.

Gutman, A. R. (2006, January 5). Deep brain stimulation for treatment-resistant depression: An expert interview with Helen S. Mayberg, MD. Retrieved February 16, 2008, from www.Medscape.com/viewarticle/520659.

Guyll, M., & Contrada, R. J. (1998). Trait hostility and ambulatory cardiovascular activity: Responses to social interaction. *Health Psychology, 17,* 30–39.

Haber, R. N. (1969, April). Eidetic images. *Scientific American,* 36–44.

Haber, R. N. (1970, May). How we remember what we see. *Scientific American,* 104–112.

Haber, R. N. (1980, November). Eidetic images are not just imaginary. *Psychology Today, 14,* 72–82.

Haberlandt, K. (1999). *Human memory: Exploration and application.* Boston: Allyn & Bacon.

Haidt, J. (2001). The emotional dog and its rational tail: A social intuitionist approach to moral judgment. *Psychological Review, 108,* 814–834.

Haier, R. J., Jung, R. E., Yeo, R. A., Head, K., &

Alkire, M. T. (2004). Structural brain variation and general intelligence. *Neuroimage, 23,* 425–433.

Haimov, I., & Lavie, P. (1996). Melatonin—A soporific hormone. *Current Directions in Psychological Science, 5,* 106–111.

Halberstam, D. (2002). *Firehouse.* New York: Hyperion.

Hall, C., (1951). What people dream about. *Scientific American, 184,* 60–63.

Hall, C. (1953/1966). *The meaning of dreams.* New York: Harper & Row/McGraw-Hill.

Hall, C. S. (1984). "A ubiquitous sex difference in dreams" revisited. *Journal of Personality and Social Psychology, 46,* 1109–1117.

Hall, M. J., Norwood, A. E., Ursano, R. J., Fullerton, C. S., & Levinson, C. J. (2002). Psychological and behavioral impacts of bioterrorism. *PTSD Research Quarterly, 13,* 1–2.

Haller, E. (1992). Eating disorders: A review and update. *Western Journal of Medicine, 157,* 658–662.

Halpern, D. F. (2002). *Thought & knowledge: An introduction to critical thinking.* Mahwah, NJ: Erlbaum.

Halpern, D. F., Benbow, C. P., Geary, D. C., Gur, R. C., Hyde, J. S., & Gernsbacher, M. A. (2007). The science of sex differences in science and mathematics. *Psychological Science in the Public Interest, 8*(1).

Halpern, D. F., Benbow, C. P., Geary, D. C., Gur, R. C., Hyde, J. S., & Gernsbacher, M. A. (December 2007/January 2008). Sex, math and scientific achievement. *Scientific American Mind, 18*(6), 44–51. [See also Halpern et al., 2007]

Hamann, S. B., Ely, T. D., Hoffman, J. M., & Clinton, D. K. (2002). Ecstasy and agony: Activation of the human amygdala in positive and negative emotion. *Psychological Science, 13,* 135–141.

Hamer, D. (1997). The search for personality genes: Adventures of a molecular biologist. *Current Directions in Psychological Science, 6,* 111–112.

Hamer, D. (2002, October 4). Rethinking behavior genetics. *Science, 298,* 71–72.

Hamer, D. H., Hu, S., Magnuson, V. L., Hu, N., & Pattatucci, A. M. L. (1993, December 24). Male sexual orientation and genetic evidence. *Science, 261,* 2863–2865.

Hamilton, L. (1989). Fight, flight or freeze: Implications of the passive fear response for anxiety and depression. *Phobia Practice and Research Journal, 2,* 17–27.

Hamlin, K., Wynn, K., & Bloom, P. (2007). Social evaluation by preverbal infants. *Nature, 450,* 557–559.

Haney, C., Banks, W. C., & Zimbardo, P. G. (1973). Interpersonal dynamics in a simulated prison. *International Journal of Criminology and Penology, 1,* 69–97.

Haney, C., & Zimbardo, P. (1998). The past and future of U.S. prison policy: Twenty-five years after the Stanford prison experiment. *American Psychologist, 53,* 709–727.

Harder, B. (2004, June 19). Narcolepsy science reawakens. *Science News, 165,* 394–396.

Harder, B. (2005, November 26). Staring into the dark: Research investigates insomnia drugs. *Science News, 168,* 344–345.

Harder, B. (2006, April 1). XXL from too few Zs? *Science News, 169,* 195–196.

Haring, M. J., Stock, W. A., & Okun, M. A. (1984). A research synthesis of gender and social class as correlates of subjective well-being. *Human Relations, 37,* 645–657.

Hariri, A. R., Mattay, V. S., Tessitore, A., Kolachana, B., Fera, F., Goldman, D., Egan, M. F., & Weinberger, D. R. (2002, July 19). Serotonin transporter genetic variation and the response of the human amygdala. *Science, 297,* 400–403.

Harlow, H. F. (1965). Sexual behavior in the rhesus monkey. In F. Beach (Ed.), *Sex and behavior.* New York: Wiley.

Harlow, H. F., & Harlow, M. K. (1966). Learning to love. *American Scientist, 54,* 244–272.

Harris, B. (1979). Whatever happened to Little Albert? *American Psychologist, 34,* 151–160.

Harris, G., Thomas, A., & Booth, D. A. (1990). Development of salt taste in infancy. *Developmental Psychology, 26,* 534–538.

Harris, J. A. (2004). Measured intelligence, achievement, openness to experience, and creativity. *Personality & Individual Differences, 36,* 913–929.

Harris, J. R. (1995). Where is the child's environment? A group socialization theory of development. *Psychological Review, 102,* 458–489.

Harrist, S. (2003). Recognition for marginalized losses. *Death Studies, 27,* 560–565.

Hart, R. A., & Moore, G. I. (1973). The development of spatial cognition: A review. In R. M. Downs & D. Stea (Eds.), *Image and environment.* Chicago: Aldine.

Hartmann, E. L. (1973). *The functions of sleep.* New Haven, CT: Yale University Press.

Hartup, W. W., & Stevens, N. (1999). Friendships and adaptation across the life span. *Current Directions in Psychological Science, 8,* 76–79.

Harvey, J. H. (1996). *Embracing their memory: Loss and the social psychology of storytelling.* Boston: Allyn & Bacon.

Harvey, J. H. (2000). *Give sorrow words: Perspectives on loss and trauma.* New York: Taylor and Francis.

Harvey, J. H., & Hofmann, W. J. (2001). Teaching about loss. *Journal of Loss and Trauma, 6,* 263–268.

Harvey, J. H., & Omarzu, J. (1997). Minding the close relationship. *Personality and Social Psychology Review, 1,* 224–240.

Harvey, J. H., & Pauwels, B. G. (1999). Recent developments in close-relationships theory. *Current Directions in Psychological Science, 8,* 93–95.

Harvey, J. H., Weber, A. L., & Orbuch, T. L. (1990). *Interpersonal accounts: A social psychological perspective.* Cambridge, MA: Basil Blackwell.

Harvey, S. M., & Spigner, C. (1995). Factors associated with sexual behavior among adolescents: A multivariate analysis. *Adolescence, 30,* 253–264.

Haslam, S. A. (2007, April/May). I think, therefore I err? *Scientific American Mind, 18*(2), 16–17.

Haslam, S. A., Salvatore, J., Kessler, T., & Reicher, S. D. (2008, April/May). The social psychology of success. *Scientific American Mind,* 24–31.

Hasler, G., Buysse D. J., Klaghofer R., Gamma, A., Ajdacic, V., Eich D., Rössler W., & Angst J. (2004). The association between short sleep duration and obesity in young adults: A 13-year prospective study. *Sleep, 27,* 661–666.

Hassebrauck, M. (1988). Beauty is more than "name" deep: The effect of women's first names on ratings of physical attractiveness and personality attributes. *Journal of Applied Social Psychology, 18,* 721–726. [See also: Brigham, 1980; Cash & Duncan, 1984; Moore et al., 1987]

Hatfield, E. (1988). Passionate and compassionate love. In R. J. Sternberg & M. L. Barnes (Eds.), *The psychology of love.* New Haven, CT: Yale University Press.

Hatfield, E., & Rapson, R. (1993). *Love, sex, and intimacy: Their psychology, biology, and history.* New York: HarperCollins.

Hatfield, E., & Rapson, R. (1998). On love and sex in the 21st century. *The General Psychologist, 33*(2), 45–54.

Hatfield, E., Rapson, R. L., & Rapson, R. (1995). *Love and sex: Cross-cultural perspectives.* Boston: Allyn & Bacon.

Hatfield, E., & Sprecher, S. (1986). *Mirror, mirror: The importance of looks in everyday life.* New York: State University of New York Press.

Hatzfeld, J. (2005). *Machete season: The killers in Rwanda speak.* New York: Farrar, Strauss, and Giroux.

Hauser, M. D., Chomsky, N., & Fitch, W. T. (2002, November 22). The faculty of language: What is it, who has it, and how did it evolve? *Science, 298,* 1569–1579.

Hawkins, S. A., & Hastie, R. (1990). Hindsight: Biased judgments of past events after the outcomes are known. *Psychological Bulletin, 108,* 311–327.

Hayes, S. C., & Heiby, E. (1996). Psychology's drug problem: Do we need a fix or should we just say no? *American Psychologist, 51,* 198–206.

Haynes, S. G., & Feinleib, M. (1980). Women, work, and coronary heart disease: Prospective findings from the Framingham Heart Study. *American Journal of Public Health, 70,* 133–141.

Hazan, C., & Diamond, L. M. (2000). The place of attachment in human mating. *Review of General Psychology, 4,* 186–204.

Hazan, C., & Shaver, P.R. (1990). Love and work: An attachment-theoretical perspective. *Journal of Personality and Social Psychology, 59,* 270–280.

Hazan, C., & Shaver, P. R. (1992). Broken attachments: Relationship loss from the perspective of attachment theory. In T. L. Orbuch (Ed.), *Close relationship loss: Theoretical approaches* (pp. 90–108). New York: Springer Verlag.

Hazeltine, E., & Ivry, R. B. (2002, June 14). Can we teach the cerebellum new tricks? *Science, 296,* 1979–1980. [See also Raymond, Lisberger, & Mauk, 1996; Seidler et al., 2002]

Headey, B., & Wearing, A. (1992). *Understanding happiness: A theory of well-being.* Melbourne, Australia: Longman Cheshire.

Heatherton, T. F., Macrae, C. N., & Kelley, W. M. (2004). What the social brain sciences can tell us about the self. *Current Directions in Psychological Science, 13,* 190–193.

Hébert, R. (2005, January). The weight is over. *APS Observer, 18*(1), 20–24.

Hébert, R. (2006, October). We love to be scared on Halloween but fears and phobias are no laughing matter. *APS Observer, 19*(10), 14–19.

Hecht, A. (1986, April). A guide to the proper use of tranquilizers. *Healthline Newsletter,* 5–6.

Heckler, S. (1994). Facilitated communication: A response by Child Protection. *Child Abuse and Neglect: The International Journal, 18*(6), 495–503.

Heeger, D. J. (1994). The representation of visual stimuli in primary visual cortex. *Current Directions in Psychological Science, 3,* 159–163.

Heine, S. J., Lehman, D. R., Markus, H. R., & Kitayama, S. (1999). Is there a universal need for positive self-regard? *Psychological Review, 106,* 766–794.

Heinrichs, R. W. (1993). Schizophrenia and the brain: Conditions for a neuropsychology of madness. *American Psychologist, 48,* 221–233.

Heller, W., Nitschke, J. B., & Miller, G. A. (1998). Lateralization in emotion and emotional disorders. *Current Directions in Psychological Science, 7,* 26–32.

Helmes, E., & Reddon, J. R. (1993). A perspective on developments in assessing psychopathology: A critical review of the MMPI and MMPI-2. *Psychological Bulletin, 113,* 453–471. [See also: Butcher et al., 1989; Butcher & Williams, 1992; Greene, 1991]

Helms, J. E. (1992). Why is there no study of cultural equivalence in standardized cognitive ability testing? *American Psychologist, 47,* 1083–1101. [See also: Garcia, 1981; Miller-Jones, 1989]

Helmuth, L. (2000, December 1). Where the brain monitors the body. *Science, 290,* 1668.

Helmuth, L. (2001a, November 2). Beyond the pleasure principle. *Science, 294,* 983–984.

Helmuth, L. (2001b, May 18). Boosting brain activity from the outside in. *Science, 292,* 1284–1286.

Helmuth, L. (2001c, March 16). Dyslexia: Same brains, different languages. *Science, 291,* 2064–2065.

Helmuth, L. (2002, June 21). A generation gap in brain activity. *Science, 296,* 2131, 2133.

Helmuth, L. (2003a, November 14). Brain model puts most complex regions front and center. *Science, 302,* 1133.

Helmuth, L. (2003b, April 25). Fear and trembling in the amygdala. *Science, 300,* 568–569. [See also: Bechara et al., 1995; Johnson, 2003]

Helmuth, L. (2003c, February 28). The wisdom of the wizened. *Science, 299,* 1300–1302.

Hendrick, S. S., & Hendrick, C. (1992). *Liking, loving, and relating* (2nd ed.) Pacific Grove, CA: Brooks/Cole.

Henig, R. M. (1998, May). Tempting fates. *Discover,* 58.

Henker, B., & Whalen, C. K. (1989). Hyperactivity and attention deficits. *American Psychologist, 44,* 216–223.

Herek, G. M. (2000). The psychology of sexual prejudice. *Current Directions in Psychological Science, 9,* 19–22.

Herrnstein, R. J., & Murray, C. (1994). *The bell curve.* New York: Free Press.

Hersh, S. M. (2004a, May 5). Torture at Abu Ghraib. American soldiers brutalize Iraqis: How far up does the responsibility go? *The New Yorker.*

Hersh, S. M. (2004b). *Chain of command: The road from 9/11 to Abu Ghraib.* New York: Harper-Collins.

Herz, R. S., & Schooler, J. W. (2002). A naturalistic study of autobiographical memories evoked by olfactory and visual cues: Testing the Proustian hypothesis. *American Journal of Psychology, 115,* 21–32.

Heston, L. L. (1970). The genetics of schizophrenic and schizoid disease. *Science, 167,* 249–256.

Hetherington, E. M., & Parke, R. D. (1975). *Child psychology: A contemporary viewpoint.* New York: McGraw-Hill.

Hetherington, M. M., Spalter, A. R., Bernat, A. S., Nelson, M. L., et al. (1993). Eating pathology in bulimia nervosa. *International Journal of Eating Disorders, 13*(1), 13–24.

Hettema, J. M., Neale, M. C., Kendler, K. S. (2001). A review and meta-analysis of the genetic epidemiology of anxiety disorders. *American Journal of Psychiatry, 158,* 1568–1578.

Heyman, K. (2006, May 5). The map in the brain: Grid cells may help us navigate. *Science, 312,* 680–681.

Hibbard, S. (2003). A critique of Lilienfeld et al.'s (2000) "The scientific status of projective techniques." *Journal of Personality Assessment, 80,* 260–271. [See also: Exner, 1974, 1978; Exner & Weiner, 1982]

Hicks, R. A. (1990). The costs and benefits of normal insomnia. Paper presented to the annual meeting of the Western Psychological Association, Los Angeles, CA.

Higgins, J. W., Williams, R. L., & McLaughlin, T. F. (2001). The effects of a token economy employing instructional consequences for a third-grade students with learning disabilities. A data-based case study. *Education and Treatment of Children, 24,* 99–106. [See also: Corrigan, 1995; Le Blanc et al., 2000; Morisse et al., 1996]

Hilgard, E. R. (1968). *The experience of hypnosis.* New York: Harcourt Brace Jovanovich.

Hilgard, E. R. (1973). The domain of hypnosis with some comments on alternative paradigms. *American Psychologist, 28,* 972–982.

Hilgard, E. R. (1992). Dissociation and theories of hypnosis. In E. Fromm & M. R. Nash (Eds.), *Contemporary hypnosis research.* New York: Guilford.

Hill, J. O., & Peters, J. C. (1998, May 29). Environmental contributions to the obesity epidemic. *Science, 280,* 1371–1374.

Hilts, P. J. (1995). *Memory's ghost: The strange tale of Mr. M. and the nature of memory.* New York: Simon & Schuster.

Hiroto, D. S. (1974). Locus of control and learned helplessness. *Journal of Experimental Psychology, 102,* 187–193.

Hirsch, J., Harrington, G., & Mehler, B. (1990). An irresponsible farewell gloss. *Educational Theory, 40,* 501–508.

Hirschfeld, L. A. (1996). *Race in the making: Cognition, culture, and the child's construction of human kinds.* Cambridge, MA: MIT Press.

Hirschfeld, R. M. A. (1999). Efficacy of SSRIs and newer antidepressants in severe depression: Comparison with TCAs. *Journal of Clinical Psychiatry, 60,* 326–335.

Hirschfeld, R. M. A., & Goodwin, F. K. (1988). Mood disorders. In J. A. Talbott, R. E. Hales, & S. C. Yudofsky (Eds.), *The American Psychiatric Press text-book of psychiatry.* Washington, DC: American Psychiatric Press.

Hobson, J. A. (1988). *The dreaming brain.* New York: Basic Books.

Hobson, J. A. (2002). *Dreaming: An introduction to the science of sleep.* New York: Oxford University Press.

Hobson, J. A., & McCarley, R. W. (1977). The brain as a dream state generator: An activation-synthesis hypothesis of the dream process. *American Journal of Psychiatry, 134,* 1335–1348.

Hobson, J. A., Pace-Schott, E., & Stickgold, R. (2000). Dreaming and the brain: Towards a cognitive neuroscience of conscious states. *Behavioral and Brain Sciences* (special issue). Retrieved on November 6, 2004, from Behavioral and Brain Sciences Web site: www.bbsonline.org/documents/a/00/00/05/44/index.html.

Hochberg, L. R., Serruya, M. D., Friehs, G. M., Mukand, J. A., Saleh, M., & Caplan, A. H. Neuronal ensemble control of prosthetic devices by a human with tetraplegia. *Nature, 442,* 164–171. [See also Nicolelis & Chapin, 2002; Taylor, Helms Tillery, & Schwartz, 2002; Wickelgren, 2003].

Hochwalder, J. (1995). On stability of the structure of implicit personality theory over situations. *Scandinavian Journal of Psychology, 36,* 386–398.

Hoffman, H. G. (2004, August). Virtual-reality therapy. *Scientific American, 291,* 58–65.

Hogan, R., Curphy, G. J., & Hogan, J. (1994). What we know about leadership: Effectiveness and personality. *American Psychologist, 49,* 493–504.

Hogan, R., Hogan, J., & Roberts, B. W. (1996). Personality measurement and employment decisions: Questions and answers. *American Psychologist, 51,* 469–477.

Hogarty, G. E., Kornblith, S. J., Greenwald, D., DiBarry, A. L., Cooley, S., Ulrich, R. F., Carter, M., & Flesher, S. (1997). Three-year trials of personal therapy among schizophrenic patients living with or independent of family, I: Description of study and effects on relapse rates. *American Journal of Psychiatry, 154,* 1504–1513.

Hoge, C. W., Castro, C. A., Messer, S. C., McGurk, D., Cotting, D. I., & Koffman, R. L. (2004). Combat duty in Iraq and Afghanistan, mental health problems, and barriers to care. *New England Journal of Medicine, 351,* 13–22.

Holden, C. (1978). Patuxent: Controversial prison clings to belief in rehabilitation. *Science, 199,* 665–668.

Holden, C. (1980a). Identical twins reared apart. *Science, 207,* 1323–1325.

Holden, C. (1980b, November). Twins reunited. *Science, 80,* 55–59.

Holden, C. (1996a, July 5). New populations of old add to poor nations' burdens. *Science, 273,* 46–48.

Holden, C. (1996b, July 19). Sex and olfaction. *Science, 273,* 313.

Holden, C. (1997, October 3). A special place for faces in the brain. *Science, 278,* 41.

Holden, C. (2000a, April 7). Global survey examines impact of depression. *Science, 288,* 39–40.

Holden, C. (2000b, July 28). The violence of the lambs. *Science, 289,* 580–581.

Holden, C. (2001a, April 27). How the brain understands music. *Science News, 292,* 623.

Holden, C. (2001b, February 9). Panel seeks truth in lie detector debate. *Science, 291,* 967.

Holden, C. (2003a, January 17). Deconstructing schizophrenia. *Science, 299,* 333–335. [See also: Lencer et al., 2000; Plomin et al., 1994]

Holden, C. (2003b, October 31). Future brightening for depression treatments. *Science, 302,* 810–813.

Holden, C. (2003c). A hard road to mental health. *Science, 302,* 1145.

Holden, C. (2003d). Posttrauma counseling questioned. *Science, 302,* 49.

Holden, C. (2004, October 29). Mystics and synesthesia. *Science, 306,* 808.

Holden, C. (2005, June 10). Sex and the suffering brain. *Science, 308,* 1574–1577. [See also: Leut-wyler, 1995; Strickland, 1992; Weissman et al., 1996]

Hollander, E. M. (2004). Am I all right? *Journal of Loss and Trauma, 9,* 201–204.

Hollis, K. L. (1997). Contemporary research on Pavlovian conditioning. *American Psychologist, 52,* 956–965.

Hollon, S. D. (1996). The efficacy and effectiveness of psychotherapy relative to medications. *American Psychologist, 51,* 1025–1030.

Hollon, S. D., Thase, M. E., & Markowitz, J. C. (2002, November). Treatment and prevention of depression. *Psychological Science in the Public Interest, 3,* 39–77.

Holloway, J. D. (2003a, March). Advances in anger management. *Monitor on Psychology, 34,* 54–55.

Holloway, J. D. (2003b, December). Snapshot from the therapy room. *Monitor on Psychology, 34*(11), 31.

Holloway, J. D. (2004a, June). Gaining prescriptive knowledge. *Monitor on Psychology, 35*(6), 22–24.

Holloway, J. D. (2004b, June). Louisiana grants psychologists prescriptive authority. *Monitor on Psychology, 35*(6), 20–21. [See also: Daw, 2002a,b; Dittmann, 2003]

Holloway, M. (1999, November). The ascent of scent. *Scientific American, 281,* 42, 44.

Holloway, M. (2003, September). The mutable brain. *Scientific American, 289*(3), 78–85.

Holmes, D. S. (1984). Meditation and somatic arousal: A review of the experimental evidence. *American Psychologist, 39,* 1–10.

Holmes, D. S. (2001). *Abnormal psychology* (4th ed.). Boston: Allyn & Bacon. [See also: Linsheid et al., 1990; Lovaas, 1977; Lovaas et al., 1974]

Holmes, T. H. (1979). Development and application of a quantitative measure of life change magnitude. In J. E. Barrett, R. M. Rose, & G. L. Klerman (Eds.), *Stress and mental disorder.* New York: Raven.

Holmes, T. H., & Masuda, M. (1974). Life change and stress susceptibility. In B. S. Dohrenwend & B. P. Dohrenwend (Eds.), *Stressful life events: Their nature and effects* (pp. 45–72). New York: Wiley.

Holmes, T. H., & Rahe, R. H. (1967). The social readjustment rating scale. *Journal of Psychosomatic Research, 11*(2), 213–218.

Holtzman, W. H. (1992). Health psychology. In M. A. Rosenzweig (Ed.), *International psychological science* (pp. 199–226). Washington, DC: American Psychological Association.

Holtzworth-Munroe, A., & Jacobson, N. S. (1985). Causal attributions of marital couples: When do they search for causes? What do they conclude when they do? *Journal of Personality and Social Psychology, 48,* 1398–1412.

Homme, L. E., de Baca, P. C., Devine, J. V., Steinhorst, R., & Rickert, E. J. (1963). Use of the Premack principle in controlling the behavior of nursery school children. *Journal of the Experimental Analysis of Behavior, 6,* 544.

Hopkins, B., & Westra, T. (1988). Maternal handling and motor development: An intracultural study. *Genetic, Social and General Psychology Monographs, 14,* 377–420.

Horgan, J. (1993, June). Eugenics revisited. *Scientific American, 268,* 122–131.

Horgan, J. (1996, November). Multicultural studies: Rates of depression vary widely throughout the world. *Scientific American, 275*(6), 24–25.

Horgan, J. (2005, June). Can a single brain cell recognize Bill Clinton? *Discover, 26*(6), 64–69.

Horney, K. (1939). *New ways in psychoanalysis.* New York: Norton.

Horney, K. (1942). *Self-analysis.* New York: Norton.

Horney, K. (1967). *Feminine psychology.* New York: Norton.

Horowitz, M. J. (1997). *Stress response syndromes: PTSD, grief, and adjustment disorders* (3rd ed.). Northvale, NJ: Jason Aronson.

Horvath, A. O., & Luborsky, L. (1993). The role of the therapeutic alliance in psychotherapy. *Journal of Consulting and Clinical Psychology, 61,* 561–573.

House, J. S., Landis, K. R., & Umberson, D. (1988).

Social relationships and health. *Science, 241,* 540–545.

Hovland, C. I., & Sears, R. (1940). Minor studies of aggression: Correlation of lynchings with economic indices. *Journal of Psychology, 9,* 301–310.

Howe, M. L., & Courage, M. L. (1993). On resolving the enigma of infantile amnesia. *Psychological Bulletin, 113,* 305–326.

Howes, C., Rodning, C., Galluzzo, D. C., & Myers, L. (1988). Attachment and child care: Relationships with mother and care-giver. *Early Childhood Research Quarterly, 3,* 403–416.

Hu, F. B., Li, T. Y., Colditz, G. A., Willett, W. C., & Manson, J. E. (2003, April 9). Television watching and other sedentary behaviors in relation to risk of obesity and Type 2 diabetes mellitus in women. *Journal of the American Medical Association, 289,* 1785–1791.

Hubel, D. H., & Wiesel, T. N. (1979, September). Brain mechanisms of vision. *Scientific American, 241,* 150–162.

Huesmann, L. R., & Moise, J. (1996, June). Media violence: A demonstrated public health threat to children. *Harvard Mental Health Letter, 12*(12), 5–7.

Huesmann, L. R., Moise-Titus, J., Podolski, C-L., & Eron, L. D. (2003). Longitudinal relations between children's exposure to TV violence and their aggressive and violent behavior in young adulthood: 1977–1992. *Developmental Psychology, 39,* 201–221. [See also: Bushman & Anderson, 2001; Johnson et al., 2001]

Hughes, G. H., Pearson, M. A., & Reinhart, G. R. (1984). Stress: Sources, effects, and management. *Family and Community Health, 7,* 47–58.

Hull, C. L. (1943). *Principles of behavior: An introduction to behavior theory.* New York: Appleton-Century-Crofts.

Hull, C. L. (1952). *A behavior system: An introduction to behavior theory concerning the individual organism.* New Haven, CT: Yale University Press.

Humphrey, T. (1970). The development of human fetal activity and its relation to postnatal behavior. In H. W. Reese & L. P. Lipsitt (Eds.), *Advances in child development and behavior (Vol. 5).* New York: Academic Press.

Humphreys, L. G. (1988). Trends in levels of academic achievement of blacks and other minorities. *Intelligence, 12,* 231–260.

Hunt, E. (1989). Cognitive science: Definition, status, and questions. *Annual Review of Psychology, 40,* 603–629. [See also: Medin, 1989; Mervis & Rosch, 1981; Rosch & Mervis, 1975]

Hunter, I. (1964). *Memory.* Baltimore: Penguin.

Huston, A. C., Watkins, B. A., & Kunkel, D. (1989). Public policy and children's television. *American Psychologist, 44,* 424–433.

Huston, T. L., Ruggiero, M., Conner, R., & Geis, G. (1981). Bystander intervention into crime: A Study based on naturally-occurring episodes. *Social Psychology Quarterly, 44,* 14–23.

Huttenlocher, J., Haight, W., Bryk, A., Seltzer, M., & Lyons, T. (1991). Early vocabulary growth: relation to language input and gender. *Developmental Psychology, 27,* 236–248.

Hwang, W. (2006). The psychotherapy adaptation and modification framework: Application to Asian Americans. *American Psychologist, 61,* 702–715.

Hyde, J. S. (2007). New directions in the study of gender similarities and differences. *Current Directions in Psychological Science, 16,* 259–263.

Hyman, I. A. (1996). Using research to change public policy: Reflections on 20 years of effort to eliminate corporal punishment in schools. *Pediatrics, 98,* 818–821. [See also: Hyman et al., 1977]

Hyman, I. A., McDowell, E., & Raines, B. (1977). Corporal punishment and alternatives in the schools: An overview of theoretical and practical issues. In J. H. Wise (Ed.), *Proceedings: Conference on corporal punishment in the schools* (pp. 1–18). Washington, DC: National Institutes of Education.

Hyman, I. E. Jr., Husband, T. H., & Billings, F. J. (1995). False memories of childhood experiences. *Applied Cognitive Psychology, 9,* 181–197.

Hyman, R. (1989). The psychology of deception. *Annual Review of Psychology, 40,* 133–154.

Iacono, W. G., & Grove, W. M. (1993). Schizophrenia reviewed: Toward an integrative genetic model. *Science, 4,* 273–276.

Ickes, W., & Layden, M. A. (1978). Attributional styles. In J. H. Harvey, W. Ickes, & R. F. Kidd (Eds.), *New directions in attri butional research (Vol. 2).* Hillsdale, NJ: Erlbaum.

Ilgen, D. R., & Bell, B. S. (2001). Informed consent and dual purpose research. *American Psychologist, 56,* 1177.

Ineichen, B. (1979). The social geography of marriage. In M. Cook & G. Wilson (Eds.), *Love and attraction.* New York: Pergamon Press.

Inglehart, R. (1990). *Culture shift in advanced industrial society.* Princeton, NJ: Princeton University Press.

Insel, T. R. (2007, August 10). Shining light on depression. *Science, 317,* 757–758.

Insko, C., et al. (1980). Social evolution and the emergence of leadership. *Journal of Personality and Social Psychology, 39,* 441–448.

Institute of Medicine. (2002). *Dietary reference intakes for energy, carbohydrate, fiber, fat, fatty acids, cholesterol, protein, and amino acids.* Washington, DC: National Institutes of Health.

International Centre for Prison Studies (2007). Prison brief—highest to lowest rates. Retrieved July 6, 2007, from www.kcl.ac.uk/depsta/rel/icps/worldbrief/highest_to_lowest_rates.html.

Isay, R. A. (1990). Psychoanalytic theory and the therapy of gay men. In D. P. McWhirter, S. A. Sanders, & J. M. Reinisch (Eds.), *Homosexuality/heterosexuality: Concepts of sexual orientation* (pp. 283–303). New York: Oxford University Press.

Ishai, A., & Sagi, D. (1995). Common mechanisms of visual imagery and perception. *Science, 268,* 1772–1774.

Ishai, A., & Sagi, D. (1997). Visual imagery: Effects of short- and long-term memory. *Journal of Cognitive Neuroscience, 9,* 734–742.

Iverson, P., Kuhl, P. K., Akahane-Yamada, R., Diesch, E., Tohkura, Y., Kettermann, A., & Siebert, C. (2003). A perceptual interference account of acquisition difficulties for non-native phonemes. *Cognition, 87,* B47–B57.

Izard, C. E. (1989). The structure and functions of emotions: Implications for cognition, motivation, and personality. In I. S. Cohen (Ed.), *The G. Stanley Hall lecture series, Vol. 9* (pp. 39–73). Washington, DC: American Psychological Association.

Izard, C. E. (1993). Four systems for emotion activation: Cognitive and noncognitive processes. *Psychological Review, 100,* 68–90.

Izard, C. E. (1994). Innate and universal facial expressions: Evidence from developmental and cross-cultural research. *Psychological Bulletin, 115,* 288–299.

Izard, C. E. (2007). Basic emotions, natural kinds, emotion schemas, and a new paradigm. *Perspectives on Psychological Science, 2,* 260–280.

Jablensky, A. (2000). Epidemiology of schizophrenia: The global burden of disease and disability. *European Archives of Psychiatry & Clinical Neuroscience, 250,* 274–283.

Jackson, D. D. (1980, October). Reunion of identical twins, raised apart, reveals some astonishing similarities. *Smithsonian,* 48–57.

Jacob, S., McClintock, M. K., Zelano, B., & Ober, C. (2002). Paternally inherited HLA alleles are associated with women's choice of male odor. *Nature Genetics, 30,* 175–179.

Jacobs, B. L. (1987). How hallucinogenic drugs work. *American Scientist, 75,* 386–392.

Jacobs, L. F., & Schenk, F. (2003). Unpacking the cognitive map: The parallel map theory of hippocampal function. *Psychological Review, 110,* 285–315.

Jacobs, M. K., & Goodman, G. (1989). Psychology and self-help groups: Predictions on a partnership. *American Psychologist, 44,* 536–545.

Jacobson, N. S., & Christensen, A. (1996). Studying the effectiveness of psychotherapy: How well can clinical trials do the job? *American Psychologist, 51,* 1031–1039.

Jacobson, N. S., Christensen, A., Prince, S. E., Cordova, J., & Eldridge, K. (2000). Integrative behavioral couple therapy: An acceptance-based, promising new treatment for couple discord. *Journal of Consulting and Clinical Psychology, 68,* 351–355.

Jacoby, L. L., Lindsay, D. S., & Toth, J. P. (1992). Unconscious influences revealed: Attention, awareness, and control. *American Psychologist, 47,* 802–809.

Jacowitz, K. E., Kahneman, D. (1995). Measures of anchoring in estimation tasks. *Personality & Social Psychology Bulletin, 21,* 1161–1166.

Jaffe, E. (2006, March). *Opening Skinner's Box* causes controversy. *APS Observer, 19*(3), 17–19.

Jaffe, E. (2007, May). Mirror neurons: How we reflect on behavior. *APS Observer, 20*(5), 20–25.

Jaffe, J., Beebe, B., Feldstein, S., Crown, C. L., & Jasnow, M. D. (2001). Rhythms of dialogue in infancy: Coordinated timing in development. *Monographs of Society for Research in Child Development, 66,* vii, 1–132.

James, W. (1950). The principles of psychology (2 vols.). New York: Holt, Rinehart & Winston. (Original work published 1890).

Janata, P., Birk, J. L., Van Horn, J. D., Leman, M., Tillmann, B., & Bharucha, J. J. (2002, December 13). The cortical topography of tonal structures underlying western music. *Science, 298,* 2167–2170.

Janis, I. (1972). *Victims of groupthink: A psychological study of foreign-policy decisions and fiascoes.* Boston: Houghton Mifflin.

Janis, I., & Mann, L. (1977). *Decision making: A psychological analysis of conflict, choice and commitment.* New York: The Free Press.

Janoff-Bulman, R. (1989). The benefits of illusions, the threat of disillusionment, and the limitations of inaccuracy. *Journal of Social and Clinical Psychology, 8,* 158–175.

Janoff-Bulman, R. (1992). *Shattered assumptions: Towards a new psychology of trauma.* New York: The Free Press.

Janoff-Bulman, R., & Frantz, C. M. (1997). The impact of trauma on meaning: From meaningless world to meaningful life. In M. Power & C. R. Brewin (Eds.), *The transformation of meaning in psychological therapies* (pp. 91–106). New York: Wiley.

Jansen, A. S. P., Nguyen, X. V., Karpitskiy, V., Mettenleiter, T. C., & Loewy, A. D. (1995, October 27). Central command neurons of the sympathetic nervous system: Basis of the fight-or-flight response. *Science, 270,* 644–646.

Janus, S. S., & Janus, C. L. (1993). *The Janus Report on sexual behavior.* New York: Wiley.

Javitt, D. C., & Coyle, J. T. (2004). Decoding schizophrenia. *Scientific American, 290,* 48–55.

Jeffery, R. W. (1987). Behavioral treatment of obesity. *Annals of Behavioral Medicine, 9,* 20–24.

Jenkins, C. D. (1976). Recent evidence supporting psychologic and social risk factors for coronary disease. *New England Journal of Medicine, 294,* 987–994, 1033–1038.

Jenkins, J. H. (1994). Culture, emotion, and psychopathology. In S. Kitayama & H. R. Markus (Eds.), *Emotion and culture: Empirical studies of mutual influence.* Washington, DC: American Psychological Association.

Jenkins, J. H., & Barrett, R. J., Eds. (2004). *Schizophrenia, culture, and subjectivity: The edge of experience.* Cambridge, U.K.: Cambridge University Press.

Jensen, A. R. (1969). How much can we boost IQ and scholastic achievement? *Harvard Educational Review, 39,* 1–123.

Jensen, A. R. (1980). *Bias in mental testing.* New York: Free Press.

Jensen, A. R. (1985). Methodological and statistical techniques for the chronometric study of mental

come and process research: Challenges leading to greater turmoil or a positive transition? *Annual Review of Psychology, 30,* 441–469.

Kosko, B., & Isaka, S. (1993, July). Fuzzy logic. *Scientific American, 269,* 76–81.

Kosslyn, S., Thompson, W., Kim, I., & Alpert, N. (1995). Topographical representations of mental images in primary visual cortex. *Nature, 378,* 496–498.

Kosslyn, S. M. (1976). Can imagery be distinguished from other forms of internal representation? Evidence from studies of information retrieval times. *Memory and Cognition, 4,* 291–297.

Kosslyn, S. M. (1983). *Ghosts in the mind's machine: Creating and using images in the brain.* New York: Norton.

Kosslyn, S. M., Cacioppo, J. T., Davidson, R. J., Hugdahl, K., Lovallo, W. R., Speigel, D., & Rose, R. (2002). Bridging psychology and biology: The analysis of individuals in groups. *American Psychologist, 57,* 341–351. [See also: Davidson, 1992a,b; 2000a,b; Heller et al., 1998]

Kotchoubey, B. (2002). Do event-related brain potentials reflect mental (cognitive) operations? *Journal of Psychophysiology, 16,* 129–149.

Koyama, T., McHaffie, J. G., Laurienti, P. J., & Coghill, R. C. (2005, September 6). The subjective experience of pain: Where expectations become reality. *Proceedings of the National Academy of Sciences, 102,* 12950–12955.

Krakovski, M. (2005, February 2). Dubious "Mozart effect" remains music to many Americans' ears. *Stanford Report.* Retrieved on September 7, 2008, from http://news-service.stanford.edu/news/2005/february2/mozart-020205.html.

Krakovsky, M. (2007, February). Unsettled scores. *Scientific American, 296*(2), 13–14.

Kramer, A. F., & Willis, S. L. (2002). Enhancing the cognitive vitality of older adults. *Current Directions in Psychological Science, 11,* 173–177.

Kramer, P. D. (1993). *Listening to Prozac: A psychiatrist explores antidepressant drugs and the remaking of the self.* New York: Viking.

Krampe, R. T., & Ericsson, K. A. (1996). Maintaining excellence: Deliberate practice and elite performance in young and older pianists. *Journal of Experimental Psychology: General, 125,* 331–359.

Krantz, D. S., Grunberg, N. E., & Baum, A. (1985). Health psychology. *Annual Review of Psychology, 36,* 349–383.

Krätzig, G. P., & Arbuthnott, K. D. (2006). Perceptual learning style and learning proficiency: A Test of the Hypothesis. *Journal of Educational Psychology, 98,* 238–246.

Kringen, J. A. (2006, April 3). How we've improved intelligence: Minimizing the risk of "groupthink." Editorial, p. A19. *Washington Post.*

Kristol, I. (1994, November 3). Children need their fathers. *The New York Times,* A15.

Krupnick, J. L., Sotsky, S. M., Simmens, S., Moyer, J., Elkin, I., Watkins, J., & Pilkonis, P. A. (1996). The role of the therapeutic alliance in psychotherapy and pharmacotherapy outcome: Findings in the National Institute of Mental Health Treatment of Depression Collaborative Research Program. *Journal of Consulting and Clinical Psychology, 64,* 532–539.

Kukla, A. (1989). Nonempirical issues in psychology. *American Psychologist, 44,* 785–794.

Kurdek, L. A. (2005). What do we know about gay and lesbian couples? *Current Directions in Psychological Science, 14,* 251–254.

Lachman, M. E., & Weaver, S. L. (1998). The sense of control as a moderator of social class differences in health and well-being. *Journal of Personality and Social Psychology, 74,* 763–773.

Lachman, R., Lachman, J. L., & Butterfield, E. C. (1979). *Cognitive psychology and information processing: An introduction.* Hillsdale, NJ: Erlbaum.

Lai, C. S. L., Fisher, S. E., Hurst, J. A., Vargha-Khadem, F., & Monaco, A. P. (2001, October 4). A forkhead-domain gene is mutated in a severe speech and language disorder. *Nature, 413,* 519–523.

Lakoff, R. T. (1990). *Talking power.* New York: Basic Books.

Lamb, H. R. (1998). Deinstitutionalization at the beginning of the new millennium. *Harvard Review of Psychiatry, 6,* 1–10.

Lamb, M. E. (1999, May/June). Mary D. Salter Ainsworth, 1913–1999, attachment theorist. *APS Observer, 32,* 34–35.

Lambo, T. A. (1978). Psychotherapy in Africa. *Human Nature, 1*(3), 32–39.

Lampl, M., Veldhuis, J. D., & Johnson, M. L. (1992). Saltation and stasis: A model of human growth. *Science, 258,* 801–803.

Landesman, S., & Butterfield, E. C. (1987). Normalization and deinstitutionalization of mentally retarded individuals: Controversy and facts. *American Psychologist, 42,* 809–816.

Landry, D. W. (1997, February). Immunotherapy for cocaine addiction. *Scientific American,* 42–45.

Lane, E. (2006, July 28). Neuroscience in the courts—A revolution in justice? *Science, 313,* 458.

Lang, F. R., & Carstensen, L. L. (1994). Close emotional relationships in late life: Further support for proactive aging in the social domain. *Psychology and Aging, 9,* 315–324.

Lang, P. J., & Lazovik, D. A. (1963). The experimental desensitization of a phobia. *Journal of Abnormal and Social Psychology, 66,* 519–525.

Langleben, D. D., Schroeder, L., Maldjian, J. A., Gur, R. C., McDonald, S., Ragland, J. D., O'Brien, C. P., & Childress, A. R. (2002). Brain activity during simulated deception: An event-related functional magnetic resonance study. *NeuroImage, 15,* 727–732.

Langlois, J. H., Kalakanis, L., Rubenstein, A. J., Larson, A., Hallam, M., & Smoot, M. (2000). Maxims or myths? A meta-analytic and theoretical review. *Psychological Bulletin, 126,* 390–423.

Langlois, J. H., & Roggman, L. A. (1990). Attractive faces are only average. *Psychological Science, 1,* 115–121.

Langlois, J. H., Roggman, L. A., Casey, R. J., Ritter, J. M., Rieser-Danner, L. A., & Jenkins, V. Y. (1987). Infant preferences for attractive faces: Rudiments of a stereotype. *Developmental Psychology, 23,* 363–369.

Langlois, J. H., Roggman, L. A., & Musselman, L. (1994). What is average and what is not average about attractive faces? *Psychological Science, 5,* 214–220.

Larson, R. (1989). Is feeling "in control" related to happiness in daily life? *Psychological Reports, 64,* 775–784.

Larson, R. W. (2000). Toward a psychology of positive youth development. *American Psychologist, 55,* 170–183.

Larson, R. W. (2001). How U.S. children and adolescents spend time: What it does (and doesn't) tell us about their development. *Current Directions in Psychological Science, 10,* 160–164.

Lash, J. (2001). Dealing with the tinder as well as the flint. *Science, 294,* 1789.

Lashley, K. S. (1950). In search of the en gram. In *Physiological mechanisms in animal behavior: Symposium of the Society for Experimental Biology (Vol. 4).* New York: Academic Press.

Latané, B., & Darley, J. M. (1968). Group inhibition of bystander intervention in emergencies. *Journal of Personality and Social Psychology, 10,* 215–221.

Laumann, E. O., Gagnon, J. H., Michael, R. T., & Michaels, S. (1994). *The social organization of sexuality: Sexual practices in the United States.* Chicago: University of Chicago Press.

Law, B. (2005, November). Probing the depression-rumination cycle. *Monitor on Psychology, 36*(10), 38–39.

Lawton, M. P. (2001). Emotion in later life. *Current Directions in Psychological Science, 10,* 120–123.

Lazar, I., & Darlington, R. (1982). Lasting effects of early education: A report from the Consortium for Longitudinal Studies. *Monographs of the Society for Research in Child Development, 47*(2–3, Serial No. 195).

Lazar, S. W., Kerr, C. E., Wasserman, R. H, Gray, J. R, Greve, D. N., Treadway, M. T., McGarvey, M., Quinn, B. T. Dusek, J. A., Benson, H., Rauch, S. L., Moore, C. I., & Fischl, B. (2005, November 28). Meditation experience is associated with increased cortical thickness. *Neuroreport, 16,* 1893–1897.

Lazarus, R. S. (1981, July). Little hassles can be hazardous to your health. *Psychology Today,* 58–62.

Lazarus, R. S. (1984). On the primacy of cognition. *American Psychologist, 39,* 124–129.

Lazarus, R. S. (1991a). Cognition and motivation in emotion. *American Psychologist, 46,* 352–367.

Lazarus, R. S. (1991b). Progress on a cognitive-motivational-relational theory of emotion. *American Psychologist, 46,* 819–834.

Lazarus, R. S. (1999). *Stress and emotion: A new synthesis.* London, U.K.: Free Association Press.

Lazarus, R. S., DeLongis, A., Folkman, S., & Gruen, R. (1985). Stress and adaptational outcomes: The problem of confounded measures. *American Psychologist, 40,* 770–779.

Leaper, C., Anderson, K. J., & Sanders, P. (1998). Moderators of gender effects on parents' talk to their children: A meta-analysis. *Developmental Psychologist, 34,* 3–27.

Le Blanc, L. A., Hagopian, L. P., & Maglieri, K. A. (2000). Use of a token economy to eliminate excessive inappropriate social behavior in an adult with developmental disabilities. *Behavioral Interventions, 15,* 135–143.

LeDoux, J. (2002). *Synaptic self: How our brains become who we are.* New York: Viking. [See also: Canli et al., 2002; Carpenter, 2001a; Craik et al., 1999; Davidson, 2002; Zuckerman, 1995]

LeDoux, J. E. (1994). Emotion, memory and the brain. *Scientific American, 270*(6), 50–57.

LeDoux, J. E. (1996). *The emotional brain: The mysterious underpinnings of emotional life.* New York: Simon & Schuster. [See also Barinaga, 1996; Singer, 1995]

LeDoux, J. E. (2000). Emotion circuits in the brain. *Annual Review of Neuroscience, 23,* 155–184.

Lee, V. E., Brooks-Gunn, J., & Schnur, E. (1988). Does Head Start work? A 1-year follow-up of disadvantaged children attending Head Start, no preschool. *Developmental Psychology, 24,* 210–222.

Leeper, R. W., & Madison, P. (1959). *Toward understanding human personalities.* New York: Appleton-Century-Crofts.

Leerhsen, C. (1990, February 5). Unite and conquer: America's crazy for support groups. *Newsweek,* 50–55.

Leichtman, M. D. (2006). Cultural and maturational influences on long-term event memory. In C. Tamis-LeMonda & L. Balter (Eds.). *Child psychology: A handbook of contemporary issues* (2nd ed.). Philadelphia, PA: Psychology Press.

Leiter, M. P., & Maslach, C. (2000). *Preventing burnout and building engagement: A complete program for organizational renewal.* San Francisco, CA: Jossey-Bass.

Lencer, R., Malchow, C. P., Trillenberg-Krecker, K., Schwinger, E., & Arolt, V. (2000). Eye-tracking dysfunction (ETD) in families with sporadic and familial schizophrenia. *Biological Psychiatry, 47,* 391–401.

Lensing, V. (2001). Grief support: The role of funeral service. *Journal of Loss and Trauma, 6,* 45–63.

Leonard, J. (1998, May–June). Dream-catchers: Understanding the biological basis of things that go bump in the night. *Harvard Magazine, 100,* 58–68.

Lepper, M. R., Greene, D., & Nisbett, R. E. (1973). Undermining children's intrinsic interest with extrinsic reward: A test of the over-justification hypothesis. *Journal of Personality and Social Psychology, 28*(1), 129–137.

Lerner, R. M., Orlos, J. R., & Knapp, J. (1976). Physical attractiveness, physical effectiveness and self-concept in adolescents. *Adolescence, 11,* 313–326.

Leshner, A. I. (1997, October 3). Addiction is a brain disease, and it matters. *Science, 278,* 45–47.

Leslie, A. M. (2001). Learning: Association or computation? Introduction to a special section. *Current Directions in Psychological Science, 10,* 124–127.

Leslie, M. (2000, July/August). The vexing legacy of Lewis Terman. *Stanford, 28*(4), 44–51.

Lesperance, F., & Frasure-Smith, N. (1996, February 17). Negative emotions and coronary heart disease: Getting to the heart of the matter. *Lancet, 347,* 414–415.

Lettvin, J. Y., Maturana, H. R., McCulloch, W. S., & Pitts, W. H. (1959). What the frog's eye tells the frog's brain. *Proceedings of the Institute of Radio Engineers, 47,* 1940–1951.

Leutgeb, S., Leutgeb, J. K., Treves, A., Moser, M-B., & Moser, E. I. (2004, August 27). Distinct ensemble codes in hippocampal areas ca3 and ca1. *Science, 305,* 1295–1298.

Leutwyler, K. (1994, March). Prosthetic vision: Workers resume the quest for a seeing-eye device. *Scientific American, 270,* 108.

Leutwyler, K. (1995, June). Depression's double standard. *Scientific American, 272,* 23–24.

LeVay, S. (1991). A difference in hypothalamic structure between heterosexual and homosexual men. *Science, 253,* 1034–1037.

LeVay, S., & Hamer, D. (1995). Evidence for a biological influence in male homosexuality. *Scientific American, 270*(5), 44–49.

Levenson, R. W. (1992). Autonomic nervous system differences among emotions. *Psychological Science, 3,* 23–27.

Leventhal, H., & Tomarken, A. J. (1986). Emotion: Today's problems. *Annual Review of Psychology, 37,* 565–610.

Levine, J. A., Eberhardt, N. L., & Jensen, M. D. (1999, January 8). Role of nonexercise activity thermogenesis in resistance to fat gain in humans. *Science, 283,* 212–214.

Levine, J. A., Lanningham-Foster, L. M., McCrady, S. K., Krizan, A. C., Olson, L. R., Kane, P. H., Jensen, M. D., & Clark, M. M. (2005, January 28). Interindividual Variation in Posture Allocation: Possible Role in Human Obesity. *Science, 307,* 584–586.

Levine, K., Shane, H. C., & Wharton, R. H. (1994). What if . . . : A plea to professionals to consider the risk–benefit ratio of facilitated communication. *Mental Retardation, 32*(4), 300–304.

Levine, L. J. (1997). Reconstructing memory for emotions. *Journal of Experimental Psychology: General, 126,* 165–177.

Levine, L. J., & Bluck, S. (2004). Painting with broad strokes: Happiness and the malleability of event memory. *Cognition & Emotion, 18,* 559–574.

Levine, L. J., & Safer, M. A. (2002). Sources of bias in memory for emotions. *Current Directions in Psychological Science, 11,* 169–173.

Levine, M., & Perkins, D. V. (1987). *Principles of community psychology: Perspectives and applications.* New York: Oxford University Press.

Levinson, D. J. (1978). *The seasons of a man's life.* New York: Knopf.

Levinson, D. J. (1986). A conception of adult development. *American Psychologist, 41*(1), 3–13.

Levinson, D. J. (1996). *The seasons of a woman's life.* New York: Knopf.

Levinthal, C. F. (2008). *Drugs, behavior, and modern society.* Boston: Pearson Education.

Levitt, S. D., & Dubner, S. J. (2005). *Freakonomics: A rogue economist explores the hidden side of everything.* New York: HarperCollins.

Levy, S. R., Stroessner, S. J., & Dweck, C. S. (1998). Stereotype formation and endorsement: The role of implicit theories. *Journal of Personality and Social Psychology, 74,* 1421–1436.

Lewinsohn, P. M., Clarke, G. N., Hops, H., & Andrews, J. A. (1990). Cognitive-behavioral treatment for depressed adolescents. *Behavior Therapy, 21,* 385–401.

Lewinsohn, P. M., & Gotlib, I. H. (1995). Behavioral theory and treatment of depression. In E. E. Beckham, & W. R. Leber (Eds.), *Handbook of depression* (2nd ed., pp. 352–375). New York: Guilford Press.

Lewinsohn, P. M., & Rosenbaum, M. (1987). Recall

of parental behavior by acute depressives, remitted depressives, and nondepressives. *Journal of Personality and Social Psychology, 52,* 611–619.

Lewinsohn, P. M., Sullivan, J. M., & Grosscup, S. J. (1980). Changing reinforcing events: An approach to the treatment of depression. *Psychotherapy: Theory, Research and Practice, 17,* 322–334.

Lewis, D. A., Cruz, D. A., Melchitzky, D. S., & Pierri, J. N. (2001). Lamina-specific deficits in parvalbumin-immunoreactive varicosities in the prefrontal cortex of subjects with schizophrenia: Evidence for fewer projections from the thalamus. *American Journal of Psychiatry, 158,* 1411–1422.

Lewis, T. L., & Maurer, D. (2005). Multiple sensitive periods in human visual development: Evidence from visually deprived children. *Developmental Psychobiology, 46,* 163–183.

Lewis-Fernández, R., & Kleinman, A. (1994). Culture, personality, and psychopathology. *Journal of Abnormal Psychology, 103,* 67–71.

Lewy, A. J., Lefler, B. J., Emens, J. S., & Bauer, V. K. (2006). The circadian basis of winter depression. *PNAS Proceedings of the National Academy of Sciences of the United States of America, 103,* 7414–7419. [See also Wehr & Rosenthal, 1989]

Lewy, A. J., Sack, R. L., Miller, S., & Hoban, T. M. (1987). Antidepressant and circadian phase-shifting effect of light. *Science, 235,* 352–354.

Li, J. (2005). Mind or virtue: Western and Chinese beliefs about learning. *Current Directions in Psychological Science, 14,* 190–194.

Li, W., Moallem, I., Paller, K. A., & Gottfried, J. A. (2007). Subliminal smells can guide social preferences. *Psychological Science. 18,* 1044–1049.

Lieberman, J. A., Stroup, T. S., McEvoy, J. P., Schwartz, M. S., Rosenheck, R. A., Perkins, D. O., Keefe, R. S. E., Davis, S. M., Davis, C. E., Lebowitz, B. D., Severe, J., & Hsiao, J. K. (2005). Effectiveness of antipsychotic drugs in patients with chronic schizophrenia. *The New England Journal of Medicine, 353,* 1209–1223.

Lieberman, M. D., & Rosenthal, R. (2001). Why introverts can't always tell who likes them: Multitasking and nonverbal decoding. *Journal of Personality and Social Psychology, 80,* 294–310.

Liegeois, F., Baldeweg, T., Connelly, A., Gadian, D. G., Mishkin, M., & Vargha-Khadem, F. (2001). Language fMRI abnormalities associated with FOXP2 gene mutation. *Nature Neuroscience, 11,* 1230–1237.

Liem, R., & Rayman, P. (1982). Health and social costs of unemployment: Research and policy considerations. *American Psychologist, 37,* 1116–1123.

Light, K. C., Grewen, K. M., & Amico, J. A. (2005). More frequent partner hugs and higher oxytocin levels are linked to lower blood pressure and heart rate in premenopausal women. *Biological Psychology, 69,* 5–21.

Lilienfeld, S. O. (2007). Psycholgical treatments that cause harm. *Perspectives on Psychological Science, 2,* 53–70.

Lilienfeld, S. O., Lynn, S. J., Kirsch, I., Chaves, J. F., Sarbin, T. R., Ganaway, G. K., & Powell, R. A. (1999). Dissociative identity disorder and the sociocognitive model: Recalling the lessons of the past. *Psychological Bulletin, 125,* 507–523.

Lilienfeld, S. O., Wood, J. M., & Garb, H. N. (2000a). The scientific status of projective techniques. *Psychological Science in the Public Interest, 1,* 27–66. [See also: Anastasi, 1988; Wood et al., 1996]

Lilienfeld, S. O., Wood, J. M., & Garb, H. N. (2000b). What's wrong with this picture? *Scientific American, 284*(5), 80–87.

Lillard, A. (1999). Developing a cultural theory of mind: The CIAO approach. *Current Directions in Psychological Science, 8,* 57–61.

Lillard, A. S. (1997). Other folks' theories of mind and behavior. *Psychological Science, 8,* 268–274. [See also: Miller, 1984; Morris & Peng, 1994]

Lindsay, D. S. (1990). Misleading suggestions can impair eyewitnesses' ability to remember event details.

Journal of Experimental Psychology: Learning, Memory, and Cognition, 16(6), 1077–1083.

Lindsay, D. S. (1993). Eyewitness suggestibility. *Current Directions in Psychological Science, 2,* 86–89.

Linebarger, D. L., Kosanic, A. Z., Greenwood, C. R., & Docku, N. S. (2004). Effects of viewing the television program "Between the Lions" on the emergent literacy skills of young children. *Journal of Educational Psychology, 96,* 297–308.

Linsheid, T. R., Iwata, B. A., Ricketts, R. W., Williams, D. E., & Griffin, J. C. (1990). Clinical evaluation of the self-injurious behavior inhibiting system (SIBIS). *Journal of Applied Behavior Analysis, 23,* 53–78.

Lipsey, M. W., & Wilson, D. B. (1993). The efficacy of psychological, educational, and behavioral treatment: Confirmation from meta-analysis. *American Psychologist, 48,* 1181–1209.

Lipsitt, L. P., Reilly, B., Butcher, M. G., & Greenwood, M. M. (1976). The stability and interrelationships of newborn sucking and heart rate. *Developmental Psychobiology, 9,* 305–310.

Liu, W., Vichienchom, K., Clements, M., DeMarco, S. C., Hughes, C., McGucken, E., Humayun, M. S., De Juan, E., Weiland, J. D., & Greenberg, R. (2000, October). A neuro-stimulus chip with telemetry unit for retinal prosthetic device. *IEEE Journal of Solid-State Circuits, 35,* 1487–1497.

Liverant, G. I., Hofmann, S. G., & Litz, B. T. (2004). Coping and anxiety in college students after the September 11th terrorist attacks. *Stress & Coping, 17,* 127–139.

Lock, J., le Grange, D., Agras, W. S., & Dare, C. (2001). *Treatment manual for anorexia nervosa: A family-based approach.* New York: Guilford.

Loftus, E. F. (1979). *Eyewitness testimony.* Cambridge, MA: Harvard University Press.

Loftus, E. F. (1984). The eyewitness on trial. In B. D. Sales & A. Alwork (Eds.), *With liberty and justice for all.* Englewood Cliffs, NJ: Prentice Hall.

Loftus, E. F. (1992). When a lie becomes memory's truth: Memory distortion after exposure to misinformation. *Current Directions in Psychological Science, 1,* 121–123.

Loftus, E. F. (1993). The reality of repressed memories. *American Psychologist, 48,* 518–537.

Loftus, E. F. (1997a, September). Creating false memories. *Scientific American, 227,* 70–75.

Loftus, E. F. (1997b). Memory for a past that never was. *Current Directions in Psychological Science, 6,* 60–65.

Loftus, E. F. (2003a). Make-believe memories. *American Psychologist, 58,* 867–873. [See also: Hyman et al., 1995; Loftus, 1997a, 1997b; Loftus & Ketcham, 1994]

Loftus, E. F. (2003b). Our changeable memories: Legal and practical implications. *Nature Reviews: Neuroscience, 4,* 231–234.

Loftus, E. F. (2004). Memories of things unseen. *Current Directions in Psychological Science, 13,* 145–147.

Loftus, E. F., & Ketcham, K. (1991). *Witness for the defense: The accused, the eyewitness, and the expert who puts memory on trial.* New York: St. Martin's Press.

Loftus, E. F., & Ketcham, K. (1994). *The myth of repressed memory: False memories and allegations of sexual abuse.* New York: St. Martin's Griffin. [See also: Loftus, 1993; Ofshe & Watters, 1994]

Loftus, E. F., & Klinger, M. R. (1992). Is the unconscious smart or dumb? *American Psychologist, 47,* 761–765.

Loftus, E. F., & Palmer, J. C. (1973). Reconstruction of automobile destruction: An example of the interaction between language and memory. *Journal of Verbal Learning and Verbal Behavior, 13,* 585–589.

Loftus, G. R., Duncan, J., & Gehrig, P. (1992). On the time course of perceptual information that results from a brief visual presentation. *Journal of Experimental Psychology: Human Perception and Performance, 18*(2), 530–549.

London, K. A., Mosher, W. D., Pratt, W. F., &

Williams, L. B. (1989, March). Preliminary findings from the National Survey of Family Growth, Cycle IV. Paper presented at the annual meeting of the Population Association of America, Baltimore, MD.

Lonner, W. J. (1990). An overview of cross-cultural testing and assessment. In R. W. Brislin (Ed.), *Applied cross-cultural psychology.* Newbury Park, CA: Sage.

Lonner, W. J., & Malpass, R. (1994). *Psychology and culture.* Boston: Allyn & Bacon.

Lott, A. J., & Lott, B. E. (1961). Group cohesiveness, communication level, and conformity. *Journal of Abnormal and Social Psychology, 62,* 408–412.

Lourenço, O., & Machado, A. (1996). In defense of Piaget's theory: A reply to 10 common criticisms. *Psychological Review, 103,* 143–164.

Lovaas, O. I. (1977). *The autistic child: Language development through behavior modification.* New York: Halstead Press.

Lovaas, O. I. (1993). The development of a treatment-research project for developmentally disabled and autistic children. *Journal of Applied Behavior Analysis, 26,* 617–630.

Lovaas, O. I., Schreibman, L., & Koegel, R. L. (1974). A behavior modification approach to the treatment of autistic children. *Journal of Autism and Childhood Schizophrenia, 4,* 111–129.

Lovibond, S. H., Adams, M., & Adams, W. G. (1979). The effects of three experimental prison environments on the behavior of nonconflict volunteer subjects. *Australian Psychologist, 14,* 273–285.

Luborsky, L., Singer, B., & Luborsky, L. (1975). Comparative studies of psycho therapies: Is it true that everyone has won and all must have prizes? *Archives of General Psychiatry, 32,* 995–1008.

Luders, E., Narr, K. L., Thompson, P. M., Rex, D. E., Jancke, L., Steinmetz, H., & Toga, A. W. (2004, July 4). Gender differences in cortical complexity. *Nature Neuroscience, 7,* 799–800. [See also: Bower, 2004a]

Lutz, C. (1988). *Unnatural emotions.* Chicago: University of Chicago Press.

Lykken, D., & Tellegen, A. (1996). Happiness is a stochastic phenomenon. *Psychological Science, 7,* 186–189.

Lykken, D. T. (2001). Parental licensure. *American Psychologist, 56,* 885–894.

Lykken, D. T., McGue, M., Tellegen, A., & Bouchard, T. J. (1992). Emergenesis: Genetic traits that may not run in families. *American Psychologist, 47,* 1565–1577.

Lynch, G., & Staubli, U. (1991). Possible contributions of long-term potentiation to the encoding and organization of memory. *Brain Research Reviews, 16,* 204–206.

Maas, J. B. (1999). *Power sleep: The revolutionary program that prepares your mind for peak performance.* New York: HarperPerennial.

Maccoby, E. (1998). *The two sexes: Growing up apart, coming together.* Cambridge, MA: Belknap Press.

Maccoby, E. (2000). Gender differentiation in childhood: Broad patterns and their implications. Address given at the American Psychological Association annual convention, Washington, DC.

Maccoby, E. E., & Martin, J. A. (1983). Socialization in the context of the family: Parent–child interaction. In E. M. Hetherington (Ed.), *Handbook of child psychology: Vol. 4, Socialization, personality, and social development* (4th ed., pp. 1–101). New York: Wiley.

Maccoby, N., Farquhar, J. W., Wood, P. D., & Alexander, J. K. (1977). Reducing the risk of cardiovascular disease: Effects of a community-based campaign on knowledge and behavior. *Journal of Community Health, 3,* 100–114.

MacCoun, R. J. (1998). Toward a psychology of harm reduction. *American Psychologist, 53,* 1199–1208.

MacLeod, C., & Campbell, L. (1992). Memory accessibility and probability judgments: An experimental evaluation of the availability heuristic. *Journal of Personality and Social Psychology, 63,* 890–902.

Macmillan, J. C. (2000). *An odd kind of fame: Stories of Phineas Gage.* Cambridge, MA: MIT Press.

MacNair, R. M. (1999). Symptom pattern differences for perpetration-induced traumatic stress in veterans: Probing the National Vietnam Veterans Readjustment Study. Doctoral dissertation, University of Kansas City, Missouri.

MacNair, R. M. (2002). *Perpetration-induced traumatic stress: The psychological consequences of killing.* Westport, CT: Praeger.

Macrae, C. N., Milne, A. B., & Bodenhausen, G. V. (1994). Stereotypes as energy-saving devices: A peek inside the cognitive toolbox. *Journal of Personality and Social Psychology, 66,* 37–47.

Maddi, S. R. (1987). Hardiness training at Illinois Bell Telephone. In J. P. Opatz (Ed.), *Health promotion evaluation* (pp. 101–115). Stevens Point, WI: National Wellness Institute.

Maddi, S. R. (2002). The story of hardiness: Twenty years of theorizing, research and practice. *Consulting Psychology Journal, 54,* 173–185.

Magee, W. J., Eaton, W. W., Wittchen, H.-U., McGonagle, K. A., & Kessler, R. C. (1996). Agoraphobia, simple phobia, and social phobia in the national comorbidity survey. *Archives of General Psychiatry, 53,* 159–168.

Maher, B. A., & Maher, W. B. (1985). Psychopathology: II. From the eighteenth century to modern times. In G. A. Kimble & K. Schlesinger (Eds.), *Topics in the history of psychology* (Vol. 2, pp. 295–329). Hillsdale, NJ: Erlbaum.

Maher, B. A., & Ross, J. S. (1984). Delusions. In H. E. Adams & P. B. Sutker (Eds.), *Comprehensive handbook of psychopathology* (pp. 383–987). New York: Plenum.

Maier, S. F., & Watkins, L. R. (1999). Bidirectional communication between the brain and the immune system: Implications for behaviour. *Animal Behaviour, 57,* 741–751.

Maier, S. F., & Watkins, L. R. (2000). The immune system as a sensory system: Implications for psychology. *Current Directions in Psychological Science, 9,* 98–102.

Maier, S. F., Watkins, L. R., & Fleshner, M. (1994). Psychoneuroimmunology: The interface between behavior, brain, and immunity. *American Psychologist, 49,* 1004–1017.

Maisto, S. A., Galizio, M., & Connors, G. J. (1995). *Drug use and abuse* (2nd ed). Fort Worth, TX: Harcourt Brace.

Majewska, M. D., Harrison, N. L., Schwartz, R. D., Barker, J. L., & Paul, S. M. (1986). Steroid hormone metabolites are barbiturate-like modulators of the GABA receptor. *Science, 232,* 1004–1007.

Malatesta, V. J., Sutker, P. B., & Treiber, F. A. (1981). Sensation seeking and chronic public drunkenness. *Journal of Consulting and Clinical Psychology, 49,* 282–294.

Malinowski, B. (1927). *Sex and repression in savage society.* London, U.K.: Humanities Press.

Malitz, S., & Sackheim, H. A. (1984). Low dosage ECT: Electrode placement and acute physiological and cognitive effects. *American Journal of Social Psychiatry, 4,* 47–53.

Manderscheid, R. W., Witkin, M. J., Rosenstein, M. J., Milazzo-Sayre, L. J., Bethel, H. E., & MacAskill, R. L. (1985). In C. A. Taube & S. A. Barrett (Eds.), *Mental Health, United States, 1985.* Washington, DC: National Institute of Mental Health.

Manfredi, M., Bini, G., Cruccu, G., Accor nero, N., Beradelli, A., & Medolago, L. (1981). Congenital absence of pain. *Archives of Neurology, 38,* 507–511.

Mann, C. C. (1994, June 17). Behavioral genetics in transition. *Science, 264,* 1686–1689.

Manning, R., Levine, M., & Collins, A. (2007). The Kitty Genovese murder and the social psychology of helping. *American Psychologist, 62,* 555–562.

Manschreck, T. C. (1989). Delusional (paranoid) disorders. In H. I. Kaplan & B. J. Sadock (Eds.), *Comprehensive textbook of psychiatry* (pp. 816–829). Baltimore, MD: Williams & Wilkins.

Manson, S. M. (1994). Culture and depression: Discovering variations in the experience of illness. In W. J. Lonner & R. Malpass (Eds.), *Psychology and culture* (pp. 285–290). Boston: Allyn & Bacon.

Maquet, P. (2001, November 2). The role of sleep in learning and memory. *Science, 294,* 1048–1052.

Marcus, G. (2004). *The birth of the mind: How a tiny number of genes creates the complexities of human thought.* New York: Basic Books. [See also: Netting & Wang, 2001; Pennisi, 2003]

Marcus, G. B. (1986). Stability and change in political attitudes: Observe, recall, and "explain." *Political Behavior, 8,* 21–44.

Marcus, G. F. (1996). Why do children say "breaked"? *Current Directions in Psychological Science, 3,* 81–85.

Maren, S. (2007, August 24). The threatened brain. *Science, 317,* 1043–1044.

Markman, H. J., & Notarius, C. I. (1993). *We can work it out.* Berkeley, CA: Berkeley Publishing Group.

Marks, J. (2004, June). Ask *Discover:* How closely related are people to each other? And how closely does our genome match up with those of other primates? *Discover, 25*(6), 17.

Markus, H. R., & Kitayama, S. (1994). The cultural construction of self and emotion: Implications for social behavior. In H. R. Markus & S. Kitayama (Eds.), *Emotion and culture: Empirical studies of mutual influence* (pp. 89–130). Washington, DC: American Psychological Association.

Markus, H. R., Uchida, Y., Omoregie, H., Townsend, S. S. M., & Kitayama, S. (2006). Going for the gold: Models of agency in Japanese and American contexts. *Psychological Science, 17,* 103–112.

Marschall, J. (2007, February/March). Seduced by sleep. *Scientific American Mind, 18*(1), 52–57.

Marsh, P. (1988). Detecting insincerity. In P. Marsh (Ed.), *Eye to eye: How people interact.* (Ch. 14, pp. 116–119). Oxford, U.K.: Oxford Andromeda.

Marshall, E. (2000, August 4). Duke study faults overuse of stimulants for children. *Science, 289,* 721.

Martin, A., Haxby, J. V., Lalonde, F. M., Wiggs, C. L., & Ungerleider, L. G. (1995). Discrete cortical regions associated with knowledge of color and knowledge of action. *Science, 270,* 102–105.

Martin, D. J., Garske, J. P., & Davis, M. K. (2000). Relation of the therapeutic alliance with outcome and other variables: A meta-analytic review. *Journal of Consulting and Clinical Psychology, 68,* 438–450.

Martin, G., & Pear, J. (1999). *Behavior modification: What it is and how to do it* (6th ed.). Upper Saddle River, NJ: Prentice-Hall.

Martin, J. A. (1981). A longitudinal study of the consequences of early mother–infant interaction: A microanalytic approach. *Monographs of the Society for Research in Child Development, 46* (203, Serial No. 190).

Martin, R. C. (2005). Components of short-term memory and their relation to language processing. *Current Directions in Psychological Science, 14,* 204–208.

Martin, S. (1999, February). Drug use appears to be easing among teens. *APA Monitor,* 8.

Martindale, D. (2005, October). One face, one neuron: Storing Halle Berry in a single brain cell. *Scientific American, 293*(4), 22, 24.

Maruyama, G., & Miller, N. (1975). *Physical attractiveness and classroom acceptance (Research Report 75–2).* Los Angeles: University of Southern California, Social Science Research Institute.

Marx, J. (2003, February 7). Cellular warriors at the battle of the bulge. *Science, 299,* 846–849.

Marx, J. (2004, July 16). Prolonging the agony. *Science, 305,* 326–329.

Marx, J. (2005). Preventing Alzheimer's: A lifelong commitment? *Science, 309,* 864–866.

Marx, J. (2006, January 20). Drugs inspired by a drug. *Science, 311,* 322–325.

Maslach, C. (1998, April). The truth about burnout. The G. Stanley Hall Lecture given at the Western Psychological Association convention in Albuquerque, NM.

Maslach, C. (2003). Job burnout: New directions in research and intervention. *Current Directions in Psychological Science, 12,* 189–192.

Maslach, C., & Goldberg, J. (1998). Prevention of burnout: New perspectives. *Applied and Preventive Psychology, 7,* 63–74.

Maslach, C., & Leiter, M. P. (1997). *The truth about burnout: How organizations cause personal stress and what to do about it.* San Francisco: Jossey-Bass Publishers.

Maslach, C., Schaufeli, W. B., & Leiter, M. P. (2001). Job burnout. *Annual Review of Psychology, 52,* 397–422.

Maslow, A. (1943). A theory of human motivation. *Psychological Review, 50,* 370–396. Retrieved April 4, 2008, from http://psychclassics.yorku.ca/Maslow/motivation.htm.

Maslow, A. H. (1968). *Toward a psychology of being* (2nd ed.). New York: Van Nostrand.

Maslow, A. H. (1970). *Motivation and personality* (rev. ed.). New York: Harper & Row.

Maslow, A. H. (1971). *Farther reaches of human nature.* New York: Viking Penguin.

Massimini, M., Ferrarelli, F., Huber, R., Esser, S. K., Singh, H., & Tononi, G. (2005, September 30). Breakdown of cortical effective connectivity during sleep. *Science, 309,* 2228–2232. [See also: Miller, 2005; Roser & Gazzaniga, 2004]

Mason, M. F., Norton, M. I., Van Horn, J. D., Wegner, D. M., Grafton, S. T., Macrae, C. N. (2007, January 19). Wandering minds: The default network and stimulus-independent thought. *Science, 315,* 393–395.

Masten, A. S. (2001). Ordinary magic: Resilience processes in development. *American Psychologist, 56,* 227–238.

Masters, W. H., & Johnson, V. E. (1966). *Human sexual response.* Boston: Little, Brown.

Masters, W. H., & Johnson, V. E. (1970). *Human sexual inadequacy.* Boston: Little, Brown.

Masters, W. H., & Johnson, V. E. (1979). *Homosexuality in perspective.* Boston: Little, Brown.

Matarazzo, J. D. (1980). Behavioral health and behavioral medicine: Frontiers for a new health psychology. *American Psychologist, 35,* 807–817.

Mather, M. (2007). Emotional arousal and memory binding: An object-based framework. *Perspectives on Psychological Science, 2,* 33–52.

Matossian, M. K. (1982). Ergot and the Salem witchcraft affair. *American Scientist, 70,* 355–357.

Matossian, M. K. (1989). *Poisons of the past: Molds, epidemics, and history.* New Haven, CT: Yale University Press.

Matsumoto, D. (1994). *People: Psychology from a cultural perspective.* Pacific Grove, CA: Brooks/Cole.

Matsumoto, D. (1996). *Culture and psychology.* Pacific Grove, CA: Brooks/Cole. [See also: Jenkins, 1994; Manson, 1994]

Matt, G. E., Vázquez, C., & Campbell, W. K. (1992). Mood-congruent recall of affectively toned stimuli: A meta-analytic review. *Clinical Psychology Review, 12,* 227–255.

Matthews, K. A. (1982). Psychological perspectives on the Type-A behavior pattern. *Psychological Bulletin, 91,* 293–323.

Matthews, K. A., Woodall, K. L., Kenyon, K., & Jacob, T. (1996). Negative family environment as a predictor of boys' future status on measures of hostile attitudes, interview behavior, and anger expression. *Health Psychology, 15,* 30–37.

Matus, A. (2000, October 27). Actin-based plasticity in dendritic spines. *Science, 290,* 754–758.

Maugh, T. H. (1988, February 23). 22-caliber surgery suicide bid cures psychological disorder, doctor reports. *Los Angeles Times,* p. 3.

Maunsell, J. H. R. (1995, November 3). The brain's visual world: Representation of visual targets in cerebral cortex. *Science, 270,* 764–769.

Mauron, A. (2001, February 2). Is the genome the secular equivalent of the soul? *Science, 291,* 831–833.

Mayberg, H. S., Lozano, A. M., Voon, V. McNeely, H. E., Seminowicz, D., Hamani, C., Schwalb, J. M., & Kennedy, S. H. (2005, March 3). Deep brain stimulation for treatment-resistant depression. *Neuron, 45,* 651–660.

Mayberry, R. I. (1994). The importance of childhood to language acquisition: Evidence from American Sign Language. In J. C. Goodman & H. C. Nusbaum (Eds.). *The development of speech perception: The transition from speech sounds to spoken words* (pp. 57–90) Cambridge, MA: MIT Press.

Mayer, D. J. (1979). Endogenous analgesia systems: Neural and behavioral mechanisms. In J. J. Bonica (Ed.), *Advances in pain research and therapy (Vol. 3).* New York: Raven Press.

Mayer, J. D. (1999, September). Emotional intelligence: Popular or scientific psychology? *American Psychological Association Monitor, 50.*

Mayer, J. D., & Salovey, P. (1995). Emotional intelligence and the construction and regulation of feelings. *Applied & Preventive Psychology, 4,* 197–208.

Mayer, J. D., & Salovey, P. (1997). What is emotional intelligence? In P. Salovey & D. J. Sluyter (Eds.), *Emotional development and emotional intelligence: Educational implications.* New York: Basic Books.

Mayer, R. E. (1983). *Thinking, problem solving, and cognition.* San Francisco: W. H. Freeman.

Mayr, E. (2000, July). Darwin's influence on modern thought. *Scientific American,* 79–83.

McAdams, D. P. (1992). The five-factor model in personality: A critical appraisal. *Journal of Personality, 60,* 239–361.

McAdams, D. P., & Pals, J. L. (2006). A new Big Five: Fundamental principles for an integrative science of personality. *American Psychologist, 61,* 204–217.

McAdams, D. P., de St. Aubin, E., & Logan, R. L. (1993). Generativity among young, midlife, and older adults. *Psychology and Aging, 8,* 221–230.

McAnulty, R. D., & Burnette, M. M. (2004). *Exploring human sexuality: Making healthy decisions* (2nd ed.). Boston: Allyn & Bacon.

McArdle, J. J., Ferrer-Caja, E. Hamagami, F., & Woodcock, R. W. (2002). Comparative longitudinal structural analyses of the growth and decline of multiple intellectual abilities over the life span. *Developmental Psychology, 38,* 115–142.

McCann, I. L., & Holmes, D. S. (1984). Influence of aerobic exercise on depression. *Journal of Personality and Social Psychology, 46,* 1142–1147.

McCann, I. L., & Pearlman, L. A. (1990). Vicarious traumatization: A framework for understanding the psychological effects of working with victims. *Journal of Traumatic Stress, 3,* 131–149.

McCarley, N., & Carskadon, T. G. (1983). Test–retest reliabilities of scales and subscales of the Myers–Briggs Type Indicator and of criteria for clinical interpretive hypotheses involving them. *Research in Psychological Type, 6,* 24–36.

McCarthy, K. (1991, August). Moods—good and bad—color all aspects of life. *APA Monitor, 13.*

McCartney, K., Harris, M. J., & Bernieri, F. (1990). Growing up and growing apart: A developmental meta-analysis of twin studies. *Psychological Bulletin, 107,* 226–237.

McClearn, G. E., Johansson, B., Berg, S., Pedersen, N. L., Ahern, F., Petrill, S. A., & Plomin, R. (1997, June 6). Substantial genetic influence on cognitive abilities in twins 80 or more years old. *Science, 276,* 1560–1563.

McClelland, D. C. (1965). Achievement and entrepreneurship: A longitudinal study. *Journal of Personality and Social Psychology, 1,* 389–392.

McClelland, D. C. (1975). *Power: The inner experience.* New York: Irvington.

McClelland, D. C. (1985). *Human motivation.* New York: Scott Foresman.

McClelland, D. C. (1987a). Characteristics of successful entrepreneurs. *The Journal of Creative Behavior, 21,* 219–233.

McClelland, D. C. (1987b). *Human motivation.* New York: Cambridge University Press. [See also: Cooper, 1983; French & Thomas, 1958]

McClelland, D. C. (1993). Intelligence is not the best predictor of job performance. *Current Directions in Psychological Science, 2,* 5–6.

McClelland, D. C., & Boyatzis, R. E. (1982). Leadership motive pattern and long-term success in management. *Journal of Applied Psychology, 67,* 737–743.

McClelland, J. L., McNaughton, B. L., & O'Reilly, R. C. (1995). Why there are complementary learning systems in the hippocampus and neocortex: Insights from the successes and failures of connectionist models of learning and memory. *Psychological Review, 102,* 419–457.

McCook, A. (2006, July 24). Conflicts of interest at federal agencies. *TheScientist.com.* Retrieved October 18, 2007, from www.the-scientist.com/news/display/24056/.

McCrae, R. R., & Costa, P. T. (1989). Reinterpreting the Myers–Briggs Type Indicator from the perspective of the five-factor model of personality. *Journal of Personality, 57,* 17–40.

McCrae, R. R., & Costa, P. T. Jr. (1997). Personality trait structure as a human universal. *American Psychologist, 52,* 509–516.

McCrae, R. R., Terraciano, A., & 78 members of the Personality Profiles of Cultures Project. (2005). Universal features of personality traits from the observer's perspective: Data from 50 cultures. *Journal of Personality and Social Psychology, 88,* 547–561.

McCullough, M. L. (2001). Freud's seduction theory and its rehabilitation: A saga of one mistake after another. *Review of General Psychology, 5,* 3–22.

McDonald, K. A. (1998, August 14). Scientists consider new explanations for the impact of exercise on mood. *The Chronicle of Higher Education,* A15–A16.

McGaugh, J. L. (2000, January 14). Memory—A century of consolidation. *Science, 287,* 248–251.

McGuire, P. A. (2000, February). New hope for people with schizophrenia. *Monitor on Psychology, 31*(2), 24–28.

McGurk, S. R., Mueser, K. T., Feldman, K., Wolfe, R, & Pascaris, A. (2007). Cognitive training for supported employment: 2–3 year outcomes of a randomized controlled trial. *American Journal of Psychiatry, 164,* 437–441. [See also: Butcher et al., 2008]

McIntosh, A. R., & Lobaugh, N. J. (2003, July 18). When is a word not a word? *Science, 301,* 322–323.

McKeachie, W. J. (1990). Research on college teaching: The historical background. *Journal of Educational Psychology, 82,* 189–200.

McKeachie, W. J. (1997). Good teaching makes a difference—and we know what it is. In R. B. Perry & J. C. Smart (Eds.), *Effective teaching in higher education: Research and practice* (pp. 396–408). New York: Agathon Press.

McKeachie, W. J. (1999). *McKeachie's teaching tips: Strategies, research, and theory for college and university teachers* (10th ed.). Boston: Houghton Mifflin.

McKhann, G. (June, 2006). No lie: Science must develop before targeting truth. *Brain in the News, 13*(7), 3.

Mcleod, F. (2008, March 8). *Bullying affects girls far more than boys.* Retrieved on September 8, 2008, from http://news.scotsman.com/bullyingatschool/Bullying-affects-girls-far-more.3857607.jp.

McNally, R. J. (1994, August). Cognitive bias in panic disorder. *Current Directions in Psychological Science, 3,* 129–132.

McNally, R. J., Bryant, R. A., & Ehlers, A. (2003). Does early psychological intervention promote recovery from posttraumatic stress? *Psychology Science in the Public Interest, 4,* 45–79.

McNamara, P., McLaren, D., Smith, D., Brown, A., & Stickgold, R. (2005). A "Jekyll and Hyde" within: Aggressive versus friendly interactions in REM and non-REM dreams. *Psychological Science, 16,* 130–136.

Medin, C., Lynch, J., & Solomon, H. (2000). Are there kinds of concepts? *Annual Review of Psychology, 52,* 121–147.

Medin, D. L. (1989). Concepts and conceptual structure. *American Psychologist, 44,* 1469–1481.

Medin, D. L., & Ross, B. H. (1992). *Cognitive psychology*. Fort Worth, TX: Harcourt Brace Jovanovich.

Meeus, W. H. J., & Raaijmakers, Q. A. W. (1986). Administrative obedience: Carrying out orders to use psychological-administrative violence. *European Journal of Social Psychology, 16,* 311–324.

Mehl, M. R., Gosling, S. D. & Pennebaker, J. W. (2006). Personality in its natural habitat: Manifestations and implicit folk theories of personality in daily life. *Journal of Personality and Social Psychology, 90,* 862–877.

Meichenbaum, D. H., & Cameron, R. (1974). The clinical potential and pitfalls of modifying what clients say to themselves. In M. J. Mahoney & C. E. Thoreson (Eds.), *Self-control: Power to the person* (pp. 263–290). Monterey, CA: Brooks-Cole.

Meier, R. P. (1991). Language acquisition by deaf children. *American Scientist, 79,* 60–70.

Meltzoff, A. N. (1998). The nature of the preverbal mind: Towards a developmental cognitive science. Paper presented at the Western Psychological Association/ Rocky Mountain Psychological Association joint convention, Albuquerque, NM.

Meltzoff, A. N., & Prinz, W. (2002). *The imitative mind.* New York: Cambridge University Press.

Meltzoff, J., & Kornreich, M. (1970). *Research in psychotherapy.* New York: Atherton.

Melzack, R. (1990, February). The tragedy of needless pain. *Scientific American, 262,* 27–33.

Melzack, R., & Wall, P. D. (1965). Pain mechanisms: A new theory. *Science, 150,* 971–979.

Melzack, R., & Wall, P. D. (1983). *The challenge of pain.* New York: Basic Books.

Menzel, E. M. (1978). Cognitive mapping in chimpanzees. In S. H. Hulse, H. Fowler, & W. K. Honzig (Eds.), *Cognitive processes in animal behavior* (pp. 375–422). Hillsdale, NJ: Erlbaum.

Merari, A. (2006). Psychological aspects of suicidal terrorism. In B. Bongar, L. M. Brown, L. Beutler, J. N. Breckenridge, & P. G. Zimbardo (Eds.), *Psychology and Terrorism,* (pp. 101–115). New York: Oxford University Press.

Meredith, N. (1986, June). Testing the talking cure. *Science 86, 7,* 30–37.

Merikle, P. M., & Reingold, E. M. (1990). Recognition and lexical decision without detection: Unconscious perception? *Journal of Experimental Psychology: Human Perception & Performance, 16,* 574–583.

Mervis, C. B., & Rosch, E. (1981). Categorization of natural objects. *Annual Review of Psychology, 32,* 89–115.

Mesulam, M. M. (1990). Schizophrenia and the brain. *New England Journal of Medicine, 322,* 842–845.

Meyer, I. H. (2003). Prejudice, social stress, and mental health in lesbian, gay, and bisexual populations: Conceptual issues and research evidence. *Psychological Bulletin, 129,* 674–697.

Meyers, L. (2007, June). Of mind and matter: Understanding consciousness. *Monitor on Psychology, 38*(6), 32–35.

Michael, R. T., Gagnon, J. H., Laumann, E. O., & Kolata, G. (1994). *Sex in America: A definitive survey.* New York: Little, Brown.

Miklowitz, D. J. (2007) The role of the family in the course and treatment of bipolar disorder. *Current Directions in Psychological Science, 16,* 192–196.

Miklowitz, D. J., Otto, M. W., Frank, E., Reilly-Harrington, N. A., Wisniewski, S. R., Kogan, J. N., Nierenberg, A. A., Calabrese, J. R., Marangell, L. B., Gyulai, L., Araga, M. Gonzalez, J. M., Shirley, E. R., Thase, M. E., & Sachs, G. S. (2007). Psychosocial treatments for bipolar depression: A 1-year randomized trial from the systematic treatment enhancement program. *Archives of General Psychiatry, 64,* 419–426.

Milgram, S. (1965). Some conditions of obedience and disobedience to authority. *Human Relations, 18,* 56–76.

Milgram, S. (1974). *Obedience to authority.* New York: Harper & Row.

Miller, A. G. (1986). *The obedience paradigm: A case study in controversy in social science.* New York: Praeger.

Miller, E. D. (2003). Reconceptualizing the role of resiliency in coping and therapy. *Journal of Loss and Trauma, 8,* 239–246.

Miller, G. (2004, April 2). Learning to forget. *Science, 304,* 34–36.

Miller, G. (2005, May 13). Reflecting on another's mind. *Science, 308,* 945–946.

Miller, G. (2006a, August 4). The emotional brain weighs its options. *Science, 313,* 600–601.

Miller, G. (2006b, October 6). An enterprising approach to brain science. *Science, 314,* 76–77.

Miller, G. (2006c, May 12). Probing the social brain. *Science, 312,* 838–839.

Miller, G. (2006d, January 27). The unseen: Mental illness's global toll. *Science, 311,* 458–461.

Miller, G. (2007, March 9). Hunting for meaning after midnight. *Science, 315,* 1360–1363.

Miller, G. A. (1956). The magic number seven plus or minus two: Some limits in our capacity for processing information. *Psychological Review, 63,* 81–97.

Miller, J. (1984). Culture and the development of everyday social explanation. *Journal of Personality and Social Psychology, 46,* 961–978.

Miller, K. E., Barnes, G. M., Sabo, D. F., Melnick, M. J., & Farrell, M. P. (2002). Anabolic-androgenic steroid use and other adolescent problem behaviors: Rethinking the male athlete assumption. *Sociological Perspectives, 45,* 467–489.

Miller, M. E., & Bowers, K. S. (1993). Hypnotic analgesia: Dissociated experience of dissociated control? *Journal of Abnormal Psychology, 102,* 29–38.

Miller, M. W. (1993, December 2). Dark days: The staggering cost of depression. *The Wall Street Journal,* B1.

Miller, N. E. (1983). Behavioral medicine: Symbiosis between laboratory and clinic. *Annual Review of Psychology, 34,* 1–31.

Miller, P. Y., & Simon, W. (1980). The development of sexuality in adolescence. In J. Adelson (Ed.), *Handbook of adolescent psychology.* New York: Wiley.

Miller, W. R., & Brown, S. A. (1997). Why psychologists should treat alcohol and drug problems. *American Psychologist, 52,* 1269–1279.

Miller-Jones, D. (1989). Culture and testing. *American Psychologist, 44,* 360–366.

Millum, J., & Emanuel, E. J. (2007, December 21). The ethics of international research with abandoned children. *Science, 308,* 1874–1875.

Milner, B., Corkin, S., & Teuber, H. H. (1968) Further analysis of the hippocampal amnesic syndrome: 14-year follow-up study of H. M. *Neuropsychologia, 6,* 215–234.

Mineka, S., Davidson, M., Cook, M., & Keir, R. (1984). Observational conditioning of snake fear in rhesus monkeys. *Journal of Abnormal Psychology, 93,* 355–372.

Mineka, S., & Zinbarg, R. (2006). A contemporary learning theory perspective on the etiology of anxiety disorders: It's not what you thought it was. *American Psychologist, 61,* 10–26.

Mintz, L. B., & Betz, N. E. (1986). Sex differences in the nature, realism, and correlates of body image. *Sex Roles, 15,* 185–195.

The mirror of your soul. (1998, January 3). *The Economist.* Retrieved on November 8, 2004, from http://search.epnet.com/direct.asp?an=35349&db=aph.

Mischel, W. (1968). *Personality and assessment.* New York: Wiley.

Mischel, W. (1973). Toward a cognitive social learning conceptualization of personality. *Psychological Review, 80,* 252–283.

Mischel, W. (1990). Personality dispositions revisited and revised: A view after three decades. In L. A. Pervin (Ed.), *Handbook of personality: Theory and research.* New York: Guilford Press.

Mischel, W. (1993). *Introduction to personality* (5th ed.). Fort Worth, TX: Harcourt Brace Jovanovich College Publishers.

Mischel, W. (2003). Challenging the traditional personality psychology paradigm. In R. J. Sternberg, (Ed.), *Psychologists defying the crowd: Stories of those who battled the establishment and won* (pp. 139–156). Washington, DC: American Psychological Association.

Mischel, W., & Shoda, Y. (1995). A cognitive-affective system theory of personality: Reconceptualizing situations, dispositions, dynamics, and invariance in personality structure. *Psychological Review, 102,* 246–268.

Miyake, K. (1993). Temperament, mother–infant interaction, and early emotional development. *Japanese Journal of Research on Emotions, 1,* 48–55.

Miyake, K., Cen, S., & Campos, J. J. (1985). Infant temperament, mother's mode of interaction, and attachment in Japan: An interim report. In J. Bretherton & E. Waters (Eds.), *Growing points of attachment theory: Monographs of the Society of Research in Child Development, 50* (1-2, Serial No. 209).

Miyashita, Y. (1995). How the brain creates imagery: Projection to primary visual cortex. *Science, 268,* 1719–1720.

Mizukami, K., Kobayashi, N., Ishii, T., & Iwata, H. (1990). First selective attachment begins in early infancy: A study using telethermography. *Infant Behavior and Development, 13,* 257–271.

Moar, I. (1980). The nature and acquisition of cognitive maps. In D. Cantor & T. Lee (Eds.), *Proceedings of the international conference on environmental psychology.* London, U.K.: Architectural Press.

Mobbs, D., Hagan, C. C., Azim, E., Menon, V., & Reiss, A. (2006, November). Personality predicts activity in reward and emotional regions associated with humor. *Proceedings of the National Academy of Sciences, 102,* 16, 496–416, 501.

Mobbs, D., Petrovic, P., Marchant, J. L., Hassabis, D., Weiskopf, N., Seymour, B., Dolan, R. J., & Frith, C. D. (2007, August 24). When fear is near: Threat imminence elicits prefrontal-periaqueductal gray shifts in humans. *Science, 317,* 1079–1083. [See also: Barlow, 2000, 2001; Maren, 2007]

Moen, P., & Wethington, E. (1999). Midlife development in a life-course context. In S. L. Willis & J. D. Reid (Eds.), *Life in the middle: Psychological and social development in middle age* (pp. 3–25). San Diego, CA: Academic Press.

Mogelonsky, M. (1996). The rocky road to adulthood. *American Demographics, 18,* 26–36, 56.

Moghaddam, F. M., Taylor, D. M., & Wright, S. C. (1993). *Social psychology in cross-cultural perspective.* New York: W. H. Freeman.

Mogilner, A., Grossman, J. A. I., & Ribary, W. (1993). Somatosensory cortical plasticity in adult humans revealed by magnetoencephalography. *Proceedings of the National Academy of Sciences, 90*(8), 3593–3597.

Molden, D. C., & Dweck, C. S. (2006). Finding "meaning" in psychology: A lay theories approach to self-regulation, social perception, and social development. *American Psychologist, 61,* 192–203.

Mombaerts, P. (1999, October 22). Seven-transmembrane proteins as odorant and chemosensory receptors. *Science, 286,* 707–711.

Monaghan, P. (1999, February 26). Lessons from the "marriage lab." *The Chronicle of Higher Education,* A9.

Moncrieff, R. W. (1951). *The chemical senses.* London, U.K.: Leonard Hill.

Mones, A. G., Schwartz, R. C. (2007). The functional hypothesis: A family systems contribution toward an understanding of the healing process of the common factors. *Journal of Psychotherapy Integration, 17,* 314–329.

Money, J. (1987). Sin, sickness, or status? Homosexual gender identity and psychoneuroendocrinology. *American Psychologist, 42,* 384–399.

Monte, C. F. (1980). *Beneath the mask: An introduction to theories of personality* (2nd ed.). New York: Holt, Rinehart and Winston.

Moore, J. S., Graziano, W. G., & Millar, M. G. (1987). Physical attractiveness, sex role orientation, and the evaluation of adults and children. *Personality and Social Psychology Bulletin, 13,* 95–102.

Moore, M. K., & Meltzoff, A. M. (2004). Object permanence after a 24-hour delay and leaving the locale of disappearance: The role of memory, space, and identity. *Developmental Psychology, 40,* 606–620.

Moore-Ede, M. (1993). *The twenty-four-hour society: Understanding human limits in a world that never stops.* Reading, MA: Addison-Wesley.

Moran, C. C. (2002). Humor as a moderator of compassion fatigue. In C. R. Figley (Ed.), *Treating compassion fatigue* (pp. 139–154). New York: Brunner-Routledge.

Moran, J. M., Wig, G. S., Adams, R. B., Jr., Janata, P., & Kelley, W. M. (2004). Neural correlates of humor detection and appreciation. *Neuroimage, 21,* 1055–1060.

Morgan, A. H., Hilgard, E. R., & Davert, E. C. (1970). The heritability of hypnotic susceptibility of twins: A preliminary report. *Behavior Genetics, 1,* 213–224.

Mori, K., Nagao, H., & Yoshihara, Y. (1999). The olfactory bulb: Coding and processing of odor molecule information. *Science, 286,* 711–715.

Moriarity, T. (1975). Crime, commitment and the responsive bystander: Two field experiments. *Journal of Personality and Social Psychology, 31,* 370–376.

Morisse, D., Batra, L., Hess, L., Silverman, R., & Corrigan, P. (1996). A demonstration of a token economy for the real world. *Applied and Preventive Psychology, 5,* 41–46.

Morrell, E. M. (1986). Meditation and somatic arousal. *American Psychologist, 41*(6), 712–713. [See also: Dillbeck & Orme-Johnson, 1987; Holmes, 1984]

Morris, M. W., & Peng, K. (1994). Culture and cause: American and Chinese attributions for social and physical events. *Journal of Personality & Social Psychology, 8,* 949–971.

Morris, W. N., & Miller, R. S. (1975). The effects of consensus-breaking and consensus-preempting partners on reduction of conformity. *Journal of Experimental Social Psychology, 11,* 215–223.

Morrison-Bogorad, M., & Phelps, C. (1997, March 12). Alzheimer disease research comes of age. *JAMA: Journal of the American Medical Association, 277,* 837–840.

Moskowitz, H. (1985). Marihuana and driving. *Accident Analysis & Prevention, 17,* 323–345.

Moss, R. (1996). *Conscious dreaming: A spiritual path to everyday life.* New York: Crown Publishing.

Mowrer, O. (1960). *Learning theory and symbolic processes.* New York: Wiley.

Mowrer, O. H., & Mowrer, W. M. (1938). Enuresis—a method for its study and treatment. *American Journal of Orthopsychiatry, 8,* 436–459.

Mroczek, D. K. (2001). Age and emotion in adulthood. *Current Directions in Psychological Science, 10,* 87–90.

MTA Cooperative Group. (1999). A fourteen-month randomized clinical trial of treatment strategies for attention-deficit/hyperactivity disorder. *Archives of General Psychiatry, 56,*1073–1086.

MTA Cooperative Treatment Group. (2004). National Institute of Mental Health Multimodal Treatment Study of ADHD Follow-up: 24-Month Outcomes of Treatment Strategies for Attention-Deficit/Hyperactivity Disorder. *Pediatrics, 113,* 754–761.

Mukerjee, M. (1995, October). Hidden scars: Sexual and other abuse may alter a brain region. *Scientific American, 273*(4), 14, 20.

Munakata, Y., McClelland, J. L., Johnson, M. H., & Siegler, R. S. (1997). Rethinking infant knowledge: Toward an adaptive process account of successes and failures in object permanence tasks. *Psychological Review, 104,* 686–713.

Munroe, R. L. (1955). *Schools of psychoanalytic thought.* New York: Dryden.

Munsey, C. (2007). Armor for the mind. *Monitor on Psychology, 38.*

Murnen, S. K., & Stockton, M. (1997). Gender and self-reported sexual arousal in response to sexual stimuli: A meta-analytic review. *Sex Roles, 37,* 135–153.

Murphy, G., & Murphy, L. B. (Eds.). (1968). *Asian psychology.* New York: Basic Books.

Murphy, J. M. (1976, March 12). Psychiatric labeling in cross-cultural perspective. *Science, 191,* 1019–1028.

Murphy, S. A., Johnson, C., & Beaton, R. D. (2004). Fire fighters' cognitive appraisals of job concerns, threats to well-being, and social support before and after the terrorist attacks on September 11, 2001. *Journal of Loss and Trauma, 9,* 269–283.

Murray, B. (1995, October). Americans dream about food, Brazilians dream about sex. *APA Monitor, 30.*

Murray, B. (1997, September). Why aren't antidrug programs working? *APA Monitor, 30.*

Murray, B. (2002, June). Writing to heal. *APA Monitor, 54–55.*

Murray, D. J., Kilgour, A. R., & Wasylkiw, L. (2000). Conflicts and missed signals in psychoanalysis, behaviorism, and Gestalt psychology. *American Psychologist, 55,* 422–426.

Murray, J. P., & Kippax, S. (1979). Children's social behavior in three towns with differing television experience. *Journal of Communication, 28,* 19–29.

Myers, D. G. (2000). The funds, friends, and faith of happy people. *American Psychologist, 55,* 56–67.

Myers, D. G. (2002). *Intuition: Its powers and perils.* New Haven, CT: Yale University Press.

Myers, D. G., & Diener, E. (1995). Who is happy? *Psychological Science, 6,* 10–19.

Myers, I. B. (1962). *The Myers–Briggs type indicator.* Palo Alto, CA: Consulting Psychologists Press.

Myers, I. B. (1976). *Introduction to type* (2nd ed.). Gainesville, FL: Center for Applications of Psychological Type.

Myers, I. B. (1987). *Introduction to type: A description of the theory and applications of the Myers–Briggs Type Indicator.* Palo Alto, CA: Consulting Psychologists Press.

Myers, I. B., & Myers, P. B. (1995). *Gifts differing: Understanding personality type.* Palo Alto, CA: Consulting Psychologists Press. [See also: Myers, 1962, 1976, 1987]

Myers, R. S., & Roth, D. L. (1997). Perceived benefits of and barriers to exercise and stage of exercise adoption in young adults. *Health Psychology, 16,* 277–283.

The mysteries of twins. (1998, January 11). *The Washington Post.* Retrieved on November 8, 2004, from www.washingtonpost.com/wpsrv/national/longterm/twins/twins2.htm.

Nahemow, L., & Lawton, M. P. (1975). Similarity and propinquity in friendship formation. *Journal of Personality and Social Psychology, 32,* 205–213.

Naigles, L. (1990). Children use syntax to learn verb meanings. *Child Language, 17,* 357–374.

Naigles, L. G., & Kako, E. T. (1993). First contact in verb acquisition: Defining a role for syntax. *Child Development, 64,* 1665–1687.

Nantais, K. M., & Schellenberg, F. G. (1991). The Mozart effect: An artifact of preference. *Psychological Science, 10,* 370–373.

Napier, A. Y. (2000). Making a marriage. In W. C. Nichols, M. A. Pace-Nichols, D. S. Becvar, & A. Y. Napier (Eds.), *Handbook of family development and intervention* (pp. 145–170). New York: Wiley.

Nash, M. R. (2001, July). The truth and the hype of hypnosis. *Scientific American, 285,* 46–49, 52–55.

Nathan, P. E. (1998). Practice guidelines: Not yet ideal. *American Psychologist, 53,* 290–299.

National Academies of Science. (2003). *The polygraph and lie detection.* Washington, DC: National Academies Press.

NICHD Early Child Care Research Network. (2000). The relation of child care to cognitive and language development. *Child Development, 71,* 960–980.

NICHD Early Child Care Research Network. (2003). Does quality of child care affect child outcomes at age 4 1/2? *Developmental Psychology, 39,* 451–469.

National Institute of Medicine (2006). Sleep disorders and sleep deprivation: an unmet public health problem. Retrieved March 19, 2008, from www.iom.edu/CMS/3740/23160/33668.aspx.

National Institute of Mental Health (NIMH). (2000). *Depression.* Retrieved on August 20, 2004, from www.nimh.nih.gov/publicat/depression.cfm#ptdep1.

National Institute of Mental Health (NIMH). (2003a). *Childhood-onset schizophrenia: An update from the NIMH.* Retrieved August 19, 2004, from www.nimh.nih.gov/publicat/schizkids.cfm.

National Institute of Mental Health (NIMH). (2003b, December 22). Mental illness genetics among science's top "breakthroughs" for 2003. Retrieved February 6, 2008, from www.nimh.nih.gov/science-news/2003/mental-illness-genetics-among-sciences-top-breakthroughs-for-2003.shtml [See also: Plomin, 2003]

National Institute of Mental Health, MTA Cooperative Group. (2004). National Institute of Mental Health multimodal treatment study of ADHD follow-up: Changes in effectiveness and growth after the end of treatment. *Pediatrics, 113,* 762–769.

National Institute of Mental Health (NIMH). (2005, April 21). Brain scans reveal how gene may boost schizophrenia risk. Retrieved February 6, 2008, from www.nimh.nih.gov/science-news/2005/brain-scans-reveal-how-gene-may-boost-schizophrenia-risk.shtml.

National Institute of Mental Health (NIMH). (2006, January). *Statistics. Questions and answers about the NIMH sequenced treatment alternatives to relieve depression (STAR*D) study—Background.* Retrieved February 5, 2008, from www.nimh.nih.gov/health/trials/practical/stard/questions-and-answers-about-the-nimh-sequenced-treatment-alternatives-to-relieve-depression-stard-study-background.shtml.

National Institute of Mental Health (NIMH). (2008a, April 3). Anxiety disorders. Retrieved April 20, 2008, from http://nimh.nih.gov/health/publications/anxiety-disorders/complete-publication.shtml#pub7.

National Institute of Mental Health (NIMH). (2008b, February). Schizophrenia. Retrieved February 6, 2008, from www.nimh.nih.gov/health/publications/schizophrenia/summary.shtml. [See also: Javitt & Coyle, 2004; Sawa & Snyder, 2002]

National Institute of Mental Health (NIMH). (2008d, February). Statistics. Retrieved February 5, 2008, from www.nimh.nih.gov/health/statistics/index.shtml.

National Institute of Neurological Disorders and Stroke (NINDS). (2007, February). Coma and persistent vegetative state information page. Retrieved December 4, 2007 from www.ninds.nih.gov/disorders/coma/coma.htm.

National Institute on Aging. (2004). Alzheimer's Disease Education & Referral Center. Retrieved on November 8, 2004, from www.alzheimers.org/generalinfo.htm.

National Press Club. (1999, Summer). Seligman on positive psychology: A session at the National Press Club. *The General Psychologist, 34*(2), 37–45.

National Public Radio. (2003a, August 19). Interview: Kenneth Kendler on study about severity of depression depends on the cause. *Morning Edition.*

National Public Radio. (2003b, March 21). Profile: Camp Pendleton Marine wives' coping strategies. *Morning Edition.*

National Public Radio. (2004, March 17). Analysis: New research may dispute theory that source of depression is in the brain. *Morning Edition.*

Neal, D. (Producer). (2000, September 20). [Television broadcast of Olympic Games]. New York: NBC. [As cited in Markus et al., 2006]

Needleman, H., Schell, A., Belinger, D., Leviton, A., & Allred, E. (1990). The long-term effects of exposure to low doses of lead in childhood: An 11-year follow-up report. *New England Journal of Medicine, 322,* 83–88.

Neimark, J. (2004, August). Are recovered memories real? *Discover,* 73–77.

Neimark, J. (2005, October). Can the flu bring on psychosis? *Discover, 26*(10), 70-71.

Neimark, J. (2007, April). Autism: It's not just in the head. *Discover, 28*(4), 33–36, 38, 75.

Neimeyer, R. A. (1995). An invitation to constructivist psychotherapies. In R. A. Neimeyer & M. J. Mahoney (Eds.), *Constructivism in psychotherapy.* Washington, DC: American Psychological Association.

Neimeyer, R. A. (1999). Narrative strategies in grief therapy. *Journal of Constructivist Psychology, 12,* 65–85.

Neimeyer, R. A., & Mahoney, M. J. (Eds.). (1995). *Constructivism in psychotherapy.* Washington, DC: American Psychological Association.

Neimeyer, R. A., Prigerson, H. G., & Davies, B. (2002). *Mourning and meaning.* American Behavioral Scientist, 46, 235–251.

Neisser, U. (1967). *Cognitive psychology.* New York: Appleton-Century-Crofts.

Neisser, U. (1991). A case of misplaced nostalgia. *American Psychologist, 46,* 34–36.

Neisser, U. (1997). Never a dull moment. *American Psychologist, 52,* 79–81.

Neisser, U., Boodoo, B., Bouchard, T. J. Jr., Boyukin, A. W., Brody, N., Ceci, S. J., Halpern, D. F., Loehlin, J. C., Perloff, R., Sternberg, R. J., & Urbina, S. (1996). Intelligence: Knowns and unknowns. *American Psychologist, 51,* 77–101.

Nelson, C. A. (1987). The recognition of facial expressions in the first two years of life: Mechanisms of development. *Child Development, 58,* 889–909.

Nelson, C. A. III, Zeanah, C. H., Fox, N. A., Marshall, P. J., Smyke, A. T., & Guthrie, D. (2007, December 21). Cognitive recovery in socially deprived young children: The Bucharest early intervention project. *Science, 318,* 1937–1940. [See also: Millum & Emanuel, 2007]

Nelson, T. D. (1993). The hierarchical organization of behavior: A useful feedback model of self-regulation. *Current Directions in Psychological Science, 2,* 121–126.

Nemecek, S. (1999, January). Unequal health. *Scientific American, 280*(1), 40–41.

Nemeroff, C. B. (1998, June). The neurobiology of depression. *Scientific American, 278,* 42–49.

Nesse, R. M., & Berridge, K. C. (1997, October 3). Psychoactive drug use in evolutionary perspective. *Science, 278,* 63–66.

Nestler, E. J. (2001, June 22). Total recall—the memory of addiction. *Science, 292,* 2266–2267.

Nestler, E. J., & Malenka, R. C. (2004, March). The addicted brain. *Scientific American, 290,* 78–85. [See also: Koob & Le Moal, 1997; Nestler, 2001]

Netting, J., & Wang, L. (2001, February 17). The newly sequenced genome bares all. *Science News, 159,* 100–101.

Neuman, S. B. (2003). From rhetoric to reality: The case for high quality compensatory prekindergarten programs. *Phi Delta Kappan, 85,* 286–291.

Neuroethics needed. (2006, June 22). *Nature, 441,* 907. [unsigned editorial]

Neville, H. J., Bavelier, D., Corina, D., Rauschecker, J., Karni, A., Lalwani, A., Braun, A., Clark, V., Jezzard, P., & Turner, R. (1998, February 3). Cerebral organization for language in deaf and hearing subjects: Biological constraints and effects of experience. *Proceedings of the National Academy of Sciences, 95,* 922–929.

Newcomb, T. M. (1943). *Personality and social change.* New York: Holt.

Newcomb, T. M., Koenig, D. E., Flacks, R., & Warwick, D. P. (1967). *Persistence and change: Bennington College and its students after twenty-five years.* New York: Wiley.

Newman, B. S., & Muzzonigro, P. G. (1993). The effects of traditional family values on the coming out process of gay male adolescents. *Adolescence, 28,* 213–226.

Newman, C. (2004, August). Why are we so fat? *National Geographic, 206,* 46–61.

Newman, R., Phelps, R., Sammons, M. T., Dunivin, D. L., & Cullen, E. A. (2000). Evaluation of the psychopharmacology demonstration project: A retrospective analysis. *Professional Psychology: Research and Practice, 31,* 598–603.

Niaura, R., Banks, S. M., Ward, K. D., Stoney, C. M., Sprio, A., & Aldwin, C. M., Landsberg, L., & Weiss, S. T. (2000). Hostility and the metabolic syndrome in older males: The normative aging study. *Psychosomatic Medicine, 62,* 7–16.

Nicholson, I. (2007, Fall). Maslow: Toward a psychology of being. *The General Psychologist, 42*(2), 25–26. [See also: Baumeister & Leary, 1995; Brehm, 1992; Hatfield & Rapson, 1993; Kelley et al., 1983; Weber & Harvey, 1994a,b]

Nickerson, R. S. (1998). Confirmation bias: A ubiquitous phenomenon in many guises. *Review of General Psychology, 2,* 175–220.

Nickerson, R. S., & Adams, M. J. (1979). Long-term memory for a common object. *Cognitive Psychology, 11,* 287–307.

Nicol, S. E., & Gottesman, I. I. (1983). Clues to the genetics and neurobiology of schizophrenia. *American Scientist, 71,* 398–404.

Nicolelis, M. A. L., & Chapin, J. K. (2002, October). Controlling robots with the mind. *Scientific American, 287*(4), 46–53.

Nicoll, R. A., & Alger, B. E. (2004, December). The brain's own marijuana. *Scientific American, 291*(6), 68–71.

Niedenthal, P. M. (2007, May 18). Embodying emotion. *Science, 316,* 1002–1005.

Niederhoffer, & Pennebaker, J. W. (2002). Sharing one's story: On the benefits of writing or talking about one's experience. In C. R. Snyder & S. J. Lopez (Eds.), *Handbook of positive psychology.* London, U.K.: Oxford University Press.

Nietzel, M. T., Speltz, M. L., McCauley, E. A., & Bernstein, D. A. (1998). *Abnormal psychology.* Boston, MA: Allyn & Bacon.

Nisbett, R. E. (1972). Hunger, obesity, and the ventromedial hypothalamus. *Psychological Review, 79,* 433–453.

Nippold, M. A., Duthie, J. K., & Larsen, J. (2005). Literacy as a leisure activity: Free time preferences of older children and young adolescents. *Language, Speech, and Hearing Services in Schools, 36,* 93–102.

Nisbett, R. E. (2000). Culture and systems of thought: Holistic versus analytic cognition in East and West. Master Lecture presented at the annual convention of the American Psychological Association, Washington, DC.

Nisbett, R. E. (2003). *The geography of thought: How Asians and Westerners think differently . . . and why.* New York: Free Press. [See also: Chua et al., 2005; Nisbett & Norenzayan, 2002; Winerman, 2006]

Nisbett, R. E. (2005). Heredity, environment, and race differences in IQ: A commentary on Rushton and Jensen. *Psychology, Public Policy, and Law, 11,* 302–310.

Nisbett, R. E., & Norenzayan, A. (2002). Culture and cognition. In D. L. Medin (Ed.), *Stevens' Handbook of Experimental Psychology* (3rd ed.). New York: John Wiley & Sons.

Nisbett, R. E., Peng, K., Choi, I., & Norenzayan, A. (2001). Culture and systems of thought: Holistic versus analytic cognition. *Psychological Review, 108,* 291–310.

Nobles, W. W. (1976). Black people in white insanity: An issue for black community mental health. *Journal of Afro-American Issues, 4,* 21–27.

Nolen-Hoeksema, S. (1987). Sex differences in unipolar depression: Evidence and theory. *Psychological Bulletin, 101,* 259–282.

Nolen-Hoeksema, S. (1990). *Sex differences in depression.* Stanford, CA: Stanford University Press.

Nolen-Hoeksema, S. (2001). Gender differences in depression. *Current Directions in Psychological Science, 10,* 173–176.

Nolen-Hoeksema, S., & Davis, C. G. (1999). "Thanks for sharing that": Ruminators and their social support networks. *Journal of Personality and Social Psychology, 77,* 801–814.

Norcross, J. C., Koocher, G. P., & Garofalo, A. (2006). Discredited psychological treatments and tests: A Delphi poll. *Professional Psychology: Research and Practice, 37,* 515–522.

Norenzayan, A., & Nisbett, R. E. (2000). Culture and causal cognition. *Current Directions in Psychological Science, 9,* 132–135. [See also: Fletcher & Ward, 1988; Miller, 1984; Triandis, 1996]

Norman, D. A., & Rumelhart, D. E. (1975). *Explorations in cognition.* San Francisco: Freeman.

Notarius, C., & Markman, H. (1993). *We can work it out: Making sense of marital conflict.* New York: G. P. Putnam's Sons.

Notarius, C. I. (1996). Marriage: Will I be happy or sad? In N. Vanzetti & S. Duck, *A lifetime of relationships.* Pacific Grove, CA: Brooks/Cole.

Nova Online. (1996). *Kidnapped by UFOs?* Retrieved August 2, 2007, from www.pbs.org/wgbh/nova/aliens/carlsagan.html.

Novak, M. A., & Suomi, S. J. (1988). Psychological well-being of primates in captivity. *American Psychologist, 43,* 765–773.

Novotney, A. (2008, March). Preventing harassment at schools. *Monitor on Psychology,* 18–20.

Nowack, K. M. (1983). The relationship between stress, job performance, and burnout in college resident assistants. *Journal of College Student Personnel, 24,* 545–550.

Nungesser, L. G. (1990). *Axioms for survivors: How to live until you say goodbye.* Santa Monica, CA: IBS Press.

Nurnberger, J. I. Jr., & Bierut, L. J. (2007, April). Seeking the connections: Alcoholism and our genes. *Scientific American, 296*(4), 46–53.

Oakland, T., & Glutting, J. J. (1990). Examiner observations of children's WISC-R test-related behaviors: Possible socioeconomic status, race, and gender effects. *Psychological Assessment, 2,* 86–90.

Oakley, D. A. (1999). Hypnosis and conversion hysteria: A unifying model. *Cognitive Neuropsychiatry, 4,* 243–265.

Oakley, D. A. (2006). Hypnosis as a tool in research: Experimental psychopathology. *Contemporary Hypnosis 23,* 3–14. [See also: Bowers, 1983; Hilgard, 1968, 1973; Miller & Bowers, 1993; Nash, 2001]

Oatley, K., & Duncan, E. (1994). The experience of emotions in everyday life. *Cognition and Emotion, 8,* 369–381.

O'Connor, E. M. (2001, December). Medicating ADHD: Too much? Too soon? *Monitor on Psychology, 32*(11), 50–51.

Oden, G. C. (1968). The fulfillment of promise: 40-year follow-up of the Terman gifted group. *Genetic Psychology Monographs, 77,* 3–93.

Oden, G. C. (1987). Concept, knowledge, and thought. *Annual Review of Psychology, 38,* 203–227.

O'Doherty, J., Dayan, P., Schultz, J., Deichmann, R., Friston, K., & Dolan, R. J. (2004, April 16). Dissociable roles of ventral and dorsal striatum in instrumental conditioning. *Science, 304,* 452–454.

Offer, D., Ostrov, E., & Howard, K. I. (1981). *The adolescent: A psychological self-portrait.* New York: Basic Books.

Offer, D., Ostrov, E., Howard, K. I., & Atkinson, R. (1988). *The teenage world: Adolescents' self-image in ten countries.* New York: Plenum Medical.

Ofshe, R., & Watters, E. (1994). *Making monsters: False memories, psychotherapy, and sexual hysteria.* New York: Charles Scribner's Sons.

Ohlsson, S. (1996). Learning from performance errors. *Psychological Review, 103,* 241–262.

Öhman, A., & Mineka, S. (2001). Fears, phobias, and preparedness: Toward an evolved module of fear and fear learning. *Psychological Review, 108,* 483–522.

Olds, M. E., & Fobes, J. L. (1981). The central basis of motivation: Intracranial self-stimulation studies. *Annual Review of Psychology, 32,* 523–574.

O'Leary, K. D. (Ed.). (1987). *Assessment of marital discord: An integration for research and clinical practice.* Hillsdale, NJ: Erlbaum.

Olton, D. S. (1979). Mazes, maxes, and memory. *American Psychologist, 34,* 583–596.

Olton, D. S. (1992). Tolman's cognitive analyses: Predecessors of current approaches in psychology. *Journal of Experimental Psychology: General, 121,* 427–428. [See also: Menzel, 1978; Moar, 1980; Olton, 1979]

Olweus. D. (1993). *Bullying at school: What we know and what we can do.* Oxford, UK: Blackwell.

Oren, D. A., & Terman, M. (1998, January 16). Tweaking the human circadian clock with light. *Science, 279,* 333–334.

Orne, M. T. (1980). Hypnotic control of pain: Toward a clarification of the different psychological processes involved. In J. J. Bonica (Ed.), *Pain* (pp. 155–172). New York: Raven Press.

Ornstein, R., & Sobel, D. (1989). *Healthy pleasures.* Reading, MA: Addison-Wesley.

Orser, B. A. (2007, June). Lifting the fog around anesthesia. *Scientific American, 296*(6), 54-61.

Ortmann, A., & Hertwig, R. (1997). Is deception acceptable? *American Psychologist, 52,* 746–747. [See also: Bower, 1998d]

Osterhout, L., & Holcomb, P. J. (1992). Event-related brain potentials elicited by syntactic anomaly. *Journal of Memory and Language, 31,* 785–806.

Ostow, M. (1973, April 27). (Untitled letter to the editor). *Science, 180,* 360–361. [See also other critiques of the Rosenhan study among other letters in the same issue.]

Overmier, J. & Seligman, M. (1967). Effects of inescapable shock upon subsequent escape and avoidance learning. *Journal of Comparative and Physiological Psychology, 63,* 23–33.

Overmier, J. B. (2002). On learned helplessness. *Integrative Behavioral and Physiological Science, 37,* 4–8.

Paffenbarger, R. S., Hyde, R. T., Wing, A. L., & Hsieh, C. C. (1986, March). Physical activity, all-cause mortality, and longevity of college alumni. *New England Journal of Medicine, 314,* 605–613.

Paikoff, R. L., & Brooks-Gunn, J. (1991). Do parent-child relationships change during puberty? *Psychological Bulletin, 110,* 47–66.

Paivio, A. (1983). The empirical case for dual coding. In J. C. Yuille (Ed.), *Imagery, memory and cognition* (pp. 307–332). Hillsdale, NJ: Erlbaum.

Paivio, A. (1986). *Mental representations: A dual coding approach.* New York: Oxford University Press.

Paller, K. A. (2004). Electrical signals of memory and of the awareness of remembering. *Current Directions in Psychological Science, 13,* 49–55.

Palmer, S. E. (2002). Perceptual grouping: It's later than you think. *Current Directions in Psychological Science, 11,* 101–106.

Pandey, J., Sinha, Y., Prakash, A., & Tripathi, R. C. (1982). Right–left political ideologies and attribution of the causes of poverty. *European Journal of Social Psychology, 12,* 327–331.

Paré, D., Quirk, G. J., & LeDoux, J. E. (2004). New vistas on amygdala networks in conditioned fear. *Journal of Neurophysiology, 92,* 1–9.

Panksepp, J. (2000). The riddle of laughter: Neural and psychoevolutionary underpinnings of joy. *Current Directions in Psychological Science, 9,* 183–186.

Park, C. L., Cohen, L. H., & Murch, R. L. (1996). Assessment and prediction of stress-related growth. *Journal of Personality, 64,* 71–105.

Parkes, C. M. (2001). *Bereavement: Studies of grief in adult life.* New York: Routledge.

Parr, W. V., and Siegert, R. (1993). Adults' conceptions of everyday memory failures in others: Factors that mediate the effects of target age. *Psychology and Aging, 8,* 599–605.

Patenaude, A. F., Guttmacher, A. E., & Collins, F. S. (2002). Genetic testing and psychology: New roles, new responsibilities. *American Psychologist, 57,* 271–282. [See also Fackelmann, 1998]

Patrick, C. J., & Iacono, W. G. (1991). Validity of the control question polygraph test: The problem of sampling bias. *Journal of Applied Psychology, 76,* 229–238.

Patterson, D. R. (2004, December). Treating pain with hypnosis. *Current Directions in Psychological Science, 13,* 252–255.

Patterson, F., & Linden, E. (1981). *The education of Koko.* New York: Holt, Rinehart and Winston.

Patterson, F. G. (1978). The gestures of a gorilla: Language acquisition in another pongid. *Brain and Language, 5,* 72–97.

Patterson, J. M. (1985). Critical factors affecting family compliance with home treatment for children with cystic fibrosis. *Family Relations, 34,* 74–89.

Patzer, G. L. (1985). *The physical attractiveness phenomena.* New York: Plenum Press.

Paulesu, E. D., Démonet, J.-F., Fazio, F., McCrory, E., Chanoine, V., Brunswick, N. Cappa, S. F., Cossu, G., Habib, M., Frith, C. D., & Frith, U. (2001, March 16). Dyslexia: Cultural diversity and biological utility. *Science, 291,* 2165–2167.

Paulus, J. (2007, April/May). Lithium's healing power. *Scientific American Mind, 18*(2), 70–75.

Paunonen, S. P., Jackson, D. N., Trzebinski, J., & Fosterling, F. (1992). Personality structure across cultures: A multimethod evaluation. *Journal of Personality and Social Psychology, 62,* 447–456.

Pavlov, I. P. (1928). *Lectures on conditioned reflexes: Twenty-five years of objective study of higher nervous activity (behavior of animals)* (Vol. 1, W. H. Gantt, Trans.). New York: International Publishers.

Pavot, W., Diener, E., & Fujita, F. (1990). Extraversion and happiness. *Personality and Individual Differences, 1,* 1299–1306.

Pawlik, K., & d'Ydewalle, G. (1996). Psychology and the global commons: Perspectives of international psychology. *American Psychologist, 51,* 488–495.

Pearlman, L. A., & Mac Ian, P. S. (1995). Vicarious traumatization: An empirical study of the effects of trauma work on trauma therapists. *Professional Psychology: Research and Practice, 26,* 558–563.

Pearman, R. R. (1991, November 13). Disputing a report on "Myers–Briggs" test. *Chronicle of Higher Education,* B7.

Pearson, H. (2006, June 22). Lure of lie detectors spooks ethicists. *Nature, 441,* 918–919. [See also: McKhann, 2006; Neuroethics Needed, 2006]

Pedersen, P. (1979). Non-Western psychology: The search for alternatives. In A. J. Marsella, R. G. Tharp, & T. J. Ciborowski (Eds.), *Perspectives on cross-cultural psychology* (pp. 77–98). New York: Academic Press.

Penfield, W. (1959). The interpretive cortex. *Science, 129,* 1719–1725.

Penfield, W. (1975). *The mystery of the mind.* Princeton, NJ: Princeton University Press.

Penfield, W., & Baldwin, M. (1952). Temporal lobe seizures and the technique of subtotal lobectomy. *Annals of Surgery, 136,* 625–634.

Penfield, W., & Jasper, H. (1954). *Epilepsy and the functional anatomy of the human brain.* Boston: Little, Brown & Co.

Penfield, W., & Rasmussen, T. (1950). *The cerebral cortex of man: A clinical study of the localization of function.* New York: Macmillan.

Penfield, W., & Roberts, L. (1959). *Speech and brain mechanisms.* Princeton, NJ: Princeton University Press.

Peng, K., & Nisbett, R. E. (1999). Culture, dialectics, and reasoning about contradiction. *American Psychologist, 54,* 741–754.

Pennebaker, J. W. (1990). *Opening up: The healing power of confiding in others.* New York: William Morrow.

Pennebaker, J. W. (1997). Writing about emotional experiences as a therapeutic process. *Psychological Science, 8,* 162–166.

Pennebaker, J. W., Barger, S. D., & Tiebout, J. (1989). Disclosure of traumas and health among Holocaust survivors. *Psychosomatic Medicine, 51,* 577–589.

Pennebaker, J. W., & Harber, K. D. (1991, April). Coping after the Loma Prieta earthquake: A preliminary report. Paper presented at the Western Psychological Association Convention, San Francisco, CA.

Pennebaker, J. W., Kiecolt-Glaser, J., & Glaser, R. (1988). Disclosure of traumas and immune function: Health implications for psychotherapy. *Journal of Consulting and Clinical Psychology, 56,* 239–245.

Pennisi, E. (2001, February 16). The human genome. *Science, 291,* 1177–1180.

Pennisi, E. (2002, October 25). Jumbled DNA separates chimps and humans. *Science, 298,* 719–720.

Pennisi, E. (2003, August 22). Gene counters struggle to get the right answer. *Science, 301,* 1040–1041.

Pennisi, E. (2006, September 29). Mining the molecules that made our mind. *Science, 313,* 1908–1913.

Pennisi, E. (2007, April 3). Genomicists tackle the primate tree. *Science, 316,* 218–221.

Peplau, L. A. (2003). Human sexuality: How do men and women differ? *Current Directions in Psychological Science, 12,* 37–40.

Peplau, L. A., Garnets, L. D., Spalding, L. R., Conley, T. D., & Veniegas, R. C. (1998). Critique of Bem's "Exotic becomes erotic" theory of sexual orientation. *Psychological Review, 105,* 387–394.

Perkins, D. F., & Lerner, R. M. (1995). Single and multiple indicators of physical attractiveness and psychosocial behaviors among young adolescents. *Journal of Early Adolescence, 15,* 268–297.

Perrin, M. A., DiGrande, L., Wheeler, K., Thorpe, L., Farfel, M., & Brackbill, R. (2007). Differences in PTSD prevalence and associated risk factors among World Trade Center disaster rescue and recovery workers. *American Journal of Psychiatry, 164,* 1385–1394.

Perry, W. G. Jr. (1970). *Forms of intellectual and ethical development in the college years: A scheme.* New York: Holt, Rinehart and Winston.

Perry, W. G. Jr. (1994). Forms of intellectual and ethical development in the college years: A scheme. In B. Puka (Ed.), *Defining perspectives in moral development: Vol. 1. Moral development: A compendium* (pp. 231–248). New York: Garland Publishing.

Pert, C. (1997). *Molecules of emotion.* New York: Scribner.

Pervin, L. A. (1985). Personality: Current controversies, issues, and directions. *Annual Review of Psychology, 36,* 83–114.

Peterson, C. (2000). The future of optimism. *American Psychologist, 55,* 44–55.

Peterson, C., Seligman, M. E. P., & Valliant, G. E. (1988). Pessimistic explanatory style is a risk factor for physical illness: A thirty-five year longitudinal study. *Journal of Personality and Social Psychology, 55,* 23–27.

Petitto, L. A., & Marent ette, P. F. (1991, March 22). Babbling in the manual mode: evidence for the ontogeny of language. *Science, 251,* 1493–1496.

Petrill, S. A., Plomin, R., Berg, S., Johansson, B., Pedersen, N. L., Ahern, F., & McClearn, G. E. (1998). Specific cognitive abilities in twins age 80 and older. *Psychological Science, 9,* 183–195.

Petrosino A., Turpin-Petrosino, C., and Buehler, J. (2003, November). "Scared Straight" and other juvenile awareness programs for preventing juvenile delinquency. (Updated C2 Review). *The Campbell Collaboration Reviews of Intervention and Policy Evaluations (C2-RIPE).* Philadelphia: Campbell Collaboration. Retrieved August 2, 2007, from www.campbellcollaboration.org/doc-pdf/ssrupdt.pdf.

Petrovic, P., Kalso, E., Petersson, K. M., & Ingvan, M. (2002, March 1). Placebo and opioid analgesia—Imaging a shared neuronal network. *Science, 295,* 1737–1740.

Pettigrew, T. F. (1998). Intergroup contact theory. *Annual Review of Psychology, 49,* 65–85.

Phelps, J. A., Davis, J. O., & Schartz, K. M. (1997). Nature, nurture, and twin research strategies. *Current Directions in Psychological Science, 6,* 117–121.

Physician's desk reference (58th ed.). (2004). Montvale, NJ: Medical Economics Company.

Pifer, A., & Bronte L. (Eds.). (1986). *Our aging society: Paradox and promise.* New York: Norton.

Pilcher, J. J., & Walters, A. S. (1997). How sleep deprivation affects psychological variables related to college students' cognitive performance. *Journal of American College Health, 46,* 121–126.

Pilisuk, M., & Parks, S. H. (1986). *The healing web: Social networks and human survival.* Hanover, NH: University Press of New England.

Pillard, R., & Bailey, M. (1991). A genetic study of male sexual orientation. *Archives of General Psychiatry, 48,* 1089–1096.

Pillemer, D. B. (1984). Flashbulb memories of the assassination attempt on President Reagan. *Cognition, 16,* 63–80.

Pilling, S., Bebbington, P., Kuipers, E., Garety, P., Geddes, J., Orbach, G., & Morgan, C. (2002). Psychological treatments in schizophrenia: I. Meta-analysis of family intervention and cognitive behaviour therapy. *Psychological Medicine, 32,* 763–782.

Pinel, J. P. J. (2005). *Biopsychology* (6th ed.). Boston: Allyn & Bacon.

Pinel, J. P. J., Assanand, S., & Lehman, D. R. (2000). Hunger, eating, and ill health. *American Psychologist, 55,* 1105–1116.

Pinker, S. (1994). *The language instinct: How the mind creates language.* New York: Morrow.

Pinker, S. (2002). *The blank slate: The modern denial of human nature.* New York: Viking.

Pinker, S. (2006, Spring). The blank slate. *The General Psychologist, 41*(1), 1–8. [Also available online at www.apa.org/divisions/div1/news/Spring2006/GenPsychSpring06.pdf]

Pinto, R. M. (2003). The impact of secondary traumatic stress on novice and expert counselors with and without a history of trauma. *Dissertation Abstracts International, Section A: Humanities and Social Sciences, 63,* 3117.

Piper, A. Jr. (1998, May/June). Multiple personality disorder: Witchcraft survives in the twentieth century. *Skeptical Inquirer, 22*(3), 44–50.

Piper, A., & Merskey, H. (2004a). The persistence of folly: A critical examination of dissociative identity disorder. Part I. The excesses of an improbable concept. *Canadian Journal of Psychiatry, 49,* 592–600.

Piper, A., & Merskey, H. (2004b). The persistence of folly: A critical examination of dissociative identity disorder. Part II. The defence and decline of multiple personality or dissociative identity disorder. *Canadian Journal of Psychiatry, 49,* 678–683.

Pitman, G. E. (2003). Evolution, but no revolution: The "tend-and-befriend" theory of stress and coping. *Psychology of Women Quarterly, 27,* 194–195.

Pittenger, D. J. (1993). The utility of the Myers–Briggs Type Indicator. *Review of Educational Research, 63,* 467–488.

Plomin, R. (1989). Environment and genes: Determinants of behavior. *American Psychologist, 44,* 105–111.

Plomin, R. (1997, August). Current directions in behavioral genetics: Moving into the mainstream. *Current Directions in Psychological Science, 6,* 85.

Plomin, R. (2000, September). Psychology in a post-genomics world: It will be more important than ever. *American Psychological Society Observer, 3,* 27. [See also Boomsma, Anokhin, & de Geus, 1997]

Plomin, R. (2003). 50 years of DNA: What it has meant to psychological science. *Observer, 16*(4), 7–8.

Plomin, R., & DeFries, J. C. (1998). The genetics of cognitive abilities and disabilities. *Scientific American, 278*(5), 62–69.

Plomin, R., & McClearn, G. E. (Eds.). (1993). *Nature, nurture, and psychology.* Washington, DC: American Psychological Association.

Plomin, R., Owen, M. J., & McGuffin, P. (1994). The genetic basis of complex human behaviors. *Science, 264,* 1733–1739.

Plous, S. (1996). Attitudes toward the use of animals in psychological research and education: Results from a national survey of psychologists. *American Psychologist, 51,* 1167–1180. [See also: Blum, 1994]

Plutchik, R. (1980). *Emotion: A psychoevolutionary synthesis.* New York: Harper & Row.

Plutchik, R. (1984). Emotions: A general psychoevo-

lutionary theory. In K. Scherer & P. Ekman (Eds.), *Approaches to emotion.* Hillsdale, NJ: Erlbaum.

Pole, N., Best, S. R., Metzler, T., & Marmar, C. R. (2005). Why are Hispanics at greater risk for PTSD? *Cultural Diversity and Ethnic Minority Psychology, 11,* 144–161.

Polefrone, J. M., & Manuck, S. B. (1987). Gender differences in cardiovascular and neuroendocrine response to stressors. In R. C. Barnett, L. Biener, & G. K. Baruch (Eds.), *Gender and stress.* New York: Free Press.

Poling, A., Gadow, K. D., & Cleary, J. (1991). *Drug therapy for behavior disorders: An introduction.* New York: Pergamon Press.

Polivy, J., & Herman, C. P. (1993). Etiology of binge eating: Psychological mechanisms. In C. G. Fairburn & G. T. Wilson (Eds.), *Binge eating: Nature, assessment, and treatment* (pp. 173–205). New York: Guilford Press. [See also: Rodin et al., 1985; Squire, 1983; Striegel-Moore et al., 1993]

Polyn, S. M., Natu, V. S., Cohen, J. D., & Norman, K. A. (2005, December 23). Category-specific cortical activity precedes retrieval during memory search. *Science, 310,* 1963–1966.

Pomerantz, J. R. (1994). On criteria for ethics in science: Commentary on Rosenthal. *Psychological Science, 5,* 135–136.

Pool, R. (1997, October). Portrait of a gene guy. *Discover,* 51–55.

Pool, R. (1998). Saviours: Someday the transplant you need may be growing on the hoof—or in a lab. *Discover, 19*(5), 52–57.

Poole, D. A., Lindsay, D. S., Memon, A., & Bull, R. (1995). Psychotherapy and the recovery of memories of childhood sexual abuse: U.S. and British practitioners' opinions, practices, and experiences. *Journal of Consulting and Clinical Psychology, 63,* 426–437.

Poon, L. W. (1985). Differences in human memory with aging: Nature, causes, and clinical implications. In J. E. Birren & W. K. Schaie (Eds.), *Handbook of the psychology of aging* (pp. 427–462). New York: Van Nostrand Reinhold.

Popejoy, D. I. (1967). The effects of a physical fitness program on selected psychological and physiological measures of anxiety. Unpublished doctoral dissertation. University of Illinois.

Popkin, B. M. (2007, September). The world is fat. *Scientific American, 297*(3), 88–95.

Posner, M. I., & McCandliss, B. D. (1993). Converging methods for investigating lexical access. *Science, 4,* 305–309.

Posner, M. I., & Raichle, M. E. (1994). *Images of mind.* New York: W. H. Freeman.

Practice Directorate Staff. (2005, February). Prescription for success. *Monitor on Psychology, 36*(2), 25–29.

Premack, D. (1965). Reinforcement theory. In D. Levine (Ed.), *Nebraska Symposium on Motivation* (pp. 128–180). Lincoln: University of Nebraska Press.

Premack, D. (1971). Language in chimpanzees. *Science, 172,* 808–822.

Premack, D. (1976). *Intelligence in ape and man.* Hillsdale, NJ: Erlbaum.

Prentice, D. A., & Miller, D. T. (1993). Pluralistic ignorance and alcohol use on campus: Some consequences on misperceiving the social norm. *Journal of Personality and Social Psychology, 64,* 243–256.

Price, D. D., Rafii, A., Watkins, L. R., & Buckingham, B. (1984). A psychophysical analysis of acupuncture analgesia. *Pain, 19,* 27–42.

Priest, R. F., & Sawyer, J. (1967). Proximity and peership: Bases of balance in interpersonal attraction. *American Journal of Sociology, 72,* 633–649.

Primavera, L. H., & Herron, W. G. (1996). The effect of viewing television violence on aggression. *International Journal of Instructional Media, 23,* 91–104.

Prinzmetal, W. (1995). Visual feature integration in a world of objects. *Current Directions in Psychological Science, 5,* 90–94.

Provine, R. R. (2004). Laughing, tickling, and the evolution of speech and self. *Current Directions in Psychological Science, 13,* 215–218.

Putnam, F. W., Guroff, J. J., Silberman, E. K., Barban, L., & Post, R. M. (1986). The clinical phenomenology of multiple personality disorder: Review of 100 recent cases. *Journal of Clinical Psychiatry, 47,* 285–293.

Qualls, S. H., & Abeles, N. (2000). *Psychology and the aging revolution: How we adapt to longer life.* Washington, DC: American Psychological Association.

Quiñones-Vidal, E., López-García, J. J., Peñaranda-Ortega, M., & Tortosa-Gil, F. (2004). The nature of social and personality psychology as reflected in JPSP, 1965–2000. *Journal of Personality and Social Psychology, 86,* 435–452.

Quiroga, R. Q., Reddy, L., Kreiman, G., Koch, C., & Fried, I. (2005, June 23). Invariant visual representation by single neurons in the human brain. *Nature, 435,* 1102–1107. [See also Horgan, 2005; Martindale, 2005]

Rabasca, L. (1999, September). High marks for psychologists who prescribe. *APA Monitor, 30*(8), 21.

Rabkin, J. G., & Struening, E. L. (1976). Life events, stress, and illness. *Science, 194,* 1013–1020.

Rachman, S. (2000). Joseph Wolpe (1915–1997). *American Psychologist, 55,* 431–432.

Rahe, R. H., & Arthur, R. J. (1978, March). Life change and illness studies: Past history and future directions. *Journal of Human Stress,* 3–15.

Raichle, M. E. (1994). Visualizing the mind. *Scientific American, 270*(4), 58–64.

Rakic, P. (1985). Limits of neurogenesis in primates. *Science, 227,* 1054–1057.

Ramachandran, V. S. (1992). Filling in gaps in perception: Part 1. *Current Directions in Psychological Science, 1,* 199–205.

Ramachandran, V. S., & Blakeslee, S. (1998). *Phantoms in the brain.* New York: William Morrow.

Ramachandran, V. S., & Hubbard, E. M. (2001). Synaesthesia—A window into perception, thought and language. *Journal of Consciousness Studies, 8,* 3–34.

Ramachandran, V. S., & Hubbard, E. M. (2003, May). Hearing colors, tasting shapes. *Scientific American (Special Edition), 16*(3), 76–83. [See also Ramachandran & Hubbard, 2001]

Ramachandran, V. S., & Oberman, L. M. (2006, November). Broken mirrors. *Scientific American, 295* (5), 62–69.

Rambo-Chroniak, K. M. (1999). Coping and adjustment in the freshman year transition. Unpublished dissertation, Northwestern University, Chicago, IL. (*Dissertation Abstracts International, 59* [June], 12-A, 4378.)

Ramey, C. T., & Ramey, S. L. (1998a). Early intervention and early experience. *American Psychologist, 53,* 109–120.

Ramey, C. T,. & Ramey, S. L. (1998b). In defense of special education. *American Psychologist, 53,* 1159–1160.

Rand, C. S., & Kuldau, J. M. (1992). Epidemiology of bulimia and symptoms in a general population: Sex, age, race, and socioeconomic status. *International Journal of Eating Disorders, 11,* 37–44.

Randerson, J. (2002, January 26). Sleep scientists discount sheep. *New Scientist,* Issue #2327. Retrieved December 8, 2007, from www.newscientist.com/article/dn1831-sleep-scientists-discount-sheep.html

Raphael, B. (1984). *The anatomy of bereavement: A handbook for the caring professions.* London, U.K.: Hutchinson.

Rapoport, J. L. (1989, March). The biology of obsessions and compulsions. *Scientific American, 263,* 83–89.

Rathus, S. A., Nevid, J. S., & Fichner-Rathus, L. (2005). *Human sexuality in a world of diversity* (6th ed.). Boston: Allyn & Bacon.

Rauscher, F. H., Shaw, G. L., & Ky, K. N. (1993, October 14). Music and spatial task performance. *Nature, 365,* 611.

Ravussin, E. (2005, January 28). A NEAT way to control weight? *Science, 307,* 530–531.

Ravussin, E., & Danforth, E. Jr. (1999, January 8). Beyond sloth—physical activity and weight gain. *Science, 283,* 184–185.

Rawlins, W. K. (1992). *Friendship matters: Communication, dialectics, and the life course.* New York: DeGruyter.

Raymond, C. (1989, September 20). Scientists examining behavior of a man who lost his memory gain new insights into the workings of the human mind. *The Chronicle of Higher Education,* A4, A6.

Raymond, J. L., Lisberger, S. G., & Mauk, M. D. (1996, May 24). The cerebellum: A neuronal learning machine? *Science, 272,* 1126–1131.

Raynor, J. O. (1970). Relationships between achievement-related motives, future orientation, and academic performance. *Journal of Personality and Social Psychology, 15,* 28–33.

Raz, S., & Raz, N. (1990). Structural brain abnormalities in the major psychoses: A quantitative review of the evidence from computerized imaging. *Psychological Bulletin, 16,* 491–402.

Raz, A., Shapiro, T., Fan, J., & Posner, M. I. (2002). Hypnotic suggestion and the modulation of Stroop interference. *Archives of General Psychiatry, 59,* 1151–1161.

Ready, D. D., LoGerfo, L. F., Burkan, D. T., & Lee, V. E. (2005). Explaining girls' advantage in kindergarten literacy learning: Do classroom behaviors make a difference? *The Elementary School Journal, 106,* 21–38.

Reber, A. S. (1993). *Implicit learning and tacit knowledge: An essay on the cognitive unconscious. (Oxford Psychology Series No. 19).* Oxford, U.K.: Oxford University Press.

Rechtschaffen, A. (1998). Current perspectives on the function of sleep. *Perspectives in Biology and Medicine, 41,* 359–390. [See also: Pinel, 2005]

Rector, N. A., & Beck, A. T. (2001). Cognitive behavioral therapy for schizophrenia: An empirical review. *Journal of Nervous & Mental Disease, 189,* 278–287.

Redding, R. E. (2001). Sociopolitical diversity in psychology: The case for pluralism. *American Psychologist, 56,* 205–215.

Redding, R. E. (2002). Grappling with diverse conceptions of diversity. *American Psychologist, 57,* 300–301.

Regier, D. A., Boyd, J. H, Burke, J. D., Rae, D. S., Myers, J. K., Kramer, M., Robins, L. N., George, L. K., Karno, M., & Locke, B. Z. (1988). One-month prevalence of mental disorders in the United States. *Archives of General Psychiatry, 45,* 977–986.

Regier, D. A., Narrow, W. E., Rae, D. S., Manderscheid, R. W., Locke, B. Z., & Goodwin, F. K. (1993). The de facto U.S. mental and addictive disorders service system: Epidemiologic Catchment Area prospective 1-year-prevalence rates of disorders and services. *Archives of General Psychiatry, 50,* 85–94.

Reinisch, J. M. (1990). *The Kinsey Institute new report on sex: What you must know to be sexually literate.* New York: St. Martin's Press.

Reis, B., & Saewyc, E. (1999). *Eighty-three thousand youth: Selected findings of eight population-based studies as they pertain to anti-gay harassment and the safety and well-being of sexual minority students.* Seattle, WA: Safe Schools Coalition of Washington. Document also retrieved online November 8, 2004, from www.safeschools-wa.org/83000youth.pdf

Rescorla, R. A. (1972). Information variables in Pavlovian conditioning. In G. Bower (Ed.), *The psychology of learning and motivation (Vol. 6).* New York: Academic Press.

Rescorla, R. A. (1988). Pavlovian conditioning: It's not what you think it is. *American Psychologist, 43,* 151–160.

Rescorla, R. A., & Wagner, A. R. (1972). A theory of Pavlovian conditioning: Variations in the effectiveness of reinforcement and nonreinforcement. In A. H. Black & W. F. Prokasy (Eds.), *Classical conditioning, II: Current research and theory* (pp. 64–94). New York: Appleton-Century-Crofts.

Resnick, S. M. (1992). Positron emission tomography in psychiatric illness. *Current Directions in Psychological Science, 1,* 92–98.

Rest, J. R., & Thoma, S. J. (1976). Relation of moral judgment development to formal education. *Developmental Psychology, 21,* 709–714.

Reuter-Lorenz, P. A., & Miller, A. C. (1998). The cognitive neuroscience of human laterality: Lessons from the bisected brain. *Current Directions in Psychological Science, 7,* 15–20.

Reynolds, C. R. (2000). Why is psychometric research on bias in mental testing so often ignored? *Psychology, Public Policy, and Law, 6,* 144–150.

Rhodes, G., Sumich, A., & Byatt, G. (1999). Are average facial configurations attractive only because of their symmetry? *Psychological Science, 10,* 52–58. [See also: Langlois & Roggman, 1990; Langlois et al., 1994]

Riccio, D. C., Millin, P. M., & Gisquet-Verrier, P. (2003). Retrograde amnesia: Forgetting back. *Current Directions in Psychological Science, 12,* 41–44.

Rich, L. E. (2004, January). Bringing more effective tools to the weight-loss table. *Monitor on Psychology, 35*(1), 52-55.

Rickgarn, R. L. V. (1996). The need for postvention on college campuses: A rationale and case study findings. In C. A. Corr & D.E. Balk (Eds.), *Handbook of adolescent death and bereavement* (pp. 273–292). New York: Springer Publishing.

Richards, J. M., & Gross, J. J. (2000). Emotion regulation and memory: The cognitive costs of keeping one's cool. *Journal of Personality & Social Psychology, 79,* 410–424.

Riessman, C. K., Whalen, M. H., Frost, R. O., & Morgenthau, J. E. (1991). Romance and help-seeking among women: "It hurts so much to care." *Women and Health, 17,* 21–47.

Riolli, L. (2002). Resilience in the face of catastrophe: Optimism, personality and coping in the Kosovo crisis. *Journal of Applied Social Psychology, 32,* 1604–1627.

Ripple, C. H., Gilliam, W. S., Chanana, N., & Zigler, E. (1999). Will fifty cooks spoil the broth? The debate over entrusting Head Start to the states. *American Psychologist, 54,* 327–343.

Ripple, C. H., & Zigler, E. (2003). Research, policy, and the Federal role in prevention initiatives for children. *American Psychologist, 58,* 482–490. [See also: Ripple et al., 1999; Schweinhart & Weikart, 1986; Smith, 1991]

Rizzolatti, G., Fogassi, L., & Gallese, V. (2006, November). Mirrors in the mind. *Scientific American, 295*(5), 54–61.

Robak, R. W., & Weitzman, S. P. (1994). Grieving the loss of romantic relationships in young adults: An empirical study of disenfranchised grief. *Omega: The Journal of Death and Dying, 30,* 269–281.

Robbins, D. (1971). Partial reinforcement: A selective review of the alleyway literature since 1960. *Psychological Bulletin, 76,* 415–431.

Robbins, J. (2000, April). Wired for sadness. *Discover, 21*(4), 77–81.

Roberts, D. F., Foehr, U., & Rideout, V. (2005). *Generation M: Media in the lives of 8–18-year-olds.* Menlo Park, CA: Kaiser Family Foundation.

Roberts, S. B., Flannelly, K. J., Weaver, A. J., & Rigley, C. R. (2003). Compassion fatigue among chaplains, clergy, and other respondents after September 11th. *Journal of Nervous & Mental Disease, 191,* 756–758.

Robins, C. J. (1988). Attributions and depression: Why is the literature so often inconsistent? *Journal of Personality and Social Psychology, 54,* 880–889.

Robins, L. N., Locke, B. Z., & Regier, D. A. (1991). An overview of psychiatric disorders in America. In L. N. Robins & D. A. Regier (Eds.), *Psychiatric disorders in America: The epidemiologic catchment area study.* New York: Free Press.

Robins, R. W. (2005, October 7). The nature of personality: Genes, culture, and national character. *Science, 310,* 62–63.

Robinson, N. M., Zigler, E., & Gallagher, J. J. (2000). Two tails of the normal curve: Similarities and differences in the study of mental retardation and giftedness. *American Psychologist, 55,* 1413–1424. [See also Baumeister, 1987; Detterman, 1999; Greenspan, 1999]

Roche, S. M., & McConkey, K. M. (1990) Absorption: Nature, assessment, and correlates. *Journal of Personality & Social Psychology, 59,* 91–101.

Rock, I., & Palmer, S. (1990, December). The legacy of Gestalt psychology. *Scientific American, 263,* 84–90.

Rodin, J. (1986). Aging and health: Effects of the sense of control. *Science, 233,* 1271–1276.

Rodin, J., & Salovey, P. (1989). Health psychology. *Annual Review of Psychology, 40,* 533–579.

Rodin, J., Striegel-Moore, R. H., & Silberstein, L. R. (1985, July). A prospective study of bulimia among college students on three U. S. campuses. Unpublished manuscript. New Haven: Yale University.

Roediger, H. L. III. (1990). Implicit memory: Retention without remembering. *American Psychologist, 45,* 1043–1056.

Roediger, H. L. III, & McDermott, K. B. (1995). Creating false memories: Remembering words not presented in lists. *Journal of Experimental Psychology: Learning, Memory, and Cognition, 21,* 803–814.

Roediger, H. L. III, & McDermott, K. B. (2000, January/February). *Psychological Science Agenda,* 8–9.

Roediger, R. (2004, March). What happened to behaviorism? *APS Observer, 17*(3), 5, 40–42.

Roesch, M. R., & Olson, C. R. (2004, April 9). Neuronal activity related to reward value and motivation in primate frontal cortex. *Science, 304,* 307–310.

Rogers, C. R. (1951). *Client-centered therapy: Its current practice, implications and theory.* Boston: Houghton Mifflin.

Rogers, C. R. (1961). *On becoming a person: A therapist's view of psychotherapy.* Boston: Houghton Mifflin. [See also: Rogers, 1951, 1980]

Rogers, C. R. (1977). *On personal power: Inner strength and its revolutionary impact.* New York: Delacorte.

Rogers, C. R. (1980). *A way of being.* Boston: Houghton Mifflin.

Rogers, C. R. (1982, July/August) Roots of madness. In T. H. Carr & H. E. Fitzgerald (Eds.), *Psychology 83/84* (pp. 263–267). Guilford, CT: Dushkin. (Originally published in *Science 82,* July/August, 1982).

Rogoff, B. (1990). *Apprenticeship in thinking: Cognitive development in social context.* New York: Oxford University Press.

Rohrer, M., et al. (1954). The stability of autokinetic judgment. *Journal of Abnormal and Social Psychology, 49,* 595–597.

Roll, S., Hinton, R., & Glazer, M. (1974). Dreams and death: Mexican Americans vs. Anglo-American. *Interamerican Journal of Psychology, 8,* 111–115.

Rollman, G. B., & Harris, G. (1987). The detectability, discriminability, and perceived magnitude of painful electrical shock. *Perception & Psychophysics, 42,* 257–268.

Rolls, B. J., Federoff, I. C., & Guthrie, J. F. (1991). Gender differences in eating be havior and body weight regulation. *Health Psychology, 10,* 133–142.

Rolnick, J. (1998, December 4). Treating mental disorders: A neuroscientist says no to drugs. *The Chronicle of Higher Education,* A10.

Rooney, S. C. (2002). Examining Redding's (2001) claims about lesbian and gay parenting. *American Psychologist, 57,* 298–299.

Rorschach, H. (1942). *Psychodiagnostics: A diagnostic test based on perception.* New York: Grune & Stratton.

Rosa, L., Rosa, E., Sarner, L., & Barrett, S. (1998). A close look at therapeutic touch. *Journal of the American Medical Association, 279,* 1005–1010.

Rosch, E. (1999). Is wisdom in the brain? *Psychological Science, 10,* 222–224.

Rosch, E., & Mervis, C. B. (1975). Family resemblances: Studies in the internal structure of categories. *Cognitive Psychology, 7,* 573–605.

Rosch, E. H., Mervis, C. B., Gray, W. D., Johnson, D. M., & Boyes-Braem, P. (1976). Basic objects in natural categories. *Cognitive Psychology, 8,* 382–439.

Rosen, J. B., & Schulkin, J. (1998). From normal fear to pathological anxiety. *Psychological Review, 105,* 325–350.

Rosenblatt, P. C. (1966). A cross-cultural study of child-rearing and romantic love. *Journal of Personality and Social Psychology, 4,* 336–338.

Rosenhan, D. L. (1969). Some origins of concern for others. In P. Mussen, J. Langer, & M. Covington (Eds.), *Trends and issues in developmental psychology.* New York: Holt, Rinehart & Winston.

Rosenhan, D. L. (1973a). On being sane in insane places. *Science, 179,* 250–258.

Rosenhan, D. L. (1973b, April 27). (Untitled letter to the editor). *Science, 180,* 360–361. [See also the critiques of Rosenhan's study among other letters in the same issue.]

Rosenhan, D. L. (1983). Psychological abnormality and law. In C. J. Scheirer & B. C. Hammonds (Eds.), *The master lecture series: Vol. 2. Psychology and the law.* Washington, DC: American Psychological Association.

Rosenhan, D. L., & Seligman, M. E. P. (1995). *Abnormal psychology* (3rd ed.). New York: Norton.

Rosenheck, R. A., Leslie, D., L., Sindelar, J., Miller, E. A., Lin, H., Stroup, T. S., McEvoy, J., Davis, S. M., Keefe, R. S. E., Swartz, M., Perkins, D. O., Hsiao, J. K., & Lieberman, J. (2006). Cost-effectiveness of second-generation antipsychotics and perphenazine in a randomized trial of treatment for chronic schizophrenia. *American Journal of Psychiatry, 163,* 2080–2089.

Rosenthal, N. E., Sack, D. A., Gillin, J. C., Lewy, A. J., Goodwin, F. K., Davenport, Y., Mueller, P. S., Newsome, D. A., & Wehr, T. A. (1984). Seasonal affective disorder: A description of the syndrome and preliminary findings with light therapy. *Archives of General Psychiatry, 41,* 72–80.

Rosenthal, R. (1994). Science and ethics in conducting, analyzing, and reporting psychological research. *Psychological Science, 5,* 127–134.

Rosenthal, R. & Jacobson, L. F. (1968a). *Pygmalion in the classroom: Teacher expectations and intellectual development.* New York: Holt.

Rosenthal, R., & Jacobson, L. F. (1968b). Teacher expectations for the disadvantaged. *Scientific American, 218*(4), 19–23.

Rosenzweig, M. R. (1992). Psychological science around the world. *American Psychologist, 47,* 718–722.

Rosenzweig, M. R. (1999). Continuity and change in the development of psychology around the world. *American Psychologist, 54,* 252–259.

Roser, M., & Gazzaniga, M. S. (2004, April). Automatic brains—interpretive minds. *Current Directions in Psychological Science, 13,* 56–59.

Ross, B. (1991). William James: Spoiled child of American psychology. In G. A. Kimble, M. Wertheimer, & C. L. White (Eds.), *Portraits of pioneers in psychology* (pp. 13–25). Washington, DC: American Psychological Association.

Ross, C. A., Miller, S. D., Reagor, P., Bjornson, L., Fraser, G. A., & Anderson, G. (1990). Structured interview data on 102 cases of multiple personality disorder from four centers. *American Journal of Psychiatry, 147,* 596–601.

Ross, C. A., Norton, G. R., & Wozney, K. (1989). Multiple personality disorder: An analysis of 236 cases. *Canadian Journal of Psychiatry, 34,* 413–418.

Ross, L., & Nisbett, R. E. (1991). *The person and the situation: Perspectives of social psychology.* New York: McGraw-Hill.

Ross, P. (2003, September). Mind readers. *Scientific American, 289,* 74–77.

Ross, P. E. (1992, July). Compulsive canines. *Scientific American, 266*(5), 24–25.

Ross, P. E. (2006, August). The expert mind. *Scientific American, 295*(8), 64–71. [See also: Bédard &

Chi, 1992; Bransford et al., 1986; Chi et al., 1982; Glaser, 1990; Greeno, 1989; Klahr & Simon, 2001]

Rothbaum, B. O., & Hodges, L. F. (1999). The use of virtual reality exposure in the treatment of anxiety disorders. *Behavior Modification, 23,* 507–525.

Rothbaum, B. O., Hodges, L. Smith, S., Lee, J. H., & Price, L. (2000a). A controlled study of virtual reality exposure therapy for the fear of flying. *Journal of Consulting & Clinical Psychology, 68,* 1020–1026.

Rothbaum, F., Weisz, J., Pott, M., Miyake, K., Morelli, G. (2000b). Attachment and culture: Security in the United States and Japan. *American Psychologist, 55,* 1093–1104.

Rothbaum, F. M., Weisz, J. R., & Snyder, S. S. (1982). Changing the world and changing the self: A two-process model of perceived control. *Journal of Personality and Social Psychology, 42,* 5–37.

Rothenberger, A., & Banaschewski, T. (2007). Informing the ADHD debate. *Scientific American Reports, 17,* 36–41.

Rotter, J. B. (1954). *Social learning and clinical psychology.* Englewood Cliffs, NJ: Prentice-Hall.

Rotter, J. B. (1966). Generalized expectancies for internal versus external control of reinforcement. *Psychological Monographs, 80* (Whole no. 609).

Rotter, J. B. (1971, June). External control and internal control. *Psychology Today, 4,* 37–42, 58–59.

Rotter, J. B. (1990). Internal versus external control of reinforcement: A case history of a variable. *American Psychologist, 45,* 489–493.

Rouhana, N. N., & Kelman, H. C. (1994). Promoting joint thinking in international conflicts: An Israeli-Palestinian continuing workshop. *Journal of Social Issues, 50,* 157–168.

Roush, W. (1996, July 5). Live long and prosper? *Science, 273,* 42–46.

Roy-Byrne, R. P., Craske, M. G., Stein, M. B., Sullivan, G., Bystritsky, A., Katon, W., Golinelli, D., & Sherbourne, C. D. (2005). A randomized effectiveness trial of cognitive-behavioral therapy and medication for primary care panic disorder. *Archives of General Psychiatry, 62,* 290–298.

Rozin, P. (1976). The evolution of intelligence and access to the cognitive unconscious. In J. M. Sprague & A. A. Epstein (Eds.), *Progress in psychobiology and physiological psychology* (pp. 245–280). New York: Academic Press.

Rozin, P. (1996). Towards a psychology of food and eating: From motivation to module to model to marker, morality, meaning, and metaphor. *Current Directions in Psychological Science, 5,* 18–24.

Rubin, D. C. (2006). The basic-systems model of episodic memory. *Perspectives on Psychological Science, 1,* 277–311.

Rubin, G. J., Brewin, C. R., Greenberg, N., Simpson, J., & Wessely, S. (2005). Psychological and behavioural reactions to the bombings in London on 7 July 2005: Cross sectional survey of a representative sample of Londoners. *British Medical Journal, 331,* 606.

Rubinstein, J. S., Meyer, D. E., & Evans. J. E. (2001). Executive control of cognitive processes in task switching. *Journal of Experimental Psychology: Human Perception and Performance, 27,* 763–797.

Ruiz-Caballero, J. A., Bermúdez, J. (1995). Neuroticism, mood, and retrieval of negative personal memories. *Journal of General Psychology, 122,* 29–35.

Rumbaugh, D. M. (Ed.). (1977). *Language learning by a chimpanzee: The Lana project.* New York: Academic Press.

Rumbaugh, D. M., & Savage-Rumbaugh, E. S. (1994). Language and apes. *The Psychology Teacher Network, 4,* 2–5.

Rushton, J. P., & Jensen, A. R. (2005). Thirty years of research on race differences in cognitive ability. *Psychology, Public Policy, and Law, 11,* 235–294. [See also Nisbett, 2005; Shiraev & Levy, 2007]

Russell, A., Mize, J., & Bissaker, K. (2002). Parent-child relationships. In P. K. Smith & C. H. Hart (Eds.), *Handbook of childhood social development.* Oxford, U.K.: Blackwell.

Rusting, C. L., & Nolen-Hoeksema, S. (1998). Regulating responses to anger: Effects of rumination and

distraction on angry mood. *Journal of Personality and Social Psychology, 74,* 790–803.

Rutter, M. (2006). *Genes and behavior: Nature-nurture interplay explained.* Malden, MA: Blackwell Publishing. [See also Bouchard, 1994; Caspi et al., 2002; DeAngelis, 1997; Gelernter, 1994; Hamer, 1997; Hamer, 2002; Lai et al., 2001; Plomin, 2003; Plomin, Owen, & McGuffin, 1994; Plomin & Rende, 1991; Saudino, 1997]

Ryan, R. M., & Deci, E. L. (2000). Self-determination theory and the facilitation of intrinsic motivation, social development, and well-being. *American Psychologist, 55,* 68–78.

Ryff, C. D. (1989). In the eye of the beholder: Views of psychological well-being among middle-aged and older adults. *Psychology and Aging, 4,* 195–210.

Ryff, C. D., & Heidrich, S. M. (1997). Experience and well-being: Explorations on domains of life and how they matter. *International Journal of Behavioral Development, 20,* 193–206.

Ryff, C. D., & Heincke, S. G. (1983). The subjective organization of personality in adulthood and aging. *Journal of Personaltiy and Social Psychology, 44,* 807–816.

Saarinen, T. F. (1987). *Centering of mental maps of the world: Discussion paper.* Tucson: University of Arizona, Department of Geography and Regional Development.

Sabin-Farrell, R., & Turpin, G. (2003). Vicarious traumatization: Implications for the mental health of health workers? *Clinical Psychology Review, 23,* 449–480.

Sackett, P. R. (1994). Integrity testing for personnel selection. *Current Directions in Psychological Science, 3,* 73–76.

Sackheim, H. A., Prudic, J., Devanand, D. P., Nobler, M. S., Lisanby, S. H., Peyser, S., Fitzsimons, L., Moody, B. J., & Clark, J. (2000). A prospective, randomized, double-blind comparison of bilateral and right unilateral electroconvulsive therapy at different stimulus intensities. *Archives of General Psychiatry, 57,* 425–434.

Sacks, O. (1995). *An anthropologist on Mars.* New York: Random House.

St. George-Hyslop, P. H. (2000). Piecing together Alzheimer's. *Scientific American, 283*(6), 76–83. [See also: Morrison-Bogorad & Phelps, 1997; Plomin, Owen, & McGuffin, 1994; Skoog et al., 1993]

Sakaki, M. (2007). Mood and recall of autobiographical memory: The effect of focus of self-knowledge. *Journal of Personality, 75,* 421–450. [See also: Blaney, 1986; Bower, 1981; Eich et al., 1997; Gilligan & Bower, 1984; Goodwin & Sher, 1993; Lewinsohn & Rosenbaum, 1987; MacLeod & Campbell, 1992; Matt et al., 1992; Ruiz-Caballero & Bermúdez, 1995]

Salovey, P., & Grewal, D. (2005). The science of emotional intelligence. *Current Directions in Psychological Science, 14,* 281–285.

Salovey, P., & Mayer, J. D. (1990). Emotional intelligence. *Imagination, Cognition, and Personality, 9,* 185–211. [See also Mayer & Salovey, 1997, 1995]

Salovey, P., Rothman, A. J., Detweiler, J. B., & Steward, W. T. (2000). Emotional states and physical health. *American Psychologist, 55,* 110–121.

Saltzstein, H. D., & Sandberg, L. (1979). Indirect social influence: Change in judgmental processor anticipatory conformity. *Journal of Experimental Social Psychology, 15,* 209–216. [See also: Deutsch & Gerard, 1955; Lott & Lott, 1961]

Sanger, M. (1971). *Margaret Sanger: An autobiography.* New York: W. W. Norton/Dover Publications. (Original work published in 1938).

Santarelli, L., Saxe, M., Gross, C., Surget, A., Battaglia, F., Dulawa, S., Weisstaub, N., Lee, J., Duman, R., Arancio, O., Belzung, C., & Hen, R. (2003, August 8). Requirement of hippocampal neurogenesis for the behavioral effects of antidepressants. *Science, 301,* 805–809. [See also: Dubuc, 2002; Vogel, 2003]

Sapolsky, R. (2002, November). The loveless man . . . who invented the science of love. *Scientific American,* 95–96.

Sapolsky, R. M. (1990). Adrenocortical function, social rank, and personality among wild baboons. *Biological Psychiatry, 28*, 1–17.

Sapolsky, R. M. (1992). *Stress: The aging brain and the mechanisms of neuron death*. Cambridge, MA: MIT Press.

Sapolsky, R. M. (1998). *Why zebras don't get ulcers: An updated guide to stress, stress-related disease, and coping*. New York: Freeman.

Sarbin, T. R., & Coe, W. C. (1972). *Hypnosis: A social psychological analysis of influence communication*. New York: Holt, Rinehart & Winston.

Satir, V. (1983). *Conjoint family therapy* (3rd ed.). Palo Alto, CA: Science & Behavior Books.

Satir, V., Banmen, J., Gerber, J., & Gomori, M. (1991). *Satir model: Family therapy and beyond*. Palo Alto, CA: Science & Behavior Books.

Sattler, J. M. (1970). Racial "experimenter effects" in experimentation, testing, interviewing, and psychotherapy. *Psychological Bulletin, 73*, 137–160.

Saudino, K. J. (1997, August). Moving beyond the heritability question: New directions in behavioral genetic studies of personality. *Current Directions in Psychological Science, 6*, 86–90.

Saufley, W. H., Otaka, S. R., & Bavaresco, J. L. (1985). Context independence. *Memory and Cognition, 13*, 522–528.

Savage-Rumbaugh, E. S. (1990). Language acquisition in a non-human species: Implications for the innateness debate. *Developmental Psychobiology, 23*, 559–620. [See also: Patterson, 1978; Premack, 1971, 1976; Rumbaugh, 1977]

Savage-Rumbaugh, S., & Lewin, R. (1994). *Kanzi: The ape at the brink of the human mind*. New York: John Wiley & Sons.

Savitsky, J. C., & Lindblom, W. D. (1986). The impact of the guilty but mentally ill verdict on juror decisions: An empirical analysis. *Journal of Applied Social Psychology, 16*, 686–701.

Sawa, A., & Snyder, S. H. (2002, April 26). Schizophrenia: Diverse approaches to a complex disease. *Science, 296*, 692–695.

Sax, B. (2002). *Animals in the Third Reich: Pets, scapegoats, and the Holocaust*. London: Continuum International Publishers.

Sax, L., & Kautz, K. J. (2003). Who first suggests the diagnosis of attention-deficit/hyperactivity disorder? *Annals of Family Medicine, 1*, 171–174.

Saxe, L. (1991). Lying: Thoughts of an applied social psychologist. *American Psychologist, 46*, 409–415.

Saxe, L. (1994). Detection of deception: Polygraph and integrity tests. *Current Directions in Psychological Science, 3*, 69–73.

Saxe, L., Dougherty, D., & Cross, T. (1985). The validity of polygraph testing: Scientific analysis and public controversy. *American Psychologist, 40*, 355–366.

Scarr, S. (1997). Why child care has little impact on most children's development. *Current Directions in Psychological Science, 6*, 143–148.

Scarr, S. (1998). American child care today. *American Psychologist, 53*, 95–108.

Scarr, S., & Weinberg, R. (1976). IQ test performance of black children adopted by white families. *American Psychologist, 31*, 726–739.

Scarr, S., & Weinberg, R. A. (1978, April). Attitudes, interests, and IQ. *Human Nature*, 29–36.

Schachter, S. (1971). *Emotion, obesity and crime*. New York: Academic Press.

Schachter, S. (1977). Nicotine regulation in heavy and light smokers. *Journal of Experimental Psychology: General, 106*, 5–12.

Schacter, D. L. (1992). Understanding implicit memory: cognitive neuroscience approach. *American Psychologist, 47*, 559-569.

Schacter, D. L. (1996). *Searching for memory: The brain, the mind, and the past*. New York: Basic Books. [See also: Anderson, 1982; Tulving, 1983]

Schacter, D. L. (1999). The seven sins of memory: Insights from psychology and cognitive neuroscience. *American Psychologist, 54*, 182–203.

Schacter, D. L. (2001). *The Seven Sins of Memory:* *How the Mind Forgets and Remembers*. Boston: Houghton Mifflin.

Schaefer, H. H., & Martin, P. L. (1966). Behavioral therapy for "apathy" of hospitalized patients. *Psychological Reports, 19*, 1147–1158.

Schafe, G. E., Doyère, V., & LeDoux, J. E. (2005). Tracking the fear engram: The lateral amygdala is an essential locus of fear memory storage. *Journal of Neuroscience, 25*, 10,010–10,015.

Schank, R. C., & Abelson, R. (1977). *Scripts, plans, goals and understanding: An inquiry into human knowledge and structures*. Hillsdale, NJ: Erlbaum.

Scharfe, E., & Bartholomew, K. (1998). Do you remember? Recollections of adult attachment patterns. *Personal Relationships, 5*, 219–234.

Schatzberg, A. F. (1991). Overview of anxiety disorders: Prevalence, biology, course, and treatment. *Journal of Clinical Psychiatry, 42*, 5–9.

Schaufeli, W. B., Maslach, C., & Marek, T. (Eds.) (1993). *Professional burnout: Recent developments in theory and research*. Washington, DC: Taylor & Francis.

Schechter, B. (1996, October 18). How the brain gets rhythm. *Science, 274*, 339–340.

Schick, T., Jr., & Vaughn, L. (2001). *How to think about weird things: Critical thinking for a new age* (3rd ed.). New York: McGraw-Hill.

Schiff, M., & Bargal, D. (2000). Helping characteristics of self-help and support groups: Their contribution to participants' subjective well-being. *Small Group Research, 31*, 275–304.

Schill, R. A., & Marcus, D. K. (1998). Incarceration and learned helplessness. *International Journal of Offender Therapy and Comparative Criminology, 42*, 224–232.

Schlenker, B. R., Weingold, M. F., Hallam, J. R. (1990). Self-serving attributions in social context: Effects of self-esteem and social pressure. *Journal of Personality and Social Psychology, 58*, 855–863. [See also: Epstein & Feist, 1988; Ickes & Layden, 1978]

Schmidt, C. (2007, May 18). Putting the brakes on psychosis. *Science, 316*, 976–977.

Schmidt, R. A., & Bjork, R. A. (1992). New conceptualizations of practice: Common principles in three paradigms suggest new concepts for training. *Psychological Science, 3*, 207–217.

Schmitt, D. P., Allik, J., McCrae, R. R., & Benet-Martínez, V. (2007). The geographic distribution of Big Five personality traits: Patterns and profiles of human self-description across 56 nations. *Journal of Cross-Cultural Psychology, 38*, 173–212. [See also: Birenbaum & Montag, 1986; Guthrie & Bennet, 1970; McCrae & Costa, 1997; Paunonen et al., 1992]

Schmolck, H., Buffalo, E. A., & Squire, L. R. (2000). Memory distortions develop over time: Recollections of the O. J. Simpson trial verdict after 15 and 32 months. *Psychological Science, 11*, 39–45.

Schneider, K., & May, R. (1995). *The psychology of existence: An integrative, clinical perspective*. New York: McGraw-Hill.

Schou, M. (1997). Forty years of lithium treatment. *Archives of General Psychiatry, 54*, 9–13.

Schreiber, F. R. (1973). *Sybil*. New York: Warner Books.

Schroeder, D. A., Penner, L. A., Dovidio, J. F., & Piliavin, J. A. (1995). *The psychology of helping and altruism*. New York: McGraw-Hill.

Schroeder, D. A., & Prentice, D. A. (1995). Pluralistic ignorance and alcohol use on campus II: Correcting misperceptions of the social norm. Unpublished manuscript, Princeton University.

Schroeder, S. R., Schroeder, C. S., & Landesman, S. (1987). Psychological services in educational settings to persons with mental retardation. *American Psychologist, 42*, 805–808.

Schulkin, J. (1994). Melancholic depression and the hormones of adversity: A role for the amygdala. *Current Directions in Psychological Science, 3*, 41–44.

Schultz, D. P., & Schultz, S. E. (2006). *Psychology and work today: An introduction to industrial and orga-* *nizational psychology* (9th ed.). Upper Saddle River, NJ: Prentice Hall.

Schulz, R. (1976). Effects of control and predictability on the physical and psychological well-being of the institutionalized aged. *Journal of Personality and Social Psychology, 33*, 563–573.

Schulz, R., & Heckhausen, J. (1996). A life span model of successful aging. *American Psychologist, 51*, 702–714.

Schuster, M. A., Stein, B. D., Jaycox, L. H., Collins, R. L., Marshall, G. N., Elliott, M. N., Zhou, A. J., Kanouse, D. E., Morrison, J. L., & Berry, S. H. (2001). A national survey of stress reactions after the September 11th, 2001, terrorist attacks. *New England Journal of Medicine, 345*, 1507–1512.

Schwartz, B. (1997). Psychology, idea technology, and ideology. *Psychological Science, 8*, 21–27.

Schwartz, B. (2004, April). The tyranny of choice. *Scientific American, 290*(4), 70–75.

Schwartz, C. E., Wright, C. I., Shin, L. M., Kagan, J., & Rauch, S. L. (2003, June 20). Inhibited and uninhibited infants "grown up": Adult amygdalar response to novelty. *Science, 300*, 1952–1953.

Schwartz, J., & Wald, M. L. (2003, March 9). Smart people working collectively can be dumber than the sum of their brains: "Groupthink" is 30 years old, and still going strong. *New York Times*. Retrieved on December 15, 2004, from www.mindfully.org/ Reform/2003/Smart-People-Dumber9mar03.htm.

Schwartz, J. M., Stoessel, P. W., Baxter, L. R., Martin, K. M., & Phelps, M. E. (1996). Systematic changes in cerebral glucose metabolic rate after successful behavior modification treatment of obsessive–compulsive disorder. *Archives of General Psychiatry, 53*, 109–116.

Schwartz, P. (1994). *Peer marriage: How love between equals really works*. New York: The Free Press.

Schwarz, N. (1999). Self-reports: How the questions shape the answers. *American Psychologist, 54*, 93–105.

Schwarzer, R. (Ed.). (1992). *Self-efficacy: Thought control of action*. Washington, DC: Hemisphere.

Schwebel, A. I., & Fine, M. A. (1994). *Understanding and helping families: A cognitive behavioral approach*. Hillsdale, NJ: Erlbaum.

Schweinhart, L. J., & Weikart, D. P. (1986, January). What do we know so far? A review of the Head Start Synthesis Project. *Young Children, 41*(2), 49–55.

Scott, K. G., & Carran, D. T. (1987). The epidemiology and prevention of mental retardation. *American Psychologist, 42*, 801–804.

Scovern, A. W., & Kilmann, P. R. (1980). Status of electro-convulsive therapy: Review of outcome literature. *Psychological Bulletin, 87*, 260–303.

Scoville, W. B., & Milner, B. (1957). Loss of recent memory after bilateral hippocampal lesions. *Journal of Neurology, Neurosurgery, & Psychiatry, 20*, 11–21. Retrieved March 10, 2008, from http://homepage.mac.com/sanagnos/scovillemilner1957.pdf

Scully, J. A., Tosi, H., & Banning, K. (2000). Life events checklist: Revisiting the Social Readjustment Rating Scale after 30 years. *Educational and Psychological Measurement, 60*, 864–876.

Seeman, T. E., Dubin, L. F., & Seeman, M. (2003). Religiosity/spirituality and health: A critical review of the evidence for biological pathways. *American Psychologist, 58*, 53–63.

Segal, M. W. (1974). Alphabet and attraction: An unobtrusive measure of the effect of propinquity in a field setting. *Journal of Personality and Social Psychology, 30*, 654–657.

Segall, M. H. (1994). A cross-cultural research contribution to unraveling the nativist/empiricist controversy. In W. J. Lonner & R. Malpass, *Psychology and culture* (pp. 135–138). Boston: Allyn & Bacon.

Segall, M. H., Dasen, P. R., Berry, J. W., & Poortinga, Y. H. (1990). *Human behavior in global perspective: An introduction to cross-cultural psychology*. Boston: Allyn & Bacon. [See also: Deregowski, 1980; Kitayama et al., 2003; Segall, 1994; Segall et al., 1966; Stewart, 1973]

Segall, M. H., Dasen, P. R., Berry, J. W., & Poortinga,

Y. H. (1999). *Human behavior in global perspective: An introduction to cross-cultural psychology* (2nd ed.). Boston: Allyn & Bacon.

Segall, M. H., Lonner, W. J., & Berry, J. W. (1998). Cross-cultural psychology as a scholarly discipline: On the flowering of culture in behavioral research. *American Psychologist, 53*, 1101–1110.

Segall, M. N., Campbell, D. T., & Herskovits, M. J. (1966). *The influence of culture on visual perception.* Indianapolis: Bobbs-Merrill.

Segerstrom, S. C., & Miller, G. E. (2004). Psychological stress and the human immune system: A meta-analytic study of 30 years of inquiry. *Psychological Bulletin, 130*, 601–630.

Seidler, R. D., Purushotham, A., Kim, S. G., Urbil, K., Willingham, D., & Ashe, J. (2002, June 14). Cerebellum activation associated with performance change but not motor learning. *Science, 296*, 2043–2046.

Selfridge, O. G. (1955). Pattern recognition and modern computers. In *Proceedings of the Western Joint Computer Conference.* New York: Institute of Electrical and Electronics Engineers.

Seligman, M. E. P. (1971). Preparedness and phobias. *Behavior Therapy, 2*, 307–320.

Seligman, M. E. P. (1973, June). Fall into helplessness. *Psychology Today, 7*, 43–48.

Seligman, M. E. P. (1975). *Helplessness: On depression, development and death.* San Francisco: Freeman.

Seligman, M. E. P. (1991). *Learned optimism.* New York: Knopf.

Seligman, M. E. P. (1995). The effectiveness of psychotherapy: The Consumer Reports study. *American Psychologist, 50*, 965–974.

Seligman, M. E. P. (1998). *Learned optimism: How to change your mind and your life.* New York: Free Press.

Seligman, M. E. P. (2002). *Authentic happiness: Using the new positive psychology to realize your potential for lasting fulfillment.* New York: Free Press.

Seligman, M. E. P., Abramson, L. Y., Semmel, A., & von Baeyer, C. (1979). Depressive attributional style. *Journal of Abnormal Psychology, 88*, 242–247.

Seligman, M. E. P., & Csikszentmihalyi, M. (2000). Positive psychology: An introduction. *American Psychologist, 55*, 5–14.

Seligman, M. E. P., & Maier, S. F. (1967). Failure to escape traumatic shock. *Journal of Experimental Psychology, 74*, 1–9.

Seligman, M. E. P., Rashid, T., & Parks, A. (2006). Positive psychotherapy. *American Psychologist, 61*, 774–788.

Seligson, S. V. (1994, November/December). Say good night to snoring. *Health, 8*(7), 89–93.

Selye, H. (1956). *The stress of life.* New York: McGraw-Hill.

Selye, H. (1991). *Stress without distress.* New York: Signet Books.

Serpell, R. (1994). The cultural construction of intelligence. In W. J. Lonner & R. Malpass, *Psychology and culture* (pp. 157–163). Boston: Allyn & Bacon.

Service, R. F. (1999, April 23). Bypassing nervous system damage with electronics. *Science, 284*, 579.

Seybold, K. S., & Hill, P. C. (2001). The role of religion and spirituality in mental and physical health. *Current Directions in Psychological Science, 10*, 21–24.

Shadish, W. R., Matt, G. E., Navarro, A. M., & Phillips, G. (2000). The effects of psychological therapies under clinically representative conditions: A meta-analysis. *Psychological Bulletin, 126*, 512–529.

Shapiro, D. H. (1985). Clinical use of meditation as a self-regulation strategy: Comments on Holmes's conclusions and implications. *American Psychologist, 40*, 719–722.

Shapiro, F. (1995). *Desensitization and reprocessing: Basic principles, protocols, and procedures.* New York: Guilford.

Shapiro, S. L., Astin, J. A., Bishop, S. R., & Cordova, M. (2005). Mindfulness-based stress reduction for health care professionals: Results from a randomized

trial. *International Journal of Stress Management, 12*, 64–176.

Sharps, M. J., & Wertheimer, M. (2000). Gestalt perspectives on cognitive science and on experimental psychology. *Review of General Psychology, 4*, 315–336.

Shatz, M., Wellman, H. M., & Silber, S. (1983). The acquisition of mental verbs: A systematic investigation of the first reference to mental state. *Cognition, 14*, 301–321.

Shaver, P., & Hazan, C. (1987). Romantic love conceptualized as an attachment process. *Journal of Personality and Social Psychology, 52*, 511–524.

Shaver, P. R., & Hazan, C. (1993). Adult attachment: Theory and research. In W. Jones & D. Perlman (Eds.), *Advances in personal relationships (Vol. 4)*, pp. 29–70. London, U.K.: Jessica Kingsley.

Shaver, P. R., & Hazan, C. (1994). Attachment. In A. L. Weber & J. H. Harvey (Eds.), *Perspectives on close relationships* (Chapter 6, 110–130). Boston: Allyn & Bacon.

Shaw, P., Eckstrand, K., Sharp, W., Blumenthal, J., Lerch, J. P., Greenstein, D., Clasen, L., Evans, A., Giedd, J., & Rapoport, J. L. (2007). Attention-deficit/hyperactivity disorder is characterized by a delay in cortical maturation. *Proceedings of the National Academy of Sciences, 104*, 19,649–19,654.

Shaywitz, S. E. (1996, November). Dyslexia. *Scientific American*, 98–104.

Shaywitz, S. E., Shaywitz, B. A., Fletcher, J. M., & Escobar, M. D. (1990). Prevalence of reading disability in boys and girls: Results of the Connecticut Longitudinal Study. *Journal of the American Medical Association, 264*, 998–1002.

Shea, C. (1998, January 30). Why depression strikes more women than men: "Ruminative coping" may provide answers. *The Chronicle of Higher Education*, 14.

Shedler, J. (2006, Fall). Why the scientist-practitioner split won't go away. *The General Psychologist, 41*(2), 9–10.

Shepard, R. N., & Metzler, J. (1971). Mental rotation of three-dimensional objects. *Science, 171*, 701–703.

Sherif, C. W. (1981, August). Social and psychological bases of social psychology. The G. Stanley Hall Lecture on social psychology, presented at the annual convention of the American Psychological Association, Los Angeles, CA.

Sherif, M. (1935). A study of some social factors in perception. *Archives of Psychology, 27*, 187.

Sherif, M., Harvey, O. J., White, B. J., Hood, W., & Sherif, C. (1961). *Intergroup conflict and cooperation: The Robbers Cave experiment.* Norman: University of Oklahoma Institute of Intergroup Relations.

Shermer, M. (2006, July). The political brain. *Scientific American, 295*(1), 36.

Sherrill, R. Jr. (1991). Natural wholes: Wolfgang Köhler and Gestalt theory. In G. A. Kimble, M. Wertheimer, & C. L. White (Eds.), *Portraits of pioneers in psychology* (pp. 256–273). Washington, DC: American Psychological Association.

Shih, M., Pittinsky, T., & Ambady, N. (1999). Stereotype susceptibility: Identity salience and shifts in quantitative performance. *Psychological Science, 10*, 80–83.

Shields, S. A. (1991). Gender in the psychology of emotion: A selective research review. In K. T. Strongman (Ed.), *International review of studies on emotion (Vol. 1)*. New York: Wiley.

Shiffrin, R. M. (1993). Short-term memory: A brief commentary. *Memory and Cognition, 21*(2), 193–197.

Shimamura, A. P. (1996, September/October). Unraveling the mystery of the frontal lobes: Explorations in cognitive neuroscience. *Psychological Science Agenda*, 8–9.

Shiraev, E., & Levy, D. (2001). *Coss-cultural psychology: Critical thinking and contemporary applications.* Boston: Allyn & Bacon.

Shizgal, P., & Arvanitogiannis, A. (2003, March 21). Gambling on dopamine. *Science, 299*, 1856–1858.

Shneidman, E. (1987, March). At the point of no return. *Psychology Today*, 54–58.

Shobe, K. K., & Kihlstrom, J. F. (1997). Is traumatic memory special? *Current Directions in Psychological Science, 6*, 70–74.

Shorter, E., & Healy, D. (2007). *Shock therapy: A history of electroconvulsive treatment in mental illness.* New Brunswick, NJ: Rutgers University Press. [See also: Glass, 2001; Holden, 2003; Hollon et al., 2002; Sackheim et al., 2000; Scovern & Kilmann, 1980]

Siegel, J. M. (1990). Stressful life events and use of physician services among the elderly: The moderating role of pet ownership. *Journal of Personality and Social Psychology, 58*, 1081–1086.

Siegel, J. M. (2001). The REM sleep–memory consolidation hypothesis. *Science, 294*, 1058–1063.

Siegel, J. M. (2003, November). Why we sleep. *Scientific American, 289*, 92–97.

Siegel, R. K. (1980). The psychology of life after death. *American Psychologist, 35*, 911–931.

Siegler, R. S. (1994). Cognitive variability: A key to understanding cognitive development. *Current Directions in Psychological Science, 3*, 1–5.

Sigelman, C. K., Thomas, D. B., Sigelman, L., & Robich, F. D. (1986). Gender, physical attractiveness, and electability: An experimental investigation of voter biases. *Journal of Applied Social Psychology, 16*, 229–248.

Silbersweig, D. A., Stern, E., Frith, C., Cahill, C., Holmes, A., Grootoonk, S., Seaward, J., McKenna, P., Chua, S. E., Schnorr, L., Jones, T., & Frackowiak, R. S. J. (1995, November 9). A functional neuroanatomy of hallucinations in schizophrenia. *Nature, 378*, 176–179.

Silver, R. L. (1983). Coping with an undesirable life event: A study of early reactions to physical disability. *Dissertation Abstracts International, 43*, 3415.

Silver, R. L., Boon, C., & Stones, M. L. (1983). Searching for meaning in misfortune: Making sense of incest. *Journal of Social Issues, 39*, 81–101.

Silver, R. L., & Wortman, C. B. (1980). Coping with undesirable life events. In J. Garber & M. E. P. Seligman (Eds.), *Human helplessness: Theory and application.* New York: Academic Press.

Simeon, D., Gross, S., Guralnik, O., Stein, D. J., et al. (1997). Feeling unreal: 30 cases of *DSM-III-R* depersonalization disorder. *American Journal of Psychiatry, 154*, 1107–1113.

Simeon, D., Guralnik, O., Hazlett. E. A., Spiegel-Cohen, J., Hollander E., & Buchsbaum, M. S. (2000). Feeling unreal: A PET study of depersonalization disorder. *American Journal of Psychiatry 157*, 1782–1788.

Simon, G. E., & Savarino, J. (2007). Suicide attempts among patients starting depression treatment with medications or psychotherapy. *American Journal of Psychiatry, 164*, 1029–1034.

Simon, H. A. (1992). What is an "explanation" of behavior? *Psychological Science, 3*, 150–161.

Simons, D. J., & Levin, D. T. (1998). Failure to detect changes to people during a real-world interaction. *Psychonomic Bulletin & Review, 4*, 644–649.

Simonton, D. K. (2001). Talent development as a multidimensional, multiplicative, and dynamic process. *Current Directions in Psychological Science, 10*, 39–43.

Simpson, J. A. (1990). The influence of attachment styles on romantic relationships. *Journal of Personality and Social Psychology, 59*, 971–980.

Simpson, J. A., & Harris, B. A. (1994). Interpersonal attraction. In A. L. Weber & J. H. Harvey (Eds.), *Perspectives on close relationships* (pp. 45–66). Boston: Allyn & Bacon.

Sinclair, R. C., Hoffman, C., Mark, M. M., Martin L. L., & Pickering, T. L. (1994). Construct accessibility and the misattribution of arousal: Schacter and Singer revisited. *Psychological Sciences, 5*, 15–18.

Singer, J. L. (1966). *Daydreaming: An introduction to the experimental study of inner experience.* New York: Random House.

Singer, J. L. (1975). Navigating the stream of consciousness: Research in daydreaming and related inner experience. *American Psychologist, 30,* 727–739.

Singer, J. L., & McCraven, V. J. (1961). Some characteristics of adult daydreaming. *Journal of Psychology, 51,* 151–164.

Singer, J. L., Singer, D. G., & Rapaczynski, W. S. (1984). Family patterns and television viewing as predictors of children's beliefs and aggression. *Journal of Communication, 34,* 73–89.

Singer, T., Seymour, B., O'Doherty, J., Kaube, H., Dolan, R. J., & Frith, C. D. (2004, February 20). Empathy for pain involves the affective but not sensory components of pain. *Science, 303,* 1157–1162

Singer, W. (1995, November 3). Development and plasticity of cortical processing architectures. *Science, 270,* 758–763.

Singhal, A., & Rogers, E. M. (2002). A theoretical agenda for entertainment—Education. *Communication Theory, 12*(2), 117–135.

Singleton, J. L., & Newport, E. L. (2004). When learners surpass their models: The acquisition of American Sign Language from inconsistent input. *Cognitive Psychology, 49,* 370–407.

Sinha, G. (2005, July). Training the brain. *Scientific American, 293*(1), 22–23.

Skinner, B. F. (1948). *Walden Two.* Indianapolis, IN: Hackett Publishing Company.

Skinner, B. F. (1953). *Science and human behavior.* New York: Macmillan.

Skinner, B. F. (1956). A case history in scientific method. *American Psychologist, 11,* 221–233. (Reprinted in S. Koch [Ed.], *Psychology: A study of a science* [Vol. 2, pp. 359–379]. New York: McGraw-Hill.)

Skinner, B. F. (1987). Whatever happened to psychology as the science of behavior? *American Psychologist, 42,* 780–786.

Skinner, B. F. (1989). The origins of cognitive thought. *American Psychologist, 44,* 13–18.

Skinner, B. F. (1990). Can psychology be a science of mind? *American Psychologist, 45,* 1206–1210. [See also: Skinner, 1987.]

Skinner, E. A. (1996). A guide to constructs of control. *Journal of Personality and Social Psychology, 71,* 549–570.

Skoog, I., Nilsson, L., Palmertz, B., Andreasson, L. A., & Svanborg, A. (1993). A population-based study of dementia in 85-year-olds. *New England Journal of Medicine, 328,* 153.

Skotko, B. G., Kensinger, E. A., Locascio, J. J., Einstein, G., Rubin, D. C., Tupler, L. A., Krendl, A., Corkin, S. (2004). Puzzling thoughts for H. M.: Can new semantic information be anchored to old semantic memories? *Neuropsychology, 18,* 756–769.

Slater, L. (2005). *Opening Skinner's box: Great psychological experiments of the Twentieth Century.* New York: W. W. Norton.

Sleek, S. (1994, April). Could Prozac replace demand for therapy? *APA Monitor,* 28.

Sleek, S. (1996, May). Shifting the paradigm for prescribing drugs. *APA Monitor, 1,* 29.

Slobin, D. I. (1985a). Introduction: Why study acquisition crosslinguistically? In D. I. Slobin (Ed.), *The crosslinguistic study of language acquisition. Vol. 1: The data* (pp. 3–24). Hillsdale, NJ: Erlbaum.

Slobin, D. I. (1985b). Cross-linguistic evidence of the language making capacity. In D. I. Slobin (Ed.), *The crosslinguistic study of language acquisition. Vol. 2: Theoretical issues* (pp. 1157–1256). Hillsdale, NJ: Erlbaum.

Small, D. M., Zatorre, R. J., Dagher, A., Evans, A. C., & Jones-Gotman, M. (2001). Changes in brain activity related to eating chocolate. *Brain, 124,* 1720–1733.

Smith, A. W. (1995). Separation-individuation and coping: Contributions to freshman college adjustment. Unpublished doctoral dissertation, University of North Carolina at Greensboro. (*Dissertation Abstracts International, 56,* 3-A, 0831.)

Smith, C. A., & Ellsworth, P. C. (1987). Patterns of appraisal and emotion related to taking an exam.

Journal of Personality and Social Psychology, 52, 475–488.

Smith, D. (2001, October). Sleep psychologists in demand. *Monitor on Psychology,* 36–39.

Smith, D. (2002a, January). Guidance in treating ADHD. *Monitor on Psychology, 33*(1), 34–35. [See also: Angold et al., 2000; Marshall, 2000]

Smith, D. (2002b). The theory heard "round the world." *Monitor on Psychology, 33*(9), 30–32.

Smith, D. (2002c, June). Where are recent grads getting jobs? *Monitor on Psychology, 33*(6), 28–32.

Smith, D. (2003a, January). Five principles for research ethics. *Monitor on Psychology, 34*(1), 56–60.

Smith, D. (2003b). *Report from Ground Zero.* New York: Penguin.

Smith, D. (2003c, January). What you need to know about the new code. *Monitor on Psychology, 34*(1), 62–65.

Smith, E. E. (2000). Neural bases of human working memory. *Current Directions in Psychological Science, 9,* 45–49.

Smith, E. E., & Jonides, J. (1999, March 12). Storage and executive processes in the frontal lobes. *Science, 283,* 1657–1661.

Smith, E. E., & Medin, D. L. (1981). *Cognitive Science Series: 4. Categories and concepts.* Cambridge, MA: Harvard University Press.

Smith, G. B., Schwebel, A. I., Dunn, R. L., & McIver, S. D. (1993). The role of psychologists in the treatment, management, and prevention of chronic mental illness. *American Psychologist, 48,* 966–971.

Smith, G. T., Spillane, N. S., & Annus, A. M. (2006). Implications of an emerging integration of universal and culturally specific psychologies. *Perspectives on Psychological Science, 1,* 211–233. [See also: Matsumoto, 1994, 1996]

Smith, M. L., & Glass, G. V. (1977). Meta-analysis of psychotherapy outcome studies. *American Psychologist, 32,* 752–760.

Smith, R. E., Haroutunian, V., Davis, K. L., & Meador-Woodruff, J. H. (2001). Expression of excitatory amino acid transporter transcripts in the thalamus of subjects with schizophrenia. *American Journal of Psychiatry, 158,* 1393–1399.

Smith, S. (1991, Spring). Two-generation program models: A new intervention strategy. *Social Policy Report of the Society for Research in Child Development, 5* (No. 1).

Smythe, J. (1998). Written emotional expression: Effect sizes, outcome types, and moderator variables. *Journal of Consulting and Clinical Psychology, 66,* 174–184.

Snyder, H. N., & Sickmund, M. (1995). *Juvenile offenses and victims: A national report.* Washington, DC: Office of Juvenile Justice and Delinquency Prevention.

Snyder, S. H. (1986). *Drugs and the brain.* New York: Scientific American Books.

Solms, M. (2004, May). Freud returns. *Scientific American, 17*(2), 28–35.

Solso, R. L. (2001). *Cognitive psychology* (6th ed.). Boston: Allyn & Bacon.

Solvason, H. B., Ghanta, V. K., & Hiramoto, R. N. (1988). Conditioned augmentation of natural killer cell activity: Independence from nociceptive effects and dependence on interferon-beta. *Journal of Immunology, 140,* 661–665.

Sommer, D. H. (2000). Relationships between sexual abuse, cognitive style, and depression among adolescent psychiatric inpatients. Doctoral dissertation, University of Texas at Austin.

Sommer, I. E. C., Aleman, A., Bouma, A., & Kahn, R. S. (2004). Do women really have more bilateral language representation than men? A meta-analysis of functional imaging studies. *Brain: A Journal of Neurology, 127,* 1845–1852.

Sow, I. (1977). *Psychiatrie dynamique africaine.* Paris, France: Payot.

Sparling, J. W., Van Tol, J., & Chescheir, N. C. (1999). Fetal and neonatal hand movement. *Physical Therapy, 79,* 24–39.

Spear, L. P. (2000). Neurobehavioral changes in ado-

lescence. *Current Directions in Psychological Science, 9,* 111–114.

Spearman, C. (1927). *The abilities of man.* New York: Macmillan.

Spelke, E. S. (2000). Core knowledge. *American Psychologist, 55,* 1233–1243.

Spelke, E. S., & Owsley, C. J. (1979). Intermodal exploration and knowledge in infancy. *Infant Behavior and Development, 2,* 13–27.

Spencer, R. M. C., Zelaznik, H. N., Diedrichsen, J., & Ivry, R. B. (2003, May 30). Disrupted timing of discontinuous but not continuous movements by cerebellar lesions. *Science, 300,* 1437–1439.

Sperling, G. (1960). The information available in brief visual presentations. *Psychological Monographs, 74,* 1–29.

Sperling, G. (1963). A model for visual memory tasks. *Human Factors, 5,* 19–31.

Sperry, R. W. (1964). The great cerebral commissure. *Scientific American, 210,* 42–52.

Sperry, R. W. (1968). Mental unity following surgical disconnection of the cerebral hemispheres. *The Harvey Lectures, Series 62.* New York: Academic Press.

Sperry, R. W. (1982). Some effects of disconnecting the cerebral hemispheres. *Science, 217,* 1223–1226.

Spiegel, D., & Cardeña, E. (1991). Disintegrated experience: The dissociate disorders revisited. *Psychological Bulletin, 100,* 366–378.

Spinweber, C. (1990). Insomnias and parasomnias in young adults. Paper presented at the annual meeting of the Western Psychological Association, Los Angeles, CA.

Spitz, R. A. (1946). Hospitalism: A follow-up report on investigation described in Volume I, 1945. *The Psychoanalytic Study of the Child, 2,* 113–117.

Spitzer, R. L. (1973). On pseudoscience in science, logic in remission, and psychiatric diagnosis: A critique of Rosenhan's "On being sane in insane places." *Journal of Abnormal Psychology, 84,* 442–452.

Spitzer, R. L., Gibbon, M., Skodol, A. E., Williams, J. B. W., & First, M. B. (1989). *DSM-III-R casebook.* Washington, DC: American Psychiatric Press.

Spitzer, R. L., Lilienfeld, S. O., & Miller, M. B. (2005). Rosenhan revisited: The scientific credibility of Lauren Slater's pseudopatient diagnosis study. *Journal of Nervous and Mental Disease, 193,* 734–739.

Sprang, G. (1999). Post-disaster stress following the Oklahoma City bombing: An examination of three community groups. *Journal of Interpersonal Violence, 14,* 169.

Sprecher, S., Barbee, A., & Schwartz, P. (1995). "Was it good for you, too?": Gender differences in first sexual intercourse experiences. *Journal of Sex Research, 32,* 3–15.

Sprecher, S., & McKinney, K. (1994). Sexuality in close relationships. In A. L. Weber & J. H. Harvey (Eds.), *Perspectives on close relationships* (pp. 193–216). Boston: Allyn & Bacon.

Springer, S. P., & Deutsch, G. (1993). *Left brain, right brain* (4th ed.). New York: W. H. Freeman.

Sprock, J., & Blashfield, R. K. (1991). Classification and nosology. In M. Hersen, A. E. Kazdin, & A. S. Bellack (Eds.), *The clinical psychology handbook* (2nd ed., pp. 329–344). New York: Pergamon Press.

Squier, L. H., & Domhoff, G. W. (1998). The presentation of dreaming and dreams in introductory psychology textbooks: A critical examination with suggestions for textbook authors and course instructors. *Dreaming: Journal of the Association for the Study of Dreams, 8,* 149–168.

Squire, L. R. (2007, April 6). Rapid consolidation. *Science, 316,* 57–58. [See also Balter, 2000; Beardsley, 1997; Bilkey, 2004; Fyhn et al., 2004; Haberlandt, 1999; Heyman, 2006; Kandel, 2001; Leutgeb et al., 2004; McGaugh, 2000; Travis, 2000a]

Squire, S. (1983). *The slender balance: Causes and cures for bulimia, anorexia, and the weight loss/weight gain seesaw.* New York: Putnam.

Srivastava, S., John, O. P., Gosling, S. D., Potter, J. (2003). Development of personality in early and middle adulthood: Set like plaster or persistent change? *Journal of Personality and Social Psychology, 84,* 1041–1053.

Stahl, S. A. (1999, Fall). Different strokes for different folks? A critique of learning styles. *American Educator, 23*(3), 27–31.

Staples, S. L. (1996). Human response to environmental noise: Psychological research and public policy. *American Psychologist, 51,* 143-150.

Stapley, J. C., & Haviland, J. M. (1989). Beyond depression: Gender differences in normal adolescents' emotional experiences. *Sex Roles, 20,* 295–308.

Stapp, J., Tucker, A. M., & VandenBos, G. R. (1985). Census of psychological personnel: 1983. *American Psychologist, 40,* 1317–1351.

Statistics Canada. (2002). *Family studies kit.* Retrieved on November 8, 2004, from www.statcan.ca/english/kits/Family/pdf/ch3_3e.pdf.

Stavish, S. (1994, Fall). Breathing room. *Stanford Medicine, 12*(1), 18–23.

Steele, C. M. (1997). A threat in the air: How stereotypes shape intellectual identity and performance. *American Psychologist, 52,* 613–629.

Steele, C. M., Spencer, S. J., & Aronson, J. (2002), Contending with group image: The psychology of stereotype and social identity threat. In Mark P. Zanna (Ed.), *Advances in experimental social psychology, Vol. 34* (pp. 379–440). San Diego, CA: Academic Press.

Steele, K. M., Bass, K. E., & Crook, M. D. (1999). The mystery of the Mozart effect: failure to replicate. *Psychological Science, 10,* 366–369.

Stein, M. B., Walker, J. R., & Forde, D. R. (1996). Public-speaking fears in a community sample: Prevalence, impact on functioning, and diagnostic classification. *Archives of General Psychiatry, 53,* 169–174.

Steinberg, L. D., & Silk, J. S. (2002). Parenting adolescents. In M. H. Bornstein (Ed.) *Handbook of parenting* (Vol. 1, pp. 103–134). Mahwah, NJ: Erlbaum.

Steketee, G., & Barlow, D. H. (2002). Obsessive compulsive disorder. In D. H. Barlow (Ed.), *Anxiety and its disorders* (2nd ed., pp. 516–550). New York: Guilford.

Stern, J. A., Brown, M., Ulett, G. A., & Sletten, I. (1977). A comparison of hypnosis, acupuncture, morphine, valium, aspirin, and placebo in the management of experimentally induced pain. *Annals of the New York Academy of Sciences, 296,* 175–193.

Sternberg, R. J. (1994). A triarchic model for teaching and assessing students in general psychology. *The General Psychologist, 30,* 42–48.

Sternberg, R. J. (1998). *Cupid's arrow: The course of love through time.* New York: Cambridge University Press.

Sternberg, R. J. (1999). The theory of successful intelligence. *Review of General Psychology, 3,* 292–316.

Sternberg, R. J. (2000). Implicit theories of intelligence as exemplar stories of success: Why intelligence test validity is in the eye of the beholder. *Psychology, Public Policy, and Law, 6,* 159–167.

Sternberg, R. J. (2001). What is the common thread of creativity? Its dialectical relation to intelligence and wisdom. *American Psychologist, 56,* 360–362.

Sternberg, R. J. (2003). It's time for prescription privileges. *Monitor on Psychology, 34*(6), 5.

Sternberg, R. J. (2004). Culture and intelligence. *American Psychologist, 59,* 325–338. [See also: Kleinfeld, 1994; Neisser et al., 1996; Rogoff, 1990; Segall et al., 1999; Serpell, 1994]

Sternberg, R. J., & Grigorenko, E. L. (1997). Are cognitive styles still in style? *American Psychologist, 52,* 700–712.

Sternberg, R. J., Grigorenko, E. L., & Kidd, K. K. (2005). Intelligence, race, and genetics. *American Psychologist, 60,* 46–59. [See also: Chorney et al., 1998; McClearn et al., 1997; Neisser et al., 1996; Petrill et al., 1998; Plomin, 1989; Scarr, 1998]

Sternberg, R. J., & Lubart, T. I. (1991). An investment theory of creativity and its development. *Human Development, 34,* 1–31.

Sternberg, R. J., & Lubart, T. I. (1992). Buy low and

sell high: An investment approach to creativity. *Current Directions in Psychological Science, 1,* 1–5.

Sternberg, R. J., Wagner, R. K., Williams, W. M., & Horvath, J. A. (1995). Testing common sense. *American Psychologist, 50,* 912–927.

Stevenson, H. W., Chen, C., & Lee, S. Y. (1993). Mathematics achievement of Chinese, Japanese, and American children: Ten years later. *Science, 259,* 53–58.

Stevenson, J., Graham, P., Fredman, G., & McLoughlin, V. A. (1987). Twin study of genetic influences on reading and spelling ability and disability. *Journal of Child Psychiatry, 28,* 229–247.

Stewart, V. M. (1973). Tests of the "carpentered world" hypothesis by race and environment in America and Zambia. *International Journal of Psychology, 8,* 83–94.

Stickgold, R., Hobson, J. A., Fosse, R., & Fosse, M. (2001). Sleep, learning, and dreams: Off-line memory processing. *Science, 294,* 1052–1057.

Stock, M. B., & Smythe, P. M. (1963). Does undernutrition during infancy inhibit brain growth and subsequent intellectual development? *Archives of Disorders in Childhood, 38,* 546–552.

Storms, M. D. (1980). Theories of sexual orientation. *Journal of Personality and Social Psychology, 38,* 783–792.

Storms, M. D. (1981). A theory of erotic orientation development. *Psychological Review, 88,* 340–353.

Strasburger, V. C. (1995). *Adolescents and the media.* Thousand Oaks, CA: Sage.

Strauss, E. (1998). Writing, speech separated in split brain. *Science, 280,* 827.

Strayer, D. L., Drews, F. A., & Johnston, W. A. (2003). Cell phone-induced failures of visual attention during simulated driving. *Journal of Experimental Psychology: Applied, 9,* 23–32.

Strickland, B. R. (1992). Women and depression. *Current Directions in Psychological Science, 1,* 132–135.

Strickland, B. R. (2000). Misassumptions, misadventures, and the misuse of psychology. *American Psychologist, 55,* 331–338.

Striegel-Moore, R. H., Silberstein, L. R., & Rodin, J. (1993). The social self in bulimia nervosa: Public self-consciousness, social anxiety, and perceived fraudulence. *Journal of Abnormal Psychology, 102,* 297–303.

Stromeyer, C. F., & Psotka, J. (1970). The detailed texture of eidetic images. *Nature, 225,* 346–349.

Stuart, R. B., & Lilienfeld, S. O. (2007). The evidence missing from evidence-based practice. *American Psychologist, 62,* 615–616.

Styron, W. (1990). *Darkness visible: A memoir of madness.* New York: Random House.

Suddath, R. L., Christison, G. W., Torrey, E. F., Casanova, M. F., & Weinberger, D. R. (1990). Anatomical abnormalities in the brains of nonpsychotic twins discordant for schizophrenia. *New England Journal of Medicine, 322,* 789–794.

Sue, S. (1991). Ethnicity and culture in psychological research and practice. In J. D. Goodchilds (Ed.), *Psychological perspectives on human diversity in America* (pp. 47–86). Washington, DC: American Psychological Association.

Sue, S., & Okazaki, S. (1990). Asian-American educational achievements: A phenomenon in search of an explanation. *American Psychologist, 45,* 913-920.

Sugarman, L. (2001). *Life-span development. Frameworks, accounts, and strategies* (2nd ed.). East Sussex, U.K.: Psychology Press.

Sulloway, F. J. (1992). *Freud, biologist of the mind: Beyond the psychoanalytic legend.* Cambridge, MA: Harvard University Press.

Sulloway, F. J. (1996). *Born to rebel: Birth order, family dynamics and creative lives.* New York: Pantheon Books.

Suls, J., & Marco, C. A. (1990). Relationship between JAS- and FTAS-Type A behavior and non-CHD illness: A prospective study controlling for negative affectivity. *Health Psychology, 9,* 479–492.

Suls, J., & Sanders, G. S. (1988). Type A behavior as

a general risk factor for physical disorder. *Journal of Behavioral Medicine, 11,* 201–226.

Swann, W. B., Jr., Hixon, J. G., & De La Ronde, C. (1992). Embracing the bitter "truth": Negative self-concepts and marital commitment. *Psychological Science, 3,* 118–121.

Swanson, J. M., Elliott, G. R., Greenhill, L. L., Wigal, T., et al. (2007a). Effects of stimulant medication on growth rates across 3 years in the MTA follow-up. *Journal of the American Academy of Child and Adolescent Psychiatry, 46,* 1015–1927.

Swanson, J. M., Hinshaw, S. P., Arnold, L. E., Gibbons, R. D., et al. (2007b). Secondary evaluations of MTA 36-month outcomes: Propensity score and growth mixture model analyses. *Journal of the American Academy of Child and Adolescent Psychiatry, 46,* 979–988.

Swartz, M., & Watkins, S. (2003). *Power failure: The inside story of the collapse of Enron.* New York: Doubleday.

Sweeney, P. D., Anderson, K., & Bailey, S. (1986). Attributional style in depression: A meta-analytic review. *Journal of Personality and Social Psychology, 50,* 974–991.

Swets, J. A., & Bjork, R. A. (1990). Enhancing human performance: An evaluation of "new age" techniques considered by the U.S. Army. *Psychological Science, 1,* 85–96.

Symond, M. B., Harris, A. W. F., Gordon, E., & Williams, L. M. (2005), "Gamma synchrony" in first-episode schizophrenia: A disorder of temporal connectivity? *American Journal of Psychiatry, 162,* 459–465.

Szasz, T. S. (1961). *The myth of mental illness.* New York: Harper & Row.

Szasz, T. S. (1977). *The manufacture of models.* New York: Dell.

Tafrate, R. C., Kassinove, H., & Dundin, L. (2002). Anger episodes in high and low trait anger community adults. *Journal of Clinical Psychology, 58*(12), 1573–1590.

Tait, R., & Silver, R. C. (1989). Coming to terms with major negative life events. In J. S. Uleman & J. A. Bargh (Eds.), *Unintended thought* (pp. 357–381). New York: Guilford Press.

Tamres, L., Janicke, D., & Helgeson, V. S. (2002). Sex diffferences in coping behavior: A meta-analytic review. *Personality and Social Psychology Review, 6,* 2–30.

Task Force on Promotion and Dissemination of Psychological Procedures. (1993). *A report adopted by the Division 12 Board—October 1993.* Washington, DC: American Psychological Association, Division 12.

Taubes, G. (1998, May 29). As obesity rates rise, experts struggle to explain why. *Science, 280,* 1367–1368.

Tavris, C. (1989). *Anger: The misunderstood emotion.* New York: Touchstone.

Tavris, C. (1991). The mismeasure of woman: Paradoxes and perspectives in the study of gender. In J. D. Goodchilds (Ed.), *Psychological perspectives on human diversity in America* (pp. 87–136). Washington, DC: American Psychological Association.

Tavris, C. (1995). From excessive rage to useful anger. *Contemporary Psychology, 40*(11), 1101–1102.

Tavris, C. (2000). *Psychobabble and biobunk: Using psychology to think critically about issues in the news.* Upper Saddle River, NJ: Prentice Hall.

Tavris, C., & Aronson, E. (2007). *Mistakes were made, but not by me.* Orlando, FL: Harcourt.

Taylor, D. M., Helms Tillery, S. I., & Schwartz, A. B. (2002, June 7). Direct cortical control of 3D neuroprosthetic devices. *Science, 296,* 1829–1832.

Taylor, S. E. (1983). Adjusting to threatening events: A theory of cognitive adaptation. *American Psychologist, 38,* 1161–1173.

Taylor, S. E. (1990). Health psychology: The science and the field. *American Psychologist, 45,* 40–50.

Taylor, S. E. (2003). *The tending instinct: Women, men, and the biology of relationships.* New York: Owl Books/Henry Holt.

Taylor, S. E. (2006). *Health psychology*. New York: McGraw-Hill.

Taylor, S. E., Kemeny, M. E., Reed, G. M., Bower, J. E., & Gruenewald, T. L. (2000a). Psychological resources, positive illusions, and health. *American Psychologist, 55*, 99–109.

Taylor, S. E., Klein, L., Lewis, B. P., Gruenewald, T. L., Gurung, R. A. R., & Updegraff, J. A. (2000b). Biobehavioral responses to stress in females: Tend-and-befriend, not fight-or-flight. *Psychological Review, 107*, 411–429.

Tedeschi, R. G., & Calhoun, L. G. (1996). The Post-traumatic Growth Inventory: Measuring the positive legacy of trauma. *Journal of Traumatic Stress, 9*, 455–471.

Teicher, M. H. (2002, March). Scars that won't heal: The neurobiology of child abuse. *Scientific American, 286*(3), 68–75.

Tellegen, A., Lykken, D. T., Bouchard, T. J., Wilcox, K. J., Segal, N. L., & Rich, S. (1988). Personality similarity in twins reared apart and together. *Journal of Personality and Social Psychology, 54*, 1031–1039.

Teller, D. Y. (1998). Spatial and temporal aspects of infant color vision. *Vision Research, 38*, 3275–3282.

Terman, L. M. (1916). *The measurement of intelligence*. Boston: Houghton Mifflin.

Terman, L., & Oden, M. H. (1959). *Genetic studies of genius: Vol. 4. The gifted group at midlife*. Stanford, CA: Stanford University Press.

Terrace, H. (1979, November). How Nim Chimpsky changed my mind. *Psychology Today*, 65–76.

Terrace, H. (1985). In the beginning was the "name." *American Psychologist, 40*, 1011–1028.

Terry, W. S. (2000). *Learning and memory: Basic principles, processes, and procedures*. Boston: Allyn & Bacon.

Tesser, A., & Brodie, M. (1971). A note on the evaluation of a "computer date." *Psychonomic Science, 23*, 300.

Thabet, A. A. M., Abed, Y., & Vostanis, P. (2004). Comorbidity of PTSD and depression among refugee children during war conflict. *Journal of Child Psychology and Psychiatry, 45*, 533–542. [See also: Horgan, 1996; Weissman et al., 1996]

Thase, M. E., Greenhouse, J. B., Reynolds F. E. III, Pilkonis, P. A., Hurley, K., et al. (1997). Treatment of major depression with psychotherapy or psychotherapy-pharmacotherapy combinations. *Archives of General Psychiatry, 54*, 1009–1015.

Thio, A. (1995). *Deviant behavior*. New York: Harper-Collins.

Thomas, F. F. (1991). *Impact on teaching: Research with culturally diverse populations*. Symposium conducted at the Western Psychological Association Convention, San Francisco.

Thompson, D. M. (1988). Context and false recognition. In G. M. Davies & D. M. Thompson (Eds.), *Memory in context: Context in memory* (pp. 285–304). New York: Wiley.

Thompson, J. K. (1986, April). Larger than life. *Psychology Today*, 38–44.

Thompson, R., Emmorey, K., & Gollan, T. H. (2005). "Tip of the fingers" experiences by deaf signers: Insights into the organization of a sign-based lexicon. *Psychological Science, 16*, 856–860.

Thompson, W. R., Schellenberg, E. G., & Husain, G. (2001). Arousal, mood, and the Mozart effect. *Psychological Science, 12*, 248–251.

Thorndyke, P. W., & Hayes-Roth, B. (1979). Spatial knowledge acquisition from maps and navigation. Paper presented at the Psychonomic Society Meeting, San Antonio, TX.

Thorpe, S. J., & Fabre-Thorpe, M. (2001, January 12). Seeking categories in the brain. *Science, 291*, 260–263.

Thorsteinsson, E. B., James, J. E., & Gregg, M. E. (1998). Effects of video-relayed social support on hemodynamic reactivity and salivary cortisol during laboratory-based behavioral challenge. *Health Psychology, 17*, 436–444.

Tienari, P., Sorri, A., Lahti, I., Naarala, M., Wahlberg, K.-E., Moring, J., Pohjola, J., & Wynne, L. C. (1987). Genetic and psychosocial factors in schizophrenia: The Finnish adoptive family study. *Schizophrenia Bulletin, 13*, 476–483.

Tirozzi, G. N., & Uro, G. (1997). Education reform in the United States: National policy in support of local efforts for school improvement. *American Psychologist, 52*, 241–249. [See also: Zigler & Muenchow, 1992; Zigler & Styfco, 1994]

Todes, D. P. (1997). From the machine to the ghost within: Pavlov's transition from digestive physiology to conditional reflexes. *American Psychologist, 52*, 947–955.

Tolin, D. F., & Foa, E. B. (2006). Sex Differences in Trauma and Post-Traumatic Stress Disorder: A quantitative Review of 25 Years of Research. *Psychological Bulletin, 132*, 959–992.

Tolman, E. C. (1932). *Purposive behavior in animals and men*. New York: Appleton.

Tolman, E. C. (1948). Cognitive maps in rats and men. *Psychological Review, 55*, 189–208.

Tolman, E. C., & Honzik, C. H. (1930). "Insight" in rats. *University of California Publications in Psychology, 4*, 215–232.

Tolman, E. C., Ritchie, B. G., & Kalish, D. (1946). Studies in spatial learning: I. Orientation and the short-cut. *Journal of Experimental Psychology, 36*, 13–24.

Tomasello, M. (2000). Culture and cognitive development. *Current Directions in Psychological Science, 9*, 37–40.

Toneatto, T., & Nguyen, L. (2007). Does mindfulness meditation improve anxiety and mood symptoms? A review of the controlled research. *The Canadian Journal of Psychiatry, 52*, 260–266.

Tononi, G., & Edelman, G. M. (1998, December 4). Consciousness and complexity. *Science, 282*, 1846–1850.

Torabi, M. R., & Seo, D. C. (2004). National study of behavioral and life changes since September 11. *Health Education Behavior, 31*, 179–192.

Torrey, E. F. (1996). *Out of the shadows: Confronting America's mental illness crisis*. New York: Wiley.

Torrey, E. F. (1997). The release of the mentally ill from institutions: A well-intentioned disaster. *The Chronicle of Higher Education*, B4–B5.

Totterdell, P. (2000). Catching moods and hitting runs: Mood linkage and subjective performance in professional sport. *Journal of Applied Psychology, 85*, 848–859.

Totterdell, P., Kellett, S., Briner, R. B., & Teuchmann, K. (1998). Evidence of mood linkage in work groups. *Journal of Personality and Social Psychology, 74*, 1504–1515.

Tracy, J. L., & Robins, R. W. (2004) Show your pride: Evidence for a discrete emotion expression. *Psychological Science 15*, 194–197.

Trainor, L. J. (2005). Are there critical periods for musical development? *Developmental Psychobiology, 46*, 262–278.

Travis, J. (2000a, October 14). Pioneers of brain-cell signaling earn Nobel. *Science News, 158*, 247.

Travis, J. (2000b, September 23). Snap, crackle, and feel good? Magnetic fields that map the brain may also treat its disorders. *Science News, 158*, 204–206.

Travis, J. (2004, January 17). Fear not. *Science News, 165*, 42–44.

Treffert, D. A., & Wallace, G. L. (2002, June). Islands of genius. *Scientific American*, 76–85.

Triandis, H. (1989). The self and social behavior in differing cultural contexts. *Psychological Review, 96*, 506–520.

Triandis, H. (1990). Cross-cultural studies of individualism and collectivism. In J. Berman (Ed.), *Nebraska Symposium on Motivation, 1989* (pp. 42–133). Lincoln: University of Nebraska Press.

Triandis, H. C. (1994). *Culture and social behavior*. New York: McGraw-Hill.

Triandis, H. C. (1995). *Individualism & collectivism*. Boulder, CO: Westview Press. [See also: Triandis, 1989, 1990, 1994; Triandis & Gelfand, 1998]

Triandis, H. C. (1996). The psychological measurement of cultural syndromes. *American Psychologist, 51*, 407–415.

Triandis, H. C., & Gelfand, M. J. (1998). Converging measurement of horizontal and vertical individualism and collectivism. *Journal of Personality and Social Psychology, 74*, 118–128.

Tronick, E., Als, H., & Brazelton, T. B. (1980). Moradic phases: A structural description analysis of infant-mother face to face interaction. *Merrill-Palmer Quarterly, 26*, 3–24.

Trope, I., Rozin, P., Nelson, D. K., & Gur, R. C. (1992). Information processing in separated hemispheres of the callosotomy patients: Does the analytic-holistic dichotomy hold? *Brain and Cognition, 19*, 123–147.

Tse, D., Langston, R. F., Kakeyama, M., Bethus, I., Spooner, P. A., Wood, E. R., Witter, M. P., & Morris, R. G. M. (2007, April 6). Schemas and memory consolidation. *Science, 316*, 76–82.

Tsai, M., & Uemura, A. (1988). Asian Americans: The struggles, the conflicts, and the successes. In P. Bronstein & K. Quina (Eds.), *Teaching a psychology of people: Resources for gender and sociocultural awareness*. Washington, DC: American Psychological Association.

Tsao, D. (2006, October 6). A dedicated system for processing faces. *Science, 314*, 72–73. [See also: Downing et al., 2001; Holden, 1997; Tsao et al., 2006; Turk et al., 2002)

Tsao, D. Y., Freiwald, W. A., Tootell, R. B. H., & Livingstone, M. S. (2006, February 3). A cortical region consisting entirely of face-selective cells. *Science, 311*, 670–674.

Tsuang, M. T., & Faraone, S. V. (1990). *The genetics of mood disorders*. Baltimore, MD: Johns Hopkins University Press.

Tulving, E. (1983). *Elements of episodic memory*. Oxford, U.K.: Clarendon Press.

Turin, L. (2006). *The secret of scent: Adventures in perfume and the science of smell*. New York: Ecco. [See also: Mombaerts, 1999]

Turk, D. C. (1994). Perspectives on chronic pain: The role of psychological factors. *Current Directions in Psychological Science, 3*, 45–48.

Turk, D. J., Heatherton, T. F., Kelly, W. M., Funnell, M. G., Gazzaniga, M. S., & Macrae, C. N. (2002, September 1). Mike or me? Self-recognition in a split-brain patient. *Nature Neuroscience, 5*, 841–842.

Turkheimer, E., Haley, A., Waldron, M., D'Onofrio, B., & Gottesman, I. I. (2003). Socioeconomic status modifies heritability of IQ in young children. *Psychological Science, 14*, 623–628.

Turkington, C. (1992, February). Depression? It's in the eye of the beholder. *APA Monitor*, 14–15.

Turkington, C. (1993, January). New definition of retardation includes the need for support. *APA Monitor*, 26–27.

Turner, E. H., Matthews, A. M., Linardatos, E., Tell, R. A., & Rosenthal, R. (2008, January 17). Selective publication of antidepressant trials and its influence on apparent efficacy. *New England Journal of Medicine, 358*, 252–260.

Turner, J. C., & Oakes, P. J. (1989). Self-categorization theory and social influence. In P. B. Paulus (Ed.), *Psychology of group influence* (2nd ed.). Hillsdale, NJ: Erlbaum.

Turner, S. G. (2001). Resilience and social work practice: Three case studies. *Families in Society, 82*, 441–448.

Turvey, M. T. (1996). Dynamic touch. *American Psychologist, 51*, 1134–1152.

Tversky, A., & Kahneman, D. (1973). Availability: A heuristic for judging frequency and probability. *Cognitive Psychology, 5*, 207–232.

Tversky, A., & Kahneman, D. (1974). Judgment under uncertainty: Heuristics and biases. *Science, 185*, 1124–1131.

Twin Oaks Intentional Community Homepage. (2007). Retrieved June 19, 2007, from www.twinoaks.org/index.html

Tyler, L. (1988). Mental testing. In E. R. Hilgard (Ed.),

Fifty years of psychology (pp. 127–138). Glenview, IL: Scott, Foresman.

Ulrich, R. E., & Azrin, N. H. (1962). Reflexive fighting in response to aversive stimulation. *Journal of the Experimental Analysis of Behavior, 5,* 511–520.

U.S. Bureau of the Census. (1997). *Statistical abstracts of the United States: 1997.* Washington, DC: U.S. Government Printing Office.

U.S. Bureau of the Census. (2002). *Statistical abstract of the United States* (122nd ed.). Washington, DC: U.S. Government Printing Office.

U.S. Bureau of the Census. (2008). *Facts for features, Mother's Day: May 11, 2008.* Retrieved July 23, 2008, from www.census.gov/Press-Release/www/releases/archives/facts_for_features_special_edition/011633.html.

U.S. Department of Health and Human Services. (2000). *Reducing tobacco use: A report of the Surgeon General.* Atlanta, GA: U.S. Department of Health and Human Services.

U.S. Department of Health and Human Services. (2002). *Hospitalization in the United States, 2002.* Retrieved February 20, 2008, from http://ahrq.gov/data/hcup/factbk6/factbk6b.htm#common.

U.S. Department of Health and Human Services. (2005). *Surgeon General's advisory on alcohol use in pregnancy.* Retrieved July 23, 2008, from www.surgeongeneral.gov/pressreleases/sg02222005.html.

U.S. Department of Justice. (1999). *Eyewitness Evidence: A Guide for Law Enforcement.* Retrieved July 14, 2007, from www.ncjrs.gov/pdffiles1/nij/178240.pdf.

U.S. Merit Systems Protection Board. (1995). *Sexual harassment in the federal workplace: Trends, progress, continuing challenges.* Washington, DC: U.S. Government Printing Office.

U.S. Senate Select Committee on Intelligence. (2004). *Report on the U.S. Intelligence Community's Prewar Intelligence Assessments on Iraq: Conclusions.* Retrieved on November 23, 2004, from http://intelligence.senate.gov/conclusions.pdf.

University of Michigan News Service. (2006, December 21). Teen drug use continues down in 2006, particularly among older teens; but use of prescription-type drugs remains high. [Press release] Retrieved December 10, 2007, from http://monitoringthefuture.org/pressreleases/06drugpr_complete.pdf.

USA Today. (1996, December). College freedom can trigger illness. *125*(1), 7.

Valenstein, E. S. (1973). *Brain control.* New York: John Wiley & Sons.

Valenstein, E. S. (Ed.). (1980). *The psychosurgery debate.* New York: Freeman.

Valenstein, E. S. (1998). *Blaming the brain: The truth about drugs and mental health.* New York: The Free Press.

Vallee, B. L. (1998, June). Alcohol in the Western world. *Scientific American, 278*(6), 80–85.

van Dam, L. (1996, October 1). Mindful healing: An interview with Herbert Benson. *Technology Review, 99*(7), 31–38. [See also: Bjork, 1991; Shapiro, 1985]

Van de Castle, R. L. (1983). Animal figures in fantasy and dreams. In A. Katcher & A. Beck (Eds.), *New perspectives on our lives with companion animals.* Philadelphia: University of Pennsylvania Press.

Van de Castle, R. L. (1994). *Our dreaming mind.* New York: Ballantine Books.

VandenBos, G. R. (1986). Psychotherapy research: A special issue. *American Psychologist, 41,* 111–112.

Van Dongen, H. P. A., Maislin, G., Mullington, J. M., & Dinges, D. F. (2003). The cumulative cost of additional wakefulness: Dose-response effects on neurobehavioral functions and sleep physiology from chronic sleep restriction and total sleep deprivation. *Journal of Sleep, 26,* 117–126.

Verbaten, M. N. (2003). Specific memory deficits in ecstasy users? The results of a meta-analysis. *Human Psychopharmacology: Clinical and Experimental, 18,* 281–290.

Vernon, P. E. (1969). *Intelligence and cultural environment.* London: Methuen.

Vernon, P. E. (1987). The demise of the Stanford-Binet Scale. *Canadian Psychology, 28,* 251–258.

Viken, R. J., & McFall, R. M. (1994). Paradox lost: Implications of contemporary reinforcement theory for behavior therapy. *Current Directions in Psychological Science, 3,* 121–125.

Vincent, K. R. (1991). Black/white IQ differences: Does age make a difference? *Journal of Clinical Psychology, 47,* 266–270.

Vincent, M., & Pickering, M. R. (1988). Multiple personality disorder in childhood. *Canadian Journal of Psychiatry, 33,* 524–529.

Viney, W. (2006, Fall). William James: "What Is Emotion?" *The General Psychologist, 41*(2), 36–37. [Electronic version available at www.apa.org/divisions/div1/newspub.html.]

Vingerhoets, G., Berckmoes, C., & Stroobant, N. (2003). Cerebral hemodynamics during discrimination of prosodic and semantic emotion in speech studied by transcranial doppler ultrasonography. *Neuropsychology, 17,* 93–99.

Vitaliano, P. P., Russo, J., Young, H. M., Becker, J., & Maiuro, R. D. (1991). The screen for caregiver burden. The Gerontologist, 31, 76–83.

Vogel, G. (1996, November 22). Illusion reveals pain locus in brain. *Science, 274,* 1301.

Vogel, G. (1997, February 28). Scientists probe feelings behind decision-making. *Science, 275,* 1269.

Vogel, G. (2003, August 8). Depression drugs' powers may rest on new neurons. *Science, 301,* 757.

Vokey, J. R. (2002). Subliminal messages. In John R. Vokey and Scott W. Allen (Eds.), *Psychological Sketches* (6th ed., pp. 223-246). Lethbridge, Alberta: Psyence Ink. Retrieved November 27, 2007, from http://people.uleth.ca/~vokey/pdf/Submess.pdf.

Volpe, K. (2004). Taylor takes on "fight-or-flight." *Psychological Science, 17,* 391.

Volz, J. (2000, February). In search of the good life. Monitor on Psychology, 31(2), 68–69.

Von Fritsch, K. (1974). Decoding the language of the bee. *Science, 185,* 663–668.

von Hofsten, C., & Lindhagen, K. (1979). Observations on the development of reaching for moving objects. *Journal of Child Psychology, 28,* 158–173.

Wade, T. J. (1991). Race and sex differences in adolescent self-perceptions of physical attractiveness and level of self-esteem during early and late adolescence. *Journal of Personality and Individual Differences, 12,* 1319–1324.

Wagar, B. M., & Thagard, P. (2006). Spiking Phineas Gage: A neurocomputational theory of cognitive-affective integration in decision making. *Psychological Review, 111,* 67–79.

Wager, T. D. (2005). The neural bases of placebo effects in pain. *Current Directions in Psychological Science, 14,* 175–179.

Wager, T. D., Rilling, J. K., Smith, E. E., Sokolik, A., Casey, K. L., Davidson, R. J., Kosslyn, S. M., Rose, R. M., & Cohen, J. D. (2004, February 20). Placebo-induced changes in fMRI in the anticipation and experience of pain. *Science, 303,* 1162–1167.

Wagner, U., Gais, S., Haider, H., Verleger, R., & Born, J. (2004, January 22). Sleep spires insight. *Nature, 427,* 352–355.

Walden, J., Normann, C., Langosch, J., Berger, M., & Grunze, H. (1998). Differential treatment of bipolar disorder with old and new antiepileptic drugs. *Neuropsychobiology, 38,* 181–184.

Walker, E. F., & Diforio, D. (1997). Schizophrenia: A neural diathesis-stress model. *Psychological Review, 104,* 667–685.

Walker, L. J. (1989). A longitudinal study of moral reasoning. *Child Development, 60,* 157–166.

Walker, L. J. (1991). Sex differences in moral reasoning. In W. M. Kurtines & J. L. Gewirtz (Eds.), *Handbook of moral behavior and development: Research* (Vol. 2, pp. 333–364). Hillsdale, NJ: Erlbaum.

Walker, L. J., & de Vries, B. (1985). Moral stages/moral orientations: Do the sexes really differ? Paper presented at the annual meeting of the American Psychological Association, Los Angeles.

Walker, L. J., de Vries, B., & Trevethan, S. D. (1987).

Moral stages and moral orientations in real-life and hypothetical dilemmas. *Child Development, 58,* 842–858.

Wallace, A. F. C. (1959). Cultural determinants of response to hallucinatory experience. *Archives of General Psychiatry, 1,* 58–69.

Wallace, B., & Fisher, L. E. (1999). *Consciousness and behavior.* Boston: Allyn & Bacon.

Wallbott, H. G., Ricci-Bitti, P., & Banniger-Huber, E. (1986). Non-verbal reactions to emotional experiences. In K. R. Scherer, H. G. Wallbott, & A. B. Summerfield (Eds.), Experiencing emotion: A cross-cultural study (pp. 98–116). *European monographs in social psychology.* New York: Cambridge University Press.

Wallis, C. (1984, June 11). Unlocking pain's secrets. *Time,* 58–66.

Walsh, R. (1984). Asian psychologies. In R. Corsini (Ed.), *Encyclopedia of psychology* (pp. 90–94). New York: Wiley.

Walster (Hatfield), E., Aronson, V., Abrahams, D., & Rottman, L. (1966). Importance of physical attractiveness in dating behavior. *Journal of Personality and Social Psychology, 5,* 508–516.

Walters, E. E., Neale, M. C., Eaves, L. J., Heath, A. C., Kessler, R. C., & Kendler, K. S. (1992). Bulimia nervosa and major depression: A study of common genetic and environmental factors. *Psychological Medicine, 22*(3), 617–622.

Wampold, B. E. (2007). The humanistic (and effective) treatment. *American Psychologist, 62,* 857–873. [See also: Barker et al., 1988; Jones et al., 1988]

Wampold, B. E., & Brown, G. S. (2005). Estimating variability in outcomes attributable to therapists: A naturalistic study of outcomes in managed care. *Journal of Consulting and Clinical Psychology, 73,* 914–923. [See also: Blatt et al., 1996; Krupnick et al., 1996]

Wampold, B. E., Goodheart, C. D., & Levant, R. F. (2007). Clarification and elaboration on evidence-based practice in psychology. *American Psychologist, 62,* 616–618.

Wardle, J., Steptoe, A., Bellisle, F., Davou, B., Reschke, K., & Lappalainen, M. (1997). Healthy dietary practices among European students. *Health Psychology, 16,* 443–450.

Warren, J. (2007). *The head trip.* New York: Random House.

Wassermann, E. M., & Lisanby, S. H. (2001). Therapeutic application of repetitive transcranial magnetic stimulation: A review. *Clinical Neurophysiology, 112,* 1367–377.

Watkins, L. R., & Maier, S. F. (2003). When good pain turns bad. *Current Directions in Psychological Science, 12,* 232–236.

Watkins, L. R., & Mayer, D. J. (1982). Organization of the endogenous opiate and nonopiate pain control systems. *Science, 216,* 1185–1193.

Watson, J. B., & Rayner, R. (2000). Conditioned emotional reactions. *American Psychologist, 55,* 313–317. (Original work published by J. B. Watson and R. Rayner, 1920, *Journal of Experimental Psychology, 3,* 1–14.)

Watson, J. D. (1968). *The double helix.* New York: The New American Library (Signet).

Watson, K. K., Matthews, B. J., & Allman, J. M. (2007, February). Brain activation during sight gags and language-dependent humor. *Cerebral Cortex, 17,* 314-324. [See also: Johnson, 2002; Mobbs et al., 2006; Moran et al., 2004]

Weber, A. L., & Harvey, J. H. (1994a). Accounts in coping with relationship loss. In A. L. Weber & J. H. Harvey (Eds.), *Perspectives on close relationships* (pp. 285–306). Boston, MA: Allyn & Bacon.

Weber, A. L., & Harvey, J. H. (Eds.). (1994b). *Perspectives on close relationships.* Boston, MA: Allyn & Bacon.

Wegner, D. M. (1989). *White bears and other unwanted thoughts.* New York: Guilford.

Wegner, D. M., Schneider, D. J., Carter, S. III, & White, T. (1987). Paradoxical effects of thought suppression. *Journal of Personality and Social Psychology, 53,* 5–13.

Wegner, D. M., Wenzlaff, R. M., & Kozak, M. (2004). Dream rebound: The return of suppressed thoughts in dreams. *Psychological Science, 15,* 232–236.

Wehr, T. A., & Rosenthal, N. E. (1989). Seasonality and affective illness. *American Journal of Psychiatry, 146,* 829–839.

Weil, A. (1998). *Eight weeks to optimum health.* New York: Ballantine.

Weil, A. T. (1977). The marriage of the sun and the moon. In N. E. Zinberg (Ed.), *Alternate states of consciousness* (pp. 37–52). New York: Free Press.

Weinberger, M., Hiner, S. L, & Tierney, W. M. (1987). In support of hassles as a measure of stress in predicting health outcomes. *Journal of Behavioral Medicine, 10,* 19–31.

Weiner, J. (1994). *The beak of the finch.* New York: Vintage Books.

Weingardt, K. R., Loftus, E. F., & Lindsay, D. S. (1995). Misinformation revisited: New evidence on the suggestibility of memory. *Memory and Cognition, 23,* 72–82.

Weisberg, R. (1986). *Creativity, genius, and other myths.* New York: Freeman.

Weiss, R. (2007, November 11). Study debunks theory on teen sex, delinquency. *Washington Post.* Retrieved December 15, 2007, from www.washingtonpost.com/wp-dyn/content/article/2007/11/10/AR2007111001271_pf.html.

Weissman, M. M., Bland, R. C., Canino, G. J., Faravelli, C., Greenwald, S., Hwu, H. G., Joyce, P. R., Karam, E. G., Lee, C. K., Lellouch, J., Lepine, J. P., Newman, S. C., Rubio-Stipec, M., Wells, J. E., Wickramaratne, P. J., Wittchen, H., & Yeh, E. K. (1996, July 24–31). Cross-national epidemiology of major depression and bipolar disorder. *Journal of the American Medical Association, 276,* 293–299.

Weissman, M. M., Merikangas, K. R., Wickramaratne, P., Kidd, K. K., Prusoff, B. A., Leckman, J. F., & Pauls, D. L. (1986). Understanding the clinical heterogeneity of major depression using family data. *Archives of General Psychiatry, 43,* 430–434.

Weissman, M. M., Neria, Y., Das, A., Feder, A., Blanco, C., Lantigua, R., et al. (2005). Gender differences in posttraumatic stress disorder among primary care patients after the World Trade Center attack of September 11, 2001. *Gender Medicine, 2,* 76–87.

Weisz, J, R., Rothbaum, F. M., & Blackburn, T. C. (1984). Standing out and standing in: The psychology of control in America and Japan. *American Psychologist, 39,* 955–969.

Wellman, H. M., & Estes, D. (1986). Early understanding of mental entities: A reexamination of childhood realism. *Child Development, 57,* 910–923.

Wells, B. E., & Twenge, J. M. (2005). Changes in young people's sexual behavior and attitudes, 1943-1999: A cross-temporal meta-analysis. *Review of General Psychology, 9,* 249–261.

Welsh, E. J., Gullotta, C., & Rapoport, J. (1993). Classroom academic performance: Improvement with both methylphenidate and dextroamphetamine in ADHD boys. *Journal of Child Psychology and Psychiatry and Allied Disciplines, 34,* 785–804.

Werblin, F., & Roska, B. (2007, April). Movies in our eyes. *Scientific American, 296*(4), 73–79.

Wertheimer, M. (1923). *Untersuchungen zur Lehre von der Gestalt, II. Psychologische Forschung, 4,* 301–350.

Wesson, D. R., Smith, D. E., & Seymour, R. B. (1992). Sedative-hypnotics and tricyclics. In J. H. Lowinson, P. Ruiz, R. B. Millman, & J. G. Langrod (Eds.), *Substance abuse: A comprehensive textbook* (2nd ed., pp. 271–279). Baltimore: Williams & Wilkins.

Westen, D. (1998). The scientific legacy of Sigmund Freud: Toward a psychodynamically informed psychological science. *Psychological Bulletin, 124,* 333–371.

Westen, D., Blagov, P. S., Harenski, K. Kilts, C., & Hamann, S. (2006). Neural bases of motivated reasoning: An fMRI study of emotional constraints on partisan political judgment in the 2004 U.S. presidential election. *Journal of Cognitive Neuroscience, 18,* 1947–1958.

Westen, D., & Bradley, R. (2005). Empirically supported complexity: Rethinking evidence-based practice in psychotherapy. *Current Directions in Psychological Science, 14,* 266–271.

Westen, D., Novotny, C. M., & Thompson-Brenner, H. (2005). EBP ≠ EST: Reply to Crits-Christoph et al. (2005) and Weisz et al. (2005). *Psychological Bulletin, 131,* 427–433.

Whalen, P. J. (1998). Fear, vigilance, and ambiguity: Initial neuroimaging studies of the human amygdala. *Current Directions in Psychological Science, 7,* 177–188.

What we learn from twins. The mirror of your soul. (1998, January 3). *The Economist.* Retrieved November 8, 2004, from http://search.epnet.com/direct.asp?an=35349&db=aph

Wheeler, D. L. (1999, January 22). Prospect of fetal-gene therapy stimulates high hopes and deep fears. *The Chronicle of Higher Education,* A13.

Wheeler, D. L., Jacobson, J. W., Paglieri, R. A., & Schwartz, A. A. (1993). An experimental assessment of facilitated communication. *Mental Retardation, 31,* 49–60.

Wheeler, J. G., Christensen, A., & Jacobson, N. S. (2001). Couple distress. In Barlow, D. H. (Ed.) *Clinical handbook of psychological disorders: A step-by-step treatment manual* (3rd ed., pp. 609–630). New York: Guilford.

Wheeler, M. E., Petersen, S. E., & Buckner, R. L. (2000). Memory's echo: Vivid re membering reactivates sensory-specific cortex. *Proceedings of the National Academy of Sciences, 97,* 11125–11129.

Whiteman, M. C., & Fowkes, F. G. R. (1997, August 16). Hostility and the heart. *British Medical Journal, 7105,* 379–380.

Whitley, B. E., Jr. (1999). Right-wing authoritarianism, social dominance orientation, and prejudice. *Journal of Personality and Social Psychology, 7,* 126–134.

Who wants to be a genius? (2001, January 13). *The Economist, 358*(8204), 77–78.

Whyte, W. F. (1972, April). Skinnerian theory in organizations. *Psychology Today,* 67–68, 96, 98, 100.

Wickelgren, I. (1997, June 27). Marijuana: Harder than thought? *Science, 276,* 1967–1968.

Wickelgren, I. (1998a, August 28). A new route to treating schizophrenia? *Science, 281,* 1264–1265.

Wickelgren, I. (1998b, May 29). Obesity: How big a problem? *Science, 280,* 1364–1367.

Wickelgren, I. (1998c, June 26). Teaching the brain to take drugs. *Science, 280,* 2045–2047.

Wickelgren, I. (1999, March 19). Nurture helps mold able minds. *Science, 283,* 1832–1834.

Wickelgren, I. (2001, March 2). Working memory helps the mind focus. *Science, 291,* 1684–1685.

Wickelgren, I. (2003, January 24). Tapping the mind. *Science, 299,* 496–499.

Wickelgren, I. (2006, May 26). A vision for the blind. *Science, 312,* 1124–1126. [See also Leutwyler, 1994; Service, 1999]

Wickelgren, W. (1974). *How to solve problems: Elements of a theory of problems and problem solving.* San Francisco: W. H. Freeman.

Wiggins, J. S. (1973). *Personality and prediction: Principles of personality assessment.* Reading, MA: Addison-Wesley.

Wilensky, A. E., Schafe, G. E., Kristensen, M. P., & LeDoux, J. E. (2006). Rethinking the fear circuit: The central nucleus of the amygdala is required for the acquisition, consolidation, and expression of Pavlovian fear conditioning. *Journal of Neuroscience, 26,* 12,387–12,396. [See also: Paré et al., 2004]

Willford, J. A. (2006). Moderate prenatal alcohol exposure and cognitive status of children at Age 10. *Alcoholism: Clinical and Experimental Research 30,* 1051–1059.

Wills, T. A. (1991). Similarity and self-esteem in downward comparisons. In J. Suls & T. A. Wills (Eds.), *Social Comparison: Contemporary Theory and Research* (pp. 51–78). Hillsdale, NJ: Erlbaum.

Wills, T. A., & DePaulo, B. M. (1991). Interpersonal analysis of the help-seeking process. In C. R. Snyder & D. R. Forsyth (Eds.), *Handbook of social and clinical psychology: The health perspective* (pp. 350–375). New York: Pergamon Press.

Wilner, D., Walkley, R., & Cook, S. (1955). *Human relations in interracial housing.* Minneapolis: University of Minnesota Press.

Wilson, E. D., Reeves, A., & Culver, C. (1977). Cerebral commissurotomy for control of intractable seizures. *Neurology, 27,* 708–715.

Wilson, E. O. (1998). *Consilience: The Unity of Knowledge.* New York: Alfred A. Knopf.

Wilson, E. O. (2004). *On Human Nature (25th Anniversary Edition).* Cambridge, MA: Harvard University Press.

Wilson, R. I., & Nicoll, R. A. (2002, April 26). Endocannabinoid signaling in the brain. *Science, 296,* 678–682.

Wilson, S. M., & Medora, N. P. (1990). Gender comparisons of college students' attitudes toward sexual behavior. *Adolescence, 25,* 615–627.

Wilson, T. D. (2002). *Strangers to ourselves: Discovering the adaptive unconscious.* Cambridge, MA: Belknap Press/Harvard University Press.

Windholz, G. (1997). Ivan P. Pavlov: An overview of his life and psychological work. *American Psychologist, 52,* 941–946.

Winerman, L. (2005a, September). The culture of memory. *Monitor on Psychology, 36*(8), 56–57.

Winerman, L. (2005b, July/August). Fighting phobias: Figuring out phobia. *Monitor on Psychology; 36*(7), 96–98.

Winerman, L. (2005c, June). Intelligence, sugar and the car-lot hustle headline WPA meeting. *Monitor on Psychology, 36*(3), 38–39.

Winerman, L. (2005d, March). "Thin slices" of life. *Monitor on Psychology, 36*(3), 54–56.

Winerman, L. (2005e, July/August). A virtual cure. *Monitor on Psychology, 36*(7), 87–89. [See also: Hoffman, 2004; Rothbaum & Hodges, 1999; Rothbaum et al., 2000]

Winerman, L. (2005f, March). What we know without knowing. *Monitor on Psychology, 36*(3), 50–52.

Winerman, L. (2006a, June). The anatomy of funny. *Monitor on Psychology, 37*(6), 66-67.

Winerman, L. (2006b, January). Brain, heal thyself. *Monitor on Psychology, 37*(1), 56–57.

Winerman, L. (2006c, April). Bringing recovery home: Telehealth initiatives offer support and rehabilitation services in remote locations. *Monitor on Psychology, 37*(4), 32–34.

Winerman, L. (2006d, February). The culture-cognition connection. *Monitor on Psychology, 37*(2), 64–65.

Winerman, L. (2006e). A laughing matter. *Monitor on Psychology, 37*(6), 58–59. [See also: Panksepp, 2000]

Winner, E. (2000). The origins and ends of giftedness. *American Psychologist, 55,* 159–169.

Winograd, E., & Neisser, U. (Eds.). (1992). *Affect and accuracy in recall: Studies of "flashbulb" memories.* New York: Cambridge University Press.

Winson, J. (1990, November). The meaning of dreams. *Scientific American, 263,* 86–96.

Winter, D. G., John, O. P., Stewart, A. J., & Klohnen, E. C. (1998). Traits and motives: Toward an integration of two traditions in personality research. *Psychological Review, 105,* 230–250.

Winters, J. (2002, January). Hey birder, this phone's for you. *Discover,* 75.

Wirth, S., Yanike, M., Frank, L. M., Smith, A. C., Brown, E. N., & Suzuki, W. A. (2003, June 6). Single neurons in the monkey hippocampus and learning of new associations. *Science, 300,* 1578–1581.

Wixted, J. T. (2005). A theory about why we forget what we once knew. *Current Directions in Psychological Science, 14,* 6–9. [See also: McClelland et al., 1995]

Wolfson, A. (2005, October 19). A hoax most cruel. *The Courier-Journal* (Louisville, Kentucky).

Wolpe, J. (1958). *Psychotherapy by reciprocal inhibition*. Stanford, CA: Stanford University Press.

Wolpe, J. (1973). *The practice of behavior therapy* (2nd ed.). New York: Pergamon.

Wolpe, J. (1985). Existential problems and behavior therapy. *The Behavior Therapist, 8,* 126–127.

Wolpe, J., & Plaud, J. J. (1997). Pavlov's contributions to behavior therapy: The obvious and the not so obvious. *American Psychologist, 52,* 966–972.

Wolraich, M. L., Wilson, D. B., & White, J. W. (1995, November 22/29). The effect of sugar on behavior or cognition in children: A meta-analysis. *Journal of the American Medical Association, 274,* 1617–1621.

Wong, M. M., & Csikszentmihalyi, M. (1991). Motivation and academic achievement: The effects of personality traits and the quality of experience. *Journal of Personality, 59,* 539–574.

Wood, J. M., Bootzin, R. R., Rosenhan, D., & Nolen-Hoeksema, S. (1992). Effects of the 1989 San Francisco earthquake on frequency and content of nightmares. *Journal of Abnormal Psychology, 101,* 219–224.

Wood, J. M., Nezworski, M. T., & Stejskal, W. J. (1996). The comprehensive system for the Rorschach: A critical examination. *Psychological Science, 7,* 3–10.

Wood, J. V., Saltzberg, J. A., & Goldsamt, L. A. (1990a). Does affect induce self-focused attention? *Journal of Personality and Social Psychology, 58,* 899–908.

Wood, J. V., Saltzberg, J. A., Neale, J. M., Stone, A. A., & Rachmiel, T. B. (1990b). Self-focused attention, coping responses, and distressed mood in everyday life. *Journal of Personality and Social Psychology, 58,* 1027–1036.

Woods, S. C., Seeley, R. J., Porte, D. Jr., & Schwartz, M. W. (1998, May 29). Signals that regulate food intake and energy homeostasis. *Science, 280,* 1378–1383.

Woodworth, R. S. (1918). *Dynamic psychology.* New York: Columbia University Press.

Woody, E., & Sadler, P. (1998). On reintegrating dissociated theories: Comment on Kirsch and Lynn (1998). *Psychological Bulletin, 123*(2), 192–197.

World Health Organization. (1973). *Report of the International Pilot Study of Schizophrenia (Vol. 1).* Geneva, Switzerland: Author.

World Health Organization. (1979). *Schizophrenia: An international follow-up study.* New York: Wiley.

Wright, E. R., Gronfein, W. P., & Owens, T. J. (2000). Deinstitutionalization, social rejection, and self-esteem of former mental patients. *Journal of Health and Social Behavior, 41,* 68–90.

Wright, K., & Mahurin, M. (1997, October). Babies, bonds, and brains. *Discover,* 74–78.

Wright, L. (1988). The Type A behavior pattern and coronary artery disease: Quest for the active ingredients and the elusive mechanism. *American Psychologist, 43,* 2–14.

Wu, C. (1998, April 4). Ritalin may work better as a purer compound. *Science News, 153,* 213.

Wurtman, R. J. (1982, April). Nutrients that modify brain functions. *Scientific American, 242,* 50–59.

Wynn, K. (1992). Addition and subtraction by human infants. *Nature, 358,* 749–759.

Wynn, K. (1995). Infants possess a system of numerical knowledge. *Current Directions in Psychological Science, 4,* 172–177.

Yacoubian, G. S. Jr., Deutsch, J. K., & Schumacher, E. J. (2004). Estimating the prevalence of ecstasy use among club rave attendees. *Contemporary Drug Problems, 31,* 163–177.

Yalom, I. D., & Greaves, C. (1977). Group therapy with the terminally ill. *American Journal of Psychiatry, 134,* 396–400.

Yamamoto, A. (Producer). (2000, October 8). *NHK Special* [Television broadcast of Olympic Games]. Tokyo: NHK. [As cited in Markus et al., 2006]

Yeaman, J. (1995). Who is resilient? Who is vulnerable? *Dissertation Abstracts International, Section A: Humanities and Social Sciences, 55,* 3110.

Yee, A. H., Fairchild, H. H., Weizmann, F., & Wyatt, G. E. (1993). Addressing psychology's problems with race. *American Psychologist, 48,* 1132–1140.

Yee, P. L., Pierce, G. R., Ptacek, J. R., & Modzelesky, K. L. (2003). Learned helplessness, attributional style, and examination performance: Enhancement effects are not necessarily moderated by prior failure. *Anxiety, Stress & Coping, 16,* 359–373.

Yerkes, R. M. (1921). Psychological examining in the United States Army. In R. M. Yerkes (Ed.), *Memoirs of the National Academy of Sciences: Vol. 15.* Washington, DC: U.S. Government Printing Office.

Young, J. R. (2003, February 14). Prozac campus. *The Chronicle of Higher Education,* A-37–A-38.

Zajonc, R. B. (1968). Attitudinal effects of mere exposure. *Journal of Personality and Social Psychology. Monograph Supplement, 9*(2, Part 2), 1–27.

Zajonc, R. B. (1980). Feeling and thinking: Preferences need no inferences. *American Psychologist, 35,* 151–175.

Zajonc, R. B. (1984). On the primacy of affect. *American Psychologist, 39,* 117–123.

Zajonc, R. B. (2001). Mere exposure effects explained . . . finally! Address given to the Western Psychological Association annual convention in Lahaina (Maui), Hawaii.

Zakowski, S. G., Hall, M. H., Klein, L. C., & Baum, A. (2001). Appraised control, coping, and stress in a community sample: A test of the goodness-of-fit hypothesis. *Annals of Behavioral Medicine, 23,* 158–165.

Zaman, R. M. (1992). Psychotherapy in the third world: Some impressions from Pakistan. In U. P. Gielen, L. L. Adler, & N. A. Milgram (Eds.), *Psychology in international perspective* (pp. 314–321). Amsterdam: Swets & Zeitlinger.

Zarit, S. H., & Pearlin, L. I. (Eds.). (2003). *Personal control in social and life course contexts: Societal impact on aging* (pp. 127–164). New York: Springer Publishing.

Zatorre, R. J., & Krumhansl, C. L. (2002, December 13). Mental models and musical minds. *Science, 298,* 2138–2139.

Zeki, S. (1992, September). The visual image in mind and brain. *Scientific American, 267,* 68–76.

Zeman, N. (1990, Summer/Fall). The new rules of courtship (Special Edition). *Newsweek,* 24–27.

Zigler, E., & Muenchow, S. (1992). *Head Start: The inside story of America's most successful educational experiment.* New York: Basic Books.

Zigler, E., & Styfco, S. J. (1994). Head Start: Criticisms in a constructive context. *American Psychologist, 49,* 127–132.

Zilbergeld, B. (1986, June). Psychabuse. *Science 86, 7,* 48.

Zimbardo, P. G. (1953). The dynamics of prejudice and assimilation among two underprivileged minority groups in New York City. *Alpha Kappa Delta, XXIV* (1), 16–22.

Zimbardo, P. G. (1973). On the ethics of investigation in human psychological research: With special reference to the Stanford Prison Experiment. *Cognition, 2,* 243–256.

Zimbardo, P. G. (1975). On transforming experimental research into advocacy for social change. In M. Deutsch & H. Hornstein (Eds.), *Applying social psychology: Implications for research, practice, and training* (pp. 33–66). Hillsdale, NJ: Erlbaum.

Zimbardo, P. G. (1990). *Shyness: What it is, what to do about it* (Rev. ed.). Reading, MA: Perseus Books. (Original work published 1977).

Zimbardo, P. G. (2002, August). Why and how normal people go mad. Address presented at the convention of the American Psychological Association, Chicago.

Zimbardo, P. G. (2004a, July). *The politics of fear.* Address given at the annual convention of the American Psychological Association, Honolulu, HI.

Zimbardo, P. G. (2004b, May 9). Power turns good soldiers into "bad apples." *Boston Globe,* D11.

Zimbardo, P. G. (2004c). A situationist perspective on the psychology of evil: Understanding how good people are transformed into perpetrators. In A. G. Miller (Ed.), *The Social Psychology of Good and Evil* (pp. 21–50). New York: Guilford Press.

Zimbardo, P. G. (2007). *The Lucifer effect: Understanding how good people turn evil.* New York: Random House. [See also: Haney et al., 1973; Haney & Zimbardo, 1998; Zimbardo, 1973, 1975; Zimbardo et al., 1999; replicated in Australia by Lovibond et al., 1979]

Zimbardo, P. G. (2008). On being "Shoe" at Yale: A study in institutional conformity. In preparation. Stanford University.

Zimbardo, P. G., Andersen, S. M., & Kabat, L. (1981). Induced hearing deficit generates experimental paranoia. *Science, 212,* 1529–1531.

Zimbardo, P. G., & Leippe, M. (1991). *The psychology of attitude change and social influence.* New York: McGraw-Hill.

Zimbardo, P. G., Maslach, C., & Haney, C. (1999). Reflections on the Stanford prison Experiment: Genesis, transformations, consequences. In T. Blass (Ed.), *Obedience to authority: Current perspectives on the Milgram paradigm* (pp. 193–237). Mahwah, NJ: Erlbaum.

Zimbardo, P. G., & Montgomery, K. D. (1957). The relative strengths of consummatory responses in hunger, thirst, and exploratory drive. *Journal of Comparative and Physiological Psychology, 50,* 504–508.

Zimmer, C. (2005, November). The neurobiology of the self. *Scientific American, 293*(5), 92–101.

Zimmerman, F. J., & Christakis, D. A. (2007). Associations between content types of early media exposure and subsequent attentional problems. *Pediatrics, 120,* 986–992.

Zimmerman, F. J., Christakis, D. A., & Meltzoff, A. N. (2007). Television and DVD/video viewing in children younger than 2 years. *Archives of Pediatrics and Adolescent Medicine, 16.* 473–479.

Zimmerman, S. (2002). *Writing to heal the soul: Transforming grief and loss through writing.* New York: Three Rivers Press/Crown Publishing.

Zucker, G. S., & Weiner, B. (1993). Conservatism and perceptions of poverty: An attributional analysis. *Journal of Applied Social Psychology, 23,* 925–943.

Zuckerman, M. (1974). The sensation-seeking motive. In B. Maher (Ed.), *Progress in experimental personality research* (Vol. 7). New York: Academic Press.

Zuckerman, M. (1978, February). The search for high sensation. *Psychology Today, 12,* 38–46.

Zuckerman, M. (1990). Some dubious premises in research and theory on racial differences: Scientific, social, and ethical issues. *American Psychologist, 45,* 1297–1303.

Zuckerman, M. (1995). Good and bad humors: Biochemical bases of personality and its disorders. *Psychological Science, 6,* 325–332.

Zuckerman, M. (2004). The shaping of personality: Genes, environments, and chance encounters. *Journal of Personality Assessment, 82,* 11–22. [See also: Zuckerman, 1995; Zuckerman et al., 1978, 1980, 1993]

Zuckerman, M., Buchsbaum, M. S., & Murphy, D. L. (1980). Sensation seeking and its biological correlates. *Psychological Bulletin, 88,* 187–214.

Zuckerman, M., Depaulo, B. M., & Rosenthal, R. (1981). Verbal and nonverbal communication of deception. *Advances in Experimental Social Psychology, 14,* 1–59.

Zuckerman, M., Eysenck, S., & Eysenck, H. J. (1978). Sensation seeking in England and America: Cross-cultural, age and sex comparisons. *Journal of Consulting and Clinical Psychology, 46,* 139–149.

Zuckerman, M., Kuhlman, D. M., Joireman, J., Teta, P., & Kraft, M. (1993). A comparison of three structural models for personality: The Big Three, the Big Five, and the Alternative Five. *Journal of Personality and Social Psychology, 65,* 575–768.

CHAPTER 1
Program Review
1. c, 2. b, 3. c, 4. c, 5. c, 6. c, 7. b, 8. b, 9. d, 10. c, 11. b, 12. b, 13. c, 14. a, 15. b, 16. b, 17. d, 18. c, 19. c, 20. b

Questions to Consider
1. The fundamental issues of psychology include the relationship of mind and body, the role of heredity and environment in determining personality and behavior, the role of the conscious and the unconscious in determining behavior, the influence of individual dispositional and external social and situational forces on behavior, the influence of early experience on later life, and the significance of individual differences and similarities.

2. Many people are not aware of the different kinds of work that psychologists do. A popular stereotype is that of the slightly nutty Freudian-style analyst depicted in popular movies of the 1930s and 1940s. As you will learn, the treatment of mental illness is only one part of psychology. Psychologists are scientists who can also help people teach more effectively and learn more efficiently. They help people improve their physical and emotional well-being, enhance communication, find the right job, quit smoking, make decisions, improve social relations, understand child development, promote world peace, and fight poverty and prejudice.

3. Observer bias influences our choices about what is relevant and what isn't. Our values, interests, and expectations can even influence our perceptions, leading us to see things that are not there and overlook things that are.

4. We can't know the future, but we're certainly at the dawning of an important era when biological and psychological phenomena can truly be seen to interact with each other. It's unlikely that we'll ever completely know how the brain and body create psychological experience or that we'll ever be able to read the intricate details of someone's thoughts just by looking at the firing patterns of neurons in their brain, but there will certainly be progress even on those fronts. For example, we already know that certain kinds of mental activity are associated with greater brain activity in certain regions. In the year 2500, psychologists will probably be required to have training in the neurosciences in order to consider themselves educated in human functioning.

5. Some studies cannot be run without keeping participants somewhat in the dark about the purpose of the research, since knowledge of the study's goals would be likely to affect their behavior and make it unlike the actual phenomenon being studied. The goal is always to be as respectful of participants as possible, never to deceive them if it is not necessary to the research, and always to debrief them after their participation is complete so that the deception is removed and any possible distress is dispelled. According to APA Guidelines, which hold the participants' welfare as primary, any likely distress must be consented to before the study begins, and a study involving deception would threaten the opportunity for truly informed consent. Psychologists acknowledge that this disallows some experiments from being conducted, but have accepted this limitation and, when possible, design other, more acceptable studies that address similar questions.

CHAPTER 2
Program Review
1. d, 2. a, 3. b, 4. c, 5. c, 6. a, 7. a, 8. d, 9. b, 10. a, 11. a, 12. b, 13. d, 14. a, 15. b, 16. b, 17. c, 18. a, 19. c, 20. c

Questions to Consider
1. Techniques such as the fMRI, EEG, CAT, MRI, and PET provide information that can be used to help distinguish between normal and abnormal brain structures and functions. The process of mapping or imaging the brain promises to help identify the chemical or structural abnormalities underlying such problems as Alzheimer's disease, schizophrenia, learning disabilities, and depression.

2. When a person has catastrophic brain injuries and sudden changes in functioning, the people who know the person best may have trouble adapting. Often this involves a sudden loss of language, spatial ability, or memory, with no real change in what they've come to know as their loved one's personality. In the case of Phineas Gage, not only were the changes he experienced unusual, so that his loved ones did not have a previous model to refer to in learning to relate to him, but his changes were in interpersonal functioning and personality, which people tend to think of as unshakeable characteristics. We can only imagine that it was very difficult for loved ones to accept the "new" Phineas and to believe that a new personality had completely replaced the old one.

3. Although we are able to determine which areas of the brain are active and may be able to argue that, for example, verbal activity or emotional activity is involved, there is no indication that we can come any closer to reading or controlling the precise thoughts that people experience.

4. With an all-or-none response, you have a physical means for detecting things, rather than forcing some higher function to decide whether a neuron has fired with a great enough strength for something to be the case (e.g., there really was a noise, I really did have a memory). You also create a system that allows for the same information to be processed, while protecting the neuron from constantly having to be in some state of firing. As for neurotransmitters, the greater number allows for greater diversity of functioning in the brain and allows for one function to be active while other, less relevant or undesired ones remain inactive.

CHAPTER 3
Program Review
1. b, 2. d, 3. d, 4. a, 5. b, 6. c, 7. c, 8. a, 9. d, 10. c, 11. b, 12. d, 13. c, 14. a, 15. b, 16. d, 17. a, 18. c, 19. b, 20. d

Questions to Consider
1. Compulsive gambling could be considered a disease and a learned behavior. An organization called Gamblers Anonymous is based on the same principles as Alcoholics Anonymous. However, analyzing compulsive gambling in terms of antecedents and consequences might suggest ways to eliminate cues that lead to gambling, thereby leading to extinction. The best policy might be to avoid all settings where gambling takes place. Because any winning would serve to reinforce gambling, the best goal for a behavior change program is no gambling at all. Because it is reinforced intermittently (on a variable ratio schedule), it may be very resistant to extinction.

2. You could provide positive reinforcement for keeping the school clean. For example, students could receive a sticker for every 50 pieces of litter they pick up. They could also be punished (e.g., with extra homework or reduced break periods) if they are caught littering. You might also try integrating other principles, such as modeling, shaping, and ideal reinforcement schedules, into your program to increase the likelihood that students' behavior will conform to your goals.

3. Intention is not always a prerequisite for learning. We learn many behaviors without setting out to do so. However, if intention can help us focus attention, learning is enhanced. One exciting aspect of learning principles is that they do not require consent or knowledge of the learner in order to work. They can work on pigeons, people who are mentally retarded, and people who are resistant to change just as well as they can work on intelligent human adults. Learning principles are truly a universal phenomenon.

4. Parents generally don't reward or punish their children's grammar. Instead, they model good grammar for their children and do what they can to understand whatever utterances their children produce. So the

learning of grammar does not depend on operant principles. Parents do, however, reward and punish other linguistic features, such as content (e.g., "That's right; that *is* a doggy") and politeness (e.g., "Did you say 'thank you'? You're such a good girl").

CHAPTER 4
Program Review
1. d, 2. c, 3. b, 4. b, 5. d, 6. a, 7. b, 8. a, 9. b, 10. b, 11. c, 12. c, 13. d, 14. a, 15. b, 16. d, 17. a, 18. a, 19. b, 20. d

Questions to Consider
1. Helpful memory strategies include paying attention, minimizing distractions and interference, and encoding information in more than one way, such as reading out loud, outlining important points, or chunking information in some personally meaningful way. It is also helpful to add meaning by linking new facts and ideas to familiar information, to use visual imagery, to review material distributed in study sessions, to study before going to sleep, and to overlearn material.
2. The schema we used as children are very different from the ones we have developed as adults. And because young children are lacking in language, which normally helps us to label and organize memories, we may find that memories from our preverbal days are sparse or nonexistent. There is also evidence that early memories may be lost due to physiological maturation. Nevertheless, many memories, particularly from later childhood, are recoverable through good cues, and most people find that cues, such as family stories or photographs, can help in reconstructing memories.
3. The ABC song offers many devices to aid retention. The letters are chunked or grouped in units that conform to the capacity of short-term memory. The letters at the end of each phrase rhyme, which is a mnemonic device. The song encodes the information in sounds as well as in movements. And the fun of it also motivates multiple rehearsals and performances.
4. Most of us are justifiably impressed with the capacity of our long-term memory. Society rewards people for good memories, starting in early childhood. Playing trivia games can set off a host of associations to events and ideas that we often don't even know we have in memory.
5. There is substantial controversy over what "leading" questions do to memories. The way a person perceives and recalls an event depends on perceptual and cognitive biases that even the eyewitness may not be aware of. Jury members are subject to their own biases when they hear and judge testimony. Jurors need to be especially alert to leading questions that might introduce details or prompt a witness to report an event in a particular way. The more informed a jury member is about how memory works, the better he or she may be able to weigh the value of testimony.

CHAPTER 5
Program Review
1. d, 2. a, 3. a, 4. c, 5. c, 6. b, 7. a, 8. d, 9. b, 10. a, 11. c, 12. a, 13. b, 14. b, 15. a, 16. d, 17. c, 18. a, 19. a, 20. c

Questions to Consider
1. Scripts might include types of activities and dress, level of education, achievement, income, social status, family patterns, interests, vacation ideas, restaurant preferences, and health status.
2. Pitfalls of problem solving include the inability to define the problem, to be illogical in situations in which emotions are involved, and the reluctance to consider opposing points of view. People also depend on certain familiar approaches and strategies and often do not recognize when these are no longer useful. Cognitive bias and mental shortcuts also cause people to draw false conclusions or make bad decisions.
3. According to the representativeness heuristic, we are prone to believe that an event is likely if it fits our stereotype of what usually happens. This makes us particularly likely to notice events that fit our stereotype, and it may lead us to overestimate how commonly stereotype-consistent instances are. Similarly, the availability heuristic can perpetuate stereotypes through the cues we provide ourselves with when conjuring up examples or "typical profiles" of the groups with whom we hold the stereotypes.
4. No. Environment still has an important influence on the expression of any trait or ability. This is obvious from studies of development in

enriched and impoverished environments. Impoverished environments lower a person's test performance. Both heredity and environment play a role.
5. It is rare for someone to be universally more capable or more intelligent than the average person. A brilliant mathematician may be kinesthetically awkward, and a person with excellent spatial skills may be average or below average on verbal measures of intelligence. Looking around at our greatest models of mathematical intelligence, body skills, and social intelligence leads to outstanding models for those specific kinds of intelligence that may show no particular excellence on any of the other scales.

CHAPTER 6
Program Review
1. c, 2. d, 3. b, 4. d, 5. c, 6. d, 7. d, 8. d, 9. b, 10. b, 11. a, 12. c, 13. d, 14. b, 15. d, 16. c, 17. c, 18. a, 19. a, 20. c

Questions to Consider
1. Lack of knowledge or inappropriate expectations can cause unnecessary frustration and misunderstanding. Some child abuse may be related to unrealistic expectations, especially in toilet training and bedwetting. In the past, parents were warned not to spoil their children by handling them too much. This was followed by a period of attentive indulgence. Currently, child-rearing advice falls somewhere between these two extremes.
2. Many very clever techniques for measuring topics, such as memory, perception, and preference, have been developed to study infants, who can have sophisticated abilities but who cannot respond to complex language or answer questions verbally. Some of these techniques can be adapted for use with other nonverbal animals, as long as their behavioral capabilities (such as grasping and looking) are well enough developed.
3. Language helps structure thought, and people use words to think, solve problems, and define and use concepts. But thinking also involves visual and sensory images. Certain cognitive operations, but not all, are dependent on language.
4. You would have a hard time raising your child without exposing him or her to any gender-typing biases. Other people your child interacts with on a day-to-day basis, including young children and even strangers, will treat your child in a manner consistent with gender roles. If you try to disguise your child's gender in order to prevent this, by careful selection of clothing and a unisex-style haircut, people may ask your child whether he or she is a boy or a girl in order to figure out what they believe to be the appropriate means of interacting, and other children might tease or reject your child for not following stereotypical dress and behavior patterns. Socialization and interaction based on gender is so strong in our culture that it is unlikely you'd be successful at your efforts.
5. Social attitudes and economic conditions determine which changes and responsibilities are considered appropriate for adult roles. For example, the age at which marriage is acceptable or at which children are expected to become self-supporting is often set by economic and social conditions in the larger society.

CHAPTER 7
Program Review
1. d, 2. c, 3. c, 4. a, 5. d, 6. a, 7. a, 8. a, 9. c, 10. c, 11. b, 12. b, 13. c, 14. b, 15. a, 16. d, 17. c, 18. a, 19. d, 20. a

Questions to Consider
1. The distinction between sensation and perception is an important one and will still be present 50 years from now. Whereas "sensation" refers to the registering of a physical stimulus on one of many different kinds of receptors, "perception" refers to one's experience of the stimulus. Sensations are translated through sophisticated neuronal structures into perceptions.
2. To improve the environment for individuals with visual deficits, one could print large labels on medicine bottles and other containers. For people with impaired balance, handrails in hallways and safety rails in bathrooms could be installed. To adjust for hearing loss, background noise could be reduced by better insulation, and blinking lights that indicate when the phone is ringing could be installed. For those with a

loss of sensitivity to smells, smoke detectors or fire alarms could be installed. And, if loss of smell is affecting appetite, special effort should go into planning a diet to enhance flavors and ensure adequate nutrition.

3. Items on the grocery shelves have labels on them so that it's easy to group by perceptual similarity. Products belonging to the same category are typically stored within the same area of the store, allowing grouping by proximity. At the checkout stand, two different customers will typically leave a perceptible space between their clusters of purchases, allowing the clerk to group the clusters by the principle of proximity. Items moving together on a clerk's conveyer belt can be grouped by the principle of common fate.

4. By training yourself to pay close attention to visual and auditory elements, you can become increasingly aware of the purposeful choices film and television directors make and how they use and combine various techniques to influence your perceptions. For example, children's toys are frequently photographed in ads so that they appear larger or sturdier than they really are. In films and television programs, dim lighting, a low camera angle, and shadows are used to create suspense or danger. Music is often used in television and film to evoke happiness, fear, or other emotions.

5. One possibility is that the tendency in primates to climb and to brachiate through trees required an extremely accurate three-dimensional perceptual system that would allow rapid navigation. Vision seems to serve this function best, although other animals who navigate at night seem to do well by using hearing, rather than vision.

CHAPTER 8
Program Review
1. c, 2. c, 3. b, 4. c, 5. d, 6. b, 7. c, 8. a, 9. d, 10. d, 11. b, 12. d, 13. b, 14. a, 15. d, 16. c, 17. b, 18. a, 19. c, 20. d

Questions to Consider
1. REM sleep is critical, and when one is deprived of it, one generally experiences rebound effects. These can take the form of particularly vivid daydreaming, more rapid onset of the first REM phase when one falls asleep again, and a longer proportion of total sleep time spent in REM sleep.

2. Illness, love, and grief can cause many changes in mental functioning typically associated with altered consciousness. Love and grief particularly can cause people to experience intense or extensive changes in consciousness and behavior.

3. Treatment should take into account social and psychological factors, as well as chemical effects and physiological factors. Drug education programs must prepare students to evaluate the social and psychological components of drug use that lead to dependence and addiction. Some drug education programs aimed at children attempt to establish a certain mind-set that counteracts peer and cultural pressures and promotes critical thinking about pro-drug messages.

4. Effects of extensive television viewing include heightened arousal and suggestibility, depression, and lowered motivation, as well as a distorted sense of time, disorientation, impulsivity, and hyperactivity, especially in children. Studies tend to be contradictory. Prolonged inactivity can lead to a kind of stimulus deprivation. Young children do not have the intellectual ability or sufficient experience and information to distinguish fantasy from reality, so they may be confused by the distortions of reality they see on television.

5. People certainly differ in their ability to be hypnotized or the ease with which they can enter meditative states. It may take some practice, but you may well find that the benefits outweigh the investment you have to make up-front to learn to do it. In both cases, exposing oneself to quiet environments, practicing without imposing inappropriate demands on oneself, and following the instructions of an expert should help.

CHAPTER 9
Program Review
1. d, 2. b, 3. b, 4. c, 5. a, 6. c, 7. c, 8. a, 9. d, 10. b, 11. a, 12. b, 13. c, 14. a, 15. d, 16. c, 17. d, 18. b, 19. a, 20. c

Questions to Consider
1. An individual's sexual script is based on a unique combination of personal, social, and cultural beliefs and attitudes. Scripts are influenced by family role models, the media, and feedback from social experiences. Boys and girls are typically treated differently during development. Cultural stereotypes tend to reinforce some personal choices and not others. Sexual scripts are often not overtly expressed and may be a source of friction and disappointment in a relationship. If couples can talk about mismatched role expectations and values, they may be able to negotiate a shared script. The threat of AIDS and other sexually transmitted diseases may change the norms governing sexual activity and thereby rewrite the social scripts that guide sexual behavior. Expect to see changes in what characterizes an acceptable mate, dating patterns, and other relationship issues.

2. How you respond might be determined by your need for achievement. If you believed you could get an A, you probably would want a grade. Your motivation to study might be reduced by the less rewarding pass/fail option. If you thought you could earn only a C, a pass/fail option might be more appealing. You would eliminate the potentially handicapping stress of working for a grade. Working for a grade might also interfere with your intrinsic motivation to learn. If you were very interested in the course but didn't want the pressure of working hard, you would not need the incentive of being graded, and a pass/fail option would be more appealing.

3. You may, for example, be perceived as overly familiar with people, expressing your affection for them in too forward a manner. Or you may be perceived as not expressive enough if, for example, you were raised to be relatively stoic and reserved but you find yourself in a demonstrative culture that expects more showy displays of love, surprise, or sadness.

CHAPTER 10
Program Review
1. c, 2. b, 3. a, 4. b, 5. a, 6. d, 7. d, 8. b, 9. c, 10. b, 11. a, 12. c, 13. d, 14. a, 15. b, 16. b, 17. a, 18. a, 19. c, 20. d

Questions to Consider
1. The id is the driving energy of our passion, curiosity, and excitement. According to Freud, it is the life force that operates on the pleasure principle. On the positive side, it is the drive for self-preservation. It is also the place where sexual urges arise, thus ensuring the survival of the species. The fantasies of the id are the basis for imagination and creative endeavors. The id also contains aggressive and destructive drives that can be turned against the self or against society.

2. Although the Internet exposes us to lots of different kinds of people from all around the world, many of the social skills used with the Internet are specific to that particular medium. For people who substitute Internet-based interaction with face-to-face interaction, other critical social skills may be underdeveloped or lost over time. They may feel isolated, awkward in social situations, and shy. This is becoming particularly important as people find that identities are easy to slip into and out of in an Internet-based culture.

CHAPTER 11
Program Review
1. a, 2. c, 3. d, 4. a, 5. b, 6. a, 7. c, 8. d, 9. a, 10. b, 11. b, 12. c, 13. d, 14. a, 15. a, 16. c, 17. b, 18. c, 19. a, 20. d

Questions to Consider
1. The participants in Milgram's research could avoid blaming themselves if they reasoned that the situation was influencing their behavior. They could rationalize that they were only following orders and did not have to accept responsibility for their behavior. Therefore, they could avoid guilt, much as the Nazis did when they claimed they were only following orders.

2. Although extreme examples of blind obedience, such as Nazi Germany or even Milgram's experiment, are easy to identify, there are many ambiguous situations in which the difference is not so clear. In schools, churches, and the workplace, cooperation is highly esteemed and compliance is usually rewarded. Efforts to undermine authority are typically considered to be a threat by the leader of the group. Parents and teachers tend to reinforce obedient behavior in children. It may be useful to cite examples of people who buck authority and to help illustrate possibilities for legitimate dissent. However, most research on so-

cial influence shows that unquestioning obedience is the norm in the presence of perceived authority figures.

3. You should artificially create a situation in which people do not feel as though they are part of a large group of people who could act. Individually identify someone and ask him or her to help you. In such a situation, it would be unlikely that he or she would fall prey to diffusion of responsibility.

4. Individuals do not respond to situations identically. Some individuals have such strong personal values and self-confidence that they do not seek social approval as much as others. Also, people usually choose what they hear and watch. They can turn off the television, ignore a program, or walk out of the movie theater. They can read selectively, actively looking for articles that support their ideas or challenge them. They can associate with people who share their beliefs and opinions or purposely expose themselves to new ideas and experiences.

5. People who are made aware of their identities and responsibilities are more likely to follow cultural norms. The deindividuation and anonymity of big cities foster irresponsible and aggressive behavior. In addition, in accordance with the principle of diffusion of responsibility, the large number of people who can intervene to help or to correct a situation tends to lower the likelihood that anyone will intervene.

CHAPTER 12
Program Review
1. d, 2. b, 3. b, 4. b, 5. d, 6. a, 7. b, 8. c, 9. d, 10. b, 11. d, 12. b, 13. c, 14. a, 15. b, 16. a, 17. d, 18. b, 19. d, 20. a

Questions to Consider
1. Courts differ on how they deal with the insanity defense. In order for a person to be excused from legal responsibility for criminal actions, the defense must demonstrate severely impaired judgment and lack of self-control. A person is not considered legally responsible if he or she is unable to distinguish right from wrong. The definition may vary from country to country, from state to state, even from court to court. It is a highly controversial issue.

2. The *Diagnostic and Statistical Manual* has been criticized for inflating disorders, basing some criteria on myth instead of empirical evidence, and for stigmatizing people. It is also, clearly, a relative assessment guide subject to cultural forces. For example, homosexuality was once characterized as a disorder. Today, the self-defeating personality has been proposed as a disorder to be included. Women's groups and others are very concerned that such a label will lead to a blaming of the victim.

3. Statistically, homosexuality is relatively less common. However, cultural standards are relative. Psychological assessments show no differences in personality or adjustment between heterosexuals and homosexuals. Today, the *DSM-IV* does not list homosexuality as a disorder. It is considered a problem only if it causes guilt or self-hate.

4. Women may be more willing to talk about distress and emotional problems. They are more often denied opportunities for independence and achievement and may feel angry, hopeless, or helpless, justifiably. There is a male bias toward traditional concepts of mental health.

5. Many psychological problems are just extreme instances of behavior that most of us exhibit at one time or another. If you are extremely worried about a certain behavior, if the behavior is disruptive to relationships, or if it has become a persistent problem, you might consider getting a professional evaluation.

CHAPTER 13
Program Review
1. c, 2. a, 3. d, 4. b, 5. a, 6. b, 7. d, 8. c, 9. c, 10. d, 11. a, 12. c, 13. b, 14. b, 15. b, 16. d, 17. c, 18. a, 19. c, 20. a

Questions to Consider
1. A given psychological problem is often associated with clear abnormalities in the functioning of the brain. We know, for example, that depression is associated with the functioning of the neurotransmitter sero-

tonin. We also know that serotonin can be affected in multiple ways, including through either direct manipulation of serotonin reuptake in the brain, as is accomplished through some antidepressants, or indirectly, through one's psychological experience. Psychotherapy is intended to provide people with the skills and experience that will allow changes in one's behavior, environment, experience, and relationships. Although it is not intended as the ultimate goal, a change in brain functioning co-occurs with these other changes. One's movement toward greater happiness and self-efficacy is reflected in one's brain.

2. Finding the right match between a problem and an approach to therapy starts with how you define the problem and your attitude or beliefs about the kind of help you need. A person might seek assistance in making the decision from a physician or person in the community who is familiar with available resources and services.

3. Program 22 describes therapies that focus on illness and problem solving, as well as on those designed to address life-management issues, self-esteem, relationships, and potential. Most people, at some time, could benefit from professional intervention.

4. In U.S. culture, there is typically a stigma associated with seeking help of any kind. Our culture emphasizes individuality, self-sufficiency, and strength, especially for men. That makes it harder to admit weakness or the need for support.

5. Although it is confrontational and can be aversive, exposure therapy is also quite an effective treatment strategy. If you are committed to facing and overcoming a phobia and you trust your therapist, you might consider this very efficient therapeutic strategy.

CHAPTER 14
Program Review
1. c, 2. b, 3. d, 4. b, 5. d, 6. c, 7. a, 8. b, 9. c, 10. d, 11. b, 12. d, 13. a, 14. c, 15. b, 16. c, 17. a, 18. d, 19. b, 20. c

Questions to Consider
1. Friends can help reduce stress in several ways. They can offer practical help. For example, when there is illness or a crisis in a family, friends can relieve temporary concerns about money, child care, food, or transportation needs. They can also offer emotional support, being there to listen and empathize with you about what you are going through and reassuring you that you are not going crazy even when you feel most vulnerable and confused. Friends may also offer advice in an unfamiliar situation, helping you to think through decisions. Social support makes people less vulnerable to stress-related problems. Social networks counteract a sense of isolation by providing a sense of belonging. In support groups, individuals help each other by providing a social reference group. They share advice, feelings, and information specific to the situation.

2. Self-defeating thoughts undermine a person's sense of self-esteem, optimism, efficacy, and control—all necessary for adequate coping.

3. Perfectionists unnecessarily stress themselves by setting impossible goals and standards. They may compare themselves with inappropriate models of achievement, never being satisfied with their own accomplishments. They may feel they have inadequate resources to measure up to their unreasonably high standards. These attitudes can create stress and can undermine their ability to perform.

4. Although the traditional gender roles for running a household have changed over the past several years, men still typically find themselves in more stressful, powerful job situations. Such work conditions are associated with poor lifestyle habits, such as caffeine, nicotine, and alcohol abuse, and with insufficient sleep and lack of exercise. Add to that a cultural tendency to foster aggression in men, and we see that such a combination puts men at risk for cardiovascular disease. Women are also at risk. In the workplace, they may find themselves in situations where they have less control than men do, making them also prone to stress-related health problems, including cardiovascular disease. And as gender roles continue to shift, women become more and more vulnerable to the traditional "male" stress-related risks.

name index